HANDBOOK OF
RESEARCH
ON WRITING

HISTORY, SOCIETY, SCHOOL, INDIVIDUAL, TEXT

HANDBOOK OF
RESEARCH ON WRITING

HISTORY, SOCIETY, SCHOOL, INDIVIDUAL, TEXT

Edited by

CHARLES BAZERMAN

University of California, Santa Barbara

NEW YORK AND LONDON

Routledge
Taylor & Francis Group
270 Madison Avenue
New York, NY 10016

Routledge
Taylor & Francis Group
2 Park Square
Milton Park, Abingdon
Oxon OX14 4RN

© 2008 by Taylor & Francis Group, LLC
Routledge is an imprint of Taylor & Francis Group, an Informa business

Transferred to Digital Printing 2009

International Standard Book Number-13: 978-0-8058-4870-0 (Softcover) 978-0-8058-4869-4 (Hardcover)

Library of Congress Cataloging-in-Publication Data

Bazerman, Charles.
    Handbook of research on writing / Charles Bazerman.
        p. cm.
    Includes bibliographical references and index.
    ISBN 978-0-8058-4870-0 (pbk. : alk. paper) -- ISBN 978-0-8058-4869-4 (hardback : alk. paper)
    1. Written communication. 2. Rhetoric. 3. Discourse analysis. I. Title.

P211.B394 2008
302.2'244--dc22
                                                                                        2007018833

Visit the Taylor & Francis Web site at
http://www.taylorandfrancis.com

Contents

Advisory Board ix
Preface xi
Acknowledgments xiii
List of Contributors xv

Introduction 1

I. HISTORY OF WRITING 5

1. Origins and Forms of Writing 7
   Denise Schmandt-Besserat and Michael Erard

2. History of Writing Technologies 23
   Brian Gabrial

3. History of Typography 35
   David Jury

4. History of the Book, Authorship, Book Design, and Publishing 65
   David Finkelstein

5. History of Reflection, Theory, and Research on Writing 81
   Paul A. Prior and Karen J. Lunsford

II. WRITING IN SOCIETY 97

6. Writing and the Social Formation of Economy 103
   Graham Smart

7. On Documentary Society 113
   Dorothy E. Smith and Catherine F. Schryer

8. Writing, Text, and the Law 129
   Peter Tiersma

9. Writing and Secular Knowledge Apart From Modern European Institutions 143
   Charles Bazerman and Paul Rogers

10. Writing and Secular Knowledge Within Modern European Institutions 157
    Charles Bazerman and Paul Rogers

11. The Collection and Organization of Written Knowledge 177
    Jack Andersen

12. Writing as Art and Entertainment 191
    Patrick Colm Hogan

13. Writing and Journalism: Politics, Social Movements, and the Public Sphere   205
    Martin Conboy

14. Writing in the Professions   221
    Anne Beaufort

15. History of Writing in the Community   237
    Ursula Howard

16. Writing, Gender, and Culture: An Interdisciplinary Perspective   255
    Mary P. Sheridan-Rabideau

17. Writing and Social Change   269
    Brenton Faber

III. WRITING IN SCHOOLING   **281**

18. History of Schools and Writing   283
    David R. Olson

19. Writing in Primary School   293
    Pietro Boscolo

20. Writing in Secondary Schools   311
    George Hillocks

21. Teaching of Writing in Higher Education   331
    Richard H. Haswell

22. Teaching of Writing and Writing Teachers Through the Ages   347
    Duane Roen, Maureen Daly Goggin, and Jennifer Clary-Lemon

23. Construct and Consequence: Validity in Writing Assessment   365
    Sandra Murphy and Kathleen Blake Yancey

24. Teaching of Writing and Diversity: Access, Identity, and Achievement   387
    John Albertini

IV. WRITING AND THE INDIVIDUAL   **399**

25. Development of Writing Abilities in Childhood   401
    Deborah Wells Rowe

26. Defining Adolescent and Adult Writing Development: A Contest
    of Empirical and Federal Wills   421
    Julie Cheville and Margaret Finders

27. The Reading–Writing Nexus in Discourse Research   435
    Nancy Nelson

28. Writing and Cognition: Implications of the Cognitive Architecture
    for Learning to Write and Writing to Learn   451
    Deborah McCutchen, Paul Teske, and Catherine Bankston

29. Writing and Communication Disorders Across the Life Span 471
Julie A. Hengst and Cynthia J. Johnson

30. Writing as Physical and Emotional Healing: Findings From
Clinical Research 485
Jessica Singer and George H. S. Singer

31. Identity and the Writing of Culturally and Linguistically Diverse Students 499
Arnetha F. Ball and Pamela Ellis

32. Multilingual Writing Development 515
Dwight Atkinson and Ulla Connor

V. **WRITING AS TEXT** 533

33. Writing and Speaking 535
Douglas Biber and Camilla Vásquez

34. Grammar, the Sentence, and Traditions of Linguistic Analysis 549
Mary J. Schleppegrell

35. Form, Text Organization, Genre, Coherence, and Cohesion 565
Christine M. Tardy and John M. Swales

36. Persuasion, Audience, and Argument 583
Carolyn R. Miller and Davida Charney

37. Seeing the Screen: Research Into Visual and Digital Writing Practices 599
Anne Frances Wysocki

Author Index 613

Subject Index 641

Advisory Board

John Albertini, *Rochester Institute of Technology*

Arnetha F. Ball, *Stanford University*

Vijay Bhatia, *City University of Hong Kong*

Suzanne Bratcher, *Northern Arizona University*

Wally Chafe, *University of California, Santa Barbara, emeritus*

Ulla Connor, *Indiana University, Purdue University, Indianapolis*

Florian Coulmas, *University of Duisburg, Germany*

Anne Haas Dyson, *University of Illinois, Urbana-Champaign*

Elyse Eidman-Aadahl, *University of California, Berkeley, National Writing Project*

Sara W. Freedman, *University of California, Berkeley*

Jack Goody, *Cambridge University, emeritus*

John R. Hayes, *Carnegie Mellon University, emeritus*

George Hillocks, *University of Chicago, emeritus*

Gunther Kress, *London Institute of Education*

James Martin, *University of Sydney*

Susan McLeod, *University of California, Santa Barbara*

Sandy Murphy, *University of California, Davis*

David R. Olson, OISE, *University of Toronto*

Anthony Pare, *McGill University*

James Pennebaker, *University of Texas, Austin*

Paul A. Prior, *University of Illinois, Urbana-Champaign*

Gert Rijlaarsdam, *University of Amsterdam*

David Russell, *Iowa State University*

Peter Smagorinsky, *University of Georgia*

Anne Frances Wysocki, *Michigan Technological University*

Preface

The last 30 years have produced a wide interdisciplinary inquiry into how people write, how we learn to write, under what conditions and for what purposes we write, what resources and technologies we use to write, how our current forms and practices of writing emerged within social history, and what impacts writing has had on society and the individual. This research has been interdisciplinary and broad-ranging, but until recently there has been little attempt to aggregate these many strands of research and bring them together into a common intellectual space. This volume is an attempt to sum up what we know about writing and the many ways we know about it.

This volume will be, I hope, of use and interest to all scholars and researchers of writing as well as to those just starting down the path of writing research. But I also hope this volume will be of interest and use to anyone who teaches writing or is just curious about writing. Writing is a powerful and complex technology that touches the lives of writers deeply, and affects the lives of all in contemporary society, but we have barely begun to perceive that power. The various chapters in this volume, in summing up our knowledge, deepen our experience and appreciation of writing in ways that will make us better teachers of writing as well as individual writers—for the knowledge here deepens our sense of what we do every time we write or attempt to expand a student's capacity to write.

In commissioning the chapters of this volume and editing them, I have learned much more than I could have ever hoped to learn, for it has put me in contact with the experience and thought of some of the top scholars that have addressed every aspect of writing. The Advisory Board includes eminent researchers from many nations and many specialties—with focus on all aspects of writing. All authors of the 37 chapters, chosen from an international range of eminent researchers, have been faithful to a charge to seek out relevant materials from diverse research traditions in all countries. Authors and board members come from disciplines as diverse as anthropology, archaeology, typography, communication studies, linguistics, journalism, sociology, rhetoric, composition, law, medicine, education, history, and literary studies.

The volume is organized in five parts. Part I considers the history of writing as a set of intertwined technologies—of symbol system, of production and distribution, of graphic design, of the book, and of reflection on these technologies. Part II surveys from an historical and social perspective the many social domains within which writing has had tran formative effect and has become part of the cognitive and material infrastructure—economy, law, government, knowledge, libraries, literature, journalism, professional work, and everyday life. Part III then considers writing instruction within the specialized institutions designed to teach people literacy—considering schools within history and at all levels, as well as the preparation of writing teachers and practices of assessment. Part IV focuses on individuals as they develop as writers throughout their life span, how cognition, affect, and identity are engaged and influenced by writing, how communication disorders affect writing, and how multilinguality provides special conditions for writing development. Part V considers specifically textual elements that each writer must make choices about, from the sentence up through the larger structure of text organization and argument, through design issues facilitated by new writing technologies.

Acknowledgments

A volume such as this relies on the contribution of countless numbers of scholars and colleagues. If I do attempt to list names, I will miss more than I catch, and still the list will go on for many pages. This volume bears the mark of all who have toiled as researchers and teachers to advance our understanding of writing and to advance student learning, helping to make our societies more literate, more communicative, more intelligently coordinated, more knowledgeable. More directly, each chapter has been improved by the many colleagues and the various authors I have consulted and who have been generous in their help. The bibliographic queries, reading of drafts, engaged conversations have been endless and uncountable. More specifically, the members of the Advisory Board and the authors of the chapters have borne much responsibility for commenting on the developing manuscripts for each chapter, so that each separate piece bears marks of the collaboration of the whole.

I single out only a few people for special mention: Naomi Silverman, my editor at Erlbaum who first proposed the volume, provided much wisdom, and supported me in all substantive decisions. She provided me the license to frame writing research as broadly as even my most grand visions could wish. I owe even greater thanks to my research assistants during the years it took for this volume to emerge: René De los Santos, Paul Rogers, and Sarah Boggs. They helped me keep this massive project in order, helped me with editorial tasks, dug through libraries, synthesized materials, and provided ideas that kept this project moving forward, despite the complexity and immensity of the undertaking. They are also part of a larger group of wonderful graduate students who have surrounded me these recent years and have kept me curious, learning, and engaged. It is to all the graduate students in the Language, Literacy, and Composition Specialization at the Gevirtz Graduate School of Education at the University of California–Santa Barbara that I dedicate this volume.

List of Contributors

John Albertini
Rochester Institute of Technology
Rochester, New York

Jack Andersen
Royal School of Library and Information Science
Copenhagen, Denmark

Dwight Atkinson
Purdue University
West Lafayette, Indiana

Arnetha F. Ball
Stanford University
Stanford, California

Catherine Bankston
University of Washington
Seattle, Washington

Charles Bazerman
University of California
Santa Barbara, California

Anne Beaufort
University of Washington
Tacoma, Washington

Douglas Biber
Northern Arizona University
Flagstaff, Arizona

Pietro Boscolo
University of Padova
Padova, Italy

Davida Charney
University of Texas
Austin, Texas

Julie Cheville
University of Maine
Orono, Maine

Jennifer Clary-Lemon
University of Winnipeg
Winnepeg, Canada

Martin Conboy
University of Sheffield
Sheffield, United Kingdom

Ulla Connor
Indiana University, Purdue University
Indianapolis, Indiana

Pamela Ellis
Stanford University
Stanford, California

Michael Erard
University of Texas
Austin, Texas

Brenton Faber
Clarkson University
Potsdam, New York

Margaret Finders
University of Wisconsin
LaCrosse, Wisconsin

David Finkelstein
Queen Margaret University College
Edinburgh, Scotland

Brian Gabriel
Concordia University
Montreal, Canada

Maureen Daly Goggin
Arizona State University
Tempe, Arizona

Richard H. Haswell
Texas A&M University
Corpus Christi, Texas

Julie A. Hengst
University of Illinois
Urbana-Champaign, Illinois

George Hillocks
University of Chicago
Chicago, Illinois

Patrick Colm Hogan
University of Connecticut
Storrs, Connecticut

Ursula Howard
University of London
London, United Kingdom

Cynthia J. Johnson
University of Illinois
Urbana-Champaign, Illinois

David Jury
Colchester Institute
Essex, United Kingdom

Karen J. Lunsford
University of California
Santa Barbara, California

Deborah McCutchen
University of Washington
Seattle, Washington

Carolyn R. Miller
North Carolina State University
Raleigh, North Carolina

Sandra Murphy
University of California
Davis, California

Nancy Nelson
Texas A & M University
Corpus Christi, Texas

David R. Olson
University of Toronto
Ottawa, Canada

Paul A. Prior
University of Illinois
Urbana-Champaign, Illinois

Duane Roen
Arizona State University
Tempe, Arizona

Paul Rogers
University of California
Santa Barbara, California

Deborah Wells Rowe
Vanderbilt University
Nashville, Tennessee

Mary J. Schleppegrell
University of Michigan
Ann Arbor, Michigan

Denise Schmandt-Besserat
University of Texas
Austin, Texas

Catherine F. Schryer
University of Waterloo
Ontario, Canada

Mary P. Sheridan-Rabideau
Rutgers, The State University of New Jersey
New Brunswick, New Jersey

George H. S. Singer
University of California
Santa Barbara, California

Jessica Singer
Arizona State University
Tempe, Arizona

Graham Smart
Carleton University
Ottawa, Ontario, Canada

Dorothy E. Smith
University of Victoria
British Colombia, Canada

John M. Swales
University of Michigan
Ann Arbor, Michigan

Christine M. Tardy
DePaul University
Chicago, Illinois

Paul Teske
University of Washington
Seattle, Washington

Peter Tiersma
Loyola Law School
Los Angeles, California

Camilla Vásquez
University of South Florida
Tampa, Florida

Anne Frances Wysocki
Michigan Technological University
Houghton, Michigan

Kathleen Blake Yancey
Florida State University
Tallahassee, Florida

Introduction

In the 21st century, literacy is part of almost every human activity. Both grandly public and personal activities are now influenced by written documents and are organized with reference to distant systems of government, law, economy, religion, news, knowledge, and entertainment. We carry out complex activities and projects that would be impossible without the recorded knowledge, planning, and coordination enabled by writing. Rockets that travel to distant space as well as the automobile on the road beside you rely on devices and components dependent on literacy for design, distribution, installation, operation, regulation, and repair.

Furthermore, in this pervasively literate world the beliefs, ideologies, stances, and prescriptions inscribed on the documents of culture, religion, and philosophy—as well as advertising—have come to guide our activities and decisions. Even our most basic biological activities that long preceded literacy are influenced by agricultural and nutritional science, philosophies and research of child care, teachings of religion and contemporary psychology, not to mention the realms of entertainment that have celebrated and conditioned our attitudes, from restaurant reviews to romantic movies.

In many cases, the very activity is carried out through writing. The bureaucracies, corporations, political groups, and communities of belief that shape our lives are held together by paperwork. Almost everyone today in the developed world is to some degree a pencil pusher or a computer nerd, even the checkout clerk at a fast-food restaurant. Literacy is a key competence for contemporary life, and is one of the key intellectual infrastructural elements differentiating our way of life from that 5,000 years ago.

One way to consider this pervasive literacy is through reading, as consumers of texts taking our place in the inscribed orders created by others. Much of the research in education has been on the reading side of the equation, to enable students to be able to gain the meanings around them, to draw on the humanly created storehouses of knowledge, wisdom, experience, and entertainment available in books, to be able to move about and frame actions in a world pervaded by texts—from the functional literacies of a train schedule and government forms to the analytic evaluation of data for managerial decision making. Literary studies has also focused on reading, on how to interpret and draw on the riches of the most complex and freighted texts produced by our society and to find entry into the rich texts of other societies. Critical analysis and cultural analysis have also focused on reading, to understand the beliefs, subject positions, coercions, identities made available in a cultures texts, to understand how we are inscribed by the texts around us. But all of these approaches leave us in a primarily passive role, as consumers, as shaped by the texts with little role in shaping them. In such a reading-focused approach to understanding literacy, our most active role is to criticize and distance ourselves from texts we question or to read creatively in order to appropriate texts for our own ends—as though the texts we read were created by mysterious others. A world in which we read but don't write is a world in which we do not have primacy agency. To gain direct agency it is necessary to be able to write, to produce the texts that will reach out to others, that will interact with others and influence them, that will mark our interests and perspectives in the literate world. It is by writing that we inscribe our place in the literate world and all the social systems that depend on literacy. This volume takes the perspective of writing, how writing has developed, what role it has taken in the formation of social systems, how schooling has taught and currently teaches writing, how people develop as writers and as people using writing, the particular linguistic resources people use in writing. In taking this writing perspective, this volume also considers what it means to be and to learn to be an active participant in contemporary systems of meaning.

There is a fundamental absurdity in teaching literacy as reading without little writing. It is like asking children to learn language only by listening and never talking. If one only listens, lack of enthusiasm, disengagement, and alienation are likely to ensue. Language becomes a tool for things to be done to you rather than a tool that enables you to do things. One does not learn to listen carefully and may even stop paying attention altogether. Only when formulating one's own statements does one start to see how powerfully language can work for you—to request what you want, to get the attention of others, to say no and to say yes. Only in speaking, in making utterances, does one start attending to the subtleties and possibilities of expression and only then does one's command of language resources grow. Even more, only then does one become engaged in increasingly complex and challenging language situations that elicit more and more advanced language production. And in that engagement one learns to listen more carefully and with more nuanced attention to the words of others, for one needs to answer them, speak to them, use what they model and what they offer substantially, exploit the opening their words create for you.

So how is it then we can separate reading education from writing, and then give writing only small attention? It is a truism that extensive reading expands one's resources for writing, but it is equally essential that as one writes one becomes more deeply engaged in reading, to enter into dialogue with the literate world.

It is interesting that in the United States, the one robust and pervasive pedagogic site for the teaching of writing, as well as research and scholarship on writing, has been in the first-year university course, out of which the field of composition has arisen. The near universality of the first-year college writing requirement contains an implicit recognition that in higher education new levels of writing and expression are demanded. Further limitation in access to higher education by reason of race, class, gender, religion, or other distinctions, has been associated with limitations in access to the advanced literacies associated with the university. Insofar as access has opened up, writing courses and other forms of writing support have been crucial in providing tools for participation for students from historically underrepresented groups. Around the world, as access to higher education has expanded, again writing has been viewed as a necessary skill for participation and success in the undergraduate years and access to the powerful social, professional, and organizational roles typically filled by university graduates and those with more advanced degrees.

This international concern for the support of university student writing in their first languages as well as those languages that mediate global interaction, particularly English, has been accompanied by robust scholarship and research. The desire to expand access to universities in the United States and around the world has also had impact on secondary writing curricula, and the teaching of writing from preschool onward. In primary and secondary literacy research, the study of writing has started expanding, though still small in comparison to the attention to reading. Within different national scholarly traditions, the precise dynamics of writing research as well as traditional forms of writing education have played out somewhat differently, but there is clearly a global renaissance in writing studies at all levels on every continent.

I hope this volume adequately reflects this international research activity with attention to writing at all levels of schooling and in all life situations, despite the inevitable limitations of my own position, coming out of a U.S. higher education focus and now located in a school of education. This volume is an attempt to synthesize what has been learned about writing in all nations in recent decades. Although the recognition of the educational importance of writing motivates a large part of the research reported here, the research goes far beyond the schoolhouse; for to understand what, why, and how we teach writing, in many different circumstances and what, why, and how diverse people learn to write, we need to look far and broad into history, societies, and the worlds constructed by literacy. Schools are important institutions with a very special charge, but to understand their functions, goals, and activities, requires us to inquire broadly. Although to the child school may seem to exist autonomously as a fact of life, schools have developed historically to serve social needs for literacy and thrive in relation to the entire social, economic, civic, and cultural landscape and schools have developed in relation to the character and capacities of the humans who gather within its walls as educators and learners.

Because writing is so multidimensional and so situated within history, society, and human capacities, the research reported here is multidisciplinary, drawing on archaeology, anthropology, technology studies, information sciences, typography, cultural history, intellectual history, religious studies, sociology, political science, law, gender studies, economics, psychology, neurology, medicine, as well as the more anticipatable linguistics, education, and composition studies. The more you look into it, writing is not just an imperative for schooling, it is a core element in human history. Every discipline in the human sciences potentially has something significant to say about writing and might well consider how writing has contributed to those aspects of human life that it studies.

The Advisory Board and the authors of the chapters also reflect this diversity of disciplines as well as international location. We hope the broad representation in this volume will foster even more interdisciplinary, international, and wide-ranging awareness of the many dimensions of writing research, and that future volumes will be able to reach far beyond the attempts here. By providing an overview of the developments in the many fields that contribute to our understanding of writing, I hope this volume will deepen our sense of the multidimensionality of writing and open up new vistas of interdisciplinary research. For though writing is as old as knowledge and as old as history—indeed it is the medium of creation of knowledge and history—still there is much we don't know. Furthermore, because no single discipline is fully committed to studying writing in its full range, many important questions and opportunities fall in interdisciplinary cracks. Appreciation of the interdisciplinarity needed to understand the human capacity for writing may lead to a greater appreciation of the importance of writing. Improved resources for advancing writing education will be only one of the many consequences that would grow from that appreciation.

The broad view of this volume is reflected in its organization. Part I places writing in a historical context, as a technology of inscribing the meanings of spoken language, developed independently in at least three locales in different historical moments and elaborating into a variety of writing systems, typographies, and handwritings. This technology has been facilitated by and incorporates many related technologies to inscribe, to replicate, to store, and to distribute. Each of these histories takes place within social history. Furthermore, as writing has emerged historically it leaves a residue of texts to be examined and reflected upon, leading to a history of thought about writing.

Part II then considers how writing has enabled and become a central element of social systems and practices over that same five millennia. The economy, law, government, documentary bureaucracy, knowledge, journalism, literature, and professions depend on and are structured around the production and distribution of texts. Writing as well interacts with the formation of gender and community and is itself a vehicle of cultural change.

Once writing is seen as part of the infrastructure of society and a medium of participation, then writing education makes a new kind of sense. Schooling is one of those systems that have emerged in society specifically to enable people to participate in all the other literate roles and activities by which society is carried out. Part III then covers what we know about the history of schools and writing, the history of writing teaching and teachers, and current practices of teaching writing at primary, secondary and tertiary levels, along with current understanding of diversity and assessment at all levels.

Individuals develop their writing within the social world available to them, and particularly in their experience of writing in school. Therefore, this considers writing development and the personal impact of writing in the context of the history and Society of schooling. Part IV of this volume, following on the sections on history, society, and schooling, is consequently devoted to issues of the individual and writing: development, cognition, affect, identity, multilinguality, health, disabilities, and disorders.

Finally, Part V explores more deeply what we know about the specific linguistic resources people deploy to carry out their purposes within their situations, social activities, and educations. This section covers what we know of the relation of written language to spoken language, grammar, syntax, larger forms of organization, and the transformations in writing facilitated by electronic tools.

The final chapter on digital writing serves to qualify the whole volume by questioning the limits of our focus on the written word. The computer, with its expanded ease with multiple dimensions of representation, has made more of the visual components of text under the control of the ordinary writer—although page design and the mixing of art with texts have always been present since the earliest days of writing. Now, as well, audio and video files along with databases and other elements can be incorporated into a text. Nonetheless, there is also a history of mathematical notation, music and dance transcription, and other multimedia elements embedded in texts. Though not all these historical and contemporary multimedia components share the direct transcription of language into symbols, they nonetheless share many of the dimensions we have come to associate with writing, including reproduction and distribution over time and space, deliberate composition, and new opportunities for social communication and organization. Since the rise of telegraphy and telephony over a century and a half ago, these capacities have been growing, but computers and the Internet have expanded opportunities for production and distribution for all users. No doubt in future volumes like this multimedia research will take on increasing presence. As the new era of electronic communication unfolds, having a clearer picture of the impact of the role of writing in the world of paper and ink may provide us clues about how to think about what changes, what stays the same, and where we are heading.

I

History of Writing

This first part provides a historical framework through which to understand the impact of writing technology as it spread and ramified throughout society. The formation of writing symbols, discussed in chapter 1, creates a technology of meaning inscription that developed independently in the Fertile Crescent, East Asia, and Mesoamerica. The writing systems, their dissemination, and use were further dependent on technologies of inscription devices and media from stylus and clay to printing press and inexpensive paper and now to computers, word-processing software, and the Internet, as presented in chapter 2.

These inscription, transmission, and reproduction technologies are further associated with histories of inscription design—in the form of handwriting, typography, and now Web design. Though Web design is too new a topic to have much of a history (although the issue is touched on in the final chapter of the volume), typography has a long scholarly history, reviewed in chapter 3. Handwriting also has a fascinating history, which we were unable to arrange to be presented in this volume, but I refer readers to two volumes: *Handwriting in America* (Thornton, 1996) and *Handwriting in the Twentieth Century* (Sassoon, 1999) as starting points.

The technologies of print, typography, and the social arrangements that support the production and dissemination of texts have come together in a new discipline of the history of the book, the work of which is presented in chapter 4.

The materiality of writing, embodied in the residue of marks on pages and clay, the grime of ink and printing presses, the feel of the bound book in the hand, the touch of the keyboard at the fingertips, and the weight of the endless pages on the shelf, has also meant that writing is something people can look upon and think about. Thus, there has also been a history of intellectual technology of reflection on writing, of which this volume is very much part. That history of scholarly reflection on writing is the subject of chapter 5.

REFERENCES

Sassoon, R. (1999). *Handwriting in the twentieth century*. London: Routledge.
Thornton, T. P. (1996). *Handwriting in America*. New Haven, CT: Yale University Press.

CHAPTER 1

Origins and Forms of Writing

Denise Schmandt-Besserat
Michael Erard
University of Texas, Austin

Writing is a system of graphic marks that represent the units of a specific language. The units to be represented (whether individual sounds, syllables, parts of words, or some combination of all three) are a function of the structure of the language, the needs and traditions of the society that uses that system, and the capabilities of the human brain. *Writing* is a general term for a visual system distinct from art, and a mode of language use that is distinguished from speaking, whereas *writing system* refers to a specific type of graphic marks that represent types of linguistic units. Other words for writing systems are *script* and *orthography*. Alphabets (such as the Roman alphabet), syllabaries (such as Cherokee or Ethiopic, which represent consonant + vowel syllables), abjads (such as Arabic, which represent only consonants), and logosyllabaries (such as Chinese, which represent words) are all types of writing systems.

Writing is a unique human achievement, and this chapter sketches some of the history of this achievement. It is distinct from art, as we discuss. We visit the three known origins of writing in Mesopotamia, China, and Mesoamerica to show how writing arose, in what forms, and how it spread. We also provide an overview of how writing systems have been studied in modern times, and we propose some ideas about what the future might hold for writing and writing systems.

ART AND WRITING

Humans created two major systems of visual symbols to express themselves and to communicate with others: art and writing. By visual symbols we mean markings standing for a meaning shared by a community. For example, in Western society, the picture of a dove evokes peace. It is a common assumption that art and writing are related and, in particular, that writing has its origin in pictures. However, both communication systems are fundamentally different, fully independent from each other, and play different roles in society.

Archaeological evidence shows that art preceded writing by some 25,000 years. The first evidence of it comes from France in the Paleolithic Aurignacian period about 30,000 BCE. The appearance of art does not coincide with any major physiological, technological, or economic human development. Therefore, it remains a mystery why image making appeared so relatively late in human cultural development. The first art creations consisted of lines, circular depressions called *cup marks*, incomplete sketches of animals, and a motif interpreted as a female vulva, all pecked with a flint axe on stone boulders (Bahn & Vertut, 1988, 1997; Leroi-Gourhan, 1971). In the Gravettian period, about 23,000 BCE, small three-dimensional sculptures representing obese women become familiar. The same repertory of shapes made with the same technique were repeated in several rock shelters of southwestern France. They attest to the existence of an extended community of Paleolithic humans who communicated meaning via complex visual symbols that were stylized in various ways. A community, dispersed in time and space, communicating with visual symbols: All of these elements underlie the development of writing as well.

What did Paleolithic cup marks mean, and why were they associated with animal designs or vulvae? We will never know for certain. However, most scholars consider them to be representing the elements of a cosmology. The images stood for ideas of utmost significance for the society, such as the creation of the world, the meaning of death, and the principle of reproduction. According to this hypothesis, visual art dealt with the supernatural, the unknown, the feared, or the wanted. It was a powerful instrument of thought to conceive ideas and bring a community to forge a common understanding of the mysteries of life. By the late Upper Paleolithic and the following Mesolithic and Neolithic periods, art had become a worldwide phenomenon: No culture is known that does not foster art.

THE ORIGINS OF WRITING

The available evidence shows that writing arose autochthonously in three places of the world: in Mesopotamia about 3200 BCE, in China about 1250 BCE, and in Mesoamerica around 650 BCE. Devising a system of graphic symbols to represent the sounds of language is, in itself, a remarkable achievement. However, the spread of this system through a society and across a geographical area is also remarkable. After all, communicating with writing is impossible if the recipient of a written message does not know the meaning of the written symbols. Thus, when we refer to the *spread of writing*, we mean not only the dissemination of the concept of representing the sounds of language with graphic symbols or the migration of those symbols, but also the dissemination of the rules and standards of what the graphic signs represent. This was as important at the beginning of writing as it will be in the future. As recently as 2005, archaeology has played an active role in informing theories about the origins of writing, and archaeologists may someday discover evidence that China, Mesopotamia, and Mesoamerica influenced each other, or that other regions or cultures influenced them. Until such evidence is uncovered, it is reasonable to treat these regions separately and the writing systems that arose as unique.

Mesopotamia

The function of writing when it came about in 3200 BCE was exclusively economic. Whereas art dealt with the numinous, each sign of writing stood for a precise unit of a specific commodity—the things of mundane life. After 10,000 BCE, art became an integral part of every culture, whereas writing remained the asset of few civilizations. Moreover, art came without precedent, whereas the signs of writing derived their shape, meaning, format, and economic function from a 4,000-year-old counting system using clay counters called *tokens*. The long evolution from counting to writing can be summarized as follows (Schmandt-Besserat, 1996).

The Token System Antecedent of Writing. The token system coincided with the Neolithic Revolution, when animals and cereals were first domesticated. About 7500 BCE, probably in a Syrian village, farmers modeled counters in clay in various specific and striking shapes that were easy to recognize, remember, and duplicate. Each shape was assigned a meaning: A cone was a small measure of grain, a sphere stood for a large measure of grain,

Figure 1.1. Some of the earliest token types from Tepe Gawra, present-day Iraq. Courtesy Denise Schmandt-Besserat, University of Texas–Austin.

a cylinder for an animal of the herd, and an ovoid for a jar of oil (Fig. 1.1) This invention was simple, but it was a great invention: It was the first visual code—the first system of artifacts created for the sole purpose of communicating information. Art communicated profound, but vague, ideas, but the tokens communicated concrete, discrete information on specific quantities of merchandise such as grain and animals.

The token system was destined to a long life remaining in use for 4,000 years. Art's evolution paralleled technological advances such as the use of copper and bronze tools, whereas the tokens were driven by the needs of an economy of redistribution. When city-states came about, in the 4th millennium BCE, the tokens became a complex system with multiple shapes and multiple markings, incised or punched, to record the products of urban workshops such as wool, textiles, garments, mats, vessels, and tools, imported goods such as metal, or processed foods such as trussed ducks, honey, and bread (Fig. 1.2). There were also new tokens to record goods with greater precision in order to satisfy the more stringent state administration, such as special tokens designating rams, ewes, and lambs (i.e., the sex and age of animals).

The token system shared with art one archaic feature. From the beginning of its use, around 7500 BCE, to the very end, around 3000 BCE, the tokens, like images, represented the number of units of goods in one-to-one correspondence. Six jars of oil were shown with 6 ovoids and 10 jars of oil with 10 ovoids. Keeping records with tokens was cumbersome and bulky.

Two-Dimensional Signs. About 3500 BCE, the temple economy of the Sumerian city of Uruk required keeping tokens in archives—perhaps to keep track of debts until they were settled. The temple administration invented envelopes consisting of small hollow clay balls in which tokens could be held together and be protected from tampering. The envelopes also offered a clay surface on which the temple officials as well as debtors could impress their seals to warrant the terms of the transaction represented by the tokens inside (Fig. 1.3).

About 3500 BCE, the envelopes were perfected to make their content visible. The tokens were impressed on the surface showing how many of what shape were included inside. This invention was a major step toward writing because the three-dimensional tokens were reduced to two-dimensional markings (Fig. 1.4).

Evidence from such cities such as Uruk in Mesopotamia, Susa in Elam, and Habuba Kabira in Syria shows tokens (dating from 3300–3200 BCE) imprinted on a solid clay ball—a tablet (Fig. 1.5). Accordingly, the signs were no longer merely duplicating actual tokens

Figure 1.2.   Complex tokens from Uruk, present-day Iraq, ca. 3300 BCE. Courtesy
Vorderasiatisches Museum, Bodestrasse 1–3, D-1020 Berlin, Germany.

held within. The tablets did altogether away with tokens, and by doing so, the signs
became independent entities. The tablets were far more convenient than envelopes filled
with tokens because they could display permanently one or even several accounts that
could be viewed at a glance.

   The Creation of Numerals.   Signs traced with a stylus, rather than impressed with
actual tokens, appeared at the Mesopotamian city of Uruk about 3100 BCE. These incised
signs had the advantage of accurately illustrating the exact shape of the most intricate
tokens and their particular markings. Incisions led to more than changed shapes, as they
also marked the introduction of numerals (Fig. 1.6). The incised signs were never repeated
in one-to-one correspondence. Numbers of jars of oil were no longer shown by the sign for
jar of oil repeated as many times as the number of units of oil to record. The sign for jar of
oil was preceded by numerals—signs for abstract numbers. Whereas the tokens fused
together inextricably the concept 1 with that of a unit of merchandise, the incised signs
abstracted the concept of *oneness* from that of the item counted.
   The units of grain were used to express such abstract numbers as 1, 2 or 3 (and upwards).
"1" was indicated by the impression of a cone token that formerly was a small measure of

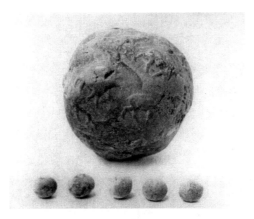

Figure 1.3.   Envelope with six spheres it contained. The animal designs are those of seals authentifying the contents, from Susa, Iran, ca. 3300 BC E. Courtesy Musée du Louvre, Départment des Antiquités Orientales, Paris.

Figure 1.4.   Inscribed Envelope. The 3 long wedges and 3 flat circular markings indicate the three cylinders and three disks held inside, from Suza, Iran, ca 3300 BC E. Courtesy Musée du Louvre, Départment des Antiquités Orientales, Paris.

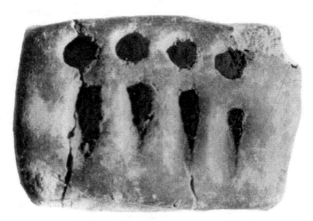

Figure 1.5.   Impressed tablet featuring an account of four large (circular markings) and four small (wedges) meausres of grain, from Godin Tepe, Iran, ca. 3100 BC E. Courtesy Dr. T. Cuyler Young, Royal Ontario Museum, Toronto, Canada.

Figure 1.6.   Pictographic tablet featuring an account of 33 measures of oil,
(circular = 10, wedges = 1) from Godin Tepe, Iran, ca. 3100 BC E.
Courtesy Dr. T. Cuyler Young, Royal Ontario
Museum, Toronto, Canada.

grain, and "10" by a sphere that represented a large measure of grain. It was a great economy of signs: 33 jars of oil were expressed by seven signs (3 × 10 + 3 × 1 + "oil")—instead of 33 (Fig. 1.6). Most important, as a result of the abstraction of numbers, the signs for goods and those for numerals could evolve in separate ways. Writing and counting generated different sign systems.

The Sound of Speech Emulated.   About 3000 BCE, the Sumerian city-state administration required recording the personal name of the individuals who gave or received the goods listed on the tablets. Phonograms—signs standing for sounds—were created. The new signs were simple, incised sketches with no concern for esthetics. They singled out things that were easy to draw that stood for the sound of the word they evoked. The drawing of a man's body stood for the sound "*lu*" and that of the mouth for "*ka*," which were the sounds of the words for *man* and *mouth* in the Sumerian language (Fig. 1.7). The syllables or words composing an individual's name were written like a rebus. For example, the modern name *Lucas* could have been written with the two signs mentioned earlier "lu - ka." The stage of pictography—writing with pictures—when the technique of writing came in its form closest to visual art, was in fact the time when writing became removed from the concrete world of logography to be formally connected with the sounds of speech by the extraordinary invention of phonograms.

The Parting From Accounting.   In 2800 BCE, 400 years after the invention of clay tablets, writing still dealt exclusively with accounting. The texts listed merchandise received or dispensed by a temple administration, stipulated land donations, or compiled signs to be used by accountants for performing their tasks. But a scribe at the court of the kings of Ur, a southern Sumerian city, in about 2700 to 2600 BCE, innovated by using a chisel to inscribe

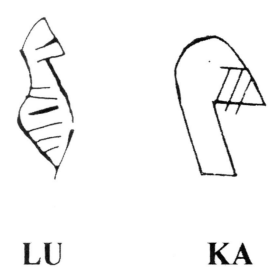

LU   KA

Figure 1.7.   Example of the rebus principle used to record names.

gold, silver, and lapis lazuli objects to be deposited in tombs (Moorey, 1982; Woolley, 1934). The royal scribe of Ur did not list quantities of goods. His inscriptions had nothing to do with accounting. They consisted of a personal name such as *Meskalamdug* wrought on a gold bowl (Fig. 1.8) or a name and a title, "Puabi, Queen," carved on a lapis lazuli seal (Burrows, 1934) (Fig. 1.9).

For the first time, this scribe put writing to work for a function other than accounting. That new purpose was funerary. The Sumerian belief that the name of a deceased individual was to be spoken aloud at regular intervals in order for his or her ghost to exist in the underworld explains the funerary texts (Bayliss, 1973; Jonker, 1995; Niditch, 1996; Scurlock, 1988). Meskalamdug's name, couched in gold, suggests that casting the sounds of a name into writing was held equivalent to a perpetual utterance for the benefit of his ghost. After 5,000 years of accounting, the second function of writing was to guarantee the survival of the dead in the netherworld (Westenholz, 1993). At this point, for the first time, art and writing became complementary. The artifact enshrined the written word.

The Sentences of Speech Emulated.   The concern for survival in the afterlife continued to bring art and writing together. About 2600 or 2500 BCE, a scribe inscribed small statues in the name of deceased individuals. He further added a prayer asking for a long afterlife to the god to whom the statue was dedicated (George, 1999). The inscription gave speech to the worshipper figure who addressed the gods in writing using sentences with subjects, verbs, and complements, bringing writing to model itself onto speech by adopting the syntax of spoken language. It was the powerful combination of sculpture and writing that was the true take-off of writing. About 2500 BCE, a Sumerian king was able to describe his victories in a lengthy text (Cooper, 1983). By 2000 BCE, writing was used for historical, religious, legal, scholarly, and literary texts, including poetry.

The Spread of Writing.   Mesopotamia and its nearest neighbors Syria and Elam, in present-day Western Iran, are unique in presenting the evidence for the synchronic stages of tokens, envelopes, and tablets (Schmandt-Besserat, 1992). But the cognitive steps that

MESKALAMDUG

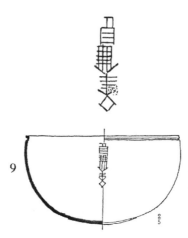

Figure 1.8.   Graphic design: Meskalamdug—inscription on gold bowl (U 10002) from the tomb of Meskalamdug (PG 755) Royal Cemetery of Ur, ca. 2700 BC E. This bowl was found in the hands of the skeleton. From C. L. Woolley, *Ur Excavations, Vol. II: The Royal Cemetery*, Oxford University Press, London, 1934, Plate 232: 9.

PUABI, QUEEN

Figure 1.9.   Name carved on Queen Puabi's seal (U10939) recovered in Royal Tomb 800 of the Royal Cemetery of Ur. From C. L. Woolley, *Ur Excavations, Vol. II: The Royal Cemetery*, Oxford University Press, London, 1934, Plate 191.

led from logography to numerals and phonograms occurred only once in Mesopotamia. The Mesopotamian writing system constitutes the prototype of the other Bronze Age writing systems of the Old World. When the Proto-Elamites created their own script, they borrowed simultaneously the concept of abstract numbers and phonetic signs from Mesopotamia (Hoyrup, 1994). Egypt, where the use of tokens in prehistory is not clearly attested, produced a full-blown writing system based on the rebus principle visibly imitating Mesopotamia. Carbon 14 dating disproves the claims for Egyptian primacy (Boehmer, Dreyer, & Kromer, 1993). About 2500 BCE, the Indus Valley Civilization devised a script that had no links with the Mesopotamian-like tokens recovered in pre-Harappan sites (Possehl, 1996). Crete probably adopted first the idea of tokens and then that of writing. This is suggested by the fact that Minoan clay counters in the shape of miniature vessels seem unrelated to the Linear A or B scripts used in the Aegean between 2200 and 1300 BCE (Poursat, 1994). The Mesopotamian tokens and writing loomed large over the process of civilization in the Old World.

The Cuneiform Script.   The Mesopotamian script reached its classical period about 2200 to 2000 BCE when scribes used a reed stylus with a triangular end that produced cuneiform's distinctive wedge patterns. Though always remaining partly logographic (one sign = one concept), the script represented ever-more syllables, not individual sounds, making the script a syllabary (Walker, 1987). This first writing system played a vast role in the diffusion of writing: In the course of the third to first millennia BCE, it was adapted to languages of various families such as Akkadian and Eblaite (Semitic); Elamite (perhaps Dravidian); Hittite and Old Persian (Indo European); and Hurrian and Urartian (whose identification as Caucasian is disputed). The cuneiform script lost ground when Aramaic, written with a flowing hand on papyrus or parchment, became prevalent in the Near East. Cuneiform writing lingered in Mesopotamia until the Christian era.

The Alphabet.   The alphabet was invented only once—which means that all the present alphabets, from Latin, Arabic, Greek, Cyrillic, Hebrew, Ethiopian, and Tamil to Navaho derive from the same first alphabet. The invention of the alphabet took place in the Near East, probably in present-day Lebanon, about 1700 BCE (Healey, 1990). Neither syllabic nor logographic, it owed nothing to the cuneiform; rather, it was a totally new system based on the identification of the distinctive sounds of a language and matching each with a specific sign. The first alphabet consisted of 22 letters, each standing for a phoneme—a single speech sound. The success of the alphabet was to streamline script. Compared to the some 600 cuneiform signs, the 22 letters were easy to learn allowing literacy to spread more widely. The letters of this first alphabet, however, only represented consonants.

The Phoenician cities that thrived on the coast of present-day Syria and Lebanon between 1000 and 300 BCE played an important role in the diffusion of the alphabet across the Mediterranean Sea, and in particular to Greece. (Markoe, 2000; Whitt, 1995). Perhaps as early as 800 BCE, the Greeks adapted the Semitic alphabet to their Indo-European language by adding letters for vowels. This resulted in a 27-letter alphabet that made it easier to transcribe the spoken word and even easier to read, because all the sounds were indicated (Cook 1987). In turn, the Etruscans, who occupied the province of Tuscany in present-day Italy, starting in the eighth century BCE adopted the Greek alphabet by slightly modifying the shape of the letters (Bonfante, 1990). When Etruria was conquered by Rome in the first century BCE, the Etruscan alphabet became that of the Romans. The diffusion of the Latin alphabet followed the conquests of the Roman armies through Europe (Reynolds, 1991).

Chinese

Among these three origins of writing, Chinese is the only one that has an unbroken record of use in the last three millennia leading up to the modern time. The earliest evidence of

Chinese characters dates to 1250 BCE. About 4,500 symbols have been identified on shards of turtle shell and cow bone, used in divination practices. Questions to an oracle were written on the shell or bone, which were then heated in the fire; the resulting cracks were read, and the answers given were also inscribed in the bone. About 1,500 of these 4,500 symbols have survived as modern Chinese characters. The oldest examples of oracle bone writing have been found in north central China in the Shang region. There is no evidence that the Shang were solely responsible for developing writing in China, but there is also no evidence of Chinese writing at any other place at an earlier time (Keightley, 1978, 1989).

From the beginning, Chinese was written vertically, the columns read right to left. (Modern conventions have also added horizontal, left-to-right reading.) Early Chinese writing had several variants. The "great seal" script, *ta chuan*, was used in 1200 to 800 BCE on bronze vessels and carved on character seals, and was also used in all other writing. Other seal scripts were the most diverse of formal writing. From 403 to 221 BCE, a number of independent states developed their own script styles, but from 221 to 206 BCE the Qin dynasty established a standard script called *hsiao chuan*, or "lesser seal script." This gave way to *li shu*, the "clerkly script," a straighter style that was easier to write, developed by the staff of the imperial democracy and used from 206 BCE to 220 CE. Around the second century CE, a third formal style, the standard script (or *kai shu*), was developed (Boltz, 1994).

Until the early 20th century, all dialects of Chinese were written in a literary dialect that dated to the late Old Chinese period, about 1100 BCE to 100 CE. This meant that literate Chinese wrote in a way they themselves did not speak. This form persisted, in part, because of the Chinese civil service's power in creating and maintaining the written standard for some 2,000 years. However, in the early 20th century, a reform movement in China adapted modern spoken Chinese as the basis for written Chinese. Now writing is done in Modern Standard Chinese, a dialect close to the Mandarin spoken in Beijing.

The most remarkable feature of Chinese writing is the size of its character set. Since around 100 CE, when the scholar Xu Shen created a dictionary of 9,353 characters, the number of characters has steadily increased to about 60,000. Most of these characters, however, are archaic words, variant characters, or proper names. For the modern Chinese writer and reader of Chinese, 1,000 characters account for 90% of all occurrences in texts, and 2,400 characters cover 99% of occurrences. In other words, only a slight fraction of the total number of characters is required to be fully literate in contemporary Chinese societies (Boltz, 1994).

In the West, a myth about Chinese writing has persisted. Because Chinese characters are written with elaborate series of pen strokes, and because Chinese calligraphy is done with brushes and ink, the characters have been considered small pictures that represent ideas. This is not the case, and numerous books have been devoted to dispelling this myth (DeFrancis, 1984). Most characters do represent speech sounds; 90% of the characters consist of a graphic element that indicates pronunciation, combined with another element that marks meaning.

Mesoamerica

In Mesoamerica—what is now southern Mexico and the countries of Central America—as many as 13 different writing systems had been developed by 900 CE by various civilizations (Lounsbury, 1989). The most visible of these is the Maya writing system, because it was written on stone on upright monuments know as *stelae*, and because major advances in Maya decipherment have been made in the last 20 years (Coe, 1999). Maya was written during the height of the civilization, from 250 to 900 CE through to the 16th century, when Christopher Columbus first encountered the Maya.

Maya characters are known as *glyphs*, about 800 of which are known to exist. Each glyph organizes several smaller elements known as graphemes and contains a main grapheme with one or more diacritics. The diacritics can appear to the left, right, top, or bottom of the main symbol. The glyphs represent morphemes (or basic units of words), syllables (consonant + vowel sequences), as well as semantic and phonological determinatives. Because there was no set standard for glyph construction, writers could present the same word in many different ways, often in the same texts, and writers took pleasure in creating these variants. Glyphs were always written in paired vertical stacks and read top to bottom, left to right, in a zig-zag fashion. The sequences of graphemes in a glyph are read, more or less, from the upper left corner to the lower right.

The Maya carved glyphs on stone stelae and painted them on ceramics and bark paper books called codices; archaeological and deciphering work is done with the stelae and other stone carvings as well as the codices. If writing in Mesopotamia is associated with economic functions, then in Mesoamerica writing is associated with calendrical calculations and the actions of kingly dynasties. Hundreds of codices existed and were used by the Maya; many were destroyed by the Europeans as pagan works; others hidden or lost by the Maya decomposed. (Since the 19th century the extant codices have been copied and photographed; though they are known by the European cities where they reside—the Dresden Codex, the Madrid Codex, the Paris Codex, and the Grolier Codex—they are now distributed worldwide via the Web.)

Despite its prominence, Maya writing was not the oldest Mesoamerican writing, and archaeologists have attempted to establish its lineage more precisely. Some markings that may be precursors date as early as 1100 BCE. The earliest writings that are recognizably antecedent to later scripts date to around 650 BCE in the states of Tabasco and Oaxaca, Mexico. In 2002, archaeologists M. Pohl, K. Pope, and C. von Nagy announced the discovery of a roller stamp and plaques with glyphs, which were found near the Olmec site of La Venta in Tabasco (Pohl, Pope, & Von Nagy, 2002; Stokstad, 2002). The discovery bolstered the theory that the Olmec had influenced other civilizations and cultures. From 400 BCE to 200 CE, three related writing systems were used in Mesoamerica. The Isthmian script (the descendent of the Olmec script and a logosyllabic script like the later Maya script) was used from the Mexican Gulf Coast through the Isthmus of Tehuantepec; the Oaxacan script was used in the Valley of Oaxaca; and the Maya script was used in an area that extended from the Yucatan peninsula to the foothills of the Guatemalan Highlands.

When Europeans arrived in Mexico, they outlawed the use of native writing systems. Indigenous Mesoamerican people have revived the use of glyphs in contemporary times as a symbol of their heritage.

Writing as Culture

The contemporary interest in the structure of writing systems is generally agreed to begin with I. J. Gelb, a philologist at the University of Chicago, whose 1952 book, *The Study of Writing*, was the first to categorize various writing systems in terms of their history and structure. Though many of his statements about writing's relationship to language have been corrected, his book sparked exploration into writing systems. Gelb even coined a name for this field: *grammatology*. (The word is perhaps better known among humanists as the title of a book by the French philosopher, Jacques Derrida—*Of Grammatology*.)

However, scholars' interest in the relationship between orality and literacy traditions began with Milman Perry in the 1920s (Jahandarie, 1999). Perry was a Harvard classicist who first showed that the texts of the ancient Greek poet Homer were primarily oral compositions. This closed a debate (ongoing at the time) about Homer's indentity and whether "Homer" was a single author or several. (Parry argued that Homer was a single, real person who assembled his unique epics from a number of essential themes and variations that had been passed down as part of an oral tradition.) Other early investigators, such as Eric Havelock (1976), sought to uncover how literacy shaped Greek society, and the impact of the alphabet on the organization of ideas, abstract, thought, and consciousness.

In the 1960s, Marshall McLuhan, a Canadian media critic, became a popular thinker on the effects of mass media and media technologies, such as television, which led him to consider how cultures that relied on aural/oral information differed from visual cultures (Mc Luhan 1962, 1964, Moos 1997, Gordon 2003). Many of McLuhan's colleagues and followers extended these ideas to thinking about the properties of cultures that did not have books or writing. Walter Ong argued that writing is a technology that restructures consciousness of individuals who use it and refocuses the energies of societies that utilize it (Ong 1982). Anthropologist Jack Goody, characterizing writing as a "technology of the intellect," tackled the oral-literate divide to show how writing influences religion, the economy, law, and commerce (Goody 1977, 1987). David Olson argues that writing, not speech, determine our ability to reflect on ourselves (Olson and Torrance 1991, Olson 1994).

For most of the 20th century, linguists did not pay much attention to forms of written language, arguing that their task was to study language as it was spoken. In the 1970s, they found renewed interest in writing systems as evidence for abstract units of language and for insight into otherwise unobservable linguistic processes. The fact that many writing systems are alphabetic (because they represent individual sounds) suggests that individual sound segments called phonemes are fundamental to human language production. However, the fact that some writing systems encode syllables suggests that syllabic units are also fundamental. Anthropological linguists have been attentive to writing, beginning in the late 19th century, due to work describing languages indigenous to the Americas and recording narratives, oral poetry, and other verbal performance. Later they theorized how transcribing spoken utterances, conversations, and oral performances altered the interpretations of spoken discourse (Bauman & Sherzer, 1974).

Late in the 20th century, the academic attention to writing systems matured. This interest led to the publication of encyclopedic works on writing systems. These were novel because they collected language, writing, and cultural experts and combined these with state-of-the-art advances in computer printing that allowed all the characters in numerous writing systems to be printed. These works included *The Blackwell Encyclopedia of Writing Systems* (1999), edited by Florian Coulmas. Because of increased interest in teaching writing systems, several textbooks have also been published, such as *Writing Systems: An Introduction to Their Linguistic Analysis* (2002) by Florian Coulmas, and *Writing Systems: A Linguistic Approach* (2005) by Henry Rogers.

Decipherment

European scholars and explorers were deciphering ancient texts written in ancient, often no longer used, writing systems long before Milman Perry and I. J. Gelb's work. Three decipherments in particular captivated European imaginations, opening up aspects of unknown civilizations: the decipherment of Egyptian hieroglyphics, of cuneiform, and of Linear B.

In the early 19th century, a number of decipherment projects were launched, the most famous of which is the translation of the trilingual text (hieroglyphic, Coptic, and Greek) of the Rosetta stone by Jean Francois Champollion. The French scholar recognized that the hieroglyphic script was fundamentally phonetic. Using the obelisk of Philae, he noted that the names of Ptolemaios and Cleopatra had four letters in common—PT—and that these letters were shown in the expected order. Other names expanded the number of characters deciphered: Alexander, Philip, Arsinoe, Berenice, Caesar, and Claudius. Starting his work in 1808, Champollion by 1822 had drawn the connection between ancient Egyptian and Coptic, identified the difference between phonograms and logograms, compiled an impressive dictionary of ancient Egyptian, and established the first elements of a grammar (Chassagnard, 2001).

Cuneiform was first encountered by Europeans in the early 17th century CE, when travelers heard of a writing system made out of narrow, nail-shaped characters. (The word *cuneiform* comes from the Latin word *cuneus*, for "wedge.") Several scholars contributed to the decipherment of the cuneiform script. Among them, Henry Creswicke Rawlinson stands out as the heroic individual who between 1835 and 1844 made paper squeezes of parts of the trilingual (Old Persian, Akkadian, and Elamite) proclamation of Darius the Great inscribed on the rock of Behistun in Western Iran. This was daring because the inscriptions were carved on a steep cliff more than 300 feet above the ground, and could only be reached either from a flimsy scaffold or dangling down from on a rope. The column of 112 lines Rawlinson copied allowed him to recognize that the Akkadian cuneiform script was polyphonic; that is, each sign could stand for several sounds (Kramer, 1963). In 1851, his publication correctly identified Akkadian, the language spoken in Babylonia, as a Semitic language and established the first rudiments of its grammar (Walker, 1987).

One long-standing decipherment problem was the script called Linear B, which came from the Aegean island Knossos and from mainland Greece at the site of Pylos. It was finally deciphered in 1953 by Michael Ventris and John Chadwick (Chadwick, 1958). The script they discovered is the oldest surviving record of a Greek dialect called Mycenaean and was used between 1500 and 1200 BCE on Crete and southern Greece. A counterpart script, called Linear A, remains undeciphered.

The excitement for decipherment among Europeans was motivated by biblical scholarship and fueled by European colonial expansion into Asia and the Middle East. As the European powers moved through northern Africa, Persia, and Mesopotamia, they encountered ancient cities, archaeological sites, and other enduring monuments of civilizations that predated the ancient Greeks. Scholars' access to artifacts in European museums and libraries aided their work. Not all decipherment is finished, however. Presently, John S. Justeson is engaged in the study of the stele of La Mojjara, Mexico, making headway toward the understanding of the Epi-Olmec Hieroglyphic writing (Justeson & Kaufman, 1993). Some writing systems have never been successfully figured out because the language they represent are unknown. Among them are the Indus Valley Script, proto-Elamite, Proto-Elamite, Linear A, Meroïtic, and Rongo Rongo. Other artifacts, such as the Phaistos Disk, bear inscriptions that may or may not be writing. In the case of Rongo Rongo, a writing system on Easter Island, it is the only example of the writing system ever found.

The Spread of Writing

In 1986, the anthropologist of science Bruno Latour proposed a materialist explanation for the impact of writing on a society. In contrast to the distinctively mentalist or cognitivist arguments of Marshall McLuhan (1962, 1964), Walter Ong (1982), Jack Goody (1977, 1987a, 1987b), David Olson (1994), and others, Latour limits his arguments to how representational devices (drawings, charts, graphs, photos, and diagrams) allow scientists to make increasingly stronger arguments about the phenomena they study (Latour, 1986, 1990). Thus, representations succeed because they enable their users to do more. Without erasing the historical details, and without subsuming diverse places into the same developmental sequence, Latour's explanation extends to Maya astronomers, Chinese oracles, and Mesopotamian merchants. Writing systems may spread through the influence of religion, military and political conquest, or economic ties, but it persists for reasons that have to do with its utility for human work and its adaptability across spheres. One might use Latour to explain that many writing systems evolve toward the alphabetic, not because the alphabetic is inherently better but because it has social advantages over the representation of ideas, words, or syllables: It may be easier to learn, more easily adapted to other languages, and more efficiently ordered.

The Future of Writing

The history of writing has marked the interplay between linguistics, socioeconomics, and the forces of technological change, an interplay that will shape the future of writing. This future may not involve creating new symbols or diffusing new ways to write down languages. However, the evolution of technology, particularly the advent of the World Wide Web, more advanced data-processing technologies, and cheap, accessible personal computers have created technical challenges.

For instance, one challenge facing writers of Chinese was inputting the large number of characters with a standard keyboard. This problem, which has existed since the advent of publishing and of the typewriter, led to several systems for writing Chinese phonetically. One system, called *Pinyin*, is used in Mainland China; another system, called *bopomofo*, is used in Taiwan. Both (which were originally developed for students to learn characters more easily) have been employed in various inputting schemes using computers, for which no standard exists. Faster computer processors and cheaper computer memory has helped widen the impact of the inputting bottleneck on writing Chinese on computers.

Another challenge that faced computer users around the world was ensuring that different computing platforms, operating systems, and software programs could swap, share, and process text data, regardless of the writing system of the text. Computers do not store, send, or process letters or characters; rather, they process strings of numbers that are encoded by software and displayed on computer screens as the appropriate letters, numerals, punctuation marks, and other symbols. As an example, when computer A sends a string of numbers to computer B, both computers must share the same formula for turning those numerical strings into the appropriate visual symbols. The development of a universal standard for text encoding with computers would therefore be an important development for the future of writing (Erard, 2003).

The earliest computers could encode only limited character sets, such as Roman and Cyrillic. As personal computers spread globally, and as the computer industry began looking for global markets, it became clear that many people in the world would purchase and use computers only if they could write their native scripts on them. In the late 1980s, computer scientists from IBM, Xerox-Parc, Apple, and other computer companies began working on a solution: a universal standard for text encoding that would be installed as part of the basic architecture of all hardware and software. This standard, now known as Unicode, contains encodings for 96,000 characters and 55 writing systems, from Chinese to Thai to Mongolian to Gothic. Approximately 70,000 of Unicode's encodings are for Chinese characters. However, about 100 writing systems, most of them used by small groups or of ancient or academic interest, remain to be encoded. These include Egyptian hieroglypic, cuneiform, Balinese, Javanese, and Tifinagh (or Berber). A group at the University of California–Berkeley, called the Universal Scripts Initiative, is working on standardizing character sets for these minority writing systems in order to make them a part of the Unicode standard as soon as possible (Erard, 2003). This will ensure that Unicode is universal and allows as many people as possible to participate in the digital age.

The future of writing will also be determined by communications technologies. The rise of e-mail, chat rooms, and bulletin boards, as well as the widespread use of text messaging on cell phones, has created new symbols in Europe, North America, and Asia. In e-mail text, users invented "emoticons," graphic symbols that inventively combined punctuation marks to add emotional or intonational context to a writer's text (such as ":-)" to denote a positive or happy remark). Users of chat rooms and text messaging on cell phones have also developed abbreviations, phonetic spellings (as in English, using "lol" for "laugh out loud," "2" for "to," and "U" for "you"), and logograms that allow them to compress messages. In Japan and China, manufacturers of cell phones have created limited symbol sets built in to phones. In one system, the message "please call me" is displayed with an icon of a telephone, followed by *kure*, which is an abbreviated word for making a request. "Would you like to go out for a drink tonight" is displayed as a picture of a mug or cup, followed by a verb ending that is typically used for extending invitations (French, 2000). These types of unique symbols will continue to evolve, particularly with communication formats and devices that are strongly identified with youth cultures.

Another future development is that more of the world's languages will be written down. According to *Ethnologue* (Grimes and Grimes, 2005), a catalog of the world's languages, there are 6,912 languages spoken in the world as of 2004. Most of these are not written down because no writing systems have been developed or adapted for them yet. Because the writing system most often adapted for them is the Roman alphabet, the future favors the Roman alphabet. Not only is technology available in the Roman alphabet, most of the language workers, many of them missionaries, who are assigning writing systems to language use the Roman alphabet. Widely used in the world already, the Roman alphabet is written by more people in the world than any other.

REFERENCES

Bahn, P., & Vertut, J. (1988). *Images of the Ice Age*. New York: Facts on File.

Bahn, P., & Vertut, J. (1997). *Journey through the Ice Age*. Berkeley: University of California Press.

Bayliss, M. (1973). The cult of the dead kin in Assyria and Babylonia. *Iraq, 35*, 115–125.

Bauman, R., & Sherzer, J. (Eds.). (1974). *Explorations in the ethnography of speaking*. London: Cambridge University Press.

Boehmer, R., Dreyer, G., & Kromer, B. (1993). Eine fruezeitliche 14C—Datierungen aus Abydos and Uruk *Mitteilungen des Deutschen Archaeologisches Instituts Abteilung Kairo, 49*, 63–68.

Boltz, W. G. (1994) *The origin and early development of the Chinese writing system*. New Haven, CT: American Oriental Society.

Bonfante, L. (1990) *Etruscan*. Berkeley: University of California Press.

Burrows, E. (1934). Inscribed material. In C. L. Woolley (Ed.), *Ur excavations: Vol. II. The royal cemetery* (Vol. 1, pp. 311–322). London: Oxford University Press.

Chadwick, J. (1958). *The decipherment of Linear B*. New York: Random House.

Chassagnard, G. (2001). *Les Freres Champollion, de Figeac aux Hieroglyphes*. Paris: Segnat Editions.

Coe, M. (1999). *Breaking the Maya code*. New York: Thames & Hudson.

Cook, B. F. (1987). *Greek inscriptions*. Berkeley: University of California Press.

Cooper, J. S. (1983). Reconstructing history from ancient inscriptions: The Lagash–Umma border conflict. *Sources From the Ancient Near East, 2*(1), 44–48.

Coulmas, F. (Ed.). (1999). *The Blackwell Encyclopedia of Writing Systems*, Oxford, England: Oxford University Press.

Coulmas, F. (2003). *Writing Systems: An Introduction to their Linguistic Analysis*. Cambridge, England: Cambridge University Press.

DeFrancis, J. (1984). *The Chinese language: Fact and fantasy*. Honolulu: University of Hawaii Press.

Derrida, J. (1976). *Of grammatology*. Baltimore: Johns Hopkins University Press.

Erard, M. (2003, September 25). For the world's A B C's, he makes 1's and 0's." *The New York Times*, p. 000.

French, H. (2000, June 8). In e-mail wrinkle, cell phones are chatterboxes. *The New York Times*, p. 000.

Gelb, I. J. (1952). *A study of writing*. Chicago: University of Chicago Press.

George, A. (1999). *The epic of Gilgamesh*. London: Penguin.

Goody, J. (1977). *The domestication of the savage mind*. Cambridge, England: Cambridge University Press.

Goody, J. (1987). *The interface between the written and the oral*. Cambridge, England: Cambridge University Press.

Goody, J. (1987). *The logic of writing and the organization of society*. Cambridge, England: Cambridge University Press.

Gordon, W. T. (Ed.). (2003). *Marshall McLuhan: Understanding media—the extensions of man*. Corte Madera, CA: Gingko.

Grimes, B., & Grimes, J. (Eds.). (2005). *Ethnologue*. Dallas, TX: Summer Institute of Linguistics.

Havelock, E. A. (1976). *Origins of Western literacy* (Monograph series 14). Toronto: Ontario Institute for Studies in Education.

Healey, J. (1990). *The early alphabet*. Berkeley: University of California Press.

Hoyrup, J. (1994). *Measure, number and weight*. Albany: State University of New York Press.

Jahandarie, K. (1999). *Spoken and written discourse: A multi-disciplinary perspective*. Stamford, CT: Ablex.

Jonker, G. (1995). *The topography of remembrance*. Leiden, Netherlands: E. J. Brill.

Justeson, J. S., & Kaufman, T. (1993). A decipherment of Epi-Olmec hieroglyphic writing. *Science, 259*, 1703–1711.

Keightley, D. N. (1978). *Sources of Shang history: The oracle-bone inscriptions of Bronze Age Chin*. Berkeley: University of California Press.

Keightley, D. N. (1989). The origins of writing in China: Scripts and cultural contexts. In W. Senner (Ed.), *The origins of writing* (pp. 171–202). Lincoln: University of Nebraska Press.

Kramer, S. (1963). *The Sumerians*. Chicago: University of Chicago Press.

Latour, B. (1986). "Visualization and Cognition: Thinking with Eyes and Hands," Knowledge and Society: Studies in the Sociology of Culture Past and Present, 6, 1–40.

Latour, B. (1990). Drawing things together. In M. Lynch & S. Woolgar (Eds.), *Representation in scientific practice* (pp. 19–68). Cambridge, MA: MIT Press.

Leroi-Gourhan, A. (1971). *Prehistoire de l'art occidental* Paris: Editions Lucien Mazenod.

Lounsbury, F. (1989). The ancient writing of middle America. In W. Senner (Ed.), *The origins of writing* (pp. 203–237). Lincoln: University of Nebraska Press.

Markoe, G. E. (2000). *Phoenicians*. Berkeley: University of California Press.

McLuhan, M. (1962). *The Gutenberg galaxy*. Toronto: A Mentor Book, University of Toronto.

McLuhan, M. (1964). *Understanding media*. New York: Mentor Book, New American Library.

Moorey, P. R. S. (1982). *Ur "of the Chaldees": A revised and updated version of Sir Leonard Wooley's "Excavations at Ur."* Ithaca, NY: Cornell University Press.

Moos, M. E. (Ed.). (1997). *Marshall McLuhan essays: Media research*. Amsterdam: Overseas Publishers Association.

Niditch, S. (1996). *Oral world and written word*. Louisville, KY: Westminster John Knox Press.

Olson, D. R. (1994). *The world on paper*. Cambridge, England: Cambridge University Press.

Olson, D. R., & Torrance, N. (1991). *Literacy and orality*. Cambridge, England: Cambridge University Press.

Ong, W. J. (1982). *Orality and literacy*. New York: Methuen.

Pohl, M., Pope, K., & Nagy, C. (2002). Olmec origins of Mesoamerican writing. *Science, 298*(5600), 1984–1988.

Possehl, G. (1996). *Indus age: The writing system*. Philadelphia: University of Pennsylvania Press.

Poursat, J.-C. (1994). Les systemes primitifs de comptabilite en Crete minoenne In P. Ferioli, E. Fiandra, G. G. Fissore, & M. Frangipane (Eds.), *Archives before writing* (pp. 247–252). Rome: Ministero per i beni Cultirali e Ambientali Ufficio Centrale per i beni Archivisti.

Reynolds, J. (1991). *Latin inscriptions*. Berkeley: University of California Press.

Rogers, H. (2005). *Writing systems: A linguistic approach*. Malden, MA: Blackwell.

Schmandt-Besserat, D. (1992). *Before writing*. Austin: University of Texas Press.

Schmandt-Besserat, D. (1996). *How writing came about*. Austin: University of Texas Press.

Scurlock, J. A. (1988). *Magical means of dealing with ghosts in ancient Mesopotamia*. Unpublished doctoral dissertation, University of Chicago.

Stokstad, E. (2002). Oldest New World writing suggests Olmec innovation. *Science, 298*(5600). Retrieved December 12, 2004, from Academic Search Premier.

Walker, C. B. F (1987). *Cuneiform*. Berkeley: University of California Press.

Westenholz, J. G. (1993). Writing for posterity: Naram-Sin and Enmerkar. In A. F. Rainey (Ed.), *Kinattutu sha darati: Raphael Kutscher memorial volume* (p. 216). Tel Aviv: The Institute of Archeology of Tel Aviv University, 1993, 205–218.

Whitt, W. D. (1995). The story of the Semitic alphabet. In J. Sasson (Ed.), *Civilizations of the ancient Near East* (Vol. 4, pp. 2379–2397). New York: Scribner's.

Woolley, C. L. (Ed.). (1934). *Ur excavations: Vol. II. The royal cemetery* (Vol. 1). London: Oxford University Press.

CHAPTER 2

History of Writing Technologies

Brian Gabrial
Concordia University, Montreal, Canada

Despite Socrates' caution that writing gave the "appearance of wisdom instead of wisdom itself" (Plato, 1988, para. 275), humans have always desired means and media to preserve and reproduce expressions of their culture and history (H. Martin, 1988). History shows that different cultures developed technologies to create these means (hardware) and media (software) to accommodate their socioeconomic needs and to extend knowledge (Fang, 1997), or, as David Sholle (2002) puts it about technologies, they "do not simply fulfill a function in meeting natural needs, but rather their develop-ment is caught up in the social construction of needs" (p. 7). The history of writing tech-nologies reveals a past, containing stories of competition and secrecy, of stability and portability, of resistance and acceptance, and of refinement and use. Although scientific observation often initiated changes in writing technologies, others appeared, as it so often happens, by sheer luck. Furthermore, some changes evolved slowly whereas others appeared rapidly. The writing stylus, for example, has kept a basic form for cen-turies, and the printing press changed little in appearance from Guttenberg's original 15th-century design until the early 19th century. As electricity's use and the development of electronics arrived, changes in technologies—in both form and function—accelerated. This chapter briefly explores significant developments in writing technologies that enabled humans to record the important, as well as the mundane, facts about their lives, and it places those developments into three somewhat permeable categories: manual, mechanical, and electrical/electronic technologies.

MANUAL TECHNOLOGIES

Long before Socrates' warning about writing, ancient civilizations were creating permanent records on stone and clay. Likely, the first writing hardware was a human finger dipped in plant juice or animal blood (Lambrou, 1989) and the first writing software a bone, a shell, or tree bark (Coulmas, 1996). Certainly, early hunter societies used animal hides for clothing, shel-ter, and writing. Still, no one knows with complete certainty who ingeniously realized some 5,000 to 8,000 years ago in Mesopotamia, China, or Egypt (H. Martin, 1988) that permanent records could be etched, stamped, or painted onto available materials. Many of these first tran-scriptions were likely a simple record-keeping shorthand useful for business transactions (D. Baron, 1999). In ancient Mesopotamia's fertile crescent of the Tigris and Euphrates Rivers, the abundance of clay and the development of a refined stylus with a wedge-shaped tip that made make fairly uniform triangular impressions led to cuneiform's development (Lambrou, 1989; Fang, 1997). These crude technologies were significant advances because they provided the first means and medium of creating and maintaining a standardized communication system that preserved and spread meaningful examples of Mesopotamian culture (H. Martin, 1988), such as the epic story of the Babylonian King Gilgamesh, a story that ancient scribes preserved on clay about 4,000 years ago (Gilgamesh, 1996/1999).

In ancient Egypt, artisans working along the Nile River serendipitously found a new medium both lighter and certainly more portable than clay. Although lacking clay's durability, papyrus, fashioned from certain river reeds, split, and hammered together, proved relatively easy to manufacture. Its popularity turned Egypt into a papyrus mill for other civilizations, such as the Greeks and the Romans, who could easily scroll and transport important documents (Coulmas, 1996). Unfortunately, papyrus's lack of durability means today that few scrolls survived into the modern era (Fang, 1997). This significant disadvantage, combined with Egypt's production monopoly, likely encouraged the literate cultures of Greece and Rome to make greater use of an already available and lasting medium made from sheepskins. Like papyrus, parchment could be produced relatively cheaply, scrolled easily, and transported from points of origin; but unlike papyrus, parchment did not crumble with age and could be reused. Parchment's obvious technological advantages led to the medium's increased use, which eclipsed that of papyrus, and led to parchment becoming the preferred writing medium of both the ancient and the medieval worlds (Coulmas, 1996). Because both sides of a parchment page could be used, the development of the modern book became possible. For example, the early Christian Gospels were fashioned as a Roman codex, a book prototype that used cut parchment sheets bound between wooden covers (Fang, 1997; Petroski, 1990). By the second century BCE, the Greeks and Romans were using parchment or vellum, a similar material made from calfskin.

Although parchment and papyrus certainly suited the needs of their cultures, their significance as writing media would never surpass that of paper, whose origins began in ancient China. There writers had already experimented with diverse media such as bones and bamboo, silk and ivory, and developed permanent inks made from soot, lamp oil, musk, and the gelatin of donkey skin or from berries or other plants (Bellis, 1997/2006; Carter, 1955/1995). However, in 105 CE, Ts'ai Lun, a high-ranking eunuch in the Han imperial court, wisely recorded for the first time that plant and animal fibers, such as mulberry or bamboo, could be separated to produce the new writing medium—paper (Carter, 1955/1995; "The Amazing History of Paper," 2001). Because paper was thin, portable, and durable, it became popular among Chinese elites who wanted its manufacturing process kept secret (Coulmas, 1996; Fang, 1997; Weaver, 1937). For centuries, then, this new technology remained in China until finally spreading to Korea and Japan by the seventh century and a century later to Arab traders, who introduced the medium to Europeans (Carter, 1955/1995). Evidence in the form of old manuscripts on paperlike, cotton-based material indicates that Europeans were using the medium as early as 1050 (Carter, 1955/1995; Martin, 2003). As for paper's inventor, Ts'ai Lun, he later killed himself after becoming involved with imperial court intrigues.

Paper, papyrus, and parchment were not the only writing media used to keep records. Elsewhere another portable and cheap, but different medium barely survived the European conquest of South America. The Incan civilization developed khipu (or quipu), which used strings tied into sequences of knots to maintain records. For many years, archaeologists have assumed these strings and knots could be a method of business record keeping, and recent scholarship now suggests khipu could be a binary system of communication strings, similar to a computer language, that, if decoded completely, might unlock the secrets of Inca civilization before the Spanish arrived (Urton, 2003; Wilford, 2003). Because no "Rosetta stone" exists to decode the surviving pieces of this complex of knots and strings, they remain mysterious mementos of Spanish conquest of the New World. Elsewhere in the Americas, other pre-Columbian records stored on the inner bark of certain trees did not survive the Spanish conquest. One 16th-century missionary wrote of finding some early "literature" of the Yucatan peoples: "We found a great number of books written with their characters, and because they contained nothing but superstitions and falsehoods about the devil, we burned them all" (Fang, 1997, p. 7).

Just as writing media (software) evolved, so, too, did their hardware. Greek and Roman writers had already modified the stylus from a device used to make triangular cuneiform impressions to one that could hold ink for writing on papyrus or parchment. Initially, reeds made suitable writing implements because they could be trimmed to make broad or fine lines with simple inks from native plants or soot, but reed brushes wore out quickly. Because of this, scribes turned to other materials such as animal horns and bones, and, even among Pompeii's ruins metal pens have been found. At some point, someone discovered that a bird feather held ink, and, this led to the quill's fashionable use around 500 CE and its eventual dominance as the stylus of choice for more than a thousand years. Like reeds, quills have natural limitations and need constant replacement (Fang, 1989; Lambrou, 1997). By the 18th century, artisans, using the quill's design, made metal ink pens available. Although quills, pens, and ink were portable, writers needed to be vigilant to prevent messy ink spills. In 1883, inventor Lewis Edson Waterman solved this problem when, after several tries with various inks, he devised the first practical fountain pen in 1883 (Lambrou, 1997). An American, J. J. Loud, invented a version of a ballpoint pen in 1888, but it could only make marks on rough surfaces (see Albus, Kras, & Woodham, 2000). Fifty-five years later, the Hungarian journalist Laslo Josef Biro, experimenting with heavier printer's ink, small ball bearings, and the fountain pen concept, patented the first ballpoint pen, and Biro's name would become synonymous for the ballpoint pen (Albus et al., 2000). Marcel Bich, a French ink maker, improved on Biro's design and founded the company that bears his name, *sans* h. Bich introduced the Bic pen in 1950 and its ubiquitous see-through, crystal version in 1958 (see http://www.Bicworld.com).

Another stylus innovation appeared about the same time as metal-tipped pens became popular in Europe and America. The modern wooden pencil, as pencil historian Henry Petroski (1990) puts it, is a "dream invention" because it "needed no liquid ink," was "relatively clean and smudge-proof," and was "erasable" (pp. 30–36). The word comes from Latin's *pencillum,* a thin paintbrush the Romans thought early pencils resembled. Early pencils were crude and potentially lethal devices that used lead not encased in wood and exposed writers to lead poisoning or *plumbism,* as it was called. By the 18th century, pencil makers developed a more prudent pencil-making recipe that combined safer graphite with clay, which was cooked and extruded into pieces cut and glued into wooden frames. In the 19th century, the best graphite or *plumbago* originated in Borrowdale, England, and, in America, Henry David Thoreau, a man better known for his stay at Walden Pond, became a master pencil maker himself (Baron, 1999). Like the first, ancient Chinese paper makers and the modern computer software developers, 19th-century pencil manufacturers kept their plumbago recipes secret. Not all pencil advancements, however, won unanimous approval. For example, some early 20th-century schoolteachers warned that erasers attached to pencils would encourage students to forget how to prepare their lessons properly.

Certainly, writing technology's improvements led to greater needs for information storage and distribution. As to distribution, the Chinese created a postal system by the 10th century BCE (Martin, 2003) and sent official news throughout the dynastic empire. The Romans had a postal service by the fourth century CE (Fang, 1997) and posted "news by decree" in official diurnals, which busy slave scribes copied for subscribers (Martin, 1988). These scribes, who produced manuscripts quickly and relatively cheaply, became the essential hardware of a flourishing slave scribe-to-buyer publishing industry that began with the Greeks in the fifth century BCE and ended a thousand years later when Rome fell (Mumby, 1930). During the Middle Ages, religious monks sitting in their scriptoriums produced lasting, beautiful works of calligraphic art and replaced the slave scribe as the major producers of written text (Kubler, 1927). As Europe entered the Renaissance, these scriptoriums became vestiges of the past (Hobson, 1970). As for storage, nearly all ancient civilizations built libraries to house written works (Fang, 1997; Khurshodov, 2001; Jacob, 2002). The Greek Ptolomies built the Great Library at Alexandria in the third century BCE that contained possibly 40,000 volumes (Fang, 1997; Hobson, 1970). Some dispute exists about who eventually destroyed the library in the fifth century CE, but it may have been the Bishop of Alexandria's order to destroy pagan temples that led to the library's eventual destruction. Centuries later, a forgetful medieval book borrower might face excommunication for failing to return an overdue monastery manuscript (Mumby, 1930).

The Chinese, who had already bested Europeans in the development of ink, paper, and postal systems, also advanced a printing technology called xylography, which eventually made *mass* communication possible. Xylography's importance cannot be understated because it *was* the "invention of printing" (Carter, 1955/1995), but pinpointing an exact date for its origin may be impossible because, as historian Thomas Francis Carter notes, its evolution "was so gradual as to be almost imperceptible" (p. 41). Another historian, Joseph Needham (1965a), asserts xylography or block printing started around 880 CE, adding that China's massive imperial "civil examination system" spurred the technique's use. Officials likely understood that the process, which transferred whole pictures and ideographic text from a carved block onto a permanent surface (Coulmas, 1996), might strengthen the central government's control by easily re-creating government-approved texts for distribution (Needham, 1965b). The oldest surviving printed book, however, is a ninth-century CE religious text called the *The Diamond Sutra* that presents Buddha's discourses on the "subject of non-existence of all things" (Carter, 1955/1995, p. 56; see also Fang, 1997; Kubler, 1927). Eventually spreading to Europe by the 12th century CE, xylography's use is evident on 15th-century Venetian playing cards (Martin, 2003).

MECHANICAL TECHNOLOGIES

Although manual writing technologies, notably the pencil, pen, and paper, remain in common use, they do not mass-produce information efficiently. Mechanical printing technologies made that possible. Of those mechanical technologies, the printing press and a system of moveable type, an idea the Chinese first developed but made little use of (Carter, 1955/1995; Gernet, 1996), transformed the literate world in the West. Johannes Gutenberg's letter press was a simple machine that resembled in form the basic wine-making press. Though history is murky about whether the German goldsmith knew much about China's block printing, Gutenberg deserves credit for revolutionizing printing technology by fashioning individual, reusable letters and setting them into a wooden frame, thus enabling any printer to duplicate a printed page as many times as desired (Fang, 1997). His system of moveable type also made infinitely more sense in Europe, whose printed languages, based on the Roman alphabet, required relatively few characters, versus in China, which, in Gernet's (1996) words, was "a world [in] one whose riches was precisely the wealth and diversity of the signs used for writing" (p. 335). Gutenberg also developed a suitable printer's ink, a combination of linseed oil and soot, which adhered cleanly to a surface and made printing possible on both sides of a page (Kubler, 1927). From about 1450 to 1455, Gutenberg and six workers completed 100 Bibles with 42 lines per page, each requiring an estimated 300 sheepskins to produce (Fang, 1997). Of the first Gutenberg Bibles, 30 were on parchment; the others were printed on paper. Like past innovators, Gutenberg desired secrecy but could not keep the knowledge of his letterpress and moveable-type system from reaching most of Europe by century's end, including England, where the printer William Caxton set up a printing press in 1476 (Mumby, 1930).

Books, especially the Bible and other sacred writings—now mass-produced in the common language or vernacular—prompted great social change in Western Europe and helped break the Roman Catholic Church's monopoly on the interpretation of important Christian texts (Curran, 2002; Eisenstein, 1983). Despite the Roman Catholic Church's reactionary efforts against what it viewed as heresies, such as the execution of printers like William Tyndale, who produced the first English Bible in 1526, the Church could not prevent the Reformation from spreading throughout Europe (Fang, 1997; Mumby, 1930). Letterpress printing technology created as well two powerful groups, the printers and stationers and greatly expanded the literate class (Curran, 2002; Lebvre & Martin, 1984). The printed book replaced the manuscripts once done by monks and created a need for such innovations as the modern title page and improved book-binding techniques (Mumby, 1930).

However, centuries passed before the first truly significant change in printing technology occurred. *Stereotyping*—a term coined in the late 18th century—eliminated lead type's constant shortage by creating an impression of a type-set page for use and reuse (Fang, 1997). In 1803, the Earl of Stanhope received one of the first patents for this process (Kubler, 1927). Other changes, such as Friedrich Koenig's steam press that printed on both sides of a sheet of paper and Richard Hoe's faster, rotary cylinder press, ushered in a new age of mass-produced, printed text. These and later press technologies, such as lithography and offset lithography, which transferred a picture of the printed page onto a metal plate, gradually replaced the labor-intensive letterpress and relegated it to arcane and artisan endeavors (Fang, 1997).

By a rare coincidence, Gutenberg's printing press appeared almost concurrently with a greater availability of paper, which was a result of a short-lived surplus of cloth rags created by the Black Death that had ravaged Europe's population. Still, printing only increased a demand for paper, and technology needed to keep pace. In the early 18th century, the French naturalist and physicist Rene de Reaumur made an important observation about certain wasps' nests, which he noted were made from a pasty woodlike substance resembling paper. Printing's reliance on expensive, handmade paper from cloth rags or parchment would come to an end when, finally, decades later, a German cleric working with Reaumur's ideas created paper from wood pulp, a cheap and abundant paper source (Hunter, 1930). In late 18th-century France, Nicholas Robert built a machine that mass-produced paper in a continuous sheet cut to appropriate lengths, and across the Channel, England's Fourdrinier brothers financed refinement of Robert's machine that now bears their name and not Robert's.

Although the typewriter ushered in portable mechanical printing technology during the 19th century, the machine's conceptualization originated decades earlier when Henry Mill received a queen's patent for "an artificial machine or method for impressing or transcribing of letters singly or progressively one after another" in 1714 (Adler, 1973, pp. 47–48; Bliven, 1954). In subsequent decades, inventors tinkered with other "proto" type-writing machines variously called the machine *tachygraphique*, *universal compositor*, and *mechanical typographer* (Lundmark, 2002). Some resembled small pianos, and most were considered mechanical ways to help the blind "read" printed pages. Although many of these early typewriters passed into history, the "Sholes and Glidden Type Writer" made history. Christopher Latham Sholes and his partners, working for the Remington gun company, developed an upstrike machine that sold for $125 (Gitelman, 1999; Lundmark, 2002). Sholes gave the machine its name and chose its easily memorized but inefficient QWERTY keyboard layout, which prevented too-quick typists from jamming the keys by forcing typists to press with weaker fingers the most frequently used letters. Because the machine's other design flaw prevented the typist from seeing the page while typing, the Sholes typewriter lost the marketing edge to its major competitor, Underwood's "frontstrike" machine. This machine solved the "typing blind" problem in 1894, and typing "visibility" became a selling point with the public and with business. As the typewriter's commercial use increased, many women found they could find work outside the home. About this Sholes is to have said, "I do feel I have done something for women who have always had to work so hard. This will enable them to more easily earn a living" (Fang, 1997, p. 59; Thurschwell, 2001). The machine also changed composition, as media technology scholar Lisa Gitelman argued, by separating the author from the text during its creation. Pamela Thurschwell similarly observes that intimacy is mediated through "teletechnologies" like the typewriter and the telegraph. Mark Twain, one first notable author-typist, typed a note to his brother on his Remington that said it "piles an awful stack of words on one page" (reprinted in Current, 1954, p. 72). To his publisher, Twain submitted the first typewritten manuscript, *Life on the Mississippi* (Lundmark, 2002). Although some technologies like the typewriter increased office jobs, others like the mimeograph machine eliminated them. The first mimeograph machine made in 1884 by Chicago inventor Albert B. Dick, quickly duplicated office documents while eliminating the need for office copyists or scriveners who had heretofore replicated them ("Antique Copying Machines," 2006).

In his book *Power of the Written Word*, Alfred Burns (1989) called the years from 1815 to 1914 the "Golden Age" of the printed word. Clearly, new printing and paper-making technologies created a new information age by making the printed word cheaper and more available to a mass 19th-century audience. As a result, the publishing industry's growth exploded along with a demand for popular literature and newspapers, especially the penny press (Fang, 1997). The penny press era, which began with Benjamin Day's New York *Sun* in 1833 and James Gordon Bennett's *New York Herald* in 1835, created a news media for the masses. The rise of the penny newspapers, which stressed scandal and human interest stories over those of commercial or partisan natures (Fang, 1997), led to the creation of the modern newsroom that separated printers from editors. New mass-communication technologies were determining newspaper content as well, leading to what press historian Donald Brazeal (2003) called the *perishability of news*.

American and European postal systems also improved to keep pace with burgeoning amounts of newspapers, business, and personal correspondence for delivery. In America, the Continental Congress created the future U.S. postal system by decreeing "that a line of posts be appointed under the direction of the Postmaster General from Falmouth in New England to Savannah in Georgia, with as many cross posts as he [sic] shall think fit" ("The Postal Service Begins, 1999–2006). In 1860, demand for fast delivery of news and correspondence from east to west led to the creation of the Pony Express (Fang, 1997), which the transcontinental railroad and telegraph abruptly turned into a romantic 19th-century artifact. In England, sending correspondence became simpler and more reliable as the country refined its postal system in the 1800s (N. Baron, 2000). In 1874, an international agreement reached in Berne, Switzerland, created the Universal Postal Union, which settled differences among nations regarding postal rates. Although not a writing technology *per se*, the simple postage stamp would symbolize America's success in quickly distributing communication. As the Industrial Age propelled the world through the 19th century, which historian Henri-Jean Martin (1988) called the "century of the communication revolution" (p.480), it ushered in the electrical and electronic age in mass-communication technology.

ELECTRICAL AND ELECTRONIC TECHNOLOGIES

In some respects, the history of electrical and electronic writing technologies is a story of technology catching up to science. The ancient Greeks and the scientists of the Enlightenment, for example, experimented with and were fascinated by electromagnetism ("A Ridiculously Brief History," 1999). Yet the idea that energy could be harnessed for communication did not happen until 1843 when Charles Wheatstone and William Cooke built the first electrical telegraph line, which paralleled England's Great Western Railroad (Fang, 1997). The telegraph made communication *instant* over long distances and turned electricity into a common carrier of communication (H. Martin, 1988). A method to standardize these electrical impulses into a universally accepted communication system developed in America when Samuel B. Morse perfected his codes of dots and dashes. Morse, after observing printers at work and noting their efficient arrangement of letters, realized that the most commonly used letters should become the most easily memorized codes (Winston, 1998). With U.S. government funding, Morse established the first U.S. telegraph line from Baltimore to Washington, DC, and sent along that wire his famous "What hath God wrought?" message to assistant Alfred Vail on May 24, 1844. Later that year, Morse warned Vail of the telegraph's misuse and cautioned Vail to "be especially careful not to give a partisan character to any information you may transmit" ("Samuel F. B. Morse Preview," 1997). Morse code eventually pushed all rival systems into the footnotes of communication history. By the 19th century's end, Guglielmo Marconi's successful experiments on England's Salisbury Plains proved that wireless, electrical communication was also possible (Fang, 1997).

Other electrical writing technologies emerged in the 19th and 20th centuries and found their way into the modern business office. One of Morse's chief competitors, Alexander Bain, patented in 1843 the first facsimile machine that re-created images with electric impulses on specially treated paper (Bellis, 2006; Fang, 1997; Meadow, 1998), and the great American inventor Thomas Edison patented the first electric typewriter by the end of the 1800s (Adler, 1973). Later, a combination of photoconductivity and human ingenuity resulted in the first photocopier. In Astoria, New York, Chester Carlson, a shy soft-spoken patent attorney, along with his assistant experimented with India ink, a lightbulb, and wax paper to develop a feasible process that Carlson called *xerography*, which in Greek meant dry writing. Carlson, whose first photocopy read "10-22-38 ASTORIA," signifying the date and place of his success, finally sold the idea to the Haloid Company of Rochester, New York, a company that became better known as the Xerox Corporation. It sold the first office-friendly photocopier, the Xerox 914, in 1959 (Fang, 1997; "Making Copies," 2004; Xerox, 1999–2006). For many office workers, *to Xerox* is an infinitive defined as the act of making a photocopy of a printed page. The same principles underlying Carlson's early photocopier are the same as those applied later to modern facsimile machines and laser printers.

As a piece of writing technology, the computer's use was more evolutionary than revolutionary. During the Renaissance, Leonardo Da Vinci envisioned a computer, and, in the 17th century, the French mathematician Blaise Pascal created an eight-digit mechanical calculator (McCartney, 1999). By the Industrial Age, the first practical computers were mechanical contraptions made for business and government use (Freiberger & Swaine, 2000). In the late 1700s, the Frenchman Joseph-Marie Jacquard designed a machine that used punch cards to repeat intricate woven patterns. Because the machine also eliminated many mill worker jobs, some incensed workers destroyed these Jacquard's looms and, thus, became participants in the anti-industrialization, antitechnology movement known as the Luddites. In 1833, Charles Babbage adapted a similar punch card method for his "Analytical Engine" and, by the century's end, Herman Hollerith built a punch card machine to tabulate the 1890 U.S. census in the remarkable span of 6 weeks (Fang, 1997; "The Jacquard Loom," 2001–2003; McCartney, 1999).

Scientists working at the University of Pennsylvania built the first truly electronic computer, the ENIAC—short for electronic numerical integrator and computer—to compute ballistic firing tables that required relatively simple decimal-based mathematical operations (Meadow, 1998; Winston, 1998). The massive device weighed some 30 tons, took up an entire room with its nearly 19,000 vacuum tubes, and required a cool, constant stream of air to keep from overheating. ENIAC and other early, similar computers were not digital and needed full-time staffs to rewire hardware to enable the machines to handle new functions (McCartney, 1999; Stern, 1981). In 1938, William Hewitt and David Packard built a computer that used binary code in a Palo Alto, California, garage ("The Digital Century," 1999).

Further computer refinements such as random access memory in 1957 (Khurshodov, 2001) and solid-state transistor technology made computers smaller and faster. The integrated circuit and the microchip further increased speed and reduced size. Beginning in the 1940s, improvements in magnetic storage meant computers could maintain larger amounts of data, and, by the 1970s, hard disk drives resembling washing machines became common in data-processing departments managing payroll and other business functions. From the start, the news media recognized the computer's potential, and, for example, CBS News used a UNIVAC computer to predict an Eisenhower presidential victory in 1952 (Fang, 1997). However, the view that computers could also be word processors required a perceptual shift about them and their use (Ernst, Oettinger, Branscomb, Rubin, & Wikler, 1993).

In 1964, International Business Machines (IBM), which defined *word processing* as "electronic ways of handling a standard set of office activities—composing, revising, printing, and filing written documents," took the lead in word processing's development. In the early 1960s, the company perfected its iconic Selectric typewriter with its unique golf ball-size typing element and stationary carriage. By 1964, IBM introduced a system called Magnetic Tape/Selectric Typewriter (MS/ST) that used reusable magnetic tape (Kunde, 1986–2001). The introductions of the floppy disk in 1972 (Ernst et al., 1993) and IBM's personal computer (PC) for home and office use in 1981 made the marriage of computers to word processing feasible and desirable. (Although Apple Computer had been selling personal computers by the late 1970s, it notably did not have IBM's marketing or financial clout.) In a rare move, IBM also contracted with Intel and Microsoft companies to manufacture PC computer microchips and disk operating software (Freiberger & Swaine, 2000), thus allowing other PC manufacturers to flourish. As a result, IBM and its clones dominated the personal computer market.

The explosion of PC clones in the 1980s created natural demands for word-processing software. One of the first, the "Electric Pencil" (Freiberger & Swaine, 2000), and early versions of Word, WordPerfect, and AppleWriter II were hardly user-friendly. One popular program, WordStar, was described as "difficult to learn" but "easy to use once the commands and the control keys become familiar" (Langman, 1998, appendix). As the word-processing market expanded, programs improved so that updated versions replaced the earlier ones with their strange codes and keystrokes (Baron, 2000). Today, word processors commonly present electronic pages to the typist just as they appear in printed and even published forms. Such innovations turned word processing into a primary computer use, and the advent of easy-to-use desktop-publishing software programs, such as the Adobe Company's PageMaker, enable anyone to produce printing house-quality documents.

True paperless, electronic communication began in the late 1960s with the simultaneous developments of the Internet and the U.S. Department of Defense's Advanced Research Project Agency's system of transferring packets of information (ARPAnet) (Sholle, 2002). By the 1980s, the early Internet was a sophisticated communication medium that used hypertext protocols to transfer whole electronic text pages to computer screens (Swiss, 2004). With electronic communication came electronic-mail delivery. Ray Tomlinson, a computer engineer working on ARPAnet's crude electronic-mail system, chose the "@" symbol to denote a Web address and sent the first e-mail message, that read, "QWERTYUIOP" (Bellis, 2006). Improvements such as the development of Hypertext Markup Language (HTML) enabled computers to share electronic documents regardless of the software application used to create them (Sellen & Harper, 2002). By the 1990s, anyone with Web design software could invite global visitors to an Internet Website, containing vast, perhaps unlimited amounts of electronically created digital material. In McLuhanesque fashion, the Internet has created new digital global villages where, according to Paul Levinson (1999), "centers are everywhere and margins are nowhere" (p. 7). Ironically, increasing electronic and digital communication has not decreased paper's use, as Abigail Sellen and Richard Harper argue in *The Myth of the Paperless Office*. Instead, they propose that the electronic age has simply switched communication's distribution from *printing-then-distribution* to electronic *distribution-then-printing*. Although the "hegemony of paper" may not be at an end, as Sellen and Harper (2002. p 5) note, the "new technologies will *shift* the role of paper rather than *replace* it" (p. 194; italics original).

The Internet as a communication technology could not have developed without previous writing and computer technologies (Sholle, 2002) and has become a hugely responsive and popular "means of communication" in the 21st century (Meadow, 1998). Advances in digital and electronic communication technologies have created a boom in knowledge-based industries, including libraries, news, and publishing, where some publications are now distributed strictly online, providing authors with new venues for their work. In newsrooms throughout the world, journalists and their editors are converging media as they update their online newspaper and broadcast editions. Even more remarkable, Michael A. Keller, the head librarian at Stanford University, has predicted the following: "Within two decades, most of the world's knowledge will be digitized and available, one hopes for free reading on the Internet, just as there is free reading in libraries today" (cited in Markoff &

Wyatt, 2004,p. A1). Powerful Internet search engines like GOOGLE enable anyone to obtain what had once been available in only printed text or to specialists. As for the mails, almost all documents once restricted to the mails (or fax) can be sent instantly in original form via e-mail attachment. Therefore, a combination of increasing computer speed, expanded memory capacity, durable and portable storage media like CD-ROMs, DVDs, the Internet (Khurshodov, 2001; Meadow, 1998) have permanently changed the nature of writing and communication. The inevitable results of such dramatic changes are still unknown.

CONCLUSION

Just as centuries ago when "new" media such as reeds and papyrus communicated human knowledge and culture, so, too, do today's "new" media of electronic bits and bytes. Furthermore, these new media do not necessarily replace old media if a need for that old media remains. It is important to understand, as Sholle (2002) notes, that "there is no clear moment at which a technology is something radically new, nor is there a definite point where a new technology eradicates previous technologies"(p. 9). Although it may happen that printed material will become what Meadow (1998) calls "technological artifacts" (p. 41), it is equally likely that readers will never completely forego printed words for electronic ones (e.g., Sellen & Harper, 2002; Swiss, 2004). Just as some observers have noted the printing press' standardizing effect on language, others have warned that electronic technologies will do the opposite. Truss (2004), the author of a popular English punctuation book, wrote: "Electronic media are intrinsically ephemeral, are open to perpetual revision, and work quite strenuously against any sort of historical perception" (p. 181). Despite her observation, it seems that no writing medium or technology has ever guaranteed permanence. The beginning of this chapter began with Socrates' warning that printing gave the "appearance of wisdom instead of wisdom itself." Although the philosopher's words are preserved on a printed page, another printed page in another book puts Socrates' warning this way: "It is no true wisdom that you offer your disciples, but only its semblance" (Plato, 1952, para. 275). Although an awkward concluding point, the comparison suggests that words merely put onto a printed page (or any other medium) hardly guarantee their immutability. As such, the effects that writing technologies—in fact all technologies—have on humans and human communication will continue as an important debate among scholars and practitioners for the present and the future.

REFERENCES

Adler, M. (1973). *The writing machine*. London: Allen & Unwin.

Albus, V., Kras, R., & Woodham, J. M.(Eds). (2000). *Icons of design! The 20th century*. Munich, Germany: Prestel.

The amazing history of paper. (2001). Retrieved Nov. 05, 2006, from http://www.tappi.org/paperu/all_about_paper/paperHistory.htm

Antique copying machines. (2006). Retrieved Nov. 5, 2006, from http://www.officemuseum.com/copy_machines.htm

Baron, D (1999). From pencils to pixels: the stages of literary technologies. In G. E. Hawisher & C. L. Selfe (Eds.), *Passions, pedagogies, and 21 technologies* (pp. 15–33). Logan: Utah State University Press.

Baron, N. (2000). *Alphabet to email: How written English evolved and where it's heading*. London: Routledge.

Bellis, M. (1997–2006). A brief history of writing instruments. Retrieved Nov. 17, 2004, from http://inventors.about.com/library/weekly/aa100197.htm

Bellis, M. (2006). History of the fax machine and Alexander Bain. Retrieved Nov. 5, 2006, from http://inventors.about.com/odbstartinventors/a/fax_machine.htm

Bellis, M. (2006). The history of the Internet. Retrieved Nov. 05, 2006, from http://inventors.about.com/library/inventors/blinternet.htm

Bliven, B., Jr. (1954). *The wonderful writing machine*. New York: Random House.

Brazeal, D. K. (2003, October). *The perishable newspapers.* Paper presented at the Symposium on the 19th Century Press, the Civil War, and Free Expression. Chattanooga, TN.

Burns, A. (1989). *The power of the written word: The role of literacy in the history of Western civilzation.* New York: Peter Lang.

Carter, T. (1995). *The invention of printing in China* (2nd ed., rev. by L. C. Goodrich). New York: Ronald. (Original work published 1955)

Coulmas, F. (1996). *The Blackwell encyclopedia of writing systems.* Oxford, England: Blackwell.

Curran, J. (2002). *Media and power.* London: Routledge Current, R. N. (1954). *The typewriter and the men who made it.* Urbana: University of Illinois Press.

The digital century: Computing through the ages. (1999). Retrieved Nov. 05, 2006, from http:// www.cnn.com/TECH/computing/9911/24/digital.century5.idg/

Eisenstein, E. L. (1983). *The printing revolution in early modern Europe.* Cambridge, England: Cambridge University Press

Ernst, M. L., Oettinger, A. G., Branscomb, A. W., Rubin, J. S, & Wikler, J. (1993). *Mastering the changing information world.* Norwood, NJ: Ablex.

Fang, I. (1997). *A history of mass communication: Six information revolutions.* Boston: Focal.

Freiberger, P., & Swaine, M. (2000). *Fire in the valley: The making of the personal computer* (2nd ed.). New York: McGraw-Hill.

Gernet, J. (1996). *A history of Chinese civilization* (2nd ed., J. R. Foster & C. Hartman, Trans.). Cambridge, England: Cambridge University Press.

Gilgamesh. (1996/1999). Retrieved Nov. 05, 1996, from http://www.wsu.edu/~dee/MESO/GILG.htm

Gitelman, L. (1999). *Scripts, grooves, and writing machines: Representing technology in the Edison era.* Stanford, CA: Stanford University Press.

Hobson, A. (1970). *Great libraries.* London: Weldenfeld & Nicolson.

Hunter, D. (1930). *Paper through eighteen centuries.* New York: Rudge.

Jacob, C. (2002). Gathering memories: Thoughts on the history of libraries. *Diogenes, 49*(4), 41–57.

The Jacquard loom. (2001–2003). Retrieved Nov. 05, 2000, from http://www.columbia.edu/acis/history/jacquard.html

Khurshodov, A. (2001). *The essential guide to computer data storage from floppy to DVD.* Upper Saddle River, NJ: Prentice-Hall.

Kubler, G. A. (1927). *A short history of stereotyping.* New York: Certified Dry Mat Corporation.

Kunde, B. (1986–2001). A brief history of word processing (through 1986). Retrieved Nov. 05, 2006, from http://www.stanford.edu/~bkunde/fb-press/articles/wdprhist.html

Lambrou, A. (1989). *Fountain pens: Vintage and modern.* New York: Sothebys.

Langman. L. (1986). *An illustrated dictionary of word processing.* Phoenix, AZ: Oryx Press.

Lebvre, L., & Martin, H. (1984). *The coming of the book: The impact of printing, 1450–1800* (D. Gerard, Trans.). London: Verso.

Levinson, P. (1999). *Digital McLuhan: A guide too the information millennium.* London: Routledge.

Lundmark, T. (2002). *Quirky Qwerty: The story of the keyboard @ your fingertips.* Sydney, Australia: University of New South Wales.

Making copies. (2004). Retrieved Nov. 05, 2006, from http://www.smithsonianmag.com/smithsonian/issues04/aug04/copies.html

Markoff, J., & Wyatt, E. (2004, December 14). Google is adding major libraries to its database. *The New York Times,* p. A1.

Martin, H. (1988). *The history and power of writing.* Chicago: University of Chicago Press.

Martin, S. (2003). Newspaper history traditions. In S. Martin & D. A. Copeland (Eds.), *The function of newspapers in society: A global perspective* (pp. 1–11). Westport, CT: Praeger.

McCartney, S. (1999). *ENIAC: The triumph and tragedies of the world's first computer.* New York: Walker & Company.

Meadow, C. (1998). *Ink into bits: A web of converging media.* Lanham, MD: Scarecrow Press.

Mumby, F. A. (1930). *Publishing and bookselling: A history from the earliest times to the present day.* London: Jonathan Cape.

Needham, J. (1965a). *Science and civilization in China* (Vol. 1). Cambridge, England: Cambridge University Press.

Needham, J. (1965b). *Science and civilization in China* (Vol. 6). Cambridge, England: Cambridge University Press.

Petroski, H. (1990). *The pencil: A history of design and circumstance.* New York: Knopf.

Plato (1952). *Phaedrus* (R. Hackforth, Trans.). Indianapolis, IN: Bobbs-Merrill.

Plato. (1988). *Phaedrus* (2nd [corrected] ed., C. J. Rowe, Trans.). Warminister, England: Aris & Rowe. The postal service begins. (1999–2006). Retrieved Nov. 05, 2006, from http://www.usps.com/postalhistory/postal_service_begins.htm

A ridiculously brief history of electricity and magnetism. (1999). Retrieved Nov. 05, 2006, from http://maxwell.byu.edu/~spencerr/phys442/node4.html

Samuel F. B. Morse preview. (1997). Retrieved Nov. 05, 2006, from http://memory.loc.gov/ammem/atthtml/morse4.html

Sellen, A., & Harper, R. H. R (2002). *The myth of the paperless office*. Cambridge, MA: MIT Press.

Sholle, D. (2002). Disorganizing the "new technology." In G. Elmer (Ed.), *Critical perspectives on the Internet* (pp. 2–26). Lanham, MD: Rowman & Littlefield.

Sosnoski, J. (1999). Hyper-readers and their reading engines. In G. E. Hawisher & C. L. Selfe

(Eds.), *Passions, pedagogies, and 21st century technologies* (pp. 161–177). Logan: Utah State University Press.

Stern, N. (1981). *From ENIAC to UNIVAC: An appraisal of the Eckert–Mauchly computers*. Bedford, MA: Digital Press.

Swiss, T. (2004). Electronic literature: Discourses, communities, traditions. In L. Rabinovitz & A. Geil (Eds.), *Memory bytes: History, technology, and digital culture* (pp. 283–304). Durham, NC: Duke University Press.

Thurschwell, P. (2001). *Literature, technology and magical thinking 1880–1920*. Cambridge, England: Cambridge University Press.

Truss, L. (2004). *Eats, shoots and leaves: The zero tolerance approach to punctuation*. New York: Gotham Books.

Urton, G. (2003). *Signs of the Inka Khipu*. Austin: University of Texas Press.

Weaver, A. (1937). *Paper, wasps and packages: The romantic story of paper and its influence on the course of history*. Chicago: Container Corporation of America.

Wilford, J. N. (2003, August 12). String and knot theory of Inca writing. i*The New York Times*, p. D1.

Winston, B. (1998). *Media Technology and society: A history from the telegraph to the Internet*. London: Routledge.

Xerox. (1999–2006). Retrieved Nov. 05, 2006, from http://www.xerox.com

CHAPTER 3

History of Typography

David Jury
Colchester Institute, Essex, United Kingdom

PRE-1500: THE INVENTION OF PRINTING AND ITS EARLY DEVELOPMENT

Early Printing: Pre-Gutenberg

The need for an exact and incontrovertible statement that can be *repeated* while maintaining the originator's intention is a basic requirement of any civilized, rule-governed society. Printing—entirely interwoven with typography since the mid-1400s—has provided this essential service.

Between 1452 and 1455, Johann Gutenberg, in Mainz, Germany, printed the first book with moveable type in Europe: a Bible, involving the use of paper or vellum, a thick, sticky ink, a wooden press, and, of course, moveable type made of metal. None of these elements were in themselves new inventions, but it appears Gutenberg first brought them together for the purpose of multiple printing of texts in Europe. Even moveable type—individual letters that can be arranged, edited, printed from, and dismantled to be reused to print again in an entirely different arrangement—often regarded as the revolutionary aspect of Gutenberg's invention, had, in fact, been developed in China four centuries earlier for much the same purpose. Although there were transcontinental trade routes during the 13th century (the Venetian Marco Polo returned from his first journey to China in 1295), there is no evidence to suggest that Gutenberg was ever aware of Chinese printing methods.

In fact, the earliest known moveable type was not used to print multiple copies, but simply to emphatically record a statement by making a set of impressions into soft clay that was then baked to make the information permanent and unalterable. Ancient Crete's Phaistos Disk, circa 1600 BC is, perhaps, the earliest example (see Fig. 3.1). Measuring 16 cm across, an ideal size for the palm of a hand, it was found in 1908 at the palace of Phaistos on Crete's southern coast. It contains 45 discrete signs that have been impressed, on both sides of the disk, starting at the bottom and reading right to left and spiraling inward. The idea of using separate punches for each syllable was possibly inspired by similar devices used to make individual, personalized wax seals.

By the 11th century, the use of moveable type for the purpose of printing had been established in China and later in Korea. The 11th-century essayist Shěn Kuò describes the process of printing from moveable type in some detail, giving the name of the first master of the process as Bì Shēng. Such type was made of ceramic or wood or cast in bronze. But this activity was never a practical proposition in the Far East because approximately 4,000 different characters—or ideographs—are required to adequately form a text. In comparison, the Latin alphabet requires, in essence, just 52 letters (capitals and texturals or upper and lowercase), 10 numerals, and a small assortment of punctuation marks.

Figure 3.1.   The Phaistos disc, a terracotta tablet displaying a continuous linear text that spirals inward to its center (Crete, circa 1600 BCE).

The other key aspect of Gutenberg's invention, the transfer of an image from one surface to another using ink or similar substance, was first achieved, and indeed perfected, in Japan around the year AD 770. However, there is no evidence that this involved the use of a press. The sheet of paper was probably laid directly onto the brush-inked surface of the combined image and text that had been cut in reverse from a flat and surface-polished block of wood, and simply rubbed by hand or with the aid of a burnisher (this is called *frotten* printing) to ensure an even transfer of the ink from the wood to the sheet.

Woodblocks had been used to print textiles in Europe from the 13th century, but their use in the printing of European books did not occur until the mid-15th century—coinciding with the time when paper was becoming easier and cheaper to obtain and, more significant, at roughly the same time that Gutenberg's Bible was completed. One can assume, therefore, that texts could also have been printed from such blocks at any time from the 13th century had there been sufficient demand for them.

The Typographic Revolution

The craft of printing spread with astonishing speed. At the height of the Renaissance, demand for secular—as distinct from religious—literature was voracious, fueled, of course, by the fact that printed books could now provide such literature. Printing made books more plentiful and much cheaper than handwritten books, which, in turn, provided additional incentives for more people to learn to read. The demand for books, including illustrated books, continued (and continues) to grow at a remarkable rate.

The sheer number and variety of books also increased the opportunity to consult and compare. Copper engraving (1446) and etching (1483) provided the opportunity to print detailed maps and scientific and biological illustrations while the basic elements of moveable type were quickly adapted to print music scores. Once images and texts, old and new, came together on the same bookshelf, a diverse range of ideas and specialist disciplines could be combined. Naturally, this kind of cross-cultural exchange was also experienced by the new occupational groupings responsible for the output of all good-quality printed books. Before a single sheet had been printed, meetings among type founders, proofreaders, translators, copyeditors, illustrators or print dealers, indexers, and others engaged in editorial work would have taken place.

Of course, a number of these roles might have been undertaken by the printer; a master printer could serve not only as publisher and bookseller, but also as indexer, abridger, translator, lexicographer, and chronicler. Printers such as Nicolaus Jenson and Aldus Manutius took great pride not only in the craft of printing, but also in the scholarship of their texts. Printing encouraged such forms of collaboration among men of various intellectual disciplines, as well as between intellectual and craft-based disciplines. As John Addington Symonds (1875–1886) explains:

> There were no short-cuts to learning, no comprehensive lexicons, no dictionaries of antiquities, no carefully prepared thesauri of mythology and history. [The early presses] employed scores of scholars, men of supreme devotion and of mighty brain, whose work it was to ascertain the right reading of senses, to accentuate, to punctuate, to commit to the press. (p. 696)

Printing may well have been called a new *art*, but many of the most beautiful books of the 15th and 16th centuries were produced under harsh workshop conditions. Although it was enthusiastically received and much influenced by the humanist scholars, printing would, in general, be rooted in commercial expansion and exploitation of the market for printed words and images, and the rationalization of production in order to provide a maximum return on investment.

Certainly, once the outcome of the process became more predictable, there were many entrepreneurs who were attracted to printing and/or publishing by the lure of profits from the publication of cheap almanacs, cookbooks, pseudoscience treatises, and the like. In fact, by the end of the 15th century, printing was already established as a mass-production industry. Certainly, from 1500 onward, the majority of printers simply replicated what was handed to them in a perfunctory manner. When no one is particularly concerned about the quality of the finished product, there is little consideration for the conditions in which it is produced. As early as the 1530s, French compositors (the men who composed the type; i.e., picked the individual characters and set them in order) went on strike to protest working conditions.

Gothic: Germany—Gutenberg, Fust, and Schöffer

Gutenberg's 42-Line Bible is the earliest book printed in the Western world to have survived. It was a huge undertaking, consisting of 1,286 pages and published in two volumes. Gutenberg is thought to have printed between 180 and 200 copies, of which 21 complete copies still exist (see Fig. 3.2).

The type Gutenberg designed and made for this, the only certified book printed by him, is generally referred to as *Fraktur* (meaning broken, angular) or Gothic and is quite condensed and closely set. Because vellum, made from calfskin, and paper were probably the most expensive materials involved in the print production process, the tightness of the setting might owe something to the need for economy. Nevertheless, Gutenberg's type simulates the kind of writing then typically used for Bibles and service books in the churches of Northern Europe. Gutenberg's letterforms could be described as upright and angular, characterized by an almost entire absence of curves. Compared with other *texturas*, Gutenberg's type is uncomplicated—so uncomplicated, in fact, that some characters are occasionally difficult to differentiate. For example, the *n* is merely two *i*s and the *m* is three *i*s placed in contact (Johnson, 1934). However, the closely spaced characters offer strong, dark lines of text that, because of their immaculate setting, provide an even rhythm and balance—a great aid to reading—that has never been surpassed.

To help him achieve this, Gutenberg used a large number of ligatures (two or more characters joined together: *fi* and *fl* are common contemporary examples) as well as perhaps six

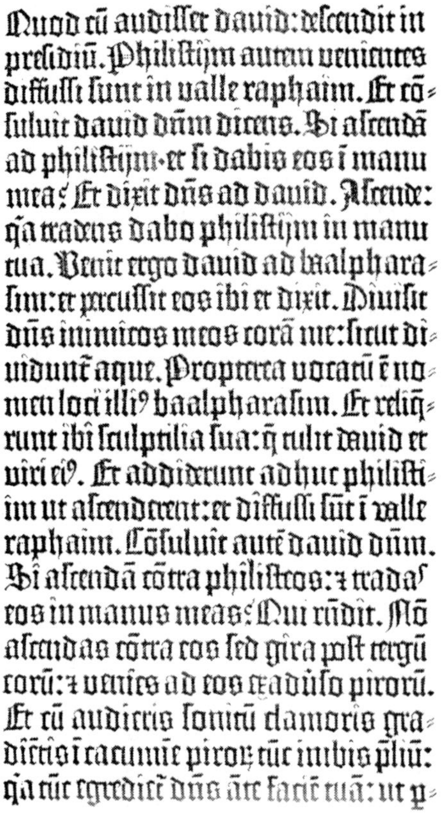

Quod cū audiſſet dauid: deſcendit in
preſidiū. Philiſtijm autem venientes
diffuſſi ſunt in valle raphaim. Et cō=
ſuluit dauid dūm dicens. Si aſcendā
ad philiſtijm: et ſi dabis eos ī manu
mea? Et dixit dūs ad dauid. Aſcende:
 qa tradens dabo philiſtijm in manu
tua. Venit ergo dauid ad baalphara=
ſim: et percuſſit eos ibi et dixit. Diuiſit
dūs inimicos meos corā me: ſicut di=
uidunt aque. Propterea vocatū e no=
men loci illi⁹ baalpharaſim. Et reliq̄
runt ibi ſculptilia ſua: q̄ tulit dauid et
viri ei⁹. Et addiderunt adhuc philiſti=
im ut aſcenderent: et diffuſſi ſūt ī valle
raphaim. Cōſuluit autē dauid dūm.
Si aſcendā cōtra philiſtteos: ʒ tradas
eos in manus meas? Qui rūdit. Nō
aſcendas cōtra eos ſed gira poſt tergū
corū: ʒ venies ad eos ex aduſo pirorū.
Et cū audieris ſonitū clamoris gra=
dietis ī cacumie piroꝛ tūc inibis pliū:
qa tūc egrediet dūs āte faciē tuā: ut p

Figure 3.2.   Johann Gutenberg's type of the *42-Line Bible*, Mainz, Germany, circa 1455.

Figure 3.3.   Punchcutter's workbench and tools.

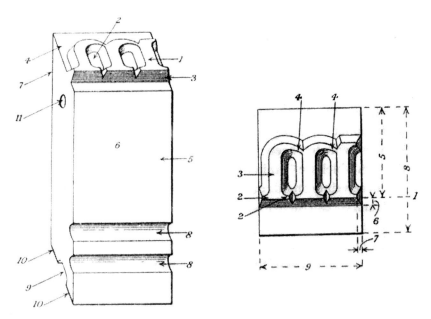

Figure 3.4.   Type for metal composition: (a) Left, isometric view of type: 1, the face; 2, the counter; 3, the neck (or beard); 4, the shoulder; 5, the st or shank; 6, the front; 7, the back; 8, the nicks; 9, the heel nick or groove; 10, the feet; 11, the pin mark or drag. (b) Right, plan view of type: 1, the line; 2, serifs, 3, main stroke; 4, hairline; 5, line to back; 6, beard; 7, side wall; 8, body; 9, set.

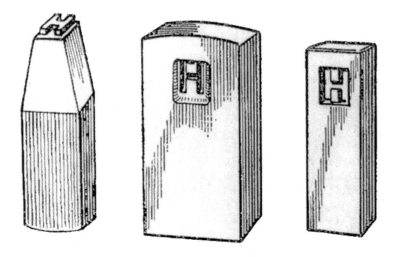

Figure 3.5.   Punch, strike, and matrix used in the manufacture of metal type.

or seven alternative versions of some characters and numerous word contractions. These alternative characters also had the advantage of providing Gutenberg's texts with a hand-rendered appearance, reminiscent of the manuscripts that preceded his invention. This was important if his printed Bible was to be a commercial success.

To enable him to research, experiment, and make the equipment and tools required to print his Bible, Gutenberg borrowed money from Johann Fust, a wealthy Mainz merchant. The loan was secured by a mortgage on Gutenberg's equipment. After further borrowing, and despite his Bible being virtually complete, the agreement was foreclosed and all his printed work, tools, and materials were forfeited to satisfy the debt (Updike, 1937). The

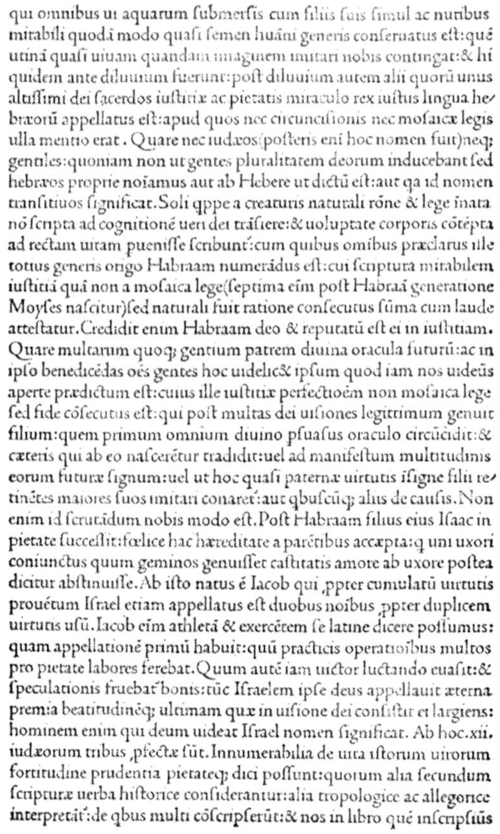

qui omnibus ut aquarum fubmerfis cum filiis fuis fimul ac nuribus
mirabili quod.i modo quafi femen huâni generis confernatus eft:quê
utinâ quafi uiuam quandam imaginem imitari nobis contingat:& hi
quidem ante diluuium fuerunt:poft diluuium autem alii quorû unus
altiffimi dei facerdos iuftitiæ ac pietatis miraculo rex iuftus lingua he-
bræorû appellatus eft:apud quos nec circuncifionis nec mofaicæ legis
ulla mentio erat . Quare nec iudæos(pofteris eni hoc nomen fuit)neq;
gentiles:quoniam non ut gentes pluralitatem deorum inducebant fed
hebræos proprie noîamus aut ab Hebere ut dictû eft:aut qa id nomen
tranfitiuos fignificat.Soli qppe a creaturis naturali rône & lege înata
nô fcripta ad cognitioné ueri dei trâfiere:& uoluptate corporis côtêpta
ad rectam uitam pueniffe fcribunt:cum quibus omibus præclarus ille
totius generis origo Habraam numeridus eft:cui fcriptura mirabilem
iuftitiâ qui non a mofaica lege(feptima eim poft Habraâ generatione
Moyfes nafcitur)fed naturali fuit ratione confecutus fûma cum laude
atteftatur.Credidit enim Habraam deo & reputatû eft ei in iuftitiam.
Quare multarum quoq; gentium patrem diuina oracula futurû:ac in
ipfo benedicêdas oés gentes hoc uidelic& ipfum quod iam nos uideûs
aperte prædictum eft:cuius ille iuftitiæ perfectioém non mofaica lege
fed fide côfecutus eft:qui poft multas dei uifiones legittimum genuit
filium:quem primum omnium diuino pfuafus oraculo circûcidit:&
cæteris qui ab eo nafcerétur tradidit:uel ad manifeftum multitudinis
eorum futuræ fignum:uel ut hoc quafi paternæ uirtutis ifigne filii re-
tinétes maiores fuos imitari conaret:aut qbufcûq; aliis de caufis.Non
enim id fcrut.idum nobis modo eft.Poft Habraam filius eius Ifaac in
pietate fucceffit:fœlice hac hæreditate a parêtibus accæpta:q uni uxori
coniunctus quum geminos genuiffet caftitatis amore ab uxore poftea
dicitur abftinuiffe.Ab ifto natus é Iacob qui ,ppter cumulatû uirtutis
prouétum Ifrael etiam appellatus eft duobus noîbus ,ppter duplicem
uirtutis ufû.Iacob eim athletâ & exercêtem fe latine dicere poffumus:
quam appellatione primû habuit:quû practicis operatioîbus multos
pro pietate labores ferebat.Quum autê iam uictor luctando euafit:&
fpeculationis fruebat´bonis:tûc Ifraelem ipfe deus appellauit æterna
premia beatitudinéq; ultimam quæ in uifione dei confiftit et largiens:
hominem enim qui deum uideat Ifrael nomen fignificat. Ab hoc.xii.
iudæorum tribus ,pfectæ fût.Innumerabilia de uita iftorum uirorum
fortitudine prudentia pietateq; dici poffunt:quorum alia fecundum
fcripturæ uerba hiftorice confiderantur:alia tropologice ac allegorice
interpretat´:de qbus multi côfcripferût:& nos in libro qué infcripfius

Figure 3.6.   Jenson's roman type used in Eusebius's *De Praeparatione Evangelica;*
Venice, 1470.

Gutenberg (or 42-Line) Bible was, therefore, finally published by Fust. The precarious
nature of Gutenberg's finances, particularly during the latter stages of production of his 42-
Line Bible, has led some to question whether Gutenberg, in fact, managed to finish the project before his considerable debts to Fust were foreclosed. D. B. Updike (1937) cautiously
describes the situation: "The *42-Line Bible* commonly ascribed to Gutenberg, but printed,
perhaps, by Fust and Schöeffer at Mainz about 1455" (p. 61; italics original).

In 1457, shortly after the appearance of Gutenberg's Bible, the Mainz Psalter (also
known as the 36-Line Bible) appeared, printed and published by Johann Fust with considerable help from Peter Schöffer, Fust's son-in-law. Schöffer, originally a calligrapher, apparently cut and cast the type for the Mainz Psalter and became Fust's working partner and
eventually his heir.

Among the notable features of the Mainz Psalter are its large, two-color printed initials,
probably accomplished by carefully preparing intercut woodblocks that could be separated, inked individually in red and blue, and reassembled to print both colors, along with
the black type, in one impression. The Mainz Psalter also includes distinctive capitals.
These are rotund in form and quite different from the typically narrow, angular lowercase
forms. Such decorative letters, known as *versals*, indicate the degree to which the earliest
printers were committed to imitating the work of the illuminators and calligraphers who
had preceded them. The lack of emphasis to capitals had clearly been a criticism of
Gutenberg's Bible because it was common practice to add, by hand, a dab of red pigment
to provide additional emphasis to his capital letters.

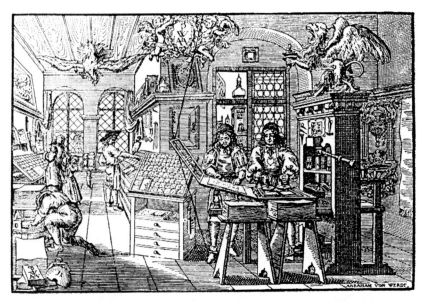

Figure 3.7.   A printshop from the 17th century. The man kneeling to the left is dampening paper. There are two men shown working at the press. The man to the left is positioning the paper, whereas the man to the right is using a pair of ink daubers. The gryphon, on top of the press, also has a pair of ink daubers in its talons.

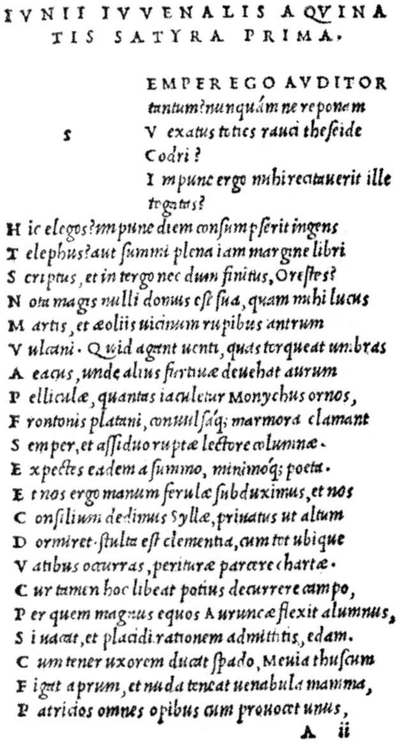

IVNII IVVENALIS AQVINA
TIS SATYRA PRIMA.

EMPER EGO AVDITOR
tantum?nunquámne reponem
S   V exatus toties rauci theseide
Codri?
I mpune ergo mihirecitauerit ille
togatus?

H ic elegos?impune diem consumpserit ingens
T elephus?aut summi plena iam margine libri
S criptus, et in tergo nec dum finitus, Orestes?
N ota magis nulli domus est sua, quam mihi lucus
M artis, et æoliis uicinum rupibus antrum
V ulcani. Quid agant uenti, quas torqueat umbras
A eacus, unde alius furtiuæ deuehat aurum
P elliculæ, quantas iaculetur Monychus ornos,
F rontonis platani, conuulsáq; marmora clamant
S emper, et assiduo ruptæ lectore columnæ.
E xpectes eadem a summo, minimóq; poeta.
E t nos ergo manum ferulæ subduximus, et nos
C onsilium dedimus Syllæ, priuatus ut altum
D ormiret-stultæ est clementia, cum tot ubique
V atibus occurras, perituræ parcere chartæ.
C ur tamen hoc libeat potius decurrere campo,
P er quem magnus equos Auruncæ flexit alumnus,
S i uacat, et placidi rationem admittitis, edam.
C um tener uxorem ducat spado, Meuia thuscum
F igat aprum, et nuda teneat uenabula mamma,
P atricios omnes opibus cum prouocet unus,
A   ii

Figure 3.8.   Aldus Manutius's *Aldine* as used in Juvenal and Persius; Venice, 1501.

The Dispersion of Typography

Violent political events that brought commercial activities to a virtual halt in Mainz account for the surprising number of German names to be found among the earliest printers all over Europe, despite difficulties of language and finances that these displaced emigrés must have faced. A mistake in the choice of subject to print, or the manner in which it is printed, to say nothing of the idiosyncrasies of the regional language, could result in disaster. These emigrés were not only typographer and printer, they were also the publisher: They had to *sell* the books they printed.

Initially, a printer would have his own font of type cut to a design of his choosing. As reference, he might provide a specimen of another printer's work and/or a favorite handwritten manuscript. However, by 1480, there is evidence that printers were selling copies of their fonts to fellow printing establishments.

A single font might consist of an alphabet (upper and lowercase) plus numerals and punctuation (all in *one* size, *one* weight, and *no* italics or small caps) and would be sufficient for the needs of a newly established print workshop for several years. Where emphasis was required, spaced capitals were commonly employed. Title pages did not exist in the early days of printing/publishing because the business of the printer was generally to print the text only, leaving the headings and ornamented capitals (as well as the covers and binding) to be supplied by the purchaser—depending on his budget.

However, as the customer expectation of cheaper books increased, printers were forced to respond by finishing their books inhouse and, in so doing, cut out the last vestige of employment for the scribe. For the printer, this meant arranging for the cutting of decorative types, much later to be called display sizes of types.

Most printers who fled Mainz went to Italy, where they found their skills were most appreciated. The Gothic influences they brought with them, plus the Arabesque influences from the East, appear to have fused effortlessly with the classical Roman characters of Italy.

Gothic to Roman: Old Style—Venice: Jenson, Ratdolt, and Aldus Manutius

"The best Roman types are to be found in Italian books printed before 1500" (Updike, 1937, p. 70). These types were modeled on humanistic characters, which in turn were revivals of the Carolingian book-hands. Nicolas Jenson, a Frenchman in Venice, produced his first book, *De Præparatione Evangelica* by Eusebius, in 1470. Updike describes Jenson's celebrated types as "mellow of form and evenness of colour in mass" (see Fig. 3.6). These characteristics are largely achieved by the fitting of letters: perfectly letter-spaced to match the spaces within the letterforms. However, another characteristic mentioned by Updike is their "lack of perfection." Scholars often comment on these (so-called) imperfections, suggesting that they add something distinctive, something wholly advantageous to the text (aesthetically) and for the reader (functionality): "The eye becomes tired when each character is absolutely perfect. Thus, the good effect of the type in mass depends, somewhat, upon the variations in, and consequent 'movement' of its integral parts" (Updike, 1937, p. 73). Stanley Morison (1924/1960) also uses the word *mellow* to describe Jenson's work: "A more mellow calligraphic appearance attaches to the work of Nicolas Jenson" (p. 18).

Debates concerning perfection or regulation became more prevalent as technological developments allowed an increasingly accurate, more even, and regular rendering of an entire font. (Digital technology, where arguably regularity is the *natural* outcome, has proved the culmination of this search for control.) In fact, the pursuit of perfection, I would suggest, has always been the aim of the type cutter and the printer; as the materials and tools improved, the type cutter would naturally want to take advantage, the sole aim being to improve the quality—meaning, for example, the regularity in the thickness (or thinness) of line and the angle of balance—of his work. There are many, however, who argue that

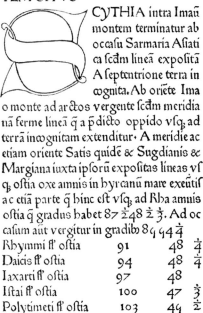

SCYTHIE INTRA IMAVM MON
TEM SITVS

CYTHIA intra Imaũ
montem terminatur ab
occafu Sarmaria Afiati
ca fcdm lineã expofitã
A feptentrione terra in
cognita. Ab oriẽte Ima
o monte ad arctos vergente fcdm meridia
nã ferme lineã q̃ a p̃dicto oppido vfq̃ ad
terrã incognitam extenditur· A meridie ac
etiam oriente Satis quidẽ & Sugdianis &
Margiana iuxta ipforũ expofitas lineas vf
q̃ oftia oxe amnis in hyrcanũ mare exeũtif
ac etiã parte q̃ hinc eft vfq̃ ad Rha amnis
oftia q̃ gradus habet 87 ½48 ½ ⅓. Ad oc
cafum aũt vergitur in gradibꝰ 84 44 ¾

Rhymmi ff' oftia	91	48 ¾
Daicis ff oftia	94	48 ¾
Iaxarti ff' oftia	97	48
Iftai ff' oftia	100	47 ⅔
Polytimeti ff' oftia	103	44 ½
Afpabotis ciuitas	102	44

Figure 3.9.   Transitional gothic to roman type: Ulm, 1482.

this regularity has been an entirely negative influence, and that such perfection equals sterility and dullness.

A similar debate relates to printing. Letterpress was the major form of commercial printing (until lithography at the end of the 18th century), and the earlier printing process required the ink to be applied to the type on the press using a pair of *daubers* (see Fig. 3. 7) while the packing of the press aimed to provide an even pressure. The minute variations in the color of the resulting pages of these early texts are often described as improving both the aesthetic *and* the reading experience. However, there can be little doubt that the pressman strained and sweated to provide the perfect (even pressure and evenly inked) page, and cursed his assistants for the imperfections some commentators now describe as "interesting."

With such tools and equipment, it is all the more remarkable that Jenson was able to print approximately 150 books in the period from 1470 to when he died in 1480, while the quality and accuracy of his scholarly work did much to establish the printed word as one that could be trusted above all else.

Two other typographers were crucial in establishing Venice as the world center for the highest standards in printing—Erhard Ratdolt and Aldus Manutius. Ratdolt, whose press-work is generally considered to be superior to both Jenson and Aldus Manutius, came from Augsburg, Germany, and began printing in Venice in 1476 (Morison, 1924/1960). His books are the first to include decorative title pages and to him is credited the earliest known type-specimen sheet (known as the *Ave Maria*) dated April 1, 1486. This document provides an interesting insight into the status and use of various types at that time, containing a Gothic letterform (derived from 14th-century manuscripts) in 10 sizes, a Roman in 3 sizes, and a single Greek letterform.

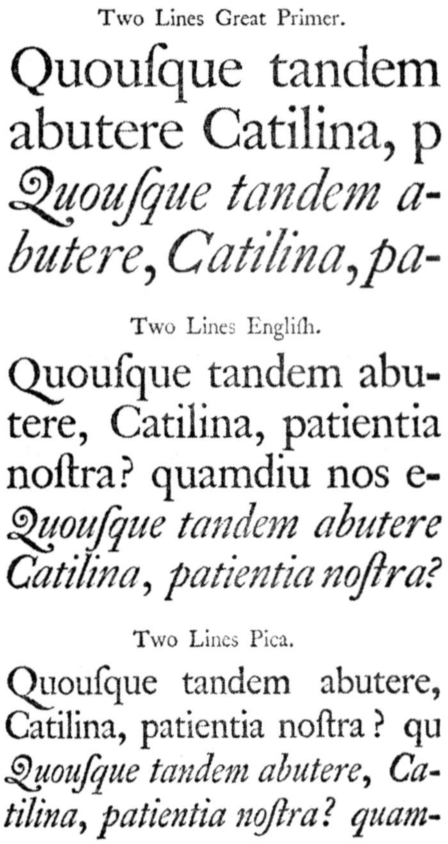

Two Lines Great Primer.

Quoufque tandem abutere Catilina, p
Quoufque tandem a-butere, Catilina, pa-

Two Lines Englifh.

Quoufque tandem abu-tere, Catilina, patientia noftra? quamdiu nos e-
Quoufque tandem abutere Catilina, patientia noftra?

Two Lines Pica.

Quoufque tandem abutere, Catilina, patientia noftra ? qu
Quoufque tandem abutere, Ca-tilina, patientia noftra? quam-

Figure 3.10.   Roman and italic from William Caslon's specimen book; England, 1763.

Manutius (Manutio), a scholar with a particular interest in Greek texts, had five or six Roman fonts cut, his best being cut by Francesco da Bologna (Griffo), including his celebrated cursive (italic). Griffo's first Roman type was used for Pietro Bembo's *De Aetna* and a revised, and much improved, version for Francesco Colonna's *Hypnerotomachia Poliphili* (*The Strife of Love in a Dream*), which was printed by Aldus in the last year of the 15th century. It is this type that Morison (1924/1960) describes as "the origin of all *Old Faces*" (p. 24; see Fig. 3.8).

By 1500, Venice was a renowned center for printing—so much so that publishers wishing to commend their books would announce in the colophon that they were printed in the *carattere Veneto*. In fact, Venice had approximately 150 printing houses. Meanwhile, for political and cultural reasons, the rest of Italy lagged far behind Venice. For example, at this time, Florence was a renowned center for the art of writing, with the famous writing schools of Niccolò dè Niccoli, Poggio Bracciolini, and others producing their best work. (It might be significant that Jenson was, at the same time, producing his finest printed work in Venice.) The libraries of Florence, including the celebrated Medici Library (opened 1444), contained thousands of books, all handwritten.

Vespasiano da Bisticci, master scribe and famous bookseller (also the largest employer of copyists in Italy), had played an important part in assembling such collections and, understandably, his views concerning the printed word were shared by the powerful owners of

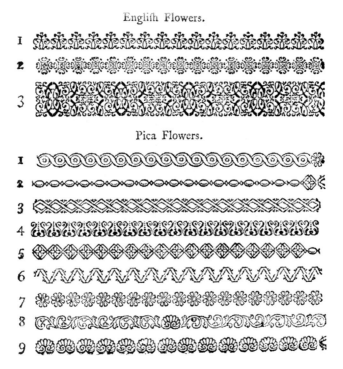

English Flowers.

Pica Flowers.

Figure 3.11. William Caslon. Ornaments from Caslon's specimen book, England 1763. The term *English* was the name for a size equivalent to 14 point. *Pica* was equivalent to 12 point.

such libraries: "[In our libraries] the books are superlatively good, all are written with the pen; and were there a single printed book it would have been ashamed in such company" (Morison, 1924/1960, p. 20). Florence—the city of Cimabue, Giotto, and Raphael—did not produce its first printed book until late 1471, almost 2 years after Jenson's *De Præparatione Evangelica*. Even more astonishing, this was only 6 years before William Caxton introduced printing to London.

The transition from Gothic to Roman type happened with surprising ease. The process began not with the typeface, but in the way it was utilized: by including additional space both between the lines of text (called *leading*, pronounced "ledding") and between the characters. Gothic fonts then appeared in books with Roman-style capital letters, followed by headlines, running heads, and folios (page numbers) being set in pure Roman capitals. Then, finally, the text face began to evolve—from Gothic to Roman—apparently all with little public concern (see Fig. 3.9). This development was similarly repeated in France, the Netherlands, Spain, and England, each of which had its own formal Gothic letterforms and all of which gave way to Roman alternatives.

The book was also transformed. Books had often been produced (both handwritten and, initially, printed) to be read aloud—usually in poor light conditions—to an audience. Because of this, it was necessary for the type to be large, which in turn meant that the book would be both bulky and heavy. Such books would often be a fixed item set on a lectern. However, as books became more plentiful, and therefore cheaper, their size, shape, and weight were all quickly reduced to allow the reader the convenience of being able to carry the book in a saddlebag or, eventually, in a coat pocket.

Aldus is considered to be one of the earliest printers to accommodate—perhaps even lead—such a change in reading habits. He was certainly aware of the convenience and pleasure a small book provided in allowing the act of reading to be a private and positively

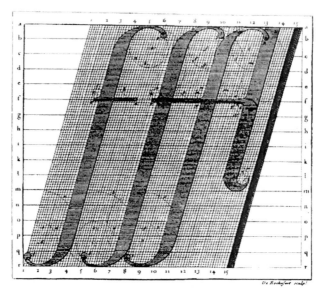

Figure 3.12.   One of the engraved designs that illustrated the report by the Academy of Sciences, from which Philippe Grandjean based his *romain de roi*, France, circa 1702.

selfish activity. The needs of the student and the scholar were much in Aldus's mind when he designed his books.

Incidentally, as more people learned to read, so more people became interested in the art of writing, and thus the 16th century was also the age of the great printed manuals of handwriting.

Aldus commissioned Griffo to cut a cursive typeface. The reason often cited is that such a typeface took up less lateral space than a typical Roman and, therefore, allowed for a smaller format and/or fewer pages. In fact, his cursive typeface saved little space and, if space were the prime concern, Aldus could have surely saved the same amount of space by a far less radical design change. It is just as likely that Aldus wished to have a font that imitated the Greek handwriting of his time for use in books concerned, appropriately, with the subject of Greek literature. Whatever his reasons, the result was the *Aldine Cursive*.

The word *italic* was first used by printers who had produced their own version of the *Aldine cursive* letterform (known in Venice as *Aldino*) despite its design being protected by patents. In such circumstances, they clearly did not wish to suggest any link between their cursive and that of the Aldine and so they called it *italico* (italic) instead.

1500 TO 1820: THE RATIONALIZATION TYPE AND TYPOGRAPHIC DESIGN

Old Style Outside Venice: France, Belgium, and England—Garamond, Estienne, Plantin, and Caslon

Aldus' books were distributed throughout Europe, and by 1500 Aldus was considered to be the greatest of all Venetian printer-publishers. Not only were his texts copied, but the types in which they were set were also copied, often successfully. One of the first and most famous type cutters to use the *Aldine cursive* as a model was Claude Garamond in Paris. Garamond's Roman and italic types (cut in several sizes between 1540 and 1545) were so widely distributed that in a comparatively short time they appeared in Venice. According to A. F. Johnson (1934), "By the end of the sixteenth century the *Garamond roman* had become the standard European type" (p. 69) and continued to be used throughout Europe for some 200 years after his death in 1561.

Claude Garamond (a pupil of the French printer, publisher, and scholar Geofroy Tory, a great enthusiast for the pure Roman letter) was one of the first and most distinguished of French letter cutters and type founders working separate from printing. It is often said that he based his renowned Roman font on Jenson's; although it would be only natural for him to have closely studied Jenson's types, he subtly gave his own types greater independence from the humanistic manuscript hand than had Jenson.

The celebrated printer, Robert Estienne, used Garamond's Roman and italic fonts on several occasions, most notably in 1549 for his *Vitæ duodecim Vicecomitum Mediolano Principum* by Paolo Giovio (with decorative initials by Tory). Estienne had been appointed the "Royal Printer" for Hebrew, Latin, and Greek (there were also Royal Printers for various Oriental languages as well as for music and mathematics), and he used Garamond's royal Greek fonts (*grecs du roi*) to good effect. Estienne's appointment was made necessary by the establishment, in 1530, of the Collège de France (also known as Collège de Trois-Langues) to encourage studies in Hebrew, Latin, and Greek classics. It was for this purpose, commissioned by François I, that Garamond cut his *grecs du roi*, circa 1541.

Whereas the majority of those printer/typographers and publishers discussed thus far would have considered their activity as "art with a dedicated purpose," Christopher Plantin was, first and foremost, a businessman, bringing together expertise and creative flair to catch the imagination of the public. Many of Plantin's books have an opulent appearance, profusely illustrated with engravings by leading artists and designed using the best available fonts of the day.

Christopher Plantin was born near Tours, France, in about 1520, but he worked and made his reputation in Antwerp, Belgium. He always had his types cut for him, notably by two fellow Frenchmen, François Guyot and Robert Grandjon, both of whom lived in Antwerp for a time. He also purchased *Garamond* types (Plantin was a voracious collector of fonts), the result being that, although he spent all his working life in Antwerp, his books maintained a distinctive French character.

Between 1568 and 1572, Plantin's printing office completed a huge commission received from Philip II of Spain: the *Biblia Regia,* an eight-volume publication printed in five languages—Hebrew, Greek, Aramaic, Latin, and Syriac. (It was also known as the *Polyglot Bible.*) The Greek and Syriac types were provided by Grandjon. The edition consisted of 13 sets printed on vellum for Philip II and 1,200 sets on paper for general sale. This huge project, his greatest achievement both technically and aesthetically, almost brought Plantin's business to its knees, but the edition was, eventually, a financial success, and he was further rewarded by the Spanish Crown by being granted the monopoly to print the service books for all Spanish churches, a commission much criticized by Spanish printers.

The perfect finale to the Old Face era is generally agreed to have been expressed in England by William Caslon I (1692–1766). England was little affected by the changes in typographic design being caused by the Imprimerie Royale (Royal Printing House) in Paris (see Transitional Style, next section), and most English books of this period continued to be printed using rather dull, imported Dutch types. This poor state of affairs had been caused, for the most part, by a 1586 decree (not lifted until 1695) that had prohibited printing outside London—with the exception of one press each at the Universities of Oxford and Cambridge—and those few given the right to print were by no means the best at their craft.

Caslon's father was an engraver and had come to England from Italy. Caslon first set up in business engraving decorations onto gun stocks, producing cutting tools and brass letter-punches for hot-pressing names, dates, and decorations onto book covers. It is also known that Caslon was in contact with fellow craftsmen at the James Foundry in London. In about 1720, he set up his own type foundry, and his first Roman fonts were used in Bowyer's 1726 edition of Selden's works. Further types were cut, and by 1734, when his celebrated type specimen sheet was published (see Fig. 3.10), his reputation was such that

PUBLII VIRGILII

MARONIS

BUCOLICA,

GEORGICA,

E T

AE N E I S.

BIRMINGHAMIAE:

Typis J O H A N N I S   B A S K E R V I L L E,

MDCCLVII.

Figure 3.13.   Title page from John Baskerville's *Virgil*, England, 1757.

his foundry, types, and ornaments (see Fig. 3.11) were recognized as the best in England, if not Europe. In fact, as Edward Rowe Mores (1776) wrote, "We may, without fear of contradiction, make the assertion that a fairer specimen can not be found in Europe; that is, not in the World" (p. 49).

Although Caslon died in 1766, he was the founder of a type-founding dynasty that stayed in his family's control until 1874, but that continued to trade under his name until 1937, when it was bought by Stephenson Blake and Co. Whereas Caslon's conservative types reflect the late and mature development of the Old Style, it seemed, well before his death, that all other significant contemporary typographic developments embodied the more conspicuous, more self-consciously imposing typography of the Transitional Style.

Transitional Style: France and England—Grandjean, Fournier, and Baskerville

In France, two other type-founding dynasties were being built: those of Fournier and Didot, both of whom are associated with the style and development of Grandjean's *Romain de roi* (see Fig. 3.12). But it is the work of another contemporary (and fellow countryman of Caslon), John Baskerville, whose types and book design dramatically and confidently cut the final links between printing and the handwritten manuscript and, simultaneously, forged the link between Old Style and Modern: the Transitional Style.

By the middle of the 16th century, there had been a general and rather sudden decline in standards of printing and type cutting across the whole of Europe. Garamond's Roman was still widely used or copied with varying degrees of success. But the nature of printing and publishing had changed. It had been 100 years since the earliest printed European book had been produced, and it can reasonably be speculated that by 1550 the traditional influence of the manuscript had evaporated, whereas the ideals of book scholars had been overtaken by business and commercial constraints. Plantin is, perhaps, an exception, but even here one cannot ignore that the activity—the business of printing and publishing—had evolved into

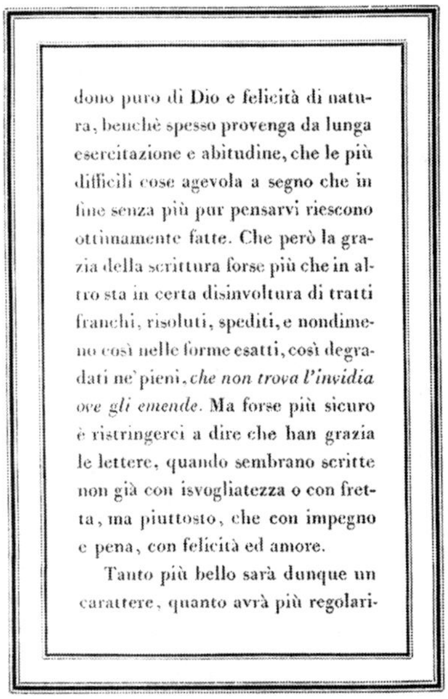

Figure 3.14.   A page from Giambattista Bodoni's *Prefazione: Manule Tipografico*, Parma, Italy, 1818.

Figure 3.15.   An auction poster that utilizes several display faces, including an altrabold "Modern" face in roman and italic and a "slab serif," Norwich, England, circa 1880–1900; (or 168 point-14 ×12 point) *Ornamented Number* 1, England, circa 1840.

something different from what it had been for Jenson and Manutius in Venice in the 15th century.

The enthusiasm with which the new art was at first received had evaporated. Printers were no longer offered rooms in palaces, monasteries, and colleges; church and state authorities, who had initially encouraged and protected printers, were now suspicious of, sometimes even hostile to, them. Wealthy members of other occupations and professions, recognizing an opportunity to make money, began to move into the art—the business—of printing. A hundred years before, great scholars had wanted to give their help and advice, and at least a few printers had been scholars. But books were rarely prized or precious objects anymore, and the people who printed them no longer held the high social status once awarded to printers. Transitional type and typography reflected Neoclassicism, so predominant a style in architecture and all the other arts at the time, and its self-consciously imposing appearance had the effect of bringing, once more, the printer and typographer back to the fore.

It had not been until Louis XIII in France established his Royal Printing House in 1640 that a renewed interest in typographic standards was established. *Garamond* fonts (originally cut 100 years earlier) were still the preferred choice, and when these were replaced it was by Jean Jannon's *Sedan*, a font so similar to *Garamond* that its true identity was not rediscovered until 1926 (by Beatrice Warde). These Old Face designs, in fact, remained in use until 1692, when Louis XIV ordered a new series of types for the exclusive use of the Royal Printing House. This project was considered by a specially selected committee appointed by the Academy of Sciences who, in a lengthy report, recommended a more rationally designed Roman alphabet constructed on a mathematical basis. The report was illustrated with geometric designs for "the perfect typeface," each traditional Roman letter being constructed using rule and compass on a grid of 2,304 squares. A trapezoidal grid was used to demonstrate the italic characters (see Fig. 3.12).

Although rationalization was a prime objective, these engraved letterforms contain numerous idiosyncrasies and inconsistencies—particularly obvious in the lowercase characters. Their designer, Jacques Jangeon, was, in fact, a maker of educational board games. Philippe Grandjean, who finally cut the punches for what would be the called the *romain du roi*, considerably refined Jangeon's design, but there remains in his font a distinct and profound change of emphasis from that of *Garamond* and the other Old Style faces that had been prevalent for so long.

By 1702, the first sizes of Grandjean's *romain du roi* were ready. Their appearance is stiffer than *Garamond*, achieved by the characters having a more pronounced vertical emphasis and by the contrasts of weight between the thick and thin strokes being more pronounced. These changes, made possible in part by improvements in both materials and tools (e.g., required to achieve the thinness of the lines), although less dramatic than those proposed in the original engraved designs, nevertheless take type design and typography in general away from its handwriting roots. It is often stated that, prior to the *romain du roi*, all Roman types are predominately humanistic (having a distinct diagonal, northwest–southeast emphasis in sympathy with natural writing techniques), whereas the *romain du roi* is rationalist (having a more vertical emphasis giving a more mechanical appearance). It is perhaps ironic that these rationalist features had first been seen in letters drawn by engravers before Grandjean cut his type. The first and possibly the best publication to use these types was the magnificent *Médailles sur les évènements du règne de Louis-le-Grand* and is "the most splendid example of the ornate and sophisticated book" (Morison, 1924/1960, p. 36).

This was by no means the first attempt to rationalize type forms; "The geometric grail: a Platonic and eternal explication of the forms of roman letters" (Chappel & Bringhurst, 1999, p. 107) had been explored (yet remained tantalizingly elusive) in Luca Pacioli's *De Divina Proportione* (Venice, 1509), Albrecht Dürer's *Underweysung der Messung* (Nürenberg, 1525), and Geofroy Tory's *Champfleury* (Paris, 1529).

The full set of 82 fonts that made up the *romain du roi* was not completed until 1745, some 31 years after Grandjean's death. (Given that the work on each character might take a day, it could take 6 months to complete a single font.)

The work was continued by Grandjean's assistants, Jean Alexandre and his son-in-law, Louis-René Luce. The *romain du roi* was admired, but the extent of its influence was restricted by the strict laws and heavy penalties enforced for copying or selling Royal designs. Luce went on to devote the last 30 years of his life to cutting his own typeface: *Poétiques*. This condensed font, which included ornaments and borders, was designed specifically to accommodate the long lines of the French *Alexandre* verse.

This was a period of great excitement and debate. Not only was the appearance of the printed letter being questioned, but also the method of its manufacture and application. A detailed exposition of a system of typographic measurement had been made for the first time by Pierre Simon Fournier in his *Manuel Typographique* (1764) and was further refined by François-Ambroise Didot, the idea being that the entire printing profession could have a fully integrated measuring system for type sizes and all subsidiary spacing material. (This ideal never fully materialized until the computer, or more specifically the Apple MacIntosh, became the standard tool for typographers worldwide in the late 20th century.) This spirit of reappraisal was naturally assisted by the French Revolution, during which ornament was suddenly abandoned because it was construed as propaganda of the *ancien régime*.

These new types, and the way they were being used, brought into question the entire nature and purpose of typography, as well as the function of the printer/typographer. This was the first time that the appearance of type had been consciously changed to reflect aesthetic taste or fashion, rather than the reading experience. These new types (and their creators) were perceived to have a brashness about them that went against the concept of type design being essentially neutral—the creation of a self-effacing means by which the author can communicate directly to his or her reader. But this was only the beginning.

John Baskerville, born in England circa 1706, was a contemporary of Caslon, although his training and background were wholly different. He was a writing master and designer (and perhaps carver) of decorative headstones. But there was one similarity: Baskerville, like Caslon, was a good businessman who amassed a modest fortune; he decided, at the age of 44, to devote himself to printing and typography. At his home in Birmingham, he established a foundry and printshop and employed John Handy to cut the types that he designed.

Baskerville's letters and the way he arranged them on the printed page celebrated the spirit of 18th-century Neoclassicism. To this end, Baskerville had set about trying to improve his entire print process, spending 7 or 8 years experimenting with various methods of making his own ink and paper and in refining his printing press. He eventually found a way of making a smooth-surfaced *wove* paper (rather than *laid* paper, which clearly displays its rippled, lined texture) and after printing subjected it to pressure between two warmed copper plates or cylinders (an entirely innovative procedure), providing the finished printed sheet with an immaculate, flat, and slightly shiny surface that left no trace of the physical stresses of the letterpress printing process. His types are elegant, are slightly lighter overall (than Caslon's), have a pronounced vertical axis (more vertical than Grandjean's *romain de roi*), and are aided by a stronger distinction between the thickest and thinnest character strokes.

The whiteness and silky finish of Baskerville's paper, the blackness of his specially formulated inks, and the austere, undecorated page layouts were highly praised in mainland Europe. However, in England, where Caslon's more conservative types were so well loved, Baskerville's printing and typography was often harshly criticized. The lack of illustration or decoration must have been particularly noticeable at the time: no illustrative plates, vignettes, tail pieces, or even ornamental letters. Instead, Baskerville was "content with the simplicity of typographic art" (De Fonenai, 1776, p. 156).

Baskerville was the first to significantly adapt conventional print methodology since Gutenberg printed his *42-Line Bible* 300 years earlier. Baskerville's first book, the Latin *Virgil*, which was published in 1757, established his reputation, and in the following year he brought out his two-volume *Milton*. He was appointed printer to the University of Cambridge and produced editions of his formidable *Bible*, which, with the *Virgil*, remained his best work. The title page of *Virgil* (see Fig. 3.13) is a *tour de force*, set in lines of widely spaced Roman and italic capitals, characteristic features of Baskerville's work.

and he wondered at her word, and a new hope sprang up in his heart that he was presently to be brought face to face with the Hostage, and that this was that love, sweeter than their love, which abode in him, & his heart became lighter, and his visage cleared.

CHAPTER XII. THEY LOOK ON THE KING OF THE GLITTERING PLAIN.

O now the women led them along up the stream, and Hallblithe went side by side by the Sea-eagle; but the women had become altogether merry again, & played and ran about them as gamesome as young goats; and they waded the shallows of the clear bright stream barefoot to wash their limbs of the seabrine, & strayed about the meadows, plucking the flowers and making them wreaths and chaplets, which they did upon themselves and the Sea-eagle; but Hallblithe they touched not, for still they feared him. They went on as the stream led them up toward the hills, and ever were the meads about them as fair and flowery as might be. Folk they saw afar off, but fell in with none for a good while, saving a man and a maid clad

79

Figure 3.16.   William Morris, *The Story of the Glittering Plain*. The typeface is *Golden*; England, 1891.

Modern Style: France and Italy—Didot, Luce, and Bodoni

If Baskerville experienced little critical success in Britain during his lifetime, his efforts were not unnoticed elsewhere, especially in France and Italy. His neoclassically designed types provided those in mainland Europe with the inspiration for a more dramatic, theatrical interpretation of the *Beau Idéal*.

The major cultural movement toward Neoclassicism had been building up during the 18th century and, by 1800, dominated all aspects of art and design. The practice of the "Grand Tour" and the excavations in and around Rome had made Roman antiquities famous. The popularization of these and other excavations, notably Pompeii and Herculaneum during the 18th century, was achieved by publications illustrating and describing them, by their depiction in contemporary painting, and by all the major city museums collecting classical sculpture, ceramics, metal work, and architectural details for display. In short, ancient Rome was considered "the unique emporium of the beautiful and the temple of taste." *Ideal* beauty could be attained only by studying antiquity—and certainly not by studying the inconsistent, unpredictable, and often chaotic state that was (and is) *real* life.

Major European cities fought to be the "new Rome," and in this quest Paris led the way by commissioning major neoclassical building projects and purchasing copious amounts of Roman monuments and Italian art. In such circumstances, it is not surprising that typographers felt it necessary to present classical literature with a type that expressed the visual qualities of antique virtue. The scholarly prestige of the Didots and the radical forms of Luce's types were instrumental in popularizing neoclassical typography (also referred to

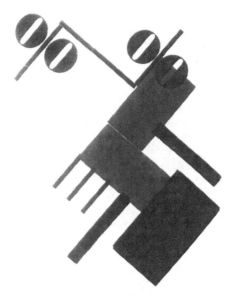

Figure 3.17.   From *The Next Call*, a magazine edited, designed, and printed by Henrik Nicolas (H. N.) Werkman, who was influenced by the Avant Garde movement. Nine issues were printed, the first in 1923; Holland.

as *Modern* by typographic historians). However, these were eclipsed, appropriately, by the work of an Italian, Giambattista Bodoni.

Bodoni was born in 1740, the son of a printer with whom he worked for a number of years and who greatly admired the work of Baskerville. Bodoni's reputation grew, and he was asked, on behalf of Ferdinand, Duke of Palma, to take charge of the Stamperia Reale at Palma. Bodoni's job was that of a private printer: producing documents required for the court or that were of interest to the Duke. With permission, he could also initiate projects of his own.

His first stock of types were bought from Paris, in fact from Pierre-Simon Fournier's foundry; using these as models, he cut his own types. Bodoni continued to produce prodigious amounts of types throughout his entire life, ranging from initial examples—early Transitional, almost Old Style in appearance—before arriving, by degrees, with his famous Modern types. These types might be characterized as having a strong distinction between thick and thin strokes, and with flat, unbracketed serifs. They are usually set with generous intercharacter and interline spaces and wide, but impeccably proportioned, margins arranged without decoration. Where borders are used, they are usually confined to simple straight-line ruling with mitered corner joints (see Fig. 3.14). The visual impact of these displays of controlled typographic bravado was designed to elicit a sense of awe in the viewer. Bodoni was, of course, aided and abetted in these aims by the indulgence and status of his employer. In fact, 20 years after first being employed by the Duke of Palma, the work of his press was so famous that it was considered an essential part of the Grand Tour for the *dilettanti* and *cognoscenti*. His specimen sheets (now extremely rare) and books were admired and collected by bibliophiles throughout the world in his own lifetime.

It is often said that Bodoni's work was designed to be looked at rather than read, a point emphasized by the criticism that his work lacked care in its scholarly detail. His books are rather like reading a long stone inscription: magnificent, but rather slow, work. His work certainly lacked intimacy or charm, but these were precisely the characteristics Bodoni made every effort to avoid. Neoclassicism required a sense of grandeur, detachment, and cool elegance, and in achieving these qualities, Bodoni's types remain a formidable presence.

1814 TO THE PRESENT: MECHANICAL POWER
AND COMMERCIAL IMPERATIVES

Display Faces: England and America

There is a tendency to equate printing with fine printing, and therefore to ignore important commercial developments of the 19th and 20th centuries that have influenced typography. From 1814 onward, the nature of printing began to change at a dramatic speed, leading, inevitably, toward automation. Printing presses became stronger, heavier, and more accurate *machines*, powered first by steam and then by electricity. The era of the handpress in commercial printing was effactually over.

Many of the new developments were stimulated by the growth of the newspaper industry. For example, an edition of the *Times* newspaper was printed on November 29, 1814, for the first time, on a double-cylinder press, designed and built by Friedrich Köring in Germany. It required several men to feed paper in by hand, but it could print 1,100 sheets per hour. However, by 1868, the *Times* was printing, in a fully automated process, 20,000 sheets per hour. The effects of the Industrial Revolution enabled print—particularly in the form of newspapers—to become a commonplace commodity in every home. This was a crucial factor in the development of the advertising industry, which, in turn, would become the primary market force in the development of new types that were quite different from any designed before.

These new types, commonly called *display*, were designed to function as image as much as type—being required to draw attention to itself through color, form, contrast, and context. For this reason, the conventions pertaining to legibility and readability are irrelevant for display types. Their designs, of necessity, were intentionally invasive, often intentionally out of keeping with their context. Competition led display types to become ever more inventive and, quite purposely, more offensive (Gray, 1938).

However, at the same time, more sober, heavier, and practicable types suddenly came into vogue. By the middle of the 19th century, the sans serif (unserifed typeface) had reemerged after its initial, unheralded appearance in a 1746 sans serif *Etruscan* font cut by William Caslon I and an 1812 sans serif Roman cut by Caslon IV (Bringhurst, 1996). Its ability to appear larger than any other type, given the same amount of space, made it a popular choice for advertisers as competition increased the need to "shout" louder, particularly on posters, which by now were a common sight in every city (see Fig. 3.15). Scale was clearly an important factor, and from about 1827, larger sizes of types became available manufactured from wood. Darius Wood, a New York printer, developed a steam-powered router to mass-produce wood type in 1827. In 1834, a pantograph mechanism was added, enabling type to be copied at any size from one master.

Display faces (any typeface cut at a size generally considered too large for normal text setting—14 point and above—often referred to as *fancy* or *exotic* types) were, at the time, greeted by many in the print trade with disdain because they turned all previously held assessment criteria for good typography on its head. However, the visual presence of, for example, extra-bold sans and slab-serifed types reflected the dramatic industrialization of the New World: Edmund Gress (1931) described such early American display fonts as reflecting "a rugged and pioneering mood: log cabins, canal boats, black plug hats, black boots, stage coaches. ... It was a period of strength of character and purpose" (p. 73).

The Arts and Crafts Movement:
England—William Morris

William Morris and the Arts and Crafts movement dominate consideration of any 20th-century craft, and printing and typography are no exception. The movement was given its name and achieved public recognition with the founding of the Arts and Crafts Exhibition

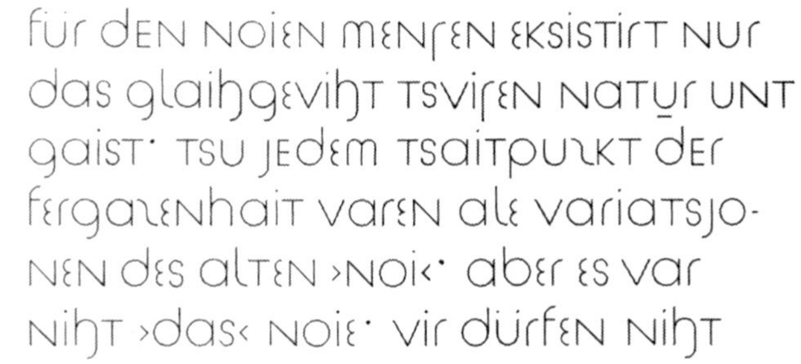

für den noien menfen eksistirt nur
das glaihgeviht tsvifen natur unt
gaist· tsu jedem tsaitpu∖kt der
ferga∖enhait varen ale variatsjo-
nen des alten ›noi‹· aber es var
niht ›das‹ noie· vir dürfen niht

Figure 3.18.   Jan Tschichold's *Single Alphabet* (phonetic version); Germany, 1929.

Society in London in 1888. William Morris and others in the movement were involved in the whole range of "minor arts" (Morris' words). These included buildings, interiors, carpets, furniture, embroideries, fabrics, wallpapers, stained glass, and, of course, books, together with all the associated crafts: letter cutting, typography, decorative engraving, illustration, calligraphy, printing, and bookbinding.

In Morris' opinion, which was shared by his typographic adviser, Emery Walker, type design and printing had been in decline since 1500. Plantin's work was considered "poor and wiry," Baskerville "misguided" and his work "false perfection," whereas the depths of "sweltering hideousness" were finally reached with the Didots and Bodoni. Meanwhile, in England, during the 1870s and 1880s, it seems that typography in all its forms was pandering to the elaborate decrepitude that was the predominant Victorian taste.

Morris' own tastes tended toward romanticism, type with the strongest possible hint of its calligraphic origins. Like so many others at this time, he was fascinated with medievalism. The artist and poet, Blake, and the poets, Byron, Coleridge, Keats, Shelley, and Tennyson, were much admired, while the artists of the Pre-Raphaelite Brotherhood, particularly Rossetti and Burne-Jones, were both personal friends and major influences, as was the critic John Ruskin.

Having been inspired by Emery Walker's lecture in November 1888, where he had seen enlarged letterforms projected onto the screen, Morris used photography to record and enlarge pages from Jenson's *Pliny* of 1476. A similar process ensued when he was drawing his first type, *Golden,* while Burne-Jones' ink drawings were transferred to wood using photography. All recurring initials and decorations were printed from electrotypes. This process, first successfully applied to printing in 1839, involved printing plate made by electrolytically depositing a thin but rigid shell of copper on top a mold of either wax, plaster, or a thermoplastic lightly but firmly pressure-molded from the original type and backed up with a lead alloy that is then planed to the correct printing height. The printing press used by Morris was still commonplace in many commercial letterpress workshops—although, by this time, rarely used—and the types drawn by Morris were cast by machine because he could see no advantage in casting by hand. Even so, a significant part of the Morris legacy was his supposed antipathy to mechanization, whose evils were discussed by the followers of the Arts and Crafts movement, interminably, well into the 1930s. This was clearly not the case; in fact, Morris was not averse to using any means necessary to achieve his goals.

The books of William Morris' Kelmscott Press were neither dogmatically traditionalist nor modernist. The fact is that they were quite unlike anything associated with printing as it was known and practiced at that time. They were designed, printed, and bound to the highest standards that Morris could achieve. No effort was spared in finding the right materials, reasoning that if the original means of producing type, paper, and ink could be reestablished, there was no doubt that the printed book could become as fine as ever before. Morris had his paper made for him, based on a Northern Italian pattern made wholly of linen using hand-woven wire molds to provide a slightly irregular texture. The

heightx⁻xheight

Figure 3.19.   Edward Johnston's *Underground Railway Sans*, designed for the London Underground transport signage syst 1926. Shown here is Johnston's original design and the recently digitized bolder version designed by Colin Banks of Banks & Miles (London) with its larger x-height.

ink was made with linseed oil, freed from grease by the use of stale bread and raw onions, rather than chemicals, then mixed with boiled turpentine and matured for 6 months before the organic, animal lampblack was ground into the mixture. Morris worked to please himself and took as much time to produce his books as was necessary to achieve his aims. The first Kelmscott book, *The Story of the Glittering Plain* (see Fig. 3.16), was completed in January 1891. Its impact was immediate and extensive. The general agreement, by the middle of that same decade, was that the Kelmscott Press, and its edition of *Chaucer* (1896) in particular, represented the most splendid book production since printing began.

The importance of Morris' work as a printer was not in his style, but in his example. By taking apart and rebuilding the print process based on best practices, printing took root in an entirely new way. In the late 1890s and 1900s, the great international revival in fine printing began, led by the Private Press movement, which, like Morris, was fueled by political and social idealism. For others, however, embracing the mechanization of the print process ensured that print matter succeeded in fulfilling its social purpose of reaching those who needed it most.

The Avant Garde: International

During the second decade of the 20th century, and while the Private Press movement was still in its prime and arguing for a return to orthodoxy, others were utilizing the printed word in a revolt against orthodoxy. Several ideologically overlapping movements were involved, each with subtly differing motivations, but all with a mission to assault the comfort of the established cultural and social norms.

In terms of communication, the printed word was the establishment. It had established the conventions, the rules, everything that made mass communication efficient (or predictable) and comfortable. Print could reflect the refinement of language. There could be no better way of displaying the determined rejection of all established—fossilized—forms of communication than by hijacking its oldest and most revered medium, the printed word (see Fig. 3.17).

Not surprisingly, this impulse for the innovative use of typography came from people outside the printing trade. These were artists intent on disrupting all of the familiar patterns that make life predictable and, therefore, controllable, including those on which the notions of art were then established. The common link among the Futurists in Italy, Spain, and Russia; the Vorticists in England; the Constructivists in Russia; the Activists in Hungary; and the International Dadaists was contempt for rational outcomes. (There can be few activities more rational than typography.) It was not surprising, then, that the typographic results achieved by these artists were completely different from anything that had been done before. Coming from outside the print establishment, these artists, of course, had little interest in standard practices; in fact, standard practice was exactly what they intended to break down. However, some conventions were maintained in order to advance the cause: The chosen medium was often the common magazine, complete with a paper and print quality that offered no pretensions. This was art for the streets and the home—in fact anywhere but the gallery.

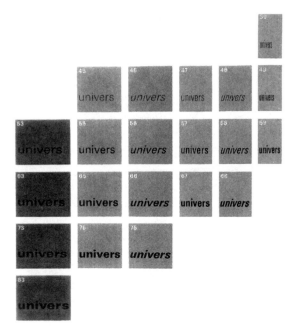

Figure 3.20.   Adrian Frutiger's fully integrated family of 21 fonts that make up *Univers*.

Bauhaus Theory and Rhetoric: Germany—Bill, Renner, and Tschichold

After the Russian Revolution, the irrational began to be replaced by a more geometric, more structured abstraction that was suggestive of functionality and a return to basic elements in a new direction known as *Constructivism*. In Germany, this work was formalized between 1919 and 1934 in the workshops of the Bauhaus, where, after an initial period inspired by the Arts and Crafts movement and the teaching strategies of the Central School of Arts and Crafts in London, Bauhaus director Walter Gropius embraced industrialization. Bauhaus typography achieved a highly recognizable style built on clarity and order (not to be confused with legibility), particularly in the work of Moholy-Nagy, Herbert Bayer, and Max Bill. Simultaneously, this approach was being explored in Germany by Jan Tschichold (see Fig. 3.18) and in the Netherlands by Piet Zwart as part of the De Stijl movement.

The Bauhaus typographers wished to distance themselves from the frippery of commercial art, but were equally determined to reject what they saw as the redundancy that is tradition. They achieved this by redefining *functionalism* (as being the exact opposite of that stated by members of the Arts and Crafts movement) by equating it to the efficiency of the mechanized process, and they went on to construct type from the simplest possible geometric elements. They admired the aesthetic of the industrial product and, considering sans serif to be the simplest form, declared it, therefore, to be *the* modernist typeface.

For the designers/teachers of the Bauhaus, the role of technology, and its perceived potential to improve the general quality of life, became a point of reference for all technical, economic, functional, and aesthetic requirements of typography. Naturally, being educationalists, this meant rewriting the rules, unlike the Avant-Gardists who were content simply to break them. Max Bill later (in 1946) described rules as *recipes*, whose sole purpose was to provide a security blanket for (he suggests) the weak-willed typographer. "We have happily freed ourselves from the *schema* of the Renaissance and do not wish to go back to it."

Figure 3.21.   *Quadraat* and *Quadraate* Sans designed by Fred Smeijers. There is also a *Quadraate* Display and *Quadraat* Sans Mono.

New Traditionalism: England—Johnson, Gill, and Morison

In Britain, the same period could also be viewed as a golden age for typography, although its design and application were based on ideas quite opposite to those held in Germany. Stanley Morison, typographic adviser at the Monotype Corporation (and later typographic adviser to the *Times* and designer of *Times New Roman*), provided New Traditionalism with a summary of his philosophy in his extended essay, *First Principles of Typography*, in 1930. Here, Morison (1930/1967) argued for the inviolability of governing typographic values such as convention, reason, and comprehension. This essay is also notable for its lack of comment concerning the work of the modernists in Germany. Morison believed that the experiments of the Bauhaus typographers had little to do with typography because they were making *art* out of something that he considered to be a *service*. This term was used also by René Hague—son-in-law of Eric Gill, with whom he ran the Hague & Gill Press— in a short text entitled "Reason and Typography" (1936):

> There is only one sort of hope, and that is in establishing a new tradition, but not a new academicism, in keeping everything plain, trying not to remember the—tenth century (filling in whatever is the fashionable number) when you are struggling with a news- paper in a tube, remembering that, finally, printing will have to be judged as printing and not as an advertisement or fine art.

New Traditionalism had its roots in the works of the Arts and Crafts movement and the private presses (notably the Doves Press, London) that followed. William Morris had strong links with education in London and had been instrumental in the appointment in 1896 of the architect W. R. Lethaby as head of the Central School of Arts and Crafts in London. The influence of this school on the function of the typographer was far-reaching, and certainly the removal of subject barriers among specialist areas of study by Lethaby later became a major aspect of the teaching philosophy at the Bauhaus.

Lethaby (1931) summed up the school's philosophy in the journal *Imprint*—a focal point for this reforming movement—thus: "Usually, the best method of designing has been to improve on an existing model … a perfect table, chair or book has to be very well bred" (p. 19). This edict became the basis of New Traditionalism. Although such ideas were sustained by historical revivalism (whereas the Bauhaus claimed to embrace the future), New Traditionalism nevertheless produced two of the most influential typefaces of the 20th century: Eric Gill's *Gill Sans* in 1927 and Edward Johnston's typeface for the London Underground Railway signage system. Conceived in 1913, and drawn between 1915 and 1916, Johnson's alphabet was based on the underlying shapes and proportions of Renaissance humanistic letterforms, and yet the final result was a sans serif. This is all the

Figure 3.22.   Wim Crouwel's *New Alphabet*; Holland, circa 1968.

more surprising when Johnston's renowned revivalist work as a calligrapher is taken into account (see Fig. 3.19).

Eric Gill had been a student at Johnston's calligraphy classes at the Central School of Arts and Crafts. Already a renowned sculptor and stone letter cutter, Gill belonged to the New Traditionalism of Morris, Lethaby, and Johnston, but was also something of a maverick. Like his Arts and Crafts colleagues, he poured scorn on industrialization and capitalism at every opportunity, and yet found ways to form partnerships (albeit on his own terms) with the "enemy" when it suited. In 1925, Gill was asked by Stanley Morison to draw an alphabet that could be reproduced as printing types for the Monotype Corporation, which, along with the Mergenthaler Linotype Company, was the key manufacturer of mechanical type-casting and setting machines. Morison had been particularly interested in the idea of going back to the stone-cut or engraved letterforms as a model for type design, sensing that something had been lost in the mechanized process of producing letterforms. The result was *Perpetua*. Shortly after, Gill became fully engaged in the drawing and production of what would be *Gill Sans*, a distinctive, humanistic sans serif typeface, based on the groundwork accomplished by Johnston's *Underground Railway Sans* alphabet.

Commercial Artists and Independent Typographers: North America—Updike, Rogers, and Goudy

After the First World War (1914–1918), the printing industry was acutely aware that many of their business clients were employing the services of the commercial artist to provide artwork often including hand-drawn lettering for advertising, magazines, and books—which could be mechanically mass-produced.

Commercial artists sometimes knew little of the printing technology, or, at least, it was common for the printer to complain that this was so. However, the artist's lack of inhibition was a distinct advantage in the necessary design of unconventional and attention-grabbing letterforms. Such material would be drawn onto a suitable surface and then transferred, via photographic film, to a metal block, into which the image would be etched in reverse. The block could then be relief-printed together with any textual material using normal letterpress printing equipment. Alternatively (especially for posters, book covers, packaging, etc.), image and lettering could be drawn (in reverse) directly onto a lithographic stone (or later onto zinc plates) and printed by lithography. This alternative process offered considerable freedom, resulting in these hand-drawn letterforms being given a distinctly calligraphic appearance. A cursory glance at any magazine produced in the first half of the 20th century reveals that the overwhelming majority of headlines are hand-drawn scripts.

If one adds to this the significant workforce dedicated to producing one-off commercial signs, tickets, posters, banners, show cards, and information or advertising on buildings and vehicles, then the extent to which the activities related to hand-rendered lettering was quite significant. Specialist lettering artists could, by this time, make a living in any major city, especially where advertising companies were based. But the level of skill reached in the United States, where demand was most voracious, was rarely bettered. A notable nucleus was formed at the Warne School in Chicago during the early 1900s, a school that included Fredrick W. Goudy, Bruce Rogers, Oswald Cooper, W. A. Dwiggins, and T. M. Cleland (Shinn, 2004).

If the commercial artist posed a threat to the printer, then the commercial (or independent) typographer was far more serious. Generally attached or commissioned on a freelance basis to advertising, or perhaps to publishing companies, these individuals—*flashy little stylists* (Beatrice Warde's term)—were deeply despised in the print trade because they were taking away a significant, perhaps the most significant, part of the craft from the printer.

A group of North American typographers shared the printers' concerns for the heritage of their craft, but were equally keen to maintain their independence from the printer in the spirit of William Morris' Arts and Crafts movement. American followers of the Private Press movement took seriously the letter William Morris wrote to the editor of the *Daily Chronicle* in London, in which he commented on the current state of typography in Europe, ending the statement "and as for American printing, it is quite abominable." Technically, American printing had been generally accepted as being superior to British printing by a considerable distance, and so it is not surprising that the editor requested verification. Morris replied:

> I do think American printing the worst from the point of view of good taste. Of course, I am aware that there are technical matters in which the American printers excel; but what is the use of that, if the result is ugly books very trying to the eyes?

Morris' strong following in North America was achieved largely through the work of Daniel Berkley Updike's Merrymount Press, established in 1893 in Boston. Updike, one of America's most distinguished printers, ran his press as a commercial concern but with impeccable standards. He is also famous as the author of his two-volume book, *Printing Types: Their History, Forms and Use* (1937).

The most important American typographer of the early 20th century, however, was Bruce Rogers, who, for a time, was an associate of Updike's, but later became the archetypal independent or freelance typographer. He worked for many publishers in a number of countries, including Cambridge and Oxford in England, one of his most famous projects being the *Oxford Lectern Bible* of 1935. He also designed two type faces—*Montaine* in 1901 and *Centaur* circa 1914—the latter based on the work of Nicolas Jenson (from *Eusebius*, 1470). *Centaur italic* (also named *Arrighi* and based on the calligrapher Arrighi's manuscripts circa 1520) was designed by another American typographer, Frederic Warde, circa 1929.

In 1903, at the age of 28, Frederic W. Goudy opened the Village Press in Park Ridge, Illinois. Goudy became one of the most prolific type designers in printing history, and his types were praised and highly popular throughout America. Elsewhere, however, his types, even his later, more sophisticated works, were considered too idiosyncratic (or overdesigned) for setting larger amounts of text. His best types might be considered to be *Deepdene* and *Kennerley*.

A consequence of the typographer working independently of the printer was that the typographer needed a method of explaining to the printer's compositor which typefaces were required and how they should be arranged. Such a plan came to be called a *type specification*. This would typically comprise a diagrammatic drawing (the layout) and the annotated typescript (the mark-up) indicating, in detail, precise descriptions (or instructions) such as style and weight of typefaces and their spatial and positional relationships, which had to be interpreted (or followed to the letter) by the compositor.

Such methods were often the cause of bitter frustration for both typographer and compositor because, for the compositor, it epitomized the deskilling of his craft and exasperation for the typographer when instructions were misinterpreted or unhelpfully corrected. Sometimes the agency-trained typographer had a limited understanding of typesetting and page-making operations; so for those involved in the printing industry, the *type-spec* was the final humiliation before the computer in the 1980s finally, and comprehensively, took all remnants of typographic craft out of their hands. A lasting legacy of this period, however, are the *Rules for Composition* written by Jan Tschichold when he was working in England for Penguin Books from March 1947 to December 1949. It is interesting to compare the work with the current "Penguin Books Rules for Composition" written by Nicky Barneby in 2002, then head of typography at Penguin Books.

Sans Serif: England, Germany, Switzerland—Gill, Renner, and Meier

Unserifed letters (often called *sans serifs, sanserif,* or just *sans*) are an ancient tradition, found on Etruscan and Greek inscriptions from the seventh century BC. Sans serif Roman printing types, however, did not appear until William Caslon IV cut a set of caps in 1816. These were initially ignored but, by the middle of the 19th century, the requirements of advertising meant that there were numerous full-font sans serif variations available, all designed specifically for display purposes only.

The design of a sans serif type for text setting was not considered until the 20th century. Key achievements toward this include Eric Gill's *Gill Sans,* 1927; Paul Renner's *Futura,* 1927; Adrian Frutiger's *Univers,* 1957 (see Fig. 3.20); Hermann Zapf's *Optima,* 1958; and Hans-Eduard Meier's *Syntax,* 1969. *Gill Sans* was the first sans serif to be designed on the humanistic model of Jenson and Aldus Manutius. Meier's *Syntax* was the second. However, none of these, initially, was issued by their foundries with the all the characters required for setting extended texts: for example, no nonlining numerals or small caps. For these reasons alone, typographers found sans serif fonts too restrictive for setting books.

During the 1990s, however, several digital foundries and individual type designers issued comprehensive sans serif fonts, some even with matching serifed fonts to provide a full typographic palette. These sans serif fonts are characterized by a distinctive calligraphic form, providing a more readable, lyrical typeface. Martin Majoor's *Scala* and Fred Smeijers's *Quadraat* (see Fig. 3.21) are good examples, both designed with a humanistic model in mind. Typical of such recent developments is Hans Eduard Meiers' *Linotype Syntax.* This is a reworked and extended version of the original (sans serif) *Syntax* and now includes *Syntax Serif, Syntax Letter,* and a display face called *Syntax Lapidar.*

The Digital Revolution

The initial pressure on graphic design studios to install computers and desktop publishing software in the early 1980s came largely from clients, rather than from designers. Buyers and employers of design expertise sought to democratize the design process, thus allowing a "more flexible, more democratic" working relationship. For this reason, many designers initially saw the computer as a threat to the integrity of their profession precisely because it appeared to eliminate the tacit, hands-on activity that many considered as defining the design process and offered the client the possibility of a more proactive role in the design process.

Before the Digital Revolution (effectively pre-1984), a typographer's studio looked and smelled very different from that of today. Commonly, a typographer would work at a drawing table with parallel motion, plus a flat surface used for cutting, sticking, and making. It would also contain stocks of various papers and boards, craft knives, scalpels, various adhesives, tapes, paints, inks, brushes, technical drawing tools, and, of course, hundreds of pencils, crayons, markers, and pens of various thicknesses. Craft skills, including hand-lettering, had been an integral part of typographic practice because a client presentation inevitably meant finding ways of "mocking up" print by other means. Such craft activities were generally considered to be an integral part of the creative process.

In 1984, the Apple MacIntosh personal computer (PC) was launched in California. In the same year—and the same state—Rudy Vanderlans (originally from Holland) and Zuzana

Licko (pronounced "Litchko," originally from Czechoslovakia) launched their typographic *fanzine Emigré*. Early dot-matrix printer technology was crude, and the use of highly refined, classic typefaces—with their subtle changes of line weight and fine serifs—only emphasized its crudity. In response, Licko designed *Oakland*, a font that utilized what the printer *could* do by restricting the appearance of the characters to elementary "jagged" right-angled "steps." The result of a similar process some years earlier, although with a different outcome, was Wim Crouwel's *New Alphabet*, 1968 (see Fig. 3.22) in response to the "horrible type" coming out of early electronic typesetting devices.

The breakthroughs for digital typography came with the improvement of printer technology and onscreen software. Apple developed the LaserWriter, which used a new language called *PostScript*, developed by Adobe, in which fonts were stored as mathematical formulas instead of bitmaps. This meant that a letterform could be increased in size and its edges would remain microdigitally smooth.

PageMaker, released in 1985, allowed text to be run out onto a page prearranged into columns (or text boxes) and, using the mouse, moved about in much the same way as one would move paper around on a desktop. That was clever enough, but PageMaker also allowed the typographer to adjust the width or length of the columns at will. Not only that, the typographer could change the size of the type in minute increments, as well as the spaces between the characters (of the whole text, line by line, or individually) and the interline spacing, and see the result in seconds. PageMaker made typography *flexible*.

The typographer could now accurately print (using an ink-jet or laser printer) what was on the screen: WYSIWYG (What You See Is What You Get). At this point, Apple began licensing real typefaces. Because PostScript could be read by other, larger machines used to transfer artwork onto film (and later directly to lithographic plates), the typographer suddenly had direct contact again with the printing press (if only in the virtual sense).

The digital age of typography had arrived. It was a revolution that in terms of technological innovation and social implications matched Gutenberg's invention of moveable type more than 500 years earlier. Until the early 1990s, the two primary manufacturers of typesetting equipment remained Monotype and Linotype. Both converted to digital foundries, but were subsequently sold. As a result, their digital inventories survive, but not the older craft connections. The Type Museum, London, holds much of the vast Monotype Corporation archive.

New digital foundries have appeared, the oldest and largest being Adobe Systems in San Jose, California; the Dutch Type Library in The Hague, Netherlands; and Fontworks, in Berlin, Germany. Each has its own version (or interpretation) of the best fonts of the past. Perhaps the most significant influence of digital technology is that it has enabled type design to become a "cottage industry," in fact, a genuinely postindustrial craft. Type designers have now been aided by the global communications network that is the World Wide Web and by competitions, conferences, lecture programs, and exhibitions that are organized by typographic organizations, such as Association Typographique Internationale (AtypI), International Society of Typographic Designers (ISTD), and New York Type Club (NYTC).

REFERENCES

Barneby, N. (2002). Rules of composition. *TypoGraphic, 58,* 14–20.

Bill, M. (2000). On typography. In *Typography papers* (Vol. 4, p. 41). Reading, England: University of Reading,

Chappell, W., & Bringhurst, R. (1999). *A short history of the printed word* (2nd ed.). Dublin, Ireland: Hartley & Marks.

De Fonenai, A. (1776). *Dictionaire des Artistes* (Vol. 1). Paris.

Gray, N. (1938). *Nineteenth century ornamented types and title pages.* London: Faber & Faber.

Gress, E. (1931). *Fashions in American typography.* New York: Harper & Brothers.

Hague, R. (1936). Reason and typography. *Typography, 1,* 33.

Johnson, A. F. (1934). *Type designs: Their history and development.* London: Grafton & Company.

Lethaby, W. R. (1931). Art and workmanship. *The Imprint, 1,* 1.

Mores, E. R. (1776). *A dissertation upon English typographical founders and foundries.* London.

Morison, S. (1960). *Four centuries of fine printing.* London: Ernest Benn. (Original work published 1924)

Morison, S. (1967). *First principles of typography.* Cambridge, England: Cambridge University Press. (Original work published 1930)

Shinn, N. (2004). T. M. Cleland. *TypoGraphic, 61,* 18–22.

Symonds, J. A. (1875–1886). *Renaissance in Italy* (7 vols.). London: Smith, Elder, & Co.

Tschichold, J. (1975). Rules of composition. In R. McLean (Ed.), *Jan Tschichold: Typographer* (pp. 94–95). London: L. Humphries.

Tschichold, J. (2000). *Typography Papers* (No. 4, p. 71). Reading, England: University of Reading.

Updike, D. B. (1937). *Printing types: Their history, forms and use* (Vol. 1, 2nd ed.). Oxford, England: Oxford University Press.

Warde, B. (1955). *The Pencil Draws a Vicious Circle* (p. 73). London: Sylvian.

CHAPTER 4

History of the Book, Authorship, Book Design, and Publishing

David Finkelstein
Queen Margaret University College, Edinburgh, Scotland

It has been argued that the history of the book in Western culture can be subdivided into three key revolutionary phases (see e.g., Anderson, 1983; Eisenstein, 1979; Johns, 1998; McLuhan, 1962/1969; Ong, 1982/2002). The first was the movement from oral to written cultures (which included such key moments as the invention of the alphabet, the development of written languages, the setting up of trade structures and economies, the creation and use of writing tools such as ink, paper, and codexes, and the setting up of systems of writing). The second involved shifts from literacy to printing, moving through manuscript culture, the invention of printing, the move of print into the center of culture and society, and the printing of books and newspapers for mass audiences thanks to technological advances during the Industrial Revolution. The third phase is one we are currently living through, moving from print to computer-mediated technology, and seeing print absorbed into a larger communication framework that includes visual and sound media.

Elsewhere in this handbook, you will find details regarding the "first revolution." Western European traditions of social communication through writing go back several millennia, to the Near East and Mesopotamia. Around 3500 to 3300 BC, it has been argued, Sumerian farming communities began forming into urban city-states. The invention of new irrigation techniques for farming the dry lands and the resulting sophisticated commercial and social transactions of urban life called for the development of shared, common legal and social structures and codes. It has been suggested that it is from these needs that writing sprang—not, as one would assume, to record language, but rather as mnemonic devices (memory aids scratched on hard surfaces such as clay tablets) to record economic communications and transactions, and to register ownership and other claims on goods and property (Assmann, 1994; Schmandt-Besserat, 1982a, 1982b).

Mesopotamia was not unique in developing script for communication purposes. Among others of note were Egyptian hieroglyphics, developed around 3000 BC; Aegean scripts (the so-called Linear A and Linear B scripts), dated around 1650 to 1200 BC; Indus Valley script, from about 3000 to 2400 BC; Chinese script, circa 1500 BC; the Greek alphabet (precursor of Western alphabets), circa 800 to 700 BC; Mayan script, occurring about 50 AD; and Aztec script, dating from 1400 AD.[1]

---

[1]It is outside the remit of this chapter to follow through on the development of written culture in other parts of the world, but further information on script and written culture as it evolved in places like South America, China, and Southeast Asia can be found in Bayly (1996), Cavallo (1999), Christin (2001), Goody (1987), Harris (1989), Havelock (1988), Lavallée (2001), Lechtman and Soldi (1981), Martin (1995), and Oliver (2001).

Egyptian hieroglyphic writing proved a more sophisticated recording system in its initial conception than Sumerian cuneiform: Its purpose was "political rather than economic communication, the recording of acts of special political significance" (Assmann, 1994, p. 18). Like Mesopotamian writing, it would become the province of an elite section of society, a "priesthood expert in medicine and magic" (Noegel, 2004, p. 135), with hieroglyphics "reserved for the 'writing of divine words,' as it is called in Egyptian, for recordings in the sacred space of permanence" (Assmann, 1994, p. 19).

Such reverence for the sacred nature of the word carried through to cultures based in the Sinai and Palestinian regions, as most notably expressed in the Hebrew Bible. This, as Scott B. Noegel (2004) points out, is not surprising, "since Israel became a cultural conduit and receptacle for Egyptian and Mesopotamian influences, and since in Canaan (which eventually would become the land of Israel) writing first appeared in cuneiform script" (p. 135).

Although there were also obvious differences and deviations between usage and development of writing systems, what united Mesopotamian, Egyptian, and Sinaitic cultures was a belief in the weight of words, both written and spoken, "a conception of words as vehicles of power, of creation by fiat, and of the oracular use of written and spoken words" (Noegel, 2004, p. 134). What this meant in practice was a careful attention to the representation of words, a practice of transcription that believed inaccuracies would violate sacred tenets and have unforeseen, dire consequences. Within such contexts, "An accurate memory is everything, copying is sacred, and knowledge of the associative subtleties embedded in a text is tantamount to secret knowledge of the divine" (Livingstone, 1986; Noegel, 2004, p. 137).

Similar sacralistic intent carried through into medieval times and Western European manuscript culture, part of the second "phase." Manuscript culture has its own trajectory and history, usually characterized as dividing into two periods—the Monastic Age, running from around 400 AD to late 1100 AD, and the Secular Age, developing at the tail end of the Monastic Age and running through to the start of the "incunabula" period of printing in the late 1400s (and leaking over beyond then). The Monastic Age gets its name from the fact that for much of the so-called Dark Ages, framed by the destruction of the Roman Empire in the 5th century until the rise of university centers in the 12th and 13th centuries, monasteries and other religious centers were at the heart of Western European book production. Intellectual life was focused on such centers, and manuscripts were produced in line with religious interest in upholding the authority of the church and its teachings.

Such monastic orders set aside portions of the day for intellectual endeavor and the copying and illuminating of sacred texts. The monastic *scriptoria* or *scriptorium,* where such work took place, was highly organized in nature: Spaces were set aside for various aspects of manuscript production (lettering, calligraphy, illumination, binding), and specific tasks were assigned to different members of the order. From the 11th century onward, monasteries also had work done by professional scriveners or scribes hired for the purpose. This piecework accelerated as demand increased for teaching texts in the "Secular Age" from the universities newly established in places like Bologna, Paris, Leuven, Basel, Cambridge, and Oxford. The demand soon outstripped monastic capacity to provide texts, and as a result a separate, commercial book industry was created, providing *peciae,* or original exemplar texts for students and interested laypeople to rent and copy from.

The founding of universities in the late 1100s onward increased interest in books, with new readers wanting a wider range of secular and nonreligious books than previously available. Initially many of these were priests attached to their chosen university or college, who along with their professors required texts of classical authors, references, commentaries, and glosses. Universities set up libraries to cater for student demand, and along with this established university-based workshops to cope with the demand for copies of essential works.

At the same time, another reading public developed from the 13th century onward, made up of the emerging bourgeois classes—lawyers, state officials, successful merchants, and medics. Their interest in books for professional activity expanded the range of texts on the market to include law, politics, science, and medicine, as well as other works of entertainment such as literary romances, translations, and poetry. The resulting rush in production of secular, "humanistic" works (all still handwritten) marked out the new era from its predecessor, where books had been focused on religious themes (although there had also been allowed certain works of ancient Latin authors such as Ovid, Virgil, Boethius, and Priscian, granted special exemption from the prevailing rules by medieval religious authorities).

GUTENBERG AND CHANGE

Johannes Gutenberg is credited with changing all this, adapting old materials to new activities—the olive oil and grape screw press, for example, proving the inspiration for the hand press; the development of moveable metal type potentially inspired by such early prototypes as Chinese wooden printing blocks. Gutenberg, born in Mainz in the 1390s, was initially a goldsmith. In 1448, after various secret experiments with lead type and press parts, he came up with the prototype of what in Western Europe is now considered to be the first printing press. The first book attributed to him was a 42-line Bible (the Mainz Bible), which appeared around 1456. Other books also attributed to his printing press between 1455 and 1460 (when he stopped printing) included a 36-line Bible, some grammatical works, a papal indulgence, at least one broadside astrological calendar, and possibly the *Catholicon* of Joannes Balbus de Jannua.

Printing took hold as Gutenberg's innovations were exported to other countries. First to take advantage of this new innovation were German towns between the 1460s and 1480s, followed by Switzerland. It would then spread across Western Europe to France, Italy, Spain, Britain, and elsewhere. It reached Buda in Hungary in 1473, Cracow in Poland, and Prague in Bohemia a few years later. The first books in Spain were printed in Valencia in 1473, and the first Portuguese printings were done in Lisbon in 1489. The first press in Scandinavia was built in Stockholm in 1483. By 1500, every significant urban center in Europe could boast of at least one printing workshop.

Printing soon reached beyond Europe: For example, a press was set up in Constantinople in 1488, and later in Salonika (Greece) in 1515. The earliest Greek types had been cut by Aldus Manutius in Venice in the 1490s. Printing did not reach areas that used the Cyrillic script until much later, with the first printed books in Moscow and Belgrade being run off in the 1550s. The English book trade would emerge earlier, when printing was brought to London by William Caxton in 1476. The concern of the Tudors to suppress seditious and heretical literature in the 16th century led to a compact between booksellers and the crown. Under Queen Mary, the London Stationers' Company were granted a monopoly charter in 1557, giving them control over London book production as well as prohibiting printing elsewhere (with the exception of the university towns of Oxford and Cambridge). The monopoly would continue through to the late 1700s when, as we see later in this chapter, it was challenged by the Scottish bookseller William Donaldson, with the results having international repercussions.

Previously, knowledge had circulated through hand-produced and handwritten texts. Information about international events would circulate in this fashion, copied and sent across borders and around small networks made up of educated laypeople, church members, and other civil authorities. What Gutenberg's development in 1450 enabled people to do was to mass-produce texts and circulate them widely in a way that hadn't been done before.

But not all welcomed this development. The development of printing in the late 15th and early 16th centuries forced through a process of cultural change that threatened privileges and areas under elitist control. A good example of such reactions is the case of the 16th-century Venetian monk who argued in the Venetian senate (to their general approval) against the adoption of Gutenberg's printing innovations. Printing needed to be resisted in favor of writing, he argued vehemently, because it corrupted texts (through circulation in poorly manufactured and incorrect editions for profit), it corrupted minds (making available immoral or dangerous texts to a general public without proper approval or consent by the church), and it corrupted knowledge (by making it freely available to the ignorant) (Chartier, 1989).

The democratizing nature of printing is evident in the way in which literacy spread in its wake, helped by the Protestant-led Reformation movement in the 1500s, which advocated, among other things, widespread literacy so as to encourage the individual reading and interpretation of the Bible and other religious works. The invention of printing drew on and accelerated the spread of reading by making such material more readily accessible. Yet it was not the only factor. Also playing a part was a general rise in economic prosperity, due in no small part to the riches uncovered and exploited on the discovery and colonization of new lands in the Indies, Asia, and America. Similarly, the rise of the Humanist movement (also known as the Renaissance) in the 17th century prompted the rediscovery of classical texts previously suppressed under the Monastic Age. The splits in the Catholic Church created by the Reformation and the reaction of the Counter-Reformation had consequences on material churned out by the presses servicing either side. Likewise the evolution of nation-states and the desire to create new, distinctive senses of nationhood through literary culture, as well as the expansion of human understanding of science and nature, all contributed to the spread of material produced and readers reading the results. Initially, printing also changed the look of book to make reading easier. New fonts were developed. Aldus Manutius in Venice pioneered a portable-size book to allow readers to dispense with lecterns or reading stands. The range of subject matter, though still dominated by the needs of religion and law, began to expand more rapidly.

EXPORTING PRINT COMMUNICATION PRACTICES

European printing technology spread with the development of imperial and overseas colonial possessions between the 16th and 19th centuries, used to service intellectual, economic, and political needs. One of the first printing presses founded in the United States, for example, was in Cambridge, Massachusetts, in 1639, begun to meet the needs of students and staff at Harvard College (itself founded in 1636). Commercial printing would gain a boost when the English printer William Bradford set up a press in Philadelphia in 1685, and then one in New York in 1693. Benjamin Franklin would make his fortune in the 1730s running a network of printing houses and newspaper presses.

Printing networks and activities would flourish or falter as per the specific needs of and levels of support by the ruling powers. Initial printing setups were usually part of missionary settlements and official print communication requirements for information purposes. New Zealand printing, for example, began in support of missionary activities between 1814 and 1845, and expanded to print newspapers and other materials for incoming colonist from the 1840s onward.

The pattern of printing development in New Zealand is one that we see replicated in other colonial territories such as the West Indies, Hawaii, Tahiti, Indonesia, Kenya, and India. In India, although trade with European powers had flourished from the 1600s onward, interestingly enough its ultimate rulers (the British) were among the last of the European powers active in India to introduce the printing press into their areas of influence, setting up a press in 1761 that had been captured from the French. It was used primarily for printing official documents and proclamations. Printing for popular consumption came much more slowly. The first newspaper in Calcutta came out in 1780, followed by one in Madras in 1785 and Bombay in 1789. By the mid-19th century, newspapers and magazines were common elements in Anglo-Indian life.

Australia had a similar history of printing development. Throughout the 19th century, there was little domestic book publishing in Australia; it would start developing after the influx of immigrants drawn by the lure of gold during the Gold Rush of the 1850s, but focus mainly on producing newspapers and magazines for this new audience. Books that were to be had were usually imported from Britain and the United States by Australian wholesale book distributors such as George Robertson of Melbourne. Australian writers who wanted to publish had to either serialize their work in various local and regional journals and newspapers, or get a London publisher to take them on and hope their work was resold in Australia, although after the 1880s matters changed with the introduction of inexpensive colonial series books aimed at British-dominated markets in India, Canada, Australia, and New Zealand.

Toward the end of 19th century, Australian booksellers would start to publish original work, often in partnership with British publishers. In general though, from the 1890s through to the 1960s, the Australian book market was dominated by British publishers, who kept tight control of books circulating around the country through scrupulous prosecutions under the terms of the Australian Copyright Act of 1912, which "ensured that overseas publishers could dictate the terms of trade and oblige retailers to obtain their supplies from prescribed sources, thus fixing prices and maintaining them at a higher level" (Kirsop, 2001, p. 326). As late as 1961, exports accounted for 40% of British books manufactured in that year, of which 25% were destined for Australia alone (Johanson, 2000).

In Canada, printing and book production started much earlier, but was equally slow in moving away from dependency on overseas suppliers to creating a nationally based industry. As one survey suggests:

> Publishing in Canada began with handwritten manuscripts, circulated privately. This gave way to the newspaper and general publishing output of printing presses using hand-set type, and thence to new technologies as they became available. Distribution of books, in the earliest years, was often by private importation of by purchase from the local printing office, before the population was great enough to support separate bookstores and distribution agents. (MacDonald, 2001, p. 92)

The development of printing moved across Canada in tandem with internal land development; the first printing press was set up in Halifax in 1751, to be followed by a printing operation in Quebec in 1764, and presses in Niagara in 1793 and Toronto in 1798. These presses on the whole worked on job printing (producing small handbills, posters, stationery, account books). They also printed official state documentation, religious texts, and newspapers. For much of its early history, through until the late 1880s, Canadian printing structure was regionalized, functionalist, and individual in nature. As one commentator adds, "It was not until consolidation began with the arrival of large non-Canadian firms at the beginning of the twentieth century that this changed" (MacDonald, 2001, p. 93).

THE AGE OF STEAM

As can be deduced from the preceding examples, for much of the period from Gutenberg's time to the 19th century, printing and publishing structures followed fairly simple business models. Early printers acted as printers, publishers, and booksellers in one. They commissioned and bought rights to works, then produced and attempted to make a profit from the finished products. As trade increased to include international links, these roles began to be separated: By the early 19th century, many Western European cities had traders specializing specifically in publishing, subcontracting to printers, illustrators, and other related production specialists to complete material work on books and other printed texts, and subsequently selling the finished products to established, specialist book retailers.

Among the first to change, partly in response to the technological advances made during the Industrial Revolution of the late 18th and early 19th centuries, were the British. After 1780, we see a shift from small, individualized firms to large, multifocused family-led corporate entities.

Similarly, we begin to see the increasing movement of print into a dominant position in the public sphere, as new technology developed in the 19th century made the business of printing faster and cheaper to run. The Koenig steam press, for example, first unveiled by the directors of the *Times* newspaper in London in 1814, revolutionized the world of print. Writing could be turned into print pages in a fraction of the time and at a fraction of the cost of previous hand-press and machine efforts. Likewise it could be sped to increasingly distant destinations by the steam trains and boats that linked counties and countries together.

Such success enabled printing to spread its products beyond national borders. From the 1830s onward, British business models would be copied in North America and in other European states: As David Reed (1997) has argued, the "second half of the nineteenth century saw a complete transformation of the printing trade" (p. 44). In the United States, as mentioned earlier, printing had formed a key part of developing U.S. national consciousness (exemplified, e.g., in the Declaration of Independence, a transformative, printed document that has since become an iconic symbol of U.S. national identity). But as David D. Hall (1996) points out, the "golden age" of U.S. publishing and printing activity occurs after 1830, when businesses adopt new processes that increase capacity and make use of the new communication structures (railways, roads, telegraphic lines) that would unite the East and West coasts. Firms such as Harpers in New York, or Carey, Lea in Philadelphia would emerge to become nationally and internationally known. Their ability to make such impact on local markets was in part due to their dominant size and ability to produce more at cheaper cost—typically, American editions were three or four times larger than British printings (which averaged about 750–1,000 copies per edition), and prices a third or a quarter less. Such cheap print runs were also helped by widespread flouting of copyright and pirating (with the main victims usually British firms and authors whose works were liberally borrowed). Until 1891, when the U.S. government reluctantly passed the Chace Act (which adopted some of the copyright legislation measures hammered out by international conventions throughout the 19th century), U.S. restrictions on non-U.S.-produced material, and its accompanying plundering of foreign sources for profitable work, would prove a major point of contention with countries, businesses, and writers affected by such practices.

But such protectionism was also part of a move by American publishers and printers to coax to life an internal mass market for their works. It would lead, for example, to early experiments in paperback productions, such as paperback "newspaper supplements" hawked by newsboys and mail-order methods in the 1840s; and paperbacks produced and sold in the 1860s through to the 1890s by the Boston-based Beadle Brothers. The concept would return in the 1930s with the launch in the UK of the groundbreaking Penguin series of cheap paperbacks, whose success would be replicated by other international publishers and whose format would become part of the general fabric of book publication activity.

Such 19th-century successes were joined by successful ventures in daily, weekly, monthly, and quarterly journal and newspaper publishing (see chap. 13), and not confined to Europe, the United States, and UK colonies alone. Among innovations tried were serializations of fiction and nonfiction, used to boost newspaper and journal sales and act as advertising for publishers' wares. From the 1840s through to the 1880s and beyond, serialization became standard fare for literary periodical and newspaper sources: Texts (either pirated or bought legally) reached international audiences through endless recycling in serialized form in different countries. Such recycling also played an important part in turning authorship into a profitable profession.

BOOKS AND AUTHORS

Let us turn our attention to authorship: How do we define *authorship*, and when did it become a significant part of our cultural milieu? It has been argued that interpretations of what authors did and what they stood for came into sharp focus during the Renaissance period (Finklestein and McCleery, 2005). This was due in no small part to the opportunities made possible by the mass reproduction of printed texts, the shift in the 15th century from a world where transcribed manuscripts circulated in small numbers to a world where works could be reproduced in large quantities. Writing became a socially recognized activity, a means of gaining individual acclaim and social status. Authors could emerge as "sellable names," signifiers attached to individual products that led to evaluation, recognition, and in some cases an enhanced reputation. It gave impetus to human desires to seek fame, if not fortune, from such work.

Printing engaged writers in a manner that was different from previous scribal activity. It also undermined previous social beliefs in authorship as part of an established, collective authority—no longer were they merely cogs in an ecclesiastical wheel. The same principles of individualized authorship could be found in other textual arenas. As Douglas Brooks (2000) points out, British playwrights, for example, were quick to gain advantages from popular interest in their printed plays, linked as they were to moves to professionalize the London theaters and stages from the 1500s onward. The result was a commercialization of playwriting that in turn fed and intensified the "preoccupation with individualized autho-rial agency" (p. xiv). Printers saw that money could be made from printed plays branded with named and known authors. Their authentication of "authoritative texts" could then be used to enhance their market value. Such examples show how printing in the early period of development shifted cultural perceptions of authorship to make it possible for individ-ual writers to emerge, completing, as Mark Rose (1994) comments, "the transformation of the medieval *auctor* into the Renaissance *author*" (p. 18; italics original).

Such changes shifted interests and activities of authors. Later in this chapter, we cover copyright and its application to authorship. Generally, the concept of copyright as a repre-sentation of authorial ownership of intellectual property did not prevail until the late 18th and early 19th centuries, when it was aggressively implemented in Britain, France, and Germany, among other places. Scholars, however, have pointed out early legal examples of literary property debates from the 1500s onward, which were linked to legal recognition of individual rights to patents on inventions (Brown, 1995; Eisenstein, 1979, Vol. 1; Rose, 1994). Cases recorded in France in 1504, for example, focus on such definitions, as in the success-ful challenge of Guillaume Cop, a well-known Parisian doctor responsible for the compila-tion of an annual almanac, against a bookseller who had been printing copies of the almanac without Cop's agreement. Cop successfully argued for an injunction against fur-ther printings and sales by the bookseller. The underlying legal point acknowledged that it was the addition of Cop's name and signature that authenticated the work, adding value and increasing sales. As Mark Rose comments, "In a sense, then, what Cop was securing was as much a right having to do with the use of his name as a right to a text" (pp. 18–20). Such cases, as Cynthia J. Brown (1995) explains, signaled a shift in perceptions about the role of authors in a commercial environment:

> Authors had become marketable commodities outside the courtly circle of wealthy benefactors, and new participants in book production—the printer, the publisher, and eventually a different, more expanded reading public—were crucial determinants in an authors' involvement in determining the physical and literary makeup of their books.

She concludes that these, and other such legal moves by late medieval writers, signaled an important shift in textual production patterns: "Indeed, the hierarchical triad of patron, poet, and scribe that characterized the manuscript culture evolved into a more balanced sharing of authority in the association of patron, poet, and publisher in the print culture" (p. 2).

Changes in copyright laws in the late 18th century would change all that. Before these changes took hold and irrevocably shifted business patterns, however, authors generally worked within the context of a highly structured patronage system. The system had evolved along with the development of a manuscript culture in the medieval era. Within this structure, "authors" found themselves trying to master the art of pleasing courtly circles of wealthy benefactors, where "through a complex set of symbolic and material transactions, patrons received honor and status in the form of service from their clients, and in return provided both material and immaterial rewards" (Rose, 1994, p. 16).

Patrons would commission, protect, encourage, and in many cases control literary production. Authors who had no independent income of their own invariably looked for powerful patrons who could offer them funds and help promote their careers. Such social systems were much in evidence throughout the 14th and 15th centuries, functioning as a gift exchange economy, where authors dedicated or presented works to potential courtly or elite sponsors (kings, knights, princes, noblemen, and noblewomen), in the hopes of securing a financial gift in return, and/or securing a sinecure post within the sponsor's household or social and political circles (Macherel, 1983; Mauss, 1954).

The system functioned in tandem with a market economy: By finding the right sponsor to dedicate a work to, an author could ensure a popular success for the work, using the sponsor's reputation to gain a wide readership among significant figures in the court and society. Such social positioning would prove particularly important from the 16th century onward, when authors found that the business of publishing often involved complex negotiations with publisher and booksellers based on assessments of their financial worth and potential (Febvre & Martin, 1976; Darnton, 1982a; Brewer and McCalman, 1999). Through to the mid-1700s, despite changes in markets and audiences, we still find authors trying to align themselves with powerful patrons.

Patronage at its worst often supported those of little talent or ambition. It demanded a price—authors could find their intellectual gifts compromised, subordinated to the whims of their sponsors. They could find themselves forced to write work supporting or praising their patrons and their social interests, or commissioned to produce material to fit particular political agendas. So we find notable English authors such as Joseph Addison, Richard Steele, William Congreve, Edward Gibbon, and Samuel Johnson, respected for their writings and statements published in the newly emerging London press, finding their independence of thought cramped and crimped by having accepted government positions or royal pensions, and so unable to refuse official demands on their time and skills. As John Brewer (1997) notes, "Most writers supported by the crown were expected to pen political polemics in favour of the king's ministers" (p. 163). Under such sponsored systems, authors could find themselves torn between their intellectual interests and financial practicalities, having to produce material in a form likely to attract and keep patrons, and if funded by the government, write discreetly enough to avoid political disapproval. As Cynthia Brown (1995) concludes, authors often had to compromise morally and creatively to carve out a living: "In the patronage system, then, the author's writing represented his personal rendition of the patron's desires, needs, or image, inspired either by some form of commission or by the hope of obtaining one" (p. 106).

AUTHORS AND COPYRIGHT

The rise of a reading public in the late 18th century (with interests in and ability to pay for printed works) created changes in the economic fortunes of authors, generating an audience outside of the patronage system from whom authors could earn money if successful in capturing their imagination. Crucially it would be the development of copyright as a legal concept that would lead to an economic revolution, a result of 18th-century legal battles in Britain between English and Scottish factions.

Interpretations of who owned the results of an author's efforts would be clarified in 1774 following a landmark legal case in London between a Scottish and English bookseller. The case was argued with the legal help of James Boswell, the literary recorder of Samuel Johnson's life. *Donaldson v. Becket* established the legal precedents and concepts of individual copyright ownership that would shape all international interpretations of copyright that followed. Initially, authors or whoever bought copyright were granted sole reproduction rights for 14, then 28 years. France followed in 1778 with its own legal interpretation of copyright protection (rights that were subsequently strengthened in 1793 with further statutes). Austria followed in 1832, as did Germany in 1835. Over the next 60 years, other nations slowly adopted similar copyright laws (with increasing lengths of time assigned for copyright protection—50, then 75 years from initial publication), but international copyright regulation was achieved only after much struggle with the ratification of the Berne convention in 1891.

But it should be noted that copyright, in the sense of exclusive control over the proceeds and process of printed texts, was something that had been part of the printing process since the late 15th century. There are legal records of Milanese publishers and printers, for example, seeking and being granted exclusive copyright privileges as early as 1481 (when Andrea de Bosiis secures publishing rights to Jean Simoneta's *Sforziade*) and 1483 (when the Duke of Milan issues a 5-year privilege to Petrus Justinus of Tolentino for rights to print Francesco Filelfo's *Convivium*). The renewal of such rights and privileges in profitable titles (some concessions could last up to 30 years) was highly contentious and frequently contested. This often led to powerful monopolies that made it difficult for newcomers to break in and establish credibility in the printing, publishing, or bookselling business.

To cover production costs, often under such schemes the printer/publisher solicited advance payments from interested readers. This then gave way to general commercial publishing practices associated with current systems of authorial interaction (royalty payments, e.g., on copies sold). Subscription publishing functioned for many years as one of the single most important methods (after patronage) of securing publication for prose and verse works. In Britain, volume subscription rose swiftly in the late 1600s until the 1730s, maintained a steady level throughout the middle of the century, then rose again during the last 20 years of the 18th century. Works subscribed in this fashion ranged from poetry, sermons, histories, medical texts, and advice manuals to biographies, mathematical works, music books, and other nonliterary texts.

Other methods of rewarding authors included the half-profits system, where authors would agree to share the risk of publication, and in return receive 50% of book sales income after costs. This was common throughout the 18th and 19th centuries, but could be abused by unscrupulous publishers doctoring and inflating printing costs at the expense of the authors' pocket. Another method of reward, in use since the beginning of printing, was the outright purchase at a fixed price of an author's copyright. Under this system, authors were paid up front but did not share in any subsequent profits from sales. A third method also in frequent use, particularly after late-18th-century copyright rulings were acted on by commercially aware authors, was the selling of copyright to a publisher for a fixed number of years, or for a stated number of editions, at the end of which the author regained ownership of the work.

Finally, there was the establishment in the 19th century of a relatively transparent system of royalty payments that continues in general form to this day. This royalty system allowed authors to gain an agreed, sliding-scale percentage of the retail price of every copy of their work sold. The system, said to have been developed first in the United States, became commonplace in Europe from the 1880s onward, some say as a result of attention paid to George Haven Putnam's arguments for the system in his *Authors and Publishers: A Manual of Suggestions for Beginners in Literature* (1883) and *The Grievances Between Authors and Publishers* (1887). Likewise, it's not until the turn of the 20th century that we see the development of the marketing and promotional strategies that are now in common use today—the rise of literary agents to handle the finances and selling of manuscripts to interested publishers; the promotional tours, readings, and signings that follow book publication; the use of other media (radio, TV, and newspapers) to generate interest in authors' works; the tie-ins between print and other media, with books often optioned and converted into films, audio cassettes, radio plays, or TV shows.

AUTHORS IN AN INDUSTRIAL AGE

Changes in legal rights happened in tandem with major technological and market innovations and change. Book production was transformed by scientific and industrial innovations that increased paper rates, speeded up print production, and altered communication systems. The invention of the mechanized Fourdrinier papermaking machine in 1801, for example, replaced hand-prepared papermaking techniques—printers were able to access more paper more quickly for less. New machines were pioneered to increase typesetting speed. Production time dropped with the use of faster, steam-driven rotary presses. Steam-driven trains and boats speeded up delivery of books and print across national and international borders. Land- and sea-based telegraph cables were laid across national, transatlantic, and international borders, which with the establishment of dependable postal services enabled quick and efficient transmission and circulation of information between authors, editors, and publishers.

Such industrialization of printing and publishing systems was part of a larger industrialization of business across Western Europe. Mechanization enlarged market potential, shifting power in the book trade at the same time. As Roger Escarpit (1966) notes:

> Faced with a developing market, printing and bookselling underwent a major change, as [a] nascent capitalist industry took charge of the book. The publisher appeared as the responsible entrepreneur relegating the printer and bookseller to a minor role. As a side effect, the literary profession began to organize. (pp. 22–23)

FROM THE 20TH CENTURY TO THE FUTURE

Such changes in legal statutes, technology, business practices, and social formations created circumstances by which printed texts, manufactured more quickly and at increasingly cheaper costs, could be sold to more people, generating larger profits for publishers, and allowing individual authors to claim more profits from work produced. During the 20th century, further changes occurred in international corporate and economic business practices and structures. To increase economies of scale, there was an increasing tendency to join publishing houses together through mergers to form large, often transnational conglomerates. This has been due in part to an acknowledgment of the internationalization of business, and to a move by some to join together different media platforms for maximum efficiency and profitability (thus bringing books, newspapers, TV, film, and music industries together under one roof). It could be argued that the "vertical integration" of books into media empires that combine visual and textual products is part of the radical restructuring of social communications (the third revolution) mentioned at the start of this chapter. Various conglomerate models have also evolved, including print-based ones operating in a number of different countries (the German-based Bertelsmann is one example); and multiple media organizations (such as the joining together of Time Warner and AOL). Small independent firms still exist, and will continue to do so, but their activities are often overshadowed by the clout and reach of their larger competitors.

MEDIA GLOBALIZATION

One could argue that such multinational trends in the book-publishing industry have led it to become an engine driving forward cultural globalization, much as it was once a force driving forward cultural change over the past 600 years of human history. The ongoing transition, driven partly by digital technologies, from publishers producing only books and, for example, studios producing only films and TV programs, to combined organizations doing both (and more) has blurred the distinction between the two types of conglomerate from the 1990s onward. The linked characteristics of media and print conglomerate industries are certainly striking: Both involve hefty capital investment, a move to generate mass-market content through mass production techniques, and moves to increase multipurpose use of cultural assets and intellectual property—books into film scripts and the like.

Recent trends in corporate mergers and acquisitions, particular in the United States since the 1960s, suggest that such conglomeration of media is rising, in particular since the 1990s. One analysis done in 1996 demonstrated a dramatic jump in such corporate activity, with more than 557 media acquisitions occurring between 1990 and 1995 alone, almost equal to the number of similar transactions recorded between 1960 and 1989 (Greco, 1995, 1996). This flurry of activity during the 1990s has resulted in major transnational media conglomerates whose activities reach across a range of cultural products. More recent examples include the highly trumpeted merger in 2000 of AOL, chiefly an Internet service provider and online-focused organization, with Time Warner, itself a media conglomerate that combined TV and film with book-publishing interests. The merger created for a period one of the largest such corporations in the world. The year 2000 also saw the merger of the French conglomerate Vivendi, whose core holdings included media and book publishing, with the U.S.-based music, film, and TV giant Universal. Other media conglomerates were pushed to follow such examples, adding digital technologies, products, and services to traditional book trade activity, with the hope that the result would cross-fertilize and offer integrated synergy through exploitation of texts and intellectual property across different media platforms. The ultimate example of business appropriation of the intellectual-property branding and copyright process first begun in the 1700s has been the successful efforts of the Disney Corporation to change and expand U.S. intellectual-property law statutes to protect its investment in Mickey Mouse and other Disney characters. Exploiting brands is no longer confined to books—it encompasses films, television, theme parks, CDs, and merchandising. Texts complete the circle of products in the form of direct publication or licensing of children's books based on the characters created in original texts (Winnie the Pooh is one classic example), or in the form of "novelizations" of films (basically amplifications of film screenplays and action), themselves based on original novels or other texts (such as comic books and graphic novels).

BOOK HISTORY AND THE COMMUNICATION CIRCUIT

With such a broad canvas of change to work with, how do we go about studying the place of books in society? Robert Darnton's groundbreaking essay, "What Is the History of Books?"—published in the early 1980s and since endlessly reproduced—focused attention on the diverse methods and avenues available to the enterprising scholar interested in the place of books in society. Darnton proposed a general model for analyzing the way in which books made their way into society, a "communication circuit" running "from the author to the publisher (if the bookseller does not assume that role), the printer, the shipper, the bookseller, and the reader" (Darnton, 1982b, p. 11). The circuit would work within and between these key players—thus allowing room, for example, for discussing how readers could influence authors' and texts (such as shown in studies on the role of audiences in influencing 19th-century authors' writing of novels serialized in literary journals), or the place of booksellers in publishing plans (as Darnton demonstrated with a case study drawn from 18th-century French print culture tracking the contraction and expansion of the French book trade through bookselling orders). Darnton's circuit derived from similar models in communication studies, but his intention was to offer book historians a way of conceiving the production of texts as a multifaceted enterprise encompassing social, economic, political, and intellectual conditions. "Books belong to circuits of communication that operate in consistent patterns, however complex they may be," he concluded. "By unearthing those circuits, historians can show that books do not merely recount history; they make it" (Darnton, 1982b, p. 22).

Since Darnton's presentation of the "communication circuit" as a focus for book history studies, the field has begun increasingly to take note of what McGann has described as the "socialization of texts": that is, the impact of books as artifacts traveling from private to public spaces. In this way, production is seen very much part of a process of, as Paul Duguid (1996) notes, "producing a public artifact and inserting it in a particular social circuit" (p. 81).

But not all have been satisfied with Darnton's (and his successors) definition of such communication circuits. In 1993, two eminent British bibliographers (Thomas R. Adams and Nicolas Barker) argued with and proposed an expansion of Darnton's model. For them, the point was to draw attention to the bio-bibliographical dimension that many steeped in bibliographic traditions felt was missing from a postprint (i.e., after 1500) perspective on book history. The answer to the questions, "What did people imagine a book was? What was it for?" involved acknowledging a deeper connection between people and texts in antiquity than might be expected. Although agreeing that Darnton's communication circuit had its uses from the perspective of social-history analysis, they critiqued its approach as too focused on explaining communication systems, ignoring the book as an artifact in its own right. They proposed a study of books based on production processes, a circuit made up of five events in the life of a text (publishing, manufacturing, distribution, reception, and survival), surrounded and affected by four zones of influence (intellectual influences; political, legal, and religious influences; commercial pressures; social behavior and taste). The result was a reversal of emphasis: "The text is the reason for the cycle of the book: its transmission depends on its ability to set off new cycles." This is a circuit that does not follow how people interact with texts, but rather one that follows texts "whose sequence constitutes a system of communication" (Adams & Barker, 1993, p. 15).

Jerome McGann (1991) has called for a slightly different tack, one grounded in studying books through social and material contexts: "One breaks the spell of romantic hermeneutics by socializing the study of texts at the most radical levels" (p. 12). McGann's "socialization of the text" would prove an influential rallying call in the development of book history research, joining Don McKenzie's "sociology of the text" (1986) as a means of underlining how book historians differentiated their areas of investigation from those that worked from a strictly literary or historical base.

In 1998, the editors of a new journal in the area used the first issue to set out ambitious parameters for the history of the book, ones broad enough to accommodate all such concerns:

> [*Book History* would be about] the entire history of written communication: the creation, dissemination, and uses of script and print in any medium, including books, newspapers, periodicals, manuscripts, and ephemera. . . . the social, cultural, and economic history of authorship, publishing, printing, the book arts, copyright, censorship, bookselling and distribution, libraries, literacy, literary criticism, reading habits, and reader responses. (Greenspan & Rose, 1998, p. ix)

Or as another scholar stated more succinctly, the history of the book "is centrally about ourselves. It asks how past readers have made meaning (and therefore, by extension, how others have read differently from us); but it also asks where the conditions of possibility for our own reading came from" (Price, 2002, p. 39). Such a broad definition is likely to be the one that finds most favor with those who study book history, given that it covers all aspects of print activity.

CONCLUSION

Two key issues have until recently informed how we understand books in society. First, there is the issue of "reproducibility." Printing shifted communication structures by being able to duplicate exact copies of texts very quickly, so allowing knowledge to be transferred more efficiently and more reliably across time and space. In the second place, this "fixing" of print would become a key factor in establishing authority and trust in the figures (authors) who produced these works. It would create a new profession (authorship), bring forth an entire industry dedicated to promoting such a profession, and place the printed word at the center of social communication.

As technology has grown increasingly sophisticated, and society has developed institutional and social filters to control and assess print outputs (publishing houses, editorial staff, periodical and literary reviews and reviewers), we have grown accustomed to placing trust in corporate identities and brands. Our dependency on and trust in the printed text has not diminished in the face of an increasing domination of the personal computer in commercial and social transactions, and the increasing diversity of information and activity now available and utilized via the World Wide Web. It is clear that as we move into an era marked by discussions of the "new" electronic revolution, the old print revolution, begun in the 15th century, assumes a clearer focus and a natural closure. Just as manuscript traditions merged with new print technologies, so too we are now seeing similar mergings and complementarities between new and old media. The embedding of visual culture into cultural formations from the 20th century onward (the advance of film, TV, the World Wide Web) has meant also a reshaping of print to accommodate such forms of communication. One has only to look at the multiple media through which humanity now communicates to see that books and printed materials are slowly being displaced from the center of social communication to the periphery, still necessary but no longer the sole form of information in an electronic age. But if the book in the future will no longer be the main form of human communication, this does not signify, as some critics would have us believe, the death of the book. Nor does it lessen the impact of print on social formations. Book history is important for what it says about human development. For well over 500 years, books have been central to the shaping of Western society, and to the transmission of its values outward (whether imposed or voluntarily) into colonized and connected societies and territories. Without the portability and reach of print, social, cultural, legal, humanistic, and religious structures would not have developed, been transmitted, or shaped beliefs and systems around the world.

REFERENCES

Adams, T., & Barker, N. (1993). A new model for the study of the book. In N. Barker (Ed.), *A potencie of life: Books in society* (pp. 000–000). London: British Library 5–43.

Anderson, B. (1983). *Imagined communities*. London: Verso.

Assmann, J. (1994). Ancient Egypt and the materiality of the sign. In H. U. Gumbrecht & K. L. Pfeiffer (Eds.), *Materialities of communication* (pp. 5–31). Stanford, CA: Stanford University Press.

Bayly, C. A. (1996). *Empire and information: Intelligence gathering and social communication in India 1780–1870*. Cambridge, England: Cambridge University Press.

Brewer, J. (1997). *The pleasures of the imagination: English culture in the eighteenth century*. London: HarperCollins.

Brewer, J., & McCalman, I. (1999). Publishing. In I. McCalman (Ed.), *An Oxford companion to the Romantic Age: British culture 1776–1832* (pp. 197–206). Oxford, England: Oxford University Press.

Brooks, D. (2000). From Playhouse to Printing House: Drama and Authorship in Early Modern England. Cambridge Studies in Renaissance Literature and Culture, 36. Cambridge: Cambridge University Press.

Brown, C. J. (1995). *Poets, patrons, and printers: Crisis of authority in late medieval France*. Ithaca, NY: Cornell University Press.

Cavallo, G. (1999). Between *Volumen* and codex: Reading in the Roman world. In G. Cavallo & R. Chartier (Eds.), *A history of reading in the West* (pp. 64–89). Cambridge, England: Polity.

Chartier, R. (1989). The Practical Impact of Writing. In R. Chartier (60). A History of Private Life III: Passions of the Renaissance. Cambridge, MA and London: Harvard University Press, 111–159.

Christin, A.-M. (Ed.). (2001). *A history of writing: From hieroglyph to multimedia.* Paris: Flammarion.

Darnton, R. (1982a). *The literary underground of the old regime.* Cambridge, MA: Harvard University Press.

Darnton, R. (1982b). What is the history of books? *Daedalus*, pp. 65–83. Reprinted 2001 in D. Finkelstein & A. McCleery (Eds.), *The book history reader* (pp. 9–26). London: Routledge.

Duguid, P. (1996). Material matters: The past and futurology of the book. In G. Nunberg (Ed.), *The future of the book* (pp. 63–102). Berkeley: University of California Press.

Eisenstein, E. (1979). *The printing press as an agent of change* (Vols. 1 & 2). Cambridge, England: Cambridge University Press.

Escarpit, R. (1966). *The book revolution.* London: Harrap.

Febvre, L., & Martin, H.-J. (1958). *L'Apparition du Livre* Translated as: Paris: Albin Michel.

Febvre, L., & Martin, H.-J. (1976). *The coming of the book: The impact of printing, 1450–1800* (D. Gerard, Trans.). London: NLB. (Reprinted 1997, London: Verso)

Finkelstein, D., & McCleery, A. (2005). *An introduction to book history.* London: Routledge.

Goody, J. (1987). *The interface between the oral and the written.* Cambridge, England: Cambridge University Press.

Greco, A. (1995). Mergers and acquisitions in the US book industry, 1960–1989. In P. G. Altbach & E. S. Hoshino (Eds.), *International book publishing: An encyclopedia* (pp. 229–242). New York: Garland.

Greco, A. (1996). Shaping the future: Mergers, acquisitions, and the U.S. publishing, communications, and mass media industries, 1990–1995. *Publishing Research Quarterly, 12*(3), 5–16.

Greenspan, E., & Rose, J. (1998). Introduction. *Book History, 1*, ix–xi.

Hall, D. D. (1996) *Cultures of print: Essays in the history of the book.* Amherst: University of Massachusetts Press.

Harris, W. V. (1989) *Ancient literacy.* Cambridge, MA: Harvard University Press.

Havelock, E. (1988). *The muse learns to write: Reflections on orality and literacy from antiquity to the present.* New Haven, CT: Yale University Press.

Johanson, G. (2000). *Colonial editions in Australia, 1842–1972.* Wellington, NZ: Elibank.

Johns, A. (1998). *The nature of the book: Print and knowledge in the making.* Chicago: University of Chicago Press.

Kirsop, W. (2001). From colonialism to the multinationals: The fragile growth of Australian publishing and its contribution to the global Anglophone reading community. In J. Michon & J.-Y. Mollier (Eds.), *Les Mutations du Livre et de L'édition dans le Monde du XVIIIe Siècle À L'an 2000* (pp. 324–329). L'Harmattan, France: Les Presses de L'Université Laval.

Lavallée, D. (2001). The Peruvian Quipus. In A.-M. Christin (Ed.), *A history of writing: From hieroglyph to multimedia* (pp. 190–191). Paris: Flammarion.

Lechtman, H., & Soldi, A.-M. (Eds.). (1981). *La Tecnologia en el Mundo Andino* [Technology in the Andean World]. Mexico City: Universidad Nacional Autonoma de Mexico.

Livingstone, A. (1986). *Mystical and mythological explanatory works of Assyrian and Babylonian scholars.* Oxford, England: Clarendon.

MacDonald, M. L. (2001). The modification of European models: English Canada before 1890. In J. Michon & J.-Y. Mollier (Eds.), *Les Mutations du Livre et de L'édition dans le Monde du XVIIIe Siècle À L'an 2000I* (pp. 84–93). L'Harmattan, France: Les Presses de L'Université Laval.

Macherel, C. (1983). Don et réciprocité en Europe [Gift Exchange and Reciprocity in Europe]. *Archives Européennes de Sociologie, 24*(1), 151–166.

Martin, H.-J. (1995). *The history and power of writing* (L. G. Cochrane, Trans.). Chicago: University of Chicago Press.

Mauss, M. (1954). *The gift: Forms and functions of exchange in archaic societies* (I. Cunnison, Trans.). London: Cohen & West.

McGann, J. (1991). *The textual condition.* Princeton, NJ: Princeton University Press.

McKenzie, D. F. (1986). *The Panizzi lectures, 1985: Bibliography and the sociology of texts.* London: British Library.

Noegel, S. B. (2004). Text, script and media: New observations on scribal activity in the ancient Near East. In R. Modiano, L. F. Searle, & P. Shillingsburg (Eds.), *Voice, text, hypertext: Emerging practices in textual studies* (pp. 133–143). Seattle: University of Washington Press.

Oliver, J.-P. (2001). Aegean scripts of the second millennium BCE. In A.-M. Christin (Ed.), *A history of writing: From hieroglyph to multimedia* (pp. 197–202). Paris: Flammarion.

Ong, W. J. (2002). *Orality and literacy: The technologizing of the word*. London: Methuen. (Original work published 1982).

Price, L. (2002, October 31). The tangible page. *London Review of Books*, pp. 36–39.

Reed, D. (1997). *The rise of the popular magazine in Britain and the United States, 1880–1960*. Toronto: University of Toronto Press.

Rose, M. (1994). Authors and Owners: The Invention of Copyright. Cambridge, MA: Harvard University Press.

Schmandt-Besserat, D. (1982a). The emergence of recording. *American Anthropologist, 84*, 871–878.

Schmandt-Besserat, D. (1982b). How writing came about. *Zeitschrift für Papyrologie und Epigraphik, 47*, 1–5.

CHAPTER 5

History of Reflection, Theory, and Research on Writing

Paul A. Prior
University of Illinois, Urbana–Champaign

Karen J. Lunsford
University of California, Santa Barbara

The history of theory and research on writing has been narrated through varied genealogies, and the scope of the field has been defined in quite diverse ways. A history of writing theory and research (e.g., Connors, 1993; Crowley, 1998; Welch, 1999) may begin with classical (explicitly oral) Greek rhetoric, take a tour through Roman and (perhaps) medieval developments, note the formation of current-traditional rhetoric (where style emerged as the dominant canon, invention morphed into arrangement, and the cultivation of literary-cultural good taste, *belles lettres,* assumed a prominent role), and finally narrate a line of research in modern rhetoric and composition studies. Other accounts (e.g., Hillocks, 1986; Nystrand, Greene, & Wiemelt, 1993; Olson, 1994) ignore pre-20th-century rhetoric, focusing on ways that modern disciplines (linguistics, psychology, anthropology, education, composition, and rhetoric) have researched writing over the past 100 years, with a marked uptick in activity beginning around the 1960s. Specific disciplines (e.g., psychology, anthropology, elementary education) also have their own ways of narrating particular lines of inquiry. In this chapter, we propose a broad, inclusive history, one that explores reflection on writing as well as recent theory and research, looks globally (not only to Europe), and seeks to bring work from multiple disciplines into dialogue.

We propose such a history for several reasons. First, histories of reflective practice remain very much alive in current writing theory and research. For example, although he believed that European rhetoric—largely a history of reflective practice—had been eclipsed by modern linguistics, semiotics, psychology, and sociology, Barthes (1988) argued that study of it remains valuable because rhetorical perspectives and concepts have become so deeply entrenched in our language and culture. European rhetoric is not the only tradition; we look to the emergence of reflection on writing across the globe, asking what conditions have prompted it and what dimensions of writing have become visible under particular regimes of cultural-historical interest and attention. We do not, for example, assume the radical ruptures of rhetoric, poetic, and epistemic that have dominated Euro-American rhetorical traditions following Aristotle, but take those divisions as a product of reflective practice shaped by certain conditions and interests. Second, we anticipate a future where multidisciplinary inquiries into writing take up an expanding array of objects of inquiry, methods, and theories. Sharp divisions between school and workplace writing, the acquisition of writing by children and its use by adults, or psychological and anthropological perspectives are ultimately neither well motivated nor theoretically tenable. Writing research should proceed as a unified, though complex, field of inquiry, with theoretical frameworks rich enough to operate across the many ecologies that writing itself occupies. What we offer in this chapter then is a prolegomenon to a history of writing studies. We certainly cannot detail that broad history in this brief chapter. Our goal is simply to motivate and map out a framework for this project and to offer some initial sketches of what such a history might offer.

DEFINING TERMS: WRITING, REFLECTIVE PRACTICE, THEORY, AND RESEARCH

What counts as *writing* in this history? Writing can signify an artifact, an individual capacity to act, a situated activity, a technology, or a mode of social organization. Writing thus might refer to the inscriptions carved into stone or scratched onto paper; the capacity of a professional novelist or novice student to write texts; exchanges among developers, managers, marketers, and end-users as they compose an instruction manual; the use of print technologies; or the evolving system of genres through which an academic community organizes its work. We are interested in phenomena at all five of these levels. As Harris (1986) argued, writing refers to conventional systems of graphic communication, in which representation of language exists simply as one option (though certainly an important one). Inscription inevitably mixes visual, tactile, and other semiotic modes. Electronic texts have accelerated and expanded this multimodality. For example, a written text may now be visually and acoustically animated, the page in effect acting more like a film than a frame (Manovich, 2001). In short, we intend *writing* to be understood expansively, in all five of its meanings and as a multimodal phenomenon.

The arc traced from practice to reflective practice to theory and research (Phelps, 1989) is initiated by development of a metadiscourse. A practice, say writing to transmit messages between individuals over a distance, first arises in activity. A metadiscourse then begins to form around it—classifying the types and parts of such "letters," offering narratives of their effects or principles to guide their composition. As a reflective practice, letter writing may now be discussed, taught, critiqued, standardized, reformed, and repurposed. Reflective practice involves sustained, collaborative attention to a phenomenon, but remains anchored in the givens of the practice at hand. At some point, it may shade into theory as the metadiscourse is increasingly reworked through collective, critical scrutiny and abstracted from the embedded assumptions of its source domains. Likewise, but in a more marked fashion, the attentive noticing of reflective practice may shift into research—planned, sustained, theorized inquiry aimed at increasing knowledge. Bazerman (1988) represents a clear case of taking up letter writing through theory and research. He examined correspondence as a means of forming scientific communities, as an intervention in laboratory methods, and as a strategically interesting site for exploring genre theory and the sociogenesis of cultural forms. In a disciplinary phase, theory and research are organized in a social enterprise with forums of communication and socialization. Finally, it is important to recognize that this arc traces a recursive, nonlinear set of relations: An active traffic continues between everyday and disciplinary domains. Over time, as the space of writing in social life has shifted, attention to writing has expanded and receded; the current broad interest in writing suggests the central place it has now assumed across many domains of social practice.

WHAT HAS MOTIVATED AND DRIVEN REFLECTION ON WRITING

As writing has emerged and evolved, so has reflection on writing. Many factors might motivate such reflection; here we point to four key centers of gravity. First, writing involves the development of a script along with technologies of inscription (tools and media) and distribution. As the first four chapters of this handbook attest, this technical dimension of writing has itself been a domain of reflective practice and research (until recently craft based) on inks, inscription devices and media, compilation (e.g., in scrolls and codexes), and collection (in libraries, files, and now electronic databases). The potential affordances of graphic signs came to be recognized (e.g., use of pictographs to represent the sound of foreign names). By making language available for repeated, slow, visual-graphic attention and by the ways that language was visualized in texts, writing opened language itself to new forms of analysis (see Harris, 1986; Olson, 1994).

Second, the need to reproduce literate technologies, practices, and resources through education, apprenticeship, and socialization leads to formalization, to systemizing literate metadiscourses as well as institutionalizing modes for transmission of writing. Discussing Akkadian literacy in the first millennium (BCE), Oppenheim (1964) notes:

> The characteristic method of training has left us countless "school tablets"—mostly small, lentil shaped disks—with a sign, word, or a short sentence in the teacher's writing on one side (or above a line) and on the reverse (or below the line) the pupil's efforts to copy the example. (p. 243)

Imitation and worksheets have persisted through the millennia. Transmission of writing also involves enculturation into values, which generates reflection on aesthetics, good taste, and cultural identity. Consider, for example, how writers and critics in Euro-American literary traditions (e.g., Johnson, 2006; Richards, 1929; Woolf, 1998) worked to define what counts as good writing. Transmission may also involve conveying notions (well or poorly grounded) about clarity (Williams, 1995)—how textual meanings can be made more transparent for various users or conversely more ambiguous or paradoxical. Transmission may also entail attention to assessment, both of writing and of the person through writing (see chap. 23, this volume).

Third, some texts achieve a mobility and permanence that prompts reflection and theory. Texts may appear without their producers in tow, in unfamiliar languages, distant in space, time, and context from their origins. In modern Europe, philology developed as a discipline to trace texts to their origins, whether to recapture the contexts that first provided their meaning (as in rebuilding the Classical corpus); to uncover deep linkages among world languages, perhaps even an ur-language; or to decipher inscription systems (such as Egyptian hieroglyphs) now lost. The mobility of writing then prompts attention to the authorship or authenticity of a text, the hermeneutic recovery of meaning from difficult texts, and questions of translation.

Finally, as written texts offer new means of representation (textual and multimedia), affording sustained and dispersed inspection of language and ideas, writing has repeatedly assumed a key place in the production and critique of discourse and knowledge in political, social, scientific, philosophical, and religious spheres. Attention to how writing mediates knowledge has been pursued by broad theorizing (e.g., Ong, 1982), close historical inquiry (e.g., Bazerman, 1988), and microanalysis of texts and practices (e.g., Myers, 1990; Prior, 1998). Whereas Plato (1989, *Phaedrus*) feared writing would diminish individuals (who would rely on externalized memory) and reduce opportunities for critical dialogue (because texts cannot answer questions), modern observers have instead emphasized the power of writing to mediate knowledge communities and govern organizations and societies.

A FRAMEWORK FOR A HISTORY OF WRITING STUDIES

The story of how writing emerged in various societies is still being written. For some ancient societies, scholars have extensive evidence and have begun to put together detailed narratives. Other scripts (see Coulmas, 2003) remain undeciphered and their histories may never be recovered. It now seems clear that writing coincided with, and contributed to, the emergence of complexly differentiated societies and social networks, often involving the appearance of multilingual communities, the need for extended political and economic governance, and the stabilization of religious and mythic traditions. Early reflection on writing is harder to trace; the evidence at this point, largely indirect. However, the development of writing technologies and the expanding functionality of writing systems testify to reflective practices and craft research.

Only in the final centuries BCE do we find more abundant evidence of how people had begun to understand writing and its reproduction. The specific conditions under which such reflections arose varied. In Greece, rhetoric emerged as a reflective practice oriented to civic participation in courts of law, public deliberation over policy, and public rites of praise and blame. As these fora were oral, writing was generally a back-stage practice, part of pedagogy and preparation, especially useful for attention to style. As literacy was increasingly imbricated in political life, a second focus of reflection, though less elaborated, addressed the social and individual consequences of writing. In China, reflective practice was less distinctly defined in a civic life oriented to rulers and the place of the literati in serving large states often in conflict. In India, writing operated in a space fixed on one side by Hindu rejection of writing as a medium for sacred texts (which had to be orally transmitted) and on the other side by Buddhism, which was more accepting of writing (sermons).

History has not unfolded inside geographically separate test tubes or on a socially and technologically stable landscape. Greek rhetorical texts and practices passed to Egypt and Persia, were taken up and transformed in Rome, were later translated and explored in the Islamic world (and then retransmitted to Europe to help trigger the Renaissance), and in modern times have spread globally through Western schooling and scholarship. Chinese texts and practices passed to Japan and Korea and after encountering Euro-American rhetorical practices are now receiving new attention in the West. The past 500 years have seen the rapid expansion of communication technologies (from the second coming of the printing press in Europe to the present age of computers linked into global networks); the expansion of scholarly and disciplinary activity (especially in the past century); global travel and trade mixed with growing social complexity; mass education; and social activities and institutions increasingly mediated by writing. Reflection on writing has been expanding, and in the last 50 years sustained programs of writing theory and research have clearly coalesced in diverse disciplinary and professional sites.

Rather than attempt a grand narrative of the emergence of writing studies over several millennia, we seek here to illustrate the value of a broad approach to writing reflection, theory, and research by offering five cases. Each case takes up a theme and sketches a few of the global, historical, and multidisciplinary engagements with that theme. These cases highlight the four motives we noted previously (technology, teaching/learning, hermeneutics/translations, and knowledge/governance); however, there is no one-to-one correspondence between themes and motives. To pull on one of these strings is to pull on others, and our goal here is simply to illustrate and motivate the framework we have proposed.

AUTHORSHIP

Because of the spiritual or temporal authority some texts wield, authorship (or authenticity) has repeatedly been an issue of significance. Pointing to Clanchy's (1993) examination of how written contracts allowed Normans to supercede the orally attested property claims of the Brits, Baron (1999) notes that authenticity of texts did not suddenly become a question with digitization. How early attention to authenticity arose is suggested by Thompson's (1994) description of a contract made between a mother and son in Ptolemic Egypt in 265 BCE, an era marked by Greek-Demotic biliteracy in public documents. The contract transferred property to the son in exchange for an allowance and other considerations, and it displayed a mix of Egyptian contractual practices (16 witnesses) and Greek (multiple written copies).

Written in demotic, the contract was once made up of 20 sheets of papyrus pasted together in a larger sheet approximately 40 cm high and three metres in width. On the back of this sheet are listed the standard sixteen witnesses to the deed, but the main body of the document contains the more remarkable feature: witnessing not just by name but by copying. Alongside the original text four of the sixteen witnesses have, in their own hands, each copied out for themselves, with only minor variants, the complete text of the contract, ending with the words: "X has written this." (Thompson, 1994, p. 80)

Authenticity of religious texts is likewise an issue. In Islam, the sayings (*hadith*) of the Prophet Muhammad became, along with the Quran, a main source of religious law. Hitti (1970) notes that political, cultural, and religious tensions in Islam "provided ample opportunity for the fabrication of hadiths and motivated their dissemination" (p. 394). To stablize Islamic law, a great effort was made to collect and codify the hadith. One key collection, Hitti notes, was produced by al-Bukhari (810–870 CE), who reportedly collected several hundred thousand sayings over 15 years. Examining their provenance, he selected just under 8,000 as possible.

Authorship became an issue of a different sort with the changing economies of print publication in Europe (Woodmansee & Jaszi, 1994). The notion of an autonomous author and of literary and scientific genius grew around economic arguments for assigning copyright protection to published texts. Indeed, much current work (e.g., Howard, 1999; A. Lunsford & Ede, 1990) has aimed at identifying the powerful effects of these cultural developments on theories of authorship. Situated or ethnographic research into writing processes along with historical and autobiographical accounts of writing have complicated simple notions of authorship, pointing to the many ways that ideas and forms of a text may be collaboratively shaped through recursive social processes of production, distribution, and reception. Research has, for example, identified complex fields of authorship in science (Biagioli & Gallison, 2003; Myers, 1990). How do you figure the relative contributions of the senior scientist who established and funded a laboratory with a particular mission, a lead scientist who conceived a particular experiment and led analysis and write-up, a bench technician who managed data collection and analysis, and a research assistant who drafted parts of the article? Studies of workplaces (e.g., Beaufort, 1999; Cross, 1994) have routinely noted various forms of ghostwriting, the use of "boilerplate," and the prevalence of unsigned texts (especially for internal use). Recent technological innovations (hypertext, digitized archives, collaborative interfaces) have punctuated the postmodern claim of the "death of the author," as readers actively (re)shape the texts they encounter.

At the intersection of histories of production and politics of representation, the notion of authorship suggests the need for equal attention to how nonauthorship (plagiarism, absence of credit, unsigned work) is achieved (Prior, 1998). Goffman (1981) helps here as he analyzed how models of communication mistakenly assume a simple, direct, linguistic dyad, in which who chooses the words, who utters or inscribes them, and whose positions are being represented coincide. In fact, those three roles are often distributed across a cast of participants. Carpenter (1981), as a librarian concerned with cataloging, also noted the different grounds (origination vs. representation, intention and work vs. responsibility) for classification of authorship and the different types of participation (writing on, writing up, writing down) that might be relevant. In fields such as anthropology, sociology, and gender studies, sharp questions have been raised about the linkage between ethical representation of others and who participates in authoring such representations (e.g., Clifford & Marcus, 1986; Latour, 2004). Clearly, taking up questions of authorship, we find phenomena that cross many cultural-historical and disciplinary boundaries.

TRANSLATION STUDIES

As texts began to circulate through space and time, issues of translation came to the fore. Not incidentally, the translation of a text often has high-stakes consequences. Treaties in two or more languages define terms of war, peace, trade, and colonization. Religious and literary texts may instigate cultural transformations. Science and specialized knowledge move across societies and through history. Instruction manuals may determine the usability and safety of products. Not only are questions of authorship (as noted earlier) intensified when the assumptions of two or more communities must be negotiated, but also the standards for what counts as an acceptable translation vary widely. Thus, translation has served as a site for intense reflection on writing since ancient times, and recently an interdisciplinary field of translation studies has arisen.

Briefly put, translation practices across history seem as varied as the communities that have employed them; however, certain issues help define these variations. One issue involves the relative value of texts and languages. For example, Jewish translation histories are punctuated by frequent arguments over which texts are worthy of a translator's attention, and which of the many Jewish languages/dialects ought to be privileged as the target, especially because the most common tongue of the Jewish diaspora—the Hebrew used in sacred texts—may not be amenable to new word coinages (Toury, 2002). Central to many traditions of translation are arguments over whether a translator should strive for a word-for-word or segment-for-segment equivalence, or whether a translator should employ a looser style to capture a text's meaning, connotations, and tone. Dryden's 17th-century preface to Ovid's epistles (2003) offers an influential, early European response to these issues. In China, Buddhist translators in the 4th century CE specified principles of good translation, some of which were codified much later in the "theory of translation promulgated by Yan Fu (1854–1921) of *xin* ('faithfulness' or 'fidelity'), *da* ('lucidity' or 'readability'), and *ya* ('elegance' or 'refinement')" (Kenan, 2002, p. 162, drawing on Ma, 1984). Likewise, beginning in the third century CE, Greek scientific and philosophical texts were translated into Syriac and Sanskrit, which (with the rise of the Islamic empire in the seventh century CE) were in turn translated into Arabic under massive, state-sponsored initiatives. Translators argued for fidelity to the texts, seeking out Greek originals for source texts and comparison, yet they also felt free to recompile works and to add extensive commentaries of their own, as did the later European translators (particularly from the 12th century CE) who converted Arabic and Greek texts into Latin (Gutas, 2000; Montgomery, 2000).

Modern work in linguistics, literary studies, and cultural studies has echoed this ancient debate over fidelity, as scholars have asked whether there are universal language/thought structures that allow the transfer of meaning from one to another language, or whether texts are so culture-specific that something is always lost in translation (Benjamin, 1996; Chomsky, 2002; House, 2002). Likewise, authors and literary scholars have asked whether a translator must be an expert in both the source and target languages. The French translator Dolet (1540) famously answered "yes," setting a standard for European translation in the Renaissance (Worth, 1988). Yet team translation has also been common, particularly in China (Kenan, 2002), where an intermediary (who knows the source language) summarizes a source text orally to allow an inscriber (who does not) to produce a written translation in the target language. Scholars (Montgomery, 2000) of scientific and technical translation have pointed out one drawback of efforts to make texts relevant to target communities: Scientific translations often employ anachronistic terms to articulate early scientific concepts, thus reinscribing the assumption that modern science stands unproblematically on the shoulders of giants. Debates also rage over machine translation, which has been pursued in part to address the demands of global signals intelligence, whose capacity to intercept, record, and store electronic communications has far outstripped human resources to translate them. Although computers often can pair a source word with a target word, a work's meaning depends on larger textual chunks and contexts that machines do not yet interpret well (see Richardson, 2002). The science fiction dream (as in the *Star Trek* TV series) of a universal translator is likely to remain a fantasy; however, computer scientists remain keenly interested in how to parse (analyze) discourse so that machines might produce even rough equivalents.

Current translation theories, shaped by social movements such as women's movements (see Hyun, 2004, on Korea) and academic trends such as postcolonialism (Venuti, 1992), have begun to value polyvocality, subversive phrasing, and the subaltern voice. Instead of assuming that a translator's work should be transparent, so that a translated text reads as though it were originally written in a target language, these views suggest that translators ought to preserve a sense of foreignness, difference, alterity (see Robinson, 1997). In part, this turn responds to the recognition in religious studies, anthropology, history, and legal studies that a number of translation wrongs have been perpetrated. For example, scholars have focused on the problems of treaties and the dangers of assuming that concepts embedded in certain legal systems readily cross cultures, particularly if one culture gains by dominating another. Fenton and Moon (2002) document such problems, including deliberately falsified terms in the translation of the Treaty of Waitangi, which effectively created New Zealand.

Like writing studies, translation studies as a distinct field of inquiry (Gentzler, 1993; Riccardi, 2002) has formed as a loosely defined amalgam of established disciplines. (In fact, both fields have drawn on many of the same disciplines.) Reflection and research on translation offer particularly rich illustrations of how complexly writing works within and across literate and social ecologies.

ORALITY AND LITERACY

In the 4th century BCE in Greece, Aristotle (1984, in *De Interpretatione*) offered an early account of the relation of orality to writing:

> Now spoken sounds are symbols of affections in the soul, and written marks symbols of spoken sound. And just as written marks are not the same for all men, neither are spoken sounds. But what these are in the first place signs of—affections of the soul— are the same for all; and what these affections are likenesses of—actual things—are also the same. (p. 25)

As Harris (1986) has noted, this account has remained common sense (and Aristotle was the first pollster of common sense) through the millennia, though it misconstrues the relation of orality to literacy as well as of signs to thoughts and the world. In any case, reflection, theory and research on orality and literacy has continued, with many initial reflections driven by concerns over the social, even spiritual, significance of literacy.

Plato's (1989) *Phaedrus* has served as a key marker of emerging anxieties over the impact of literacy. In it, Socrates expresses concerns over the negative consequences of writing on individual mental faculties, especially memory, and on society, as knowledge is separated from its human sources. In the *Letters* (1989, *XII*), Plato dramatizes the superficiality of the knowledge of people who learn from writing by comparing such knowledge to a suntan. As Too (1995) documents, when Isocrates wished to promote writing, he had to work against deep concerns about its morality as well as its efficacy, answering Alcidemas' claims (in *Against the Sophists*) that professional speech writers had a negative effect on the courts and public deliberation because their speeches could unduly inflate a speaker's case and speakers could not effectively engage in dialogue beyond their texts. Ghosh (2002) traces the late and somewhat attenuated appearance of literacy in India in the 3rd century BCE (though an earlier Indus Valley script existed, died out, and remains undecipherable) to the Hindu belief that instruction in the holy *Rig Veda* should be strictly oral, with learning from written texts viewed as an abomination.

The issue of orality-literacy has formed one key nexus for multidisciplinary investigation of writing, bringing together scholars in classics, rhetoric, anthropology, and psychology. With varying nuances, Havelock (1963), Goody (1977), Olson (1977), and Ong (1982) forwarded what came to be called the great-divide theory—that deep differences separate oral from literate peoples (or more controversially people), with literacy associated with "advanced" forms of social life (e.g., complex organization) and cognitive processes (e.g., logic). Scribner and Cole's (1981) ethnographic experiments with the Vai of Liberia in the 1970s proved seminal in these debates. Taking advantage of the natural laboratory of the Vai culture, with its varied forms of literacy, to untangle the cognitive, behavioral, and ideological consequences of schooling, modern life, and literacy, they found that literacy per se did not have general consequences. Instead, specific literate practices were associated with specific consequences: a certain kind of memorization (incremental), for example, being associated with Quranic literacy; syllogistic reasoning, with schooled English literacy; and certain kinds of verbal integration, with Vai.

Following Scribner and Cole's findings, attention has generally shifted to exploring specific practices. Yunis (2003), for example, introduces an edited collection in the classics by stating that the essays will not concern themselves with orality and literacy per se or their presumed cognitive or social consequences, that the book will instead be "concerned with understanding how specific cultural practices in Greece were affected when people engaged in those practices began to use written texts" (pp. 10–11). In anthropology, Besnier (1995) and Schieffelin (2000) explored cultural transitions as nonindigenous literacies introduced by Western or Western-trained missionaries were taken up in the Pacific islands. Besnier documented ways the Polynesians on Nukulaelae Atoll used literacy for a broad array of interpersonal, personal, and familial purposes, through such genres as letters, invitations, sermons, genealogies, minutes of meetings, song lyrics, slogans woven into mats for decoration, and graffiti. Schieffelin's study of the introduction of literacy to Kaluli in Papua New Guinea focused on the way texts and school-based practices altered Kaluli language, genres, and forms of social knowledge. Linguistics has likewise complicated simple classifications of orality and literacy, noting that orality includes formal lectures and speeches as well as extemporaneous small talk, and writing includes grocery lists and notes passed by children to classmates as well as carefully edited essays and books (see chaps. 33 and 34, this volume). Studies in anthropology, education, and composition have also examined ways writing is drafted, negotiated, and received through talk. Kalman (1999) explored ways that scribes and their clients in Mexico City produced varied documents (e.g., contracts, tax forms, school assignments, love letters, petitions) through dictation and joint oral composition as well as ways that social identities shaped participation in these practices. Dyson (1997) and Kamberelis (2001) offered close analyses of how classroom talk (often talk that recontextualized mass media) shaped young students' writing. K. Lunsford (2002) identified marked dialogic complexity as high school students in a summer program struggled to understand terms, texts, and tasks across contexts (classroom lectures, peer groups, and small instructor-led groups). Examining a 2-hour response to a dissertation prospectus in a sociology seminar, Prior (1994, 1998) traced ways that complex oral arguments, often grounded in everyday experiences and politics, led to significant revisions of the text and the research. In short, broad theories that distinguish orality from literacy are giving way across disciplines to careful analyses of specific oral and textual practices and ways that literate activity routinely blends multiple modes.

BEYOND COMPARATIVE RHETORICS

Aristotle has cast a heavy shadow on conceptualizations of rhetoric, perhaps commensurate with the strong light he focused on certain dimensions of communicative practice. Aristotle's *Rhetoric* (1984) defined a vocabulary for the study of persuasion and divided rhetoric from poetic and dialectic (logic). He provided a kind of early survey of common sense (of what people count as good, neutral, and bad) as a resource for making arguments. Grounded in the literate and oral practices of ancient Greece, Aristotle's rhetoric focused heavily on public speech (with writing primarily as a method for composition and polishing style) and on the judicial, deliberative, and civic spaces of the Greek *polis*. In this sense, he made *rhetoric* a visible, ordered practice for study and instruction, but even in the

Western tradition, this particular disposition has rendered other dispositions difficult to articulate (see chap. 22, this volume). Sophistic rhetoric has been the object of repeated rescue attempts, not only from the explicit critiques of Plato, Aristotle, and others, but also from the counterweight of Aristotle's system (see e.g., Haskins, 2004; Too, 1995; Welch, 1999). Hawhee (2004) offers a more radical rereading, as she examines the roots of rhetorical education in athletics and recovers a pedagogy grounded in models of embodied habit and agonistic responsive struggle. Moving to a later period, Camargo (1995) notes that "the medieval schoolmen did not recognize rigid distinctions among the various 'arts of discourse' that modern scholars have sought to impose in retrospect" (p. 30). The *ars dictaminis* (in manuals of letter writing and notary) mark a key development as they were directed at written end products. (In the *Institutio Oratoria* (circa 95 CE, Quintilian, 1920, had extolled the value of writing, but still saw oratory as the main product.) Consisting primarily of multiple model texts, these manuals also countered Aristotle's abstraction. Woods (2001) points out that the instructional order of the five canons was noncanonical: Repeated exercises in style, memory, and delivery served as the basis for arrangement and ultimately invention (rather than the other way around). Modern rhetorics also must do some heavy lifting to get beyond Aristotle. The reintegration of epistemic issues as rhetorical (e.g., Perelman & Olbrechts-Tyteca, 1968; Toulmin, 1958), Burke's (1950) shift toward identification and his introduction of Marxist themes, the development of rhetorics embedded in particular disciplines (e.g., McCloskey, 1985), and the introduction of empirical methods of inquiry, ranging from Flower and Hayes's (1981) cognitive process protocols to Eubanks's (2000) use of focus groups to analyze of the tropes of international trade, all must struggle not only to be viewed as legitimate revisions of Aristotelian rhetoric, but to not slip into some other category altogether (becoming literary, philosophical, linguistic, or social scientific rather than "rhetorical").

This resistance to alternative formulations is nowhere clearer than in the case of Chinese thought and practice. Kennedy's (1998) account of comparative rhetorics offers a serious and valuable attempt to honor diverse rhetorical traditions across the globe and throughout history. However, Kennedy renders global rhetorics intelligible through very Western, hence quite Aristotelian, lenses. In the chapter on rhetoric in ancient China, he seeks, for example, to identify the Chinese "sophists" and instances of "deliberative rhetoric." Lu (1998) observes that Western students of rhetoric have struggled with the fluid metadiscourse of the Chinese traditions—with their integration of rhetoric, poetic, politics, and dialectic; and with their transmittal of persuasive practice through documented narratives. In her philosophical account of ancient Chinese rhetoric, Lu portrays a far more complex set of distinctions and practices. Considering the classic text *Intrigues of the Warring States* (compiled in the first century BCE; Crump, 1970), Lu highlights use of metaphors, a mix of deductive and inductive reasoning, and a focus on psychological and instrumental appeals. Key to this text are the contexts of its stories—literati advising rulers, often in private, sometimes in writing (with extended examples of letters and other texts presented), and often through conversational dialogues (or a mix of genres and modes) rather than through monologues. The *Intrigues* offers something quite different from Western rhetorical traditions, something more like a narrative archive of rhetorical situations in which participants choose among diverse means and genres (cf. Shipka's, 2005, account of a multimodal, activity-based theory of composing) to achieve their goals, sometimes succeeding, sometimes failing. One story, for example, entitled "Sun-tzu is first dismissed and then reinvited, but declines with a letter and a *fu*" (Crump, 1970, pp. 268–269), presents two retainers offering different arguments to a king. The first retainer's argument leads the king to dismiss Sun-tzu (who goes to advise a neighboring ruler), whereas the second's leads the king to invite Sun-tzu to return. Sun-tzu, not very impressed with this fickle king, declines the offer with an extended letter followed by a *fu*, a poem.

Finally, though Lu (1998) does not address this issue, China's history of literate practice was strongly marked by the tradition of the civil examination. From perhaps as early as 600 BCE, the examination system became a way to certify the literati for service to the rulers. In

China then, we find writing shaped and informed by millennia of high-stakes testing. Civic rhetoric in this context came to be strongly tied to the classical canon of Confucian texts. Looking at the Ming and Ching periods (1368–1911), Elman (2000) describes a sophisticated social machinery designed to prepare and examine the literati. Test takers, for example, were segregated in special compounds and searched to prevent cheating. The texts were first drafted and then finalized in black ink. The examiners would make them anonymous as they copied them in red ink (examiners' marks were sometimes made in green ink). Guy (1994) describes the *Ch'in-ting Ssu-Shu-wen* (Manual of Examination Essays on the Four Books) by Fang Pao (1737), which included a historical sampling of several hundred essays (written over about 270 years) with commentary on their strengths and weaknesses. Fang Pao's work could be usefully read against the much later Western literature on writing assessment (see chap. 23, this volume). A global history of reflection on writing could differ from the present project of comparative rhetoric by taking up whatever local frameworks and terms have been developed in whatever domains of practice rather than by using Greek, largely Aristotelian, rhetoric as the metric of all things.

WRITING, SCIENCE, AND SOCIETY

Bazerman's (1988) analysis of the historical emergence of scientific report genres around the *Philosophical Transactions* suggests the key role that textual exchanges played in remaking both laboratory practices and forging a collective, progressive social enterprise focused on theorized findings rather than (as initially) recipes and marvels. Perhaps the centrality of writing to scientific and technical practices helps explain why early ethnographic studies of laboratories (e.g., Knorr-Cetina, 1981; Latour & Woolgar, 1979) focused such detailed attention on texts. Knorr-Cetina examined the processes of drafting and revising scientific reports, surprisingly finding that the textual story reversed the order of events that happened in the laboratory. Latour and Woolgar identified cascading chains of inscriptions (bench notes, measurements, labels, printouts, drafts, published articles, grant applications, vitas) that marked the journey of scientific objects from ambiguous phenomena (e.g., a series of spikes registered on a meter) at the laboratory bench to debatable scientific claims in technical articles to accepted facts and objects to be traded. Russell (1997) sketches interlocking *genre systems* (Bazerman, 1994) across interwoven activity systems (Engeström, 1993) in college biology. A lab report for a biology class, for example, is linked to the wider world of lab reports and other scientific genres on one side, but also to instructional and institutional genres (teacher response, letters of recommendation, grades, graduation documents).

Scientific and disciplinary texts have been analyzed to identify the linguistic and rhetorical features that mark them (Martin & Veel, 1993; Myers, 1990; Swales, 1990, 2004). Philosophers and rhetoricians (see Baake, 2003) have questioned the role that metaphors and other figurative language play in scientific work, whether a metaphor is constitutive of knowledge, a distortion of fact, a method of conveying what is already known in one domain to a novice or to an expert in another domain, or some combination of all these. Likewise, psycholinguists (e.g., Lakoff, 1987), information scientists (e.g., Bowker & Star, 1999), philosophers (e.g., Hacking, 1995), and compositionists (e.g., Berkenkotter, 2001) have explored ways in which categories of information reflect and constitute social and material worlds.

Exploring the ways writing mediates knowledge points to the intersection of writing with modes of social organization as well as to how knowledge mediates society (see chaps. 9, 10, and 11, this volume). Early examples of writing point to the mundane record keeping that facilitated organization of large social networks (Bowman & Woolf, 1994; Oppenheim, 1964; see also chap. 1, this volume). To account for the reach and power of modern social organizations, Latour (1987) has noted the way literate artifacts can act as immutable mobiles that are brought together in centers of calculation. His flat, networked focus on specific practices resonates with elaborations (e.g., Bennett, 2003) of Foucault's

(1991) notion of governmentality as well as with Smith's (1990) accounts of the social organization of textual/documentary reality:

> Our knowledge of contemporary society is to a large extent mediated to us by texts of various kinds. The result, an objectified world-in-common vested in texts, coordinates the acts, decisions, policies and plans of actual subjects as the acts, decisions, policies and plans of large-scale organizations. . . . The realities to which action and decision are oriented are virtual realities vested in texts and accomplished in distinctive practices of reading and writing. (pp. 61–62)

Research on scientific and sociotechnical workplaces has highlighted complexly situated literate practices. Yates (1989) traces the historical development of communication technologies and internal genres to the emerging need to manage large, geographically dispersed organizations. Bazerman (1999) details the *heterogeneous symbolic engineering* that Thomas Edison engaged in, not only to fabricate an incandescent device, but also to fund that activity, obtain patents, and begin fashioning the electrified world he envisioned, in which the light would only be the first of many devices. Studying one center of calculation (the operations center of the London Underground) in Edison's electrified world, Heath and Luff (2000) track the intricate management of talk and text as workers sit side-by-side at multimedia consoles, watching screens that bring computer-mediated displays of data from global networks, talking face-to-face and over phones or radios, and typing information onto screens and into databases.

CONCLUSION: TOWARD A PARLIAMENT OF DISCIPLINES

The five cases we have sketched suggest the value of taking a global perspective on the historical emergence of reflection on writing as well as of looking to theory and research pursued within and across many disciplinary communities. In each case, we find research explicitly focused on writing or literate practice coming into fruitful dialogue with other work that offers what amounts to "found studies" of writing (e.g., historical research on the development of copyright in Europe or civil examinations in China; situated studies of science or bureaucracy wherein the place of writing ultimately looms large). The cases point to the rich disciplinary mix of current studies of writing, including educational research at all levels, anthropology, sociology, psychology, communication disorders, literary and cultural studies, linguistics, applied and sociolinguistics, critical discourse analysis, classics, history, art history and graphic design, media studies, information science, rhetoric, writing and literacy studies, and interdisciplinary endeavors such as Internet studies, translation studies, genre studies, and cultural-historical activity theory. The diversity and breadth of these lines of inquiry—in terms of their objects, methodologies, and theoretical orientations—suggest the complexity of an ecologically valid unit of analysis for the study of writing. Writing studies will not relocate all of these enterprises under a new institutional shingle; however, it might serve as a central exchange (referencing an old communication technology) for multidisciplinary dialogue, a structure to open up lines of interaction and resist the pressure for studies to become encapsulated in narrow disciplinary and institutional frames.

The emergence in the last 40 years of a field devoted to theory and research on writing, with its strongest centers of gravity in English and education departments in the United States and in applied linguistics departments elsewhere in the world offers a foundation for future work in writing studies. Interestingly, a seminal moment in this development occurred in the 1960s in the United States as practical pressures on literacy education ramped up in response to social and technological change and international conflict, and as a confluence of reflection, theory, and research focused attention on the writing process. A series of interviews with famous literary figures in *The Paris Review* (see Cowley, 1958) prompted new attention to the complex, concrete practices of writers that the romanticism of current-traditional rhetoric had buried under notions of individual genius. If the literary geniuses were finding writing so hard, so filled with false starts and frustrations, then perhaps the work of invention warranted fresh attention. This attention to process combined with efforts within rhetoric to overthrow current-traditional approaches by the recovery of richer classical frameworks, with challenges to the unity of authorship emerging within literary studies, and with psychological theories that gave new weight to process and culture (see Crowley's, 1998, account of these developments). Emig's (1971) study of the writing processes of high school students in the United States, and Britton, Burgess, Martin, McLeod, and Rosen's (1975) of students' writing in British schools fused these developments together and led to rapid disciplinary formation (new journals, books, graduate programs, conferences, and institutes). A focus on processes of writing, on textual practices rather than texts, remains a distinctive feature of research in writing studies.

At present, writing studies is reaching out to better understand how writing is implicated in the development of personal and social identities (see e.g., Brandt, 2001; Finders, 1997; Ivanic, 1998; Prendergast, 2003; Sheridan-Rabideau, 2001). It is also struggling to come to grips with the recognition that texts (as artifacts) and writing (as activity) are both fundamentally multimodal. There is a growing understanding of the need to approach writing as a committed interest within a broader semiotic framework, a call Witte (1992) issued with characteristic clarity. Elkins's (1999) evocation of an art history that takes up all kinds of visual artifacts, Lemke's (1998) identification of multimedia genres in print and electronic technologies, Bolter and Grusin's (1999) attention to repurposing and remediation in old as well as new media, Bruce's work (e.g., 2003) on technologies of inquiry, Iedema's (2003) studies of resemiotization in institutional planning (movements across talk, text, and material objects), and Wysocki and her colleagues' work on graphic design and new media (Wysocki, Johnson-Eiola, Selfe, & Sirc, 2004), all represent this new confluence around a semiotic framework for studies interested in writing. Selfe and Hawisher's (2004) call for detailed studies of "literate lives in the information age" draws together these issues of identity, technology, semiotics, and sociohistoric practice.

Writing is a complex, diverse, and important phenomenon, whether viewed historically in its global manifestations over the last five millennia or functionally as it appears today in forms entangled with so many personal and social motives, significations, and consequences. Writing crops up as a part of disciplines and professions, in everyday lives at home and in the community, in the work of large social organizations. The complexity of society and challenges of coordination, communication, storage, and education continue to expand rapidly, pushed by electronic and other new technologies, global economic and political entanglements, and rapid expansion of scientific, technical, and cultural enterprises. Theoretically, the unit of analysis is under interesting pressures as researchers, theorists, and practitioners ask how writing relates to reception and distribution and how it operates across semiotic modes. We should, thus, expect expanded pressure to understand writing, to improve writing instruction, to enhance the clarity of texts, and to embed effective means (formal and/or informal) of acquiring writing practices and genres within social organizations. Proposing a history of writing reflection, theory, and research that is global, historical, and multidisciplinary represents a claim that our present and future needs and visions will best be served by opening up our lenses to capture writing with the widest field and finest detail possible.

REFERENCES

Aristotle. (1984). *The complete works of Aristotle: The revised Oxford translation* (J. Barnes, Ed.; Bollingen Series LXXI). Princeton, NJ: Princeton University Press.

Baake, K. (2003). *Metaphor and knowledge: The challenges of writing science.* Albany: State University of New York Press.

Baron, D. (1999). From pencils to pixels: The stages of literacy technologies. In G. Hawisher & C. Selfe (Eds.), *Passions, pedagogies, and 21st century technologies* (pp. 15–33). Logan: Utah State University Press.

Barthes, R. (1988). *The semiotic challenge* (R. Howard, Trans.). Berkeley: University of California Press.

Bazerman, C. (1988). *Shaping written knowledge: The genre and activity of the experimental article in science.* Madison: University of Wisconsin Press.

Bazerman, C. (1994). Systems of genres and the enactment of social intentions. In A. Freedman & P. Medway (Eds.), *Genre and the new rhetoric* (pp. 79–101). London: Taylor & Francis.

Bazerman, C. (1999). *The languages of Edison's light.* Cambridge, MA: MIT Press.

Beaufort, A. (1999). *Writing in the real world: Making the transition from school to work.* New York: Teachers College Press.

Benjamin, W. (1996). The task of the translator (Harry Zohn, Trans.). In M. Bullock & M. Jennings (Eds.), *Walter Benjamin: Selected writings, Volume 1, 1913–1926* (pp. 253–263). Cambridge, MA: Belknap Press of Harvard University Press.

Bennett, T. (2003). Culture and governmentality. In J. Bratich, J. Packer, & C. McCarthy (Eds.), *Foucault, cultural studies, and governmentality* (pp. 47–66). Albany: State University of New York Press.

Berkenkotter, C. (2001). Genre systems at work: DSM–IV and rhetorical recontextualization in psychotherapy paperwork. *Written Communication, 18,* 326–349.

Besnier, N. (1995). *Literacy, emotion, and authority: Reading and writing on a Polynesian atoll.* Cambridge, England: Cambridge University Press.

Biagioli, M., & Galison, P. (Eds.). (2003). *Scientific authorship: Credit and intellectual property in science.* New York: Routledge.

Bolter, J., & Grusin, R. (1999). *Remediation: Understanding new media.* Cambridge, MA: MIT Press.

Bowker, G., & Star, S. (1999). *Sorting things out: Classification and its consequences.* Cambridge, MA: MIT Press.

Bowman, A., & Woolf, G. (1994). Literacy and power in the ancient world. In A. Bowman & G. Woolf (Eds.), *Literacy and power in the ancient world* (pp. 1–17). Cambridge, England: Cambridge University Press.

Brandt, D. (2001). *Literacy in American lives.* Cambridge, England: Cambridge University Press.

Britton, J., Burgess, T., Martin, N., McLeod, A., & Rosen, H. (1975). *The development of writing abilities.* London: Macmillan

Bruce, B. (Ed.). (2003). *Literacy in the information age: Inquiries into meaning making with new technologies.* Newark, DE: International Reading Association.

Burke, K. (1950). *A rhetoric of motives.* Berkeley: University of California Press.

Camargo, M. (1995). *Medieval rhetorics of prose composition: Five English artes dictandi and their tradition.* Binghampton, NY: Medieval Texts and Studies.

Carpenter, M. (1981). *Corporate authorship: Its role in library cataloguing.* Westport, CT: Greenwood.

Chomsky, N. (2002). *On nature and language* (A. Belletti & L. Rizzi, Eds.). Cambridge, England: Cambridge University Press.

Clanchy, M. (1993). *From memory to written record, England 1066–1307* (2nd ed.). Oxford, England: Blackwell.

Clifford, J., & Marcus, G. (1986). *Writing culture: The poetics and politics of ethnography.* Berkeley: University of California Press.

Connors, R. (1993). *Composition-rhetoric: Backgrounds, theory, and pedagogy.* Pittsburgh: University of Pittsburgh Press.

Coulmas, F. (2003). *Writing systems: An introduction of their linguistic analysis.* Cambridge, England: Cambridge University Press.

Cowley, M. (1958). *Writers at work: The* Paris Review *interviews.* New York: Viking.

Cross, G. (1994). *Collaboration and conflict: A contextual exploration of group writing and positive emphasis.* Cresskill, NJ: Hampton Press.

Crowley, S. (1998). *Composition in the university: Historical and polemical essays.* Pittsburgh: University of Pittsburgh Press.

Crump, J. (Trans.). (1970). *Chan-Kuo Ts'e.* Oxford, England: Clarendon.

Dolet, É. (1540). *La maniere de bien traduire d'une langue en autre. D'advantage. De la punctuation de la langue francoyse. Plus. Des accents d'ycelle* [The technique of translating well from one language to another. Further, of the punctuation of the French language. Also, of the accents pertaining to such.] Lyons, France: Estienne Dolet.

Dryden, J. (2003). Preface to *Ovid's epistles translated by several hands.* In K. Walker (Ed.), *John Dryden: The major works* (pp. 155–164). Oxford, England: Oxford University Press.

Dyson, A. (1997). *Writing superheroes: Contemporary childhood, popular culture, and classroom literacy.* New York: Teachers College Press.

Elkins, J. (1999). *The domain of images.* Ithaca, NY: Cornell University Press.

Elman, B. (2000). *A cultural history of civil examination in late Imperial China.* Berkeley: University of California Press.

Emig, J. (1971). *The composing processes of twelfth graders*. Urbana, IL: National Council of Teachers of English.

Engeström, Y. (1993). Developmental studies of work as a test bench of activity theory: The case of primary care medical practice. In S. Chaiklin & J. Lave (Eds.), *Understanding practice* (pp. 64–103). Cambridge, England: Cambridge University Press.

Eubanks, P. (2000). *A war of words in the discourse of trade: The rhetorical constitution of metaphor*. Carbondale: Southern Illinois University Press.

Fenton, S., & Moon, P. (2002). The translation of the treaty of Waitangi: A case of disempowerment. In M. Tymoczko & E. Gentzler (Eds.), *Translation and power* (pp. 25–44). Amherst: University of Massachusetts Press.

Finders, M. (1997). *Just girls: Hidden literacies and life in junior high*. New York: Teachers College Press.

Flower, L., & Hayes, J. (1981). A cognitive process theory of writing. *College Composition and Communication, 32*, 365–387.

Foucault, M. (1991). Governmentality. In G. Burchell, C. Gordon, & P. Miller (Eds.), *The Foucault effect: Studies in governmentality* (pp. 87–104). Chicago: University of Chicago Press.

Gentzler, E. (1993). *Contemporary translation theories*. London: Routledge.

Ghosh, S. (2002). *Civilization, education, and school in ancient and medieval India, 1500 B.C –1757 A. D.* Frankfurt, Germany: Peter Lang.

Goffman, E. (1981). *Forms of talk*. Philadelphia: University of Pennsylvania Press.

Goody, J. (1977). *The domestication of the savage mind*. Cambridge, England: Cambridge University Press.

Gutas, D. (2000). *Greek philosophers in the Arabic tradition*. Aldershot, England: Ashgate/Variorum.

Guy, K. (1994). Fang Pao and the Ch'in-ting Ssu-shu-wen. In B. Elman & A. Woodside (Eds.), *Education and society in later Imperial China, 1600–1900* (pp. 150–182). Berkeley: University of California Press.

Hacking, I. (1995). *Rewriting the soul: Multiple personality and the sciences of memory*. Princeton, NJ: Princeton University Press.

Harris, R. (1986). *The origin of writing*. London: Duckworth.

Haskins, E. (2004). *Logos and power in Isocrates and Aristotle*. Columbia: University of South Carolina Press.

Havelock, E. (1963). *Preface to Plato*. Cambridge, England: Cambridge University Press.

Hawhee, D. (2004). *Bodily arts: Rhetoric and athletics in ancient Greece*. Austin: University of Texas Press.

Heath, C., & Luff, P. (2000). *Technology in action*. Cambridge, England: Cambridge University Press.

Hillocks, G. (1986). *Research on written composition: New directions for teaching*. Urbana, IL: National Conference on Research in English and ERIC.

Hitti, P. (1970). *History of the Arabs* (10th ed.). New York: St. Martin's Press.

House, J. (2002). Universality versus culture specificity in translation. In A. Riccardi (Ed.), *Translation studies: Perspectives on an emerging discipline* (pp. 92–110). Cambridge, England: Cambridge University Press.

Howard, R. M. (1999). *Standing in the shadow of giants: Plagiarists, authors, collaborators*. Stamford, CT: Ablex.

Hyun, T. (2004). *Writing women in Korea: Translation and feminism in the colonial period*. Honolulu: University of Hawaii Press.

Iedema, R. (2003). *Discourses of post-bureaucratic organization*. Amsterdam: John Benjamins.

Ivanic, R. (1998). *Writing and identity: The discoursal construction of identity in academic writing*. Amsterdam: John Benjamins.

Johnson, S. (2006). *Samuel Johnson's lives of the poets* (4 vols; R. Lonsdale, Ed.). Oxford, England: Oxford University Press.

Kalman, J. (1999). *Writing on the plaza: Mediated literacy practices among scribes and clients in Mexico City*. Cresskill, NJ: Hampton.

Kamberelis, G. (2001). Producing heteroglossic classroom (micro)cultures through hybrid discourse practice. *Linguistics and Education, 12*, 85–125.

Kenan, L. (2002). Translation as a catalyst for social change in China. In M. Tymoczko & E. Gentzler (Eds.), *Translation and power* (pp. 160–183). Amherst: University of Massachusetts Press.

Kennedy, G. (1998). *Comparative rhetoric: An historical and cross-cultural introduction*. New York: Oxford University Press.

Knorr-Cetina, K. (1981). *The manufacture of knowledge*. Oxford, England: Pergamon.

Lakoff, G. (1987). *Women, fire, and dangerous things: What categories reveal about the mind*. Chicago: University of Chicago Press.

Latour, B. (1987). *Science in action: How to follow scientists and engineers through society*. Cambridge, MA: Harvard University Press.

Latour, B. (2004). *Politics of nature: How to bring the sciences into democracy* (C. Porter, Trans.). Cambridge, MA: Harvard University Press.

Latour, B., & Woolgar, S. (1979). *Laboratory life: The social construction of scientific facts*. Princeton, NJ: Princeton University Press.

Lemke, J. (1998). Multiplying meaning: Visual and verbal semiotics in scientific text. In J. Martin & R. Veel (Eds.), *Reading science: Critical and functional perspectives on discourses of science* (pp. 77–113). London: Routledge.

Lu, X. (1998). *Rhetoric in ancient China, fifth to third century B.C.E.: Comparison with classical Greek rhetoric.* Columbia: University of South Carolina Press.

Lunsford, A., & Ede, L. (1990). *Singular texts/plural authors: Perspectives on collaborative writing.* Carbondale: Southern Illinois University Press.

Lunsford, K. (2002). Contextualizing Toulmin's model in the writing classroom: A case study. *Written Communication, 19*(1), 109–174.

Ma, Z. (1984). *Zhongguo fanyi jian shi* [A brief history of translation in China up to the May Fourth Movement of 1919]. Beijing: China Publishing Corporation of Translations.

Manovich, L. (2001). *The language of new media.* Cambridge, MA: MIT Press.

Martin, J., & Veel, R. (Eds.). (1998). *Reading science: Critical and functional perspectives on discourses of science.* London: Routledge.

McCloskey, D. (1985). *The rhetoric of economics.* Madison: University of Wisconsin Press.

Montgomery, S. L. (2000). *Science in translation: Movements of knowledge through cultures and time.* Chicago: University of Chicago Press.

Myers, G. (1990). *Writing biology: Texts in the social construction of scientific knowledge.* Madison: University of Wisconsin Press.

Nystrand, M., Greene, S., & Wiemelt, J. (1993). Where did composition studies come from? An intellectual history. *Written Communication, 10,* 267–333.

Olson, D. (1977). From utterance to text: The bias of language in speech and writing. *Harvard Educational Review, 47,* 257–281.

Olson, D. (1994). *The world on paper: The conceptual and cognitive implications of writing and reading.* Cambridge, England: Cambridge University Press.

Ong, W. (1982). *Orality and literacy: The technologizing of the word.* London: Metheun.

Oppenheim, A. L. (1964). *Ancient Mesopotamia: Portrait of a dead civilization.* Chicago: University of Chicago Press.

Perelman, C., & Olbrechts-Tyteca, L. (1968). *The new rhetoric: A treatise on argumentation* (J. Wilkinson & P. Weaver, Trans.). Norte Dame, IN: Norte Dame University Press.

Phelps, L. (1989). Images of student writing: The deep structure of teacher response. In C. Anson (Ed), *Writing and response: Theory, practice, and research* (pp. 37–67). Urbana, IL: National Council of Teachers of English.

Plato. (1989). *The collected dialogues, including the letters* (Bollingen Series LXXI) (E. Hamilton & H. Cairns, Eds.). Princeton, NJ: Princeton University Press.

Prendergast, C. (2003). *Literacy and racial justice: The politics of learning after* Brown v. Board of Education. Carbondale: Southern Illinois University Press.

Prior, P. (1994). Response, revision, disciplinarity: A microhistory of a dissertation prospectus in sociology. *Written Communication, 11*(4), 483–533.

Prior, P. (1998). *Writing/disciplinarity: A sociohistoric account of literate activity in the academy.* Mahwah, NJ: Lawrence Erlbaum Associates.

Quintilian. (1920). *Institutio oratoria* (4 vols.; Harold Butler, Trans.). Cambridge, MA: Harvard University Press.

Riccardi, A. (Ed.). (2002). *Translation studies: Perspectives on an emerging discipline.* Cambridge, England: Cambridge University Press.

Richards, I. (1929). *Practical criticism: A study of literary judgment.* San Diego, CA: Harcourt Brace.

Richardson, S. (2002). *Machine translation: From research to real users.* Berlin: Springer.

Robinson, D. (1997). *What is translation? Centrifugal theories, critical interventions.* Kent, OH: Kent State University Press.

Russell, D. (1997). Rethinking genre in school and society: An activity theory analysis. *Written Communication, 14,* 504–554.

Schieffelin, B. (2000). Introducing Kaluli literacy: A chronology of influences. In P. Kroskrity (Ed.), *Regimes of language: Ideologies, politics, and identities* (pp. 293–328). Santa Fe, NM: School of American Research Press.

Scribner, S., & Cole, M. (1981). *The psychology of literacy.* Cambridge, MA: Harvard University Press.

Selfe, C., & Hawisher, G. (2004). *Literate lives in the information age: Narratives of literacy from the United States.* Mahwah, NJ: Lawrence Erlbaum Associates.

Sheridan-Rabideau, M. (2001). The stuff that myths are made of: Myth building as social action. *Written Communication, 18,* 440–469.

Shipka, J. (2005). A multimodal task-based framework for composing. *College Composition and Communication*, *57*(2), 277–306.

Smith, D. (1990). *The conceptual practices of power: A feminist sociology of knowledge*. Toronto, Canada: University of Toronto Press.

Swales, J. (1990). *Genre analysis: English in academic and research settings*. Cambridge, England: Cambridge University Press.

Swales, J. (2004). *Research genres: Exploration and applications*. Cambridge, England: Cambridge University Press.

Thompson, D. (1994). Literacy and power in Ptolemaic Egypt. In A. Bowman & G. Woolf (Eds.), *Literacy and power in the ancient world* (pp. 67–83). Cambridge, England: Cambridge University Press.

Too, Y. L. (1995). *The rhetoric of identity in Isocrates: Texts, power, pedagogy*. Cambridge, England: Cambridge University Press.

Toulmin, S. (1958). *The uses of argument*. Cambridge, England: Cambridge University Press.

Toury, G. (2002). Translation and reflection on translation: A skeletal history for the uninitiated. In R. Singerman (Ed.), *Jewish translation history: A bibliography of bibliographies and studies* (pp. ix–xxxi). Amsterdam: John Benjamins.

Venuti, L. (Ed.). (1992). *Rethinking translation: Discourse, subjectivity, ideology*. London: Routledge.

Welch, K. (1999). *Electric rhetoric, orality, and a new literacy*. Cambridge, MA: MIT Press.

Williams, J. (1995). *Style: Toward clarity and grace*. Chicago: University of Chicago Press.

Witte, S. (1992). Context, text, intertext: Toward a constructivist semiotic of writing. *Written Communication*, *9*, 237–308.

Woodmansee, M., & Jaszi, P. (1994). *The construction of authorship: Textual appropriation in law and literature*. Durham, NC: Duke University Press.

Woods, M. C. (2001). The teaching of poetic composition in the later Middle Ages. In J. Murphy (Ed.), *A short history of writing instruction: From ancient Greece to modern America* (pp. 123–144). Mahwah, NJ: Lawrence Erlbaum Associates.

Woolf, V. (1998). *A room of one's own, and three guineas* (M. Shiach, Ed.). Oxford, England: Oxford University Press.

Worth, V. (1988). *Practising translation in Renaissance France: The example of Étienne Dolet*. Oxford, England: Clarendon.

Wysocki, A., Johnson-Eiola, J., Selfe, C., & Sirc, G. (2004). *Writing new media: Theory and application for expanding the teaching of composition*. Logan: University of Utah State Press.

Yates, J. (1989). *Control through communication: The rise of system in American management*. Baltimore: John Hopkins University Press.

Yunis, H. (2003). Introduction: Why written texts? In H. Yunis (Ed.), *Written texts and the rise of literate culture in ancient Greece* (pp. 1–15). Cambridge, England: Cambridge University Press.

II

Writing in Society

The appearance of writing transformed existing social systems by increasing the ease of communication across space and time, by supporting an enduring and stable record, by allowing relative uniformity in multiple copies aligning multiple audiences, by making communications visible and inspectable, and perhaps by other processes we only dimly understand. Belief, knowledge, law, economy, and government all took on new force when mediated through writing. Literate modes of organization supported new social systems, linking people over distance and through time in textually mediated activities.

Writing began in relation to economic activity, and writing' reorganizing effect on the economy is the subject of chapter 6. Writing facilitated accounting of goods, making contractual arrangements, forming of large and extended economic enterprises, developing of economic theories to guide action and policy, and ultimately constructing a conceptual system called the economy within which people make concrete economic choices.

Writing from early on has played a major role in the formation of government bureaucracies by which people's lives are inscribed in ruling orders. Chapter 7 presents studies of the workings of documentary society. Writing also has transformed law from the oral invocation of tradition and the dictates of community leaders to a written code, applied and adjudicated by literate experts. Chapter 8 examines the history of the transformation of law from an oral practice where writing served only as evidence of what people said to its current literate foundation where the law and agreements are embodied in texts, with particular focus on the Anglo-American tradition.

Although the formation of scriptural religions historically followed early developments in economic, governmental, and legal writing, it has been one of the most visible and pervasive forces in the spread of literacy, the spread of schooling, and the organization of people's daily lives around the written word. Jack Goody (1986) even argues that the modern idea of religion depended on the production of scriptures to define, bound, stabilize, and allow shared commitment to a set of beliefs identifiably distinct from beliefs inscribed in other scriptures. Unfortunately, we have not been able to provide a chapter on this important topic for this handbook. However, at the end of this part introduction, we provide some starting points for those who wish to explore this topic more deeply.

Much knowledge was originally subsumed within scriptural religions, but over time distinct traditions of secular knowledge arose, inscribed, stored, and disseminated in texts around which knowledge-focused institutions arose. Three chapters are devoted to chronicling the relation of writing to secular knowledge. Chapter 9 examines the production and dissemination of knowledge and related institutions prior to or outside the ambit of the Western university. Chapter 10 turns to the development and spread of secular knowledge arising out of the European experience of the last thousand years, now globalized through Western knowledge practices and institutions. Chapter 11 focuses on the institutions devoted to organizing, preserving, and making available the knowledge texts—namely archives, libraries, and reference works.

Within the world of writing, literary writing (that writing that is produced to be enjoyed as entertainment or artistic expression) has in recent centuries held a privileged place. Literary writing goes back as far as *Gilgamesh* and now encompasses a wide variety of texts, both canonical and vernacular. As these texts, their histories, their contexts, their diffusion, and their interpretation are the focus of many scholars in literary and cultural studies internationally, the scholarship on these texts far exceeds by several orders of magnitude the scholarship on writing in all other domains reported in this part and volume. Chapter 12 does not attempt to provide an overview of all scholarship on canonical and vernacular literary texts, but rather attempts to help us understand this domain as parallel to the other domains presented in this part.

In the last several centuries, journalism has also emerged to become closely associated with the writer's craft, along with being associated with political processes and the emergence of a public sphere. Chapter 13 examines the rise of journalism and its role in the formation of publics and social movements.

The restructuring of the economy, work, and knowledge has resulted in the emergence of new forms of knowledge-based work, often associated with powerful institutions, in what are called the *professions*. Writing in the professions has itself become a major focus of scholarly study in large part to support and direct programs to teach professionals the skills they need to carry out their work effectively. Chapter 14 examines what this research has told us. Simultaneously, forms of writing have emerged as part of the everyday world or as expressions of peoples outside those powerful institutions. Chapter 15 on writing in the community examines what we have learned about writing in this more domestic sphere.

Writing not only has helped form many social spheres, it helps carry out fundamental processes that cut across social spheres. Chapter 16 looks at writing and the formation of gender, and chapter 17 considers how writing can be a vehicle of social change.

REFERENCE

Goody, J. (1986). *The logic of writing and the organization of society.* Cambridge, England: Cambridge University Press.

WRITING AND SCRIPTURAL RELIGIONS

(with the assistance of Sarah Boggs)

Unfortunately we are unable to provide a chapter written by an area specialist addressing writing in the context of religion and for this we apologize. Nevertheless it is an important area, and we provide the following entry points for people who wish to pursue work in this area. The foundational work in writing and religion, as well as in all topics covered in this section, is Goody's *The Logic of Writing and the Organization of Society*. As part of his larger argument that writing contributes to the formation of modern society, Goody begins by noting how the modern concept of religion depends on scriptures to define, stabilize, and facilitate shared commitment to a set of beliefs identifiably distinct from beliefs inscribed in other scriptures. Scriptural religions and their dependence upon the written word restructured prior belief and the surrounding practices. Institutions and elite priestly classes emerged to administer the divine word and thereby to organize and regulate the communities of adherents. In identifying belief as inscribed in the sacred texts, religions could be spread with the book and peoples could be converted by allegiance to the book. The words of the book inscribed a moral universalism which could be at odds with the state. Differing interpretation of the scriptures could also lead to internal division of theological dispute, factionalism, heresy, and sectarian splits. Probst's "The Letter and the Spirit: Literacy and Religious Authority in the History of the Aladura Movement in Western Nigeria" provides an interesting case study of how these processes have played out in the formation of a new religious society.

The great preponderance of scholarly work on literacy in scriptural religions has focused on reading, as the writing or inspiration of significant texts is associated with divinity, and the human responsibility is to attend—to read or hear the divine word. Issues of authorship, authority, and authorial intent have been often subsumed into issues of divinity. Several collections and monographic works contain studies of historical and contemporary reading practices within Christian, Jewish, and Islamic contexts, along with the scribal reproduction of divine texts: Boyarin's *Ethnography of Reading*; Cavallo & Chartier's *History of Reading in the West*; Graff's *Literacy and Social Development in the West*; Gamble's *Books and their Readers in the Early Church: A History of Early Christian Texts*; and Hassan's *Art and Islamic Literacy Among the Hausa of Nigeria*. Other historical volumes focusing on religious and political history discuss the spread and use of texts as part of the story, such as Edwards' *Religion and Society in Roman Palestine*; Eaton's *The Rise of Islam and the Bengal Frontier*; Kapstein's *The Tibetan Assimilation of Buddhism*. Graham's *Beyond the Written Word: Oral Aspects of Scripture in the History of Religion* considers how the written word was transmitted orally. Another entry point to the relation of religion and literacy is through examining how the motive to read the scriptures led to the development of schooling (see this volume, chapter 18 and Gordon & Gordon's *Literacy in America*).

More writing focused studies of literacy and religion have centered around those who have been authorized to speak for the divine word—the preachers, translators, and evangelists. Preaching, though an oral practice, is often scripted, and within the Christian world there is a long tradition of homiletics offering rhetorical principles for sermon writing (for historical treatments see Kennedy's *Classical Rhetoric and its Christian and Secular Tradition from Ancient to Modern Times*, Murphy's *Rhetoric in the Middle Ages: A History of Rhetorical Theory from Saint Augustine to the Renaissance*, and Osborn's *Folly of God: The Rise of Christian Preaching*. Besnier's *Literacy, Emotion and Authority: Reading and Writing on a Polynesian Atoll* presents an anthropological study of how sermon writing practices are organized on one island community, and how those practices are tied to other social identities and processes.

There is a large literature on the history of the translation of Old and New Testaments and its relation to proliferation of religions and sects as well as proselytizing and missionary work, almost all of it with a Christian focus. Much of this literature is tied to histories or theologies of specific sects or examinations of particular cultural or historical moments, much of it focused on Reformation and Post Reformation Christianity. Nonetheless, one somewhat synoptic collection (still from an instrumentalist sectarian perspective) is Stine's *Bible Translation and the Spread of the Church: The Last Two Hundred Years.*

Christian Evangelism also produced much writing, both in the production of documents to spread the faith and in accounts of the conversion of various populations. Two studies of these texts and their relation to the societies of the time are Wyss's *Writing Indians: Literacy, Christianity, and Native Community in Early America* and Brown's *The Word in the World: Evangelical Writing, Publishing, and Reading in America, 1789-1880.*

One more democratically available writing practice associated with religions has been the spiritual autobiography, which has both a deep history and a current popularity. Among the many literary studies of individual texts, are several that take a more synoptic perspective, such as Hindmarsh's *The evangelical conversion narrative : spiritual autobiography in early modern England*, Ibsen's *Women's spiritual autobiography in colonial Spanish America*, Shea's *Spiritual autobiography in early America*, and Leigh's *Circuitous Journeys: Modern Spiritual Autobiography.*

WORKS CITED

Besnier, N. (1995). Literacy, emotion and authority: reading and writing on a Polynesian atoll. Cambridge: Cambridge University Press.

Boyarin, J. (Ed.). (1993) The ethnography of reading. Berkeley: University of California Press.

Brown, C. G. (2004). The Word in the world: Evangelical writing, publishing, and reading in America, 1789-1880. Chapel Hill: The University of North Carolina Press.

Cavallo, G. & Chartier, R. (Eds.). (1999). History of reading in the West. Cambridge: Polity Press,

Eaton, R. M. (1993). The rise of Islam and the Bengal frontier. Berkeley: University of California Press.

Edwards, D. R. (Ed.). (2004). Religion and society in Roman Palestine. New York: Routledge.

Gamble, H. Y. (1995). Books and their readers in the early Church: A history of early Christian Texts. New Haven: Yale University Press.

Goody, J. (1986). The logic of writing and the organization of society. Cambridge: Cambridge University Press.

Gordon, E. E. & Gordon, E. H. (2003). Literacy in America. Westport CN: Praeger.

Graff, H. (Ed.). (1981). Literacy and social development in the West. Cambridge: Cambridge University Press.

Graham, W. A. (1987). Beyond the written word: Oral aspects of scripture in the history of religion. Cambridge: Cambridge University Press.

Hassan, S. M. (1992). Art and Islamic literacy among the Hausa of Nigeria. Lewiston NY: Edwin Mellen Press.

Hindmarsh, D. B. (2005). The evangelical conversion narrative: spiritual autobiography in early modern England. Oxford: Oxford University Press.

Ibsen, K. (1999). Women's spiritual autobiography in colonial Spanish America. Gainesville: University Press of Florida

Kapstein. M.T. (2000). The Tibetan assimilation of Buddhism. Oxford: Oxford University Press.

Kennedy, G.A. (1999). Classical rhetoric and its Christian and secular tradition from ancient to modern Times (2nd ed.). Chapel Hill: The University of North Carolina Press.

Leigh, D. J. (2000). Circuitous Journeys: Modern spiritual autobiography. NY: Fordham University Press.

Murphy, J.J. (1974). Rhetoric in the Middle Ages: A history of rhetorical theory from Saint Augustine to the renaissance. Berkeley: University of California Press.

Osborn, R.E. (1999). Folly of God: The rise of Christian preaching. St. Louis: Chalice Press.

Probst, P. (1993). The letter and the spirit: Literacy and religious authority in the history of the Aladura movement in Western Nigeria. In B. Street (Ed.). Cross-cultural approaches to literacy (pp. 198-219). Cambridge: Cambridge University Press.

Shea, D. B. (1988). Spiritual autobiography in early America. Madison: University of Wisconsin Press.

Stine, P. (Ed.). (1990). Bible translation and the spread of the Church: The last two hundred years. Leiden: E. J. Brill.

Wyss, H. E. (2000). Writing Indians: Literacy, Christianity, and native community in early America. Amherst: University of Massachusetts Press.

CHAPTER 6

Writing and the Social Formation of Economy

Graham Smart
Carleton University, Ottawa, Ontario, Canada

This chapter draws on scholarship from several different fields to construct an account of the role of writing in the social formation of economy. The account explores three facets of this topic: We begin by considering the part that writing has played throughout recorded history in the development of objects, practices, and institutions that have enabled and organized human economic activity. Next, we turn to the modern academic/professional discipline of economics, tracing its discursive origins and subsequent evolution through a series of landmark theoretical texts, and then examining the discourse of the discipline from a rhetorical and social constructionist perspective. And finally, we look at how the science of economics produced through this disciplinary discourse has over the last two centuries become an essential conceptual and analytical resource for government policymaking as well as for corporate and individual action.

THE ROLE OF WRITING IN ENABLING AND ORGANIZING ECONOMIC ACTIVITY

Writing has, over the millennia, supported the development of increasingly complex and geographically far-reaching forms of economic activity. Throughout this history, newly invented texts and functions for writing have facilitated innovative economic practices. In turn, the use of particular kinds of texts in economic activity led to their early and widespread development, ahead of other forms of writing.

The story begins some 5,000 years ago in Mesopotamia and Egypt, the world's first literate cultures, when embryonic writing practices enabled individuals and collectives to conduct transactions involving property and goods through increasingly elaborate systems of exchange, production, distribution, and trade—with this economic activity extended over time and space in ways not possible prior to the existence of writing (Goody, 1986, 2004). In southern Mesopotamia, the specialization of farming, hunting, and fishing in the countryside and the contemporaneous appearance of craft manufacturing in urban centers led to a loss of individual economic self-sufficiency and to the consequent need for exchanges of goods together with the affordance of credit in return for payment of interest. This cultural development occurred jointly with the emergence of a written system of Sumerian cuneiform inscriptions on clay tablets that along with texts such as numerical tables, accounts, and receipts provided both a credible sign of legitimacy for agreements and transactions as well as a reliable method of recording them (Van de Mieroop, 2005).

Subsequently, these and other new texts such as contracts guaranteeing future deliveries and repayment of loans supported the growth of a merchant class and the expansion of commerce on a broader scale, with increased long-distance trade and the creation of networks for importing and exporting goods (Goody, 1986, 2004). Later, in both Mesopotamia and Egypt other new texts such as census lists, taxation rolls, bookkeeping ledgers, and auditing tools allowed an emergent state, following in the steps of the temple bureaucracy and its management of the priesthood's economic affairs, to take an increasingly central place in economic life through taxation and spending and, later, through support and control of regional and international trade (Goody, 1986, 2004).

We see a similar relationship between new texts and more complex and distance-spanning forms of economic activity in China. In the seventh century, officials of the Tang dynasty developed a document-based legal system to negotiate commercial disputes between their Chinese subjects and inhabitants of other lands along the Silk Road trade route (Hansen, 2005). Later, during the Song dynasty of the 11th century, the Chinese, aided by technological innovations in papermaking and printing, invented paper money and established the first reliable system of government-assured paper currency, a reflection of the growing role of the state in business and trade as it moved to control the amount of money in circulation in order to encourage stable prices and sufficient supplies of goods (Goetzmann & Köll, 2005; Von Glahn, 2005). From these beginnings, other forms of paper-based financial instruments were created, including monetary vouchers—in effect an early form of traveler's checks—that were used by traveling government officials to pay their expenses and also by military officers as compensation for goods requisitioned during war (Von Glahn, 2005).

Throughout this history, as well as in later periods, we can see the reciprocal relationship between writing and economic activity. New forms and functions for writing allowed for increased complexity in economic affairs—a greater volume of more complicated and reliable business transactions became possible, and information could be stored over time and transported textually from one locale to another, thereby enabling commerce to transcend the constraints of human memory, social trust, and geography (Bazerman, 2006b). At the same time, we see that those particular kinds of writing that were employed in commerce and trade and in the economic practices of the state—such as lists, numerical tables, bookkeeping records, accounts, and contracts—tended to develop at a faster pace and over a greater geographical range than those forms of writing that did not—for example, texts conveying narratives, descriptions, and arguments (Goody, 1986, 2004). Similarly, on a broad societal level, new networks for circulating monetary currency and early networks for circulating other texts overlapped and were mutually reinforcing (Stock, 1983).

In medieval and Renaissance Europe, with the further expansion of commerce and trade as well as the need to finance city-state activities such as building construction and military campaigns, other newly invented forms of writing provided the basis for a sophisticated system of commercial law that regulated business transactions and debt payments and also provided mechanisms for adjudicating disputes among individuals and groups. Contracts, land deeds, wills, standardized textual procedures, highly literate legal specialists—all contributed to the operation of a legal system that provided the underpinning for increasingly sophisticated economic activity (Bazerman, 1999). Concurrently, European scholars contributed new mathematical tools that were combined with texts to calculate and represent financial entities such as present value, compound interest, and profit allocation (Goetzmann, 2005). From the 12th century onward, in related developments in northern Italy, particularly in Pisa, Bologna, Milan, Venice, and Florence, the widespread use of letters to acknowledge sales, loans, monetary exchanges, receipt of money and goods, contractual commitments, and credit arrangements led to the eventual evolution of these letters into more specialized financial instruments such as paper currency, bonds, stocks, cheks, and promissory notes (Bazerman, 1999; Pezzolo, 2005).

From their origins in Renaissance Europe and over the centuries since, networks of national and international financial markets have emerged to meet the needs of commerce, industry, and trade for loans and capital investment. These financial markets have arisen in tandem with a variety of supporting institutions including commercial banks, brokerage houses, insurance companies, accounting firms, and stock exchanges, the latter first created in 17th-century Holland for trading in securities needed to finance the overseas commercial activities of the Dutch East India Company. New literate practices and textual forms have played an essential role in the development and social organization of these financial markets and institutions, which have spawned—and rely on—a vast web of spreadsheets, financial statements, stock reports, shareholder newsletters, and myriad other texts (Gunnarsson, 2000, 2004; Neal, 2005). In more recent times, of course, this intertextual web has extended beyond the printed page, migrating to electronic networks enabled by computer technologies and the Internet (Bazermen, 2006a; Goetzmann & Williams, 2005; Levy, 2001).

The growth of the modern business corporation constitutes another strand in this history. We can trace the development of the corporation from the prominent trading houses of Renaissance Italy, through to the emergence in 16th-century England of joint stock companies such as the Company of Mineral and Battery Works, and on to the rise in the 17th century of organizations linked to European colonization, such as the Dutch East India Company and the British East India Company. It was in post–Industrial Revolution Britain and North America, however, that corporations began to grow into the large multinational entities we know today (Bakan, 2004). In American railroad and manufacturing companies of the late 1800s and early 1900s, capitalist owners and business managers developed novel organizational systems for monitoring, operational analysis, and communication employing newly invented technologies—the telegraph, mimeograph machine, typewriter, and vertical filing cabinet—and new forms of writing such as the progress report, interoffice memorandum, and analytical report (Yates, 1989). (During this period, through a somewhat unlikely turn of events, a series of judicial decisions in the United States granted the corporation the legal status of "personhood"—with all the rights of free speech and action accorded to individuals under the law [Bakan, 2004]). In the 20th century, the corporate sector, led by insurance companies needing to store and manipulate vast amounts of data, pioneered the development of automated information-processing technologies with a host of new related electronic texts (Yates, 2005).

Alongside private-sector financial institutions and business corporations arose a parallel sphere of governmental organizations—national regulatory bodies and statistical agencies, ministries of finance, central banks, and international institutions such as the World Bank and the International Monetary Fund (De Vries, 2006; Lavoie & Seccareccia, 2004; Peet, 2003; Wood, 2005). And once again, throughout the history of these governmental organizations we see the growth of new functions and forms of writing as well as the reciprocal relationship between the invention of new types of texts and the development of increasingly complex and geographically distributed networks of economic activity (Harper, 1998; Smart, 2006).

THE MODERN DISCIPLINE OF ECONOMICS

The Discursive Origins and Development of Modern Economics

The discursive origins of the modern academic/professional discipline of economics—as a field of research, theory, and practice taking as its purview the realm of human economic affairs—can be traced back to the publication in 1776 of Adam Smith's *An Inquiry Into the Nature and Causes of the Wealth of Nations*. Smith's work is strikingly rhetorical: He labors mightily to enroll his readers into a vision of the world in which a capitalist free-market economy, with its clearly delineated division of labor and limited instrumental role for government, generates wealth for all and advances the prosperity and social harmony of the nation (Bazerman, 1993). Here Smith presents the first discursive and conceptual depiction of the capitalist economy, a world of social arrangements, symbolic meanings, and productive actions, while also providing—through the trope of "the invisible hand"—an explanation for the human motivations animating this world. In Smith's laissez-faire landscape of landowners and renters, capitalists and laborers, goods and services, money and prices, supply and demand, we can see the precursor of contemporary microeconomic theory.

In the decades following Adam Smith, the discursive system of (what later came to be called) "classical economics" originating in *Wealth of Nations* was further developed in a series of widely read theoretical texts that included David Ricardo's *On the Principles of Political Economy and Taxation* (1817), Thomas Malthus' *Principles of Political Economy Considered With a View to Their Practical Application* (1820), John Stuart Mill's *Principles of Political Economy With Some of Their Applications to Social Philosophy* (1848), William Stanley Jevons's *The Theory of Political Economy* (1871), Friedrich von Hayek's *Prices and Production* (1931), and Joseph Schumpeter's *The Theory of Economic Development* (1934). In addition to their theoretical advances, these texts also contributed a series of new mathematical tools to economic discourse (Heilbroner, 1999). In a parallel ideological space, the publication of the first volume of Karl Marx's *Das Kapital* in 1867 (Marx, 1867/2000) initiated a theoretical countercurrent of anticapitalist discourse (Desai, 2002; Heilbroner, 1985; Screpanti & Zamagni, 2005).

In 1936, the publication of John Maynard Keynes's *The General Theory of Employment, Interest and Money* revolutionized the theoretical discourse of Western economics (Skidelsky, 2005). The Keynesian perspective, with its distrust of unfettered market forces and a faith in the ability of governments to take the lead in promoting economic growth and employment, exerted a strong shaping influence on the discipline over the next four decades. In the mid-1970s, however, the monetarist theory developed by Milton Friedman and his colleagues at the University of Chicago in texts such as *Counter Revolution in Monetary Policy* (1970), with its belief in the capacity of unrestrained markets and free competition to allocate society's resources effectively and its suspicion of government regulation and spending, began to displace the Keynesian view. A decade later, a variation of monetarism known as neoclassical economics—as posited in Robert Lucas' *Studies in Business-Cycle Theory* (1981), with its concepts of rational expectations in decision making and the natural rate of unemployment—took center stage, where it has remained since.

Although the neoclassical discourse has dominated the discipline of economics over the last three decades, critics within the field have pointed to limitations common to both the neoclassical and Keynesian perspectives, viewing them as jointly constituting a mainstream economics with shared epistemological, theoretical, and methodological foundations. Paul Ormerod, for example, argues in *Butterfly Economics* (1999) against the mechanistic representation of economic reality that is inherent in this discourse, with the economy is seen as "a machine," rather as a "living organism." For Omerod, another limitation of the mainstream economic discourse is its depiction of the human being as "Rational Economic Man"—an isolated individual characterized by obsessive self-interest and hyperrationality. Ormerod claims that the dominant discourse is further limited by an overreliance on formal mathematics, as, for example, with the widespread use of mathematics-based economic models for forecasting future trends, a position also taken by David Colander in *Why Aren't Economists as Important as Garbage Men?* (1991).

Another critique of mainstream economic discourse comes from feminist economists. In *Feminist Economics Today* (2003), Marianne Ferber and Julie Nelson reproach the mainstream discourse for its "androcentric bias," as manifested in the problems chosen for inquiry, the underlying assumptions held, the methods of research, and the approaches to interpreting findings—a state of affairs that they attribute to the traditional male control of the profession. In the orthodox economic discourse, Ferber and Nelson see a world in which the experience of women and families is either absent or distorted, so that, for example, childrearing and housework are accorded little economic value and the connection between poverty and gender is largely ignored. In *Counting for Nothing* (1999), Marilyn

Waring extends this critique to the international sphere. Waring argues that by focusing solely on the economic activity of the marketplace, the United Nations' system of national accounts—used as an analytical tool by prominent agencies such as the World Bank and the International Monetary Fund—renders invisible women's labor in the household, thereby institutionalizing the exploitation of women.

A final line of critique of the mainstream economic discourse comes from a number of well-known figures within the discipline who have taken issue with the assumptions and values underlying the economic policies of the major financial institutions that anchor globalization—the International Monetary Fund, the World Bank, and the World Trade Organization. Nobel laureate Joseph Stiglitz, for example, contends in *Globalization and Its Discontents* (2003) that globalization can potentially be a positive force, particularly for developing nations, but only if the major financial institutions change the way they think and act—reforming policies designed primarily to serve the interests of the industrialized nations and the financial markets and displaying a broader socioeconomic vision. This theme has also been taken up by other prominent economists such as Jeffery Sachs in *The End of Poverty* (2005), Jagdish Bhagwati in *In Defense of Globalization* (2004), and Paul Krugman in *The Return of Depression Economics* (2000).

RHETORICAL AND SOCIAL CONSTRUCTIONIST VIEWS OF ECONOMIC DISCOURSE

Historically, the discipline of economics has exhibited considerable self-reflexivity regarding the written discourse employed in the development of economic thought. This is a tradition that we can follow from the aspersions of Alfred Marshall (1881) and John Maynard Keyes (1933) on the writing style of Francis Edgeworth, to the economist Deidre McCloskey's (1987) praise for the writing of Keynes, Joseph Schumpeter, and Milton Friedman, and through to a study by Andrea Fracasso, Hans Genberg, and Charles Wyplosz (2003) on transparency in the writing of central bankers and to Richard Parker's (2005) tribute to the lucid prose of John Kenneth Galbraith.

On a broader plane, scholars in several different fields have examined the multifaceted character of the discourse of contemporary economics, where knowledge is produced and communicated through texts combining written language with mathematical equations, statistics, and visual representations such as charts and graphs (Henderson, Dudley-Evans, & Backhouse, 1993; Klamer, McCloskey, & Solow, 1988; Samuels, 1990; Smart, 2006; Swales, 1993). The economist Deidre McCloskey (1985) argues that because the pseudoscientific methodologies employed in economics fail to offer any real certainty, knowledge making in the discipline depends on persuasion achieved through the effective marshaling of arguments (1985). As McCloskey (1990) puts it, economics "is rhetoric, human argument, all the way down" (p. 8). Similarly, economist Arjo Klamer (1990) advocates looking beyond the knowledge claims of economists to examine the "discursive practice[s]" and "rhetorical devices" they employ (p. 130). Taking up this approach himself, Klamer subjects economic texts to rhetorical readings that demonstrate how economists work to create a scientific ethos for their methods and knowledge claims. In the same vein, McCloskey (1990) points to the widespread use of narrative and metaphor underlying the discipline's empirical methodologies and scientific posture. She sees the discourse of economics as being organized around a "rhetorical tetrad" of "fact, logic, metaphor, and story" (pp. vii, 1).

Social constructionism has also made inroads into the study of economic discourse. The economic historian Vivienne Brown (1993) argues that "instead of seeing the development of economics as the steady march of progress towards a scientific understanding of the real economy," we need to look at "the ways in which economic knowledge is produced within specific discursive conditions, and how it comes to be culturally inscribed and socially constructed" (pp. 69, 64). For Brown, written texts "are constitutive of ways of seeing the economy" (p. 70). Similarly, the economist Robert Heilbroner (1990) points to the "ideological nature of economic inquiry" (p. 104), defining ideology as "the frameworks of perception by which all social groups organize and interpret their experience" (p. 103), and claims that, accordingly, "economics [must be] understood as a belief system" (p. 104).

To this point in the chapter, the term *the economy* has been used as if it referred to an objective phenomenon, something that exists "out there" in the world as a tangible material entity. This of course is not really the case. From the arguments of Brown and Heilbroner described previously, it is but a short step to suggest that *the economy*, as an object of study and analysis, must seen as socially constructed through discourse. Indeed, Brown (1993) herself articulates this view:

> The real economy is not knowable as a direct or brute fact of existence independently of its discursive construction. The economy is represented as an object of analysis by a set of discourses which constitute it as such; it is these discourses that provide the economic concepts, modes of analysis, statistical estimates, econometric methods and policy debates that constitute the different analytic understandings of the economy. (p. 70)

Interestingly, Bruno Latour (1990) offers a similar perspective on the economy as a social construct:

> It is of course impossible to talk about the economy of a nation by looking at "it." The "it" is plainly invisible, as long as cohorts of enquirers and inspectors have not filled in long questionnaires, as long as the answers have not been punched onto cards, treated by computers, [and] analyzed.... Only at the end can the economy be made visible inside piles of charts and lists. Even this is still too confusing, so that redrawing and extracting is necessary to provide a few neat diagrams that show the Gross National Product or the Balance of Payments. (p. 38)

Such a socially constructed economy is a cultural tool that supports and shapes the collaborative activity and thinking of the particular group of economists who have created it for use in their work. As cultural tools, however, economies are not all cut from the same discursive cloth; their specific character is determined by location and use. Professional economists are always situated somewhere, either in universities or in public-sector, private-sector, or nongovernmental organizations (NGOs). The occupational setting—university department, government agency, labor union, business corporation, trade association, economic forecasting firm, environmental NGO—determines the specific version of the economy that is constructed there, reflecting the organization's mandate, goals, history, theoretical assumptions, bureaucratic practices, technological systems, and so on. For economists in any given professional site, the discursive creation of their particular version of the economy is a means to an end: The economists use its structure of conceptual categories—such as household consumption, commodity prices, exports, and government expenditures—and the dynamic relationships among these conceptual categories to analyze empirical data and produce stories that identify and explain current economic developments and expected future trends (McCloskey, 1985; Smart, 2006).

Economics as a Resource for Government Policy and for Corporate and Individual Action

The modern science of economics—that is, the ensemble of theoretical concepts and analytical tools that has been developed within the discipline from the late 17th century to the present—has become an essential resource for government policymakers as well as for corporate and individual actors. We can see an early example of the influence of economic science on government policymaking in the British and U.S. legislatures' ongoing embrace during the 1800s of the capitalist free-market model developed through the theoretical writings of the classical economists of the late 1700s and the 19th century—Adam Smith, David Ricardo, Thomas Malthus, John Stuart Mill, and William Stanley Jevons.

Adam Smith provided the impetus for the up-take of economic science by policymakers with his magnum opus *Wealth of Nations*. Published in 1776, the book argues for the material and social benefits of a free-market capitalist economy in which landowners, renters, workers, managers, and stockholders interact within the rules of a competitive game defined by a minimal set of government policies and laws—an argument that rejected the trade protectionism and state intervention in economic affairs advocated by mercantilism, the dominant economic ideology in Europe from the 16th to the 18h centuries. During the 19th century, as the capitalist model introduced by Smith and elaborated through the writings of Ricardo, Malthus, Mill, Jevons, and others was inscribed in British and U.S. legislation, it increasingly came to impose an attendant set of ideological imperatives on policymakers (Fetter, 1965, 1980; Fetter & Gregory, 1973; Haakonssen, 1981).

Another stage in the growing influence of economic science on government policymaking began with the publication in 1936 of John Maynard Keynes' *The General Theory of Employment, Interest and Money*. In addition to its ideological dimension—the vision of a demand-driven national economy with a much-expanded active role for government—*The General Theory* also introduced an innovative analytic framework comprising new concepts, economic indicators (data categories), mathematical methods of measurement, and technical lexicon (Skidelsky, 2005). Keynes' theoretical prescriptions for the effective functioning of national economies had a decisive impact on government policies in Europe and North America over the succeeding four decades, whereas his analytical framework was taken up by economists in government bureaucracies around the world.

Keynes' analytical framework was elaborated by economists such as Holland's Jan Tinbergen (1951), Norway's Trygve Haavelmo (1944), and the Americans Paul Samuelson (1947) and Lawrence Klein (1976) to create the approach known as econometrics, in which theory, mathematics, and statistics are brought together in economic models that allow economists to empirically test, extend, and apply theoretical concepts (Bodkin, Klein, & Marwah, 1991; Epstein, 1987; Pesaran, 1987). This technical advance eventually led, through the 1960s and 1970s, to the development of computer-run macroeconomic models comprising systems of mathematical equations representing entire national economies (Smart, in press). These models, which have become stock-in-trade tools for the economic staffs who advise policymakers in finance ministries, other government departments, and central banks, are typically employed in combination with writing to analyze statistical data and generate narratives about current economic developments as well as forecasts of future economic activity. One such computer-run model employed by economists at the Bank of Canada, that country's central bank, is used together with a set of written discourse genres to create knowledge about the Canadian economy that is applied by the organization's senior decision makers in directing national monetary policy (Smart, 2006).

The discourse of economic science, with its repertoire of theories and analytical methods, has also become a key resource in the private sector. Business corporations, trade associations, commercial banks, economic forecasting firms, large nonprofit organizations—all typically employ staff economists who use theoretical concepts from their discipline along with analytical tools such as economic indicators, macroeconomic models, and forecasting techniques (Bodkin et al., 1991; Daub, 1987). And again, these concepts and analytical tools are invariably used in combination with writing to produce texts that provide an organization's managers with specialized knowledge for making decisions in the areas of strategic planning, finance, marketing, research and development, investment, and recruitment (Cooper, 2005).

Finally, and most obvious to the lay person, there is the socially constructed economy that is continuously being projected into the public domain by print and electronic media. Newspapers, magazines, and other publications, television, radio, and the Internet all communicate daily news about government budgets, inflation estimates, interest rates, forecasts of economic growth, unemployment figures, consumer spending, trade balances, and the hour-to-hour movements of stock markets (Bazerman, 2006a). The composite representation of the economy that is projected through this plethora of media and texts is used by individual entrepreneurs and households (and those who advise them about financial matters) as a touchstone for decisions involving investing, spending, borrowing, hiring, and retiring. Increasingly, this media-generated abstract economy has become an essential reference point for all of us as we attempt to navigate our way among the financial byways of contemporary life. Indeed, this projected economy has become so central to our Western culture that one might view it as an iconic centrepiece on the high altar of capitalist consumerism, with economic science serving as a theology and The Market as a god (Loy, 2000).

A FINAL WORD

From their origins some 5,000 years ago, through the medieval era and the Renaissance to modernity and the present, writing and texts have facilitated and organized human activity within the multiple social formations—of governance, law, religion, education, science, cultural life, economy—that mediate collective human experience, with writing and texts themselves created and shaped through this activity (Bazerman & Russell, 2003). And at least on the level of material subsistence, one could argue that the role of writing and texts in the social formation of economy lies at the very center of this story. From cuneiform inscriptions on clay tables in ancient Mesopotamia to paper currency in 11th-century China and legal contracts in Renaissance Italy, through to cyber-inscriptions in the electronic financial networks of our own times, humans have continued to develop innovative literate practices to serve our need, as Kenneth Burke's (1978) symbol-using animals, to generate symbolic realms of shared meaning and value as we act and urge others to act in the world of economic affairs.

REFERENCES

Bakan, J. (2004). *The corporation: The pathological pursuit of profit and power*. Toronto, Canada: Penguin.

Bazerman, C. (1993). Money talks: The rhetorical project of the *Wealth of Nations*. In W. Henderson, T. Dudley-Evans, & R. Backhouse (Eds.), *Economics and language* (pp. 173–199). London: Routledge.

Bazerman, C. (1999). Letters and the social grounding of differentiated genres. In D. Barton & N. Hall (Eds.), *Letter writing as a social practice* (pp. 15–30). Amsterdam: Benjamins.

Bazerman, C. (2006). Persuasive economies. Foreword to *Writing the economy: Activity, genre and technology in the world of banking*, by G. Smart. London: Equinox.

Bazerman, C. (2006). The writing of social organization and the literate situating cognition: Extending Goody's social implications of writing. In D. Olson & M. Cole (Eds.), *Technology, literacy and the evolution in society: Implications of the work of Jack Goody* (pp. 000–000). Mahwah, NJ: Lawrence Erlbaum Associates.

Bazerman, C., & Russell, D. (2003). Introduction. In C. Bazerman & D. Russell (Eds.), *Writing selves/writing societies: Research from activity perspectives* (pp. 1–6). Fort Collins, CO: The WAC Clearinghouse and *Mind, Culture, and Activity* (http://wac.colostate.edu/books/selves_societies).

Bhagwati, J. (2004). *In defense of globalization*. New York: Oxford University Press.

Bodkin, R., Klein, L., & Marwah, K. (1991). *A history of macroeconometric model-building*. Cheltenham, England: Edward Elgar.

Brown, V. (1993). Decanonizing discourses: Textual analysis and the history of economic thought. In W. Henderson, T. Dudley-Evans, & R. Backhouse (Eds.), *Economics and language* (pp. 64–84). London: Routledge.

Burke, K. (1978). *Language as symbolic action: Essays on life, literature and method*. Berkeley: University of California Press.

Colander, D. (1991). *Why aren't economists as important as garbage men? Essays on the state of economics*. New York: Sharpe.

Cooper, C. (Ed.). (2005). *The Blackwell encyclopedia of management*: Malden, MA: Blackwell.

Daub, M. (1987). *Canadian economic forecasting: In a world where all's unsure*. Montreal, Canada: McGill-Queen's University Press.

Desai, M. (2002). *Marx's revenge: The resurgence of capitalism and the death of statist socialism*. London: Verso.

de Vries, W. (2006). *The organization of official statistics in Europe*. United Nations Department of Economic and Social Affairs. Retrieved March 2006 from http://unstats.un.org/unsd/goodprac/bpform.asp?DocId=125&KeyId=21

Epstein, R. (1987). *A history of econometrics*. New York: Elsevier.

Ferber, M., & Nelson, J. (2003). *Feminist economics today: Beyond economic man*. Chicago: University of Chicago Press.

Fetter, W. (1965). *Development of British monetary orthodoxy: 1797–1875*. Cambridge, MA: Harvard University Press.

Fetter, W. (1980). *The economist in Parliament: 1780–1868*. Durham, NC: Duke University Press.

Fetter, W., & Gregory, D. (1973). *Monetary and financial policy*. London: Irish University Press.

Fracasso, A., Genberg, H., & Wyplosz, C. (2003). *How do central banks write? An evaluation of inflation reports by inflation-targeting central banks*. London: International Center for Monetary and Banking Studies.

Friedman, M. (1970). *Counter revolution in monetary policy*. London: Institute of Economic Affairs.

Goetzmann, W. (2005). Fibonacci and the financial revolution. In W. Goetzmann & G. Rouwenhorst (Eds.), *The origins of value: The financial innovations that created modern capital markets* (pp. 123–143). New York: Oxford University Press.

Goetzmann, W., & Köll, E. (2005). Venture shares of the Dutch East Indian Company. In W. Goetzmann & G. Rouwenhorst (Eds.), *The origins of value: The financial innovations that created modern capital markets* (pp. 91–103). New York: Oxford University Press.

Goetzmann, W., & Williams, L. (2005). From tallies and chirographs to Franklin's printing press at Passy: The evolution of the technology of financial claims. In W. Goetzmann & G. Rouwenhorst (Eds.), *The origins of value: The financial innovations that created modern capital markets* (pp. 105–121). New York: Oxford University Press.

Goody, J. (1986). *The logic of writing and the organization of society*. Cambridge, England: Cambridge University Press.

Goody, J. (2004). *Capitalism and modernity: The great debate*. Cambridge, England: Polity.

Gunnarsson, B.-L. (2000). Discourse, organizations and national cultures. *Discourse Studies, 2*, 5–33.

Gunnarsson, B.-L. (2004). The multilayered structure of enterprise discourse. *Information Design Journal, 12*, 36–48.

Haakonssen, K. (1981). *The science of a legislator: The natural jurisprudence of David Hume and Adam Smith*. Cambridge, England: Cambridge University Press.

Haavelmo, T. (1944). The probability approach in econometrics. *Econometrica, 12*(Suppl.), 1–115.

Hansen, V. (2005). How business was conducted on the Chinese Silk Road during the Tang dynasty, 618–907 (Part I: The resolution of an international dispute on the Silk Road, ca. 670). In W. Goetzmann & G. Rouwenhorst (Eds.), *The origins of value: The financial innovations that created modern capital markets* (pp. 43–53). New York: Oxford University Press.

Harper, R. (1998). *Inside the IMF: An ethnography of documents, technology and organizational action*. London: Academic Press.

Heilbroner, R. (1985). *The nature and logic of capitalism*. New York: Norton.

Heilbroner, R. (1990). Economics as ideology. In W. Samuels (Ed.), *Economics as discourse: An analysis of the language of economists* (pp. 101–116). Boston: Kluwer Academic.

Heilbroner, R (1999). *The wordly philosophers: The lives, times, and ideas of the great economic thinkers*. New York: Simon & Schuster.

Henderson, W., Dudley-Evans, T., & Backhouse, R. (Eds.). (1993). *Economics and language*. London: Routledge.

Jevons, W. S. (1871). *The theory of political economy*. London: Macmillan.

Keynes, J. M. (1933). *Essays in biography*. Toronto, Canada: Macmillan.

Keynes, J. M. (1936). *The general theory of employment, interest and money*. London: Macmillan.

Klamer, A. (1990). The textbook presentation of economic discourse. In W. Samuels (Ed.), *Economics as discourse: An analysis of the language of economists* (pp. 129–154). Boston: Kluwer Academic.

Klamer, A., McCloskey, D., & Solow, R. (Eds.). (1988). *The consequences of economic rhetoric*. Cambridge, England: Cambridge University Press.

Klein, L. (1976). *Econometric model performance: Comparative simulation studies of the U.S. economy*. Philadelphia: University of Pennsylvania Press.

Krugman, P. (2000). *The return of depression economics*. New York: Norton.

Latour, B. (1990). Drawing things together. In M. Lynch & S. Woolgar (Eds.), *Representation in scientific practice* (pp. 19–68). Cambridge, MA: MIT Press.

Lavoie, M., & Seccareccia, M. (Eds.). (2004). *Central banking in the modern world: Alternative perspectives*. Northampton, MA: Edward Elgar.

Levy, D. (2001). *Scrolling forward: Making sense of documents in the digital age*. New York: Arcade.

Loy, D. (2000). The religion of the market. In H. Coward & D. Maguire (Eds.), *Visions of a new earth: Religious perspectives on population, consumption, and ecology* (pp. 15–27). Albany: State University of New York Press.

Lucas, R. (1981). *Studies in business-cycle theory*. Cambridge, MA: MIT Press.

Malthus, T. (1820). *Principles of political economy considered with a view to their practical application*. London: John Murray.

Marshall, A. (1881). Review of Francis Edgeworth's *Mathematical Psychics*. *The Academy*, p. 457.

Marx, K. (2000). *Das kapital* (Vol. 1). Moscow: Progress. (Original work published 1867)

McCloskey, D. (1985). *The rhetoric of economics*. Madison: University of Wisconsin Press.

McCloskey, D. (1987). *Writing of economics*. London: Macmillan.

McCloskey, D. (1990). *If you're so smart: The narrative of economic expertise*. Chicago: University of Chicago Press.

Mill, J. S. (1848). *Principles of political economy with some of their applications to social philosophy*. London: John W. Parker.

Neal, L. (2005). Venture shares of the Dutch East Indian Company. In W. Goetzmann & G. Rouwenhorst (Eds.), *The origins of value: The financial innovations that created modern capital markets* (pp. 165–175). New York: Oxford University Press.

Ormerod, P. (1999). *Butterfly economics: A new general theory of social and economic behavior*. New York: Basic Books.

Parker, R. (2005). *John Kenneth Galbraith: His life, his politics, his economics*. New York: Farrar, Straus & Giroux.

Peet, R. (2003). *Unholy trinity: The IMF, World Bank and WTO*. London: Zed Books.

Pesaran, M. H. (1987). Econometrics. In J. Eatwell, M. Milgate, & P. Newman (Eds.), *The new Palgrave: A dictionary of economics* (pp. 8–22). London: Macmillan.

Pezzolo, L. (2005). Bonds and government debt in Italian city-states, 1250–1650. In W. Goetzmann & G. Rouwenhorst (Eds.), *The origins of value: The financial innovations that created modern capital markets* (pp. 145–163). New York: Oxford University Press.

Ricardo, D. (1817). *On the principles of political economy and taxation*. London: John Murray.

Sachs, J. (2005). *The end of poverty: Economic possibilities for our time*. New York: Penguin.

Samuels, W. (1990). *Economics as discourse: An analysis of the language of economists*. Boston: Kluwer Academic.

Samuelson, P. (1947). *Foundations of economic analysis*. Cambridge, MA: Harvard University Press.

Schumpeter, J. (1934). *The theory of economic development: An inquiry into profits, capital, credit, interest, and the business cycle* (R. Opie, Trans.). Cambridge, MA: Harvard University Press.

Screpanti, E., & Zamagni, S. (2005). *An outline of the history of economic thought* (2nd ed.). London: Oxford University Press.

Skidelsky, R. (2005). *John Maynard Keynes: 1883–1946: Economist, philosopher, statesman*. New York: Penguin.

Smart, G. (2006). *Writing the economy: Activity, genre and technology in the world of banking*. London: Equinox.

Smith, A. (1776). *An inquiry into the nature and causes of the wealth of nations*. London: W. Stahan & T. Cadell.

Stiglitz, J. (2003). *Globalization and its discontents*. New York: Norton.

Stock, B. (1983). *The implications of literacy: Written languages and models of interpretation in the eleventh and twelfth centuries*. Princeton, NJ: Princeton University Press.

Swales, J. (1993). The paradox of value: Six treatments in search of the reader. In W. Henderson, T. Dudley-Evans, & R. Backhouse (Eds.), *Economics and language* (pp. 223–239). London: Routledge.

Tinbergen, J. (1951). *Econometrics*. London: Allen & Unwin.

van de Mieroop, M. (2005). The invention of interest: Sumerian loans. In W. Goetzmann & G. Rouwenhorst (Eds.), *The origins of value: The financial innovations that created modern capital markets* (pp. 17–30). New York: Oxford University Press.

von Glahn, R. (2005). The origins of paper money in China. In W. Goetzmann & G. Rouwenhorst (Eds.), *The origins of value: The financial innovations that created modern capital markets* (pp. 65–89). New York: Oxford University Press.

von Hayek, F. (1931). *Prices and production*. London: Routledge & Sons.

Waring, M. (1999). *Counting for nothing: What men value and what women are worth* (2nd ed.). Toronto, Canada: University of Toronto Press.

Wood, J. (2005). *A history of central banking in Great Britain and the United States*. Cambridge, England: Cambridge University Press.

Yates, J. (1989). *Control through communication: The rise of system in American management*. Baltimore, MD: Johns Hopkins University Press.

Yates, J. (2005). *Structuring the information age: Life insurance and the technology of the twentieth century*. Baltimore, MD: Johns Hopkins University Press.

CHAPTER 7

On Documentary Society

Dorothy E. Smith
University of Victoria, British Colombia, Canada

Catherine F. Schryer
University of Waterloo, Ontario, Canada

The term *documentary society* does not have a definition predating this handbook. Part of the aim of this chapter is to define the term to enable those working in the field of writing and literacy to relate it to other more fully developed and familiar topics. Although the term *documentary society* loosely refers to research that investigates the ways written documentary practices such as record keeping, reporting, and policy and procedure development contribute to organizations and institutions, as a scholarly region, the area of documentary society is not well articulated or circumscribed. Hence, definition proceeds not by formulation, but by engaging the reader with some of the ways in which the significance of texts and documents for society has been theorized and by finding the differences and convergences that help to locate the concept. Rather than constructing a theoretical model, we are attempting to locate the phenomenon and make it more observable.

Our aim, then, is to identify distinctive aspects of our contemporary world that the concept of documentary society brings into view. This does not mean, of course, that contemporary society can be reduced to or equated with the notion. Rather, we discover herein how such a concept can explicate social dimensions that otherwise remain in the tangled knots of the various theorizings of the information age or society (Beniger, 1986; Mosco, 1988; Nunberg, 1996; Schiller, 1988), global communication (McChesney, 1998), cybernetic or virtual capitalism (Dawson & Foster, 1998), virtual society (Woolgar, 2002), or the ruling relations (Smith, 1990b, 1999). The aim is not to arrive at an alternative meta-theory, but to develop a conceptualization that applies ostensively—that is, that says something like: "Here's a phenomenon; let's investigate it."

Writing

Commitment to a definition intended to open up a new region has meant drawing on the work of various theorists to extract from them some key themes that their thinking sediments.We start with the general distinction between societies primarily organized orally and those in which writing has developed. This is the primary distinction with which Jack Goody (1986) works. He is interested in the effects of writing on various institutions—religion, the state and bureaucracy, commerce, and law being his primary foci. Writing, in his view, supports the differentiation and specialization of institutional functions as it promotes "the autonomy of organizations that have developed their own modes of procedure, their own corpus of written tradition, their own specialities and possibly their own system of support" (p. 90).

Goody's main evidential bases are the ancient Near East and colonial and immediately pre-colonial West Africa. His view is complemented by Mark Eward Lewis's (1999) study of the transformation of China from the period of the Warring States (fifth to second century BCE) to empire. His study follows the progressive dominance of writing in the organization of the imperial state that enabled "the creation of specialized institutions such as administration and law, the preservation of the past and of tradition, poetry, and so on" (p. 287).

More generally, according to Goody, writing promotes the public explication of norms and rules as, "a process of universalization, of generalization" (p. 166). He aligns Talcott Parsons's contrast between patterns of particularism and universalism with the shift from orally based societies to societies based on writing. Although careful to disclaim a simple determinism, his formulation depends on a dichotomy between societies characterized by writing and those based on oral cultures, and thus relies on an implicit theory of historical progression in which writing plays a key role. In such a view, modernism may be characterized by functionally specialized institutions that are vested in records, universalized norms, and explicit rules, whereas premodernism lacks these features.

Textuality

Any formulation of documentary society must connect with concepts of text and textuality. The latter is the focus of Christopher Leigh Connery's (1998) study of writing and authority in early imperial China. He complicates the formulation of writing and its role in society as described by Goody (1986) and Lewis (1999). The production of texts in Literary Sinitic—a form of nonphonetic writing independent of regional differences in language—made possible the emergence of a textual regime that transgressed regional linguistic differences. Though recognizing its significance for the emergence of empire, Connery insists that the textual goes beyond its association with governance. Of course, official texts existed and these served political ends, but he argues "that textual production must also be read as autonomous—as serving to constitute and strengthen its own authority" (p. 7). Textual authority existed, writes Connery, "with a logic and ordering principles beyond that of political authority" and led to "textual excess" (p. 7). Classic texts survived beyond the imperial period in which they originated, and over time poetry, belles lettres, and other genres expanded textual authority even further. He observes:

> Textualization becomes the medium for increasingly diverse aspects of social and nonofficial life, and one consequence of this is the rise of textual genres and sub genres creating what I would call "the subjectivity effect" as conditioned by texts and the institutions that produced the texts. (p. 12)

A category or class of people with a specialized education and differentiated from the rest of the population then emerged to sustain this textual authority.

Connery fuses his conception of textual authority to Brian Stock's (1990) concept of the textual community. The notion of a textual community absorbs both terms of what Smith (2005) has called the text–reader conversation. Stock uses the term *textual community* to draw attention to the formation of groups oriented to a text or texts and sharing practices of reading and interpretation. This move to link textuality to social organization releases a dimension of reading to complicate the undifferentiated general category of writing. It reminds us that writing has no effect without reading and readers, and it uncouples textuality from the tendency to reduce its significance to the institutional order of governing. On the one hand, texts/documents can play significant roles in governance, particularly of administrative and managerial processes, and, on the other hand, certain forms of textuality defined by readers and readership cannot be folded into a defined organization. As we approach the developed concept of documentary society, these two forms of organization and their relations reappear as essential components in understanding the term.

THE MATERIALITY OF DOCUMENTS/TEXTS

Connery's (1998) link between the documentary, the textual, and the formation of society rests on the materiality of texts. As Chartier (1994) notes:

> We need to remember that there is no text apart from the physical support that offers it for reading (or hearing), hence there is no comprehension of any written piece that does not at least in part depend upon the forms in which it reaches its reader. (p. 9)

The materiality of documents has been of major significance in organizing continuities over time. This aspect of documentary society has received relatively little attention in contemporary research though its earlier significance has been fully recognized (Goody, 1986; Stock, 1983). Material documentation, for example, is clearly of major significance in the constitution of the legal right to intellectual property even when what is owned is legally described as an intangible.

New technologies of writing and reading create new possibilities for coordinating work and other activities. Extraordinary transformations followed on the invention of printing and the adoption of paper in the 14th and 15th centuries (Eisenstein, 1979; Martin, 1988). Technologies that produce what Bruno Latour (1990) calls immutable mobiles (p. 26) have been of special significance in enabling new forms of social relations because they make possible the reproduction of the same forms of words or images in multiple different sites and at different times. David Olson (1994) expands on Goody's (1986) association of the textual with objectivity in associating the objectification of meaning with the emergence of a world on paper—detaching words from the immediacy of interpersonal communication, creating forms of representation in which the meaning of words can appear as generalized ideas and concepts. In her concept of textually mediated social organization, Smith (1984, 1990b, 1999, 2002, 2005) has also drawn attention to the emergence of forms of organizing society that are distinctively translocal; that is, they coordinate work and other activities across local sites. These she calls the ruling relations, emphasizing that the term identifies the social relations that rule rather than forms of authority or domination. As the ruling relations have evolved (and technologies have enabled and promoted their evolution), they have progressively supplanted localized forms of organization and those based exclusively on direct relationships among individuals[1] (Chandler, 1962; Veblen, 1954).

The various theoretical versions of documentary society–virtual society, information age, ruling relations–all involve exploiting technologies that reproduce texts in material forms. Whether the topic is science and scientific discovery, the extension of law, the emergence of mass media, or the organizational transformations of corporations, all depend in their contemporary and still-emerging forms on technologies creating material forms in which the same message is or can be replicated many times over. They make possible what Jannis Kallinikos (1995) calls "action at a distance." As he explains:

> The mode of being and the organization of the contemporary social world are inextricably connected to the ability of its institutions to transcend the limited spatio-temporal coordinates of immediate contexts and to act on signs or cues that represent absent states of the world, i.e., states extending beyond the here and now. Instrumental action and accomplishment are very much concerned with the codification, ordering and mastery of absence, a task rendered manageable through the confluence of cognitive and material techniques which enact, in abbreviated forms, absent states of the world and provide the physical connexions [sic] that enable action at a distance. (pp. 117–118)

---

[1] Weber's (1947) focus on shifts from forms of "imperative coordination" based on individual relationships as in patrimonial forms of governance to rational-legal-based forms traces the same historical transformation.

Since the slow but ever advancing radicalization following on the discoveries of print and paper, other technologies reproducing words and images across multiple local sites and over time such as radio, film, television, and finally the computer have expanded the forms of standardized coordination of people's actions that print made possible.

The various nomenclatures cited previously—information age, global communication, virtual society, or capitalism—emphasize different aspects of document/text-mediated society. Smith's (1990b) concept (referred to earlier) of a text-mediated society and later of the ruling relations (1999) provides a more general formulation. In her view, the contemporary world is marked by social relations and organization in which replicable texts play an essential part. They are distinctive in that they coordinate work and other actions in local settings that then organize them translocally. For example, technologies of print and more recently of computers replicate texts in settings not otherwise connected to one another and play a key role in coordinating people's activities at a distance. Note that this does not imply that identical texts are read as the same or in the same way. Coordinating people's doings through the multiplication of identical texts takes for granted that a given text will be interpreted in different local contexts. Texts penetrate and organize the very texture of daily life as well as the always-developing foundations of the social relations and organization of science, industry, commerce, and the public sphere.

DIMENSIONS OF DOCUMENTARY SOCIETY

Though it is doubtful that any simple set of categories is adequate to identify different aspects of documentary society, the course we have taken through anthropological and historical thinking and research suggests a useful contrast between two types—the documentary forms of governance and those of textual communities. Goody's work emphasizes the significance of texts and documents for governance; Connery, however, extracts another dimension, sharing with Stock—the discovery of social relations mediated by texts that connect people as communities. This distinction is pursued in what follows: first in an examination of documentary governance as a major dimension of documentary society, and second in a similar treatment of textual communities, particularly those generated by contemporary mass media.

Documentary Governance

Max Weber was, perhaps, the first to attend to the significance of documents for governance. He emphasizes the keeping of written records of decision processes, of decisions, and of written rules. He views the "combination of written documents and a continuous organization of official functions" (Weber, 1947, p. 332) as constituting the "office." Weber's major focus is on government and on change from forms of government based on particular individuals and relationships to forms of rationally organized and legitimated governance. More generally, he took the view that the office, as the central organizational device that constituted organizations independent of particular individuals, was, critical to corporate action at the turn of the 19th and 20th centuries. A more contemporary study of documents/texts in government and corporate organizations would focus on texts as integral to the characteristic modes in which those institutional forms exist (Smith, 2001; Turner, 2002, 2003; Iedema, 2003) Further, as computerized modes of organizing increasingly predominate, the forms of authority and control described by Weber are being displaced. Shoshana Zuboff (1988) provides an elegant formulation of the distinctive character of the production controls that computers have achieved. She observes:

> The devices that automate by translating information into action also register data about those automated activities, thus generating new streams of information. ... The same systems that make it possible to automate office transactions also create a vast overview of an organization's operations. (p. 9)

Starting with this radical transformation that translates process into information accessible in textual form on a computer, we can track back to Alfred Chandler's (1977) account of textual controls in railroad company management. Laborious documentation as means of control were "the first modern, carefully defined, internal organizational structure used by an American business enterprise" (p. 97). For example, James Beniger's (1986) account of the bureaucratic technologies (his term) introduced by one railroad company emphasizes the informational feedback process. Those working at ground level, stationmasters and conductors, "passed up to the regional hierarchies a continual flow of data" (p. 224). Division heads had to keep journals and make formal monthly reports to the company's main office. Those directly responsible for operating trains were "programmed" (Beniger's term) by rules that were so detailed that these workers "became little more than programmable operators" (p. 224). The documentary possibilities of standardization made possible the expansion of corporate organization into multiple sites "an identity of service and practice across [its] distributed operations" (Hughes, Rouncefield, & Tolmie, 2002, p. 249).

Though the logic of control through document-mediated forms of organization and through computers is similar, computerized control processes can be more standardized, detailed, calculable, reliable, and fast. In informated (Zuboff, 1988, p. 9) systems, forms schedules and feedback are built right into the system. In fact, the transformation to informated systems as described by Zuboff dispenses with the labor and time involved in technologies of paperwork. Paperwork technologies created written documents that had to be translated into other written or typed forms. This mediating informational work, much of which was performed by women, disappears in Zuboff's informated systems. The labor of organization based in paperwork meant the interpositioning of people at every point.[2] In what has been called the "virtual organization" (Hughes et al., 2002, p. 248), the concrete realities of the documentary and documenting process are computerized and people and places, hence distances and time, appear to be suspended.

It would, however, be a mistake to travel with theorists such as Steve Woolgar (2002) who see in the technological possibilities created by computerized modes of coordination a transition to a totally virtual society. A very different picture is drawn by students of literacy in the workplace such as Belfiore, Deoe, Flinsbee, Hunter, and Jackson (2004). The pressures of a highly competitive market have promoted new approaches to management that combine "two highly developed concepts: Continuous Improvement and Quality Performance. Both rely heavily on intensive record keeping on paper, much of it maintained by front-line workers" (Jackson, 2004; p. 9). Whether by hand or by computer, "speaking with data" depends on the literacy practices of front-line workers (Jackson, 2004, p. 9), imposing a self-regulated scrutiny of the detail of their work. Analogous observations have been made in the context of the imposition of international standards of certifying food quality or organic food production (see for example), Wagner, (2005) has described the complex paperwork required of small organic farmers to achieve certification of their product as organic.

Whether largely computerized or a mix of paperwork and computers, the contemporary forms of documentary governance are simply much more deeply penetrated with writing than ever before. It is indeed hard to realize the extent to which our activities are coordinated textually.

Textual Communities, Mass Media and the Public Sphere

Since Stock's (1990) identification of textual communities occurring in the medieval period, technological changes have transformed the character of the textual or documentary. Walter

---

[2] We can think of Melville's "Bartleby the Scrivener" (a short story of Wall Street), Gogol's "The Overcoat," Dickens's *Christmas Carol*, and Stevie Smith's *A Novel on Yellow Paper*. See also David Lockwood's *The Black-Coated Worker*, a study of male clerical workers in the 1950s.

Benjamin's (1936/1968) study of art in the age of mechanical reproduction identifies the technological innovations first of lithography and then of photography in extracting a work of art from its local and historically saturated setting. Multiple copies float the image free of time, place, and particular social relations. In Stock's conception of textual communities, groups form around floating texts or documents, that is, texts that do not have a defined relationship with the government or church or that are not part of large-scale organization such as business corporations. Rather, floating texts are sources of authority independent of organized forms of power. People are connected through shared interpretations of the floating text; they are collected as individuals from a population, creating what we might describe as collectivities of adherents lacking distinctive institutional form. As the Bible became available in the vernacular and as literacy expanded, such textual communities formed around specific interpretations. Fans of *The Lord of the Rings* or the series of Harry Potter books are contemporary examples of textual communities based on print. Such collectivities of adherents based on a variety of technologies are a general feature of contemporary society.

Thus historical distance and the transformations wrought by technological change do not remove the relevance of Stock's (1990) conception. Indeed, his insight directs us to co sider the social dimensions of the technological innovations of the past 100 years.Telecommunications, radio, film, television, the recording of music, the computer, and the Internet have extended the reach of floating texts deep into the everyday lives of ordinary citizens. The replication of the visual in film, television, advertisements, and computer games creates radically new forms of text-mediated social relations; radio and recorded music have created audio-oral forms without previous parallels. In all the regions enabled by these new technologies, the linkage to documentary society emerges when we consider them as the bearers of texts on which textual communities are based.

Drawing in Michel Foucault's (1972a, 1972b) conception of discourse is useful here. He used the term *discourse* to reject the traditional notion that texts represent the intentional thought of their authors. The concept of discourse located systems of knowledge and knowledge making independent of particular individuals. Rather than tracing continuities and influences, he directed inquiry to discursive events—that is, spoken or written statements (1972a, p. 28)—and to the distinctive forms of power that discourse represents. He ascribed to discourse an order prior to any given moment of the making of a statement. The speaker's or writer's intention is never purely expressed. What can be said or written is subject to the regulation of the discourse within which it is framed.

Foucault's conception of discourse displaces the traditional basis of knowledge from individual perception and locates it externally to particular subjectivities as an order that imposes on them. The documentary dimensions of discourse do not interest him— documents, in his view, "say in silence, something other than what they actually say" (Foucault 1972a, p. 7). He does not theorize discourse as organizing social relations. Yet the presence of texts and social relations are implicit in his account of the order of discourse (1972b, 1981). He describes this order as regulating how people's subjectivities are coordinated—what can be uttered, what must be excluded, and what is simply not made present.

Contemporary mass media have expanded the region of the floating text. Mass communications are, of course, a major focus of both theory and research. Our focus on documentary society is more specialized because we are locating those dimensions of the textual that are implicated in social organization or relations. Jürgen Habermas's (1989) classic account of the historical emergence of the public sphere in Western societies focuses on transformations in social and political life based on the rapid expansion of print-media newspapers, journals, and books during the 17th and 18th centuries. Herbert Blumer's (1946, 1948) concept of "publics" provides us with a useful resource for explicating a contemporary public sphere now mediated electronically. He rejected the generalized notion of public opinion, proposing rather a concept of publics rather than the public. Publics are defined by their shared interest in a topic or issue. Publics, for Blumer (1946), are groups of individuals who "are confronted by an issue, who are divided in their ideas about how to meet the issues, and who are engaged in discussion over the issue" (p. 189). Add in the textual mediation of the process—which Blumer, as is general among sociologists, ignores—and his concept of publics is similar to Stock's (1990) conception of textual communities. Smith's (1990b) account of "femininity as discourse" extends Michel Foucault's (1972a, 1972b) conception of discourse to explore another contemporary form of "communities" oriented to floating texts. She argues that the discourses that formulate femininity "must not be isolated from the practices in which they are embedded and which they organize" (p. 165). Women's magazines and advertisements, for example, articulate the standardized images against which women compare themselves. As she explains:

> Discourse also involves the talk women do in relation to such texts, the work of producing oneself to realize the textual images, the skills involved in going shopping, in making and choosing clothes, in making decisions about colors, styles, makeup, and the ways in which these become a matter of interest among men. [The concept of discourse] locates the social relations of a "symbolic terrain." (p. 163)

Web sites also become bases for textual communities, as, for example, the formation of a textual community based in Web sites devoted to polyamory, referring to practices of sexual attachment among more than two partners (McLuskey, 2005). Chat among participants elaborates the shared experience, the sense the concept can make, and presumably feeds back into participants' sense of comfort in sexual relationships falling outside the traditional—there are others like themselves out there.

Though the notion of community is clearly attenuated when it is applied to such phenomena, nonetheless a clear historical continuity exists between Stock's (1990) textual communities that share interpretations of floating texts and the social organization and relations that arise in relation to the textuality of the mass media. We have only to think of the transition of sports from local communities into televised spectacles that create textual communities of sports fans. Fans are knowledgeable about the sports they follow; they can pick up conversations with strangers on the basis of current games; televised sports events provide for companionable drinking in bars. The expansion of what Connery (1998) calls textual authority beyond the intelligentsia constitutes a dramatic shift in how technological changes in the forms, extent, and powers of textual media have transformed society.

More general implications of contemporary mass media in the formation of textual communities are suggested by linking the topics raised here with issues raised by Paul Starr (2004) in his study of the "political origins of modern communications" in the United States. His study explores the implications for democracy of the interrelations of technology, changing regulatory forms, and commerce. He notes that "traditional conceptions of liberal democracy had assumed and exalted a press that was not only free from state control but also at the service of public discussion, readily accessible to contending parties and interests" (p. 388). Starr reveals the emergence of a new regime of communications, a regime mediated by documents and their electronic analogues. He asks how is it that the media has developed under the control of commercial interests that are deeply at odds with the ideals of democracy, and whether "the commercially driven media and new techniques of mass persuasion so distort public knowledge and degrade public discussion as to make popular self-government impossible?" (p. 388). Connecting such questions to the topic of documentary society suggests lines of inquiry that explore the social organization implicit in such notions as public knowledge and public discussion.

METHODS OF RESEARCH

The concluding sentence of the previous section makes an appropriate transition into issues of research methods into documentary society. These appear sparser than might be expected. Of course, major techniques such as content analysis or semiotics address the content of the textual. These, however, are research strategies that take the materiality of the floating text for granted and do not reach into the social relations in which it is implicated.

Focus on content is an effect of the treatment of the textual or documentary as cultural phenomena in which semiotics and some varieties of discourse analysis go to work. In the context of conceptualizing documentary society, however, the notion of culture cuts the textual off from the social processes, organization, and relations that the dimensions of governance and of textual community have claimed. In what follows, two different research approaches are considered: (a) ethnographic and (b) discourse analysis.

Ethnographic Methods

Recently there has been a slender but growing interest in texts and documents in social research.[3] For the most part, the use of documents in social research had oriented not to the documents as such or how they participate in the social, but on their uses as information sources about past events or the culture that generated them. Early ethnographic attention to texts and documents as integral to the social originates with the innovations in sociological ethnographies associated with Aaron Cicourel (1964) and the nascence of ethnomethodology. Cicourel's (1976) study of juvenile justice describes the transition from the talk and work of police and probation officers into documentary forms of representation. Don Zimmerman's (1969) study of the processing of welfare claimants, though less clearly focused on the documentary, also displays the significance of texts and the textualization of people's lives in the construction of the facts recognized by a welfare agency.

Tim May's (2001) discussion of conceptualizing documents in the context of social research makes an important move in stressing the importance of seeing texts and documents as "mediating between the local and the general in social relations" (p. 184). Although other ethnographic research in which documents or texts appear as integrated into the substance of ethnography are rare, some do exist. One important study is Sauer's (2003) investigation into the role of technical documentation in hazardous mining environments. Her work traces the transformation of localized, shifting information into various forms of technical documentation that come back to affect local situations. Another is De Montigny's (1995) study of social workers' professional practice of the documentary representation of clients, showing how the latter's voice is displaced in the institutional processes of child protection agencies. The role of medical documentation has also been a key focus of a growing body of work (Atkinson, 1995; Berg, 1997; McCarthy, 1991; Schryer, 1993).

Genre researchers in professional communication have also been investigating the roles that documentation processes play in fields such as engineering (Winsor, 2000), midwifery (Spoel & James, 2003), insurance (Schryer, 2000), and city planning (Wegner, 2004). This research owes much to Miller's (1984) fundamental insight that genres are forms of social action and not simply classification systems, and her work has encouraged these researchers to investigate the effects of document types on organizations. Originally more descriptive of discursive practices in workplace settings, this tradition has evolved into one offering powerful critiques of documentation processes (Giltrow, 2002; Paré, 2002; Schryer, 1993, 2000). For example, reflecting Bakhtin's (1986) insights, Schryer has identified the way certain genres such as medical records (1993) and letters produced within an insurance company (2000) produce world views or chronotopes that constrain the space/time of their readers and writers. Using Bazerman's (1994) work on genres as existing in interrelated systems, she and her research associates (Schryer, Lingard, & Spafford, 2005; Schryer, Lingard, Spafford, & Garwood, 2003) have also traced out the way record-keeping processes find their way into the oral practices of health care education—especially those practices related to case presentations.

Research approaches that recognize texts as an integral component of the social are put forward by Rod Watson (1997), who developed for ethnomethodology an approach that

---

[3] Tim May (2001), in his discussion of the use of documents in social research, comments on the absence of treatment of texts and documents in social research.

preserves a text's "active" character and situates it in local courses of action. He proposes analyses of a text in terms of its implications, looking for those aspects that orient themselves to future action. In analyzing the data that he and John Lee collected doing fieldwork in street settings, he observed people waiting for a bus. He noticed how, as a bus approached, its number led to some standing back and others moving forward in line. Different numbers sorted the group into those who wanted and those who did not want the bus route that the number identified. He introduces the notion of the "duplex-action" of the text of the bus number. He noted that "the first 'moment' of this is parties' monitoring of the sign(s), and the second 'moment' is the incorporation of the sign into 'further' action" (p. 93).

Watson's (1997) observations and proposed method of analysis are promising for exploring ethnographically (or ethnomethodologically) how texts are taken up locally. The method does not, however, respond to the extralocal dimension of textually mediated forms of coordination that are called for in ethnographic explorations of institutions. Institutional relations are present in the every day, but the translocal connections cannot be tracked using the traditional observational approaches of ethnography and ethnomethodology. Texts have a capacity for a dialogic or dual coordination, one as they enter into how the course of action in which they occur is coordinated and the other as coordinators of a local and particular course of action with social relations extending both temporally and spatially beyond the text. Just take the number 16 on the front of Lee and Watson's bus as an example. Reading a bus number as information presupposes organization beyond the text itself. Watson's analysis shows us the local practices of reading and action of those waiting for the bus; it does not, however, open up other kinds of connections such as the design of bus routes and how such routes are organized in relation to the layout of the city, passenger flows, and peak times; the work of bus drivers, mechanics, and others who get the bus to the bus stop on time; and beyond that, the organization of the bus company, including clerical workers and managers.

A research approach analogous to Watson's is recommended in an ethnographic approach called institutional ethnography (Smith, 2005). Incorporating texts and documents into ethnographic practice is an integral part of this method, which explores institutional levels beyond the observable. Texts and documents are seen as essential to the very existence of institutions and large-scale organizations (Smith, 2002). Smith's research approach is based on recognizing discourse as an actually happening, performed, local organizing of consciousness among people. Drawing on Liza McCoy's (1995) investigation of the "reading" of a photographic text and Susan Turner's (2002, 2003) study of a municipal council's "reading" of a proposed development map, Smith introduces the notion of a text–reader conversation as a way to insert texts or documents into actual sequences of action. She notes, "We are actively engaged with texts as we read them, or as we continue to carry on a silent conversation with what we have read" (Smith, 1990a, p. 18). Furthermore, she says:

> Textual materials on the shelves, in files (whether in computer directories or in file cabinets), or otherwise out of action, exist in potentia but their potentiating is in time and in action, whether in ongoing text-reader conversations or in how the "having read" enters into the organization of what is to come. (Smith, 2002, p. 18).

She proposes that the text–reader conversations can be investigated ethnographically by finding out how texts are taken up and drawn on in actual settings (Smith, 2005, 2006). Her interest, however, is not, as Watson's was, in finding the part played by the text in a sequence of action, but, beyond that, in how a given organizational/institutional text or document connects a local setting into a larger regulatory organization. As she observes:

> The capacity of the replicable text to standardize at least one term of the text–reader conversation and hence the organizational/institutional input into whatever course of action that conversation is embedded in, is a regulatory device essential to the existence of the large-scale corporation or to the multi-situated character ascribed to institutions. (Smith, 2002, p. 18)

Thus, Smith (2005) emphasizes how to incorporate texts fully into the sequential organization of local activities, articulating the local organization to what she calls the intertextual hierarchy of regulatory texts.

The most recent comprehensive treatment of texts and documents in social research is Lindsay Prior's (2003) thoughtful treatment based on the concept of "documents in action," a concept analogous to Smith's (1990b) notion of "texts in action." Prior proposes that documents should be explored for the part they play in people's activities. He argues that we must move away from the conception of documents as "stable, static, and pre-defined artefacts. Instead we must consider them in terms of fields, frames and networks of action" (p. 2). He takes J. L. Austin's concept of performative as a model. "People do things with documents" (p. 68), he tells us, and it is for the researcher to find out how they are used. In fact, the status of things as "'documents' depends precisely on the ways in which such objects are integrated into fields of action, and documents can only be defined in terms of such fields" (p. 2). Prior illustrates his points with ethnographic accounts of how documents are used in institutional settings. For example:

> [His own research] examined how the identities of "patients," "clients," and the criminally insane are structured through documentation, how forms of documentation can be used as warrants for action or as props in interaction, and how "organization" is made evident "performed"—through the written record. (p. 67)

In order to investigate documentary society, Prior suggests researchers should follow how a document is "enrolled" in routine activity, its function, how it differs in different contexts, and its role in constituting a phenomenon (p. 68). Although the document is linked to activity, his aim appears to be to produce an account that detaches the document and its uses, functions, or role (Prior uses all three terms) from how it enters into the social (Smith, 2005) or coordinates people's activities. Action is ascribed to documents, but how people are implicated in that action and, more particularly, what part the documentary plays in the social are not a research focus.

Discourse Analysis

Discourse analysis may be viewed as an extension of ethnographic research that shifts from observation of the social to the texts or documents themselves. Discourse analytical approaches are many (e.g., Halliday & Hasan, 1985; Hoey, 2001; Tannen, Schiffrin, & Hamilton, 2001; Titscher, Meyer, Wodak, & Vetter, 2000; Wetherell, Taylor, &Yates, 2001, among others). Many focus on the more general meaning of text that applies to any "communicative event" whether documentary, in the sense used here, or in ongoing social interaction isolated as discrete events by audio or video recording. Our discussion, however, focuses exclusively on that approach known as critical discourse analysis largely because it does focus, though not exclusively, on the documentary type of text and because it systematically addresses the relation between text and the social. Critical discourse theory or critical discourse analysis (CDA) distinguishes itself from other forms of discourse analysis in that its analysis is directed toward social concerns and social issues, particularly those involving inequality and relations of dominance (Van Dijk, 1993, p. 252).

Analysis of the texts of a discourse gives access to an important dimension of the sociopolitical that is analogous to ethnographic access to people's everyday worlds. As Hodge and Kress (1993) note, "the grammar of a language is its theory of reality" (p. 7). By a close analysis of syntax or register, CDA researchers can identify consistent patterns of usage that indicate specific ideological discourses. Thus, ideological commitments in policy (Fairclough, 2001), news, and other public communicative events (Fowler, Hodge, Kress, & Trew, 1979) can be explored as they are located in texts rather than located in people's heads as "ideas," "beliefs." Though the latter are directly or indirectly connected to—if not originating in—documents and texts, the conceptual practices of the social sciences have institutionalized a separation of mind and body for which we may hold Descartes responsible (Ryle, 1949). The documentary dimensions of the social become invisible (Smith, 2005). CDA, however, engages directly with the texts that mediate social order whether conceived as context or underlying structure. It focuses critically on the symbolic resources that control public communications (Van Dijk, 1996). For example, many studies that appear in *Discourse and Society*, a journal that represents this interest, provide careful analysis of how the texts of a discourse reproduce racial and gender inequities. In general, CDA makes visible the documentary dimensions of the social, particularly with respect to how documents and texts constitute and reconstitute social identities, coordinate social relations, and regulate organizations.

Norman Fairclough (1992, 1995, 2000, 2001, 2003) analyzes texts such as a conversation between doctor and patient, a television talk, or a statement by a political figure as specific communicative events. Whereas analysis of the surface of the text attends to its linguistic features, Fairclough's focus is on what is to be learned from the text about the discourse or interdiscursivity in which it participates and that it reproduces. Texts as communicative events can be analyzed linguistically, at one level, as actual spoken or written sequences. Thus, linguistic strategies, such as those describing degrees of abstraction and concreteness, the practices of inclusion and exclusion, and what is assigned to foreground or background (Van Leeuwen, 1993, 1995), have been used to focus on the surface of the document. At another level, the discourse or interdiscursivity that produces and interprets the text can also be explicated and examined in context as a social practice, linking the text particularly to power dimensions. Thus analyses of texts reveal forms of ideological hegemony, and these forms are reproduced in the language of the public sphere. Fairclough's (2001, 2005) most recent work explicitly develops a complementarity between the analysis of discourse and sociological theorizing, proposing in particular a dialectical relation between critical discourse analysis and contemporary work on governance (see Fairclough's 2000 study of the new language of the Labour government under Tony Blair).

CDA is a rich and developing field of investigation. For example, some recent CDA-influenced studies (Sarangi, 1998; Schryer 2000) have combined ethnographic accounts of reading and writing practices together with CDA analysis of documentary texts such as case reports and insurance decisions. The kinds of developments pioneered by Fairclough that aim to bring CDA into a strongly dialectical relationship with the theorizing and study of contemporary governance is clearly congenial to explorations into the field that we have been defining in this chapter. True, our strategy of defining the scope of what might be meant by documentary society has leaned toward defining it through assembling the ways in which it has been recognized empirically. As we have developed the concept, the orientation has been empirical rather than theoretical and concepts have been introduced and elaborated to account for the problem of making observable changing social realities. This tendency has given our research orientation a strongly ethnographic emphasis, one that is extended in the work of critical discourse analysis that incorporates the documentary and textual, the defining phenomena of documentary society.

SUMMARY

Our chapter has sought to define the concept of *documentary society* by ranging over more than one region of exploration and engaging with scholarly historical, anthropological, and sociological resources, to identify the distinctive properties of organization that rely on documents or texts (in the sense of written or printed rather than communicative events in general). We have emphasized the materiality of the documentary or textual and its significant replicability as an essential dimension in the development of forms of documentary society over the past 200 years. Our range has extended the documentary to include the new documenting technologies of radio and television and the recent and rapid development of computer technologies. Some might find the inclusion of the latter incongruous. The concept of document has connotations of fixity, weight, and solidity that computers and communicative events mediated by computers do not have. But our conception of documentary society has been developed in the context of a handbook on writing, and in such a context, electronic media that facilitate both reading and writing (often simultaneously) cannot be ignored for their social implications.

In examining the various scholarly sources that differentiated societies and social forms in relation to the presence/absence or different forms of literacy, we identified two major themes. The first emphasizes the significance of documents/texts for bureaucracy, administration, and management; and the second emphasizes their significance for the cultural dimension of documentary society. We have used this conceptual differentiation to track two dimensions of documentary society: documentary governance and textual communities (Stock, 1990). Each develops and transforms with changing documentary technologies and yet has internal continuity. Of course, we do not imagine we have provided a comprehensive theoretical framework for the conceptual appropriation of contemporary documentarity and textually mediated forms of social organization. Our method explored the work of other scholars as well as drawing on our own, and it is exploration that we hope to encourage. This exploration might track one or other of the dimensions we have identified. It might build on Smith's conception of the significance of texts for the organization of institutions, health care, science, education, government, and business corporations. It might complicate the simplification of our two-dimensional analysis by proposing that we view such major functional complexes within what she calls the ruling relations as intersections of the two foundational forms—governance and textual community. This exploration might also attempt to combine CDA analysis together with ethnographic accounts of institutional reading and writing practices. Our aim in general has been to bring into focus what we view as a major and generally neglected dimension of contemporary society.

In writing this chapter, we are aware that we are actively participating in the documentary society we have attempted to make observable. Its dimensions, its distinctive orderings, its forms of power are ones that are only beginning to be explored. Though giving the concept of documentary society definition, we are also reserved about our or anyone's ability, at this time, to provide a comprehensive treatment. As can be seen, our sources derive from many fields of study that have only this in common—that they have paid attention to what is ignored by most people in the social sciences: the forms of documentary mediation that coordinate people's activities and that dominate contemporary society. The objective has been to give documentary society a distinct scholarly presence. Its potential as a research resource to be mined and uncovered is rich. We have indicated relevant methods of investigation, but we anticipate exciting methodological as well as substantive discoveries as exploration goes forward.

REFERENCES

Atkinson, P. A. (1995). *Medical talk and medical work*. London: Sage.

Bakhtin, M. (1986). The problem of speech genres (V.W. McGee, Trans.). In C. Emerson & M. Holquist (Eds.), *Speech genres and other late essays* (pp. 60–102). Austin: Texas University Press.

Bazerman, C. (1994). Systems of genres and the enactment of social intentions. In A. Freedman & P. Medway (Eds.), *Genre and the new rhetoric* (pp. 79–101). London: Taylor & Francis.

Belfiore, M. E., Deoe, T. A., Flinsbee, S., Hunter, J., & Jackson, N. S. (2004). *Reading work: Literacies in the new workplace*. Mahwah, NJ: Lawrence Erlbaum Associates.

Beniger, J. R. (1986). *The control revolution: Technological and economic origins of the information society*. Cambridge, MA: Harvard University Press.

Benjamin, W. (1968). The work of art in the age of mechanical reproduction. In H. Arendt (Ed.), *Illuminations* (pp. 217–251). New York: Schocken. (Original work published 1936)

Berg, M. (1997). *Rationalizing medical work: Decision-support techniques and medical Practices*. Cambridge, MA: MIT Press.

Blumer, H. (1946). *Collective behavior*. New York: Barnes & Noble.

Blumer, H. (1948). Public opinion and public opinion polling: Rejoinder to Woodward and Newcombe. *American Sociological Review, 13*(5), 554.

Chandler, A .D. (1962). *Strategy and structure: Chapters in the history of the industrial enterprise*. Cambridge, MA: MIT Press.

Chandler, A. D. (1977). *The visible hand: The managerial revolution in American business*. Cambridge, MA: Harvard University Press.

Chartier, R. (1994). *The order of books: Readers, authors, and libraries in Europe between fourteenth and eighteenth centuries*. Stanford, CA: Stanford University Press.

Cicourel, A. V. (1964). *Method and measurement in sociology*. New York: The Free Press.

Cicourel, A.V. (1976). *The social organization of juvenile justice*. London: Heineman.

Connery, L. C. (1998). *The empire of the text: Writing and authority in early imperial China*. Boulder, CO: Rowman & Littlefield.

Dawson, M., & Foster, J. B. (1998). Virtual capitalism. In R. W. McChesney & E. M. Wood (Eds.), *Capitalism and the information age: The political economy of the global communication revolution* (pp. 51–67). New York: Monthly Review Press.

de Montigny, G. A. J. (1995). *Social working: An ethnography of front-line practice*. Toronto, Ontario, Canada: University of Toronto Press.

Eisenstein, E. (1979). *The printing press as an agent of change: Communication and cultural transformation in early modern Europe*. Cambridge, England: Cambridge University Press.

Fairclough, N.. (1992). *Discourse and social change*. Cambridge, England: Polity.

Fairclough, N. (1995). *Critical discourse analysis*. London: Longman.

Fairclough, N. (2000.) *New Labour, new language?* London: Routledge.

Fairclough, N. (2001). *Language and power* (2nd ed.). London: Longman.

Fairclough, N. (2003). *Analyzing discourse: Text analysis for social research*. London: Routledge.

Foucault, M. (1972a). *The archaelogy of knowledge* (A. M. Sheridan-Smith, Trans.). New York: Pantheon.

Foucault, M. (1972b). The discourse on language. In M. Foucault (Eds.), *The archaelogy of knowledge* (A. M. Sheridan-Smith, Trans.; pp. 000–000). New York: Pantheon, 215–237.

Foucault, M. (1981). The order of discourse. In R. Young (Ed.), *Untying the text: A poststructuralist reader* (pp. 51–78). London: Routledge.

Fowler, R., Hodge, B., Kress, G., & Trew, T. (1979). *Language and control*. London: Routledge & Kegan Paul.

Giltrow, J. (2002). Meta-genre. In R. Coe, L. Lingard, & T. Teslenko (Eds.), *The rhetoric and ideology of genre: Strategies for stability and change* (pp. 187–205). Cresskill, NJ: Hampton.

Goody, J. (1986). *The logic of writing and the organization of society*. Cambridge, England: Cambridge University Press.

Habermas, J. (1989). *The structural transformation of the public sphere: An inquiry into a category of bourgeois society* (T. Burger & F. Lawrence, Trans.). Cambridge: MA: MIT Press.

Halliday, M. A., & Hasan, R. (1985). *Language, context and text: Aspects of language in a social-semiotic perspective*. Oxford, England: Oxford University Press.

Hodge, R., & Kress, G. (1993). *Language as ideology*. London: Routledge.

Hoey, M. (2001). *Textual interaction: An introduction to written discourse analysis*. London: Routledge.

Hughes, J. A., Rouncefield, M., & Tolmie, P. (2002). The day-to-day work of standardization: A sceptical note on the reliance on IT in a retail bank. In S. Woolgar (Ed.), *Virtual society: Technology, cyberbole, reality* (pp. 247–263). New York: Oxford University Press.

Iedema, R. (2003). *Discourses of post-bureaucratic organization*. Amsterdam: John Benjamins.

Jackson, N. S. (2004). Introduction: Reading work. In M. E. Belfiore, T. A. Deoe, S. Flinsbee, J. Hunter, & N. S. Jackson (Eds.), *Reading work: Literacies in the new workplace* (pp. 1–15). Mahwah, NJ: Lawrence Erlbaum Associates.

Kallinikos, J. (1995). The architecture of the invisible: Technology as representation. *Organization: The Interdisciplinary Journal of Organization, Theory and Society, 2*(1), 117–140.

Latour, B. (1990). Drawing things together. In M. Lynch & S. Woolgar (Eds.), *Representation in scientific practice* (pp. 19–68). Cambridge, MA: MIT Press.

Lewis, M. E. (1999). *Writing and authority in early China*. Albany: State University of New York Press.

Martin, H.-J. (1988). *The history and power of writing*. Chicago: University of Chicago Press.

May, T. (2001). *Social research: Issues, methods and process*. Buckingham, England: Open University Press.

McCarthy, L. P. (1991). A psychiatrist using *DSM–III*: The influence of a charter document in psychiatry. In C. Bazerman & J. Paradis (Eds.), *Textual dynamics of the professions: Historical and contemporary studies of writing in professional communities* (pp. 358–378). Madison: University Press of Wisconsin.

McChesney, R. W. (1998). The political economy of global communication. In R. W. McChesney, E. M. Wood, & J. B. Foster (Eds.), *Capitalism and the information age: The political economy of the global communication revolution* (pp. 1–26). New York: Monthly Review Press.

McCoy, L. (1995). Activating the photographic text. In M. Campbell & A. Manicom (Eds.), *Knowledge, experience, and ruling relations: Essays in the social organization of knowledge* (pp. 181–192). Toronto, Ontario, Canada: University of Toronto Press.

McLuskey, K. (2005). *Expressing polyamory: The language of loving more.* Unpublished manuscript, University of Victoria, British Columbia, Canada.

Miller, C. R. (1984). Genre as social action. *Quarterly Journal of Speech, 70,* 151–167.

Mosco, V. (1988). Introduction: Information in the pay-per society. In V. Mosco & J. Wasko (Eds.), *The political economy of education* (pp. 3–26). Madison: University of Wisconsin Press.

Nunberg, G. (1996). Farewell to the information age. In G. Numberg & U. Eco (Eds.), *The future of the book* (pp. 103–133). Berkeley: University of California Press.

Olson, D. R. (1994). *The world on paper: The conceptual and cognitive implications of writing and reading.* Cambridge, England: Cambridge University Press.

Paré, A. (2002). Genre and identity. In R. Coe, L. Lingard, & T. Teslenko (Eds.), *The rhetoric and ideology of genre: Strategies for stability and change* (pp. 57–71). Cresskill, NJ: Hampton Press.

Prior, L. (2003). *Using documents in social research.* London: Sage.

Ryle. G. (1949). *The concept of mind.* Chicago: University of Chicago Press.

Sarangi, S. (1998). Interprofessional case construction in social work: The evidential status of information and its reportability. *Text, 18*(2), 241–270.

Sauer, B. (2003). *The rhetoric of risk: Technical documentation in hazardous environments.* Mahwah, NJ: Lawrence Erlbaum Associates.

Schiller, D. (1988). How to think about information. In V. Mosco & Wasko (Eds.), The political economy of information. (pp. 27–43). Madison, WI: University of Wisconsin Press.

Schryer, C. F. (1993). Records as genre. *Written Communication, 10,* 200–234.

Schryer, C. F. (2000). Walking a fine line: Writing "negative news" letters in an insurance company. *Journal of Business and Technical Communication, 14*(4), 445–497.

Schryer, C. F., Lingard, L., & Spafford, M. (2005). Techne or artful science and the genre of case presentations in healthcare settings. *Communication Monographs, 72*(2), 234–260.

Schryer, C. F., Lingard, L., Spafford, M., & Garwood, K. (2003). Structure and agency in medical case presentations. In C. Bazerman & D. R. Russell (Eds.), *Writing selves/writing society* (pp. 62–96). Fort Collins, CO: The WAC Clearinghouse and Mind, Culture and Activity (http://wac.colostate.edu/books/selves_society/).

Smith, D. E. (1984). Textually-mediated social organization. *International Social Science Journal, 36*(1), 59–74.

Smith, D. E. (1990a). *The conceptual practices of power: A feminist sociology of knowledge.* Boston: Northeastern University Press.

Smith, D. E. (1990b).*Texts, facts and femininity: Exploring the relations of ruling.* London: Routledge.

Smith, D. E. (1999). The ruling relations. In *Writing the social: Critique, theory and investigations* (pp. 171–190). Toronto, Ontario, Canada: University of Toronto Press.

Smith, D. E. (2002). Texts and the ontology of organizations and institutions [Special issue]. *Studies in Cultures, Organizations and Societies, 7*(2), 159–198.

Smith, D. E. (2005). *Institutional ethnography: A sociology for people.* Lanham, MD: AltaMira.

Smith, D. E. (2006). Incorporating texts into ethnographic practice. In D. E. Smith (Ed.), *Institutional ethnography as practice* (pp. 000–000). Lanham, MD: AltaMira.

Spoel, P., & James, S. (2003). The textual standardization of midwives' professional relationships. *Technostyle, 18*(ii), 3–29.

Starr, P. (2004). *The creation of the media: Political origins of modern communications.* New York: Basic Books.

Stock, B. (1983). *The implications of literacy: Written language and models of interpretation in the eleventh and twelfth centuries.* Princeton, NJ: Princeton University Press.

Stock, B. (1990). *Listening for the text: On the uses of the past.* Philadelphia: University of Pennsylvania Press.

Tannen, D., Schiffrin, D., & Hamilton, H. E. (Eds.). (2001). *Handbook of discourse analysis.* Oxford, England: Blackwell.

Titscher, S., Meyer, M., Wodak, R., & Vetter, E. (2000). *Methods of text and discourse analysis* (B. Jenner, Trans.). London: Sage.

Turner, S. M. (1995). Rendering the site developable: Texts and local government decision making in land use planning. In M. Campbell & A. Manicom (Eds.), *Knowledge, experience and ruling relations: Essays in the social organization of knowledge* (pp. 234–248). Toronto, Ontario, Canada: University of Toronto Press.

Turner, S. M. (2002). Texts and the institutions of municipal planning government: The power of texts in the public process of land development. *Studies in Cultures, Organizations, and Societies, 7*(2), 297–325.

Turner, S. M. (2003). *Municipal planning, land development and environmental intervention: An institutional ethnography.* Unpublished doctoral dissertation, University of Toronto, Ontario, Canada.

Turner, S. M. (2006). Mapping institutions as work and texts. In D. E. Smith (Ed.) *Institutional ethnography as practice*, Lanham, MD: Rowman & Littefield, 139–161.

van Dijk, T. A. (1993). Principles of critical discourse analysis. *Discourse and Society, 4*(2), 249–283.

van Dijk, T. A. (Ed.). (1996). *Introduction to discourse analysis.* London: Sage.

van Leeuwen, T. (1993). Genre and field in critical discourse analysis. *Discourse & Society, 4*, 193–223.

van Leeuwen, T. (1995). Representing social action. *Discourse & Society, 6*(1), 81–106.

Veblen, T. (1954). *Absentee ownership and business enterprise in recent times.* New York: Viking.

Wagner, K. (2005). *Organic farming: An institutional ethnography.* Unpublished manuscript, University of Victoria, British Columbia, Canada.

Watson, R. (1997). Ethnomethodology and textual analysis. In D. Silverman (Ed.), *Qualitative research: Theory, method and practice* (pp. 80–98). London: Sage.

Weber. (1947). *The theory of social and economic organization* (A. M. Henderson & T. Parsons, Trans.) New York: The Free Press.

Wegner, D. (2004). The collaborative construction of a management report in a municipal community of practice: Text and context, genre and learning. *Journal of Business and Technical Communication, 18*(4), 411–451.

Wetherell, M., Taylor, S., & Yates, S. (Eds.). (2001). *Discourse as data: A guide for analysis.* London: Sage.

Winsor, D. (2000). Ordering work: Blue-collar literacy and the political nature of genre. *Written Communication, 17*, 155–184.

Woolgar, S. (Ed.). (2002). *Virtual society: Technology, cyberbole, reality.* New York: Oxford University Press.

Zimmerman, D. (1969). Record-keeping and the intake process in a public welfare agency. In S. Wheeler (Ed.), *On records: files and dossiers in American life* (pp. 319–354). New York: Russell Sage Foundation.

Zuboff, S. (1988). *In the age of the smart machine: The future of work and power.* New York: Basic Books.

CHAPTER 8

Writing, Text, and the Law

Peter Tiersma
Loyola Law School, Los Angeles

WRITING LAW IN THE ANCIENT WORLD

Mesopotamia

It is generally agreed that cuneiform, the earliest known writing system, emerged in present-day Iraq around 5,000 years ago (see chap. 1, this volume). Cuneiform texts include a substantial number of legal documents. Indeed, the oldest legal texts known to exist were made in Mesopotamia in the early third millennium BCE and involved the sale of land (Ellickson & Thorland, 1995).

Private legal documents such as these were generally inscribed on clay tablets, which were often placed in a clay envelope. On the envelope was a copy of the text contained on the tablet inside. The purpose was to deter one of the parties from changing the text because the text in the envelope remained inaccessible. The documents normally had to name the witnesses who were present, and the parties had to indicate their consent to the agreement by making an impression in the clay using a cylinder seal, signet ring, or some other object (VerSteeg, 2000).

Not too much later, the first law collections, or codes, began to appear. The oldest is ascribed to King Ur-Nammu and dates from around 2100 BCE. A few hundred years afterward came the renowned Code of Hammurabi, which—consistent with its public nature—was inscribed on large stone stelae. These laws covered areas such as trial procedure, property, the military, agriculture, principal and agent, debt, family law, personal injury, wages, and slaves (VerSteeg, 2000).

Although the exact nature of the legal codes from the Mesopotamian period remains disputed, it is generally agreed that they were not legislation in the modern sense. Mesopotamian law remained essentially unwritten despite being inscribed in stone or on clay. In the many extant documents and reports of disputes from the period, there is apparently not a single case in which the wording of a law is quoted. The Mesopotamian codes seem, for the most part, to have been descriptions of rules and practices that already existed, along with some embellishments and improvements, rather than attempts to legislate by means of written text (VerSteeg, 2000; Westbrook, 1994).

Egypt and Israel

The Egyptian hieroglyphic writing system arose at about the same time that the Mesopotamians began to make cuneiform inscriptions. By the end of the Old Kingdom, around 2150 BCE, legal decrees and important private contracts appeared in writing and sometimes also on stone stelae. Court procedures seem to have made extensive use of writing. Material from the Old Kingdom includes records of proceedings, as well as evidence of the use of documents and the citation of precedent and statutes in courts. The Egyptians also had written wills. Unlike the Babylonians, however, the ancient Egyptians do not seem to have created codes of law similar to that of Hammurabi, although there is at least one demotic code (Baines, 1983).

Writing in the ancient Hebrew world was, of course, heavily religious, as evidenced by the Bible. The most lawlike parts of the Bible include the *Covenant Code* in Exodus, chapters 21 to 23, and Deuteronomy, chapters 21 to 25. The Covenant Code shows a number of similarities to the Babylonian codes that were briefly discussed earlier (Westbrook, 1994). It has been suggested that one function of written law among the Hebrews was to limit the power of the monarchy (Jackson, 2000), similar to concerns in ancient Greece. The Bible also contains indications of writing being used to evidence private legal transactions (Jeremiah 32:9–14).

Greece

Alphabetic writing arose in Greece around the eighth century BCE and by 700 BCE had made its way to the island of Crete. It was soon put to use in the city of Dreros for the inscription of laws. A more extensive code has survived from the city of Gortyn, also on Crete. It consists of 600 lines divided into 12 columns. The magistrate at Gortyn was required to follow this written law if it contained an applicable rule. Nonetheless, the code addressed only a small part of their legal system, which suggests that the rest of the law remained oral or customary. Witnesses and remembrancers continued to play a critical role in civil life, acting as living records of important events. Legal transactions were performed orally before witnesses, and if a dispute arose the witness had to come to court to testify; written evidence was not admissible (Robb, 1994).

Written law was taken a step further in Athens. According to tradition, Draco wrote the first Athenian laws in 621 BCE. His law on homicide, which contained famously "draconian" penalties, has been preserved from a later reinscription. With the exception of the law on homicide, Draco's laws were superseded by those of Solon, but none has survived in Solon's own wording. As with the earlier Cretan codes, these were not legislation, but a record of law that existed independently (Robb, 1994).

By the beginning of the fourth century BCE, however, the primacy of written law was well established. Magistrates were forbidden to enforce any other type of law. Moreover, the decrees of the counsel or assembly could not prevail over a law inscribed in stone, which signals an early appreciation of the concept of the rule of law. This appreciation is also reflected in the efforts, beginning in 410 BCE, to inscribe all existing Athenian law in stone (Robb, 1994).

There is evidence not only that the Athenians required that law be written down, but that they enacted written text. Demosthenes records that, in the early fourth century, the Athenians had developed a procedure for examining and ratifying existing laws. Citizens apparently had the right to propose laws to the Assembly, writing them on a white board that was publicly displayed in the Agora until the Assembly could meet and take a vote (Arnaoutoglou, 1998; see also Robb, 1994).

Early in fourth-century Athens, the text of inscribed laws was being used to decide cases. Sections of the law would sometimes be read aloud at trials. Someone would go to the public inscription of the law, make a copy of the relevant provision, and bring it to the clerk of the court. These developments suggest that the Greeks did not just require that laws be written, which might have exclusively an *evidentiary* function, but were beginning to view the law as *consisting* of written text. The law was no longer something that resided in the memory of the individual or community; it was something that has been authoritatively written down. At that point, the law was literally "set in stone" (Robb, 1994, p. 140).

As in Egypt and Babylonia, the Athenians used writing for private legal transactions. During the fourth century, written contracts and wills were introduced into evidence in Athenian courts, although they were valid only if they were drawn up before witnesses and secured in a sealed vase (Robb, 1994). Mortgages were sometimes inscribed in stone and placed on the land to which they pertained (Thomas, 2001).

Rome

Writing was an important aspect of Roman law, especially in later periods. The earliest written Roman law of any importance is the Twelve Tables. They were a collection of rules compiled by a group of men known as the *Decemviri* and were enacted by an assembly, the *Comitia Centuriata,* around 450 BCE. Although the complete text did not survive, we know from extant fragments that the tables mostly reflected ancient Roman custom, but there may also have been some innovation. The Twelve Tables were a type of fundamental law that stated general principles, rather than being a comprehensive code of conduct. During the later Republic, the making of laws (*leges*) was generally the province of popular assemblies. Another important source of law were the edicts issued by magistrates. Custom, or *ius*, also played a significant role (Buckland, 1966).

In the imperial period, the Senate, which could originally only invalidate legislation, acquired the function of making laws, called *senatusconsulta*. Most power resided in the emperor, however, who would propose legislation in a speech known as an *oratio*. The Senate could only accept or reject it. Initially, the emperor seems to have delivered the oratio orally, but it was soon replaced by a written oratio. Eventually, the emperor's oratio came to be viewed as constituting the law itself, rather than being merely a request or proposal (Buckland, 1966).

By the end of the third century, the emperor was the sole legislator and governed by means of constitutions, edicts, decrees, letters, and other documents. Clearly, writing had come to take on tremendous importance in running an empire that covered a large part of the known world. Although writing was extremely useful, however, it was not essential. Because the emperor had so much power, he could use any form he wished to make law, and any utterance he made was considered binding (Buckland, 1966).

Writing law became almost an obsession for a later emperor, Justinian, who ruled over the eastern empire. The large volume of Roman law had become increasingly unwieldy. In 529, he published a code meant to consolidate existing codes, omit what was out of date, and correct and restate the law. He also published a digest, which was a collection of extracts from juristic writings. (The Jurists, such as Gaius and Ulpian, were highly regarded lawyers who expounded on the law.) An interesting feature of Justinian's digest is that the extracts, or the paragraphs within them, were numbered for ease of reference, and they indicated the original source of the extract, thus showing a relatively advanced literary mentality. Finally, Justinian's *Institutes* was a book of law for students. After his original code became outdated, Justinian published a second code in 534. Despite his prodigious efforts, Justinian's laws were not always applied, and appear to have had limited relevance in more remote areas (Buckland, 1966; Johnston, 1999). Justinian's laws did have a great impact on legal education, however (see chap. 10, this volume).

Roman private law likewise came to be heavily influenced by literary practices. Many legal transactions were originally effectuated by means of ritualistic ceremonies. *Mancipatio,* for instance, was an ancient and formal way of transferring ownership of property. The claimant would say specified ritual words before witnesses, at the same time striking a piece of copper on a scale. This ceremony was later replaced, or at least supplemented, by the production of a written document (Buckland, 1966).

A related transaction is the transfer of ownership to property at death. Before the empire, Romans could make a will orally before the assembly. Later the *testamentum per aes et libram* developed. It involved a written will that was prepared beforehand. The testator then engaged in a ceremony similar to the mancipatio. At some point the necessity of the ceremony seems to have disappeared, and the writing sufficed.

New forms of the will were developed in the fifth century. One type involved a will that was entered on the rolls of the court and did not need witnesses at all. The other was the tripartite will, made before seven witnesses, and subscribed by the testator (who put his seal on the will, along with his name and the word *subscripsi*). At around the same time, Roman law accepted holographic wills, which were written in the handwriting of the testator and required no additional formalities (Buckland, 1966). All of these developments show an increasing acceptance of writing, where the written word supported by literary conventions replaced formulaic spoken language supported by ritualistic actions (see also Tiersma, 1988).

A detailed examination of the role of writing in Roman law, particularly writing on waxed wooden tablets, is presented in Meyer (2004). The text, of course, was on the waxed side, and it was customary to attach two or three tablets together with hinges. A string could be bound around it as a type of seal, and it became customary to write a duplicate of the text on the outside of the tablet to guard against alterations, similar to clay envelopes in Mesopotamia.

Writing also played an important role in litigation. In early times, the parties brought a dispute before the magistrate by means of the *legis actio*. If it was a case of contested ownership, the plaintiff placed his hand on the object and uttered prescribed ritual words, then touched the disputed item with a wand. The magistrate and defendant had to utter ritualistic language of their own. The matter was then referred to a judge, who reviewed the evidence and decided the outcome. During the classical period, the *formulary* system developed. Instead of reciting fixed words, the parties agreed to a written formula, which had to be approved by the magistrate, and which stated the nature of the controversy and how it was to be decided. This written formula was then sent to the judge for a decision (Buckland, 1966; for an actual formula, see Johnston, 1999).

China

Written law seems to have appeared in China at roughly the same time as in Europe. The first clear indication of such laws are "books of punishment" that a prime minister of a Chinese state ordered to be inscribed on a set of bronze tripod vessels in 536 BCE. Although the vessels themselves have been lost, they are known from a surviving letter by another high official who protested the inscription. His prescient concern was that if laws were written, people would stop following accepted norms of behavior and would instead "make their appeal to the written word, arguing to the last over the tip of an awl or knife" (Bodde & Morris, 1973, pp. 16–17).

By the time of the Tang Dynasty (619–906 CE), the Chinese had an extensive body of written law, including the Tang Code, statutes, regulations, and ordinances. The Tang Code was very influential and many of its provisions were incorporated into the legal codes of subsequent dynasties (Johnson, 1979). The Chinese codes were primarily concerned with criminal matters. Nonetheless, they did have written private legal texts (Scogin, 1990). Written agreements or contracts can be traced back around two millennia to the Han dynasty. Many of them involve the sale of land. Surviving examples were mostly written on durable media like stone, brick, metal, and jade. They typically named the parties and the place where the transaction occurred, the identity of the witnesses, and a recitation of the performance of formalities (such as partial payment of the price or the drinking of wine). Although it is sometimes thought that private transactions in ancient China were governed mainly by custom, Scogin argues that these contracts had formal legal status, in the sense that they could be enforced in court.

Of all these ancient legal systems, that of the Romans had the greatest influence on later developments in continental Europe, which we consider at the end of this chapter. It had less of an impact on the common law of England.

WRITING AND THE COMMON LAW

The common-law system arose in England and was later extended via the British Empire to many other parts of the world, including the United States. Its distinctive feature is that the opinions of judges are an authoritative source of law, known as *precedent*.

Although the writing of laws and legal transactions developed in the ancient world more than 4,000 years ago, and was briefly introduced to the British Isles during the Roman occupation, the practice of writing largely disappeared when the Romans left. The Anglo-Saxons, who arrived soon thereafter, were mostly illiterate. Writing returned to England with the advent of Christian missionaries around 600 CE, and before long legal texts began to appear in both Latin and Anglo-Saxon (Tiersma, 1999).

After the Norman invasion in 1066, Latin became the sole language of written legal documents. Starting around 1275, however, French gained ground as a legal language, although writs and official court records continued to be in Latin. Statutes were in French until around 1480, and the legal profession continued to use French as a written language into the 17th century. The extent to which the profession ever spoke French is debatable. Throughout much of its history, therefore, the English legal profession was trilingual, using English as a spoken language and French or Latin for writing (Tiersma, 1999).

In the rest of this section, we consider the role of writing with respect to a number of different types of texts. We begin with private legal texts, including wills, deeds, and contracts, and then move on to consider public documents like statutes and judicial opinions.

Wills

When the Anglo-Saxons arrived in England, wills would necessarily have been made orally in the presence of witnesses. After the arrival of Christianity, people began to give property by will to religious orders or churches. Members of those orders, who were usually literate, had an interest in preserving evidence of the gift, and began to write down the terms of the will. Several of these texts have survived (Whitelock, 1930).

Written wills of this period were not what lawyers today would call *dispositive* or what linguists might call *performative* documents. Rather, they were entirely evidentiary: records of oral transactions. Observe that the Old English word for a will, *cwide,* derives from the verb *cweðan,* whose primary meaning is "to speak." The testator did not sign or seal the document. The witnesses also did not sign. Their job was to keep the contents of the will in their memory. The written documents, even though they are called "wills," were merely evidentiary of those oral events, and were at first not considered particularly strong evidence (Danet & Bogoch, 1994; Hazeltine, 1930).

By the 13th century, as the English became more comfortable with literacy, the written text gradually took on greater significance. Written wills, which were previously viewed with a measure of mistrust, were now preferred. Witnesses no longer testified to the contents of the will, but simply guaranteed their authenticity (Clanchy, 1993). The essential act was no longer the oral expression of a person's will, but the execution of the document. Testators began to affix a seal to signal the document's authenticity (Sheehan, 1963). These developments culminated in the Statute of Wills of 1540, which required written evidence of wills transferring land. Whereas the Statute of Wills required simply that there be written evidence of the testator's intentions, something that could be done by making a memorandum after the fact, the Statute of Frauds (1677) went a step further by making the execution of a written document the essential act. A will was no longer something in the testator's mind, but words on paper or parchment. This remains the situation today.

Conveyances

Conveyances, which involve the immediate transfer of interests in property (as opposed to delayed transfer at death) share many similarities with wills. Transfers of land in early England were originally oral, usually accompanied by a ritual like the handing over of a clod of dirt, and—like wills—often came to be evidenced by a writing. This was particularly true of a type of land known as book-land, which, as the name clearly shows, involved the process of writing. Likewise, transfers by charter, a word that derives from the Latin *charta* (a piece of papyrus or a letter), obviously required writing (Robertson, 1956).

Just as forgery was a problem in the ancient world, the medieval English were concerned about fraudulent changes being made to records on parchment. A solution was the final concord, or *fine*, which was evidenced in a document called a *tripartite indenture*. Parties who wanted undisputable evidence of a transfer of land would initiate a fictitious lawsuit, in which the buyer would claim land occupied by the seller. The seller would admit that the buyer owned the land, and the court would order that the transaction be memorialized in a final concord, which recited the names of the parties, described the land being conveyed, the price, and so forth. The text was written three times on a single piece of parchment. A knife was used to cut a wavy line that divided the parchment into separate documents, one for each party, and one (the "foot of the fine") to be kept in the archives. In case of dispute, the indented sides had to match, or the forgery would be detected (Plucknett, 1956).

Modern conveyances are by *deed*. It must generally be signed by the seller, and delivered to the buyer or his or her agent. There are various types of deeds, including *grant deeds* (in which the owner transfers an interest in land, using operative words like "I grant and have granted") and *quitclaim deeds* (in which the owner surrenders any interest she or he might have in the property, generally using a dispositive phrase similar to "I release, remise and forever quitclaim"). It is critical that the words indicate a present intent to convey an interest in property, which is usually but not always signified by the use of the present tense (Natelson, 1992). Thus, as with wills, a modern deed is not merely evidentiary, but an authoritative or dispositive text that, by being properly executed (and also delivered), performs the act of conveying.

Contracts

Contracts, at least as they are currently conceptualized (as an exchange of promises), are a relatively late development in the common law. One might therefore think that they would be quintessentially written documents. In actuality, contracts can be surprisingly oral. This is in sharp contrast to wills or deeds, which can only be in writing, and which are so closely identified with writing that the words *will* and *deed* have come to refer to a type of document, not the intentions or acts of the legal actor. The word *contract*, on the other hand, is ambiguous. It can refer either to the agreement in the minds of the parties or to the document in which it is embodied.

As mentioned, a contract can be completely oral. In fact, vast numbers of oral agreements are made every day. The main reason is convenience. It is faster and easier to make an oral contract than to write one. Of course, if the parties do not trust each other, or if there is much at stake, it becomes worthwhile to spend the additional effort required to create a writing.

It is therefore not unusual to make an oral contract, and later to create a written record that contains some or all of the terms. In contract law, this is generally called a *memorandum*. For example, a person might go to a store and orally agree to buy a refrigerator, to be delivered in a week. The only writing might be a sales receipt that states "refrigerator—$500" or something similar. Like an oral Anglo-Saxon will whose terms are written down by a monk, this is an oral agreement; the sales receipt does not create the contract, but is merely evidence of the oral event. Under the Statute of Frauds, certain types of contracts (e.g., those dealing with sale of an interest in land) are enforceable only if there is a memorandum of this kind (Farnsworth, 1990).

In the alternative, the parties to a contract might decide to create an authoritative text of their agreement. Lawyers call this an *integrated* agreement. A contract may be either partially or fully integrated. If the parties decide to write down certain terms of their contract and intend those terms to be final, the agreement is partially integrated. Because it is only partially integrated, additional oral terms might still be considered part of the contract, but such oral terms, or any other writing outside of the contract, cannot be used to contradict the text of the writing (Farnsworth, 1990). With a partially integrated agreement, the text is final, but only as far as it goes.

On the other hand, the parties might decide to reduce their entire agreement to writing, creating a fully integrated agreement. If so, any possible terms that are not included in the writing, whether spoken or written, become legally irrelevant. In deciding what the agreement was between the parties, a judge can look only at the text itself. The writing has become the "exclusive repository of their agreement" (Murray, 1990, p. 381). Thus, a fully integrated contract is an authoritative text very much like a will or statute.

Statutes

Various Anglo-Saxon kings had codes of laws made in their names, beginning with the laws of King Æthelberht of Kent, composed shortly after the first Christian missionaries arrived (Oliver, 2002). Many of these early codes were little more than lists of fines or compensation required to be paid for specified offenses. Anglo-Saxon compilations of laws therefore served mainly to record or memorialize laws or customs that already existed. Later Anglo-Saxon codes reveal an emerging appreciation for the rule of law, as evidenced by King Edgar's Wihtbordesstan code, which provided that multiple copies should be made and that they should be sent "in all directions" so that the law should be known to rich and poor alike (Wormald, 1999, p. 317).

The earliest Norman kings likewise did not produce legislation in any systematic way. In fact, legislation enacted by or approved by a parliament was rare until roughly the 13th century, when laws began to appear under the name of *assizes* or *provisions* or *constitutions*. Even then, it was possible for kings to legislate orally, followed by proclamation of the law throughout the realm (Clanchy, 1993). Eventually, however, statutes became the exclusive form of lawmaking. By the year 1407, it became settled that legislation should be enacted by having the commons and lords each approve a proposal, and then obtaining the assent of the king (Baker, 1990).

Legislation of this period, although it was now written, was not yet authoritative text in the modern sense. Statutes remained essentially oral decisions made by the king and Parliament. According to legal historian J. H. Baker (1990), medieval legislation was "not a text which had been pored over word for word by the lawmakers, with debates upon the wording" (p. 236). Often the drafting of the text was done by clerks and judges after Parliament had given its assent. As a result, "Medieval courts had no authentic texts available to them, and argument in court rarely turned on the precise wording of a statute" (p. 236).

During the course of the 15th century, legislation in England underwent an important transition. It became "the deliberate adoption of specific proposals embodied in specific texts" (Plucknett, 1944, p. 248). In other words, the written document was no longer merely evidence of the law, but constituted the law itself. The term *statute*, which once referred to something that had been established or decided, now referred to the text that expressed that decision in writing.

Although the text of statutes now had greater authority than ever before, courts nonetheless continued to interpret them quite loosely. Although the king and Parliament expressed their intentions in writing, it was difficult to obtain an exact copy of the text. As Plucknett (1956) observed:

> The wording of a statute is not at first taken very seriously. Copies used by the profession were only approximately accurate; even government departments and the courts were no better off; the recording of statutes in the national archives was by no means regular. (p. 340)

As a consequence, interpretation "could not be precise" because "there was no sacrosanct text" (p. 340).

The invention of printing created the potential for making available to the legal profession a large number of identical copies of statutes, something that in the long run would greatly promote the authority of the text. The first printed statutes were published in 1484. Printers soon produced more and more compilations of statutes. Yet the earliest printings of legislation were private profit-making ventures, and the quality was often questionable. It was only during the 18th century that accurate printed copies of statutes became widely available (Allen, 1964).

It is probably not coincidental that at around the same time, English courts began to interpret statutes in a very literal or acontextual way. Judges felt that they had to interpret statutes based solely on the text itself. Only if it was obviously ambiguous would they consider nontextual clues regarding the intentions of the legislature. This principle of literal interpretation is sometimes known as the *Plain Meaning Rule*. Until recently, it was the dominant principle of statutory interpretation in England (Plucknett, 1956).

In the United States, legislation has been written from the beginning. Although the Constitution does not specifically require Congress to enact written text into law, its reference to "bills" in Article 1, Section 7, and the requirement that they be presented to the president for "signature," clearly presuppose the enactment of written text.

Originally, the text of federal statutes was printed in major newspapers. At the end of the 18th century, Congress authorized a printer to publish all the statutes it adopted, but only after ensuring that the printed version matched the original rolls (Surrency, 1990).

The American legal profession has therefore had access to accurate versions of the exact text of American statutes for more than 200 years. Unlike the English, however, American judges did not adopt a strictly textual approach to statutory interpretation. Some judges did indeed adhere to the plain-meaning rule, but others felt no compunction about referring to sources outside the text, particularly records of congressional proceedings, including statements made by proponents or reports by committees (collectively known as *legislative history*; Solan, 1998).

Although the plain-meaning rule appeared to be dying out during the course of the 20th century, it has recently been reinvigorated by Justice Antonin Scalia of the U.S. Supreme Court, who has declared that in his view, legislative history and most other nontextual sources of information about the legislature's intent should not be used in the process of interpretation (Scalia, 1997).

The debate between followers of Scalia's approach (often called *textualists*) and those who oppose them (sometimes called *intentionalists*) refuses to go away. To a large extent, it can be viewed as a natural outgrowth of the development of highly literate conventions in the legal world, especially those pertaining to statutes. When a legislature lays down the law in the form of written text that it has carefully drafted and thoroughly debated, there seems to be a strong tendency for those who read the resulting highly autonomous text to interpret it in a relatively acontextual or literal fashion. We might say, therefore, that textualist judges use a relatively written mode of interpretation. At the same time, our culture remains predominantly oral. With most human communication, especially the spoken variety, we do not fixate on the exact words that were used, but try instead to determine the meaning that the speaker intended to convey. Thus, intentionalist judges tend to read statutes in a way that could be described as more oral. The American experience with statutes shows that although the development of highly accurate and authoritative copies of legal texts can promote a literal mode of interpretation, as it did in England, this result is not inevitable.

Judicial Opinions and the Concept of Precedent

Statutes are one of the two main sources of law in the common-law system. The other is the common law itself, which is the law made by judges and expressed in judicial opinions (usually called *judgments* in England). Although both statutes and opinions are sources of law, they differ in some fundamental ways. The most important distinction is that statutes are considered written law, whereas the common law is traditionally considered unwritten (Hale, 1971). Of course, when judges had to decide a case, they would often articulate in words the rule or principle that they were applying, thus creating a precedent that should be followed in later cases. And those precedents would often be written down. But the essence of the common law was, and to some extent still is, conceptual rather than textual.

One reason that the common law has remained relatively unwritten is that, until quite recently, English judges did not write their opinions. Rather, they pronounced their judgments orally in open court. Lawyers who were present took notes that they used to produce a report of the case (usually a summary of what the lawyers and judges said). Originally used as a learning device, these reports gradually came to be viewed as sources of law, and they consequently began to concentrate more on what the judges said and eventually dropped all references to the arguments of the lawyers. Critically, however, the words in the reports were a synopsis by the reporter, not a verbatim record. Lawyers searching for the rule or principle of a case could therefore not focus too intently on the exact words of the report. To determine the principle of the case (its *holding* or *ratio decidendi*), they had to analyze the issue before the court and the outcome of the case, and then formulate a rule or principle necessary to reach that result. This analytical process is generally known as *legal reasoning*.

Moreover, the quality of reports was sometimes very poor. Although some reporters had an excellent reputation for accuracy, others were held by later judges to be of questionable authority, or even downright wrong. Thus, reports of opinions were at the time deemed to be merely *evidence* of the common law, and sometimes were not very good evidence (Megarry, 1973). The accuracy of case reports improved during the 18th century, and since the mid-19th century, highly reliable reports have been available to English lawyers.

Even today, however, many appellate decisions in England are delivered *extempore* (i.e., the judgment is delivered orally after the lawyers finish their arguments). Moreover, although many English appellate judges now write their opinions, they have largely preserved the practice of delivering opinions *seriatim*, or one after the other. Thus, even with written opinions, English judges usually each write a separate opinion, stating how they would decide the case and why. There could thus be three or four opinions that reach the same result, but for somewhat different reasons. In that event, which is quite common, there is no single authoritative text. The rule or principle of the case must be synthesized by analyzing all the opinions, and it is therefore relatively abstract and somewhat malleable. In large part because of its oral history, the English common law therefore remains relatively conceptual.

Although the United States inherited the common-law system from England, the American notion of precedent has become considerably more textual. Most American jurisdictions require that appellate judges formulate their opinions in writing. Although seriatim opinions were used early in the republic, they were soon abolished. Multiple opinions are certainly possible in the United States, but courts generally strive to produce a single opinion that speaks for the entire majority.

The writing style of American opinions has also become more autonomous. A hundred years ago, American judges would express the holding of a case by using prefatory words that referred to their mental state, such as "we believe that ..." or "it is our opinion that ..." Currently, that relatively conceptual formulation has largely been displaced by a more textual one: "We hold that, ..." often followed by a rule-like statement of the principle of the case.

As the common law—especially in the United States—becomes more textual, it is increasingly difficult to suggest that it is unwritten, in contrast to statutory law. The two sources of law remain distinct, of course. But judicial opinions are clearly becoming less conceptual, and the process of legal reasoning is gradually becoming more literate, using less analytical or analogical reasoning, and focusing more on the text.

THE CIVIL LAW

The term *civil law* has various meanings. We use it here to refer to the system of law that developed on the continent of Europe. Being based to a large extent on Roman law, civil law began with a tradition in which writing played a prominent role. In the following relatively brief discussion, we concentrate on some of the major differences between civil and common law in terms of writing.

Private Legal Texts

Like the common law, the civil law requires that certain types of transactions (such as wills and certain categories of contracts) be evidenced by a writing. In the common law, such a writing is normally made by the person or persons subject to the agreement, or by a lawyer drafting the document on behalf of, and in the voice of, the legal actor. Thus, an English or American will speaks in the first person, even if drafted by a lawyer. Contracts are often in the third person, but nonetheless are conceptualized as having been written by, and as speaking on behalf of, the parties.

In the civil-law tradition, private writings by the parties are certainly possible, but there are also specified transactions that must be written by a notary, who is not a lawyer but may have significant legal training (unlike the American notary public, who normally has no such training and merely authenticates documents or signatures). The European notary's job is not just to authenticate the identity of the parties, but to ascertain their intentions, to write down those intentions clearly and accurately, and to keep a record of the transaction. Notaries are also expected to explain the nature of the transaction and its consequences. Tellingly, the documents or acts that they produce record the transaction in the third person. As opposed to an American will, which often begins with a statement along the lines of "I, [name of testator], declare that this is my will," a notarial act typically begins with a phrase like the following: "I, [name of notary], living in [location], state that [name of testator] appeared before me and declared his will as follows ..." (Zweigert & Kötz ,1992, pp. 393–340).

The various civil-law systems have differing requirements regarding whether and what type of writing is required for the various types of private legal transactions. In Germany, for instance, sales for any amount of money are valid whether or not there is a writing, but sales of land require written evidence. Austria, in contrast, allows oral contracts for the sale of land, but requires a notarial writing to record the transfer of ownership in official records. A promise of a gift must evidenced by a notarial writing in Germany or Austria, but a private writing is sufficient in Switzerland (unless it involves a gift of land) (Zweigert & Kötz, 1992).

It has been suggested that private legal documents in the civil-law system are considerably shorter than similar documents in common-law countries. Claire Hill and Christopher King (2004) make this point with respect to German commercial contracts. The same appears to be true of public legal texts, including codes of law. Overall, legal documents in the civil-law system are written in a somewhat more abstract and general style than equivalent English or American texts. It may be that the less adversarial nature of the civil-law system makes it less necessary for lawyers to try to anticipate and prevent every possible way in which the other party to an agreement might attempt to wiggle out of it, enabling them to draft documents in broader and more general language.

The Codes

Unlike common-law systems, where precedent is an important source of law, the civil law does not consider the opinions of judges to be authoritative in the same sense. Thus, the main source of public law in those countries is legislation. Civil-law countries are distinguished by the degree to which they have codified their legal systems.

The great modern proponent of codification was the English philosopher Jeremy Bentham. His idea was to compile the totality of the law in codes, one for each subject area, which are logically organized and readily accessible to those who need to consult them. Bentham's ideas had very little success in his native land. Codification was partially implemented in some American states, but it was even more enthusiastically embraced on the continent of Europe.

Codification had been known in Europe since the time of Justinian, but the concept fell into disuse and was later reinvigorated, partly through Bentham's influence. The archetypical code is, of course, the French *Code Napoléon*. Although heavily influenced by Roman Law, the Code was intended to revolutionize and exhaustively state the entire law, and to this end all prior law was repealed. The aim was to state the law so clearly that an ordinary citizen could read the code and determine what his or her rights and responsibilities were. Lawyers would become superfluous. Judges would be more constrained, because the Code was supposed to be so clear as not to need interpretation. In terms familiar to those involved in the study of literacy, it was meant to be completely autonomous. Many of these goals were not accomplished, especially those relating to comprehensibility, but the *Code Napoléon* was widely imitated throughout Europe and other parts of the world (Merryman, 1985).

As in the common-law system, there is no single approach to how European legislation should be interpreted. The aim of some of the earlier codes, to state the law as clearly as possible, was meant not only to educate the citizenry, but also to reduce the interpretive discretion of judges. According to Merryman (1985), the folklore that judges merely apply the law, without interpretation, has had a "surprising persistence" in the civil law world.

In reality, continental judges must fill gaps and resolve ambiguities, just as they do in England and the United States. The methods they use include textual or grammatical analysis, structural or contextual interpretation, historical interpretation, and teleological approaches that concentrate on the apparent goal or purpose of the legislation (Brugger, 1994). Despite the widespread codification of the civil law, and the common perception that judges merely apply the exhaustive provisions of the codes to the factual situation before them, civil-law lawyers and judges approach statutes in much the same way that their colleagues do in England and other common-law jurisdictions.

CONCLUSION

Laying down the law and memorializing private legal transactions were among the earliest uses of writing. The relative permanence of writing and its ability to communicate over large distances makes it particularly appropriate for legal purposes. Before long, additional advantages of writing the law became evident. Most important, people began to realize that written law can serve as a bulwark against arbitrary decisions by rulers and magistrates. Of course, law does not inevitably have to be in writing, and literacy does not necessarily promote democracy. Yet the practice of writing the law not only has practical advantages for those who govern, but also is an important component of the rule of law, which safeguards those who are governed.

ACKNOWLEDGMENTS

I would like to thank to Janet Ainsworth and Jeff Atik for their helpful comments, and Summer Kern for research assistance. I retain full responsibility for errors.

REFERENCES

Allen, C. K. (1964). *Law in the making*. Oxford, England: Clarendon.

Arnaoutoglou, I. (1998). *Ancient Greek laws: A sourcebook*. London: Routledge.

Baines, J. (1983). Literacy and ancient Egyptian society. *Man, 18*, 572–599.

Baker, J. H. (1990). *An introduction to English legal history* (3rd ed.). London: Butterworths.

Bodde, D., & Morris, C. (1973). *Law in imperial China*. Philadelphia: University of Pennsylvania Press.

Brugger, W. (1994). Legal interpretation, schools of jurisprudence, and anthropology: Some remarks from a German point of view. *American Journal of Comparative Law, 42*, 395–421.

Buckland, W. W. (1966). *A text-book of Roman law from Augustus to Justinian* (3rd ed., rev. by P. Stein). Cambridge, England: Cambridge University Press.

Clanchy, M. T. (1993). *From memory to written record: England 1066–1307* (2nd ed.). Oxford, England: Blackwell.

Danet, B., & Bogoch, B. (1994). Orality, literacy, and performativity in Anglo-Saxon wills. In J. Gibbons (Ed.), *Language and the law* (pp. 100–135). London: Longman.

Ellickson, R., & Thorland, C. (1995). Ancient land law: Mesopotamia, Egypt, Israel. *Chicago-Kent Law Review, 71*, 321–411.

Farnsworth, E. A. (1990). *Contracts* (2nd ed.). Boston: Little, Brown.

Hale, M. (1971). *The history of the common law of England* (C. M. Grey, Ed.). Chicago: University of Chicago Press.

Hazeltine, H. D. (1930). Comments on the writings known as Anglo-Saxon wills. In D. Whitelock (Eds.), *Anglo-Saxon wills* (pp. vii–xi). Cambridge, England: Cambridge University Press.

Hill, C., & King, C. (2004). How do German contracts do as much with fewer words? *Chicago-Kent Law Review, 79*, 889–926.

Jackson, B. S. (2000). Literal meaning: Semantics and narrative in Biblical law and modern jurisprudence. *International Journal for the Semiotics of Law, 13*, 433–457.

Johnson, W. (1979). *The T'ang code*. Princeton, NJ: Princeton University Press.

Johnston, D. (1999). *Roman law in context*. Cambridge, England: Cambridge University Press.

Megarry, R. (1973). *A second miscellany-at-law: A further diversion for lawyers and others*. London: Stevens & Sons.

Merryman, J. H. (1985). *The civil law tradition* (2nd ed.). Stanford, CA: Stanford University Press.

Meyer, E. A. (2004). *Legitimacy and law in the Roman world: Tabulae in Roman belief and practice*. Cambridge, England: Cambridge University Press.

Murray, J. E., Jr. (1990). *Murray on contracts*. Charlottesville, VA: Michie.

Natelson, R. G. (1992). *Modern law of deeds to real property*. Boston: Little, Brown.

Oliver, L. (2002). *The beginnings of English law*. Toronto, Ontario, Canada: University of Toronto Press.

Plucknett, T. F. T. (1944). Ellesmere on statutes. *Law Quarterly Review, 60*, 242.

Plucknett, T. F. T. (1956). *A concise history of the common law*. Boston: Little, Brown.

Robb, K. (1994). *Literacy and paideia in ancient Greece*. Oxford, England: Oxford University Press.

Robertson, A. J. (1956). *Anglo-Saxon charters*. Cambridge, England: Cambridge University Press.

Scalia, A. (1997). *A matter of interpretation: Federal courts and the law*. Princeton, NJ: Princeton University Press.

Scogin, H. T., Jr. (1990). Between heaven and man: Contract and the state in Han Dynasty China. *Southern California Law Review, 63*, 1325.

Sheehan, M. M. (1963). *The will in medieval England*. Toronto, Ontario, Canada: Pontifical Institute of Mediaeval Studies.

Solan, L. M. (1998). Law, language, and lenity. *William & Mary Law Review, 40*, 57–144.

Surrency, E. C. (1990). *A history of American law publishing*. New York: Oceana.

Thomas, R. (2001). Literacy in ancient Greece: Functional literacy, oral education, and the development of a literate environment. In D. R. Olson & N. Torrance (Eds.), *The making of literate societies* (pp. 68–81). Malden, MA: Blackwell.

Tiersma, P. (1988). Rites of passage: Legal ritual in Roman law and anthropological analogues. *Journal of Legal History, 9*, 3–25.

Tiersma, P. (1999). *Legal language*. Chicago: University of Chicago Press.

VerSteeg, R. (2000). *Early Mesopotamian law*. Durham, NC: Carolina Academic Press.

Westbrook, R. (1994). Biblical and cuneiform law codes. In A. Dundes Renteln & A. Dundes (Eds.), *Folk law: Essays in the theory and practice of lex non scripta* (Vol. 1, pp. 495–511). Madison: University of Wisconsin Press.

Whitelock, D. (1930). *Anglo-Saxon wills*. Cambridge, England: Cambridge University Press.

Wormald, P. (1999). *The making of English law: King Alfred to the twelfth century*. Oxford, England: Blackwell.

Zweigert, K., & Kötz, H. (1992). *An introduction to comparative law* (2nd ed.; T. Weir, Trans.). Oxford, England: Clarendon.

CHAPTER 9

Writing and Secular Knowledge Outside Modern European Institutions

Charles Bazerman
Paul Rogers
University of California, Santa Barbara

Knowledge is a large, vague term often considered coterminous with civilization. In this first section, we narrow the scope of the term to suggest that much of what we think of as knowledge is embedded in literate institutions and associated with particular forms of writing. This chapter and the next then review the forms of written knowledge and the institutions by which this knowledge has been produced and disseminated in various societies. A third chapter (11) then examines the institutions created to archive, maintain, organize, and index knowledge.

By knowledge, we mean concepts and information shared with other people rather than personal certainties. Some knowledge is shared through physical guidance and imitation, often supported by language, to orient people toward perceptions and tasks. Other forms of knowledge, however, are realized in the statements. Such declarative knowledge can be passed down by oral traditions, but holding knowledge stable in oral cultures is labor intensive and constrained by the kinds of devices that keep them stable, such as narrative, imagery, sound patterning (e.g., rhythm, rhyme, alliteration, or assonance), and ritual performance (Rubin, 1995). Oral memory may also be supported by drawings, monuments, and architectural arrangements (Renfrew & Scarre, 1999).

The invention of writing made knowledge more readily and reliably remembered, transported across time and space, and shared, by copying, among multiple people and sites. This shared knowledge forms common reference points for those who have access and who attend to it. It forms "what everyone knows" and what dissenters dissent from. At times the knowledges available in a time and place are harmonious and at times they may be contending or contradictory, representative of different interests and peoples. Also the advance of knowledge may be built on organized contestation among claimants in structured forums based on mutually recognized criteria, as in the contemporary academy.

Jack Goody (1977, 1987), Eric Havelock (1982), and Walter Ong (1982), among others, further suggested that writing facilitates organizing information into lists and charts, aggregating multiple instances into general categories, constructing abstractions apart from instances, and reasoning about them. Writing also holds stable procedures, rituals, formulae, recipes, and experiments, thereby allowing comparison of the consequences of repeated behaviors. Writing facilitates inspecting exact wording to hold authors accountable for what was said, as well as comparing accounts for inconsistencies, differences, and contradictions. Although these tasks can be carried out in oral contexts, and none are a necessary consequence of the acquisition of literacy, these facilitations nonetheless are consistent with historically observed changes occurring with literacy. One interesting aspect of the inspectibility of writing and its potential for reflectiveness about language is that in most societies discussed herein, some form of linguistics emerged early in the wake of literacy.

Sylvia Scribner and Michael Cole (1981), in investigating the three forms of literacy of the Vai people in Africa (in Koranic Arabic, in Western schooled languages, and in an indigenous script), noted that differences in thought came from the social practices and institutions associated with each form of literacy rather than as a general consequence of literacy. Thus, the impact of literacy on thought and knowledge should be understood within particular social, cultural, and historical circumstances and practices. Writing in turn reshapes the forms of social and cultural organization within which literacy is practiced (Goody, 1986). Schooling, for example, developed to meet needs for literacy training. In turn, the conditions of schooling removed from other daily practices changed the distribution and production of knowledge—with impact on other social institutions such as the state, which came to rely on schooling to prepare functionaries. Literacy also extended communicative networks among people interested in advancing knowledge; philosophic and scientific communities formed around the inscribed (and later printed) text. (For sociological analyses of how such communities take shape, thrive, move to abstraction, differentiate, and fragment, see Collins, 1998; Kaufer & Carley, 1993.) Literacy knowledge and associated social arrangements became intertwined with each other (Bazerman, 2006; Goody, 1986).

This chapter and the next give a synoptic overview of that intertwined story. This chapter reaches backward to the earliest production of written knowledge in the Fertile Crescent, the Middle East, the Mediterranean, China, India, and Mesoamerica and leaves off in each region just before the introduction of modern Western universities and accompanying structures of modern scholarship. For Europe, that means this chapter ends with the fall of the Roman Empire; for the rest of the world, this chapter continues until just prior to European colonization, Westernization, or integration into a global knowledge economy. In these chapters, we further narrow our scope to look at secular knowledge, in contrast to the sacred knowledge of scriptural religions. The sacred–secular distinction is admittedly a whiggish one, in that we look backward from contemporary knowledge systems and social organization to find traces in earlier periods and other geographic regions where those things we might call secular knowledge may have been bound up with sacred knowledge. Furthermore, although these two chapters touch on law and the economy, the focus is primarily on the kind of knowledge currently associated with academic research and the universities. It is only from the perspective of the modern university that we would identify the subject matter of this chapter as secular knowledge abstracted from both religious belief and daily affairs.

We have one further prefatory comment concerning the sources cited. Intellectual and cultural histories of the various global societies have documented and analyzed, extensively and in detail, the contents of knowledge-bearing documents. In these histories, knowledge-bearing texts serve as evidence of what individuals and cultures knew, believed, or discovered, but only rarely has the production and circulation of texts been given central focus. Such a concern for the role of writing itself has been most evident in the study of the rhetoric of modern science and modern disciplines. Where such literature is available we draw directly on it. For the most part, however, we glean from the more traditional intellectual and cultural historical literature for indications about the nature of the writing and texts. We also present uncited, widely known facts of intellectual history. We hope that our sketchy story of how writing has had an influence on the production of knowledge will spur further investigations.

EARLY FORMS OF INSCRIBED KNOWLEDGE

The origins of written language in the impressing of tokens into clay envelopes are closely linked to the inscription and storage of knowledge about plant and animal produce (see chap. 1, this volume). This invention in the Fertile Crescent soon led to aspects of Sumerian religious, governmental, and business affairs being transcribed to facilitate activities stretching over time and space, and over many parties. Sumerian cuneiform dominated the region from the middle of the third millennium to the middle of the first millennium BCE even when spoken Sumerian was long dead. It was used by the Akkadians, Hittites, Elamites, and even the 18th Egyptian dynasty in the latter half of the second millennium when it ruled the East (Vanstiphout, 1995).

Sumerian cuneiform was taught in the Eduba—or tablet houses—of the Mesopotamian basin. In these schools, the primary knowledge taught was the written language. Sumerian cuneiform not only inscribed knowledge of this dead language, but also became the vehicle for knowledge of the spoken languages such as Akkadian (Vanstiphout, 1995). The school was organized on a craftsman apprentice model (Vogelzang, 1995), where the central activity was the copying of vocabulary, grammar, and mathematics lists. Beyond the lists of common words and names, students copied word lists and documents largely pertaining to administrative, diplomatic, contractual, and legal matters, thereby simultaneously tutoring them in knowledge of administration, commerce, and the law. The archives of tablets at these schools may also be repositories of such knowledge, though it is unclear from archaeological evidence which documents were true archival information and which were student exercises.

Curriculum also included literary texts, which were largely narratives about the great deeds of gods and heroic leaders or poems of praise to them. Some reflective wisdom literature, lyric love poetry, elegies, and complaints as the civilization collapsed also became part of this knowledge of the scribal classes (Vanstiphout, 1995). These literary texts provided knowledge of both their contents and the styles they were realized in. These literary texts also became the basis of bibliographic information about them through catalogs. The knowledges recorded and gathered in the Eduba seemed to stay close to the Eduba, which became the center of an educated elite cultural life.

Two of the more widely circulated domains of knowledge concerned the law and the accomplishments attributed to the great leaders. Though we have tablets of legal code from prior to 2000 BCE, Hammurabi's code of the mid-18th century BCE is the first we have clear evidence of having wide circulation. Hammurabi, who created the empire of Old Babylonia, ordered his legal code inscribed on stone stelae in temples. This public presence of his laws, even though intelligible only to the scribal classes, may have aided administration of and respect to a uniform law. As well, it may have served as a monument to leadership by establishing and maintaining a rule of law. Accounts of royal accomplishments of other leaders, such as prowess in battle and prosperity of their state, were inscribed on city and palace walls, as well as placed on decorative cones. This public recorded knowledge served to create fealty and obedience in subjects and respect and fear in others, as we can see in the opening lines of *Gilgamesh*, which we take as the first extended instance of literature (see also Kramer, 1981).

SCRIBAL EGYPT

In the bureaucratic state of ancient Egypt, complicated economic and social systems depended on writing. Scribes held distinguished positions within Egyptian administrative, political, and learned professions, and new scribes were trained principally to enter civil service. Although some children of the highest class were educated at the palace along with the royal princes, most were taught at home, by their own fathers or in schools associated with the temple or office for which their fathers worked. Access to education was largely limited to those from the scribal and elite classes (Silverman, 1997). Advanced teaching was on an apprenticeship model, mentored by senior officials (Lichtheim, 1976).

The scribal craft embraced an ideal of the knowledgeable man, to measure, count, and record (Claggett, 1989). One instruction book from the New Kingdom (late second millennium BCE) presents the scribe as the most desirable of occupations: "The scribe he alone records the output of all of them" (Lichtheim, 1976, p. 170). Scribal employment was extremely diversified; one list of scribes indicates 58 distinct scribal positions (Clagget, 1989). The home of learning was in the temples where departments called "House of Life" contained libraries and scriptoria. Letter writing was a prominent feature of scribal activity, whereas Egyptian knowledge making most often took the form of the list (Silverman, 1997).

Surviving texts consist in large part of funerary forms, such as offering lists, the prayer for offerings, and other writing on the walls of tombs. The written word gave specific identity to pictorial representations, naming the tomb owner, his family, titles, and ranks plus the offerings he was to receive. From these funerary texts evolved many other genres of writing including the autobiography. Surviving administrative, business, and legal contracts (common forms include leases, loans, freight contracts, divorce contracts, deeds, deposits, apprenticeship contracts, receipts, judicial records, legal decrees, and letters of recommendation) cumulatively indicate an extensive government structure protecting contracts and collecting taxes. Surviving lists of prices, ships, soldiers, taxes, and food stuffs suggest the vitality of the economy. Lists and charts also record geographic, hydrologic, calendric, and astronomic information revealing an extensive, practical knowledge of movements of stars and planets. Numerous texts also display measurement practices and decimal recording for applied purposes (Silverman, 1997).

Surviving medical texts, dating back to the late Middle Kingdom, consist largely of prescriptions or recipes for treatment, but there is no evidence of organized anatomical inquiry. Nonetheless, though referencing some religion and magic, the texts show concern for "regular and predictable phenomenon with relatively little supernatural involvement" (Bernal, 1992). One late text during Ptolemaic era, shows a continuity of old Egyptian traditions, knowledge, and experience, within Alexandrine Greek culture (Reymond, 1976). Although controversies continue over the extent of Egyptian and Phoenician influence on the origins of Greek culture in the Middle and Bronze ages, some definite exchange did occur between these ancient cultures (O'Conner, 1996).

RECORDED KNOWLEDGE IN MESOAMERICA

Though historically and geographically discontinuous with Sumer or Egypt, the uses and forms of written knowledge in Mesoamerica bear some similarities to those in the early Middle East. The oldest sample of Mesoamerican writing, Mayan calendar inscriptions on buildings in San José Mogote in the Oaxaca Valley, have been carbon-dated from circa 650 BCE (Flannery & Marcus, 1983). Early samples of this writing, which developed from prior symbols and iconography, are found on stone stelae, lintels, masks, jade plaques, and cliff carvings (Coulmas, 1996). Mayan glyphs were also painted on codices made of either deer hide or bleached fig-tree paper, which were then covered with a thin layer of plaster and folded accordion-style. Most nonarchitectural Mayan writing did not survive natural deterioration and the burning of Mayan texts during the 16th-century Spanish invasion. The loss of these texts demonstrates the importance of writing in preserving and transmitting knowledge, and the difficulty of re-creating that knowledge without such texts.

From the beginning, the Maya used writing to reinforce a ruler's military power and to legitimize his descent from noble ancestors and the gods. Inscribed on public buildings, tombs, and stelae are ruler reigns and genealogies, rituals, religious ceremonies, and state and military histories, including conquests, dates, place names, and captives conquered and then sacrificed. Writing from later periods increasingly concerned wars and conquest of neighboring states (Schele & Matthews, 1998). The Maya considered writing to be a sacred gift from the gods and use of it was reserved to elite scribal classes who claimed to have sole authority to mediate between the gods and the common people (Boone, 1994). Nonetheless, the public nature of the monumental writing, wall carvings, and paintings suggests they may have been read and interpreted publicly. Moreover, the codices bearing on daily life would likely have been regularly consulted, although it is unclear whether this would have been mediated by scribal elites. Scribes also composed several types of manuscripts, which were housed in libraries, including maps, financial accounts, tribute payments, and legal records as well as astronomical/astrological records, genealogical accounts, and chronicles (Berdan, 2005; Boone, 2000). Although we know little of Mayan education, Aztec male children of the nobility received formal education in schools called *calmecac*. This education extended from basic literacy to study of military mechanical, astrological, religious, and legal texts (Berdan, 2005).

PEOPLE OF THE BOOK: HEBREWS

Although the date of origin and final redaction of the Torah, or the five books of Moses, are in dispute, from the time of Moses in the 15th century BCE until after the 6th century BCE Babylonian Exile, it is clear that the 10 commandments and other laws embedded within it provided the central principles and governing law from the earliest days. The textual organization of individual and communal life was further strengthened after the destruction of the second temple in 70 CE and the recording of the oral law, the Mishnah, in 200 CE and the writing of commentaries over the next three centuries, together forming the Talmud. Both in ancient times and currently in observant Jewish communities, all learning, law, government, commerce, hygiene, agriculture, food selection and preparation, and other aspects of daily life were regulated by these texts and in the educational, governmental, judicial, and religious institutions that grew up around them. Similarly, all philosophic influences from the peoples they lived among were considered within this scriptural community. Furthermore, the sacred books sacralized the knowledge of history. During the Diaspora, it became a religious obligation of all to participate in this learning through lifelong study of the sacred texts. With no physical land and no access to the means of regional government, commitment to the sacred books held the Jews together as a people.

Because all practical and empirical knowledge of the world was made sacred by bringing it under the divine law, it is difficult to identify a distinctive secular knowledge even though many topics that might otherwise be considered secular are encompassed within it. Even modern commentary on the knowledge held by the ancient community is complicated by a strong motive to read that knowledge in sacred contexts. As Jews lived and participated among other peoples for more than 2,000 years, many pursued knowledges outside the sacralization of the holy books. Although secular learning usually was often encouraged or at least not proscribed and although the culturally developed practices of textual scholarship that arose from the universal obligation to study sacred texts provided skills and tools for those Jews who engaged in secular learning, the secular learning remained outside Jewish identity. For example, Moises ben Maimon, who lived in 13th-century Cordoba, was famous with in both the Jewish and the secular world for his medical skill, but within the sacred tradition his identity is distinctly that of the great talmudic commentator and philosopher Maimonides. The tensions arising from allegiance to both secular and sacred knowledge systems were to become increasingly problematic for both individuals and communities with the development of European knowledge in the 18th century and after. That tension is now evident in the modern secular state of Israel and in other countries with sizable populations who have a similar relation to their scriptures.

WRITING AND KNOWLEDGE CREATION IN ANCIENT INDIA

Writing was widespread in ancient India from at least 500 BCE, the time of the great linguist Panini, but because few, if any, inscriptions or written records are left of the civilization in the Indus valley between 2500 and 1500 BCE, it is not definitely known when the art of writing evolved in India. Yet since the birth of the oldest Vedic poetry, religious texts were central to the culture and even nonreligious texts had religious ends. The term *Veda* comes from the root *Vid* and designates sacred lore as a branch of literature. Inscriptions on stone and copper, the palm leaf records of the temples, and in later days, the widespread manufacture of paper, all alike indicate the common use of the art of writing. Furthermore, Buddhist Vinaya texts, the Mhavagga, and the Vighanga refer to the occupation of the clerk or scribe as a source of livelihood (Mookerji, 1969). Scribes, nonetheless, had low status and the texts they wrote were judged to be less reliable than what was transmitted orally.

This textually transcribed knowledge was transmitted orally, directly from a teacher to his students in small domestic schools with students in residence with the teacher's family or Brahmacharya. Teaching was recitation, and learning was by memorization (viewed as necessary, but not sufficient). The written word was valued as a teaching aid for those too dull to remember. Systematic education, available only to the three higher castes (Brahman, Kshatria, and Vaisia) but not to the Sudra or the untouchables, was based on the direct and personal relationship between a teacher and his pupils. In the Vedas, *education* was defined as the transmission of life from life to life: "Every literary man of ancient Indian was himself a living library, so to speak each man a book" (Mookerji, 1969, p. 78). Even today, access to traditional knowledge of subjects like art, music, grammar, or philosophy is widely held to require a direct oral transmission from master to pupil.

Indeed, the first great accomplishment of Indian written secular knowledge, Panini's analysis of the prosody, syntax, and grammar of Sanskrit, appears to be a gathering and codification of a highly developed set of principles developed and transmitted orally for the purposes of proper recitation of classic texts. The ancient Hindu texts thus went through a period of initial invention, inscription, and compilation and then were highly codified and preserved through an elaborate and diffuse system of oral transmission. The phase following the creation of these original sacred texts was marked by a shift from the hymns themselves to a focus on commentary and the priestly work of ritual, reserved to the Brahman class. This gave rise to a system of "higher education" focused primarily on the work of the priests and the ritual systems. It has been argued that the shutting up of knowledge work to the Brahman caste slowed the development of writing activity in India in the centuries that were to follow their initial creation (Perrett, 1999). The system of oral tradition was as much the characteristic of Buddhist as Brahmanical education, though the causes of its adoption might be different in the two cases (Mookerji, 1969).

The development of a complex ritual structure by the Brahman caste also created a stable location of early speculative reflection, from which connections can be made to Upanishadic speculation and philosophy (Houben, 2000). Mathematics and astronomy were central in Vedic studies, for without acknowledgment of astronomy and mathematics one could not perform the sacrifices, and the construction of sacrificial altars of various sizes and shapes involved the knowledge of geometry and geometric figures. Pythagoras is even said to have been familiar with the Upanishads, which contains in Baudhayana's Sutra, an early statement of the Pythagorean Theorem.

By the sixth century CE, Indian astronomers had made significant discoveries concerning planetary motion: Aryabhata described the earth as a sphere that rotated on its own axis, provided a model of planets orbiting elliptically around the sun, correctly explained solar and lunar eclipses, and deduced that the moon and planets shined by reflected sunlight. He also propounded the heliocentric theory of gravitation, predating Copernicus by almost a thousand years. His work, which was translated into Latin in the 13th century, acquainted European mathematicians with methods for calculating the areas of triangles and volumes of spheres, as well as square and cube roots. The use of the decimal system and the concept of zero—which originated in India—were essential in facilitating large astronomical calculation and allowed such seventh-century mathematicians as Brahmagupta to estimate the earth's circumference at about 23,000 miles.

Similarly, the beginnings of biological and medical knowledge in ancient India are buried in polemical texts that are not normally thought of as scientific. For example, the Vedic literature demarcated the body parts of plants into roots, shoot, leaves, branches, flower, and fruit. Furthermore, plants were grouped in flowering and nonflowering groups. Practical biological knowledge continued to grow, such as a treatise on bovine animals, which play a significant role in the Indian economy. Also horses and elephants, because of their military importance from ancient times, were the subject of a number of veterinary works. There is an extensive written legacy of Indian writers on the subject of medicine, particularly Ayurveda—a health-oriented regimen having its origins in the ancient Rig Veda. Buddhist literature from the Vinaya texts downward evidences progress in medicine and surgical operations. The progress of medical science is further testified by the first-century BCE Milinda Panha, which names the oldest teachers of medical science, each renowned for a treatise of his own (Mookerji, 1969).

WRITING IN THE GREEK AND ROMAN WORLD

Despite Plato's distaste for writing, expressed by Socrates in the *Phaedrus*, the written legacy from the Greek and Roman world has been formative for Western culture, to the point where the contributions of other traditions have until recently been obscured. The knowledge texts of Greece and Rome have a distinctive character. The prior forms of secular knowledge we have noted in this chapter have been embedded in religious practice and/or immediate practical concerns, such as regulating agriculture, collecting taxes, or establishing the might and authority of rulers, but authors of Greece and Rome also offer texts at some philosophic remove from immediate ends—questioning, critiquing, or refining the knowledge arising from practice or taking up objects of inquiry with little immediate practical or religious relevance. Thus, from ancient Greece we gain redaction, collection, and comparison of regional religious stories; histories that stretch beyond the accomplishments of the current ruler and adopt a more critical perspective to events; and descriptions, measurements, and theories about plant and animal life, the physical world, and social life. Furthermore, there are analyses and evaluations of various forms of literary and linguistic practices, including the proper and allowable sequencing of statements that are to follow from one another (i.e., logic). We also have inquiries into various forms of life and government and how one might behave apart from asserted moral directives. Havelock (1963, 1978, 1982) has argued these developments are the direct consequence of literacy, and the collection, inspection, and comparison of texts. Perhaps these intellectual developments may have had other or contributing causes in the cosmopolitan character of seafaring people close enough to learn from Near Eastern empires but far enough away to follow their own path, geographic conditions encouraging communication and movement of individuals among city-states but discouraging centralization of power, the formation of prosperous city-state economies and leisured classes resting on slavery, the formation of guild classes of wandering specialists to take advantage of these conditions, the presence of competing views fostering debate, or transient political conditions that distributed power and decision making. Whatever the causes, in Greece between the sixth and fourth centuries BCE an intense philosophic life flourished producing texts representing several schools of thought that continued within the literate culture in Rome. Together these two cultures produced texts of philosophic inquiry into all areas of life that are still considered foundational for our current knowledge and modes of inquiry (Brunschwig & Lloyd, 2000).

The early work of the wandering presocratic philosophers, sophists, and rhetoricians is known only through short and fragmentary documents and by the report in the writings of later philosophers. The founding of Plato's Academy in a suburb of Athens and his composition of the Socratic dialogues mark the robust organization and production of knowledge and knowledge texts. Although the teaching within the academy remained oral, the texts of the dialogues spread the fame of the school. The dialogues discuss issues such as the nature and guiding principles of law and government, the nature of virtue and love, the sources of truth and knowledge, and the development of the individual spirit.

Plato's student Aristotle established a school at the Lyceum, outside Athen's walls, already a gathering place for philosophic debate. There he collected books for study purposes. His student Theophrastus continued the school and the library, which was then to continue, though with disruptions, for almost 600 years into the third century CE (Lynch, 1972). The learning in the Lyceum was more closely linked to writing than in Plato's Academy, as many of the 30 surviving texts of Aristotle appear to be notes for his lectures, whereas others appear to be more polished treatises. His works and the curriculum apparently covered all aspects of life from metaphysics and ethics to the earth sciences and biology. Three of his treatises are particularly concerned with the art and science of using language: the *Poetics*, the *Rhetoric*, and the *Organon*. The *Organon* consists of six works on logic (Categories; On Interpretation; Prior Analytics; Posterior Analytics; Topics; On Sophistical Refutations) concerned with how knowledge can be formulated in language and what one can properly say following on one's premises. Much of the remainder of Aristotle's work is based on empirical observation, which is then reported, organized, and theorized within the treatises.

Epicurus and the Stoics also founded schools in Athens in the fourth century BCE and produced many books, but we have only fragments and secondhand reports. We have only complete works from the Roman period and not much knowledge about the workings of their schools.

With the writings of the fifth-century-BCE Herodotus, history emerged from traditions of genealogy, mythic narrative, and geographic description. His contemporary, Thucydides, developed a more critical approach based on examination of documents and interviews with participants in events. He attempted a more neutral, objective stance, thereby separating history from the accounts written in the service of the state or religion. Following the footsteps of these two were many Greek and Roman historians including Xenophon, Polybius, Arrian, Plutarch, Flavius Josephus, Sallus, Livy, and Tacitus.

Greek medicine is usually associated with Hippocrates in the fifth century BCE, to whom more than 60 volumes have been attributed, but they were likely written by others following in his wake, including the Hippocratic Oath, which embodies the ideals of his practice. These 60 volumes along with other works provided learning that Galen built on through his own practice. A second-century-CE Greek physician from Pergamon who went to Rome to serve at the Imperial court, Galen, wrote the 17-volume *On the Usefulness of the Parts of the Human Body* that was to dominate the instruction of medicine through the Renaissance.

Greek learning also flourished in Hellenized Egypt, particularly in Alexandria, founded around 334 BCE and that became home of the great library (see chap. 11, this volume). The textual work of compilation and extension carried out by Euclid and Ptolemy there produced books that were to be viewed as founding modern mathematics and astronomy. Euclid, who arrived in Alexandria within a few years after its founding, compiled the *Elements*, based on the work of earlier mathematicians, placing them in a coherent framework and filling out missing proofs. This work established the foundations for geometry to follow and remained as an authoritative textbook to the current day, only in the past century to be set beside what is called non-Euclidean geometry based on alternative postulates. Euclid, in addition to other works on geometry, wrote a geometrically grounded volume on optics, containing the elements of perspective.

Ptolemy in the second century CE compiled the astronomical knowledge of the Greek and Middle Eastern world in *Hè Megalè Syntaxis*, translated into Arabic as *al-kitabu-l-mijisti*, or the great book, and then Latinized as the *Almagest*. He relied heavily on the work of Hipparchus of three centuries prior, whose star catalog he updated and incorporated. His synthesis of astrology, the *Tetrabiblos*, was also taken as authoritative through the Renaissance. Ptolemy's work on geography was as well compiled from Roman, Middle Eastern, and other sources. In addition, his *Harmonika* synthesized competing approaches to music–the Pythagorean based on mathematics and physics and the Harmonist based on auditory experience, whose leading proponent was Aristoxenos.

The wide learning available as Rome took over political and cultural leadership of the Mediterranean set the ground for continuing interest in synthesis and compilation. The first-century-BCE Varro was considered the most learned of all Romans and compiled a widely used (though now lost) nine-volume encyclopedic work called *Disciplinae*. Pliny the Elder of the first century CE in addition to writing histories compiled his *Naturalis Historiae*, finished posthumously by his nephew. In preparing this 37-volume encyclopedia that covers geography, peoples, cultures, physiology, zoology, botany, medicine, and mineralogy, he consulted many hundreds of volumes. His contemporary Strabo wrote in Greek an encyclopedic 17-volume *Geographika*.

Whereas the Roman period is notable for its many technological advances in building and construction, mining and metallurgy, hydrology, and transportation, these seem to have been developed and transmitted primarily in material practice. Vitruvius's 10 volumes of *de Architectura* seems to be a unique exception and serves to document much of contemporary practical knowledge of machinery, hydrology, and materials as well as construction and architecture. Vitruvius, however, seems to have a more learned and literate vision than his colleagues, as he considers the architect to need theoretical knowledge of mathematics, rhetoric, history, philosophy, medicine, and law. The one practical area that seems to have developed numerous manuals and compilations is agriculture, as in Palladius' handbook *Opus Agriculturae*.

Roman education was largely private and reserved for upper-class males, aimed at making them effective public orators. Rhetoric, following Greek models, was at the center of education, incorporating written exercises in imitation of rhetorical models (known as *progymnasmata*). The anonymous *Rhetorica ad Herrenium* (ca. 84 BCE) is the earliest extant Latin rhetoric manual. Cicero at about the same time added his own rhetorical treatises, culminating in *De Oratore* (55 BCE), which is cast as a guide to rhetorical education. Quintillian, in *Institutio Oratoria* (95 CE), set out a course for the development of boys into orators; he views wide reading of admirable texts, along with written composition of orations and other imitative exercises to be cornerstones of the education of a respected public person—"the good man speaking well."

CHINA'S IMPERIAL BUREAUCRACY

As the largest, most stable empire throughout human history, China has over millennia developed an extensive learning, based on a cultural heritage of classic texts. Indeed, the entire national order was built on an administration trained in and valuing classical learning and its ideals, and institutionally regulated by the imperial civil service examinations that lasted over two millennia, until the final collapse of Imperial power in the early 20th century. First instituted in the Han dynasty (206 BCE–220 CE), the exams defined the aims of schooling, the prized texts, and the literate development of every individual seeking power and place (Connery, 1998). State-sponsored schools usually trained students for the exams, although at times private academies, often little more than the extended following of a renowned teacher, flourished. These private schools periodically were seen as training grounds for political opposition and sedition, and were banned. Whether schools were governmental or private, the examinations and the canon of texts needed for the examinations remained at times constant. Furthermore, the need for objectivity of evaluation led to a narrowing of the canon of texts concerned, a formalization of the questions, and a ritual patterning of expected answers in the notorious eight-legged essay based on eight matched pairs of opposing concepts. Because the most valuable knowledge was that which would provide advantage on the examinations, much scholarly production was summary, commentary, and interpretation of the classic texts. Some of these commentaries in turn became part of the examined canon. Confucius (551–479 BCE) had synthesized the ideal for this education from earlier sources as self-improvement, ethical growth, and moral perfection for the sake of a harmonious self and a harmonious society. The five classic Confucian arts that became the heart of the curricula were rites, archery, chariot, writing, and mathematics, each embodied in canonical texts, although the canon was modified to reflect political and ideological changes during different dynasties. The sixth classic Confucianist art, music, did not enter the educational canon. Taoism and Buddhism also influenced the exams and curriculum. Within this examination culture, knowledge of the key texts and of the expected form of the essay soon outweighed substantive understanding of the specifics of knowledge, values, and arts expressed within the texts (Lee, 2000).

The anti-intellectual and centralizing acts of the preceding Qin dynasty (221–207 BCE) ironically established some of the core concerns and practices of the Han educational and civil services reform. The Qin, to silence the Confucianist opposition, ordered all books in the empire to be burned and all the varying scripts of principalities to be replaced with a common script. With the collapse of the Qin, scholars set about recovering and editing remaining books as well as translating the terms written in older scripts. This philology and lexicography became one of the chief forms of knowledge production and the core of knowledge disseminated. Collections of words that were glosses on ancient texts, analysis of ideographs, lexicography of dialects, and phonological study, aided by a rhyming form of spelling, formed the basis of an extensive linguistics and literary study.

Although throughout this 2,000-year period, there was great consistency in the kind of ethical, philological, literary, and aristocratic knowledge valued in the civil service, the exams and the schools that prepared candidates also at times supported learning in the law, medicine, astronomy and mathematics, and military arts in preparation for appropriate civil service roles. These forms of knowledge allowed for centralized control and maintenance of the economy and national welfare. Detailed astronomical records were kept and compared from observatories in the capital and provinces, but these were collected for the office of the astronomical directorate and existed only in small numbers, concentrated in palace and governmental collections, even after the invention of printing. This astronomical knowledge was considered a state secret facilitating the control of floods and agriculture—a key to dynastic legitimacy. Only a few fragments have survived. Meteorology and civil engineering with a focus on hydrology also helped manage and maintain the extensive agricultural basis of the society. More popular farmer's calendars dating from as early as the fifth century BCE, however, were widely spread, including astronomical information to establish dates. These calendars, often government produced, appeared frequently for more than 2,000 years (Ronan & Needham, 1981). Mathematics, as a classic Confucianist art as well as an underpinning of the other sciences and accounting of the bureaucracy, also flourished, with imperial sponsorship and production of treatises.

Medical specialists (to serve the nobility and officials) had from the second century BCE been monitored for proficiency. By the sixth century CE, medicine had become a high-level bureaucratic specialty with officers of the seventh rank, professorships at the imperial college, and written examinations. A medical literature became the basis for these examinations and training, bringing together the collected knowledge of medicinals, anatomy, acupuncture, and related arts. Moreover, the clinical practice of the civil service physicians was recorded and monitored for success (Needham & Lu, 1970a, 1970b). Thus, there was established the social infrastructure of an empirically grounded medical literature.

However, whereas these knowledge domains of use to the state had some coherent development and expanding literature, other areas of knowledge were sporadic with little organized distribution of texts or institutional support. So although a stable history and a prosperous gentry created the leisured conditions for many observations and inventions related to physics, biology, and engineering, these did not aggregate in coherent sciences.

Even medicine was restricted to interests of training, certification, and administrative practice, such as forensics.

The many technological advances made in agriculture, textile manufactures, mining, fishing, construction, weaponry, explosives, mechanical and civil engineering, shipbuilding, and other arts and crafts were developed largely by artisans, workers, craftspeople, or people in the lowest rungs of the state bureaucracy, even though the work may have been supervised by higher level administrators trained in the classics. Thus, its promulgators were neither educated and highly literate nor had access to the means of publication and text distribution. The work tended to be atheoretic and did not attempt much articulation with the dominant educated thought systems of Confucianism, Taoism, and Buddhism. Sometimes inventions and discoveries remained local and sporadic because of the lack of textual transmission. When this practical knowledge did spread it was through objects and practices; in these concrete forms, much of this knowledge diffused to India, the Islamic world, and Europe (Needham, 1970).

Whereas in Europe the invention of the printing press was to foster in the hands of its entrepreneurial printers novel texts, new communities of knowledge seekers and producers, and new disciplines of learning, in China the much earlier invention of printing (block printing at the eighth century CE or before and movable type ca. 1041–1048; Carter, 1955) led to much less diversity of new knowledge, as the control of the press remained largely in the hands of the state and monasteries (Luo, 1998). As a result, most mass-produced and widely circulated print documents reflected bureaucratic functions of the state, the literary classics and commentaries associated with examination, religious scriptures, and government-issued paper money. Sometimes leisured elites used the government press for publication of special-interest limited editions of their poetry and avocations. When private printing flourished (often based in private academies), it too was dominated largely by the culture of the classically based examination system. Only during the Ming (1368–1644) and Qing (1644–1911) dynasties did private printing of vernacular texts (such as popular novels and tales, books on crafts and technology, and gazetteers) appear on a large scale. However, most private printing remained devoted to such ritual artifacts as New Year pictures and funerary money. Thus, the printing press largely supported and participated in the same world of knowledge fostered by the government civil service and examinations.

Before leaving the topic of knowledge in China, we should address the question of why the greatness of Chinese civilization did not produce a scientific revolution of the sort that appeared in the West. This question motivated Needham's massive historical project of 21 volumes of *Science and Civilization*, beginning in 1954 and still not finished. This question also pervades most contemporary historical work on Chinese science and technology. Many reasons have been proposed along with redefinitions of scientific revolution. Without repeating or evaluating here the arguments that range from religious to economic, it is noteworthy that a number of the factors raised have to do with the character of writing and handling of texts: the nature of ideographic writing; the ambiguity of signs; the lack of syntax in the Western sense; the writing style fostered by the examination system of uncritical citation and extended commentaries within a limited domain of interests; the philosophic styles and reigning ideologies within classical prose, particularly fostering a taste for dualities and balances rather than critical debate; the control of astronomical texts as state secrets; the state control of large-volume printing; and the intellectual and professional enlistment of all highly literate people into the state system (Bodde, 1991; Huff, 2003).

THE ISLAMIC CROSSROADS OF LEARNING

After the decline of the great Mediterranean empires, the Middle Eastern world became a repository and crossroads for the knowledge books of both the classical and the Asian world—preserving, translating, keeping alive, and contributing to the knowledge recorded in these books. The transmission of Greek texts began as early as Alexander's conquests in the fourth century BCE and continued throughout the Middle Ages through the Roman outpost of the Byzantine empire. Nestorians (Christians in Persia who dominated the medical profession in Syria) were particularly active in transmitting and translating Greek texts into Syriac. With Mohammed's death in 632, the Umayyad dynasty ruled the Islamic world from Damascus, with the aid of educated Syrians and Persians such as the Nestorians. When the Abassid dynasty gained power in 749 they built and inhabited the new capital of Baghdad. The Caliph al-Mansur (754–775) created schools for bureaucracy and medicine drawing on the same educated groups, with the knowledge and texts they brought with them. Caliph Harun al Rashid (786–809) later sent agents to Byzantium to collect texts, and his son Caliph Al-Ma'mun (813–833) founded a research institute (House of Wisdom) in Baghdad. Nestorian Christian and Arab Hunayb ibn Ishaq (808–873) headed the House of Wisdom and translated the medical texts of Galen and Hippocrates into Syriac and Arabic. However, to understand this medical knowledge scholars were drawn to translate the Greek philosophy, mathematics, and astronomy underlying it. By the end of the first millennium, Arabic translations existed for almost all Greek texts on medicine, natural philosophy, and mathematical sciences. Several Indian works on medicine and therapeutics were translated into Arabic from 786 to 809 CE.

Beyond the universal appeal of medical knowledge, the Islamic way of life also deeply supported astronomy, mathematics, and related mathematical sciences, such as optics. Learned scholars became deeply versed in the classic philosophic texts and advanced knowledge in their model. The 9th-century Al Kindi and the 11th-century Ibn al Haytham and Ibn Sina (Avicenna) starting from Greek knowledge contributed to philosophy, optics, astronomy, and other areas of knowledge—including extending and correcting details of the Ptolemaic system. Other notable astronomers such as Al-Farghani (ca. 861), Thabit ibn Qurra (d. 901), and Al Battani (d. 929) improved star charts and found new values of solar and lunar motions. The ninth-century Muslim mathematician al-Khwarazmi adopted the Indian innovation of zero and was the vehicle for the concept's transmission to the West. He also was the author of the first work on algebra built on Greek and Indian predecessors. The philosophers al-Karaji and Khayyam further advanced knowledge of algebra in their works.

The need to recite, teach, and interpret the Koran correctly led to an extensive study of language, with a focus on Arabic phonology and lexicography (of which al-Khalil, d. 791, is viewed as the founder) and grammar (of which Sîbawayho, d. 793, is viewed as the founder). The philosopher al-Farabi attempted to reform Arabic linguistics based on Aristotelian logical principles, but the field remained formalist and largely separate from philosophic concerns, consistent with the Koran becoming the center of education (Versteegh, 1995).

This secular knowledge constituted an initial rationalist movement among Islamic scholars and educational institutions; however, by the end of the ninth century religious traditionalists came to dominate the Islamic world, and Koranic knowledge became the core of learning. By the 10th century, *madrasas* (Islamic institutions of higher learning) were formed by the addition of residential colleges to mosques. The curriculum was organized around dialectic to determine proper legal opinion based on scripture and authoritative theological interpretation. Only with the license granted by this education could one take on a judicial-clerical position. Makdisi (1981) has argued, however, that this guild model of licensure through apprenticeship in dialectic within an approved institution of higher education influenced the formation of the medieval European university.

After being unseated by the Abassids, the Umayyads moved their center of power to Spain, where Caliph al-Hakam (d. 976) built and stocked libraries in Cordoba and Toledo. During the Christian reconquest of Spain, these libraries and the philosophers associated with them, such as Averroes (ibn Rushd) made possible Europe's rediscovery of Greek knowledge as well as Indian. Similarly, Arabic and Persian translations of Greek and Egyptian scientific texts found their way to India.

Muslim learning, texts, and schools spread with the Islamic empire both throughout North Africa and to the edge of the South Asia subcontinent by the eighth century. With trade, Islamic learning was to expand across the South Asian subcontinent into Southeast Asia and across the southern Sahara and down the east coast of Africa. In Africa, one of the most prominent centers of learning formed at Timbuktu, the seat of the Songhay Empire. By the 14th century a center of learning developed around the Sankore Mosque. This university was said to include faculties of law, medicine and pharmacology, letters, grammar, geography, and industrial arts. Indigenous learning also emerged as African medical practices entered into the medical texts. Local histories and biographies were also written. The lively book trade that surrounded the school at Sankore resulted in a number of substantial private book collections over the next several centuries. The late-16th-century conquest by Morocco marked the end of the university, the book trade, and the production of new written knowledge. Nonetheless, a number of the private family libraries have survived and are now being restored (Hunwick, 1991).

The Greeks and Romans had created a new stage in knowledge formation in developing substantial domains of knowledge, texts, and communication outside the needs and networks of the church or state. Although the control and motives for knowledge in the Abassid Islamic world were brought back under a religious state, in the Umayyad caliphate, the condition of full access to secular knowledge combined with an interest in philosophy and the philosophic advance of the individual. As in the Greco-Roman world, this interest in philosophic knowledge was accompanied by a desire to collect and make available in libraries all knowledge. Because the Islamic world drew on great knowledge and text-producing societies of Asia and Europe, their collections were international in scope, gathering the texts of the entire literate world. This rich resource was to provide the motive and material for the founding of new knowledge institutions, practices, communities, and texts in post-Roman Europe.

REFERENCES

Bazerman, C. (2006). The writing of social organization and the literate situating of cognition. In D. Olson & M. Cole (Eds.), *Technology, literacy, and the evoluton of society* (pp. 215–240). Mahwah, NJ: Lawrence Erlbaum Associates.

Berdan, F. (2005). *The Aztecs of central Mexico: An imperial society*. Belmont, CA: Thomson Wadsworth.

Bernal M. (1992). Animadversions on the origins of Western science. *Isis, 83*(4), 596–607.

Bodde, D. (1991). *Chinese thought, society, and science: The intellectual and social background of science and technology in pre-modern China*. Honolulu: University of Hawaii Press.

Boone, E. (1994). In E. Boone (Ed.), *Aztec pictorial writing: Writing without words* (pp. 50–77). Durham, NC: Duke University Press.

Boone, E. (2000). *Stories in red and black*. Austin: University of Texas Press.

Brunschwig, J., & Lloyd, G. D. (Eds.). (2000). *Greek thought: Guide to classical knowledge*. Cambridge, MA: Harvard University Press.

Carter, T. F. (1955). *The invention of printing in China and its spread westward* (2nd ed.; rev. by L. C. Goodrich). New York: Ronald.

Claggett, M. (1989). *Ancient Egyptian science: A source book* (Vol. 1). Philadelphia: American Philosophical Society.

Collins, R. (1998). *The sociology of philosophies: A global theory of intellectual change*. Cambridge, MA: Harvard University Press.

Connery, C. L. (1998). *The empire of the text*. Lanham, MD: Rowman & Littlefield.

Coulmas, F. (1996). *The Blackwell encyclopedia of writing systems*. Oxford, England: Blackwell.

Flannery, K., & Marcus, J. (1983). *The cloud people: Divergent evolution of the Zapotec and Mixtec civilizations*. New York: Academic Press.

Goody, J. (1977). *The domestication of the savage mind*. Cambridge, England: Cambridge University Press.

Goody, J. (1986). *The logic of writing and the organization of society*. Cambridge, England: Cambridge University Press.

Goody, J. (1987). *The interface between the written and the oral*. Cambridge, England: Cambridge University Press.

Havelock, E. (1963). *Preface to Plato*. Cambridge, MA: Harvard University Press.

Havelock, E. (1978). *The Greek concept of justice: From its shadow in Homer to its substance in Plato*. Cambridge, MA: Harvard University Press.

Havelock, E. (1982). *The literate revolution in Greece and its cultural consequences*. Princeton, NJ: Princeton University Press.

Houben, J. (2000). The ritual pragmatics of a Vedic hymn. *The Journal of the American Oriental Society, 120,* 499–536.

Huff, T. E. (2003). *The rise of early modern science: Islam, China, and the West*. Cambridge, England: Cambridge University Press.

Hunwick, J. (1991). *West Africa and the Arab world : Historical and contemporary perspectives*. Accra: Ghana Academy of Arts and Sciences.

Kaufer, D., & Carley, K. (1993). *Communication at a distance: The influence of print on sociocultural organization and change*. Mahwah, NJ: Lawrence Erlbaum Associates.

Kramer, S. N. (1981). *History begins at Sumer*. Philadelphia: University of Pennsylvania Press.

Lee, T. H. C. (2000). *Education in traditional China: A history* (Handbook of Oriental Studies, Vol. 13). Leiden, Netherlands: Brill.

Lichtheim, M. (1976). *Ancient Egyptian literature* (Vol. 2). Berkeley: University of California Press.

Luo, S. (1998). *An illustrated history of printing in ancient China*. Hong Kong: City University Press.

Lynch, J. P. (1972). *Aristotle's school: A study of a Greek educational institution*. Berkeley: University of California Press.

Makdisi, G. (1981). *The rise of colleges: Institutions of learning in Islam and the West*. Edinburgh, Scotland: Edinburgh University Press.

Mookerji, K. R. (1969). *Ancient Indian education: Brahmanical and Buddhist*. London: Macmillan.

Needham, J. (1970). The unity of science: Asia's indispensible contribution. In J. Needham et al. (Eds.), *Clerks and craftsmen in China and the West* (pp. 14–29). Cambridge, England: Cambridge University Press.

Needham, J., & Lu, G. (1970a). Medicine and Chinese culture. In J. Needham et al. (Eds.), *Clerks and craftsmen in China and the West* (pp. 263–293). Cambridge, England: Cambridge University Press.

Needham, J., & Lu, G. (1970b). China and the origin of qualifying examinations in medicine. In J. Needham et al. (Eds.), *Clerks and craftsmen in China and the West* (pp. 379–395). Cambridge, England: Cambridge University Press.

O'Conner, D. (1996). Egypt and Greece: The Bronze Age evidence. In M. Lefkowitz & G. Rogers (Eds.), *Black Athena revisited* (pp. 49–61). Chapel Hill: University of North Carolina Press.

Ong, W. J. (1982). *Orality and literacy: The technologizing of the word*. New York: Methuen.

Perrett, R. W. (1999). History, time, and knowledge in Ancient India. *History and Theory, 38*(3), 307–321.

Renfrew, C., & Scarre, C. (Eds.). (1999). *Cognition and material culture: The archaeology of symbolic storage*. Cambridge, England: McDonald Institute.

Reymond, E. (Ed.). (1976). *A medical book from Crocodilopolis*. Vienna, Austria: Verlag Brüder Hollinek.

Ronan, C. A., & Needham, J. (1981). *The shorter science & civilization in China* (Vol. 2). Cambridge, England: Cambridge University Press.

Rubin, D. C. (1995). *Memory in oral traditions*. Oxford, England: Oxford University Press.

Schele, L., & Mathews, P. (1998). *The code of kings: The language of seven sacred Maya temples and tombs*. New York: Simon & Schuster.

Scribner, S., & Cole, M. (1981). *The psychology of literacy*. Cambridge, MA: Harvard University Press.

Silverman, D. (Ed.). (1997). *Ancient Egypt*. New York: Oxford University Press.

Vanstiphout, H. L. J. (1995). On the old Babylonian Eduba curriculum. In J. W. Drijvers & A. A. MacDonald (Eds.), *Centres of learning: Learning and location in pre-modern Europe and the Near East* (pp. 3–16). Leiden, Netherlands: Brill.

Versteegh, K. (1995). *Landmarks in linguistic thought: III. The Arabic linguistic tradition*. London: Routledge.

Vogelzang, M. E. (1995). Learning and power during the Sargonid period. In J. W. Drijvers & A. A. MacDonald (Eds.), *Centres of learning: Learning and location in pre-modern Europe and the Near East* (pp. 17–28). Leiden, Netherlands: Brill.

CHAPTER 10

Writing and Secular Knowledge Within Modern European Institutions

Charles Bazerman
Paul Rogers
University of California, Santa Barbara

After the collapse of the Roman Empire, the seats of learning moved to Constantinople and Baghdad. With few texts, poorly distributed in Europe, learning was thin and static for over five centuries. Yet within this bleak landscape, the reintroduction of the texts of the world produced institutions, practices, and forces that were to be the basis of modern learning, knowledge production, and scholarly communication that now encompass the globe.

THE EUROPEAN MIDDLE AGES AND THE BIRTH OF THE UNIVERSITY

In the early European Middle Ages, classical knowledge was limited to a few Latin texts and compendia derived from them, such as Isidore of Seville's (560–632) encyclopedic *Etymologies* and Boethius' (ca. 480–ca. 525) Latin translations of Aristotle's works on logic. Some chronicles, most notably Gregory of Tours' (d. 595) *History of the Franks,* documented newly powerful peoples and political structures. Extant texts were housed in monastic and other church collections with only small, sporadically consulted holdings. Beyond the brief accomplishments of Alcuin during the eighth-century Carolingian Renaissance, few institutions supported instruction in these texts, so the vitality of knowledge depended on individual scholars.

Developments in the 11th and 12th centuries increased the available stock of knowledge texts and expanded organized access to them. When Umayyad Islamic culture in Spain met the Christian reconquest, Europe regained access to classic Greek and Roman texts preserved by Islamic scholars. Ptolemy's synthesis of the work of Greek astronomers, for example, became known through its Arabic translation *al-Majisti,* translated into Latin as the *Almagest.* Many of Aristotle's works were recovered, including his works on medicine and biology, as was Plato's *Timaeus,* Euclid's *Elements,* and Galen's medical works. The taste for texts held in the Islamic world led to interest in other texts available in Constantinople as well as the work of Islamic scholars such as Al-khwarizimi's *Algebra* and Avicenna's commentaries on medicine and philosophy.

Scholars translating and studying these works created a vital intellectual life in the monasteries and larger cities of Europe. Students gathered around scholars lecturing on classic texts, usually beginning with a passage following with an interpretation (Ridder-Symoens, 1991). Generally courses focused on works of moral and natural philosophy along with metaphysics. As available texts increased and scholars gathered in greater numbers, teachers and students organized themselves in guild structures to form the bases of modern universities. These universities first formed in the south, in Italy and Spain, with additional centers around Paris and London. By the end of the 12th century, universities existed at Salerno, Bologna, and Reggio, and soon others emerged at Vicenza, Palencia, Paris, Oxford, Montpelier, Arrezo, Salamanca, Padua, and Naples, with around 20 by the year 1300. By 1500, more than 60 universities were active throughout Europe, from Uppsala in the north to Catania in Sicily in the south, from Lisbon in the west to Cracow in the east (Verger, 1991). The universities varied in size from those that could accommodate over 1,000 students simultaneously (such as, at times, Paris, Orleans, Toulouse, Avignon, Bologna, Oxford, and Cambridge) to those that barely accommodated 100. Nonetheless, from the middle of the 14th until the start of the 16th, approximately three quarters of a million students matriculated throughout Europe, as Schwinges (1991) conservatively calculates.

Curricula were soon standardized under Vatican authority, and degrees granted were held to be valid and equivalent throughout Christendom, although certain faculties were recognized as superior. There were four faculties or disciplines at these universities (theology, law, medicine, and liberal arts), although only a few universities had all four. These disciplines were each defined by a list of authorities or standard texts; studies and authors not included in this classification were in most cases excluded from formal study (Verger, 1991).

The mode of instruction consisted of lecture on passages from authoritative texts (in Latin translation) and debate on general propositions conducted on the basis of those same authoritative texts. Consequently, books in Latin were at the heart of the curriculum, and the shared learning was based on the core disciplines of language and interpretation—the liberal arts trivium (composed of grammar, logic, and rhetoric), although logic and grammar at times took a speculative turn into philosophy, particularly as the Greek and Arabic texts were translated into Latin. The new texts also put new life, substance, and interest into the quadrivium of arithmetic, geometry, astronomy, and music, which gained increasing presence in the universities during the late medieval period (Leff, 1991), in response to the availability of new texts (North, 1991).

In addition to the liberal arts of the trivium and quadrivium, medieval universities contained more specialized faculties. The faculty of medicine distinguished its graduates from the many nonuniversity-trained medical practitioners through the study of Greek and Islamic texts translated into Latin, particularly works attributed to Hippocrates and Galen along with the Islamic encyclopedic works of Avicenna, Haly Abbas, ar-Razi, and Albucasis. These were largely taught through lecture and disputation as were the liberal arts, although supplemented with some practice, apprenticeship, and dissection—guided by the same texts. Surgery, using texts of more recent vintage incorporating practical experience along with Galen, was not part of all medical faculties, and was in fact excluded from Paris (Siraisi, 1991).

The faculty of law, teaching both canon and civil law, was also based on commentary of authoritative texts. The authoritative texts of canon law or *corpus iuris canonici* were of more recent vintage, being 12th-century and later summations of church law, decrees, and rulings, supplemented by contemporary additions to church law. The *corpus iurus vilis* was based on Justinian's code, dating from the end of the Roman Empire, which had been in continuous circulation in Europe since then. This was supplemented by more recent constitutions of German emperors and contemporary commentary. Legal works were sometimes translated and taught in the vernacular. Thus law seemed more closely attached to contemporary situations and institutions. Furthermore, as clerics needed to write legal documents, contracts, and the bureaucratic correspondence of the church, training in writing practice through *ars dictaminis* and *ars notaria* became part of the curriculum, at least in some Italian universities. Nonetheless, law remained taught through lecture and disputation, with the logic and organization of the classic legal canon taking priority over any contemporary code operative in the jurisdiction in which the university was located. This system of legal training as a form of scholastic learning remained universal in Europe through the 17th century. In some countries, law is still studied as a form of liberal art and logic through university lecture (Garcia, 1991).

The fourth faculty of theology taught specifically religious knowledge, exegisis of sacred texts, and philosophic disputation of questions of religion. Relevant to secular knowledge is that many of the fundamental disputes of theology had to do with whether attention or authority should be given to pagan philosophers or whether theology should proceed only on the basis of the testaments and the church fathers. That tension between sacred and secular texts of course continued through Renaissance humanism and the transformation of natural philosophy into modern science. The place of theology within universities moving to secular sponsorship has been a continuing question, particularly in the United States, where state sponsorship has been accompanied by the legal separation of church and state.

THE PRINTING PRESS AND CHANGING NETWORKS OF KNOWLEDGE IN EUROPE

During the Middle Ages, the close nexus of the universities, the church, scriptoria, and education for church careers kept universities at the center of the knowledge maintenance, dissemination, and production. In the 15th century, however, knowledge moved out into the world. The moveable-type printing press, along with related inventions and social arrangements (see chap. 2, this volume), made books available in increasing quantity, no longer tying the scholar to the university or monastery library and freeing the scholar from supervision within church-supported activities. Reformation religious division and struggle did not fundamentally change the church bound character of the universities, although changing some allegiances and disrupting the Vatican's universal curricular authority.

Even more, the printing houses proliferating across Europe, often near university towns, no longer came under a single religious jurisdiction and therefore could not be uniformly censored or controlled, nor did they serve a single international organization. Separate states had neither wealth nor jurisdictional reach to keep the production of texts subservient to their needs, as China had done. Rather, learning became a competitive force that could enhance the status and power of monarchs, starting with the great merchant princes of Italy who patronized such scholars as da Vinci and Galileo (Biagioli, 1993). Monarchs throughout Europe patronized scholars and brought them to court to bring grandeur and luster, if not the vision of a new world, as in the court of Rudolph of Austria (Evans, 1973). In the free city of Magdeburg, Otto von Guericke rose to power in part on his demonstrations of learning, which he then turned to the benefit of the state (Bazerman, 1993). Printing houses saw themselves as beyond the force of any state and began to fashion themselves as a Republic of Letters, spreading cosmopolitan thoughts and ideals (Eisenstein, 1979). Gaining knowledge of each other through books, scholars across Europe engaged in lively correspondence networks.

Multiple copies of books and the ability to compare editions led to textual scholarship to establish definitive editions (Grafton, 1991). The multiplication of contemporary and ancient books led to vigorous debates over the value of classical and contemporary learning in what became known in England as the battle of the books (Jones, 1965; Levine, 1991).

WRITTEN KNOWLEDGE AND PROFESSIONAL PRACTICES:
MEDICINE, LAW, AND COMMERCE

Medicine had strong motive to reach beyond the books to incorporate practical knowledge gained through surgery, which had been kept at the margins of universities by its craft nature and the church prohibition of dissection. During the 15th and 16th centuries, university medical studies combined medical and surgical cures, relating books and embodied practice more closely. By the 17th century, the new discipline of anatomy mixed books with skeletons, bodies, and models to give order to discoveries and to become a cornerstone of medicine (Pedersen, 1996). Two centuries later, anatomy was to be brought in relation to knowledge of infectious agents, and shortly thereafter to chemical knowledge of the pharmacopia, biochemistry, and now genetics. Each of these extensions of relevant knowledge recontextualized understanding of the operation and regulation of the body, as seen through textually inscribed orders, principles, and empirical findings. This bookish part of medical education is then reinforced and applied in situ (Lingard et al., 2002); it also organizes and directs the professional vision by which experts come to see the world in knowledgeable ways (Goodwin, 1994). New medical tools, expanding the kinds and amount of inscribed data available, have now combined with electronic manipulatable multimedia texts to bring about new levels of integration between the body and the book. Although anatomy and other studies preliminary to medical practice continued to be taught in the universities, the central site of medical education moved to the teaching hospitals, which mix the book learning, bodies, practice, and formation of new knowledge in the production of research.

As national legal codes elaborated and commercial interests expanded, the faculties of law included more contemporary law in their curricula still dominated by Roman Law (Brockliss, 1996; Pedersen, 1996). In England, however, the adherence to common law and the collection of texts of laws and customs led to a break with Roman Law; legal education left the universities and organized around the courts with their libraries that informed both education and practice. This separation of law from the humanistic and philosophic grounds of the university has led to a substantially separate system of legal knowledge in the Anglo-American world, in both the profession and legal education, reflected in the specialization of law libraries and the limited legal collections in libraries where there is not a law school. There is a separate world of publication, circulation, use, and even radically different citation. Much of legal education has to do with navigating, interpreting, and applying this alternative documentary system for purposes of communicating, staking claims, and adjudicating within this textualized world that regulates rights and obligations in the material and social world of daily life (see chap, 8, this volume).

Commercial growth also made commercial information more valuable. Although the keeping of financial records was as ancient as writing (see chap. 1, this volume), only in 14th-century Italy did the rights of private ownership, volume of trade and capital, and the development of money and financial instruments (see chap. 6, this volume), combined with advances in arithmetic, come together in the new advance of double-entry bookkeeping (attributed to Benedetto Cotrugli and widely disseminated through the 1494 treatise of Luca Pacioli), which is generally taken to be the founding of the accountancy profession (Littleton, 1933). Proprietary financial information generally stayed with the commercial venture or estate of the wealthy person except for government intervention or regulation, particularly with the rise of publicly traded corporate stock in the 18th and 20th centuries. In the last two centuries, to keep track of the complexities of large corporations and geographically dispersed enterprises new modes of knowledge organization (first the pigeonhole desk, then the file folder and the filing cabinet, then electronic storage and retrieval), new means of inscription and reproduction (typewriter, rexograph, and punch card and data entry systems), and new genres (memo, report, corporate charts, and databases) were invented (Yates, 1989, 2005).

New commerce also required information about foreign markets and trade at urban centers. The earliest newspapers in England in the early 17th century arose out of letters by agents circulating information about commercial markets to gentry in the provinces (Andrews, 1968; Bourne, 1887; Raymond, 1996). The Fugger family in Europe also had a chain of correspondents to provide commercial news (Sommerville, 1996). From these arose the earliest newspapers (see chap. 13, this volume), and ever since newspapers have had a strong component of business and financial news, whether reports of sailings and arrivals, latest market prices, or corporate restructurings. With industrial and corporate and financial market growth in more recent centuries, a robust specialized financial and industrial journalism has developed, often organized around industries and job categories. Market prices have come to be seen as valuable information. With the need for instantaneous knowledge, such markets have become the sites of the development of new communicative and information technologies, whether the ticker tape of the late 19th century or the Internet a century later.

Knowledge of the specific arts on which commerce was based also became of great value. The origins of technical writing have been traced to the printed books of instruction in practical arts farming, silkworm production, beekeeping, estate management, home management, and cooking that appeared in the Renaissance (Brockmann, 1998; Tebeaux, 1997). In the medieval period, many of the practical crafts and arts were held as orally transmitted secrets within the guild system. But some of the arts were so complex as to require extensive documents closely held among the adept, such as apothecaries and herbalists, lens makers, and alchemists.

Another means of maintaining monopoly was a royal letter of patent, granted to guilds and individuals. In England in 1624, the royal abuse of such grants was restricted, leaving only the possibility of temporary monopoly for the inventor of a new good. This led to the development of the modern system of patent, whereby new inventions are registered and made public in return for a temporary monopoly (now 14 years; Bugbee, 1967; Federico, 1929). By the 19th century, all patents were published and made widely available in national repositories. The archives of the patents have become an organized body of knowledge to be consulted in the preparation of new patents and in litigation involving patent rights. Currently, patent applications include a review of prior art as revealed in the patent archives. During the 19th century, a series of treaties coordinated the patent systems of many countries, culminating in the 1883 Paris Convention for the Protection of Industrial Property and revised periodically since then. It now is signed by 169 nations, with more than 150,000 patents granted annually, over half emanating from the United States.

With the Industrial Revolution and the formation of large corporations, technological and industrial development became closely intertwined; currently about 85% of patents are granted to corporations. Control is exerted more through a constant flow of new patents than by secrecy. Nonetheless, papers presenting industrially sponsored scientific work that has not yet eventuated in patent ownership often are restricted in publication and distribution. Particularly, the emergence of the biotech industry in partnership with universities has raised questions about restrictions of scientific publication, hampering scientific advance and sheltering embargoed work from peer criticism and evaluation of the work (Etzkowitz, Webster, & Healey, 1998; Lievrouw, 2004).

One final wrinkle on this subject has been the recognition that information and knowledge themselves are commercially valuable commodities, especially as we move into what has been called an information economy. The economic value of texts was established by the extension of patent monopoly to copyright in the 18th century. As the length of the copyright monopoly has been extended, largely under an ideology of author's rights, more extended ownership of the knowledge instantiated in texts has been made possible, and ownership has aggregated in publishing houses. As modern society has become more dependent on knowledge, the economic value of many sorts of information and the texts that bear them has increased, particularly with the advent of electronic communication and the Internet, so that the purchaser may gain only transient use of the purchased knowledge product, the permanent and authoritative copy of which still resides solely in the possession of the owner. We are starting to see the consequences in industry and the academy as a few corporations are gaining ownership of large segments of the knowledge our society depends on.

KNOWLEDGE OF EXPLORATION, COLONIES, AND NATIONS

During the 15th and 16th centuries, other knowledges moved from the universities out into the world. The age of exploration expanded the need for astronomy, the arts of navigation, and map making; geographic documents were spread by the growing print industry (Ruegg, 1996). Exploration and trade also brought natural and cultural wonders from around the world, collected in wonder cabinets, and illustrated and described in volumes (Impey & Macgregor, 1985). Colonial conquest created needs for documentary control of the colonies, with such results as the Archivo General de Indias in Seville becoming the repository for more than 45 million documents from the Spanish colonization of the new world. The colonial archives of the various European empires contained geographical, geological, mineralogical, anthropological, botanic, zoological, agricultural, and economic knowledge, as well as political and legal documents defining the colonial order and economic exploitation. This massive expansion of recorded knowledge of the world, however, was accessible only to ruling elites, of the church, the throne, or commercial organizations.

Within Europe, expanding commerce combined with print images, descriptions, and tales to increase knowledge of the peoples, customs, lands, and arrangements throughout the continent. This knowledge of human, geographic, zoologic, and botanic variety also expanded national and regional awareness (Eisenstein, 1979). Knowledge of national histories and national cultures, including literatures, became important forms of citizenship identification and affiliation (Anderson, 1983; Helgerson, 1992). In the later 19th century and 20th century, such knowledge entered curricula of schooling and universities.

As the publications and knowledge of each nation came to be understood as part of the heritage and vitality (economic, cultural, and spiritual of each region), the language of publication switched from Latin, the previous international language of scholarship, to the local national vernacular. This had been largely accomplished in the 17th century, and was typically followed by a movement for standardization and purification of the prestige dialects of the national capitals used in publication. This once again provided motive and tasks for further development of linguistic knowledge, with a prescriptive intent. In 1612, the Florentine Accademia della Crusca published its *Vocabulario della Crusca*, helping define the Italian language. In 1647, Claude Favre de Vaugelas, an early member of the Académie Française, published his influential *Remarques sur la langue française*. And in 1755, Samuel Johnson's *Dictionary of the English Language* attempted to regularize English. Each established a standard for publication and editorial improvement. The languages became associated with national genius, and knowledge of them became marks of refinement and dedication to the culture so that each nation that wanted to achieve full status would need to produce its monumental dictionary, such as Noah Webster's *American Dictionary of the English Language* in 1828 and the Grimm brothers' *Deutsches Wörterbuch* begun in 1838 but not finished until 1960. Advancement of knowledge of national languages as well as the national cultures and literatures produced within them became a matter for state support (McArthur, 1986). To this day, nationalist movements are often accompanied by attempts to revivify and purify a national language, to spread literacy in it, and to create familiarity with the texts considered the national heritage.

Access to texts of the classical world inspired visual, architectural, and verbal arts on ancient models as well as provided models for the political revolutions to follow in the 17th and 18th centuries. Starting with the Puritan Revolution in England, formation of states became increasingly based on philosophic grounds. Texts of political and social philosophy became widely circulated controversial documents, as societies sought for the grounds of order outside church doctrine or monarchical authority. Hobbes, Locke, Hume, Montaigne, and Rousseau, among others, pervaded a new public sphere that sought explicit rational justifications and designs for their constitutions, most notably during the American and French Revolutions. Each of these new political formations created institutions for the advance of knowledge, as well as the collection and distribution of texts (Fliegelman, 1993; Warner, 1990).

Though this age of political thought was fostered in an international climate of freedom and exchange, this movement was to become fractured by national identities and national languages. Consequently, distinctive national traditions, affecting what scholars were likely to read, developed in philosophy, humanities, and social thought—and even to some degrees the natural sciences (see e.g., Guerlac, 1981). Furthermore, insofar as scholarship remained international, competition ensued to be the leading language in any area of study, with French and German each having domains of dominance until the general dominance of English from the middle of the 20th century on. This language situation, in turn, led to an expectation that any person of learning (even in areas of little language contact, as in the United States) needed familiarity with several European languages. This expectation still resides in undergraduate and graduate language requirements, though now reinterpreted through business and cultural-diversity motives.

PRINT AND THE FORMATION OF SCIENCE

Science, previously called natural philosophy, is closely associated with consequences of the printing press: easier access to classic texts; wide and rapid dissemination of new data, observations, and theories; the reproduction of exact descriptions, tables, illustrations, and maps that allowed the comparison and aggregation of astronomic, geographic, botanic, zoological, and anatomic data; the impetus to criticism, commentary, taxonomy, and theory based on the access to multiple sources that then could be compared to new results; and the impetus for improved maps, illustrations, tables, and taxonomies to meet the book-buying market (Eisenstein, 1979). Publishers were instrumental in creating cultures of trust that allowed readers to rely on the authority of editions untainted by piracy and other forms of immorality and amorality (Johns, 1998). Although universities, scriptoria, and monasteries formed communities of trust within which books could be selected, shared, interpreted, and evaluated, the proliferation of copies of printed books seemed to set them free of social context, which needed to be re-created around the networks of publishers, authors, collectors, and sponsors. These new communities of knowledge, communicating across national and religious boundaries, challenged the authority and legitimacy of at least one state, England, in the 17th century (Shapin & Schaffer, 1985), and the restored monarchy needed to position itself warily with respect to natural philosophic inquiry, which it sequestered apart from public discourses of faith and royal legitimacy (Jacob, 1976).

In urban areas where new learning thrived outside the walls of universities or government, societies of learned people formed to share their readings, thoughts, and discoveries, as well as to support and criticize their new claims to knowledge. These societies, often enjoying patronage of rich families or royalty, became the centers of learning. The Scholarly Societies Project (http://www.scholarly-societies.org) has identified 30 such societies prior to 1600. The earliest that specifically turned its attention to natural philosophy appears to be the Accademia dei Segreti founded by Giambattista della Porta in 1560 in Naples and lasting 20 years until shut down by ecclesiastical opposition. Among the other early scientific societies were the Accademia dei Lincei in Rome (1603–1630), Accademia degli Investiganti (ca. 1650–1670 in Naples), and the Accademia del Cimento (1657–1667 in Florence). In 1660, the Royal Society of London, the oldest scientific society in continuous existence, were organized from a series of informal meetings. At first, communication among scientists across Europe was facilitated by active letter writing with some individuals becoming the centers of correspondence, such as Marin Mersenne (whose correspondents were to form the basis of the Académie Royale des Sciences) and Henry Oldenburg (who was secretary of the Royal Society of London). Out of these two networks were to form in 1665 the first scientific journals, *Journal de Scavans* and the *Philosophical Transactions of the Royal Society*. Although the earliest journal issues carried the trappings of letter correspondence, this was to rapidly evolve into distinctive authored articles. An illustrated overview of the history of scientific journals can be found at http://www.fathom.com/course/21701730/index.html (see also Kronick, 1976, for a catalog of early scientific journals). By 1790, more than 1,000 scientific journals had appeared, at least briefly, of which three fourths presented original contributions and/or were society proceedings (Kronick, 1976). Currently the Scholarly Societies Project indexes more than 4,000 societies.

The interest in nature was coupled by a desire for language appropriate for communicating about nature. The wide availability of detailed descriptions and illustrations of botanic species, for example, vexed prior taxonomy, as principles were needed to aggregate and organize these many species in collections (Slaughter, 1982). Bacon in *The Advancement of Learning* argued that we often mistake words for things and lose sight of the things themselves; words come to us filled with unconsidered and unsubstantiated associations; and words sometimes name things that do not exist or that are ill-defined. Bacon expressed a desire for a method of notation that would not be deluded by what he called the Idol of the Marketplace. His critique inspired projects for universal languages that could be used to record and organize all knowledge in its true form—the best known of which is Bishop Wilkins's *Essay Towards a Real Character and a Philosophic Language*. Bacon's description of Solomon's house in the *Novum Organum* set out a communal project for the gathering, inscription, and interpreting of knowledge of nature that inspired the Royal Society. Thomas Sprat's 1667 hyperbolic description of *The History of the Royal Society* sees language purification at the heart of the society's project. Despite hopes for a language that transcended rhetoric, scientific writing was always to remain persuasive and argumentative (Pera, 1994; Pera & Shea, 1991), but the grounds of the argument were to shift to accounts of empirical experience (Bazerman, 1988; Dear, 1985). A plainer style, less reliant on ornaments, was to influence pages of the new scientific journals. Nonetheless, figures of speech and thought (such as antithesis, series, and repetition) were to remain an essential part of scientific writing (Fahnestock, 1999).

Journal publication and society meetings created new forums for scientific arguments that had previously been published in books that were publicly contestable only years later in new books. Further books contained such a myriad of details and claims that it would be difficult to focus a specific disagreement across books. At society meetings, such as at the Royal Society, however, the heart of the argument was a physical demonstration of an empirical reality. As such, much effort went into the creation of apparatus that could experimentally demonstrate phenomena (Shapin & Schaffer, 1985). Issues of detail could be directly debated. Furthermore, the rapid response available in journals allowed for controversies to be argued with many rounds of responses. But as journals could contain only accounts of demonstrations, to be read by distant audiences, the credibility of the witnesses and the impressiveness of the described apparatus carried persuasive value. At first, credibility drew on earlier social resources for gentlemanly credibility, but over time scientific expertise became the source of credibility (Shapin, 1994). Credibility also came to be enhanced by the scientific credibility of the editor of the journal and the people who were to assist in the evaluation, criticism, and selection of the articles in what emerged as a system of referees by the mid-18th century. These social changes were accompanied by transformation of a more gentlemanly style for a more overtly contestative and professional one (Atkinson, 1999; Gross, Harmon, & Reidy, 2002), expressing evaluations through facts, use of the literature, and irony, rather than overt first-person judgments (Gunnarsson, 2001; Myers, 1989, 1990a). This professional discourse had unique features that set it apart from languages in other social domains and made it increasing difficult for nonspecialist and amateur reading (Batalio, 1998; Halliday & Martin, 1993). Differing historical, social, cultural, and economic circumstances in different countries led to distinct kinds of journals and forms of articles (Gross et al., 2002; Gunnarsson, 1997).

Controversy was to erupt on the pages of the journal as natural philosophers questioned each other's results. More detailed accounts of the conditions and actions that led to the results soon followed, as did quantification and precision in reporting the results. More extensive reasoning connecting theory and research design and results led to theoretical claims being supported through experimental and other methodologically focused empirical evidence (Bazerman, 1988). Changing ideological beliefs about the value of collective experiences along with the mounting accumulation of empirical results led to the development of modern practices of citation and reviews of literature in the latter part of the 18th century (Bazerman, 1991). Many of the rewards and values associated with participation in science developed in conjunction with journal publication and served to reinforce participation within the journal system (Bazerman, 1988; Merton, 1973). Recurrent violation of these values in terms of misrepresentation of parts of the experiments and results, plagiarism, lack of supervision, collusion, or self-delusion serves to illustrate how strongly rewards are tied to values and the periodic scandals and calls for self-policing indicate how much hangs on the reliability of the system threatened by such acts (Broad & Wade, 1982; LaFollette, 1992). The current increasing alliance among government, industry, and science presents challenges to the kind of open communication of results and debate that is at the heart of scientific evaluation.

The systems of publication and authorship grew hand in hand with the formation of modern science: emerging forms of journal publication focused and directed the work of scientists aiming to contribute; roles of editors, critical readers, and referees emerged around journal production; communal values became formulated around the publication process; and the literature came to stand for the accumulated accomplishment of the sciences. Within that simultaneously cooperative and agonistic social system, the concept of the individual scientific authorship to be granted credit and reward arose along with accountability for claims (Merton, 1973), although authorship is now being transformed through the emergence of large collaborative science (Biagioli & Galison, 2003). Furthermore, within the social organization of reviewing, criticism, publication, and uptake, even the singly authored article is a social accomplishment (Myers, 1990b).

As sciences expanded and proved useful for many activities, in the late 18th and early 19th centuries, scientific specialties, societies, and journals proliferated, at first in England. The Society of Civil Engineers was founded in 1771 and became the Institution of Civil Engineers in 1818; the Entomological Society, 1806; the Geological Society, 1807; the Royal Astronomical Society, 1820; the Zoological Society of London, 1826; and the Chemical Society of London in 1841. Specialized societies on the continent soon followed. The membership of these societies was military engineers and officers, other government employees, and employees of industry. The proliferation of these societies continues to this day, although since the late 19th century membership has shifted to academics. Johnson (2006), using as example the charcoal iron industry in the United States between 1760 and 1860, examines the process by which embodied technological practices become professionalized by written technical communication.

Whereas since the early years of printing in the West, the new knowledge being published was to some degree read by more popular audiences than it was intended for (Chartier, 1987). In the 18th century reliance of industry and social progress on science created a substantial popular audience for the dissemination of knowledge and self-improvement. Encyclopedias and other reference volumes began being written for this audience (Darnton, 1979; see also chap. 11, this volume). In the mid-19th century, with decreasing print and paper costs, nonspecialist and industry journals presented the latest in science and technology along with basic instruction, such as *Scientific American* founded in 1845. Bazerman (1999) documents such developments in the United States around the telegraphic and electrical industries. The fields of popular science writing and science journalism have thrived since then and now have their own societies and forms of professional training, including specializations in medical and health writing, nature writing, and environmental writing. Also, many divisions of technical and professional writing have developed to serve the internal needs of knowledge-reliant disciplines (see chap. 14, this volume).

In the 19th and early 20th centuries, specialized knowledge became important for public-policy decisions, corporate and financial planning, and analysis of social problems accompanying urban industrialization. Quantification became useful for representing projects, problems, and various aggregate states of affairs. Writing about economics, markets, bureaucratic policy, public works, insurance, and social problems took on an increasing statistical and mathematical character. Ted Porter (1986, 1995) argues that quantification was a persuasive rhetorical tactic, giving an appearance of objectivity to controversial policies and advancing the authority of forms of expertise.

MILITARY KNOWLEDGE

The military has long seen knowledge as providing strategic advantage and has long been producer and consumer of knowledge. In ancient India, veterinary science developed to treat militarily important horses and elephants. Egyptian documents, in another example, list logistic support for specific campaigns (Gardiner, 1964). Manuals of military strategy date back at least to Sun Tzu's *Art of War* (ca. 500 BCE), with other notable Chinese martial manuals being Chiang Chi's *The Myriad Stratagems* (ca. 225 CE), Li Chüan's *Manual of the Martial Planet* (759 CE), and Tsêng Kung-Liang's *Collection of Military Techniques* (1044 CE). In the West, histories such as of Thucydides, Caesar, and Tacitus contained information on tactics and strategy, as well as glorification of the leaders and forces. Dedicated manuals of war in the West date back to Frontinus' *Strategemata* from the latter part of first century CE and Arrian's *Ars Tactica* in the early second century.

Although much military technology was embodied in unwritten and secret craftwork, the political conditions of Europe in the latter Middle Ages and Renaissance encouraged the production and distribution of military knowledge. Nations in frequent conflict on economic, national, and religious grounds created a distributed market for military books. The first printed book on fortifications (e.g., Albrect Durer's 1527 *Etliche Unterricht zu Befestigung der Stett, Schloss und Flecken Nürnberg*) arose within the highly contested world of Germany. Italy was also a site of fortification technology. Treatises on shipbuilding technology, of importance for military and colonial conquest, date from Mathew Baker's work circa 1580. Gunnery and ballistics was a strong motive in the development of mechanics from the time of Galileo and Thomas Harriot in the early 17th century, although useful practical calculations that incorporated air resistance were not available until the 20th century.

As science demonstrated its military potential, governments began to enlist it to produce new weapons, as when the bureaucracy of the French revolutionary government in 1793 authorized the chemist Claude Louis Berthohellet to develop secret explosives (Gillispie, 1992). This case exemplified several of the features of texts that were to recur in the alliance of government and science. First, government and bureaucratic documentary systems intersected with science in the authorization, funding, and accountability for the project. Bureaucratic texts authorized the initial allocation of resources for facilities and materials, and granted permission for scientists to go forward. Routine meeting minutes, policy statements, injury reports, and descriptions of employees were documented. Letters within the government, between ministers and ministries, and with Berthohellet, were crucial in project development, administration, and monitoring. Tests, reports, diagrams, and descriptions of accomplishments all flowed from the researchers back to the bureaucracy. Second, the projects were initiated by scientists, in the initial scientific papers and communications with the government about military potential. Third, much of the crucial information was kept secret: that concerning government decisions and operations; substance of the scientific advance; details of the technology design, operations, and testing; and deployment. Fourth, public access to knowledge was limited or delayed, though some scientific papers and patents resulted. Descriptions of new tactics made people aware of the existence of the knowledge and its consequences but not the detailed substance, with a consequence for perceptions of security, fear, and national strength. This limited knowledge also restricted the open scientific advance. Over time, more information became available through declassification of documents, personal accounts, and the science advancing to the point where the technology became more obvious. Fifth, a further series of documents arose concerning use and maintenance of the technology, much of it remaining secret within the military. Sixth, documents tied industry to both the government and scientists, defining financial arrangements for manufacture, knowledge of the technology, and procedures of production. Finally, the massiveness of the undertaking and its bureaucratic organization meant that it required regular government attention.

Advances in cartography, communication and transportation (such as telegraphy and rail), propulsion (steam and internal combustion), armaments (such as the machine gun), and shipbuilding (ironclads and steampower) were of military interest. Engineers became important members of the military, with military education often leading engineering education and the formation of professional engineering societies, as in the founding of the British Society of Civil Engineers in 1771 (Watson, 1989), its successor Institution of Civil Engineers in 1818, the Royal Swedish Academy of War Sciences in 1796, and the British Society of Telegraph Engineers in 1871.

During World War I, the military, both axis and allied, became interested in applications of new technologies, and industry saw potential profit in producing new means of war. In the United States, this alliance of industry, science, and the military manifested itself in two new government civilian agencies: the Naval Consulting Board and the National Research Council (Hughes, 1989). The chemist Haber persuaded an initially reluctant German military to pursue chemical weapons, but once the military understood the character of trench warfare, it became committed to the weapon, as did all the major axis and allied powers. By the end of the war, more than 1,500 university-trained scientists and around 4,000 scientists with lesser qualifications were engaged in chemical warfare-related research on all sides. These researchers generated "an enormous mass of paper on the details of offensive warfare" (Haber, 1986, p. 107). The complex production of documents followed much as in the gunpowder case of a century before, with a few new wrinkles. First, the massiveness of the project meant greater planning and centralization with the formation of several large government-sponsored laboratories, which themselves required management and planning documents. Second, industry was drawn into the planning, production, and secrecy processes. Third, a closer communication between technologic knowledge and its field uses developed, with a consequence that field experience identified specific knowledge needs the scientists needed to fulfill. Fourth, scientists saw that the development and funding of military technology would not be of benefit just to the nation but to the general funding of science. As the size and complexity of the project grew, the aggregation of existing knowledge in literature reviews also identified application opportunities and needs for knowledge. Finally, the production of knowledge became so extensive as to make useful the production of secret bulletins and journals that circulated among the scientists on each side; in fact, these journals fell into the hands of enemy counterparts, so that there was a scientific literature known to the military scientists of both sides, but secret from the public and nonmilitary-engaged scientists.

From the beginning of World War II, both sides invested heavily in technological development. Nuclear weaponry, which both sides worked on, was the most dramatic, with its realization marking the end of the war. Major advances also occurred in aviation and rocketry, aerial bombing, motorized vehicles and tanks, radar and other telemetry, encryption, and computing. The last three specifically concerned the production, communication, and management of information, laying the groundwork for many postwar developments in information technologies. All these technologies involved massive research, development, and design operations with the same kind of documentary support seen in the earlier instances of explosives and chemical warfare. Furthermore, like chemical warfare, all except the most secret operations of nuclear weaponry and cryptography involved major industrial partners. The two exceptions involved major collaboration between the military and academic scientists. At the war's end, academic scientists had achieved higher status in the eyes of governmental and industrial leaders, and money poured into university-based research projects, which would coalesce in the ensuing years as a military–industrial–academic complex. In U.S. President Eisenhower's farewell address, his well-known warning about the military–industrial complex, it should be noted, is immediately followed by a warning about scientific research becoming beholden to government contract (Eisenhower, 1961). Currently, most academic research in the United States is funded by the federal government, with about 60% of it, on average, being defense related. Much of those funds are administered by the Department of Defense, which has developed an elaborate congressionally regulated system for developing projects, calling for and receiving proposals, and forming contracts with academic and industrial vendors. This system forms tight communicative relations among universities, corporations, and the military (Van Nostrand, 1997).

The American Vannevar Bush's engagement with these developments is iconic. After serving during World War I on the National Research Council, Bush became a professor of electrical engineering at the Massachusetts Institute of Technology and was a cofounder of the electronic equipment manufacturer, the American Appliance Company, soon renamed Raytheon after its first successful product. In 1939, as war broke out in Europe, he was named chair of the National Advisory Committee on Aeronautics. The year after, he became chair of the National Defense Research Committee, and in 1941 the director of the Office of Scientific Research and Development, which oversaw wartime scientific research, including the Manhattan Project to develop the atomic bomb. Out of that war experience of managing such massive knowledge-based projects, he wrote two documents making proposals that were to fundamentally change the production and distribution of knowledge. First, and most directly, "Science, the Endless Frontier," a 1945 report prepared at the request of President Roosevelt, articulated the role of scientific development in both national security and industrial prosperity, and led to the formation in 1950 of the National Science Foundation (NSF). The second, an article "As We May Think" in the June 1945 *Atlantic Monthly*, proposed a device for managing microfilm information called the Memex, which inspired the development of hypertext and underlay the design of the World Wide Web.

In the ensuing cold war, continuing relationships among science, the military, and industry became institutionalized. Whereas previously military engagement with science had been limited to wartime mobilization, a state of permanent warfare made the military an enduring partner with science. Furthermore, as scientifically based military technology was produced by private manufacturers, this system of knowledge production became deeply intertwined with the interests of corporations. At the end of the war and as the cold war emerged, secrecy issues surrounding nuclear weaponry came to a head in the United States. Scientists argued that all wartime restrictions imposed on the communication of scientific knowledge should be lifted and all discoveries be made part of the open scientific literature, both to support scientific advance and to allow informed civilian democratic decision making over the future of nuclear weaponry. The military and government argued for continuing secrecy in the name of national security. The resulting compromise provided only limited public access and civilian oversight through the Atomic Energy Commission. Public stakes in access to knowledge became evident as concern grew in the early 1950s over fallout from hydrogen bomb tests. In response to the government not providing sufficient details to satisfy citizens' concerns, a popular movement was initiated by the St. Louis Citizen's Committee for Nuclear Information to develop independent scientific information in the public interest. Out of this movement grew networks of scientifically based publications directed toward issues of public concern, around which advocacy movements have formed, including environmentalism (Bazerman, 2001). Issues of community access to independently produced knowledge as well as to the knowledge produced and used by governments have become heightened as more aspects of the information society are viewed as matters of national security.

THE MODERN RESEARCH UNIVERSITY

Although some creators of knowledge in the 15th through 18th centuries were university trained and held university posts, the main advances occurred outside universities and were largely disseminated outside university networks. Galileo is a case in point; although studying medicine at the University of Pisa, he left without a degree to study mathematics under a military engineer. He then taught mathematics, astronomy, mechanics, and fortification in the cities of Siena, Pisa, and Padua, but only in part at universities. He left universities entirely when he gained the patronage of the Medicis.

Gradually, several universities made some curricular adjustments and hosted chairs in new specialisms (such as the Lucasian Chair in Mathematics that Newton occupied at Cambridge), yet the university curriculum generally remained conservative, aimed at the moral formation and intellectual discipline of leadership classes, principally clergy, lawyers, and physicians. The Reformation did not bring secularization, autonomy, or research to the university, but only changed the religious auspices, to which national sponsorship was sometime added. The largest exceptions were the 18th-century Scottish universities, with secular charters and the dissident academies in England (although not fully accredited universities) that provided practical education for emerging business classes. Also, some higher education for practical professions developed in the service of governments, as with the British military academy at Sandhurst.

In France, the Enlightenment, Revolution, and Napoleonic reorganization, abolishing the colleges of the *ancien régime*, created conditions for new secular professional schools. Research was, nonetheless, supported in nonuniversity institutes and centers, such as the botanic and zoological gardens. This model of reform held some influence over mid-19th-century universities elsewhere in Europe. Prussia, following the ideas of Kant, Fichte, Schliermacher, and Humboldt, developed another model of university reform at Göttingen, Halle, and Berlin based on scholarly research professorships and advanced research seminars and degrees. Whereas the professorships initially were in philosophy and theology, these soon became differentiated into philology, history, economics, and the sciences. This model spread to the rest of Germany, particularly after unification, as well as to Austria, Russia, and the rapidly expanding educational system of the United States. By the turn of the 20th century, it influenced the more traditional systems of England and southern Europe, as well as the French bureaucratic system (Charle, 2004; Ruegg, 2004).

The research university provided an institutional framework for the university to be again associated with the forefront of knowledge. Professors of theology such as Friederich Schleiermacher and Georg Frederich Creuzer turned to philology and textual studies, soon to be directed at classical texts and to contemporary languages and literatures, in part motivated by ideas of national heritages embodied in cultural works. Leopold Ranke, appointed to a professorship at Berlin in 1825, espoused a history grounded in archives, taking advantage of the new national archives being established, and set the terms for the foundation of the academic discipline. It should be noted that both philology and history, two of the core founding disciplines in the university, were founded on the study of texts. Furthermore, the pedagogic innovation of the seminar associated with the research university brought with it a disciplinary-based writing-to-learn pedagogy in the form of the seminar paper (Kruse, 2006).

Philosophers of political economy, society, human nature, and language also found employment in universities and turned their philosophical inquiries into empirical social sciences. German chairs in national or political economy were established in the mid-19th century, and by 1895 the London School of Economics was founded. Whereas Auguste Comte (1798–1857) was a public philosopher and never obtained an academic position, by the time of Durkheim (1858–1917), sociology was an academic profession and he was to found the first French academic journal in sociology in 1898. Wilhelm Wundt, appointed to a professorship in philosophy at Leipzig in 1875, laid the groundwork for academic experimental psychology, founding the first psychological experimental lab and the first journal of experimental psychology. In the 20th century, linguistics, anthropology, and political science were also to define themselves as modern scientific disciplines with distinctive networks of departments, societies, journals, and publications.

The French and German universities provided a particularly welcoming environment for mathematics and sciences. The French concern for practical arts led to large infusions of mathematics, chemistry, physics, and astronomy into university curricula. However, in France, much of the biological sciences research remained at nonuniversity government institutions, such as museums, gardens, and academies, where both Claude Bernal and Louis Pasteur were to work. The German research model fostered university sciences more broadly, fostering the careers of major researchers such as Franz Neumann, Gustav Kirchoff, Herman von Helmholtz, Max Planck, Justus von Liebig, and Robert Wilhelm Bunsen. The British and Scottish universities adopted a research focus in the latter half of the 19th century, with the institution of new professorships and laboratories—but not in time for such greats as Charles Darwin, Charles Lyell, and James Hutton, who supported and published their science privately. The initial debates over Darwin's theories were carried out in the public sphere, where they still in part remain, despite the robust growth of academic biology, which carries out a distinctively different discussion. Engineering education, fostered by industrial dependence on technology, was to be established within university curricula across Europe in the latter half of the 19th century. Scientific and technological journals also became increasingly professional throughout the 19th century.

WESTERN UNIVERSITIES, TEXTS, AND KNOWLEDGE GLOBALLY

As Europeans colonized the New World, they brought for themselves (although not for indigenous populations) traditional universities. The earliest colonial universities in the Spanish Americas were on the model of and chartered by the University of Salamanca, with the universities of Santo Domingo, Lima, and Mexico City all founded in the sixteenth century run by the Dominican order. By the early 19th century, about two dozen universities in the Spanish Americas educated clergy and elites. Only in the second half of the 20th century were Latin American universities to evolve more practical and research-based missions.

Anglophone North America took its models from Cambridge, with Harvard founded in 1636 and chartered in 1650, William and Mary founded in 1693, and Yale chartered in 1745, with others soon thereafter. After the American Revolution, these universities stayed much the same until the latter half of the 19th century, when two changes transformed them. First, in 1862, the Morrill Act granted states land to establish publicly funded secular universities aimed at advancing practical arts and industry. This widened access to higher education and established more practical ends of education (Veysey, 1965), creating different curricula and career paths for students related to agriculture, manufactures, and engineering. Second, the German research university model was enthusiastically imported along with the research-oriented PhD, and a redefined role of professor as publishing researcher. As faculties were reorganized along disciplinary departmental lines, researchers formed national organizations, published journals, and constituted research communities. The sciences also gained strength from engineering education, which required their courses. Economics and other social sciences, as well, formed as areas of professional expertise removed from amateur engagement in social-improvement projects (Furner, 1975). The humanities also reorganized along disciplinary lines, with a focus on philology and literary studies, leaving behind the practical concerns for communication and rhetoric (i.e., text production) that had previously dominated the humanities (Graff, 1987; Parker, 1967). Disciplinary majors, graduate degrees, and advanced specialized courses created markets for advanced specialized texts. After World War II, university student access again expanded, so that currently more than 15 million students are enrolled in higher education at any time and about 30% of the population has completed a 4-year degree. The accompanying expansion of the research enterprise, in large part funded by federal national security initiatives, has made U.S. universities the leading producers of international scientific publications.

Australia and New Zealand in the latter half of the 19th century, although still sparsely populated, also established British-style universities. Education in colonies other than these outposts of English and Spanish emigration, however, was not sponsored to the level of university. The single exception was in India, where the strong interest in Western education by Indian mercantile classes was satisfied by the founding of three universities (Calcutta, Bombay, and Madras) in 1857, only in the wake of the political unrest of the Indian Rebellion of that year. For the most part, students from the colonies had to travel to Europe for access to higher education, at a cost prohibitive to all but the highest elites (Shils & Roberts, 2004). Only in the closing years of colonialism did the European powers who ruled through Africa, the Middle East, and South and Southeast Asia make any but minimal gestures to providing higher education or bibliographic and archival resources. Even those late and limited gestures lacked the resources to foster serious research.

Nor for a long time did countries independent of European domination show more than limited interest in Western knowledge. China had contact with modern science, but undertook no fundamental institutional changes in education until the early 20th century. The Ottoman Empire banned the printing press from the 15th until the early 20th century, and in Istanbul a university was established only in 1900. Until the mid-19th century, Japan remained closed to the West, but founded Tokyo University in 1869 and the Imperial University of Kyoto in 1897 in a self-conscious process of modernization (Huff, 2003).

The mid-20th-century independence of former colonial nations marked the growth of national university systems throughout Asia, Latin America, the Middle East, and Africa with some attempt to expand access beyond elites. Though serving educational needs of these countries, these new universities have also provided the beginnings of research infrastructure producing knowledge of local value and expressing non-European perspectives, particularly in the social sciences and humanities, where disciplines are more closely tied to regional experiences (see Hayhoe & Pan, 2001; Porter & Ross, 2003).

KNOWLEDGE AND WRITING AT THE START OF THE 21ST CENTURY

The expansion of research universities worldwide in conjunction with the increasing reliance of all social domains on the production of knowledge has accelerated the growth of knowledge along disciplinary lines. The Web of Science currently indexes a selected sample of almost 10,000 significant journals across the arts and humanities, social sciences, and sciences. The relations among disciplines have become matters of issue, and interdisciplinary publication has become a major force in the last several decades (Klein, 1990), although disciplinary reintegration is limited (see e.g., Bazerman, 2005; Ceccarelli, 2001).

This rapid growth of scholarly and scientific publication has been accompanied by specialized genres and discourses, often obscure to educated people in other disciplines (MacDonald, 1994; Swales, 1998, 2004), and has increased the literacy demands of undergraduate and graduate students (Blakeslee, 2001; Prior, 1998), as the Writing Across the Curriculum movement and the related scholarship on writing in the disciplines has addressed (see chap. 22, this volume; see also Bazerman et al., 2005). Researchers in various fields have also critically examined their fields' writing practices. Anthropology, for example, has analyzed the legacies of colonialism in ethnographic writing and has been redirecting its discourses accordingly (Clifford & Marcus, 1986; Geertz, 1988). In economics, Weintraub (2002) has examined the mathematicization of discourse, and McCloskey (1985) has questioned whether that mathematicization has obscured argument over policy issues. Psychologists have come to question the role of language in framing psychological categories and the psychological subject (Graumann & Gergen, 1996; Shotter & Gergen, 1989; Soyland, 1994).

In the latter half of the 20th century, English became the dominant language of science and scholarship (Benfield & Howard, 2000), as well as the medium of instruction at many universities in countries where English is not the first language (Wilson, 2002). This has placed additional obstacles in the way of scholarship and learning in the non-Anglophone world and also challenges the development of other languages as vehicles for intellectual thought (Flowerdew, 1999; Swales, 2004). However, there are some indications that non-native English speakers are gaining support and presence in Anglophone journals (Flowerdew, 2001), and that scholars are making strategic and disciplinary choices about which work is of regional interest and best published in the local language (Peterson & Shaw, 2002).

Economic inequalities of nations that do not support the conditions necessary for the production of knowledge also challenge full participation in and access to knowledge (Canagarajah, 2002). Rising costs of commercially produced research publications have also affected access in both developing and developed worlds (Wellcome Trust, 2003). At the same time, desktop publication and the Internet are making possible new means of distribution of knowledge, crystallized in a movement for free, public, open access to scholarly publications (Chesler, 2004; Velterop, 2004). This is a period of ferment, and it is unclear what the system of scholarly publication and distribution will be within a few years. The electronic revolution has also increased the incorporation of graphic, audio, and other data, including dynamically accessible databases within research publications (Kostelnick & Hassett, 2003). This is leading to a changing definition of both the form and substance of contributions to knowledge, requiring new skills for writing and reading such texts, as well as sorting out and selecting from the mass of available information. Understanding and making strategic use of organizing tools, search engines, and selective interfaces are likely to be crucial research skills.

The greatest challenge to knowledge, its inscription, and its circulation may the great value that it has come to have. On one side is the recognition of its value by powerful institutions with interests in controlling production and access. As governments and military see knowledge and information as crucial to national security and as universities are increasingly supported by corporate providers with their own proprietary concerns for information secrecy and ownership, the texts bearing significant knowledge may not be available for public circulation, examination, and use. On the other side is the emergence of the modern university and the associated scholarly networks devoted to the open production and circulation of knowledge. Accordingly, people in the university community tend to hold values for knowledge, its evaluation, and use that are to some degree independent of political, governmental, economic, religious, national, or military concerns. To the degree the university as a research and educational community is able to maintain some autonomy, it will provide an alternative means to know the world and evaluate human actions, partisan only in its commitment to the advancement and distribution of knowledge.

REFERENCES

Anderson, B. (1983). *Forms of nationhood*. London: Verso.

Andrews, A. (1968). *The history of British journalism* (Vols. 1 & 2). London: Haskell House.

Atkinson, D. (1999). *Scientific discourse in sociohistorical context: The philosophical transactions of the Royal Society of London, 1675–1975*. Mahwah, NJ: Lawrence Erlbaum Associates.

Batalio, J. T. (1998). *The rhetoric of science in the evolution of American ornithological discourse*. Stamford, CT: Ablex.

Bazerman, C. (1988). *Shaping written knowledge: The genre and activity of the experimental article in science*. Madison: University of Wisconsin Press.

Bazerman C. (1991). How natural philosophers can cooperate. In C. Bazerman & J. Paradis (Eds.), *Textual dynamics of the professions* (pp. 13–44). Madison: University of Wisconsin Press.

Bazerman, C. (1993). Forums of validation and forms of knowledge: The magical rhetoric of Otto von Guericke's sulfur globe. *Configurations, 1*, 201–228.

Bazerman, C. (1999). *The languages of Edison's light*. Cambridge, MA: MIT Press.

Bazerman, C. (2001). Nuclear information: One rhetorical moment in the construction of the information age. *Written Communication, 18*, 259–295.

Bazerman, C. (2005). Practically human: The pragmatist project of the interdisciplinary journal *Psychiatry*. *Linguistics and the Human Sciences, 1*, 15–38.

Bazerman, C., et al. (2005). *Writing across the curriculum* (Reference Guides to Rhetoric and Composition). West Lafayette, IN: Parlor Press and WAC Clearinghouse.

Benfield, X., & Howard, X. (2000). The language of science. *European Journal of Cardo-Thoracic Surgery, 18*, 642–648.

Biagioli, M. (1993). *Galileo courtier: The practice of science in the culture of absolutism*. Chicago: University of Chicago Press.

Biagioli, M., & Galison, P. (Eds.). (2003). *Scientific authorship: Credit and intellectual property in science*. New York: Routledge.

Blakeslee, A. M. (2001). *Interacting with audiences: Social influences on the production of scientific writing*. Mahwah, NJ: Lawrence Erlbaum Associates.

Bourne, H. R. F. (1887). *English newspapers: Chapters in the history of journalism* (Vol. 2). London: Chatto & Windus.

Broad, W., & Wade, N. (1982). *Betrayers of the truth*. New York: Simon & Schuster.

Brockliss, L. (1996). Curricula. In Hilde de Ridder-Symoens (Ed.), *A history of the university* (Vol. 2, pp. 565–620). Cambridge, England: Cambridge University Press.

Brockmann, R. J. (1998). *From millwrights to shipwrights to the twenty-first century*. Cresskill, NJ: Hampton.

Bugbee, B. W. (1967). *Genesis of American patent and copyright law*. Washington, DC: Public Affairs Press.

Canagarajah, A. S. (2002). *A geopolitics of academic writing*. Pittsburgh: University of Pittsburgh Press.

Ceccarelli, L. (2001). *Shaping science with rhetoric: The cases of Dobzhansky, Schrodinger and Wilson*. Chicago: University of Chicago Press.

Charle, C. (2004). Patterns. In W. Ruegg (Ed.), *A history of the university* (Vol. 3, pp. 33–74). Cambridge, England: Cambridge University Press

Chartier, R. (1987). *The cultural uses of print in early modern France*. Princeton, NJ: Princeton University Press.

Chesler, A. (2004). Open access: A review of an emerging phenomenon. *Serials Review, 30*, 292–297.

Clifford, J., & Marcus, G. E. (Eds.). (1986). *Writing culture*. Berkeley: University of California Press.

Darnton, R. (1979). *The business of enlightenment: A publishing history of the Encyclopédie, 1775–1800*. Cambridge, MA: Belknap.

Dear, P. (1985). Totius in verba: Rhetoric and authority in the early royal society. *Isis, 76*, 145–161.

Durer, A. (1527). *Etliche Unterricht zu Befestigung der Stett, Schloss und Flecken* Nürnberg [Some instructions on the fortification of city castle and town]. Nürenberg

Eisenhower, D. D. (1961, January 17). *Farewell radio and television address to the American people*. Retrieved 3/16/2006, from http://www.eisenhower.archives.gov /farewell.htm

Eisenstein, E. L. (1979). *The printing press as an agent of change*. Cambridge, England: Cambridge University Press.

Etzkowitz, H., Webster, A., & Healey, P. (Eds.). (1998). *Capitalizing knowledge: New intersections of industry and academia*. Albany: State University of New York Press.

Evans, R. J. W. (1973). *Rudolf II and his world*. Oxford, England: Oxford University Press.

Fahnestock, J. (1999). *Rhetorical figures in science*. New York: Oxford University Press.

Federico, P. J. (1929). Origin and early history of patents. *Journal of the Patent Office Society, 11*, 292–305.

Fliegelman, J. (1993). *Declaring independence: Jefferson, natural language, and the culture of performance*. Palo Alto, CA: Stanford University Press.

Flowerdew, J. (1999). Problems in writing for scholarly publication in English: The case of Hong Kong. *Journal of Second Language Writing, 8*(3), 243–264.

Flowerdew, J. (2001). Attitudes of journal editors to non-native contributions. *TESOL Quarterly, 35*, 121–150.

Furner, M. (1975). *Advocacy and objectivity: A crisis in the professionalization of American social science, 1865–1903*. Lexington: University Press of Kentucky.

Garcia, A. (1991). The faculties of law. In H. de Ridder-Symoens (Ed.), *A history of the university* (Vol. 1, pp. 388–408). Cambridge, England: Cambridge University Press.

Gardiner, A. H. (1964). *Egyptian hieratic texts* (Part 1). Hildesheim, Germany: Georg Olms.

Geertz, C. (1988). *Works and lives: The anthropologist as author*. Stanford, CA: Stanford University Press.

Gillispie, C. C. (1992). Science and secret weapons development in revolutionary France, 1792–1804. *Historical Studies in the Physical and Biological Sciences, 23*, 35–152.

Goodwin, C. (1994). Professional vision. *American Anthropologist, 96*(3), 606–633.

Graff, G. (1987). *Professing literature: An institutional history*. Chicago: University of Chicago Press.

Grafton, A. (1991). *Defenders of the text: The traditions of scholarship in an age of science, 1450–1800*. Cambridge, MA: Harvard University Press.

Graumann, C. F., & Gergen, K. (Eds.). (1996). *Historical dimensions of psychological discourse*. Cambridge, England: Cambridge University Press.

Gross, A. G., Harmon, J. E., & Reidy, M. (2002). *Communicating science: The scientific article from the seventeenth century to the present*. New York: Oxford University Press.

Guerlac, H. (1981). *Newton on the continent*. Ithaca, NY: Cornell University Press.

Gunnarsson, B. L. (1997). On the sociohistorical construction of scientific discourse. In B. L. Gunnarsson, P. Linell, & B. Nordberg (Eds.), *The construction of professional discourse* (pp. 99–126). London: Longman.

Gunnarsson, B. L. (2001). Expressing criticism and evaluation during three centuries. *Journal of Historical Pragmatics, 2*, 115–139.

Haber, L. F. (1986). *The poisonous cloud: Chemical warfare in the First World War*. Oxford, England: Clarendon.

Halliday, M. A. K., & Martin, J. R. (1993). *Writing science: Literacy and discursive power*. London: Falmer.

Hayhoe, R., & Pan, J. (Eds.). (2001). *Knowledge across cultures*. Hong Kong: University of Hong Kong Press.

Helgerson, R. (1992). *Forms of nationhood: The Elizabethan writing of England*. Chicago: University of Chicago Press.

Huff, T. E. (2003). *The rise of early modern science: Islam, China, and the West*. Cambridge, England: Cambridge University Press.

Hughes, T. P. (1989). *American genesis: A century of invention and technological enthusiasm*. New York: Viking Penguin.

Impey, O., & MacGregor, A. (Eds.). (1985). *The origins of museums: The cabinet of curiosities in sixteenth- and seventeenth-century Europe*. Oxford, England: Oxford University Press.

Jacob, M. C. (1976). *The Newtonians and the English Revolution, 1689–1720*. Ithaca, NY: Cornell University Press.

Johns, A. (1998). *The nature of the book: Print and knowledge in the making*. Chicago: University of Chicago Press.

Johnson, C. S. (2006). Prediscursive technical communication in the early American iron industry. *Technical Communication Quarterly, 15*, 171–189.

Jones, R. F. (1965). *Ancients and moderns: A study of the background of the battle of the books* (2nd ed.). Berkeley: University of California Press.

Klein, J. T. (1990). *Interdisciplinarity: History, theory, and practice*. Detroit, MI: Wayne State University Press.

Kostelnick, C., & Hassett, M. (2003). *Shaping information: The rhetoric of visual conventions*. Carbondale: Southern Illinois University Press.

Kronick, D. A. (1976). *A history of scientific & technical periodicals: The origins and development of the scientific and technical press, 1665–1790*. Metuchen, NJ: Scarecrow.

Kruse, O. (2006). The origins of writing in the disciplines. *Written Communication, 23*(3), 331–352.

LaFollette, M. (1992). *Stealing into print: Fraud, plagiarism and misconduct in scientific publishing*. Berkeley: University of California Press.

Leff, G. (1991). The trivium and the three philosophies. In H. de Ridder-Symoens (Ed.), *A history of the university* (Vol. 1, pp. 307–336). Cambridge, England: Cambridge University Press.

Levine, J. M. (1991). *The battle of the books: History and literature in the Augustan Age*. Ithaca, NY: Cornell University Press.

Lievrouw, L. A. (2004). Biotechnology, intellectual property, and the prospects for scientific communication. In S. Barman (Ed.), *Biotechnology and communication: The meta-technologies of communication* (pp. 145–172). Mahwah, NJ: Lawrence Erlbaum Associates.

Littleton, A. C. (1933). *Accounting evolution to 1900*. New York: American Institute Publishing.

MacDonald, S. P. (1994). *Professional academic writing in the humanities and social sciences*. Carbondale: Southern Illinois University Press.

McArthur, T. (1986). *Worlds of reference: Lexicography, learning, and language from the clay tablet to the computer*. Cambridge, England: Cambridge University Press.

McCloskey, D. (1985). *The rhetoric of economics*. Madison: University of Wisconsin Press.

Merton, R. K. (1973). *The sociology of science: Theoretical and empirical investigations*. Chicago: University of Chicago Press.

Myers, G. (1989). The pragmatics of politeness in scientific articles. *Applied Linguistics, 10*, 1–35.

Myers, G. (1990a). The rhetoric of irony in academic writing. *Written Communication, 7*, 419–455.

Myers, G. (1990b). *Writing biology*. Madison: University of Wisconsin Press.

North, J. (1991). The Quadrivium. In H. de Ridder-Symoens (Ed.), *A history of the university* (Vol. 1, pp. 337–359). Cambridge, England: Cambridge University Press.

Parker, W. R. (1967). Where do English departments come from? *College English, 28*, 339–351.

Pedersen, O. (1996). Tradition and innovation. In H. de Ridder-Symoens (Ed.), *A history of the university* (Vol. 2, pp. 451–488). Cambridge, England: Cambridge University Press.

Pera, M. (1994). *The discourses of science*. Chicago: University of Chicago Press.

Pera, M., & Shea, W. (Eds.). (1991). *Persuading science: The art of scientific rhetoric*. Canton, MA: Science History Publishers.

Peterson, M., & Shaw, P. (2002). Language and disciplinary differences in a biliterate context. *World Englishes, 21*, 357–374.

Porter, T. M. (1986). *The rise of statistical thinking 1820–1900*. Princeton, NJ: Princeton University Press.

Porter, T. M. (1995). *Trust in numbers: The pursuit of objectivity in science and public life*. Princeton, NJ: Princeton University Press.

Porter, T. M., & Ross, D. (Eds.). (2003). *The Cambridge history of science: Vol. 7. The modern social sciences*. Cambridge, England: Cambridge University Press.

Prior, P. (1998). *Writing/disciplinarity*. Mahwah, NJ: Lawrence Erlbaum Associates.

Raymond, J. (1996). *The invention of the newspaper: English newsbooks, 1641–1649*. Oxford, England: Clarendon.

Ridder-Symoens, H. (1991). Mobility. In H. de Ridder-Symoens (Ed.), *A history of the university* (Vol. 1, pp. 280–304). Cambridge, England: Cambridge University Press.

Ruegg, W. (1996). Themes. In H. de Ridder-Symoens (Ed.), *A history of the university* (Vol. 2, pp. 3–42). Cambridge, England: Cambridge University Press.

Ruegg, W. (2004). Themes. In W. Ruegg (Ed.), *A history of the university* (Vol. 3, pp. 3–32). Cambridge, England: Cambridge University Press.

Schryer, C. F., Lingard, L., Spafford, M., & Garwood, K. (2002). Structure and agency in medical case presentations. In C. Bazerman & D. Russell (Eds.), *Writing selves/writing societies: Research from activity perspectives*. Fort Collins, CO: WAC Clearinghouse.

Schwinges, R. C. (1991). Admission. In H. de Ridder-Symoens (Ed.), *A history of the university* (Vol. 1, pp. 171–194). Cambridge, England: Cambridge University Press.

Shapin, S. (1994). *A social history of truth: Civility and science in seventeenth-century England*. Chicago: University of Chicago Press.

Shapin, S., & Schaffer, S. (1985). *Leviathan and the air-pump: Hobbes, Boyle, and the experimental life*. Princeton, NJ: Princeton University Press.

Shils, E., & Roberts, J. (2004). The diffusion of European models outside Europe. In W. Ruegg (Ed.), *A history of the university* (Vol. 3, pp. 163–230). Cambridge, England: Cambridge University Press.

Shotter, J., & Gergen, K. (Eds.). (1989). *Texts of identity*. London: Sage.

Siraisi, N. (1991). The faculty of medicine. In H. de Ridder-Symoens (Ed.), *A history of the university* (Vol. 1, pp. 360–387). Cambridge, England: Cambridge University Press.

Slaughter, M. M. (1982). *Universal languages and scientific taxonomy in the seventeenth century*. Cambridge, England: Cambridge University Press.

Sommerville, C. J. (1996). *The news revolution in England*. New York: Oxford University Press.

Soyland, A. J. (1994). *Psychology as metaphor*. London: Sage.

Swales, J. (1998). *Other floors, other voices: A textography of a small university building*. Mahway, NJ: Lawrence Erlbaum Associates.

Swales, J. (2004). *Research genres*. Cambridge, England: Cambridge University Press.

Tebeaux, E. (1997). *The emergence of a tradition: Technical writing in the English Renaissance, 1475–1640*. Amityville, NY: Baywood.

van Nostrand, A. D. (1997). *Fundable knowledge: The marketing of defense technology*. Mahwah, NJ: Lawrence Erlbaum Associates.

Velterop, J. (2004). Open access: Science publishing as science publishing should be. *Serials Review, 30*, 308–309.

Verger, J. (1991). Patterns. In H. de Ridder-Symoens (Ed.), *A history of the university* (Vol. 1, pp. 35–74). Cambridge, England: Cambridge University Press.

Veysey, L. R. (1965). *The emergence of the American university*. Chicago: University of Chicago Press.

Warner, M. (1990). *The letters of the Republic: Publication and the public sphere in eighteenth-century America*. Cambridge, MA: Harvard University Press.

Watson, G. (1989). *The smeatonians: The society of civil engineers*. London: Telford.

Weintraub, E. R. (2002). *How economics became a mathematical science*. Durham, NC: Duke University Press.

Wellcome Trust. (2003). *Economic analysis of scientific research publishing*. London: Author. Retrieved Oct. 25, 2004, from http://www.wellcome.ac.uk/scipublishing

Yates, J. (1989). *Control through communication*. Baltimore: Johns Hopkins University Press.

Yates, J. (2005). *Structuring the information age: Life insurance and information technology in the 20th century*. Baltimore: Johns Hopkins University Press.

CHAPTER 11

The Collection and Organization of Written Knowledge

Jack Andersen
Royal School of Library and Information Science
Copenhagen, Denmark

Writing makes social, cultural, and cognitive capital available for posterity. To this end, institutions such as archives and libraries have developed to collect, organize, and make synopses of knowledge. The earliest archives or libraries were affiliated with a palace, temple, or some kind of learning institution. State-funded public libraries, open to a general public, appeared later when widespread citizen education became an issue of national interest. This chapter takes a look at how different forms of collecting and organizing written knowledge historically have been carried out.

THE COLLECTION OF TEXTS IN THE ANCIENT WORLD

The archive is the product of state and governmental institutions using texts to document their activities, so as to legitimate their practices. Archives in ancient times consisted of clay tablets and papyri, depending on the geographical location. Ernst Posner (1972) enumerates six kinds of documents regularly in ancient archives: (a) the laws of the land; (b) records created and retained as evidence of past administrative action (e.g., the "royal skins" of the Persian kings or the registers of the popes); (c) financial and other accounting records to administer a ruler's domain and its resources (e.g., records of palace and temple economies of the ancient Near East); (d) records of the ruler or other authority to assure his income from land and people (e.g., land surveys, land records establishing legal ownership of areas of land, or records establishing tax obligations); (e) records facilitating control over people; and (f) notarial records of state agencies or state-authorized people.

Theses six invariants of ancient archives show an overt concern for control and documentation of activities by means of the administrative use of writing, as examined by Goody (1986). They stored and retrieved information, pursued state-authorized activities, and then provided a legitimating and preservative record, dialectically advancing new state activity. The use of writing in various forms of state and governmental activities created a need to store writings in order to be able to continue and maintain these activities.

Libraries have an historical origin connecting them with the activity of transmitting culture. Wright (1977) argues that the first Greek libraries emerged during the transition of the Greek culture from a primary oral culture to a culture based on a written tradition. The

Homeric tradition of oral transmission of culture and the library's mediation of written texts are similar in informational function despite their different cultural points of departure. Thereby, Wright (1977) points to how an understanding of the notion of libraries as storehouses of knowledge and experience for the purpose of out that oral societies also have means for preserving and transmitting cultural heritage (cf. Andersen, 2002). Nonetheless, the *activity* of writing transforms the organization, communication, and formation of knowledge. With writing, a textual space is created that allows for an externalization of the organization of knowledge. In primary oral cultures, organizing knowledge was restricted to the people possessing it and the oral genres they employed to communicate. The oral genres were at once a mode of communication *and* a mode of organizing the cultural and cognitive heritage of a particular culture and society, thus holding the position as a kind of an oral archive. With its capability of storing and recording more permanently the knowledge of a particular society, writing makes possible a separation of the communication and organization of knowledge. It creates different kinds of genres for organizing knowledge such as lists and tables (Goody, 1977, 1986).

BIBLIOGRAPHIES

Although the term *bibliography* is relatively new (see Blum, 1980, for a history of the term and the concept), the function dates back at least to the Greek collection at Alexandria. The Alexandrian library was the first to explicitly make lists of literature and authors (Blum, 1991) for purposes of acquisition, management, and textual criticism (Casson, 2001). Bibliographic writing at the Alexandrian library structured, produced, and shaped written literary and scholarly knowledge and contributed in this way to the core activities of the library. Thus, writing was both the substance collected and the means of management and organization.

The first director of the library was Zenodotus, said to have been the first to adopt alphabetization as a mode of organizing the library's collection (Casson, 2001). According to Blum (1991), however, Callimachus is the first bibliographer to exist because he created both a systematic bibliographical survey of Greek literature arranged in relation to literary form or scholarly disciplines and a list of the holdings of the Alexandrian library, the famous *Pinakes*. Callimachus divided writers into prose writers and poets. These two divisions were then divided according to subject groups, with authors arranged alphabetically in each group. Furthermore, a biographical account of the writers was followed by a list of their writings. This way of organizing writings has had a modeling effect to this day. Blum and others (e.g., Casson, 2001) consider the *Pinakes* the first systematic bibliography.

All this suggests alertness to the library's objective to promote culture and scholarship. Compared to a palace library such as Arshupanibal's library supporting the king, the Alexandrian library is the first library deliberately making texts and knowledge available for scholars affiliated with the library.

Besides the *Pinakes*, historians of bibliography also agree that Galen's, a court physician in the Rome of Marcus Aurelius, *De libris propriis liber* (a book about my own books), published in the second century, also represents a first form of bibliography (Besterman, 1968). In addition, many of the first bibliographies to appear were a combination of biographies of writers and a list of their writings, a biobibliography (Besterman, 1968; Blum, 1991), suggesting that the lives of writers were not yet viewed as separate from their literary productions.

Bibliography is referred here to by such terms as *compilation, description,* and *listing of books or literature* (see e.g., Besterman, 1968; Blum, 1980; Schneider, 1934). Whereas libraries and archives represent a response to textual activities by means of a physical location, bibliographies are not a response to textual activities in terms of a physical location. Rather, they may be considered a textual response to a textual activity. That is why bibliographies have been named *libraries without walls* (see Chartier, 1994). In fact, many bibliographies have invoked the notion of a library by including the term *bibliotheca* in their title—for instance, Konrad Gesner's famous bibliography, *Bibliotheca Universalis*, published in 1545. In most of Europe, bibliography was, up until the mid-19th century, part of what was named *historia litteraria* (Blum, 1980; Murray, 1917; Schneider, 1934; Woledge, 1983), an area concerned with the history of knowledge and of disciplines and their literature, not the history of belle lettres.

Thus, in the formation of knowledge, writing not only created a variety of written genres, but the writing activity also created a distinct genre that registers writings—that is, the bibliography. German historian of bibliography Georg Schneider recognized this when he stated that bibliography's relationship to human endeavor is to be understood only through publications (Schneider, 1934). This situates the understanding of bibliographies in connection with writing and the social, political, and intellectual activities that produce writings for their particular purpose(s). Besterman (1968) notes, for instance, that St. Jerome (fourth century CE), in his *De viris illustribus*, "looked upon his compilation as a piece of theological propaganda" (p. 9). At the beginning of his bibliography, St. Jerome pronounces, "his intention of showing the enemies of the church how many good writers she had already produced" (Balsamo, 1990, p. 8). Furthermore, Balsamo also points out that early bibliographies were "to supply information for cultural or other purposes, such as the defense of his own scientific worth in the case of Galen" (p. 8). Bibliographies seek to influence, persuade, and inform their reading audiences about the existence, value, and meaning of various forms of writings and their authors/producers.

INSTITUTIONS AND PRACTICES OF KNOWLEDGE WRITING AND DISSEMINATION IN THE EARLY WORLD

Long before the fall of Rome, monasteries began to appear in the eastern Mediterranean and North Africa, in many cases founded and driven by particular people. The earliest monastery library known was Coptic, founded by Pachomius (d. 346) in Tabennis in Egypt. Origen, theologian and biblical scholar, in 231 founded a school at Caesarea in Palestine containing a library of his work and other Christian literature (Humphreys, 1994). In Bethlehem, Jerome, as he founded a monastery, advised the monks to write in order to make available reading for other monks. The library collection was based on Jerome's own collection of Christian and biblical writings, which he used to produce a new Latin translation of the Bible (the Vulgate) (Humphreys, 1994).

By the fall and division of the Roman Empire in 395 CE, the *idea* of collecting writings for use, that is, the idea of a library, had been established and practiced for centuries, although the sponsorship had shifted from pagan elites to the Christian church. Christianity was in the beginning dependent on the literary heritage provided by the classical authors, as Christians had not yet produced adequate and acceptable literary substitutions. In addition, in order to make Christianity appealing to the literate pagan, Christians had to show that concepts provided by the new religion could be discussed as equal to the work of classical authors (Reynolds & Wilson, 1968). After the fourth century, classical literature and its dissemination faced a hard time as Christian libraries in churches and monasteries prioritized their limited storage capacity to preserve Bibles and theological and religious books. Pagan authors slowly disappeared and with them much Roman culture. On the European continent, St. Benedict's Monastery was founded in 529 at Monte Cassino, Italy. St. Benedict's rules required monks to read regularly, necessitating a collection of books in a library. Monks from Monte Cassino established monasteries throughout Western Europe on the basis of the Rules of St. Benedict, thereby advancing collections of books. These collections motivated the founding of scriptorias of professional copyists in a kind of writing factory (Humphreys, 1994).

Although classic texts were being lost in Western Christendom, library, learning, and collection activities flourished in the Byzantine Empire (Thompson, 1939/1967). The Emperor Diocletian is said to be the first to have founded an imperial library at Nicomedia around 300, but according to Harris (1995), little is known about it. The Roman Emperor Constantine Christianized Byzantium and with that followed an upsurge in the collection and preservation of Christian writings in the churches and monasteries of the eastern part of the Mediterranean. Between 330 and 336, Constantine established the Imperial Library in the capital of the Byzantine Empire, Constantinople. Constantine demanded that his agents search the Empire for Christian books, as well as Greek and Latin secular writings (Harris, 1995). This suggests an explicit motivation and interest in collecting writings.

The significance of Constantinople and its libraries in the production and dissemination of written knowledge is demonstrated with the compilation and codification of the Roman law code, The Justinian Code, which was done in Constantinople by the Emperor Justinian. The Justinian Code formed the *Corpus Juris Civilis,* which became "the basis of all civil law in western Europe throughout the Middle Ages and into the modern era" (Harris, 1995, p. 73). Such a compilation was, in effect, dependent on collections of law writings, Harris argues, because the compilation was produced by scholars appointed by Justinian summarizing and studies of nearly 2,000 volumes of legal works, including works going far back in Roman history. The effect of this work was further demonstrated with the establishment of a law school in Constantinople based on the *Corpus Juris Civilis.* The school turned later on into a legal university in the 11th century.

The rise of monasteries gave Christianity and its written mediation an institutionalized context vital to its practice. The work of writing was in these times, therefore, characterized by its sacred aura and was restricted to a limited number of literate people and institutions. The church was able to control what kind of knowledge was distributed and promoted, paradoxically managing to make illiterate people believe in the written word: the Bible. Jack Goody (1986) comments: "The Bible does not represent the writing down of an oral religion so as much as the creation of a literate one" (p. 39). In creating a literate religion, the church could subjugate the illiterate population through recitation of the recorded holy word. A challenge to this paradigm did not appear until the translation of the Bible into vernacular languages.

TEXTUAL INSTITUTIONS IN THE MUSLIM
WORLD AND CHINA

Christianity was not alone, however, in shaping knowledge by means of writing in the Mediterranean in this premodern period. Because it was obligatory for Muslims to know and study the Koran, literacy became a religious obligation and schools were founded. Furthermore, scholars and priests were needed and became affiliated with the mosques that were in charge of the institutions of higher education. Because Muslims were required not only to study the Koran, but also to make it available to others, a copying industry formed around the Koran. In connection with this, the first cultural and learning center of the Muslim world was founded in Damascus by the Umayyid dynasty, which was in power from 661 to 750 (Harris, 1995). This dynasty held an interest in learning and established a royal library that also contained the archives of the state and of the church (Harris, 1995). The archives were divided in circa 690 into two parts: a palace library with literary and religious works and a House of Archives. The palace library was open to use by students and scholars, and it obtained books from all parts of the known world by means of copying. Moreover, the Muslims also acquired Greek books from Constantinople through trade connections.

The apex of Muslim literature and learning was during Abbasid Caliphat, from circa 750 to 1050. Baghdad became the new capital of the Muslim world and it had both public and scholarly libraries. The former was open to those who could read. Cairo, in Egypt, had during the 10th and 12th centuries developed into a Muslim cultural center. Caliph al-Aziz

(975–996) established a royal library for the poets and scholars he protected. Consequently, a catalog of this and other libraries in Cairo were then compiled. In addition, subject bibliographies covering the then known branches of knowledge were also produced (Harris, 1995, p. 80).

As Islam spread to North Africa, to Sicily, and, in particular, to Spain and Portugal, learning centers with libraries were established. In particular, the cities of Cordoba, Sevilla, and Toledo became powerful centers of learning in the Mediterranean area. Cordoba had not only a noted Muslim university, but also several large libraries, including a royal library. In the 10th century, there were reported around 70 libraries in Muslim Spain. Private libraries also burgeoned in Muslim Spain, and Cordoba is said to have housed the largest book market in the Western world around this time (Harris, 1995). Muslim culture reached Sicily, Sardinia, and Corsica in the 9th and 10th centuries. From these islands, and from Spain, writings of translated classical authors, preserved by the Muslims, found their way to Western Europe. A significant characteristic of Muslim libraries was that they acquired almost anything except religions works of other faiths, including Greek and Latin classics, Sanskrit philosophy, Egyptian history, Hindu epics, and medieval French love poems, as well as scientific and biographical texts (Harris, 1995). This suggests a curiosity in and an appreciation for writing, much more so than in the Christian West. The Muslim preservation, organization, and dissemination of written knowledge, as well as the Muslim libraries and the trade through Constantinople, became the means by which these texts were reintroduced into Europe.

In early and premodern China, collections developed connected to the existence of the various dynasties. From the Shang dynasty (16th–11th century BCE), evidence suggests that the earliest written records were inscribed on oracle bones and bronzeware (Seymor, 1994). In the Chinese dynasties, the imperial libraries served as both archives and depositories of national literature. The primary intended audience of these libraries was the imperial family, high officials, and scholars. They were not open to the general public. It was only during the Song, Yuan, and Ming dynasties that the libraries gradually became open to students as well (Lin, 1998).

MEDIEVAL AND EARLY RENAISSANCE EUROPEAN TEXTUAL INSTITUTIONS

In Western Europe, Frankish Emperor Charlemagne (742–814), reflecting his interest in scholarship, began to gather books and learned men at his court. Charlemagne hired the influential English monk and scholar Alcuin (735–804) to run the school at his court in Aachen. Alcuin subsequently established the palace library, which permitted copying for other libraries, expanding holdings in France, Switzerland, and Germany. Furthermore, books from Italy and Spain were copied for the palace library (Johnson, 1966). These texts were copied in the new style of writing, the Carolingian minuscule. These collections, however, were eventually destroyed by the Danish and Viking invasions (Harris, 1995).

The monasteries faced a troubled time after the ninth century, and consequently their role in the production, distribution, use, and collection of books was reduced. Book collection now occurred in the cathedral, the headquarters for bishops or archbishops. Contrary to the rural monasteries, cathedrals were urban, with a different audience and a different purpose. Moreover, cathedral libraries also contained more secular books because cathedrals were also concerned with educational reading (Harris, 1995). However, the library collections of the cathedrals and monasteries up to the 13th century were not large and did not claim a separate room. Books were kept in book chests (*armariums*), small closets, or, in connection with the scriptoriums, the writing factories. A book market had not fully developed yet, and literacy was restricted to a few. This meant that library acquisitions in the medieval library were not systematic, but rather dependent on what was copied in the scriptorium, gifts, or occasional purchases (Harris, 1995). In the closing stages of the Middle Ages in the 14th and 15th centuries, the number of books in both cathedral and monastic libraries increased, resulting in the construction of separate library buildings. With independent library buildings, writing and written knowledge now had an explicit social and material context devoted to the organization of written knowledge.

The medieval university may be regarded as an outgrowth of the cathedral schools and learning centers (cf. Vickery, 2000). The scholars at the universities had their own book collections and students could borrow from these (Vickery, 2000). Students were, however, required to acquire authentic texts. For this purpose, the medieval universities created the *stationarii* to control the book trade and ensure the distribution and lending of authentic texts. The student groups, or nations, also owned books communally for shared use in the groups. But due to the emphasis on book learning, universities over time developed more elaborate libraries: "libraries that would not only preserve the heritage of the past but also open it up to general use" (Harris, 1995, p. 107). Medieval university libraries thus transformed collections from mere preservation to active use.

The collection of books in the early Renaissance differed from the prior epochs as private people rather than institutions were responsible for gathering books. The humanists were ardent book collectors and consequently many private libraries were established. Petrarch (1304–1374), one of the leading figures of the early Renaissance and the humanist movement, was known as an enthusiastic book collector and by the help of informants Petrarch gathered classical writings from all over Europe for his private library. Because of Europe's dedicated interest in classical writings, a book trade slowly developed, which provided for learning outside the domain of the church. The private libraries of the feudal nobility in many cases formed the basis for the libraries that were to come, that is, municipal, state, and national libraries (Harris, 1995). The library of the Medici family in Florence represents one of the most important Italian book collections of the early Renaissance. Cosimo de Medici (1389–1464) hired people to collect books for his library. Compared to the standards of the time, Cosimo de Medici had an exceptional collection of books, which consisted of several copies of the Bible, religious commentaries, medieval writers, works of church fathers, and quite a few classical works in philosophy, history, poetry, and drama (Harris, 1995). This book-collection activity of the Medicis suggests that the formation and organization of knowledge had moved beyond the walls of the churches and monasteries, and thus had a different purpose.

Through the activities and institutions of collection in the Middle Ages and early Renaissance, much, although definitely not all, of the knowledge of the ancient world is preserved. Our knowledge today of ancient writers is a function of the writings that have been organized, stored, and transmitted through various institutional arrangements of the libraries of the Middle Ages and early Renaissance.

TEXTUAL INSTITUTIONS AFTER GUTENBURG

The development of printing in Europe changed the scope and character of collecting (Eisenstein, 1983). Printing not only multiplied books and increased people's contact with them, it provided a new sense of what a book was. As Bolter (2001) comments, "Western culture came more and more to anthropomorphize books, to regard each book as a subject with a name, a place (in the library), a voice, and a bibliographic life of its own" (p. 79). Before printing, a conception of the book as a subject with a name could not be upheld because there was no fixed idea of an edition, among other things.

In the 16th and 17th centuries, the number of national libraries increased in Europe, in many instances based on the collections of private libraries and private book collectors. The task of national libraries was to ensure the cultural heritage of a given nation, combining the Renaissance interest in the past with the beginning nationalism also furthered by the printing press (see e.g., Anderson, 1983; Eisenstein, 1983). Because of the interest in preserving cultural heritage, legal deposit laws were passed in many countries, ensuring every national library one copy of every book published in the respective country. Besides obtaining free copies of books, national libraries also gained financial support from governments. Thereby, national governments gained power to oversee and control the production and dissemination of written knowledge.

The Reformation dissolution of monastery libraries in the 16th century and after meant both that research and university libraries inherited books from the monastic libraries and that the collections of research and university were restructured from a secular perspective. though many manuscript collections containing ancient and theological literature were destroyed, many of the books hidden away in monastery libraries were released.

THE GROWTH OF PUBLIC LIBRARIES AND ENCYCLOPEDIAS FOR THE PUBLIC IN 19TH-CENTURY EUROPE

Nineteenth-century Europe witnessed a beginning democratization of access to written knowledge not seen hitherto. Public libraries emerged in several European countries. "Public" libraries in ancient and Roman times, in the Middle Ages, and in the Renaissance were mostly privately owned and open only to a select elite. For instance, the Renaissance public libraries were, according to Lerner (1998), intended for the use of scholarly gentlemen. National and university libraries may have been public in the sense of being open and supported by the state. But their use was not intended for the general public because the purpose behind these libraries was not to educate and enlighten the growing reading public of 19th-century Europe. In the 19th century, however, attention was paid to the growing public outside the court or palaces and the role the public plays in forming civic life. The idea of a public library in Europe took shape in countries such as France, England, Germany, Italy, and Russia, each within diverse historical and political circumstances and enjoying differing degrees of state support. Nonetheless governmental concern behind the development of public libraries in the 19th and early 20th centuries sent a universal message that knowledge is a common good, worthy of state support. In this perspective, public libraries are to be understood in connection with the development of other kinds of public institutions and democratic arrangements taking place in 19th-century Europe such as public schools, public opinion, and public spheres. Public libraries may be seen as part of the growing nation-states and their interest in institutionalizing democratization and invoking the ideals of Enlightenment thought. Free, tax-supported public libraries nonetheless shaped popular reading habits by controlling what books were made readily available.

Another activity of the 19th century that affected the use and dissemination of written knowledge was the publishing of encyclopedias for the general public. Encyclopedias of the 19th century had, however, important antecedents. The British encyclopedist Ephraim Chambers published in 1728 the *Cyclopaedia; or An Universal Dictionary of Arts and Sciences* (Encyclopedia, n.d.). Chambers emphasized easy-to-read articles, included articles on the arts and summaries of philosophical systems, and was the first to use cross-references (Katz, 1998). The *Cyclopedia* inspired the French encyclopedists because Diderot and d'Alembert's *L'Encyclopedie* actually started as a translation of the *Cyclopedia* into French. *L'Encyclopedie* was an explicitly political project as it tried to communicate the ideology of the French enlightenment, which meant, among other things, a de-emphasis of the role of religion in society in favor of the primacy of reason, science, and technology in society. *L'Encyclopedie* was deliberately conceived of by Diderot and d'Alembert as a means of changing society, and achieved some degree of success in this ambition as it gained popularity in intellectual circles of Europe and among the rising middle classes of Europe (Katz, 1998).

The conceptual underpinnings of encyclopedias had from their beginning been that they had to display the universe of knowledge. Readers using an encyclopedia would thus gain an insight into how knowledge and its parts were related. All this was to change, however, with the encyclopedias of the 19th century, as encyclopedias shifted from "didactic 'trees of knowledge' into the fact-filled, up-to-date ready reference works we know today" (Headrick, 2000, p. 144). Thus, both *Encyclopædia Britannica* and the *Grand Dictionnaire Universel du XIX siecle,* published in 15 volumes between 1865 and 1876 by Pierre Larousse (1817–1875), expressed a similar concern for everyday knowledge. Moreover, Larousse introduced a new approach to organization as it made use of short informative articles about topics, in contrast to long articles, organized under a specific entry term (Katz, 1998). The concern for everyday matters in encyclopedia contents, as expressed by the Britannica and Larousse in the 19th century, may explain why one of the great encyclopedia undertakings of the century, the *Encyclopedia Metropolitana,* went wrong as it continued to employ a scholarly systematic arrangement at the expense of alphabetical order. The shift from thematic organization to alphabetical order, even though preceded much earlier by the Byzantine encyclopedia *Suida,* is a shift not only in terms of a change in worldview but also in modes of reading (Collison, 1966; see also Burke, 2000).

NEW TECHNOLOGIES AND ACCESS TO KNOWLEDGE

Partly due to the scientific and industrial revolutions, the 19th and 20th centuries witnessed a growth of knowledge, particularly specialized knowledge. This growth challenged the existing means of describing, registering, and providing access to scientific knowledge. Early bibliographical initiatives such as the Royal Society's *Catalogue of Scientific Papers* (1867–1902, covering the whole 19th century) and its *International Catalogue of Scientific Literature* (1901–1914) paved the way for large bibliographic projects.

One of the most influential bibliographical projects of the late 19th and early 20th century was the *documentation movement,* in particular personified by two Belgians, Paul Otlet and Henri LaFontaine. The documentation movement was particularly interested in written knowledge and its bibliographic organization on both national and international levels and in the social effects of bibliographic organization. The movement is known for the 1895 founding of the *Institut Internationale de Bibliographie* (changed to *Federation Internationale de Documentation* [FID] in 1935) and for introducing the classification system Universal Decimal Classification (UDC; see also http://www.udcc.org/). The documentalists, as they were called, were not concerned with traditional library activities such as collection management and the enlightenment of a public. Rather, they were concerned with providing access to scientific knowledge by registering books by "the monographic principle" (Rayward, 1994), perhaps inspired by the German bibliographical institute Die Brücke (Hapke, 1998).

The idea behind the monographic principle is that all facts from scientific documents can be extracted and expressed in phrases and stored on index cards. For this purpose, the UDC fulfilled an important function as it was (and is) able to express detailed classifications of documents. The ideology behind such organization of knowledge was that the sciences had to cooperate if they were to play a role in society. One means of such cooperation was to distill the facts from the various scientific documents produced in the world and register them bibliographically on both national and international levels.

The founders of the European documentalists movement, Otlet and LaFontaine, had been in contact with Melvil Dewey—the founder of the American classification system, the Dewey Decimal Classification (DDC)—to see if he was interested in cooperation. It ended up that there was little cooperation and eventually the documentalists went on to create their own system, inspired by the DDC (McIlwaine, 1997; Rayward, 1975).

The DDC has a different story than the UDC. Throughout history there have been attempts to classify knowledge (e.g., Aristotle, Bacon, and Leibniz). The usual story goes that there are clear *and* strong connections between the movements of the 18th and 19th centuries to classify knowledge and the sciences and library classification. Though he agrees that there is some connection, Miksa (1996) questions this strong connection concerning library classification in general and the DDC in particular. The attempts to classify knowledge and the sciences in the 19th century were mainly characterized by a quest for the acceptance of science in society. Science, as part of its social and discursive institutionalization, had to demonstrate and explain its social value and its knowledge production. Classification was one instrument in this process (see Dolby, 1979; cited in Miksa, 1998). Library classification, in contrast, was concerned with practical issues of book classification to locate the position of the book in the universe of knowledge (Miksa, 1998). Therefore, although library classification to some extent relied on the classification of knowledge and the sciences, library classification did not have to be concerned with producing an argument in order to legitimize its activity.

According to Wiegand (1998), Dewey adapted his basic structure of the DDC from a classification system devised by William Torrey Harris, responsible for the St. Louis Public School Library and superintendent of the St. Louis Public Schools from 1868 to 1880. This classification system was inspired by Francis Bacon's original structure with memory, imagination, and reason as the basic outline, but built on Hegel's inversion of it. Consequently, the DDC held a very minor philosophical basis in Hegel (see e.g., Graziano, 1959; Olson, 2004).

But in order to define and identify a hierarchy of division and sections for his system, Dewey looked elsewhere. According to Wiegand (1998) this elsewhere is the socio-institutional context of Amherst College, where Dewey was a student and later on librarian. Guidance as to the identification and arrangement of divisions and sections came, Wiegand (1998) argues, from two sources: (a) the Amherst College tradition and curriculum, and (b) the Amherst faculty and the texts used in the courses.

The Amherst College tradition had strong ties to orthodox Christianity and was interested in disciplining students and exposing them to Western culture and classics. This matched the worldview of Dewey, as he was more concerned with superimposing simplicity and efficiency and Harris's divisions made a sound foundation for doing so. Because Dewey, along with the other students at Amherst, was not taught to question the Amherst curriculum, there was nothing that Dewey could, or would, object to. Thus, Dewey's way of thinking about his classification system can be attributed to the sociocultural context that Dewey was part of as a student, defined by the Amherst faculty and the textbooks used in the courses Dewey took (Wiegand, 1998). At least two textbooks, one in physics and one in psychology, and their arrangement corresponded more or less perfectly with how Dewey subdivided physics and psychology in his classification system. As a result, the construction of the first edition of DDC contributed to "framing and cementing a worldview and knowledge structure taught on the tiny Amherst College campus between 1870 and 1875 into what became the world's most widely used library classification" (Wiegand, 1998, p. 188).

Another means that developed to give access to written knowledge was indexing and abstracting services. These services evolved as a particular textual response to the increased amount of scholarly literature produced. There are traces of abstracting and indexing activities back to antiquity and the Middle Ages serving, among other things, as annotations to the literature covered (Witty, 1973). Moreover, the two first scientific journals—the first English scientific journal, *Philosophical Transactions* (1665), and the first French scientific journal, *Journal des Sçavans* (1665)—included in their beginning years reviews, extracts, and abstracts of books and not primary scientific articles.

The more systematic publication of an abstract journal containing abstracts of scientific literature is a relatively recent invention beginning to take shape the 18th century, primarily as a response to the growth in journal literature (see e.g., Kronick, 1976; Manzer, 1977). The activity of the early abstracting journals consisted of individual editors summing up or reprinting selected articles from other periodicals. The abstract journals of the 18th century were general, not focusing on particular subject areas. During the 19th century and from the early 20th century on, abstract journals turned into discipline-oriented journals as part of the growing specialization among of the scientific disciplines (Vickery, 2000). A further development of abstracting and indexing services is the use of computers for this purpose beginning in the 1960s. Printed abstract and index journals were now also issued as online databases, making it possible to conduct electronic searches using descriptors, searching in titles and in abstracts. Thus, the whole bibliographic enterprise has undergone a development from being the product of a single dedicated individual producing a bibliography, abstract, or index journal to an organized bibliographic industry.

The construction and production of citation indexes is also to be understood in this light. Although Weinberg (1997) reports on some earlier Hebrew citation indexes from the 16th century, it was a law citation index, *Shepard's Citations* (1873), that Eugene Garfield, the founder of the citation indexes, was inspired by when he construed the citation indexes (Wouters, 1999). The citation indexes are construed on the assumption that subject retrieval can be improved when using references as subject terms (Garfield, 1979). It is believed that the reference lists of documents can reveal something about the subject matter of the citing documents and about the semantic (or rhetorical?) relationship between citing and cited documents.

In the 20th century, storage and retrieval of knowledge through the use of computers was also envisioned by the American scientist Vannevar Bush in 1945 (Bush, 1945) and computer scientist Ted Nelson in 1965 (Nelson, 1965). Bush described an imaginary storage and retrieval system called *MEMEX*, whose retrieval function was to be based on associative trails because, as Bush argued, that was the way the human mind works. However, Bush's MEMEX system never materialized because it was technologically impossible. The concept of hypertext was introduced by Ted Nelson in 1965 in connection with his XANADU project. According to Nelson, hypertext was a notion for nonsequential writing, that is, the nonlinear text. The basic idea, then, in hypertext is that the reader/user, by the use of links, is allowed to jump in texts or in between systems of texts. Hence, Nelson's distinction between two forms of hypertext—the docuplex (document complex), referring to the way a document was hypertextually organized internally, and the docuvers (document universe), referring to the way various documents are connected to each other in a hypertextual network. XANADU was essentially a database of all kinds of texts connected by the use of links, thus creating an associative network in between texts. According to later commentators, the concept of *associative indexing (trails)* was the predecessor of hypertext. But as both Buckland (1992) and Rayward (1994) argue, the history of hypertext ideas can be traced back to Paul Otlet and the Russian Emanuel Goldberg working in the 1920s and 1930s as they both developed thoughts about electronic retrieval technologies that anticipated the thoughts of Bush and Nelson.

Looked at from the perspective of the history of writing and the formation of knowledge, the new information and communication technologies (ICT) both break with and continue past forms of the production, dissemination, and organization of knowledge. In particular, the Internet and the World Wide Web (WWW) provide a kind of a writing space (cf. Bolter, 2001). Writing on the Web emphasizes a relationship between the production and retrieveability of text not necessarily present in print culture. In print, the production of text and making it retrieveable, that is, describing and registering it in some kind of information system, are two separate activities, at least functionally. This is not the case when writing on the Web. The retrieveability of a written document in old print culture was not (primarily or necessarily) part of the document's rhetorical activity because the writing space did not allow for or was concerned with the retrieval aspect. Now, writing and publishing a Web document necessarily means that the writer is interested in the fact that this document is being retrieved in the new writing space, which the Web creates, entailing that genre performance on the Web includes recognition of the retrieval aspect. The retrieval feature becomes a significant part of the literate activity on the Internet as indicated by the fact that many Web sites have a search function. Web sites are in fact constituted by a database feature, turning the database into a new cultural form (Manovich, 2001).

Moreover, the Internet has also given rise to emergent compendia and archival functions such as Wikipedia, search engines, or Web archives. They all empower users of written knowledge but at the same time they challenge users' form of literacy. Wikipedia is the encyclopedic project of the Internet and reflects and remediates the old encyclopedic thinking of preserving and synthesizing human knowledge. But what is different from previous encyclopedia projects in history is that the knowledge to be presented is not subjected to editing by some kind of authority. The authority of Wikipedia is in the hands of the users. All users can post an article about a particular subject or they can comment on, criticize, add to, or modify already published articles in the Wikipedia. In this way, Wikipedia allows users at once to produce and shape the knowledge included in Wikipedia, a feature of the production and use of written knowledge not seen hitherto in human history.

Like Wikipedia, search engines have their precursors in databases, indexes, and bibliographies. But unlike databases, indexes, and bibliographies, search engines are not necessarily restricted to cover, for instance, particular subjects or national areas. When searching the Internet by use of search engines like Google, the result of a search is a variety of documents (e.g., syllabus, organization site, personal Web site, records from a library catalog, etc.) in a variety of formats (e.g., ppt, pdf, doc) belonging to a variety of domains (e.g., org, edu, gov, etc.). Almost anything on the Internet holds a textual (or written) attribute. The organization presenting itself on the Internet through a Web site is a text and not a physical place. A government agency presents itself by the production of a text explaining and describing its activity. The personal homepage introduces itself by means of a text. Thus, we can say that searching on the Internet is like searching in the archives of a variety of forms of textually mediated social organization (Smith, 1984). This generates a view of knowledge "as collections of (verbal and visual) ideas that can arrange themselves into a kaleidoscope of hierarchical and associative patterns" (Bolter, 2001, p. 91), and it shapes written knowledge in a particular way as it reinforces the role of texts and genres in producing, using, and organizing knowledge.

The search engines represent a dominating form of knowledge organization on the Internet. Because many people for many different purposes use search engines, there are also many interests connected to them and their knowledge organization practice. Introna and Nissenbaum (2000) argue that search engines represent a political matter, not just a technical one, with regard to what to organize and retrieve, because search engines systemically exclude certain sites and certain types of sites at the expense of others. Search engines, Introna and Nissenbaum argue, have an ideological function, pretending to be helping users find relevant information whereas in effect its is the user who helps the search engine find what is of interest to it, that is, profit. Search engines do this because they are dependent on commercial interests in order to function, thereby also pointing to how politics shapes the organization and use of knowledge on the Internet.

The Internet and the Web also provide opportunities for archiving. Several archiving initiatives are taking place on the Web. The nongovernmental Internet Archive (www.archive.org), for instance, seeks to preserve Web pages in terms of snapshots—that is, to archive Web pages as they looked like a particular moment during their Web history. Consequently, the way the Internet Archive organizes its texts is similar to considering and preserving them as one would photographs to be put in a photo album. The presence of the Internet Archive (and other Internet-based archival activities) suggests how electronic written culture holds an interest in preserving the knowledge that the Internet at once mediates, materializes, and organizes. In this view, the Internet is not just yet another medium transmitting culture. The Internet is considered *as* culture with its (own) cultural artifacts and means and modes of structuring knowledge. The Internet textual practices thus hold a view on knowledge, which is almost equal to how nations consider their traditional cultural heritage; that is, as knowledge materialized in artifacts, and considered essential to civilization and its collective memory.

The consequences of the digitization have of course also affected libraries, as all other previous information and communications technologies (ICTs) in history have done. The notion of electronic libraries can be traced back to the 1970s when the first electronic bibliographic databases appeared. Digital libraries are a continuation of this development. But they are not only an enlarged version of electronic databases. Digital libraries are also an extended version, some may even say a replacement, of the physical library. The books and other materials are digitized or are only published electronically and, with this, digital libraries represent a renewal of the library without walls and new library functions and tools. The label "the library without walls" is, however, historically attached to bibliographies. By employing such a label for digital libraries, the textual character of digital libraries is enforced because it is the architecture of digital libraries that is of a highly textual nature. The effect of this is that digital libraries and their role in society and culture can be understood from the perspective of texts.

For that reason, the formation of digital libraries brings about an understanding of libraries as more than physical spaces and physical structures. With hypertext as one means of organizing knowledge in digital libraries, they come to look more like systems of interconnected texts and genres. Physical libraries may, of course, be viewed in such a perspective too. But digital libraries are a place on the Web. As Bolter (2001) says with regard to Web pages, "Web pages function as ordinary text, but they also function as places along a path" (p. 28). That is, digital libraries are not dependent on a physical placement but occupy instead a textual place in a new textual infrastructure. This textualization of digital libraries leads to new library functions and tools and new conceptions of these functions and tools. The digital library has a textual function on the Web and our knowledge and use of digital libraries come close to the knowledge we bring to (printed) texts and to our conception of texts in professional as well as everyday life. The way we use a digital library is more than recognizing it as a search-and-retrieval tool. Clearly, this aspect is important, but it cannot stand alone. The digital library's occupation of a textual space on the Web requires that we understand what we can expect of it compared to other similar tools (e.g., Amazon or Google) on the Web that offer related search possibilities. Thus, how we master and approach a digital library as a tool depends on the genre knowledge we have regarding other similar Web genres and how they perform in the genre ecology of digital libraries on the Web. Such an understanding is more than recognizing particular search-and-retrieval facilities; the provision of new library functions and tools demands a literate activity similar to the one we are involved in when using texts because the organization of knowledge carried out by the hypertextual nature of digital libraries is comparable to intertextuality. The successful use of the new library tools is proportionate to an understanding of how texts rely on other texts in order to perform some communicative activity in the human life world. This intertextual function of digital libraries indicates how digital libraries underpin the role of written knowledge in society and culture as it (re-)invokes our textual consciousness and our literacy skills. Furthermore, digital libraries form written knowledge because the rationale behind them is not just to provide access to texts and the knowledge materialized in them and act as a mere storehouse of knowledge but to connect a variety of texts. By doing this, digital libraries contribute to shaping an understanding of written knowledge as being interconnected on both a local and global level and not as atomistic pieces of nature and culture.

The WWW and its contribution to social textualization contribute to other difficulties, however. The division of labor between publishers, journals, and libraries is undergoing dramatic changes because of this. It is, for instance, not unusual by now that the individual publishers also act as a library on their Web sites. They offer search possibilities, maintaining author or subject indexes, or providing samples of particular journal issues. By doing this, the publishers remediate and challenge the library genre, so to speak. Likewise it is with electronic journals (e-journals); that is, those journals with no counterpart in print. E-journals are part of the open-access movement and as such they challenge both publishers and libraries. Open-access movements constitute a response to the rise in the price of scholarly journals and through this to the power of publishers. The principle behind open-access journals is that all readers with Internet access can freely read and use these journals. Readers gain free access to public knowledge and scholars are still ensured the quality of articles as the peer-review system is maintained. But e-journals also challenge libraries, because as the e-journals, like the publisher Web sites, also maintain library functions as well as provide search possibilities and access to full text. This change in the division of labor between publishers, journals, and libraries represents a change in the organization of knowledge because the means and modes of access change. Libraries can, of course, still practice their meta-textual activity but they have to do it in a way that demonstrates how libraries fulfill a role in the knowledge-organizing ecology of our times.

Such a role and its social and cultural significance is dependent on what kind of expectations citizens have toward publishers, e-journals, and libraries and on how citizens recognize what these agents are performing in terms of their handling of written knowledge.

CONCLUSION

This historical narrative illustrates how writing and written knowledge throughout history is accompanied by activities and practices that try to control writing by means of organizing it. This suggests a picture where writing is more than putting words, symbols, or numbers on a page. Writing is also a tool for managing, structuring, and retrieving writings and it gives rise to such means and modes of storing, collecting, and organizing written knowledge such as libraries, bibliographies, or encyclopedias. By providing a historical outlook on how writing and written knowledge have been handled during the history of mankind, we are shown not only how writing shapes human activity but also how various human activities dealing with the collecting and organization of writing shape our conception of what writing can do and what we can do with writing. A historical consciousness of our means and modes of organizing and storing the world of writing provides us with a sense of what the various knowledge organization activities are doing and how they are doing it. Having such a consciousness seems to be a compulsory part of being a literate person in our late modern society where we are surrounded by activities, in both professional and everyday life, that collect and organize various sorts of information, documents, and/or knowledge. Alertness to what motivates these activities may help us recognize their agendas.

REFERENCES

Andersen, J. (2002). Communication technologies and the concept of knowledge organization. A medium-theory perspective. *Knowledge Organization, 29*(1), 29–39.

Anderson, B. (1983). *Imagined communities: Reflections on the origin and spread of nationalism*. London: Verso.

Besterman, T. (1968). *The beginnings of systematic bibliography* (Vol. 2, rev. ed.). New York: Franklin.

Blum, R. (1980). *Bibliographia: An inquiry into its definition and designations* (M. V. Rovelstad, Trans.). Chicago: American Library Association.

Blum, R. (1991). *Kallimachos: The Alexandrian library and the origins of bibliography* (H. H. Wellisch, Trans.). Madison: University of Wisconsin Press.

Bolter, J. D. (2001). *Writing space: Computers, hypertext and the remediation of print* (2nd ed.). Mahwah, NJ: Lawrence Erlbaum Associates.

Buckland, M. K. (1992). Emanuel Goldberg, Electronic document retrieval, and Vannevar Bush's Memex. *Journal of the American Society for Information Science, 43*(4), 284–294.

Burke, P. (2000). *A social history of knowledge: From Gutenberg to Diderot*. Cambridge, England: Polity.

Bush, V. (1945). As we may think. In J. M. Nyce & P. Kahn (Eds.), *From Memex to hypertext: Vannevar Bush and the mind's machine* (pp. 85–110). Boston: Academic Press.

Casson, L. (2001). *Libraries in the ancient world*. New Haven, CT: Yale University Press.

Chartier, R. (1994). *The order of books: Readers, authors and libraries in Europe between the fourteenth and eighteenth centuries*. Cambridge, England: Polity.

Collison, R. (1966). *Encyclopaedias: Their history throughout the ages; a bibliographical guide with extensive historical notes to the general encyclopaedias issued throughout the world from 350 B.C. to the present day* (2nd ed.). New York: Hafner.

Eisenstein, E. L. (1983). *The printing revolution in early modern Europe*. Cambridge, England: Cambridge University Press.

Encyclopaedia. (n.d.). *Encyclopædia Britannica*. Retrieved July 5, 2005, from Encyclopædia Britannica Online, http://search.eb.com/eb/article?tocId=32031

Frohmann, B. (2000). Discourse and documentation: Some implications for pedagogy and research. *The Journal of Education for Library and Information Science, 42*, 13–28.

Garfield, E. (1979). *Citation indexing and its theory and application in science, technology, and humanities*. New York: Wiley.

Goody, J. (1977). *The domestication of the savage mind*. Cambridge, England: Cambridge University Press.

Goody, J. (1986). *The logic of writing and the organization of society*. Cambridge, England: Cambridge University Press.

Graziano, E. E. (1959). Hegel's philosophy as basis for the decimal classification schedule. *Libri*, 9, 45–52.

Hapke, T. (1999). Wilhelm Ostwald, the "brücke" (bridge), and connections to other bibliographic activities at the beginning of the twentieth century. In M. E. Bowden, T. B. Hahn, & R. V. Williams (Eds.), *Proceedings of the 1998 Conference on the History and Heritage of Science Information Systems* (pp. 139–147). Medford, NJ: Information Today. Available at: http://www.chemheritage.org/explore/ASIS_documents/ASISbook.pdf

Harris, M. H. (1995). *History of libraries in the Western world* (4th ed.). Metuchen, NJ: Scarecrow.

Headrick, D. R. (2000). *When information came of age: Technologies of knowledge in the age of reason and revolution, 1700–1850*. Oxford, England: Oxford University Press.

Humphreys, K. W. (1994). Christian libraries, early. In *Encyclopedia of library history* (pp. 138–139). New York: Garland.

Introna, L. D., & Nissenbaum, H. (2000). Shaping the Web: Why the politics of search engines matters. *Information Society*, 16, 169–185.

Johnson, E. D. (1966). *Communication: An introduction to the history of writing, printing, books and libraries*. New York: Scarecrow.

Katz, B. (1998). *Cuneiform to computer: A history of reference sources*. Lanham, MD: Scarecrow.

Kronick, D. A. (1976). *A history of scientific & technical periodicals: The origins and development of the scientific and technical press* (2nd ed.). Metuchen, NJ: Scarecrow.

Lerner, F. (1998). *The story of libraries: From the invention of printing to the computer age*. New York: Continuum.

Lin, S. C. (1998). *Libraries and librarianship in China*. Westport, CT: Greenwood.

Manovich, L. (2001). *The languages of the new media*. Cambridge, MA: MIT Press.

Manzer, B. M. (1977). *The abstract journal, 1790–1920: Origin, development and diffusion*. Metuchen, NJ: Scarecrow.

McIlwaine, I. C. (1997). The Universal Decimal Classification: Some factors concerning its origins, development, and influence. *Journal of the American Society for Information Science*, 48(4), 331–339.

Miksa, F. L. (1998). *The DDC, the universe of knowledge, and the post-modern library*. Albany, NY: Forest.

Murray, D. (1917). *Bibliography: Its scope and methods; with a view of the work of a local bibliographical society*. Glasgow, Scotland: Maclehose.

Olson, H. A. (2004). The ubiquitous hierarchy: An army to overcome the threat of a mob. *Library Trends*, 52(3), 604–616.

Posner, E. (1972). *Archives in the ancient world*. Cambridge, MA: Harvard University Press.

Rayward, W. B. (1975). *The universe of information: The work of Paul Otlet for documentation and international organization* (FID Pub. No. 520). Moscow: All-Union Institute for Scientific and Technical Information.

Rayward, W. B. (1994). Visions of Xanadu: Paul Otlet (1868–1944) and hypertext. *Journal of the American Society for Information Science*, 45, 235–250.

Reynolds, L. D., & Wilson, N. G. (1968). *Scribes and scholars: A guide to the transmission of Greek and Latin literature*. London: Oxford University Press.

Seymor, S. (1994). China, People's Republic of. In W. A. Wiegand & D. G. Davis (Eds.), *Encyclopedia of library history* (pp. 133–138). New York: Garland.

Smith, D. E. (1984). Textually-mediated social organization. *International Social Science Journal*, 36, 59–75.

Thompson, J. W. (1967). *The medieval library*. New York: Hafner. (Original work published 1939)

Vickery, B. C. (2000). *Scientific communication in history*. Lanham, MD: Scarecrow.

Weinberg, B. H. (1997). The earliest Hebrew citation indexes. *Journal of the American Society for Information Science*, 48(4), 318–330.

Wiegand, W. A. (1998). The "Amherst method": The origins of the Dewey Decimal Classification scheme. *Libraries & Culture*, 33(2), 175–194.

Witty, F. J. (1973). The beginnings of indexing and abstracting: Some notes towards a history of indexing and abstracting in antiquity and the Middle Ages. *The Indexer*, 8(4), 193–198.

Woledge, G. (1983). Bibliography and documentation: Words and ideas. *Journal of Documentation*, 39(4), 266–279.

Wouters, P. (1999). The creation of the *Science Citation Index*. In M. E. Bowden, T. B. Hahn, & R. V. Williams (Eds.), *Proceedings of the 1998 Conference on the History and Heritage of Science Information Systems* (pp. 127–136). Medford, NJ: Information Today. Available at: http://www.chemheritage.org/explore/ASIS_documents/ASISbook.pdf

Wright, H. C. (1977). *The oral antecedents of Greek librarianship*. Provo, UT: Brigham Young University Press.

CHAPTER 12

Writing as Art and Entertainment

Patrick Colm Hogan
University of Connecticut, Storrs

LEARNING TO WRITE: VARIETIES OF UNIVERSALS AND THE AUTONOMY OF LITERATURE

Work in linguistics over the past half century has shown that what initially appeared to be a limitless diversity of languages is in fact a collection of highly constrained variants on a single set of universal principles. The differences that appear so important to us are superficial (see e.g., Chomsky, 2000). Some more recent research suggests that there are many universals in literature as well (see Hogan, 2003). But before literary study can benefit from the study of universals, drawing inspiration from linguistics, it is important to understand the linguistic use of the term *universal*.

In linguistics, universal does not mean that a particular feature is to be found everywhere. A feature is universal if it occurs more frequently across unrelated languages than is predicted by chance. If a feature recurs in all languages, then it is an *absolute universal*. Otherwise, it is a *statistical universal*. Moreover, if sets of features tend to co-occur in distinct subsets of languages (e.g., if noun/adjective order tends to be correlated with verb/object order, the use of prepositions, etc.), then we have a *typological universal*. In some cases, the distinction between absolute or statistical universals, on the one hand, and typological universals, on the other, is a residue of the way we define our domain. An absolute universal for one domain may be understood as typological when shifted to a more encompassing domain. Consider the domain of verbal art, which includes orature and literature. An absolute universal of literature may also be an absolute universal of verbal art. However, if an invariant property of literature does not apply to orature, then it is an absolute universal of literature, but only a typological universal of verbal art (i.e., it applies to only one *type* of verbal art—literature).

In a discussion of writing as art and entertainment, it is obviously important to distinguish between the properties shared by all verbal art, on the one hand, and the properties shared by specifically literary works, on the other. But a complication arises here, for the division between orature and literature is not as sharp as one might initially imagine. There is a period of transition from orality to literacy. Indeed, Walter Ong speaks of "residual orality" affecting apparently literate societies for millennia (see Ong, 1971). Perhaps the best way to treat this issue of overlap is to distinguish three periods, employing a criterion slightly different from that used by Ong. The first is the period before the invention of writing, the second is a transition period, and the third is a period of what might be called *technological autonomy*. When any new technology is developed, there is often a period in which its applications are unclear. Its use is confined by ideas or imaginations that preceded its development. Gradually, however, people begin to think of the technology in terms of its own independent possibilities.

For a certain time, then, writing is an adjunct to what preceded writing—primarily memory and speech. As an adjunct to memory, it serves as a way of recording whatever is important that one might otherwise forget. Thus merchants find a use for writing in inventories (see e.g., Lawall & Mack, 2002, on the Middle East) and rulers find a use for writing in memorials and decrees (for Egyptian cases, see Lichtheim, 1973). As an adjunct to speech, writing allows a sort of continuous repetition. When writing is new, a text may be treated as an unending utterance, rather than a mere physical thing that may guide utterance when read. Thus, one early use of writing is for the inscription of prayers. The written text suggests a continual repetition of the prayer. Indeed, it suggests repetition even when the supplicant is dead—hence the use of at least certain tomb inscriptions. For example, two of the earliest uses of writing in ancient Egypt were for the inscription of prayers and "autobiography," which is to say memorial eulogy (see Lichtheim, 1973). Along the same lines, O'Connor (1996) explains that, at the end of the Middle Bronze Age (ca. 1500 BCE), Proto-Sinaitic inscriptions were "religious, specifically votive" (p. 90).

After this period of adjuncthood, however, people begin to recognize a wider range of possibilities for writing. Writing develops not simply as a way of enhancing speech and memory, but as a set of novel techniques or tools that open up new possibilities for thought and action. This is not to say that adjunct or dependent uses of writing disappear. They do not. In some cases, they may even be extended. More generally, the distinction between the transition period and the autonomous period is not a distinction between residually oral and fully literate societies. Residual orality remains well after writing begins to follow its own autonomous development.

WHAT TO WRITE AND HOW TO DO IT: PROTOTYPES AND DEVELOPMENT PRINCIPLES

The period of chirographic autonomy is, of course, the crucial period for the study of literature as such. Written verbal art arises initially in the transition period. But, prior to chirographic autonomy, literature is, first of all, transcribed orature. A good example of this may be found in the *Iliad* and the *Odyssey*, assuming Albert Lord is correct about the dictation of these poems (see Lord, 1976).

But what exactly is the difference between autonomously developed literature, on the one hand, and transcribed orature, on the other? To clarify this, we need to distinguish between the general structures that organize verbal art and the development principles that serve to specify those structures. Whether we are producing a literary work or trying to understand and enjoy it, we evidently begin with prototypes. (*Prototype* is a technical term from cognitive science. It refers to a complex of features that defines a standard or average case.) Thus, a writer composing a narrative poem on love begins with prototypes of poems and love (thus the standard properties of poems and love). But clearly that is not all there is to it. The poet has to produce a particular poem, not some general structure. Thus, in addition to prototypes, the poet has a set of development principles, procedures by which he or she may produce a specific poem from the prototypical structure. For instance, if the prototypical structure involves two lovers who are separated by society, the poet needs ways of defining just who the lovers are and how they are separated.

Prototypes do, of course, vary culturally. Nonetheless, there are remarkable patterns across traditions. Moreover, it seems that many central prototypes remain remarkably constant historically—from oral composition, across the transition period, and through the autonomous period. A striking case of this is general narrative structure. The most common generic prototypes are almost certainly heroic, romantic, and sacrificial tragic-comedy. The heroic structure involves an internal disruption of social hierarchy (e.g., a usurpation of the rightful monarch) and a threat to society from an external enemy. The romantic structure involves the separation of lovers due to some social disapproval. The sacrificial structure involves a communal disaster due to some ethical violation and the necessity of a communal sacrifice to rectify the situation. (For a full explanation of these prototypes and an account of the evidence for their universality, see Hogan, 2003b.) The relative frequency of these genres varies. But they appear to dominate both enduring literary canons and ephemeral popular literature cross-culturally.

The situation with development principles is different. They are transformed radically in the transition to the autonomous use of writing. To a great extent, the differences between orature and literature result from this change.

FLUID EXPRESSION, HALTING REVISION: THE SHIFT IN DEVELOPMENT PRINCIPLES

The change in development principles is best understood in relation to the differences between oral performances and written texts. Oral performances of any given story or poem are re-creations of that story or poem. If recorded, they would produce unique, if closely related texts. Rubin (1995) has discussed the development principles for these oral recreations. Performers, he argues, enact a system of cues and constraints. While a bard is reciting, one sequence will cue options for the following sequence while simultaneously constraining that sequence within fairly tight limits. At any given point in a tale, the bard will have relatively few choices for how to continue. This method of development is necessitated by the fact that the performer must remake the poem rapidly. As Rubin points out, this account of composition predicts the development of various characteristics of oral composition, such as the use of formulas and epithets.

The situation with writing is obviously very different. Thus, the development principles are very different as well. First, the system of cues and constraints is not only unnecessary for written composition, but in many ways deleterious. The system serves rapid production and is simultaneously sustained by rapid production. Long, repeated interruptions for writing would almost certainly cause a bard to falter. The basic principle here is similar to remembering one's Social Security number. If asked about the penultimate digit in their Social Security number, most people recite the entire thing. If stopped in the middle, they have to begin again. This method becomes cumbersome, to say the least, when production involves inscription, not merely speech. The point is clear even for those of us who use a keypad to type an alphabetic script into a word processor. Early writing materials were not so easy to manipulate, and early scripts were more complex to produce. The pauses for writing could be lengthy. In this context, cues and constraints are almost entirely unworkable. In addition, the products of cues and constraints (i.e., the resulting literary works) would be variants on a small set of stories. Such variants are valuable in oral composition, where each past recitation of a poem has disappeared forever. They are not valuable in a written composition, where the earlier variants are all still around to be read.

Of course, writing not only eliminates the use of cues and constraints as a primary development principle, it necessarily fosters the use of other development principles. Needless to say, these do not arise fully formed, but take time to be worked out. This is one function of the transition period. To some extent, the autonomous period may be understood as beginning with the formation of development principles particular to writing.

Chirographic development principles form implicitly at first. But they may subsequently be articulated and refined in explicit accounts of composition. Some striking cases of this may be found in works by the important Chinese literary theorists, Lu Ji (261–303 CE; see Lu, 1966) and Liu Xie (465–522 CE; see H. Liu, 1959). The principles they articulate may at first seem a matter of common sense, unnecessary descriptions of spontaneous practices. But they are not. The practices at issue require study. They are part of learning to use a technology. Specifically, these theorists urge prospective writers first to familiarize themselves with the great writings of the past—in other words, the canonized works, particularly the classics. They also urge the cultivation of life experience. They then suggest that the writer set aside the books in a gesture designed to foster some degree of novelty. After this, the author should jot down ideas, subsequently organizing them into a sort of outline. Once the author has written a draft, he or she needs to return to the text, making sure that there are summary sentences inserted at key points. The entire composition must be cut and cast, which is to say, excesses must be removed and the remaining passages given a clear organization. Revision involves attention to word choice, paragraphing, and so forth.

Note that these development principles rely heavily on the specific properties of writing. Writing allows the retention of a wide range of ideas for a literary work. It allows for selection and outlining in a relatively unconstrained manner. Perhaps most strikingly, it allows for revision. The processes of systematic revision are virtually impossible in the case of oral composition. Certainly a poet may learn from past mistakes. But it is not possible to scrutinize a lengthy, ephemeral utterance at every level from overall structure through various subunits (e.g., paragraphs) all the way down to word choice. (Parallel points apply to the reader. The ability of a reader to reread clearly affects the constraints placed on the author, thus on his or her development principles.)

TYING UP THE LOOSE ENDS: THE STRICTNESS OF WRITING

Systematic differences in development principles lead to systematic differences in properties across particular works. Specifically, researchers in orality and literacy have isolated a number of distinct patterns in written texts, as opposed to oral compositions (see e.g., Ong 1982). We may organize these by reference to three major components of a literary work: language, events, and characters.

As to language, literature involves a decline in the use of epithets and formulaic phrases. In orature, such phrases facilitate the rapid production of successive lines with the right metrical or other properties. In writing, however, these are unnecessary, as that ongoing, fluid production has no particular value. Moreover, though epithets and formulae facilitate rapid production, they inhibit stylistic novelty. As we discuss later, novelty tends to be prized in literature, certainly more so than in orature. This too, then, works against the continued use of formulas. Of course, oral tendencies do not entirely disappear from language use in literature. In some cases of residual orality, writing may actually be recruited to enhance the number of fixed phrases available to authors (see Ong, 1977). However, even in these cases, the development principles are entirely different from those of oral composition. Searching a hefty collection of commonplaces does not contribute to fluid performance. Moreover, the number and variety of the commonplaces enhance the possibilities for using them in novel ways. Indeed, a writer might not only draw on little-known commonplaces, he or she might alter these commonplaces through rephrasing (which would undermine their purpose in oral composition) or juxtapose them in ways that are unlikely to arise in the cues and constraints framework of oral composition.

Turning to events, we find that literature-specific development principles, from outlining to revision, allow authors to tighten plots. In writing, it is much easier to streamline the occurrences in a story so that the causal sequence is not only clear and rigorous, but also minimal. One can make sure that points in the sequence are not left out, and that nothing irrelevant enters. This is not to say that looser plot sequences disappear. They do not. But researchers in the field argue that the development of tight plot structures is a distinctive feature of literature (see Ong, 1982).

Finally, writing fosters the development of a complex internal life for literary characters (see Ong, 1982). In oral composition, characters tend to be defined by one or two predominant traits, given in epithets. They rarely if ever have the sort of multifaceted psychological complexity that we find in a range of written works. This is due in part to the usual possibilities for elaborative revision that come with script. It may also derive from the way writing, in contrast with oral composition, tends to associate the making of stories with privacy or isolation. Moreover, through journals, letters, and the like, writing may augment a writer's articulate awareness of his or her own complex inner states.

THE GREAT-WORKS PROGRAM: CANONS, CLASSICS, AND SCRIPTURES

The transition to autonomous literature not only affects the content of particular works (through the change in development principles). It also alters the status of particular works. Put simply, literary works stick around. This is a radical change from orature, and the effects of this change accumulate over time.

A fully oral society simply has no works of verbal art in the sense in which a literate society has literary works. There are, rather, processes of creation and re-creation that are continually changing with no fixed reference text. Oral poets have a hierarchy of more or less abstract structures from which they produce the particular poems they speak. Some of the structures are very general—including the universal prototypes discussed previously. Others are more specific. Thus a bard would have prototypes for particular scenes in the *Iliad*, for particular actions or events within those scenes, and so forth. Every time he or she would retell those scenes, he or she would produce a new particular poem. The crucial point here is that, in this context, particular poems exist only as ephemeral tellings. What is (relatively) constant is the poet's complex of hierarchized prototypes and development principles, not the poems he or she produces using those structures.

The situation is, obviously, different in writing. When a poem or story is written, the result is an enduring particular. Thus, in a literate culture, something happens that cannot happen in an oral culture. Over time, a body of particular literary works accumulates. The consequences of this simple fact are extensive. Two seem particularly significant.

First, due to the longevity of writing, individual works may be reread. This renders retellings of those works redundant, except in cases where the retelling is such an improvement that it renders the prior work redundant. Proprietary considerations also make retellings complex—for the existence of enduring particulars encourages a sense of ownership. The general tendency of all this is to push toward the valorization of novelty. This is true even in cultural traditions where novelty is officially denigrated.

The second result of the endurance of writing is in a sense the opposite of the first. Though writing allows us to read the same work many times, it also leads to a situation in which we cannot read many works even a first time. Specifically, as new works are produced, the set of available works grows. Eventually, these become so numerous that they cannot all be read by any one person. This leads to the selection of works, not only individually, but socially. In other words, it leads to the formation of canons. (The universality of canonization has been argued by Kuipers, 2003.) By *canon formation*, I do not mean the establishment of a consensus of taste. Rather, I mean the institutionalization of a particular hierarchy. Because writing involves some people (writers) making things (literary works) for other people (readers), it necessarily involves systems of production and distribution. Canonization is most important a matter of what gets produced and distributed. Moreover, because writing is a technology, it requires some system of education, which itself is a crucial component in the network of production and distribution. Indeed, a major part of canon definition derives from educational structures and practices—what is read in schools, what is required for passing government examinations, and so forth.

But even canons are unwieldy. As a result, they are commonly structured in such a way as to make them more manageable. First, they are often segmented, for example, by genre or nation. As a result, canonization does not have the same consequences for all individual works. Works are understood and evaluated differently depending on where they are located in the canon—nationally, generically, and so forth.

Second, beyond segmentation, canons are themselves hierarchized. A few works become preeminent. These are not only canonical; they are paradigmatic. Shakespeare and Milton are paradigms; Webster and Dryden, though canonical, are not. At the very pinnacle of this hierarchy, we find works that are not only paradigms, but in some sense sacred. These become a crucial source for subsequent literature. Thus we find the Confucian Classics, the Torah, the Bible, the Qur'-n, the great Hindu sacred epics (the *R-m-yana* and the *Mah-bh-rata*) serving as a sort of common currency in their respective traditions. They become center-pieces of traditional education and tend to be the most widely distributed and most widely familiar works.

ART AND ENTERTAINMENT: REWRITING THE CLASSICS

Paradigmatic works are not only recopied and reprinted. They are rewritten in new works. Indeed, a great deal of literature involves the direct literary development of parts of the par-adigmatic works. Thus, much Christian literature is devoted to the elaboration of biblical sto-ries. An entire group of storytellers, the qussas, developed in Islam largely to recount stories suggested in the Qur'-n (see Waines, 1995). Retellings of all or part of the Hindu epics are numberless (see Richman, 1991). Moving outside sacred texts to other paradigmatic works, we find Greek authors developing elements from Homer and Japanese writers drawing out episodes from *The Tale of the Heike*.

The rewriting of classics (in the sense of paradigmatic works) appears to go against the general tendency of literature to value innovation. In order to understand this, we need to distinguish two types of paradigm revision. First, rewriting may serve to familiarize read-ers with socially consequential works (e.g., scriptures or paradigmatic epics bearing on national identity). The value of this work is in the way it gives readers access to—and thus, in effects repeats—the precursor work (e.g., the biblical story). Second, rewriting may com-ment on or otherwise respond to such works. In cases of this sort, the value of the new work is based on its difference from, not its similarity to, the precursor.

In keeping with this emphasis on difference, the second variety of revision may be pos-itive or negative. In other words, the new work may preserve the reverence accorded the original or it may be irreverent, engaging in parody or critique. One particularly signifi-cant form of irreverence is writing back (see Ashcroft, Griffiths, & Tiffin, 1989). Writing back is the reworking of some precursor text so as to dispute its status and, more impor-tant, to challenge or correct its social and political implications. Writing back is usually viewed as a practice peculiar to 20th-century anticolonial authors, when they respond to canonical European texts that have supported colonialism. However, it is common cross-culturally and transhistorically. For example, Gilbert and Gubar (1979) treat numerous instances of women writing back to patriarchal precursors. Similarly, Paula Richman's research shows that there are countless oppositional revisions of the *R-m-yana*, revisions that alter the original in such a way as to radically transform its social implications (see Richman, 1991).

The broad distinction between revisions that repeat classics and revisions that respond to those classics implies a parallel distinction among readers. Specifically, it suggests a dis-tinction between those who are not familiar with the classics and those who are. Again, as a technology, writing requires education. That education extends from the mechanics of writing and reading to familiarity with relevant canons as these are formed. In connection with the latter, most traditions develop a concept of an individual who has adequate famil-iarity with the canon and is therefore able to understand the similarities and differences between a new work and its canonical precursors. In Sanskrit, this is the sahrdaya or connoisseur (see Ingalls, 1990); in Arabic, the ad-b or littérateur (see Allen, 2000) fulfills this function; in Chinese, the chün tzu or gentleman, though broader, incorporates this idea (see Lau, 1979); in recent European theory, this figure is sometimes called the *ideal reader* (see e.g., Brooks, 2001). (Of course, all these ideal readers have other attributes as well, some of which carry over from forms of expertise important for understanding and appreciating orature.)

Needless to say, distinctions in readership are not confined to revising the classics. Any author may aim either at ideal readers—connoisseurs, littérateurs, and so on, who are familiar with the canon—or at readers who lack familiarity with the canon. Indeed, this division in projected readership roughly defines the division between art and popular literature or entertainment. (Entertainment would usually be understood as a form of popular literature lacking a didactic function. Thus, the work of the qussas might be viewed as popular, but not as entertainment. For simplicity, however, I use *entertainment* and *popular literature* interchangeably.) In other words, art is work that is aimed at and succeeds in pleasing ideal readers, thus readers who are familiar with the canon generally and the classics in particular. Entertainment is work that is aimed at and succeeds in pleasing readers who are not familiar with the canon or the classics. It is important to note that the two categories are not mutually exclusive. An author may aim a work at both sorts of reader, and may even succeed with both. Indeed, some of the most revered canonical works—such as the plays of Shakespeare—are successful as both art and entertainment.

IMAGINING A READERSHIP, AND A MARKET

Clearly, the division just outlined has some basis in fact. There are readers who are familiar with a particular canon and readers who are not familiar with that canon. Moreover, this makes a difference for both the production and reception of literature. Yet there are some serious problems with the opposition between ideal and popular readers. Perhaps most important, popular literature presupposes knowledge, sometimes a great deal of knowledge. There is an ideal reader for Tupac Shakur's lyrics as much as there is for W. B. Yeats'. In this way, a fixed opposition between ideal and popular is largely a matter of prestige, in the manner set out by Bourdieu (1984). Moreover, the situation of real readers is much more complex than being familiar or unfamiliar with the canon. Everyone's knowledge is partial. Additionally, everyone's knowledge is different. As a result, no one is a truly ideal reader for any work.

But if there are these difficulties, why does such a dichotomization arise and why is it sustained? A number of factors seem to contribute to this. For our purposes, the most important derive from the specific characteristics of writing. Perhaps most obviously, the division between art and entertainment bears on sales. Texts are marketed to groups. The separation of art and entertainment serves to isolate groups for marketing. This separation develops with particular intensity in connection with the mass production of texts that follows the shift from chirographic to print technologies. It continues to develop through postprint media such as film.

But that is not all. Writers are forced to imagine their readership in ways that oral poets are not. An oral poet is faced with an audience. He or she is able to gauge the reaction of the audience in the course of the poem, adjusting as seems necessary. In contrast, "the writer's audience is always a fiction" (to cite the title of a well-known essay by Walter Ong; see Ong, 1977, pp. 53–81). A crucial part of an author's fictive imagination of his or her readers is an imagination of their familiarity with other literary and nonliterary works. Because an author cannot go through the entire catalog of extant writings and all possible, individual readers, he or she must rely on broad generalizations—specifically, prototypes. The ideal reader is one such prototype.

SACRED METAPHORS: MODELING AND ALLUSION

The preceding sections may seem to imply that the primary use of classical works is in rewriting, the explicit refashioning of those works through elaboration, parody, or whatever. But, in fact, such rewriting is limited. In keeping with the claims of the preceding section, Northrop Frye (1982) has argued that the Bible constitutes the great code for understanding Western literature after Christianization. But Frye did not mean that the bulk of Western literature is like *Paradise Lost* in directly developing biblical tales.

In fact, the most common uses of classics, especially sacred classics, are in modeling and allusion. Put differently, the most common uses are, roughly, metaphorical rather than literal. An author models one story on another when he or she develops a tacit parallel between the new story and the prior story. The point of the modeling is for the reader to think of the new situation in relation to the canonical situation. Thus, numerous Western works draw parallels between the suffering of a tragic hero and the Passion of Jesus. Similarly, in the central paradigmatic work of Sanskrit drama, *Abhijñ-na-kuntalam*, K-lid-sa repeatedly models the actions of his hero and heroine on R-ma and S-t-from the *R-m-yana*. In each case of this sort, the author is, in effect, asking the reader to look at the events in the new story through the lens of the sacred precursor (or, in some cases, to look at the precursor through the lens of the new story).

Allusion has much the same function. It too operates as an instruction to the reader that he or she should think about the present work in terms of the prior work (or vice versa). The difference between modeling and allusion is twofold. First, allusion is more localized. Modeling develops a fuller sequence of parallels between the precursor work and the new work. In this way, the precise nature of the connections is often easier to interpret in modeling than in allusion. On the other hand, this deficit in allusion is compensated by the fact that allusion is often easier to identify. Allusion commonly relies on some direct verbal link between the new work and the precursor, as when a Hindi poem repeats a line from the *Bhagavad G-t-*. Looser allusive connections may be defined by distinctive semantic echoes, even where there is no direct quotation, as when Arabic poets draw on Qur'-nic imagery (see Allen, 2000).

Note that precise verbal links are far more likely to arise in literature than in orature. This is not because orature lacks well-known statements. It is, rather, because well-known statements tend to assume the character of autonomous commonplaces when they cannot be linked definitively to a source text. Phrases that operate as allusions in literary works are likely to operate as more generalized proverbs or idioms in orature. Indeed, literature has the opposite tendency. When a proverb or idiom appears in a canonical work—especially in a paradigmatic work—subsequent uses may come to be viewed as allusions to that work.

There are two common reasons for the use of models or allusions, the same reasons that most often motivate the use of metaphors. The first is emotional. The second is interpretive or thematic. As to the former, allusions and models frequently enhance the impact of one work by associating it with the reader's emotional response to an earlier work (e.g., by linking a reader's feelings about the new work's protagonist with his or her compassion for the suffering of Jesus). As to themes, an author often inflects our understanding and evaluation of events or characters by developing parallels with paradigmatic forebears (e.g., by linking the relation between two characters in the new work with the relation between Jesus and Judas). Here, as elsewhere, the target of the emotional or interpretive effect is most often the new work. However, in some cases, it may be the precursor.

TENDENTIAL TYPOLOGIES: WRITING
SYSTEMS AND THEIR MEDIA

We have been considering patterns that apply to literature generally, at least following the emergence of technological autonomy. Needless to say, there are universal typological patterns—or, perhaps more properly, universal correlational tendencies—as well. The most important of these, for our purposes, concern writing systems. Certainly, some properties are shared by all well-developed writing systems. Nonetheless, writing systems differ, and their differences are consequential for literature (as, e.g., Powell, 2002, has discussed). The easiest and most common way of treating these differences is by invoking the well-known triad of logographic, syllabic, and alphabetic scripts. But, in fact, things are more complex than this implies. The issues bearing on literature are probably best understood by considering two variables that are related, but not reducible to that triad.

The more crucial variable is how much learning it takes to become literate in a given script. This is in part a function of the number of symbols in a script, thus whether the script is logographic, syllabic, or alphabetic. But it is also related to the ease with which reading occurs once the symbols of the script have been learned. The Roman script used in English has fewer letters than, say, the devan-gar- syllabary. However, some of the advantages of this are qualified by the fact that letters are often ambiguous signals of sound in English. Thus one has to learn a series of peculiar usages and a number of individual exceptions to general principles. This is much less true in devan-gar-. In any case, the crucial factor is not simply whether the script elements represent words, syllables, or consonants and vowels. Rather, it is the degree to which a large number of people can readily learn the script in such a way as to function as readers or writers. Needless to say, societies can have low literacy rates even when the script is readily learnable, or high literacy rates even when the script is difficult. However, the learnability of the script does facilitate the development of a range of writers and a range of readers. This necessarily affects the generation and reception of literature. Literary works tend to follow different patterns when there is a large readership of ordinary people and when there is only a small, elite readership. For example, in the second case, the distinction between art and entertainment may be virtually absent among works directed at readers. Instead, it might arise primarily or even solely in connection with works aimed at oral performance and thus accessible to nonliterate people (see e.g., J. Liu, 1972, on the traditional Chinese view of drama).

A second, almost equally important variable is ease of reproduction and dissemination. As technological changes allow works to reach a larger readership, the author's imagination of his or her readership changes. Moreover, the definition, segmentation, and hierarchization of canons change as well. This is particularly clear when these material and technological changes are linked with economic alterations in production and distribution (e.g., the shift from a patronage system to a system of sales on an open market; on the broad effects of political economy on literature, see Hauser, 1957).

Perhaps the most radical change of this sort comes with the invention of printing. Printing allows for the exact reproduction of many copies of a work both quickly and cheaply. It vastly extends the possibilities for the physical production and distribution of literary works, thus transforming the possible readership for literature, the practices of that readership, the authors' imagination of readership, and so forth. For example, it is now virtually a commonplace that print has had significant effects on genre and, at least in the West, is bound up with the development of the novel (see Benjamin, 2000; McKeon, 1987; Watt, 1957).

Postprint media have given rise to still further changes (discussed most famously by McLuhan, 1964)—including the development of new genres and subgenres, such as the situation comedy. Here the reproducibility of texts is extended to the reproducibility of performances. It is often remarked that there is a secondary orality that develops with electronic media. This is due in part to the fact that a great deal of what is written in the electronic age is written to be watched and heard, not read. This requires changes in a writer's development principles, perhaps leading to the incorporation of some oral elements.

A striking feature of the new media is that they extend the reach of particular sorts of literature to nearly everyone. For example, even the most impoverished and illiterate people across the globe may see movies or a television program. Of course, this expansion is almost entirely in the realm of entertainment. However, the new media have greatly extended dissemination of classics (e.g., through Shakespeare films or the televised *R-m-yana* in India). This, in turn, has helped to create a large audience/readership with a fairly extensive, if indirect and unsystematic knowledge of canonical literature. In other words, it has created a range of sporadically, idiosyncratically, partially ideal readers.

At the same time, the new media have intensified a number of the problems that arose with writing and print, in particular problems associated with durability. These, in turn, have affected the very idea of an ideal reader. Specifically, in the past century, film, video, and related media have generated an unfathomable range of recorded literary works, reproduced in exact copies of performances. Moreover, the same period has seen an equally unfathomable production of books. In this context, it becomes more difficult to have a sense of an ideal reader for either entertainment or art. Again, increasing numbers of people are familiar with some canonical works. But that familiarity is often haphazard and indirect (e.g., a matter of adaptations that one happens to have seen on TV). The classics, especially the sacred classics, remain fairly well established. But the broader canon is much less certain. This is true not only in popular understanding and electronic media, but in the educational system as well. The subparadigmatic canon has become increasingly fragmented, often along the lines of identity categories or (what is sometimes the same) academic specializations. Of course, canons were always fragmented. It is simply that we had gotten used to fragmentation by nation, but not, for example, by ethnicity.

Finally, digital technology is transforming the production and reception of texts themselves, through electronic books, the World Wide Web, hypertext editions of canonical works, new works written specifically for hypertext, and so on (see McGann, 2001). However, these trends have begun so recently that it is impossible to gauge their outcomes.

THE DIFFERENCE IDENTITY MAKES: CULTURAL TRADITIONS AND THEIR CANONS

Any general discussion of literature is bound to focus on universals. The topic of literature as such requires a treatment of broad patterns, not cultural or individual specificity. In contrast, a discussion of French, Chinese, or Zulu literature would focus on the particularities of those traditions. Similarly, an essay on K-lid-sa or Chinua Achebe would address the individual characteristics of these writers. Nonetheless, there are some general points to make about cultural traditions (and about individual idiosyncrasy, to which we turn in the next section).

Cultural traditions are, first of all, traditions of influence. More technically, they are historical trajectories of learning in which prototypes and development principles are acquired by one generation of writers and readers from preceding generations of writers and readers. These prototypes and development principles alter in the course of transmission to new generations and they differ somewhat from individual to individual within a given generation. However, they retain some complex of characteristics that are—or, at least, are taken to be—distinctive of the tradition in question.

At a general level, traditional principles are communicated via a hierarchized canon that provides models and exemplars of culturally accepted standards. Thus, canons are both a source and a product of the prototypes that guide traditional practice. But cultural traditions are more than this, and that is shown in canons as well. Specifically, cultural traditions and the canons that crystallize them are not only a matter of practical literary activity. They are equally a matter of self-conscious identity. Thus we define our traditions and our canons largely on the basis of identity categories—religious, national, ethnic, and so forth. Historically, the first criterion for the definition of the highest canonical level has been religious. The pinnacle of the canon tends to be the greatest sacred work or works—the Bible, the R_m_yana, the Qur'-n. But nationally definitive works have not been far behind. Indeed, the secular works that generate rewritings tend to be just those works that have national significance. Moreover, we tend to categorize traditions in national, not religious terms.

The link between national identity and canon formation is particularly clear in colonial situations where colonized people work self-consciously to establish a national canon.

Ireland provides an obvious case. Anticolonial writers revived ancient Irish epics and set out to complement these with new, nationalist drama, poetry, and fiction. Developments of the same sort occurred in India and Africa. But the intertwining of national self-concepts and literary paradigms is not confined to modern, anticolonial societies. The writing and reading of such Persian works as the *Shâhnâme* were spurred by anti-Arab nationalism. The high canonical status of the Chinese *Three Kingdoms* is bound up with its place in Chinese national self-understanding. "Bardolatry" is historically inseparable from Shakespeare's role in English patriotism. Even some works we think of as religious—for example, the Torah—are almost equally nationalistic.

The development of subnational canons is simply an extension of the same principle. We see examples of this in the formation of an Afrocentric canon by some African Americans or even the institution of various minority studies programs (e.g., Asian-American studies). In a similar way, feminists have worked to establish a canon of women writers.

Again, identity categories define not only canons, but cultural traditions more generally. Indeed, the preceding definition of *tradition*, with its emphasis on the practical matter of influence, is not quite in keeping with the way the term is usually used. In its standard employment, tradition does not refer to all forms of influence on an author. It refers only to the influences that fit within his or her religious, national, racial, or other identity categories. Thus, if I am influenced by both Aristotle and Abhinavagupta, most people would view the former as an influence from "within my tradition," while judging the latter to be an influence from "outside my tradition." This has nothing at all to do with familiarity or the internalization of prototypes and development principles. No matter how well I understand and use Abhinavagupta, no matter how badly I understand and use Aristotle, most people would be inclined to continue characterizing Abhinavagupta as outside my tradition and Aristotle as inside my tradition.

In keeping with this, a great deal of cultural criticism has been devoted to establishing identity-based traditions, which is to say, chains of influence across writers within a given identity category—the tradition of women's writing, African American writing, and so forth. Of course, work of this sort is often undertaken in response to the implicit limitation of earlier canons and literary histories. For example, prior to recent, revisionist efforts by women and ethnic minorities, hegemonic canons and histories were confined almost entirely to a few dominant identity categories, prominently *male* and *white*.

But there are problems with identity-based notions of tradition, as my example of Abhinavagupta suggests. First, individual authors draw their prototypes and development principles from a wide range of sources. Often these sources belong to distinct traditions, in the identity-based sense of the term. This is particularly true today, but it was true in the past as well. For example, Ferdowsi's Persian nationalist epic was pervaded by Arabic influence. More important, the dilemma is not confined to isolated individuals. The traditions are hopelessly mixed. China deeply influenced Japan. India influenced both China and Greece. Greece influenced India. Such paradigmatic European authors as Goethe read Middle Eastern and South Asian works with great engagement. The influence of these foreign works undoubtedly affected, not only Goethe himself, but Goethe's influence on subsequent writers.

Of course, this is not to say that there are no broad patterns, that it does not make sense to speak of European or Chinese traditions. There are indeed rough trajectories for the standard literary lineages. European literature is more influenced by the Bible and Homer than by the Upanisads and V-lm-ki. Moreover, once they are institutionally established, traditions and their associated canons tend to be self-perpetuating. There are influences from outside the identity-defined tradition. But, most often, these do not radically change the production and distribution of works; they do not fundamentally alter general reading practices or educational curricula.

On the other hand, this does not mean that traditions proceed smoothly and without any disruption. It does sometimes happen that there is significant change in production and distribution networks. Sometimes educational curricula are altered substantively. Most often, this too is identity based, precipitated by social and political conflict surrounding identity categories or a significant change in the social structure bearing on identity categories. Colonial conquest is an obvious case of this sort, as is national independence. But the same effects may result from internal social rebellion, such as the civil rights and feminist movements in the United States. In each of these cases, the hegemonic identity-based tradition is challenged on the basis of a nonhegemonic identity category.

THE BURDENED POET

Beyond the cultural specification of universals in literary traditions, there is another important level of particularism—poetic individuality, what is sometimes called "voice." As we have already noted, writing encourages readers and authors to value innovation. Written literature stays around. In an oral society, a poet has to compete only with other living bards. In a literate society, a poet has to compete, not only with the living, but with the dead (Bate, 1970). Already in the Egyptian Middle Kingdom, this "burden of the past" (in Bate's phrase) became a topic for poetry. Thus, almost 4,000 years ago, Khakheperre-Sonb lamented that he could do nothing but repeat the phrases of his ancestors, lacking anything new (see Lichtheim, 1973).

This is not to say that all literate cultures claim to value innovation. They do not. Some cultures see conservative as good and innovative as bad. Others have no higher praise than to call something revolutionary. But, whatever a literate culture affirms about innovation, it values innovation in a way that oral culture does not. A culture that did not value writing something new would not value writing anything—for there is no point in repeating what is already available.

This is not to say that literate societies value radical change. Research in human cognition suggests that we like the stimulation that accompanies novelty, but we dislike disorientation and confusion (see chap. 1 of my *Cognitive* and citations). This is true for the highly literate readers of a modern novel and for the preliterate auditors of a bard's performance. The nature of our preferences in this regard is constant (though our rhetoric may vary, as when we use *revolutionary* as a term of praise for even mildly innovative works). The situation is well described by Hans Robert Jauss (1982), who argued that the "horizons of expectation" of readers alter historically. New works have to violate just enough of those expectations to be stimulating, but not so many as to produce an unpleasant disorientation.

More exactly, our sense of what is familiar and comprehensible is historically and culturally variable. Changes in comprehensibility are largely a matter of the cognitive models and skills we bring to reading (e.g., our experience of recently developed literary techniques, such as interior monologue, makes those techniques less confusing). Changes in familiarity are, first of all, a matter of what works exist and how they are distributed. But there is a complication here. Novelty may be opposed to either banality or imitation. We judge a work to be banal if it does what many other works have done previously. But we judge an author to be imitative or "derivative" if he or she has drawn on innovations of a previous author. What is curious here is that we stop counting an author as derivative if the innovations of the precursor are taken up by a large enough group of writers. Suppose one person writes a successful novel combining realism and magic. Then a second person writes a work that is realistic but includes elements of magic. In this case, we are likely to see the second author as derivative. But suppose more writers take up this technique. At a certain point, we are likely to stop counting any of these writers as derivative. Rather, we are likely to count them all as members of a movement, and we will view a number of them as innovative.

Our apparently contradictory responses to innovation and derivativeness result from ordinary cognitive processes. When we read the first magical realist novel, we relate it to the closest prototype available (perhaps one for the modernist novel). Faced with discrepancies, we class the nonprototypical properties as distinctive features of this work or its author. On reading a second magical realist novel by another author, we cannot class the nonprototypical properties as individually distinctive of this author as well. Rather, we continue to class them as distinctive of the first author, categorizing the second author as derivative. This is in part a product of writing, for writing allows us to identify an original and an imitation by reference to publication dates. Writing also allows instances of a particular type to accumulate. When we have read enough magical realist novels, we implicitly and spontaneously form them into a prototype. This prototype, then, becomes the tacit reference point for all those novels, changing their status accordingly.

WRITING ABOUT WRITING: THE UBIQUITY OF THEORY

The durability of writing has consequences not only for imaginative literature per se, but also for the analysis of and reflection on imaginative literature. As various traditions accumulated works, they began to articulate ways of thinking systematically about those works. In other words, they developed literary criticism and theory. This resulted from practical pressures (e.g., to form principles of canonization) as well as broad, intellectual curiosity.

Criticism and theory may be divided into four branches. These treat interpretation (of individual works), literary structure (shared by sets of works), aesthetical value, and ethical or political value. Though the emphases vary, all traditions that have left a large archive of literary works—European, Middle Eastern/North African, South Asian, East Asian—have paid some attention to each branch of criticism and theory. (For an overview of non-European theories, see Hogan & Pandit, 2005.)

Unsurprisingly, identity categories enter here as well. Theories are often viewed as having great worth within their own traditions but no particular utility outside those traditions. However, insofar as any theory has value as a theory, it should be applicable to a range of texts across traditions. In fact, one of the greatest benefits of writing is that it facilitates the communication of literary ideas across cultures. That communication is what allows us to understand, not only different cultural traditions and an increased number of individual idiosyncrasies, but literary universals as well.

REFERENCES

Allen, R. (2000). *An introduction to Arabic literature*. Cambridge, England: Cambridge University Press.

Ashcroft, B., Griffiths, G., & Tiffin, H. (1989). *The empire writes back: Theory and practice in postcolonial literatures*. London: Routledge.

Bate, W. J. (1970). *The burden of the past and the English poet*. Cambridge, MA: Harvard University Press.

Benjamin, W. (2000). The storyteller. In M. McKeon (Ed.), *Theory of the novel: A historical approach* (pp. 77–93). Baltimore: Johns Hopkins University Press.

Bourdieu, P. (1984). *Distinction: A social critique of the judgement of taste* (R. Nice, Trans.). Cambridge, MA: Harvard University Press.

Brooks, C. (2001). The formalist critics. In V. B. Leitch (Ed.), *The Norton anthology of theory and criticism* (pp. 1366–1371). New York: Norton.

Chomsky, N. (2000). *New horizons in the study of language and mind*. Cambridge, England: Cambridge University Press.

Frye, N. (1982). *The great code: The Bible and literature*. New York: Harcourt Brace.

Gilbert, S., & Gubar, S. (1979). *The madwoman in the attic: The woman writer and the nineteenth-century literary imagination*. New Haven, CT: Yale University Press.

Hauser, A. (1957). *The social history of art* (Vol. 1; Stanley Godman, Trans.). New York: Vintage.

Hogan, P. C. (2003). *The mind and its stories: Narrative universals and human emotion*. Cambridge, England: Cambridge University Press.

Hogan, P. C., & Pandit, L. (2005). Ancient theories of narrative (non-Western). In *Routledge encyclopedia of narrative theory* (pp. 14–19). London: Routledge.

Ingalls, D. (Ed.). (1990). *The Dhvany-loka of -nandavardhana with the Locana of Abhinavagupta* (D. Ingalls, J. Masson, & M. V. Patwardhan, Trans.). Cambridge, MA: Harvard University Press.

Jauss, H. R. (1982). *Toward an aesthetic of reception* (T. Bahti, Trans.). Minneapolis: University of Minnesota Press.

Kuipers, C. M. (2003, December 29). *The will to anthologize: The universality of canonization.* Paper presented at the annual convention of the Modern Language Association, San Diego, CA.

Lau, D. C. (1979). Introduction. In D. C. Lau (Ed. & Trans.), *Confucius: The analects* (pp. 9–55). New York: Penguin.

Lawall, S., & Mack, M. (Eds). (2002). *The Norton anthology of world literature* (2nd ed., Vol. A). New York: Norton.

Lichtheim, M. (1973). *Ancient Egyptian literature: Vol. 1. The Old and Middle Kingdoms.* Berkeley: University of California Press.

Liu, H. (1969). *The literary mind and the carving of dragons* (V. Y. Shih, Trans.). New York: Columbia University Press.

Liu, J. (1972). Introduction. In J. Liu (Ed. & Trans.), *Six Yüan plays* (pp. 7–35). New York: Penguin.

Lord, A. B. (1976). *The singer of tales.* New York: Atheneum.

Lu C. (1966). Rhymeprose on literature: The *Wên-fu* of Lu Chi (A.D. 261–303) (A. Fang, Trans.). In J. Bishop (Ed.), *Studies in Chinese literature* (pp. 527–561). Cambridge, MA: Harvard University Press.

McGann, J. (2001). *Radiant textuality: Literature after the World Wide Web.* New York: Palgrave.

McKeon, M. (1987). *The origins of the English novel 1600–1740.* Baltimore: Johns Hopkins University Press.

McLuhan, M. (1964). *Understanding media: The extensions of man.* New York: McGraw-Hill.

O'Connor, M. (1996). Epigraphic Semitic scripts. In P. T. Daniels & W. Bright (Eds.), *The world's writing systems* (pp. 88–107). New York: Oxford University Press.

Ong, W. J. (1971). *Rhetoric, romance, and technology: Studies in the interaction of expression and culture.* Ithaca, NY: Cornell University Press.

Ong, W. J. (1977). *Interfaces of the word: Studies in the evolution of consciousness and culture.* Ithaca, NY: Cornell University Press.

Ong, W. J. (1982). *Orality and literacy: The technologizing of the word.* London: Methuen.

Powell, B. B. (2002). *Writing and the origins of Greek literature.* Cambridge, England: Cambridge University Press.

Richman, P. (1991). Introduction: The diversity of the *R-m-yana* tradition. In P. Richman (Ed.), *Many R-m-yanas: The diversity of a narrative tradition in South Asia* (pp. 3–21). Berkeley: University of California Press.

Rubin, D. C. (1995). *Memory in oral traditions: The cognitive psychology of epic, ballads, and counting-out rhymes.* New York: Oxford University Press.

Waines, D. (1995). *An introduction to Islam.* Cambridge, England: Cambridge University Press.

Watt, I. (1957). *The rise of the novel: Studies in Defoe, Richardson and Fielding.* Berkeley: University of California Press.

CHAPTER 13

Writing and Journalism: Politics, Social Movements, and the Public Sphere

Martin Conboy
University of Sheffield, UK

This chapter chronicles research into the area of social writing referred to broadly as journalism. Journalism, in all its written forms, has always had a strong social function not least because of its ever-present economic imperative to make money by appealing to and even constructing social readerships.

THE EMERGENCE OF SOCIALLY ORIENTED RESEARCH INTO JOURNALISM

Academic research into journalism has lagged behind the historical development of its subject, certainly compared to other fields. Perhaps this has been because of the perceived lowly status of a form of writing that foregrounds the transitory. A sneaking contempt for journalism is wittily captured in a 19th-century comic dialogue that opens: "What, Warnford! corrupting your style by studying a newspaper?" (Traill, 1884, p. 436). Furthermore, the United States had to wait until 1810 for Thomas' *The History of Printing in America* and it was not until the middle of the Victorian era that Britain produced A. Andrews' (1859/1998) *The History of British Journalism*.

These accounts celebrated a version of journalism history as a gradual and indeed inevitable triumph of democratic involvement in contemporary political affairs over the vested interests of the powerful. The 19th century also saw the start of the great man style of hagiography with regard to journalists, editors, and owners, which detracts from the social context of their productions. In America, this produced notable early examples such as *The Life of Horace Greeley* (1855) and *The Life and Times of Benjamin Franklin* (1864), both by Parton.

Journalism in the United States 1690–1872 by Hudson (1873), set the standard for developmental exposition, which was to dominate the field continuing until well into the 20th century with Mott's *American Journalism* (1941). Such books provided an account in which journalism assisted social progress by providing more citizens with basic political opinion and information while serving the secondary purpose, of building communities through a readership.

The explicit acknowledgment of the social role of this form of writing in the early 20th century as a paradigm shift in research methodologies brought journalism into focus as an area worthy of investigation for the first time. Robert E. Park's "The Natural History of the Newspaper" (1925) was the first to foreground the social conditions and institutional structures that created the journalism of a particular age. A similar engagement with the social implications of journalism in Britain came in Angell's *The Press and the Organisation of Society* (1922), which was written from an explicitly socialist perspective. A. M. Lee's *The Daily Newspaper in America: The Evolution of a Social Instrument* (1937) stresses the social and economic factors that come together in journalism to make it an effective political instrument and eschews the influence of individuals other than as socially motivated factors themselves.

The late 20th and early 21st century sees the consolidation of a distinctly social perspective from which a more skeptically focused and politically suspicious research has emerged. Carey (1974), for instance, rejects the "Whig" teleology of journalism that implies the unfolding of an inevitable progression of journalism and insists instead on a cultural reading of how journalism has shaped the understanding of reality itself and how this has been woven together with questions of social and political power. It has destabilized many of the platitudes of developmental histories of journalism. More recently, W. D. Sloan and Williams (1994) have returned to the early years of American journalism to explore the impact of early journalism on society. Nord (2001) explores a wide historical range of the community-building aspects of journalism in America from the 17th to the 20th century and stresses the part that communicating to a specific public plays in maintaining a sense of identifiable community. He uses reader response literature and survey material to identify who the readers actually were.

Hanno Hardt (1979) had produced an exploration of theories of the press that aligns it with prevailing social and political philosophies from both an American and a German perspective. Altschull (1990) adds to this tradition by providing an intellectual history of the ideas that lay behind the development of journalism in the United States.

From a British perspective, Herd (1952) demonstrates that developmental accounts had not been entirely superseded. One has only to consider his title *The March of Journalism* to infer the celebratory approach. By1978, Cranfield was to provide a history of journalism in its social context. Berridge (1978) also published work that examined the nature of the social expectations of journalism as the reach of news spread during the early industrializing period of the 19th century. Most subsequent historical studies continue to stress the changing nature of journalism as it sought to capitalize on an expanded social audience. Robson (1995) concentrates on how the *Daily Telegraph* incorporated readers' views for the first time into a campaign around the issue of prostitution building an extended community of readership among the lower middle class. Baldastay (1992) gives an American contextualization of the consequences of the commercialization of news and draws similar conclusions to those subsequently arrived at by Chalaby (1998) in a later British context. The latter argues that it was the commercialization of the new print media of the middle of the 19th century in search of specific readerships that actually created the form that we identify as journalism today. Conboy (2004) has written a contemporary history that attempts to take a discursive approach to journalism as a genre that has drawn heavily on miscellany in order to secure its social and national readerships.

EARLY JOURNALISM FORMS

Having identified the paradigm shift in journalism research from a developmental, even teleological celebration, to a more socially orientated engagement, we must now return chronologically to explorations of the social implications of journalism from its earliest manifestations in England in the late 16th century.

From this period, early forms of public print culture provided the precursor to journalism in Europe. Despite the claims of Chalaby (1998) and K. Campbell (2000), this era produced the template for many of its defining characteristics. In turn, these textual features form part of the broader development of modernity, drawing together issues of social representation, broadening demands for political democracy, and the importance of market forces in the trading of information as a commodity. Siebert (1965) has written the classic articulation of the emergence of the freedom of the press in England as a political negotiation with the power elite in society. Frank (1961) and Raymond (1996, 1999a, 1999b) have contributed accounts of the formation of the variety of textual practices that constituted early journalism in England. Voss (2001) provides a revisionist reading of the late Elizabethan quartos as the authentic first stirrings of journalistic creativity in England whereas Dooley and Baron (2001) put the development of journalism in a pan-European context of communication politics. Indicative of the radical skepticism of contemporary historiography with regard to journalism, Sommerville (1996) provides an in-depth account of the formation of journalism from a range of textual experimentation. Economic pressures have meant that the collection and presentation of news has developed to conform to a predetermined style that has increasingly foregrounded brevity and clarity. Sommerville concludes that this has not enhanced our appreciation of the complexity of social reality.

JOURNALISM AND MODERNITY

Journalism has had a key role in the formation of modernity through the creation and control of a public sphere that has been defined by power relationships within society. The debate fostered within this sphere has sometimes enhanced democratic developments on behalf of rising social classes and on other occasions journalism has been deployed to close down debate just as successfully within authoritarian regimes.

A key contributor to the debate on how journalism has functioned as a force within modernity is B. Anderson (1986), who has foregrounded the role of print journalism in the creation of imagined national spaces. He interprets journalism as one of the formative factors that enabled individuals to imagine themselves as participants in a wider project of empathetic nationhood. Sherman (1996) also highlights aspects of time in his work on the impact of diurnality on textual from in English. K. Campbell (2000), too, argues that journalism, particularly in its early 19th-century combination of high and low culture, was a dominant factor in the consolidation of modernity's claims to cultural hegemony.

PUBLIC SPHERE

The power implications of the relationship between journalism and the public have meant that there has been no straightforward trajectory to mass involvement in democratic participation through journalism but rather a constant renegotiation of the relationships within dominant social forces at particular times. Newspapers began by assuming that their readership was reasonably homogeneous. This unifying vision gave rise to the power of a middle-class public from the beginning of the 18th century across parts of Western Europe. Habermas (1989) links the rise of the bourgeoisie explicitly to its ability to negotiate a public sphere located between the interests of itself as a social class and the interests of the state. As an addition to this theory, Eagleton (1991) provides an illuminating commentary on how this public sphere came to represent the emergent aesthetic and cultural tastes of a new political class that occluded that on which its identity depended for its existence: private property.

Nevertheless, the world that the language of these early papers projected was a bourgeois and a male domain and both women (McDowell, 1998) and the laboring classes (Harris & Lee, 1978) were excluded from it. Over time and under political and market pressures from both social audiences and business interests, it developed a broader range of language for specifically targeted readerships. The style of language within journalism has therefore evolved over time to conform to the demands of this variety.

JOURNALISM AS CATALYST FOR SOCIAL AND POLITICAL CHANGE

One of the factors that distinguishes American from British histories of journalism is that American histories unsurprisingly see the newspaper as an essential tool in the liberation of America from British colonial rule and thereafter the building of a new American nation. There has been much excellent work in the field establishing the role of the early printers in forging social ideologies of democracy and political critique. Schlesinger (1958) is notable in this tradition of establishing the centrality of journalism to the propaganda war for the hearts and minds of an American people. Most histories stress this social reality, including most recently Copeland (2000), who provides a discussion of the role of the press in the formation of an independent and cohesive sense of American identity.

In the French tradition, there is also much that foregrounds the role of journalism as a tool that shaped a revolutionary public, such as Darnton (1996) and Popkin (1990). Popkin, in a second book (2001), takes this style of interpretation into a later period, 1830–1835. He shows how the regional press in Lyon was able to articulate a complex range of social identities for the industrializing urban France of the period. The variety of these new imagined communities in print, workers, women, and self-conscious members of an older bourgeoisie eroded the conventional establishment myth of the existence of one public, as the press redefined the complexity of European public sphere, defining the *public space of modernity*.

In an English context, Thompson (1969) is eloquent in his claims that the radical press helped to foster a new way of identification for working people in the early years of the 19th century. Hollis (1970) can be read as companion piece to Thompson, highlighting, as she does, the inadequacies of the early phase of radical journalism. At a time that saw the press become capitalized and therefore cut off from radical intent, Curran (1977) shows the paradox between the freedoms of capitalism and the mechanism of social control that the press had become. Berridge (1978) has plowed a similar furrow, delineating the cultural and political restrictions that the particular forms of popular journalism that emerged in the mid-19th century placed on their readers.

The ability of journalism to articulate the concerns of radical and alternative communities persists in the margins of the public sphere today. Sometimes these communities are outside the dominant Anglophone media traditions of Western capitalism and can be best considered as in Said (1994) as part of a postcolonialist tradition. The political and cultural span of such an area of research is vast, but readers can consider some of the following as portals for consideration of the complexities of this rich vein of discussion on the role of journalism as a public communicator between imperial power and colonized peoples.

Copeland and Martin (2003) place contemporary debate concerning the function of newspapers into a wider historical context that includes sustained discussion of the relationship between a broad range of different types of society and the medium of the newspaper in the Arab world, Africa, Asia, and the Pacific Rim. Potter (2003) considers the role of the British imperial press as significant in shaping the structure and understanding of the position of Britain in the world both for its own educated population as well as for large sections of the peoples under British dominion.

Ainslie (1967) provides one of the earliest and most widely referenced accounts of the historical and political development of newspapers in Africa, both Anglophone and Francophone, from their colonial origins to their role in national liberation struggles. Prior to the formation of political parties in the British West African colonies in the 1930s, newspapers were the main channel for both nationalist agitation and the drive for political independence. Coker (1968), Jones-Quarty (1974), and Kasoma (1988) provide historical accounts of Nigeria, Ghana, and Zambia, respectively. Lamb (1981) is the first to convincingly chart the political and economic decline of much of the African press and to place it within the context of the postcolonial frustrations of much of the continent.

Ayalon (1995) charts the history of journalism across the varied terrain of the Arab Middle East between 1800 and 1945 and considers the role of the press in the development of modern variants of Arabic culture and political formation.

Kaul (2003) provides an extremely focused account of the ways in which reporting of the British Empire in India formed a growing part of the popular understanding of Britain's role in an imperial context between 1880 and 1922. Indigenous accounts of the longer development of the press in India include Natarajan (1962), George (1967), and Krishnamurty (1966), all of whom contribute to our understanding of how journalism grew in India from British missionary fervor and desire for political control, to provide a wide platform for political identification across the continent.

Marshall (1995) provides a starting point for investigating the rich tradition of the English-language press of Latin America, which maintains an interesting function even in postcolonial times. Meyer (1996) considers the ways in which a Spanish press developed the specific cultural identity of Mexicans between 1880 and 1920. González-Pérez (1993) looks more broadly across Spanish-speaking newspapers to consider how this variety of journalism enabled a specific sense of Spanish–American narrative to emerge. Chasteen and Castro-Klaren (2003) begin by exploring the role of Anderson's thesis on the imagined community of newspapers in the formation of cultural identities but extend their range of cultural forms beyond the press to consider how it was interrelated to a wide selection of other equally dynamic literary and other communicative formats. On a contemporary note, Weisbord (2000) looks at the role of journalism as watchdog and guarantor of democratic accountability in contemporary Latin America.

Other research has looked more broadly within Western cultures for significant opposition to the political or economic status quo. Downing (2000), for instance, roots his work in the history of the media deployed by social outsiders. He is eclectic in his range of media examples but contributes to debates on the social use of journalism by radical groups. Rodriguez (2001) and Atton (2002) also belong to this tradition of exploring how different publics can claim their rights as citizens through alternative media. They are particularly strong on new social movements and the role of activist-journalists within them.

JOURNALISM AND URBAN SPACES

We have read how Anderson has created a framework for the role that journalism played in the normalizing of nationalism. Social psychologist Billig demonstrates the continuing pervasiveness of nationalism throughout our daily newspaper culture in *Banal Nationalism* (1995) together with an assessment of the default perspective of North American political values in much mainstream British media. P. J. Anderson and Weymouth (1999) recount how the British press represent issues of vital importance to the future of the British state with regard to Europe to the detriment of a good understanding of the relevant issues, and argue that, in doing so, they impoverish the comprehension of this national community that risks becoming defined by its ignorance about European and global politics.

Splichal (1994) is invaluable in providing an overview of how journalism has provided a means of articulating the aspirations and complexities of emerging national identities in the new publics of postcommunist eastern and central Europe that have suddenly been confronted with new paradigms of association.

In terms of charting the construction of Black American communities of journalism, Hutton (1993) traces a variety of approaches that Black newspapers took toward the aspirations of urban middle-class Black communities. As a corrective to the assimilationist tendencies within these mainstream Black publications, we have Hutton and Reed (1995), who provide a view of alternatives. In contemporary terms, although Newkirk's contribution

(2000) is not written as a research monograph, it is nevertheless a major contribution to exploring the representation of Black people in the American media from the perspective of the Black journalists within a White establishment. It places contemporary experiences within a historical context.

FOURTH ESTATE

One of the comfortable myths associated with journalism is that it has, as a form of public writing, enabled an informed citizenship to emerge from the shackles of authoritarian modes of communication control. The most celebrated historical account of this process in England is Siebert's (1965). Yet for all its historical richness and textual detail, Siebert's account is challenged by the more skeptical work of authors such as Boyce (1978) who see the whole concept of the Fourth Estate, the watchdog function of the press, as obscuring the relationship between the power bloc and the press throughout its history. Boyce argues that journalism would understand itself and its place in society better if it was more candid about the nature of its integration within power structures.

Despite their long reliance on a factual reporting style, newspapers are relatively new to the concept of objectivity as a professional ideal. The 18th- and 19th-century press were notorious for their overt support for the political and commercial positions and interests that paid them directly for their support. Economic success that meant that they did not need to curry direct political favor came relatively late to newspapers. This meant that it was only at the start of the 20th century that newspapers began to consistently adhere to a certain common perception of objectivity as a means of promoting their own rigor and political independence. Schudson (1978) and Schiller (1981) look at objectivity as rooted not only in the social and cultural conditions of the development of the newspaper but also in the technologies that changed the shape and content of journalism. Certainly, they stress the ways in which journalism created audiences within a market economy as social and increasingly stratified communities while it claimed for itself an increasingly professionalized set of standards of production, including objectivity.

Herman and Chomsky (1988) have explored the relationship between elite groups and community of readers that informs a propaganda model that is not solely dependent on distortion or bias but on the implicit self-interest of those with access to primary information and the ways that these can actively filter out what is inconvenient to their preferred agenda at a structural and routine level. Such has been the influence of this model that professional commitment to high ideals of service to the reading public have been voiced (Lichtenberg, 2000; Schudson, 2001). This riposte indicates, as in all areas of journalism research, that revision and opposition to dominant theses are a healthy sign of active debate within the field.

Research concentrating on skeptical views of journalism has led some, in antidotal fashion, to call for a "journalism of attachment," which is clear about the location of the sympathies of both journalist and institution. One key protagonist in the debate is a journalist himself, M. Bell (1998). This development is of importance because it contests what has been a dominant theme within the orthodoxy of journalism over the 20th century—that of objectivity. Particularly in war situations, the journalism of attachment insists on an honest, ethical engagement. This is one of the pragmatic reconfigurations within the discourses of journalism that has the potential, at least, to offer a reconstitution of social writing, and it is one that is given technological impetus by the fragmentation of conventional markets for journalism through the Internet and is particularly noticeable in new public writing practices such as blogs.

As early as 1927, Dewey identified the inability of the public to communicate its needs to the political elite other than through the prism of commercial media interests as being *the* problem of the public. In this publication, Dewey first alerts us to the problematic relationship between press and the public on whose behalf it claims to speak.

There is currently a resurgence of interest in alternative ways of engaging with the public in a civic involvement that attempts to transcend the merely commercial aims of audience identification by the press, leading to campaigns for public journalism that enables genuine engagement of service to a specific community.

Both Glasser (1999) and Merritt (1995) promote an idea of journalism as broadening out the participation of the public, going beyond the conventions and even the professional norms of contemporary practice, enabling a greater degree of involvement from the public in social matters, more context to news, and a more explicit realization of the journalist as a participant in the democratic process.

The contemporary study of the ethics of journalism is also part of the reaction to concerns about journalism's public functions and professional obligations. McManus (1994) is characteristic of the trend with his analysis of the impact of market-driven journalism, summarized in his subtitle *Let the Citizen Beware!* This ethical concern is also an aspect of research on the social function and obligations of contemporary journalism to its public and how the ethical quality of journalism impacts on that public. Belsey and Chadwick (1992), Christians (1995), Kieran (1997), Starck (2001), and Harcup (2002) have all provided indicative reviews of the field.

THE LINGUISTIC TURN

Newspaper language plays a major part in the construction of what Berger and Luckman (1976) have referred to as the social construction of reality. Newspapers assist in the creation of a set of public discourses through their selection of narratives and the language they employ to project them. Just as language continues to vary in its content and structure to adapt to the variety of social and cultural demands made on it in differing circumstances, so too has the language of newspapers.

In Britain, the pioneering work of the Birmingham School with Hall, Critcher, Jefferson, Clarke, and Roberts (1978) led to the foregrounding of linguistic analysis in studies of the news. This takes one form in the content analysis of the Glasgow Media School, another in the close textual readings of critical discourse analysis, including work emanating from the Netherlands by Van Dijk (1991), and in Britain by Fowler (1991), Fairclough (1989), and Hodge and Kress (1993).

Within the range of linguistic style of the newspaper, there is a diversity and differentiated social target. Matheson has charted the historical emergence of this feature of audience targeting in the prose and layout of newspapers. One characteristic of this new discourse of news (Matheson, 2000) was the way that the reporting of facts and opinions, often from partisan perspectives within newspapers, become replaced by the central component of the story (Smith, 1978). Each newspaper has developed and indeed created an ideal audience within the language that it uses and the stories that it tells. Each newspaper must look for an opportunity to present its own angle that ties in with a relatively stable identity and lexicon (Cameron, 1996). The language style of each newspaper is, in fact, no more and no less than an exercise in audience design (A. Bell, 1984). Bell has, in fact, gone further, claiming that newspapers are "language-forming institutions" (A. Bell, 1994, p. 000), which means that their language connects with and is influenced by broader linguistic trends. Much newspaper language is driven as never before by the economic imperative to retain an audience within a densely competitive news media environment and to achieve this by refining its construction of social audiences through writing style.

Newspapers routinely reduce the complexity of the world and they often lack context because of constraints on space and the narrowness of their focus on idealized readerships as market segment. They provide very much a model of the mosaic culture described by McLuhan (1995). News values that represent an unwritten set of criteria that classify events in terms of the interests of the newspaper and its idealized reader are constructed very much in terms of social categories:

The media do not simply and transparently report events which are "naturally" newsworthy *in themselves.* "News" is the end-product of a complex process which begins with a systematic sorting and selecting of events and topics according to a socially constructed set of categories. (Hall et al., 1978, p. 000; italics original)

CRITIQUES OF POPULAR JOURNALISM

As journalism has developed, it has been targeted at larger audiences. One of the pressures of maintaining large-scale readerships is to consistently reproduce something that claims to speak on behalf of ordinary people and their interests. Historical accounts have emerged including Huntzicker's (1999) exploration of the penny press between 1833 and 1865 that locate the central issues involved in the expansion of journalism's markets to include increasingly members of lower socioeconomic groups and the political and textual implications of these developments. In many ways, popular newspapers attempt to create and maintain a consistent appeal to ordinary people. Bessie (1938) provides a snapshot of a particular era in the still-fresh and stimulating account of *Jazz Journalism*. Stevens provides an account of an earlier era of the penny press in the way that it sought to define public mood in terms of ever-increasing levels of sensationalism (1991), but stresses the negativity of the construction of these blue-collar communities in the populist exploitation of the fears of their readers. Bird (1992) takes a view of popular journalism as a form of anthropological index of the American people. It is far from a pessimistic view and encourages us to appreciate the dynamism and diversity of contemporary popular journalism. A similar exploration of the relationship between readers and the sensational end of the journalism market that reveals as much about the readers as the producers from the era of the early penny press can be found in Tucher (1994). Sloan (2001), from the perspective of a former tabloid editor, attempts to place the social practice of contemporary tabloids in a cultural context.

W. J. Campbell (2001) combats what he sees as the attitude of contempt around the term, the practice, and the readers of the "yellow press" to give a rounder picture of how it emerged and what traditions of journalism it grew out of and how it maintains its cultural place within its readers' affections today. It is particular important in its brief survey of the demographics of this sort of journalism.

The work of Hoggart (1958) on popular journalism was seminal in influencing future developments in the field in Britain. He was the first to take a social perspective of the meanings of working-class print-media consumption. This provided the intellectual springboard for a particularly British yet extremely influential paradigm of research into the social consumption of popular journalism. The first to continue this work exclusively in the context of the social audiences for popular journalism was Williams (1961). Smith (1975) provides a stimulating exploration of the textual construction of social audiences in two very different British popular newspapers either side of World War II, whereas James (1976) charts a longer history of the involvement of ordinary people and their political concerns in the history of popular print. Sparks and Swedish scholar Dahlgren (Dahlgren & Sparks, 1992) have continued the serious investigation from a wide range of political perspectives on the ways in which popular journalism textually constructs a worldview for its readers. Dahlgren encourages us to see the meaning of popular journalism, in particular in the associated networks of meanings in which it operates for its target readership. Connell (1992) provides some very provocative insights into how the television celebrity culture was integrated within popular journalism and Gripsrud (1992) locates such narratives with work on melodrama, indicating the rich potential for interdisciplinary work within explorations of popular journalism and its audiences.

Hartley (1996) broadens the project started by Hoggart and Williams to integrate a wide range of popular journalism text into a postmodern and intertextual reading of how contemporary society uses journalism as one cultural means of making sense of the world.

Conboy (2002) understands popular journalism less in terms of a real social readership than as a form of rhetorical performance that, despite its reproduction of a highly stylized popular vernacular, remains rhetorical and not otherwise linked with any real conditions of the existence of ordinary people. Brumm (1980) in Germany began the process of examining the country's most successful daily newspaper and came to the conclusion that it was acting as a sounding board for the views and prejudices of a large number of ordinary Germans. Sparks, this time in conjunction with Tulloch (Sparks & Tulloch, 2002), has given the study of tabloids a useful global comparative perspective as well as providing some more useful historical context to the study of the social implications of tabloid journalism.

JOURNALISM AND CRISIS DEFINITION

Research into the relationship between state, press, and society tends to move in cycles from propaganda to hegemony and back again. Much recent journalism research has shifted from a narrative of social consolidation and development to one that depicts a society in crisis (Raboy & Dagenais, 1992). This crisis is either articulated as the West under political or military threat from outside forces, most notably fundamentalism and terrorism, or as a crisis in political credibility among indigenous populations.

In the latter, the crisis can be interpreted as emanating from a logical progression within journalism and its relationship with the state (Keeble, 1997) or big business (Hermann & Chomsky, 1988). The more intensively journalism has intruded into political life, the more intense the scrutiny of the relationship between journalism and politics has become. This is particularly the case as it appears that their proximity has led to a codependence that has tended to draw journalism away from impartial scrutiny and closer to an interpretation of a set of complex processes of which it itself is a formative part. This has led to a crisis felt by the public in political communications, especially as mediated through journalism (Blumler & Gurevitch, 1995). These authors have applied the talk of crisis to domestic politics in Britain. They have tracked both political coverage and audience reception of this coverage during British general elections and argue that the decline in politically mature media debate of policies has drastic implications for the quality of political communication in the country.

From the perspective of the North American news media, Hermann and Chomsky (1988) have developed an influential set of paradigms that demonstrate how the dominant news media do not have to resort to anything as crude as lying or propaganda to establish structures of social reception that favor the representation of the world from viewpoints favorable to a conservative status quo. They have elaborated theories on such key concepts as *gate-keeping* and privileged primary news definers. Building on this work, and in ways more inflected toward a European Marxist perspective and the work of Gramsci, writers such as Keane (1991), Raboy and Dagenais (1992), and Keeble (1997) have explored the hegemonic operation of the news media in times of self-defined crisis and militarist intervention.

WOMEN'S JOURNALISM

Because much of the journalism intended for female consumption has taken the form of the magazine, it is no surprise that much research has tended to focus on this output. Much of this research considers how women have been constructed as a gendered audience by the print media directed at them. Some early work (White, 1970) concentrates exclusively on women's magazines and is useful in providing a developmental chronology of journalism that sought to appeal to a readership that was changing over time. Other work stresses the female authors who were instrumental in this work (Adburgham, 1972). An early demonstration of the impact of feminist scholarship explored the relationship that straightforward chronologies of the writing of women's journalism had tended to overlook. Ballaster, Beetham, Frazer, and Hebron (1991) examine the relationship between ideological constructs such as *femininity* and how the worldview of women's magazines conforms to patriarchal views of the world. A notable exploration of the social construction of bourgeois women in the 18th century press based on close textual observation can be found in Hunter (1977) as part of the generic development of journalism from newsletters to newspapers. Shevelow (1989) is an exception to this concentration on the generic patterns of the women's magazine, preferring to place women, more specifically, at the heart of centuries of endeavor within print culture and as instrumental in creating communities of readers identifiable and differentiated as women.

This tendency to include women in broader cultural involvement within print culture in general, as owners, distributors, and writers, has become more prevalent. McDowell (1998) provides a detailed chronology of the ways in which women were steadily marginalized from the routines of print ownership and production and steered into the confines of a restricted political arena of magazine journalism. Nevitt (1999) provides an interesting specific insight into the work of one particular woman, "Parliament Joan," in early propagandizing during the English civil war and sets her into the broader context of women's role in the early construction of communities of political allegiance through print.

McCracken (1993) has continued work on contemporary women's magazines from a broadly feminist perspective whereas Beetham (1996) has dealt with the complexities surrounding issues of feminine desire and domesticity across the 19th and early 20th centuries again, reflecting the instabilities and changes as well as the ideological continuities in these themes over time. Easley (2000), Shattock (2000), and K. Jackson (2000), in an invaluable survey of the construction of social identities in the print media of the 19th century (Brake, Bell, & Finkelstein, 2000), provide brief but insightful views of individual authors such as Martineau and Oliphant as well as providing a more in-depth analysis of the deliberately feminized tone of the New Journalism as it appealed to a greater market share of women readers in the last decade of the 19th century. K. Jackson (2001) later takes this up in a book-length study. An interestingly different take on the magazine format, which certainly has implications for feminist interest in journalism but that explores the construction of explicitly male readerships, comes from P. Jackson, Stevenson, and Brooks (2001). It considers the recent phenomenon of the "LadMag" culture in Britain and the representation of women as part of its appeal to its highly gendered audience.

In terms of research on women's journalism in the United States, we have certain significantly different contributions. Of note historically, Bennion also chooses to focus on periodical journalism in her *Equal to the Occasion: Women Editors of the Nineteenth-Century West* (1990). Russo and Kramarae also take a view broader than concentrating on individuals to look at broader patterns of women's journalism as a contribution to social change in *The Radical Women's Press of the 1850s* (1990), and more specific to generic patterns of representation of women in the press, Hoffert (1995) examines the coverage of women's conventions within mainstream newspapers and the ways suffragettes exploited a hostile press to their own provocative ends.

The journalistic representation of women is key to the development of a society in which discrimination becomes steadily combated and eroded. Therefore journalism has the potential, according to the analysis of Tuchman, Daniels, and Bénet (1978), to re-create a more gender-balanced set of professional communities. Van Zoonen (1994) disputes the transparency of this model and points out that it is a far more complex cultural and hegemonic process. She sets out the argument that in many ways journalism always assumes a male reader in its traditions and practice and is therefore a thoroughly androcentric product.

Hermes' work (1995) is intriguing in the way that it uses interview material rather than purely text-based analysis for its research method, articulating very much the thoughts of a community of readers on magazines aimed at them. It looks in an anthropological fashion at the uses women make of magazines in their everyday lives, creating a distinctive women's public sphere. Meyers (1997) looks at the ways in which women are routinely reported in news about violence and therefore the ways in which newspapers routinely construct a set of negative stereotypes about women. It draws on U.S. examples and also highlights the double representative discrimination of women of color who fall victim to male violence in United States. As in most research on issues of social discrimination, this draws the conclusion that the fault lies not in individual journalists' attitudes but within larger and older patterns of misogyny and patriarchy that are embedded within the practices of journalism as a social communicator.

Carter, Branston, and Allen (1998) take a broad-ranging view of the ways in which a whole network of traditions of practices, institutional patterns of behavior, and social realities of women's lives are drawn together to create a specifically female audience and draws on a range of feminist criticism to look at and challenge the limitations of the community that is constructed.

NEW TECHNOLOGIES AND JOURNALISM

As the technological delivery systems for journalism have become more diverse, so too has research tried to keep pace with these developments. In particular, the impact of these technologies on the social aspects of journalism has given rise to a fascinating range of interpretations. These may have started with explorations of the impact of broadcasting and later the Internet, but they have also begun to reach back and consider the nature of print technology and media themselves with relation to journalism. From McLuhan (1995) to Baudrillard (1983) and Kittler (1997), we can see a trend toward analyses that claim to chart the fragmentation of the public and the anarchic destabilization of journalism through the Internet. Bourdieu (1990) is determined to retain something of the social with his idea of the fields in which journalism and communities coexist, formed by commercial and political interests at the same time. Drawing on professional as well as philosophical considerations of the changing interrelationship between journalism and the social, Altheide and Snow (1991) and Bardel (1996) have all queried the social role of journalism as it becomes increasingly indistinguishable from the technologies that drive the information that it requires and draw radical conclusions about what this means for conventional notions of the social and the civic in this process.

In terms of the implications of the Web on journalism and its communities of consumption, much has been written that is based more on speculation than empirical evidence. In terms of political communities, Grossman (1996) provides an early celebration of the potential enhancement of participation through online access, but since then most research has been more cautious or even dismissive of issues of access and reliability or too premature to perceive any clear differences or trends. This trend has moved many commentators to view the destabilizing potential of the new technology on older paradigms of relationship between producers and consumers of social writing. Of particular interest is Pavlik (2001), particularly on the relationship between journalism and its publics and, for our purposes, the two-way system that allows citizens to directly access sources. He is optimistic of the democratic implications of this flow in terms of refined relationships between journalists and their publics.

The other side of this dynamic has been charted embryonically by Serfaty (2004), who provides an overview of developments in American blog communities. She traces the tradition of writing as a form of self and communal identification and explores how the Internet allows a wider community of exchange to be formed within such traditionally intimate practices as diary writing—reflecting on the impact of these on broader American society.

CONCLUDING COMMENTS

What emerges in this brief overview is a field of research that is contributing to our general understanding of how journalism adds to the range of ways in which writing constructs and describes different social groupings. Journalism has always had a profoundly social orientation and this has become more emphatic as the genre has diversified in terms of technology to embrace both radio and TV. Online developments mean that the complexities of journalism as a branch of social writing are opening up new ways of identifying communally and politically. More research into this emergent field will certainly continue to enhance not only our understanding of the potential of contemporary journalism but also a deeper appreciation of how this new impetus sheds light on its historical antecedents.

REFERENCES

Adburgham, A. (1972). *Women in print: Writing women and women's magazines from the Restoration to the accession of Victoria.* London: Allen & Unwin.

Ainslie, R. (1967). *The press in Africa: Communications past and present.* New York: Walker & Coy.

Altheide, D., & Snow, R. (1991). *Media worlds in the postjournalism era.* New York: de Gruyter.

Altschull, J. H. (1990). *From Milton to McLuhan: The ideas behind American journalism.* London: Longman.

Anderson, B. (1986). *Imagined communities.* London: Verso.

Anderson, P. J., & Weymouth, A. (1999). *Insulting the public? The British press and the European Union.* Harlow, England: Addison Wesley Longman.

Andrews, A. (1998). *The history of British journalism: From the foundation of the newspaper press in England to the repeal of the Stamp Act in 1855, with sketches of press celebrities* (Vols. 1 & 2). London: Routledge/Thoemmes. (Original work published 1859)

Angell, N. (1922). *The press and the organisation of society.* London: Labour.

Atton, C. (2002). *Alternative media.* London: Sage

Ayalon, A. (1995). *The press in the Arab Middle East: A history.* New York: Oxford University Press.

Baldasty, G. J. (1992). *The commercialization of news in the nineteenth century.* Madison: University of Wisconsin Press.

Ballaster, R., Beetham, M., Frazer, E., & Hebron, S. (1991). *Women's worlds: Ideology, femininity and the women's magazine.* Basingstoke, England: Macmillan.

Bardel, J. (1996). Beyond journalism: A profession between information society and civil society. *European Journal of Communication, 11*(3), 283–302.

Baudrillard, J. (1983). The ecstasy of communication. In H. Foster (Ed.), *The anti-aesthetic: Essays on postmodern culture* (pp. 126–134). Seattle, WA: Bay.

Beetham, M. (1996). *A magazine of her own? Domesticity and desire in the women's magazine 1800–1914.* London: Routledge.

Bell, A. (1984). Language style as audience design. *Language in Society, 13,* 145–204.

Bell, A. (1994). *Language in the news.* Oxford, England: Blackwell.

Bell, M. (1998). The journalism of attachment. In M. Kieran (Ed.), *Media ethics* (pp. 15–22). London: Routledge.

Belsey, A., & Chadwick, R. (Eds). (1992). *Ethical issues in journalism.* London: Routledge.

Bennion, S. C. (1990). *Equal to the occasion: Women editors of the nineteenth-century West.* Reno: University of Nevada Press.

Berger, P. L., & Luckman, T. (1976). *The social construction of reality.* London: Penguin.

Berridge, V. (1978). Popular Sunday papers and mid-Victorian society. In G. Boyce, J. Curran, & P. Wingate (Eds.), *Newspaper history from the seventeenth century to the present day* (pp. 247–264). London: Constable.

Bessie S, (1938). *Jazz journalism.* New York: Dutton.

Billig, M. (1995). *Banal nationalism.* London: Sage.

Bird, S. E. (1992). *For enquiring minds: A cultural study of supermarket tabloids.* Knoxville: University of Tennessee Press.

Blumler, J., & Gurevitch, M. (1995). *The crisis in public communication.* London: Routledge.

Bourdieu, P. (1990). *On television and journalism.* London: Pluto.

Boyce, G. (1978). The Fourth Estate: The reappraisal of a concept. In G. Boyce, J. Curran, & P. Wingate (Eds.), *Newspaper history from the seventeenth century to the present day* (pp. 19–40). London: Constable.

Brake, L., Bell, B., & Finkelstein, D. (Eds.). (2000). *Nineteenth-century media and the construction of identities.* Basingstoke, England: Palgrave.

Brumm, D. (1980). Sprachohr der Volksseele? [Spokepiece of soul of the people]. In M. W. Thomas (Eds.), *Porträts der deutschen Presse* (pp. 127–143). Berlin: Spiess.

Cameron, D. (1996). Style policy and style politics: A neglected aspect of the language of the news. *Media, Culture and Society, 18,* 315–333.

Campbell, K. (2000). Journalistic discourses and constructions of modern knowledge. In L. Brake, B. Bell, & D. Finkelstein (Eds.), *Nineteenth century media and the construction of identities* (pp. 40–53). Basingstoke, England: Palgrave.

Campbell, W. J. (2001). *Yellow journalism: Puncturing the myths, defining the legacies.* Westport, CT: Praeger.

Carey, J. (1974). The problem of journalism history. *Journalism History, 1,* 3–5, 27.

Carter, C., Branston, G., & Allen, S. (Eds.). (1998). *News, gender and power.* London: Routledge.

Chalaby, J. K. (1998). *The invention of journalism.* Basingstoke, England: Macmillan.

Chasteen, J. C., & Castro-Klaren, S. (2003). *Beyond imagined communities: Reading and writing the nation in nineteenth-century Latin America.* Baltimore: Johns Hopkins University Press.

Christians, C. G. (1995). Review essay: Current trends in media ethics. *European Journal of Communication, 10*(4), 545–558.

Coker, I. H. E. (1968). *Landmark of the Nigerian press: An outline of the Nigerian press and development of the origins and development of the newspaper press in Nigeria 1859–1965.* Laos, Nigeria: National Press Limited.

Conboy, M. (2002). *The press and popular culture.* London: Sage.

Conboy, M. (2004). *Journalism: A critical history.* London: Sage.

Connell, I. (1992). Personalities in the popular media. In P. Dahlgren & C. Sparks (Eds.), *Journalism and popular culture* (pp. 68–43). London. Sage.

Copeland, D. A. (2000). *Debating the issues in colonial newspapers.* Westport, CT: Greenwood.

Copeland, D. A., & Martin, S. E. (2003). *The function of newspapers in society.* Westport, CT: Praeger.

Cranfield, G, (1978). *The press and society: From Caxton to Northcliffe.* London: Longman.

Curran, J. (1977). Capitalism and the control of the press. In J. Curran, M. Gurevitch, & J. Woollacott (Eds.), *Mass communication and society* (pp. 51–75). London: Arnold and Open University Press.

Dahlgren, P., & Sparks, C. (Eds.). (1992). *Journalism and popular culture.* London: Sage.

Darnton, R. (1996). *Forbidden fruit.* London: HarperCollins.

Dewey, J. (1927). *The public and its problems.* Denver, CO: Swallow.

Dooley, B., & Baron, S. (Eds.). (2001). *The politics of information in early modern Europe.* London: Routledge.

Downing, J. D. (2000). *Radical media: Rebellious communication and social movements.* London: Sage.

Eagleton, T. (1991). *The function of criticism: From the spectator to post-structuralism.* London: Verso.

Easley, A. (2000). Authorship, gender and power in Victorian culture: Harriet Martineau and the periodical press. In L. Brake, B. Bell, & D. Finkelstein (Eds.), *Nineteenth-century media and the construction of identities* (pp. 154–164). Basingstoke, England: Palgrave.

Fairclough, N. (1989). *Language and power.* London. Longman.

Fowler, R, (1991). *Language in the news.* London: Routledge

Frank, J. (1961). *The beginnings of the English newspaper.* Cambridge, MA: Harvard University Press.

Franklin, B. (1997). *Newszack and news media.* London: Arnold.

George, T. J. S. (1967). *The provincial press in India.* New Dehli: Press Institute of India.

Glasser, T. (Ed). (1999). *The idea of public journalism.* New York: Guilford.

González-Pérez, A. (1993). *Journalism and the development of Spanish American narrative.* Cambridge, England: Cambridge University Press.

Gripsrud, J. (1992). The aesthetics and politics of melodrama. In P. Dahlgren & C. Sparks (Eds.), *Journalism and popular culture* (pp. 84–95). London: Sage.

Grossman, L. K. (1996). *The electronic republic: Reshaping democracy in the information age.* New York: Penguin.

Habermas, J, (1989). *The structural transformation of the public sphere.* Cambridge, England: Polity.

Hall, S., Critcher, C., Jefferson, T., Clarke, J., & Roberts, B. (Eds.). (1978). *Policing the crisis: Mugging, the state and law and order.* London: Macmillan.

Harcup, T. (2002). Journalists and ethics: The quest for a collective voice. *Journalism Studies, 3*(1), 101–114.

Hardt, H. (1979). *Social theories of the press: Early German and American perspectives.* London: Sage.

Harris, M., & Lee, A. J. (Eds). (1986). *The press in English society from the seventeenth to the nineteenth century.* London: Associated University Presses.

Hartley, J. (1996). *Popular reality.* London: Arnold.

Herd, H. (1952). *The march of journalism: The story of the British press from 1622 to the present day.* London: Allen & Unwin.

Herman, E., & Chomsky, N. (1988). *Manufacturing consent.* New York: Pantheon.

Hermes, J. (1995). *Reading women's magazines*. Cambridge, England: Polity.

Hodge, R., & Kress, G. (1993). *Language as ideology*. London: Routledge.

Hoffert, D. E. (1995). *When hens crow: The women's rights movement in antebellum America*. Bloomington: Indiana University Press.

Hoggart, R. (1958). *The uses of literacy*. London: Penguin.

Hollis, P. (1970). *The pauper press*. Oxford, England: Oxford University Press.

Hudson, F. (1873). *Journalism in the United States from 1690–1872*. New York: Harper & Row.

Hunter, J. (1977). The lady's magazine and the study of Englishwomen in the eighteenth century. In D. H. Bond & R. McLeod (Eds.), *Newsletters to newspapers: Eighteenth century journalism* (pp. 103–117). Morgantown: West Virginia University Press.

Huntzicker, W. E. (1999). *The popular press 1833–1865*. Westport, CT: Greenwood.

Hutton, F. (1993). *The early Black press in America, 1827 to 1860*. Westport, CT: Greenwood.

Hutton, F., & Reed, B. S. (1995). *Outsiders in 19th-century press history: Multicultural perspectives*. Bowling Green, OH: Popular.

Jackson, K. (2000). George Newnes and the "Loyal Tit-Bitites"—editorial identity and textual interaction in tit-bits. In L. Brake, B. Bell, & D. Finkelstein (Eds.), *Nineteenth-century media and the construction of identities* (pp. 11–26). Basingstoke, England: Palgrave.

Jackson, K. (2001). *George Newnes and the new journalism in Britain 1880–1910*. Aldershot, England: Ashgate

Jackson, P., Stevenson, N., & Brooks, K. (2001). *Making sense of men's magazines*. Cambridge, England: Polity.

James L, (1976). *Print and the people*. London: Lane.

Jones-Quarty, K. A. B. (1974). *A summary of the Ghana press: 1822–1960*. Accra: Ghana Information Services Department.

Kasoma, F. P. (1988). *The press in Zambia*. Lusaka, Zambia: Multimedia Productions.

Kaul, C. (2003). *Reporting the Raj: The British press and India 1880–1922*. Manchester, England: Manchester University Press.

Keane, J. (1991). *The media and democracy*. Cambridge, England: Polity.

Keeble, R. (1997). *Secret state, silent press*. Luton, England: University of Luton Press.

Kieran, M (1997). *Media ethics: A philosophical approach*. Westport, CT: Praeger.

Kittler, F. (1997). Media wars: Trenches, lightning, stars. In J. Johnson (Ed.), *Literature media information systems* (pp. 117–129). Amsterdam: G & B Arts International.

Krishnamurty, N. (1966). *Indian journalism*. Mysore, India: Prasanranga.

Lamb, D. (1981). *The Africans*. New York: Random House.

Lee, A. M. (1937). *The daily newspaper in America: The evolution of a social instrument*. New York: Macmillan.

Lichtenberg, J. (2000). In defense of objectivity. In J. Curran & M. Gurevitch (Eds.), *Mass media and society* (pp. 238–254). London: Arnold.

Marshall, O. (1995). *The English-language press in Latin America: An annotated bibliography*. New York: Institute of Latin American Studies.

Matheson, D. (2000). The birth of news discourse: Changes in news language in British newspapers, 1880–1930. *Media, Culture and Society, 22*(5), 557–573.

McCracken, E. (1993). *Decoding women's magazines: From* Mademoiselle *to* Ms. Basingstoke, England: Macmillan.

McDowell, P. (1998). *The women of Grub Street*. Oxford, England: Oxford University Press.

McLuhan, M. (1995). *Understanding media*. London: Routledge.

McManus, H. R. (1994). *Market driven journalism: Let the citizen beware*. London: Sage.

Merritt, D. (1995). *Public journalism and public life: Why telling the news is not enough*. Hillsdale, NJ: Lawrence Erlbaum Associates.

Meyer, D. (1996). *Speaking for themselves: Neomexicano cultural identity and the Spanish Language press 1880–1920*. Albuquerque: University of New Mexico Press.

Meyers, M. (1997). *News coverage of violence against women: Engendering blame*. Thousand Oaks, CA: Sage.

Mott, F. L. (1941). *American journalism: A history of newspapers in the US through 250 years 1690–1960*. New York: Macmillan.

Natarajan, J. (1962). *A history of the press in India*. New York: Asia Publishing House.

Nevitt, M. (1999). Women in the business of revolutionary news: Elizabeth Alkin, "Parliament Joan," and the Commonwealth Newsbook. In J. Raymond (Ed.), *News, newspapers and society in early modern Britain* (pp. 84–108). London: Cass.

Newkirk, P. (2000). *Within the veil: Black journalists, White media*. New York: New York University Press.

Nord, D. P. (2001). *Communities of journalism: A history of American newspapers and their readers*. Urbana: University of Illinois Press.

Park, R. E. (1923). The natural history of the newspaper. In R. E Park, E. W. Burgess, & R. D. McKenzie (Eds.), *The city* (pp. 273–290). Chicago: University of Chicago Press.

Parton, J. (1855). *The life of Horace Greeley.* Mason Bros. New York.

Parton, J. (1864). *The life and times of Benjamin Franklin.* Mason Bros. New York.

Pavlik, J. V. (2001). *Journalism and the new media.* New York: Columbia University Press.

Popkin, J. D. (1990). *Revolutionary news: The press in France 1789–1799.* Durham, NC: Duke University Press.

Popkin, J. D. (2001). *Press, revolution and social identities in France 1830–35.* University Park: Pennsylvania State University Press.

Potter, S. J. (2003). *News and the imperial world: The emergence of an imperial press system.* Oxford, England: Clarendon.

Raboy, M., & Dagenais, B. (1992). *Media, crisis and democracy.* London: Sage.

Raymond, J. (1996). *The invention of the newspaper, English newsbooks, 1641–1649.* Oxford, England: Oxford University Press.

Raymond, J. (Ed). (1999a). *News, newspapers and society in early modern Britain.* London: Cass.

Raymond, J. (1999b). The newspaper, public opinion, and the public sphere in the seventeenth century. In J. Raymond (Ed.), *News, newspapers and society in early modern Britain* (pp. 109–140). London: Cass.

Robson, J. M. (1995). *Marriage or celibacy? The Daily Telegraph on a Victorian dilemma.* Toronto, Ontario, Canada: University of Toronto Press.

Rodriguez, C. (2001). *Fissures in the media landscape: An international study of citizens' media.* Cresskill, NJ: Hampton.

Russo, A., & Kramarae, C. (1990). *The radical women's press of the 1850s.* New York: Routledge.

Said, E. (1994). *Culture and imperialism.* New York: Vintage.

Schiller, D. (1981). *Objectivity: The public and the rise of commercial journalism.* Philadelphia: University of Pennsylvania Press.

Schlesinger, M. (1958). *Prelude to independence: The newspaper war on Great Britain, 1764–1776.* New York: Knopf.

Schudson, M. (1978). *Discovering the news: A social history of American newspapers.* New York: Harper.

Schudson, M. (2001). The objectivity norm in American journalism. *Journalism, 2*(2), 149–170.

Serfaty, V. (2004). *The mirror and the veil: An overview of American online diaries and blogs.* Amsterdam: Rodopi.

Shattock, J. (2000). Work for women: Margaret Oliphant's journalism. In L. Brake, B. Bell, & D. Finkelstein (Eds.), *Nineteenth century media and the construction of identities* (pp. 165–176). Basingstoke, England: Palgrave.

Sherman, S. (1996). *Telling time: Clocks, diaries and English diurnal form.* Chicago: University of Chicago Press.

Shevelow, K. (1989). *Women and print culture.* London: Routledge.

Siebert, F. S. (1965). *Freedom of the press in England 1476–1776: The rise and fall of government control.* Urbana: Illinois University Press.

Sloan, B. (2001). *"I watched a wild hog eat my baby!" A colourful history of the tabloids and their cultural impact.* New York: Prometheus.

Sloan, W. D., & Williams, J. H. (1994). *The early American press 1690–1783.* Westport, CT: Greenwood.

Smith, A. D. (1975). *Paper voices.* London: Chatto & Windus.

Smith, A. D. (1978). The long road to objectivity and back: The kinds of truth we get in journalism. In G. Boyce, J. Curran, & P. Wingate (Eds.), *Newspaper history from the past to the present* (pp. 153–171). London: Constable.

Sommerville, J. (1996). *The news revolution.* Oxford, England: Oxford University Press.

Sparks, C., & Tulloch, J. (Eds). (2000). *Tabloid tales.* Lanham, MD: Rowman & Littlefield.

Splichal, S. (1994). *Media beyond socialism.* Boulder, CO: Westview.

Starck, K. (2001). What's right/wrong with journalism ethics research? *Journalism Studies, 2*(1), 133–152.

Stevens, J. (1991). *Sensationalism and the New York press.* New York: Columbia University Press.

Thomas, I. (1810). *The history of printing in America.* New York: Munsell.

Thompson, E. P. (1969). *The making of the English working class.* London: Penguin.

Traill, H. D. (1884, October). Newspapers and English: A dialogue. *Macmillan's Magazine,* pp. 436–445.

Tucher, A. (1994). *Froth & scum: Truth, beauty, goodness and the ax murder in America's First mass medium.* Chapel Hill: University of North Carolina Press.

Tuchman, G., Daniels, A., & Bénet, J. (Eds.). (1978). *Hearth and home: Images of women in the mass media.* New York: Oxford University Press.

van Dijk, T. (1991). *Racism and the press.* London: Routledge.

van Zoonen, L. (1994). *Feminist media studies*. London: Sage.

Voss, P. J. (2001). *Elizabethan news pamphlets*. Pittsburgh, PA: Dusquesne University Press.

Weisbord, S. (2000). *Watchdog journalism in South America: News, accountability and democracy*. New York: Columbia University Press.

White, C. L. (1970). *Women's magazines 1693–1968*. London: Joseph.

Williams, R. (1961). *The long revolution*. London: Penguin.

CHAPTER 14

Writing in the Professions

Anne Beaufort
University of Washington, Tacoma

Writing research took a turn in the late 1970s and early 1980s. Although there had been some early research and theorizing about technical writing (Brockmann & Farr, 1998; Connors, 1982), in the late 1970s and early 1980s, researchers in literacy studies and composition studies began to take a particular interest in the writing that takes place in workplace and professional contexts. This work has contributed considerably both to an enlarged view of writing literacies in multiple contexts, and also to an enlarged view of a continuum of life-long learning for writers. In particular it has explored four major themes: (a) the importance and pervasiveness of writing in the workplace, (b) processes and practices that support writing in the workplace, (c) the role of changing technologies in workplace writing, and (d) the impact of workplace writing on employees, institutions, and society. Themes overlap, of course, but for purposes of some orderliness to this review, they appear separate.

IMPORTANCE AND PERVASIVENESS OF WRITING IN THE WORKPLACE

Several early survey studies established the value placed on writing by management-level employees in a variety of professions. Faigley and Miller (1982) reported, for example, that white-collar professionals in six occupations wrote an average of 23% of the work week. Another survey (Harwood, 1982) at the same time found that a typical graduate wrote once or twice a day, and perhaps more important, as income rose, so did frequency of writing.

Subsequent to these early studies, there has been a continual stream of research on workplace writing activities, looking both at professional writing and at blue-collar writing activities (see chaps. 8 and 13, this volume). Blue-collar workers' writing skills have become increasingly important as technologies have driven more record keeping and decision making to those who are directly involved in manufacturing, information-processing, and care-giving activities. A good overview of some of the research on blue-collar writing practices on-the-job is provided in Hull's edited collection, *Changing Work, Changing Workers: Critical Perspectives on Language, Literacy, and Skills* and Gowen's (1992) ethnography of hospital workers, *The Politics of Workplace Literacy: A Case Study*. As these two titles suggest, the views of workplace writing in recent research are particularly sensitive to the social and political power (or lack of power) associated with writing acts within institutions. For example, Jolliffe (1997) analyzes rhetorical strategies upper-management authors evoke in addressing workers in company documents and argues that workers' identities need to be considered in shaping such texts. Hart-Landsberg and Reder (1997) analyze the effect of writing processes on teamwork in a manufacturing firm.

PROCESSES AND PRACTICES THAT SUPPORT
WORKPLACE WRITING

Managing the Writing Process

In the wake of composition research's interest during the late 1970s and early 1980s in the composing processes of writers, a number of researchers of professional writing studied whether the same recursive process of composing as identified by Flower and Hayes (1981) was evidenced among seasoned writers in the workplace. A few expanded on the Flower and Hayes model. For example, Doheny-Farina (1986) found that, among writers in a small computer firm, "stored writing plans" meant a rich and specific understanding of complex social issues that would affect the writer's decision-making process in composing texts. Hovde (2001) documented the extensive generative nature of the research process technical writers needed to undertake as part of the process of being able to write software documentation and Spilka (1988) also found generating content to be an important part of the composing process. In a year-long ethnography following six engineers composing a variety of documents, she found more successful engineers spending more of their energies on content than on arrangement or style.

But several studies convincingly argued that composing processes of writers varied depending on the nature of the genre and other situational variables found in workplace settings. Broadhead and Freed (1986) documented a very linear composing process of two management consultants who used boilerplate formulas supplied by their company to write proposals to clients. The government proposal, on the other hand, could be a daunting genre to tackle. In another study, one writer, after suffering through a very laborious, anxiety-ridden round of proposal writing, approached the same task a year later, wiser for her earlier experiences, in her own methodical way: typing out the request for proposal (RFP) to internalize what the grantors were requesting; creating manila folders for each section of the proposal where she could place notes, relevant information, and rough drafts of the section for later assemblage into the whole. She wrote sections nonsequentially as well, according to what seemed easiest to tackle first, and so on (Beaufort, 1999). Schumacher, Scott, Klare, Cronin, and Lambert (1989), in an experiment with journalism students, found that under one writing condition—composing a news story—the writers needed to spend less time planning, given the preestablished structure of the genre, whereas when writing editorials, which have a more open format, writers spent more time reaching decisions as they wrote.

Couture and Rymer (1993) and Beaufort (1999) documented the influence of situational factors—the amount of time available, and whether or not the writing situation was routine—on writers' degree of attention to planning and revising. Writers in one nonprofit organization (Beaufort, 1999) were found to vary their writing processes depending not only on the nature of the genre being written, but also on the physical realities of the workplace—one writer wrote easy things on Mondays and Fridays, when there were a lot of interruptions, and the more difficult projects on Tuesdays, Wednesdays, and Thursdays, when there were greater opportunities for concentrated effort but still numerous interruptions, which in themselves became part of the writing process.

Several other variables that influenced the writing processes of workplace writers also demonstrate richly varied composing processes: A number of studies (Beaufort, 1999; Johns, 1989; Selzer, 1993; Winsor, 1989) point to the effect of intertextuality in workplace writing (portions of texts freely borrowed from other texts) on writers' processes. For example, one writer in a nonprofit agency (Beaufort, 1999) organized various boilerplate texts for business letters she frequently wrote into file folders on her desktop computer, labeled according to type of letter: rejection letter, request for donation, and so on. Other researchers (Allen, 1993; Dorff, 1989; Witte & Haas, 2001) further complicate conceptions of writing process by observing various forms of collaborative writing the Flower and Hayes (1981) model cannot account for. For example, Witte and Haas (2001) demonstrate the intertwining of different areas of expertise ("distributed cognition") of city workers and engineers in the process of documenting and revising technical documents, and ways in which gestures and diagrams operated in the composing process as pretexts. Allen, Atkinson, Morgan, Moore, and Snow (1987) were able to document specific processes that best facilitated collaborative writing: preserving divergent points of view of group members, shared decision making about documents, and so forth.

Collaborative writing (sometimes also referred to as *document cycling*) could also lead writers to feel less ownership of texts and less immediacy in terms of the rhetorical situation. Not only is the image of the solo writer as creator often not apropos in workplace writing situations, but the resulting effects on writers' sense of authorship (or lack of it) spawned by these writing practices have also been documented. It seems most writers have to go through a period of psychological adjustment to the loss of control of their texts (Anson & Forsberg, 1990; Beaufort, 1999; Doheny-Farina, 1989; Henry, 1995; Winsor, 1993), and in one case (Henry, 1995), this loss of sense of ownership of text also affected the writers' abilities to imagine the real audience for the texts, as internal readers and editors were the most immediate audience. As one writer (a public relations writer within an engineering firm) said, "Neither our native tongue nor our professional language is ever entirely our own. We must constitute ourselves in texts that we do not wholly control" (Winsor, 1993, p. 194). For a bibliography of studies on collaboration in technical writing, see Jorn (1993).

Efficiency with the writing process was a factor in workplace settings as well: Front-line supervisors who didn't have a good handle on the writing process were losing money for the company with their inefficiencies (Mabrito, 1997). One Silicon Valley company (MsIsaac & Aschauer, 1990) formed a Proposal Operations Center to review proposals as part of the writing process to improve not only efficiency in the writing process, but effectiveness of the proposals as well (proposals, in this case, for large military contracts, were often 1,000 pages in length and involved a 52-step process; anywhere from 42 to 100 individuals could be involved in writing of the proposals). The writing process for these documents included storyboarding (scribble sheets; i.e., early drafts of sections of text) pinned to walls for viewing and a Red Team that simulated readers' reactions to early drafts. In some settings, workplace writing processes resembled an assembly line.

INSTITUTIONAL STRUCTURES AND THE EFFECT ON WRITING ACTIVITY

A number of studies have examined the ways in which organizational culture influenced writers' behaviors. Brown and Herndl (Brown, 1986) found that social hierarchies within an organization influenced writers' sense of what linguistic features and even what genres were appropriate. Specifically, through interviews and analysis of writing samples of two writing groups (those considered outstanding writers within the organization and those considered average), the authors found that superfluous use of nominalizations was greater among the "average" writers, causing their writing to be muddy and verbose, and these traits increased if the writing was for upper management or for powerful people outside the corporation and decreased when writing down the corporate hierarchy. Nominalizations also increased with a sense of job insecurity: Writers felt such linguistic features conveyed a greater sense of authority. Similarly, Henry (1995) found writers' use of nominalizations, passive voice, and other less direct stylistic choices in a military organization resulted from the layers of approvals (what they referred to as the *chop chain*) that removed them from any sense of audience or personal investment in the writing. Others have documented similar stylistic choices made by writers in response to the social milieu in which they wrote (Odell, 1983; Orlikowski, 1994).

The effect of gender differences on practices in written business communications have, unfortunately, not been a subject of much research. Tebeaux (1990) did one study with technical-writing students who had workplace experience and found that both men and women who had worked in jobs requiring interpersonal communications had used both masculine and feminine approaches to communication as specific situations warranted either. From this study and her review of gender research, Tebeaux argues for business writers to have androgynous writing strategies to meet a variety of communication situations. Barker and Zifcak (1999) argue for a similar position, almost 10 years later, based on studies or oral communications in the workplace.

THE ROLE OF CHANGING TECHNOLOGIES IN WORKPLACE WRITING

The impact of technology on composing processes has only begun to be investigated and is not exclusive to workplace research. There have been a number of investigations in this arena, generally along two lines of questioning: (a) how technologies affect writers' processes (or don't), and (b) how technologies spawn new genres or new communicative patterns (or don't).

An experimental study of professional and advanced graduate students composing press releases on the computer or with paper and pencil, as well as revising and editing press releases under the same conditions, revealed advantages and disadvantages of composing with computers: On the one hand, writers spent less time planning and felt free to write spontaneously and creatively with the computer. They also made five times more changes to the text on the computer than with paper and pencil and more changes at the whole-sentence level. On the other hand, the physical limitations of the computer screen interfered with making whole-text-level structural changes, which were more readily made on the paper-and-pencil version, when the whole text could be spread out (Lutz, 1987). Haas (1989) also documented the difficulty for writers of reading their texts on computer screens. Other researchers (Sellen, 2002), looking at writing at the International Monetary Fund, found that managers drafted and did final editing on computers, but collaborating on revisions was done on paper and accounted for 71% of the writing time. Managers needed to spread papers on tables, mark them, share pages, and so on before making changes in the computer. Paper also seems to serve other cognitive functions in critical-thinking and composing processes. The author states:

> Knowledge workers rarely store and file paper documents or refer back to the information they do keep. Rather, it is the process of taking notes that is important in helping them to construct and organize their thoughts. The information that they do keep is arranged around their offices in a temporary holding pattern of paper documents that serves as a way of keeping available the inputs and ideas they might have use for in their current projects. (p. 63)

Gladwell (2002) reports a study by Mackay, a computer scientist, of air traffic controllers making similar use of online technologies and paper. The researcher found that air traffic controllers used little strips of paper to make notes on airplane locations and worked with the slips of paper and the radar images on their computer screens to manage air traffic. It appears that computers aid aspects of the writing process and old-fashioned paper and pencil aid other aspects of the composing process. On the one hand, digital processing of texts facilitates storing and accessing large amounts of information, display of multimedia documents, fast full-text searches, quick links to related materials, and dynamic modifying or updating of content. But hard copy of text facilitates quick, flexible navigation through and around documents, reading across more than one document at once, marking up a document while reading, and interweaving reading and writing (Daiute, 1983; Harper, 2002).

In addition to the influence of technology on reading/writing practices, research has documented the shifting of social roles in relation to written communications in the workplace as a result of technological changes. Dictation has nearly disappeared as even top executives have turned to desktop computers, and conversely, secretaries have become more than typists, often doing revising and editing of others' documents online (Dautermann, 1996). Other roles, too, have changed as a result of the ready accessibility of digital technologies. Cook-Gumperz and Hanna (1997) found that the social status of nurses in the hospital hierarchy increased when they started using bedside computer terminals to chart patients' conditions and accessing database tools for patient assessment.

More radical perhaps than word processing are several other technical media: personal digital assistants (PDAs), structured document processors (SDPs), instant messaging (IM), and hypertext. PDAs, as exemplified in Geisler's (2001) self-study, may blur the boundaries between personal and work-related writing. Geisler's self-study of a 97-minute composing session also demonstrated the multilayered, multitasking possibilities that Internet technology, computers, and PDAs allow: She was using all three interchangeably as she composed. IM has transformed written communication to nearly match the synchronicity of oral communication and, like PDAs, is a newer technology warranting further research.

Researchers point to the alteration of the concept of *authoring* as well when writing tools such as these are employed. Reader–writer relationships are affected by new media. Hypertext enables readers, in a sense, to become coauthors with writers (Wenger, 1994) and presents additional organizational possibilities and problems for writers: Nonlinear organizational patterns such as trees, cycles, grids, and stars can be created that verbal rhetorical devices do not allow (Horton, 1991). Also, information can be layered for different audiences. Fortune (1989) also presents a case for the use of computer drawing programs as another tool for aiding critical thinking and prewriting in the composing process.

The second line of investigation of technology–writing connections has been an examination of changes in writing styles, genres, and communications patterns as a result of new technologies. Yates' (1989) historical study of the rise of business communications reveals a fascinating intertwining of human and material factors that spawned new genres and new communications practices. Her study helps to set current technological changes that affect writing in perspective. Some predicted the telephone would diminish or eliminate written communications, but other tools—the telegraph, the typewriter, carbon paper, and vertical filing cabinets—all increased the ease and functionality of written communications. For example, the genre of the internal memo evolved, gradually, from the more formal business letter: The standard headings of the memo were created for efficiency of referencing documents and allowed dropping unnecessary courtesies such as "yours very truly." The information in the headings of memos in turn led to adopting the use of vertical files for easy retrieval of documents.

E-mail, which took off as a communications medium in the late 1980s, has been examined as a new genre. Although early on some researchers raised the question whether e-mail was really a genre (Spooner, 1996), most of the research suggests that e-mail is a hybrid between oral and written communications and has been developing a set of regularized textual features unique enough to warrant considering it a genre in its own right—for example, more use of incomplete sentences, a preference for coordinated rather than subordinated ideas, and use of specialized vocabulary and graphical symbols to convey emotions (Baron, 2000; Gimenez, 2000; Sims, 1996; Yates et al., 1999). Yates et al. also found, in an extensive study of organizational culture, a number of mail subgenres—for example, *official announcement* and *dialogue*.

Changes in organizational structure and patterns of communication as a result of new computer technologies such as e-mail have also been examined. Researchers found that communications with new customers began as standard business letters, but as relationships became established, e-mail became the preferred medium of communication (Murray, 1987). As the memo encouraged more informality than the business letter, likewise, e-mails have increased both the informality and personal nature of business communications (Gimenez, 2000). Yet Yates et al. (1999), studying use of e-mail in two different divisions of a Japanese manufacturing firm, found that corporate cultures in the divisions differed and as a result, norms for e-mail communications also differed, suggesting that it is not the medium, but the genre features as shaped by social context that vary the form of communications. The researchers offer this cautionary note: "The migration of existing communication patterns to new media may, however, lead users simply to apply ineffective habits of use form old technologies to new ones" (p. 100). They call for deliberate consideration of genres and genre repertoires in specific contexts for communication.

A final note on technology's influence on writing that has a bearing in particular on workplace environments and business communications: Bernhardt (1993) gives a good overview of the ways in which hypertext is changing acts of reading and writing. Although he does not give empirical evidence of readers' and writers' behaviors with hypertext media, he does a thorough textual analysis, pointing out the features of hypertext that influence the ways writers and readers interact around such texts: Hypertexts are interactive, a reader can be active rather than passively absorbing information, hypertexts are functionally mapped (text displayed in ways that cues readers what can be done with it), hypertexts are modular, hypertexts are navigable (reader can move across large pools of information in different directions for different purposes), hypertexts are hierarchically embedded, hypertexts are spacious (unconstrained by physicality), and hypertexts are graphically rich.

INTERRELATIONSHIPS OF TEXTS AND VISUALS IN NEW TECHNOLOGIES

As I mentioned already, the physicality of the new genre of hypertext has altered reading and writing processes and meaning making (Bernhardt, 1993; Haas, 1989). Others have documented the pervasiveness of visual symbols side by side with written text in home and workplace settings (Hull, 1997; Medway, 2000; Rose, 2003; Witte, 1992). Witte even raises the question: What is writing versus nonwriting? Several studies suggest the richness of this area of investigation. Bernhardt (1986) offers an excellent analysis of the interaction of visual and verbal rhetoric in a brochure published by a wetlands agency. Horton (1993) documents research on the culturally specific meanings of graphics, text layouts, and even colors. Brumburger (2002), in an experimental study, found that subjects consistently assigned personality types to certain typefaces. Medway (2000) analyzes, in an extensive case study, the use of tools—visual and textual—in an architecture student's critical-thinking process as he worked on a building design. Early conceptual thinking was done in words, but later design ideas had to be represented with visual symbols.

Document design has become a subspecialty within rhetoric, drawing on perception studies in psychology, reading studies (how readers process texts), and linguistic anthropology (what symbols mean in context). An example of such research is the study by Zimmerman and Schultz (2000) of two medical questionnaires filled out by cancer patients—one a standard form and the other asking for the same information, but employing the principles of information design. Ninety percent of the questions in the designed form elicited better information than the questions on the standard form, demonstrating the efficacy of applying known principles of document design to strategic documents. It appears, however, that there has been limited empirical research into the effects of other sign systems on writers' processes, on genres themselves, and on the social dynamics of text usage, in spite of calls for such research (Schriver, 1989). For a good bibliography on visual design, see Albers and Lisberg (2002). For an overview of the field of information design, see Redish (2000) and Schriver (1997). There have been advances, however, in research methods for studying the effects of document design: Instead of relying on abstract readability formulas, for example, researchers now examine readers' actual comprehension and use of documents and have expanded their definition of which aspects of documents to evaluate (Schriver, 1997).

EFFECTS/IMPORTANCE OF WORKPLACE WRITING

Turning to more large-scale effects of recent writing practices in workplace settings, one study in particular exemplifies the interface of technologies, writing practices, and social structures in the workplace: Nurses' use of bedside computers to chart patients' conditions and access databases for diagnostic purposes (Cook-Gumperz & Hanna, 1997) both depersonalized the writing for the nurses ("I cannot even see my own signature on the chart," p. 329) and raised the visibility of the nurses' observations to the rest of the medical staff. The use of the new technologies even enabled the patients to be more involved in their own medical planning and healing processes.

Although Cook-Gumperz and Hanna's study revealed mixed effects of writing technologies in the workplace, social factors can also have a negative effect on writers. Pare (2000) documented the ways in which social workers tried to circumvent legal and social constraints on the types of information they could put into case reports on juvenile delinquents. Similar studies in the field of psychiatry (Berkenkotter, 2001; McCarthy, 1991, 1994) have documented the ways in which the *Diagnostic and Statistical Manual of Mental Disorders* (3rd ed., *DSM–III*, and 4th ed., *DSM–IV*) pushes psychiatrists into codifying clients' behaviors for billing and social accountant purposes, potentially restricting the actual practice of therapy. Schryer (1993) documented similar constraints on social dynamics between veterinarians and pet owners, given the professional standards for forms of documentation.

Stygall (1991) documents the ways in which jury instructions can interfere with the jury's understanding of the legal process, and Schryer (2000) documented the ways in which particularly dense boilerplate text (off the charts in readability indexes) in an insurance company's letters turning down clients' disability claims was a major factor in the number of appeals the insurance company received to negative letters (over 60% were appealed). When the researcher presented her evidence to the company (she was hired as a consultant to help them reduce the number of appeals of negative letters) there was a reluctance to turn dense legal prose into plain English. Even more disconcerting, Sauer (1994) demonstrates that the linear, sequential model of cause-and-effect prose used in accident reports of large government agencies fails to account for the multidimensional nature of accidents. Herndl, Fennel, and Miller (1991) do a thorough rhetorical analysis of memos that led to both the Three Mile Island nuclear accident and the deaths of eight astronauts aboard the Challenger flight. They demonstrate, through careful rhetorical analysis of memos and an examination of the social context of the two divisions of the company involved in the Challenger decision, that the engineering division was arguing that past performance and some limited data about cold temperatures affecting O-rings warranted canceling the flight, but management discounted the engineers' data. Herndl et al. say, "The managers reasoned at the level of contracts and programs—successful flights. The warrants of each set of interests, or social groups, were insufficient to the other" (p. 302).

Fortunately, writing practices can also have a positive influence on work activities within organizations. One of the earliest studies (Doheny-Farina, 1986) documents the ways in which the drafting of a business plan in a small, start-up computer company in fact shaped the direction of the company. More recently, Katz (1998) documented one writer's social agency within an organization through her acumen and self-confidence as a writer.

Another vein of research in workplace writing on the interrelationship of social context and texts concerns the features of texts as they evolve in relation to their social functions within organizations. Bazerman's (1981) pioneer article comparing the rhetorical approaches of three academic disciplines—sociology, biology, and literature—led to a number of other rich analyses of the ways in which genre conventions arise out of socially constrained or socially motivated situations and enact certain epistemological assumptions—what counts as truth, evidence, and so forth. There is a substantial body of work now on the rhetorical (i.e., nonobjective) nature of science writing (Bazerman, 1982; Blakeslee, 2001; Fahnestock, 1986; Myers, 1985; Paul and Davida, 1995). In addition, Fahnestock and Secor

(1991) explicate the rhetorical motives and moves of literary scholars and in business settings, Smart (1993), Orlikowski and Yates (1994), and Devitt (1991) similarly document the interrelationships of genre features (evolving, nonstatic, dialogic) and the social purposes to which the texts attend. Segal (1993) analyzed more than 200 articles written over a 10-year period, in various medical publications, to examine the rhetoric of medicine. She found medical writing to be paternalistic and that authority was established through extensive use of citations and nominalizations. She concluded, "Physicians are locked within scientific medicine's frame of reference because of the nature of language itself" (p. 84). Beaufort (1999) found that a single genre, the grant proposal, varied considerably in its genre features depending on the goals, values, and communications processes of different discourse communities using the genre: Grant proposals for private foundations had different requirements from those for local government agencies, and grant proposals for federal agencies had yet another set of features particular to the communicative context. Social status can also be at issue in formation of text types, as Munger (2000) demonstrates in a historical review of the evolution of reporting forms for emergency medical technicians. The more the form evolved from narrative to checking off boxes or fill-in-the-blank type reporting, the less social status EMTs felt they had within the medical profession.

SOCIALIZATION PROCESSES FOR WRITERS AND SCHOOL–WORK TRANSITIONS

Also of interest is how writers learn in workplace settings, where instruction is usually informal, self-motivated, and indirect. Although early research in workplace settings captured only what writers were doing or thinking in a given interview or survey, or in single texts, by the late 1980s researchers began to use ethnographic techniques to take a longer view of workplace scenes for writing. From these studies came increased awareness of the socialization processes of writers making the transition from academic writing to business and professional writing. Doheny-Farina (1989, 1992) followed a student doing a writing internship in a nonprofit and documented her process of coming to realize the importance of understanding the political context of the organization in order for her writing to be useful to the organization. Anson and Forsberg (1990) also documented the psychological adjustment of students doing writing internships—coming to see the community's viewpoint as paramount, rather than their own.

Beaufort (1999) followed the trajectory of four writers at a nonprofit over several years as they gradually adapted their writing behaviors and gleaned knowledge in five areas associated with writing expertise that were crucial to successful written communications both internal and external to the organization. Although there was no formal training program for writers new to the organization, managers were teaching as they worked with the writers, staging growth by assigning low-risk tasks (routine business correspondence, or small sections of grant proposals) that were gradually replaced by high-risk writing tasks (grant applications, etc.), by giving feedback on drafts in face-to-face coaching situations, and by treating novices as already part of the professional community they were working in. From the writers' vantage points, learning to write successfully on the job involved constant observation of others' language practices (oral and written), finding out who was the best grammarian to solicit editing help from, and so on. All possible resources for learning on the job were marshaled to accomplish the writing tasks. Although mistakes were made and the learning environment was by no means ideal, in this ethnographic study, many of the features of what Lave and Wenger (1991) term *cognitive apprenticeships* or *legitimate peripheral participation* were present. Dias, Freedman, Medway, and Pare (1999) also document the role of cognitive apprenticeships and distributed cognition in workplace sites for learning.

THEORETICAL IMPACT OF WORKPLACE RESEARCH

Theorists in composition studies and literacy studies have drawn from and expanded their work in the last 20 years by looking at the empirical and descriptive research in workplace and professional writing practices reported here. A number of key people come to mind: Bazerman (1994), Berkenkotter and Huckin (1995), Gee (1989), Russell (1995), Swales (1990), and Witte (1988). The work of Orlinkoski and Yates (1994) in management communications theory has followed a similar trajectory. Drawing from social constructionist theories, literary theories, rhetorical theory, sociolinguistics, and the new literacy studies, as well as drawing on their own rhetorical analyses of written communications in these contexts, or through ethnographic work (their own and others'), these researchers have, collectively, greatly expanded the understanding of written communications. These theorists have added theoretical understanding specifically to matters of writing acquisition and use.

Cope and Kalantzis (2000) employ the term *multiliteracies* to describe the wide variations in literate behaviors in out-of-school settings. Here is their definition of the term:

> We decided that the outcomes of our discussions could be encapsulated in one word, multiliteracies—a word we chose because it describes two important arguments we might have with the emerging cultural, institutional, and global order. The first argument engages with the multiplicity of communications channels and media; the second with the increasing salience of cultural and linguistic diversity. (p. 5)

They argue, as do others (Beaufort, 2000; Heath, 1982; Hull, 2001; Rose, 2003), that there can be no one standard for what counts as writing proficiency or expertise. In a similar vein, Gee (1989) states that true literacy in a discourse is possible only outside of one's primary (home) discourse because literacy requires the meta-knowledge of what the discourse is doing socially and that's not possible until one has a secondary discourse with which to critique the primary discourse. So, in essence, whether a writer is working in a school or workplace setting, she or he is outside the home discourse and immersed in other social, political, and cultural contexts that shape the nature of the writing in multiple ways. What is correct or good depends on the social context—the activity system, discourse community, or genre at hand (Nystrand, 1986). To conceptualize more specifically how writers and the texts they produce function socially, others have applied activity theory to written communications in workplace and professional contexts (Bazerman, 1988; Russell, 1997) and explored the concept of discourse community (Beaufort, 1997; Killingsworth & Gilbertson, 1992; Olsen, 1993; Swales, 1990, 1992), an activity system that focuses specifically on written communication (and the interface with oral and visual communications). Examining the goals, values, communicative patterns, genre sets, and epistemologies for establishing arguments that particular discourse communities espouse (e.g., nonprofit agencies, government agencies, biologists, stamp collectors, physicists, literary scholars, etc.) can illuminate what is going on in individual writers' behaviors and in individual texts and groups of texts within discourse communities.

Closely related to theories of activity systems and discourse communities but not as broad in scope are the expanded theories of genre, genre systems, and intertextuality that have grown from and been employed in understandings of workplace and professional communications practices. Bazerman's (1982) work in scientific genres, Devitt's (1991) in the genres employed by tax accountants, Berkenkotter's and McCarthy's (2001) on the formation of the *DSM–III* and *DSM–IV* in psychiatry, Schryer's (1993) examination of veterinary records, and Yates' (1989) historical work on the rise of the business memo, to name a few studies, have added to conceptions of genres as socially situated and interactive with social forces over time, both influencing and being influenced by those forces.

Devitt (1991) broke new ground theoretically by demonstrating the interrelationships of sets of genres employed by an accounting firm. She found two types of intertextuality— referential (one text referring to another explicitly) and functional (one text linked by function to another). She states, "In examining the genre set of a community, we are examining the community's situations, its recurring activities and relationships" (p. 340). She also observed that "the stabilizing power of genres, through the interaction of texts within the same, genre … increases the efficiency of creating the firm's products" (p. 342).

Others likewise have documented the occurrence of interconnected genres that work in concert within given social contexts: in the legal system (Bazerman, 1994), in banking (Smart & Spilka, 1993), and in interoffice e-mail communications (Orlikowski & Yates, 1994). How texts function in cultures is an ongoing subject of scholarship in business communications, in composition studies, and in linguistic anthropology, in large part as a result of the workplace research in the last 20 years reported here. Arguments for the social construction of knowledge can be instantiated by the research reported here as well.

Some studies in workplace and professional writing have also taken a cognitive perspective and add to sociocognitive theories of composing and to general understandings of distributed cognition as well. Dias et al. (1999), drawing on theories of situated cognition and situated learning, point to the sociocognitive aspect of collaborative writing processes, common in workplace settings. In banking (Smart, Dias, & Pare, 2000) and in engineering (Witte & Haas, 2001), examples abound of overlapping and specialized knowledge that is shared, leading to "robustness of decision making " in connection with written texts. Knowledge and thinking processes in acts of composing are shared and interactive. Collaborative writing is not just a division of labor; rather, it entails interactive cognitive processes among writers, editors, and managers.

In addition to adding to sociocognitive views of composing processes of writers, workplace studies have instantiated socially situated views of learning, and in particular, cognitive apprenticeships and legitimate peripheral participation of novice writers in workplace and professional discourse communities(Beaufort, 2000; Freedman et al., 2000). Interactive composing sessions, employing cultural tools at hand (model texts, electronic resources, etc.), and tangible results from writing projects are commonplace in workplace and professional settings and suggest an alternative model of learning processes than those typical of formal instructional settings.

CONCLUSION

A review of research such as this will hopefully spur further research and theorizing based on empirical findings. What might next steps be for research in workplace and professional settings? Areas that appear important for further investigation include:

- Effects of current and evolving technologies on composing processes of writers, reader–writer relations, genres, and discourse community practices.
- Interactions of visual and written rhetoric.
- Gendered differences in workplace communications.
- Transfer of learning issues (what transfers from school to work or from any discourse community to another and what aids or hinders transfer).
- Learning/socialization processes in workplace settings.

I would also make a brief comment on research methodologies. Early research in workplace settings typically employed surveys and brief interviews. There was much self-reporting by writers and a lack of triangulation of data to increase validity. As several have pointed out (Faigley & Hansen, 1985; Spilka, 1993; Stratman & Duffy, 1990), analyses of social contexts is important: Looking at a text or talking solely to the individual writer cannot fully explain what is going on in terms of social roles and discourse community goals, purposes, and ideologies as they impact acts of writing. In 1986, two ethnographies of writing in workplace settings were published (Brown & Herndl, 1986; Doheny-Farina, 1986) and numerous others have followed. For a detailed explanation of ethnographic methods employed in a workplace setting, see Beaufort (1999, chap. 8).

Odell and Goswami (1983), among the earliest scholars to conduct workplace research, developed a new method for getting at writers' tacit knowledge of social contexts, genres, and so on, that they called *discourse-based interviews*. They found examples in the writers' texts of supporting statements for an argument and asked, for example, if the writer would be willing to eliminate the statement. Writers' answers revealed much about the context for writing and the writer's conceptual thinking. They also tried writing the legislative report their informants were writing and then had the informants (legislative analysts) comment on their writing to get further information on the "norms" in the context for writing. This method is used frequently now in ethnographic studies, usually in combination with interviews, observation, and textual analysis.

Although qualitative and naturalistic studies or textual analyses have been used more commonly in recent years in workplace research, it is worth a reminder that a number of researchers have developed experimental designs that have yielded interesting findings. Think-aloud protocols (Blyer, 1989) and manipulating writing conditions (Freedman, 1984) have also yielded important findings, and Debs (1993) also recommended visualizing methods (networks, maps, and Q-sorts) as other ways of investigating workplace writing. In addition, Geisler (2001) employed state-of-the-art screen-capture technology (set at one frame per second) to capture data for a self-study of her composing process. This and other technologies to come could provide other means, as well, for understanding writers' composing processes.

In all, studies of writing in the social contexts of business and the professions has yielded a rich basis for understanding (and theorizing) the social features of language, genres, and acts of composing. Olson's (1993) review of studies of legal and medical writing illustrates what the impact of this collective body of research has been:

> These studies show that there is indeed an effect—and often a profound effect—of the context and the values of the community of readers and listeners on the content and form of a document. Perhaps more unexpectedly, a few of the studies also suggest that there is sometimes an effect of the content and form of a document on the context, including helping to define the sense of community and to project its set of values and attitudes (Olsen & Spilka, 1993).

Not only those in literacy studies and professional and technical communications fields, but also those in organizational development and economic development, would do well to heed this field of research as it impacts their endeavors.

REFERENCES

Albers, M. J., & Lisberg, B. C. (2002). Information Design: A Bibliography. *Technical Communication, Second Quarter*, 170–176.

Allen, N., Atkinson, Dianne, Morgan, Meg, Moore, Teresa, Snow, Craig. (1987). What Experienced Collaborators Say about Collaborative Writing. *Journal of Business and Technical Communication, 1*(2), 70–90.

Allen, N. J. (1993). Community, Collaboration, and the Rhetorical Triangle. *Technical Communication Quarterly (TCQ), 2*(1).

Anson, C. M., & Forsberg, L. L. (1990). Moving beyond the academic community: Transitional stages in professional writing. *Written Communication, 7*(2), 200–231.

Barker, R. T., & Zifcak, L. (1999). Communication and Gender in Workplace 2000: Creating a Contextually-Based Integrated Paradigm. *Journal of Technical Writing and Communication, 29*(4), 335–347.

Baron, N. S. (2000). *Alphabet to Email: How Written English Evolved and Where It's Headed.* London: Routledge.

Bazerman, C. (1981). What written knowledge does: Three examples of academic discourse. *Philosophy of the Social Sciences, 2,* 361–387.

Bazerman, C. (1982). Scientific writing as a social act. In P. Anderson (Ed.), *New essays in technical and scientific communication* (pp. 156–184). Farmingdale, N.Y.: Baywood.

Bazerman, C. (1988). *Shaping written knowledge: The genre and activity of the experimental article in science.* Madison: University of Wisconsin Press.

Bazerman, C. (1994a). *Constructing experience.* Carbondale, IL: Southern Illinois University Press.

Bazerman, C. (1994b). Systems of Genres and the Enactment of Social Intentions. In A. Freedman & P. Medway (Eds.), *Genre and the New Rhetoric* (pp. 79–100). London: Taylor & Francis.

Beaufort, A. (1997). Operationalizing the concept of discourse community: A case study of one institutional site of composing. *Research in the Teaching of English, 31*(4), 486–529.

Beaufort, A. (1999). *Writing in the Real World: Making the Transition from School to Work.* New York: Teachers College Press.

Beaufort, A. (2000). Learning the trade: a social apprenticeship model for gaining writing expertise. *Written Communication, 1*(2), 185–223.

Berkenkotter, C. (2001). Genre Systems at Work: DSM-IV and Rhetorical Recontextualization in Psychotherapy Paperwork. *Written Communication, 18*(3), 326–349.

Berkenkotter, C., & Huckin, T. N. (1995). *Genre knowledge in disciplinary communication: Cognition/culture/power.* Hillsdale, NJ: Lawrence Erlbaum.

Bernhardt, S. A. (1986). Seeing the Text. *College Composition and Communication, 37*(1), 66–78.

Bernhardt, S. A. (1993). The Shape of Texts to Come: The Texture of Print on Screens. *College Composition and Communication, 44*(2), 151–175.

Blakeslee, A. M. (2001). *Interacting with Audiences: Social Influences on the Production of Scientific Writing* (Hardcover ed.). Mahwah, NJ: Lawrence Erlbaum Associates Inc.

Blyer, N. R. (1989). Purpose and Professional Writers. *The Technical Writing Teacher, 16*(1).

Broadhead, G. J., & Freed, R. C. (1986). *The variables of composition: Process and product in a business setting.* Carbondale: Southern Illinois University Press.

Brockmann, R. J. (1998). *From millwrights to shipwrights to the twenty-first century: explorations in a history of technical communication in the United States* (Hardcover ed.). Cresskill, New Jersey: Hampton Press, INC.

Brown, R. L., & Herndl, C. G. (1986). An ethnographic study of corporate writing: Job status as reflected in written text. In B. Couture (Ed.), *Functional Approaches to Writing: Research Perspectives* (pp. 11–28). London: Frances Pinter.

Brumburger, E. R. (2002). The Rhetoric of Typography: The Persona of Typeface and Text. *Technical Communication, 50*(2).

Connors, R. J. (1982). The Rise of Technical Writing Instruction in America. *Journal of Technical Writing and Communication, 12*(4), 329–352.

Cook-Gumperz, J., & Hanna, K. (1997). Nurses' Work, Women's Work: Some Recent Issues of Professional Literacy and Practice. In G. Hull (Ed.), (pp. 316–334). Albany, NY: State University of New York Press.

Cope, B., & Kalantzis, M. (2000). *Multiliteracies: Literacy Learning and the Design of Social Futures.* London: Routledge.

Couture, B., & Rymer, J. (1993). Situational Exigence: Composing Processes on the Job by Writer's Role and Task Value. In R. Spilka (Ed.), *Writing in the Workplace: New Research Perspectives* (pp. 4–20). Carbondale, IL: Southern Illinois Universith Press.

Daiute, C. (1983). The Computer as Stylus and Audience. *College Composition and Communication, 34,* 134–145.

Dautermann, J. (1996). Writing with Electronic Tools in Midwestern Businesses. In P. Sullivan & J. Dautermann (Eds.), *Electronic Literacies in the Workplace: Technologies of Writing* (pp. 3–22). Urbana, IL: National Council of Teachers of English.

Debs, M. B. (1993). Reflexive and Reflective Tensions: Considering Research Methods from Writing-Related Fields. In R. Spilka (Ed.), *Writing in the Workplace: New Research Perspectives* (pp. 238–252). Carbondale: Southern Illinois University Press.

Devitt, A. J. (1991). Intertextuality in tax accounting: Generic, referential, and functional. In C. Bazerman & J. Paradis (Eds.), *Textual Dynamics of the Professions: Historical and Contemporary Studies of Writing in Professional Communities* (pp. 336–357). Madison, WI: University of Wisconsin Press.

Dias, P., Freedman, A., Medway, P., & Pare, A. (1999). *Worlds Apart: Acting and Writing in Academic and Workplace Contexts.* Mahwah, NJ: Lawrence Erlbaum Associates.

Doheny-Farina, S. (1986). Writing in an emerging organization. *Written Communication, 3,* 158–185.

Doheny-Farina, S. (1989). A case study of one adult writing in academic and nonacademic discourse communities. In C. B. Matalene (Ed.), *Worlds of writing: Teaching and learning in discourse communities of work* (pp. 17–42). New York: Random House.

Doheny-Farina, S. (1992). The Individual, the Organization, and Kairos: Making Transitions from College to Careers. In S. P. Witte, N. Nakadate & R. D. Cherry (Eds.), *A Rhetoric of Doing: Essays on Written Discourse in Honor of James L. Kinneavy* (pp. 293–309). Carbondale: Southern Illinois University Press.

Dorff, D. L., & Duin, A. H. (1989). Applying a Cognitive Model to Document Cycling. *The Technical Writing Teacher, 16*(3), 234–.

Fahnestock, J. (1986). Accommodating science: The rhetorical life of scientific facts. *Written Communication, 3*(3), 275–296.

Fahnestock, J., & Secor, M. (1991). The rhetoric of literary criticism. In C. Bazerman & J. Paradis (Eds.), *Textual dynamics of the professions: Historical and contemporary studies of writing in professional communities* (pp. 76–96). Madison: University of Wisconsin Press.

Faigley, L., & Hansen, K. (1985). Learning to write in the social sciences. *College Composition and Communication, 34*, 140–149.

Faigley, L., & Miller, T. P. (1982). What we learn from writing on the job. *College English, 44*(6), 555–569.

Fortune, R. (1989). Visual and Verbal Thinking: Drawing and Word Processing in Writing Instruction. In G. E. Hawisher & C. L. Selfe (Eds.), *Critical perspectives on computers and composition instruction* (pp. 145–161). New York: Teachers College Press.

Freedman, A., & Adam, C. (2000). Write Where You Are: Learning to Write in University and Workplace Settings. In P. Dias & A. Pare (Eds.), *Transitions: Writing in Academic and Workplace Settings* (pp. 31–60). Cresskill, NJ: Hampton Press, Inc.

Freedman, S. W. (1984). The Registers of Student and Professional Expository Writing: Influence on Teachers' Responses. In R. Beach & L. S. Bridwell (Eds.), *New Directions in Composition Research* (pp. 334–347). New York: Guilford Press.

Gee, J. P. (1989). Literacy, Discourse, and Linguistics: Introduction. *Journal of Education, 171*(1), 5–17.

Gee, J. P. (2000). The New Literacy Studies: From 'socially situated' to the work of the social. In D. Barton, M. Hamilton & R. Ivanic (Eds.), *Situated Listreacies: Reading and Writing in Context* (pp. 180–196). London: Routledge.

Geisler, C. (2001). Textual Objects: Accounting for the Role of Texts in the Everyday Life of Complex Organizations. *Written Communication, 18*(3), 296–325.

Gimenez, J. C. (2000). Business e-mail communication: some emerging tendencies in register. *English for Specific Purposes, 19*, 237–251.

Gladwell, M. (2002). The Social Life of Paper: Looking for method in the mess. *The New Yorker*, 92–96.

Haas, C. (1989). Seeing It on the Screen Isn't Really Seeing It: Computer Writers' Reading Problems. In G. E. Hawisher & C. L. Selfe (Eds.), *Critical Perspectives on Computers and Composition* (pp. 16–29). New York: Teachers College Press.

Hart-Landsberg, S., & Reder, S. (1997). Teamwork and Literacy: Teaching and Learning at Hardy Industries. In G. Hull (Ed.), *Changing Work, Changing Workers* (pp. 350–382). Albany: State University of New York Press.

Harwood, J. T. (1982). Freshman English ten years after: Writing in the world. *College Composition and Communication, 33*(3), 281–283.

Heath, S. B. (1982). What no bedtime story means: Narrative skills at home and school. *Language in Society, 11*, 49–76.

Henry, J. (1995). Workplace Ghostwriting. *Journal of Business and Technical Communication (JBTC), 9*(4), 425–445.

Herndl, C. C., Fennel, B. A., & Miller, C. R. (1991). Understanding Failures in Organizational Discourse: The Accident at Three Mile Island and the Shuttle Challenger Disaster. In C. Bazaerman & J. Paradis (Eds.), *Textual Dynamics of the Professions: Hisotrical and Contemporary Studies of Writing in Professional Communities* (pp. 279–395). Madison, WI: University of Wisconsin Press.

Horton, W. (1991). Is Hypertext the Best Way to Document Your Product? An Assay for Designers. *Technical Communication Quarterly, First Quarter*, 20–32.

Horton, W. (1993). The Almost Universal Language: Graphics for International Documents. *Technical Communication, 40*(Fourth Quarter), 682–693.

Hovde, M. R. (2001). Research Tactics for Constructing Perceptions of Subject Matter in Organizational Contexts: An Ethnographic Study of Technical Communicators. *Technical Communication Quarterly (TCQ), 10*(1), 59–95.

Hull, G. (Ed.). (1997). *Changing Work, Changing Workers: Critical Perspectives on Language, Literacy, and Skills.* Albany, NY: State University of New York Press.

Hull, G., & Schultz, K. (2001). Literacy and learning Out of School: A Review of Theory and Research. *Review of Educational Research, 71*(4), 575–611.

Johns, L. C. (1989). The file cabinet has a sex life: Insights of a professional writing consultant. In C. B. Matalene (Ed.), *Worlds of Writing: Teaching and Learning in Discourse Communities of Work* (pp. 153–187). New York: Random House.

Jolliffe, D. (1997). Finding Yourself in the Text: Identity Formation in the Discourse of Workplace Documents. In G. Hull (Ed.), *Changing Work, Changing Workers* (pp. 335–349). Albany, NY: State University of New York Press.

Jorn, L. A. (1993). A Selected Annotated Bibliography on Collaboration in Technical Communication. *Technical Communication Quarterly, 2*(1), 105–115.

Katz, S. M. (1998). *The Dynamics of Writing Review: Opportunites for Growth and Change in the Workplace* (Hardcover ed. Vol. 5). Stamford, Connecticut: Ablex Publishing Corporation.

Killingsworth, M. J., & Gilbertson, M. K. (1992). *Signs, genres, and communities in technical communication.* Amityville, NY: Baywood.

Lave, J., & Wenger, E. (1991). *Situated learning: Legitimate peripheral participation.* Cambridge: Cambridge University Press.

Lutz, J. A. (1987). A Study of Professional and Experienced Writers Revising and Editing at the Computer and with Pen and Paper. *Research in the Teaching of English, 21*(4), 398–421.

Mabrito, M. (1997). Writing on the Front Line: A Study of Workplace Writing. *Business Communication Quarterly, 60*(3), 58–70.

McCarthy, L. (1991). A Psychiatrist Using DSM-III: The Influence of a Charter Document in Psychiatry. In C. Bazaerman & J. Paradis (Eds.), *Textual Dynamics of the Professions* (pp. 358–377). Madison , WI: University of Wisconsin Press.

McCarthy, L., & Gerrig, J. (1994). Revising Psychiatry's Charter Document, DSM-IV. *Written Communication, 11*, 147–192.

McIsaac, C., & Aschauer, M. A. (1990). Proposal writing at Atherton Jordan, Inc. *Management Communication Quarterly, 3*(4), 527–560.

Medway, P. (2000). Writing and Design in Architectural Education. In P. Dias & A. Pare (Eds.), *Transitions: Writing in Academic and Workplace Settings* (pp. 89–128). Creskill, NJ: Hampton Press, Inc.

Munger, R. (2000). Evolution of the Emergency Medical Services Profession: A Case Study of EMS Run Reports. *Technical Communication Quarterly, 9*(3), 329–346.

Murray, D. E. (1987). Requests at Work: Negotiating the Conditions for Conversation. *Management Communication Quarterly, 1*, 58–83.

Myers, G. (1985). The social construction of two biologists' proposals. *Written Communication, 2*(3), 219–245.

Nystrand, M. (1986). *The Structure of Written Communication: Studies in Reciprocity between Writers and Readers.* New York: Academic Press.

Odell, L., Goswami, D., & Herrington, A. (1983). The discourse-based interview: A procedure for exploring the tacit knowledge of writers in nonacademic settings. In P. Mosenthal, L. Tamor & S. Walmsley (Eds.), *Writing Research: Methods and Procedures.* NY: Longman.

Odell, L., Goswami, D., Herrington, A., & Quick, D. (1983). Studying writing in non-academic settings. In P. B. Anderson, R. J. Brockman & C. R. Miller (Eds.), *New essays in technical and scientific communication: Research, Theory, Practice* (Vol. 2, pp. 17–40). Farmingdale, N. Y.: Baywood Publishing.

Olsen, L. A. (1993). Research on Discourse Communities: An Overview. In R. Spilka (Ed.), *Writing in the Workplace* (pp. 181–194). Carbondale, IL: Southern Illinois University Press.

Orlikowski, W. J., & Yates, J. A. (1994). Genre Repertoire: The Structuring of Communicative Practices in Organizations. *Administrative Science Quarterly, 39*(4), 541–574.

Pare, A. (2000). Writing as a Way into Social Work: Genre Sets, Genre. In P. Dias & A. Pare (Eds.), *Transitions: Writing in Academic and Workplace Settings* (pp. 145–166). Cresskill, NJ: Hampton Press, Inc.

Paul, D., & Charney, D. (1995). Introducing Chaos (Theory) into Science and Engineering. *Written Communication, 12*(4), 396–438.

Redish, J. C. (2000). What is Information Design? *Technical Communication, Second Quarter*, 163–166.

Rose, M. (2003). Words in Action: Rethinking Workplace Literacy. *Research in the Teaching of English, 38*(1), 125–128.

Russell, D. (1995). Activity theory and its implications for writing instruction. In J. Pegralia (Ed.), *Reconceiving writing, rethinking writing instruction* (pp. 51–77). Mahwah, NJ: Erlbaum.

Russell, D. R. (1997). Rethinking Genre in School and Society: An Activity Theory Analysis. *Written Communication, 14*(4), 504–554.

Sauer, B. (1994). The dynamics of disaster: A 3 dimensional view of a tightly regulated industry. *Technical Communication Quarterly (TCQ), 3*, 393–419.

Schriver, K. A. (1989). Document Design from 1980 to 1989: Challenges That Remain. *Technical Communication Quarterly, 36*(Fourth Quarter), 316–333.

Schriver, K. A. (1997). *Dynamics in Document Design*. New York: John Wiley & Sons.

Schryer, C. F. (1993). Records as Genre. *Written Communication, 10*(2), 200–234.

Schryer, C. F. (2000). Walking a Fine Line: Writing Negative Letters in an Insurance Company. *Journal of Business and Technical Communication, 14*(4), 445–497.

Schumacher, G. M., Scott, B. T., Klare, G. R., Cronin, F. C., & Lambert, D. A. (1989). Cognitive Processes in Journalistic Genres: Extending Writing Models. *Written Communication, 6*(3), 390–407.

Segal, J. Z. (1993). Writing and Medicine: Text and Context. In R. Spilka (Ed.), *Writing in the Workplace: New Research Perspectives* (pp. 84–97). Carbondale, IL: Southern Illinois University Press.

Sellen, A. J., & Harper, R. H. R. (2002`). *The Myth of the Paperless Office*. Cambridge, MA: MIT Press.

Selzer, J. (1993). Intertextuality and the Writing Process: An Overview. In R. Spilka (Ed.), *Writing in the Workplace: New Research Perspectives* (pp. 171–180). Carbondale, IL: Southern Illinois University Press.

Sims, B. R. (1996). Electronic Mail in Two Corporate Workplaces. In P. Sullivan & J. Dautermann (Eds.), *Electronic Literacies in the Workplace: Technologies of Writing* (pp. 41–64). Urbana, IL: NCTE.

Smart, G. (1993). Genre as Community Invention: A Central Banks' Response to Its Executives' Expectations as Readers. In R. Spilka (Ed.), *Writing in the Workplace: New Research Perspectives* (pp. 124–140). Carbondale, IL: Southern Illinoise University Press.

Smart, G. (2000). Reinventing Expertise: Experienced Writers in the Workplace Encounter a New Genre. In P. Dias & A. Pare (Eds.), *Transitions: Writing in Academic and Workplace Settings* (pp. 223–252). Cresskill, NJ: Hampton Press, Inc.

Spilka, R. (1988). Studying Writer-Reader Interactions in the Workplace. *The Technical Writing Teacher, XV*(3), 208–221.

Spilka, R. (Ed.). (1993). *Writing in the Workplace: New Research Perspectives*. Carbondale, ILL: Southern Illinois University Press.

Spooner, M., & Yancey, K. (1996). Postings on a Genre of Email. *College Composition and Communication, 47*(2), 252–278.

Stratman, J. F., & Duffy, T. M. (1990). Conceptualizing research on written management communication: Looking through a glass onion. *Management Communication Quarterly, 3*(4), 429–451.

Stygall, G. (1991). Texts in Oral Context: The 'Transmission' of Jury Instructions in an Indiana Trial. In C. Bazerman & J. Paradis (Eds.), *Textual Dynamics in the Professions: Historical and Contemporary Studies of Writing in Professional Communities* (pp. 234–253). Madison, WI: University of Wisconsin Press.

Swales, J. M. (1990). *Genre analysis: English in academic and research settings*. Cambridge: Cambridge University Press.

Swales, J. M. (1992). Re-Thinking Genre: Another Look at Discourse Community Effects. Carleton University Conference on Genre: Unpublished Paper.

Tebeaux, E. (1990). Toward an Understanding of Gender Differences in Written Business Communications: A Suggested Perspective for Future Research. *Journal of Business and Technical Communication, 4*(1), 25–43.

Wenger, M. J., & Payne, D. G. (1994). Effects of Graphical Brower on Readers' Efficiency in Reading Hypertext. *Technical Communications, Second Quarter*, 224–233.

Winsor, D. (1993). Owning Corporate Texts. *Journal of Business and Technical Communication, 7*(2), 179–195.

Winsor, D. A. (1989). An engineer's writing and the corporate construction of knowledge. *Written Communication, 6*(3), 270–285.

Witte, S. P. (1988). Some contexts for understanding written literacy: unpublished paper.

Witte, S. P. (1992). Context, text, intertext: Toward a constructivist semiotic of writing. *Written Communication, 9*(2), 237–308.

Witte, S. P., & Haas, C. (2001). Writing as an Embodied Practice: The Case of Engineering Standards. *Journal of Business and Technical Communication, 15*(4), 413–457.

Yates, J. (1989). *Control through communication: The rise of system in American management*. Baltimore: The Johns Hopkins University Press.

Yates, J., & Orlikowski, W. J. (1992). Genres of organizational communication : A structurational approach to studying communication and media. *Academy of Management Review, 17*(2), 299–326.

Yates, J. A., Orlikowski, W. J., & Okamura, K. (1999). Explicit and Implicit Structuring of Genres in Electronic Communication: Reinforcement and change of Social Interaction. *Organization Science, 10*(1), 83–103.

Zimmerman, B. B., & Schultz, J. R. (2000). A Study of the Effectivness of Information Design Principles Applied to Clinical Research Questionnaires. *Technical communication, Second Quarter*, 177–194.

CHAPTER 15

History of Writing in the Community

Ursula Howard
University of London

This chapter explores the unbidden learning and practice of writing by ordinary people in disempowered communities, mostly during the 19th and 20th centuries in mainly, but not only, Britain. Writing in the community has long historical roots. It burgeoned in the early 19th century as the patterns of community life changed and the status and levels of literacy rose. During the 19th century, community-based writing developed as a social practice, in a tense and constantly evolving relationship with official and school literacies, whereas the establishment sought to discourage, contain, or assimilate it. Empirical research and cultural theories, together with first hand accounts, are used to illuminate this relationship. It is also important to celebrate the fertility of writing as a creative, social, and practical expression of the culture of communities.

Writing in the community is generated in, supports, and expresses that community. Communities contextualize and determine people's lives and identities (Hannon, Pahl, Bird, Taylor, & Birch, 2003). As Vincent (2000) suggests, skills-dominated mass literacy came about through a historical process in which "literacy was made distinct from other modes of daily practice," although "it was embedded in the structures of deprivation and opportunity, fear and aspiration which conditioned the struggle for existence" (p. 25). The concept of *ideological literacy*, the "New Literacy Studies," and social practice theory (Barton, Hamilton, & Ivanic, 2000; Street, 1984) have enabled a community-focused way of understanding literacy, encouraging the excavation of the writing practices and aspirations of those Olsen (1978) called "silenced ... their beings consumed in the hard, everyday essential work of maintaining human life. Their art ... anonymous, refused respect, recognition; lost" (p. 000). Social division has been a major factor in the production and visibility of writing, explored, for example, in the theoretical work of Williams (1984) and Bourdieu (1993).

Historical research has focused on writing in families and in local educational, cultural, and religious organiszations. The uses of writing for practical, financial, and legal uses have been documented. Attention has also been given to writing in social and political movements and in informal associations, special-interest groups, and networks (Barton & Hamilton, 1998; Mitch, 1992; Rose, 2001). The fluidity of historical contexts and the multiple meanings of writing practices and the concept of community are apparent in the particular — in familial, work-based, and social networks—and at local level, among family, friends, allies, neighbors, fellow believers, fellow workers, and members of organizations (Vincent, 1989). However, the history of writing remains an underresearched area compared with reading, despite plentiful primary sources (Brandt, 2001; Gillespie, 2001; Wright & Halloran, 2001).

In the research on writing in the community, a number of themes recur. One is the significance of writers' connections, long-standing and short-lived, with intermediaries or sponsors (Brandt, 2001) who influenced their learning and practice of writing. These included teachers, preachers, political activists, family members, community leaders, and itinerant strangers. Another is the role of writing in addressing separation, dispersal, and loss, which have always been part of life in communities. People come and go, temporarily and permanently, without ceasing to belong to their community or maintaining a significant presence within it. Belonging is a critical element of writing in the community.

Death, or the anticipation of death, was a significant occasion for writing in the community, moving against the invisibility of working-class lives, and what E. P. Thompson (1968) called the "enormous condescension of posterity" (p. 13) to the lives of people with no public voice. Over the last 30 years, oral history, as well as cultural, labor, feminist, and social history, has begun to address this deficit.

Writing in communities has enabled the realization of self-hood and agency for individuals and organizations. Research has confirmed the power of writing in communities, both material and mythical, that literary figures such as Dickens recognized. Research has also revealed the personal costs of writing to individuals, families, and communities (Bate, 2001; Howard, 1991; Vincent, 1982). The difficulties and obstacles associated with learning and practicing writing are now well known. Communities and families were not consistently benign forces. Opposition was also evident, particularly in women's accounts of conflict about their writing activity (Howard, 1991; Swindells, 1985).

THE ROOTS OF WRITING IN THE COMMUNITY

Writing practices became significant in daily life and work from the sixth century, when Benedictine monks began to copy ancient manuscripts and to train scribes, thus beginning a long history of teaching writing. In the 10th century, texts in English began to emerge from monastic communities in England, such as Cerne Abbas. In Eynsham, Aelfric produced homilies, books on gardening, grammars, and lives of the saints (Crystal, 2004). Informal early writing practices are difficult to reconstruct. Michael Clanchy (1979) argues that the arrival of state schooling in the late 19th century has distorted our picture of how literacy developed over the preceding 10 or more centuries as an activity in what he calls *lay* households. The term *lay* is significant because it derives from "leici," which meant illiterate. The plethora of historical accounts of increasing literacy rates and usages in the 19th and 20th centuries has obscured the gradual development over preceding centuries of literacy as part of daily life in communities. However, from the 11th century, practical literacy began to grow in communities independently of the bureaucratic literacies of church and state. Translation into English and the invention of print also enabled wide circulation of texts, with the Bible as core reading (Clanchy, 1979; Crystal, 2004).

The drives toward universal literacy in the 19th century had their roots in the shift from sacred script to practical literacy. As a response to the "harsh exactitude" of the Norman officials who created the "Domesday Book," ordinary people, the "leity," began during the 11th to 13th centuries to adopt their literacy practices as part of their lives (Clanchy, 1979). New elements of literate communication and transaction were the possession of a seal, comparable to a signature in the 19th century, and the dating of documents (Clanchy, 1979). Clanchy argues that the rapid development of commercial forms of literacy in and between local communities is evidenced by unprecedented numbers of written records of transactions. This made the 11th to 13th centuries a critical stage in the development of lay literacies. Dates, contracts, and seals are fundamental to the history of ownership and power relationships in communities. Writing became the trusted medium of transaction and property ownership became much easier to identify with writing.

Crystal (2004) argues that "writing became increasingly visible to all" by the 12th century, and its significance became clear to "the illiterate majority whose lives were governed by it"

(p. 135). Literacy development became a priority, and the number of schools rapidly increased. This was the first epoch during which literacy and schooling became closely connected, and grew separately from literacy as a set of social, community, and transactional practices. Literacy was also part of social movements. Shakespeare suggested in *Henry VI* (part 2) that Jack Cade's 15th-century rebellion was a conflict that put oppressive uses of literacy at the heart of the rebels' grievances (Crystal, 2004). From the 16th century, cheap publications such as chapbooks, ballads, popular literature, and poems became part of the public culture of community, often political and social in content. These forms increased significantly in the 17th century. Political and social upheavals in 17th-century Britain made literacy activity in communities surge. Growth and change in community uses of literacy from the 14th century have been strongly associated with periods of social and political change (Crick & Walsham, 2003; A. Hughes, 2004). By 1700, nearly half the male and a fourth of the female population of England were able to read and write. As literacy levels rose, laborers, girls, and women were least likely to be offered the opportunity to learn to write. Indeed, for the 17th-century laboring classes, working life started at age 7, about the age writing instruction began (Spufford, 1979; 1981). The expansion of the reading public was an essential foundation for the growth of writing (Graff, 2001).

The 18th century witnessed the further growth of popular and street literature and greater numbers of local schools. The Industrial Revolution and the accompanying political and social unrest saw the motivation for and use of literacy rise steeply in the decades that straddled the two centuries.

THE 19TH CENTURY

Scholars have debated the extent and significance of literacy practices in 19th-century communities and their impact on individuals, society, and the economy. Graff argues that external demand for literacy was limited and that it had little relevance either to the vast majority of people or to economic growth. Others have argued that the social movements and interest groups in which literacy was widely practiced made their importance greater than the actual numbers of schools or colleges attended, and that participation in education "effected psychological changes" in the relationship of working-class people to literacy (Sanderson, 1991; Vincent, 2000). However, apart from quantitative research on literacy levels, scholarship has concentrated largely on reading and qualitative accounts. Quantitative instruments, prior to compulsory schooling, offer too little to assess numerically the real extent or impact of writing.

Raymond Williams argued that the first half of the 19th century was the moment of change following 2,000 years of "cultural division" during which writing was known only to a minority. In this period, a majority of people rapidly achieved at least "minimal access to writing", giving rise to a "confusion of developments", a confusion exacerbated by a continuous relocation of the boundaries that keep the social divisions in education, cultural production, and life chances intact (Williams, 1981).

This was also a period of state formation in which formal uses of writing grew to unprecedented levels. Institutional, scientific, bureaucratic, commercial, regulatory, systemic, literary, and legislative literacy provided constraints and opportunities. The growth in public literacy also enabled alternative literacies to develop. Writing, whether practical, communicative, or creative, became increasingly part of social experience, human identity, community activity, and aspirations for change.

Signatures and Numbers: Official Emblems of Community Writing

Signatures are an emblematic feature of 19th-century writing in the community. To write a signature in a marriage register was a voluntary act, in the presence of family, friends, and community, made to seal an oral commitment. By the 19th century, signatures had fully replaced seals as marks of identity for transactional purposes. There is evidence of the sense of empowerment, identity, and agency engendered by this act of writing: naming yourself rather than being named by others (Vincent, 1982, 1989). Signatures also represented the power of writing to control individuals, demanded by authorities to identify and measure their populations. Literacy was a key element of social control to which measurement and counting of people were central (Johnson, 1970; W. B. Stephens, 1987). Population censuses, which began in 1790 in the United States and in 1801 in Britain, were initially resisted as an infringement of personal liberty. Self-identity through literacy remains emblematic of the two-way power relationship in the development and practice of writing skills.

In many countries, signatures were replaced by the end of the century as the official state vehicle for counting literacy. The creation of the international Universal Postal Union in 1974 heralded the measurement of literacy growth by counting letters. Community writing practices were thus recorded, though sheer numbers say little about the real purposes and meaning of writing to the "silent witnesses of the past" (Vincent, 2003, p. 417).

Learning and Practicing Writing in the Community

State and established church schools gradually replaced the tapestry of informal, community, and educational organizations, many based in nonconformist churches and religious groups. This shift was achieved through the educational drives of the established church as well as successive waves of government-sponsored directives, inspection, legislation, and a series of parliamentary inquiries (Vincent, 1989, 2000). Until at least 1860, however, it was difficult for working-class families to develop their literacy purely through school. Time was scarce, childhood short, working hours long, and family responsibilities heavy. Reading and writing materials were expensive, and the culture of learning in communities patchy. Research nevertheless shows that many thousands of people managed to learn and practice writing.

Vincent (1982) and Rose (2001) provide much evidence of the variety of reasons why people were prepared to undertake the painstaking work of learning to write in their communities, with precious few available hours, tools, or teachers. A comprehensive annotated three-volume bibliography (Burnett , Vincent, & Mayall, 1984–1989) includes more than 1,000 extant 19th-century working-class autobiographies in Britain and Ireland, published and unpublished, and a similar number in the 20th century. Vincent's study of hundreds of 19th-century male autobiographies (1982) finds that one major motivation is to leave a trace of one's life before dying. Anthony Errington wrote that "the Reason of my Wrighting ... is to inform my family and the world" (cited in Vincent, 2000, p. 27). In the United States, scholarship has identified this aspect as significant in slave narratives (Graff, 2001; Halloran & Wright, 2001). Obscurity was associated with a lack of literacy. Autobiographers identify this sense of the obscurity of their ancestors with the lack of any handwriting to evidence their existence. Death is a common theme, evidenced by epitaphs, memorials, testimonies, and life stories. Nineteenth-century Sunday school records reveal the considerable extent of such practices (Lacqueur, 1976). The memoir books of religious organizations sought to immortalize the short lives of devout young aspirants to literacy by extolling their writing practices (Howard, 1994).

From the 18th century, locally run schools were the main means of community learning in Britain. Gardner (1984) analyzed the multitude of private working-class schools, often termed *dame schools*, that flourished before compulsory state schooling in the 1890s. These organizations were based in, and funded by, communities through fees. Reading, spelling, and basic arithmetic were taught by lay teachers, alongside skills relevant to local industries or domestic life. Colls (1976) offers a study of one such school in a Northumberland mining village and its organic relationship to the community. In Ireland, *hedge schools* flourished, often literally conducted among fields and hedgerows (Vincent, 2000). The teaching of writing generally followed reading and in the brief spells of time available to learners, it remained a luxury, excluding many young people who could not afford the materials, had already started work, or were fully occupied caring for younger siblings, particularly girls. Writing was sometimes taught in dedicated writing schools. The silk weaver John Castle described his attendance at a writing school as so brief that he "filled only two copy books" (Howard, 1994, p. 304).

Detailed historical accounts describe the role of such schools in communities and the systematic attacks on them by the establishment in the process of establishing state education (Colls, 1976; Gardner, 1984; Horn,1978; M. Johnson, 1970; Vincent, 1989). The statist, as well as the economic case against informal schooling, is articulated in the reports of Her Majesty's Inspectorate from the 1840s, and in evidence to a series of parliamentary inquiries (Gardner, 1984; Vincent, 2000).

Although in Britain periods of attendance at community schools were brief and intermittent (Vincent, 1989), many supplemented their few weeks of school learning and practiced writing at home, with parents, siblings, relatives, and outsiders as teachers, or at Sunday schools and adult schools. People also learned by themselves, using what literacy material was at hand. Graveyard epitaphs were a common source of text for copying (Howard, 1994). Because paper and pens were costly, people gathered learning materials from any available source: pieces of chalk, stones, scraps of sugar paper, roof slates, walls, sand, cloth, and pins. Autobiographical accounts of ingenious ways of assembling the materials for learning are testimony to the high levels of motivation against considerable odds. John Clare's account is typical (cited in Bate, 2003). Autobiographical accounts of learning to write are often more detailed and vivid than those of learning to read, with claims that the writing materials of one's young self as aspiring writer have been carefully kept, offering inspiration for subsequent acts of writing.

Sunday schools were important institutions for learning to write. Rose (2001) argues that "most nineteenth century Sunday schools were indigenous working-class self-help institutions" (p. 62). Even the Chartists, with their very different ideology and aims, approved, if only because Sunday schools were instrumental in creating an actively literate working class. Historians have debated learners' motivations for learning to write: Lacqueur (1976) argued that social mobility was a key driver, in a challenge to E. P. Thompson (1968), who emphasized the role of literacy in the emerging working-class consciousness of the early 19th century. Sanderson (1991) argued that aspiration, whether for individual gain or the collective good, was a major motivational factor.

In the early decades of the 19th century, there was considerable debate about the teaching of writing on Sundays, which was opposed by the powerful Methodist hierarchy (M. Hamilton, 1996; Lacqueur, 1976). Opposition to writing reflected broader fears about teaching the working classes skills that could upset the social order. Access to writing skills could invite forgery and ambition for worldly gains. In several towns in northern England, notably in Bolton, street protests opposed the ban. Thousands of learners decamped to schools that taught writing and by the 1830s, writing was routinely taught (Musgrave, 1865 The Origin of Methodism in Bolton). Although writing instruction won the battle, debates about what should be taught and how continued for decades as the establishment sought to contain it.

According to Samuel Bamford, radical weaver and chronicler of the Peterloo Massacre of 1819, Sunday schools enabled working men "to become readers, writers and speakers in the village meetings for parliamentary reform" (Rose 2001, p. 62). Like dame schools, Sunday schools were organic to communities. Their teachers were mostly local people, their buildings attached to local churches. In 1852, 91.8% of workers in 12 Manchester mills had attended and significantly, by 1881 nearly 20% of the entire population of Great Britain were enrolled (Harrison, 1961; Lacqueur, 1976; Rose, 2001). What emerges from most narratives are the interventions of community members who enabled one short learning episode to be linked to the next. Active networks of mentors and informal teachers based in church, workplace, or extended family are repeatedly emphasized in autobiography (Brandt, 2001; Howard, 1991; Vincent, 1982) along with eulogies to the brief and basic literacy education on offer in communities across industrializing England (Howard, 1994).

Charles Shaw exemplified thousands of learners as cofounder of a Mutual Improvement Society. These learning associations had writing at the heart of their activity. They sometimes took the form of a more advanced Sunday school (Rose, 2001). Samuel Smiles was the philosopher of such self-help organizations, emphasizing the power of mutuality (M. D. Stephens & Roderick, 1983). Smiles borrowed the term *self-help* from the Owenite cooperator George J. Holyoake, promoter of literacy education for working people. Mutual Improvement Societies were sometimes political, but their core purpose was to satisfy the educational aspirations and intellectual curiosity of members, enabling a culture of autodidactism to flourish. Typically, Saturday night meetings blended writing, group discussion of essays on agreed subjects, and self-study (Howard 1991; Rose, 2001). The high ambition of the Mutual Improvement Societies in community learning is well documented (Graham, 1983; Harrison, 1961; Rose, 2001). Firsthand accounts write of intense motivation, and aspirations to higher levels of learning undaunted by technically low reading and writing skills.

Libraries and reading rooms flourished. Those who could read and write often taught those who could not. The Northumberland Chartist Robert Lowery claimed that over half the 20 members of his Mutual Improvement Society became authors and public speakers. Although some societies received support from middle-class benefactors, they remained largely autonomous if ephemeral, community organizations. Writing was part of their constitution as well as their curriculum. One at Hebden Bridge in West Yorkshire with 131 members was set up in an empty cottage: "We met and stood in a circle, one holding the candle while we deliberated, another wrote out the resolutions on loose paper" (Rose, 2001, p. 64).

Mechanics Institutes were prototype vocational colleges, founded by local communities. Unlike Mutual Improvement Societies, middle-class benefactors increasingly controlled their curriculum. But the Institutes remained community-managed ventures that helped many people develop their literacy and vocational skills including clerical skills, essay writing, and later in the century, shorthand (Ferreira-Buckley & Horner, 2001; Tylecote, 1957). Women as well as men attended Mechanics Institutes and working men's colleges, which flourished in Australia and other British colonies, and engaged in writing activities, although not without struggle (Purvis, 1989).

From the late 18th century, writing was taught at the Quaker-led adult schools and in classes run by local nonconformist groups such as Primitive Methodist classes and the Band of Hope. These institutions grew and flourished in urban areas until the First World War. The first half hour of Sunday morning instruction in literacy and Bible studies was dedicated to writing. Writing class sizes often exceeded 100 learners (Rowntree & Binns, 1903; Currie Martin, 1924). Adult schools were a part of an independent culture of education and community life dedicated to temperance, family health, and the well-being of the poor. They worked with women who often saw little of their husband's wages. Moral and social imperatives were addressed through practical skills development.

Graff (2001) describes a similar patchwork of informal and formal learning in U.S. communities, including migrant and immigrant groups. Their activity was overtaken, as in England, by the rush to formal state schooling and stronger social control. Graff acknowledges the persistence of communities in engaging in learning despite his argument that the economic gains were few. Black people's experience was different, however, with literacy levels remaining low, although Graff suggests that the drive for literacy in Black communities was markedly different, associated with liberation and the will to establish autonomous Black organizations in communities. In his view, although reading and writing did not lead to economic gain, the achievements in literacy by Black communities were impressive despite the opposition they faced. There is evidence, for example, from Frederick Douglass' (1986) autobiography, that learning to write was severely discouraged by the establishment as potentially subversive.

Using Writing in 19th-Century Communities: Practices and Meanings

Working Life, Self-Help, and Social Protest.   By the mid-19th century, there had been growing demand for literacy in the workplace, though researchers debate its extent. Mitch (1992) noted that advertisements for carters and barmaids in the United States asked for a man "who can write plainly" and required written applications and numeracy skills. E. P. Thompson (1968) similarly argues that writing skills were demanded by employers. However, Graff (1979) argues that there was little economic or social demand for literacy, and that even justices of the peace were not required to be able to sign their name. Workplaces in which people used writing included local cooperatives or friendly societies, which needed minute writers, secretaries, and treasurers. Some Mutual Improvement Societies began at work, with factory workers clubbing together to learn after hours.

The extent of evidence of writing in the workplace challenges the dominant view that "poverty is a poor place to write poetry in" (Vicinus, 1974, p. 3), and that only rural working environments could inspire imaginative expression. The routines of factory or mill life have rarely been the subject of poetry. Yet research shows that significant numbers of manual workers wrote creatively in and about the workplace, inspired by relationships at work, and the noises and rhythms of the factory. R. M. Fox and Ethel Carnie are two among many (Burnett et al., 1984–1989; Howard, 1994).

Even early in the century, however unrealistic, the aspiration for most working-class children to learn clerical skills to secure stable employment was widespread (Lacqueur, 1976; Sanderson, 1991). John Clare's parents despaired of his determination to write poetry rather than become a clerk. As the century progressed, and clerical work expanded, writing became a highly practical as well as desired skill, for women as well as men (Purvis, 1987).

Writing about work was an element of workers' joint action, including circulars and petitions to prevent a factory closure, or negotiation about wages and conditions. Careful thought was given to the effectiveness of the style of writing in negotiation with powerful employers: whether to perfect the grammar and spelling or whether, conversely, the authenticity of ungrammatical, unpolished language might elicit a more sympathetic response. Individuals also used writing to seek employment, through patrons and intermediaries (Howard, 1994; Vincent, 1989).

In the politically repressive early decades of the 19th century, meetings in communities, for example, any form of trade union activity, were proscribed as subversive. Writing in secret (including signed oaths) became a hallmark of gatherings and activities. Corresponding societies became an important organizational form, promoting social and political progress (E. P. Thompson, 1968). Indeed, from the late 18th century, writing became increasingly central to community-based organization for change. Vincent (2000) attributes "the institutionalisation of protest" during the 19th century to the increased use of writing, which enabled effective organization, communication, and action. Writing was a key element in organizing protests such as bread riots, in Luddite action in industrial centers in 1811 to 1812, and the later "Swing" riots and rick burnings in rural communities. These actions were a response to the mechanization of work processes, as well as to unemployment, poverty, and rising prices.

At issue was the traditional right to earn a livelihood and defend the customs and practices of employment against the imperatives of the new factory system (Binfield, 2004; Hay et al., 1988; Hobsbawm & Rude, 1973; E. P. Thompson, 1971). The threatening letter, the "gazetting" of grievances in local newspapers, or notices pinned to trees were common forms of protest against local employers. Writing played a key part in a long continuum of social protest, not only in the machine breaking and arson seen of the early 19th-century movements. Writing could be the expression of intent to take action as redress, but was also a traditional form of intervention in a process of negotiation for better conditions. Skilled workers and their unions organized peaceful bargaining through letters. From Luddites through to 20th-century trade unionists, bargaining and protest entailed posters, banners, proclamations, songs, and poems. Together they offered locally varied "rich texts," and discourses that included petitioning for better wages, suffrage, and other radical political reform.

The act of naming was critical to the identity of a protest, the creation of a single emblematic collective signature. Writing was a collective act of community self-interest and a practical defense. Anonymous letters presented grievances in a form that protected individuals through a collective demand and avoided the retaliation that meetings, or real signatures, could provoke. E. P. Thompson (1968) argued that these acts of writing can be read as the individual's or group's desire to solemnify an act, stamping authority and purpose on even the most desperate action. Writing in this local, community context ritualizes, dramatizes, and makes permanent what were often improvised and uncoordinated actions.

Letter Writing as a Community Practice.   From the mid-18th century, the separation of community members, temporarily and permanently, increased dramatically, particularly where the rural population declined, as industrializing urban communities grew, or in countries where immigration and emigration were significant. In Britain, cottage industries, smallholdings, family concerns, the common use of land, and the traditional dependent relationships between landowners and laboring people, which E. P. Thompson (1971) called the *moral economy*, were gradually replaced by private ownership, traveling to work, factory production, and the impersonal, precarious nature of the wage economy. As autobiographies and letters record, people left home for diverse reasons: to seek work; to undertake the journeyman years of mastering trades and crafts, to join the army or navy, to go into domestic service, or as a result of eviction and destitution. Others moved to escape persecution, in particular from Eastern Europe to North America and Britain, or sought a better life in the colonies or elsewhere.

Mobility increased the need to communicate through letters sent via friends, carriers, and embryonic postal services (Vincent, 1982, 1989). Autobiographies relate in detail the painful or laborious efforts at writing letters, the sharpness of memories, and the language suggesting that writing itself was a step into unfamiliar and daunting territory (Howard, 1994).

Writings expressed the difficulty of separation from families and loved ones, but also the power of writing to diminish distance, to maintain a sense of belonging, and to accomplish practical transactions. Writing was the means of sustaining old relationships and a sense of belonging during prolonged absences. Moves away from communities were matched by the advent of newcomers. Writers witness the coming and going of strangers: migrant workers, itinerants, peddlers, scribes, preachers, and the part they played in the culture of communities. From the point of view of old communities, they amount to a typology of strangers. There are many examples of people in liminal positions, lived between old and new lives. Thomas and Znaniecki's (1984) study of Polish immigrants to the United States, first published in 1919, pioneered scholarship on migrant communities and their multiple allegiances, revealing an intense culture of letter writing as part of complex identities in lives transplanted to an unfamiliar world. The lives and extensive writing practices of early convicts in Australia have been documented by Robert Hughes (1987).

Official statistics about letter writing are telling. In 1839, sixty-five million letters were delivered in England and Wales (E & W), 8 million in Scotland (Sc), and 9 million in Ireland (Ire). By 1850, numbers had risen to 276 million (E & W), 35 million (Sc), and 35 million (Ire); and by 1872, to 737 million (E & W), 82 million (Sc), and 66 million (Ire) (Vincent, 1989). Before the Penny Post was introduced in the UK in 1840, payment was made by the addressee, and the costs were often prohibitive. Poverty caused letters to be refused or not written in the first place: "I did not like to saddle them with the postage and, for my part, I had no money to spare" (Howard, 1994, p. 216). Many letters failed to arrive for want of properly written addresses. Many letters were turned away because just knowing they had arrived (sometimes blank sheets) was enough to know the correspondent was alive and well (Howard, 1994; Vincent, 2000).

Although evidence to parliamentary inquiries about the extent of letter writing in Britain was contradictory, much evidence suggests that it spread fast after 1840. Other evidence from parliamentary papers and autobiography suggests that the increase in letter writing after postal reforms was not as spectacular as claimed because the widespread and often ingenious evasions of postal charges before 1840 had been underestimated. The "Dead Letter Office" also recorded many thousands of letters so sketchily addressed they could not be delivered. They retain traces of the oral communication practices that writing superceded and the investing of magical properties in written communication systems, barely grasped by new writers: "to my dear father in Yorkshire at the white house with the green palins" (Howard, 1994; Smith, 1908; Vincent, 2000). By the mid-century, letter writing was being embraced in communities as a practical form of communication, but was also experienced as a deep code of magical passwords. Letters could either connect and empower, or underline personal isolation and the fragmentation of communities.

Writing enabled more efficient passing on of practical information, helping to end the practice of walking many miles, often fruitlessly, in search of work, on the basis of oral chains of information. As reported to a Parliamentary Select Committee in 1838, "This tramping would not take place if the persons could write to other workmen in those places, to inquire if there was a frame to let, or they could get employment" or "If the postage were low, they would write first and know whether they were likely to succeed" (Howard, 1994, p. 211). Autobiographies testify to the growth in letters of application. These changes in practice helped to break down rural isolation through networks of information dispersal (Rose, 2001; Vincent 1982).

Greeting cards became increasingly popular vehicles for writing, subject to changing fashions. Valentine's Day cards ranged at different times from the discreet to the comic to the obscene (F. Thompson, 1939). Picture postcards arrived in the late 19th century. They took off rapidly, encouraged across Europe by a change in the Postal Union rules in 1897. By 1913, five billion were sent each year (Briggs, 1988; Vincent, 2003). Postcards, reflective of the growth of leisure, also widened access to writing: The style was informal, the words required to convey the desired messages few (Vincent, 2003).

Remarkable similarities in writing practice exist across time and place. Besnier's anthropological study of a Polynesian atoll of Nukulaelae examines letter-writing practices there from the late 19th century. Letters were written to known people from the community. Their language was influenced by external influences: here, the use of English words. Letters bore traces of oral traditions and were often dispatched with oral messages. Practices were gendered and strongly expressive of emotion and vulnerability (Besnier, 1995). Letters were also seen as potentially subversive and a dangerous medium: they were sometimes read by others with harsh consequences for writers who transgressed customs and norms.

The Role of Scribes.   Scribes undertook much letter writing in 19th-century communities. Families and communities relied on their own members. The mother of Joseph Arch, a prominent trade unionist and autobiographer, taught her son to write:

> [And she] was a splendid hand at writing letters. A great many of the poor people who had children and relatives away from home, but could not write to them, used to come to my mother and ask her to write their letters for them. (Howard, 1994, p. 217)

Postmen and post offices performed interlinked social functions, including scribing, supporting a range of writing practices, and sharing their information and skills. One autobiographer, a village postmistress in the late 19th century, described writing letters for itinerant Irish harvesters when they sent money orders home (F. Thompson, 1939). Postman, poet, and political activist John Bedford Leno wrote of his power as a scribe, relishing "like a crafty statesman, the possession of secret knowledge" he gained (Howard, 1994, p. 221). After the introduction of compulsory schooling, children's skills began to surpass their parents' and young people increasingly acted as family scribes, generating awkward feelings and sometimes conflict over status and roles (T. Thompson, 1981).

Writing in Community Organizations.   A culture of writing was embedded in community organizations. Self-help and mutual organizations, clubs, and businesses sprang up in communities in the wake of the Poor Law of 1834, which replaced direct poverty alleviation in communities with the workhouse system. Such organizations worked to foster independence and self-reliance in communities. They generated an industry of constitutional, practical, and transactional writing that played a central part in their sustained success. The cooperative movement, which started in Rochdale, is the most prominent of these. Friendly Societies, reading rooms, libraries, trade unions, nonconformist religious groups, working men's clubs and institutes, women's organizations, and special-interest clubs such as allotment associations are among organizations from which there is a wealth of surviving evidence of the intensity of formal and informal writing practices. In many organizations, educational activities supported the need for competent writers to draw up rules, order stock, and carry out other writing tasks: minutes of meetings, records of transaction, keeping accounts, or writing for newsletters, magazines, and yearbooks. Membership organizations generated much writing in recruitment campaigns. Autobiographies record letters "coming in by the gross" as trade unions rapidly grew toward the end of the century (Howard, 1994, p. 211). Research shows that a dense web of literacy activities continues to keep social activity in communities buoyant (Barton & Hamilton, 1998; Brandt, 2001). Some organizations extended their social, economic, or religious goals into cultural and educational activities. The cooperative movement established libraries as well as educational and leisure activities for their members (Harrison, 1960).

In the late 19th and early 20th centuries, organizational journals and magazines proliferated as important vehicles for writing. Articles, poems, life stories, essays, practical advice, and emotional conversion narratives sat side by side, written by grassroots members and community-based or social-movement leaders whose writing appeared in several. They were characterized by a diversity of writing, but also a shared purpose of social and moral improvement and the alleviation of poverty. Yearbooks and other publications were important vehicles for writing in organizations. Their output grew well into the 20th century.

Working-class organizations grew their own intellectuals, some of whom specifically supported the development of writing for social and political purposes. William Cobbett, the cooperator George J. Holyoake, and the Chartist William Lovett were among those who fit Gramsci's concept of "organic intellectuals." Each wrote a popular grammar with guidance on writing techniques and pedagogic approaches. In the early 20th century, R. H. Tawney and G. D. H. Cole, prominent academics as well as tutors for the Workers' Education Association's (WEA) "tutorial classes," published practical advice on essays and other forms of writing in *The Highway*, the WEA's journal (Cole & Mansbridge, 1912; Stock, 1953).

Meaning and Difference in 19th-Century Writing Practices: Themes and Issues

Conversion and Self-Improvement: Writing as Proselytising in the Interests of Community.   Personal testimony was a common form of writing, from the journals of religious and political movements to the sensationalist press. This took the shape of stories, declarations of innocence and defense, betrayal, religious conversion, the last-minute confessions of condemned criminals, and the correspondence of prisoners with their families and supporters. Publication enabled public debate from the point of view of those affected. The significance of the process of writing itself is manifest in narratives. Magazines, articles, memoirs, and letters commonly describe the gaining of literacy skills as a central element of the conversion to sobriety, rectitude, and self-improvement (Currie Martin, 1924; Howard, 1994; Vincent, 1982).

Gender, Race and Class: Writing in the Private and Public Spheres. Women's writing in the 19th and 20th centuries suggests that the learning and practicing of writing in the community has been different for men and women. Men's accounts of learning to write in the 19th century tended to emphasize publicly social and aspirational learning, whereas women's memories express more individual, secretive, and transgressive experiences. Men dominated informal learning of writing (Howard, 1994). Writing practices reflect wider gender divisions between public and private spheres. Gender differences continued into the 20th century (Brandt, 2001; Howard 1991). One difference in the 19th century was that boys were encouraged by the possibility, however remote, of earning a better living from writing (Mitch, 1992; Sanderson, 1991). Clerical work did not open up to women until the last quarter of the century, when girls routinely learned writing skills in the higher standards of the school curriculum. Marianne Farningham, Janet Bathgate, Hannah Mitchell, and Louise Jermy, all brought up in poverty, persisted with learning to write despite family opposition and went on to achieve clerical or teaching careers. All were active in social/political organizations and published autobiographies.

Young women who were forced into domestic service or caring roles in the family also used writing to express negative feelings and to precipitate a change in their circumstances. Women writers often encountered fierce opposition from parents and stepparents, mothers and fathers. Conflictual relationships are later presented in self-justifying terms. Working women autobiographers could thus become the heroines of their own stories, in which writing events are high among the transformational processes of their lives. Autobiographer Janet Bathgate was sent away to become a farmworker as a totally illiterate girl. Using scraps of text she had collected to practice reading, she pricked out letters onto a piece of cloth with a pin. She was brought home and sent to school. After years of pleading, Marianne Farningham learned to write in secret, at night, away from the displeasure of her father (Howard, 1991; Swindells, 1985).

In the United States, writing also follows gendered patterns. White boys were encouraged to learn to write, whereas girls and Black people were not. Wright and Halloran argue that for Black communities in the United States and the British Caribbean colonies, the prospects of gaining literacy hardly improved from the well-documented accounts of slave narratives (Wright & Halloran, 2001).

Research shows the ways in which American women, from both middle-class and Black communities, engaged in literacy as part of public practice. Some Black women's communities have had a different response, embracing a more public practice through club movements. Shirley Wilson Logan, editor of an anthology of 19th-century African American women's writing (1999), studied the experience of Black women in 19th-century American club and church movements. She develops the theme of writing as empowerment in the context of oppositional forces and concentrates on writing in the public sphere. She links writing with rhetoric and public speaking in a "persuasive discourse" that sought social change, analyzing essays and letters as well as speeches on, for example, anti-lynching, and examines the discourses associated with women's organizations in religious communities.

Anne Ruggles Gere's (1997) study of American clubwomen contrasts the practices of different communities of women and sees their literacy as part of the culture of women's clubs, addressing, for example, contesting versions of Americanization such as urbanization and the impact of immigration. She argues that Black clubwomen often used writing to document the effects of racism, producing reports from their own surveys of households in deprived districts and inspections of schools. In working women's clubs, including Jewish clubs, literacy practices were an attempt to create a new identity that "need no longer be as dull as the materials with which they labour." Gere argues that clubwomen were "constructing independence through their texts, asserting the integrity of their positions rather than focusing all their energies on trying to leave the working class" (pp. 59–65, 82–88). Improving writing skills was a focus, including talks and advice on learning to write English for immigrant groups.

For Jacqueline Jones Royster (2000), the writing of African American women in the 19th century constituted resistance against oppression. Citing some of the same writers and speakers as Wilson Logan, Royster draws on periodicals and journals that promoted social change to highlight the literacy practices of elite Black women, educators, and clubwomen. Gere and Royster both place emphasis on the links between rhetoric and writing, public speaking and publishing as the critical instruments of the aspirational activity among 19th-century American women, and the significance of their entry into a stream of public discourse—not as exceptional or unique members of their communities but as much more typical than mainstream judgments have allowed. Eldred and Mortenson (2002) also explore the links between rhetoric and composition in the development of women's literacy in the United States from the Revolution to the Civil War, drawing on a range of women's writing from novels and essays to diaries. The role of writing in women's active engagement with civic life challenges notions of women in this period as contained within the private sphere. Rhetoric is a field of study in which composition and writing in the community interestingly converge.

Significant Others.   Studies of learning to write in 19th-century communities uncover an inventory of significant others: agents, brokers, supporters, and opponents of literacy. Deborah Brandt has developed the notion of "sponsors" into a conceptual framework for literacy learning, in particular writing. Sponsors are the qualitative reflection of statistics such as those that record the numbers of Sunday school teachers in urban communities. The social map of sponsors includes Sunday school teachers, family members, letter carriers, literate artisans, journeymen and masters, male and female scribes, middle-class patrons, quack doctors, and itinerants. They frequently appear as complete strangers whose gestures and actions triggered a desire to learn to write and whose appearance and disappearance mark lives more usually led in familiar and tight relationship circles (Brandt, 2001; Mitchell, 1977). Autobiographical writers regularly invoke the names of sponsors as their stories illuminate the complex informal patterns of learning to write in communities and the social interactions that characterized learning to practise literacy.

THE 20TH CENTURY: CHANGE AND CONTINUITY

The transition between 19th- and 20th-century literacies started with the advent of compulsory state education, which changed attitudes to literacy and saw the steady erosion of associational cultures of writing in communities. For many of their activists, like Joseph Lawson, state education was a mixed blessing: "There is something wrong with education when the years of school education are increased and there is less desire for knowledge" (Howard, 1994, p. 201). Many writers regretted the colder climate for writing and the loss of community involvement in children's learning, eloquently criticizing those architects of standardisation who had derided working-class cultural practices (Bourne, 1984; Vincent, 2003).

The assumption of universal literacy followed universal schooling. Across Europe and America, literacy was estimated as reaching uniformly high levels in the early 20th century and differentials between women and men diminished (Furet & Ozouf, 1982; Vincent, 2003). The First World War was a watershed, with enlisted men expected to read instructions and millions of letters to and from home evidence of writing practices across class, gender, and age.

There is evidence that writing remained a strong motivational and practical feature of community life. In Britain, the mass observation (MO) movement, founded in 1937, started as a "people's ethnography" (Sheridan, 1993, p. 17). It offers ordinary people the opportunity to take part in an ongoing writing project, which is amassed and analyzed at national level, but written by volunteers in communities. Large numbers of ordinary people write diaries, letters, and life-story documents, as well as views and reflections on centrally directed MO themes. This writing is by women (mainly) and men who work alone exposing hidden lives (Barton et al., 1993; Mace, 1998). Writers are known as correspondents, to reflect a "sense of mutual relationship" (Sheridan, 1996, p. 30). MO offers significant evidence of the continuity of community writing practices: MO writers represent themselves, but also their communities, adopting a "sense of responsibility for ... writing down a particular set of experiences" (Sheridan, 1993, p. 18).

From 1907, writing transformed formal adult education in communities, initially through the Women's Educational Association (WEA) tutorial-class movement for working men and women. University-based extramural education had offered lectures for the previous half century, but largely failed to attract working-class participation (Rowbotham, 1981). The WEA learner's pledge to regular writing assignments was the key to the success of this educational initiative in working-class communities (Stock, 1953; Tawney, 1914). The classes were pioneered in industrial communities: Rochdale, Longton, and Reading, towns steeped in the cultural and community activism of the previous century. More widely, the post-World War I reconstruction effort gave adult education the opportunity to become widely accessible to working-class communities and to women (Yeo, 1976, p. 235–251). Recent scholarship has explored the flourishing culture and democratising forces around writing in working-class communities and elsewhere in the 1920s and 1930s (Hilliard, 2006).

Since the 1950s, there has been active debate about working-class uses of literacy in the 20th century. Richard Hoggart in his influential study of literacy in working-class communities (1957) and J. F. C. Harrison (1961) argued that the active culture of self-education and literacy practices was lost after 1914. Popular literacy and the media had turned communities into consumers debased by an impoverished mass culture. This view was largely unchallenged, until the 1970s. Hoyles's *The Politics of Literacy* (1977) pointed to communities in the 1940s and 1950s where reading magazines and newpapers did not preclude diary keeping, scrapbook making, and other literacy practices.

In the 1970s, adult literacy was revealed as a public-policy issue, linked to the rediscovery of poverty and inequality in some Western countries. Literacy movements flourished in developing countries too, marked by social change and new cultural movements that promoted the voices of the culturally excluded (Freire, 1972). At the same time, repoliticized community activism, feminism, and new approaches to social and cultural history were coupled with a renewed focus on writing in local communities. The extent of writing practices became apparent and much writing by women and working-class writers was collected. It formed the basis of community writing events and the publication of many autobiographies, oral histories, and poetry (Morley & Worpole, 1982; Yeo, 1986).

In the UK, the Federation of Worker Writers and Community Publishers, established in 1976, is the umbrella organization for autonomous community writing and publishing, set up to support the writing of marginalized groups to help them to become cultural producers with a public voice. The initial focus was on working-class writing (Woodin, 2001). Adult literacy groups were part of this movement, creating texts that were used for reading practice and as stories in their own right (Gillespie, 2001; Mace, 1979). The writing and publishing movement met opposition (Morley & Worpole, 1982) from the arts establishment and from scholars of working-class origin, including Hoggart, who argued against what they considered cultural relativism (Woodin, 2005a). What emerges from research is the sense of the Federation's participants as cultural outsiders, preferring informal, community-based learning to education and with diverse reasons for writing. What distinguishes the writing practice is the community-based workshop form, which Gregory (1991) called "collective self-education" (p. 130), a descendant of the mutual improvement society tradition. A further distinction is the consciousness and purpose of the "Fed," which aims to challenge cultural power imbalances. O'Rourke's (2005) study of creative-writing groups as part of local adult education shows the value of "local cultures of writing" or "socialised creative writing" (pp. 231–233), neither mere subject nor just a hobby; and the importance of distancing community writing from the pressures of educational standardization.

Woodin (2005b) draws on Williams' (1981) analysis to argue that the result of community writing activity includes the widespread use of life-history writing in publishing and the media, making "the idea of oppositional cultures appear more blurred and deeply implicated in mainstream culture" (p. 577). Diversification has changed the mainstream, but this is largely about reshaping a (slightly larger) elite without dismantling fundamental cultural divisions (Woodin, 2006). However, there is also a collective pride, as there was among the alumni of 19th-century mutual improvement societies and in the success of individual Federation writers, and the adherence to democratic and inclusive cultural practices remains a core purpose. The idea that everyone can be a writer remains a core value. Class remains a key issue in understanding cultural production in communities as does the question of whose stories are recorded for history (Woodin, 2005a, 2005b; Yeo, 1986).

The work of contemporary women writers groups in the United States, from disadvantaged rural and urban districts, has been conceptualized by Gere (2001). She argues that the history of writing as composition has been either "inside the classroom walls," rooted in the history of rhetoric, or understood as extracurricular in the sense of literary societies, part of mainstream academic institutions. For writers from disempowered communities, of whom "nobody ever asked … opinions about anything," Gere proposes the concept of "the extracurriculum of composition," which is explicitly located in community-based, informal settings. The concept embraces the diversity of gender race and class, nurtures self-belief and opportunities for collective feedback, and aims for varieties of publications relevant to the multiple contexts of people's lives. The "extracurriculum" offers an active interface between composition as part of the education system and composition as a community-focused activity, nurturing "the aspirations and imaginations of its participants." She poses a challenge to the historians of writing, or composition, to embrace writing beyond the historiography of formal education (pp. 275–289).

Similarly, Peck, Flower, and Higgins (2001) examine writing practices in a Pittsburgh community center working with young African American men, exploring the need for an alternative discourse for "community literacy." Writing notes and petitions are part of "composing" action in the interests of self and community in support of social change, or "collaborative problem solving in the community" (pp. 575–583). The Peck et al. concept of "learning to take literate action in the face of conflict" is comparable to the work of Edmondson (2003). In *Prairie Town*, Edmondson similarly sees literacy as a way of composing change and developing independent discourses for community self-determination. She examines how rural communities disempowered by economic change need to move beyond traditional literacies, reject neoliberal discourses, and seek to redefine their world in their own terms, regenerating community through, in this case, a Prairie Renaissance project. This work echoes the emancipatory approaches to writing in the 19th century, proposing that the broadest concept of literacy is needed to practice local autonomy in a new global age.

Ethnographic literacy research in the United States also suggests, differently, that writing practices had become more transactional and utilitarian in communities by the mid to late 20th century than previously, and less significant than reading in family and community discourses, echoing the 1950s debates in Britain. Shirley Brice Heath's study of three U.S. communities also demonstrates a continuum of fluid change in literacy practices. More women than men were practicing writing, with more positive attitudes to and usages of writing observed in the Black community than either the White or the professional communities. The most extended writings in the rural White community were redolent of the 19th century, based around cooperative writing efforts within church organizations, with more family and social writing in the Black community where "every letter writer is part of a familiar unbroken chain of linkages between relatives and/or friends" (Brice Heath, 1983, pp. 213–214). More recent studies of family literacy practices include Rogers' (2003) detailed ethnographic research with families in a U.S. community that argues for the importance of linking literacy with local life to empower people to direct "their own social circumstances."

Research also suggests that clear differences have developed in American communities between men's and women's literacy, and between reading and writing (Brandt, 2001). Brandt found that early memories of writing in 20th-century experience were ambivalent and uncomfortable compared with memories of reading. This relates interestingly to the memories of 19th-century writers, where women often associated learning to write with personal progress achieved in the face of difficulty and conflict. Woodin (2005a, 2005b) also argued that trauma has continued to motivate writing in the late 20th century.

Other continuities with earlier epochs appear to persist. Significant others, or sponsors, remain influential in literacy practice (Padmore, 1994). Barton and Hamilton (1998) have revealed a continuing culture of writing in communities, showing the value still placed on detailed, accurate records in organizational proceedings among the diversity of writing practices in one small city. Researchers have suggested that the autodidactic tradition did not survive the two world wars (Harrison, 1961). But much recent research on informal learning as well as community writing and publishing suggests otherwise. Despite the availability of formal, postcompulsory education, many prefer independent, informal learning and literacy practices.

Letter writing, increasingly through e-mail, has also increased, as has the need for it. As the mobility and displacement of people has increased, letter writing is as relevant as ever. Scribes continue to be an essential part of writing in the community, as Mace and Kalman demonstrate. The role of scribe is complex, operating on a spectrum, from alienated composition on behalf of the writer to receiver of dictation. As Kalman's (1999, 2005) studies in present-day Mexico show, the relationship of scribe can be much more cooperative, an act of "shared composition," which Mace (2002) terms "the give and take of writing" (pp. 157–158).

CONCLUSION

Writing in the community has offered people who practiced literacy beyond the practicalities of daily life the power of speaking with authority not only for self, but for locality and community. Research also uncovers the ways in which writing in the community has the capacity to disturb life, materially and psychologically. The act of writing, particularly the aspiration to be a writer, have created a distance between writers and their communities, even when, or especially when, they aspired to speak for their community. To write about circumstances objectifies and abstracts them. Writing has set people apart from their communities. As an Irish migrant railway worker put it, "I was working on a shift they did not understand" (Howard, 1994, p. 300).

Evidence shows that writing in the community continues to proliferate. There remains awkwardness and difficulty in interactions with powerful and official literacies (Barton & Hamilton, 1998; Brice Heath, 1983). However, new forms of written communication continually develop, exploiting the resources of new technologies. Gunther Kress (2002) has argued that the shift to digital and mobile media, and more visual forms of communication are fast changing the nature of writing. Glynda Hull (2004) has illustrated the power of story writing through multimedia initiatives in the community, such as "DUSTY' in Oakland, California, and argues for openness to new definitions of literacy in the digital age (Hull & Schulz, 2002). Blogging, chatrooms, and other writing media echo past practices, oral and written, and they are dramatically increasing the volume of writing in virtual communities. Fanzines, which express particular communities of interest, still flourish: Their roots lie in 19th-century U.S.-based literacy groups. Writing through the Internet enables connectivity on an unprecedented scale, creating new communities. The resilience of writing practices in communities, supported by ever-changing technologies and new forms of community keep alive the possibilities for the democratization of cultural practices.

REFERENCES

Barton, D., Bloome, O., Sheridan, D., Street, B. (1993) Ordinary People Writing: The Lancaster and Sussex Writing Research Projects. Papers Lancaster: Lancaster University.

Barton, D., & Hamilton, M. (1998). *Local literacies: Reading and writing in one community.* London: Routledge

Barton, D., Hamilton, M., & Ivanic, R. (Eds.). (2000). *Situated literacies: Reading and writing in context.* London: Routledge.

Bate, J. (2003). *John Clare: A biography.* London: Picador.

Besnier, N. (1995). *Literacy, emotion and authority: Reading and writing on a Polynesian atoll.* Cambridge, England: Cambridge University Press.

Binfield K. (Ed). (2004). *Writings of the Luddites.* Baltimore: Johns Hopkins University Press.

Bourdieu, P. (1993). *The field of cultural production.* London: Polity.

Bourne, G. (1984). *Change in the village.* London: Harmondsworth.

Brandt, D. (2001). *Literacy in American lives.* Cambridge, England: Cambridge University Press.

Brice Heath, S. (1983). *Ways with words: Language, life and work in the communities and classrooms.* Cambridge, England: Cambridge University Press.

Briggs, A. (1988). *Victorian things.* London: Batsford.

Burnett, J., Vincent, D., & Mayall, D. (1984–1989). *The autobiography of the working class* (3 vols.). Brighton, England: Harvester.

Clanchy, M. T. (1979). *From memory to written record: England 1066–1307.* London: Arnold.

Cole, G. D. H., & Mansbridge, A. (1912). Higher education of working men. *The Highway,* vol. 4 No. 47 pp. 166–167

Colls, R. (1976). "Oh happy English children!": Coal, class and education in the North East. *Past and Present,* 73, 75–99.

Crick, J., & Walsham, A (Eds.). (2003). *The uses of script and print 130–1700.* Cambridge, England: Cambridge University Press.

Crystal, D. (2004). *The stories of English.* London: Lane.

Currie Martin, G. (1924). *The adult school movement: Its origins and development.* London: National Adult School Union.

Douglass, F (1986). *Narrative of the life of Frederick Douglass: An American slave (1845).* London: Harmondsworth.

Edmondson, J. (2003). *Prairie town: Redefining rural life in the age of globalisation.* Lanham, MD: Rowman & Littlefield.

Eldred, J. C., & Mortensen, P. (2002). *Imagining rhetoric: Composing women of the early United States.* Pittsburgh: University of Pittsburgh Press.

Ferreira-Buckley, L., & Horner, W. B. (2001). Writing instruction in Great Britain: The eighteenth and nineteenth centuries. In J. J. Murphy (Ed.), *A short history of writing instruction* (pp. 173–212). Mahwah, NJ: Lawrence Erlbaum Associates.

Freire, P. (1972). *Cultural action for freedom.* London: Harmondsworth.

Furet, F., & Ozouf, J. (1982). Reading and Writing: Literacy in France from Calvin to Joles Ferry. Cambridge: Cambridge University Press.

Gardner, P. W. (1984). *The lost elementary schools of Victorian England.* Beckenham, England: Croome Helm.

Gere, A. R. (1997). *Intimate practices: Literacy and cultural work in US women's clubs 1880–1920.* Urbana: University of Illinois Press.

Gere, A. R. (2001). Kitchen tables and rented rooms: The extracurriculum of composition. In E. Cushman, M. Rose, B. Kroll, & E. Kintgen (Eds.), *Literacy: A critical sourcebook* (pp. 275–289). Boston: Bedford/ St. Martin's.

Gillespie, M. (2001). Research in writing: Implications for adult literacy education. In J. Comings, B. Garner, & C. Smith (Eds.), *Review of adult learning and literacy* (Vol. 2, pp. 63–100). Mahwah, NJ: Lawrence Erlbaum Associates.

Graff, H. J. (1979). *The literacy myth: Literacy and social structure in the nineteenth century city.* New York: Academic Press.

Graff, H. J. (2001). The nineteenth century origins of our times. In E. Cushman, M. Rose, B. Kroll, & E. Kintgen (Eds.), *Literacy: A critical sourcebook* (pp. 211–233). Boston: Bedford/St. Martin's.

Graham, B. (1983). *Nineteenth century self-help in education—manual improvement societies* (Case Study: The Carlisle Working Men's Reading Rooms, Vol. 2). Nottingham, England: University of Nottingham Press.

Gregory, G. (1991). Community publishing as self-education. In D. Barton & R. Ivanic (Eds.), *Writing in the community* (pp. 109–142). Newbury Park, CA: Sage.

Hamilton, M. (1996). Literacy and adult basic education. In R. Fieldhouse et al. (Eds.), *A history of modern British adult education* (pp. 142–165). Leicester, England: National Institute of Adult Continuing Education.

Hannon, P., Pahl, K., Bird, V., Taylor, C., & Birch, C. (2003). *Community-focused provision in adult literacy, numeracy and language: An exploratory study.* London: National Research and Development Centre for Adult Literacy and Numeracy.

Harrison, J. F. C. (1961). *Learning and living (1790–1960).* London: Routledge & Kegan Paul.

Hay, D., et al. (1988). *Albion's fatal tree.* London: Harmondsworth.

Hilliard, C. (2006). *To exercise our talents: The democratisation of writing in Britain.* Cambridge, MA: Harvard University Press.

Hobsbawm, E., & Rude, G. (1973). *Captain swing.* London: Harmondsworth.

Hoggart, R. (1957). *The uses of literacy.* London: Harmondsworth.

Horn, P. (1978). *Education in rural England 1810–1914.* Dublin, Ireland: Gille Macmillan.

Howard, U. (1991). *Self, education and writing in 19th century English communities* [In reply to: Barton, D. & Ivanic, R., (eds.), *Writing in the Community.*] Newbury Park, CA: Sage.

Howard, U. (1994). *Writing and literacy in 19th century England: Some uses and meanings.* Unpublished doctoral dissertation, University of Sussex, England.

Hoyles, M. (Ed.). (1977). *The politics of literacy.* London: Writers & Readers.

Hughes, A. (2004). TITLE OF BOOK. Oxford, England: Oxford University Press.

Hughes, R. (1987). *The fatal shore.* London: Collins Harvill.

Hull, G. (2004). *Beyond instrumental literacy: Fashioning narratives of self through multiple media and modes.* Paper presented to NRDC for Adult Literacy and Numeracy. London, 2004: Published on website at www.brde.org.uk

Hull, G., & Schulz, K, (2002). *School's out! Bridging out-of-school literacies with classroom practice.* New York: Teachers College Press.

Johnson, M. (1970). *Derbyshire village schools in the nineteenth century.* Newton Abbot, England: David & Charles.

Johnson, R. (1970). Educational policy and social control. *Past and Present, 49,* 96–119.

Kalman, J. (1999). *Writing on the plaza.* Cresskill, NJ: Hampton.

Kalman, J. (2005). *Discovering literacy: Access routes to written culture for a group of women in Mexico.* Hamburg, Germany: UNESCO Institute for Education.

Kress, G. (2002). *Literacy in the new media age.* London: Multilingual Matters.

Lacqueur, T. W. (1976). *Religion and respectability: Sunday schools and working class culture 1780–1850.* New Haven, CT: Yale University Press.

Mace, J (1979). *Working with words: Literacy beyond school.* London: Writers & Readers.

Mace, J. (1998). *Playing with time: Mothers and the meaning of literacy.* London: UCL Press.

Mace, J. (2002). *The give and take of writing: Scribes, literacy and everyday life.* Leicester, England: National Institute of Adult Continuing Education.

Mitchell, H. (1977). The Hard Way Up. The autobiography of Hannah Mitchell, Suffragette and Rebel. London: Virago.

Mitch, D. F. (1992). *The rise of popular literacy in Victorian England: The influence of private choice and public policy.* Philadelphia: University of Pennsylvania Press.

Morley, D., & Worpole, K. (Eds.). (1982). *The republic of letters: Working class writing and local publishing.* London: Comedia.

Musgrave, J. (1865). The Origin of Methodism in Bolton. Bolton.

Olsen, T. (1980). *Silences.* London: Virago.

O'Rourke, R. (2005). *Creative writing: Education, culture and community.* Leicester: National Institute of Adult Continuing Education.

Padmore, S. (1994). Guiding lights. In M. Hamilton, D. Barton, & R. Ivanic (Eds.), *Worlds of literacy* (pp. 143–156). London: Multilingual Matters.

Peck, W. C., Flower, L., and Higgins, L. (2001) Community Literacy. In Cushman, E., Kintgen, E. R., Kroll, B. M., Rose., M.: Literacy. A Critical Sourcebook. Boston: Bedford St. Martins.

Purvis, J. (1989). *Hard lessons: The lives and education of working class women in nineteenth century England.* Cambridge, England: Polity.

Rogers, R. (2003). *A critical discourse analysis of family literacy practices: Power in and out of print.* Mahwah, NJ: Lawrence Erlbaum Associates.

Rose, J. (2001). *The intellectual life of the British working classes.* New Haven, CT: Yale University Press.

Royster, J. J. (2000). *Traces of a stream: Literacy and social change among African American women.* Pittsburgh, PA: University of Pittsburgh Press.

Rowbotham, S. (1981). Travellers in a strange country: Responses of working class students to the University Extension Movement—1873–1910. *History Workshop Journal, 12(1),* 62–95.

Rowntree, J. W., & Binns, H. B. (1903). *A history of the adult school movement.* London: Headley Brothers.

Sanderson, M. (1991). *Education, economic change and society in England 1780–1870.* London: Macmillan.

Sheridan, D. (1993). Writing for ... Questions of representation, representativeners, authorship and audience. In D. Barton, D. Bloome, D. Sheridan, & B. Street (Eds.), *Ordinary people writing: The Lancaster and Sussex Writing Research Projects*. Paper 51 (pp. 17–23). Lancaster: Lancaster University.

Sheridan, D. (1996). *"Dammed anecdotes and dangerous confabulations": Mass observation as life history* (MO Occasional Paper No. 7). Brighton, England: University of Sussex Library.

Smith, G. R. (1908). *Half a century in the Dead Letter Office*. Bristol, England: Hemmonsa.

Spufford, M. (1979). First steps in literacy: The reading and writing experiences of the humblest seventeenth century spiritual autobiographers. *Social History, 4,* 407–435.

Spufford, M. (1981). *Small books and pleasant histories: Popular fiction and its readership in seventeenth century England*. Cambridge, England: Cambridge University Press.

Stephens, M. D., & Roderick, G. W. (Eds). (1983). *Samuel Smiles and nineteenth century self-help in education*. Nottingham, England: University of Nottingham.

Stephens, W. B. (1987). *Education, literacy and society, 1830–1970: The geography of diversity in provincial England*. Manchester, England: Manchester University Press.

Stock, M. (1953). *The WEA, the first 50 years*. London: Allen & Unwin.

Street, B. V. (1984). *Literacy in theory and practice*. Cambridge, England: Cambridge University Press.

Swindells, J. (1985). *Victorian writing and working women*. Cambridge, England: Polity.

Tawney, R. H. (1914). An experiment in democratic education. *The Political Quarterly, 2,* 62–84.

Thomas, W. I., & Znaniecki, F. (1984). *The Polish peasant in Europe and America*. Urbana: University of Chicago Press.

Thompson, E. P. (1968). *The making of the English working class*. London: Harmondsworth.

Thompson, E. P. (1971). The moral economy of crowd. *Past and Present, 50, 76–136.*

Thompson, F. (1939). *Larkrise to Candleford*. London: Harmondsworth.

Thompson, T. (1981). *Edwardian childhoods*. London: Routledge & Kegan Paul.

Tylecote, M. (1957). *The Mechanics Institutes of Lancashire and Workshire before 1851*. Manchester, England: Manchester University Press.

Vicinus, M. (1974). *The industrial muse*. London: Croome Helm.

Vincent, D. (1982). *Bread, knowledge and freedom: A study of nineteenth century working class autobiography*. London: Methuen.

Vincent, D. (1989). *Literacy and popular culture: England 1750–1914*. Cambridge, England: Cambridge University Press.

Vincent, D. (2000). *The rise of mass literacy: Reading and writing in modern Europe*. Cambridge, England: Polity.

Vincent, D. (2003). The progress of literacy. *Victorian Studies, 45*(3), 405–431.

Williams, R. (1981). *Culture*. Glasgow, Scotland: Fontana.

Williams, R. (1984). *Writing and society*. London: Hogarth.

Wilson Logan, S. (1999). *"We are coming": The persuasive discourse of nineteenth century Black women*. Carbondale: Southern Illinois University Press.

Woodin, T. (2001). Social class and life writing. In M. Jolly (Ed.), *Encyclopedia of life writing* (pp. 816–818). London: Fitzroy Dearborn.

Woodin, T. (2005a). Building culture from the bottom up: The educational origins of the Federation of Worker Writers and Community Publishers. *History of Education, 34*(4), 345–363.

Woodin, T. (2005b). "More writing than welding": Learning in worker writing groups. *History of Education, 34*(5), 561–578.

Wright, E. A., & Halloran, S. M. (2001). From Rhetoric to Composition: The Teaching of Writing in America to 1900. In J. J. Murphy (Ed.), *A short history of writing instruction* (pp. 213–246). Mahwah, NJ: Lawrence Erlbaum Associates.

Yeo, S. (1976). *Religion and Voluntary Organisations in Crisis*. London, Croom Helm.

Yeo, S. (1986). Whose story? An argument from within current historical practice in Britain. *Journal of Contemporary History, 21*(2), April, 1986, pp. 295–320.

CHAPTER 16

Writing, Gender, and Culture:
An Interdisciplinary Perspective

Mary P. Sheridan-Rabideau
Rutgers, The State University of New Jersey, New Brunswick

Within the long histories of feminism and composition, contemporary gender and writing research emerged from the cultural moment of the late 1960s. During that time, open admissions flooded universities with students who had not traditionally been able to attend institutions of higher learning. The subsequent informal and published research that investigated how to teach these students shaped the current instantiation of composition studies. Concurrently, the U.S. women's movement burst onto the public stage, calling for academic research on gender in many disciplines, including what would become composition studies.

Although many women who might later be read as feminists (e.g., Mina Shaughnessy, Janet Emig, Ann Berthoff, and Andrea Lunsford) were pivotal to the founding of composition work, early published gender and writing scholarship was somewhere between scant and episodic, making the term "gender and writing scholars" a retrospective term rather than one that a group of scholars would have used during the time. In fact, it was not until Elizabeth Flynn's (1988) "Composing as a Woman" that gender-focused work began to be published regularly. In this article, Flynn argued that writing scholars should systematically engage with feminist theory and research in a sustained manner, a practice long overdue given the value placed on feminist theory and research in the academy. Despite this late 1980s public engagement between feminism and writing scholarship, many academics continued to detail the difficulties of being a feminist in the classroom (Bauer, 1990; Eichhorn et al., 1992; Schmidt, 1998). These difficulties echoed the extended cultural moment of the 1990s when terms like *feminazi* were used openly and often in public discussions and when younger generations simultaneously valued feminist ideas but fled from the feminist label.

More recently, the scope of writing research focusing on gender has expanded greatly. No longer synonymous with females in the classroom, contemporary gender and writing research examines the writing of males and females in and out of the classroom. This shift expanded the typical methods and sites of research from personal reflections on the classroom to include ethnography, case study, and archival research focusing on both in- and out-of-school sites. Within these changes, what remains constant is that scholars seek to understand how/why gender remains a powerful cultural category and writing a privileged practice.

Although this history of gender and writing is often circumscribed within the disciplines of English and education—perhaps because these departments teach writing—the history of contemporary gender and writing research is highly interdisciplinary. The following sections describe these interdisciplinary contributions and in so doing sketch a broadened history of gender and writing research.

AN INTERDISCIPLINARY HISTORY OF WRITING
RESEARCH ON GENDER

This interdisciplinarity of gender and writing research is hardly surprising given the range of disciplines interested in questions about gender and about writing. For example, since at least the 1970s, the feminist movement called researchers to explore feminist tenets within their particular disciplines. These researchers shared a goal of understanding and validating how gender is a difference that makes a difference. In slow-to-change institutions such as universities, gender and writing scholars initially needed to rely as much on their interdisciplinary colleagues pursing gender-based inquiries as they did on their disciplinary colleagues pursuing more traditional writing research. In addition, as composition scholars challenged understandings of writing as discrete coding/decoding skills, these scholars needed to draw on theories of learning and writing from cognitive psychology to oral history. These interdisciplinary influences shaped the history of gender and writing research today.

Initial Steps in Literacy/Literary Study: Making
Visible the Invisible

Like other disciplines, education and English were influenced by the feminist movement in a variety of ways. First, by the early 1970s, the professional organizations devoted to studying writing overtly responded to the women's movement: The National Council for the Teachers of English (NCTE) established the Committee on the Role and Image of Women, whereas the Modern Language Association (MLA) developed a Commission on the Status of Women in the Profession. By soliciting women's experiences, these commissions sought to make visible the problems and structures that worked against women. After assessing how women fared in these fields, NCTE and MLA offered policy suggestions to redress sexism and sexist language, such as NCTE's (1976) *Position Statement: On Awareness of Racism and Sexism* and the many publishing guidelines for nonsexist language.

Second, education and English journals on writing showed feminism's influences. In 1972, the *English Journal,* a publication geared primarily toward K–12 language arts teachers, published "The Undiscovered," Robert A. Bennett's NCTE presidential address from the previous year. In his address, Bennett called on NCTE to publicly recognize the existing contributions of women and girls and other undiscovered people to nurture their potential. In a similar vein, *College English,* a publication geared predominantly toward postsecondary teachers, published two special issues (1971, 1972) addressing the dilemmas female students faced in academe. These articles focused on a lack of literary and institutional resources as well as the debilitating societal assumptions about women's inferiority—assumptions many male and female teachers and students shared. Articles from both of these special issues proved key resources for literature and writing teachers who struggled to enact feminist projects, such as modeling women's texts as exemplary or valorizing the personal in discourse (e.g., Howe, 1971; Rich, 1972).

Third, there was sporadic scholarly attention to gender-based research, examining whether men and women wrote differently (Farrell, 1979), whether writing styles were gendered (Annas, 1985; Hiatt, 1978), or whether feminist theories could transform classroom practices (Howe, 1971; Junker, 1988). In this research, teachers generally reflected on their classroom to ground their arguments about raising student consciousness and empowering (female) students (Bolker, 1979; Taylor, 1978). Teachers focused on using the personal as a site of authority in order to engage others and spark action, ideas prevalent in feminist consciousness raising and in expressivist pedagogy of the time. This focus on the personal often translated into an expressivist pedagogy that valued the personal narrative, a genre that remains important to writing researchers focusing on gender issues, as evidenced in oft-cited individual articles such as Lynn Bloom's (1992) personal narrative about the poor working conditions women face in composition or in special editions of leading journals such as the "Special Focus: Personal Writing" volume of *College English* (2001) that addressed the place of personal writing in composition.

Although few men explicitly wrote about gender differences in writing research, many male pedagogues of the time such as Peter Elbow, Ken Macrorie, and Donald Murray forwarded early articulations of expressivist pedagogy (Elbow, 1973; Macrorie, 1980; Murray, 1968). Not only would these scholars be retroactively read as protofeminist (Ritchie & Boardman, 1999), but also a range of pedagogical ideas such as nurturing students, collaboration, and decentering the classroom championed during this time would later be associated with feminist pedagogy. In these ways, the intense feminist and feminist-friendly activity of the 1970s laid the groundwork for future pedagogy and scholarship that would be read as explicitly feminist.

Despite these three important trends, there were few sustained discussions in print: Hardly any explicitly gender-focused arguments were published in the prominent academic journals, such as *English Journal, College English*, and *College Composition and Communication*, during the 1970s and 1980s. Although retrospective personal accounts of writing scholars argue that feminism dramatically influenced the teaching of writing during this time (cf. Caywood & Overing, 1987; Jarratt & Worsham, 1998; Phelps & Emig, 1995), feminism's influence was barely apparent in the public accounts of writing research of this period. Because academic journals provide an important forum to make and share knowledge, the absence of this scholarship indicates the lack of validated interaction between those publishing on writing and the rise of feminist, gender-focused scholarship. To bolster their gender-informed scholarship, writing turned to (and informed) other disciplines.

Linguistics and Communication: The Language Bind

The late 1970s and early 1980s saw several groundbreaking feminist works that shaped gender and writing research. In linguistics, Robin Lakoff's (1975) *Language and Woman's Place* and in linguistics/speech communication, Dale Spender's (1980) *Man Made Language* exposed how language systems are constructed to serve those in power, primarily men. Both texts argued that women are in a double bind, forced to communicate in language systems that serve men and work against women. At times, however, Lakoff argued that women are partially to blame for using the expected ladylike language that does them a disservice, an argument similar to that of gender and writing researcher Joan Bolker. In "Teaching Griselda to Write," Bolker (1979) reflected on the "good girls" in her classes, competent writers who receive good grades yet who have internalized traditional academic discourses to the extent that they have lost their voice. Bolker called on teachers to help these "good girls" break the stifling academic and societal conventions and find their own voice.

Unlike Lakoff, Spender directed her blame squarely on patriarchal practices and expectations. Spender pointed out that patriarchal stereotypes are given more credence than women's actual practices, leading women to distrust what they know to be occurring in order to maintain the accepted stereotypes as truth. In "The Feminine Style: Theory and Fact," Mary Hiatt's (1978) *College Composition and Communication* essay, Hiatt anticipated Spender's argument. After analyzing 400 student essays, Hiatt noted stylistic differences between men's and women's writing. However, unlike the stereotype of women as emotional or talkative, Hiatt found that women's writing style is "conservative, structurally sound, and balanced" (p. 226). Spender and Hiatt used language-based analyses of women's actual practices to expose and challenge the assumptions that do not serve women well.

A decade later, gender scholars in composition returned to the "language bind." Despite the fact that scholars had repeatedly detailed how women are disadvantaged by academe's agonistic tenor, women in the academy were judged by their competence in adopting this assumed-to-be-masculinist communication style of academic writing (Frey, 1990). The question for gender-focused research became what should teachers do about this: Is it more effective/better to prepare women to engage these agonistic academic structures as they are, or is it possible/better to create alternatives that might be more suited to women's language practices? In "Feminism and Composition: The Case for Conflict," Susan C. Jarratt (1991) took the former position. Challenging the expressivist pedagogies that reigned in the late 1980s, Jarratt argued that writing teachers need to spend less time having students focus on personal reflection and developing/discovering an authentic voice and to spend more time preparing women to engage in conflict-based argumentation. Not to do so, according to Jarratt, is a disservice to female students, who are often less prepared for this public discourse. Contrasting this argument, Catherine E. Lamb (1991) in "Beyond Argument in Feminist Composition" claimed that writing teachers need to help students find alternative ways to engage audiences beside conflict. Echoing a critique similar to what Sally Miller Gearhart (1979) had earlier, and more stridently, called the conquest/conversion mentality of rhetorical argumentation, Lamb sought to develop "the beginning of a feminist pedagogy" (p. 11) of argumentation by teaching students how to collaborate, cooperate, and negotiate with their readers. This, Lamb hoped, would provide an alternative to the one-sided communication that Lamb finds all too common in typical notions of argumentation. Although Lamb (1996) later revised this position to recognize how conflict is a part of argumentation, these early articles represent the difficulties of negotiating female students' needs within institutional and societal contexts that do not validate their strengths.

Writing scholars' concern about the language bind extended beyond females to include those whose language socialization did not match the valued language of school, whether due to vernacular, class, religious, gender, and/or other reasons. In this way, gender and writing scholars' engagement with the language bind indexes their connection to a range of interdisciplinary research on access and equity, power and representation, in schooling and beyond.

Psychology: Finding and/or Constructing New Voices

Throughout the 1980s, gender and writing researchers drew heavily on work out of psychology, such as Nancy Chodorow's (1979) *The Reproduction of Mothering: Psychoanalysis and the Sociology of Gender* and Mary Belenky, Nancy Goldberger Clinchy, Blythe Field, and Jill Tarule's (1986) *Women's Ways of Knowing: The Development of Self, Voice, and Mind.* Perhaps the most notable among these many works is Carol Gilligan's (1982) *In a Different Voice: Psychological Theory and Women's Development.* In this work, Gilligan challenges Lawrence Kohlberg's theory for the stages of moral development. Claiming that research on a sample of only Harvard male students does not reflect a universal stage of moral development, Gilligan focuses on how women's voices have been excluded. Women reason "in a different voice" and this difference should not be translated as a deficiency, as was the prevailing assessment. Gilligan's use of voice resonated with conversations within feminism and within writing research. This research was often associated with essentialist perspectives that held that there was something essential to being a woman (the usual term under discussion) and, at least initially, often anchored this ahistorical, acultural fixed position in biology. Whether linking to essentialist or expressivist pedagogies about finding one's voice or linking to dialogic or constructivist pedagogies about mediating multiple voices (Bridwell-Bowles, 1992; Zawacki, 1992), the voice metaphor became and continues to be central in feminist and writing research.

In addition to an American focus on voice that would later be read as pragmatic, essentialist, or focused on personal experience (cf. Phelps & Emig, 1995), French feminists such as Julia Kristeva, Helene Cixous, and Luce Irigaray provided a theoretically dense attention to voice. Despite their many theoretical differences, these French feminists are associated with *ecriture feminine* or a feminine writing that ruptures the masculinist language systems readily available today. Drawing heavily on Lacan's idea of phallocentricism (the privileging of the masculine—the phallus—when learning to use language and to enter into social relations) and Derrida's idea of logocentricism (the idea that speech is prior to and more important than writing), French feminists argue that when people learn to use language they enter a language-made-world that privileges masculinist ways, or what they call the phallogocentric order of the West. French feminists share the pragmatic American idea that women must tell their own stories, but French feminists have a denser theoretical project of shifting how the feminine relates to the possibilities of personhood available through language and therefore through the Symbolic social order.

Some composition scholars applied *ecriture feminine* to the classroom with the goal of opening new ways of writing, of relating to language, and of shaping existing social relations (Junker, 1988). Others, such as Lynn Worsham (1991), argue that compositions' attempts to harness *ecriture feminine* have been misguided: Either *ecriture feminine*'s call for dismantling phallocentrism will dismantle the university; or, more likely, composition goals of teaching academic discourse—a profoundly phallocentric practice—will domesticate and therefore dramatically alter *ecriture feminine*. The powerful influence of *ecriture feminine* was short lived largely due to the trouble writing scholars had in finding ways to make this language-based rupture useful in the writing classroom (cf. De Beaugrande, 1988). Nonetheless, these dense theoretical French feminist ideas for imagining new ways of approaching language anticipated other posttheories that were taken up in the 1990s (see later discussion).

The conversations about a feminine voice indexed what would become a central tension in writing research on gender during the early 1990s: essentialism versus social constructionism. Countering essentialist positions, social constructionists believed that women thought and acted the way they did based on how society treated them: People were constructed by the ways they were socialized. Researchers from psychology and beyond examined the linguistic, social, and political gendering that shaped these constructions. As essentialism became a denigrated term, many scholars moderated their strong positions taken in these early works. For example, Elizabeth Flynn (1990, 2003) later modified her earlier, allegedly essentialist position in her foundational *College Composition and Communication* article "Composing as a Woman," even as she continued to argue that she needed this strong stance simultaneously to interrupt the erasure of women and to facilitate what Flynn calls a Kuhnian-like paradigm shift that would incorporate women's perspectives as valid (2003).

Too often these essentialist–social constructionist debates lost sight of how much these positions could inform each other. To move beyond this seeming dichotomy, Joy Ritchie (1990) and others called for pragmatic attention to how writing research on gender should be based in theory and practice. Gender and writing scholars responded to this call in part by examining alternative ways to write, hoping these alternatives could challenge or circumvent sexist practices associated with the traditional, agonistic academic style. For example, in "Rhetoric in a New Key: Women and Collaboration," Andrea Lunsford and Lisa Ede (1990) advocated for dialogic, collaborative forms of writing to be valued in addition to the hierarchical single-authored works. In "Discourse and Diversity: Experimental Writing Within the Academy" Lillian Bridwell-Bowles (1992) similarly advocated a dialogic relationship, this time between students' academic knowledge and the extensive knowledge students bring to the academic setting. For Bridwell-Bowles, experimenting with seemingly surface-level language conventions provides a way to get at deeper-level issues where language, knowledge, and culture interact. Grounding her argument in the need to bring the personal into the academic setting—a long-standing feminist belief and writing pedagogy—Bridwell-Bowles encouraged alternative styles of writing to help students develop this dialogic relationship.

Questions about how new forms of writing relate to the gendered expectations and the gendered style of academic writing resurfaced forcefully when computer-mediated communication (CMC) became increasingly common in writing classrooms during the 1990s. Early CMC research investigated whether anonymous postings, an altered classroom interaction structure, or other CMC practices could level gendered power differentials. These hopes quickly proved illusory (Selfe & Hawisher, 1991; Takayoshi, 1994) as CMC generally reproduced the power differentials in the world outside of CMC where deference and attention are given to those with higher status based on factors such as professional rank, gender, race, and sexuality (Addison & Hilligoss, 1999; Kramarae, 1993; Selfe & Meyers, 1991). More recent research notes how hypertexts may encourage a writer's many voices, may help individuals explore their relationship with their community, and may even be a forum for personal empowerment (LeCourt & Barnes, 1999; Sullivan, 1999), arguments that echo earlier feminist goals evident in a variety of fields.

Challenging "Objectivity" in the Sciences: Creating Feminist Methods

Also during the 1980s, scientific frameworks, such as those coming out of the cognitive sciences, were academically powerful and scholars outside of the sciences, such as writing scholars, drew on these frameworks (cf. Flower & Hayes, 1980, 1981). Feminists, however, challenged the calls for objectivity that often accompanied this scientifically informed research. For example, philosopher Sandra Harding's *Whose Science, Whose Knowledge?: Thinking From Women's Lives* (1991) and her edited collection *Feminism and Methodology* (1987) contested the claim that a researcher could be a detached observer, an idea central to science's claims of objectivity. Rather, Harding argues, researchers must admit their investments in the research and in the research design, investments that have historically privileged men's (White, moneyed men) ways of knowing in seemingly invisible ways. Responding to this critique, feminists developed research methodologies, such as feminist ethnography (Oakley, 1981) and feminist oral history (Gluck & Patai, 1991), that sought to have women heard more in their own voices.

Scholars studying gender and writing employed similar theories and methods. For example, Patricia A. Sullivan's (1992) "Feminism and Methodology in Composition Studies" challenged the fairness of supposedly androcentric standards prevalent in composition. Sullivan called on researchers "to understand issues of gender difference and sexual politics" (p. 58) that infuse composition research, a move that Sullivan, like Flynn before her, believed composition had yet to do. Pursuing alternative methods that foregrounded participants' voices, gender and writing scholars increasingly used ethnography, case studies, and oral histories. Certainly these methods were not entirely new. Janet Emig's (1971) foundational text *The Composing Processes of Twelfth Graders* is based on several case studies with the central case study focusing on a girl. Yet Emig's work does not privilege gender as a central factor. Generally in writing research, it wasn't until the 1980s and beyond that researchers used ethnographies, case studies, and oral histories to foreground how and if gender plays a role in the composing processes and literate practices of a range of readers and writers. These methodologies encouraged researchers to explore their invested relationships with their research participants (Kirsch & Ritchie, 1995) and to acknowledge the dilemmas and difficulties of the research process, a process more complicated than the smoothly written reports that generally make it to publication (Kirsch 1999; Mortensen & Kirsch, 1996).

In the last decade, rhetorical and archival research with a gender focus has seen a surge in scholarly publication. Scholars revised rhetorical traditions to include and value women's politically and socially efficacious writing (Bizzell & Herzberg, 2000; Gere, 1998; Glenn, 1997; Logan, 1999; Lunsford, 1995; Ritchie & Ronald, 2001; Royster, 2000). Taking up earlier feminist work that challenged the detached knower–known relationship between researchers and those researched, these scholars articulated what Patricia Bizzell (2000) sees as feminist archival methods that called researchers to acknowledge their invested relationship with their material and with those who benefit from it today (cf. Royster, 2000). In all of these methods, researchers explicitly looked at and not through the seemingly invisible structures that shape what counts as knowledge and who counts as knowledgeable.

Post Theories: Breaking In and Breaking Up

In the 1990s, writing scholars became highly invested in posttheories, from postmodernism to postcolonialism. This was particularly the case in English departments where high theory became the coin of the realm. Postmodern feminist theorists, among others, argued against a coherent woman identity and for hybrid, multiple identities. These works unhinged stable categories in order to examine the complexities and diverse investments various stakeholders had in maintaining or undermining gender norms.

Writing researchers used postmodern theories to investigate how gender, identity, and writing are constructed and constructing, key concerns within and outside of the classroom (cf. Jarratt & Worsham, 1998). For example, during and after the identity politics of the late 1980s and early 1990s, many scholars examined how gender, race, and other identity categories intersected in complicated ways (Lunsford, 1998), pursuing paths forged by postmodern theorists such as Gloria Anzaldua's (1990) work on the multiple intersections of identity in her concept of the *mestiza*. Similarly, gender and writing scholars constantly cited Judith Butler's work—especially her work in *Gender Trouble* (1990) where she compared gender to an intricate, ritualized drag performance—as a way to challenge how gender and sexuality are performed in the academy and in writing contexts more particularly (Kopelson, 2002). Computer and composition scholars took up Donna Haraway's "Cyborg Manifesto" (1991) to examine how technology naturalizes gendered identity options (Hawisher & Sullivan, 1999; see also Balsamo, 1996). By decade's end, writing scholars were citing postcolonial theorists like Trinh Minh-ha as they addressed the complexities of writing about and representing others (Jarratt, 1998).

Despite this work to deconstruct stable identity and gender categories, many teachers found these identity/gender categories helpful in understanding their classrooms and the everyday patterns they faced. These teachers feared that deconstructing these categories would obfuscate the very real biases that women in the academy still face. Many teachers felt theorists remained in obtuse abstraction, citing how dense postmodern writings were difficult for nonspecialists to read let alone apply. On the other hand, theorists felt practitioners relied on folk understandings of classroom practice that missed the complexity of the way both gender and writing function in the world.

Although not as dichotomous as perhaps just represented, this teacher–theorist split is salient enough to contribute to what is widely considered composition's feminized status. This status reflects composition as less powerful than other fields; it is on the subjugated female side of the male–female binary. Certainly composition's feminized status is partially due to the high percentage of women who teach in the language arts and composition classrooms from kindergarten through college (Lauer, 1995). In addition, *within* these fields there is a feminization associated with those who teach as opposed to those who publish in the leading journals (Enos, 1997; Lauer, 1995). Theorizing and publishing earn their authors scholarly status; teaching writing is viewed as service work where teachers are metaphorically constructed in the gendered roles of nurses or midwives who do the grunt work of caring for others (Schell, 1992; Schell & Stock, 2000). Postmodern theories provided a touchstone that highlighted this teacher–theorist tension, an important tension in how writing research is generally read.

Beyond Women in the Classroom: Girls and Boy Studies, the Men's Movement, and the Extracurriculum

Since the 1990s, there has been a steady expansion in the sites that writing researchers explore and the people they study. Although the classroom is still privileged and the term *gender* still triggers associations with females, these trends are changing. Research on gender more explicitly attends to powerful social forces that impact both males and females. In addition, researchers more regularly attend to how writing functions outside the classroom. Anne

Ruggles Gere (1994) calls this the *extracurriculum* or the everyday self-sponsored writing motivated by economic or social consequences and not by academic assignments. Writing scholars are increasingly recognizing the importance of examining extracurricular writing both for how it impacts the classroom and for its own sake.

In education, these moves were evident in the rise of girls' and boys' studies. Girls' studies comprised two main groups of interdisciplinary scholars already attending to girls. One group of scholars largely from psychology and education focused on girls' development, generally chronicling how girls were victims of a "girl poisoning culture" (Pipher, 1994), "hostile [school] hallways" (American Association of University Women [AAUW], 1993), and "schools that shortchanged them" (AAUW, 1992; Sadker & Sadker, 1994), especially in the fields of math, science, and technology (AAUW, 2000). A second strand of girls' studies largely comprised cultural studies' scholars redressing this field's historical omission of girls. This strand centered on girls' assertion of agency, often linking this agency to girls' complicated relationships with representation and consumer culture (McRobbie, 1991). Outside the academy, girls published about these issues in unprecedented ways, from writing and editing entire collections (Shandler, 1999) to contributing to foundational third-wave texts (Gilbert-Levin, 2002; McCarry, 2002).

Writing scholars picked up both strands of girls studies. This spike in research on girls' literate practices primarily focused on girls' engagement with magazines, the revitalized zines movement, and Web-based communications such as chat rooms, Web sites, and blogs. As scholars examined the writing and reading practices girls pursued, it became clear that girls used texts and text-centered activities to help them negotiate their uptake of culturally defined gender roles (Sheridan-Rabideau, 2001). Like others, girls read and write in certain ways in order to represent themselves and construct their identities, identities shaped by (and shaping) their understandings of race, class, and most certainly gender (Finders, 1997).

All this attention to girls encouraged and grew alongside a call for increased attention to boys. The writing research on boys and young men's literacy practices (e.g., Newkirk, 2002) often exposed the complex ways literacy practices intersect with factors that are valued in out-of-school contexts but not in school (Mahiri, 1998). For example, in *Reading Don't Fix No Chevy's: Literacy in the Lives of Young Men*, Michael Smith and Jeffrey D. Wilhelm (2002) argue that boys often find school-based reading and writing to be feminizing. Not surprisingly, boys opt out of school-based literacy practices, preferring literacy practices such as reading sports or mechanics texts that reaffirm their gendered identity. Complicating and at times complementing the conversations that pitted males versus females—a particularly common trope in cross-over academic-popular books like linguist Deborah Tannen's *You Just Don't Understand: Men and Women in Conversation* (1990) or popular-press books about men's and women's inability to communicate as illustrated in titles such as *Men Are From Mars and Women Are From Venus* (Gray, 1992)— this academic work detailed how youth use reading and writing as important cultural practices to negotiate their gendered identities. Through ethnographies and case studies of both the classroom and the extracurriculum, girls and boys studies scholars were finding a far more rich and complex range of literacy practices than traditional studies had illustrated.

Just as writing researchers were drawing on girls and boys studies, they were also drawing on the men's movement. Like the prominent discussions of masculinity that activist feminists were having (e.g., Faludi, 1999), academics explored the impact of gendered expectations on male teachers and students. These expectations had typically been privileged and normed, and therefore not investigated. Two oft-cited articles that draw on the men's movement were published in the same 1996 *College English* journal: Bob Connors's "Teaching and Learning as a Man" and Lad Tobin's "Car Wrecks, Baseball Caps, and the Man-to-Man Defense: The Personal Narratives of Adolescent Males." Notably, both Connors and Tobin partially ground their arguments through personal narratives that reflect on their classroom, a move prominent in the early gender and writing research from the 1970s. In these articles, both Connors and Tobin methodologically and theoretically acknowledge their indebtedness to feminist theorizing of gender as constructed by societal forces, a fact equally true for boys and men as it is for girls and women.

Global Concerns: Writing as Advocacy, Public Policy, and Business Practice

Today, as the sites of gender and writing research continue to expand, writing scholars increasingly engage with fields addressing issues associated with globalization. For example, in their edited collection, *Just Advocacy? Women's Human Rights, Transnational Feminisms, and the Politics of Representation,* Wendy Kozol and Wendy Hesford (2005) draw on visual rhetoric, transnational feminism, and human rights discourses to examine the implications of textual and visual representations of women in global contexts. Other writing scholars examine how changing information and communication technologies alter present and future writing needs of students, often with gendered effects. For example, in *Persuasion and Privacy in Cyberspace: The Online Protests Over Lotus Marketplace and the Clipper Chip,* Laura Gurak (1997) draws on the fields of law and business to investigate both privacy rights on the Internet and what gender and other identity features might mean when writing in cyberspace. Similarly, in "Rhetoric, Feminism and the Politics of Textual Ownership," Andrea Lunsford (1999) draws on business and law, as well as feminist theory and personal reflection on her earlier gender and writing scholarship to argue against the recent trend that defines knowledge as intellectual property. As varied as this research is, these gender and writing scholars all examine the ways knowledge, gender, and writing in the information age are being reshaped in ways that are both unique to the current conditions and troublingly reminiscent of gendered exclusions of the past. By drawing on research that addresses human rights, information technology, law, business, and a host of other interdisciplinary foci, these scholars highlight the continuing interdisciplinarity of writing research that addresses gender issues.

AN INTERDISCIPLINARY PRESENT AND FUTURE IN THE NEW MEDIA AGE

It now seems as if writing research that focuses on gender has made it: Gender research is represented in national journals, collected in anthologies (Addison & McGee, 1999; Kirsch, Maor, Massey, Nickoson-Massey, & Sheridan-Rabideau, 2003), presented at the biannual Feminism(s) and Rhetoric(s) Conference, and published in academic presses that specifically focus on gender research. Despite these important accomplishments, research on new media both points out the continuation of disturbing trends (e.g., a loss of feminists' works) and reinflects ongoing questions (e.g., what do *gender* and *writing* mean in virtual environments?). An analysis of new media, then, provides a useful opportunity for assessing the present and imagining the future of gender and writing research.

Publishing's Material Conditions

Historically, community and academic feminists have been denied access to publication. To circumvent sexist publishing practices, feminists from Emma Goldman and Margaret Sanger (Reed, 1984)[1] to Shulamith Firestone (1968) and the Boston Women's Health Collective (1973) turned to do-it-yourself (DIY) methods to self-publish. This, however, was not enough. Feminists also had to start presses and open bookstores to distribute their work. Contemporary gender and writing researchers have benefited from these practices in concrete and material ways. The tremendous research on gender that is available at bookstores and online is a testament to that earlier work. Even so, the late date of Flynn's

---

[1] Thanks go to Laura Anatale and her honors research on DIY ethics in women's health movement.

(1988) foundational composition article attests to the recent difficulty writing scholars focusing on gender have felt in finding a publisher for their work. Similarly, the closing of the *Feminist Review of Books* in 2004, after 22 years of publishing, exposes how market pressures continue to make the viability of feminist and gender work a challenge. These internal biases within writing scholarship and external market forces highlight the enduring obstacles gender and writing researchers face when publishing their work.

A related concern in contemporary publishing practices is the push to digitize previously published work. In "Oxidation Is a Feminist Issue," Carol Poster (1996) argues that as libraries digitize their collections, and as our students come to read and research primarily what is easily digitized, the fact that gender research (among others) is not being digitized at nearly the rate of other materials means that to our students this material seems not to exist. Digitization of early feminist writing is particularly pressing because the process of oxidation is destroying the cheap paper on which women's and feminist works of the previous century were written. In a literal and material sense, digitization is central to ensuring that another generation of feminist work will not be lost. Google's recent decision to digitize entire academic holdings only heightens the importance of attending to this issue. For gender scholars, the new media age may mean addressing old obstacles in a new form.

Gender and Writing in a Technological Environment: Categories Up for Grabs

Technological changes are altering the ways people read and write, often in gendered ways. These changes demand gender and writing scholars rethink contemporary understandings of writing and of gender. For example, as globalized workplaces require reading and writing online documents, *writing* means not only composing text, but also creating images and designing page layout. Within this changing understanding, writing scholars are investigating why certain writing practices are gendered. For example, paralleling speech communication theorist Cheris Kramarae's (1988) exploration of the gendering of everyday technologies almost two decades ago, Pam Takayoshi (2004) examines the gendering of everyday technologies today. In particular, Takayoshi examines how *tween* girls spend untold hours every day writing to each other on instant messenger (IM). Although this *texting* consumes far more time than what girls spend on writing in any other context, neither the girls nor many academics consider this writing. What, then, is this practice and its relation to what these participants see as writing? Why is this practice so gendered? What does this indicate about how writing constructs and maintains gendered identities in the increasingly technologically driven world?

Unlike most research from two decades ago, contemporary writing and gender research, particularly in new media, addresses these questions within international frameworks. For many youth, international exchange is a common practice, as evidenced in online fan sites that cross national boundaries. For example, the increasingly popular fan sites for shojo—girl-centered Japanese comics, movies, and television programs like *Sailor Moon* or *The Revolutionary Girl Utena*—expose how youth from around the world negotiate what it means to be a girl or what it means to write in certain ways that reflect this gendering. In a text-based world where girls shun adult male intrusion for a variety of material and discursive reasons, how do fans textually perform their girly-ness in order to be viewed as viable on these often girl-centric sites? What is essential about these textual representations? What is gendered and what is culturally authentic? How do participants use writing in these contexts to accept and rebuke assumptions about race, class, and sexuality within the cross-cultural contexts that shape so much of today's consumer-driven new media?

For gender and writing scholars, these questions about gender and writing are both new and quite familiar. To address them, gender and writing researchers need to better understand how writing in electronic environments both reflects and participates in the shaping of cultural norms such as gendered identities in electronic environments. As with previous gender and writing research, in this project of understanding, writing in the new media age challenges researchers to rethink why gender remains a powerful cultural category and writing a privileged cultural practice.

REFERENCES

Addison, J., & Hilligoss. S. (1999). Technological fronts: Lesbian lives "on-the-line." In K. Blair & P. Takayoshi (Eds.), *Feminist cyberscapes: Mapping gendered academic spaces* (pp. 21–40). Stamford, CT: Ablex.

Addison, J., & McGee, S.J. (1999). *Feminist empirical research: Emerging perspectives on qualitative and teacher research*. Portsmouth, NH: Heinemann.

American Association of University Women. (1992). *How schools shortchange girls: The AAUW report*. Washington, DC: AAUW Educational Foundation Research.

American Association of University Women. (1993). *Hostile hallways: The AAUW survey on sexual harassment in American schools*. Washington, DC: AAUW Educational Foundation Research.

American Association of University Women. (2000). *Tech savvy: Educating girls in the new computer age*. Washington, DC: AAUW Educational Foundation Research.

Annas, P. J. (1985). Silences: Feminist language research and the teaching of writing. *College English, 47*, 360–371.

Anzaldua, G. (1990). *Making face, making soul: Haciendo caras*. San Francisco: Aunt Lute Foundation.

Balsamo, A. (1996). *Technologies of the gendered body: Reading cyborg women*. Durham, NC: Duke University Press.

Bauer, D. (1990). The other "f" word: The feminist in the classroom. *College English, 52*, 385–396.

Belenky, M. F., Clinchy, B. M., Goldberger, N. R., & Tarule, J. M. (1986). *Women's ways of knowing: The development of self, voice, and mind*. New York: Basic Books.

Bennett, R. A. (1972). NCTE presidential address: The undiscovered. *English Journal, 61*, 351–357.

Bizzell, P. (2000). Feminist methods of research in the history of rhetoric: What difference do they make? *Rhetoric Society Quarterly, 30*, 5–17.

Bizzell, P., & Herzberg, B. (2001). *The rhetorical tradition: Readings from classical times to the present*. Boston: Bedford/St. Martin's.

Bloom, L. Z. (1992). Teaching college English as a woman. *College English, 54*, 818–825.

Bolker, J. (1979). Teaching Griselda to write. *College English, 40*(8), 906–908.

Boston Women's Health Collective. (1973). *Our bodies, ourselves* (2nd ed.). New York: Simon & Schuster.

Bridwell-Bowles, L. (1992). Discourse and diversity: Experimental writing within the academy. *College Communication and Composition, 43*(3), 349–368.

Butler, J. (1990). *Gender trouble: Feminism and the subversion of identity*. New York: Routledge.

Caywood, C., & Overing, G. (Eds.). (1987). *Teaching writing: Pedagogy, gender, and equity*. Albany: State University of New York Press.

Chodorow, N. (1979). *The reproduction of mothering: Psychoanalysis and the sociology of gender*. Berkeley: University of California Press.

College English. (1971). Volume 32.

College English. (1972). Volume 34.

College English. (2001). Special Focus: Personal Writing. Volume 64(1).

Connors, R. (1996). Teaching and learning as a man. *College English, 58*, 2: 137–157.

De Beaugrande, R. (1988). In search of feminist discourse: The "difficult" case of Luce Irigaray. *College English, 50*, 253–272.

Eichorn, J., Farris, S., Hayes, K., Hernandez, A., Jarratt, S. C., Powers-Stubbs, K., et al. (1992). A symposium on feminist experiences in the composition classroom. *College Communication and Composition, 43*, 297–322.

Elbow, P. (1973). *Writing without teachers*. New York: Oxford University Press.

Emig, J. (1971). *The composing processes of twelfth graders*. Urbana, IL: National Council of Teachers of English.

Enos, T. (1997). Gender and publishing scholarship in rhetoric and composition. In G. A. Olson & T. W. Taylor (Eds.), *Publishing in rhetoric and composition* (pp. 57–74). Albany: State University of New York Press.

Faludi, S. (1999). *Stiffed: The betrayal of the American man*. New York: Morrow.

Farrell, T. (1979). The female and male modes of rhetoric. *College English, 40*, 909–921.

Finders, M. (1997). *Just girls: Hidden literacies and life in junior high*. New York: Teachers College Press.

Firestone, S. (1968). *Notes from the first year*. New York: New York Radical Women.

Flower, L. S., &. Hayes, J. R. (1980). The cognition of discovery: Defining a rhetorical problem. *College Composition and Communication, 31*, 21–32.

Flower, L. S., &. Hayes, J. R. (1981). A cognitive process theory of writing. *College Communication and Composition, 32,* 365–387.

Flynn, E. (1988). Composing as a woman. *College Composition and Communication, 39,* 423–435.

Flynn, E. (1990). Composing "composing as a woman": A perspective on research. *College Composition and Communication, 41,* 83–89.

Flynn, E. (2003). Contextualizing "composing as a woman." In G. Kirsch, F. S. Maor, L. Massey, L. Nickoson-Massey, & M. P. Sheridan-Rabideau (Eds.), *Feminism and composition: A critical sourcebook* (pp. 339–341). Boston: Bedford/St. Martin's.

Frey, O. (1990). Beyond literary Darwinism: Women's voices and critical discourse. *College English, 52,* 507–526.

Gearhart, S. M. (1979). The womanization of rhetoric. *Women's Studies International Quarterly, 2,* 195–201.

Gere, A. R. (1994). Kitchen tables and rented rooms: The extracurriculum of composition. *College Composition and Communication, 45,* 75–92.

Gere, A. R. (1997). *Intimate practices: Literacy and cultural work in U.S. women's clubs, 1880–1920.* Urbana: University of Illinois University Press.

Gilbert-Levin, E. (2002). Class feminist. In B. Findlen (Ed.), *Listen up: Voices from the next feminist generation* (2nd ed., pp. 165–172). Seattle, WA: Seal.

Gilligan, C. (1982). *In a different voice: Psychological theory and women's development.* Cambridge, MA: Harvard University Press.

Glenn, C. (1997). *Rhetoric retold: Regendering the tradition from antiquity through the Renaissance.* Carbondale: Southern Illinois University Press.

Gluck, S. B., & Patai, D. (1991). *Women's words: The feminist practice of oral history.* New York: Routledge.

Gray, J. (1992). *Men are from Mars, women are from Venus: A practical guide for improving communication and getting what you want in your relationships.* New York: HarperCollins.

Gurak, L. J. (1997). *Persuasion and privacy in cyberspace: The online protests over Lotus MarketPlace and the Clipper chip.* New Haven, CT: Yale University Press.

Haraway, D. (1991). Cyborg manifesto: Science, technology, and socialist-feminism in the late twentieth century. In D. Haraway (Eds.), *Simians, cyborgs and women: The reinvention of nature* (pp. 149–181). New York: Routledge

Harding, S. (1987). *Feminism and methodology: Social science issues.* Bloomington: Indiana University Press.

Harding, S. (1991). *Whose science, shoes knowledge? Thinking from women's lives.* Ithaca, NY: Cornell University Press.

Hawisher, G. E., & Sullivan, P. A. (1999). Fleeting images: Women visually writing the web. In G. E. Hawisher & C. L. Selfe (Eds.), Passions pedagogies and 21st century technologies (pp. 268–291). Logan, VT. Utah State Press and NCTE.

Hiatt, M. P. (1978). The feminine style: Theory and fact. *College Composition and Communication, 27,* 222–226.

Howe, F. (1971). Identity and expression: A writing course for women. *College English, 32,* 863–871.

Jarratt, S. C. (1991). Feminism and composition: The case for conflict. In P. Harkin & J. Schilb (Eds.), *Contending with words: Composition and rhetoric in a postmodern age* (pp. 105–123). New York: Modern Language Association.

Jarratt, S. C. (1998). Beside ourselves: Rhetoric and representation in postcolonial feminist writing. *JAC: A Journal of Advanced Composition, 18,* 57–75.

Jarratt, S. C., & Worsham, L. (Eds.). (1998). *Feminism and composition studies: In other words.* New York: Modern Language Association.

Junker, C. (1988). Writing (with) Cixous. *College English, 50,* 424–436.

Kirsch, G. E. (1999). *Ethical dilemmas in feminist research: The politics of location, interpretation, and publication.* Albany: State University of New York Press.

Kirsch, G. E., Maor, F. S., Massey, L., Nickoson-Massey, L., &. Sheridan-Rabideau, M. P. (2003). *Feminism and composition: A critical sourcebook.* Boston: Bedford/St. Martin's.

Kirsch, G. E., & Ritchie, J. (1995). Beyond the personal: Theorizing a politics of location in composition research. *College Communication and Composition, 46,* 7–29.

Kopelson, K. (2002). Dis/integrating the gay/queer binary: "Reconstructed identity politics." *College English, 65,* 17–35.

Kozol, W., & Hesford, W. (2005). *Just advocacy? Women's human rights, transnational feminism, and the politics of representation.* New Brunswick, NJ: Rutgers University Press.

Kramarae, C. (1988). Gotta go Myrtle, technology's at the door. In C. Kramarae (Ed.), *Technology and women's voices* (pp. 1–14).London: Routledge.

Kramarae, C. (1993). Women and information technologies: Creating a cyberspace of our own. In H. J. Taylor, C. Kramarae, & M. Ebben (Eds.), *Women, information technology, and scholarship.* Urbana: University of Illinois, Center for Advanced Study.

Lakoff, R. (1975). *Language and woman's place*. New York: Harper.

Lamb, C. (1991). Beyond argument in feminist composition. *College Communication and Composition, 42*, 11–24.

Lamb, C. (1996). Other voices, different parties: Feminist responses to argument. In D. Berrill (Ed.), *Perspectives on written argument* (pp. 257–269). Cresskill, NJ: Hampton.

Lauer, J. (1995). The feminization of rhetoric and composition studies? *Rhetoric Review, 13*, 276–286.

LeCourt, D., & Barnes, L. (1999). Writing multiplicity: Hypertext and feminist textual practices. *Computers and Composition, 16*, 55–71.

Logan, S. (1999). *"We are coming": The persuasive discourse of nineteenth-century Black women*. Carbondale: Southern Illinois University Press.

Lunsford, A. (1995). *Reclaiming rhetorica: Women in the rhetorical tradition*. Pittsburgh, PA: University of Pittsburgh Press.

Lunsford, A. (1998). Toward a mestiza rhetoric: Gloria Anzaldúa on composition and postcoloniality. *JAC: A Journal of Composition Theory, 18*(1), 1–29.

Lunsford, A. (1999). Rhetoric, feminism, and the politics of textual ownership. *College English, 61*, 529–544.

Lunsford, A., & Ede, L. (1990). Rhetoric in a new key: Women and collaboration. *Rhetoric Review, 8*, 234–241.

Macrorie, K. (1980). *Telling writing*. Rochelle Park, NJ: Hayden.

Mahiri, J. (1998). *Shooting for excellence: African American and youth culture in new century schools*. Urbana: National Council of Teachers of English.

McCarry, S. (2002). Selling out. In B. Findlen (Ed.), *Listen up: Voices from the next feminist generation* (2nd ed., pp. 247–250). Seattle, WA: Seal.

McRobbie, A. (1991). *Feminism and youth culture*. New York: Routledge.

Moffett, J. (1992). *Active voice: A writing program across the curriculum* (2nd ed.). Portsmouth, NH: Boynton/Cook.

Mortensen, P., & Kirsch, G. (1996). *Ethics and representation in qualitative studies of literacy*. Urbana, IL: National Council of Teachers of English.

Murray, D. (1968). *A writer teaches writing: A practical method of teaching composition*. Boston: Houghton Mifflin.

National Council of Teachers of English. (1976). *Position statement: On awareness of racism and sexism*. Urbana, IL: Author.

Newkirk, T. (2002). *Misreading masculinity: Boys, literacy, and popular culture*. Portsmouth, NH: Heinemann.

Oakley, A. (1981). Interviewing women: A contradiction in terms? In H. Roberts (Ed.), *Doing feminist research* (pp. 30–61). New York: Routledge.

Phelps, L. W., & Emig, J. (Eds.). (1995). *Feminine principles and women's experience in American composition and rhetoric* (Pittsburgh series in composition, literacy, and culture). Pittsburgh, PA: University of Pittsburgh Press.

Pipher, M. (1994). *Reviving Ophelia: Saving the lives of adolescent girls*. New York: Putnam.

Poster, C. (1996) Oxidation is a feminist issue: Acidity, canonicity, and popular Victorian female authors. *College English, 58*, 287–306.

Reed, J. (1984). *The birth control movement and American society: From private vice to public virtue* (2nd ed.). Princeton, NJ: Princeton University Press.

Rich, A. (1972). When we dead awaken: Writing as re-vision. *College English, 34*, 18–25.

Ritchie, J. (1990). Confronting the "essential" problem: Reconnecting feminist theory and pedagogy. *JAC: A Journal of Advanced Composition, 10*, 249–273.

Ritchie, J., & Boardman, K. (1999). Feminism in composition: Inclusion, metonymy, and Disruption. *College Communication and Composition, 50*(4), 585–606.

Ritchie, J., & Ronald, K. (2001). *Available means: An anthology of women's rhetoric*. Pittsburgh, PA: University of Pittsburgh Press.

Royster, J. J. (2000). *Traces of a stream: Literacy and social change among African American women*. Pittsburgh, PA: University of Pittsburgh Press.

Sadker, D., & Sadker, M. (1994). *Failing at fairness: How America's schools cheat girls*. New York: Scribner.

Schell, E. E. (1992). The feminization of composition: Questioning the metaphors that bind women teachers. *Composition Studies/Freshman English News, 20*, 55–61.

Schell, E. E., & Stock, P. (2000). *Moving a mountain: Transforming the role of contingent faculty in composition studies and higher education*. Urbana, IL: National Council of Teachers of English.

Schmidt, L. Z. (1998). *Women-writing-teacher*. Albany: State University of New York Press.

Selfe, C., & Hawisher, G. (1991). The rhetoric of technology and the electronic writing class. *College Composition and Communicatio, 42*(1), 55–65.

Selfe, C., & Meyers, P. (1991). Computer-based forums for academic discourse: Testing the claims for on-line conferences. *Written Communication, 8*(2), 163–192.

Shandler, S. (1999). *Ophelia speaks: Adolescent girls write about their search for self*. New York: HarperCollins.

Sheridan-Rabideau, M. P. (2001). The stuff that myths are made of: Myth building as social action. *Written Communication, 18*(4), 440–469.

Smith, M. W., & Wilhelm, J. D. (2002). *Reading don't fix no Chevy's: Literacy in the lives of young men*. Portmouth, NH: Heinemann.

Spender, D. (1980). *Man made language*. New York: Routledge.

Sullivan, P. A. (1992). Feminism and methodology in composition studies. In G. Kirsch & P. A. Sullivan (Eds.), *Methods and methodology in composition research* (pp. 37–61). Carbondale: Southern Illinois University Press.

Takayoshi, P. (1994). Building new networks from the old: Women's experiences with electronic communications. *Computers and Composition, 11*(1), 21–35.

Takayoshi, P. (2004, March). *Girl talk online*. Paper presented at the Conference on College Composition and Communication, San Antonio, TX.

Tannen, D. (1990). *You just don't understand: Men and women in conversation*. New York: HarperCollins.

Taylor, S. O. (1978). Women in a double bind: Hazards of the argumentative edge. *College Communication and Composition, 29*, 385–389.

Tobin, L. (1996). Carwrecks, baseball caps, and man-to-man defense: The personal narratives of adolescent males. *College English, 58*, 2: 158–176.

Worsham, L. (1991). Writing against writings: The predicament of ecriture feminine in composition studies. In P. Harkin & J. Schilb (Eds.), *Contending with words: Composition and rhetoric in a postmodern age* (pp. 82–104). New York: Modern Language Association.

Zawacki, T. M. (1992). Recomposing as a woman—an essay in different voices. *College Communication and Composition, 43*, 32–38.

CHAPTER 17

Writing and Social Change

Brenton Faber
Clarkson University

OVERVIEW

In social communities such as organizations, institutions, and communities of work, writing enables people to achieve specific activities. This chapter explores how writing enables such groups to initiate, manage, and stabilize sociocultural change. The chapter discusses the interrelationship between writing and social change, emphasizing that writing simultaneously constitutes and reflects social practices. First, I provide an overview of the current research and theory on writing and cultural change in social systems, primarily organizations. This research has been instrumental in helping scholars better understand and empirically document the function of written texts in contexts of social change. I explain that change occurs as a transitional process in which advocates will initially destabilize a current context, introduce new elements into that context, and then restabilize that context with new meanings and practices.

Next, the chapter introduces research that has attempted to better examine and understand the motivation or the rationale for change. To pursue these questions, researchers have turned to the cultural-rhetorical concepts of image and identity, theorizing that rhetorical perception can play a central role in the reasons why social groups will go through processes of social and cultural change. The chapter presents narratives as key organizational genres that functionally allow agents to challenge and replace a social group's image and identity. Finally, the chapter concludes by presenting discourse-based research that has attempted to characterize the process of change at the linguistic level. This work has highlighted specific syntactic and pragmatic discursive features that appear to help texts create causal connections between old and new social contexts.

Throughout the chapter, I draw on the case of the marketization of university education for examples to demonstrate various theoretical and pragmatic concepts. I chose this backdrop in part because it has been a prominent part of the discourse studies and writing research literature on social change and because I have assumed that it would be a generally interesting backdrop for an academic audience.

WRITING REFLECTS AND CONSTITUTES SOCIAL SYSTEMS

A key feature of modernity has been the dominant role written communication has come to play in both constituting and reflecting social practices (Chouliaraki & Fairclough, 1999). In the chapter 1 of this volume, Schmandt-Besserat and Erard described a materialist orientation toward writing that emphasizes the social activity that is enabled by writing. Citing Latour's

(1990) studies of the function of writing within scientific communities, Schmandt-Besserat and Erard claimed that written representations "succeed because they enable their users to do more." Thus, in areas of science (Latour, 1990; Lyotard, 1979) and cultural production (Jameson, 1991), and in the emergence and cultural dominance of organizational and professional life (Burrell, 1988; Foucault, 1973, 1979), written communication has functioned as a constitutive form of legitimacy and social power (Ong, 1982) as it has enabled users to accomplish significant activities. The constitutive power and utility of written communication has been especially prominent in the creation and regulation of modern organizations and the varied and conflicting identities of those who work within these organizations (Zachry & Thralls, 2006).

Although social change is often associated with external, material conditions such as economic factors, environmental conditions, or technological innovations, studies of the intersection of writing and social change have shown social change to be a multiformed process involving a complex interplay of discursive, material, and social conditions. Legally, but also socially and culturally, modern organizations and professions are the products of written communication. As Mumby and Clair (1997) claimed, "Organizations exist only in so far as their members create them through discourse" (p. 181). This discourse functions "simultaneously as both an expression and a creation of organizational structure" (p. 181). Similarly, Alvesson and Kärreman (2000) pointed out that throughout the social sciences, researchers have come to understand that "societies, social institutions, identities, and even cultures may be viewed as discursively constructed ensembles of texts" (p. 137). As researchers have come to understand social groups and organizations as products of written communication, further studies have shown that social and cultural changes within such organizations are also combinations of social and textual activities. For example, researchers have documented the textual and rhetorical activities that have enabled conceptual changes in scientific fields (Bazerman, 1984; Hull, 1988; Myers, 1990; Vande Kopple, 1998, 2002; see Faber, 2006, for discussion). David Hull goes so far as to find that despite the process and chronology of scientific discovery, the written rationale for conceptual change is typically (re)ordered to assert causality and consistency with existing practices and research within the same field (p. 116). It is important to note here that Hull's finding does not suggest impropriety or falsified data. Instead, this process is akin to the tension Deleuze and Guattari (1987) describe between planes of organization and consistency (p. 270), or to the sort of retrospective regroupings by which Foucault (1972) characterized discipline formation and promotion. Knowledge is built in often chaotic and stochastic relations and formations. The interpretation of these formations reaggregate the material conditions in stable, coherent accounts, creating this necessary tension.

(DE)STABILIZATION: CHANGE AS A TRANSITIONAL SOCIAL-TEXTUAL PROCESS

Paul Feyerabend (1991), writing about changes in knowledge within academic groups, argued that change in disciplinary communities occurs primarily through a process of argumentation. Using the term *transition*, Feyerabend argues that a successful transitional argument must coherently link from the existing to the new, "protect" the new system from "misinterpretation," and convince (condition) adopters that the new is vital and important (p. 18). This model emphasizes the creation of the new from within existing and disputed contexts. In other words, this concept of *transitional change* occurs in increments or linked steps as prior existent knowledge is disrupted and eventually displaced by small additions that ultimately build into new formations.

Feyerabend's (1991) concept of transitional change was expanded by Bazerman (1999) in his work on Thomas Edison's development and introduction of electric lighting technology (for a comparison of Feyerabend's and Bazerman's models of change, see Vanburen Wilkes, 2002). Unlike Feyerabend's concept, Bazerman's examination is overtly rhetorical. He argued that both the technological discovery and the eventual widespread acceptance of electric lighting were dependent on Edison creating specific and varied social conditions that would welcome this new technology. Edison's project was equally rhetorical (discursive) as it was technical. It was also strategic in that genres, like patent applications, necessitated a written discourse that was strategically and generically different from, but could still work within the same contexts as, other key written products (newspaper reports, consumer guides, advertisements). Bazerman introduced a useful vocabulary to describe this process whereby Edison's technology, in concert with his various discourses, introduced significant social and cultural changes. Using the metaphor of *stability*, he noted that written documents will create "stabilized representations" that articulate the final transition within a changing social context. It is important to note that the concept of stability also assumes that initial discursive activities will *destabilize* current contexts. Thus, the coherent link that Feyerabend describes often occurs as a subversive displacement. Written communication can provide a coherent link between old and new, but such a link can also be used to displace and destabilize older (current) concepts and practices. This destabilization creates the conditions necessary for change.

Once a social context has become destabilized, writing will help to introduce emergent and competing alternatives (representations) and thereby introduce and stabilize the emerging system. In such a context, written communication can become highly strategic, controversial, and negotiated at various levels as agents pursue competing and diverse representations. In this transitioning context, the emergent system requires protection (as Feyerabend [1991] suggests) to ensure that older practices do not reemerge/restabilize. In addition, advocates of various alternatives will use writing (and other discourses) to protect and thereby attempt to stabilize their own systems.

Written communication will enable the stabilization of new practices and assist in their ongoing maintenance by positioning and inscribing various representations of the new within the transitioning culture. To use Bazerman's (1999) terms, proponents must create "stabilized representations" (p. 308) that compete with and eventually displace accepted concepts, meanings, and interpretations (Faber, 2003). As older meanings are displaced, new meanings will congeal into what Bazerman called a "unitary social fact" (p. 144). Bazerman wrote that the new system will aggregate together "its own core of meanings, which draw the various other relevant discursive systems together in a new configuration" (p. 144). In other words, the various competing discourses eventually aggregate together into a new model, which is represented as a core concept. This core concept then provides the basis for interpreting and perceiving other discourses and integrating them within the new system.

Example of Destabilizing Discourses: Commodifying Higher Education

For example, the culture of university education in the United States and the UK has recently been contested by discourses of business and capitalism (for discussion, see Connell & Galasinski, 1998; Faber, 2003; Fairclough, 1992; Lemke, 1995; White, 2000). Gee, Hull, and Lankshear (1996) described this encroachment of capitalist values into education as the activities of new capitalism whose advocates do not limit market-based practices to business transactions but view the totality of human life through the lens of the market. The new capitalism is not based on material, goods, or exchange but on values. Gee et al. wrote that the values of the new capitalism are "profoundly imperialistic, seeking to take over practices and social identities that are (or were) the terrain of other discourses connected to churches, communities, universities, and governments" (p. 26). In education, new capitalist discourses have aggregated together the core concept of *educational market* and have used this concept to articulate new systematic roles that restructure other discourses of the university under this core concept. In this aggregation, students become customers, faculty become retailers, research becomes a commodity, university administration becomes management, and university facilities become resources. Fairclough showed that this market-based educational discourse has imposed a discourse of commodities onto learning, writing that:

> [The discourse] is dominated by a vocabulary of skills, including not only the word "skill," and related words like "competence," but a whole new wording of the processes of learning and teaching based upon concepts of skill, skill training, use of skills, transfer of skills, and so forth. (p. 209)

Fairclough's (2004) analysis showed that this vocabulary of skills emerged from within the core concept (educational market) with new meanings and assumptions that carry specific normative and objective criteria that differentiate the commodified "skill" from the liberal humanist notion of skill (individual ability). Fairclough has shown that this process often is accomplished through "co-hyponyms," in which certain words (skills/knowledge; training/education) are made equivalent under the core concept. In the perspective formed by the core concept *educational market*, skills/knowledge are gained from "normalized [education/training] procedures" and they are "[taught/transferred] across contexts, occasions, and users" (Fairclough, 2004, p. 209). As the new discourse stabilizes transitional terms (clients, retailers, commodities, management, resources) other, more radical terms (standardization, efficiency, cost containment) can be introduced legitimately.

NARRATIVES: GENRES OF IMAGE AND
IDENTITY CONSTRUCTION

Students of classical rhetoric and sophistic education (Jarratt, 1992; Kennedy, 1991; Rankin, 1983) will see concepts and assumptions from these schools embedded within this model of a competitive and constitutive discursive process of change. Inasmuch as rhetorical debate and sophistic perspectives played key roles in forming, maintaining, and changing the Greek city-state, these same principles continue to enhance our understanding of the functional role of written communication in the contexts of modern organizational change. But, to better examine and understand the motivation or the rationale for change, researchers have turned to the cultural-rhetorical concepts of image and narrative, theorizing that rhetorical perception can play a central role in the reasons why social groups will go through processes of social and cultural change. Using the metaphor of a mirror, organization studies scholars Dutton and Dukerich (1981) theorized that organizations present images to their members and to external audiences to build and reflect specific perceptions of the organization and its products and services. These perceptions enable employees and other organizational stakeholders (customers, suppliers) to define and identify themselves as part of the organization (Dutton, Dukerich, & Harquail, 1994). Dutton and Dukerich argued that image integrates how members identify with the organization and the extent to which they perceive that the organization shares common values. As Hardy, Lawrence, and Phillips (1998) wrote, this image-driven concept of identity is important, "not only because it affects others' valuations, but because it affects action: identity has been found to be a key factor in influencing whether issues are noticed, considered legitimate and important and, hence, acted on by different organizational members" (p. 70).

An organizational image, a product of written communication, provides a way for an organization's members to identify with the organization and to assess their level of participation with various organizations. A similar concept, organizational narrative, has also been developed by rhetorical scholarship to identify a parallel process of identity construction within organizations (Boyce, 1996). Mumby (1987, 1993) showed that organizational narratives are key to constructing social contexts within organizations. He argued that narratives are important devices for meaning making within organizations as they enable people to understand and explain their complex and often contradictory roles. Narratives are forms of social reality, describing what Robert Heath (1994) simply called "why we do things we do" (p. 60). As stories of daily life, organizational history, historical events, or even rumors and gossip, the utility of the narrative is found not in its factual status but in the interpretation and the meaning it has for its teller and its audience (Gabriel, 1998). Thus, like image, narrative also helps to define and reflect an organizational self (Perkins, & Blyler, 1999). These stories, especially when codified in written form, present an organization's identity, its values, and the way it appears and is interpreted by various groups within and outside of its stakeholder community. Gee et al. (1996) described this function of narrative *enactive* because these texts are written (often by business leaders) to enact or call into being a specific vision of a new organization.

The preceding discussion reviewed various writing researchers who have posited that change occurs when discourses become destabilized. This theory can be further elaborated by suggesting that this destabilization occurs when an organization's narratives and images no longer support or construct a viable identity. Narratives and images will ideally work together to construct an organization's identity—providing complementary discourses in stories and symbols that present a coherent, stable interpretation of the organization. However, when an organization produces conflicting or contradictory narratives, or when the "image in the mirror" (Dutton & Dukerich, 1981) conflicts with the stories the members of an organization are telling, the organizational identity becomes destabilized.

Image and Narrative in Destabilized Contexts of Higher Education

This destabilization and disruption creates the discursive conditions for organizational change by creating a rationale for change. When the discourses that construct and reflect a desired identity are no longer functional, identity is disrupted. In such a context, an organization's identity must be re-formed by creating new images and narratives. These images and narratives may be constructed and situated by members of the organization—or, recalling the system model discussed previously, they may be constructed and situated by competing agents. The forces promoting the marketization of higher education gained legitimacy and prominence at a time when many universities were struggling to define and defend their basic narratives. Throughout the 1980s and 1990s, educationalists and representatives of higher education came to realize that the university experience had been constructed in ways that alienated and disenfranchised large social groups. Research was demonstrating that large numbers of minority groups were actively being discriminated against by university entrance requirements and standardized exams, course curriculum and testing procedures, and campus community and residential activities (Giroux, 1988, 1992; Rose, 1990; Spivak, 1993). The scholarship emerging from these issues and discussions recognized that the meta-narratives that had informed liberal education were dysfunctional. Even authors defending historical methods and content of education claimed that the narratives and images of higher education had become destabilized and dysfunctional (Bloom, 1988).

During this time, when scholars and university administrators were attempting to reconstruct the narratives of higher education, economic pressures from government in the form of declining financial support for university operating budgets and declining support for research (especially in the arts and humanities) placed increased strain on colleges and universities. The image of universities reflected in the mirrors of governments, conservative think-tanks, popular media, and even in the arguments of well-intentioned scholars attempting to relegitimize higher education, portrayed places of exploitation, bias, and most crucially, of mixed and unclear educational messages and purposes. As a result, many universities became unable to successfully tell their story or present a coherent and positive image of themselves to their communities and their stakeholder groups.

Into this context of destablized educational narratives, advocates of market-based education began creating and situating their own narratives of education. These new narratives of market-based education directly challenged the faltering narratives of traditional higher education. For example, Hein (1999), writing about McDonald's Hamburger University, a corporate learning center often sited as a model of market-based (corporate) education, claimed that corporate education better responds to and integrates students' diverse cultural and economic backgrounds. Hein wrote, "Being that McDonald's managers come from a variety of educational and cultural backgrounds, they must be taught the essentials of running a franchise" (p. 75). Describing this intercultural context at Hamburger University, he wrote, "Half the students wear headphones as linguistic experts in glass rooms translate the instructors' words into one of five different languages" (p. 75). The narrative created here tells the story of a corporation taking the education of its future multicultural managers into its own hands. As Fairclough noted (1992; see previous discussion), the narrative focuses on *skills* and *skill training*, but these meanings are shifted from traditional dualisms (skill vs. knowledge; training vs. education) to aggregate new narrative in which *skill* represents opportunity, *training* is advancement, and *culture* is a corporate identity shared by all employees regardless of economic, racial, or gender differences.

The narratives created by advocates of market-based education echo issues similar to those raised by Giroux, Rose, and Spivak. In this way, the narratives of market-based education speak directly to the identity struggles experienced by traditional university educators. The advocates of market-based education structured their narratives within the space contested by higher education to argue that the corporate university is more egalitarian, merit based, efficient, and practical than traditional higher education.

GENRE KNOWLEDGE: ENABLING TRANSITIONS FROM THE FAMILIAR TO THE NEW

Contesting narratives demonstrate that in contexts of change, written communication often functions to inscribe and situate perceptions in situations where utility is more important than truth or accuracy. On a functional and semantic level, written narratives compete for situational meaning and legitimacy. At the same time, structurally and pragmatically, these narratives are part of what Berkenkotter and Huckin (1995) called *genre knowledge* because these texts use conventions (narratives, images, vocabulary) from within the targeted social group to attempt to make changes (disrupt, destabilize, restabilize) within that same group. Genre knowledge is central to understanding the process of change because, as Graham (2004) argued, the "level of genre is where institutional ructions are first expressed" (p. 62). It is at this level that the text, discourse, and social mediation intersect and contest extant knowledge and practice.

In conditions of change, writers must be able to strategically utilize the predominant genres of the social context in an attempt to change that same context. Berkenkotter and Huckin (1995) noted that "genres are inherently dynamic rhetorical structures that can be manipulated according to the conditions of use" and that "for writers to make things happen ... they must know how to strategically utilize their understanding of genre" (p. 3). Thus, if narrative and image provide the means for disrupting social contexts and creating dysfunctional identities within an organization or social group (the subversive displacement of meaning), genres are the key mechanisms through which various representations become (re)stabilized.

Genres enable transitional change because they are dynamic, situational, and strategically value-oriented. Genres elicit and solicit social expectations. As Graham (2004) noted, "Because they are patterned ways of producing expectations, genres link social pasts with the present, and with possible futures" (p. 54). Another way to characterize genre patterns is to view genres as objects of social and community regulation. Genres are regulated because they emerge from a consensus of everyday practice and are recognized and trusted as a relatively formal part of that structure. Yet, genres are still performed improvisationally (Schryer, 2000), and it is this characteristic that enables agents to use genres for transitional purposes. The functional tension between regulation and improvisation makes genres powerful written instruments of change. As familiar representations, genres inspire trust and are linked to the symbolic capital of social groups (Bourdieu, 1977). As forms of symbolic capital, or what Bourdieu also called *credit*, the genre is part of a system of belief and trust within social groups (Bourdieu, 1991; Bourdieu & Wacquant, 1992). This trust can be leveraged to create acceptance during the social-change transition. Genres provide writers sufficient stability and trust to link to the old while simultaneously restructuring (reaggregating) the new.

Berkenkotter and Huckin (1995) described the product of this reaggregation as a *generic blend* when writers combine features from two or many subgenres to create a new genre or stabilize an existing one. Alternatively, a new aggregation could be identified as a *hybrid* genre (Latour, 1999; Spinuzzi, 2003; Winsor, 2003), a combination of different structures and events that produce a distinctly new approach or event while still resembling the parent genres that produced them (Spinuzzi, 2003). Genre hybridity is especially relevant from an activity perspective (Graham, 2004) because, as Fairclough (2004) argued, "Social change is change in the networking of social practices" (p. 112). Those practices that constitute (new) genres are often formed in networks of necessary activities because of the limitations of current forms of action (Graham, 2004; Spinuzzi, 2003). Fairclough (2004) used the term *order of discourse* to describe "a particular articulation or configuration of genres, discourses, and styles" (p. 112). Further noting the reciprocal relationship between language and social context, he wrote that orders of discourse are the "social structuring of semiotic difference or variation" (p. 112) that is mediated by interdiscursive links among various texts. Thus, a particular mix of genres, discourses, and styles is evident in specific text features but also in the way the text works as a social practice (Fairclough, 2004). In this way, social practice may elevate specific texts, diminish others, and leave others vulnerable to collocation and hybridity.

Genre Knowledge and Generic Hybridity in Corporate University Contexts

This process, whereby generic hybridity is constructed from orders of discourse, was described by Connell and Galasinski (1998), who traced the creation of academic mission statements in UK universities (HEIs). They noted that the mission statement is a socially powerful genre that has emerged from market-based ideology and they anticipated that some may see the imposition of mission statements within higher education "as another symptom of the 'marketization' of post-compulsory education, of its incorporation 'into the commodity market ... and the general reconstruction of social life on a market basis" (p. 457). However, Connell and Galasi•ski showed how the writers they studied created hybrid documents that used the genre of the mission statement but advocated for the independence and authority of the university apart from the market. They wrote that:

> [The statements] did not always, nor did they only, set out to represent academic affairs as "business like." There is evidence that the Statements both acknowledged *and* negotiated the political-ideological context. In some cases, at least, while they made lexical concessions to what may be regarded as commercial discourses, they still represented core academic affairs much as they have always represented them. (p. 476)

This hybrid discourse combined discourses of the market with discourses of traditional academic practice to create a negotiated stance that Connell and Galasinski wrote was based primarily on strategic ambiguity and an absence of precision. They argued that "excellence is about the only state which the HEIs are prepared to say they have achieved and will maintain .... Yet the (deliberate) uncertainty about what will be delivered and when allows them to keep their options open, for who knows what their paymasters will expect of them in future" (pp. 476–477). Other writing researchers have noted that the *strategic ambiguity* described by Connell and Galasinski is a common feature of texts claiming to initiate social change especially in contexts driven by market-based assumptions and practices (Swales & Rogers, 1995) and in the texts constructed by advocates of market-based higher education policies (Faber, 2003).

DISCOURSE-BASED STUDIES OF THE TEXT-OF-CHANGE

Focusing on more micro and specific textual features, like strategic ambiguity, represents a relatively recent but growing interest among researchers who are examining the syntactic and pragmatic features of specific texts of change. Such examinations of the text-of-change have suggested key grammatical and pragmatic features of change-enacting texts. Specifically, researchers have examined grammatical metaphor, theme–rheme relationships, modality, and presupposition as textual features commonly associated with social change. Such work has emerged from a relatively new effort within writing research to combine systemic functional linguistics (SFL; Halliday, 1978, 1994) with critical discourse analysis (CDA; Fairclough, 1992, 1995; Van Dijk, 1998; Wood & Kroger, 2000). (On combining SFL with CDA, see Fairclough, 1989; Fowler, Hodge, Kress, & Trew, 1979; Martin, 2000; Young & Harrison, 2004.)

Combining CDA with SFL provides a robust analytical framework for examining the interconnectedness of language and social context and specifically the interactions of language, social context, and social change. Such studies have pointed to specific semiotic, syntactic, and pragmatic features found in texts of change and may eventually help to detail specific discursive conditions that enable social change. Hasan (2004) noted that a major task for this work will be to determine the relationship between discursive variation and social change. Understanding variation will enable researchers to place specific activities of change within specific types of discursive variation. However, as Hasan claimed, research has not yet explained this relationship. She wrote that there is "next to no reliable account of how the 'genres of power' grow" (p. 43), and no real understanding of how specific forms of language use have given rise to specific states of affairs. To better attain this knowledge, researchers must examine systemic stability and how it is maintained. She wrote, "To understand stability is to know what hinders change; to understand system is to understand why process so overwhelmingly tends the way it does" (p. 45). Furthermore, Bartlett (2004) cautioned that a linguistic description of change cannot be formed from a few examples of variables in use. When coding linguistic variables that appear to be associated with discourses of change, researchers must be careful to locate large numbers of uses and from these uses identify common meanings and functions that unite such use. This caution is important because, in contexts of change, texts and social contexts are always in reciprocal relations. Fairclough (2004) has reminded, in contexts of change, that "the 'overdetermination' of language by other social elements becomes massive" (p. 116). This makes it extremely difficult and problematic to state with certainty that specific linguistic features determine certain social actions or specific social actions have initiated specific textual features.

Given these limitations and cautions, several researchers have attempted to articulate and empirically demonstrate specific discursive variables associated with changing social contexts. These studies either assume or demonstrate the theoretical perspective outlined earlier, that change occurs as the resolution of strategic ambiguity. However, the questions informing this work focus on how such ambiguity is discursively constructed, how such texts and their writers achieve and maintain systemic stability, and how to empirically identify the discursive features that enable or support this process.

For example, Harrison and Young (2004) reported on major announcements made by a senior manager in a government of Canada department (Health Canada) regarding changes he was instituting to the department. The communication (memo) was the manager's attempt to stabilize the changes he had made within the department and introduce the future direction of the new branch. Harrison and Young's study showed that the memo emerged as a hybrid of egalitarian and command-and-control managerial genres. The discourse worked by using egalitarian genres to introduce strategic ambiguity and then solidifying the social change through the powerful command-and-control genre. Harrison and Young's analysis pointed to four specific discursive features that can be associated with the resolution of strategic ambiguity: verb choice (verbs associated with completed processes; passive verbs combined with nominalizations that together entailed background decisions but removed agency from those decisions), grammatical metaphor (nominalized processes in the subject position that obscured agency, made activities appear completed, and concealed a lack of staff input in process), theme construction with given information (new information was assumed to be taken for granted), and genre hybridity (bureaucratic texts contained traces of advertising and promotional genres within bureaucratic discourse).

This discursive creation of strategic ambiguity, as presented by Harrison and Young (2004), was also prominent in Harvey's (2004) study of transformational leadership discourse. Examining speeches by Steve Jobs of Apple Computer, Harvey claimed that Jobs' transformational rhetoric initially created a sense of ambiguity that was then resolved "by appealing to followers' self-concept" (p. 248). Specifically, Jobs used " 'do' + Range," which, as Harvey explained, weakened the representation of the the "goings-on" that relate to the verb (p. 252) (do *this*, do *something*, do *nothing*; Bloor & Bloor, 1995, p. 258). In addition, Jobs frequently used metaphors to construct processes, which added to the clausal ambiguity (we have to *drive a stake in the ground*). These metaphors characterized change as inevitable and irresistible, referencing "windows of opportunity," required activities, and "certain realities" (Harvey, 2004, p. 252). Finally, Jobs used collective pronouns (we), which deemphasized agency and made the accountability for change more ambiguous.

As these strategies created contextual ambiguity (destabilizing the current context), Jobs restabilized the changing context by appealing to his followers' own efficacy and self-worth (Harvey, 2004). Discursive stability was accomplished by appealing to (in)capacity, tenacity, normality (fate), and social esteem. Harvey wrote that Jobs created distinct camps for his followers, those who would succeed (overcome) and those who would fail. She wrote, "It is here that the organizational identity breaks down into individuals; Jobs is not prepared to tolerate faintheartedness, i.e. insecurity, and the talk of failure is not an option" (p. 257). After constructing situational ambiguity, Jobs forced followers to make a decision to embrace his leadership and his changes or give in to failure. In this choice, followers were forced to resolve the strategic ambiguity for themselves but in ways that ultimately supported Jobs' vision and plan.

DISCOURSE OF STRATEGIC AMBIGUITY AS TECHNOCRATIC DISCOURSE

The discursive resolution described in this research is characteristic of what Lemke (1995) described as "technocratic discourse" (pp. 58–79; see also Fairclough, 1996, 2004). Lemke wrote that technocratic discourse is a characteristic of discourses that are transformed from discourses of knowledge to discourses of social policy, from descriptive texts to texts seeking specific types of action. The problem with such texts, according to Lemke, is that they present issues of choice as if they were dictated by fact and they deflect and elide issues of value, morality, accountability, or personal choice. Lemke wrote that the grammatical features of technocratic discourse include few processes of direct action, nominalized themes and agents (grammatical metaphor), agentless passive clause structures, and a dominant use of third-person forms. The effect of technocratic discourse is the minimization of interpersonal exchange and subjective forms. Instead, the discourse appears as a value-neutral, objective reporting. Functionally, Lemke argued that these features "serve to establish and maintain a social élite, its claims of privilege and its access to power" (p. 61). Although these strategies were often associated with scientific and technical discourse, they are more commonly associated with social texts and with texts of change.

For example, Faber (2003), in a study of 30 articles advocating the expansion of corporate universities into academic higher education, found that strategic ambiguity was created through modality. Writers used the dual possibilities of intrinsic (permission, obligation, and volition) and epistemic (possibility, necessity, and prediction) modality to assert different reasons for corporate involvement in education. This ambiguity between extrinsic and epistemic modality was resolved in the same sentence by presuppositions that provided an ideological key by which readers could interpret the ambiguous modality. Faber contrasted policy claims with definitional claims about corporate universities. As Lemke would predict, the contrast showed that the policy claims employed modal ambiguity and ideological presuppositions in 54.5% of occurrences, whereas definitional claims used the combination in 5.3% of occurrences. Faber concluded that the presuppositions embedded specific social assumptions within the process of textual comprehension. To fully comprehend the text, readers needed to admit the presupposition and (at least temporarily) agree with the imposed ideology. This form of technocratic discourse demonstrated linguistically how writers have attempted to simultaneously create and then resolve strategic ambiguity in texts advocating social change.

CONNECTING THE MICROFEATURES WITH MACROTHEORIES OF CHANGE

These studies of specific linguistic features associated with change have started to document linguistic processes that enable writers to create ambiguities (to destabilize/displace an existing social context) and then resolve these ambiguities in ways that introduce specific social changes (aggregating concepts into a unitary guiding discourse). In a study of the promotion of genetically modified foods, Lassen (2004) hypothesized given/new relationships in texts of change, suggesting that the interplay between theme/rheme and given/new may form a transitional textual path for social change. Halliday (1994) characterized theme as the information in a clause that precedes the verb and rheme as the information that pertains to the subject of the clause but comes after the verb. Typically, themes will present given information (information that is assumed to be known or familiar to the readers) whereas information that is assumed to be new for the reader is presented in the rheme. Examining texts about genetically modified food, Lassen showed that clauses "developed their Themes by frequently resuming an earlier Rheme as a Theme in a new sentence" (p. 270). Writers introduced new material in the rheme and once introduced, the new material was used to construct new themes in the text. Lassen argued that treating information that is new in one sentence as given information in a subsequent sentence "has the effect that its information can no longer be challenged" (p. 270). Furthermore, Lassen noted that ideational grammatical metaphors were used to resume the rheme as a theme in the subsequent sentences. In other words, rhemes were nominalized and their agency was eliminated to make the assertion appear completed in the thematic position. For example, the rheme "are part of the company's ongoing commitments to global agricultural research" was turned into the theme "Monsanto's commitment" in a later sentence. This strategy enabled the author of change to achieve cohesion across a transitional text and create a coherent link between old and new ideologies.

In examining the function of written communication in contexts of change, researchers have stressed the important function of written discourse in influencing cognition and perception within social systems. This research has shown that social change occurs as a combination of material and discursive events. The social realm is always mediated by this interplay. But, recognizing a role for material and contextual elements in the process of change should not lead researchers to discount the role of language and the symbolic in these same processes. Though material conditions may initiate disruptions in social systems, discursive activity in the form of symbolic activity, written communication, and speech provides the necessary means for perceiving, interpreting, and acting on the material disruption. Such symbolic activity is crucial to reconstituting the disrupted and dysfunctional social system.

REFERENCES

Alvesson, M., & Kärreman, D. (2000). Taking the linguistic turn in organizational research: Challenges, responses, consequences. *Journal of Applied Behavioral Science, 36*(2), 136–158.

Bazerman, C. (1984). Modern evolution of the experimental report in physics: Spectroscopic articles in *Physical Review* 1893–1980. *Social Studies of Science, 14,* 163–196.

Bazerman, C. (1999). *The languages of Edison's light.* Cambridge, MA: MIT Press.

Berkenkotter, C., & Huckin, T. (1995). *Genre knowledge in disciplinary communication: Cognition/culture/power.* Hillsdale NJ: Lawrence Erlbaum Associates.

Bloom, H. (1988). *The closing of the American mind.* New York: Simon & Schuster.

Bloor, T., & Bloor M. (1995). *The functional analysis of English: A Hallidayan approach.* London: Arnold.

Bourdieu, P. (1977). *Outline of a theory of practic* (R. Nice, Trans.). Cambridge, England: Cambridge University Press.

Bourdieu, P. (1991). *Language & symbolic power* (J. Thompson, Ed.; G. Raymond & M. Adamson, Trans.). Cambridge, MA: Harvard University Press.

Bourdieu, P., & Wacquant, L. (1992). *An invitation to reflexive sociology.* Chicago: University of Chicago Press.

Boyce, D. (1996). Organizational story and storytelling: A critical review. *Journal of Organizational Change Management, 9*(5), 5–26.

Burrell, G. (1988). Modernism, postmodernism, and organizational analysis: II. The contribution of Michel Foucault. *Organization Studies, 9*(2), 221–235.

Chouliaraki, L., & Fairclough, N. (1999). *Discourse in late modernity: Rethinking critical discourse analysis.* Edinburgh, Scotland: Edinburgh University Press.

Connell, I., & Galasinski, D. (1998). Academic mission statements: An exercise in negotiation. *Discourse and Society, 9*(4), 457–479.

Deleuze, G., & Guattari, F. (1987). *A thousand plateaus, capitalism and schizophrenia* (B. Massumi, Trans.). Minneapolis: University of Minnesota Press.

Dutton, I., & Dukerich, J. (1981). Keeping an eye on the mirror: Image and identity in organization adaptation. *Academy of Management Journal, 34*(3), 517–554.

Dutton, I., Dukerich, J., & Harquail, C. (1994). Organizational images and member identification. *Administrative Science Quarterly, 39*(2), 239–263.

Faber, B. (2003). Creating rhetorical stability in corporate university discourse: Discourse technologies and change. *Written Communication, 20*(4), 391–425.

Faber. B. (2006). Written popular media representations of nanoscale science & technology 1986–1999. *Technical Communication Quarterly, 15*(2), 141–169.

Fairclough, N. (1992). *Discourse and social change.* Cambridge, England: Polity.

Fairclough, N. (1995). *Critical discourse analysis: The critical study of language.* London: Longman.

Fairclough, N. (1996). Technologization of discourse. In R. Caldas-Coulthard & M. Coulthard (Eds.), *Texts and practices: Readings in critical discourse analysis* (pp. 71–83). London: Routledge.

Feyerabend, P. (1991). *Three dialogues on knowledge.* Oxford, England: Basil Blackwell.

Foucault, M. (1973). *The archaeology of knowledge and the discourse on language* (A.M. Sheridan Smith, Trans.). New York: Pantheon.

Foucault, M. (1979). *Discipline and punish: The birth of the prison* (A. Sheridan, Trans.). New York: Vintage.

Foucault, M. (1994). *The birth of the clinic: An archaeology of medical perception* (A. Sheridan, Trans.). New York: Vintage.

Fowler, R., Hodge, R., Kress, G., & Trew, T. (Eds.). (1979). *Language and control.* London: Routledge & Kegan Paul.

Gabriel, Y. (1998). Same old story or changing stories? Folkloric, modern and postmodern mutations. In D. Grant, T. Keenoy, & C. Oswick (Eds.), *Discourse and organization* (pp. 84–103). London: Sage.

Giroux, H. (1988). *Schooling and the struggle for public life: Critical pedagogy in the modern age.* Minneapolis: University of Minnesota Press.

Giroux, H. (1992). *Border crossings: Cultural workers and the politics of education.* New York: Routledge.

Graham, P. (2004). Prediction, propagation, and mediation: SFL, CDA, and the inculcation of evaluative-meaning systems. In L. Young & C. Harrison (Eds.), *Systemic functional linguistics and critical discourse analysis: Studies in social change* (pp. 53–67). London: Continuum.

Hardy, C., Lawrence, T., & Phillips, N. (1998). Talk and action: Conversations and narrative in interorganizational collaboration. In D. Grant, T. Keenoy, & C. Oswick (Eds.), *Discourse & organization* (pp. 65–83). London: Sage.

Hasan, R. (1999). The disempowerment game: A critique of Bourdieu's view of language. *Linguistics and Education, 10*(1), 443–459.

Heath, R. (1994). *Management of corporate communication: From interpersonal contacts to external affairs.* Hillsdale NJ: Lawrence Erlbaum Associates.

Hein, K. (1999). Class culture. *Incentive, 17*(9), 75–78.

Hull, D. (1988). *Science as a process: An evolutionary account of the social and conceptual development of science.* Chicago: University of Chicago Press.

Jameson, F. (1991). *Postmodernism, or the cultural logic of late capitalism.* Durham, NC: Duke University Press.

Jarratt, S. (1992). *Rereading the Sophists: Classical rhetoric refigured.* Carbondale: Southern Illinois University Press.

Kennedy, G. (1991). Prooemion. In Aristotle, *On rhetoric: A theory of civic discourse* (G. Kennedy, Trans. & Ed.) (pp. i–xiii). London: Oxford University Press.

Latour, B. (1990). Drawing things together. In M. Lynch & S. Woolgar (Eds.), *Representation in scientific practice* (pp. 19–61). Cambridge, MA: MIT Press.

Latour, B. (1999). *Panora's hope: Essays on the reality of science studies.* Cambridge, MA: Harvard University Press.

Lemke, J. (1995). *Textual politics: Discourse and social dynamics.* London: Taylor & Francis.

Lyotard, J. F. (1979). *The postmodern condition: A report on knowledge* (G. Bennington & B. Massumi, Trans.). Minneapolis: University of Minnesota Press.

Martin, J. (2000). Close reading: Functional linguistics as a tool for critical discourse analysis. In J. Martin & R. Veel (Eds.), *Researching language in schools and communities, functional linguistics perspectives* (pp. 3–14). London: Routledge.

Mumby, D. (1987). The political function of narrative in organizations. *Communication Monographs, 54,* 113–127.

Mumby, D. (Ed.). (1993). *Narrative and social control: Critical perspectives.* Newbury Park, CA: Sage.

Mumby, D., & Clair, R. (1997). Organizational discourse. In T. van Dijk (Ed.), *Discourse as social action (Discourse studies: A multidisciplinary introduction)* (Vol. 2, pp. 181–205). London: Sage.

Myers, G. (1990). *Writing biology: Texts in the social construction of scientific knowledge.* Madison: University of Wisconsin Press.

Ong, W. (1988). *Orality and literacy: The technologizing of the word.* London: Routledge.

Rankin, H. D. (1983). *Sophists, socratics, and cynics.* Kent: Croom Helm.

Rose, M. (1990). *Lives on the boundary.* New York: Penguin.

Schryer, C. (2000).Walking a fine line: Writing negative letters in an insurance company. *Journal of Business and Technical Communication, 14*(4), 445–497.

Spinuzzi, C. (2003). *Tracing genres through organizations: A sociocultural approach to information design.* Cambridge, MA: MIT Press.

Spivak, G. (1993). *Outside in the teaching machine.* London: Routledge.

Swales J., & Rogers, P. (1995). Discourse and the project of corporate culture: The mission statement. *Discourse & Society, 6,* 223–242.

Vanburen Wilkes, G. (2002). XML and the new design regime: Disputes between designers, application developers, authors, and readers in changing technological conditions and perceptions of social and professional need. *ACM Journal of Computer Documentation, 26,* 33–42.

Vande Kopple, W. (1998). Relative clauses in spectroscopic articles in the *Physical Review:* Beginnings and 1980. Some changes in patterns of modification and a connection to a possible shift in style. *Written Communication, 15*(2), 170–202.

Vande Kopple, W. (2002). From the dynamic style to the synoptic style in spectroscopic articles in *Physical Review:* Beginnings and 1980. *Written Communication, 19*(2), 227–264.

van Dijk, T. (1998). Discourse and ideology [Editorial]. *Discourse and Society, 9*(3).

White, G. (Ed.). (2000). *Campus Inc.: Corporate power in the ivory tower.* Amherst, NY: Prometheus.

Winsor, D. (2003). *Writing power: Communication in an engineering center.* Albany: State University of New York Press.

Wood, L., & Kroger, R. (2000). *Doing discourse analysis: Methods for studying action in talk and text.* Thousand Oaks, CA: Sage.

Young, L., & Harrison C. (Eds.). (2004). *Systemic functional linguistics and critical discourse analysis: Studies in social change.* London: Continuum.

Zachry, M., & Thralls, C. (Eds.). (2006). *Communicative practices in workplaces and the professions: Perspectives on the regulation of discourse and organizations.* Amityville, NY: Baywood.

III

Writing in Schooling

As social institutions became more dependent on literacy, schools developed to fill the need for literates. The earliest schools were tied to needs of the state and religions to administer their extended domains, and to promulgate their core texts, whether sacred or legal. Schools also became attached to economic activity as well as the collection and dissemination of knowledge. In contemporary society, the need for high degrees of literacy and knowledges transmitted through writing is so high that almost all countries have extended periods of mandatory education, and opportunities for higher education are being extended to large parts of the population, particularly in countries with developed economies.

Schools, in fulfilling their educational missions, have developed into semiautonomous institutions with their own set of literacy practices, somewhat distinct from the literate practices of the surrounding societies for which students are being prepared. Distinctive school-based literacy practices have both pedagogic and institutional rationales. Much of writing research consists of investigating the workings and value of the pedagogic and institutional practices that define writing instruction and provide opportunities for student learning. Chapter 18 presents how writing has been tied up with the history of schooling, and how distinctive school-based practices have developed. Chapter 22 examines how teachers of writing have been prepared and advised to assist students in learning to write.

As a consequence of the institutional division of contemporary schooling into primary, secondary, and tertiary (or higher) education, the research on writing teaching and learning also falls into three distinct divisions, with only limited overlap of focus and method of inquiry. Accordingly, chapters 19, 20, and 21 tell distinct stories of the state of research at each level of writing education, with only limited attention to the entire trajectory of writing education or issues of transition from one level to the other. Given current trends in educational attention, we hope that in a few years research will be able to say more about teaching and learning that extends across institutional boundaries.

Though assessment is part of classroom practice, as teachers evaluate what students have learned and where they would still gain from instruction, assessment is also a very significant part of the institutional life of schools, to place students in appropriate classes, to certify student competence, to monitor the quality of instruction and student accomplishment, and to establish the effectiveness of the institution. The tension between institutional needs to have efficient and consistent means of assessments and the classroom needs to support actual learning of writing has vexed a large literature on validity in assessment, reviewed in chapter 23.

Classrooms can contain many different kinds of students, a fact that education has become increasingly sensitive to in recent decades, as society has become increasingly inclusive. Diversity is particularly an issue for writing as writing calls on such a large complex of skills and abilities as well as is so tied up with student experiences, identities, and expression. Chapter 24 presents research on diversity in the classroom and how it can be supported for the enrichment of all.

CHAPTER 18

History of Schools and Writing

David R. Olson
University of Toronto, Ottawa, Canada

Schools are quintessentially literate institutions. They are literate institutions not only in virtue of the fact that they have a virtual monopoly over the teaching of the skills of reading and writing but also because they are organized by means of written documents—laws, mandates, curricula, texts, and tests. Thus, there are reasons beyond their specific responsibilities as to why schools are such predominantly literate institutions. First, they inherit some of this reliance on writing from the other literate institutions of the society as they provide the training needed for participating in those larger institutions, whether of science, literature, government, or the economy. Second, the history of school is a reflection of the historical development of a literate society. Third, schools in the modern age have become mass institutions, designed to deal with large numbers and consequently have developed group methods of instruction that put a new emphasis on writing as a convenient means of dissemination and surveillance, that is, for keeping track of the academic activity and learning of a large group of learners. Fourth, schools provide for the development of specialized cognitive competencies that are, arguably, by-products of learning to write and otherwise deal with the specialized genres of written language. And fifth, historical shifts in assumptions about the relation between writing and literacy altered the uses of texts and writing in the school. These five factors provide the structure for this chapter.

SCHOOLS AS LITERATE INSTITUTIONS

Schools are defined by written legal statutes, they are regulated by published government directives, they are organized bureaucratically through formal curricula, and they are evaluated in terms of documented criteria. The value of schooling to the larger society is taken to be sufficiently obvious that public education is near the top of the political agenda of most developed nations and has been named by the United Nations as a universal human right (UNESCO, 1995). Whether or not schooling and literacy have the advertised effects on economic and social development (Graff, 1986), both parents and governments believe so, and employers routinely prefer high school graduates to nongraduates even for jobs requiring low levels of literacy. That is, it is widely assumed that successful functioning in the school is a good indication of successful functioning in a modern literate society. Because the larger society is organized along lines specified in written documents and organized by written procedures, high levels of literacy are socially valued and schools are mandated to achieve those levels through its programs and its control over the awarding of credentials.

The activities within the school are also organized around written documents, including courses of study, daily plans, posted rules and regulations, blackboard directives, scribblers and notebooks, and the ubiquitous textbooks. Student writing ranges from listing assignments in a daily ledger, filling in forms, keeping informal notes of materials read or discussed, drafting private memos, and producing public documents for posting on the classroom walls or submitted to the teacher as the basis for evaluation. Although modern classrooms are often reported to be noisy, verbal environments, writing is the predominant and official mode of communication in the school. Talk tends to be around documents and texts, rather than alternatives to them.

THE GROWTH OF LITERATE SOCIETIES

The role of literacy in the school reflects quite directly the roles that literacy has played in the larger society. Reading and writing in antiquity tended to be restricted to records of business transactions and only later of historical chronicles (Gaur, 1987). Learning to read was seen as a valued skill only in relation to those particular functions. Those functions determined not only what there was to be read but also who learned to read. In Western Christendom, that tended to be the Bible and other ecclesiastical works. Protestantism brought with it an emphasis on reading the word of God for oneself and sponsored a dramatic increase in reading and literacy. Reading spread much more rapidly than writing, which in feudal society was taught by a special guild. But literacy became more or less universal with the growth of a secular society and an increasingly large reading public.

Q. D. Levis (1932) was perhaps the first to show how the growth of a reading public contributed to the rise of the diversity of forms of writing found in modern societies and to the increased need for schooling. The Elizabethans (roughly the 17th-century British) read very little. The publics were community based and relied primarily on talk and song as basic modes of communication. Levis writes: "In the sixteenth and even the seventeenth centuries it was music that filled the leisure of rich and poor and the working hours of the people" (p. 83). Such prose writing as appeared showed "an insulting disregard of the readers' convenience" (p. 88) and consequently took a secondary role relative to the theater and the sermon.

The reading public was too narrow to be segmented into highbrow and lowbrow (pop) writing and journalism had yet to explore the diverse possibilities of the written word. Writers addressed the community at large, some claiming that their books were "profitable for Gentlemen, lawyers, Merchants, Citizens, Farmers, Masters of Households, and all sorts of servants, and delightful for all men to read" (Levis, 1932, p. 94). Such writing as there was, was written to be read orally in public partly because not everyone could read and partly because of the pervasive oral culture into which writing was being inserted.

Puritanism defined the next period of writing and reading. Puritanism preserved the Lutheran goal of allowing readers to consult the word of God for themselves as private, often silent, readers rather than as public auditors. In addition to Bibles published in the vernacular language, most people read only Bunyan (not Paul) and Milton. If three books were found in a home, they were likely to be the *Holy Bible, Paradise Lost,* and *Pilgrim's Progress.* The adventures of Mr. Badman and Mr. Worldly Wiseman contributed to what has been called "improving reading" reading, which did not merely inform but aspired to improve one as a person. Quite different but in the same period came Defoe's *Robinson Crusoe,* which is widely regarded as the first modern novel. Defoe "wrote as he spoke" (Levis, 1932, p. 103) and was able to reach a broad readership because his interests were "identical with his readers." The availability of works by Bunyan and Defoe, along with the Bible, often more than made up for the absence of a formal education. In 18th-century England, it was possible for even the poorest children to learn to read if they chose, whether from parents, companions, or a "dame school," and the rest they could do for themselves. The many autobiographies of self-educated men of the period reveal an education gained through reading and study of just those books. Thus, the availability of printed works made it possible to educate oneself. Indeed, several self-taught and self-made men wrote their autobiographies. A typical case is *The Life of Thomas Cooper. Written by Himself* (1872).

The sudden growth of the British reading public between 1753 and 1775, a period in which sales of daily newspapers doubled and that saw the growth of lending libraries, resulted from this new match between the skills of the writer and the needs and interests of the readers. The style of writing, developed by Defoe and shaped by such publications as the *Tatler* and the *Spectator*, established a "taste of polite writing" (Levis, 1932, p. 122), writing that was based on ordinary speech rather than oratory or sermonizing. The result was a "lucid, easy, uncoloured prose" (Levis, 1932, p. 122). Such writing was addressed to a "discerning public," neither highbrow nor lowbrow, and dominated the novels, journals, and correspondence for more than a century. In the hands of the Royal Society of London and the French Academy, prose with a "mathematical plainness of style" (Olson, 1994, p. 196) became the normative standard for educated writing. The essay and the sermon became distinctive genre.

A century later, by the mid-19th century, writing had split into clearly highbrow and lowbrow sensationalist bestsellers. The popular press contributed to the breakup of the Puritan tradition by addressing new interests and reaching new readers. The working urban poor, a product of industrialization, formed a new reading public that was created and addressed by such writers as Dickens, who could speak directly to his readers. But at the same time it led to what Levis (1932, p. 150) called the *disintegration* of the reading public, that is, a sharp divide between the fiction directed to the general reader as did Dickens, from that directed to the educated reader as did Henry James. To inoculate beginners from the excesses of popular media, schools designed programs of required reading and defined the canon, the standard works that would provide a model for learners own thinking and writing. In so doing, of course, it created a textual tradition that was and remains inaccessible to a not insignificant proportion of the student body.

To reach new readers, writers found ways of writing that spoke to them in their language and about subjects that interested them. This dimension of *audience directedness* is perhaps the biggest shift in modern literature. Rather than writing for a general reader, writers in the 20th and 21st centuries address particular readers with particular interests and purposes. Students are such audiences and the design of books and textbooks for children and for different grade levels is now a major facet of the publishing industry (Chall & Squire, 1991).

LITERACY AND SCHOOLS IN MASS SOCIETY

Modern schools are mass institutions, instruments of a mass industrial society modeled on the factory and the military. The class, not the individual, becomes the primary unit of instruction. The fact that schools are mass public institutions gives the school many of its conspicuous properties (Olson, 2003). In many social contexts prior to the Industrial Age, schooling was restricted to a small percentage of the population and teaching relied on individual methods such as tutorials and apprenticeships. Even if several children attended the school, instruction tended to be on an individual basis. Etchings of classrooms from the 14th and 15th centuries show the schoolmaster teaching a single student while others watched or milled around. A Jan Steen painting from the early 17th century, "A School for Boys and Girls," depicts the range of activities some 20 or 30 students engaged in while the teacher at the desk taught a single child:

> In the seventeenth-century classroom shown in the painting a certain amount of chaos and disorder is balanced by evidence of hard work—islands of calm, concentration, and absorbed interest are interspersed among the foolery, laziness, and discord apparent in the other parts of the picture. Two of the boys at the table in the right foreground are absorbed in writing and reading, while a less industrious group behind them make faces behind the teacher's back, and tease the school mascot, a pet owl. (J. H. Astington, 2002, p. 97)

Chartier and Hebrand (2001) pointed out that the group method of instruction was introduced in the 18th century by De la Salle as the *simultaneous system*. He abandoned individual teaching not only to cope with increasing enrollments, but because, as he said, individual methods caused a lack of discipline and an intolerable level of background noise in the classroom. Group methods allowed one teacher to teach a whole group and the increasing abundance of paper and written materials made it possible for students to work on their own. When taught in large groups, didactic methods permitted some monitoring of student learning but teachers relied increasingly on written assignments that permitted an appraisal of the performance of individual students. Hence, writing came to serve as the primary criterion for judging competence, assigning learners to grade levels, and awarding credentials.

Whereas the study of children learning to read and write is a subject of considerable research, the entry of children into the more general literate environment of this mass institution, the school, remains largely unexamined. One of these early lessons is the ascendancy and authority of the written. Student perceptions and understandings come to be treated as serious information only when they are entered into the ledger, when they are written down in the notes or on the blackboard, or when they are found in the textbook. Children learn that talk is cheap; what gets written down is important. It is important because one may be asked or examined about it. Correspondingly, student competence is judged on the basis of their written, rather than their oral, productions. This was not always the case. As Chartier (2004) points out that not until the mid-19th century did the pedagogical practice of connecting reading with saying (oral reading) yield pride of place to that of connecting reading with writing, as in using a text to answer set questions in an exercise book or in taking written exams. Whereas in the 18th century teachers and monitors could keep track of student progress in learning to read through their responses to oral questions, by the 19th they did it primarily through marking notebooks and exams. Today, ironically, children's reading ability is assessed almost exclusively through writing, that is, through written tests. This has the advantage of permitting some objectivity and the establishment of norms and reading levels.

THINKING FOR WRITING

Writing is not merely an aid to memory; it is the technology for making utterances and thoughts real. Once documented, ideas may be revisited, consulted, revised, and criticized. A written document is as much a part of the external world as any other physical object. Furthermore, casting ideas into written form requires that thought take a special form. Slobin (2003) has argued that the old question of the relation between language and thought should be recast as the question of how one must organize one's thoughts to talk about them. Thoughts are wild; speaking requires that one impose some structure or discipline on them. For oral language, that involves suiting the utterance to the needs and expectancies of one's interlocutor, choosing some object of thought as the topic of the utterance, choosing what is to be added as new information, deciding when one has said enough, and the like. These decisions are summarized in what Grice (1989) called the cooperative principle—be relevant, informative, brief, and apposite. Thinking for writing requires that one reformulate one's ideas in a number of new dimensions. Obvious ones include typographical—do I use printing or cursive script?—lexical—can I end a sentence with "you know"?—grammatical—do I use a capital letter at the beginning of every line or every sentence (indeed, what is a sentence)?—what is my main point? Is it to be expressed in a topic sentence? And so on. But in addition, one must address textual issues as well such as organizing an account as a narrative or as an argument. Learning to write and to organize one's thoughts for writing requires reading, teaching, and a great deal of practice. Consciousness of language is in part a consequence of learning to deal with written text whether in reading or writing (Morais & Kolinsky, 2004).

TEXTS AS MODELS FOR WRITING: THE COMPOSITION

Textbooks are not merely convenient repositories of accessible knowledge; they provide a model for correct or acceptable student writing. This is true not only at the linguistic level of spelling, grammar, and punctuation but also at the textual level, what is labeled as *composition*. Textbooks exemplify prose structure of claim–evidence relations: The claim is the main point whereas examples may serve as evidence for the main point. Other structures such as the five-paragraph essay are uniquely associated with the school. In an extended form, the essay has remained a staple of university composition courses for more than a century. Proctor (2002) examined the syllabus for the teaching and testing of composition at the University of Toronto for the past century. The primary requirement, the essay, seems to be a contrivance of the school rather than a genuine form of written discourse because it is written for one reader, the professor (although that reader must not be acknowledged in the text itself). The pretended audience is "the general reader," the reading public. It is assumed that the essay is a model for sustained thought and for integrating diverse information into a coherent form, although school essays are more often reflections of a single point and point of view. In a series of studies with undergraduates, Perry (1970) discovered that as students become more educated they move from a naive, uncritical approach to presented information to a more critical, perspectival stance. It is possible that this growth reflects the pedagogical practices involved. Some religious schools, for example, may be less encouraging of any moves toward a more critical and more relativistic stance valued by secular schools.

LEARNING HOW AND WHEN TO USE WRITING

One function of writing in the school is as an aid to memory. How children learn to construct useful written artifacts is itself worthy of study. Eskritt and Lee (2002) had children play the game Concentration, a game modeled on "Kim's game," in which they had to remember the identity and location of overturned cards. Eskritt investigated if and how children would use writing to help them win the game. One child used writing as an admonition to herself "Remember the cards"; others, older, used writing to make notes indicating object and locations. It was concluded that learning to write is not merely learning a skill but a function. One of the reasons children fail to use writing as an aid to memory is that, as Flavell (1977) earlier had shown, young children massively overestimate their abilities to remember. Note taking becomes the critical form of writing for more advanced students, a form widely practiced but little understood (see Olson, 2003). Studies comparing note taking versus no note taking are inconclusive—presumably because it is not whether or not one makes a note that is important; it is whether one makes the correctly useful note, as Eskritt's study showed. Writing is a function, not simply a skill.

LEARNING WHEN TO CONSULT A TEXT

In a preliminary study, Kathy Bell (1990) asked children, working in groups, to make a drawing corresponding to a written description. Children's drawings based on the same text were often quite different. Attempts to reconcile differences consisted mostly of arguments against each other based on a superficial reading of the text. Only rarely did children carefully examine the text to find the source of their misinterpretations. They tended to assume that all readers saw the same thing in the texts. Horowitz and Olson (2006) reported a series of studies on how children consulted and used written textual materials in their own writing. The tendency of early writers to simply copy a text is what leads teachers to the routine injunction to "use your own words". Learning to use a variety of speech act verbs, such as *claim, assert, deny, allege,* and the like, come to be used by writers only as they learn to distinguish their own views from those of the authorities they consult (Astington & Olson, 1990). Students tend to regard texts as authoritative and increasingly rely on published sources to adjudicate disputes. Although students' uncritical trust in the reliability of the written record is now considered a problem, it is perhaps the case that trust is necessary to get learners to take their content seriously.

LITERACY AND KNOWLEDGE

A refrain going back to the 14th century (de Bury, 1345; see Olson, 2003) is that "All knowledge is contained in books." Thus, again in the 19th century, Cuissart (1865, cited in Chartier, 2004) writes, "All human knowledge can be found in books." The commitment to knowledge is a commitment to book learning. Reading is never merely the acquisition of a skill but rather a commitment to the knowledge and experience that one gains through the reading of particular texts. Schools in Luther's Germany encouraged literacy because of the unmediated access it provided to Scripture. Nation-states such as France and Germany developed public education, emphasizing literacy and numeracy, to create citizens who were loyal to the state and capable of contributing to the economy. Textbooks of grammar, mathematics, and history not only conveyed information but provided the normative standards against which a learner's competence could be judged. As they embodied the standard, they were treated as authoritative. Consequently, the textbooks provide a normative standard; they are taken to be up-to-date expressions of accepted truth and more important, they are the standard against which student performance is to be judged.

Because textbooks are required to provide an authoritative standard for knowledge, they take on some characteristic properties. First, they tend to be written impersonally so as not to be seen as merely the expression of some individual but rather as the society's authorized knowledge. Teachers gain some of their authority from the fact that they are exponents of the information contained in those books. Textbooks are taken to be above criticism (Olson, 1988). The existence of authorized textbooks is often seen as contributing to student's passive, uncritical attitude and reformers such as Dewey took aim at book-centered teaching. Indeed, such criticism led to the rewriting of textbooks, as we see later.

Because textbooks are taken as authorized versions of the society's knowledge, the task of fixing their contents is widely disputed, with every sectarian interest vying for mention if not endorsement—thus the battles over creationism, but also over *whose* history (Cody, 1990; Zimmerman, 2002). Although experts in every discipline have the right (and responsibility) to decide what constitutes knowledge in their domain and therefore what appears in textbooks in those subjects, other domains such as literature remain open to more local cultural and sectarian concerns. Because textbooks frequently serve as embodiments of the curriculum, they help to define what students will be held responsible for.

There is an important and somewhat neglected link between the knowledge of a society and its written records, its archives. A major dimension of school reform is textbook reform, bringing texts up-to-date with advancing fields of knowledge. Schooling is largely a matter of making contact with the society's valid knowledge. The history of schooling, in part, is the history of those books, first choosing them, later creating them, and still more recently, revising the assumptions about knowledge and writing.

Changing assumptions about the relation between knowledge and writing have, in fact, affected the choice of textbooks. In her study of textbook selection in Ontario, Canada, from the mid-18th century to the 1950s, Parvin (1965) noted that, although textbooks have long held a place as "the most popular instrument of instruction" (p. 102), the reliance on textbooks has often been challenged. Textbooks are considered indispensable by some and as an impediment to learning by others. Parvin takes a middle ground, treating them as a useful tool, and examines the political and educational grounds for their adoption, publication, and distribution. In Canada, early texts were often adopted directly from Ireland, as a sort of compromise between the forces advocating increasing ties to England and those advocating closer ties to the United States.

At the beginning of mass public education in Canada, texts and curriculum were treated as synonymous. Competence would be judged in terms of mastery of critical texts. Texts served much the same role in public schools that Scripture had played in religious schools. In the 1930s, educational reforms, influenced by Progressivism, led to the introduction of new courses of study and a new attitude to texts—namely, "an expanded list of books." The text was to have a new role: It was no longer to be the fount of all wisdom but a spur to the pupil to search out information and "do for himself" (Parvin, 1965). School libraries became an essential resource. Although knowledge was no longer assumed to lie in any particular book, the commitment to books as sources of knowledge never wavered. According to Lazare (2005), Canadian history classrooms today are most commonly structured around the history textbook. These textbooks, however, are not monological, but offer a plurality of perspectives and multiple accounts of events (McKeown & Beck, 1994). Although the student is left to form his or her own view, the course of study mandates certain outcomes that again tend to reflect authoritative texts and particular forms of written discourse.

Venezky (1984, 1991, 1992), too, argued that the history of textbook selection, writing, adoption, and use provides a degree of insight into the history of the society. Textbooks, or books used as textual objects of study, have always been both the goal and the means of education. However, textbooks came increasingly to be objects of scrutiny, not on the basis of their pedagogical advantages but rather on the basis of how well they expressed the special concerns of various groups, whether those of powerful commercial interests, national interests, or religious and ethnic interests. Those interests determined the goals of schooling that were expressed through the selection of the content of schooling. Reading, writing, and calculating were not separated out as skills so much as they were involved in the pursuit of more general goals such as selection for the clergy, increasing piety, or preparing one for clerical and business tasks.

Through all these transformations, the relation between the text, teacher, and student remained much the same. An impersonal style (Barzun, 1945), in which "the truth drones on with the muffled sound of one who is indeed speaking from a well" (p. 66), is furthered by the fact that textbooks are often the product not of authors, but of committees. As noted, the texts are bearers of authority, approved by the state, and used as the standard against which student productions are evaluated. The role of the teacher hovers between that of mediating between text and learner in which the text is dominant, and that of using the text to mediate between child and teacher in which the authority resides primarily in the teacher. The contemporary attempt to design programs and materials that determine the outcome of instruction tends to further subordinate the teacher to the program.

EVOLUTION OF MODERN TEXTBOOKS AS KNOWLEDGE TOOLS

Venezky (1992) provided a brief summary of the history of the social, economic, and pedagogical factors involved in the production of the modern textbook. He noted that the term *textbook* is a recent one, dating to the end of the 18th century. Yet as mentioned, from the outset, the use of particular texts as standard works for various subjects has defined schools. In the Middle Ages, Boethius' *De Musica*, Cassiodorus' *On the Liberal Arts and Sciences*, along with works by Aristotle were standard texts. Before the rise of print (Eisenstein, 1979) scribal houses, centered around universities, made copies of important manuscripts, and sustained an active book trade among professors, students, and an emerging reading public.

Books designed explicitly for schooling and accompanied by pictures began in the late 15th century in Italy and Germany. Christopher Hueber, a teacher, included pictures in his ABC book of 1477. The Moravian cleric John Amos Comenius' *Orbis Sensualium Pictus* appeared in Germany in 1657 and was soon translated into a dozen European languages, including English. English textbooks served as models for American ones until the early

19th century and made some concessions to the interests and abilities of learners, though sometimes premised on questionable theories. The history of textbooks and especially textbooks for teaching reading is a thriving research domain summarized in standard works by Nietz (1961, 1966) and Smith (1965). Until the mid-18th century, children's books tended to be indistinguishable from textbooks but gradually came to be distinguished. Again today, many reading programs rely heavily on children's books rather than on reading series. Libraries tend to ignore textbooks, but excellent collections exist in the U.S. Library of Congress, the British Museum, New York University, Columbia University, and the Osborne Collection of the Toronto Reference Library.

Venezky (1992) summarized the evolution of textbooks in the United States through five periods: colonial (1639–1782), early national (1783–1837), pre–Civil War (1838–1865), early modern (1866–1920), and modern (1921–present). Chall and Squire (1991) examine the close links between the publishing industry and textbooks in the United States. Chartier (2004) examined changes in schooling and especially in the teaching of reading in Europe over this period and Olson (1975, 161–2; 2003) examined how textbooks mediated the relation between institutional forms and pedagogical practices. Kumar (2004) examined the use of textbooks in Hindi and English schools in India and pointed out that mathematics is often taught in a second language, thereby making the content needlessly difficult to grasp. Although textbooks are essential constituents of schooling, their evolution and roles in pedagogy remain relatively unexamined.

IMPROVING TEXTUAL MATERIALS

Research on the content, structure, and use of textual materials in the schools was initiated some half century ago. In introducing one analysis, *Text Materials in Modern Society,* Cronbach (1955) wrote:

> Very little research has examined the contribution of text materials: this work has been scattered, inconclusive, and often trivial. Philosophical study of texts has led to equally insubstantial results. We have today no comprehensive modern view of what texts should try to do, what limitations they have, and how they might contribute more in school. (p. 188)

A survey of progress in the analysis of the issues involved in textbook production and use through the 1990s was published as a yearbook of the National Society for the Study of Education (NSSE) under the title *Textbooks and Schooling in the United States* (Elliott & Woodward, 1990). Although no comprehensive modern view of texts was developed there or elsewhere, some more specific research has been done on designing usable texts. The collection of papers published in Duffy and Waller (1985) provide a useful analysis of how texts address or fail to address readers and users of those texts. That book was a response to the belief, widespread in the 1980s, that electronic media would replace textbooks unless they were made more accessible. By emphasizing usability, the articles in that volume show how texts may be designed to better achieve their varied functions. Chapters focus on issues of the relation between the cognitions of the users and the design of the texts including the management of textual, linguistic, and typographic design. There is a good treatment of how texts mediate a writer and a reader, of how texts allow a distancing between writers and readers thereby granting a degree of autonomy to the text. That autonomy of texts is in part responsible for the authority that readers assign to the text beyond that attributed to the writer him or herself (Olson, 1985).

Although it is clear that many documents are difficult for readers to follow and that documents can be shaped to better serve specific functions, it has proven difficult to do so. This is presumably because when they are written to serve many diverse and unspecified functions and texts tend to revert to a general didactic style that emphasizes informational content at the expense of readability. Thus, texts come to be written to be searched rather than read. Searching a text calls for somewhat different cognitive skills than does reading one, but that difference has not been carefully examined. Trends in testing, it may be argued, encourage such search strategies rather than reading strategies, in that short-answer tests require specific, fixed answers rather than summaries or criticisms.

The attempts at text design in the last century, like the modern attempts to design the perfect reading program, tended to assume that if only information was correctly expressed and appropriately convincing, it would produce a specific and reliable effect on a reader. With the postmodern shift from writers to readers, it has come to be more widely accepted that there is little or no way to guarantee any particular uptake of a text. Rather, texts have come to be regarded as objects from which readers can draw, some would say invent, anything they like. There is little sympathy for the more traditional, so-called modernist view that books transmit knowledge; the hope of designing the perfect text is now seen as illusory. Wide reading and writing of many texts is now preferred to the mastery of any single text. Yet oral discourse and tests of comprehension tend to highlight a single, standard interpretation.

The historical study of how and why texts are the chosen instruments of curriculum or of why texts, once chosen, have such authority has only begun. Schools are premised on the assumption that learners lack knowledge and that that knowledge exists primarily in books. When schools were operated by the church, there was an obvious premium on respecting and learning Scripture. Texts, today, sustain at least the three functions we have discussed. They continue to be seen as analogous to Scripture, providing a definitive stance on what is taken as true and valid in the larger society. Second, texts serve as a resource or set of resources that students can draw upon in formulating their own understandings. And third, they serve as a model of writing and thinking that provides a standard against which student productions can be evaluated. By virtue of their long and successful career in serving these functions, we can be quite sure that texts will continue to find a central place in educational practice.

ACKNOWLEDGMENTS

This chapter was drafted in collaboration with friend and colleague Richard Venezky, whose untimely death deprived our field of a distinguished historical perspective on educational thought.

REFERENCES

Astington, J. H. (2002). Letters and pictures in seventeenth-century education. In J. Brockmeier, M. Wang, & D. R. Olson (Eds.), *Literacy, narrative and culture* (pp. 97–110). Richmond, England: Curzon.

Astington, J. W., & Olson, D. R. (1990). Metacognitive and metalinguistic language: Learning to talk about thought. *Applied Psychology, 39*(1), 77–87.

Barzun, J. (1945). *Teacher in America*. Indianapolis, Indiana: Liberty Press.

Bell, K. (1990). *Negotiating meaning*. Unpublished master's thesis. Toronto, Ontario, Canada: Ontario Institute for Studies in Education, University of Toronto.

Chall, J. S., & Squire, J. R. (1991). The publishing industry and textbooks. In R. Barr, M. Kamil, P. Mosenthal, & P. D. Pearson (Eds.), *Handbook of reading research* (Vol. 2, pp. 120–146). New York: Longman.

Chartier, A.-M. (2004). Teaching reading: A historical approach. In P. Bryant & T. Nunes (Eds.), *Handbook of children's literacy* (pp. 511–538). Dordrecht, the Netherlands: Kluwer.

Chartier, A.-M., & Hebrand, J. (2001). Literacy and schooling from the cultural historian's point of view. In T. Popkewitz, B. Franklin, & M. Pereyra (Eds.), *Cultural history and education: Critical essays of knowledge and schooling* (pp. 263–288). New York: Routledge.

Cody, C. (1990). The politics of textbook publishing, adoption and use. In D. Elliott & A. Woodward (Eds.), *Eighty-ninth yearbook of the National Society for the Study of Education: Part I. Textbooks and schooling in the United States* (pp. 127–145). Chicago: National Society for the Study of Education.

Cronbach, L. J. (1955). The text in use. In L. J. Cronbach (Ed.), *Text materials in modern education* (pp. 188–216). Champaign: University of Illinois Press.

Duffy, T. M., & Waller. R. (Eds.). (1985). *Designing usable texts*. New York: Academic Press.

Eisenstein, E. (1979). *The printing press as an agent of change*. Cambridge, UK: Cambridge University Press.

Elliott, D. L., & Woodward, A. (Eds.). (1990). *Eighty-ninth yearbook of the National Society for the Study of Education: Part I. Textbooks and schooling in the United States*. Chicago: National Society for the Study of Education.

Eskritt, M., & Lee, K. (2002). "Remember where you saw that word "Children's use of external symbols as a memory aid. Developmental Psychology, 38 (pp. 254–266, April). *Children's production and evaluations of notations*. Poster presentation at the meeting of the Society for Research in Child Development, LOCATION.

Flavell, J. (1977). *Cognitive development*. Englewood Cliffs, NJ: Prentice-Hall.

Gaur, A. (1987). *A history of writing*. London: The British Library.

Graff, H. (1986). *The legacies of literacy: Continuities and contradictions in Western society and culture*. Bloomington: Indiana University Press.

Grice, P. (1989). *Studies in the ways with words*. Cambridge, MA: Harvard University Press.

Horowitz, R., & Olson, D. R. (2007). Texts that talk: The special and peculiar nature of classroom discourse and the crediting of sources. In R. Horowitz (Ed.), *Talking texts: How speech and writing interact in shcool learning*. Mahwah, NJ: Lawrence Erlbaum Associates.

Kumar, K. (2004). Literacy, socialization and the social order. In P. Bryant & T. Nunes (Eds.), *Handbook of children's literacy* (pp. 711–720). Dordrecht, the Netherlands: Kluwer.

Lazare, G. (2005). *A feeling for the past: Adolescents' personal responses to studying history*. Unpublished doctoral dissertation, Ontario Institute for Studies in Education, University of Toronto, Ontario, Canada.

Levis, Q. D. (1932). *Fiction and the reading public*. London: Chatto & Windus.

McKeown, M., & Beck, I. (1994). Making sense of accounts of history: Why young students don't and how they might. In G. Leinhardt, I. L. Beck, & C. Stainton (Eds.), *Teaching and learning in history* (pp. 1–26). Hillsdale, NJ: Lawrence Erlbaum Associates.

Morais, J., & Kolinsky, R. (2004). The linguistic consequences of literacy. In P. Bryant & T. Nunes (Eds.), *Handbook of children's literacy* (pp. 599–622). Dordrecht, the Netherlands: Kluwer.

Nietz, J. A. (1961). *Old textbooks*. Pittsburgh, PA: University of Pittsburgh Press.

Nietz, J. A. (1966). *The evolution of American secondary school textbooks*. Rutland, VT: Tuttle.

Olson, D. R. (1975). "Review of Toward a literate society" edited by J. B. Carroll and J. Chall, New York: McGraw-Hill. In Proceedings of the National Academy of Education, Vol. 2. Stanford, CA: National Academy of Education.

Olson, D. R. (1985). On the designing and understanding of written texts. In T. M. Duffy & R. Waller (Eds.), *Designing usable texts* (pp. 3–15). New York: Academic Press.

Olson, D. R. (1988). On the language and authority of textbooks. In S. de Castell, A. Luke, & C. Luke (Eds.), *Language, authority and criticism: Readings on the school textbook* (pp. 233–244). London: Falmer.

Olson, D. R. (1994). *The world on paper*. Cambridge, England: Cambridge University Press.

Olson, D. R. (2003). *Psychological theory and educational reform*. Cambridge, England: Cambridge University Press.

Parvin, V. E. (1965). *Authorization of textbooks for the schools of Ontario, 1846–1950*. Toronto, Ontario, Canada: University of Toronto Press.

Perry, W. G. (1970). *Forms of intellectual and ethical development in the college years*. New York: Holt, Rinehart & Winston.

Proctor, M. (2002). The essay as a literary and academic form: Closed gate or open door? In J. Brockmeier, M. Wang, & D. R. Olson (Eds.), *Literacy, narrative and culture* (pp. 170–183). Richmond, England: Curzon.

Slobin, D. (2003). From "thought and language" to "thinking for speaking." In J. J. Gumperz & S. C. Levinson (Eds.), *Rethinking linguistic relativity* (pp. 70–96). Cambridge, England: Cambridge University Press.

Smith, N. B. (1986). *American reading instruction*. Newark, N J :

UNESCO (1995). World Symposium on family literacy. Paris: VNESCO.

Venezky, R. (1984). The history of reading research. In P. D. Pearson (Ed.), *Handbook of reading research* (Vol. 1, pp. 3–38). New York: Longman.

Venezky, R. (1991). The development of literacy in the industrialized nations of the West. In R. Barr, M. Kamil, P. Mosenthal, & P. D. Pearson (Eds.), *Handbook of reading research* (Vol. 2, pp. 46–67). New York: Longman.

Venezky, R. L. (1992). Textbooks in school and society. In P. W. Jackson (Ed.), *Handbook of research on curriculum* (pp. 436–461). New York: Macmillan.

Zimmerman, J. (2002). *Whose America? Culture wars in the public schools*. Cambridge, MA: Harvard University Press.

CHAPTER 19

Writing in Primary School

Pietro Boscolo
University of Padova, Italy

Over the past three decades, many important aspects and problems of the teaching and development of writing in primary school, including kindergarten, have been intensively investigated, from emergent literacy to early writing to the development of composition skills in various genres. Moreover, these multiple issues have been analyzed from both the cognitive and the social-constructivist perspectives. The cognitive approach emphasizes the complexity of writing as a basically solitary enterprise, whereas the social-constructivist approach underlines the social and cultural dimensions of writing as closely related to other literate practices in classroom activities. However, studies of teaching of writing during these years have tended to examine the focus of instruction rather than the mode, as Hillocks (1986) distinguished between the content of instruction and the teacher's role in planning and carrying out instructional activity.

Nevertheless, a few dimensions emerge as recurrent in recent writing research, namely, continuity, complexity, and social activity. Reflecting a shift of writing research paradigms over the past three decades, these dimensions challenge traditional views of the teaching of writing in primary school. The present chapter reviews this research around three dimensions in which there has been a major change of perspective.

THREE DIMENSIONS AND CHALLENGES FOR THE TEACHING OF WRITING

Traditional instructional strategies of many teachers of language skills in primary school rest on the belief that writing is an academic ability, a discipline itself, whose rules and skills are to be learned/taught starting from Grade 1, basically distinct from the other school subjects. This belief has been questioned, over the past three decades, by studies showing that preschool children are frequently engaged in reading and writing activities prior to the formal acquisition of literacy in school, and that those activities predict children's acquisition of formal literacy. The acquisition of writing, in particular, develops through different phases, whose sequence has been found relatively similar across different countries and languages. Thus, a first dimension of changed perspective concerns the *continuity* of writing in children's school and life experiences.

Continuity does not mean linearity: The child's transition from drawing and scribbles to correctly spelled words and sentences does not represent only the development of the ability to produce written language, but should be seen as interwoven development of various symbolic systems—drawing, oral speech, sound—through which the child learns to express him or herself and communicate with others (Dyson, 1995, 2002). In late elementary school years, the development of writing consists not only of the student's steps toward the appropriate use of strategies and skills, but of his or her progressive understanding of the functions and meanings of writing.

The second dimension regards the *complexity* of writing. This cognitive and linguistic complexity may be so great as to exceed the processing capacity of a young or novice writer (e.g., Bereiter & Scardamalia, 1982, 1987; Berninger, Fuller, & Whitaker, 1996; Harris & Graham, 1992; McCutchen, 1996). Research has also shown that becoming a writer not only involves cognitive and linguistic processes, but also motivational aspects related to a student's degree of interest and self-efficacy in writing (Bruning & Horn, 2000; Hidi & Boscolo, 2006, 2007). What is challenged, in this case, is the traditional product-based view of writing, in which writing is evaluated in terms of the quality of the written text, whereas a process-based view emphasizes the development of writing competence in terms of the child's acquisition of cognitive and self-regulation strategies.

The third dimension regards writing as a *social activity*. Few adjectives have been so frequently used as *social* in literacy studies: for example, writing as a social dialogue (Dyson, 1999, 2000), as peer collaboration in the classroom (McLane, 1990), as a way of interacting (Spivey, 1997), or as a tool for becoming a member of a community of practice (Kamberelis, 1999). All these approaches emphasize that writing activity is related to children's classroom and life social experiences, and writing is a tool for making them members of the classroom community. This challenges the traditional belief that writing is a solitary ability; rather, writing is a social activity that can represent a source of engagement for a child, who perceives it as meaningfully connected to his or her multiple experiences in the classroom community.

Of course, these three dimensions—continuity, complexity, and sociality—are not independent of each other. Viewing learning to write as a continuous experience beginning before schooling means recognizing the various social experiences through which children learn to give meaning to written language as well as the processes in which they are involved. Reciprocally, the learning of specific writing skills is facilitated by meaningful writing tasks and contexts in which children are allowed to interact.

LEARNING TO WRITE

Although a crucial step in the acquisition of literacy, early learning to write has been given little attention from researchers. On the one hand, literacy studies have more focused on the processes of learning to read; on the other, the development of writing research has in general privileged the high-level processes of composition and neglected those of orthographic coding. This section examines three topics related to learning to write: emergent writing, the debate on phonics versus the whole-language approach, and Berninger's studies on early writing.

Emergent Writing

Literacy studies over the past three decades have shown that the acquisition of literacy is a developmental continuum that originates early in a child's life (see chap. 25, this volume). Emergent literacy is the name given to the child's various contacts and relations with printed matter and related activities in kindergarten, and in his or her family life prior to schooling, that are the developmental precursors of formal literacy. Although the first use of this phrase goes back to the mid-1960s (Clay, 1967), only at the end of the 1970s did interest in the children's informal reading and writing activities develop. Bissex (1980), describing how a child—her son—acted as a writer, was one of the first scholars to argue that reading and writing activities are closely interwoven and influence each other. After Bissex, scholars from different countries and languages have analyzed and classified the form of writing of preschool children: for example, Spanish (Ferreiro & Teberosky, 1982), English (De Goes & Martlew, 1983, in England; Sulzby, 1986, in the United States), Hebrew (Tolchinsky Landsmann & Levin, 1987), French (Gombert & Fayol, 1992), and Italian (Pontecorvo & Zucchermaglio, 1990). Although with some difference, the developmental sequence of the writings appears to be similar across the different languages. Sulzby (1986) reported six major categories of children's handwriting: drawing,[1] scribbling, letterlike forms, well-learned units, invented spelling, and conventional orthography. In well-learned units, a child writes a word or wordlike and then reorders the letters in various ways to form different words. This is what Ferreiro and Teberosky called the *principle of variation of characters*: According to the child, to mean different things, what is written must differ. Writing via invented spelling is characterized by different degrees of letter–sound correspondence, and implies phonological awareness.

Despite the numerous studies on preschool literacy, few have investigated the relationship between these forms of writing and the subsequent achievement of literacy in school. In a study conducted in Israel, Levin, Share, and Shatil (1996) showed that kindergarten children's early informal writing predicted their formal acquisition of reading and writing. Children's writings and concepts about print were tested at the end of kindergarten, and 1 year later the same children were tested for spelling, oral reading, and reading comprehension. The writing test consisted of asking a child to write four pairs of words, chosen to represent various contrasts (e.g., *elephant-ant*, referring to objects of different size). The spelling test included dictation of common and homophone words. Early writing—the point of the developmental sequence from scribbles to invented spelling at which each child was located—predicted all the first-grade measures, in particular spelling. Aram and Levin (2001, 2004) studied the contribution of maternal mediation of writing to literacy in kindergarten and in early grades of elementary school. The mother's mediating role consisted of helping her child write four pairs of words of the same types of those used in the Levin et al. study and names (a list of guests to be invited to a children's party). From analyses of the videotaped mother–child writing activities, two aspects of mediation were considered: literate and print mediation. Literate mediation included grapho-phonemic mediation and reference to orthographic rules. Grapho-phonemic mediation regarded the level of the encoding processes, and was measured through a 6-point scale, where the lowest value represented the mother's writing the letter for the child and the highest score represented the mother's encouragement or help for her child to retrieve a phonological unit and link it to a letter name. Reference to orthographic rules was also measured in terms of the degree of mother's intervention. Printing mediation was the degree of autonomy allowed or encouraged by the mother and assumed by the child in retrieving and writing the letters. Correlations emerged between the literate and print mediation measures, on the one hand, and all literacy measures assessed in school, on the other. The correlations remained when controlling for socioeconomic status (SES). By highlighting the role of maternal mediation, Aram and Levin's studies make an important contribution to research concerning the relationship between emergent and formal literacy, showing that the various ways in which an adult—in this case, the mother—helps a child write have positive effects in his or her future literacy learning.

What do studies in emergent literacy suggest for the teaching of writing? A preliminary distinction should be made between studies conducted in the Piagetian and those in the Vygotskian perspectives. From a Piagetian perspective, the child is a partner in cognition, who develops hypotheses on written language that he or she adapts and modifies with age. The scholars following this approach are not concerned with the development of child's writing competence, but with his or her construction of written language. For instance, E. Ferreiro, a leading exponent of this approach, has several times criticized the

---

[1] Some authors (e.g., Gombert & Fayol, 1992; Levin, Share, & Shatil, 1996) do not include drawing among writing forms, arguing that chldren do not use drawing for writing.

behavioristic attitude of teachers who view the learner as a passive spectator/receptor and the writing system as an object of contemplation that children should look at and repro-duce, not being allowed to experiment and/or transform it (e.g., Ferreiro, 1986, 1990; Ferreiro & Teberosky, 1982; Vernon & Ferreiro, 1999). Consistently, she is not concerned with what is the best method for the teaching of literacy (e.g., phonics vs. whole-language approach), although she underlines the importance of putting children in a rich literacy environment. An instructional implication of this approach is that the first-grade teacher should not ignore what the child already knows about written language when entering school, and particularly the phase of the sound–letter relationship (syllabic, alphabetic-syllabic, or alphabetic) that he or she is at when entering first grade. This tolerant attitude is reflected in the assessment of children's early literacy acquisition, where the teacher is more an observer than an evaluator.

Studies conducted with a Vygotskian approach stress the active role of the teacher in helping children develop writing. This active role can assume the form of scaffolding in specific phases of literacy learning, as in the cited studies of Aram and Levin (2001, 2004), where the adult mediation turned out to be effective for the child's subsequent learning. However, the teacher's function in kindergarten as well as, in general, in early learning of writing, is not only to give specific support but making writing a meaningful activity for children. Although preschool writing is usually a free activity, it is important to give children the idea that writing is a goal-oriented activity. As Teale and Martinez (1989) argued, "The reasons for children's continuing motivation to write after discovering they can make marks on paper is that they see writing as a new way of achieving objectives pre-viously achieved in other ways" (p. 183). Children learn to view writing as a tool for get-ting things done: for instance, making a menu or a shopping list, or writing an invitation or fixing an appointment. Another aspect to be stressed regards the connections between reading and writing. The stories children read in the classroom may stimulate various responses, and in particular writing. Asking children to read what they write is important for helping them see themselves as writers, but also for enabling teachers to understand children's concepts of writing. For instance, Sulzby (1985) developed a scale to assess the different levels of children's ability to reread their story compositions. Reading one's own writing can also be useful for the other members of the classroom. Individual children read what they wrote to the peers, give and receive comments, and discuss. Thus, they learn to view writing as a form of social interaction.

Also stressing the social and cultural dimension of writing, Dyson (1993, 1995, 2002) has studied children's oral and written use of diverse cultural resources, including the family and peer-group cultures and the culture of the school. Dyson's question is: How does writ-ing come to be a tool in children's negotiation of their complex social worlds? From this perspective, the developmental goal is not the construction of an "autonomous" text (Olson, 1977), but the child's understanding of the social complexity of writing.

A Long Debate: Phonics Instruction Versus Whole-Language Approach

Although the sound–letter correspondence is a basic requisite of the acquisition of formal literacy, there is not a general agreement among scholars and teachers on how children should be taught to decode and encode words. The debate on this question has been kept alive for decades by advocates of the phonics instruction, on the one hand, and of the whole-language approach, on the other. Phonics instruction may be considered any approach in which the teacher does and/or says something to help children decode words (Stahl, 2002). This quite generic definition is accompanied by a list of instructional strategies, from the direct teaching of sound–symbol correspondence to making children manipulate sounds in oral and letters in written words. Similarly, the whole-language approach is a generic label, and the approach is better defined by reference to a few broad criteria regarding the teacher's attitude and the learning environment (Dahl, Scharer, Lawson, & Grogan, 1999).

According to this approach, reading and writing are viewed as meaningful activities, related to children's personal experiences and interests. Children learn to read and write in a rich literate environment, being provided with various print sources and encouraged to share their reading and writing experiences with peers. Advocates of this approach do not deny the importance of phonics, but view it as one of the cueing systems children use in reading and writing.

The debate on the two approaches reflects two broad contrasting perspectives on literacy learning—literacy as a pattern of skills to be taught by direct intervention versus a set of practices to be taught/learned in meaningful and interactive contexts. However, in recent years the debate seems to be less heated, thanks to studies that have questioned the rigidity of the distinction. On the one hand, there are new approaches to phonics instruction based on constructivist principles (Stahl, 2002): The view of the child as actively constructing his or her knowledge, usually supporting the whole-language approach, is now adopted also by phonics authors (Stanovich, 1994). On the other hand, first-grade teachers adopting the whole-language approach often tend to using instructional strategies related to phonics. In a study conducted with six "analytic" and six "wholist" first-grade teachers, Boscolo and Cisotto (1999) found that the distinction between the two methods regarded two aspects in particular: the first phase of learning to write, in which the analytic teachers introduce sounds, whereas the wholist teachers are more concerned with preparing the ground for the acquisition of writing; and the role of practice, more stressed by analytic teachers. However, an unexpected result of the study was the low frequency of opposite instructional actions, that is, preferred by one group of teachers and rejected by the other.

Recently, Dahl, Scharer, Lawson, and Grogan (1999, 2003), in a 1-year study conducted with nine teachers and 178 first graders, analyzed the role of phonics in reading and writing activities carried out in whole-language classrooms. The assessment of student phonics achievement was conceptualized as including two significant dimensions: whether the task was presented in isolation or in context, and whether it focused on decoding or encoding. The researchers acted as participant-observers who took field notes in the classrooms. The observed teaching and learning events were analyzed by means of eight categories of teacher actions and teacher and student interactions through which students were given knowledge about specific phonic concepts, skills, and strategies. Four categories regarded writing:

- Shared writing, consisting of collaborative teacher–student generation of sentences, with the teacher serving as scribe.
- Writing demonstration, when the teacher guides students by explicit actions. An example of demonstration is the teacher's writing of a sentence, involving children in the spelling of the words.
- Interactive writing, consisting of joint writing of a text on large chart paper. The final result is a combination of words written by the teacher and individual students.
- Individual writing instruction, when a teacher meets with individual students, who read their writing aloud to him or her.

Results show that a large part of phonics instruction (about 45%) occurred in the writing activities. The authors recognized that the writing task used for pre- and postassessment asked for encoding in and out of context, and did not include the production of true texts. In spite of this limitation, the Dahl et al. (2003) study is an important contribution to study of the role of phonics instruction in writing, because it describes the ways in which children are taught to encode words during writing activities.

Over the past decade and a half, a few relevant studies have addressed the relationship between phonics and writing development. For instance, Varble (1990) found that second graders in the whole-language approach wrote better texts than did children of traditional classrooms, but without any significant difference in mechanics. Freppon, McIntyre, and Dahl (1995) found that children in the whole-language approach used more text structures. However, more research is needed on the relationship between teachers' strategies in early phases of writing instruction and the development of writing.

A Simple View of Writing

Important contributions to this research field have been given by Berninger's studies, in which the cognitive, developmental and neuropsychological perspectives are integrated. Berninger and Swanson (1994) reformulated Hayes and Flower's (1980) model in developmental terms by modifying the translation component, that is, the phase in which ideas generated from long-term memory are written on paper or the keyboard. In the original model, this phase had scarce relevance in comparison to the cognitive components of planning and revising. According to Berninger and Swanson (1994), translation includes two components: text generation and transcription. Text generation is the translation of ideas generated by the writer in the planning phase into language representations in the writer's working memory; transcription is the transformation of those representations into orthographic symbols through pen or keyboard. Deficits in transcription skills can interfere with development of text generation. The more automatic the transcriptions skills are, the more working-memory capacity is available for high-level composing skills. Thus, a primary instructional objective is to develop accurate and automatic transcription (handwriting and spelling) and fluent text generation, and to transfer these low-level skills to higher-level composing (Berninger et al., 1997, 1998).

In collaboration with S. Graham and K. Harris' research team, Berninger has developed a model of simple writing, which expands Juel's (1988) simple view of writing as composed of two factors, spelling and ideation. Berninger's model is graphically represented by a triangle. At the base vertexes are, respectively, the transcription skills (letter production and spelling, or word production) and emerging executive functions for planning, monitoring, and revising. These two fundamental components support text generation at the top vertex, the main writing goal of the beginning writer. The interior of the triangle represents the working-, short-term, and long-term memory processes (Wong & Berninger, 2004).

A recent intervention study of Berninger and collaborators tests this conceptualization of writing. Berninger et al. (2002) analyzed the effects of four treatments to third graders who showed low compositional fluency, that is, wrote little under time constraints. The four treatments were: spelling, composition, spelling and composition, and control. In the spelling treatment, the alphabetic principle was explicitly taught and practiced by children until automaticity. In the composition treatment, children had to write informational (e.g., "Describe a computer to a child who cannot see it") and persuasive essays (e.g., "Should children be able to decide when they go to bed?"). In this treatment group, children engaged in discussion with peers: For instance, they were encouraged to brainstorm or debate ideas in the lessons devoted to planning, and to review their texts in the reviewing lessons. In the combined spelling-and-composition treatment, all writing was teacher directed and carried out individually by students. Last, in the control treatment children were initially given keyboard training, then were asked to type dictated alphabetic letters. Subsequently, they practiced writing on various topics, without any explicit instruction. The measures included verbal IQ, handwriting automaticity (printing the alphabetic letters from memory quickly and correctly), spelling of content and structure words, compositional fluency, and compositional quality (relatedness to the topic for the informational essay, and argumentative structure for the persuasive). Results show that all treatment groups increased spelling but not compositional quality. The composition and the composition-plus-spelling groups increased compositional quality of persuasive essays. Overall, only the combined condition, including low-level transcription and high-level composition skills, showed improvement for both transcription and composition. The authors' conclusion was that effective teaching of writing may incorporate multiple components such as phonics, self-regulation, reflection, and composition practice.

TEACHING THE WRITING PROCESSES

Over the past three decades, the word *process* has been extensively used in two phrases related to writing, with different although partially overlapping meanings: process approach and writing processes. The process approach indicates a method of teaching writing widely adopted in elementary school, emphasizing prewriting and revising. On the other hand, *process* suggests the cognitive approach to writing (see chap. 28, this volume), which initially represented the process as divided into phases (planning, translating, and reviewing). However, the relations between the instructional and the cognitively oriented approaches are more complex than a simple overlapping. The process approach includes many aspects of writing that are difficult to organize in a unitary framework. The cognitively oriented approach, although still characterized by attention to processes, looks now rather different from the early conceptualization of writing. The process approach is briefly described in the next subsection, whereas studies on the teaching/learning of writing conducted from the cognitive perspective are analyzed in the section Writing as a Cognitive Process.

The Process Approach

Process approaches (as Applebee [1986] rightly points out, there is a large variability in process-based instruction in the classrooms) are characterized by instructional strategies aiming at making students organize their ideas before writing and revise their written texts. The origin of the approach is to be found in Rohman's (1965) model. At the beginning of the 1970s, Emig (1971), on the basis of an observational study of eight 12th graders who spoke aloud while composing, criticized Rohman's model of writing, arguing that the composing process is not linear, but recursive. The process approach to writing was proposed to teachers of language skills by several authors, foremost Graves (1983) and Murray (1985). In addition, the process approach presents the following basic features. First, lectures are minimized and small-group work is valued, with an emphasis on concrete materials, problem solving, and students' engagement in writing. Second, children should be allowed to choose the topics on which to write, at least in elementary school, as this is believed to have a motivating effect. Third, the teacher is not an evaluator, but an audience who gives feedback through conferences with students. Through conferences, he or she shows how to write by posing questions that help planning, by reformulating children's ideas when writing, and by soliciting a new development of a story or new information for a report. Thus, the teacher is a facilitator and a model. Fourth, the social dimension of writing is emphasized, because students often work in small groups, and what they write is a product that is made available to other children.

In his seminal meta-analysis of modes and foci of writing instruction, Hillocks (1986) defined and contrasted the natural process mode (or process approach) with three other modes: presentational (or teacher-based), environmental, and individualized. In fact, the most effective turned out to be the environmental, a version of the process approach in which the teacher provides students with structured materials and activities. In particular, Hillocks contrasted the presentational and natural mode in relation to argumentative writing. In the presentational mode, the teacher shows the features and qualities of good argumentative writing, and provides one or more examples to be examined through discussion in the classroom. Then the teacher assigns a topic or asks students to choose one on which to write an argumentative text that will be evaluated. In the process approach, the teacher is likely to begin with asking students to find a question or problem on which different points of view (e.g., of a student and his or her peers) are to be expressed. Following this comparison, students list as many features as they can. Then they are asked to establish a focus and begin a draft for a certain audience. During these phases students share their writing in conferences with peers and teachers.

The process approach embodies a view of writing as motivated, personal, reflective activity, in which the teacher gives children guidance and feedback, and provides them with optimal conditions for writing. In spite of these positive aspects and great success in schools, the approach has been widely criticized, particularly in the 1990s, for reasons including the rigidity of the prewriting writing, rewriting sequence (Petraglia, 1999), the scarce attention to audience (Williams, 1998), and the oversimplified view of the teaching of writing (Newkirk & Tobin, 1990). In different periods, Applebee (1986) and Russell (1999) pointed out the variability of writing functions and activities: The dynamics of prewriting and rewriting are appropriate for some writing tasks but not for others. If, as Applebee argued, the teacher does not make clear to students the link between the problems (a specific writing task) and the process (the way to solve it), the approach may end up by becoming formulaic.

More recently, a group of functional linguists primarily from Australia (Cope & Kalantzis, 1993) have severely criticized this progressivist pedagogy for favoring students belonging to the literate culture of power in industrial society: Because a basic feature of the approach is emphasis on students' expression of personal voices in writing, these voices may reflect the unequal value of voices in the world outside the school. The position of these scholars on genres is analyzed in a later section.

Writing as a Cognitive Process

Cognitively oriented approaches to writing have changed significantly over the past two decades from the original focus on the adult writer's access to knowledge in long-term memory and planning and revising as fundamental processes in written production. Bereiter and Scardamalia, in the mid-1980s, introduced a developmental perspective in the cognitive approach to writing, emphasizing the constraints of novice writers' processing. Simultaneously, writing contexts, particularly in relation to peer collaboration, started to be investigated, under the influence of Vygotsky's thought and in response to the development of computer technology. In addition, studies on motivational aspects of writing started at the end of the 1980s. In general, what characterizes the recent studies in the cognitively oriented approach is attention to the ways in which the mode of instruction—the features of instructional settings and writing tasks—influence the writing processes.

Bereiter and Scardamalia (1982, 1987) with their collaborators at the Ontario Institute for Studies in Education constructed a model of writing development based on two theoretical key points. The first key point was a neo-Piagetian view of children as constrained by processing limitations imposed by a communication system—writing—requiring the autonomous production of text (Olson, 1977). According to this view, the difficulties young writers have to deal with (especially in producing argumentative and expository text) depend on their limited capacity for synthesizing information into integrated schemes. The second key point regarded the differences between novice and expert writers in terms of two ways or styles of writing: knowledge telling and knowledge transforming. Knowledge telling is a writer-based text production, basically aiming at fulfilling the writing assignment by linearly exposing one's knowledge; knowledge transforming is a mature way of subordinating knowledge to a rhetorical goal. In this section, we focus on the developmental aspect, and particularly on procedural facilitation.

Bereiter and Scardamalia (1982, 1987) assume that, for any composition task, children have to use an executive or self-regulatory procedure available for dealing with it; however, children often fail to use these procedures. Procedural facilitation, such as explicit attention to planning and revision, is well performed by an expert writer, but not by a novice one. To facilitate novice children writers in carrying out procedures intentionally, they are provided with external supports or teachable routines for reducing the processing burden. The procedure is useful not only for complex processes, as revision, but also for helping children write texts that may imply difficulties for them. When asked to expose his or her knowledge on a topic in written form, a child has no causal or chronological schema available as for narratives, and a source of difficulty is to sequence information. Boscolo (1990a) adopted a procedural facilitation strategy for helping second, fourth, and sixth graders children plan and write expository text. The facilitation consisted of separating, in children's production, *inventio* from *dispositio:* Children dictated their ideas to an adult who wrote them on cards. Then, the cards were given back to the students, who used them to write a text.

Procedural facilitation in Bereiter and Scardamalia's (1982, 1987) theory is different from facilitation in the process approach, where the teacher is a facilitator that should arrange a rich and interesting writing environment for students, by eliminating or at least limiting the conditions that traditionally make writing a compelled activity. In the cognitive-developmental approach, facilitation is a way to simplify the complex dynamics of writing, on the one hand, and to help students learn self-regulating strategies, on the other (Boscolo, 1990b; Scardamalia, Bereiter, & Fillion, 1981). Bereiter and Scardamalia (1987) argued that writing, particularly expository writing, offers students an opportunity to work with their knowledge. Students and teachers should be made aware, even in elementary school, that writing means transforming knowledge. This dimension of composition should be modeled by the teacher, who can show the planning processes of which students may be unaware. The authors underlined that procedural facilitation should be used in early writing, when students need to learn complex executive processes. However, they also underlined that students should be made aware of the complexity of these processes; otherwise they are likely to adopt only superficial aspects: For instance, when asked to review their texts, young children often make wrong changes because they have learned that revision usually implies changing the text.

In the 1990s, more interest was given to the effects of various instructional strategies on writing performance. S. Graham, K. Harris, and their collaborators have conducted intensive research to analyse the writing difficulties of students with learning disabilities, and to devise, test, and apply self-regulation strategies that can enable novice students, mainly those with writing difficulties, to produce acceptable writing. What distinguishes competent from less competent and struggling writers seems to be a repertoire of strategies that the former can flexibly use when planning, composing, and revising their texts. According to Harris and Graham (1996), cognitive-strategies instruction helps students develop the writing abilities that the process approach implies. In fact, when involved in social activities of the process approach, such as conferencing, minilessons, and brainstorming, children may not learn the strategies. Thus, a basic objective of writing instruction is making cognitive processes such as planning, writing management, and revising strategies a part of students' writing competence. The authors' approach consists of developing minilessons in which strategies are taught through modeling, discussion, and collaboration.

In the self-regulated strategy development (SRSD) approach, there are six basic stages of instruction of the use of a strategy, which are not to be considered as a mandatory sequence:

1. Developing background knowledge and skills: For instance, in the case of expository writing, this phase regards the activation of previous knowledge on a topic.
2. Discussing: The students and teacher discuss on the relevance of a strategy, and the teacher helps students establish the advantages of the strategy.
3. Modeling: The teacher or a peer models the strategy.
4. Memorizing the steps of the strategy: This is particularly important for students who experience writing difficulty.
5. Supporting or scaffolding students' strategy use: During this phase, students begin to apply the strategy autonomously.
6. Independent performance: Procedures are continued, but can be gradually faded.

The SRSD model has been used in many studies conducted with students of different school grades, particularly for teaching revising strategies (MacArthur, Graham, & Harris, 2004). In a study by Graham and MacArthur (1988), elementary school students were taught to check their persuasive texts for clarity, number of supporting reasons, and coherence. The strategy improved revision ability and also students' self-efficacy for writing.

Harris and Graham's (1996) model is a paradigmatic example of the integration of different theoretical perspectives that characterize the new cognitive approach to writing instruction: Whereas the initial activation of students' previous knowledge reflects the cognitive approach, emphasis on teacher's modeling, scaffolding, and peer collaboration are contributions from the sociocognitive perspective. A similar integration also can be found in the project CSWI (Cognitive Strategy Instruction in Writing; Englert, 1992; Englert, Raphael, Anderson, Anthony, & Stevens, 1991; Raphael & Englert, 1990). The project aims at helping elementary school students integrate information from multiple sources and write meaningful syntheses. It includes procedural facilitation (the use of "think sheets," through which strategies for improving reading and writing, such as questions and graphic organizers, are reminded to students), as well as teacher modeling of writing and collaborative dialogue between students and teachers.

This integration, which also can be found in the prescriptive guidelines recently elaborated by several authors from writing research (e.g., Benton, 1997; Wong & Berninger, 2004), is consistent with the emphasis of the early cognitive approach on the cognitive complexity of writing. Helping children deal with this complexity and write better means supplying them with tools that are no less fruitful and effective for their coming from different theoretical perspectives.

GENRE

If we ask an elementary school teacher why different text types or genres are taught to children—usually narratives in early years, followed by academic text types or genres such as report and explanation—his or her answer would most probably be that writing different text types serves two educational purposes. First, through text types, children learn to put order in their experiences and knowledge, and to express and communicate thoughts and feelings. Second, practice with text types has a preparatory function for the complex academic writing in subsequent school levels.

This view of text types as a tool for developing a general ability to write has a few instructional corollaries. A first corollary is that there is a limited number of text types to be taught—the modes of discourse of classical rhetoric: description, narration, exposition, and argumentation (Nelson & Kinneavy, 2003)—or at least introduced in elementary school. These text types are classifiable into clear and well-defined categories. A second corollary is that text types have prototypical structures, basically immutable, whose traits or components are to be emphasized in school, particularly for most complex text types. Composition in different text types can be facilitated by use of scaffolds, such as writing frames, that consist of outlines or guides that facilitate the student's search for information and its disposition in the text according to the features of a specific text type (Riley & Reedy, 2000).

The concept of genre has assumed great relevance in writing research over the past decade and half (Clark, 2003). In the following sections, two recent perspectives on the teaching of genres are presented. The first is the Australian perspective, which agrees with the aforementioned hypothetical teacher on the explicit teaching of genres. The second is the social-constructivist perspective, which contrasts it. The term *text type* has been used so far to indicate a "school-based" view of text structure; *genre* is used in relation to recent conceptualizations of text production.

Genre as a Social and Formal Category

Genres were basically neglected by the process approach, more interested in making students express their voices in composition than learn text structures. On the other hand, the cognitively oriented research has intensively investigated the production of various text types, particularly those more appropriate to highlight, also from a developmental perspective, the processes and difficulties of planning and revising. Bereiter and Scardamalia's

(1987) developmental model, for instance, is supported by data of children's expository and argumentative writing. The scarce attention to genre represented a major criticism to the process approach coming from a group of Australian scholars. In particular, those scholars argued that many working-class children, taught to write according to that approach, missed the opportunity to learn genres relevant in middle-class culture that might enable them to access social success. According to these scholars, genres are social processes, patterned in reasonably predictable ways, that reflect various forms of social interaction and that should be explicitly taught in school. The first paragraph of Cope and Kalantzis' (1993) introduction to *The Powers of Literacy* is a manifesto of this view of genre teaching:

> A genre approach to literacy teaching involves being explicit about the way language works to make meaning. It means engaging students in the role of apprentice with the teacher in the role of expert on language system and function. It means an emphasis on content, on structure and on sequence in the steps that a learner goes through to become literate in a formal educational setting. It means a new role for textbooks in literacy learning. It means teaching grammar again. (p. 1)

This theory of genre has been translated into practice through various instructional models, the first of which, applied in the 1980s in the Disadvantaged Schools Program in Sydney, was a teaching–learning cycle represented as a wheel (Callaghan, Knapp, & Noble, 1993). The model is divided into three phases, through which students are made aware of the social purpose and text structure of a range of identified text types or genres. The first stage of the cycle is modeling, in which students are provided with models, text structure, and language features of the genre to be examined. At the second stage, joint negotiation, students collect and organize through research and discussion the information to be used in writing a text. The teacher acts as a scribe and helps turn students' ideas into an approximation of the genre. The degree of approximation depends on students' familiarity with the genre and their language development. If necessary, the teacher comes back to the modeling phase and presents further model texts. Last, the phase of independent construction involves preparation of a draft, conferring, editing, and evaluating. A further step is making students explore the possibilities of the genre by working creatively within and beyond it.

An example of genre teaching in elementary school is provided by the writing of a report following a thematic unit of lessons on various jobs aiming at caring people: teacher, nurse, doctor, and veterinarian (Christie, 1993). After a first lesson, in which children's interest in the occupations was aroused, the teacher stimulated children to read, search for information, and discuss those occupations. Then the teacher directed the children's attention to veterinarians. After reading and commenting on several books, the teacher and the students discussed the various stages of a report and their functions, then they wrote a report. The first paragraph of the text anticipated the elements of the text that would follow; then a description of the treatment of animals followed, then a description of a veterinarian's clothes. The conclusion was a comparison between a veterinarian and a medical doctor.

In framing the stages or parts of the text, the teacher pointed out to the children the close relationships between the content (the veterinarian's job) and the linguistic choices, such as the use of an opening topical theme ("the vet"), the functions of a specialist language, and the use and role of description in the text.

Genre as a Typified Response

In the social-constructivist perspective, genre is viewed as a typified rhetorical action based in response to recurrent situations (Bakhtin, 1986; Bazerman, 1988; Berkenkotter & Huckin, 1993; Freedman, 1995; Freedman & Medway, 1994; Miller, 1984). Unlike the Australian perspective, which minimizes the individual's contribution to genre, the social-constructivist underlines the variation related to time, place, and situation. As social facts, genres include not only social roles in interaction, but also individuals' beliefs and affective states related to this interaction. Thus, a view of genre as an empty structure, as a set of textual features, ignores the role of individuals in using and making meaning. Genre changes with time, and so does genre understanding (Bazerman, 2004). In this perspective, teaching a genre is not providing students with formal definitions and lists of essential features, but helping them progressively understand that a genre is a set of rhetorical choices.

Early development of this understanding was analyzed by Chapman (1994, 1995), who integrated the social-constructivist and the emergent literacy perspectives in a study on the genres embedded in and growing out of the writing workshop in a first-grade classroom. The study focused on the writing of six first graders. Chapman conducted a functional analysis to infer the children's purposes of writing. She identified several functions of children's writing divided into two main categories: action/event-oriented and object-oriented. In the action/event-oriented genres, children wrote about actions or events of their experience or in an imaginative world. In the object-oriented genres, children wrote about things that were part of children's real or imaginative world.

From a developmental perspective, the writing changed both quantitatively and qualitatively. As the school year progressed, the number of genres used by the focal children increased; qualitatively, the writing became more complex. The pedagogical implications of the study regarded the role of the teacher in providing examples of different genres and opportunities for the children to explore written language independently and collaboratively. Chapman (1995) emphasized the need for analyzing the development of genres in a variety of context within classroom, in reading–writing relationships, in longitudinal studies. Moreover, because different contexts for writing incorporate different genres, she underlined the need for providing a variety of contexts for writing and expanding children's repertoire of genres, including simple forms of academic writing, often neglected in the teaching of writing in primary school[2] As the author argued, the genres teachers emphasize may become the genres children believe to be the most valued.

In late primary school, an example of genre learning and teaching from a social-constructivist perspective is provided by a social studies learning unit on the Maya in a sixth-grade class (Bazerman, 2004). The unit, which lasted 6 weeks, included other subjects and activities, such as language arts and video production. Each student produced a genre set, consisting of a variety of written texts: notes, informational reports, outlines, reflections on what he or she had learned. In the set, graphical materials and videos produced by students individually and collaboratively also were included. In the unit, the students made two basically different learning experiences. The final reports of many students were mere collections of information taken from various handbooks and encyclopedias: This depended on the type of assignment, which asked students to reproduce specific information without elaborating on it. In contrast, on the final exam students had to respond to questions such as, "What qualities do you think gave strength to the Mayan Empire?" This second type of assignment was related to a different genre, requiring a different student response: to think in causal and evaluative terms.

The learning unit on the Maya provides a nice example of how different genres can be used in the classroom. First, there is not just one genre, but a multiplicity (genre set), though which students learn to relate information from various sources, and recognize the utility of synthesizing and posing questions. Second, writing is closely related to different activities in the classroom: making a chart, drawing a map, recording comments and reflections, preparing a draft of a report to be discussed and reviewed with peers, and so on. Thus, students become aware that writing is not limited to composition, but is a pervasive activity in the classroom. Third, students learn that a genre is a way to tell/write things, and that its use is related to classroom activities: For instance, preparing a final report may be a matter of retrieving and writing learned information or, instead, of reorganizing one's

---

[2] In a study conducted with 20 first-grade classrooms, Duke (2000) showed that only 3.6 minutes per day were spent for informational text, and that was mostly for teacher read-aloud.

knowledge. The difference is not, or not only, in the quality of the product, more or less fragmented or textually organized and cohesive; the difference is that in the second case, students can engage in a task that is meaningful to them, in that it requires understanding, negotiating meaning with the teachers and peers, reframing or transforming knowledge, and giving it new meanings. Even in elementary school, making children progressively aware of genres does not mean to give (or dictate to!) them a list of features to be consulted when carrying out a writing assignment, but to help them reflect on the operations carried out and on the different uses—and difficulties—of writing. Also in a social-constructivist perspective, Allal (2004) has developed an integrated approach to genre instruction, in which basic skill activities are included within writing sequences. For example, in an instructional sequence involving the composition of a historical narrative, the basic skills may regard the coordinate use of verb tenses appropriate to this genre. Each writing instruction sequence includes two situations of text production on the same genre but different topics: Both situations are situated in authentic contexts of communication. In Situation A, there is the definition of the writing project (what to write, in what genre, for whom). Students read texts of the same genre as the one to be produced, and discover the features of the genre, which are noted on charts for future reference. The ideas for the text to be written are generated in small groups, discussed, and listed. The teacher helps students construct a guide to be used during the writing task, which includes basic skill objectives. Then (Situation B), each student uses the knowledge he or she has acquired in Situation A for the production of a second text. For instance, in second grade the students compose and revise recipes for a witch's brew, to be collected in a "Magic Recipe Book" for the class library. The basic-skill objective may concern in this case the use of the suffix *s* in plural nouns and adjectives (in French). Situation B regards the production of another regulative text—for example, instructions for a disguise using various objects and articles of clothing. The texts, once written and revised, are exchanged among students, who try to draw the disguises described by their classmates. Exchange of students' texts for revision and feedback from the intended audience assures "interactive regulation" of students' writing. At the end of the sequence, the students express orally and/or in writing their reflections on what they learned and the aspects of writing they still need to work on.

By becoming aware of the multiple functions of writing in the classroom, children learn to view it as a meaningful activity: meaningful as a tool for expressing and communicating their personal experiences, for writing a script to be played in the classroom, and also for "playing with language" (e.g., for composing, starting from old narrative texts, new, amusing, but significant stories). Moreover, in various activities across the curriculum—for example, history and science—writing can be viewed by children as a tool for recording important comments and reflections, formulating hypotheses, making comments on contrasting documents or phenomena, and expressing changes of beliefs and explanations (Boscolo, 2002; Boscolo & Mason, 2001; Mason & Boscolo, 2000). By engaging in writing activities that make sense, children become aware that they are members of a community of writers, and this has a high motivational potential (Nolen, 2001, in press; for more on genre, see chap. 35, this volume).

CONCLUSION

At the beginning of this chapter, three dimensions emerging from recent and current research on writing were identified: the continuity of writing experience in children's life, the cognitive complexity of writing, and its social nature. These dimensions had a conceptual function. On the one hand, in front of heterogeneous instructional questions of the teaching of writing in elementary school and different or conflicting theoretical perspectives, they could provide a framework for giving unity to, if not integrating, the findings of writing research relevant for instruction; on the other, they might be viewed as challenges to the traditional approach to literacy learning and the beliefs of many teachers viewing writing as an academic, and basically solitary ability.

The challenge, however, does not regard only teachers' beliefs on the nature of writing and on the best ways to teach it. Constructivist theories of learning over the three past decades have persuasively shown that the teaching of a subject—and writing in school is usually considered a subjec—includes not only the instructional activities aiming at making students learn relevant knowledge and skills, but also the construction of students' attitude to the subject. In the case of writing, the students' attitude includes their implicit beliefs (e.g., on the various functions of writing, its perceived utility, the features of a good text, etc.) as well as their disposition, or motivation, to writing. Elementary school teachers are usually more concerned with children's acquisition of writing skills than with their beliefs on writing. However, learning to be a good writer also means acquiring a positive attitude or disposition to writing. From this perspective, the dimensions of writing research can represent a source of positive beliefs not only for teachers but also for students. Thus, stressing continuity of writing means making children progressively aware of their developmental steps as writers; complexity means that learning to write requires a wide repertory of expressive and communicative tools and the use self-regulation strategies. As for the social dimension, it seems important to let children understand that by writing they not only communicate, but also construct with the teacher and peers their identities as writers. A difficult and challenging question for future research on the teaching of writing could be how to help teachers create and/or change children's beliefs about writing.

REFERENCES

Allal, L. (2004). Integrated writing instruction and the development of revision skills. In L. Allal, L. Chanquoy, & P. Largy (Eds.), *Revision: Cognitive and instructional processes* (pp. 139–155). Dordrecht, the Netherlands: Kluwer.

Applebee, A. N. (1986). Problems in process approaches: Toward a reconceptualization of process instruction. In A. R. Petrosky & D. Bartholomae (Eds.), *The teaching of writing. Eighty-fifth yearbook of the National Society for the Study of Education* (Part 2, pp. 95–113). Chicago: National Society for Studies in Education.

Aram, D., & Levin, I. (2001). Mother–child joint writing in low SES: Sociocultural factors, maternal mediation, and early literacy. *Cognitive Development, 16*, 831–852.

Aram, D., & Levin, I. (2004). The role of maternal mediation of writing to kindergartners in promoting literacy in school: A longitudinal perspective. *Reading and Writing: An Interdisciplinary Journal, 17*, 387–409.

Bakhtin, M. (1986). *Speech genres and other late essays* (V. W. McGee, Trans.; C. Emerson & M. Holquist, Eds.). Austin: University of Texas Press.

Bazerman, C. (1988). *Shaping written knowledge. The genre and activity of the experimental article in science.* Madison: University of Wisconsin Press.

Bazerman, C. (2004). Speech acts, genres, and activity systems: How texts organize activity and people. In C. Bazerman & P. Prior (Eds.), *What writing does and how it does it* (pp. 309–339). Mahwah, NJ: Lawrence Erlbaum Associates.

Benton, S. L. (1997). Psychological foundations of elementary writing instruction. In G. D. Phye (Ed.), *Handbook of academic learning* (pp. 235–264). San Diego, CA: Academic Press.

Bereiter, C., & Scardamalia, M. (1982). From conversation to composition: The role of instruction in a developmental process. In R. Glaser (Ed.), *Advances in instructional psychology* (Vol. 2, pp. 1–64). Hillsdale, NJ: Lawrence Erlbaum Associates.

Bereiter, C., & Scardamalia, M. (1987). *The psychology of written composition.* Hillsdale, NJ: Lawrence Erlbaum Associates.

Berkenkotter, C., & Huckin, T. N. (1993). Rethinking genre from a sociocognitive perspective. *Written Communication, 10*, 475–509.

Berninger, V. W., Fuller, F., & Whitaker, D. (1996). A process model of writing development across the life span. *Educational Psychology Review, 8*, 193–218.

Berninger, V. W., & Swanson, H. L. (1994). Modifying Hayes and Flower's model of skilled writing to explain beginning and developing writing. In E. Butterfield (Ed.), *Children's writing: Toward a process theory of development of skilled writing* (pp. 57–81). Greenwich, CT: JAI.

Berninger, V. W., Vaughan, K., Abbott, R., Abbott, S., Brooks, A., Rogan, L., et al. (1997). Treatment of handwriting fluency problems in beginning writing: Transfer from handwriting to composition. *Journal of Educational Psychology, 89,* 652–666.

Berninger, V. W., Vaughan, K., Abbott, R. D., Begay, K., Coleman, K. B., Curtin, G., et al. (2002). Teaching spelling and composition alone and together: Implications for the simple view of writing. *Journal of Educational Psychology, 94,* 291–304.

Berninger, V. W., Vaughan, K., Abbott, R., Brooks, A., Abbott, S., Rogan, L., et al. (1998). Early interventions for spelling problems: Teaching spelling units of varying size within a multiple connections framework. *Journal of Educational Psychology, 90,* 587–605.

Bissex, G. L. (1980). *Guys at work: A child learns to write and read.* Cambridge, MA: Harvard University Press.

Boscolo, P. (1990a). The construction of expository text. *First Language, 10,* 217–230.

Boscolo, P. (1990b). *Insegnare i processi della scrittura nella scuola elementare* [Teaching the writing processes in elementary school]. Firenze, Italy: La Nuova Italia.

Boscolo, P. (2002). *La scrittura nella scuola dell'obbligo: Insegnare e motivare a scrivere* [Writing in compulsory school: Teaching writing and motivating to write]. Roma, Italy: Laterza.

Boscolo, P., & Cisotto, L. (1999). Instructional strategies for teaching to write: A Q-sort analysis. *Learning and Instruction, 9,* 209–221.

Boscolo, P., & Mason, L. (2001). Writing to learn, writing to transfer. In P. Tynjälä, L. Mason, & K. Lonka (Eds.), *Writing as a learning tool* (pp. 83–104). Dordrecht, the Netherlands: Kluwer.

Bruning, R., & Horn, C. (2000). Developing motivation to write. *Educational Psychologist, 35,* 25–37.

Callaghan, M., Knapp, P., & Noble, G. (1993). Genre in practice. In B. Cope & M. Kalantzis (Eds.), *The powers of literacy* (pp. 179–202). London: Falmer.

Chapman, M. L. (1994). The emergence of genres: Some findings from an examination of first grade writing. *Written Communication, 11,* 348–380.

Chapman, M. L. (1995). The sociocognitive construction of written genres in first grade. *Research in the Teaching of English, 29,* 164–192.

Christie, F. (1993). Curriculum genres: Planning for effective teaching. In B. Cope & M. Kalantzis (Eds.), *The powers of literacy* (pp. 154–178). London: Falmer.

Clark, I. L. (2003). *Concepts in composition: Theory and practice in the teaching of writing.* Mahwah, NJ: Lawrence Erlbaum Associates.

Clay, M. M. (1967). The reading behaviour of five-year-old children: A research report. *New Zealand Journal of Educational Studies, 2,* 11–31.

Cope, B., & Kalantzis, M. (1993). Introduction: How a genre approach to literacy can transform the way writing is taught. In B. Cope & M. Kalantzis (Eds.), *The powers of literacy* (pp. 1–21). London: Falmer.

Dahl, K. L., Scharer, P. L., Lawson, L. L., & Grogan, P. R. (1999). Phonics instruction and student achievement in whole language first-grade classrooms. *Reading Research Quarterly, 34,* 312–341.

Dahl, K. L., Scharer, P. L., Lawson, L. L., & Grogan, P. R. (2003). Student achievement and classroom case studies of phonics in whole language first grades. In J. Flood, D. Lapp, J. R. Squire, & J. M. Jensen (Eds.), *Handbook of research on teaching the English language arts* (2nd ed., pp. 314–338). Mahwah, NJ: Lawrence Erlbaum Associates.

De Goes, C., & Martlew, M. (1983). Young children's approach to literacy. In M. Martlew (Ed.), *The psychology of written language* (pp. 217–235). New York: Wiley.

Duke, N. K. (2000). 3.6 minutes per day: The scarcity of informational texts in first grade. *Reading Research Quarterly, 35,* 202–224.

Dyson, H. A. (1993). *Social worlds of children learning to write in an urban primary school.* New York: Teachers College Press.

Dyson, H. A. (1995). Writing children: Reinventing the development of childhood literacy. *Written Communication, 12,* 4–46.

Dyson, H. A. (1999). Coach Bombay's kids learn to write: Children's appropriation of media material for school literacy. *Research in the Teaching of English, 33,* 367–402.

Dyson, H. A. (2000). On reframing children's words: The perils, promises, and pleasures of writing children. *Research in the Teaching of English, 34,* 352–367.

Dyson, H. A. (2002). Writing and children's symbolic repertoires: Development unhinged. In S. B. Neuman & D. K. Dickinson (Eds.), *Handbook of early literacy research* (pp. 127–141). New York: Guilford.

Emig, J. (1971). *The composing process of twelfth graders.* Urbana, IL: National Council of Teachers of English.

Englert, C. S. (1992). Writing instruction from a sociocultural perspective: The holistic, dialogic, and social enterprise of writing. *Journal of Learning Disabilities, 25,* 153–172.

Englert, C. S., Raphael, T. E., Anderson, L. M., Anthony, H. M., & Stevens, D. D. (1991). Making writing strategies and self-talk visible: Cognitive strategy instruction in writing in regular and special education classrooms. *American Educational Research Journal, 28*, 337–372.

Ferreiro, E. (1986). The interplay between information and assimilation in beginning literacy. In W. H. Teale & E. Sulzby (Eds.), *Emergent literacy: Writing and reading* (pp. 15–49). Norwood, NJ: Ablex.

Ferreiro, E. (1990). Literacy development: Psychogenesis. In Y. M. Goodman (Ed.), *How children construct literacy* (pp. 59–98). Newark, DE: International Reading Association.

Ferreiro, E., & Teberosky, A, (1982). *Literacy before schooling.* Exeter, NH: Heinemann.

Freedman, A. (1995). The what, where, when, why, and how of classroom genres. In J. Petraglia (Ed.), *Reconceiving writing, rethinking writing instruction* (pp. 121–144). Hillsdale, NJ: Lawrence Erlbaum Associates.

Freedman, A., & Medway, P. (Eds.). (1994). *Learning and teaching genre.* Portsmouth, NH: Boynton/Cook.

Freppon, P., McIntyre, E., & Dahl, K. (1995). A comparison of young children's writing products in skills-based and whole-language classrooms. *Reading Horizons, 36,* 151–165.

Gombert, J. E., & Fayol, M. (1992). Writing in preliterate children. *Learning and Instruction, 2,* 23–41.

Graham, S., & MacArthur, C. A. (1988). Improving learning disabled students' skills at revising essays produced on a word processor: Self-instructional strategy training. *Journal of Special Education, 22,* 133–152.

Graves, D. H. (1983). *Writing: Teachers and children at work.* Portsmouth, NH: Heinemann.

Harris, K. H., & Graham, S. (1992). Self-regulated strategy development: A part of the writing process. In M. Pressley, K. H. Harris, & J. T. Guthrie (Eds.), *Promoting academic competence and literacy in school* (pp. 277–309). San Diego, CA: Academic Press.

Harris, K. H., & Graham, S. (1996). *Making the writing process work: Strategies for composition and self-regulation.* Cambridge, MA: Brookline.

Hayes, J. R., & Flower, L. S. (1980). Identifying the organization of writing processes. In L. Gregg & E. R. Steinberg (Eds.), *Cognitive processes in writing* (pp. 3–30). Hillsdale, NJ: Lawrence Erlbaum Associates.

Hidi, S., & Boscolo, P. (2006). Motivation and writing. In C. MacArthur, S. Graham, & J. Fitzgerald (Eds.), *Handbook of writing research* (pp. 144–157). New York: Guilford.

Hidi, S., & Boscolo, P. (Eds.). (in press). *Writing and motivation.* Oxford, England: Elsevier.

Hillocks, G., Jr. (1986). *Research on written composition.* Urbana, IL: National Council on Rehabilitation Education.

Juel, C. (1988). Learning to read and write: A longitudinal study of 54 children from first to fourth grades. *Journal of Educational Psychology, 80,* 437–447.

Kamberelis, G. (1999). Genre development: Children writing stories, science reports and poems. *Research in the Teaching of English, 33,* 403–460.

Levin, I., Share, D. L., & Shatil, E. (1996). A qualitative–quantitative study of preschool writing: Its development and contribution to school literacy. In C. M. Levy & S. Ransdell (Eds.), *The science of writing* (pp. 271–293). Mahwah, NJ: Lawrence Erlbaum Associates.

MacArthur, C. A., Graham, S., & Harris, K. H. (2004). Insight from instructional research on revision with struggling writers. In L. Allal, L. Chanquoy, & P. Largy (Eds.), *Revision: Cognitive and instructional processes* (pp. 125–137). Dordrecht, the Netherlands: Kluwer.

Mason, L., & Boscolo, P. (2000). Writing and conceptual change. What changes? *Instructional Science, 28,* 199–226.

McCutchen, D. (1996). A capacity theory of writing: Working memory in composition. *Educational Psychology Review, 8,* 299–325.

McLane, J. B. (1990). Writing as a social process. In L. C. Moll (Ed.), *Vygotsky and education* (pp. 304–318). Cambridge, England: Cambridge University Press.

Miller, C. (1984). Genre as social action. *Quarterly Journal of Speech, 70,* 151–167.

Murray, D. (1985). *A writer teaches writing* (2nd ed.). Boston: Houghton Mifflin.

Nelson, N., & Kinneavy, J. L. (2003). Rhetoric. In J. Flood, D. Lapp, J. R. Squire, & J. M. Jensen (Eds.), *Handbook of research on teaching the English language arts* (2nd ed., pp. 786–798). Mahwah, NJ: Lawrence Erlbaum Associates.

Newkirk, T., & Tobin, L. (Eds.). (1994). *Taking stock: The writing process movement in the '90s.* Portsmouth, NH: Boynton/Cook.

Nolen, S. B. (2001). Constructing literacy in the kindergarten: Task structure, collaboration and motivation. *Cognition & Instruction, 19,* 95–142.

Nolen, S. B. (2007). The role of literate communities in the development of children's interest in writing. In S. Hidi & P. Boscolo (Eds.), *Writing and motivation* (pp. 241–255) Oxford, England: Elsevier.

Olson, D. R. (1977). From utterance to text: The bias of language in speech and writing. *Harvard Educational Review, 47,* 257–281.

Petraglia, J. (1999). Is there life after process: The role of social scientism in a changing discipline. In T. Kent (Ed.), *Post-process theory: Beyond the writing process paradigm* (pp. 49–64). Carbondale: Southern Illinois University Press.

Pontecorvo, C., & Zucchermaglio, C. (1990). A passage to literacy: Learning in a social context. In Y. M. Goodman (Ed.), *How children construct literacy* (pp. 59–98). Newark, DE: International Reading Association.

Raphael, T. E., & Englert, C. S. (1990). Reading and writing: Partners in constructing meaning. *The Reading Teacher, 43,* 388–400.

Riley, J., & Reedy, D. (2000). *Developing writing for different purposes: Teaching about genre in the early years.* London: Chapman.

Rohman, D. G. (1965). Pre-writing: The stage of discovery in the writing process. *College Composition and Communication, 16,* 106–112.

Russell, D. (1999). Activity theory and process approaches: Writing (power) in school and society. In T. Kent (Ed.), *Post-process theory: Beyond the writing process paradigm* (pp. 80–95). Carbondale: Southern Illinois University Press.

Scardamalia, M., Bereiter, C., & Fillion, B. (1981). *Writing for results: A sourcebook of consequential composing activities.* Toronto, Ontario, Canada: OISE Press.

Spivey, N. N. (1997). *The constructivist metaphor: Reading, writing, and the making of meaning.* San Diego, CA: Academic Press.

Stahl, S. A. (2002). Teaching phonics and phonological awareness. In S. B. Neuman & D. K. Dickinson (Eds.), *Handbook of early literacy research* (pp. 333–347). New York: Guilford.

Stanovich, K. E. (1994). Constructivism in reading education. *Journal of Special Education, 28,* 259–274.

Sulzby, E. (1985). Kindergarteners as writers and readers. In M. Farr (Ed.), *Advances in writing Research: Vol. 1. Children's early writing development* (pp. 127–199). Norwood, NJ: Ablex.

Sulzby, E. (1986). Writing and reading: Signs of oral and written language organization in the young child. In W. H. Teale & E. Sulzby (Eds.), *Emergent literacy: Writing and reading* (pp. 50–89). Norwood, NJ: Ablex.

Teale, W. H., & Martinez, M. G. (1989). Connecting writing: Fostering emergent literacy in kindergarten children. In J. A. Mason (Ed.), *Reading and writing connections* (pp. 177–198). Boston: Allyn & Bacon.

Tolchinsky Landsmann, L., & Levin, I. (1987). Writing in four to six year-old representation of semantic and phonological similarities and differences. *Journal of Child Language, 14,* 127–144.

Varble, M. E. (1990). Analysis of writing samples of students taught by teachers using whole language and traditional approaches. *The Journal of Educational Research, 83,* 245–251.

Vernon, S. A., & Ferreiro, E. (1999). Writing development: A neglected variable in the consideration of phonological awareness. *Harvard Educational Review, 69*(4), 395–415.

Williams, J. D. (1998). *Preparing to teach writing: Research, theory, and practice* (2nd ed.). Mahwah, NJ: Lawrence Erlbaum Associates.

Wong., B. Y., & Berninger, V. W. (2004). Cognitive processes of teachers in implementing composition research in elementary, middle, and high school classrooms. In B. S. Shulman, K. Apel, B. Ehren, E. R. Silliman, & A. Stone (Eds.), *Handbook of language and literacy development and disorders* (pp. 600–624). New York: Guilford.

CHAPTER 20

Writing in Secondary Schools

George Hillocks
University of Chicago

Composition is a relative newcomer to the school curriculum. It was preceded by grammar, rhetoric, and even literature. The oldest grammar, by Dionysios of Thrace, was produced more than 2,100 years ago and was antedated only by Euclid's book on geometry (Casson, 1985). This early grammar was a tool used to help decode the archaic words found in ancient texts. However, together with later Greek grammars, it became the foundation for Latin grammars of two premedieval grammarians, Donatus and Priscian, whose works dominated school grammar study throughout the Middle Ages to the Renaissance. By the Middle Ages, grammar had gone far beyond the status of mere tool. It had become the foundation of all knowledge. The beginning point of education in the seven liberal arts was the word. Grammar became, for most of the Middle Ages, the chief subject of the trivium (grammar, rhetoric, and logic), which was key to the quadrivium. The *Oxford English Dictionary* explains that in the Middle Ages, grammar meant Latin grammar and was "often used as synonymous with learning in general, the knowledge peculiar to the learned class." Not only was grammar viewed as the "gateway" to all of knowledge, it was thought to "discipline the mind and the soul at the same time, honing the intellectual and spiritual abilities" that would enable reading and speaking "with discernment" (Huntsman, 1983, p. 59). In the 18th century, this idea of honing intellectual abilities seems to have been appropriated by the Scottish Common Sense philosophers who specialized in rhetoric and belles-lettres. By the end of the 19th century, according to Applebee (1974), "The pedagogical theory of mental discipline . . . held that the purpose of education was to exercise and train the mental faculties, in particular, the faculties of 'memory' and 'reason'" (p. 6). By the time that English grammar (rather than Latin) began to be accepted for use in schools, it too was justified in terms of its power to train the faculty of reason.

One result of that idea is that grammar has been seen as foundational to composition with the effect that nearly all middle and high school textbooks providing instruction in writing also provide instruction in grammar. The two are joined at the hip without any question. In what was a famous study in its day, Lynch and Evans's (1963) *High School English Textbooks: A Critical Examination* devotes about 200 pages to literature anthologies and 200 pages to grammar and composition books. The authors examine 54 textbooks for Grades 9 to 12 by every major publisher at the time. All the series examined bear copyright dates from 1949 to 1961. The space devoted to grammar, mechanics, and usage far exceeds the pages devoted to composition and rhetoric. For example, the Harcourt Brace Grade 12 volume that we know as Warriner includes 351 pages on grammar, usage, and mechanics but only 133 pages on composition and rhetoric.

Curiously, Lynch and Evans (1963) do not question the joining together of grammar and composition in a single text, nor do they question the disparity in the pages devoted to the two. Grammar had come to be seen as a prerequisite to writing. The knowledge taught about language is intended for student use in writing. For example, in the volumes examined by Lynch and Evans:

> Typical treatments [of the sentence include] definition of the sentence, explanatory comments, examples of basic sentence patterns, discussion of subject and predicate, exercises designed to practice or test "sentence sense" and coverage of additional matters relevant to the problem of distinguishing the sentence, as sentence, from all other units. (p. 261)

Most of the series have the purpose of "making the idea of the sentence and its essential components as simple and clear as possible for students who *will use the information in their writing*" (p. 268; italics added). The idea that grammar makes writing possible is an old one and appears to be responsible for what has been called a *building block theory of writing development*.

Bernard McCabe (1971) describes this theory as based on the assumption that: Compositions can be best described [as resulting]

> from combining elements that are hierarchical in character. Letters are linked together in strings to produce words; words, to produce sentences; sentences, to produce paragraphs; and paragraphs, to produce longer compositions.
>
> Acting on the basis of this conception, a teacher may read a set of papers and notice that some papers contain run-on sentences or sentence fragments. Despite the fact that the same papers contain many more well-formed sentences, the teacher may accept the few errors as evidence that the students "cannot write sentences." All work on superordinate structures in the hierarchy is then delayed while the class is taught a number of lessons dealing with "sentence sense." (p. 509)

McCabe goes on to explain that the same happens with paragraphs that teachers believe have failed to follow the rules for paragraph development so that when teachers spot paragraphs without topic sentences, they again delay instruction for several textbook lessons on proper paragraph development.

I suspect, however, that teachers do not proceed from an analysis of student writing to decide on the course of their teaching, but rather proceed automatically on the assumption that students must first learn to write correct sentences, then paragraphs, and then some sort of longer theme, which, more often than not, turns out to be a five-paragraph theme (the 5P). More on the 5P later.

This model of what composition is continues to hold sway. It explains why grammar is strongly associated with writing and why our textbooks on writing devote so many more pages to grammar and usage than to rhetoric and writing. Interestingly, Lynch and Evans (1963) indicate that 32 of the 54 volumes they examine put activities for rhetoric, writing, listening, and speaking first in the text with material on grammar following. Only six volumes place the grammar handbook first, including all four of the Harcourt Brace volumes known as Warriner. Though it would appear that most publishers had attempted to de-emphasize grammar and usage by positioning it last, the Harcourt Brace series by John Warriner that places grammar first is thought to be the best-selling textbook ever (Hillocks, 2002).

Furthermore, according to Braddock, Lloyd-Jones, and Schoer (1963), at the time of their review, "One of the most heavily investigated problems in the teaching of writing concerns the merits of formal grammar as an instructional aid" (p. 37). Finally, it is interesting to note that some schools continue to formulate their writing programs on the basis of the McCabe (1971) model outlined earlier. For example, teachers in Oregon talk of focusing on the paragraph in the 9th grade and moving to the 5P in the 10th grade and to more expansive writing later in the 11th and 12th grades. They indicate that the sentence would have been taught in the middle school, even though the middle school teachers in the same district were requiring full compositions that were not of the 5P variety (Hillocks, 2002).

Several other ideas about writing and what it is come to us from the 18th century. According to James Berlin (1984), "Eighteenth-century rhetoric was eventually modified at the end of the nineteenth century to become the dominant paradigm for composition instruction in American colleges of the twentieth century" (p. 9). Furthermore, Berlin says, "Nineteenth-century thinking in America was completely dominated by Campbell, Blair, and Whately" (p. 19), three 18th-century Scottish inventors of a new rhetoric that set out to be appropriate for the new science (of Newton) that placed observation rather than syllogistic reasoning at the heart of science.

In addition, they argued for the importance of the discourse types that have prevailed in American secondary schools. Berlin (1984) states, "Campbell is...among the first to argue for forms of discourse: exposition appealing to understanding; narration, description, and poetry to imagination; argumentation to reason; and persuasion to all of these, but especially to the emotions and the will" (pp. 7–8). "Rhetoric becomes concerned with adapting the message to the faculties of the audience" (p. 8). Blair's "basic assumption is that effective writing is learned through studying examples of effective writing" (p. 25), an assumption that continues to dominate instruction in secondary schools at the beginning of the 21st century.

Berlin (1984) argues that because this 18th-century rhetoric was in reaction against classical rhetoric that operated through deductive logic, the invention or discovery so important to classical rhetoric was dumped by Campbell and others:

> [They] relegat[ed] it to the new logic of science, the method of a particular discipline (most commonly the scientific).... Campbell had not specified how what had been discovered outside the composing process was to be used in the rhetorical act. Whately filled the gap by providing a new inventio of management to replace the classical inventio of discovery. (p. 29)

According to Berlin:

> Managerial invention [took] the shape of forms of discourse—description, narration, exposition, and persuasion. Rhetoric, it is asserted, cannot teach the discovery of the content of discourse, but it can teach students to manage it, once found, so that it appeals to the appropriate faculty. This new invention is thus made part of arrangement. Since language must be chosen to embody the content of thought, the study of diction and sentence structure becomes an abiding concern, both resting on eighteenth century theories of language. (p. 64)

Invention, as management, then, had the effect of divorcing instruction in writing from the examination of the content of writing so that writing courses come to be focused on the form that writing is to take rather than the content that will make it up.

From the colleges, these conceptions of writing migrated straight to the high school, where we also see emphasis on form, descriptions of the forms with models for study in the 18th-century discourse types of narration, description, exposition, and persuasion.

Indicating that the material on composition and rhetoric is "virtually the same in a majority of texts" (p. 312), Lynch and Evans (1963) provide a summary of instruction on the paragraph that illustrates the common focus on form. Lynch and Evans summarize instruction on paragraphs as including a definition of the paragraph as a "group of sentences developing a single topic...set off by indenting the first word"; a definition of a topic sentence as one that "tells the main idea of a paragraph"; exercises in identifying topic sentences in paragraphs provided and in the students' textbooks for history or science; exercises in selecting and writing appropriate topic sentences; a "presentation of 'kinds' of paragraphs—explanation, description, argumentation, and narration—involving use of topic sentences and actual writing of illustrative paragraphs"; a "list of transitional words and phrases with exercises in using them"; and a list of rules about what constitutes a good paragraph (pp. 312–313). The problem of invention as discovery, or how to find the ideas that will make up a paragraph, is entirely ignored in all of the series.

Lynch and Evans (1963) comment that "the core of the composition program" is "expository writing in the forms of paragraph and essay" (p. 323). They state, "The main strength of most textbooks with regard to instruction in the principles and techniques of composition lies in their treatment of the paragraph—and, we believe, appropriately so" (p. 326). However, they make no comments on the adequacy of the rules presented as governing paragraph form. We know from Richard Braddock's (1974) research that the rules presented provide an inappropriate analysis of the reality of paragraphs. (For example, in the corpus of 25 essays that Braddock examined, only 37% of the paragraphs contained the kind of sentences that the textbooks present as topic sentences. See p. 297.)

Lynch and Evans (1963) comment that "most series devote much space in each volume to such topics as 'Writing Effective Sentences,' 'Variety—The Spice of Sentence Life,' 'Metaphor Makes Meaning Vivid,'" (p. 332) and so forth. Furthermore, they state:

> From our point of view, these approaches to effective composition are directly opposed to that approach which regards composition as the *development of idea*. The textbooks exhort students to use the devices of effective composition in word and sentence, and they set exercises requiring students to use these devices. Thus composition becomes an exercise in using devices for effectiveness. But, in truth, "real" writers do not write in order to use the devices of effectiveness; they write to express ideas and in the process of expressing these ideas they come upon the need for specific words, all kinds of figures of speech, for sentence patterns that accurately reflect meaning and emphasis, etc. (p. 333; italics in original)

TEACHING WRITING IN THE SCHOOLS

Applebee (1981, 1984) studied writing in American secondary schools across a variety of subject matters, including English, foreign language, science, math, social science, business education, and special education. The study consisted of three parts: 309 observations of class sessions in two Midwestern high schools, a questionnaire study of a stratified random sample of 9th- and 11th-grade teachers in 196 schools, and case studies of students in the schools observed.

Although writing was a major presence in all subject matters, taking up "an average of 44% of the observed lesson time" (Applebee, 1981, p. 30), researchers found that:

> Students were spending only about 3% of their school time—in class or for homework—on writing of paragraph length or longer. On the other hand, students were engaged in a variety of related activities that involved writing but not composing: fill-in-the-blank exercises, worksheets requiring only short responses, translation from one language to another, and the like.
>
> Even in those contexts where students were being asked to write at some length, the writing often served merely as a vehicle to test knowledge of specific content, with the teacher functioning primarily as an examiner. (Applebee, 1984, p. 2)

For the most part, as Applebee (1984) explains:

> Even when students were asked to write an essay, the essays were treated as tests of previous learning. The task for the student was one of repeating information that had already been organized by the teacher or textbook, rather than of extending or integrating new learning for themselves. (p. 3)

The teacher tests do not test the ability to make an analysis but simply to regurgitate one. Applebee points out that the topics assigned are a good indication of this approach to writing: "In many cases students were asked to write on topics that were in a real sense impossible" (p. 3). He provides an example from social science that asks students to "describe the political, economic, social and cultural changes that Europe was going through at the time of the Reformation." Applebee comments, "Books could be written in response to such a question. It becomes a possible topic for school writing only because it serves to index bodies of previously presented information" (p. 4).

Applebee (1981) found that the teaching of writing involved little more than the making of assignments: "In the observational studies, the amount of time devoted to prewriting activities amounted to just over three minutes. That included everything from the time the teacher started introducing the topic until the first student began to write" (p. 74). He indicates that there were five common methods of teaching writing:

1. The "most popular technique of helping students get started was to have them begin their writing in class, so that they could ask questions about what was expected if they found themselves in difficulties" (p. 78).
2. The survey indicated that model pieces of writing were used in 29% of the classes as a means of "introducing new forms of writing" (p. 78).
3. "Brainstorming…was reported in use by some 3% of English teachers, and by no more than 14% in any of the other subject areas" (p. 80).
4. Just under 33% of teachers asked for more than a single draft.
5. "The major vehicle for writing instruction, in all subject matter areas, was the teacher's comments [on] and corrections of completed work. Errors in writing mechanics were the most common focus of these responses; comments concerned with the ideas the student was expressing were the least frequently reported" (pp. 90–91).

As we might expect, the textbooks appear to support these findings. Applebee (1984) examined three of the most popular of the textbooks in each of the subject areas studied. He found that:

> The writing experiences provided in high school textbooks are narrow and limiting, whether one examines the role of the activity within the learning process or the kind of writing task the student is being asked to undertake. …
>
> The types of activities suggested were also limited. Textbooks in all subjects seemed to be constructed around a base of exercises that required only minimal writing: fill-in-the-blank exercises, short answer responses, and the like. Some subjects—literature and the social sciences in particular—supplemented this base of restricted activity with more extensive writing tasks. (p. 35)

For example, one asks students to write their own blues song, presumably after they have read some in the literature text. Another suggests that students write a modern version of a story in which a character sells his soul to the devil. Though the writing tasks here are more extensive, the preparation is minimal, simply reading examples of the type.

Has the teaching of writing changed over the past 25 years or so? There has been no study comparable to that of Applebee (1981, 1984). However, Hillocks (2002) makes some comparisons possible. His goal was to determine the impact of state writing tests on the teaching of writing. He did not observe classes as Applebee did. Nor did he include teachers in disciplines other than English. He studied the impact of state assessments intensively in five states—Illinois, Kentucky, New York, Oregon, and Texas—through examination of state documents and other materials prepared to help students and schools do better on the tests and through interviews with more than 60 teachers and more than 20 administrators or supervisors in each state in six school districts.

Teachers and supervisors described their practices in considerable detail. In the 20 years between the Applebee (1981, 1984) and Hillocks (2002) studies, there appears to be considerable change in the teaching of writing. Whereas Applebee indicates that only 3% of the time spent on writing was devoted to work on pieces of a paragraph or more, nearly all teachers interviewed for the Hillocks study tell only about teaching multiparagraph compositions, even at the elementary level. If there are teachers insisting on short writing of a sentence or less, such a focus did not surface in the interviews. In many districts, the focus was on writing 5Ps, thus imposing a limit of sorts. But it is very clear that, as a result of the state assessments, students in Illinois, Kentucky, New York, Oregon, and Texas, and probably in all states that collect writing samples as part of their assessments, students are writing far more than they did 20 years ago.

Second, teachers in the Hillocks (2002) study indicate that they spend far more time in preparation for writing. Most claim to use strings of activities in preparing students to write. They claim to ask students to read and study several models of writing, analyze their characteristics in class, and brainstorm for ideas, all before writing. Interviews make it clear that such strings of activities take several class sessions.

Third, there is greater attention to audience, or, at least greater seeming attention to audience. Most of the state assessments use topics that allude to some audience (your principal, your senator, the mayor of your town, other students) and teachers use such allusions in their assignments. But what effect naming such audiences in assignments has is not at all clear.

Fourth, across the five states Hillocks (2002) examined, an average of 78 % of the language arts teachers interviewed used model pieces of writing or more abstract descriptions of the kinds of writing students were to do, nearly two and a half times the number Applebee (1981, 1984) found. Furthermore, in the national survey Applebee asked about instructional procedures that teachers felt were important. Only slightly more than 37% of English teachers mentioned brainstorming. Hillocks found that over five states, an average of slightly more than 71% mentioned using such activities as brainstorming as a prewriting activity. Applebee indicates that 26.4% of English teachers reported using class time for students to read each other's writing. Hillocks found that 65.8% report using peer response regularly.

On the other hand, across the states there was virtually no change in the uses of revision. Whereas Applebee (1981, 1984) found that 59.3% of English teachers thought that writing more than one draft was important in teaching, Hillocks (2002) found that an average of 60.4% talked about revising as an important instructional technique. However, the percentages differ widely by state. In Kentucky, with a portfolio assessment, the percentage of teachers emphasizing revision was 81 and in Oregon, with a 3-day, three-class-period assessment, 84% emphasized revision. The three other states with assessments calling for students to sit down and write in a single time period, the average percentage of teachers emphasizing revision was only 45.7, an indication of how the kind of test in state assessments influence teaching.

Despite these apparent advances, there is an underlying similarity in the way writing is taught during the two periods. In both periods, teachers and curriculum makers assume that the knowledge necessary for effective writing is general knowledge of a few principles that are applicable to all or most writing: knowing the form that the piece of writing is to take; brainstorming for ideas before writing; knowing that effective writing requires more than one draft, and so forth (see Smagorinsky & Smith, 1992, for a discussion of the problem of general vs. specific knowledge in learning to write).

What happened to grammar? We have seen that textbooks had a very heavy emphasis on grammar, but Applebee and his team (1981, 1984) make only passing reference to grammar, usually in connection with teachers' comments on compositions. Even in the chapter on writing instruction, there is no mention of grammar as a means of teaching writing. I suspect that Applebee made a decision to study actual writing and not grammatical exercises. In the late 1990s, when Hillocks (2002) conducted his study, he found that across the five states studied, only about 5% of teachers talked about grammar as the major focus of their instruction. However, more than 70% held it as a secondary focus. Thus, although there is a considerable focus on grammar, it does not appear to be so intense as formerly.

STUDIES OF WRITING PROCESSES

Following the recommendation of Braddock et al. (1963), researchers set out in the 1970s to find out what is involved in the act of writing. Researchers studied older and younger writers, problem writers and expert writers. Most of the early studies of process were concerned with what writers do during prewriting, what they do during pauses, their rate of writing, and what writers do when they stop. For most of the studies, researchers selected writers according to some criteria, gained their cooperation, and asked them to write, usually in the presence of an observer. Some used audiotaping or videotaping as subjects "composed aloud." One of the most well-known of these studies is Emig (1971), a study of the composing processes of eight 12th graders. She and other researchers found that prewriting times were relatively short, though shorter for weaker writers than for stronger (Stallard, 1974), running between a little over 1 and a little over 4 minutes. In some studies, researchers asked writers what they were thinking about during prewriting. Emig states that during prewriting, "Most of the elements that will appear in the piece are present" (p. 83). In most studies, researchers report that writers composed rapidly and suggest that the rapid composing is possible because the writers have the basic ideas in mind at the beginning, even though they do not follow the popular textbook advice to develop an outline.

Matsuhashi (1981) suggests that the writers have "years-long familiarity with a script for narratives of personal experience" (p. 129) and that when confronted with a task of writing about an experience, they can simply call on this script. She notes, however, that when it comes to writing prose that involves argument and explanation, the case is different, and students are often lost, perhaps because they lack scripts or schemata for generalizing and supporting assertions. Matsuhashi found significant differences for mean pause lengths for different types of discourse. Pauses prior to t-units (minimally terminable unit; Hunt, 1964) in generalizing were greater than pauses prior to t-units in persuading, which were greater than pauses prior to t-units in reporting, indicating decreasing complexity in decision making across these discourse types.

Another group of researchers, led by Graves (see 1980; see also Atwell, 1987) observed primary schoolchildren as they wrote in classrooms. A third group including Hayes and Flower (see 1980, e.g.; Hayes 2000) and Bereiter and Scardamalia (1987) provided much careful and insightful research on the cognitive aspects of writing.

All of these studies had the impact of bringing the notion of writing process to the forefront of thinking about how to teach writing and gave it a place in the writing curriculum. This was a very important change from what Applebee (1981, 1984) was finding in the schools at nearly the same time as these studies were being developed.

Another group of researchers in the 1960s and 1970s began to study the syntactic development of writers across grade levels. Hunt (1964) developed a standard measure to avoid the problems that had been endemic to using the sentence as a unit of measure called the t-unit, or minimally terminable unit—a main clause and all of its modifiers. (Endlessly compounded simple sentences might be very long but did not seem a good measure of mature syntax.) This was used in dozens of studies. The researchers discovered that as students became older, their mean t-unit length increased.

Mellon (1969) did one of the first studies of sentence combining, a procedure that asks students to combine simpler sentences to make longer sentences. Dozens of studies followed Mellon's. In some, the means of combination were cued and in others they were not. (See Strong, 1986, for examples of sentence combining.)

THE EVALUATION OF INSTRUCTION

Although Applebee (1981, 1984) does not report on systematic programs for improving writing, a number existed and were being or had been researched by 1981. Most of these entailed considerable time in preparing students for writing, though not, perhaps, for particular assignments. But they were used with the idea of affecting writing performance at some point. Indeed, they made use of pre- and posttests to determine how the program had affected student writing.

In 1986, Hillocks reviewed nearly 500 quasi-experimental studies of writing instruction conducted between 1963 and 1983 and selected those that met criteria for strong research design principles (Campbell & Stanley, 1966) in order to conduct a meta-analysis or research synthesis, which permits the comparison of results across studies (H. Cooper & Hedges, 1994). Traditional reviews of studies of instruction use a vote-tabulating method, showing merely how many studies favor one teaching approach over another. The problem is that a simple tabulation does not take into account either the size of the sample or the size of the differences between group gains in the individual studies. The research synthesis deals with both and also allows us to consider the variability of results.

To be included in the meta-analysis, the studies had to be studies of sustained instruction. Studies of the effects of certain conditions on one or two pieces of writing were not included, for example, Bridwell (1980), which examined the revisions made by high school students. Requirements for inclusion in the meta-analysis were use of a scale of writing quality; minimal control for teacher bias (if teachers did not teach all treatments, then at least two different teachers had to be included in both the experimental and control treatments); control for differences among students usually by administering both pre- and posttests to all students; "Compositions must have been scored under conditions which help to insure validity and reliability" (Hillocks, 1986, p. 109); and finally, results had to be reported in such manner that means and standard deviations for pre- and posttest measures could be extracted. The application of these criteria eliminated about 80% of the studies and resulted in the inclusion of 60 studies with a total of 73 experimental treatments.

The team of researchers coded the salient features of all experimental and control treatments along several dimensions: duration of study, level of study, mode of instruction, and focus of instruction. The duration of studies did not result in significant differences. The level of the study (elementary, high school, college) had no significant impact.

Both mode and focus of instruction revealed significant differences. Mode of instruction "refers to the role assumed by the classroom teacher, the kind and order of activities present, and the specificity and clarity of objectives and learning tasks." In contrast, focus refers to the dominant content of instruction, for example, sentence combining, grammar, or the study of model pieces of writing (Hillocks, 1986).

Because various studies use different scales for judging writing, it is necessary to compute standard scores for all control and experimental groups. These are the difference between the control- and the experimental-group gains, from pretest to posttest, divided by the pooled standard deviation for all groups' posttest scores. The results indicate by what proportion of standard deviation the experimental groups outperformed or underperformed the control groups in the same study. This result is called the effect size.

MODE OF INSTRUCTION

Coding on this dimension indicated four clear modes of instruction. In the first of these, the teacher dominates the classroom, presenting information in lecture and recitation and from textbooks, setting assignments, explaining objectives to students, outlining criteria for judging writing, and so forth. Nystrand with Gamoran, Kachur, and Prendergast (1997) observed 451 lessons (class periods) in 58 eighth-grade language arts classes and 54 ninth-grade English classes. Nystrand writes of the findings:

When teachers were not lecturing, students were mainly answering questions or engaged in seatwork. On average 85% of each class day in both eighth- and ninth-grade classes was devoted to a combination of lecture, question-and-answer recitation, and seatwork. Discussion and small-group work were rare. On average, discussion took 50 seconds per class in eighth grade and less than 15 seconds in grade 9; small-group work, which occupied about half a minute a day in eighth grade, took a bit more than two minutes a day in grade 9. (p. 42)

The essential feature of this mode is that teaching is presenting information. Hillocks (1986a) calls it *presentational*. It is sometimes referred to as a *transmissive* model of teaching and sometimes as teacher centered. It appears to be the kind of instruction that Applebee (1981, 1984) finds in schools.

The second mode of instruction, natural process, is quite different. Teachers in this mode encourage students to write on topics of their own choice, receive feedback from peers, and revise writing. Most of these make use of small, student-led discussion groups but avoid structured problem solving. Several of the studies examining this mode of instruction refer to Piaget and the idea that development precedes learning, that learning will occur as the child matures and pursues her or his own goals, an idea frequently referred to as student-centered instruction.

The third mode of instruction is individualized writing conferences between teacher and student. Generally, the studies do not explore the nature of the conferences. The major differentiating factor is that the teacher conferences with one student at a time outside the classroom, at least during some parts of a course.

Hillocks calls the fourth mode of instruction environmental because it places student, materials, activities, teacher, and learning task in balance. To be included in this category, a treatment had to stipulate the use of student-led small-group discussions focused on solving problems that involve specifically stated dimensions such as judging pieces of writing according to specific criteria and revising some or all of them according to suggestions generated through use of the criteria, or discussing materials in order to make an analysis or classification, or interpretation. Hillocks (1999) presents a long profile of an 11th-grade teacher using such teaching methods along with actual class discussion that meets the criteria for discussion set by Nystrand et al. (1997).

Students in the environmental groups (mean effect = .44) outperform those in the natural process groups (mean effect = .19) and those in individualized treatments (mean effect = .17). The progress by students in presentational groups is nearly nonexistent (mean effect = .02). Even when we examine gains from pretest to posttest for all 32 presentational treatments used in both experimental and control conditions, the progress (.18) is only one fourth that for environmental groups examined in the same way (.75).

FOCUS OF INSTRUCTION

Focus of instruction refers to the dominant content of instruction occurring prior to assignment and teacher response to the writing. In most experimental classroom studies, it is common to focus on teaching a particular content, such as grammar or model pieces of writing. In this meta-analysis, six foci were the subject of five or more studies each: grammar, study of model pieces of writing, sentence combining, the use of scales for judging and revising writing, inquiry, and freewriting.

Studies in the grammar category concentrate on teaching grammatical concepts from traditional school grammar (TSG), except in one case that made use of generative grammar. Grammatical concepts include such TSG concepts as parts of speech and parts and kinds of sentences, rather than prescriptions about items of usage, for example, the simple past tense of *see* or a double negative. The stated goal of such study is to understand how language works, a goal frequently assumed to be instrumental in learning to write.

The category labeled *models* includes studies of the effect of asking students to read and analyze finished pieces of writing or abstract representations (e. g., five blocks representing the 5P) to help students understand the characteristics of the kind of writing assigned. It is common in secondary schools (cf. Applebee 1981, 1984; Hillocks, 2002).

Sentence-combining treatments ask students to combine sets of usually prewritten sentences in certain ways (ee Strong, 1986, for a complete description of a variety of approaches to sentence combining). It focuses on the procedures of putting phrases, clauses, and sentences together in a variety of ways.

Studies in the scales category made use of criteria to help students judge and revise pieces of writing by others. In one such study, Sager (1972) taught fairly simple writing scales to sixth graders, which they used to rate pieces of writing by others not known to them. Following the ratings, they revised the low-rated pieces to meet higher level criteria.

Inquiry appears in several treatments and was operationally defined for this meta-analysis as focusing on sets of data and "activities designed to help students develop skills or strategies for dealing with the data in order to say or write something about it" (Hillocks, 1986a, p. 211). Inquiry is discussed at length or exemplified in several chapters of Hillocks (1995) and of McCann, Johannessen, Kahn, Smagorinsky, and Smith (2005).

Freewriting is a technique that asks students to write whatever they have on their minds in journals, which may remain inviolate, or as preparation for sharing ideas and experiences with others. This approach views freewriting as a means of helping students discover what they have to say and their own voices for saying it.

The results for focus of instruction indicate that the mean effect size for grammar is −.29, well below the impact of any other teaching focus. The negative finding results from the fact that students focused on TSG or generative grammar made only tiny gains that were not statistically significant whereas their counterparts in control groups made fairly substantial gains. The study of models results in gains (mean effect = .22) smaller than the average gain for all experimental treatments. Freewriting makes even less headway (mean effect = .16). The most powerful treatments are sentence combining (mean effect = .35), scales (mean effect = .36), and inquiry (mean effect = .56). It is interesting to note that all of these approaches are significantly stronger than teaching of TSG. It certainly upholds the 1963 conclusion of Braddock et al. that:

> In view of the widespread agreement of research studies based upon many types of students and teachers, the conclusion can be stated in strong and unqualified terms: the teaching of formal grammar has a negligible, or because it usually displaces some instruction and practice in actual composition, even a harmful effect on the improvement of writing. (pp. 37–38)

The treatments with the largest gains (sentence combining, scales, and inquiry) all focus on teaching procedural knowledge, knowledge of how to do things. Although freewriting engages students in procedures that they already know, it does not help students learn new, specifiable procedures. Both grammar and models focus on learning what Hillocks (1986b, 1995, 1999) calls declarative knowledge, knowledge of what, rather than knowledge of how.

For this review, few experimental or quasi-experimental studies turned up in searches of literature on secondary school writing. One confirms the findings of the meta-analysis. Yeh (1998) studied the teaching of argument to minority middle school students in two experimental groups and two comparison groups with a total of 110 students. All groups worked on writing argument and shared a book that involved issues (e.g., "throw[ing] toxic wastes into the ocean") and related information for debate. All students read the materials and were engaged in debate teams to make presentations to their classmates, after which they each wrote an essay on the issue, writing eight essays in the course of 10 weeks. All groups also pursued the writing process from prewriting to revision and final draft. In the experimental groups, students were taught explicitly how to use a "heuristic" for developing an argument based on Toulmin's (1958) model of argument. The comparison groups were encouraged to develop their ideas through the use of a web, "(concept map), with the opinion (main claim) in the middle and branches for an introduction, three supporting reasons and a conclusion" (Yeh, 1998, p. 62), which sounds suspiciously like a 5P.

The experimental group outperformed the comparison groups from pre- to posttests by a margin comparable to those in the inquiry group of the meta-analysis. If we disaggregate the data that Yeh (1998) presents (in Table 2), it is possible to calculate the experimental control effect size. The mean gain for the experimental group is .65, for the comparison group .11, with a pooled standard deviation of .73. Thus, the experimental control effect size is .74.

THE IMPACT OF WRITTEN COMMENT

There have been several studies of the impact of the assignment and many studies that attempt to discover the impact of teacher-written feedback on student writing. Applebee (1981) commented that "the major vehicle for writing instruction, in all subject matter areas, was the teacher's comments [on] and corrections of completed work" (p. 90). Hillocks (1986a) reviewed several studies of the impact of teacher comment at all levels from elementary school to college. He comments:

> The results of all these studies strongly suggest that teacher comment has little impact on student writing. None of the studies of teacher comment...show statistically significant differences in the quality of writing between experimental and control groups. Indeed, several show no pre-to-post gains for any groups, regardless of the type of comment. ...

> However, a comparison of the studies suggests that in most of them the comments by teachers are diffuse; they range over substance, development, organization, style, mechanics, and so forth. The variables examined have to do with negative versus positive, frequent versus infrequent, [or] marginal versus terminal. (p. 165)

For example, in one of these studies, Gee (1972) conducted an experiment with 139 high school juniors whom he divided into high-, middle-, and low-ability groups. One third of each group received praise, one third received negative criticism, and one third received no comment on each of four compositions written to topics assigned over a 4-week period. There was no particular instruction provided other than the assignments and the teacher feedback.

Students in the praise and criticism groups received five to eight comments on each paper. In the praise group, comments dealt with originality of ideas, thoroughly developed ideas, and good grammar. Papers in the criticism group were marked for spelling, usage, grammar, and organization. Suggestions for improvement were also provided and the papers were returned the following week just prior to writing the next essay. Students were asked to examine the papers to determine how they might improve the next.

Gee (1972) found no differences in the quality of the writing from the first to the fourth paper, but he did find that the groups wrote fewer t-units. The praised group wrote slightly under two fewer from the first to the last papers whereas the criticism and the no-comment groups wrote six and five fewer, respectively. He also found that the praised group had significantly more positive attitudes toward their writing than either of the other groups.

We can infer that the teacher's lack of comment or negative comment results in less enthusiasm for writing and, therefore, less writing.

Some researchers have examined the effects of comments for degree of change on revision. Beach (1979) examined the effects of evaluations between drafts on revisions. He used three groups of students randomly assigned to three conditions: no intervening comments, teacher rating and comment, and student evaluation of their own writing. Teacher ratings were made on a form that included five 5-point scales: focus, sequence, support, overall quality, and need-for-change. Students who evaluated their own writing used a form that paralleled the teacher form. The teacher evaluation group received significantly higher degree-of-change ratings and significantly higher quality ratings for support than either of the other groups.

Working with seventh- and eighth-grade students, Hillocks (1982) studied the interaction of instruction, teacher comment, and revision, and their effect on personal narrative writing. Three teachers used four classes each for the study, one each in one of four instructional patterns: (a) observational activities, assignment, teacher comment, revision; (b) observational activities, assignment, teacher comment, no revision; (c) assignment, teacher comment, revision; and (d) assignment, teacher comment, no revision. Observational activities engage students in observing objects, pictures, or even sounds; discussing them; and finally writing about them with the goal of becoming more specific and elaborate in providing rich detail in personal narratives (cf. Hillocks, 1995, for a description of activities).

Students in each of the 12 classes were randomly divided into two groups. One group received short comments consisting of at least one compliment and one or more brief suggestions for increasing specificity or focus. Cooperating teachers were asked to keep short comments to 10 or fewer words. The second group received long comments of one or more compliments and very specific suggestions for improvement.

The results of this experiment indicate that focused comments coupled with the assignment and revision produced a significant quality gain, as did the assignment-with-no-revision condition. However, the gain for students doing revision (1.57) was nearly twice that for students receiving comments but doing no revision (.89). Furthermore, analysis of covariance revealed a significant interaction between comment length and instructional pattern ($p < .009$). For students engaged in observational activities and writing, the gains for students receiving longer comments were greater—but not significantly. For students who did not engage in observational activities, however, longer comments were less effective than shorter comments. Indeed, for the classes doing the writing assignments only, the short comments were twice as effective as the long comments (1.12 vs. .55, $p < .02$).

The available research suggests that teaching only by written comment on compositions is generally ineffective. Later studies reveal why that is. Freedman's (1987) study of response to writing is one of the most important in terms of both breadth and depth. Freedman set out to examine the nature of response teachers make and the impact that response has on student writing. She does this by conducting a survey of 560 teachers nominated as successful teachers of writing by National Writing Project site directors, a survey of selected students of those teachers, and ethnographies of two skilled teachers of ninth-grade academic writing. She redefines response to writing to include teacher- and peer-written as well as oral response, not only to final products but to drafts in progress, and most important to the thinking that students do as they participate in discussion and generation of ideas in preparation for writing. The latter is not usually thought of as response to writing, but it may be the most important kind. The surveys and ethnographies illustrate and support three conditions for successful response to student writing: "Successful teachers...resist taking over the writing of their students"; they "communicate high expectations for all students"; and they provide plentiful help and support for students during the writing process (p. 160).

Sperling and Freedman (1987), in a case study of a student included in Freedman (1987), examine the question of why even very promising students misunderstand and or misconstrue a teachers' written comments even when a class engages in conferences, peer-group response , and whole-class discussion of responses. They examine the responses of a high-achieving ninth-grade girl to her teacher's comments on segments of text of a character study developed over several drafts. They categorize the teacher comments as either reflecting information made explicit by the teacher in class or not. In all of the student's drafts, many of the teacher's comments had no in-class referents. In every such case, the student's attempts at revision failed in some way. Sperling and Freedman report that the student has no problems processing the teacher's comments with in-class referents, about half of which are positive reinforcements and half indicate a need for revision. When the teacher compliments word choice or the use of detail, the student notes it and tries to produce more in the next piece of writing. When the student attempts to revise for comments suggesting changes, even when they have in-class referents, the student's attempts are often complicated by differences between the teacher's and student's values and knowledge. This study helps to explain the effectiveness of positive short, focused comments that are tied to ongoing instruction in Hillocks (1982).

Sperling (1990) provides an analysis of one teacher's conferences with students about their writing. She says that "participating in the explicit dialogue of teacher–student conversation, students collaborate in the often implicit act of acquiring and developing written language" (p. 282). She indicates that the conferences she examined had a range of purposes: "to plan future text, ...to clarify the teacher's written comments..., to give feedback on texts on which there were no written comments, ..." and "to cover concerns tangential ... to those above" (p. 289). Sperling presents an analysis of the number of units of discourse initiated by the focal students or teacher and completed by the students or teacher to show that the conferences are collaborations and represent a "context for dialogic learning to blossom" (p. 318). From what we have seen of the emphasis on form in the teaching of writing, it is easy to imagine that the conferences might focus primarily on form. However, every conference quoted in the study has a substantive focus. That is, they develop the potential content of the writing.

ASSESSMENTS OF WRITING

At a 1963 conference called "Research Designs and the Teaching of English," Paul Diederich of Educational Testing Services reported that he was particularly "wary of experiments in English composition when the reliability of grading the test essays may be assumed to be at the usual level of .5" (Diederich, 1964, p. 59). Later in the paper, he says that "reliability of a single essay in field studies is usually between .3 and .4" (p. 62). Furthermore, he states, "I honestly believe that almost all experiments concerning English composition that rely on essay grades have been conducted with tape measures printed on elastic" (p. 60). He goes on later in the paper to recommend that researchers use "objective tests" for "the initial equating of experimental and control groups," namely, "reading comprehension, vocabulary, and ability to detect common errors in standard written English" (p. 63). However, he points out that such tests could not be used as the final criterion measure because, as he says:

> If they were given at the beginning of an experiment, and if students understood that parallel forms of the same tests were to be given at the end as the criterion of their success, it would be difficult to get anyone to write anything during the experiment. (p. 66)

Godshalk, Swineford, and Coffman (1964), in a research monograph for the College Entrance Examination Board, make similar claims. But both Godshalk et al. and Diederich go on to discuss the possibilities for attaining higher reliabilities (i.e., .7) by taking time to train raters and provide practice in using rating scales.

By the 1970s, several researchers had developed different kinds of scales for assigning ratings to student writing with high reliability. C. Cooper (1977), for example, indicates that the scales he describes can attain reliability as high as .9. He claims that "since holistic evaluation can be as reliable as multiple-choice testing and since it is always more valid, it should have first claim on our attention when we need scores to rank-order a group of students" (p. 4). Some researchers see the drive for agreement as problematic in that it may obscure qualities that researchers and teachers need to attend to (Huot, 1990). But it is clear that the attainment of high reliability has ended the old reliance on multiple-choice testing.

Three kinds of scales have been used with high rater agreements in experimental studies and in large scale testing. One kind of scale is called holistic because it represents the quality of a piece of writing as a whole. It is usually guided by a scoring rubric listing criteria for assigning scores for each level of quality (see C. Cooper, 1977).

White (1985) argues that holistic ratings have the virtue of representing the piece as a whole as opposed to analyzing the parts in a reductionist way and that such scoring has "satisfied reasonable demands for both economy and reliability and ha[s] led the way to restoring the role of writing in testing" (p. 37) by allowing us to avoid the reductionism of multiple-choice tests. However, such scoring can only rank-order the writing in a given test, providing little specific information about the characteristics of a particular piece of writing.

More specific information can be provided by primary-trait scales (Lloyd-Jones, 1977). White (1985) suggests that holistic scales are "conceptually the same" as primary-trait scales, the difference being that the primary-trait scales define the criteria more explicitly in terms of specific aspects of writing. For example, it might allow scoring the use of specific imagery in narrative writing and exclude attention to mechanics, sentence structure, and spelling and other matters not relevant to specific imagery. As White points out, writing is so complicated that many teachers concentrate on the specific features of writing, one at a time, for example, the use of evidence in making a case or argument.

Most scales in state assessments are holistic. Few use primary-trait scales. Some use what are called analytic scales. These differ from holistic and primary-trait in asking raters to judge several important traits of the writing individually, usually on subscales. The Illinois State Board of Education (1994) uses an analytic scale with ratings for organization, elaboration, mechanics, and so forth. The paper score is the sum of ratings on the subscales.

WRITING AND THE NATIONAL ASSESSMENT OF EDUCATIONAL PROGRESS

For several decades, the major source of data indicating how well American students write has been the National Assessment of Educational Progress (NAEP), which tests writing every few years. It is a nationally representative sample survey of achievement in writing as determined by the extent to which students in Grades 4, 8, and 12 across the nation reach certain standards of achievement set by the "National Assessment Governing Board as part of its statutory responsibilities" (NAEP, 2002, p. xi). These tests purport to examine achievement in three kinds of writing: narrative, informative, and persuasive. Students receive writing tasks that are supposed to generate responses in each of these types. Eighth- and 12th-grade tasks for informative and persuasive writing in 2002 provide some sort of the material to which students are supposed to respond in 25 or 50 minutes. NAEP uses as many as 20 writing prompts at each grade level to test thousands of students. The 2002 NAEP Writing Report Card reports testing "approximately 276,000 students in 11,000 schools" (p. xii). Results presented in the Report Card are for the 25-minute samples.

For both the 1998 and 2002 assessments, the writing produced by students was scored by trained raters using a 6-point scale (Unsatisfactory, Insufficient, Uneven, Sufficient, Skillful, and Excellent) with the criteria for judgment differing somewhat by grade level.

The Nation's Report Card: Writing 2002 (NAEP, 2002) explains that the 1988 NAEP legislation created a National Assessment Governing Board whose specific directive was to develop a set of "appropriate student achievement levels" (p. 7). The standards were set by a "cross-section of educators and interested citizens" who were asked to "judge what students should know and be able to do relative to a body of content reflected in the NAEP assessment framework for writing" (p. 8). The three levels of achievement are basic, proficient and advanced.

It is possible to compare NAEP scores from 1998 to 2002 (although not from earlier years) and across various groupings of the data: geographical areas, states, type of community, students' eligibility for the reduced-price or free lunch program, ethnic group, and gender. NAEP (2002) indicates that both 8th and 12th grades show gains in the percentage of students scoring at the level of proficient or above from 1998 to 2002, with 8th grade moving from 27% to 31% and 12th graders moving from 22% to 24%. At the same time, the percentage of 12th graders scoring at basic or above dropped from 78 to 74, a significant change. Although American students need not meet high standards for support, elaboration, or precise language, only about one fourth of them score at the level of proficient.

IEA STUDIES OF WRITTEN COMPOSITION

Gorman, Purves, and Degenhart (1988) and Purves (1992) describe the writing assessment conducted by the International Association for the Evaluation of Educational Achievement (IEA). Researchers developed a variety of writing tasks based on a model of school writing built to take "a balanced account of the three major factors that influence writing: (a) aims of writing including purpose and audience, (b) level of cognitive processing involved in writing, and (c) the content (topic) of writing" (Purves, 1992, p. 11). In order to examine writing curricula, writing tasks were limited to those that appeared to resonate with school curricula. Researchers selected nine tasks to be used with three different populations, elementary (ages 10–12), secondary (ages 15–17), and preuniversity (ages 17–19). The team collected three writing samples, each based on a different task, from each student. This sampling resulted in 43,563 students and 116,597 pieces of writing drawn from Chile, England, Finland, Hamburg, Hungary, Indonesia, Italy, Netherlands, New Zealand, Nigeria, Sweden, Thailand, and the United States.

Given that diversity, it was necessary to devise a scale that could be viewed as common for all participating countries and particular to each. These processes and the resulting scales are explained in detail in Gorman et al. (1988). Purves (1992) attributes variation in the scales and their use to differences in cultural norms. In addition, he reports that although "each system's scoring had its own integrity" (p. 129), the scoring from center to center was organized differently enough that "we cannot assert that the scores mean precisely the same thing across all situations" (p. 129), thereby rendering direct comparisons of achievement across countries impossible.

However, in a later study, Connor and Lauer (1988) rescored a sample of 150 persuasive compositions from three English-speaking countries including the United States. Their results indicate that American writers scored significantly lower than their counterparts in England and New Zealand. Indeed, the U.S. students fall over a full standard deviation below the English and over two thirds a standard deviation below the New Zealanders.

STATE WRITING ASSESSMENTS

In the 1980s, in the United States, certain states began the direct testing of writing, using samples of writing rather than objective tests. At present, nearly all but 2 or 3 of the 50 states require such writing exams. Though it is arguable that this nationwide testing has had a major impact on the teaching of writing across the country, little research has been conducted to examine its effect.

According to Hillocks (2002), nearly all state assessments require that students write on demand in a limited time period on prompts that provide minimal information. A few states require portfolios of writing, but they are not used as part of an assessment. Only in Kentucky is the portfolio score a major component in the formula for assessment of individual schools.

The NAEP tests of writing involve three kinds of writing at three levels of schooling. It should be no surprise that nearly all states do the same with slight variations. Nearly all announce that students at various levels should be prepared to write narrative, expository, or persuasive prose. Some add descriptive. Most offer no or only very shallow rationales for the choices. The Kentucky portfolio assessment is based on the theory of discourse advanced by Britton, Burgess, Martin, McLeod, and Rosen (1975). Writing for the portfolio must include several types of writing including literary (poems, stories, children's books, plays, etc.), personal (narratives, memoirs, etc.), transactional (arguments, proposals, historical pieces, research-focused papers, etc.), and a piece reflecting on the writer's views of his or her development as a writer or the specific papers in the portfolio or some other dimension of the writing. The result is that Kentucky students appear to have the richest writing experience of students in all states.

Directors of state assessments in Illinois, Oregon, and Texas say that they cannot hold students responsible for content, that is, specific knowledge. The result is that the prompts are general (a Texas prompt: Should students be forced to do 1 year of public-service work after graduation from high school?) and compositions are scored according to very general criteria. For example, for persuasive writing in Texas and Illinois, scoring guides contain sample papers at all tested grade levels and at all levels of evaluation, providing a scoring rubric for teacher use in guiding instruction. Hillocks argues that the benchmark papers and commentary used to illustrate and explicate the rubric, reveal that nearly anything suffices for elaboration, that there is no method for evaluating what should count as evidence, that the rubrics ignore commonsense logic, that very low levels of writing suffice to pass the exam, and that even what states identify as strong writing is quite weak (see Hillocks, 2002, for an analysis of the problem in Texas).

As though to ensure that students learn ineffective practices in writing, the states then recommend that the teachers use models from the scoring guides as examples, and most teachers say they use them. It is obvious that students are receiving a diet of poor writing that cannot provide appropriate nourishment for their growth as writers.

STUDIES OF ASSESSMENT RESULTS

A number of studies have been based on data collected in assessments, either on the scores attained or on the writing samples themselves. One group of studies has examined the various test score gaps in attempts to determine what the causes might be and whether they persist. Others have attempted to determine what factors might account for the quality ratings of holistic and primary trait scores.

Test Score Gaps

The assessments themselves and other researchers have identified three kinds of gaps between various segments of the general population: race and ethnicity, social class, and gender. These differences are substantial, on the order of a full standard deviation or more (Jencks & Phillips, 1998). Jencks and Phillips indicate that similar results hold for Hispanics and Native Americans.

The test score gap holds for writing as well. The NAEP Writing Report Card for 1998, for example, indicates that whereas only 10% of White eighth graders score at the lowest level of writing skill, 28% of Blacks and 31% of Hispanics do. Conversely, whereas 32% of White eighth graders score at the proficient level, only 8% of Black and 11% of Hispanic eighth graders do. Hedges and Nowell (1998) argue that, although the test score gap has narrowed, it remains large. In examining the data from NAEP writing tests from 1984 to 1994, they found that the differences between Blacks and Whites in writing ranged from .86 to .67 standard deviations. According to Cohen (1977), differences of .2 standard deviations are small, of .5, medium, and of .8 and over, large. By that criterion, the differences in writing scores are substantial. If we examine the NAEP results for 2002, the gaps appear to have remained large (for more information, see Table 3.3 of NAEP, 2002).

A second kind of gap appears in relation to variables that attempt to measure some aspect of socioeconomic status (SES). The NAEP uses three indices of SES: eligibility for free or reduced-price lunch, participation in Title I schools, and student-reported highest level of parent education. As one might expect, all three indices appear strongly related to how well students perform on the writing assessment.

Eighth graders and 12th graders not classified in the lower SES groups score at proficient or above nearly two and a half times as frequently as students in the lower groups. Even so, it seems remarkable that only 43% of 8th graders and only 32% of 12th graders who say their parents graduated from college, score at the level of proficient or above. If their reports are true, these students are likely to be in the highest income brackets, suggesting that a large proportion of our most advantaged students do not respond well to the writing assessment. The IEA studies indicate similar results for the countries included (Purves, 1992).

A third startling subgroup comparison is that between boys and girls. In NAEP writing assessment for 2002, 21% of eighth-grade boys scored at or above proficient, whereas twice as many girls scored at the same level, 42%. Results for 12th graders are similar, but the gap is greater: 14% of boys score at proficient or advanced whereas 33% of girls do. Purves (1992) in reporting the IEA results states that "there is a widespread gender bias favoring girls that cuts across languages, cultures, and stages of economic development" (p. 146). In 83 comparisons, girls' scores are superior to those of boys. Only in Hungary, among 17- to 19-year-olds, do boys have a significant advantage over girls in argument. But in every other kind of writing, Hungarian girls have a significant edge over the boys.

Hedges and Nowell (1995) studied gender differences in mental test scores including the NAEP writing test scores from 1960 to 1992. Across the areas of reading, mathematics, science, and writing, they examine the difference between boys' and girls' scores as effect sizes (the difference divided by the standard deviation of the population). They comment:

> Average sex differences were small [they cite the aforementioned Cohen criterion] except for writing, in which females performed substantially better than males in every year. Although average sex differences in mathematics and science have narrowed over time, differences in reading and writing scores have not. (p. 44)

They view this situation with alarm: "The large sex differences in writing ability suggested by the NAEP trend data are alarming…. The data imply that males are, on average, at a rather profound disadvantage in the performance of this basic skill" (p. 44).

I know of no studies that have examined the impact of all three indices of race/ethnicity, SES, and gender. But it is not difficult to guess that White female offspring of college graduates would have far and away the highest scores and that Black boys from poor families would trail far behind. It seems to me a problem that we ignore at our peril.

REFERENCES

Applebee, A. N. (1974). *Tradition and reform in the teaching of English: A history*. Urbana, IL: National Council of Teachers of English.

Applebee, A. N. (1981). *Writing in the secondary school: English in the content areas* (NCTE Research Report No. 21). Urbana, IL: National Council of Teachers of English.

Applebee, A. N. (1984). *Contexts for learning to write*. Norwood, NJ: Ablex.

Atwell, N. (1987). *In the middle: Writing, reading, and learning with adolescents*. Portsmouth, NH: Heinemann.

Beach, R. (1979). The effects of between—draft teacher evaluation versus student self-evaluation on high school students' revising of rough drafts. *Research in the Teaching of English, 13,* 111–119.

Bereiter, C., & Scardamalia, M. (1987). *The psychology of written composition*. Hillsdale, NJ: Lawrence Erlbaum Associates.

Berlin, J. (1984). *Writing instruction in nineteenth-century American colleges*. Carbondale: Southern Illinois University Press.

Braddock, R. (1974). The frequency and placement of topic sentences in expository prose. *Research in the Teaching of English, 8,* 287–302.

Braddock, R., Lloyd-Jones, R., & Schoer, L. (1963). *Research in written composition*. Urbana, IL: National Council of Teachers of English.

Bridwell, L. (1980). Revising strategies in twelfth-grade students' transactional writing. *Research in the Teaching of English, 14,* 197–222.

Britton, J. N., Burgess, T., Martin, N., McLeod, A., & Rosen, H. (1975). *The development of writing abilities.* London: Macmillan Education.

Campbell, D. T., & Stanley, J. C. (1966). *Experimental and quasi-experimental designs for research.* Boston: Houghton Mifflin.

Casson, L. (1985). Breakthrough at the first think tank. *Smithsonian, 16*(3), 158–168.

Cohen, J. (1977). Statistical power analysis for the behavioral sciences. New York: Academic Press.

Connor, U., & Lauer, J. (1988). Cross cultural variation in persuasive student writing. In A. C. Purves (Ed.), *Writing across languages and cultures: Issues in contrastive rhetoric* (pp. 138–159). Newbury Park, CA: Sage.

Cooper, C. (1977). Holistic evaluation of writing. In C. Cooper & L. Odell (Eds.), *Evaluating writing: Describing, measuring, judging* (pp. 3–32). Urbana, IL: National Council of Teachers of English.

Cooper, H., & Hedges, L. V. (Eds.). (1994). *The handbook of research synthesis.* Washington, DC: Brookings Institution Press.

Diederich, P. (1964). Problems and possibilities of research in the teaching of written composition. In D. H. Russell, E. J. Farrell, & M. J. Early (Eds.), *Research design and the teaching of English: Proceedings of the San Francisco conference* (pp. 52–73). Urbana, IL: National Council of Teachers of English.

Emig, J. (1971). *The composing processes of twelfth graders.* Urbana, IL: National Council of Teachers of English.

Freedman, S. W. (1987). *Response to student writing* (NCTE Research Report No. 23). Urbana, IL: National Council of Teachers of English.

Gee, T. C. (1972). Students' responses to teacher comments. *Research in the Teaching of English, 6,* 212–221.

Godshalk, F. I., Swineford, F., & Coffman, W. E. (1964). *The measurement of writing ability.* New York: College Entrance Examination Board.

Gorman, T. P., Purves, A. C., & Degenhart, R. E. (Eds.). (1988). *The international writing tasks and scoring scales: The international study of achievement in writing.* Oxford, England: Pergamon.

Hayes, J. R., & Flower, L. S. (1980). Identifying the organization of writing processes. In L. W. Gregg & E. R. Steinberg (Eds.), *Cognitive processes in writing* (pp. 3–30). Hillsdale, NJ: Lawrence Erlbaum Associates.

Hedges, L. V., & Nowell, A. (1995). Sex differences in mental test scores, variability, and numbers of high-scoring individuals. *Science, 269,* 41–45.

Hedges, L. V., & Nowell, A. (1998). Black–White test score convergence since 1965. In C. Jencks & M. Phillips (Eds.), *The Black–White test score gap* (pp. 149–181). Washington, DC: Brookings Institution Press.

Hillocks, G. (1982). The interaction of instruction, teacher comment, and revision in teaching the composing process. *Research in the Teaching of English, 16,* 261–278.

Hillocks, G., Jr. (1986a). *Research on written composition: New directions for teaching.* Urbana, IL: National Conference on Research in English/ERIC Clearinghouse on Reading and Communications Skills.

Hillocks, G., Jr. (1986b). The writer's knowledge: Theory, research and implications for practice. In A. Petrosky & D. Bartholomae (Eds.), *The teaching of writing: 85th Yearbook of the National Society for the Study of Education, Part II* (pp. 71–94). Chicago: National Society for the Study of Education.

Hillocks, G., Jr. (1995). *Teaching writing as reflective practice.* New York: Teachers College Press.

Hillocks, G., Jr. (1999). *Ways of thinking, ways of teaching.* New York: Teachers College Press.

Hillocks, G., Jr. (2002). *The testing trap: How state assessments of writing control learning.* New York: Teachers College Press.

Hunt, K. (1965). *Grammatical structures written at three grade levels* (NCTE Research Report No. 3). Urbana, IL: National Council of Teachers of English.

Huntsman, J. F. (1983). Grammar. In D. L. Wagner (Ed.), *The seven liberal arts in the Middle Ages* (pp. 58–95). Bloomington: Indiana University Press.

Huot, B. (1990). The literature of direct writing assessment: Major concerns and prevailing trends. *Review of Educational Research, 60,* 237–263.

Illinois State Board of Education. (1994). *Write on, Illinois!* Springfield, IL: Author.

Jencks, C., & Phillips, M. (1998). The Black–White test score gap: An introduction. In C. Jencks & M. Phillips (Eds.), *The Black–White test score gap* (pp. 1–52). Washington, DC: Brookings Institution Press.

Lloyd-Jones, R. (1977). Primary trait scoring. In C. Cooper & L. Odell (Eds.), *Evaluating writing: Describing, measuring, judging* (pp. 000–000).Urbana, IL: National Council of Teachers of English.

Lynch, J. J., & Evans, B. (1963). *High school English textbooks: A critical examination.* Boston: Little, Brown.

Matsuhashi, A. (1981). Pausing and planning: The tempo of written discourse production. *Research in the Teaching of English, 15,* 113–134.

McCabe, B. J. (1971). Traditions in composition teaching . In G. Hillocks, Jr., B. J. McCabe, & J. F. McCampbell (Eds.), *The dynamics of English instruction: Grades 7–12* (pp. 503–515). New York: Random House.

McCann, T., Johannessen, L., Kahn, E., Smagorinsky, P., & Smith, M. W. (2005). *Reflective teaching, reflective learning: How to develop critically engaged readers, writers, and speakers.* Portsmouth, NH: Heinemann.

Mellon, J. (1969). *Transformational sentence combining: A method for enhancing the development of fluency in English composition* (NCTE Research Report No. 10). Urbana, IL: National Council of Teachers of English.

Mischel, T. (1974). A case study of a twelfth grade writer. *Research in the Teaching of English, 8,* 303–314.

National Assessment of Educational Progress. (2002). *The nation's report card: Writing 2002.* Washington, DC: National Center for Education Statistics.

Nystrand, M., with Gamoran, A., Kachur, R., & Prendergast, C. (1997). *Opening dialogue: Understanding the dynamics of language and learning in the English classroom.* New York: Teachers College Press.

Pianko, S. H. (1979). A description of the composing processes of college freshman writers. *Research in the Teaching of English, 13,* 5–22.

Purves, A. C. (Ed.). (1992). *The IEA study of written composition: Education and performance in fourteen countries.* Oxford, England: Pergamon.

Sager, C. (1972). *Improving the quality of written composition through pupil use of rating scale.* Unpublished doctoral dissertation (Boston University, 1971), University Microfilms, Ann Arbor, MI.

Smagorinsky, P., & Smith, M. W. (1992). The nature of knowledge in composition and literary understanding: The question of specificity. *Review of Educational Research, 62,* 279–305.

Sperling, M. (1990). I want to talk to each of you: Collaboration and the teacher–student writing conference. *Research in the Teaching of English, 24,* 279–332.

Sperling, M., & Freedman, S. W. (1987). A good girl writes like a good girl: Written responses to student writing. *Written Communication, 9,* 343–369.

Stallard, C. K. (1974). An analysis of the writing behaviors of good student writers. *Research in the Teaching of English, 8,* 206–218.

Strong, W. (1986). *Creative approaches to sentence combining. Theory and research into practice book.* Urbana, IL: ERIC/National Council of Teachers of English.

Toulmin, S. E. (1958). *The uses of argument.* Cambridge, England: Cambridge University Press.

White, E. M. (1985). *Teaching and assessing writing.* San Francisco: Jossey-Bass.

Yeh, S. S. (1998). Empowering education: Teaching argumentative writing to cultural minority middle-school students. *Research in the Teaching of English, 33*(1), 49–83.

CHAPTER 21

Teaching of Writing in Higher Education

Richard H. Haswell
Hass Professor Emeritus, Texas A & M University, Corpus Christi

How do students keep learning to write in college? Before World War II, even before the mid-1960s, the question rarely attracted researchers, but since then investigations and methodologies have burgeoned. A survey of that research is the aim of this chapter. Perforce the chapter dwells mainly on U.S. studies, because in tertiary institutions elsewhere formal writing instruction hardly exists to be studied. In German, French, and British universities, and in universities of countries whose educational systems are patterned after them, courses in composition usually cease with secondary schooling. Therefore, to study writing in college doesn't "make sense," as one German professor put it (Foster, 2002, p. 192). In one sense, however, the mystery is even greater where direct instruction in writing skills is lacking, for how then are the skills acquired? The research interest in student writing deepens, moreover, the further institutions depart from the narrow entrance selectivity of the prestigious European institutions. Research into the connections between college writing and college teaching is fast making a respectable place for itself, for instance, in the provincial and urban universities of Great Britain, Canada, and Australia—and of course has long had a place in every country where university English is written as a second language.

This chapter focuses on tertiary instruction in writing of first-language English speakers, and the formal research into that instruction. By formal, it means any study whose method of investigation and data collection is systematic and exact enough that the study can be tested, replicated, and extended. The definition excludes a vast amount that has been written on the subject. Specifically the chapter does not cover rhetorical history; intuitive discussions of curriculum or of classroom practice; or philosophical, political, and theoretical analysis. The chapter also excludes several research areas covered by other chapters: argumentation, style and discourse analysis, composing and cognitive processes, evaluation and assessment, as well as issues of diversity, teacher education, faculty writing, and state of textbooks. There is now online bibliography of all this literature, including the formal research. For 1939–1999, see Haswell and Blalock (2005); for 1984–1999, see Conference on College Composition and Communication (2005); and for 2000–current, see Modern Language Association (2005).

So narrowed, the scope of this chapter covers formal research into college writing instruction and outcomes of the research. Historically, the research modes have tended to be nondistinctive and rather conservative. Historical trends have followed trends elsewhere in the social sciences. Roughly, the object of study has expanded from textual feature, to cognitive process, to social or cultural context, to embodied or material activity, and the research methodology has shifted from formalistic textual analysis, to behavioral experimentation, to naturalistic or hermeneutic studies. A synoptic history of postsecondary composition research is yet to be written (for an overview of the research methodologies, see Lauer & Asher, 1988). Theories supporting the research or aiding interpretation of its findings appear even more trendy. Kenneth Burke lost favor with the decline of semantic analysis in the 1960s, only to regain favor with cultural analysis in the 1990s. Taken as a whole, the research has an air of bricolage, with researchers taking up whatever methods, theories, and participants lie readily at hand. There are few large-scale research projects, few extended research lines, few replication studies, even few systematic reviews of research. Long-range studies such as Stormzand and O'Shea (1924) or Hunt (1970), which place college writing in the context of school and postgraduate data, have been largely replaced with a myriad of tightly focused studies, locally easier to interpret but difficult to synthesize and, as we see herein, perhaps construing the instructional enterprise of college composition more pessimistically than it deserves. Periodically, commendable efforts have been made to forge some meaningful patterns: Braddock, Lloyd-Jones, and Schoer (1963), Sherwin (1969), Hillocks (1986), Tate (1987), and Durst (2006).

This chapter's own humble attempt to impose some order maps college-writing research spatially by learning site or instructional space. The assumption is that in postsecondary institutions writing is performed and studied through a number of distinct settings, at once material and constructed. The focus is on seven sites: the composed paper, the classroom, the office conference, the computer, the writing center, the curriculum, and the institution. The spaces progress roughly from most context-stripped to most context-laden. They are not mutually exclusive. For instance, a student can conference at a writing center via e-mail with a peer tutor majoring in literary studies over a paper the student wrote for a teacher in nursing. But each site stands as a distinct spatialization, encouraging and constraining the conception and production of writing in different ways and accommodating to different procedures of formal investigation (Nagelhout & Rutz, 2004).

PAPER MARGINS

In the United States, often the earliest writing that students undertake for their postsecondary education serves for placement, usually machine-scored response to items associated with verbal skills, or sometimes a brief impromptu essay scored by a testing-firm employee or computer software. Such placement testing is a routine undertaking of around four fifths of colleges, unevenly successful, unevenly researched, and happily set aside by this chapter. Chapters 20 and 23 of this volume detail how evaluative procedures sometimes determine the kind of instructional writing space students first occupy in college—perhaps a remedial classroom or a writing center pod. In whatever instructional space students are placed, however, they will have their writing responded to once again, over and over in fact, with the intent to better their writing skills during the course. The course locus of paper commentary can be as constricted as a placement examination. The paper may be returned by a teacher to the student with only a grade, which aids learning as little as the College Board mailing the student an SAT verbal-proficiency percentile score. Composition teachers now universally condemn the grade-only comment, but what else they do varies. As we see herein, research shows that the narrow margins and narrower interlinear spaces of a student paper can expand to encompass a large and complex arena of writer–reader interaction (Anson, 1989).

Commentary on student writing has been much studied. An overriding question is whether the student paper can serve as a space where reader response may further writing improvement. Little gain in writing has been associated either with total absence of commentary (Sherwin, 1969, pp. 156–167) or with teacherless commentary such as automated grammar and style checkers (Brock, 1995). Unfortunately, it is time consuming for teachers to serve as rhetorical audience or writing coach rather than just as judge. Commenter time-on-task averages about 7 minutes a page. No wonder the history of instructional commentary on student writing is a restless trying of methods deemed more efficient: (in rough chronological order) using evaluation scales, using other students to respond, using a projector to evaluate student writing in class, relying on checklists, holding single or group conferences to respond, recording comments on audiotape, responding only to praiseworthy accomplishments, having students evaluate their own essays, attaching commentary to the student's digital text with word-processing footnotes or hypertext frames. Empirical comparisons support only a few methods over the others, and usually the advantage is minimal: using checklists, praising good effects rather than infelicities, making only task-specific points (for a review, see Sperling, 1998).

Part of the problem may be that teacher response is notoriously unreliable. Mitchell (1994), for instance, found that it took only 17 cross-campus faculty members, reading independently, to award a paper grades from B to F. Careful studies of teacher response have also found a surprising portion of error left unmarked or mislabeled (Connors & Lunsford, 1988) or of comments uninterpretable by the student (Cohen, 1987). A number of studies show teachers often think they are positively emphasizing important qualities such as reasoning and audience awareness whereas in fact the bulk of their commentary dwells negatively on syntax, word choice, and surface error. Finally, teacher response may be influenced by the student's handwriting, keyboarding, gender, attractiveness, ethnicity, personal background, status as student, and formality of syntax and diction—as well as by the teacher's own personality type, political leaning, academic field, employment status, and years teaching (Speck, 1998, provides excellent annotations of all this research).

It seems teachers operate from scores of messy and often idiosyncratic criterial sets, features ranging from punctuation to assigned-topic fit (Broad, 2003). To make matters worse, the students' evaluative sets may be quite different from the teachers'. For instance, students tend to interpret detail realistically, teachers emblematically and literarily; students prefer an oral style, teachers a professionally written style; students look on writing options as right or wrong or else as an endless shelf of choices with no way to choose, teachers as rhetorical options shaping the best strategy. In one eye-opening study of student and English-teacher reading predilections, students preferred the obvious and familiar, teachers the unusual and new; students overt meanings, teachers unstated; students explicit organization with headings, teachers implicit organization; students a bland tone, teachers an emotionally enhanced tone; students a high register, teachers a middle register (Newkirk, 1984).

In summary, the older textual research cast doubts that paper commentary will much help students move their writing forward. Recent studies of teacher commentary are more optimistic. They look closely at situational processes such as the revisions a student makes under the pressure of specific teacher comments as well as institutional processes such as the acquisition of disciplinary styles and conventions. These investigations picture a highly individual dynamic of resistance and acceptance, of misunderstanding and efforts to understand, as in Herrington's (1992) case study of a student complying with a teacher deletion at one point in her revisions and at another point sneaking the idea back in, to both maintain and reshape her academic identity.

Instructionally, the white space available for commentary on student papers may be much larger than it looks. That should not be surprising because teacher response fuses many interpersonal energies, the intricacies of a reader making sense of a text, the struggle of a mentor encouraging a sometimes resistant apprentice, the difficulties of two people trying to collaborate on a task, and, perhaps most basic of all, the uncertainties of two strangers sizing up one another within a social context.

CLASSROOM WALLS

That social context, of a teacher deciding what to do with a piece of student writing, almost always lodges within the more complex arena of the academic course, with its instructional syllabus and strategies, its peer students, and its material conditions of learning apparatus, walls, windows, seat arrangement, and so on. How does this lodgment further the learning of writing? One example of the research, though not exactly typical, gives a sense of the variety and restlessness of teaching practices that have characterized writing classrooms for decades. In 1974, four composition teachers tried responding to students with praise alone—to essays, reading logs, and classroom activities. They also gave students a choice from a variety pack of instructional techniques to meet course goals, including (listed alphabetically) gaming for decision making, group work, individualized writing projects, mastery-learning programs, peer-student teaching, role playing, sensitivity exercises, and simulations. They report that students grew in self-concept whereas their essays grew in length and cohesion (Goodman, 1975). Though eccentric in course plan and questionable in research design, the study illustrates the classroom habitus that has distinguished U.S. writing courses for decades: the experimentation with teaching techniques, the anxiety over improvement during the course, the wavering between writer attitude or writing performance as a measure of that improvement, and the recognition that many factors, social and psychological as well as cognitive and situational, constrain classroom interventions (Connors, 1997; Russell, 2002, cover the 19th- and 20th-century history of college composition practices).

As ethnomethodological research has shown, the actual ecology contained within the four walls of a writing classroom may surprise teachers, even those long dwelling there. Classroom patterns in student discussion follow ethnic, gender, class, and age lines, yet sometimes it is the silent student who is most comfortable and remembers the most. The whispering in the back row is more often in response to teacher-initiated points than teachers think (Brooke, 1987), yet teachers also imagine that their own talk takes up less of the hour than it really does, that the wait time they allow between their question and any answer is much longer than it really is, and that their questions are polite and open-ended when students readily interpret them as content-directive, authoritative, and middle class (Wootton-Don, 2000).

Can activites within the writing classroom foster writing improvement? Ironically, skepticism runs most strongly within the community of composition teachers and researchers themselves. They argue that the most important writing skills are the most difficult to quantify (e.g., awareness of reader, or recognition of conflicting validity claims), and that measurable traits of writing, such as syntactic features, mature so slowly in writers that their growth may not record between the start and end of an academic course. They note that change in writing skill may be episodic during the course, or worse that most student performance on a sequence of writing tasks will show periodic regression (Hayes, Hatch, & Silk, 2000). They also point to a chain of research that investigated but found no statistically significant improvement during writing courses. In consequence, pre–post gain studies have dwindled in composition studies since the 1980s (Haswell, 2005b). But that is only in straight-composition courses. Elsewhere across campus, teachers usually take the reasonable position that if good writing can be graded it can be measured, and that a course teaching good writing along with content might be expected to document better writing at the end of it. Outside English departments, in courses where writing is assigned and novel teaching strategies are applied, studies comparing early-course and late-course writing are still common (Bazerman et al., 2005).

Particular strategies for teaching writing at the tertiary level are normally shared across disciplines but not necessarily with the same enthusiasm. Table 21.1 inventories the teaching strategies of first-language writing classrooms as recorded in 2,373 data-based, teacher intervention studies. Strategies concerned with error, grammar, and sentence structure are more studied in straight-composition courses than in content courses, whereas journal keeping and problem solving are relatively more often studied in content courses. Otherwise, the popularity of strategies is roughly the same. Table 21.1 looks only at strategies designed to improve writing, not at strategies in which writing is used to learn content. Write-to-learn methods have long been a staple of writing-across-the-curriculum

TABLE 21.1

Data-Based Studies of the 16 Most Common Writing Strategies in Tertiary Institutions Used in Writing Courses and in Content Courses (Exclusive of ESL Instruction)

Teaching Strategy	Writing Courses		Content Courses	
	N	Percent	N	Percent
Revising or drafting	348	16.7%	22	7.5%
Error correction or detection	263	12.6%	20	6.8%
Audience awareness	187	9.0%	16	5.5%
Collaboration, including coauthoring and group discussion	175	8.4%	22	7.5%
Grammar instruction	174	8.4%	7	2.4%
Peer evaluation	165	7.9%	32	10.9%
Editing or proofreading	164	7.9%	27	9.2%
Journal writing	135	6.5%	80	27.3%
Prewriting, including heuristics, outlining, and concept mapping	126	6.1%	14	4.8%
Sentence combining	85	4.1%	2	0.7%
Programmed, modular, or self-paced instruction (not computer-assisted)	50	2.4%	3	1.0%
Problem solving	49	2.4%	19	6.5%
Imitation of models	48	2.3%	4	1.4%
Freewriting	44	2.1%	7	2.4%
Workshopping	39	1.9%	7	2.4%
Talk-write	28	1.3%	11	3.6%
Total	2080	100.00%	293	99.90%

(WAC) programs, especially in mathematics, psychology, history, science, and literature courses (Klein, 1999).

Some of the strategies listed in Table 21.1 may seem of recent invention, but all in one form or another have long heritages. In the 19th century, peer evaluation was used in Commonwealth universities and freewriting methods in some U.S. schools. Truly contemporary methods, however, show up in a list not reported in Table 21.1, of less frequent methods that have been tried and tested: case method, paragraph reordering, synetics, simulation, role playing, visual aids, grade manipulation, no grade, no textbook, Gestalt therapy, musical analogy, pictorial analogy, error tracking, extracurricular experience, free topic choice, and a long kite tail of others. Nearly all of the more traditional methods have empirical support, in the sense that, at one time or another, they can show documented pre–post writing gain. The gain most often occurs when the classroom intervention is clear and concrete and when the measurement of writing accomplishment focuses analytically on traits associated with the teaching method. The meta-analysis of Hillocks (1986), which includes studies of school as well as postsecondary instruction, found a much larger effect size for the environmental mode of writing instruction—that is, for strategies with tightly defined writing objectives involving small-group tasks. Other teaching modes, ones stressing writing processes and individualized mastery learning, also recorded an overall positive effect size in skill during courses. Some strategies have quite strong research histories of instructional success at the tertiary level, such as sentence combining (Connors, 2000), writing to learn (Bangert-Drowns, Hurley, & Wilkinson, 2004), revising (Fitzgerald, 1992), and some kinds of collaboration (Speck, Johnson, Dice, & Heaton, 1999).

Other popular teaching strategies admit more ambivalent records of success. Use of grammar exercises to improve writing has an extended research history, much of it showing doubtful effect. Peer evaluation, although probably the most widespread addition to the teaching repertoire during the last 20 years, shows some unwelcome outcomes under close observation. When students critique one of their peer's papers, the actual revisions made may be superficial, only superior students may benefit, weak and minority students may feel stigmatized, group talk may be off task, and exclusivist small-group power structures may emerge (for reviews, see DiPardo & Freedman, 1988; Dochy, Segers, & Sluijsmans, 1999).

As a result, as we have seen with marginal commentary, there may be considerable miscommunication between the goals teachers and students bring to the classroom. Teachers may stress essay organization and writing to learn whereas students favor stylistic effects and the expression of personal meaning. Part of the problem is that as an instructional site, the classroom is not as closed-door as it may look. As can be seen in following sections, multiple connectors run in and out of the room, to the very different backgrounds and learning predilections of individual students, to other learning sites on campus, to other academic disciplines with quite different standards of written form and writing skills, to years of personal writing development both before and after college.

OFFICE CONFERENCE

When a teacher and a student move to the teacher's office, these kinds of classroom miscommunication are not automatically resolved. A scheduled tête-à-tête seems an opportunity for teacher and student to learn about one another's background and personal style, and often it does. Generally, research into the one-on-one office visit shows that one of its presumed benefits—the individualization of instruction—actually happens there. The privacy of the teacher's office brings in contextual factors that the classroom closes off with its agonistic and peer-pressured space. That office privacy, however, may also allow even more play to the interpersonal dynamics that sometimes thwart teacher–student understanding.

The privacy of the teacher's personal space might also be one reason the teacher conference has been so little researched—less than any of the other instructional sites chosen for this chapter. Yet the office conference bears the longest history of university writing-instruction practice. The one-on-one master–apprentice consultation goes back as far as writing can be construed as a profession. It is still institutionalized in the tutorial system at Oxford and Cambridge, where the student reads aloud an assigned paper in the rooms of the residential tutor, who then critiques it. Lerner (2005) identifies four shifts in U.S. conferencing practice, each motivated by historical jumps in student enrollments: from individual teacher-office visits in the 1880s, to "writing laboratories" supervised by tutor assistants in the 1930s, to individualized classroom instruction through worksheets or programmed learning in the 1950s, to writing center personnel and peer or group evaluation in the 1970s. The small body of formal investigation into conferencing has focused on the one-on-one teacher-office visit, which has remained current since the 19th century, and on the writing center tutorial (see later discussion).

Surveys of opinion show composition teachers naming individual conferencing as the most effective method of teaching, yet assigning the least amount of instructional time to it. Students also rate it highly and evaluate the courses that use it more highly than those that do not (Walker & Elias, 1987). Studies analyzing audiotape transcripts of teacher tutorial sessions find good things happening to student drafts: ideas promoted, intentions clarified, inauthentic arguments exposed, and obscurities clarified. Compared with classroom discussion, in conference talk, the student does take more control, interrupting the teacher more often, and the teacher does turn over more control, indulging in longer wait time to questions (Freedman & Katz, 1987). The general teacher impression that the office conference prompts kinds of learning untapped in classroom settings has some empirical backing.

The same transcripts, however, often expose problems of which the participants are largely unaware. Teachers can be oblivious to points the student is trying to make, students uncomprehending of the teacher's recommendations. Newkirk (1995) had teachers and students comment on the tapes of their conference, and uncovered the "cross purposes, the resistances, the concealed feelings and attitudes—the unsaid and unsayable" (p. 195) that underlie office efforts to get some mutual understanding, even of terminology as fundamental as *specifics*. As in peer-evaluation sessions, in teacher conferences, the weak, minority, and female writers often speak and learn the least. The low proportion of office-conference talk generally owned by students is a sign of another common problem—the way teachers preempt the conversation by setting the agenda and imposing their version of an ideal text on the student's draft (Mlynarczyk, 1996). Working teachers, even those who would be discouraged to hear how authoritative they are in audiotapes, are still convinced that one-on-one conferences do improve student writing in ways the classroom does not. The problem is documenting it. So far there are too few investigations yet to draw safe conclusions.

COMPUTER SPACE

For the teaching of writing in college, the digital revolution has meant rapid changes not only in writing tools, but in instructional space. In spring 1978, Briand presented a survey of the technology then available to help teach writing. All were located in traditional classrooms or language labs: filmstrips on grammar, slide presentations of writing techniques, overhead projection of student writing, electric typewriters hooked up to a TV screen to illustrate sentence structure, mastery learning packages on mainframe computers, and computer analysis of writing that locates surface errors and counts parts of speech (Briand, 1978). Today the list sounds as outdated as a museum of medieval armory and as claustrophobic. Our inventory would add interactive software networking students at workstations; e-mail, blogs, and Wiki pages accessible from classrooms, dorm rooms, and teachers' homes; battery-run laptops with wireless Internet and printer connections; and instant messaging transmitted on cell phones. The technological explosion has exploded, among other things, the traditional writing classroom.

During the years since Briand's (1978) talk, writing teachers have had a hard enough time keeping their traditional territory intact, but what about the researchers investigating their teaching? The question touches not only on the currency of the research, but on its methodology and interpretability as well. An obvious issue is the lag time between technological innovation, instructional use of it, formal study of it, and publication of the findings. Compared with investigators of print technology, some features of which have remained unchanged for centuries, computer researchers may well see the technology replaced before their findings are placed. Something of the rapid turnover in technology can be seen in the relatively quick responding dissertation: The general inquirer was first studied in 1967, machine scoring of essays in 1971, computer-assisted heuristics in 1979, word processing in 1980, e-mail in 1983, style checkers (WriteAid) in 1986, electronic bulletin boards in 1988, hypertext (NoteCard) in 1990, Usenet in 1992, chatrooms (Daedalus) in 1994, Listservs in 2000, Internet instructional software (WebCT) in 2001, instant messaging in 2003, and blogs in 2004. Inman (2002) studied the technological ecology of his classroom and counted 56 different kinds of electronic equipment in use while students were composing.

Technology often comes in rescue of itself, of course, and has shortened the publication delay with online research journals such as *Kairos* and *Across the Disciplines*. But what can't be delayed is the technology. By the time Labercane, Bright, and Hunsberger (1986) published their study of an "electronic letter writing project," which established pen pals between elementary students and preservice education majors and for which the letters were hand carried on floppy disks between the school and the college, true e-mail was in educational use. For a good historical sense of this relentless stream of instructional technology in college writing, see Hawisher, Selfe, Moran, and LeBlanc (1996). Inman (2002, chap. 2) fills in the decades before 1980.

The transitional nature of the technology allowed easy dismissal of findings that did not meet early hopes. Students revising with a line editor made restricted changes not affecting the overall quality of their essays; students often took longer to revise and had more difficulty reading whole-essay organization on a small screen than with pen and paper; written chatroom discussion sometimes encouraged expression of adolescent sexism and unreflective group consensus. In the 1980s, screen versus pen-and-paper studies interested researchers partly because the outcomes did not always favor the computer, but the approach became more and more questionable as it became harder to find college students who found writing by hand as natural as on a word processor. By the same token, rapid change in technology also have questioned early findings supporting computer use, such as increases in fluency, increases in number of revisions and arguments, lowering writing apprehension, and elevating positive attitudes toward writing (for interim reviews of the research, see Bordia, 1997; Hawisher, 1989). The most persistent effect across technological venues has been the benefits of voice recognition with learning-disabled students (Raskind & Higgins, 1995).

Around 1990, a mild crisis could be sensed among researchers involved with computers and college writing. There were calls to abandon studies of instructional gain and turn to descriptions of discourse practices, inside and outside the classroom. Susser (1998) documents a steady decline in number of articles on word processing during the 10 years after the peak of research interest in 1986, Haswell (2005a) a parallel decline in study of automated text-checkers, and probably the same fadlike pattern could be seen with other technologies such as Usenet and hypertext. But a second generation of technology researchers has not abandoned the classroom. Fruitful instructional writing research continues, following the direction that technology seems to be heading, away from the isolated typewriter toward a more dispersed and interconnected discourse context, embracing both social praxis and individual singularity. Findings can be surprising. McKee (2002) analyzed interviews with an affirmative-action discussion group and transcripts of their interinstitutional posts, and found that interracial flaming was sometimes an attempt to educate whereas other seemingly innocuous posts were more alienating. On study of a classroom asynchronous interchange, Yagelski (2000) found he had successfully pushed one female student toward critical reflection much more online than face to face.

Taking advantage of the capability of computers themselves to handle the output, for instance, to deal with voluminous keystroke data or with pausal data in think-aloud protocols, researchers have studied online expression of gender and ethnicity, underuse of system capabilities, digital coauthorship, Internet researching and plagiarism, access via class and race, peer evaluation in networked environments, and computer scoring of examinations and out-of-class essays in many disciplines (there is no comprehension literature review). Among other findings, research into computer practices shows how writing instruction, computerized or not, is wired to all instructional aspects of campus life.

WRITING CENTER INTERSECTIONS

One of the first instructional spaces literally wired was the writing center. It was a step in accord with the history of writing centers that they have written for themselves. Supposedly around 1975, the space changed residence conceptually, from clinic to center. To the first kind of site, remedial students were sentenced by their teachers for fix-up cures; and now to the second site, writers at all academic levels freely walk in for advice. These two sites, however, have co-occured for nearly a century. In 1943, Mallam described an operation at Iowa State College that more than once has been cited as an exemplar of the notorious clinic, where students were assigned to watch their errors being corrected. Yet the same year, and only 100 miles away at the State University of Iowa, Stanley described a system much in tune with contemporary center philosophy, where any student can freely drop in for help drafting papers.

The simple dichotomy of clinic and center belies the complexity of writing centers as learning sites. Even when the scrutiny is on the most characteristic practice of writing centers, the face to face or conference between one student and one tutor, the interaction is still highly diffused, at least in terms of institutional organization. The computer classroom has at least four interacting factors—the student, the teacher, the administrator, and the technology. The writing center adds a fifth factor, the tutor, and that more than doubles the possible interactions among constituents. What happens when one interposes a writing center tutor into the teacher–student dialogue—it is a much discussed interruption—or attaches an ancillary learning center course to the lecture teacher's classroom? Spatially, technology has further expanded writing centers by means of online autotutorials and tutor conferencing, grammar hotlines, and telecourses of all kinds (Hobson, 1998).

Perhaps because of this instructional diaspora, of all the learning sites discussed so far, writing centers are the most self- or site-conscious. The reasons are at once historical and political, and they influence the kind of research that writing centers have generated. All teaching of writing in college has long been represented as a subaltern role. The received axiom, with the tacit and contradictory force of ideology, has not changed one bit since the 19th century—that by entrance into college, the student should need no further instruction in writing. Those students who do—and the contradiction is such that most teachers believe that this applies to the majority—are taught by means that are conceptualized in terms of catch-up, remediation, or immaturity. Teachers of college writing then fall within the custodial or repair role. All the worse for the people working in writing centers, who deal with the left-outs of such instruction (for some of the history underpinning this view of writing center work, see Carino, 1995).

All this, it has to be emphasized, is representation with no necessary relationship to the actual bodies that meet in writing center work spaces, usually with benefit to one other. But representation as much as reality drives research into writing. It helps explain the scarcity of writing center research, a phenomenon much lamented and only recently marking a reverse of course (e.g., Pemberton & Kincaid, 2004). Most of the disciplinary conversation, heard in journals such as the *Writing Lab Newsletter* and the *Writing Center Journal*, is anecdotal, pragmatic, or theoretical. The representation also helps explain what methods of hard research have been popular. Half of it is descriptive of the site, as if the first order of business is still to establish the institutional location. Another third describes writing center practices, as if the second order of business is to defend its ways. Inquiry focused on educational impact, most often in the form of case studies and much less frequently in the form of follow-up studies, form only around one fifth of hard research into college writing centers (the most substantial bibliography is Murphy, Law, & Sherwood, 1996).

That fifth shows the center as intriguingly complex. Clark (1993), for instance, documents the confusion when a first-year writing program added a holistically scored portfolio exit examination, with writing center administrators caught short with a semester-end upsurge in traffic, tutors frustrated because their training had been in invention and the students were concerned with revision, and teachers unsure about what constituted legitimate tutor assistance. This study is unusual in that most research findings counter the image of writing center work as peripheral or mere damage control. Strong evidence has been found for growth in literacy skill with tutors as well as tutees, for improvement in attitude and self-concept of both, for success of peers as tutors, for the ability of e-mail tutoring to reduce apprehension of students who have been judged remedial, and for the benefit of ancillary or stretch courses taught within centers. For instance, Patthey-Chavez (1994) observed that tutors working as computer consultants were finely sensitive to degrees of expertise with opposite-sex student novices and commanded a linguistic virtuosity in manipulating register and voice of authority. The detailed transcription analysis of Thonus (2002) finds tutor–tutee interactions filled with small talk, shared laughter, friendly overlaps, and softening of directives, all correlating with the student's evaluation of successful learning. Rehabilitation of the writing center image may lie in the direction of more research into its unique space on campus.

CURRICULUM COMPARTMENTS

In a study long due for replication, Lange (1948) analyzed papers written by the same first-year students the same semester for different courses. Half of the students judged to be writing at a remedial level by their content-course papers were not so judged by their composition-course papers. The unhappy students said their content teacher should have warned them that their papers were going to be "read for English" (p. 197). The students were locating themselves in an instructional space much discussed since Lange, the conflicted arena of postsecondary curriculum.

Curriculum *is* a site, albeit multiple and highly constructed. Students *enter* academic programs, teachers instruct in their *fields*, and departments engage in *turf* wars over general-education courses. In terms of educational experience, however, in terms of concurrent, interdisciplinary writing expectations and practices, curriculum has not always been so conflicted for the student. Historically, three massive curricular shifts lie behind the present situation in U.S. institutions: the gradual 19th-century replacement of a homogenous liberal course-of-studies with departmentalized disciplinary programs, the rapid switch in the last two decades of the 19th century from writing instruction embedded in courses throughout the curriculum and throughout the 4 years to a general or straight composition course usually confined to the first year, and the diffuse 20th-century installment of general-education requirements to counter the specialization of the 19th-century shifts (see Russell, 2006, for a survey of historical studies of postsecondary composition). For typical college students today, the result is a 4-year tiptoe through an instructional minefield. Each new field of study seems to function out of a different epistemology requiring a different set of writing skills—unfamiliar composing processes, novel genres and tasks, shifting standards and expectations. The sense of alienation works both ways, of course. Both the student facing the unpredictable writing expectations of the next course and the English teacher teaching business writing to accounting majors have been likened to Moses exiled in Egypt, a "stranger in a strange land" (McCarthy, 1987; Robertson, 1981).

From the perspective of teachers, the problem is least tractable in the general, first-year writing course. General writing skills exist only in the abstract, yet how is a teacher then to respond—as a botanist, an accountant, a social worker? Discourse analysis of intellectual disciplines (chap. 35, this volume) shows that academic fields differ in the way they regulate every aspect of writing, from usage as minute as the function of the colon in titles to usage as pervasive as the way evidence is respected, gathered, and presented. Take hedging (much studied; e.g., Markkanen & Schroder, 1997). Typically, there is a paucity of it in first-year student writing. Should a teacher praise such certainty, following the style of political discourse; recommend more formal qualification, after the style of philosophical argumentation; recommend more hedging in the presentation of data, after the style of scientific reports; or recommend more in the claims, after the style of history and other humanities studies? The problem does not disappear after the first year, nor is it restricted to U.S. universities. Students at two British universities, hopping from program to module to course unit, were aware of what the researchers call *course switching*, after the linguistic concept of code-switching: "Everybody seems to want something different. It's very different to A levels, where we used dictated notes for essay writing" (Lea & Street, 1998, p. 164). Meanwhile their tutors struggled to explain the subtle strategies of disciplinary style with abstract terms such as *unity* and *structure*.

Students face other contradictions. Investigations comparing teachers in separate academic fields inevitably find differences—in gravity assigned to common errors, in weight put on writing-to-learn goals, in meaning attached to response terminology, in attention given to technical expertise, in relative importance attached to content or style; in genres and tasks assigned, in writing processes taught (science teachers are especially inclined to part-by-part composing), in response methods applied (social science teachers especially rely on grading scales), in paths of intellectual growth envisioned, and in importance ascribed to truthfulness, confidentiality, register, format, evidence, and authorial point of view (Anson, Schwiebert, & Williamson, 1993, is a good entry for this research). Studies of the plight of students make compelling and uncomfortable reading, from either side of the Atlantic. At London's Open University, environmental science students, not sure how professionals handle uncertainty in the data, attributed the uncertainty of their own data to the educational situation and wrote their environmental-impact statement as if their data and conclusions were certain (Pardoe, 2000). At Carnegie-Mellon University, some students in sociology just made up data for their survey reports (Nelson, 1990).

In the last three decades, these curricular problems in course switching, ungrounded criteria, and sliding standards have been the concern of several popular writing program initiatives, although all are less new than revitalized (see Russell, 2002). Interdisciplinary programs or learning communities link writing courses with content courses through shared assignments and sometimes team teaching. More ambitious, with institution-wide curricular reform and faculty retraining, WAC programs uncenter writing instruction from the English department and spread it across departments and academic years, often with upper division writing-intensive courses required in the major and writing-to-learn assignments added to courses all along the way. Writing-in-the-discipline (WiD) and service-learning programs further infuse the curriculum with discourse processes and standards attuned to real-world professional and workplace practices. Survey and validation studies of these programs—of which there are scores—uncover a wealth of problems and promise. The problems range from student confusion, to teacher resistance and administrative support, to program burnout (Yancey & Huot, 1997). The problems, however, seem largely outweighed by the benefits, but here the evidence is spotty. Faculty enthusiasm and communication across departments seem to increase. Beneath the surface disagreement over conventions and forms, sometimes a surprising concordance is found in the way different faculties appraise pieces of student writing (Smith, 2003). And there is fairly consistent evidence that the writing itself improves under new WAC, WiD, service-learning, or learning-community conditions (e.g., Harris & Schaible, 1997). Interdisciplinary linking of courses holds an especially strong but scant record.

These cross-disciplinary programs may represent the most productive advance in tertiary composition pedagogy during the last half century. The lesson seems to be that meeting new and conflicting standards and tasks within disciplinary fields is a natural step in the development of both students and their writing. Theoretically this curricular lesson might seem, then, to call for the abolition of the 1st-year straight composition course—another initiative that has been heard off and on for a century—but such a position needs confirmation from studies that look at student writing beyond the course, that is, within the institution at large, over the 4 institutional years, and beyond.

INSTITUTION PATHWAYS

How do students learn writing in college? It may be more accurate to ask how do they learn writing-in-college? While they are gaining study skills and becoming academically socialized, more fundamentally they are learning to negotiate the literacy practices of the place (Brodkey, 1987; Jones, Turner, & Street, 1999). Students are "at university" or "in college," and the idiomatic dropping of the article in the phrase, British or American, is telling. As thoroughly as they would be "at home" or "at work," they are embedded in the institution (*in* + *statuere*, situated in).

The postsecondary institution as a locus, its function *in loco parentis*, has been a primary factor of much research into the academic performance of students, but not much of it deals systematically with student writing. We know little about the ways that the compositional motives, choices, and processes of students are influenced by their extracurricular work, financial aid, living group, study environment, concurrent coursework, peer support outside of classes, continued involvement with family, and dozens of other dynamics of their academic surround. Only intriguing and unconnected scraps of information have emerged. Institutions with a humanities orientation may enhance the belief of seniors that their writing has improved (Astin, 1997). Institutions that students feel stress critical-thinking skills tend to require more writing instruction (Tsui, 2002). Those with strong policy statements against plagiarism experience less of it (Brown & Howell, 2001.

Most of the research into the interaction of institution and writing touches upon institutional factors only secondarily because it focuses on writing and group identities, most often on age, sexual orientation, social class, minority status, second-language status, and learning or personality styles. It is a rich area of research. Only a few repeated findings are summarized here because the topics are covered in other chapters. By college age, women as a group have lost most of the edge they held in writing performance over men during the school years, though they still do better in institutionalized rites of passage such as proficiency tests and writing-course grades. At the same time, they tend to grow resistant to academic ways they perceive as patriarchal or masculine, such as the formal research paper and mixed-sex collaborative assignments. Minority students find their writing abilities poorly appraised by item tests and feel silenced in a host of institutional situations where the majority can wield public discursive power, for instance, in class discussion, group work, and student publications. First-generation college students write as well as continuing-generation but take less well to college life and have a higher dropout rate. All these minority groups tend to be more apprehensive about writing, anxieties that steer them toward majors like engineering and business and away from others like journalism and sociology. Finally, from ethnographic studies, we know that the two writing groups most alienated by the tertiary institution are working-class students and older women—groups who find essayist literacy opaque, academic identity alien, and composing time and space at home hard to manage. Yet these are also students who discursively can operate inside institutional practices with unusual shrewdness, determination, and savoir-faire, if the teacher will only recognize it (e.g., Lillis, 2001).

The most pervasive effect that the postsecondary institution has on students may be the graduation requirement of total hours. Students have to pass, course by course, but they also have to last the 4 years. How does their writing fare under this extended pedagogical treatment? The question is understudied. Typically earlier investigations took a cross-sectional approach, comparing different academic levels at the same point in time, a research design that may have helped spread the false notion that student writing does not improve during college. Kitzhaber (1963) compared the writing of first-year and senior students as they responded to quite different academic tasks, and he recorded a decline in many text features when he may have been measuring just the importance that the students attributed to the assignment. But whenever cross-sectional studies are careful to match ability level and writing task, seniors outwrite first-year students in most essay traits. The largest gains are seen in maturity of vocabulary, logical organization, argumentative reasoning, composing strategies, and sophisticated kinds of syntax such as appositives and final free modification (Flowers, Osterlind, Pascarella, & Pierson, 2001; Haswell, 1991; Hunt, 1970).

Cross-sectional methodology is vulnerable to the charge that the growth it measures may be a sampling effect, merely reflecting the retention of better writers in college, yet its findings of gain in writing skill are supported by longitudinal studies. Haswell (2000), for instance, found that a random sample of juniors improved their placement essays from first to third year in eight of nine traits, including vocabulary, local cohesion, free modification, substantiation and elaboration of ideas, and establishment of logical boundaries. All told, it is perhaps the longitudinal case study that provides the most convincing evidence of undergraduate advance in conception and execution of institutional writing tasks. The changes often are eccentric, erratic, and marked by periods of quiescence and even backsliding, but students leap ahead when they decide on a major (Sternglass, 1998), develop a more realistic sense of authorship and academic voice (Haas, 1994), and discursively construct a more viable interface between private and public identities (Herrington & Curtis, 2000). Would there were many such studies.

And many more that would stretch the longitudinal measure through college into the years after college. With this reach, even case studies are rare, yet the potential for revisionary findings is good. Nelms (1992) ran across a woman who had been a participant in a case study of high school writing process some 20 years earlier. Since then she had graduated from college and law school and become a practicing lawyer who wrote with surety and detailed outlining, in no way like the person who in high school composed in one unplanned draft, or the person who, she said, was taught in college only to be insecure as a writer. Beaufort (1999) investigated four women writing in a job replacement center. When she asked three of them to comment on papers they had written in college and on their growth in writing, their judgment was mixed. They had learned to "show off" and follow the "weird agendas" of their teachers, and yet they also had learned to write about ideas, back them up, and thereby start acquiring a sense of authority.

Finally, postgraduate opinion surveys provide a similar retrospect over writing and the undergraduate years. The findings are sketchy, surprisingly positive, and not yet systematically reviewed, and therefore perhaps a fit place to end this chapter. Technical and professional employees often name their writing classes as the most useful courses they took as undergraduates, sometimes more useful than any disciplinary course. More generally yet even more consistently, across degrees and across a wide range of institutions, graduates name "writing effectively" as one of the top two or three most useful or most improved skills they acquired in college (usually along with "learning independently" and "solving problems"), beating out other skills connected, for instance, with science, the environment, and group cooperation (e.g., Krahn & Silzer, 1995). Postgraduation studies support what may be the central insight of this chapter's survey of the research, that the longer and the more contextual our view of college writing, the more positive a sense we seem to get of it.

REFERENCES

Anson, C. M. (Ed.). (1989). *Writing and response: Theory, practice, and research.* Urbana, IL: National Council of Teachers of English.

Anson, C. M., Schwiebert, J. E., & Williamson, M. M. (1993). *Writing across the curriculum: An annotated bibliography.* Westport, CT: Greenwood.

Astin, A. W. (1997). *What matters in college: Four critical years revisited* (2nd ed.). San Francisco: Jossey-Bass.

Bangert-Drowns, R., Hurley, M. M., & Wilkinson, B. (2004). The effects of school-based writing-to-learn interventions on academic achievement: A meta-analysis. *Review of Educational Research, 74,* 29–58.

Bazerman, C., Little, J., Chavkin, T., Fouquette, D., Bethel, L., & Garufis, J. (2005). *Writing across the curriculum.* West Lafayette, IN: Parlor.

Beaufort, A. (1999). *Writing in the real world: Making the transition from school to work.* New York: Teachers College Press.

Bordia, P. (1997). Face-to-face versus computer-mediated communication: A synthesis of the experimental literature. *Journal of Business Communication, 34*(1), 99–120.

Braddock, R. R., Lloyd-Jones, R., & Schoer, L. (1963). *Research in written composition.* Champaign, IL: National Council of Teachers of English.

Briand, P. L. (1978). *Technology in the teaching of composition.* Paper presented at the annual meeting of the Conference on College Composition and Communication, Denver, CO. (ERIC Document Reproduction Service No. ED162324)

Broad, B. (2003). *What we really value: Beyond rubrics in teaching and assessing writing.* Logan: Utah State University Press.

Brock, M. N. (1995). Computerised text analysis: Roots and research. *Computer Assisted Language Learning, 8*(2–3), 227–258.

Brodkey, L. (1987). *Academic writing as social practice*. Philadelphia: Temple University Press.

Brooke, R. (1987). Underlife and writing instruction. *College Composition and Communication, 38*(2), 141–153.

Brown, V. J., & Howell, M. E. (2001). The efficacy of policy statements on plagiarism: Do they change students' views? *Research in Higher Education, 42*(1), 103–118.

Carino, P. (1995). Early writing centers: Toward a history. *Writing Center Journal, 15*(2), 103–116.

Clark, I. L. (1993). Portfolio evaluation, collaboration, and writing centers. *College Composition and Communication, 44*(4), 515–524.

Cohen, A. D. (1987). Student processing of feedback on their compositions. In A. Wenden & J. Rubin (Eds.), *Learner strategies in language learning* (pp. 57–69). New York: Oxford University Press.

Conference on College Composition and Communication. (2005). *The CCCC bibliography of composition and rhetoric 1984–1999*. Retrieved May 30, 2006, from http://ibiblio.org/cccc/

Connors, R. J. (1997). *Composition-rhetoric: Backgrounds, theory, and pedagogy*. Pittsburgh, PA: University of Pittsburgh Press.

Connors, R. J. (2000). The erasure of the sentence. *College Composition and Communication, 52*(1), 96–128.

Connors, R. J., & Lunsford, A. A. (1988). Frequency of formal errors in current college writing, or Ma and Pa Kettle do research. *College Composition and Communication, 39*(4), 395–409.

DiPardo, A., & Freedman, S. W. (1988). Peer response groups in the writing classroom: Theoretic foundations and new directions. *Review of Educational Research, 58*(2), 119–149.

Dochy, F., Segers, M., & Sluijsmans, D. (1999). The use of self-, peer and co-assessment in higher education: A review. *Studies in Higher Education, 24*(3), 331–350.

Durst, R. K. (2006). Writing at the postsecondary level. In P. Smagorinsky (Ed.), *Research on composition: Multiple perspectives on two decades of change* (pp. 78–107). New York: Teachers College Press.

Fitzgerald, J. (1992). *Towards knowledge in writing: Illustrations from revision studies*. New York: Springer-Verlag.

Flowers, L., Osterlind, S., Pascarella, E., & Pierson, C. T. (2001). How much do students learn in college? Cross-sectional estimates using the College BASE. *Journal of Higher Education, 72*(5), 565–583.

Foster, D. (2002). Making the transition to university: Student writers in Germany. In D. Foster & D. R. Russell (Eds.), *Writing and learning in cross-national perspective: Transitions from secondary to higher education* (pp. 192–241). Mahwah, NJ: Lawrence Erlbaum Associates.

Freedman, S. W., & Katz, A. M. (1987). Pedagogical interaction during the composing process: The writing conference. In Matsuhashi (Ed.), *Writing in real time: Modelling production processes* (pp. 58–80). Norwood, NJ: Ablex.

Goodman, A. D. J. (1975). *Utilization of positive feedback in a classroom environment of acceptance to promote enhanced learner self-concept and improved written performance*. Unpublished doctoral dissertation, University of Michigan, Ann Arbor. (ERIC Document Reproduction Service No. ED120794)

Haas, C. (1994). Learning to read biology: One student's rhetorical development in college. *Written Communication, 11*(1), 43–84.

Harris, D. E., & Schaible, R. (1997). Writing across the curriculum can work. *Thought and Action, 13*(1), 31–40.

Haswell, R. H. (1991). *Gaining ground in college writing: Tales of development and interpretation*. Dallas, TX: Southern Methodist University Press.

Haswell, R. H. (2000). Documenting improvement in college writing: A longitudinal approach. *Written Communication, 17*(3), 307–352.

Haswell, R. H. (2005a). Automated text-checkers: A chronology and a bibliography of commentary. *Computers and Composition Online*. Retrieved May 30, 2006, from http://www.bgsu.edu/cconline/haswell/haswell.htm

Haswell, R. H. (2005b). NCTE/CCCC's recent war on scholarship. *Written Communication, 22*(2), 198–223.

Haswell, R. H., & Blalock, G. (2005). *CompPile: An ongoing inventory of publications in post-secondary composition, rhetoric, ESL, and technical writing, 1939–1999*. Retrieved May 30, 2006, from http://comppile.tamucc.edu/

Hawisher, G. E. (1989). Research and recommendations for computers and composition. In G. E. Hawisher & C. Selfe (Eds.), *Critical perspectives on computers and composition instruction* (pp. 44–69). New York: Teachers College Press.

Hawisher, G. E., Selfe, C. L., Moran, C., & LeBlanc, P. (1996). *Computers and the teaching of writing in American higher education, 1979–1994: A history*. Norwood, NJ: Ablex.

Hayes, J. R, Hatch, J. A., & Silk, C. M. (2000). Does holistic assessment predict writing performance? Estimating consistency of student performance on holistically scored writing assignments. *Written Communication, 17*(1), 3–26.

Herrington, A. J. (1992). Composing one's self in a discipline: Students' and teachers' negotiations. In M. Secor & D. Charney (Eds.), *Constructing rhetorical education* (pp. 91–115). Carbondale: Southern Illinois University Press.

Herrington, A. J., & Curtis, M. (2000). *Persons in process: Four stories of writing and personal development in college*. Urbana, IL: National Council of Teachers of English.

Hillocks, G., Jr. (1986). *Research on written composition: New directions for teaching*. Urbana, IL: National Conferences on Research in English.

Hobson, E. H. (Ed.). (1998). *Wiring the writing*. Logan: Utah State University Press.

Hunt, K. W. (1970). Syntactic maturity in school children and adults. *Monographs of the Society for Research in Child Development, 35*(1).

Inman, J. A. (2002). *Computers and writing: The cyborg era*. Mahwah, NJ: Lawrence Erlbaum Associates.

Jones, C., Turner, J., & Street, B. V. (Eds.). (1999). *Students writing in the university: Cultural and epistemological issues*. Amsterdam: John Benjamins.

Kitzhaber, A. R. (1963). *Themes, theories, and therapy: Teaching of writing in college*. New York: McGraw-Hill.

Klein, P. D. (1999). Reopening inquiry into cognitive processes in writing-to-learn. *Educational Psychology Review, 11*(3), 203–270.

Krahn, H., & Silzer, B. J. (1995). A study of exit surveys: The graduand survey at the University of Alberta. *College and University, 71*(1), 12–23.

Labercane, G. D., Bright, G. W., & Hunsberger, M. (1986). *Responses of prospective language arts teachers to an electronic letter writing project*. (ERIC Document Reproduction Service No. ED282209)

Lange, P. C. (1948). A sampling of composition errors of college freshmen in a course other than English. *Journal of Educational Research, 42*, 191–200.

Lauer, J. M., & Asher, J. W. (1988). *Composition research: Empirical designs*. New York: Oxford University Press.

Lea, M. R., & Street, B. V. (1998). Student writing in higher education: An academic literacies approach. *Studies in Higher Education, 23*(3), 157–172.

Lerner, N. (2005). The teacher–student writing conference and the desire for intimacy. *College Composition and Communication, 68*(2), 186–208.

Lillis, T. M. (2001). *Student writing: Access, regulation, desire*. London: Routledge.

Mallam, D. (1943). A writing clinic at Iowa State College. *School and Society, 57*, 51–53.

Markkanen, R., & Schroder, H. (Eds.). (1997). *Hedging and discourse: Approaches to the analysis of a pragmatic phenomenon in academic texts*. New York: de Gruyter.

McCarthy, L. P. (1987). A stranger in strange lands: A college student writing across the curriculum. *Research in the Teaching of English, 21*(3), 233–265.

McKee, Heidi. (2002). "YOUR VIEWS SHOWED TRUE IGNORANCE!!!": (Mis)communication in an online interracial discussion forum. *Computers and Composition, 19*(4), 411–434.

Mitchell, F. (1994). Is there a text in this grade? The implicit messages of comments on student writing. *Issues in Writing, 6*(2), 187–195.

Mlynarczyk, R. (1996). Finding Grandma's words: A case study in the art of revising. *Journal of Basic Writing, 15*(1), 3–22.

Modern Language Association. (2005). *MLA international bibliography*. Retrieved May 30, 2006, from http://edina.ac.uk/mla/

Murphy, C., Law, J., & Sherwood, S. (1996). *Writing centers: An annotated bibliography*. Westport, CT: Greenwood.

Nagelhout, E., & Rutz, C. (Eds.). (2004). *Classroom spaces and writing instruction*. Cresskill, NJ: Hampton.

Nelms, G. (1992). *An oral history of Janet Emig's case study subject "Lynn."* (ERIC Document Reproduction Service No. ED345277)

Nelson, J. (1990). This was an easy assignment: Examining how students interpret academic writing tasks. *Research in the Teaching of English, 24*(4), 362–398.

Newkirk, T. (1984). How students read student papers: An exploratory study. *Written Communication, 1*(3), 283–305.

Newkirk, T. (1995). The writing conference as performance. *Research in the Teaching of English, 29*(2), 193–215.

Pardoe, S. (2000). A question of attribution: The indeterminacy of "learning from experience." In M. R. Lea & B. Stierer (Eds.), *Student writing in higher education: New contexts* (pp. 125–146). London: Open University Press.

Patthey-Chavez, G. G. (1994). Producing the authoritative voice in a computer lab. *Text, 14*(1), 77–111.

Pemberton, M. A., & Kinkead, J. (Eds.). (2004). *The center will hold: Critical perspectives on writing center scholarship*. Logan: Utah State University Press.

Raskind, M. H., & Higgins, E. (1995). Effects of speech synthesis on the proofreading efficiency of postsecondary students with learning disabilities. *Learning Disability Quarterly, 18*(2), 141–158.

Robertson, L. R. (1981, July). *Stranger in a strange land, or stimulating faculty interest in writing across the curriculum*. Paper presented at the annual meeting of the Wyoming Conference on Freshman and Sophomore English, Laramie, WY. (ERIC Document Reproduction Service No. ED211996)

Russell, D. R. (2002). *Writing in the academic disciplines: A curricular history* (2nd ed.). Carbondale: Southern Illinois University Press.

Russell, D. R. (2006). Historical studies of composition. In P. Smagorinsky (Ed.), *Research on composition: Multiple perspectives on two decades of change* (pp. 243–276). New York: Teachers College Press.

Sherwin, J. S. (1969). *Four problems in teaching English: A critique of research.* Scranton, PA: International Textbook Company.

Smith, S. (2003). What is "good" technical communication? A comparison of the standards of writing and engineering students. *Technical Communication Quarterly, 12*(1), 7–24.

Speck, B. W. (1998). *Grading student writing: An annotated bibliography.* Westport, CT: Greenwood.

Speck, B. W., Johnson, T. R., Dice, C. P., & Heaton, L. B. (1999). *Collaborative writing: An annotated bibliography.* Westport, CT: Greenwood.

Sperling, M. (1998). Teachers as readers of students' writing. In N. Nelson & R. C. Calfee (Eds.), *The reading–writing connection* (pp. 131–152). Chicago: National Society for the Study of Writing.

Stanley, C. E. (1943). The game of waiting: A study in remedial English. *College English, 4*(7), 423–428.

Sternglass, M. S. (1998). *Time to know them: A longitudinal study of writing and learning at the college level.* Mahwah, NJ: Lawrence Erlbaum Associates.

Stormzand, M. J., & O'Shea, M. V. (1924). *How much English grammar?* Baltimore: Warwick & York.

Susser, B. (1998). The mysterious disappearance of word processing. *Computers and Composition, 15*(3), 347–372.

Tate, G. (Ed.). (1987). *Teaching composition: Twelve bibliographic essays.* Fort Worth: Texas Christian University Press.

Thonus, T. (2002). Tutor and student assessments of academic writing tutorials: What is "success"? *Assessing Writing, 8*(2), 110–135.

Tsui, L. (2002). Courses and instruction affecting critical thinking. *Research in Higher Education, 40*(2), 185–200.

Walker, C. P., & Elias, D. (1987). Writing conference talk: Factors associated with high- and low-rated writing conferences. *Research in the Teaching of English, 21*(3), 266–285.

Wootton-Don, L. (2000). *Authority discourse: An examination of one classroom's authority structure.* (ERIC Document Reproduction Service No. ED446031)

Yagelski, R. P. (2000). Synchronous networks for critical reflection: Using CMC in the preparation of secondary writing teachers. In S. Harrington, R. Rickly, & M. Day (Eds.), *The online writing classroom* (pp. 339–368). Cresskill, NJ: Hampton.

Yancey, K. B., & Huot, B. (Eds.). (1997). *Assessing writing across the curriculum: Diverse approaches and practices.* Greenwich, CT: Ablex.

CHAPTER 22

Teaching of Writing and Writing Teachers Through the Ages

Duane Roen
Maureen Daly Goggin
Arizona State University

Jennifer Clary-Lemon
University of Winnipeg

> It is a sign of the person who knows and of the one who does not know, that the former can teach, and therefore we think art more truly knowledge than experience is; for artists can teach, and people of mere experience cannot.

> —Aristotle (I.1, 367 BCE/1994)

For Aristotle, teachers are artists distinguishable from others "as being wiser not in virtue of being able to act, but of having the theory for themselves and knowing the causes" (I.1). Teachers, in other words, are those who *know* their knowing. Given this theoretical perspective, we ask: How do teachers come to know? Who teaches the teachers? Where and when do teachers learn? In this chapter, we explore these questions historically as they relate to rhetoric and writing teachers, sketching from antiquity through today some of the teacher mentors as well as programs and organizations designed to prepare such teachers.

ADVICE TO RHETORIC TEACHERS IN THE CLASSICAL PERIOD CIRCA 460 BCE TO 410 CE

Writing in a scribal tradition certainly existed in antiquity but it was not at the center of education. In ancient Greece, for example, logographers such as Isocrates wrote speeches for others to deliver in courts, at ceremonies, and at political assemblies. However, when we look at teachers of rhetoric of this period, we need to be careful to understand that they are more often theorizing rhetoric as spoken rather than written. Indeed, some rhetoricians, such as Plato, distrusted writing altogether (see Plato, ca. 370 BCE/1993). Nonetheless, it was on top of this existing tradition of rhetorical education that a writing education developed, and rhetoric as an area of study has remained a major component of writing pedagogy. Examining the ways Western rhetoricians of antiquity paid homage to their mentors allows us to imagine the kinds of advice these mentors may have dispensed and provides a window onto the multiple pedagogical traditions that then emerged in rhetoric.

Corax from the fifth-century Greek colony of Syracuse in Sicily was named by Aristotle, Cicero, and Quintilian as the first *master* teacher of rhetoric who, along with his student Tisias, was among the earliest to systematize the study of rhetoric (Conley, 1990; Enos, 1993, 2001; Katula & Murphy, 1995). Tisias also became a renowned teacher, with Gorgias numbering among his most famous pupils. One of Gorgias's students, Isocrates, outlines a philosophy of education in both "Against the Sophists" (390 BCE/2001a) and the *Antidosis* (353 BCE/2001b) that has the goal of developing ethical citizens whose civic actions are informed by practical wisdom. For Isocrates, rhetorical education was contingent on three major factors: natural talent, sustained practice, and direct instruction. As Isocrates writes in "Against the Sophists":

> The student must not only have the requisite aptitude but he must learn the different kinds of discourse and practice himself in their use; and the teacher, for his part, must so expound the principles of the art with the utmost possible exactness...and, for the rest, must in himself set such an example of oratory that the students who have taken form under his instruction and are able to a pattern after him will...show in their speaking a degree of grace and charm which is not found in others. (p. 74)

In short, one learned to create effective discourse through emulation and consistent practice in various contexts with teachers instructing students in principles of the art of rhetoric and by serving in the role of virtuous audience for students' rhetorical efforts (Bizzell & Herzberg, 2001).

Isocrates' competitor, Plato, also provides evidence of his own pedagogical practices and that of his mentor, Socrates, in dialogues such as the *Gorgias* (386 BCE/1952) and the *Phaedrus* (370 BCE/1993). For Plato, certain truth was the only proper goal of rhetoric, and teachers bore the heavy responsibility for training truth-seeking rhetors via dialectical encounters. Teaching meant engaging in, and thus modeling, patterns of questions to strive for the truth on any topic whatsoever. Of those who attended Plato's academy, Aristotle is perhaps the most widely recognized rhetorician and teacher. His *"Art" of Rhetoric* reads as a series of lectures that theorize rhetorical practice. In contrast to his mentor Plato—who debated whether rhetoric might even be defined as an art and insisted on a dialectical process—Aristotle defined rhetoric as an art of discovering available means of persuasion and dissertated at length on the topic. Of all the classical Western teachers of rhetoric now known to us, George Kennedy (1995) identifies Hermagoras as "the most influential Hellenistic teacher of rhetoric" (p. 67). Hermagoras is credited with inventing stasis theory in the second century BCE, a powerful four-stage heuristic designed to establish the grounds of an argument. His distinctive pedagogy, and that of the many who followed his lead, consisted of training students in stasis theory and coaching them in rhetorical practices.

Historians have long credited male teachers with systematizing the study and teaching of Hellenistic rhetoric; however, sifting through these master teachers' veiled references to pedagogical contributions recovers important women teachers of rhetoric in antiquity. For instance, Sappho, the great poet and teacher of women, was paid tribute to by Plato, Aristotle, and Strabo (Glenn, 1997). In a similar vein, Plato's Socrates in the *Symposium* (360 BCE/1892) turns to Diotima for instruction in matters of love, with love serving as a trope for rhetoric. Finally, Aspasia, who was known to and praised by Socrates, Plato, and Xenonphon, influenced succeeding generations of rhetoricians. Cicero, for instance, "uses Aspasia's lesson on induction as the center piece for his argument chapter" in *De Inventione* (Glenn, 1997, p. 43; see also Bizzell & Herzberg 2001). Thus, women rhetoricians in ancient Greece exerted powerful influences that had both immediate and long-term effects (Glenn, 1997; Ritchie & Ronald, 2001; Wertheimer, 1997).

Although Hellenistic rhetoric had long flowered in the Greek colonies of southern Italy, it entered Roman culture in the waning years of the first century BCE as Rome came to conquer those colonies (Enos, 1995). Several important figures for rhetorical education emerged at this time, most notably Cicero and Quintilian. Although Cicero was never a teacher in the strictest sense of that word—he served as a Roman orator, advocate, statesman, and rhetorician—his *De Inventione* (86 BCE/1976) and *On Oratory and Orators* (55 BCE/1986) offered clear pedagogical advice. In the former treatise, Cicero advocates as the cornerstone of rhetorical study the five canons of rhetoric: invention, arrangement, style, memory, and delivery. In his latter work, *On Oratory and Orators*, Cicero places rhetoric at the center of an education that requires broad humanistic learning. For Cicero, the ideal orator must learn "the acuteness of the logicians, the wisdom of the philosophers, the language almost of poetry, the memory of lawyers, the voice of tragedians, the gesture almost of the best actors" (I.xxviii, p. 37). Teachers, then, required a strong background in these many subjects, and imparted them through modeling and direct instruction. Indeed, his *On Oratory and Orators*, arranged as a dialogue between two principal participants Antonius and Crassus, functions as a model of eloquent rhetoric to serve teachers and students alike. Cicero's two works were central to rhetorical instruction well into the 19th century.

As influential as Cicero was on succeeding generations of rhetoric and writing teachers, "the *magnus opus* of rhetoric's paideutic tradition is Quintilian's *Instituio Oratoria*" (Fleming, 1998, p. 178). In his *Instituio Oratoria*, Quintilian (360 BCE/1968)—whom Bizzell and Herzberg (2001) name "the last greatest rhetorician of the classical period" (p. 38)— lays out a life-long program of education necessary for producing the good (Ro)man speaking well. In 12 books, Quintilian provides rhetorical pedagogy that covers cradle-to-grave. Quintilian advocated formal education in speaking Greek, and reading and writing Latin; as such, he was the first to provide an extended treatment of writing. In book X of his *Instituio Oratoria*, Quintilian promotes the importance of writing. He observes: "In writing are the roots, in writing are the foundations of eloquence; by writing resources are stored up, as it were, in a sacred repository, whence they may be drawn forth for sudden emergency or as circumstances require" (X.iii.2). Although learning rhetoric is a life-long project for Quintilian, he outlines formal schooling for the young—a practice he recommended over home schooling. The first stage of formal study was in grammar where students were to master "correctness, perspicuity, elegance, and standard spelling and punctuation" (Bizzell & Herzberg, 2001, p. 361) through various imitation exercises called *progymnasmata*. The second stage focused on rhetoric during which students would complete more advanced exercises in speaking and writing in preparation for writing and delivering their own speeches. Recitation was the preferred pedagogy of the day; teachers served as harsh judges ready to correct even minor infelicities, as documented in Linanius' Progymnasta. Quintilian challenged this pedagogical approach, arguing that teachers should inspire love of learning in their students. Furthermore, teachers should provide good models and teach the principles of the art of rhetoric, including the five canons, and the three genres of forensic, deliberative, and ceremonial rhetoric. Students also required broad learning in a variety of subjects. Above all, the ideal orator was the "good man speaking well." For Quintilian, both morals and rhetorical skill could, and should, be learned with the teacher playing a central role in that development.

Quintilian's pedagogy continued to influence future generations. For instance, Libanius' student Aphthonius left a *Progymnasmata* (fl. ca. 400) that became "a standard one in Byzantine schools, mainly (as later commentators tell us) because of its clear exposition and inclusion of sample versions for each exercise" (Conley 1990, p. 60).

ADVICE TO WRITING TEACHERS IN THE
MEDIEVAL PERIOD CIRCA 410 TO 1300

As Kennedy (1980) has noted, the medieval period of rhetoric can be trisected: From the 5th through the 8th centuries (the early medieval period), classical rhetoric persisted in monastic schools; from the 9th through the 12th centuries, Ciceronian rhetoric and the liberal arts predominated; and in the 13th and 14th centuries (the late medieval period), rhetoric focused on practical needs. These three periods yielded differing emphases and pedagogies, and it is during the latter part of the medieval period that the hegemony of the spoken word is displaced by that of the written word (Clanchy, 1988).

Widely considered the most popular textbook during the first half of the Middle Ages, Martianus Capella's *The Marriage of Philology and Mercury* (429/1977) included the seven liberal arts—the trivium (grammar, rhetoric, and dialectic) and the quadrivium (arithmetic, geometry, astronomy, and music) (Cordasco, 1976). The trivium, in the early part, was largely defined by classical rhetoricians and the great master teachers of antiquity.

One way to unearth medieval advice for teachers of writing is to examine what and how they taught. As Graves (1916) notes, the curriculum included the trivium (grammar, rhetoric, and dialectic), and students commonly studied practical texts such as official letters, legal documents, and forms. Teachers thus began to rely on models, and the kinds of speaking and writing attended to shifted. Because the church and the state required effective communication, three forms of rhetoric emerged in the late Middle Ages—letter writing (*ars dictaminis*), preaching (*ars praedicandi*), and poetics (*ars poetriae*) (Camargo, 1995; Morgan, 1996; J. J. Murphy, 1974). Teachers organized rhetorical education beginning with style (*elocutio*), followed by the study of arrangement (*dispositio*), and finally focusing on invention (*inventio*) (Woods, 1990). Common instructional methods included question-and-answer, dictation, memorization, and lecture (Graves, 1916). As Kennedy (1980) notes, the *progymnasmata* remained popular in the Middle Ages.

ADVICE TO WRITING TEACHERS IN THE RENAISSANCE CIRCA 1300 TO 1700

Pedagogical practices and concerns from antiquity through the Middle Ages reemerged, often with new twists, in the Renaissance. Teaching rhetoric in the Renaissance is said to have begun with Francesco Petrarcha (1304–1374), a scholar of the Italian Humanist movement. Humanism, the basis of a liberal arts education, produced scholars who approached the trivium of grammar, dialectic, and rhetoric in stark contrast to those of the high Middle Ages. Given the rise of grammar handbooks and teachers who were paid more to teach *grammatica speculativa*, speculative grammar, rather than literary grammar, in the 13th-century, prehumanist thought assumed that perfect spoken and written discourse would emerge out of perfect rules of grammar. This perspective changed with the advance of Italian humanism, which jettisoned grammar and a closed system of scholastic logic, returning to and emphasizing classical letters and literature of Cicero and Quintilian (Kimball, 1986). Furthermore, this model stressed stages of learning that coincided with students' ages and academic levels, and encouraged a close teacher–student mentor relationship.

As a result of the emphasis on such classical rhetoricians as Quintilian, the focus for teachers of rhetoric was again on the production of a good and moral citizen through classical learning, from the earliest age possible. Rhetoric teaching emerged, as J. J. Murphy (2001) asserts, in two places: English grammar schools and Jesuit colleges. Although some scholars, such as Agricola (1444–1485) sought to change the teacher–student relationship of Italian humanists by asserting that rhetoric may be "reduced to a teachable method" through textbook cases (Bizzell & Herzberg, 2001, p. 566), this idea remained relatively unpopular until the late 16th century. Desiderius Erasmus (1469–1536) was committed to the idea that teachers of grammar, rhetoric, and dialectic were obligated to improve the personalities and moral standards of the youth in their charge in order to produce upstanding citizens, and specifically citizens eloquent in Latin (J. J. Murphy, 2001). As a result, the beginning of the 16th century was marked by a shift that emphasized "*imitatio* as the principal method of learning" (p. 157), with Cicero, Quintilian, and Erasmus serving as the most popular Latin models. Yet these models as a basis of teaching and learning were challenged by Peter Ramus (1515–1572), who not only eschewed the logic of scholasticism, but also critiqued the humanists' dependence on antiquated texts and classical thought, producing works that attacked Aristotle, Quintilian, and Cicero (Bizzell & Herzberg, 2001). Ramus moved away from Petrarch's attachment to the Ciceronian ideal of perfect eloquence, effectively removing rhetoric from the epistemic realm held by philosophy and logic, and narrowly reducing rhetoric to the study of style.

ADVICE TO WRITING TEACHERS IN THE 18TH CENTURY

Eighteenth-century rhetoric teachers continued to be caught between the contradictory Humanist and Scholastic schools of thought. Classical rhetoric, primarily Ciceronian, heavily influenced rhetorics used in schools, as texts such as John Holmes' (1739) *The Art of Rhetoric Made Easy*, John Lawson's (1758/1972) *Lectures Concerning Oratory*, and John Ward's (1759/1969) *A System of Oratory* show. However, the classical model began to change for some rhetoric scholars, when both stylistic and elocutionary elements of the classical model received expanded treatment in texts such as John Stirling's (1733/1764) *A System of Rhetoric*, Thomas Gibbons' *Rhetoric; or, a View of Its Principal Tropes and Figures* (1767), James Burgh's (1761/1775) *The Art of Speaking*, and Thomas Sheridan's (1762/1968) *A Course of Lectures on Elocution*. These texts call attention to the divide that then occurred between oral rhetoric, the focus of elocutionary rhetorics, and more text-based rhetorics focusing primarily on style. This bifurcation shows up also in other influential rhetorics, for example, Joseph Priestly's (1777) *Course of Lectures on Oratory and Criticism*, Adam Smith's (1750/1985) *Lectures on Rhetoric and Belle Lettres*, and Hugh Blair's (1783/1965) *Lectures on Rhetoric and Belles Lettres*. The turn of attention to belles lettres extended the scope of rhetoric to other genres such as literature not previously treated within rhetoric, and placed the focus for some more squarely on reading and criticizing text-based rhetorics. For others, such as George Campbell's (1776) *The Philosophy of Rhetoric*, the focus was on theorizing the mind of the rhetor with an eye toward creating both oral and written discourse.

Thus, rhetoric teachers had to balance classicism and rationalism (Bizzell & Herzberg, 2001) in their teaching methods. Students studied both Latin and English texts, and engaged in language exercises that paid close attention to correctness in diction and usage as well as mechanics. Emphasis was also placed on students' conversational abilities (J. J. Murphy, 2001). However, by the end of the century, the belletristic tradition emerged, introducing a variety of literary texts for study within the rhetoric classroom and spawning new pedagogical practices that would find their fullest expression in the next century.

ADVICE TO WRITING TEACHERS IN THE 19TH CENTURY

Due to industrialization, an increasing middle class, a radical shift from an apprenticeship practice to a credentializing one for professions, and the proliferation of print media, teachers in North America and the British Isles were faced with new pressing demands for different kinds of literacy and with more students than ever before. As utility became a more important goal for teachers in this period, there was a gradual move away from the classical languages and toward national language (J. J. Murphy, 2001). Into this mix, English departments and the writing class were born in North America.

The 19th century saw the birth of separate intellectual disciplines and departments to disseminate disciplinary knowledge. For English departments, disciplinary knowledge narrowed to mean the study of literature (Goggin & Beatty, 2000). Hence, English teachers at all levels were trained almost exclusively in literary studies even though from elementary education through higher education the bulk of a teacher's responsibility would be in the teaching of writing. This situation had an enormous impact on the training of teachers of English well into the next century.

In conjunction, with print more widely available, there was a shift in rhetorical focus from oratory to the written word, although *elocutio*, delivery, remained popular (J. J. Murphy, 2001).

Teaching methods during this time ranged from classical-language exercises (translation from English to Latin, imitation, paraphrasing, correcting faulty mechanics), to lecture halls in which students took dictated notes from a professor (notes that often took the place of a text-book), and written examinations and themes (J. J. Murphy, 2001). During this time, more so than ever before, teachers gave thematic writing prompts, and for the first time, were faced with an abundance of student writing that required response. Most teacher response "was a matter of correction rather than appraisal, and more often than not it was oral" (J. J. Murphy, 2001, p. 188), due to the logistics of student–teacher ratios sometimes numbering as much as 200 to 1. Textbooks were greatly relied on when they could be afforded, often serving as surrogate master teachers.

As detailed by Berlin (1984), Connors (1997), N. Johnson (1991), and Kitzhaber (1953/1990), the 19th century witnessed an explosion of published work in rhetoric and the teaching of writing and speaking, although many continued to rely on works published a century ear-lier. Among the most influential were *Philosophy of Rhetoric* (Campbell, 1776/1963), *Lectures on Rhetoric and Belles-Lettres* (Blair, 1783/1965), and *Elements of Rhetoric* (Whately, 1828/1963). Campbell, who treated rhetoric more as a science, de-emphasized invention and emphasized adapting messages to audiences, especially to affect emotions. Blair, who saw rhetoric more as art, advocated instruction that focused on the study of effective writing, especially the styl-istic features of belletristic texts. Whately recommended that teachers encourage students to write about topics that interested them, and suggested composing processes that included revising and editing.

Other popular 19th-century texts included *English Composition and Rhetoric* (Bain, 1866), which drew connections between figures of speech and mental operations; *Grammar of Rhetoric and Polite Literature* (Jamieson, 1818), which emphasized belletristic taste; *Practical System of Rhetoric* (Newman, 1834), which advocated thinking critically about ideas; *Science of Rhetoric* (D. J. Hill, 1877), which drew connections between language and psychology; *Elements of the Art of Rhetoric* (Day, 1866), which focused on invention and content; *The Practical Elements of Rhetoric* (Genung, 1886), which highlighted invention and style; and *The Principles of Rhetoric* (A. S. Hill, 1895), which emphasized usage and style. Although classi-cal rhetoric informed some of these textbooks, others were heavily influenced by faculty psychology. For the latter, the "modes of discourse [were understood to]...correspond to mental faculties" (Bizzell & Herzberg, 2001, p. 12). Many of the rhetorical textbooks written in this period would go on to be the basis of writing instruction for the next hundred years (Kitzhaber, 1953/1990; J. J. Murphy, 2001). These publications are important because during the 19th century writing textbooks took on a radically new role, serving to train both teacher and student alike. For many teachers in the 19th and well into the 20th century, their only preparation for teaching writing came from these textbooks. And as this brief review of diverse textbooks suggests, such preparation led to widely divergent pedagogical practices. Despite their diverse approaches, however, 19th-century textbooks generally served as "repositories of what their authors (who in most cases were teachers) believed were the practices that would best help students, as whatever level of schooling, to inhabit the intel-lectual space in which they would learn to compose" (Carr, Carr, & Schultz, 2005, p. 150).

In the credentialing society that emerged in the 19th century, professional programs of study for teachers were born. The hallmark of these was the birth of the Normal school, a college focusing on the education of teachers. Hence, in elementary and secondary schools in the 19th century, as Schultz (1999) and Carr et al. (2005) describe in detail, teachers were influenced not only by the aforementioned college-level rhetorics, but also by more general educational theorists. For instance, the Swiss educational reformer Johann Heinrich Pestalozzi, who was influenced by Locke and Rousseau, argued that children should pur-sue their interests through activities and through the exploration of objects and events (Pestalozzi, 1801/1973). This child-centered approach to education meant that teachers felt free to encourage students to write about the activities and objects that interested them most, which included asking "students to compose text generated by their observation of real-life objects or their observation of the details in an illustration" (Carr et al., 2005, p. 188).

Schultz also notes that a handful of age-appropriate composition textbooks influenced many elementary and secondary teachers: Richard Green Parker's (1832) *Progressive Exercises in Composition*, Charles Morley's (1838) *A Practical Guide to Composition*, John Frost's (1839) *Easy Exercises in Composition*, Charles Northend's (1848) *Young Composers*, Amos R. Phippen's (1854) *Illustrated Composition Book*, and F. Brookfield's (1855) *First Book of Composition*.

The most influential books in 19th-century elementary schools, the six McGuffey's readers, which sold an estimated 122 million copies between 1836 and 1920, offered along with its readings questions to guide writing.

With the rise of teacher preparation and certificate programs in the 20th century, the paths elementary and secondary education teachers took toward learning their craft was vastly different from that of postsecondary teachers. Thus, we divide our treatment of the 20th century into two major sections, one focusing on elementary and secondary teachers, and the other on postsecondary education teachers.

ADVICE TO WRITING TEACHERS IN THE 20TH CENTURY: ELEMENTARY AND SECONDARY EDUCATION TEACHERS

As Robin Varnum (1986) has documented, perceived literacy crises have surfaced in the United States frequently since the middle of the 19th century. Usually the product of political, military, or economic threats, these perceived crises have led to public outcries for more effective teaching and more thorough preparation of teachers—especially at the secondary level. Among the most salient perceived crises are those that have coincided with the following moments in U.S. history: (a) the heavy influx of immigrants in the late 19th century, (b) World War I, (c) World War II, (d) the launch of Sputnik, (e) the Vietnam War, and (f) imported products, such as automobiles and electronics from Japan and Germany in the 1980s. Each of these external threats led to calls for greater attention to standard written and spoken English; and some of them led to legislation requiring that the language of instruction be English rather than the immigrant languages.

During the cold war, the launch of Soviet satellite Sputnik on October 4, 1957, led to the National Defense Education Act (NDEA) of 1958, which substantially increased funding for mathematics and science education in the United States. Shortly thereafter, *The National Interest and the Teaching of English* (Allen et al., 1961) successfully argued for additional NDEA funding to support the teaching of English, including writing. Much of that support appeared in the form of summer workshops and institutes. One of the most prominent programs in changing the teaching of writing in primary and secondary schools has been the National Writing Project (NWP), begun as the Bay Area Writing Project at the University of California–Berkeley in 1974. The NWP's mission is to improve the teaching of writing by developing and sustaining university-based writing projects. Through partnering university teachers with teachers in Grades K to 16 via in-service and workshop settings, the NWP currently exists as "the only national program that focuses on writing as a means to improve learning in America's schools" (NWP & Nagin, 2003, p. 5). As of the turn of this century, NWP had established 189 sites across all 50 states, Puerto Rico, and the U.S. Virgin Islands that conduct summer institutes serving more than 100,000 teachers of writing annually. Through professional-development networking opportunities, the NWP sought to change the perception of writing in American schools from relying on "back-to-basics" drills of grammar and mechanics to a real understanding of writing as an important, complex, process-oriented activity. For an in-depth and representative discussion on English teaching at the secondary level in the 1960s, see Squire and Applebee's (1968) *High School English Instruction Today: The National Study of High School English Programs*. Such a bleak picture is in stark contrast with today's NWP publications such as Winter and Robbins' (2005) *Writing Our Communities: Local Learning and Public Culture*, M. Smith and Juska's (2001) *The Whole Story: Teachers Talk about Portfolios*, or Robbins and Dyer's (2004) *Writing America: Classroom Literacy and Public Engagement*.

At about the same time that the NWP was taking root, the writing process moment emerged in the United States. Considered the major catalyst for the process movement, *The Composing Processes of Twelfth Graders* (Emig, 1971) led to a flurry of research activity and plethora of publications that provided ample guidance for teachers at all levels. In the 1970s and 1980s, National Council of Teachers of English's (NCTE's) journals *Language Arts, English Journal, English Education, College Composition and Communication,* and *Research in the Teaching of English* published numerous articles on composing processes that were thought to have a major impact on the teaching of writing, shifting the focus from product to process. For a more detailed treatment of the process movement, see Perl (1994). For an in-depth description of the transformation from product-driven to process-driven pedagogy, see Hairston (1982).

Examining some general secondary English methods books from the mid- and late 20th century suggests some ways in which writing has been valued, as well as the guidance that has been available to secondary teachers. For instance, J. N. Hook's popular *The Teaching of High School English* (1950), which consists of 16 chapters, includes no chapter on teaching writing even though it does include chapters on teaching students how to write sentences, how to punctuate, how to spell, and how to develop vocabulary. In his chapter "What Is a Teacher of English," Hook offers a list of secondary English teachers' "abilities and skills," which includes "skill in improving students' oral and written English. The negative approach—the mere elimination of errors—is inadequate. Students need to be helped to learn to use language effectively as a tool for the expression of organized thoughts" (p. 21).

A decade later Harvard education professor Edwin H. Sauer published *English in the Secondary School* (1961), which reflected the current knowledge of 1961. In his preface, Sauer notes, "I have tried to take proper cognizance of the new emphases in the teaching of English, and of course, the major of these is composition" (p. vi). In his chapter "Writing is for *All*: A Practical Program," Sauer advises teachers to teach writing to all students, not just the college bound, and he notes some mistaken notions: "Altogether too many of our teachers of English still have the scientifically fallacious notion that a great deal of reading or abundant drill work in grammar will produce effective writing" (p. 82).

Another decade later, Robert Parker, Jr., and Maxine Daly published *Teaching English in the Secondary School* (1973), which captures some of the widely held views of the day. For instance, the authors recommend that "the teacher should encourage a constant stream of imaginative personal writing, not worrying about how he will find the time to correct it" (p. 126). They add that from a "climate of encouragement, freedom, and experimentation, disciplined work emerges naturally" (pp. 126–127).

In the 1980s, Arthur N. Applebee collaborated with other scholars to conduct several major studies of writing in secondary schools: *Writing in the Secondary School* (1981) and *Contexts for Learning to Write* (1984). Although not effusive, Applebee (1981) does use the results to offer some explicit advice in his chapter "Improving the Teaching of Writing" in *Writing in the Secondary School:* that teachers should ask students to write frequently, that writing should "serve as a tool for learning rather than as a means to display acquired knowledge" (p. 101), that teachers should engage students in composing processes, and that teachers should foster "contexts in which writing serves…natural purposes" (p. 105). In addition, elementary and secondary teachers could find inspiration for teaching writing in such book-length publications as *Writing: Teachers and Children at Work* (D. H. Graves, 1983), *Lessons From a Child: On the Teaching and Learning of Writing* (Calkins, 1983), *The Art of Teaching Writing* (Calkins, 1986), and *In the Middle: Writing Reading and Learning With Adolescents* (Atwell, 1987). Other popular teacher preparation books followed with titles such as *Teaching Writing as Reflective Practice* (Hillocks, 1995), *Blending Genre, Altering Style* (Romano, 2000), and *In the Middle: Writing, Reading, and Learning With Adolescents* (Atwell, 1998).

For nearly four decades, the National Assessment of Educational Progress (NAEP) has studied 4th-, 8th-, and 12th-grade student achievement in many areas, including writing. In addition to examining what students know and what students can do, the NAEP publications have also noted what students *should* know and be able to do. Although guidance for writing teachers has varied from one report to another, each report has implicitly or explicitly recommended particular curricular and pedagogical advice. As Mary Kennedy notes in her major 1998 study of the preparation of writing teachers, "In the United States in the 1980s and 1990s, reformers have wanted teachers to help students learn strategic processes that enable them to achieve their purposes" (p. 12). The influence of reformers, though, has been limited: "Despite the fact that the current reform movement has been under way for at least two decades, teachers participating in the TELT study were far more likely to be concerned about students' compliance with prescriptions than about any other aspect of writing" (p. 169).

Although the NWP and other similar initiatives along with abundant research and books on teaching composition have contributed to teacher preparation in teaching writing, particularly for secondary education English teachers, Robert Tremmel (2001) nevertheless notes that in the 20th century, "English education, while not totally ignoring composition, certainly marginalized it" (p. 9). He observes that:

> English teacher educators have yet to settle on a full commitment to viewing themselves as professional writing teacher educators. For one thing, some courses and programs fall short of fully representing the discipline by under-representing theory and over-balancing toward practice. (p. 17)

Smagorinsky and Whiting (1995) suggest that consistent guidance on writing methods is difficult to find and that some "courses in the teaching of writing served more as writing workshops than as courses in how to teach English" (p. 8).

T. S. Johnson, Thompson, Smagorinsky, and Fry (2003) consider the persistence of the five-paragraph essay in secondary schools and some postsecondary institutions, withstanding decades of attack from scholars. Johnson et al. attribute this persistence to numerous factors, including: the persistence of some traditional textbooks; teacher education programs that "emphasize literature at the expense of writing pedagogy" (p. 139); teachers' lack of experience as writers; poor working conditions that encourage teachers to "take shortcuts" (p. 140); and external pressures, including standardized testing.

ADVICE TO WRITING TEACHERS IN THE 20TH CENTURY: POSTSECONDARY EDUCATION TEACHERS

In the 20th century, in contrast, the preparation of postsecondary writing teachers flourished. First, professional organizations emerged to serve college writing teachers after the Modern Language Association (MLA) distanced itself from writing pedagogy at the turn of the 20th century (Douglas, 1985; Stewart, 1985). Although pedagogy held a central place as one of only five major sections that originally made up the MLA and accounted for well over 10% of the articles published in the *PMLA*, the section was disbanded just two decades later in 1903 (Franklin, 1984; Goggin, 2000; Parker, 1953, 1967).

In part to fill the pedagogical void, the NCTE was formed in 1911. With its primary goal of improving the teaching of English at all levels, from primary school through to college, pedagogy generally and writing instruction more specifically held a central place in the conferences and journals sponsored by NCTE. Given the breadth of NCTE, however, college writing teachers were soon frustrated by limited space on the conference programs and in the journals *English Journal* and its 1938 spin-off *College English*. In 1948, a formal petition to NCTE for a spring conference devoted to college writing was submitted and approved; that first conference, held in April 1949, led to the formation of the Conference on College Composition and Communication (CCCC) and its journal *College Composition and Communication* (CCC; Bird, 1977; Goggin, 2000). To more fully address the complexities of teaching, administering, and studying writing instruction, special-interest groups formed throughout the following decades, establishing affiliated organizations under the umbrella of the NCTE and the CCCC: the Two-Year College English Association (TYCA) in 1972, the Council of Writing Program Administrators (WPA) in 1977, the Association of Teachers of Advanced Composition (ATAC) in 1979, the Conference on Basic Writing (CBW), the International Writing Centers Association (IWCA) in 1983, Computers and Composition in 1983, and the Association of Teachers of Technical Writing (ATTW) in 1992.

Second, graduate programs in rhetoric and composition developed in the 1970s. Although a 1901 MLA study on the feasibility of graduate programs in rhetoric and composition conducted by Fred Newton Scott, then president of the MLA Pedagogical Section, indicated support for developing such programs at the turn of the last century, virtually all departments of English chose to design graduate programs in literary studies (Goggin, 2000). In a rare exception, Fred Newton Scott established a graduate program in rhetoric at the University of Michigan, moving it out of the English department in 1903 to form a separate department. It survived 30 years until Scott retired; the program was then dismantled in the late 1930s (Stewart & Stewart 1997). A decade later, Porter Perrin developed a short-lived graduate program in rhetoric and composition at the University of Washington in the late 1940s (Gage, 1990). Among his most famous graduates was Albert Kitzhaber, whose well-thumbed 1953 dissertation *Rhetoric in American Colleges, 1850–1900* (1953/1990) is one of the first histories of our field. Graduate work in rhetoric and composition was thus scarce until the late 1970s by which time some 15 doctoral programs in the field had been founded. Over the next decade, as Brown, Meyer, and Enos (1994) report, the number of doctoral programs in rhetoric and composition mushroomed to over 70. Today there are roughly the same number of programs focusing solely on the field, although if one were to count the numbers of graduate programs, especially in literary and cultural studies, that include courses or concentrations in rhetoric and composition studies, that number would be much higher (Brown, Jackson, & Enos, 2000). With little graduate work available in the field, few master teachers were available until the middle of the last century. It was during this period that some of the most influential publications for postsecondary teachers appeared, including *A Writer Teaches Writing* (Murray, 1968), *Errors and Expectations* (Shaughnessy, 1977), and *Writing With Power* (Elbow, 1981).

A third crucial space where college writing teachers have been able to learn their craft have been writing centers. Writing centers emerged in the 1930s to serve student writers who were characterized as remedial. In their early inception, they were often called *labs* or *clinics*, appropriate terms because, as Robert H. Moore noted in 1950, the clinic was used to diagnose students' problems with writing and then prescribe treatment; the lab was a space in which students labored to fix their problems under the direct supervision of the "class instructor, tutor, or clinician" (p. 4). This medical metaphor drove writing centers from 1930s through until the end of the 1960s; during this time, writing center faculty labored under a current-traditional view that equated a good product with a correct one (Murphy & Law, 1995, p. xi). Over the next two decades, the expressivist and social constructionist movements gave rise to a different sort of writing center, whose goals were "to produce better writers, not necessarily—or immediately—better texts" (North, 1984, p. 80). Under these perspectives, tutors were taught to focus on the writer rather than the writing. This was also a period of professionalization for writing center directors and faculty as evidenced by the founding of two important journals: the *Writing Lab Newsletter* in 1976 and *The Writing Center Journal* in 1980. The late 1980s and 1990s saw an emergence of a theoretical body of literature about writing centers and the work that went on in them; as a result, ideology guiding writing centers moved from "conservative, to liberal, to liberatory" (Murphy & Law, 1995, p. xii). Although still today those who direct and teach in writing centers continue to battle myths about their role and students (Harris, 1990; Leahy & Fox 1989), the writing center is a space in which many tutors and future writing teachers are finding valuable field experience.

TRENDS IN PREPARING TEACHERS OF WRITING IN FIRST-YEAR COMPOSITION PROGRAMS

In the scheme of things, formal preparation of teachers of writing in first-year composition programs via teaching assistant (TA) training workshops, seminars and other types of courses is a relatively new endeavor, not beginning in earnest until well into the 20th century. An anecdote from Frederick Scott Newton's life as a writing teacher serves to illustrate what was until at least the middle of the last century the lowly state of affairs in college teacher preparation:

> On August 1, 1889, President Angell appointed Scott instructor in English. He was now ready to embark on a professional career. But, superbly prepared as he was, he was not without misgivings. According to Jean Paul Slusser, artist and professor of art at Michigan, as Scott saw Gayley depart the Ann Arbor station for the University of California, he realized that he had not asked Gayley for any advice in getting ready to teach his first class. He called to Gayley, "What should I do? I've never taught before. How do I conduct myself until I acquire some experience in teaching?" Gayley yelled back, as the train pulled out: "Don't let them make fun of you!" (Stewart & Stewart, 1997, p. 14)

"That was," as Stewart and Stewart note, "the only preparation for teaching that Scott ever received" (p. 14).

Resistance to pedagogy ran deep within departments of English. After the pedagogical section of MLA was disbanded in 1903, practica and colloquia for new teachers of college writing vanished with rare exceptions such as Harvard's practicum titled English 67 for new TAs that began in 1912 and Columbia University's graduate course in composition pedagogy offered by Donald Clark in the mid-1920s (Connors, 1997). More often than not, however, underprepared graduate students were handed a teaching schedule and a composition textbook under the assumption that anyone can teach writing. By the mid-20th century, somewhat more formalized programs to train new teachers and teaching assistants in writing pedagogy started to blossom; publications on TA training began to appear more frequently on conference programs and in professional journals. Not all the discussions were favorable, however. For example, the first essay on this topic to appear in *CCC* came out in 1951 and was titled "A Training Course for Teachers of Freshman Composition." In it, Robert Hunting recommended that teachers devote little time to the writing classroom so that they could reserve most of their energies for research and publication, and that those who train TAs design noncredit practica that would take little time away from their students' graduate studies (see also Ede, 1999; C. Murphy, 1997). Others offered more positive testimonies describing TA training workshops and courses they conducted. In 1955 and again in 1963, clusters of articles on preparing TAs appeared in *CCC*. By the following decade, however, teacher preparation in writing instruction would take a serious turn.

A sure sign that the field was taking the training of writing teachers, and especially TAs, seriously came with the publication of Richard Gebhardt's (1977/1999) essay "Balancing Theory With Practice in the Training of Writing Teachers," which won the Braddock Award in 1978. Gebhardt had scarce resources to draw on in building his argument. The only text he cites for preparing writing teachers is Hook, Jacobs, and Crisp's (1970) *What Every English Teacher Should Know.*

Over the next 10 years, however, TA training soon gained a strong footing and became more formalized. By the early 1980s, textbooks on the teaching of writing suitable for TA courses and workshops began to appear in earnest. Among the earliest were Gary Tate's (1976) *Teaching Composition: Ten Bibliographical Essays* (revised and enlarged to 12 essays in 1987), Gary Tate and Edward Corbett's (1981) *The Writing Teacher's Sourcebook,* and Erika Lindemann's (1982) *A Rhetoric for Writing Teachers.* Over the next two decades, preparing teachers of writing gained status such that in most universities graduate students were given course credit for TA workshops and seminars. As Brown et al. (2000) found in their study of doctoral programs in rhetoric and composition, today "surveys indicate that graduate assistant training programs are increasingly more sophisticated, offering graduate assistants multiple venues for reading and discussing theory and practice, teaching, reflecting on teaching, and working with experienced mentors" (p. 237). Anthologies of competing theories of composition pedagogy abound now to help faculty guide graduate students through the maze of conflicting advice and their own competing theoretical positions (e.g., Hedengren, 2004; T. R. Johnson & Morahan, 2002; Tate, Corbett, & Myers, 1994; Tate, Ruppier, & Schick, 2001; Wilhoit, 2003). So prevalent are such graduate courses that some composition textbook publishers have capitalized on the industry of TA training. Bedford/St. Martin's, for example, publishes a series of professional resources on the teaching and tutoring of writing (e.g., Bizzell, Herzberg, & Reynolds, 2003; Glenn, Goldthwaite, & Connors, 2003; Gottschalk & Hjortshoj, 2004; C. Murphy & Sherwood, 2003; Ryan, 2002; White, 1999). Allyn & Bacon has followed suit, recently publishing *The Allyn & Bacon Teaching Assistant's Handbook: A Guide for Graduate Instructors of Writing and Literature* by Stephen W. Wilhoit (2003). Both of these publishers (and others) maintain Web sites loaded with professional resources and advice, usually available to those who have been granted a password by virtue of adopting one of their textbooks.

It is no accident that these courses and the print and digital materials to support them rapidly grew in numbers and sophistication throughout the latter part of the 20th century, for they emerged alongside the swift rise of graduate programs in rhetoric and composition that gave an ample supply of faculty to develop (and appreciate the need for) rigorous TA preparation programs.

MAJOR SCHOOLS OF THOUGHT FOR PREPARING TEACHERS OF WRITING

The nature of TA preparation programs is contingent on the institutions in which they take place and on the ideological position of those who design and run them. It is impossible to generalize about the state of such preparation; indeed, TA preparation is a highly contested arena. Yet, all those who develop such programs face similar questions. What is the role of TA preparation? Whom does such preparation serve—the graduate students, the undergraduate students they teach, or the institutions in which they work? What role should theory play in such preparation? Which theories, if any, should be taught in these programs? To what degree should TA preparation serve a larger role of professionalizing graduate students regardless of their disciplinary focus? Different responses to these crucial questions lead to very different schools of thought regarding TA preparation. These can be loosely classified as: functional, organic, conversion, and multiphilosophical. (Haring-Smith, 1985, provides an alternative categorization of TA programs: (a) a basic training approach, (b) an observation/apprenticeship approach, and (c) an advanced writing seminar approach.) A functional approach focuses almost exclusively on the nuts and bolts of teaching: a "what-to-do-on Monday morning" endeavor. As Wilhoit (2002) notes, this school of thought has been on the wane over the last 30 years or so. Ever since Tori Haring-Smith's (1985) landmark essay "The Importance of Theory in the Training of Teaching Assistants" ignited the debate over the role of theory in TA preparation—a debate that continues unabated today—the functional approach has been challenged from many different quarters. Yet, as Catherine Latterell (1996) reports on her survey of graduate programs, although at a good number of schools there is substantive preparation for TAs, including theory seminars, in-service practica, teaching journals, and teaching portfolios, many more still offer practice-oriented experience. Those following this school of thought would be apt to answer the earlier questions as: TA preparation is meant to serve the institution, theory should play little if any role, and professional training is not the responsibility of graduate education. Furthermore, though Nedra Reynolds' (1994) caution that some programs can "take the form of 'policing' the teaching of TAs rather than developing it" (p. 202) might be applied to any program regardless of its school of thought, those shaped by a functional view are perhaps more likely to err on the side of policing.

The organic approach favors an apprenticeship model for TA preparation. In *A Writer Teaches Writing*, Donald Murray (1985) exemplifies one strand of this school of thought when he states, "Your students will teach you how to teach" (p. 248). Others with a more Deweyian pragmatist view of learning (i.e., learning by doing) advocate role playing, team teaching with a mentor, and learning on the job (E. Smith & Smith, 1989; Hansen, Snyder, Davenport, & Stafford 1993; Hayes, 1987). The collection of programs that might be classified as organic are by no means uniform; they are grounded in very different philosophies of pedagogy and writing. Yet, these programs would be apt to answer the questions posed earlier as: TA preparation serves graduate students, theory may or may not play an important role, and professionalization is a useful goal.

A conversion approach typically holds that TAs need to learn, and teach by, the theory and philosophy on which a particular writing program is built. Sally Barr Ebest's (2002) theorizing of TA resistance in teaching preparation programs offers a good example of this school of thought. For Ebest, TA preparation involves a conceptual change on the part of many graduate students. Those who resist the change—a change that is in line with the departmental or writing program philosophy of learning and writing—are either unwilling or unable to see that "their conceptions are erroneous" and need to be motivated "to understand new ways of thinking" (p. 31). Theory is a cornerstone of the conversion school of thought. Where such programs diverge is in the theories they advocate. Programs under this approach would be likely to answer the earlier questions as: TA preparation should ultimately serve undergraduate programs, theory plays a key role, and professionalization may be a useful by-product but not a central goal of such programs.

Finally, a multiphilosophical approach has been gaining steam in recent years, building on the diverse theoretical premises and philosophical assumptions with which TAs enter teacher preparation programs. McKinney and Chiser-Strater's (2003) description of their TA preparation program offers a good example of this school of thought:

> Our seminar was not set up for conversions but for each new instructor to create a teaching philosophy consistent with his or her practice and beliefs about teaching and which drew upon the strengths each brought to the program from her or his own previous training and disciplinary interests. (p. 12)

Those who celebrate diversity, viewing it as a strength, are likely to offer divergent responses to the questions posed previously: TA preparation should serve graduate students, undergraduate students and/or the institution; theories—with an *s*—are central to such preparation; and professionalization may or may not be a necessary goal.

Of course, the reality of TA preparation is far messier and more complex than the four categories suggest. As Stephen Wilhoit (2002) points out, "Today TA in-service programs must balance three related needs: to educate TAs in composition theory and pedagogy, to maintain a theoretically coherent writing program, and to respect TAs own theories of writing" (p. 18). These are difficult and competing needs that require skillful balance. There is no one correct approach or school of thought.

LOOKING BACK TO LOOK FORWARD: PREPARING WRITING TEACHERS IN THE 21ST CENTURY

In this history, the disparity between the ways in which elementary and secondary education teachers of English are prepared as compared with first-year writing teachers is evident. Why is it the case that there have been, and continue to be, so many more opportunities and sites for preparing college teachers of writing as there are for those who teach Grades K to 12? What does this situation suggest about political and social constraints on public education and on the competing value systems within elementary, secondary and higher education? We suggest here that there are no quick answers that encompass the wide range of pedagogical action that constitutes being a writing teacher today in elementary, secondary, and postsecondary education—but suggest instead that our preparation as teachers is filtered through a long and complex series of events, of political and social constraints, of competing value systems.

Although methods for learning how to teach writing have radically changed over time, some of the goals of antiquity remain the same. Today, among the most important pedagogical goals are those articulated by our rhetorical ancestors: to prepare ethical citizens for civic action. Of course, as the social, political, and economic structures evolve, the preparation of writing teachers needs to follow suit. Our history suggests that it will follow suit even though it cannot predict what forms it will take.

REFERENCES

Allen, H. B., Henry, G. H., Hook, J. N., Marckwardt, A. H., Meade, R. A., Mersand, J., et al. (1961). *The national interest and the teaching of English: A report on the status of the profession.* Urbana, IL: National Council of Teachers of English.

Applebee, A. N. (1981). *Writing in the secondary school: English and the content areas.* Urbana, IL: National Council of Teachers of English.

Applebee, A. N. (1984). *Contexts for learning to write: Studies of secondary school instruction.* Norwood, NJ: Ablex.

Aristotle. (1994). *Art of rhetoric* (J. H. Freese, Trans.). Cambridge, MA: Harvard University Press. (Original work published ca. 483 BCE)

Atwell, N. (1987). *In the middle: Writing, reading, and learning with adolescents.* Portsmouth, NH: Boynton/ Cook-Heinemann.

Atwell, N. (1998). *In the middle: Writing, reading, and learning with adolescents* (2nd ed). Upper Montclair, NJ: Boynton/Cook.

Bain, A. (1866). *English composition and rhetoric: A manual.* London: Longmans, Green.

Berlin, J. A. (1984). *Writing instruction in nineteenth-century American colleges.* Carbondale: Southern Illinois University Press.

Bird, N. K. (1977). *The Conference on College Composition and Communication: A historical study of its continuing education and professionalization activities, 1949–1975.* Unpublished doctoral dissertation, Virginia Polytechnic Institute and State University, Blacksburg, VA.

Bizzell, P., & Herzberg, B. (Eds.). (2001). *The rhetorical tradition: Readings from classical times to the present* (2nd ed.). Boston: Bedford/St. Martins.

Bizzell, P., Herzberg, B., & Reynolds, N. (2003). *The Bedford bibliography for teachers of writing* (6th ed.). Boston: Bedford/St. Martin's.

Blair, H. (1965). *Lectures on rhetoric and belles lettres* (H. F. Harding, Ed.). Carbondale: Southern Illinois University Press (Original work published 1783)

Brookfield, F. (1855). *First book of composition.* New York: Barnes.

Brown, S. C., Jackson, R., & Enos, T. (2000). The arrival of rhetoric in the twenty-first century: The 1999 survey of doctoral programs in rhetoric and composition. *Rhetoric Review, 18,* 233–242.

Brown, S. C., Meyer, P.R., & Enos, T. (1994). Doctoral programs in rhetoric and composition: A catalog of the profession. *Rhetoric Review, 12,* 240–389.

Burgh, J. (1775). *The art of speaking* (4th ed.). Philadelphia: R Aitken. (Original work published 1761)

Calkins, L. M. (1983). *Lessons from a child: On the teaching and learning of writing.* Portsmouth, NH: Heinemann.

Calkins, L. M. (1986). *The art of teaching writing.* Portsmouth, NH: Heinemann.

Camargo, M. (1995). Between grammar and rhetoric: Composition teaching at Oxford and Bologna in the late Middle Ages. In W. B. Horner & M. Leff (Eds.), *Rhetoric and pedagogy: Its history, philosophy, and practice* (pp. 83–94). Mahwah, NJ: Lawrence Erlbaum Associates.

Campbell, G. (1963). *The philosophy of rhetoric* (L. F. Bitzer, Ed.). Carbondale: Southern Illinois University Press. (Original work published in 1776)

Capella, M. (1977). The marriage of philology and Mercury. In S. Stahl, R. Johnson, & E. Burge (Eds.), *Martianus Capella and the seven liberal arts* (pp. 3–389). New York: Columbia University Press. (Original work published in 429)

Carr, J. F., Carr, S. L., & Schultz, L. M. (2005). *Archives of instruction: Nineteenth-century rhetorics, readers, and composition books in the United States*. Carbondale: Southern Illinois University Press.

Cicero. (1976). *De inventione, De optimo genere, Oratorum, Topica* (H. M. Hubble, Trans.). Cambridge: Harvard University Press. (Original work published ca. 86 BCE)

Cicero (1986). *On oratory and orators* (J. S. Watson, Trans). Carbondale: Southern Illinois University Press. (Original work published ca. 55 BCE)

Clanchy, M. T. (1988). Hearing and seeing and trusting writing. In E. R. Kintgen, B. M. Kroll, & M. Rose (Eds.), *Perspectives on literacy* (pp. 135–58). Carbondale: Southern Illinois University Press.

Conley, T. M. (1990). *Rhetoric in the European tradition*. New York: Longman.

Connors, R. J. (1997). *Composition-rhetoric: Backgrounds, theory, and pedagogy*. Pittsburgh, PA: University of Pittsburgh Press.

Cordasco, F. (1976). *A brief history of education*. Towata, NJ: Littlefield, Adams.

Day, H. N. (1866). *Elements of the art of rhetoric*. New Your: Barnes & Burr.

Douglas, W. (1985). Accidental institution: On the origin of modern language study. In G. Graff & R. Gibbons (Eds.), *Criticism in the university* (pp. 35–61). Evanston, IL: Northwestern University Press.

Ebest, S. B. (2002). When graduate students resist. *WPA, 26*, 27–43.

Ede, Lisa. (1999). Reading—and rereading—the Braddock essays. In L. Ede (Ed.), *The Braddock essays 1975–1998* (pp. 1–27). Boston: Bedford/St. Martin's.

Elbow, P. (1973). *Writing without teachers*. New York: Oxford University Press.

Elbow, P. (1981). *Writing with power: Techniques for mastering the writing process*. New York: Oxford University Press.

Emig, J. (1971). *The composing processes of twelfth graders*. Urbana, IL: National Council of Teachers of English.

Enos, R. L. (1993). *Greek rhetoric before Aristotle*. Prospect Heights, IL: Waveland.

Enos, R. L. (1995). *Roman rhetoric: Revolution and the Greek influence*. Prospect Heights, IL: Waveland.

Enos, R. L. (2001). Ancient Greek writing instruction. In J. J. Murphy (Ed.), *A short history of writing instruction: From ancient Greece to modern America* (pp. 9–34). Mahwah, NJ: Lawrence Erlbaum Associates.

Fleming, D. (1998). Rhetoric as a course of study. *College English, 61*, 169–191.

Franklin, P. (1984). English studies: The world of scholarship in 1883. *PMLA, 99*, 356–370.

Frost, J. (1839). *Easy exercises in composition* (2nd ed.). Philadelphia: Marshall.

Gage, J. T. (1990). Introduction. In J. T. Gage (Ed.), *Rhetoric in American colleges, 1850–1900 by Albert Kitzhaber, 1953* (pp. vii–xxii). Dallas, TX: Southern Methodist University Press.

Gebhardt, R. C. (1999). Balancing theory with practice in the training of writing teachers. In L. Ede (Ed.), *The Braddock essays 1975–1998* (pp. 68–76). Boston: Bedford/St. Martin's. (Original work published 1977)

Genung, J. F. (1886). *The practical elements of rhetoric*. Boston: Ginn.

Gibbons, T. (1767). *Rhetoric; or, a view of its principal tropes and figures*. London: Oliver.

Glenn, C. (1997). *Rhetoric retold: Regendering the tradition from antiquity through the Renaissance*. Carbondale: Southern Illinois University Press.

Glenn, C., Goldthwaite, M. A., & Connors, R. (2003). *The St. Martin's guide to teaching writing*. Boston: Bedford/St. Martin's.

Goggin, M. D. (2000). *Authoring a discipline: Scholarly journals and the post–World War II emergence of rhetoric and composition*. Mahwah, NJ: Lawrence Erlbaum Associates.

Goggin, M. D., & Beatty, S. (2000). Accounting for "well-worn grooves": Composition as a self-reinforcing mechanism. In M. D. Goggin (Ed.), *Inventing a discipline: Rhetoric scholarship in honor of Richard E. Young* (pp. 29–66). Urbana: National Council of Teachers of English.

Gottschalk, K., & Hjortshoj, K. (2004). *The elements of teaching writing: A resource for instructors in all disciplines*. Boston: Bedford/St. Martin's.

Graves, D. H. (1983). *Writing: Teachers and children at work*. Exeter, NH: Heinemann.

Graves, F. P. (1916). *A student's history of education*. New York: Macmillan.

Hairston, M. (1982). The winds of change: Thomas Kuhn and the revolution in the teaching of writing. *College Composition and Communication, 33*, 76–88.

Hansen, K., Synder, P. A., Davenport, N., & Stafford, K. (1993). Collaborative learning and teaching: A model for mentoring TAs. In K. G. Lewis (Ed.), *The TA experience: Preparing for multiple roles* (pp. 251–59). Stillwater, OK: New Forums.

Haring-Smith, T. (1985). The importance of theory in the training of teaching assistants. *ADE Bulletin, 82*, 33–39.

Harris, M. (1990). What's up and what's in: Trends and traditions in writing centers. *The Writing Center Journal, 11*(1), 15–25.

Hayes, D. L. (1987). Integrating supervision, evaluation, and training: Graduate student internships in teaching composition. In N. van Note Chism (Ed.), *Institutional responsibilities and responses in the employment and education of teaching assistants* (pp. 227–229). Columbus: Ohio State University for Teaching Excellence.

Hedengren, B. F. (2004). *The TA's guide to teaching writing in all disciplines.* Boston: Bedford/St. Martin's.

Hill, A. S. (1895). *The principles of rhetoric.* New York: American Book.

Hill, D. J. (1877). *Science of rhetoric: An introduction to the laws of effective discourse.* New York: Sheldon.

Hillocks, G., Jr. (1995). *Teaching writing as reflective practice.* New York: Teachers College Press.

Holmes, J. (1739). *The art of rhetoric made easy: Or, the elements of oratory briefly stated, and fitted for the practices of the studious youth of Great-Britain and Ireland: In two books* (2nd ed.). London: Hitch & Hawes.

Hook, J. N. (1950). *The teaching of high school English.* New York: Ronald.

Hook, J. N., Jacobs, P., & Crisp, R. (1970). *What every English teacher should know.* Urbana, IL: National Council of Teachers of English.

Hunting, R. S. (1951). A training course for teachers of freshman composition. *College Composition and Communication, 2,* 3–6.

Isocrates (2001a). Against the sophists. In P. Bizzell & B. Herzberg (Eds.), *The rhetorical tradition: Readings from classical times to the present* (G. Norlin, Trans.) (2nd ed., pp. 72–75). Boston: Bedford/St. Martin's. (Original work published ca. 390 BCE)

Isocrates (2001b). From *Antidosis.* In P. Bizzell & B. Herzberg (Eds.), *The rhetorical tradition: Readings from classical times to the present* (G. Norlin, Trans.) (2nd ed., pp. 75–79). Boston: Bedford/St. Martin's. (Original work published 353 BCE)

Jamieson, A. (1818). *Grammar of rhetoric and polite literature.* New York: Armstrong.

Johnson, N. (1991). *Nineteenth-century rhetoric in North America.* Carbondale: Southern Illinois University Press.

Johnson, T. R., & Morahan, S. (Eds.). (2002). *Teaching composition: Background readings.* Boston: Bedford/St. Martin's.

Johnson, T. S., Smagorinsky, P., Thompson, L., & Fry, P. G. (2003). Learning to teach the five-paragraph theme. *Research in the Teaching of English, 38,* 136–176.

Katula, R. A., & Murphy, J. J. (1995). The sophists and rhetorical consciousness. In J. J. Murphy & R. A. Katula (Eds.), *A synoptic history of classical rhetoric* (2nd ed., pp. 17–50). Davis, CA: Hermagoras.

Kennedy, G. A. (1980). *Classical rhetoric and its Christian and secular tradition from ancient to modern times.* Chapel Hill: University of North Carolina Press.

Kennedy, G. A. (1995). Attitudes toward authority in the teaching of rhetoric before 1050. In W. B. Horner & M. Leff (Eds.), *Rhetoric and pedagogy: Its history, philosophy and practice* (pp. 65–71). Mahwah, NJ: Lawrence Erlbaum Associates.

Kennedy, M. M. (1998). *Learning to teach writing: Does teacher education make a difference?* New York: Teachers College Press.

Kimball, B. A. (1986). *Orators and philosophers: A history of the idea of liberal education.* New York: Teachers Collective Press.

Kitzhaber, A. R. (1990). *Rhetoric in American colleges, 1850–1900.* Dallas, TX: Southern Methodist University Press. (Original work published 1953)

Latterell, C. G. (1996). Training the workforce: An overview of GTA education curriculum. *WPA, 19,* 7–23.

Lawson, J. (1972). *Lectures concerning oratory* (E. N. Claussen & K. R. Wallace, Eds.). Carbondale: Southern Illinois Press. (Original work published 1758)

Leahy, R., & Fox, R. (1989). Seven myth-understandings about the writing center. *The Writing Lab Newsletter, 14*(1), 7–8.

Libanius. (ca. 400). *Progymnasmata.* Retrieved December 9, 2004, from http://www.leeds.ac.uk/classics/resources/rhetoric/prog-lib.htm

Lindemann, E. (1982). *A rhetoric for writing teachers.* New York: Oxford University Press.

McKinney, J. G., & Chiser-Strater, E. (2003). Inventing a teacherly self: Positioning journals in the TA seminar. *WPA, 27,* 59–74.

Moore, R. H. (1950). The writing clinic and the writing laboratory. *College English, 11,* 388–393.

Morgan, A. (1996). Medieval rhetoric. In T. Enos (Ed.), *Encyclopedia of rhetoric and composition: Communication from ancient times to the information age* (pp. 429–435). New York: Garland.

Morley, C. (1838). *A practical guide to composition.* New York: Robinson, Pratt.

Murphy, C. (1997). Breaking the print barrier: Entering the professional conversation. In G. A. Olson (Ed.), *Publishing in rhetoric and composition* (pp. 5–18). Albany: State University of New York Press.

Murphy, C., & Law, J. (Eds.). (1995). *Landmark essays on writing centers*. Davis, CA: Hermagoras.

Murphy, C., & Sherwood, S. (2002). *The St. Martin's sourcebook for writing tutors* (2nd ed.). Boston: Bedford/St. Martin's.

Murphy, J. J. (1974). *Rhetoric in the Middle Ages: A history of rhetorical theory from St. Augustine to the Renaissance*. Berkeley: University of California Press.

Murphy, J. J. (Ed.). (2001). *A short history of writing instruction: From ancient Greece to modern America* (2nd ed.). Mahwah, NJ: Lawrence Erlbaum Associates.

Murray, D. M. (1968). *A writer teaches writing: A practical method of teaching composition*. Boston: Houghton Mifflin.

Murray, D. M. (1985). *A writer teaches writing* (2nd ed.). Boston: Houghton Mifflin.

National Writing Project, & Nagin, C. (2003). *Because writing matters: Improving student writing in our schools*. San Francisco: Jossey-Bass.

Newman, S. P. (1834). *A practical system of rhetoric*. New York: Dayton & Newman.

North, S. M. (1984). The idea of a writing center. *College English, 46*, 433–446.

Northend, C. (1848). *Young composers*. Portland, ME: Sanborn & Carter.

Parker, R. G. (1832). *Progressive exercises in composition*. Boston: Davis.

Parker, R. P., & Daly, M. E. (1973). *Teaching English in the secondary school*. New York: The Free Press.

Parker, W. R. (1953). The MLA, 1883–1953. *PMLA, 68*, 3–39.

Parker, W. R. (1967). Where do English departments come from? *College English, 28*, pp. 339–357.

Perl, S. (1994). Writing process: A shining moment. In S. Perl (Ed.), *Landmark essays on writing process* (pp. xi–xx). Davis, CA: Hermagoras.

Pestalozzi, J. H. (1973). *How Gertrude teaches her children: An attempt to help mothers to teach their own children and an account of the method* (E. Cooke, Ed.; L. E. Holland & F. C. Turner, Trans.). London: Swan Sonnenschein. (Original work published 1801)

Phippen, A. R. (1854). *Illustrated composition book*. New York: Phippen.

Plato (1892). Symposium. In B. Jowett (Ed., Trans.), *The dialogues of Plato translated into English with analyses and introductions* (3rd ed., Vol. 1, pp. 513–594). London: Oxford University Press. (Original work written 360 BCE)

Plato (1952). *Gorgias* (W. C. Hembold, Trans.). New York: Macmillan. (Original work published ca. 386 BCE)

Plato (1993). *Phaedrus* (R. Hackforth, Trans.). Cambridge, England: Cambridge University Press. (Original work published ca. 370 BCE)

Priestly, J. (1971). *A course of lectures on oratory and criticism*. New York: Garland (Original work published 1777).

Quintilian. (1968). *Institutio Oratoria* (4 vols.) (H. E. Butler, Trans.). Cambridge, MA: Harvard University Press. (Original work published 95 CE)

Reynolds, N. (1994). Graduate writers and portfolios: Issues of professionalism, authority and resistance. In L. Black, D. A. Daiker, J. Sommers, & G. Stygall (Eds.), *New directions in portfolio assessment* (pp. 201–209). Portsmouth, NH: Boynton/Cook.

Ritchie, J., & Ronald, K. (Eds.). (2001). *Available means: An anthology of women's rhetoric(s)*. Pittsburgh, PA: University of Pittsburgh Press.

Robbins, R., &. Dyer, M. (2004). *Writing America: Classroom literacy and public engagement*. Berkeley: National Writing Project & Teachers College Press.

Romano, T. (2000). *Blending genre, altering style: Multigenre papers*. Portsmouth, NH: Boynton/Cook.

Ryan, L. (2002). *The Bedford guide for writing tutors* (3rd ed). Boston: Bedford/St. Martin's.

Sauer, E. H. (1961). *English in the secondary school*. New York: Holt, Rinehart & Winston.

Schultz, L. M. (1999). *The young composers: Composition's beginnings in nineteenth-century schools*. Carbondale: Southern Illinois University Press.

Shaughnessy, M. (1977). *Errors and expectations: A guide for the teacher of basic writing*. New York: Oxford University Press.

Sheridan, T. (1968). *A course of lectures on elocution*. New York: Blom. (Original work published 1762)

Smagorinsky, P., & Whiting, M. E. (1995). *How English teachers get taught: Methods of teaching the methods class*. Urbana, IL: Conference on English Education & National Council of Teachers of English.

Smith, A. (1985). *Lectures on rhetoric and belle letters* (J. C. Bryce, Ed.). Indianapolis: University of Indiana Press. (Original work published 1750/1760)

Smith, E., & Smith, M. (1989). A graduate internship in teaching. *Teaching English in the Two-Year College, 16*, 197–200.

Smith, M., & Juska, J. (2001). *The whole story: Teachers talk about portfolios*. Berkeley, CA: National Writing Project.

Squire, J. R., & Applebee R. (1968). *High school English instruction today: The national study of high school English programs*. New York: Appleton–Century–Crofts.

Stewart, D. C. (1985). Some history lessons for composition teachers. *Rhetoric Review, 3,* 134–144.

Stewart, D. C., & Stewart, P. L. (1997). *The life and legacy of Fred Newton Scott.* Pittsburgh, PA: University of Pittsburgh Press.

Stirling, J. (1764). *A system of rhetoric, in a method entirely new* (7th ed.). London: Rivington. (Original work published in 1733)

Tate, G. (Ed.). (1976). *Teaching composition: Ten bibliographical essays.* Fort Worth: Texas Christian University Press.

Tate, G. (Ed.). (1987). *Teaching composition: Twelve bibliographical essays* (rev. ed.). Fort Worth: Texas Christian University Press.

Tate, G., & Corbett, E. P. J. (Eds.). (1981). *The writing teacher's sourcebook.* New York: Oxford University Press.

Tate, G., Corbett, E. P. J., & Myers, N. (Eds.). (1994). *The writing teacher's sourcebook* (3rd ed.). New York: Oxford University Press.

Tate, G., Rupier, A., & Schick, K. (Eds.). (2001). *A guide to composition pedagogies.* New York: Oxford University Press.

Tremmel, R. (2001). Seeking a balanced discipline: Writing teacher education in first-year composition and English education. *English Education, 34*(1), 6–30.

Varnum, R. (1986). From crisis to crisis: The evolution toward higher standards of literacy in the United States. *Rhetoric Society Quarterly, 16*(3), 145–165.

Ward, J. (1969). *A system of oratory.* London: Lubrecht & Cramer. (Original work published 1759)

Wertheimer, M. M. (Ed.). (1997). *Listening to their voices: The rhetorical activities of historical women.* Columbia: University of South Carolina Press.

Whately, R. (1963). *Elements of rhetoric* (D. Ehninger, Ed.). Carbondale: Southern Illinois University Press. (Original work published 1828)

White, E. M. (1999). *Assigning, responding, and evaluating: A writing teacher's guide* (3rd ed.). Boston: Bedford/St. Martin's.

Wilhoit, S. (2002). Recent trends in TA instruction: A bibliographic essay. In B. P. Pytlik & S. Liggett (Eds.), *Preparing college teachers of writing: Histories, theories, programs, practices* (pp. 17–27). New York: Oxford University Press.

Wilhoit, S. W. (2003). *The Allyn & Bacon teaching assistant's handbook: A guide for graduate instructors of writing and literature.* New York: Longman.

Winter, D., & Robbins, S. (Eds.). (2005). *Writing our communities: Local learning and public culture.* Berkeley, CA: National Writing Project.

Woods, M. C. (1990). The teaching of writing in medieval Europe. In J. J. Murphy (Ed.), *A short history of writing instruction: From ancient Greece to twentieth-century America* (pp. 77–94). Davis, CA: Hermagoras.

CHAPTER 23

Construct and Consequence: Validity in Writing Assessment

Sandra Murphy
University of California, Davis

Kathleen Blake Yancey
Florida State University

In approaches to writing assessment, the United States differs from many, if not most, other countries. Outside the United States, written examinations are a well-established part of the culture (Foster & Russell, 2002). European countries, for example, use examinations involving extended writing for school purposes, both to screen students for admission to college and to test them for content knowledge once they arrive there. The BAC (baccalaureate) exam series in France, the A-level examinations in England, and the *Abitur* examinations in Germany all require extended writing and serve as gatekeepers to higher education. And in most European countries, "extended writing is the main—often the only—method of examining students" (Foster & Russell, 2002, p. 25).

In the United States, extended writing was once widely used in college admission decisions. For example, in order to gain admission to Harvard in 1874, students were required to write essays on topics drawn from a prescribed list of literary works. On the West Coast, the University of California–Berkeley and Stanford University followed Harvard's approach (Traschel, 1992). In the late 1930s, however, the College Entrance Examination Board began a series of changes in assessment methods that typifies U.S. developments in writing assessment more generally. Issues surrounding the reliability of scoring as well as the high cost of administering written exams led the Board to shift to multiplie-choice tests (Traschel, 1992). Thus, although essay components have been added to several important admission tests within the last decade and a half, including the Graduate Record Exam (GRE), the Medical Colleges Admissions Test (MCAT), and most recently the American College Testing (ACT) college entrance exam and the Scholastic Aptitude Test (SAT), this early shifting from a direct measure with claims on validity to an indirect measure with claims on reliability forecasts much of the history of U.S. writing assessment.

Reliability refers to the reproducibility of a test's results. As Heubert and Hauser (1999) explain, "A test is highly reliable if a student taking it on two different occasions will get two very similar if not identical scores. The key issue of reliability…is to establish that *something* is being measured with a certain degree of consistency" (p. 71).

Because early efforts to score essay tests were often unreliable (Breland, 1983), the field of writing assessment initially focused on ways to improve reliability (Huot, 2002). Ultimately, however, enhanced (some would say "tightly scripted") training procedures led to acceptable levels of reliability. As a result, reliability has been less of interest in the literature than it was in earlier years. More recently, the assessment field has turned its attention to the issue of validity.

"The key issue of validity," according to Heubert and Hauser (1999), "is to determine... whether the test measures what it purports to measure and what meaning can be drawn from the results" (pp. 71–72). Although the measurement community appeared to favor objective tests because they could be scored reliably, scholars and teachers in the field of English education and composition objected to their use, noting that they focused on low-level and rule-governed, mechanical aspects of literacy and failed to address the essentially situated nature of literacy practice, as well as its creative dimensions (Trachsel, 1992; Witte, Flach, Greenwood, &Wilson, 1995). Other challenges to the use of indirect (multiple-choice) assessments rested on the argument that the best way to assess an individual's ability to perform a task is to elicit and evaluate an actual performance. Diedrich (1974) put the argument this way:

> People who uphold the view that essays are the only valid test of writing ability are fond of using the analogy that, whenever we want to find out whether young people can swim, we have them jump into a pool and swim. (p. 1)

Traditional educational and psychological measurement theory has addressed, chiefly, three types of procedures for evaluating the validity of assessments: procedures for evaluating content validity, criterion-related validity, and construct validity (Williamson, 1993). According to Williamson, the most critical concept for writing assessment is *construct validity*, because "it examines the extent to which an assessment tool conforms to a theory of writing" (p. 13). In contemporary definitions of validity, content and criterion validity are subsumed under the aegis of construct validity (Messick, 1989).

A second critical concept for writing assessment is the idea of *contextual validation* (Williamson, 1993). In part, contextual validation involves the purpose of the assessment. As Linn, Baker, and Dunbar (1991) explain, "It has long been recognized that validity is not simply a property of the measure. A measure that is highly valid for one use or inference, may be quite invalid for another...the criteria for judging the assessment must correspond to the purpose, regardless of the nature or form of the assessment" (p. 20). In a similar vein, Williamson argues that assessment developers should demonstrate "the validity of procedures for the particular contexts in which they are used" (p. 15).

A third critical concept for writing assessment is the notion of *authenticity*, defined as "the degree of correspondence of the characteristics of a given language test task to the features of a target language use...task" (Bachman & Palmer, 1996, p. 23). Briefly, writing tasks should represent the type of writing that examinees will be expected to employ in the context for which the assessment is designed.

A fourth, critical concept is the notion of *consequence as a facet of validity*. Messick (1989) maintains that appraisal of both potential and actual social consequences of an assessment should be undertaken in any effort to determine the validity of an assessment. For writing assessment, an effective argument for validity means, ideally, a positive influence on the teaching and learning of writing. Not least, the validation process demands "that we take responsibility to research our own assessments" (Huot, 2002, p. 156).

Arguments for or against the validity of particular methods are often based on competing theories about the nature of the writing construct—as a set of discrete skills, as a cognitive (or instructional) process that takes place over time, and more recently, as a meaning-making and highly social activity that varies across contexts and purposes for writing. As methods for assessing writing have evolved, so have arguments about the values of each approach. In the pages that follow, we introduce some of those arguments and review relevant research. Because of limitations on length, we discuss only a few of the many research studies on writing assessment, we mention only a few of the nation's tests, and we focus on the writing of adolescents and college students. Our goal is simply to provide starting points for readers interested in further exploration.

APPROACHES TO THE ASSESSMENT OF WRITING

Although all tests, whether writing samples are collected or not, are indirect indicators of underlying abilities (Messick, 1994), the terms *direct* and *indirect* have been used to distinguish between two general approaches to the assessment of writing. Indirect assessments estimate *probable* writing ability through observations of specific kinds of knowledge and skills associated with writing. They require passive recognition of error and selection of best examples as opposed to active generation of text. In direct assessments, an examinee produces one or more texts evaluated by one or more assessors. Direct assessments treat writing as an active, generative sociocognitive process in which a variety of skills are orchestrated to make meaning and to communicate with others. Direct assessments can consist of single (or multiple) impromptu samples of writing generated under timed, controlled conditions, or multiple samples of writing generated in a natural context (e.g., the classroom) supported by instruction and feedback (e.g., portfolios).

Challenges to the Validity of Indirect Assessments of Writing

Messick (1989, 1994) identifies two major threats to construct validity: "construct underrepresentation" and "construct-irrelevant variance." When a "test is too narrow and fails to include important dimensions or facets of the construct" the construct is said to be underrepresented. Construct-irrelevant variance occurs when a "test contains excess reliable variance, making items or tasks easier or harder for some respondents in a manner irrelevant to the interpreted construct" (1989, p. 7). Indirect (multiple-choice) assessments of writing have been challenged on both of these grounds.

The validity of multiple-choice tests may be weak because, like other tests, they are prone to "construct-irrelevant variance." Extraneous factors and subjective interpretation on the part of the test taker—including, for instance, obedience to testing rules and confusion induced by item formats—can invalidate the multiple-choice test taker's response (Haney & Scott, 1987). Indirect assessments have also been challenged on the grounds of "construct underrepresentation." Some scholars have charged that they fail to address the cognitive and reflective processes involved in creating a text—such as making plans for writing, generating and developing ideas, and making claims and providing evidence (e.g., Camp, 1983; Odell, 1981).

In the measurement community, however, well-designed multiple-choice tests have been supported because they demonstrate concurrent validity. For example, Godshalk, Swineford, and Coffman (1966) found that a multiple-choice test of grammar provided a better prediction of criterion scores (summed scores on several short essays) than was provided by a single, holistically scored writing sample. In replicating and updating the Godshalk study, Breland, Camp, Jones, Morris, and Rock (1987) came to a similar conclusion, namely, that "very good predictions of writing ability could be made through combination of essay and non-essay assessments" (p. 59). The compromise involved combining multiple-choice tests with the collection of a timed, impromptu writing sample.

However, other studies supported the argument that indirect and direct assessment methods tap *different* skills. Factor analyses in a study conducted by Carlson, Bridgeman, Camp, and Waanders (1985) indicated that direct and indirect measures were not measuring identical skills, even though the correlations between performances on the two measures were high. Other research has demonstrated that students would be placed differently by the two methods (Olson & Martin, 1980). Several studies have also called into question the predictive validity of indirect measures of writing (see e.g., Hughes & Nelson, 1991).

Indirect assessments have also been challenged on the grounds that they lack consequential validity. Several scholars have explored relationships between teaching to such tests and narrowing of the curriculum (see e.g., Corbett & Wilson, 1991; Murphy, 2003; M. L. Smith, 1991). Existing research suggests that large-scale, high-stakes multiple-choice tests affect writing curriculum in two ways: (a) actual writing begins to disappear from the curriculum, and (b) the curriculum begins to take the form of the test. For instance, Murphy found that when a direct assessment was changed to an indirect multiple-choice format, teachers spent less time teaching writing, more time teaching grammar and usage, and put more emphasis on grammar and usage in their comments on student work. Similarly, Smith observed that teachers shifted from a writing process curriculum to "worksheets covering grammar, capitalization, punctuation, and usage" (p. 10) when their district's test date neared, because those activities were better aligned with the test.

Such findings point to a troubling irony: Despite the call for rigorous standards in recent years, the most common format used in large-scale accountability systems is the multiple-choice format (Quality Counts, 2002; cited in Hamilton, 2003), yet as noted earlier, such tests do not measure important skills required for actual composing (Camp, 1983).

Challenges to the Validity of the Timed, Impromptu Writing Sample

Research on direct assessment has demonstrated that a variety of factors influence the way writing samples are evaluated—including the nature and subject of the writing task; the scale and scoring procedures used; the characteristics of the texts; the raters; the knowledge, culture, and linguistic background of the writers; and various contextual factors (S. W. Freedman, 1981; Hamp-Lyons, 1990; Weigle, 2002). Such variation is problematic, because a goal in positivistic assessment is to reduce or eliminate variation that can be attributed to factors other than the candidate's writing abilities (Weigle, 2002)—what Messick (1989) called *construct-irrelevant variance*.

Writers

For some students, some writing tasks may be more difficult than others for reasons quite separate from their ability to write.

Knowledge of the Subject. Langer (1984) found a strong and consistent relationship between topic-specific background knowledge and writing quality as measured by holistic score on a 5-point scale. Students who had more knowledge about the subject of a prompt wrote better and more coherent essays. Langer's study has two implications for the design and impact of assessment prompts. First, prompts vary in the degree to which they tap knowledge available to writers, and second, writers who have less knowledge about the particular subject are less likely to perform well. Consequently, test designers often turn to general knowledge topics presumed to be accessible to the broadest range of participants. However, even the best general-knowledge topic may disadvantage some students, particularly those from a nonmainstream culture. For these writers, prompts that draw on their specific expertise may ultimately be more fair than some general-knowledge prompts, although the evidence on this is issue is mixed (e.g., Hamp-Lyons, 1990; Tedick, 1990).

Linguistic and Cultural Background. The background of the writer appears to be another important source of variability in score. Studies have demonstrated contrastive patterns at different linguistic and stylistic levels, across diverse student populations (e.g., Basham & Kawachka, 1991; Sullivan, 1997). When the linguistic and rhetorical patterns of the students' home culture differ in important ways from the expectations of readers and the patterns that scoring rubrics value, students' scores may be adversely affected.

Task Interpretation. Research suggests that how a writer interprets the task can influence the score he or she receives. Murphy, Carroll, Kinzer, and Robyns (1982) documented differences among the ways that students and the teachers who scored their papers interpreted the same personal-experience writing task. Keech and McNelly (1982) documented differences between the evaluative criteria employed by students and English teachers, showing that writers and raters may not have the same perception of what constitutes a successful completion of the task. English as a second language (ESL) students and/or students with reading disabilities face particular challenges in this regard; they may interpret a topic differently than a general community of readers in ways that can adversely affect their scores.

Raters

Several studies have shown that rater characteristics may influence the scores that writers receive. Variability has been demonstrated between raters who differ in their level of experience (Song & Caruso, 1996; Weigle, 1999), in their disciplinary or teaching background (Bridgeman & Carlson, 1983; Santos, 1988; Song & Caruso, 1996), in their linguistic background (A. Brown, 1995; J. D. Brown, 1991; Chalhoub-Deville, 1995; Santos, 1988; Song & Caruso, 1996), and in their cultural background (Kobayashi & Rinnert, 1999). Studies also link variability in raters' scores to specific characteristics in students' responses (see Cumming, 1997). Such variability represents an underlying disagreement about the nature of the construct underlying the assessment.

Disciplinary Background.   In an early study of essay characteristics influencing holistic scores, S. W. Freedman (1979) found that development exerted the strongest effect, followed by organization and mechanics; sentence structure wielded no significant effect. Subsequent studies of the rating patterns of English and composition teachers support Freedman's findings (Breland & Jones, 1984; Huot, 1993). Faculty from non-English departments value other essay characteristics. Bridgeman and Carlson (1983) found that whereas English faculty ranked the top three criteria as (a) paper organization, (b) development of ideas, and (c) paragraph organization, faculty from engineering and science departments ranked the top three criteria as (a) quality of the content, (b) success in satisfying assignment requirements, and (c) the degree to which the response addressed the prompt. ESL faculty, in contrast, appear to value particularly English-language proficiency, especially as reflected in absence of error, although the evidence is mixed. In some studies, ESL and English raters appear to value the same criteria (e.g., Song & Caruso, 1996), but in others not (e.g., J. D. Brown, 1991).

Language and Cultural Background.   Language and cultural background of both rater and writer appear to play a role in raters' judgments, although again, the evidence is mixed. Research by Janopoulos (1992) suggests that professors in the university at large judge more leniently sentence-level errors in the writing of non-native English speakers than comparable errors made by native speakers. Erdosy (2004) summarizes two other relevant studies, suggesting that their mixed results in fact stem from the raters' awareness of the consequences of the assessment. Native-speaker raters in one study (J. D. Brown, 1991) had to determine whether the candidates they assessed qualified for membership in their profession, whereas in a second study (Santos 1988), the ratings of the native speaker had no practical consequences for the writers.

Experience in the Teaching and Evaluation of Writing.   Raters' experience (or lack of experience) in the teaching and evaluation of writing may also influence rating patterns. Song and Caruso (1996) and Weigle (1999) found that raters with more experience scored L2 (second-language) writing more leniently than did raters with less experience, although Sweedler-Brown (1985) found that experienced trainers "tended to grade more harshly" than less experienced readers. Weigle (1999) found that inexperienced raters valued traditional formats, whereas experienced raters tended to reward writers who approached their essays in more original and creative ways. Keech and McNelly (1982) found differentiated scoring practices among high school students (lower), novice teachers (middle), and expert teachers (higher).

Research also suggests that raters adjust their ratings during the rating process. Hamp-Lyons and Matthias (1994) found that raters tend to award higher scores to essays written by L2 writers when they judged the student-selected topic to be more difficult. In contrast, Erdosy's (2004) study found just the opposite: Raters of ESL writing did not compensate for perceived biases in topics related to writing difficulty.

Taken together, these studies suggest that in any scoring session, complex interactions taking place between rater, task, and product influence scores students receive. As Erdosy (2004) points out, it is likely that inconsistencies in findings in studies of rating stem from a "preoccupation with a limited set of factors at the expense of others that may have also influenced behavior" (p. 6).

Context Effects

In an early study of the influence of contextual factors on scores, S. W. Freedman (1981) found the source of the largest variance to be the trainers. More thoroughly trained raters generally gave higher scores than raters whose trainers simply discussed the meaning of a topic. Likewise, the order of essays influences ratings—a composition will receive a higher score if preceded by weak compositions rather than strong ones, a problem that can be difficult to eradicate (Sweedler-Brown, 1993).

Topic Choice.   Evidence on the issue of topic choice is mixed. Some studies suggest that having a choice may give students an advantage (e.g., Polio & Glew, 1996), particularly when writing is used to assess subject matter learning (Allen, Holland, & Thayer, 2005). Other research, however, suggests that students may not choose topics that enable them to perform well. Evans (1979) found that more able students chose topics that gave them a positive advantage whereas less able students chose topics that disadvantaged them further. It was not clear, however, whether the poorer students would have fared any better had they chosen the prompts selected by the better students.

Scoring Systems.   The merits of contrasting approaches to scoring have been widely debated. Whereas some scholars consider holistic scoring an effective way to evaluate essays (e.g., White, 1984), critics argue that it is less likely to influence teaching and learning positively because it conflates the complex traits and skills involved in writing and provides no diagnostic information (Hamp-Lyons, 1991). Equally to the point in the context of our discussion of validity, Williamson (1993) challenges the validity of holistic scoring, because it defines a global measure of writing ability although research "continues to suggest that writing is not a single, global ability" (p. 21).

Researching analytic scoring systems, Jacobs, Zinkgraf, Wormuth, Hartfiel, and Hughey (1981) assert that they focus raters' attention on particular features of a composition, thus minimizing the differences in raters' disciplinary and experiential backgrounds that might lead them to apply different standards. One study supports this claim (Song & Caruso, 1996): When essays were scored holistically, experience of the raters influenced scores, but when essays were scored analytically, experience of the raters did not significantly influence scores.

A final and important issue concerns the connection of the scoring system to a site of activity other than the testing context itself (Haswell, 1998). Building on W. L. Smith's (1993) theory of expert readership—an expertise developed in the practice of teaching a specific writing curriculum—Haswell argues that model raters are expert in a local sense, authoritative about the relationship between a student and a specific course, one that the teacher-rater has very recently taught. Conceived of this way, reliability is more a function of rater experience with a specific curriculum than a function of agreement, directed or otherwise, among raters.

The idea that a single scoring approach can be equally valid in all contexts and for all purposes has also been challenged. An early study (Winters 1978) compared patterns of results produced by four essay scoring systems—an analytical scale, the Diederich expository scale (an approach that combines elements of analytic scales and general impression scoring), t-unit analysis (analysis of syntactic complexity), and general-impression scoring. Although each of the systems produced reliable results, they produced different *patterns* of results for the four groups of students in the study (high school and college writers of low and high ability). Carr (2000) found that changing the rating scale of a subtest altered the emphasis of the test as a whole. Results such as these suggest that choice of scoring system is an important dimension of test validity. In making that choice, purpose is an especially important consideration, and as Smith's (1993) research demonstrates, the most valid scales are appropriate for the particular purpose and context in which they are used.

Time and the Writing Context.   Research suggests that the circumstances governing the writing performance—for example, whether samples are regular classroom assignments or collected in a timed, impromptu writing test—impact the judgments made about students' abilities. A test's validity is diminished when time is a serious factor for most of the test population, or for particular groups within that population. In such cases, a test's results speak more to who can perform a task within an allotted time and less to who is capable of performing the task. Several studies support the view that increased time for writing may provide a more valid picture of ESL students' writing abilities (Cho, 2003; Hilgers, 1992; Polio, Fleck, & Leder 1998). Increased time for writing influences the scores of native speakers as well. Powers and Fowles (1996), for example, found that students' writing performance on the 60-minute version of the trial GRE essay test was significantly better than on the 40-minute version. Herman, Gearhart, and Baker (1993) found that raters' scores for students' portfolios of classroom work were higher than those for a standard writing assessment in which the students were given 30 to 40 minutes to write a story. Livingston (1987), however, also found that proficient writers were more able to take advantage of extra time on a timed test than less proficient writers. In a comparison of timed writing samples and portfolio collections, J. Simmons (1992) found that the weakest writers and writers from the poorest schools were disadvantaged by the timed test.

Taken together, these studies indicate that time impacts the quality of a writer's performance, and affects some writers' performance more than others. The validity of timed, impromptu assessments has also been challenged because they fail to provide information about students' ability to manage other, more extended kinds of tasks and because they are not well-aligned with contemporary views of effective writing instruction (Camp, 1983).

The Writing Task

Camp (1983) questioned the validity of using a single writing sample to assess writing ability because this approach rests on a questionable assumption: that "the skills involved in writing are the same, whatever its purpose or circumstances" (Camp, 1983, p. 6). Subsequent studies have supported Camp's argument, showing that task variables can influence both process and product (Ruth & Murphy, 1988).

Rhetorical Specification.   Different rhetorical purposes appear to require different processes. Witte and Cherry (1994) showed that writers' composing processes differed not only across two broad purposes for writing (to inform or explain and to persuade), but also across different writing tasks within each purpose. Using observational data (pause time and hand movement), Matsuhashi (1982) found differences in composing processes for reporting and generalizing.

Textual features also vary across writing done for different purposes and audiences. For example, comparing the textual features associated with two prompt types—(a) comparing/contrasting and (b) taking a position, describing and interpreting a chart or graph—Reid

(1990) found significant differences across the prompt types: in length, in vocabulary, and in the use of pronouns. Crowhurst and Piche (1979) found that argumentative essays composed by 6th and 10th graders contained more complex syntax than either descriptive or narrative essays at both grade levels. When asked to write for audiences of high, medium, and low intimacy, 10th graders (but not 6th graders) produced texts with significant semantic and syntactic differences. K. Black (1989), finding that college students who were given information about the audience wrote more persuasive papers than writers in a control group, argues that conscious use of ideas about an audience (audience awareness) to create or revise text may be a factor that helps to explain differences in writing ability, and Crowhurst and Piche's work suggests that development plays a role as well.

Although some studies have failed to find significant differences in score due to rhetorical features of the task (Brossell, 1983), other studies have, particularly in relation to the mode or genre of the writing task. In an early study, Godshalk et al. (1966) reported significant variation in ratings assigned to texts responding to prompts involving four genres: an imaginative story, an argumentative essay supporting a position, an opinion essay , and a character analysis. Godshalk et al. observed, "If the five topics had been assigned as alternate topics from which one or two could be chosen by students, a student's rating might depend more on which topic he chose than on how well he wrote" (p. 13). A. Freedman and Pringle (1981) found that students were far more successful in enacting the conventional schema for story structure than for the structure of an argument: 98% of the students employed narrative structure in their stories, but only 12.5% could use the classical argument patterns. Quellmalz, Capell, and Chou (1982), in contrast, found that lower ratings were assigned to narrative essays than to expository essays. Although these studies are mixed in results about the impact of specific genres, collectively they provide evidence that levels of writing performance vary on tasks representing different writing purposes.

Wording and Stimulus Material.   Results on the influence of the wording of prompts on score are mixed. Golub-Smith, Reese, and Steinhaus (1993) found that higher scores were awarded to prompts that provided explicit directions, as opposed to prompts in which directions were left implicit. In contrast, Greenberg (1981) found no significant differences in the holistic scores awarded to prompts worded differently in an attempt to vary cognitive and experiential demand. The results of studies of stimulus material are also mixed. W. L. Smith et al. (1985) studied three prompt structures: an open structure asking students to draw on personal knowledge and experience, a response structure giving students a single short passage to read, and a second response structure requiring students to read three passages. The results indicate that the different prompt structures led to essays of different quality, but also that each prompt structure distinguished low-, average-, and high-ability students in different ways. Whereas Advanced Writing students performed best on the open-structure prompt, General Writing students and Basic Writing students performed best in response to the prompt with three reading passages. The results contradict the often-held assumption that general knowledge prompts enable less proficient writers.

In contrast, in a repeated-measures design, J. D. Brown, Hilgers, and Marsella (1991) found no significant differences in the scores awarded to essays written to personal experience prompts versus prompts that required approximately 1½ pages of reading. The various prompt sets, however, did produce differences in scores, leading the researchers to speculate that students knew more about the subjects of some of the prompts than others. Their explanation corresponds with research outlined previously showing that writers' knowledge of the subject of the prompt influences the scores they receive.

Despite the mixed results, these studies taken together suggest that writing performance across situations and tasks varies in important ways. As Anastasi (1986) explains, early views of traits "as fixed, unchanging, underlying causal entities" (p. 9) have been challenged by social theorists because behavior varies across situations. A growing consensus is emerging, she says, that "in order to identify broad traits, we have to assess individuals across situations and aggregate the results" (p. 9), a position affirmed by the Conference on

College Composition and Communication (1995). This consensus challenges the construct validity of impromptu, single-sample assessments.

The authenticity of single-sample, impromptu assessments has been challenged, because such assessments are unable to represent the variety of types of writing that examinees will be expected to employ in the context for which the assessment is designed. For example, research has demonstrated that students in college are assigned a wide variety of writing tasks, that they vary on a number of rhetorical and practical dimensions, and that their frequency varies across disciplines and graduate and undergraduate levels (e.g., Bridgeman & Carlson, 1983; Hale et al., 1996). Yet many placement tests sample a single type of writing, one that may not align in important ways with the kinds of tasks that students in college may be asked to do.

Finally, single-sample writing tests have been challenged on the grounds that they negatively influence the educational environment, particularly when high stakes are attached. Evidence on this issue is mixed. Some research suggests that teachers are likely to increase the time students spend writing when an assessment includes a writing sample (Almasi, Afflerbach, Guthrie, & Schafer, 1995; Koretz & Hamilton, 2003; Koretz, Mitchell, Baron, & Keith, 1996; Stecher, Barron, Kaganoff, & Goodwin, 1998). However, other studies demonstrate a narrowing effect on the curriculum (O'Neill, Murphy, Huot, & Williamson, 2004; Scherff & Piazza, 2005; Wallace, 2002), a turn toward formulaic teaching (Hillocks, 2002; Johnson, Smagorinsky, Thompson, & Fry, 2003) and a negative effect on student attitudes (Ketter & Poole, 2001; Loofbourrow, 1994).

O'Neill et al. (2004) found that the teaching of writing in Georgia was aligned with the format of the state test: Teachers were likely to assign persuasion, the tested genre, to assign single-draft, short pieces of writing, and to require that the writing be turned in the same day. In Hillocks's (2002) study of five state-mandated writing assessments criteria and testing format were the critical factors. In states with better tests, criteria called for evidence, and benchmark papers displayed their use. In states where students had more time, they were able to find information and develop evidence for their writing.

Collectively, these findings demonstrate that the impact of assessment on classroom practice, although assured, is no means consistent.

Challenges to the Validity of Portfolios

As an assessment method, portfolios appear to address many of the concerns discussed previously about the validity of using timed, impromptu, single-sample assessments to assess writing ability. Advocates argue that task interpretation is less problematic when questions can be asked and expectations made transparent via classroom instruction, that time and support for writing gives students a better chance to do their best, and that good instruction can be mirrored in the assessment because writing can be treated as a recursive process and revisited for revision. Portfolios also offer opportunities to broaden the assessment construct by sampling a range of genres, to engage students more directly in the assessment process in ways that give them responsibility for evaluating their own learning, and to collect samples under more natural and authentic conditions that are directly linked to instruction.

However, because they reflect curricula and the web of beliefs, goals, and assumptions that undergird education, portfolio programs vary widely in theoretically important ways (Murphy, 1994; Murphy & Underwood, 2000). In some projects, students are encouraged to choose what their portfolios will contain. In others, teachers decide. In some projects, students submit evidence of the processes they engaged in along with the work; in others, only final, polished pieces. In some projects, students are asked to reflect on their work, their learning, and/or their processes for producing work. In others, not. All of these basic differences in assessment design reflect at some level different views about the construct of writing that the assessment purports to measure.

These differences also exist because, like other assessment methods, portfolios are used for different purposes. Within the classroom, portfolios are often used to involve students in the analysis of their own learning. But portfolios have also been used to influence classroom practice, to hold schools and teachers accountable, to monitor progress, and to provide information for program evaluation. In these cases, administrators may be more concerned with the need to obtain particular kinds of information efficiently and to meet standards for technical adequacy (regarding, e.g., reliability and generalizability) than with the impact of assessment on learning (Murphy & Underwood 2000).

Early concerns of the U.S. measurement community about portfolios as an assessment measure, like other assessment methods, focused on reliability, which many scholars have viewed as an essential component of validity (see e.g., Henning, 1991; L. S. Smith, Winters, Quellmalz, & Baker, 1980). Reliable scoring of portfolios is generally perceived to be more difficult than the scoring of individual texts, especially if the collections of work contain different kinds of assignments. In some studies, test administrators have reported difficulty in training portfolio scorers to agree (Despain & Hilgers, 1992; Hamp-Lyons & Condon, 1993), and in some others, interrater reliabilities have fallen below acceptable levels for decisions of consequence about individuals or programs (Koretz, McCaffrey, Klein, Bell, & Stecher, 1992; Nystrand, Cohen, & Dowling, 1993). One explanation offered for low reliabilities has been the lack of standardization of tasks. However, several portfolio projects have been able to demonstrate acceptable interrater reliability without standardizing portfolio contents. The Pittsburgh Public School District (LeMahieu, Eresh, & Wallace, 1992) scored writing portfolios on three dimensions—accomplishment, process/resources, and growth/engagement— that cut across the individual pieces of evidence in writing portfolios. Spearman correlations varied between .74 and .87 depending on the scores of the examined dimensions and the grade level of the portfolio (LeMahie, Eresh, & Wallace, 1992). Using somewhat different scoring systems, other projects have approached or exceeded the rates achieved in Pittsburgh (e.g., Herman et al., 1993; Underwood & Murphy, 1998).

Although portfolio assessments have been able to achieve acceptable levels of interrater reliability, the ultimate answer to the question raised by Herman et al.—"Can portfolios be scored reliably?" (p. 202) might best be answered by "It depends." The reliability of portfolio assessment is subject to concerns about the same factors as single-sample assessments, for example, the many rater and scoring factors that may lead to variability in scores.

Because portfolios are collections of classroom work, their validity has been challenged in other ways. Nystrand et al. (1993) pointed out that "variability over assignments may inadvertently penalize some students if the tasks included in a portfolio are ones on which they perform poorly" (p. 69). Gearhart, Herman, Baker, and Whittaker (1993), identifying authorship as a matter of concern, raised the question: Whose work is it? Proponents of portfolio assessment, in contrast, counter that teachers monitor the production of classroom work; explicit monitoring is a feature of the successful interinstitutional Washington State portfolio program. Nonetheless, if individuals other than the students are actually doing the work, the argument for the validity of portfolios is diminished.

Consequential Validity of Portfolios.

Studies of large-scale portfolio assessment programs have demonstrated positive effects on the educational environment. Nearly three fourths of the principals interviewed in a study of Vermont's portfolio assessment program reported that the portfolio program produced positive changes, including "an increased emphasis on higher order thinking skills"; "lessened reliance on textbooks and worksheets; an increase in writing overall and more integration of writing with other subjects; [and] more work in cooperative groups" (Koretz, Stecher, Klein, & McCaffrey, 1994, p. 31). Locally developed classroom and school portfolio assessments provide evidence that teachers develop higher expectations for students and put more emphasis on individual growth and development (see e.g., Jennings, 2002; Shepard, 1995).

Evidence in the literature also suggests that participation in scoring sessions for curriculum-embedded assessments such as portfolios may contribute to teachers' knowledge and expertise and to curriculur reform. For example, using and triangulating a number of data sources, Gearhart and Wolf (1994) found that teachers increased their understanding of the narrative genre and their capacity to provide focused, genre-based comments about children's narratives. Storms, Sheingold, Nunez, and Heller (1998) found that teachers learned about the qualities of student work from the conversations that occurred during scoring sessions, and Sheingold, Heller, and Paulukonis (1995) found that teachers changed their practices in substantive ways.

Portfolio assessments, however, have not exerted uniformly positive effects, in part because the design of portfolio assessment systems can work against instructional reform goals. One study, for example, found that because so many different types of writing were required, students had few opportunities to practice and refine any one type, had few decisions to make about the relative quality of different pieces of their work, and were thus unable to reflect on individual progress and goals (Murphy, Bergamini, & Rooney 1997). Similarly, though Kentucky with its statewide portfolio system fared much better overall than other states in Hillocks' (2002) study of the impact of statewide assessments on curriculum, Callahan's research (1999) has revealed several problems, including (a) that high school English teachers see the portfolios "primarily as a stressful administrative task...imposed from outside"; and (b) that although teachers believed the yearly scoring workshops "helped them understand how to evaluate writing and made them more confident writing teachers," the narrow focus of the meetings undermined the opportunities to "explore the teaching and learning theories behind portfolio pedagogy." Callahan also noted that some portfolios were accepted despite questions about the origin of some of the texts they contained. In studying the perceptions of first-year students who all completed the University of Kentucky's compulsory 12th-grade portfolios, Spaulding and Cummins (1998) found that "two-thirds of the students stated that compiling the portfolio was not a useful activity" (p. 191). Researching the same program, Scott (2005) found discrepancies between the claims students made in their reflective letters and what they said when interviewed about their writing.

Taken together, the findings of these studies suggest that the policies that surround the assessment, as well as the form of the assessment itself, play a critical role in the ultimate impact of any assessment on teachers and students.

Formative and Self-Assessment

The educational field at large has grown more aware of the sociocultural aspects of learning and assessment (see e.g., the work of Broadfoot, 1996; C. Gipps, 1998; Vygotsky, 1978). From a sociocultural perspective, learning and the processes of learning are best assessed in the social setting in which they occur, in the case of schools, in the classroom. From this perspective, students should have a role in negotiating the content and outcomes of the assessment. Promoting that role, it is believed, may encourage students to monitor and reflect on their own performance, and in the process, become self-monitoring, self-regulating, and self-assessing learners (Broadfoot, 1996; Camp, 1992; Yancey, 1996).

Formative and self-assessment are seen as critical accompaniments to such learning. As defined by Gielen, Dochy, and Dierick (2003), the term *formative assessment* "is only used for assessment that is directed at giving information to students with and after completing an assignment, and that is explicitly directed at supporting, guiding and monitoring their learning process" (p. 48). Reviews of research on formative assessment indicate that active engagement of the learner and frequent, precise, and constructive feedback from teachers leads to substantial learning gains (P. Black & Wiliam, 1998). Feedback also appears to be important in students' acquisition of metacognitive skills. Initially teachers give feedback and scaffold students' reflections on what they have produced or learned. As students become more capable, they evaluate their own efforts, drawing conclusions about the quality of their work after or during the process of production (Geilen et al., 2003).

Proponents of assessment reform believe that alternative forms of assessment will encourage teachers to spend more time on activities that cultivate complex understandings

(Mitchell, 1992; Simmons & Resnick, 1993) and encourage students to become self-directed learners (Wolf, 1989). These alternative forms would thus contribute to the validity of the assessment. A common argument for using portfolios in both instruction and assessment, then, is that in explicitly linking them, teachers can provide students with opportunities to engage in reflection and formative self-evaluation. For this reason, in many portfolio classrooms in the United States, the student's participation in reflecting on, and in making decisions about the contents of his or her portfolio, is considered of critical importance (Camp, 1992; Paulson, Paulson, & Meyer, 1991).

In their review of research on self-assessment, Hilgers, Hussy, and Stitt-Bergh (2000) comment that whereas some researchers "began to report that self-observation by itself was leading to behavior change (Kanfer & Phillips, 1966)," results from other studies "suggested that it was not self-monitoring alone that was the agent for behavior change. Some suggested that the personal value, or valence, assigned a particular behavior played a large role in shaping any behavior change associated with self-monitoring" (p. 3). Another factor was frequency. Hilgers et al. also explain how:

> [Self-monitoring] provides an individual with feedback that allows the individual to discriminate between his or her current level of behavior and some significant social or individual standard, thus leading the individual to reward or punish him- or herself at each future self-monitored occurrence.

Hilgers et al. also cite research showing a link between the efficacy of self assessment and its interruption of routine behavior, a view corresponding with other scholars' observations about the sequence of interruption-and-observation (Schon, 1987; Schulman, 1996). To encourage such self-assessment, portfolio advocates have asked students to reflect on their work: to provide a "biography of a paper" (Camp 1992); an explanation of revising practices, in general or with reference to one specific text; and/or comments on how they have grown as writers (Yancey, 1996). Advocates of self-assessment also argue that a portfolio assessment is enhanced by the views of multiple stakeholders, including the "insiders" or composers (Yancey, 1996), and in the case of program assessment, of those who direct programs (Williamson, 1997).

Some research on student reflective texts has focused on students' perceptions of informal assessments like teacher response and grading practices (Baker, 2001). Other research has investigated whether the reflections themselves provide an index of student competence in writing: Morgan and Yancey (1999) found (a) that stronger writers used a sense of genre to help them draft and revise, whereas weaker writers saw writing as universal and global; (b) that stronger writers described the audience as differentiated and as specific readers, whereas weaker writers described an audience coidentical with themselves; and (c) that stronger writers perceived a dichotomy between personal/creative writing and academic writing, especially when they talked about revising. The last finding corresponds with recent research on the perceptions of college writers as they move into their major areas of study and as college graduates move into sites of workplace writing (e.g., Beaufort, 1999). One form of self-assessment is explicitly purpose and institutionally driven: directed self-placement (DSP), a placement practice that allows informed students to make decisions about their placement into 1st-year college composition (Royer & Gilles, 2003). Some evidence suggests that such systems can work effectively. Blakesley, Harvey, and Reynolds (2003) developed a DSP procedure to allow students to choose their own best placement into 1st-year composition. In terms of both pass rates and retention, students who placed themselves into a longer version of a basic writing course outperformed their colleagues who had placed themselves in a standard, shorter course.

Other research on reflection and self-assessment examines the effect of student use of scoring guides on their performance in writing. Research on student use of scoring guides for self-assessment at Washington State University indicates that students enrolled in courses in which a guide was used received significantly higher ratings than students in courses in which the guide was not used (Washington State Critical Thinking Project, 2004). In a study of urban middle-school students, Harvard Project Zero found that students using a genre-specific scoring guide to evaluate their own writing received significantly higher scores on one of three essays (Andrade, 1998). In a second project, when a teacher-guided process of self-assessment exerted a positive effect on girls' writing but had no effect on boys' writing. Andrade points out that this finding is consistent with research on sex differences in how boys and girls respond to feedback; it corresponds as well with reports of gender differences in student portfolio reflections (e.g., L. Black, Daiker, Sommers, & Stygall, 1994).

Taken together, these studies suggest that involving students in the act of assessment produces better writing; they also raise questions about how self-assessment actually functions and in what ways it affects classroom practice. In addition, these studies suggest that validation procedures ought to involve the participation of the writer.

EVOLVING WAYS TO WARRANT VALIDITY

Interest in alternative approaches to assessment has prompted challenges to traditional concepts of validity and reliability on theoretical and epistemological grounds. Carini (1994) emphasized the importance of context, both social and historical, in evaluation, criticizing impersonal assessment procedures that remove writing from the contexts within which they are created, and from their location "within a body of works, spanning time and genre, and the relationship of these works to a person—a self history in the making" (p. 63). In her view, assessment should be personal, contextual, and descriptive in order to acknowledge the links between writing, personal history, and identity.

Several theorists have proposed that the field concentrate on developing models and explanations to support a move away from exclusive reliance on traditional psychometric evidence to the use of constructivist, expert reader, or hermeneutic social-negotiation procedures (Broad, 2003; Gitomer, 1993; Moss, 1992, 1994). For example, Moss (1994) argued that traditional statistical measures should "be treated as only one of several possible strategies serving important epistemological and ethical purposes" (p. 5). Indeed, from a hermeneutic perspective, the most credible judges are those who are most knowledgeable about the context in which a performance occurred, and about the nature of the performance itself. Their judgments are grounded in the richest contextual and textual evidence available, including the observations of others in the interpretive community. Moss (1994) offered several ways to warrant a hermeneutic approach to assessment:

> "extensive knowledge of the learning context; multiple and varied sources of evidence; an ethic of disciplined, collaborative inquiry that encourages challenges and revisions to initial interpretations," and "the transparency of the trail of evidence leading to the interpretations, which allows users to evaluate the conclusions for themselves" (p. 7).

In a similar vein, Gitomer (1993) proposed ways to warrant the dependability of judges' scores, including gathering information about what sort of interactions went on among the judges during the scoring process, how well they understood the context in which the performance was done, who they were, and what their relationship to the individuals being assessed was.

Theorists have also called for the development of a new or expanded set of quality criteria for assessment (Frederiksen & Collins, 1989; Gielen et al., 2003; P. Gipps, 1994; Linn et al., 1991). For example, Frederiksen and Collins maintain that systemically valid assessment systems should be designed to "induce curricular and instructional changes in education systems (and learning strategy changes in students) that foster the development of the cognitive traits that the tests are designed to measure" (p. 27). For proponents of alternative assessment methods, such changes would promote complex and deep understanding of content and self-regulation.

Nonetheless, at the same time that we witness interest both within the United States and internationally in alternative approaches to assessment and validation, we also, ironically, see increasing emphasis on accountability and centralization. In the United States, this emphasis appears in legislation such as No Child Left Behind; in the United Kingdom, in an increasing centralization of curriculum and assessment. As Beard (2000) explains, "The last 15 years of the twentieth century saw British schools increasingly influenced by central government through a National Curriculum, new statutory assessment arrangements at 7, 11 and 14 and increased inspection arrangements" (p. 4). A challenge for the future, especially relevant to the consequential validity of assessments, will be to balance the demands of accountability with the development and validation of assessments that enhance learning and the educational environment as a whole. One step in that direction would be to acknowledge, as Frederiksen and Collins (1989) point out, that "the efficiency in current testing practices is greatly outweighed by the cost of using a system that has low 'systemic' validity—one that has a negative impact on learning and teaching" (p. 32). Reemphasizing consequential validity could lead to writing assessment systems that better support the improvement of teaching and learning. The success of any accountability system, however, depends on multiple factors; at present, the field is just beginning to develop a knowledge base on this assessment topic (see e.g., Hamilton, 2003).

Technology and the Future

Another significant challenge for assessment systems involves technology. It takes three forms: (a) how to evaluate new texts that are already being created, (b) what if any is the appropriate role for automated scoring, and (c) how the current constructs of writing (and thus assessment) will be changed by digitized writing.

The first issue centers on digital texts. The fact that students are writing texts digitally—even when they are submitted in print—means that writing assessment has yet another concern about validity. If students are writing digitally in classrooms, and if the validity of an assessment is in part a function of its fit with real-world or classroom practice, can assessments completed in print be considered valid? There is also some question whether it is possible to evaluate print compositions and some forms of digital text (e.g., hypertext) with the same criteria (see e.g., Moran & Herrington, 2003).

A second issue concerns automated scoring. Measurement experts and entrepreneurs in the business of computerized writing assessment have applauded automated scoring, in part for its efficiency (see e.g., Page & Petersen, 1995; Shermis & Burstein, 2003); and the Web-based promotion for machine scoring programs such as Educational Testing Service's (2004) CriterionSM, the College Board's (2004) ACCUPLACER tests using WritePlacer *Plus*, and Knowledge Analysis Technologies' (2004) Intelligent Essay Assessor. Writing specialists have deplored it (see e.g., the Position Statement adopted by the Conference on College Composition and Communication, 2004). Williamson (2003) reviews the issue with a particular focus on consequential validity, defining validity in local terms "as existing in a particular use of a test, in a particular context, at a particular time" (p. 97); he argues that the defining issue "is whether the scores help make better decisions about students than the current procedures used by a particular college or university" (p. 98). Recent research provides empirical evidence that challenges the predictive (and instructional) validity of automated scoring (Ericsson & Haswell, 2006).

A third, basic, and yet complex issue is that of the construct of writing: Simply put, what difference, if any, does digital writing make to the construct of writing, and how might that affect validity? Scholars have studied this question: One of the current views requires that a new construct of writing directly related to computer-processing skills be defined. For example, Duran (2003), noting that "the skill set in writing extended text with paper and pencil may gradually become obsolete, to be replaced by a skill set which makes use of technology" (p. 16), recommends the development of such a construct for the National Assessment of Educational Progress Similarly, researchers creating new writing tasks for the National Assessment of Adult Literacy are enlarging current constructs of writing in two ways: (a) by including as sites of writing activity the home and the workplace as well as the school, and (b) by including both print and digital technology (K. Yancey, personal communication, January 1, 2005).

This interest in validity, as reflected in the discussion of electronic writing, carries forward the field's epistemological and ethical concern that assessment in writing measure what it claims to measure and that it be used to support the learning of writers. As writing assessment continues to develop and become even more complex in the 21st century that interest is likely to remain at the center of the field.

REFERENCES

Allen, N., Holland, P., & Thayer, D. (2005). Measuring the benefits of examinee-selected questions. *Journal of Educational Measurement, 42*(1), 27–34.

Almasi, J., Afflerbach, P., Guthrie, J., & Schafer, W. (1996). *Effects of a statewide performance assessment program on classroom instructional practice in literacy* (Reading Research Report No. 32). University of Georgia: National Reading Research Center.

Anastasi, A. (1986). Evolving concepts of test validation. *Annual Review of Psychology, 37*, 1–15.

Andrade, H. G. (1998). *Rubrics and self assessment project*. Retrieved December 31, 2004, from http://www.pz.harvard.edu/Research/RubricSelf.htm

Bachman, L. F., & Palmer, A. S. (1996). *Language testing in practice*. Oxford, England: Oxford University Press.

Baker, T. (2001). Identifying and negotiating conflict in the classroom: Reflections of freshman composition students. *Teaching English in the Two-Year College, 29*(2), 179–192.

Basham, C. S., & Kwachka, P. E. (1991). Reading the world differently: A cross-cultural approach to writing assessment. In L. Hamp-Lyons (Ed.), *Assessing second language writing in academic contexts* (pp. 37–49). Norwood, NJ: Ablex.

Beard, R. (2000). *Developing writing 3–23*. London: Hodder & Stoughton.

Beaufort, A. (1999). *Writing in the real world: Making the transition from school to work*. New York: Teachers College Press.

Black, K. (1989). Audience analysis and persuasive writing at the college level. *Research in the Teaching of English, 23*(3), 231–253.

Black, L., Daiker, D., Sommers, J., & Stygall, G. (1994). Writing like a woman and being rewarded for it: Gender, assessment and reflective letters from Miami University's student portfolios. In L. Black, D. Daiker, J. Sommers, & G. Stygall (Eds.), *New directions in portfolio assessment: Reflective practice, critical theory, and large-scale scoring* (pp. 235–247). Portsmouth, NH: Heinemann.

Black, P., & William, D. (1998). Assessment and classroom learning. *Assessment in Education, 5*(1), 7–74.

Blakesley, D., Harvey, E., & Reynolds, E. (2003). Southern Illinois Carbondale as an institutional model: The English 100/101 stretch and directed self placement program. In R. Giles & D. Royer (Eds.), *Directed self placement: Principles and practices* (pp. 207–143). Cresskill, NJ: Hampton.

Breland, H., Camp, R., Jones, R., Morris, M., & Rock, D. (1987). *Assessing writing skill*. New York: College Entrance Examination Board.

Breland, H. H., & Jones, R. J. (1984). *Perceptions of writing skill* (College Board Report No. 88-3; Educational Testing Service Research Report No. 82-47). New York: College Entrance Examination Board.

Breland, H. M. (1983). *The direct assessment of writing skill: A measurement review* (College Board Report No. 83-6; ETS Research Report No. 83-32). New York: College Entrance Examination Board.

Bridgeman, B., & Carlson, S. (1983). *Survey of academic writing tasks required of graduate and undergraduate foreign students* (TOEFL Research Report No. 15; ETS Research Report No. 83–18). Princeton, NJ: Educational Testing Service.

Broad, R. (2003). *What we really value: Beyond rubrics in teaching and assessing writing*. Logan: Utah State University Press.

Broadfoot, P. (1996). *Education, assessment and society*. Buckingham, England: Open University Press.

Brossell, G. C. (1983). Rhetorical specification in essay examination topics. *College Composition and Communication, 45*, 165–173.

Brown, A. (1995). The effect of rater variables in the development of an occupation-specific performance test. *Language Testing, 12,* 1–15.

Brown, J. D. (1991). Do English and ESL faculties rate writing samples differently? *TESOL Quarterly 25,* 587–603.

Brown, J. D., Hilgers, T., & Marsella, J. (1991). Essay prompts and topics: Minimising the effect of mean differences. *Written Communication, 8*(4), 533–556.

Callahan, S. (1999). All done with best of intentions: One Kentucky high school after six years of state portfolio tests. *Assessing Writing, 6*(1), 5–40.

Camp, R. (1983, April). *Direct assessment at ETS: What we know and what we need to know.* Paper presented at the meeting of the National Council on Measurement in Education, Montreal.

Camp, R. (1992). Portfolio reflections in middle and secondary school classrooms. In K. B. Yancey (Ed.), *Portfolios in the writing classroom* (pp. 61–79). Urbana, IL: National Council of Teachers of English.

Carini, P. F. (1994). Dear Sister Bess: An essay on standards, judgement and writing. *Assessing Writing, 1,* 29–65.

Carlson, S. B., Bridgeman, B., Camp, R., & Waanders, J. (1985). *Relationship of admission test scores to writing performance of native and non-native speakers of English* (TOEFL Research Report No. 19). Princeton, NJ: Educational Testing Service.

Carr, N. (2000). A comparison of the effects of analytic and holistic composition in the context of composition tests. *Issues in Applied Linguistics, 11,* 207–241.

Chalhoub-Deville, M. (1995). Deriving assessment scales across different tests and rater groups. *Language Testing, 12,* 16–33.

Cho, Y. (2003) Assessing writing: Are we bound by only one method? *Assessing Writing, 8*(3), 165–191.

College Board. (2004). *WritePlacer Plus.* Retrieved May 5, 2004, from http://www.collegeboard.com/highered/apr/accu/accu_wpp.html

Conference on College Composition and Communication. (1995). Retrieved December 31, 2004, from http://www.ncte.org/groups/cccc/positions/115775.htm

Conference on College Composition and Communication. (2004). Position statement. Retrieved December 31, 2004, from http://www.ncte.org/cccc/resources/positions/123773.htm

Corbett, H. D., & Wilson, B. L. (1991). *Testing, reform, and rebellion.* Norwood, NJ: Ablex.

Crowhurst, M., & Piche, G. L. (1979). Audience and mode of discourse effects on syntactic complexity in writing on two grade levels. *Research in the Teaching of English, 13,* 101–109.

Cumming, A. (1997). The testing of second-language writing. In C. Clapham (Ed.), *Language assessment: Vol. 7. Encyclopedia of language and education* (pp. 51–63). Dordrecht, the Netherlands: Kluwer.

Despain, L., & Hilgers, T. (1992). Readers responses to the rating of non-uniform portfolios: Are there limits of portfolios' utility? *Writing Program Administration, 16*(1), 24–37.

Diederich, P. (1974). *Measuring growth in English.* Urbana, IL: National Council of Teachers of English.

Duran, R. (2003). *Implications of electronic technology for the NAEP assessment* (NCES Working Paper No. 200316). Retrieved December 31, 2004, from http://nces.ed.gov/pubsearch/pubsinfo.asp?pubid=200316

Educational Testing Service. (2004). *Criterion SM.* Retrieved May 5, 2004, from http://www.ets.org/criterion/

Erdosy, M. U. (2004). *Exploring variability in judging writing ability in a second language: A study of four experienced raters of ESL compositions* (TOEFL Research Report No. 70). Princeton, NJ: Educational Testing Service.

Ericsson, P. G., & Haswell, R. H. (2006). *Machine scoring of student essays: Truth and consequences.* Logan: Utah State University Press.

Evans, P. J. A. (1979). Evaluation of writing in Ontario: Grades 8, 12, and 13. *Review and Evaluation Bulletins, 1*(2).

Foster, D., & Russell, D. (2002). *Writing and learning in cross-national perspective: Transitions from secondary to higher education.* Urbana, IL: National Council of Teachers of English.

Fredericksen, J., & Collins, A. (1989). A systems approach to educational testing. *Educational Researcher, 18*(9), 27–32.

Freedman, A., & Pringle, I. (1981). *Why students can't write arguments.* Unpublished manuscript, Carleton University, Ottawa, Canada.

Freedman, S. W. (1979). How characteristics of student essays influence teachers' evaluations. *Journal of Educational Psychology, 71,* 328–338.

Freedman, S. W. (1981). Influences on evaluators of expository essays: Beyond the text. *Research in the Teaching of English, 15*(3), 245–255.

Gearhart, M., Herman, J., Baker, E., & Whittaker, A. (1993). *Whose work is it? A question for the validity of large-scale portfolio assessment* (CSE Tech. Rep. No. 363). Los Angeles: CRESST Institute on Education and Training, University of California.

Gearhart, M., & Wolf, S. (1994). Engaging teachers in assessment of their students' narrative writing: The role of subject matter knowledge. *Assessing Writing, 1*, 67–90.

Gielen, S., Dochy, F., & Dierick, S. (2003). Evaluating the consequential validity of new modes of assessment: the influence of assessment on learning, including pre-, post- and true assessment effects. In M. Segers, F. Dochy, & E. Cascallar (Eds.), *Optimising new modes of assessment: In search of qualities and standards* (pp. 37–54). Dordrecht, the Netherlands: Kluwer Academic.

Gipps, C. (1998). Socio-cultural aspects of assessment. In P. D. Pearson & A. Iran-Nehad (Eds.), *Review of research in education* (Vol. 23, pp. 335–393). Washington, DC: American Educational Research Association.

Gipps, P. (1994). *Beyond testing: towards a theory of educational assessment*. London: Falmer.

Gitomer, D. (1993). Performance assessment and educational measurement. In R. Bennett & W. Ward (Eds.), *Construction versus choice in cognitive measurement: Issues in constructed response, performance testing, and portfolio assessment* (pp. 241–293). Hillsdale, NJ: Lawrence Erlbaum Associates.

Godshalk, F., Swineford, E., & Coffman, W. (1966). *The measurement of writing ability*. New York: College Entrance Examination Board.

Golub-Smith, M., Reese, C., & Steinhaus, K. (1993). *Topic and topic type comparability on the test of written English* (TOEFL Research Report No. 42). Princeton, NJ: Educational Testing Service.

Greenberg, K. (1981). *The effects of variations in essay question format on the writing performance of CUNY freshmen*. Unpublished manuscript, City University of New York Instructional Resource Center.

Hale, G., Taylor, C., Bridgeman, B., Carson, J., Kroll, B., & Kantor, R. (1996). *A study of writing tasks assigned in academic degree programs* (TOEFL Research Report No. 54). Princeton, NJ: Educational Testing Service.

Hamilton, L. (2003). Assessment as a policy tool. In R. Floden (Ed.), *Review of research in education, 27* (pp. 25–68). Washington, DC: American Educational Research Association.

Hamp-Lyons, L. (1990). Second language writing: Assessment issues. In B. Kroll (Ed.), *Second language writing: Research insights for the classroom* (pp. 69–87). New York: Cambridge University Press.

Hamp-Lyons, L. (1991b). Scoring procedures for ESL context. In L. Hamp-Lyons (Ed.), *Assessing second language writing in academic contexts* (pp. 241–276). Norwood, NJ: Ablex.

Hamp-Lyons, L., & Condon, W. (1993). Questioning assumptions about portfolio-based assessment. *College Composition and Communication, 44*, 176–190.

Hamp-Lyons, L., & Matthias, S. (1994). Examining expert judgments of task difficulty on essay tests. *Journal of Second Language Writing, 3*(1), 49–68.

Haney, W., & Scott, L. (1987). Talking with children about tests: An exploratory study of test item ambiguity. In R. O. Freedle & R. P. Duran (Eds.), *Cognitive and linguistic analysis of test performance* (Vol. 22, pp. 298–369). Norwood, NJ: Ablex.

Haswell, R. (1998). Rubrics, prototypes, and exemplars: Categorization and systems of writing placement. *Assessing Writing, 5*(2), 231–268.

Henning, G. (1991). Issues in evaluating and maintaining an ESL writing assessment program. In L. Hamp-Lyons (Ed.), *Assessing second language writing in academic contexts* (pp. 279–291). Norwood, NJ: Ablex.

Herman, J., Gearhart, M., & Baker, E. (1993). Assessing writing portfolios: Issues in the validity and meaning of scores. *Educational Assessment, 1*(3), 201–224.

Heubert, J. P., & Hauser, R. M. (Eds.). (1999). *High stakes: Testing for tracking, promotion, and graduation*. Washington, DC: National Academy Press.

Hilgers, T. (1992, March). *Improving placement exam equitability, validity, and reliability*. Paper presented at the Conference on College Composition and Communication, Cincinnati, OH.

Hilgers, T., Hussey, E., & Stitt-Bergh, M. (2000). The case for prompted self-assessment. In J. Smith & K. B. Yancey (Eds.), *Self-assessment and development in writing* (pp. 1–25). Cresskill, NJ: Hampton.

Hillocks, G., Jr. (2002). *The testing trap: How states writing assessments control learning*. New York: Teachers College Press.

Hughes, R. E., & Nelson, C. H. (1991). Placement scores and placement practices: An empirical analysis. *Community College Review, 19*(1), 42–46.

Huot, B. (1993). The influence of holistic scoring procedures on reading and rating student essays. In M. Williamson & B. Huot (Eds.), *Validating holistic scoring for writing assessment: Theoretical and empirical foundations* (pp. 206–232). Cresskill, NJ: Hampton.

Huot, B. (2002). *(Re)articulating writing assessment for teaching and learning*. Logan: Utah State University Press.

Jacobs, H. L., Zinkgraf, S. A., Wormuth, D. R., Hartfiel, V. F., & Hughey, J. B. (1981). *Testing ESL composition: A practical approach*. Rowley, MA: Newbury House.

Janopoulos, M. (1992). University faculty tolerance of NS and NNS writing errors: A comparison. *Journal of Second Language Writing, 1*(2), 109–121.

Jennings, C. (2002). *Aligning writing instruction in secondary and post secondary institutions. League for innovation in the community college.* Retrieved December 31, 2004, from http://www.league.org/leaguetlc/express/inn0207.htm

Johnson, T. S., Smagorinsky, P., Thompson, L., & Fry, P. G. (2003). Learning to teach the five-paragraph theme. *Research in the Teaching of English, 38*, 136–176.

Kanfer, F., & Phillips, J. (1966). Behavior therapy: A panacea for all ills or a passing fancy? *Archives of General Psychiatry, 15*, 114–128.

Keech, C. L., & McNelly, M. E. (1982). Comparison and analysis of rater responses to the anchor papers in the writing prompt variation study. In J. R. Gray & L. P. Ruth (Eds.), *Properties of writing tasks: A study of alternative procedures for holistic writing assessment* (pp. 260–315). Berkeley: University of California, Graduate School of Education, Bay Area Writing Project. (ERIC Document Reproduction Service No. ED230576)

Ketter, J., & Pool, J. (2001). Exploring the impact of a high-stakes direct writing assessment in two high school classrooms. *Research in the Teaching of English, 35*, 344–393.

Knowledge Analysis Technologies. (2004). *Intelligent essay assessor.* Retrieved May 5, 2004, from http://www.knowledge-technologies.com

Kobayashi, H., & Rinnert, C. (1996). Factors affecting composition evaluation in an EFL context: Cultural rhetorical pattern and readers' background. *Language Learning, 46*, 397–437.

Koretz, D., & Hamilton, L. (2003). *Teachers' responses to high-stakes testing and the validity of gains: A pilot study* (Center for the Study of Evaluation Tech. Rep. No. 610). Los Angeles: National Center for Research on Evaluation, Standards, and Student Testing.

Koretz, D., McCaffrey, D., Klein, S., Bell, R., & Stecher, B. (1992). *The reliability of scores from the 1992 Vermont Portfolio Assessment Program: Interim report* (Center for the Study of Evaluation Tech. Rep. No. 350). Santa Monica, CA: Rand Institute on Education and Training.

Koretz, D., Mitchell, K., Barron, S., & Keith, S. (1996). *Perceived effects of the Maryland School Performance Assessment Program* (Tech. Rep. No. 409). Los Angeles: National Center for Research on Evaluation, Standards, and Student Testing.

Koretz, D., Stecher, B., Klein, S., & McCaffrey, D. (1994). *The evolution of a portfolio program: The impact and quality of the Vermont program in its second year (1992–93)* (Center for the Study of Evaluation Tech. Rep. No. 385). Los Angeles: National Center for Research on Evaluation, Standards, and Student Testing.

Langer, J. (1984). The effects of available information on responses to school writing tasks. *Research in the Teaching of English, 18*(1), 27–44.

LeMahieu, P., Eresh, J., & Wallace, R. (1992). Using student portfolios for a public accounting. *The School Administrator, 49*(11), 8–15.

Linn, R., Baker, E., & Dunbar, S. B. (1991). Complex, performance-based assessment: Expectations and validation criteria. *Educational Researcher, 20*(8), 15–21.

Livingston, S. (1987, April). *The effects of time limits on the quality of student-written essays.* Paper presented at the annual meeting of the American Educational Research Association, Washington, DC. (ERIC Document Reproduction Service No. ED286936)

Loofbourrow, P. (1994). Composition in the context of the CAP: A case study of the interplay between composition assessment and classrooms. *Educational Assessment, 2*(1), 7–49.

Matsuhashi, A. (1982). Explorations in the real-time production of written discourse. In M. Nystrand (Ed.), *What writers know: The language, process, and structure of written discourse* (pp. 269–290). New York: Academic Press.

Messick, S. (1989). Meaning and values in test validation: The science and ethics of assessment. *Educational Researcher, 18*(2), 5–11.

Messick, S. (1994). The interplay of evidence and consequences in the validation of performance assessments. *Educational Researcher, 23*(2), 13–23.

Mitchell, R. (1992). *Testing for learning: How new approaches to evaluation can improve American schools.* New York: The Free Press.

Moran, C., & Herrington, A. (2003). *Evaluating academic hypertexts* (pp. 246–257). Boston: Houghton Mifflin.

Morgan, M., & Yancey, K. B. (1999). Reflective essays, curriculum, and the scholarship of administration. In S. Rose & I. Weiser (Eds.), *The writing program administrator as researcher* (pp. 81–94). Portsmouth, NH: Heinemann.

Moss, P. (1992). Shifting conceptions of validity in educational measurement: Implications for performance assessment. *Review of Educational Research, 62*(3), 229–258.

Moss, P. (1994). Can there be validity without reliability? *Educational Researcher, 23*(2), 5–12.

Murphy, S. (1994). Portfolios and curriculum reform: Patterns in practice. *Assessing Writing, 1*(2), 175–207.

Murphy, S. (2003). That was then, this is now: The impact of changing assessment policies on teachers and the teaching of writing in California. *Journal of Writing Assessment, 1*(1), 23–45.

Murphy, S., Bergamini, J., & Rooney, P. (1997). The impact of large-scale portfolio assessment programs on classroom practice: Case studies of the New Standards field-trial portfolio. *Educational Assessment, 4*(4), 297–333.

Murphy, S., Carroll, K., Kinzer, C., & Robyns, A. (1982). A study of the construction of the meaning of a writing prompt by its authors, the student writers, and the raters. In J. R. Gray & L. P. Ruth (Eds.), *Properties of writing tasks: A study of alternative procedures for holistic writing assessment* (pp. 386–468). Berkeley: University of California, Graduate School of Education, Bay Area Writing Project. (ERIC Document Reproduction Service No. ED230576)

Murphy, S., & Underwood, T. (2000). *Portfolio practices: Lessons from schools, districts, and states.* Norwood, MA: Christopher-Gordon.

Nystrand, M., Cohen, A., & Dowling, N. (1993). Addressing reliability problems in the portfolio assessment of college writing. *Educational Assessment, 1*(1), 53–70.

Odell, L. (1981). Defining and assessing competence in writing. In C. Cooper (Ed.), *The nature and measurement of competency in English* (pp. 95–138). Urbana, IL: National Council of Teachers of English.

Olson, M., & Martin, D. (1980, April). *Assessment of entering student writing skill in the community college.* Paper presented at the annual meeting of the American Educational Research Association, Boston. (ERIC Document Reproduction Service No. ED235845)

O'Neill, P., Murphy, S., Huot, B., & Williamson, M. (2004, November). *What high school teachers in three states say about high stakes writing assessments.* Paper presented at the annual conference of the National Council of Teachers of English, Indianapolis.

Page, E., & Petersen, N. S. (1995). The computer moves into essay grading: Updating the ancient test. *Phi Delta Kappan, 76*, 561–565.

Paulson, F. L., Paulson, P. P., & Meyer, C. A. (1991). What makes a portfolio a portfolio? *Educational Leadership, 48*(5), 60–63.

Polio, C., Fleck, C., & Leder, N. (1998). "If I only had more time": ESL learners' changes in linguistic accuracy on essay revisions. *Journal of Second Language Writing, 7*(1), 43–68.

Polio, C., & Glew, M. (1996). ESL Writing assessment prompts: How students choose. *Journal of Second Language Writing, 5*(1), 35–49.

Powers, D. E., & Fowles, M. E. (1996). Effects of applying different time limits to a proposed GRE writing test. *Journal of Educational Measurement, 33*(4), 433–452.

Quality counts. (2002). *Education week, 21*(17). Retrieved October 29, 2005, from http://www.edweek.com/sreports/qc02/

Quellmalz, E., Capell, F., & Chou, C. (1982). Effects of discourse and response mode on the measurement of writing competence. *Journal of Educational Measurement, 19*(4), 241–258.

Reid, J. (1990). Responding to different topic types: A qualitative analysis from a contrastive rhetoric perspective. In B. Kroll (Ed.), *Second language writing: Research insights for the classroom* (pp. 191–210). New York: Cambridge University Press.

Royer, D., & Gilles, R. (2003). Introduction: FAQ. In R.Giles & D. Royer (Eds.), *Directed self placement: Principles and practices* (pp. 000–000). Cresskill, NJ: Hampton.

Ruth, L., & Murphy, S. (1988). *Designing writing tasks for the assessment of writing.* Norwood, NJ: Ablex.

Santos, T. (1988). Professors' reactions to the academic writing of nonnative-speaking students. *TESOL Quarterly, 22*(1), 69–90.

Scherff, L., & Piazza, C. (2005). The more things change, the more they stay the same: A survey of high school students' writing experiences. *Research in the Teaching of English, 39*(3), 271–304.

Schon, D. A. (1987). *Educating the reflective practitioner.* San Francisco: Jossey-Bass.

Schulman, L. (1996, February). *Course anatomy: The dissection and transformation of knowledge.* Plenary presented at the American Associaton of Higher Education Faculty Roles and Rewards Conference, Atlanta.

Scott, T. (2005). Creating the subject of portfolios: Reflective writing and the conveyance of institutional prerogatives. *Written Communication, 22*, 3–35.

Sheingold, K., Heller, J., & Paulukonis, S. (1995). *Actively seeking evidence: Teacher change through assessment development* (Manuscript No. 94-04). Princeton, NJ: Educational Testing Service.

Shepard, L. (1995). Using assessment to improve learning. *Educational Leadership, 54*(5), 38–43.

Shermis, M. D., & Burstein (Eds.). (2003). *Automated essay scoring: A cross-disciplinary perspective.* Mahwah, NJ: Lawrence Erlbaum Associates.

Simmons, J. (1992). Don't settle for less in large-scale writing assessment. In K.Goodman, L. B. Vird, & Y. M. Goodman (Eds.), *The whole language catalog: Supplement on authentic assessment* (pp. 160–161). Santa Rosa, CA: American School Publishers.

Simmons, W., & Resnick, L. (1993). Assessment as a catalyst of school reform. *Educational Leadership, 50*(5), 11–15.

Smith, L. S., Winters, L., Quellmalz, E. S., & Baker, E. L. (1980). *Characteristics of student writing competence: An investigation of alternative scoring systems* (Research Report No. 134). Los Angeles: Center for the Study of Evaluation. (ERIC Document Reproduction Services No. ED217074)

Smith, M. L. (1991). Put to the test: The effects of external testing on teachers. *Educational Researcher, 20*(5), 8–11.

Smith, W. L. (1993). Assessing the reliability and adequacy of using holistic scoring of essays as a college composition placement technique. In M. Williamson & B. Huot (Eds.), *Validating holistic scoring for writing assessment: Theoretical and empirical foundations* (pp. 142–205). Cresskill, NJ: Hampton.

Smith, W. L., Hull, G., Land, R. E., Moore, M. T., Ball, C., Dunham, D. E., et al. (1985). Some effects of varying the structure of a topic on college students' writing. *Written Communication, 2*(1), 73–89.

Song, B., & Caruso, L. (1996). Do English and ESL faculty differ in evaluating the essays of native-English speaking and ESL students? *Journal of Second Language Writing, 5*, 163–182.

Spaulding, E., & Cummins, G. (1998). It was the best of times. It was a waste of time: University of Kentucky students' view of writing under KERA. *Assessing Writing, 5*(2), 167–200.

Stecher, B. M., Barron, S. I., Kaganoff, T., & Goodwin, J. (1998). *The effects of standards-based assessment on classroom practices: Results of the 1996–97 RAND survey of Kentucky teachers of mathematics and writing* (Center for the Study of Evaluation Tech. Rep. No. 482). Los Angeles: Center for Research on Evaluation, Standards, and Student Testing.

Storms, B. A., Sheingold, K., Nunez, A., & Heller, J. (1998). *The feasibility, comparability, and value of local scorings of performance assessments* (Tech. Rep.). Princeton, NJ: Educational Testing Service, Center for Performance Assessment.

Sullivan, F. (1997). Calling writer's bluffs: The social production of writing ability in university placement-testing. *Assessing Writing, 4*(1), 53–82.

Sweedler-Brown, C. O. (1985). The influence of training and experience on holistic essay evaluation. *English Journal, 74*(5), 49–55.

Sweedler-Brown, C. O. (1993). ESL essay evaluation: The influence of sentence-level and rhetorical features. *Journal of Second Language Writing, 2*(1), 3–17.

Tedick, D. J. (1990). ESL writing assessment: Subject matter knowledge and its impact on performance. *English for Specific Purposes, 9*, 123–143.

Trachsel, M. (1992). *Instituionalizing literacy: The historical role of college entrance examinations in English.* Carbondale: Southern Illinois University Press.

Underwood, T., & Murphy, S. (1998). Interrater reliability in a California middle school English/language arts portfolio assessment program. *Assessing Writing, 5*(2), 201–230.

Vygotsky, L. (1978). *Mind in society.* London: Harvard University Press.

Wallace, V. L. (2002). Administrative direction in schools of contrasting status: Two cases. In G. Hillocks, Jr. (Ed.), *The testing trap: How state writing assessment control learning* (pp.93–102). New York: Teachers College Press.

Washington State Critical Thinking Project. (2004) Retrieved December 31, 2004, from http://wsuctproject. ctlt.wsu.edu/rf.htm

Weigle, S. C. (1999). Investigating rater/prompt interactions in writing assessment: Quantitative and qualitative approaches. *Assessing Writing, 6*(2), 145–178.

Weigle, S. C. (2002). *Assessing writing.* Cambridge, England: Cambridge University Press.

White, E. (1984). Holisticism. *College Composition and Communication, 35*(4), 400–409.

Williamson, M. (1993). An introduction to holistic scoring. In M. Williamson & B. Huot (Eds.), *Validating holistic scoring for writing assessment: Theoretical and empirical foundations* (pp. 206–232). Cresskill, NJ: Hampton.

Williamson, M. (1997). Pragmatism, positivism, and program evaluation. In K. B. Yancey & B. Huot (Eds.), *Assessing writing across the curriculum: Diverse approaches and practices* (pp. 237–259). Greenwich, CT: Ablex.

Williamson, M. (2003). Validity of automated scoring: Prologue for a continuing discussion of machine scoring student writing. *Journal of Writing Assessment, 1*(2), 85–105.

Winters, L. (1978). *The effects of differing response criteria on the assessment of writing competence.* Washington, DC: U.S. Government Printing Office. (ERIC Document Reproduction Service No. ED212659)

Witte, S., & Cherry, R. (1994). Think-aloud protocols, protocol analysis, and research design: An exploration of the influence of writing tasks on writing processes. In P. Smagorinsky (Ed.), *Speaking about writing: Reflections on research methodologies* (pp. 20–54). Thousand Oaks, CA: Sage.

Witte, S., Flach, J., Greenwood, C., & Wilson, K. (1995). More notes toward an assessment of advanced ability to communicate. *Assessing Writing, 2*(1), 21–66.

Wolf, D. P. (1989). Portfolio assessment: Sampling student work. *Educational Leadership, 46,* 35–39.

Yancey, K. B. (1996). Dialogue, interplay, and discovery: Mapping the role and the rhetoric of reflection in portfolio assessment. In R. C. Calfee & P. Perfumo (Eds.), *Writing portfolios in the classroom: Policy and practice, promise and peril* (pp. 83–102). Mahwah, NJ: Lawrence Erlbaum Associates.

CHAPTER 24

Teaching of Writing and Diversity: Access, Identity, and Achievement

John Albertinti
Rochester Institute of Technology

Diversity becomes an issue in the teaching of writing when students from an underrepresented group must learn to write in a classroom designed by able-bodied, English-speaking, Euro-centric educators. Such a classroom may be less accessible to economically disadvantaged students, students of color, students whose home language is not English, female students, lesbian, gay, bisexual, transgender, and gender-questioning students, and students with disabilities. In this brief review of research in the teaching of writing to such students, we focus on three background variables: ethnicity (including class and race), gender, and disability. Under disability, we consider students with hearing, vision, and learning disabilities. Though distinctions among variables are necessary for purposes of discussion, they are of course arbitrary when applied to real individuals. As the research shows, students bring multiple identities to school (Kubota, 2003), and so a female deaf student from a Spanish-speaking home who uses American Sign Language (ASL) and considers herself culturally deaf will likely challenge traditional approaches to teaching writing in mainstream classrooms.

The goal of this review is to reach an understanding of how diverse students fare in mainstream writing classes with various instructional approaches. Although non-native speakers of English are the focus of chapter 32 in this volume, research on second-language learners is included here because second-language learners are culturally and linguistically marginalized in American society. We are interested here in how background, interactions, and environment affect the writing achievement of these students. Does background limit access to instruction? Which instructional approaches in second-language or regular language arts (RLA) classes appear promising? To what extent is the cultivation of a mainstream writing voice an issue for these students? Do researchers and teachers take into account student motivation and attitude on the one hand and tolerance of individual and cultural expression on the other? In other words, should students be encouraged to cultivate a voice in writing that may be unacceptable to the academy?

An understanding of diversity in writing classrooms is particularly important today when war, terrorism, and poverty lead members of a society to fear and distrust those different from themselves. Yet, dislike for the "others" in our midst has been voiced often in our history. In 1751, Benjamin Franklin interrupts his projections about the future of the new world in a pamphlet on population growth to complain about German immigration into Pennsylvania: "Why should the *Palatine Boors* be suffered to swarm into our Settlements, and by herding together establish their Language and Manners to the Exclusion of ours" (Wood, 2004, p. 71). Today the "others" are the Hispanic woman in the boardroom, the gay bishop in the diocese, or the Islamic family in the neighborhood. As educators we must do more that simply acknowledge, respect, or celebrate differences among our students. We must understand how these differences affect student learning, our teaching, and our scholarship.

ETHNICITY, CLASS, AND RACE

The key issue in this chapter is the role that ethnicity, language background, class, race, gender, and disability play in the teaching and learning of writing. We take the view, now commonplace, that learning to write and to construct meaning is largely a social activity. Similarly, development of an individual's identity is influenced by interactions with other people. Whatever biological, physical, or environmental factors are involved—whether a person is born Black, White, deaf, hearing, male or female, gay or straight; or whether a person is born into an English-speaking or Spanish-speaking home—the relative prominence such background characteristics assume in a student's view of him or herself will vary depending on that individual's social relations and discourse communities (Kubota, 2003; Royster, 1992). The crucial questions for teachers of writing then become: How do our understanding of writing and the way we teach it affect a student's developing proficiency and identity as a writer? Is the notion of voice discussed in U.S. language arts classes and 1st-year composition courses culturally determined? If so, what is the meaning of such notions for second-language learners in American schools?

Race

For African American educators like Jacqueline Jones Royster, encounters with racism, sexism, classism, and ethnocentrism in academic environments shape their identities as people and as writers. For her, the words William E. B. Du Bois used in 1903 describe the internal polarization she and other marginalized people feel:

> [It is] this sense of always looking at one's self through the eyes of others, of measuring one's soul by the tape of a world that looks on in amused contempt and pity. One ever feels his twoness—an American, a Negro; two souls, two thoughts, two unreconciled strivings; two warring ideals in one dark body, whose dogged strength alone keeps it from being torn asunder. (Du Bois, 1903/1969, p. 45)

In their study of a group of African American students participating in a precollege enrichment program, Welch and Hodges (1997) describe another kind of twoness. In their students, they observe a clash between academic identity and racial identity. For these students, attending college feels like "standing outside on the inside." In terms of writing and definitions of discourse, Gee (1989) and Delpit (1995) disagree on whether students can or even should learn a mainstream discourse, which by Gee's broad interpretation presents the student with a conflict in identity, worldview, and values. For Delpit, a decision to deemphasize the superficial trappings of discourse (grammar, form, style) and to develop the students' writing within the language and style of the students' home (vernacular) discourse is a decision *not* to teach (p. 161).

Class

Ashley (2001) presents narrative data that lead one to question Gee's (1989) concern about identity conflict and "much of the theorizing by and about working-class academics that emphasizes loss" (p. 493). A prominent theme in the auto-ethnographies of writing by four working-class women in college (one Dominican American and three Euro-American women), is "playing the school game." This means using the voice or discourse that will get the grade. Learning how to play the game means learning "general schooled discourse" and conforming to particular teachers' expectations. The women's recurrent references to gaming and to tricking the teacher, their critical stance and even parody of academic writing suggest a sense of agency and an awareness of themselves as writers "in a contact zone" (p. 493). The picture formed of these proficient undergraduate writers is not one of loss or confusion but rather one of confident "double-voicedness" (p. 516).

Their sophistication—and pragmatism—as writers allow them to play with discourse. For them, it seems, the conflict between authentic voice and acculturation is not an issue. For them, learning an academic voice did not mean giving up an identity class, race, or gender; rather, they developed an objectivity or agency that allowed them to select a use and style depending on the audience and situation. Ashley (2001) does not suggest that the submerged critical stance of these women be considered a goal of instruction. She simply points out that it is a reality for some students. Her study points out that developing agency as a writer means more than developing a unique voice. By investigating the different discourses in their lives (home, school, sports) and experimenting with them in their writing, students may become more aware of context, culture and reader expectation: the need for multiple voices.

Ethnicity

Recent research presents a complex picture of how ethnic diversity affects writing ability and attitude toward writing. For example, Knudson (1993) found that ethnicity interacted with age and gender with regard to students' attitude toward writing and views of themselves as writers. Though her data showed a general trend for girls to have a more positive attitude toward writing than boys, significant differences occurred only among Anglo-American and Hispanic students (Grades 4–8). Boys and girls in the Black and Asian groups did not differ significantly. Older students across all groups had a less positive attitude toward writing than did younger students. Anglo-American students had significantly more positive views of themselves as writers than Hispanic students; and Black and Asian students fell in between the Anglo-American and Hispanic. In terms of writing quality, Engelhard, Gordon, and Gabrielson (2001) found that the performance of eighth-grade students on statewide assessments of writing in Georgia significantly related to the writing task and whether the students were Black, White, male or female. The writing tasks varied by mode of discourse (narrative, descriptive, expository) and experiential demand (direct experience, imagined experience, outside knowledge). The hierarchy of difficulty was as expected for all students: Tasks eliciting narrative and direct experience produced higher quality writing than did tasks eliciting expository and outside knowledge. In terms of student characteristics, girls did better than boys and White students did better than Black students.

Starfield (2002) illustrates the difficulty that non-native English speakers have in establishing an authoritative writer's voice in his detailed textual analysis of two first-year sociology essays at a university in South Africa. The writer of the first essay, a White, middle-class English-speaking man, inserts summary and analysis appropriately into the text and establishes his authority and identity as author of the essay. The second writer, a Black man from a township who has learned English as a second language, overuses the words of authorities in an apparent attempt to compensate for his second-language status. The result of his attempt to mimic academic prose is censure for plagiarism and a loss of credit on his essay. Here an unskilled attempt to borrow authority results in condemnation and loss of self-esteem.

Second-Language Learners

A certain level of language proficiency and experience are necessary to establish one's authority as a writer and to achieve the double-voicedness of Ashley's (2001) working-class women. Language proficiency distinguishes learners of English as a second language (ESL), learners of English as a second dialect, and, as we see later in this chapter, deaf and hard-of-hearing students from the other types of student discussed in this chapter. In a study of middle-grade learner essays, Reynolds (2004) demonstrates the relationship between control of specific grammatical and lexical features of English and fluency in academic writing. In his study, he extends the work of Reppen (2001), who investigated how students' language varied according to age (fifth grade vs. adult), mode (oral vs. written), and rhetorical purpose (e.g., genre and topic).

Reynolds takes essays from a narrower age range (10–13, fifth and sixth grades), looks only at written discourse (two essays), and introduces the variable of linguistic proficiency (that of second-language learners). In comparing the essays of fifth- and sixth-grade U.S. students in ESL and RLA classes, he finds similar variation by grade level and topic, but marked differences in information density, lexical diversity, and engagement of the reader (primarily through the use of *you*). In other words, he finds that students in the RLA group are developmentally ahead in their ability to pack information into their writing, use diverse vocabulary, and draw the reader into the writer's point of view. By way of explanation, Reynolds suggests that grammatical competency and experience writing for different purposes account for the superiority of the RLA writers.

In writing classes for second-language learners, it seems, a focus on linguistic accuracy is widespread. In one study of language instruction for newcomers to Canada, both teachers and students report an almost exclusive focus on writing for language practice activities, such as answering reading comprehension questions (Currie & Cray, 2004). Teachers reported that the way to learn to write in a second language was through instruction in language structures, drill, and error correction. According to the teachers' reports, classroom writing activities did not relate to the literacy practices students reported doing outside the classroom (e.g., for immigration, banking, insurance, medical, and educational purposes). For these learners, a gap exists between classroom literacy practices and practices outside of the classroom. Writing instruction that focuses on grammatical accuracy typically does not emphasize writing as a socially situated activity, influenced by topic, audience, and purpose.

Studies of tutoring interaction with native and non-native English-speaking students reveal conflicting goals and expectations on the part of the tutors and tutees. As Williams (2004) and Thonus (2004) report, writers come to writing centers wanting their papers corrected, whereas, tutors "have wider aims—to help writers improve their writing" (Williams, 2004, p. 173). Negotiation between tutor and tutees may lead to positive results, but also frustration. Despite wide variation in effect of tutor suggestions, certain patterns emerged in Williams' study: The focus of discussion is usually the focus revision, surface-level features are more likely to get revised than text-based problems, and writer response (e.g., making note of the tutor's suggestions) is predictive of the session's impact on revision. In general, the impact of the sessions is greater when the suggestions are direct, when tutees actively participate in the discussion, and when the tutees write down plans during the session. In addition, "scaffolding moves" (e.g., the marking of critical features and modeling) were shown to be effective.

Differing expectations lead to frustration. Whereas the tutor has the goal of the writing center in mind—to improve the overall writing skill and independence of the writer—and may favor an inductive approach with the tutee, the tutee often has a more immediate short-term goal of completing an assignment. Another expectation seems related to cultural background and pedagogical approach. As Thonus (2004) points out, current writing pedagogy promotes providing guidance without taking ownership of the writing. The expectation of some second-language students is, however, to be told by an expert what to do. Having a tutor ask a tutee what he or she thinks should be done is ultimately unsatisfying for these students.

One tool to foster independence among writers simultaneously learning a second language is the use of large databases of authentic language. Yoon and Hirvela (2004) report favorable reaction to the use of corpora in writing instruction. They trained students in the use of Collins' COBUILD Corpus. Here a student types in a word and receives lines of text fragments with the target word in the center of each line ("concordance output") and statistical summaries of how often the target word occurs with specific, surrounding words ("collocate output") (p. 258). Students report that this information on the lexical and grammatical usage of words increased their confidence in writing.

The development of independence, confidence, and a sense of agency is as important for second-language writers as native speakers. Development of a perceptible identity or an authorial presence in writing is often described as a writer's "voice" (Hirvela & Belcher, 2001). Inquiry into the relationship between second-language writing and voice underscores the social nature of learning to write. Writers learning a second language learn to write by aligning themselves "in acceptable discourses" and "by reinventing ideas and linguistic expressions created by others" (Kubota, 2003, p. 40). As we have seen in the case of Starfield's (2002) South African students, this may be difficult even for proficient users of the language.

Ramanathan and Kaplan (1996) argue that common textbook descriptions of voice and audience are simplistic in assuming that they are universal. The notion of voice as presentation of a strong and an individualized self is largely a Western notion, and one that is not necessarily relevant to students from other cultures. Furthermore, Hirvela and Belcher (2001) argue that teaching non-native writers who already have established professional voices requires a wholly different approach. Although these students are hardly voiceless, they nevertheless have difficulty constructing a voice or identity in the second language. For second-language writers in freshman composition courses, Ramanathan and Kaplan advise taking a discipline-specific approach to teaching voice and audience. With more experienced writers, Hirvela and Belcher suggest a focus on the development of multiple voices.

GENDER AND GENDER IDENTITY

As we saw in Knudson's assessment of fourth to eighth graders' attitudes, Anglo-American and Hispanic girls had a more positive attitude toward writing than did their male counterparts. What role does gender identity play in access to writing instruction, encouragement by teachers, writing proficiency, and the development of an identity as a writer? Gender as a dynamic and changing cultural construct (Kubota, 2003) is acquired by a child through interaction with family members, peers, teachers, role models, and others in the community. "Gender, as socially constituted identity, is not monolithic, immutable, or always patriarchal" (Anderson, 2002, p. 391). In adolescence, a clash between a developing sense of individuality and societal norms may be particularly difficult for lesbian, gay, bisexual, transgender, and questioning (LGBTQ) youth. These and other writers from marginalized groups believe they are writing "in a contact zone" (Pratt, 1999, as cited in Ashley, 2001, p. 496), where "meaning is constructed through negotiation between author subjectivities and reader expectations" (Kubota, 2003, p. 40).

For women writing in a second language (e.g., Japanese women learning English), acquiring a gendered norm places one in an inferior position in male–female situations. However, not acquiring a socially appropriate norm makes female–female situations awkward or even inaccessible (Kubota, 2003). Ali (2003) argues that race and gender are not "ontological states of being" for the 8- to 11-year-old girls in a multiethnic working-class school in London. Rather, they are "states of becoming, a process that changes with time, and which is materialized through discourse" (p. 281).

What about achievement? If one looks at gender without ethnicity, the picture seems clear. National literacy test results in the UK, Australia, Canada, and the United States consistently show gender imbalances in favor of girls (Gambell & Hunter, 2000). In the United States, "females up to grade 11 have outscored males on national writing proficiency assessments since 1984" (p. 713). In Canada, results since at least 1994 have been virtually identical.

Canadian data from French-language instruction, teacher-assigned marks, graduation rates, and university enrollment create a pattern of superior female performance (Gambell & Hunter, 2000). In New York State, females showed superior high school achievement and better first-year college test outcomes, which, however, did not translate into higher eligibility for scholarship awards.

To explain the gender differences in these literacy test results, Gambell and Hunter (2000) used parallel questionnaire findings from the 1994 study and five models: division of family labor, character personification, classroom interaction, assessment bias, and identification with genre. All of the models presumed a social construction of gender difference. Analysis of the questionnaire data revealed background differences in experience and expectation according to gender. "The genre model and the character-personification model appear to be the best fit because of the distinct difference in reading interests of girls and boys across Canada" (p. 714). In Canada and the United States, at least, it is the male high school students who are in trouble.

DISABILITY

Writing in school presents exceptional challenges to students who are blind or have low vision (henceforth, blind), have learning disabilities (henceforth, LD), or are deaf or hard of hearing (henceforth, deaf). For blind and deaf students, access to either the spoken or written form of the language has been restricted since early childhood. LD students have difficulty deciphering and organizing ideas in written form because of some type of neurological impairment. (For a discussion of writing and acquired communication disorders, see chap. 29, this volume).

Blind Students

Little research has been conducted on the writing abilities of blind people (Watson, Wright, Syse, & DeL'Aune, 2004). This may in part be due to the expectation that normal hearing and unrestricted access to speech will lead blind children to acquire their first languages in ways similar to their sighted peers. The main issue regarding literacy for blind people and their teachers is independent access to print. Today access is achieved primarily through the use of Braille and print-to-voice technologies (Koenig, 1992). For the past 50 years, teachers have taught reading to children and adults using contracted Braille (Herzberg, Stough, & Clark, 2004). This is a system that consists of characters representing individual letters of the alphabet and additional characters representing groups of letters and whole words. Thus, a child learning to read via Braille must learn to decode more characters than a sighted child.

Although many blind children have achieved reading proficiency by means of contracted Braille, it appears to be particularly challenging for blind children who may also have learning disabilities (Herzberg, Stough, & Clark, 2004). For this reason, some educators now advocate the use of uncontracted (purely alphabetic) Braille to teach reading—and presumably writing—to these students. In diverse classrooms where ESL is taught, writing instruction in Braille may need to occur along with language instruction (Guinan, 1997). Experience and research indicate that, with the appropriate tools and instruction, students with visual impairments can learn literacy on an equitable basis with their normally sighted peers (Koenig, 1992).

Students With Learning Disabilities

According to the National Center for Learning Disabilities (2001), a learning disability (LD) is "a neurological disorder that affects the brain's ability to receive, process, store and respond to information." The term *LD* refers to a group of disorders that all involve "the difficulty a person of at least average intelligence has in acquiring basic academic skills" (National Center for Learning Disabilities, 2001). Although estimates vary, the literature on college students with LD indicates that the majority also experience writing difficulties (LD/WD) (Li & Hamel, 2003). These difficulties range from correct use of writing and grammar to the production of coherent and well-organized texts. Writers with LD typically spend more time writing, produce less output, and become very frustrated (Bardine, 1997).

A recent analysis of 13 studies of effective teaching practices confirms previous findings that LD students show demonstrable gains in content and mechanics when instruction focuses explicitly on steps in the writing process and on mechanics (i.e., spelling and handwriting; Baker, Gersten, & Graham, 2003). Generally, three steps in the process are thought to be critical: prewriting, writing, and rewriting (Baker, Gersten, & Graham, 2003; Li & Hamel, 2003). Varying types of support and mnemonics are suggested depending on the age of the LD writer. The use of "think sheets" for prewriting, prompt cards for feedback sessions, and mnemonics, such as POWER (Plan, Organize, Write, Edit, and Revise), seem to help students structure and talk about the process (Baker et al., 2003). Dialogue between student and teacher and among peers is also seen as an important strategy for LD students. Indeed, Baker et al. conclude that, "it may be less important to teach all the steps in the writing process than to engage in dialogue that will encourage a level of self-reflection in the student" (p. 114).

Spelling and handwriting consume an inordinate share of cognitive processing time for students with LD. Some research is available on the use of word processors and other assistive technologies to reduce processing time required for the mechanics of writing and thus allow the writer to focus more on planning and organizing content. Though improvements in mechanics and content have been documented in a few studies of writing with word processors, the effect of the technology is difficult to separate from those of practice and instruction provided in conjunction with the technology (Li & Hamel, 2003; MacArthur, Ferretti, Okolo, & Cavalier, 2001). Zhang (2000) reports on the use of a computer program called ROBO-Writer in a case study of five 5th-grade students who were reluctant writers because of their severe writing difficulties. The audio feedback provided as the students wrote purportedly improved recognition of misspelled words and meaningless sentences while increasing self-confidence and motivation. Here again, however, the effect of the technology is impossible to separate from the lab instruction provided by preservice mentors. Studies of speech recognition and speech synthesis technologies are promising but to date limited in size and scope.

Deaf Students

Because a large number of deaf people consider themselves members of a cultural and linguistic minority, use of the term *disability* with deaf students is problematic. Traditionally, a disability is defined in medical terms as physical or mental abnormality within an individual. Medical professionals diagnose and recommend treatment to ameliorate the disability, but responsibility for development of the skills and strategies necessary to adapt to the environment rests within the individual (Foster, 2001). In 1990, however, the U.S. Congress passed the Americans With Disabilities Act (ADA), a law that guarantees deaf people and other people with disabilities certain rights regarding communication access, public accommodations, and employment. This bill acknowledged a new view of disability, one defined as much by traditional attitudes and practices in society as by characteristics within an individual. From a sociopolitical viewpoint, then, disability (like ethnicity, race, class, and gender) may be defined as the result of an interaction between characteristics within an individual and the environment in which that person lives.

Although deaf and hard-of-hearing people worked alongside citizens with other disabilities for passage of ADA, those who consider themselves culturally and linguistically deaf consider the traditional medical model of deafness to be the root of oppression and continued misunderstanding. (For discussions of the history, cultural identity, and experiences of deaf people as a minority, see Lane, 1992; Padden & Humphries, 1988; Parasnis,

1996.) Unlike most disability groups, including blind and LD students who prefer *people with disabilities*, deaf people who consider ASL their native language and who belong to cultural organizations for the deaf prefer to be called *deaf* (or *Deaf*). Simply put, culturally, deaf people do not regard deafness as a disability.

Regardless of cultural affiliation, deaf students' writing achievement typically lags behind that of their hearing peers. In the United States, high school-age students typically write on par with hearing students in the fourth or fifth grade (Paul, 1998, 2001). The writing samples of these students resemble those of hearing students learning ESL (Berent, 1996; Langston & Maxwell, 1988), in that it contains word-level (inflectional, derivational) and sentence-level (subordination) errors that are common to hearing learners of English. Vocabulary is restricted, and deaf children use fewer cohesive markers (De Villiers, 1991) and a limited set of lexical devices to signal cohesion (Maxwell & Falick, 1992). Yet despite grammatical anomalies and a limited repertoire of discourse markers, analyses of stories and narratives written by older deaf students indicate that they are as coherent and well structured as those written by hearing peers (Albertini, 1990; Marschark, Mouradian, & Halas, 1994). Some deaf college students, whose writing may require grammatical editing, nevertheless possess a sophisticated sense of agency and voice as writers (Albertini, Meath-Lang, & Harris, 1994).

For some students, grammatical, lexical, or discourse errors may be attributable to a learning disability. But to date only one study has attempted to isolate the effects of language disability in students' writing from effects associated with normal language learning and deafness (Berent, Samar, & Parasnis, 2000). In this study, experienced teachers of the deaf identified difficulties in spelling, organizing sentences coherently, and the confusion of the meanings of time/space prepositions such as *before, after,* and *between* as characteristics of the writing of deaf students with learning disabilities.

As to the question of achievement, that is, whether process approaches can improve lexical and grammatical expression as well as fluency, content, and organization in deaf students' writing, research results have been mixed. In one 2-year investigation of the use of dialogue journals, student gains in grammatical complexity as well as overall quality of writing were noted (Kluwin & Kelly, 1992). In another, use of a writing rubric as a means of focusing students on product as well as process showed gains in content and organization but not in vocabulary, structure, and mechanics (Schirmer, Bailey, & Fitzgerald, 1999). Use of local-area computer networks and cross-age tutoring for language practice and writing instruction yielded positive effects on students' ability to write formal academic prose (Peyton, 1989); yet frequent network interaction produced essays written in a more conversational style (Bartholomae, 1993).

CONCLUSION

The research reviewed in this chapter has demonstrated that achievement, access to instruction, and identity development as a writer often relate to ethnicity, race, gender, and disability. It also suggests some direction for teachers of students who by virtue of belonging to one or more or these groups, we have called *diverse*. With regard to race, class, and ethnic background, the proficiency of Ashley's (2001) working-class students provides one answer to the Gee–Delpit debate over whether diverse students *can* learn mainstream discourse. The subjects of her study learned to play the game and produce acceptable general schooled discourse. With regard to proficiency and self-perception among African American, Hispanic, and Anglo-American youth, Anglo-American students scored higher than African American students and had more positive views of themselves as writers than did African American, Asian, and Hispanic students.

For second-language learners, learning the cultural aspects of writing in the target language may be as challenging if not more so than learning the grammar and vocabulary of that language. Recent scholarship suggests that the notion of voice in writing and the options of expression (i.e., multiple voices) available to a writer are to a certain extent culturally determined. Therefore, according to Ramanathan and Kaplan (1996), voice needs to be explicitly taught to second-language learners. Their view is that this may be most effectively done in the context of discipline-specific writing instruction.

Recent national assessments of writing tell us that, in addition to the continued inequality of access to scholarship aid for girls entering college, we should focus attention on the writing achievement levels of boys. It seems that boys, and perhaps LGBTQ youth, do not write as well as girls because of gender stereotyping and culturally determined preferences in reading and writing practices. Royster (1992) and Welch and Hodges (1997) prompt us to consider whether we as teachers allow gender and role stereotypes, together with our conceptions about the nature of writing, limit our students' experimentation and learning.

The main issue in literacy instruction for blind students is independent access to print, and the teaching of Braille (whether contracted or uncontracted) is complicated in diverse classrooms when a child has a learning disability or is learning ESL. Students with LD seem to benefit from instruction that focuses their attention on steps in the writing process and on mechanics. Dialogue is suggested as a technique to encourage reflection on the process; and voice recognition software may help students spot mechanics problems (the effect of using the software is difficult to separate from the effects of instruction and practice). For deaf students in American classrooms, access to spoken (and thus written) English is restricted, so their writing in many ways resembles that of hearing students learning ESL. For those students from a culturally deaf background (where ASL is used), finding an identity as a writer of English is also an issue.

As we have seen, learning to write convincingly in acceptable discourses, is extremely difficult for students marginalized by ethnicity, race, class, gender identity, or disability. Sensitivity to the developing individual and group identities of our students and a sociopolitical view of disability and diversity in general will help teachers and students define physical and attitudinal barriers in the classroom. In this regard, the experiences and views of the student can provide much insight.

Facing the complexity of today's classrooms, research suggests that teachers use those methods that encourage and accommodate individual learning styles. Writing in different genres for different audiences may help to cultivate multiple writing voices and nurture agency so that a student can develop a repertoire of writing styles and strategies. Research with deaf students indicates that surface grammatical and mechanical abilities in writing are distinct from the ability to organize coherent prose. Research with students who are blind, deaf, or have an LD indicates that teachers need to focus on the mechanics of writing as well as content and organization. Though teaching students steps in the writing process seems widely favored, teaching writing as a process should not neglect the teaching of grammatical and stylistic conventions. Finally, the study of diversity in writing classrooms points up the challenge to all teachers of writing. As is clear from the previous discussion, the groups discussed here are heterogeneous; they are composed of individuals who have unique identities and sets of affiliations. The challenge for the writing teacher is to allow each student to express his or her unique view in writing that is comprehensible and effective for the reader.

REFERENCES

Albertini, J. A. (1990). Coherence in deaf students' writing. In J. Kreeft Peyton (Ed.), *Students and teachers writing together: Perspectives on journal writing* (pp. 127–136). Alexandria, VA: Teachers of English to Speakers of Other Languages.

Albertini, J. A., Meath-Lang, B., & Harris, D. P. (1994). Voice as muse, message, and medium: The views of deaf college students. In K. Yancey (Ed.), *Voices on voice: Perspectives, definitions, inquiry* (pp. 172–190). Urbana, IL: National Council of Teachers of English.

Ali, S. (2003). "To Be a Girl": Culture and class in schools. *Gender and Education, 15,* 269–283.

Anderson, D. (2002). Casting and recasting gender: Children constituting social identities through literacy practice. *Research in the Teaching of English, 36*, 391–427.

Ashley, H. (2001). Playing the game: Proficient working-class student writers' second voices. *Research in the Teaching of English, 35*, 493–524.

Baker, S., Gersten, R., & Graham, S. (2003). Teaching expressive writing to students with learning disabilities: Research-based applications and examples. *Journal of Learning Disabilities, 36*, 109–124.

Bardine, B. (1997). *Working with learning disabled writers: Some perspectives. Research to practice* (Report No. 039-0200-0019). Kent: Ohio Literacy Resource Center. (ERIC Document Reproduction Service No. ED406554)

Bartholomae, D. (1993). "I'm talking about Alan Bloom": Writing on the network. In B. Bruce, J. K. Peyton, & T. Batson (Eds.), *Network-based classrooms* (pp. 237–262). New York: Cambridge University Press.

Berent, G. P. (1996). The acquisition of English syntax by deaf learners. In W. Ritchie & T. Bhatia (Eds.), *Handbook of second language acquisition* (pp. 469–506). San Diego, CA: Academic Press.

Berent, G. P., Samar, V. J., & Parasnis, I. (2000). College teachers' perceptions of English language characteristics that identify English language learning disabled deaf students. *American Annals of the Deaf, 145*, 342–358.

Currie, P., & Cray, E. (2004). ESL literacy: Language practice or social practice? *Journal of Second Language Writing, 13*, 111–132.

Delpit, L. (1995). *Other people's children.* New York: The New Press.

DeVilliers, P. (1991). English literacy development in deaf children: Directions for research and intervention. In J. F. Miller (Ed.), *Research on child language disorders: A decade of progress* (pp. 349–378). Austin, TX: Pro-Ed.

Du Bois, W. E. B. (1969). *The souls of Black folk.* New York: New American Library. (Original work published 1903)

Engelhard, G., Gordon, B., & Gabrielson, S. (2001). Writing tasks and gender: Influences on writing quality of Black and White students. *Journal of Educational Research, 87*, 197–209.

Foster, S. (2001). Examining the fit between deafness and disability. *Research in Social Sciences and Disability, 2*, 101–123.

Gambell, T., & Hunter, D. (2000). Surveying gender differences in Canadian school literacy. *Journal of Curriculum Studies, 32*, 689–719.

Gee, J. P. (1989). What is literacy? *Journal of Education, 171*, 18–25.

Guinan, H. (1997). ESL for students with visual impairments. *Journal of Visual Impairment & Blindness, 91*, 555–563.

Herzberg, T., Stough, L. M., & Clark, C. M. (2004). Teaching and assessing the appropriateness of uncontracted braille. *Journal of Visual Impairment & Blindness, 98*, 773–779.

Hirvela, A., & Belcher, D. (2001). Coming back to voice: The multiple voices and identities of mature multilingual writers. *Journal of Second Language Writing, 10*, 83–106.

Kluwin, T. N., & Kelly, A. B. (1992). Implementing a successful writing program in public schools for students who are deaf. *Exceptional Children, 59*, 41–53.

Knudson, R. (1993). Effects of ethnicity in attitudes toward writing. *Psychological Review, 72*, 39–45.

Koenig, A. J. (1992). A framework for understanding the literacy of individuals with visual impairments. *Journal of Visual Impairment & Blindness, 86*, 277–283.

Kubota, R. (2003). New approaches to gender, class, and race in second language writing. *Journal of Second Language Writing, 12*, 31–47.

Lane, H. (1992). *The mask of benevolence: Disabling the deaf community.* New York: Knopf.

Langston, C. A., & Maxwell, M. M. (1988). Holistic judgement of texts by deaf and ESL students. *Sign Language Studies, 60*, 295–312.

Li, H., & Hamel, C. (2003). Writing issues in college students with learning disabilities: A synthesis of the literature from 1990 to 2000. *Learning Disability Quarterly, 26*, 29–46.

MacArthur, C., Ferretti, R., Okolo, C., & Cavalier, A. (2001). Technology applications for students with literacy problems: A critical review. *Elementary School Journal, 101*, 273–301.

Marschark, M., Mouradian, V., & Halas, M. (1994). Discourse rules in the language productions of deaf and hearing children. *Journal of Experimental Child Psychology, 57*, 89–107.

Maxwell, M. M., & Falick, T. G. (1992). Cohesion & quality in deaf & hearing children's written English. *Sign Language Studies, 77*, 345–372.

National Center for Learning Disabilities. (2001). *LD at a glance.* Retrieved May 14, 2005, from http://www.ncld.org/LDInfoZone_FactSheetIndex.cfm

Padden, C., & Humphries, T. (1988). *Deaf in America: Voices from a culture.* Cambridge, MA: Harvard University Press.

Parasnis, I. (Ed.). 1996. *Cultural and language diversity and the deaf experience.* New York: Cambridge University Press.

Paul, P. V. (1998). *Literacy and deafness*. Boston: Allyn & Bacon.

Paul, P. (2001). *Language and deafness* (3rd ed.). San Diego, CA: Singular.

Peyton, J. K. (1989). Cross-age tutoring on a local area computer network: Moving from informal interaction to formal academic writing. *The Writing Instructor, 8,* 57–67.

Pratt, M. L. (1999). Arts of the contact zone. In D. Bartholomae & A. Petrosky (Eds.), Ways of reading: An anthology for writers (pp. 581–600). Boston: Bedford/St. Martin's.

Ramanathan, V., & Kaplan, R. (1996). Audience and voice in current L1 composition texts: Some implications for ESL student writers. *Journal of Second Language Writing, 5,* 21–34.

Reppen, R. (2001). Register variation in student and adult speech and writing. In S. Conrad & D. Biber (Eds.), *Variation in English: Multi-dimensional studies* (pp. 187–199). Harlow, England: Longman.

Reynolds, D. (2004). Linguistic correlates of second language literacy development: Evidence from middle-grade learner essays. *Journal of Second Language Writing, 14,* 19–45.

Royster, J. J. (1992). Looking from the margins: A tale of curricular reform. In L. Bridwell-Bowles & S. Batchelder (Eds.), *Diversity and writing: Dialogue within a modern university; Proceedings of the First Annual Conference, April 1990* (pp. 1–57). Minneapolis: Center for Interdisciplinary Studies of Writing, University of Minnesota.

Schirmer, B. R., Bailey, J., & Fitzgerald, S. M. (1999). Using a writing assessment rubric for writing development of children who are deaf. *Exceptional Children, 65,* 383–397.

Starfield, S. (2002). "I'm a second-language English speaker": Negotiating writer identity and authority in Sociology One. *Journal of Language, Identity, and Education, 1,* 121–140.

Thonus, T. (2004). What are the differences? Tutor interactions with first- and second-language writers. *Journal of Second Language Writing, 13,* 227–242.

Watson, G., Wright, V., Wyse, E., & De l'Aune, W. (2004). A writing assessment for persons with age-related vision loss. *Journal of Visual Impairment & Blindness, 98,* 160–167.

Welch, O., & Hodges, C. (1997). *Standing outside on the inside*. Albany: State University of New York Press.

Williams, J. (2004). Tutoring and revision: Second language writers in the writing center. *Journal of Second Language Writing, 13,* 173–201.

Wood, G. (2004). *The Americanization of Benjamin Franklin*. New York: Penguin.

Yoon, H., & Hirvela, A. (2004). ESL student attitudes toward corpus use in L2 writing. *Journal of Second Language Writing, 13,* 257–283.

Zhang, Y. (2000). Technology and writing skills of students with learning disabilities. *Journal of Research on Computing in Education, 32,* 467–478.

IV

Writing and the Individual

Deborah Brandt, in *Literacy in American Lives*, tellingly makes the case of how much our development as writers depends on the time, place, and social relations we find ourselves in and the social networks that provide support, sponsorship, and opportunities for development. School is an important part of that social and historical picture. So it is appropriate to consider the relation of writing and the individual only after we have considered the larger social, historical, and educational settings that define one's writing possibilities and experiences. This development of writing within social and educational circumstances comes through very clearly in chapters 25 and 26, which are explicitly devoted to writing development in various life stages. We cannot extricate learning to write during one's childhood and adolescence from one's family and schooling literacy experiences. Nor can we extricate one's adult development as a writer from the variety of life experiences, the various programs, and the economic conditions one finds oneself participating in. In some sense, therefore, these two chapters echo the chapters in the previous part on schooling, in attending to the pedagogical practices and institutional circumstances of learning to write. Nonetheless, by focusing on development of writers as individuals these chapters present a different story.

Just as we cannot separate writing from the circumstances it is learned and used in, we cannot separate it from reading, for reading and writing together comprise literacy. We read what we write as we write, and every time we write we offer up something for another potentially to read. Reading and writing employ some of the same knowledge of language and meaning. They also use some of the same mental operations—even though perhaps with significant differences. Furthermore, every text we write is embedded within and draws on texts we read, and thus every time we right we draw on our reading. Chapter 27 presents what we know about the reading–writing nexus.

Biological and psychological characteristics of human beings are also significant in understanding writing. After all, writing instruments are designed to fit the human hand; letters and characters are typically drawn large enough to be seen by the human eye and small enough that many can be surveyed when inscribed on an object held at the length of an arm comfortably bent. Similarly, writing has developed within the constraints and processes of human memory, choice making, and conceptual organization that comprise our cognitive capabilities. Chapter 28 reviews the research on writing and cognition. Chapter 29, in reviewing research on writing and communication disorders, not only tells us much about writing in the atypical circumstances of disability or disorder and how people cope with cognitive limitations, but helps us see the complexity of what comes together in more typical cognitive circumstances.

Not only does our writing draw on who we are and depend on our capacities, it also seems to transform who we are. One of the more remarkable findings about writing in recent decades is that it can impact our biomedical well-being. A substantial and continuingly refined research program, reviewed in chapter 30, has developed to explore this powerful finding that suggests writing affects our individual selves so deeply as apparently to influence our nervous and autoimmune systems.

The selves we bring to writing and affect how we present ourselves through writing are also affected by the ethnic and cultural affiliations and experiences we bring with us, as well as the several languages we may have learned. Chapters 31 and 32 review what we know about writing and identity as well as the impact of multilinguality on learning to write. In considering the diverse experiences individuals have with respect to writing, the last four chapters represent some of the same issues raised in chapter 24, but from the perspective of the individual rather than the classroom.

REFERENCE

Brandt, D. (2001). *Literacy in American lives*. Cambridge, England: Cambridge University Press.

CHAPTER 25

Development of Writing Abilities in Childhood

Deborah Wells Rowe
Vanderbilt University

My goal in this chapter is to use seminal and current research to sketch a trajectory for writing that begins long before children produce conventional letters or words. Specifically, this review focuses on *what* young children know and can do with writing beginning at birth and continuing through ages 9 or 10. By starting with the youngest children and continuing into the early years of formal schooling, my goal is to highlight links between children's first marks and later more conventional writing.

THEORETICAL PERSPECTIVES ON WRITING IN EARLY CHILDHOOD: CONVENTION, INTENTION, PARTICIPATION

In the last century, there have been several different answers to the question of when writing begins. The reading readiness perspective, prominent from the 1920s to the 1980s, located the beginnings of writing at the point when children start to write words *conventionally*. Because this view assumed children first learned to read and then to write, there was little interest in writing (except for letter formation or handwriting) until children were reading conventionally in the primary grades (See Teale & Sulzby, 1986 for a historical review).

Beginning in the late 1960s and continuing to the present, the emergent literacy perspective has dramatically altered researchers' understandings of the beginnings of writing (Clay, 1975; Ferreiro & Teberosky, 1982; Goodman, 1986; Harste, Woodward, & Burke, 1984; Teale & Sulzby, 1986). According to this perspective, literacy development begins long before formal schooling, and, furthermore, children begin to learn about writing and reading simultaneously in their everyday experiences. By observing children's playful uses of pens and paper and by talking with them about their work, researchers have demonstrated that "scribbles" carry meaning despite their unconventional form (Harste et al., 1984). This work challenged the notion of convention as the watershed criterion for identifying the beginnings of writing, replacing it, instead, with the construct of *intention*. For example, in her work on the "roots of literacy," Yetta Goodman (1986) defined *reading* and *writing* as "human interaction with print when the reader and writer *believe* that they are making sense of and through written language" (p. 6; italics added). Drawing on theories from cognitive psychology and semiotics, preschoolers' literacy learning was reframed as constructive and multimodal. This theoretical shift provided a vantage point for asking new research questions: What hypotheses do preschoolers form about writing prior to school entry? How do children's interactions with others affect these hypotheses. How do children orchestrate multiple sign systems?

By turning research attention to the graphic activities preceding conventional writing, the emergent literacy perspective opened preschool writing as a new area of study and allowed researchers to connect this work to ongoing research on writing in the elementary school years. As a result, an extensive research base describing children's cognitive hypotheses about writing has been developed. Because preschoolers' texts are so unconventional, it is difficult to understand their writing intentions without also observing their interactions during writing. As a result, researchers have broadened their focus beyond the text and child, to include the impact of social interaction on children's hypotheses about writing. The first section of this chapter reviews the contributions of researchers studying childhood writing from a sociocognitive perspective. This work focuses on: (a) writing forms, (b) form–meaning links, (c) connections to other communication systems, (d) knowledge of written genre, (e) individual writing processes, and (f) the impact of social interaction on children's writing processes.

Recently, some researchers (e.g., Dyson, 2000; Whitmore, Martens, Goodman, & Owocki, 2004) have begun to examine childhood writing through the lens of sociocultural theories of literacy (e.g., Gee, 1999; Street, 1995). When seen through this lens, learning to write is fundamentally about social participation (Gee, 2003). As soon as children are drawn into the writing practices of their discourse communities, they begin to learn what textual intentions, procedures, and reading/writing processes are valued for use in specific kinds of literacy events.

From this perspective, writing begins when children participate in social practices related to writing—the valued ways of "doing" writing in a particular community (Barton & Hamilton, 2000; Lave & Wenger, 1991; Lemke, 1995; Solsken, 1993). Although writing practices are, in part, characterized by observable behaviors involving print, they also involve values, feelings, and social relationships (Barton & Hamilton, 2000; Street, 1995). Writing practices include definitions of text and writing, ways of talking about writing, ideological views of literacy, and participants' socially constructed identities. Power relations embedded in writing practices determine the use and distribution of texts and who has access to various positions in writing events.

When sociocultural theories are applied by researchers studying preschool and elementary school writing, research attention is turned to observing the nature of children's social participation in local writing events and the ways these events are structured by race, class, and gender in the larger society (Dyson, 2000). Research questions have included: What cultural models of literacy are explicit or implicit in events children participate in? What roles, procedures, literacy processes, and textual intentions are valued in local literacy events? What positions are available to children of different ages, genders, ethnicities, and social classes? What forms of agency do children exercise? How do they accept, resist, and transform writing practices and social positions? This work is reviewed in the sections of this chapter devoted to: (a) cultural- and class-based features of home writing practices, (b) children's participation in classroom writing practices, (c) writing and identity, and (d) writing as a gendered practice.

SCOPE OF THE REVIEW

Given the purpose of this chapter, I have included both seminal and more recent work. However, to ensure the most current research was included, I conducted electronic searches for studies of preschool and elementary writing during the last 15 years and augmented this method with hand searches of eight prominent literacy research publications (i.e., *Early Childhood Research Quarterly, Journal of Early Childhood Literacy, Journal of Literacy Research, Language Arts, Reading Research Quarterly, Reading Teacher, Research in the Teaching of English,* and *Yearbook of the National Reading Conference*).

The majority of the studies reviewed here were conducted in natural settings—usually either homes or classrooms. Though some researchers wrote and talked with children in their roles as participant-observers, most studies were designed to record what children usually did in their classrooms and homes rather than to assess their reactions to literacy interventions. An impressive number of studies recorded children's writing over extended time periods lasting from a few months to a year or more. A second, smaller group of studies recorded children's responses to standard writing tasks. Many of these studies also recorded children's talk during writing. Studies using standard tasks often used either causal comparative designs to track the impact of age, or experimental designs to compare the written texts students produced in response to different writing conditions.

SOCIOCOGNITIVE PERSPECTIVES ON CHILDHOOD WRITING: YOUNG CHILDREN'S PURPOSES FOR WRITING

One of the most important breakthroughs in our understanding of preschoolers' writing is that, despite its unconventional form, it is purposeful. Lancaster (2001) and Baghban (1984) have shown that 1- and 2-year-olds engage in writing to explore the characteristics of writing materials and to engage in positive interactions with parents and teachers. Whereas toddlers are just beginning to learn about the communicative potentials of writing, it is well established that older preschoolers' scribbles are not random, but instead are often characterized by intentionality—the desire to communicate a linguistic message (Clay, 1975; Goodman, 1986; Harste et al., 1984). In literacy-rich homes and classrooms, preschoolers and elementary children write to take part in literacy activities with adults and to form friendships with peers (Ballenger, 1999; Dyson, 1989, 2001; Kenner, 2000; Rowe, 1994; Wiseman, 2003). They also continue to explore the tools of literacy by investigating the effects that can be produced with paper, writing instruments, computers, and other literacy-related materials (Kress, 1997; Labbo, 1996; Pahl, 1999; Rowe, 1994). However, they also begin to write for specific communicative purposes, including producing conventional symbols (e.g., alphabet letters and numerals), labeling people and objects, and producing messages (Dyson, 1985).

As children progress through elementary school, writing purposes are increasingly influenced by writing tasks that are included as part of the curriculum or introduced in instructional interventions. In general, research shows that, with instruction, elementary students can use writing for purposes that reflect what they have been taught (Tower, 2005). Examples of writing purposes fostered by instruction include: text-centered and reader-centered responses to literature (Wollman-Bonilla & Werchado, 1995), expressing and comparing ideas in science (Many, Fyfe, Lewis, & Mitchell, 1996; Mason & Boscolo, 2000; Tower, 2005), conducting research (Many et al., 1996), and critically analyzing social problems (Heffernan & Lewison, 2003).

Overall, research suggests that before formal instruction begins, preschoolers are exploring the social, communicative, and linguistic features of writing. There is some evidence to suggest that very young children's writing purposes are more related to the amount of exposure and types of experiences with writing than to such factors as socioeconomic status (SES) or even age (Harste et al., 1984). After school entry, it appears that children learn what they are taught. When teachers focus on teaching children to use writing for functional purposes such as responding to literature or learning science, students are able to produce written texts that serve these purposes.

FORMS USED BY BEGINNING WRITERS

Because writing is, in part, a visual medium, it is not surprising that research on the forms of children's writing has a long history and continues to be of interest for current researchers. Only a few researchers have studied the writing forms (or any other aspect of writing) used by children between birth and age 3. However, Lancaster's (2001) analysis of a 23-month-old child's writing suggests that very young children may show little concern for the forms or products they create, but instead focus on the processes of marking and interacting with others around writing. However, because research on infant and toddler experiences with writing is so limited, such conclusions are extremely tentative and await further research.

In contrast, there is an extensive research base exploring the writing forms produced by older preschoolers. In general, Hildreth's (1936) seminal report of patterns in 3- to 6-year-olds' name writing has been confirmed many times over (e.g., Clay, 1975; Dyson, 1985; Ferreiro & Teberosky, 1982; Green, 1998; Harste et al., 1984; Kenner, 2000). Writing begins with scribbles that are largely undifferentiated and over time moves in a general trajectory toward forms that have more writinglike characteristics including linearity, appropriate directional patterns, and individual units. As children move from masses of scribbles, they often produce linear zigzags—a form of "personal cursive" (Ferreiro & Teberosky, 1982; Harste et al., 1984). As they notice that print contains individual marks, children produce individual scribble units, mock letters, and, eventually, conventional letters. Clay (1975) has noted that, at certain points in their development, young writers may purposefully experiment with altering the forms of known letters, perhaps to gauge the limits of flexibility of conventional letter forms. As children learn that long messages contain many symbols, they often create linear strings composed of one or more symbols from their current repertoire (Clay, 1975; Kenner, 2000). Children also experiment with spatial arrangement of text on the page (Kenner, 2000; Sipe, 1998; Zecker, 1999).

Among researchers, there remains a debate about whether children move sequentially through a predictable series of stages, each with a characteristic form rooted in a particular hypothesis about written language. Data from individual interviews conducted by Piagetian researchers (Besse, 1996; Ferreiro, 1990; Ferreiro & Teberosky, 1982; Grossi, 1990; Kamii, Long, & Manning, 2001; Pontecorvo & Zuccermaglio, 1990) have tended to support stage theory, whereas naturalistics' observations have revealed more variability in the forms that children produce at any point in time (Clay, 1975; Green, 1998; Kenner, 2000; Sulzby, 1996). The latter group of studies supports a rough progression toward more conventional writing forms, but also suggests children continue to produce a variety of forms. When children add new forms to their repertoires, old ones are not necessarily abandoned (Sulzby, 1996). A number of studies have documented the influence of situational and task characteristics on young writers' choice of forms (Borzone de Manrique & Signorini, 1998; Zecker, 1999).

Looking across data from clinical interviews and naturalistic observations, it is possible to construct a broad trajectory for early writing forms. However, naturalistic research counters predictions that children's growth proceeds sequentially or in a smooth progression from less to more sophisticated forms. Instead, current data suggest variation is the norm. Children produce different forms in response to differences in writing contexts, genres, and task difficulty.

FORM–MEANING LINKS

For the youngest writers, a crucial understanding is that marks can represent language—an understanding Clay (1975) has termed the message concept. Children also realize that they are capable of using marks to record messages and that those marks can be read by others. Beginning with these basic understandings, early literacy researchers have documented the progression in children's hypotheses about orthography beginning before and after they develop the alphabetic principle (i.e., a letter stands for a sound).

A number of Piagetian researchers, working with different language groups, have provided support for Ferreiro and Teberosky's (1982) description of a sequenced progression of hypotheses culminating with the construction of the alphabetic hypothesis. Earlier hypotheses in this sequence include expectations that there will be correspondence between the size of the word and its referent, that words will be objectively different (i.e., words are sets of *different* letters), and that letters stand for syllables rather than sounds. Using Piagetian interview techniques, researchers have documented a similar progression through these stages for children learning Italian and Spanish (Ferreiro & Teberosky, 1982), French (Besse, 1996), Portuguese (Grossi, 1990), and English (Branscombe & Taylor, 1996; Kamii et al., 2001).

A related focus of research has been children's formation of the concept of word as expressed in the ways they separate word units in writing. As with other aspects of written language, children develop a series of hypotheses about the nature of words and how they are divided with spaces in print. This aspect of writing is complicated by the fact that words are not necessarily distinguished in speech by a pause (Tunmer, Bowey, & Grieve, 1983) and that word units do not always correspond to linguistic units (e.g., articles are written as separate words in English, but not in Hebrew or Italian; Temple, Nathan, Temple, & Burris, 1993). Although children initially write letter strings without divisions between words, as they begin to form hypotheses about words, they also begin to experiment with spacing between words—although their decisions about spacing and means of separating words (e.g., a dash or filled-in circle) are often unconventional (Clay, 1975; Harste et al., 1984). As in reading (Meltzer & Herse, 1969), word class impacts the ways children initially divide their writing into units. Content words such as proper nouns, nouns, and verbs are more likely to be written with spaces between them. Function words such as articles or auxiliaries to verbs are more likely to be combined with the words to which they refer (Tolchinksy, 2006). Concept of word continues to develop for some time. Even at the end of first grade, when children have begun to learn to read words, they do not necessarily have a stable and unified concept of word (Roberts, 1992).

Because children have an intensely personal interest in their names, name writing appears to be an important context for young children's explorations of both forms and form–meaning relationships (Bloodgood, 1999; Martens, 1999). Children's names often serve as the first stable written form that has meaning for them. Several researchers have recently explored whether the forms children produce in name writing are related to more general understandings about print. Results indicate that 3- to 5-year-olds' name writing is positively correlated with a number of measures of emergent literacy including letter identification and concept of word (Haney, Bissonnette, & Behnken, 2003; Welsch, Sullivan, & Justice, 2003). Findings are mixed as to whether name writing is related to phonological awareness (Haney et al., 2003; Welsch et al., 2003).

With regard to spelling, there is considerable consensus that development occurs in a fairly predictable way with children constructing a series of qualitatively different hypotheses about how speech is represented in print (Fresch, 2001; Henderson & Beers, 1980; Korkeamaki & Dreher, 2000; Mayer & Moskos, 1998). However, there is some debate about the best scheme for dividing and labeling spelling stages (Bear & Templeton, 1998; Gentry, 2000). In general, research shows that children progress from spellings where there is no link between letters and sounds to spellings where letters are used to represent some or all of a word's sounds. Next, children begin to use orthographic rules and visual strategies. In a final stage, conventional spelling becomes well established.

Concept of word has been found to be related to the types of spellings children construct (Roberts, 1992; Temple et al., 1993), perhaps because early attempts to spell words with letter–sound correspondence require holding a word in mind and switching back and forth between the word, its sounds, and the letters that represent those sounds. A stable concept of word may be necessary if children are to develop more conventional spelling strategies (Temple et al., 1993).

Despite differences in method, many studies support a developmental progression in learning to spell. As in other areas of writing, there is debate about the extent to which this progression represents distinct stages versus the building of a progressively more sophisticated repertoire of spelling strategies (Gentry, 2000).

CONNECTIONS BETWEEN WRITING AND OTHER COMMUNICATION SYSTEMS

Also of interest to literacy researchers have been the ways children both differentiate and connect writing to other communication systems. Perhaps because adults often assume that very young children's unconventional marks are drawing rather than writing, early work in this area focused on establishing whether preschoolers distinguish writing from drawing (e.g., Ferreiro & Teberosky, 1982; Harste et al., 1984). Initial and subsequent research has supported the conclusion that by age 3 many children have different action plans for writing and drawing (Brenneman, Massey, Machado, & Gelman, 1996; Harste et al., 1984).

A more recent interest of researchers has been describing the multimodal nature of young children's writing. Kress (1997) observes that "multimodality is an absolute fact of children's semiotic practices" (p. 137)—an observation supported by many other studies (e.g., Dyson, 2001; Kenner, 2000; Lancaster, 2001; Pahl, 1999; Rowe, 1994; Williams, 1999). Whereas adults tend to view writing as print, young children initially see the boundaries between writing and other sign systems as more permeable (Kress, 1997). For young children, writing is inextricably interwoven with talk, vocalization, gesture, gaze, and bodily action (Lancaster, 2001).

For preschool and early elementary children, then, writing is not just making marks. For both hearing (Lancaster, 2001) and deaf/hard-of-hearing (Williams, 1999) preschoolers, writing involves bodily action. Young children perform their early writings with gesture, facial expression, and pantomime. Embodied practices such as gaze and body posture carry important meanings, and are closely monitored by adults who interact with young writers (Lancaster, 2001). Multimodal authoring practices are also strongly influenced by the physical materials that are available in the environment (Kress, 1997).

Both seminal and more recent studies document children's flexible interweaving of semiotic systems. Most often described have been authoring practices that combine writing, art, and oral language (Hubbard, 1989; Newkirk, 1989; Olson, 1992), but researchers have also noted children's connections among writing, music, dance, dramatic play, and drama (Dyson, 1989; Gallas, 1994; Rowe, 1994; Upitis, 1992). They argue that multimodal writing practices allow children to draw on meanings formed in a variety of sign systems and to gain access to writing events using nonlinguistic forms of communication (Clyde, 1994; Harste, 2000). This appears to be particularly important for beginning and struggling writers (Harste, 2000; Rowe, Fitch, & Bass, 2001).

Overall, there is abundant evidence that young writers naturally combine talk, writing, drawing, and other modes of communication. Studies of elementary writers have also demonstrated that symbolic flexibility and recontextualization processes are key authoring processes (Dyson, 2001, 2003b). Children borrow and remix familiar cultural material (e.g., images, songs, cartoon characters) in ways that combine sign systems and link school and nonschool practices.

For some researchers, the multimodality of early writing is seen as a precursor to the production of "decontextualized" texts. However, Kress (1997) and Dyson (2000, 2001) argue against considering multimodality an immature practice that will one day be replaced with writing-only practices. Children's multimodal authoring appears to be a natural outgrowth of societal connections between writing and other symbol systems (Kenner, 2000; Pahl, 1999). New technologies are currently creating an increasingly multimodal environment for learning and authoring, and young children's multimodal authoring activities appear to reflect these experiences (Kress, 1997).

Several researchers have described transmediation—movement of meanings across sign systems—as an important part of multimodal authoring activities (Kress, 1997; Siegel, 1995). Because there is often no one-to-one match between sign systems, as children combine and move between them, they are encouraged to reflect on both the meanings and forms they use in their writing (Dyson, 2000; Rowe et al., 2003).

Overall, research has shown that young children begin to make distinctions between art and writing quite early. However, throughout the early years, children's authoring continues to be multimodal. Children adapt and transform cultural resources, and weave together a variety of sign systems.

GENRE KNOWLEDGE

Kress (1997) has argued that learning to write is not a generic process, but instead involves learning the demands and potentials of different genres. Growing from the observation that young writers' texts vary by task and genre, researchers have devoted a growing amount of attention to studying preschool and elementary children's knowledge and production of written genres. There is considerable evidence that preschoolers construct texts that reflect syntactic and semantic features of a variety of genres such as stories, lists, labels, signs, letters, and e-mails (Bissex, 1980; Harste et al., 1984; Wollman-Bonilla, 2003; Zecker, 1999). Children appear to build genre knowledge through social interaction and then appropriate cultural forms of writing and rework them to create hybrids that fit specific tasks and audience (Chapman, 1995; Power, 1991; Solsken, Willett, & Wilson-Keenan, 2000; Wollman-Bonilla, 2000).

Genre knowledge appears to begin developing early and becomes more complex as children grow older (Chapman, 1995; Donovan, 2001; Kamberelis, 1999; Kamberelis & Bovino, 1999; Smolkin & Donovan, 2004). Much of the existing research has focused on children's writing of information and story genres. As with research on more general characteristics of children's writing forms, it may be possible to identify a loose trajectory for children's genre-related development by describing a series of intermediate forms of story and information writing that differ in genre features and organizational complexity (e.g., for information texts: labels, statements, attribute lists, etc.; Donovan, 2001). However, existing evidence does not suggest that genre knowledge develops as a linear progression toward more complex forms (Chapman, 1995). As in other areas of writing development, children continue to use and explore multiple genre forms simultaneously. Additionally, it appears that children's written texts vary not only because of differences in their understanding of genre features, but also depending on their aims in writing them (Donovan & Smolkin, 2002).

In general, elementary children's stories were more conventional than information writing (Kamberelis & Bovino, 1999; Smolkin & Donovan, 2004), and children's abilities to write well-structured texts in both genres increased across the elementary years (Smolkin & Donovan, 2004). Even 6- and 7-year-olds have been shown to have considerable implicit knowledge of microlevel features of story and information genre (Kamberelis & Bovino, 1999), including cohesion, tense, vocabulary, and word order (Donovan, 2001). However, beginning writers' oral readings of their texts often reveal a more sophisticated understanding of the genre than is demonstrated by their written products alone (Donovan, 2001; Donovan & Smolkin, 2002; Zecker, 1999). Smolkin and Donovan (2004) found that elementary children's ability to write stories and information texts with appropriate features was only moderately correlated with their ability to consciously discuss genre features. Additionally, children who produced texts with similar organizational structures did not necessarily have the same level of conscious genre knowledge (Donovan & Smolkin, 2002). For the youngest children, the complexity of stories or information pieces is not related to the level of conventional spelling (Donovan, 2001). Several studies found that children showed the most growth in story and information writing from Kindergarten through Grade 2, with only small gains in the upper elementary years (Donovan, 2001; Langer, 1986).

To summarize, although preschool children's written forms and meanings are not always conventional, they are clearly related to the intended genre, indicating that children are sensitive to the demands and potentials of different genre. For older students, their command of genre features appears closely tied to experience and instruction (Riley & Reedy, 2005; Wollman-Bonilla, 2000).

INDIVIDUAL WRITING PROCESSES

Research on elementary children's writing processes has been heavily influenced by authoring cycle (Short, Harste, & Burke, 1996) and process writing (Calkins, 1994; Graves, 1994) approaches to writing instruction. Educators working from these perspectives have attempted to create classroom environments (e.g., reading/writing workshops) that support elementary students in engaging in the same kinds of writing activities reported by adult authors including: drafting, revising, seeking audience feedback, editing for convention, and publishing. Not surprisingly, researchers studying writing workshop classrooms have been interested in topic choice, drafting, revision, audience awareness, and student roles during authoring. Graves and his colleagues (Calkins, 1980, 1994; Graves, 1983, 1984; Sowers, 1985) conducted a number of early studies of elementary children's writing processes in writers workshop classrooms. Subsequent studies have extended their observations. A general finding is that the parts of the writing processes (i.e., drafting, revising, etc.) are recursive and interwoven across time, rather than sequential (Graves, 1983, 1984; Sowers, 1985).

Existing research documents developmental patterns in several aspects of young children's writing processes. First, over time, children's writing processes shift from external to internal (Graves, 1984). Young children often talk with others and draw as they compose (Dyson, 1997, 1998; Schneider, 2003; Wiseman, 2003). Their stories are often not planned in advance, but develop as they interact with others around their writing. As children gain experience as writers, they become more able to solve problems of topic and information choice internally (Abbott, 2000; Graves, 1984; Jones, 2003).

The use of drawing as part of the rehearsal and drafting process also varies for writers of different experience levels. For younger children, rehearsal (i.e., conscious or unconscious planning for writing) often occurs as children draw or talk about their ideas just prior to writing. Young writers, then, often draw before or during writing, whereas more experienced writers may not draw at all (Graves, 1983, 1984) or add drawings as illustrations only after their texts are complete (Tower, 2005). However, it may be that drawing retains its usefulness for older writers when they receive instruction in how to use it strategically for rehearsal (Norris, Reichard, & Mokhtari, 1997).

Regarding topic choice, Graves (1983) found that first-grade writers chose topics quickly without much thought, whereas more experienced writers sometimes experienced difficulty in choosing topics because of self-consciousness about pleasing their audience. As children in his study gained experience as writers, they began to collect ideas for composing and often considered future topics while finishing a current piece. Older elementary students used conversations with peers as opportunities to get ideas for writing (Baker, Rozendal, & Whitenack, 2000; T. J. Burns, 2001; Schultz, 1997).

The aspect of elementary students' writing processes that has garnered the most research attention is revision. A common finding is that beginning writers focus on getting their meanings down and revise little, if at all (Bradley, 2001; Graves, 1979, 1984; Schneider, 2003; Sowers, 1985). Once children begin to revise, they focus primarily on mechanics (e.g., spelling, handwriting, conventions such as punctuation), making few if any changes in information or structure (Calkins, 1980; Graves, 1979; Perez, 2001; Sipe, 1998). With experience, elementary children begin to revise more flexibly (e.g., before, during, and after writing; Perez, 2001).

Research has also shown that audience awareness can affect topic selection and choice of sign systems, as well as revision (Baker et al., 2000; T. J. Burns, 2001). Instructional factors such as the availability of computers for word processing (Baker et al., 2000) and specific instruction in revision strategies (Bradley, 2001) may have an important influence on amounts and types of revision.

Overall, young children's writing occurs in the moment. There is little preplanning or revising. As children gain experience in using their texts for a variety of purposes and interacting with peers around writing, they begin to engage in both rehearsal and revision, with an eye toward pleasing their audience.

SOCIAL INTERACTION AND WRITING

Dyson (1989) has argued that there is a dialectical relationship between cognitive and social aspects of authoring. Literacy strategies are developed to accomplish social purposes, and those social purposes in turn shape the strategies children construct (Heath, 1991). To study the impact of social interaction on children's texts and writing processes, researchers have produced fine-grained descriptions of children's interactions with parents, siblings, classmates, and teachers.

With regard to adult interaction styles, research shows that when adults exerted less control during writing events, 5- and 6-year-olds expressed more interest in writing, produced more forms of emergent writing (Fang, 1999; Gutman & Sulzby, 2000), and initiated more verbal interaction (M. S. Burns & Casbergue, 1992; Zuccermaglio & Scheuer, 1996). However, they also produced less conventional texts than when adults used a controlling style. Differences in adult style had less impact on the conventionality of children's texts after they entered kindergarten perhaps because they were already focused on conventions (DeBaryshe, Buell, & Binder, 1996). Adults were found to scaffold toddlers', preschoolers', and kindergarteners' writing by tracking the child's progress and meanings and matching their contributions to the child's current needs and independent writing level (DeBaryshe et al., 1996; Lancaster, 2001; Lysaker, 2000). When preschool and early elementary-age children interacted with parents and other familiar adults during writing, there was a relational component to their authoring processes. Adult–child interactions often included physical closeness, shared rituals, and celebrations of writing progress (Lysaker, 2000).

Peer interactions also supported writing in important ways. Gregory's (2001) study of siblings' writing interactions in a home setting found that both siblings benefited. When elementary students wrote with their peers at school, they engaged in writing to initiate and maintain friendships with peers and to communicate with present and absent audiences (Rowe, 1994; Wiseman, 2003; Wollman-Bonilla, 2001b). Dyson (2000) observed that social processes were central to the writing of the second and third graders she studied. Through writing, students affiliated, resisted, created distance, or negotiated social relations with their peers. A number of researchers have observed that elementary writers negotiate their relationships with peers by including them as characters in their stories (Dyson, 2003a; Schultz, 1997; Wiseman, 2003).

Researchers have also described the roles that hearing (Condon & Clyde, 1996; Dyson, 1989; Labbo, 1996; Rowe, 1994; Rowe et al., 2001; Wiseman, 2003) and deaf children (Troyer, 1991; Williams, 1999) took when writing with peers. When children were free to talk and write with others, they took a variety of interactive roles including observing other authors; providing assistance to another author by scribing, providing spellings, or ideas; mirroring other author' texts and processes; sharing different parts of a writing task to complete a single text; and working collaboratively to coauthor texts. Children used talk to negotiate and define their roles 'to request and provide help and information' and to challenge and question peers' authoring practices (Jones, 2003; Rowe, 1994; Schultz, 1997; Sipe, 1998; Williams, 1999).

Another way social interaction has been shown to impact children's writing processes is by providing demonstrations of culturally appropriate writing forms, processes, and meanings (Chapman, 1996; Harste et al., 1984; Rowe, 1994; Wollman-Bonilla, 2001b). A frequent finding was that children linked their texts to those of other authors with whom they interacted. Kress (1997) and others (Dyson, 1989; Newkirk, 1989; Rowe, 1994) have argued that even in cases where children's authoring processes appeared imitative, they involved constructive work, rather than copying (Kress, 1997). Instead, children analyzed others' texts through the frames provided by their current hypotheses and reconstructed the forms, meanings, and functions in their own way. What young authors chose to appropriate from a demonstration was motivated by their current hypotheses (Harste et al., 1984), individual purposes (Dyson, 1989), and social interest (Kress, 1997).

Social interaction also appears to play an important role in children's construction and testing of literacy hypotheses. First, children used interaction as a means of confirming their existing literacy hypotheses (Rowe, 1994). Second, peer questions and comments challenged their understandings, pushing young writers to clarify, expand, and refine their intended meanings and the forms used to represent them (Condon & Clyde, 1996; Rowe, 1994). Third, children shifted stances to consider the audience's perspective and monitor the effectiveness and appropriateness of their texts (Graves, 1984; Rowe, 1994; Wollman-Bonilla, 2001a).

Overall, these studies show that social interaction plays an important role in children's writing processes. For preschoolers, social relationships with adults motivate participation in writing. Adults' interactive styles may work to support or suppress emergent forms of writing. As children enter school, writing becomes intertwined with peer relationships. Social interaction offers information about writing in the form of demonstrations, opportunities to ask for and receive help, and a social nudge to consider audience perspectives on one's writing.

SOCIOCULTURAL PERSPECTIVES ON CHILDHOOD WRITING

Most of the research reviewed thus far has viewed writing as an "in head" phenomenon, albeit one that is shaped by people and social situations. Recently, researchers interested in sociocultural aspects of authoring have challenged this notion of writing as an individual mental act, suggesting, instead, that writing occurs *between* people as they negotiate authoring processes, meanings, and textual forms as part of their everyday activities.

Culture- and Class-Based Writing Practices

When writing is seen as a socially situated act, it is no longer possible to discuss the writing process as if it were a generic characteristic of mind. Instead, young children's authoring must be investigated as it occurs within the social practices of particular communities (Gee, 2001).

Culturally based variation in writing practices has been an important focus of research. Heath's (1983) classic study of variation in the literate practices of three communities in the Piedmont Carolinas is a seminal study in this area. In Trackton, a Black working-class community, preschoolers observed others reading and writing to fulfill a variety of home and community tasks, but parents did not create writing tasks for their children or consciously model writing behaviors. Children experimented with writing under the indirect supervision of older children. In Roadville, a White working-class community, parents read books to their children as early as age 6 months, but children were allowed to use crayons and pencils only under adult supervision–mostly in coloring books and work books. Children too young to complete these structured activities were not encouraged to "just scribble" (Heath, 1983, p. 391).

Heath's findings can be contrasted to reports provided by several middle-class parent/researchers (Baghban, 1984; Martens, 1996; Schickedanz, 1990) who have described the writing experiences they made available to their preschool children. A common thread in these case studies was availability of many opportunities for young children to observe adults reading and writing and to explore writing themselves. Baghban, Martens, and Schickedanz each report providing their children with easy access to writing materials beginning as soon as the child showed interest around age 1. Parents and other adults were frequently present to supervise and interact with children around their writing. Children's unconventional texts were met with parental approval and interest. Both children and parents referred to children's scribbles as writing or drawing.

Heath (1983) linked Trackton, Roadville, and mainstream children's home literacy experiences to their differential engagement and success with reading and writing when they entered school. She argued that the close match between school and home literacy practices for mainstream children provided a smooth transition to school not provided by Trackton and Roadville children's home literacy experiences. A number of more recent studies support the idea that home literacy practices affect children's understandings about writing (Purcell-Gates, 1995, 1996; Senechal, LeFevre, Thomas, & Daley, 1998). For example, Purcell-Gates' (1996) study of low-SES families found that low-SES children who observed and had opportunities to participate in many uses of written language were more likely to understand that print is symbolic and can be used for a variety of purposes.

Other researchers have also studied culture and class-based variation in family literacy practices—including writing. A recent study by Korat and Levin (2002), for example, showed a relationship between SES background and maternal beliefs and interactions about writing. Low-SES mothers engaged in more talk about spelling, were more concerned about spelling accuracy, and used a more directive style than did high-SES mothers—regardless of whether their children were good spellers.

Although different writing practices appear related to different patterns of literacy knowledge, research findings also suggest that categories such as ethnicity and SES should be used cautiously as predictors of child or family literacy practices. Researchers have observed considerable variation in the writing practices of low-income and minority homes (Purcell-Gates, 1996; Taylor & Dorsey-Gaines, 1988; Teale, 1986). Families who share similar ethnic or social-class backgrounds may not share the same values, beliefs, and practices related to writing.

Participation in Classroom Writing Practices

In addition to studies of home writing practices, researchers have also investigated the nature of young children's participation in classroom writing communities (Larson, 1999; Larson & Maier, 2000; Manyak, 2001; Power, 1991). The focus of this work is on understanding how social participation structures give children access to roles and knowledge needed to become members of the classroom writing community (Larson & Maier, 2000). It appears that some classroom literacy events are accomplished through participation structures that allow children and teachers to flexibly shift between roles as experts and novices (Manyak, 2001), and as teacher, author, coauthor, overhearer, and so on (Larson, 1995, 1999; Larson & Maier, 2000). Larson (Larson & Maier, 2000) suggests that these shifts in participation allow the social distribution of knowledge about writing, and give children access to central roles in writing events well before they can take them up independently. Through participation, children learn valued relations to text, to other participants, and to the world.

Writing and Identity

From a sociocultural perspective, writing is also seen as an act of self-definition. Learning to write involves much more than adding new skills to children's cognitive repertoires. It requires that children take on new cultural identities and affects their sense of self in profound ways (Dyson, 2001; Manyak, 2001; Rowe et al., 2001; Solsken, 1993). Elementary classrooms are intercultural sites for writing (Lemke, 1995) and identity construction. Because children are simultaneously positioned in the overlapping communities of official and peer cultures (Dyson, 1993; Rowe et al., 2001), the same writing activities often have very different meanings for their identities as students in the official world and as friends in the peer world. In elementary classrooms where students select their own topics, confer about their writing, publish their finished texts, and use writing for a variety of purposes, writing involves assuming a "social voice" (Dyson, 2001). For example, children's choices to write about insects or video games position them in particular ways in relation to their peers, the ongoing dialogue in their classroom, and to the texts and practices of the larger society (Dyson, 2001, 2003a; Heffernan & Lewison, 2003; Van Sluys, 2003).

Children's writing functions as much to establish "who I am in relation to you" as to serve other communicative purposes (Van Sluys, 2003). Dyson's (1995, 2000) research with second and third graders has demonstrated that elementary writers use texts to construct social affiliations with their peers, as well as to accept and resist the ways they are positioned by others. Students sometimes try on new identities and experiment with crossing cultural, racial, and gender boundaries in their writing (Heffernan & Lewison, 2003).

Writing as Gendered Practice

Several researchers have also conducted ideological analyses of the gendered nature of authoring practices and the ways writing may reify or transform the social positions occupied and available to young authors. Solsken (1993) has explored the ways children's orientations toward literacy were framed by gender and class relations in their families and the larger society. The middle-class boys in her study preferred writing over reading, both because it was less directly identified with their mothers and because it provided more opportunities for initiative and productivity. Girls invested in writing in ways that were consistent with female qualities, using it to maintain bonds of affection and nurturance and to entertain themselves and others.

Both Gallas (1998) and Henkin (1995, 1998) have reported that gender and ethnicity strongly influenced the ways children were positioned in authoring events by their peers, with girls and ethnic outsiders sometimes having limited access to powerful roles. At the same time, boys may be marginalized by writing activities that do not connect well with male interests and predispositions (Blair & Sanford, 2004).

Another research approach to understanding the gendered nature of elementary students' writing has been analysis of the gender roles displayed in children's written texts. Research findings document consistent gender differences in writing (Newkirk, 2000). For example, boys tend to write about adventure and other topics outside of their immediate experience. They also focus on action as part of physical and social contests, write about characters that act alone, include violence, include more male and fewer female characters, position females in traditionally passive roles, and cast males in roles of authority (Anderson, 2003; Dyson, 1995; Graves, 1973; Gray-Schlegel & Gray-Schlegel, 1995–1996; McAuliffe, 1994; Newkirk, 2000; Simmons, 1997). Girls, in contrast, tend to write about topics related to their immediate experiences with parents and friends at home and school. Girls' stories are less likely to include violence and more likely to focus on social relationships and to present characters who work collectively (Anderson, 2003; Dyson, 1995; Fleming, 1995; Graves, 1973; Gray-Schlegel & Gray-Schlegel, 1995–1996; McAuliffe, 1994). When fourth graders were asked to describe boys' and girls' stories, many of these same features were mentioned (Peterson, 2001).

Despite this picture of gendered writing practices, several researchers also report ways in which girls challenged gender boundaries, suggesting that writing can become an opportunity to explore multiple positions and alternate definitions of power (Dyson, 1995; MacGillivray & Martinez, 1998). Whereas most analyses of elementary children's gendered writing practices have, at least implicitly, negatively interpreted the violence and gender inequities observed in boys' texts, Newkirk (2000) argues that these writing patterns do not necessarily result from antisocial values. Instead, boys may be appropriating violence for nonviolent ends.

Overall, defining writing as social practice has helped to establish that writing is neither generic nor politically neutral. Children learn situated ways of making meaning with print that vary according to the literacy practices of their homes and classrooms. When children write, they take up, adapt, or resist positions in existing systems of power relations. Negotiating their places in these cultural systems is a key part of writing.

SUMMARY AND CONCLUSIONS: A PORTRAIT OF CHILD WRITERS

The portrait of young writers presented in this chapter calls on adults to look at children and their scribbles with a new eye. By age 3, and perhaps before, young children are beginning to explore the purposes and forms of writing. For the most part, they do this as part of their play. Children become intrigued with the tools of literacy—print, pens, paper, computers, staplers, tape and so on—when they see others using them. They are drawn to learning about writing because print and the materials that produce it are socially meaningful in their homes and communities. As we have seen, the extent to which young children have opportunities to access writing materials for their own uses varies depending on availability and on parental and caregiver beliefs about appropriate writing experiences for preschoolers. How adults interact with children affects their writing, as well. However, if given the chance, young children experiment with making marks and playfully begin to produce texts that display some of the characteristics of the lists, letters, signs, and storybooks they see in their environment. They experiment with differences in writing and drawing and with the ways that different sign systems can be purposefully combined. They use common tasks like name writing as an opportunity to learn foundational concepts such as what a word is or that letters represent sounds. However, these concepts are not learned all at once as fully formed understandings. Instead, as with oral language, children construct a series of hypotheses about words, form–meaning relationships, spelling, genre characteristics, and so on. It is these unconventional hypotheses, rather than random marking or inattention to detail, that gives young writers' texts their characteristic appearance. With experience, children's hypotheses and the resulting texts become more conventional.

As children move into elementary school, writing instruction builds on many of the understandings and skills that (some) children have formed as preschoolers. Children who have experimented with scribbles use their understandings of the text production potentials of paper and pencils and their initial observations about writing purposes, forms, directionality, and form–meaning relationships as the basis for participating in school writing activities. Of course, the nature of elementary school writing instruction varies depending on educators' beliefs about writing and curricular mandates. But when children attend writing workshop classrooms where they are invited to compose stories, information pieces, and other texts for functional purposes, they begin to develop not only more sophisticated understandings of print conventions, but also strategies for choosing writing topics, rehearsing ideas for writing, composing text, revising, and considering the perspectives of their audiences. As with other aspects of learning to write, children's writing processes become more sophisticated with experience.

At both the preschool and elementary levels, children use writing as a way of interacting with others. In process-writing classrooms where children share their finished pieces, children use writing not only to fulfill school assignments but also to negotiate friendships with peers. Peer and teacher interactions provide students with needed help and with opportunities to see how readers respond to their texts. By having an audience, children learn to consider audience perspectives while they are composing.

The portrait being developed here is not a generic, one-size-fits-all depiction of childhood writing, however. Children learn about writing through experiences in local events at home and school. In both locations, their experiences are bounded by culture- and class-based uses of writing and beliefs about what roles are appropriate for children of their age and gender. Children learn to write from the vantage points afforded by their positions in writing events. As children participate in writing at home and school, they appropriate cultural values and materials that form the basis for their writing responses in other contexts.

For educators, there are three important conclusions that may be drawn from this portrait of childhood writing. First, preschoolers' experiences with writing matter. As young children play with writing, they are building foundational understandings about print functions, forms, and content. Second, in supportive instructional environments, elementary writers can go far beyond traditional expectations that they will learn conventions such as spelling and punctuation. They can engage in the writing processes of planning, composing, revising, and presenting their texts to outside audiences and, with experience, do so in increasingly sophisticated ways. Third, learning to write is a local process. What and how children learn depends on home and school writing practices. Culture-, class-, and gender-based variation is an expected part of the picture.

This portrait of childhood writing also allows us to see some areas that are in need of further research. First, there is little research on children's experiences with print before the age of 3. Because writing materials and activities are present in many children's homes beginning at birth, it is likely that some preschoolers' first writing experiences occur before age 3. To more fully understand how children develop as writers, we need to investigate children's earliest experiences. Also of interest are caregiver beliefs and interactions with infants and toddlers around writing. Second, we need to continue to develop the recent line of research on sociocultural variation in children's writing experiences. A good deal of the existing research on childhood writing has been conducted with middle-class children or in mainstream school contexts. This leads to the possibility that mainstream writing practices and patterns of development are implicitly seen as the norm. Given the increasing diversity of school populations in the United States and abroad, it is crucial to understand culturally based writing practices and the resources they provide.

REFERENCES

Abbott, J. A. (2000). "Blinking out" and "having the touch": Two fifth-grade boys talk about flow experiences in writing. *Written Communication, 17*(1), 53–92.

Anderson, M. (2003). Reading violence in boys' writing. *Language Arts, 80*(3), 223–230.

Baghban, M. (1984). *Our daughter learns to read and write: A case study from birth to three.* Newark, DE: International Reading Association.

Baker, E. A., Rozendal, M. S., & Whitenack, J. W. (2000). Audience awareness in a technology-rich elementary classroom. *Journal of Literacy Research, 32*(3), 395–419.

Ballenger, C. (1999). *Teaching other people's children. Literacy and learning in a bilingual classroom.* New York: Teachers College Press.

Barton, D., & Hamilton, M. (2000). Literacy practices. In D. Barton, M. Hamilton, & R. Ivanic (Eds.), *Situated literacies. Reading and writing in context* (pp. 7–15). London: Routledge.

Bear, D., & Templeton, S. (1998). Explorations in spelling: Foundations for learning and teaching phonics, spelling, and vocabulary. *Reading Teacher, 52,* 222–242.

Besse, J. M. (1996). An approach to writing in kindergarten. In M. Orsolini, B. Burge, & L. B. Resnick (Eds.), *Children's early text construction* (pp. 127–144). Mahwah, NJ: Lawrence Erlbaum Associates.

Bissex, G. (1980). *GYNS at work: A child learns to read and write.* Cambridge, MA: Harvard University Press.

Blair, H. A., & Sanford, K. (2004). Morphing literacy: Boys reshaping their school-based literacy practices. *Language Arts, 81*(6), 452–460.

Bloodgood, J. (1999). What's in a name? Children's name writing and name acquisition. *Reading Research Quarterly, 34,* 342–367.

Borzone de Manrique, A. M., & Signorini, A. (1998). Emergent writing forms in Spanish. *Reading and Writing: An Interdisciplinary Journal, 10,* 499–517.

Bradley, D. H. (2001). How beginning writers articulate and demonstrate their understanding of the act of writing. *Reading Research and Instruction, 40*(4), 273–296.

Branscombe, N. A., & Taylor, J. B. (1996). The development of Scrap's understanding of written language. *Childhood Education, 72*, 278–281.

Brenneman, K., Massey, C., Machado, S. F., & Gelman, R. (1996). Young children's plans differ for writing and drawing. *Cognitive Development, 11*, 397–419.

Burns, M. S., & Casbergue, R. (1992). Parent–child interaction in a letter-writing context. *Journal of Reading Behavior, 24*, 289–312.

Burns, T. J. (2001). Being "social": Expanding our view of social interaction in writing workshops. *Language Arts, 78*(5), 458–466.

Calkins, L. M. (1980). Children's rewriting strategies. *Research in the Teaching of English, 14*, 331–341.

Calkins, L. M. (1994). *The art of teaching writing*. Portsmouth, NH: Heinemann.

Chapman, M. L. (1995). The sociocognitive construction of written genres in first grade. *Research in the Teaching of English, 29*(2), 164–192.

Chapman, M. L. (1996). More than spelling: Widening the lens on emergent writing. *Reading Horizons, 36*, 317–339.

Clay, M. (1975). *What did I write?* Auckland, New Zealand: Heinemann.

Clyde, J. A. (1994). Lessons from Douglas: Expanding our visions of what it means to "know." *Language Arts, 71*, 22–33.

Condon, M., & Clyde, J. A. (1996). Co-authoring: Composing through conversation. *Language Arts, 73*, 587–596.

DeBaryshe, B. D., Buell, M. J., & Binder, J. C. (1996). What a parent brings to the table: Young children writing with and without parental assistance. *Journal of Literacy Research, 28*, 71–90.

Donovan, C. A. (2001). Children's development and control of written story and informational genres. Insights from one elementary school. *Research in the Teaching of English, 35*, 394–447.

Donovan, C. A., & Smolkin, L. B. (2002). Children's genre knowledge: An examination of K–5 students' performance on multiple tasks providing different levels of scaffolding. *Reading Research Quarterly, 37*(4), 428–465.

Dyson, A. (1985). Individual differences in emerging writing. In M. Farr (Ed.), *Advances in writing research: Children's early writing development* (Vol. 1, pp. 59–125). Norwood, NJ: Ablex.

Dyson, A. (1989). *Multiple worlds of child writers: Friends learning to write*. New York: Teachers College Press.

Dyson, A. (1993). Social worlds of children learning to write in an urban primary school. NewYork: Teachers College Press.

Dyson, A. (1995). The courage to write: Child meaning making in a contested world. *Language Arts, 72*(5), 324–333.

Dyson, A. (1997). *Writing superheroes. Contemporary childhood, popular culture, and classroom literacy*. New York: Teacher College Press.

Dyson, A. (1998). The children's forum: Linking writing, drama, and development of community in an urban classroom. In B. J. Wagner (Ed.), *Educational drama and language arts: What research shows* (pp. 148–172). Portsmouth, NH: Heinemann.

Dyson, A. (2000). On reframing children's words: The perils, promises, and pleasures of writing children. *Research in the Teaching of English, 34*(3), 352–367.

Dyson, A. (2001). Where are the childhoods in childhood literacy? An exploration of (outer) school space. *Journal of Early Childhood Literacy, 1*, 9–39.

Dyson, A. (2003a). *The brothers and sisters learn to write. Popular literacies and school cultures*. New York: Teachers College Press.

Dyson, A. (2003b). Popular literacies and the "all" children: Rethinking literacy development for contemporary childhoods. *Language Arts, 81*(2), 100–109.

Fang, Z. (1999). Expanding the vista of emergent writing research: Implications for early childhood educators. *Early Childhood Education Journal, 26*, 179–182.

Ferreiro, E. (1990). Literacy development: Psychogenesis. In Y. Goodman (Ed.), *How children construct literacy: Piagetian perspectives* (pp. 12–25). Newark, DE: International Reading Association.

Ferreiro, E., & Teberosky, A. (1982). *Literacy before schooling*. Portsmouth, NH: Heinemann.

Fleming, S. (1995). Whose stories are validated? *Language Arts, 72*(8), 590–596.

Fresch, M. J. (2001). Journal entries as a window on spelling knowledge. *Reading Teacher, 54*(5), 500–513.

Gallas, K. (1998). *"Sometimes I can be anything": Power, gender, and identity in a primary classroom*. New York: Teachers College Press.

Gallas, K. (1994). The languages of learning: How children talk, write, dance, draw, and sing their understanding of the world. NewYork: Teachers College Press.

Gee, J. P. (1999). *An introduction to discourse analysis: Theory and method*. London: Routledge.

Gee, J. P. (2001). Foreward. In C. Lewis (Ed.), Literacy practices as social acts. Power, status and cultural norms in the classroom (pp. xi–xiv). Mahwah, NJ: Lawrence Erlbaum Associates.

Gee, J. P. (2003). A sociocultural perspective on early literacy development. In S. B. Neuman & D. Dickinson (Eds.), *Handbook of early literacy research* (pp. 30–42). New York: Guilford.

Gentry, J. R. (2000). A retrospective on invented spelling and a look forward. *Reading Teacher, 54*(3), 318–332.

Goodman, Y. (1986). Children coming to know literacy. In W. Teale & E. Sulzby (Eds.), *Emergent literacy* (pp. 1–14). Norwood, NJ: Ablex.

Graves, D. (1973). Sex differences in children's writing. *Elementary English, 50*(7), 1101–1106.

Graves, D. (1979). What children show us about revision. *Language Arts, 65*, 312–318.

Graves, D. (1983). The growth and development of first-grade writers. In A. Freedman, I. Pringle, & J. Yalden (Eds.), *Learning to write: First language/second language* (pp. 54–66). New York: Longman.

Graves, D. (1984). A case study observing the development of primary children's composing, spelling, and motor behaviors during the writing process. In D. Graves (Ed.), *A researcher learns to write. Selected articles and monographs* (pp. 141–165). Exeter, NH: Heinemann.

Graves, D. (1994). *A fresh look at writing*. Portsmouth, NH: Heinemann.

Gray-Schlegel, M. A., & Gray-Schlegel, T. (1995–1996). An investigation of gender stereotypes as revealed through children's creative writing. *Reading Research and Instruction, 35*(2), 160–169.

Green, C. R. (1998). This is my name. *Childhood Education, 74*(4), 226–231.

Gregory, E. (2001). Sisters and brothers as language and literacy teachers: Synergy between siblings playing and working together. *Journal of Early Childhood Literacy, 1*, 301–322.

Grossi, E. P. (1990). Applying psychogenesis principles to the literacy instruction of lower-class children in Brazil. In Y. Goodman (Ed.), *How children construct literacy: Piagetian perspectives* (pp. 99–114). Newark, DE: International Reading Association.

Gutman, L. M., & Sulzby, E. (2000). The role of autonomy-support versus control in the emergent writing behaviors of African-American kindergarten children. *Reading Research and Instruction, 39*(2), 170–184.

Haney, M. R., Bissonnette, V., & Behnken, K. L. (2003). The relationship among name writing and early literacy skills in kindergarten children. *Child Study Journal, 33*(2), 99–114.

Harste, J. C. (2000). Six points of departure. In B. Berghoff, K. Egawa, J. C. Harste, & B. Hoonan (Eds.), *Beyond reading and writing: Inquiry curriculum and multiple ways of knowing* (pp. 1–16). Urbana, IL: National Council of Teachers of English.

Harste, J. C., Woodward, V. A., & Burke, C. L. (1984). *Language stories and literacy lessons*. Portsmouth, NH: Heinemann.

Heath, S. B. (1983). *Ways with words*. Cambridge, England: Cambridge University Press.

Heath, S. B. (1991). The sense of being literate: Historical and cross-cultural features. In R. Barr, M. Kamil, & P. D. Pearson (Eds.), *Handbook of reading research* (Vol. 2, pp. 3–25). New York: Longman.

Heffernan, L., & Lewison, M. (2003). Social narrative writing: (Re)constructing kid culture in the writer's workshop. *Language Arts, 80*(6), 435–443.

Henderson, E., & Beers, J. (1980). *Developmental and cognitive aspects of learning to spell: A reflection of word knowledge*. Newark, DE: International Reading Association.

Henkin, R. (1995). Insiders and outsiders in first grade writing workshops: Gender and equity issues. *Language Arts, 72*(6), 429–434.

Henkin, R. (1998). *Who's invited to share? Using literacy to teach for equity and social justice*. Portsmouth, NH: Heinemann.

Hildreth, G. (1936). Developmental sequences in name writing. *Child Development, 7*, 291–303.

Hubbard, R. (1989). *Authors of pictures, draughtsmen of words*. Portsmouth, NH: Heinemann.

Jones, I. (2003). Collaborative writing and children's use of literate language: A sequential analysis of social interaction. *Journal of Early Childhood Literacy, 3*(2), 165–178.

Kamberelis, G. (1999). Genre development and learning: Children writing stories, science reports, and poems. *Research in the Teaching of English, 33*(4), 403–463.

Kamberelis, G., & Bovino, T. D. (1999). Cultural artifacts as scaffolds for genre development. *Reading Research Quarterly, 34*(2), 138–170.

Kamii, C., Long, R., & Manning, M. (2001). Kindergarteners' development toward "invented" spelling and a glottographic theory. *Linguistics and Education, 12*, 195–210.

Kenner, C. (2000). Symbols make text: A social semiotic analysis of writing in a multilingual nursery. *Written Language and Literacy, 3*(2), 235–266.

Korat, O., & Levin, I. (2002). Spelling acquisition in two societal groups: Mother–child interaction, maternal beliefs and child's spelling. *Journal of Literacy Research, 34*(2), 209–236.

Korkeamaki, R.-L., & Dreher, M. J. (2000). Finnish kindergarteners' literacy development in contextualized literacy episodes: A focus on spelling. *Journal of Literacy Research, 32*(3), 349–393.

Kress, G. (1997). *Before writing: Rethinking the paths to literacy*. London: Routledge.

Labbo, L. (1996). A semiotic analysis of young children's symbol making in a classroom computer center. *Reading Research Quarterly, 31*(4), 356–385.

Lancaster, L. (2001). Staring at the page: The function of gaze in a young child's interpretation of symbolic forms. *Journal of Childhood Literacy, 1*(2), 131–152.

Langer, J. (1986). *Children reading and writing: Structures and strategies.* Norwood, NJ: Ablex.

Larson, J. (1995). Talk matters: The role of pivot in the distribution of literacy knowledge among novice writers. *Linguistics and Education, 7,* 277–302.

Larson, J. (1999). Analyzing participation frameworks in a kindergarten writing activity: The role of over-hearer in learning to write. *Written Communication, 16,* 225–257.

Larson, J., & Maier, M. (2000). Co-authoring classroom texts: Shifting participant roles in writing activity. *Research in the Teaching of English, 34*(4), 468–497.

Lave, J., & Wenger, E. (1991). *Situated learning. Legitimate peripheral participation.* Cambridge, England: Cambridge University Press.

Lemke, J. (1995). *Textual politics.* London: Taylor & Francis.

Lysaker, J. (2000). Beyond words: The relational dimensions of learning to reading and write. *Language Arts, 77*(6), 479–484.

MacGillivray, L., & Martinez, A. M. (1998). Princesses who commit suicide: Primary children writing within and against gender stereotypes. *Journal of Literacy Research, 300,* 53–84.

Many, J. E., Fyfe, R., Lewis, G., & Mitchell, E. (1996). Traversing the topical landscape: Exploring students' self-directed reading-writing-research processes. *Reading Research Quarterly, 31*(1), 12–35.

Manyak, P. (2001). Participation, hybridity, and carnival: A situated analysis of a dynamic literacy practice in a primary-grade English immersion class. *Journal of Literacy Research, 33,* 423–465.

Martens, P. A. (1996). *I already know how to read: A child's view of literacy.* Portsmouth, NH: Heinemann.

Martens, P. A. (1999). "Mommy, how do you write 'Sarah'?" The role of name writing in one child's literacy. *Journal of Research in Childhood Education, 14*(1), 5–15.

Mason, L., & Boscolo, P. (2000). Writing and conceptual change. What changes? *Instructional Science, 28,* 199–226.

Mayer, C., & Moskos, E. (1998). Deaf children learning to spell. *Research in the Teaching of English, 33,* 158–180.

McAuliffe, S. (1994). Toward understanding one another: Second graders' use of gendered language and story styles. *Reading Teacher, 47*(4), 302–310.

Meltzer, N. S., & Herse, R. (1969). The boundaries of written words as seen by first graders. *Journal of Reading Behavior, 1*(3), 3–14.

Newkirk, T. (1989). *More than stories: The range of children's writing.* Portsmouth, NH: Heinemann.

Newkirk, T. (2000). Misreading masculinity: Speculations on the great gender gap in writing. *Language Arts, 77*(4), 294–300.

Norris, E. A., Reichard, C., & Mokhtari, K. (1997). The influence of drawing on third graders' writing performance. *Reading Horizons, 38,* 13–30.

Olson, J. L. (1992). *Envisioning writing: Toward an integration of drawing and writing.* Portsmouth, NH: Heinemann.

Pahl, K. (1999). *Transformation. Children's meaning making in a nursery.* Stoke on Trent, England: Trentham Books.

Perez, S. (2001). Revising during writing in a second grade classroom. *Educational Research Quarterly, 25*(1), 27–32.

Peterson, S. (2001). Gender identities and self-expression in classroom narrative writing. *Language Arts, 78*(5), 451–457.

Pontecorvo, C., & Zucchermaglio, C. (1990). A passage to literacy: Learning in a social context. In Y. Goodman (Ed.), *How children construct literacy: Piagetian perspectives* (pp. 59–98). Newark, DE: International Reading Association.

Power, B. M. (1991). Pop-ups: The rise and fall of one convention in a first grade writing workshop. *Journal of Research in Childhood Education, 6,* 54–65.

Purcell-Gates, V. (1995). *Other people's words: The cycle of low literacy.* Cambridge, MA: Harvard University Press.

Purcell-Gates, V. (1996). Stories, coupons, and the *TV Guide: Relationships between home literacy experiences and emergent literacy knowledge. Reading Research Quarterly, 31*(4), 406–428.

Riley, J., & Reedy, D. (2005). Developing young children's thinking through learning to write argument. *Journal of Early Childhood Literacy, 5*(1), 29–51.

Roberts, B. (1992). The evolution of the young child's concept of word as a unit of spoken and written language. *Reading Research Quarterly, 27,* 124–139.

Rowe, D. W. (1994). *Preschoolers as authors: Literacy learning in the social world of the classroom.* Cresskill, NJ: Hampton.

Rowe, D. W., Fitch, J. D., & Bass, A. S. (2001). Power, identity, and instructional stance in the writers' workshop. *Language Arts, 78*, 426–434.

Schickedanz, J. A. (1990). *Adam's righting revolutions: One child's literacy development from infancy through grade one*. Portsmouth, NH: Heinemann.

Schneider, J. J. (2003). Contexts, genres, and imagination: An examination of the idiosyncratic writing performances of three elementary children within multiple contexts of writing instruction. *Research in the Teaching of English, 37*(3), 329–379.

Schultz, K. (1997). "Do you want to be in my story?": Collaborative writing in an urban elementary classroom. *Journal of Literacy Research, 29*(2), 253–287.

Senechal, M., LeFevre, J.-A., Thomas, E. M., & Daley, K. E. (1998). Differential effects of home literacy experiences on the development of oral and written language. *Reading Research Quarterly, 33*(1), 96–116.

Short, K. G., Harste, J. C., & Burke, C. L. (1996). *Creating classroom for authors and inquirers* (2nd ed.). Portsmouth, NH: Heinemann.

Siegel, M. (1995). More than words: The generative power of transmediation for learning. *Canadian Journal of Education, 20*(4), 455–475.

Simmons, J. (1997). Attack of the killer baby faces: Gender similarities in third-grade writing. *Language Arts, 744*(2), 116–123.

Sipe, L. (1998). Transitions to the conventional: An examination of a first grader's composing process. *Journal of Literacy Research, 30*, 357–388.

Smolkin, L. B., & Donovan, C. A. (2004). Developing conscious understanding of genre: The relationship between implicit and explicit knowledge during the five-to-seven shift. In J. Worthy, B. Maloch, J. V. Hoffman, D. L. Schallert, & C. M. Fairbanks (Eds.), *53rd yearbook of the National Reading Conference* (pp. 385–399). Oak Creek, WI: National Reading Conference.

Solsken, J. (1993). *Literacy, gender, and work in families and in school*. Norwood, NJ: Ablex.

Solsken, J., Willett, J., & Wilson-Keenan, J.-A. (2000). Cultivating hybrid texts in multicultural classrooms: Promise and challenge. *Research in the Teaching of English, 35*(2), 179–212.

Sowers, S. (1985). Learning to write in a workshop: A study in grades one through four. In M. Farr (Ed.), *Advances in writing research. Children's early writing development* (Vol. 1, pp. 297–342). Norwood, NJ: Ablex.

Street, B. V. (1995). *Social literacies. Critical approaches to literacy development, ethnography and education*. London: Longman.

Sulzby, E. (1996). Roles of oral and written language as children approach conventional literacy. In C. Pontecorvo, M. Orsolini, B. Burge, & L. B. Resnick (Eds.), *Children's early text construction* (pp. 25–46). Mahwah, NJ: Lawrence Erlbaum Associates.

Taylor, D., & Dorsey-Gaines, D. (1988). *Growing up literate. Learning from inner-city families*. Portsmouth, NH: Heinemann.

Teale, W. (1986). Home background and young children's literacy development. In W. Teale & E. Sulzby (Eds.), *Emergent literacy* (pp. 173–206). Norwood, NJ: Ablex.

Teale, W., & Sulzby, E. (1986). Introduction. Emergent literacy as a perspective for examining how young children become writers and readers. In W. Teale & E. Sulzby (Eds.), *Emergent literacy* (pp. vii–xxv). Norwood, NJ: Ablex.

Temple, C., Nathan, R., Temple, F., & Burris, N. A. (1993). *The beginnings of writing* (3rd ed.). Boston: Allyn & Bacon.

Tolchinsky, L. (2006). The emergence of writing. In C. A. MacArthur, S. Graham, & J. Fitzgerald (Eds.), *Handbook of writing research* (pp. 83–95). New York: Guilford.

Tower, C. (2005). What's the purpose? Students talk about writing in science. *Language Arts, 82*(6), 472–483.

Troyer, C. (1991). From emergent literacy to emergent pedagogy: Learning from children learning together. In J. Zutell, S. McCormick, L. Caton, & P. O'Keefe (Eds.), *Learner factors/teacher factors: Issues in literacy research and instruction* (pp. 119–126). Chicago: National Reading Conference.

Tunmer, W. E., Bowey, J. A., & Grieve, R. (1983). The development of young children's awareness of the word as a unit of spoken language. *Journal of Psycholinguistic Research, 12*, 567–594.

Upitis, R. (1992). Can I play you my song? The compositions and invented notations of children. Portsmouth, NH: Heinemann

van Sluys, K. (2003). Writing and identity construction: A young author's life in transition. *Language Arts, 80*(3), 176–184.

Welsch, J. G., Sullivan, A., & Justice, L. M. (2003). That's my letter!: What preschoolers' name writing representations tell us about emergent literacy knowledge. *Journal of Literacy Research, 35*(2), 757–776.

Whitmore, K. F., Martens, P., Goodman, Y., & Owocki, G. (2004). Critical lessons from the transactional perspective on early literacy research. *Journal of Early Childhood Literacy, 4*(3), 291–325.

Williams, C. L. (1999). Preschool deaf children's use of signed language during writing events. *Journal of Literacy Research, 31,* 183–212.

Wiseman, A. M. (2003). Collaboration, initiation, and rejection: The social construction of stories in a kindergarten class. *The Reading Teacher, 56*(8), 802–810.

Wollman-Bonilla, J. E. (2000). Teaching science writing to first graders: Genre learning and recontextualization. *Research in the Teaching of English, 35,* 35–65.

Wollman-Bonilla, J. E. (2001a). Can first-grade writers demonstrate audience awareness? *Reading Research Quarterly, 36,* 184–201.

Wollman-Bonilla, J. E. (2001b). Family involvement in early writing instruction. *Journal of Early Childhood Literacy, 1,* 167–192.

Wollman-Bonilla, J. E. (2003). E-mail as genre: A beginning writer learns the conventions. *Language Arts, 81*(2), 126–134.

Wollman-Bonilla, J. E., & Werchado, B. (1995). Literature response journals in a first-grade classroom. *Language Arts, 72*(8), 562–570.

Zecker, L. B. (1999). Different texts, different emergent writing forms. *Language Arts, 76*(6), 483–490.

Zucchermaglio, C., & Scheuer, N. (1996). Children dictating a story: Is together better? In C. Pontecorvo, M. Orsolini, B. Burge, & L. Resnick (Eds.), *Children's early text construction* (pp. 83–98). Mahwah, NJ: Lawrence Erlbaum Associates.

CHAPTER 26

Defining Adolescent and Adult Writing Development: A Contest of Empirical and Federal Wills

Julie Cheville
University of Maine

Margaret Finders
University of Wisconsin, LaCrosse

In this chapter, we address perspectives, pedagogies, and policies that currently shape the development of adolescent and adult writers. In the case of adolescent writers, we review research that indicates how a biologically driven model of development has negated identities that are, or might be, the basis for writers' engagement. In addition, we suggest how policy debates concerning adolescent literacy restrict the nature and function of writing in classrooms. In the case of adult writers' development, we focus on writing in adult literacy education (ALE), examining the past and present development of low-literate writers. Although the developmental needs of adolescent and low-literate adult writers are distinct and although the research traditions that inform investigations of their writing do not entirely converge, we claim common features. For both, historically, pedagogical approaches have calibrated to curricula rather than to learner needs. For both, currently, federal educational and labor policy sanctions models of writing development increasingly challenged by sociocultural research.

THE DEVELOPMENT OF ADOLESCENT WRITERS

This section addresses developmental and instructional tensions associated with a prevailing biological model of adolescence. Following an introduction to the assumption that adolescence is a life stage, we review studies that suggest how a universalizing conception of adolescence predisposes teachers to overlook students' concealment and performance of identity in text and in context. We conclude by examining how federal interest in adolescent literacy risks limiting the frequency and function of writing in classrooms.

Adolescence as a Life Stage

Like literacy, *adolescence* is an ambiguous and contested term. Before we can address developmental models of writing, it Is important to analyze adolescence as a construct—namely, because how we construct adolescence inevitably frames writing development. Mainstream discourses characterize this stage as one of turbulence and transition with little or no recognition of the ways in which adolescent experience is shaped by race, class, ethnicity, and other experiences (Finders, 1997, 1998–1999). Adolescence as a biological life stage emerged from the discourses of developmental psychology, educational policy, and teacher education among others and has rendered a singular account of adolescence resistant to change. Normal adolescent development is characterized as a process that features uncontrollable hormones, romantic impulses and behaviors, aggression and resistance, and severed adult relations. Adolescents, as well as their parents and teachers, typically accept these features as both universal and biologically determined (Finders, 1997). The view that insists all adolescents display and need the same things holds dramatic implications for writing pedagogy and development. Writers' workshop as a pedagogical practice, for example, has been expressly offered as a means to meet the needs and engage the interests of all students, yet such an approach fails to take into account the sociocultural experiences that students bring to the classroom (Finders, 1997; McCarthy & Moje, 2002).

Examining the historical, social, and cultural narratives that shape the ways in which adolescence has been constructed, Lesko (2001) sets out to disrupt notions of adolescence as a natural developmental period. According to Lesko, many of the troubles of youth can be found in the authoritative discourses and public policies that surround this developmental stage. Adolescence must be understood as situated within an ever-evolving complex sociopolitical climate. In his collection of studies of urban youth, for example, Mahiri (2004) notes that adolescence "comes at a time when youth in general and youth of color particularly have often been represented in a society as dangerous Others" (p. 14). Alvermann, Hinchman, Moore, Phelps, and Waff (1998) argue that literacies in the lives of adolescents must be understood as "multilayered, shifting and relational" (p. xvii). In *Reconceptualizing the Literacies in Adolescents' Lives*, Alvermann et al. (1998) claim that (a) adolescent literacy is more complex and sophisticated than what is traditionally considered in school, (b) adolescents engage in multiple literacies and multimodal texts, (c) literacy plays an important role in the development of adolescents' individual and social identities, and (d) adolescents need spaces in schools to explore and experiment with multiple literacies and receive feedback from peers and adults (see also Moje, Young, Readence, & Moore, 2000). The contribution of sociocultural research has been the recognition that prevailing models of knowledge and identity formation regulate the experience of writing in classrooms. To view adolescent identity as fluid (Gee, 2002; Stevens, 2005) is central to investigations of writing as a socially situated process (Finders, 1997; Mahiri, 2004; Moje, 2000).

Representing Adolescence in Literacy Research

Increasingly, studies of adolescent writing address the ways in which one's gender shapes writing experiences (Chandleer-Olcott & Mahar, 2003; Finders, 2005; Gilbert, 1997), how technological tools mediate writing (Beach & Bruce, 2002), how race and ethnicity cannot be ignored (Fecho, 1998; Mahiri & Sablo, 1996; Willis, 1995), and how class shapes writing and school experiences (Gee & Crawford, 1998). Furthermore, the ways in which researchers choose to represent adolescents are rooted in multiple and often conflicting conceptions of identity. For instance, McCarthy and Moje (2002) explain the complexities of representing adolescents: "That is something I have struggled over in writing about youth. I can paint two or three different portraits of the same teen depending on relationships and interactions in the youth's life I chose to examine" (p. 230).

In recent years, more attention has been given to the dichotomous nature of in-school and out-of-school literacies for adolescents (Alvermann et al., 1998; Hull & Schultz, 2002; Rymes, 2001). Alvermann (1998) posed the question, "How is it that schooled literacy makes the other literacies in adolescents' lives less valuable or less commendable—especially given that it is the nonacademic literacies that are most likely to sustain students' interests in further schooling?" (p. 355). She added, "School literacy is assumed to be more desirable than nonacademic literacies, at least by educators' standards and perhaps by some adolescents as well" (p. 356).

Understanding the "third space" extends studies of adolescent writing in productive ways. Gutiérrez, Baquedano-López, Alvarez, and Chiu (1999) and Moje et al. (2004), among others, have described the third space as a potentially productive site to bring together the intersections and disjunctures between everyday and school literacies. Moje et al. describe the third space in the following way:

> We call this integration of knowledges and Discourses drawn from different spaces the construction of "third space" that merges the "first space" of people's home, community, and peer networks with the "second space" of the Discourses they encounter in more formalized institutions such as work, school, or church.... What is critical to our position is the sense that these spaces can be reconstructed to form a third, different or alternative, space of knowledges and Discourses. (p. 41)

Disrupting the binary between in school and out of school, this third space may serve as a site where adolescent writing practices can be examined in productive ways. Drawing on the third space may be particularly important for understanding adolescent writers who actively engage with print and nonprint literacies in work and play, contexts that King and O'Brien (2002) suggest are devalued by educators, particularly those who use the term *play* to dismiss students' active extracurricular engagement with digital literacies in comparison with school-sanctioned literacies that are most often print based (p. 42).

Competing Conceptions of Adolescent Literacy

Practitioners and researchers who work with adolescents express a growing concern that by focusing attention on early reading programs federal and state legislation will divert attention from the needs of adolescents and devalue literacy as a multimodal practice (Alvermann, 2001). Though in current literature of adolescent literacy, definitions of literacy have been expanding to include reading, writing, viewing in multiple contexts in and out of school, with print and nonprint texts, some of the most recent work seems to be narrowing the field. Literacy is often reduced to mean only reading, and reading in school. In a review of current research in adolescent literacy, Alvermann (2004) notes that what is missing is writing, "not one of the programs under review demonstrated an overt concern for developing the multiple and nuanced nonschool literacies youth use on a regular basis" (pp. 295–296). An American Association of Colleges for Teacher Education (2002) report expresses concern that No Child Left Behind legislation will force states to adopt a "one-size-fits-all approach ... [to the] ... unnecessary exclusion of other sound approaches that can build strong literacy skills with the diverse groups of students represented in our classroom today" (p. 3). The American Association of Colleges for Teacher Education (AACTE) also argues that this legislation "excludes or undermines writing as part of literacy" (p. 3).

On October 13, 2004, the Alliance for Excellent Education held a forum to discuss the findings of *Reading Next: A Vision for Action and Research in Middle and High School Literacy* (Biancarosa & Snow, 2004). The publication identifies the elements of effective adolescent literacy programs and details an overall approach to implementing programs that will seek to improve both student achievement and educators' knowledge base. This report offers comprehensive and sound strategies for the teaching of reading and advocates "intensive writing, including instruction connected to the kinds of writing tasks students will have to perform well in high school and beyond" (Biancarosa & Snow, 2004, p. 4). The report argues for the increased frequency of writing, the increased quality of writing instruction and assignments, and attention to writing development (Biancarosa & Snow, 2004). Interestingly, although this report clearly addresses writing as a literacy practice, it does not offer the same depth of attention for struggling writers as it does for struggling readers, nor does it characterize what "quality writing instruction and assignments" might look like. The report also fails to address the kinds of multiple and nonschool literacies youth use on a regular basis.

What is needed are more studies of adolescents writing in multiple contexts, studies in school and out to determine what instructional and infrastructures would best support adolescents' writing in multiple contexts with multiple tools. As Alvermann (2004) explains, "Having presented a case for being more inclusive of what counts as literacy, I must acknowledge that the extent to which new media and interactive communications technologies effectively support literacy teaching and learning in the classroom is largely unknown"(p. 296). Any return toward a more narrow definition of adolescent literacy holds grave implications for future work, for researchers, and for adolescents themselves. As Lonsdale and McCurry (2004) write of definitions of literacy:

> It has implications for governments, workplaces and institutions, for which aspects of literacy are favoured and supported, which research is funded, how literacy is measure and valued and the teaching and learning approaches adopted. How we define literacy can lead to different conclusions about the extent of illiteracy. (p. 13)

THE DEVELOPMENT OF ADULT LOW-LITERATE WRITERS

In this section, we focus specifically on developmental and instructional issues associated with low-literate adults. Because composition research has not traditionally informed the work of practitioners and researchers in ALE and because reading carries particular weight in ALE curricula, research on the writing development of low-literate adults has only begun to emerge. The narrow research base has left ALE curricula and pedagogies particularly vulnerable to recent federal legislation. Labor policy, in particular, has disrupted the emergence of developmental models that recognize knowledge, identity, and writing development as interrelated processes situated in social activity.

From Education to Employability: Key Features of Welfare-to-Work Legislation

The developmental needs of low-literate adult writers are distinct and pose particular dilemmas for adult literacy educators. Prior to the enactment of welfare reform in the mid-1990s, participation in adult basic education (ABE) programs was voluntary, open to those 16 years or older who lacked a high school diploma. During the 1990s, federal workforce legislation assigned specific ABE provisions to the U.S. Department of Labor, and by 1998, programs dependent on federal funding were required to provide compulsory education to low-literate welfare recipients, to implement writing instruction aimed at their rapid employability, to administer skill assessments, and to upload program performance data on a computerized National Reporting System that guides the allocation of federal funding. In a striking response to the federal Workforce Investment Act of 1998, a climactic moment in the transition from voluntary to compulsory adult education, nearly half of the state ABE directors resigned (McLendon, 2002).

"Work first" federal policies hold enormous implications for how ALE instructors conceive the development of low-literate adults enrolled in federally funded ALE classes. To begin, we identify key features of welfare-to-work legislation before examining its impact on three developmental models that have framed writing instruction. In the context of rapid employability, we explain the resurgence of basic-skills instruction. Finally, we examine the results of Purcell-Gates, Degener, and Jacobson's (1998) study of ALE pedagogies, which offers a disturbing prognosis for critical literacy instruction.

In 1995, prior to welfare reform, the National Adult Literacy Survey (NALS) indicated that nearly half of the nation's welfare recipients performed at the lowest literacy level on a five-tier scale; an additional one third performed at the second-lowest level (NALS, 1995; cited in Barton & Jenkins, 1995). In 1996, the Urban Institute reported that, among recipients of Aid for Dependent Children, more than 90% of families were headed by single mothers and, of these, 37% were White, 36% were African American, 20% were Hispanic, and 6% were from other groups (Urban Institute, 1996). In response to these data, work-first logic suggested that the sooner low-literate welfare recipients entered the job force, the more quickly they would acquire specialized writing skills and secure earnings that surpassed prior public-assistance payments. In so doing, they would experience incentives associated with meaningful employment, thus becoming long-term contributors to both individual and national economic productivity. Adult literacy providers were understood as intermediary agents, ensuring that low-literate adults possessed the basic reading and writing skills needed for the acquisition of workplace literacies.

In 1996, Congress enacted the Personal Responsibility and Work Opportunity Reconciliation Act (PRWORA), granting the U.S. Department of Labor oversight. Under the bill, welfare recipients deemed employable had 24 months to locate work or begin participating in work activities that included job preparation, job training, community service, vocational education, and secondary-level instruction for those under 20 (L. Martin & Fisher, 1999). States received block grant funds to orient ABE programs to required work activities that did not include ALE instruction. In the Welfare-to-Work Program of 1997, also under the authority of the U.S. Department of Labor, welfare recipients least ready to assume jobs were mandated to pursue education *concurrent* with employment. For these participants, basic-skills training and ESL instruction occurred only at the onset of job placement. The Workforce Investment Act of 1998 had the greatest impact on federally funded adult literacy programs, mandating that states develop performance indicators and assessment models so as to register performance data on a computerized National Reporting System (NRS). The U.S. Department of Labor was granted authority for overseeing states' development of performance indicators that would demonstrate learners' improvement in reading, writing, oral language, numeracy, and problem solving. Individual assessments included pre- and posttests upon program entrance and departure, as well as follow-up measures documenting either long-term performance in the workplace or postsecondary education.

Work-first legislation largely ignored sociocultural dilemmas mitigating the educational success of low-literate learners, including racism, poverty, inadequate child and health care, personal and social challenges, and inadequate transportation. In effect, the legislation invoked a color-blind perspective long a feature of ABE programs themselves (Johnson-Bailey & Cervero, 2000). The legislation also ignored trends in global capitalism, namely the outsourcing of manufacturing jobs, the lack of affordable child care, the restriction of job growth to a minimum-wage service sector, and the reduction of employee benefits. Hayes (1999) has argued that "strategies concentrating on moving people into jobs quickly are effective only at helping more welfare recipients find work, not at increasing their wages and moving them out of poverty" (p. 4).

The Influence of Welfare Legislation on Models of Adult Literacy Development

The revised design and delivery of adult basic education has had obvious consequences for existing models of adult writing development. Because higher-skilled welfare recipients are placed directly into jobs or work activities, ALE programs have oriented to lower-skilled welfare recipients, those ordered both to learn and to work. For all welfare recipients, the employment deadline of 24 months has necessitated that literacy, employment, and social-services providers reach consensus on those basic literacy skills sufficient for the acquisition of more specialized workplace literacies. In addition to new clientele and collaboration, ALE practitioners must tailor instruction to outcomes measurable on large-scale assessments that meet National Reporting System guidelines. In the following section, we discuss the specific impact of welfare-to-work legislation on models that emphasize writing development in terms of basic skills, functional literacies, and critical literacies.

Writing Development as Skills Acquisition

Basic-skills instruction, the predominant ALE approach, assumes that although patterns of error may vary for native and non-native speakers of English, low-literate writers share the same developmental needs and problems as struggling elementary students (Kazemak, 1988; Sticht, 1988). Accordingly, low-literate learners progress through graduated levels of instruction, shifting from discrete skills associated with reading (phonics, phonemic awareness, decoding, word recognition) to those associated with writing (spelling, error patterns, and generic conventions of the sentence, paragraph, and whole text). In turn, the mastery of basic skills in reading, writing, and numeracy supports subject-area study and successful completion of a high school equivalency test. Sticht suggests that this traditional approach has had less to do with the development of functional skills than the credentialing of adult learners. Others challenge the behaviorist assumption that decontextualized instruction supports the implicit transfer of skills to contexts of personal, civic, postsecondary, and workplace literacy (Beder & Medina, 2001; Harman, 1987; Kazemek & Rigg, 1983; Meyer, 1987).

Basic-skills instruction has proven notoriously unsuccessful in attracting and retaining low-literate learners. In a study published in 1995, Stein notes that median retention rates for federally funded ABE programs range from less than 60 hours per learner to 35 hours for native English speakers with the lowest skill levels. Despite chronic problems associated with didactic instruction, the emphasis on rapid employment of low-literate writers invites expediency in all areas of classroom practice and management, particularly among ALE practitioners who remain unfamiliar with writing process instruction. In a recent study sponsored by the National Center for the Study of Adult Learning and Literacy, Beder and Medina (2001) documented the instructional methods, materials, and curricula featured in 20 adult literacy classes across eight states. Through direct classroom observation, the researchers identified basic-skills instruction as the most prevalent pedagogical approach and noted these features: a sequential progression of reading and writing skills based on curricular rather than learner needs; isolated skill instruction in single lessons and units; assumed portability of mastered skills across contexts of use; a predominant IRE pattern (Mehan, 1979) in classroom discourse; lower order thinking; reliance on decontextualized commercial materials; and a low degree of learner-to-learner interaction (Beder & Medina, 2001).

The Test of Adult Basic Education (TABE) is used by more ALE programs than any other standardized test to assess writing proficiency (Ehringhaus, 1991; Kutner, Webb, & Matheson, 1996). The on-demand assessment is criterion-referenced and includes a battery of multiple-choice subtests that assess reading, writing, and numeracy. The assessment of writing is represented by a language subtest that assesses vocabulary, word definition (synonyms and antonyms), phonemic knowledge (affixes, vowels, consonants), usage, syntax, paragraph structure and development, and spelling (Kruidenier, 2002). The multiple-choice TABE corresponds closely with the guidelines of the computerized National Reporting System, and its relatively easy administration and scoring are particularly attractive to ALE programs. Given that 89% of ABE practitioners are part-time employees in programs that depend heavily on volunteers for additional support services (McLendon, 2002), the level of expertise among practitioners discourages the application of alternative assessments (Krudenier, 2002).

Although research investigating the processes of college-level basic writers has long challenged skill-driven instruction, ALE research began its critique relatively late. According to Kazemak (1988), "Much of adult literacy education is based on misconceived notions of literacy, inappropriate methodology, and a naiveté concerning political and social realities" (p. 464). At the onset of congressional deliberation in the mid-1990s, ALE researchers had only begun to assemble a research base that acknowledged writing process theory and practice. As a result, congressional policymakers had little context for questioning a framework that has invited, if not necessitated, the transmission of only those basic literacy skills.

Writing Development and the Acquisition of Competencies

One outcome of the Economic Opportunity Act of 1966 was federal sponsorship of ABE research, particularly investigations of the relationship between literacy and workplace performance. During the 1970s, interest in competency-based education shifted attention from basic-skills instruction to the assessment of performance in literacy tasks that were context specific. What popularized the movement among civilian and military patrons was the integration of assessment tools and information management systems that made the large-scale documentation of competencies possible (Sticht, 2002). As a result, an individual's functional literacy could be understood within the broader context of human resource development and economic productivity. The connection between functional literacy and socioeconomic growth has prevailed as a feature of the rhetoric of crisis underlying calls for state and federal literacy initiatives (Kazemak, 1988; Shor, 1986; Sticht, 1988), Interestingly, a UNESCO study of functional literacy education in Third World countries suggests that literacy education did not necessarily lead to improved economic conditions (Hamadache & Martin, 1987). Though literacy is clearly a factor in economic development, its influence is diminished when other troublesome socioeconomic indicators for the low-literate are ignored.[1]

One challenge for competency-based ALE programs has involved not just defining but assessing writing as a specific task performance. The Adult Performance Level Project (APL), an early program funded under the auspices of the U.S. Office of Education, targeted the domains of "consumer economics, occupational knowledge, community resources, and government and law" (Beder, 2004, p. 15) and among these competencies assessed writing using performance indicators and an assessment tool widely criticized for conceptual flaws (Cervero, 1980; Griffith & Cervero, 1977; Kazemek, 1988; Levine, 1982; cited in Beder, 2004). The Comprehensive Adult Student Assessment System (CASAS) functional writing test is an on-demand assessment involving three writing tasks: description of a scene in a picture prompt, completion of an employment form, and description of a process. Most recently, the Equipped for the Future Project (EFF) was developed by the National Institute for Literacy (NIL). EFF is a standards-based reform initiative that emerged from an NIL survey of ABE enrollees asked to identify the educational outcomes *they* most valued. Survey results highlight access to information, the ability to articulate ideas that will effect change, and the capacity to engage in independent problem solving and decision making (Stein, 2000). Based on these learner-centered needs, NIL engaged ABE practitioners and researchers in 17 states

---

[1]Meeting the literacy needs of adult learners has proven difficult. Though national literacy surveys continue to indicate achievement gaps between White and African American adults, the IEA Reading Literacy Study sponsored by the U.S. Department of Education reported that when confounding variables associated with race and ethnicity were eliminated, gaps in literacy achievement among racial/ethnic groups were much less significant (U.S. Department of Education, 1996). As researchers suggest, the notable conclusion is that adult illiteracy involves a constellation of mitigating factors (Snow, Barnes, Chandler, & Hamphill, 1991; cited in Martin & Fisher, 1999).

in the creation of Adult Performance Standards that "define what adults need to know and be able to do in order to carry out their roles as parents and family members, citizens and community members, and workers" (Equipped for the Future, 1998, p. 3). EFF is currently designing developmental skill matrixes that will guide the assessment of writing.

Like the basic-skills approach, competency-based writing instruction and assessments orient closely to what Fairclough (1995) terms an *ideology of appropriateness.* Where skill-driven approaches restrict learners' awareness of language to correctness in word, sentence, and whole-text composing, functional approaches promote appropriate conventions for specific task performances. As Fairclough argues, exclusive emphases on prescription and description presume language is determinate, constant, and uncontestable. The skills-driven approach asserts these features to be universally true whereas the functional approach holds them to be characteristic of domain-specific writing tasks.

Writing Development and Critical Literacies

Since the earliest translation of his work, Paulo Freire has been widely cited in the field of adult literacy education despite the fact that programwide implementation of his critical pedagogy in the United States is rare (Beder, 2004). In *Pedagogy for the Oppressed* (1970), Freire provides a model for adult education based on his work with low-literate adults in Brazil. In *Literacy: Reading the Word and the World* (1987), Freire elaborates the specific features of emancipatory literacy. For decades, researchers in literacy and curriculum studies have underscored the implications of his work for practitioners in First World countries (Giroux, 1981; Lankshear, 1993; Lankshear & McLaren, 1993; McLaren & Lankshear, 1994; McLaren & Leonard, 1993; Shor, 1987). During this same period, researchers in conventional and critical discourse analysis (CDA) and critical language awareness (CLA) inclined toward sociocultural theories of language.

Differences in Freirean and sociocultural traditions certainly exist. The Freirean model adheres closely to Hegelian philosophy in its characterization of the dialectic mediation between self and other, oppressed and oppressor, word and world, and other key constructs. Postmodern researchers have suggested that Freire's dichotomies are reductive and, thus, less helpful in fleshing out specific identity and contextual features associated with emancipatory learning (Bowers, 1984; Ellsworth, 1989; Martin, 2001). Those who draw on sociocultural theories of language tend to destabilize notions of text and subjectivity, noting how contexts of socially situated and embodied practices complicate learners' knowledge construction and identity presentation.

From a teleological standpoint, however, Freirean and sociocultural models are clearly compatible, and it is their shared concern for critical literacy practice as a vehicle to emancipatory outcomes that has interested some ALE researchers and practitioners. Learning to write involves more than acquisition of basic and functional literacies skills and includes awareness of how conventions can be manipulated in situated contexts to challenge the conditions that jeopardize one's personal, social, and economic well-being (Barton & Hamilton, 1998; Barton, Hamilton, & Ivani_, 2000; New London Group, 1996). Both Freirean and sociocultural traditions highlight the role of the teacher as a cultural worker who assists students to recognize the role of language in reinforcing and resisting hegemonic social practices. In addition, both models emphasize that collective and critical reflection must precede action if learners are to identify the problems most susceptible to redress, to negotiate the writing strategies and genres that constitute the best option for oppositional discourse, and to accurately anticipate the consequences that may result from contestation. Drawing on Freire, CLA researchers Janks and Ivani_ (1992) write:

> Practising emancipatory discourse involves having some principle you want to uphold, deciding how important it is to you, knowing whether others are currently engaged in the same struggle, knowing how powerful the people are you are communicating with,

knowing how sympathetic they may be to your resistance, and knowing what you have to lose if they aren't. (p. 317)

Johnson-Bailey and Cervero (1997, 2000) note that traditional ABE programming avoids the complicating factor of race. Brookfield (2003) has argued the need to "racialize criticality" so as to study how "race intersects with those learning tasks of adulthood—challenging ideology, overcoming alienation, contesting hegemony, and unmasking power" (p. 156). Although critical adult educators respond to their students' lived experiences of disempowerment, they frame analysis and discussion of these conditions so as to disclose their place in a broader constellation of racist, sexist, classist, and homophobic discoursal practices. Such critical language awareness is central if low-literate adults and their teachers are to analyze and challenge the restrictive identities and cultural practices reserved for them (Clark & Ivanic, 1991; Clark, Fairclough, Ivanic, & Martin-Jones, 1991; Fairclough, 1992; Ivanic, 1994; Janks & Ivanic, 1992).

FUTURE TRENDS IN ADULT LITERACY EDUCATION

Critical pedagogical approaches are clearly incompatible with workforce legislation that mandates low-literate adults "learn for work not for life" (Sparks, 1999). The pressure of rapid employability in federally funded centers, as well as the lack of material and human resources, invites the transmission of basic skills and functional literacies. In addition, accountability measures that dictate the progression of low-literate adults from classroom to workplace override a basic premise of emancipatory literacy, namely that "exact outcomes cannot be stipulated before the process commences" (Beder, 2004, p. 13).

In a study of instructional practices evident in 271 programs across 42 states, Purcell-Gates et al. (1998) noted that "only a very few programs attempted to take Freirean theory to heart and create programs rooted in the lives of the participants and directed largely by their input and choices" (p. 19). Using a critical literacy frame, these researchers documented the nature of adult literacy pedagogies along two dimensions: (a) life-contextual/ decontextual, representing the relevance of curriculum materials to learners' personal and civic lives; and (b) dialogic/monologic, representing that discursive character of classroom interaction. Data collection and analysis were limited to holistically coded information garnered from a questionnaire sent to ALE administrators. The survey was created to solicit evaluative data that would inform the subsequent design of a family literacy study. Despite its methodological limitations (Purcell-Gates et al., 1998), the study represents an initial attempt to document the pedagogical features of ALE instruction across the country. A key finding is the sobering statistic that 73% of ALE programs relied on instructional practices and resources that were "somewhat or highly decontextualized" and "somewhat to highly teacher-directed" (p. 14).

The effective engagement of adult learners is of particular interest to those who investigate participatory learning (Anderson, 1998; Campbell, 1995; Fingeret & Jurmo, 1989), joint parent–child reading encounters (Anderson-Yockel & Haynes, 1994; Baker, Scher, & Mackler, 1997; Dickinson & DeTemple, 1998; Hammer, 2001), and intergenerational literacy practices (Auerbach, 1989, 1995; Heath, 1983; Orellana, Reynolds, Dorner, & Meza 2003; Purcell-Gates, 1996; Taylor & Dorsey-Gaines, 1988; Valdés, 1996). For these researchers, the conditions of literacy acquisition, as opposed to formal learning, invite the kind of collaborative activity, participation structures, and joint ownership central to the emotional investment of adults, not just children. As noted in chapters 30 and 31, the relation of writing, emotion, and identity is constituted socially and materially and is central to the composing process (Cranton, 1994; Dirkx, 2001; Fingeret, 1991; Tisdell, 2000), to adults' reinvention of themselves as writers and readers (R. Martin, 2001), and to their academic persistence over time (Comings, Parella, & Soricone, 2000).

CONCLUSION

Since the passage of Goals 2000 and welfare-to-work legislation, federally supported K to 12 schools and ALE centers face enormous pressure to engage in skills instruction. For both adolescents and adults, states have designed widely different and highly restrictive standards and accountability measures for assessing writing, a problem evident in the reform of ALE as well (Belzer, 2003; Hillocks, 2002). Given the implementation of large-scale standardized writing assessments, test developers market instructional resources that jeopardize the legitimacy of professional literature (Hillocks, 2002). ETS Technologies, for example, licenses a skill-driven automated scoring program to secondary and postsecondary institutions seeking to improve writing performances on these tests (Cheville, 2004). The obvious tension between how researchers conceptualize adolescent and adult writing development and how political and commercial agents monitor and market writing makes consensus on any single developmental model unlikely. As many researchers and practitioners begin to document global literacy, including digital technologies and their respective multiliteracies, First World governments continue to view economic competitiveness as dependent on basic skills that, over time, have changed little in their definition and delivery. As Carmen Luke (2002) suggests, "In Australia, the United States and the United Kingdom, the principal public debates over education have been declining standards of traditional print literacy" (p. 195). Indeed, reform efforts in both adolescent and adult literacy education suggest we may be back where we started, a focus on the production of inauthentic print texts with remediation reserved for those who fail.

REFERENCES

Alvermann, D. (1998). Imagining the possibilities. In D. Alvermann, K. Hinchman, D. Moore, S. Phelps, & D. Waff (Eds.), *Reconceptualizing the literacies in adolescents' lives* (pp. 353–372). Mahwah, NJ: Lawrence Erlbaum Associates.

Alvermann, D. E. (2004). Viewpoint: Seeing and then seeing again. *Journal of Literacy Research, 3,* 289–302.

Alvermann, D. E. (2001). *Effective literacy instruction for adolescents* (Executive Summary and Paper Commissioned by the National Reading Conference). Chicago: National Reading Conference. Retrieved September 19, 2004, from http://www.coe.uga.edu/reading/faculty/alvermann/effective.pdf

Alvermann, D. E., Hinchman, K. A., Moore, D. W., Phelps, S. F., & Waff, D. R. (Eds.). (1998). *Reconceptualizing the literacies in adolescents' lives.* Mahwah, NJ: Lawrence Erlbaum Associates.

American Association of Colleges for Teacher Education. (2002). *Research-based literacy Instrucion: Implications for teacher education* (A White Paper of the American Association of Colleges for Teacher Education. Focus Council on Literacy). Retrieved September 19, 2004, from http://www.aacte.org/Membership_Governance_literacy.pdf

Anderson, G. (1998). Toward authentic participation: Deconstructing the discourses of participatory reforms in education. *American Educational Research Journal, 35*(4), 571–603.

Anderson-Yockel, J., & Haynes, W. (1994). Joint picture-book reading strategies in working-class African American and White mother–toddler dyads. *Journal of Speech, Language, and Hearing Research, 37,* 583–593.

Auerbach, E. (1989). Toward a social-contextual approach to family literacy. *Harvard Educational Review, 59*(2), 165–181.

Auerbach, E. (1995). Deconstructing the discourse of strengths in family literacy. *Journal of Reading Behavior, 27,* 643–661.

Baker, L., Scher, D., & Mackler, K. (1997). Home and family influences on motivation for reading. *Educational Psychologist, 32,* 69–82.

Barton, D., & Hamilton, M. (1998). *Local literacies: Reading and writing in one community.* London: Routledge.

Barton, D., Hamilton, M., & Ivanic, R. (2000). *Situated literacies: Reading and writing in context.* London: Routledge.

Barton, P., & Jenkins, L. (1995). *Literacy and dependency: The literacy skills of welfare recipients in the United States.* Princeton, NJ: Educational Testing Service. (ERIC Document Reproduction Service No. ED385775)

Beach, R., & Bruce, B. (2002). Using digital tools to foster critical inquiry. In D. Alvermann (Ed.), *Adolescents and literacies in a digital world* (pp. 147–163). New York: Lang.

Beder, H. (2004). *Quality instruction in adult literacy education.* Unpublished manuscript.

Beder, H., & Medina, P. (2001). *Classroom dynamics in adult literacy education.* Cambridge, MA: National Center for the Study of Adult Learning and Literacy.

Belzer, A. (2003). *Living with it: Federal policy implementation in adult basic education: The cases of the Workforce Investment Act and welfare reform.* Cambridge, MA: National Center for the Study of Adult Learning and Literacy.

Biancarosa, G., & Snow, C. E. (2004). *Reading next—a vision for action and research in middle and high school literacy: A report from Carnegie Corporation of New York.* Washington, DC: Alliance for Excellent Education. Retrieved October 20, 2004, from http://www.all$ed.org/publications/ReadingNext/ReadingNext.pdf

Bowers, C. (1983). Linguistic roots of cultural invasion in Paulo Freire's pedagogy. *Teachers College Record, 84*(4), 935–953.

Brookfield, S. (2003). Racializing criticality in adult education. *Adult Education Quarterly, 53*(3), 154–169.

Campbell, P. (1995). Participatory literacy practices: Exploring social identity and relations. *Adult Basic Education, 6,* 127–141.

Cervero, R. (1980). Does the Texas Adult Performance Level Test measure functional competence? *Adult Education, 30,* 152–165.

Chandleer-Olcott, K., & Mahar, D. (2003). "Tech-savviness" meets multiliteracies: Exploring adolescent girls' technology-mediated literacy practices. *Reading Research Quarterly, 38,* 356–385.

Cheville, J. (2004). Automated scoring technologies and the rising influence of error. *English Journal, 93*(4), 47–52.

Clark, R., Fairclough, N., Ivanic, R., & Martin-Jones, M. (1991). Critical language awareness: Part II. Towards critical alternatives. *Language and Education, 5,* 41–54.

Clark, R., & Ivanic, R. (1991). Consciousness-raising about the writing process. In P. Garrett & C. James (Eds.), *Language awareness in the classroom* (pp. 168–185). London: Longman.

Comings, J., Parella, A., & Soricone, L. (2000). Helping adults persist: Four supports. *Focus on Basics, 4*(A), 2–11.

Cranton, P. (1994). *Understanding and promoting transformative learning: A guide for educators of adults.* San Francisco: Jossey-Bass.

Dickinson, D., & DeTemple, J. (1998). Putting parents in the picture: Maternal reports of preschool literacy as a prediction of early reading. *Early Childhood Research Quarterly, 13*(2), 241–261.

Dirkx, J. (2001). The power of feelings: Emotion, imagination, and the construction of meaning in adult learning. In S. Merriam (Ed.), *The new update on adult learning theory* (pp. 63–72). San Francisco: Jossey-Bass.

Ehringhaus, C. (1991). Teachers' perceptions of testing in adult basic education. *Adult Basic Education, 1*(3), 138–154.

Ellsworth, E. (1989). Why doesn't this feel empowering? Working through the repressive myths of critical pedagogy. *Harvard Educational Review, 59*(3), 297–324.

Equipped for the Future Project. (1998). *EFF: A new framework for adult learning* (Field Development Institute Manual). Washington, DC: Author.

Fairclough, N. (Ed.). (1992). *Critical language awareness.* London: Longman.

Fairclough, N. (Ed.). (1995). The appropriacy of "appropriateness." In N. Fairclough (Ed.), *Critical language awareness* (pp. 33–57). London: Longman.

Fecho, B. (1998). Crossing boundaries of race in a critial literacy classroom. In D. Alvermann, K. Hinchman, D. Moore, S. Phelps, & D. Waff (Eds.), *Reconceptualizing the literacies in adolescents' lives* (pp. 75–102). Mahwah, NJ: Lawrence Erlbaum Associates.

Finders, M. J. (1997). *Just girls: Hidden literacies and life in junior high.* New York: Teachers College Press.

Finders, M. J. (1998–1999). Raging hormones: Stories of adolescence and implications for teacher preparation. *Journal of Adolescent and Adult Literacy, 42,* 2–13.

Finders, M. J. (2005). "Gotta be worse": Literacy, schooling and adolescent youth offenders. In J. Vadeboncoeur & L. P. Stevens (Eds.), *Reconstructing the adolescent: Sign, symbol and body* (pp. 97–122). New York: Lang.

Fingeret, A. (1991). Meaning, experience, literacy. *Adult Basic Education, 1,* 1–11.

Fingeret, A., & Jurmo, P. (1989). *Participatory literacy education.* San Francisco: Jossey-Bass.

Gee, J. P. (2002). Millennials and bobos, Blue's Clues and Sesame Street: A story for our times. Using digital tools to foster critical inquiry. In D. Alvermann (Ed.), *Adolescents and literacies in a digital world* (pp. 51–67). New York: Lang.

Gee, J. P., & Crawford, V. M. (1998). Two kinds of teenagers: Language, identity and social class. In D. Alvermann, K. Hinchman, D. Moore, S. Phelps, & D. Waff (Eds.), *Reconceptualizing the literacies in adolescents' lives* (pp. 225–246). Mahwah, NJ: Lawrence Erlbaum Associates.

Gilbert, P., (1997). Discoursed on gender and literacy. In S. Muspratt, A. Luke, & P. Freebody (Eds.), *Constructing critical literacies* (pp. 69–75). Cresskill, NJ: Hampton.

Giroux, H. (1981). *Ideology, culture, and the process of schooling*. London: Falmer.

Griffith, W., & Cervero, R. (1977). The Adult Performance Level program: A serious and deliberate examination. *Adult Education, 7*, 209–224.

Gutiérrez, K., Baquedano-Lopez, P., & Tejeda, C. (1999). Rethinking diversity: Hybridity and hybrid language practices in the third space. *Mind, Culture, & Activity: An International Journal, 6*, 286–303.

Gutiérrez, K., Baquedano-Lopez, P., Alvarez, H., & Chiu, M. (1999) Building a culture of collaboration through hybrid language practices. *Theory into Practice 38*(2), 87–93.

Hamadache, A., & Martin, D. (1987). *Theory and practice of literacy work: Polices, strategies and examples.* New York: United Nations Educational.

Hammer, C. (2001). "Come sit down and let Mama read": Book reading interactions between African-American mothers and their infants. In J. Harris, A. Kamhi, & K. Pollock (Eds.), *Literacy in African American communities* (pp. 21–43). Mahwah, NJ: Lawrence Erlbaum Associates.

Harman, D. (1987). *Illiteracy, a national dilemma.* New York: Cambridge University Press.

Hayes, E. (1999). Policy issues that drive the transformation of adult literacy. In L. Martin & J. Fisher (Eds.), *The welfare-to-work challenge for adult literacy educators* (pp. 3–14). San Francisco: Jossey-Bass.

Heath, S. (1983). *Ways with words.* New York: Cambridge University Press.

Hillocks, G., Jr. (2002). *The testing trap: How state writing assessments control learning.* New York: Teachers College Press.

Hull, G., & Schultz, K. (2002). *School's out: Bridging out-of-school literacies with classroom practice.* New York: Teachers College Press.

Ivanic, R. (1994). I is for interpersonal: Discoursal construction of writer identities and the teaching of writing. *Linguistics and Education, 6*, 3–15.

Janks, H., & Ivanic, R. (1992). CLA and emancipatory discourse. In N. Fairclough (Ed.), *Critical language awareness* (pp. 305–331). London: Longman.

Johnson-Bailey, J., & Cervero, R. (2000). The invisible politics of race in adult education. In A. Wilson & E. Hayes (Eds.), *Handbook of adult and continuing education* (pp. 147–159). San Francisco: Jossey-Bass.

Kazemek, F. (1988). Necessary changes: Professional involvement in adult literacy programs. *Harvard Educational Review, 58*(4), 464–487.

Kazemek, F., & Rigg, P. (1983). Treating men like boys: Pedagogy at a Job Corps center. *Urban Education, 18*, 335–347.

King, J. R., & O'Brien, D. G. (2002). Adolescents' multiliteracies and their teachers need to know: Toward a digical détente. In D. Alvermann (Ed.), *Adolescents and literacies in a digital world* (pp. 40–67). New York: Lang.

Kruidenier, J. (2002). Literacy assessment in adult basic education. In *The Annual Review of Adult Learning and Literacy* (Vol. 3, pp. 84–151). San Francisco: Jossey-Bass.

Kutner, M., Webb, L., & Matheson, N. (1996). *A review of statewide learner competency and assessment systems.* Washington, DC: Pelavin Research Institute.

Lankshear, C. (1993). Functional literacy from a Freirean point of view. In P. McLaren & P. Leonards (Eds.), *Paulo Freire: A critical encounter* (pp. 90–118). London: Routledge.

Lankshear, C., & McLaren, P. (Eds.). (1993). *Critical literacy: Politics, praxis, and the postmodern.* Albany: State University of New York Press.

Lesko, N. (2001). *Act your age! A cultural construction of adolescence.* New York: Routledge Falmer.

Lonsdale, M., & McCurry, D. (2004). *Literacy in the new millennium.* Adelaide, SA, Australia: NCVER. Retrieved November 14, 2004, from http://www.ncver.edu.au/research/proj/ nr2L22/Longsdale& McCurry.pdf

Luke, C. (2002). Re-crafting media and ICT literacies. In D. Alvermann (Ed.), *Adolescents and literacies in a digital world* (pp. 132–146). New York: Lang.

Mahiri, J. (2004). *What they don't learn in school: Literacy in the lives of urban syouth.* New York: Lang.

Mahiri, J., & Sablo, S. (1996). Writing for their lives: The non-school literacy of California's urban African American youth. *Journal of Negro Education, 65*, 164–180.

Martin, R. (2001). *Listening up: Reinventing ourselves as teachers and students.* Portsmouth, NH: Boynton/Cook.

Martin, L., & Fisher, J. (Eds.). (1999). *The welfare-to-work challenge for adult literacy educators: New directions for adult and continuing education series, No. 83* (pp. 15–28). San Francisco: Jossey-Bass.

McCarthey, S., & Moje, E. B. (2002). Identity matters. *Reading Research Quarterly, 37*, 228–237.

McLaren, P., & Lankshear, C. (Eds.). (1994). *Politics of liberation: Paths from Freire.* London: Routledge.

McLaren, P., & Leonard, P. (Eds.). (1993). *Paulo Freire: A critical encounter.* London: Routledge.

McLendon, L. (2002). The year 2000 in review. In *The annual review of adult learning and literacy* (Vol. 3, pp. 1–9). San Francisco: Jossey-Bass.

Mehan, H. (1979). *Learning lessons: Social organization in the classroom.* Cambridge, MA: Harvard University Press.

Meyer, V. (1987). Lingering feelings of failure: An adult student who didn't learn to read. *Journal of Reading, 21*, 218–221.

Moje, E. B. (2000). "To be part of the story": The literacy practices of "gangsta" adolescents. *Teachers College Record, 102*, 652–690.

Moje, E. B., Ciechanowski, K. M., Kramer, K., Ellis, L., Carrillo, R., & Collazo, T. (2004). Working toward third space in content area literacy: An examination of everyday funds of knowledge and discourse. *Reading Research Quarterly, 39*(1), 38–71.

Moje, E. B., Young, J., Readence, J. E., & Moore , D. W. (2000). Reinventing adolescent literacy for new times: A commentary on perennial and millennial issues in adolescent literacy. *Journal of Adolescent and Adult Literacy, 43,* 400–411.

New London Group. (1996). A pedagogy of multiliteracies: Designing social futures. *Harvard Educational Review, 66*(1), 60–92.

Orellana, M., Reynolds, J., Dorner, L., & Meza, M. (2003). In other words: Translating or "paraphrasing" as a family literacy practice in immigrant households. *Reading Research Quarterly, 38*(1), 12–34.

Purcell-Gates, V. (1996). Stories, coupons and the *TV Guide:* Relationships between home literacy experiences and emergent literacy knowledge. *Reading Research Quarterly, 31*, 406–428.

Purcell-Gates, V., Degener, S., & Jacobson, E. (1998). *U.S. adult literacy program practice: A typology across dimensions of life-contextualized/decontextualized and dialogic/monologic* (National Center for the Study of Adult Learning and Literacy Report No. 2). Cambridge, MA: Harvard University Press.

Rymes, B. (2001). *Conversational borderlands: Language and identity in an alternative urban high school.* New York: Teachers College Press.

Shor, I. (1986). *Culture wars: School and society in the conservative restoration, 1969–1984.* New York: Routledge & Kegan Paul/Methuen.

Shor, I. (Ed.). (1987). *Freire for the classroom.* Portsmouth, NH: Boynton/Cook.

Sparks, B. (1999). Critical issues and dilemmas for adult literacy programs under welfare reform. In L. Martin & J. Fisher (Eds.), *The welfare-to-work challenge for adult literacy educators: New directions for adult and continuing education series, No. 83* (pp. 15–28). San Francisco: Jossey-Bass.

Stein, S. (1995). *Equipped for the future: A reform agenda for adult literacy and lifelong learning.* Washington, DC: National Institute for Literacy.

Stein, S. (2000). *Equipped for the future content standards: What adults need to know and be able to do in the 21st century.* Washington, DC: National Institute for Literacy.

Stevens, L. P. (2005). Youth, adults, and literacies: Texting subjectivities within and outside schooling. In J. Vadeboncoeur & L. Stevens (Eds.), *Re/constructing "the adolescent": Sign, symbol and body* (pp. 49–68). New York: Lang.

Sticht, T. (1988). Adult literacy education. *Review of Research in Education, 15*, 59–96.

Sticht, T. (2002). The rise of adult education and literacy system in the United States: 1600–2000. In *The annual review of adult learning and literacy* (Vol. 3, pp. 10–43). San Francisco: Jossey-Bass.

Taylor, D., & Dorsey-Gaines, C. (1988). *Growing up literate: Learning from inner-city families.* Portsmouth, NH: Heinemann.

Tisdell, E. (2000). Spirituality and emancipatory adult education in women adult educators for social change. *Adult Education Quarterly, 50*(4), 308–335.

The Urban Institute. (1996). *A general profile of the welfare population.* Washington, DC: Author.

Valdés, G. (1996). *Con respeto: Bridging the distances between culturally-diverse families and schools, an ethnographic portrait.* New York: Teachers College Press.

Willis, A. I. (1995). Reading the world of school literacy: Contextualizing the experience of a young African American male. *Harvard Educational Review, 65*, 30–49.

CHAPTER 27

The Reading–Writing Nexus in Discourse Research

Nancy Nelson
Texas A&M University, Corpus Christi

The term *nexus* in the title of this chapter refers not only to connection but also to core, and both meanings are relevant because the connections discussed *are* the core of written discourse. They include the shared cognitive aspects of reading and writing, the participant relations among readers and writers who shape the discourse, and the intertextual relations effected by people who, as readers and writers, engage in discourse practices in sociocultural and historical contexts. The chapter focuses on these connections as they have been investigated since the 1970s, when important epistemological developments challenged disciplinary, curricular, and theoretical schisms separating reading and writing as academic areas and as research emphases (Nelson & Calfee, 1998). Even today an integrative review like this requires some traversal between *reading* research that addresses aspects of writing and *writing* research that addresses aspects of reading.

THE COGNITIVE CONNECTION

When the "cognitive revolution" of the 1970s overturned the behaviorist paradigm, reading comprehension became a major focus of interdisciplinary research. Texts were analyzed, comprehension products were also analyzed, and the two were compared for replications and changes that might be attributed to cognitive processing. Not long after the cognitively oriented reading research began, attention also went to the process of writing, which often meant analyzing not only the composition products but also other verbal products, such as think-aloud protocols. Researchers and theorists of both processes posited mental constructs to explain cognitive phenomena and considered mental factors that had been relegated to an unknowable "black box" during the behaviorist era. This new way of conceptualizing, and talking about, reading led eventually to questions about relations between the discourse knowledge used in reading and that used in writing.

Reading, Writing, and Meaning Making

The attention to reading comprehension helped facilitate connections with writing, because comprehension was being viewed as the *making*, instead of the reception, of meaning. Readers were portrayed as building mental products of semantic meaning from textual cues, and reading was shown to be a process characterized by transformations that were organizational, selective, and connective in nature. Undergirding much of this work

435

was Bartlett's (1932) constructivist theory, which was appropriated and elaborated (e.g., Anderson, Reynolds, Schallert, & Goetz, 1977; Bransford & Johnson, 1972; Kintsch & Van Dijk, 1978). Although much of the early research used text recalls to provide data, other approaches included study of eye movement patterns and think-aloud protocols.

This was a time of innovation—developing new ideas and critiquing old conceptions. Artificial intelligence provided some terminology, and graphic representations in flow-chart form illustrated components of the process and their interrelationships. Interestingly, some of what was new in the cognitive approach came from discovering old ideas in other fields and applying them in the empirical work. An example was Rumelhart's (1975) importation of story grammar, an approach of a Russian formalist, Propp (1928/1968), into the cognitive research investigating comprehension of narrative discourse. The 1970s were a time for redirection in various intellectual domains and for challenges to received views. Besides this cognitive, constructivist perspective that dominated much of the research, there were other new ways to think about reading, such as those associated with literary studies. These included reader response theories that also emphasized readers' contributions and poststructuralist challenges to established theory that were coming from France.

The emphasis on comprehension as a constructive process made theoretical links with writing more apparent when the writing process was being described and studied. Both reading and writing came to be viewed as generative processes, and a composing model of reading was even proposed (Tierney & Pearson. 1983). The two could no longer be viewed as simple inverses with one strictly generative and the other strictly receptive.

An influential description of the cognitive process of writing was developed by Flower and Hayes (1981)—Flower, a rhetorician from English studies, and Hayes, a cognitive psychologist. The two researchers applied the problem-solving approach associated with cognitive science to the process of composing and made claims based on data from think-aloud studies. They used the notion of rhetorical situation to set up their question about the nature of composing—Is this really how writing works?—and the model of writing was their response. This was a nonlinear, recursive, and hierarchical portrayal of writing, in which planning, translating, and reviewing appeared as the major components.

The cognitive aspects of planning and reviewing, in particular, have received much research attention. In planning, writers generate and organize material as they build meaning for their texts in accordance with their goals and task interpretations. Reviewing, which entails reading one's own text, seems to have at least two major functions in the composing process. First, it leads the writer to generate additional text—text that fits with what came before—and, second, it leads to revision because, when reading one's own writing, one evaluates it. Studies of revising, some of which preceded publication of the Flower–Hayes (1981) model, have shown different sorts of revisions at varying points in the composing process and differences between expert and novice writers—confirmation of the importance of critical reading in writing (e.g., Bridwell, 1980; McCutchen, Francis, & Kerr, 1997).

Some of what is now known about writing comes from studies considered *reading* research, and some knowledge about reading comes from studies considered *writing* research. Whether a study is considered reading research or writing research has often been a function of the community to which the researcher belongs, the forum in which the report is published, and how the study is framed. For instance, a reading study reported by Schnotz in 1984 examined the effectiveness of two ways of writing a comparison, and the results showed that different readers did better with different versions. High-knowledge readers did better with one version and low-knowledge readers with the other. That was reading research, but it can be considered writing research too. The previous year, Witte (1983) had reported a writing study that had important implications for reading. College writers in the study all revised the same text so that it would be easier to understand but retain its character as informative discourse. The superior revisions were produced by writers who, as readers, made inferences about relations among topics and cued those relations to their own readers.

Although *cognitive* and *social* have sometimes been considered dichotomous categories in composition studies, it is important to acknowledge the attention to social matters in the discourse research that is considered cognitive (cf. Bracewell, Frederiksen, & Frederiksen, 1982; Smagorinsky & Smith, 1992). Besides considering tasks and immediate contexts, attention has been directed to various kinds of discourse knowledge. Although this knowledge is obviously cognitive, it is acquired socially—a point that cognitivists have made repeatedly through their attention to acquisition and development and through their comparisons of different social groups and cultures. Moreover, it is applied socially—pragmatically—in acts of communication. Included here would be basic linguistic knowledge, such as sound–symbol correspondence and syntactic patterns; knowledge about texts, including such matters as conventional organizational patterns, approaches to staging particular content, and devices for connecting one idea to another; knowledge of authorial devices for guiding the reader, sometimes called metadiscourse; social cognition, which includes awareness of the perspectives of others; procedural knowledge, especially knowing how and when to put particular strategies to use; and metacognition, which includes awareness and control of one's own mental processes.

For more than three decades, research into the cognitive aspects of reading has continued to expand. Cognitive operations are specified in increasing detail, and attention is given to increasingly complex aspects of the reading process and of reading materials (e.g., Bransford, Brown, & Cocking, 2000). Moreover, links have been made with neuroscience, as cognitive claims become increasingly physiological, and various new network conceptions for cognition have been developed. Although cognitive research in writing has not seen as much expansion, the body of knowledge regarding the writing process continues to grow (e.g., Kellogg, 1999). It should be noted that much of the current work in the cognitive aspects of writing is being conducted by an active community of writing researchers in Europe (e.g., Allal, Chanquay, & Largy, 2004; Van den Bergh & Rijlaarsdam, 1999).

Acquiring and Applying Discourse Knowledge

The attention to cognition gave rise to questions about how various aspects of reading and writing are related. No doubt both processes rely on a repertoire of discourse knowledge that has some shared components and is acquired from both activities. Is development in a particular aspect of reading accompanied by development in a related aspect of writing, and vice versa? How strong are the relations between abilities in both, or, put another way, can performance in one predict performance in the other? Two major approaches taken in the 1970s and 1980s to examine relations were intervention studies and correlational studies, as Stotsky (1983) pointed out in her review. The intervention approach meant examining the effect of instruction in one (either reading or writing) on the other and thus concluding that the knowledge acquired in one was applied in the other. For instance, a study might show that a syntactical aspect of reading was improved by practice in written sentence combining or that organization of writing improved after students experienced a reading program focused on text patterns. The correlational approach examined statistical relations between measures of reading ability and writing ability. Published studies have reported significant correlations, although the relations are not always strong for all individuals (e.g., Langer, 1986). A major contributor to correlational research has been Shanahan, who in his 1984 study performed a canonical correlation analysis with multiple measures of reading and multiple measures of writing from elementary students, and found that variation in one set could explain almost half of the variance in the other set. In a subsequent study in 1986, Shanahan and Lomax used a linear structural relations (LISREL) procedure to test the direction of the influence from one set to another. These researchers concluded from their analyses that an interactive configuration (writing influencing reading *and* reading influencing writing) fit the data better than configurations that had a one-way influence, either reading on writing or writing on reading.

A third way to examine relations between reading and writing abilities has been to see if—and, if so, to what extent—writers acquire new discourse features for their own texts from reading texts with those features. Rhetorical models, which were a conventional component of pedagogy for centuries but have had an on-again/off-again pattern in contemporary times, are grounded in the premise that imitation, *mimesis*, is an effective means of learning. An experimental approach was taken by Bereiter and Scardamalia (1984), who had students of various ages read different kinds of texts, such as restaurant reviews, write their own versions, and list the features. The results showed that specification was exceeded by imitation, because participants applied more features than they could list. The researchers themselves pointed out the limitations of their own one-shot approach, acknowledging that people would need much more exposure for full adoption of new discourse features. Other studies (e.g., Charney & Carlson, 1995), providing more extensive learning experiences, have shown individuals of various ages acquiring a particular form of discourse as they read representative texts.

Contextualizing Cognition

Thus far in this piece, attention has been on research called *cognitive*, which focuses on the mental processes of individuals. Before moving to the next major topics, participant relations and intertextual relations, let us consider a socially oriented perspective on the locus of knowledge—a perspective that has informed much of the recent work discussed in the next two sections of this chapter. Beginning in the mid-1980s much discourse research began to take a "social turn," as many researchers came to see cultural groups as meaning makers, collectively constructing knowledge and understandings. Accordingly, knowledge and meaning were located in their activities and practices, and attention was also directed to the social positioning and power relations that influence communicative acts (e.g., Lankshear, 1999; Smagorinsky, 2001).

The notion of *discourse community* has provided a way of talking about shared assumptions, conventions, and communication forums associated with particular groups (cf. Porter, 1986). And, when describing cognition, *situated* and *distributed* have become important concepts: Cognition is thought to be situated in community practices (J. Brown, Collins, & Duguid, 1989; Lave & Wenger, 1991) and to be distributed across participants in collaborative endeavors (Salomon, 1986). The emphasis here is on the unity of mind with activity as it occurs in context (including the larger cultural and historical context). Important influences on this work are activity theory (e.g, Leontiev, 1947/1981; Vygotsky, 1934/1986, 1978), dialogism (Bakhtin, 1981), functional grammar (Halliday, 1985), and practice theory (Bourdieu, 1977).

The socially oriented research has focused on, among other things, genres associated with academic writing. Instead of portraying genres as conventional forms of texts, Miller (1984) argued that they are "typified rhetorical actions based in recurrent situations" (p. 159), and are subject to change—"open rather than closed" (p. 155). Likewise, Lemke (1988) has seen them as "patterns of action, activity structures" that "specify regular sequencing of types of action, of the functional constituents of an overall activity" (p. 82). Reading and writing (along with oral uses of language) are ways in which these patterns are enacted. Much of the research taking this perspective has focused on academic practices, such as reporting research and critiquing the writing of others—aspects of discourse discussed in more detail in the final section of this chapter.

THE PARTICIPANT CONNECTION

Studies of participant relations, especially those between writers and their readers, have dominated much of the research in reading–writing connections. Some researchers have given their attention to writers—writers' efforts to accommodate their readers and their collaborations with other writers, not only coauthorship but also the kind of support that goes by the name *response*. Other researchers have examined participant relations from the other end, focusing on readers' relations with writers of the texts they read. The importance of the participant connection was emphasized by Nystrand (1986), who pointed to the reciprocity that is required for communication, and, earlier on, by Volosinov (1973), who claimed that the "word is a two-sided act. It is determined equally by whose word it is and for whom it is meant" (p. 86). It was also highlighted by Knorr-Cetina (1981), who took a community perspective when saying that a text can be considered "co-produced by the authors and by members of the audience to which it is directed" (p. 106). These are the matters discussed next: writers' relations with their readers, their relations with collaborators, and readers' relations with writers.

Writing for Readers

Writing is an intentional act; writers intend their texts to have particular effects on their audience of readers. In descriptions of writing, from classical rhetoric to current conceptions, attention has gone to the impact and influence of audience, which might be immediate, distant, known, unknown, one person, many people, supportive, resistant, even if the audience is conceptualized as belonging to the writer's own discourse community (Nelson & Kinneavy, 2003). In general, writers can be said to "read" their readers—to consider readers and the ways in which those readers might understand, misunderstand, or even refute their texts. Not only do they read their readers but they also, in a sense, "write" (invent or construct) their readers. Even if the readers are people they know well, writers still work with their perceptions of audience, because they do not have a direct path into others' thought. They make assumptions about what their readers know, what they want or need to know, and what will influence them in the intended ways (cf. Schriver, 1992). Audience seems to have much heuristic value, because writers can generate material for their texts through anticipating possible responses, and also epistemic value, because writers must learn (if they do not already know) much of what their audience might know.

Within the field of composition, the author–audience relation was a critical issue long before empirical investigations began. It became a research issue in the 1970s and 1980s, and studies were conducted to examine writers' ability to consider and accommodate the needs of their readers. This was a particular kind of cognition—*social* cognition—that had been theorized mainly by Piaget (1923/1932) and Flavell (1966). The term *social cognition*, mentioned briefly in the previous section, refers to the ability to consider perspectives of others and to make assumptions about what they will want to gain from the reading (Rubin, 1984). Studies of students' writing have shown developmental differences in social cognition as evidenced in the ability to adapt a text to an audience. Kroll (1986) described three major research approaches: (a) having writers of different ages produce the same kind of text for the same audience and then analyzing the clarity of the writing (and presumably the writers' ability to meet the needs of their readers), (b) having writers of different ages write the same messages for two or more audiences that differ in some respect, such as age, and then seeing if complexity is modified across the two versions, and (c) having writers of different ages rewrite extant texts so that they are appropriate for a particular audience and seeing if the complexity of the original is changed. He himself took the latter approach, having people of various ages rewrite a linguistically complex story for a young audience, and he found that older students did better in reducing lexical and syntactic complexity, thereby increasing reading ease for their young readers.

Research into writer–reader relations has often focused on practices associated with disciplinary discourse (e. g., Bazerman & Paradis, 1991; Blakeslee, 2001). For scholarly texts, such as research articles, members of the audience are considered to be knowledgeable readers who are potentially skeptical with respect to the knowledge claims being made;

thus, disciplinary writers use various textual means to foster relationships with them. Hyland (2000, 2001, 2002), who has conducted numerous studies into this facet of writing, has underscored the importance of audience: "Readers can always refute claims, and this gives them an active and constitutive role in how writers construct such claims" (Hyland, 2001, p. 549) and "To be convincing, arguments must anticipate readers' expectations, difficulties and responses, as writers seek to balance their claims for the significance, originality and certainty of their work against the possible convictions or confusions of their audience" (Hyland, 2002, p. 531). Disciplinary authors employ various audience-oriented features. For instance, first-person pronouns can mark inclusion of readers, hedges can help to ward off objections and show respect for readers' possible disagreement, and evaluations can guide readers to the same conclusions the writer reached. It is important to note, however, that there are important disciplinary and genre differences in the extent to which these and other devices are used.

With respect to participant relations, there is another situation to consider: What happens to writer and reader when the text is hypertext—when the text is electronic and non-linear and its readers have much choice regarding *when* and *if* something is read? The most dramatic response here is that the reader *becomes* author because the boundary between the two is blurred. Bolter (1991) argued that readers of hypertext *are* writers, making decisions about the nature of text, and Landow (1992) spoke of a hypertextual convergence between reader and writer. Bolter's and Landow's argument is that the nonlinear nature of hypertext empowers the reader, whose choices create a unique text, and this contrasts with the linear-print experience, which does not present such options. The potential benefits of the new textuality have been much discussed. For example, the flexibility provided by hypertext seems to enhance certain kinds of reading and learning, according to the cognitive flexibility theory developed by Spiro and his colleagues (e.g., Spiro, Feltovich, Jacobson, & Coulson, 1992). There has also been discussion of the challenges of reading hypertext, particularly the disorientation that one can experience when moving through material by choosing associative links and not having the same authorial guidance that is provided for print text (e.g., Nielsen, 1990).

Writing Collaboratively

Explorations into the social aspects of discourse have also focused on collaborations among people who contribute to the writing as the text is being produced. Sometimes they are coauthors in that they share responsibility and credit for the text, and other times they fill other roles. It seems that writing is much more collaborative than it sometimes appears in a culture that celebrates the individual author; numerous studies have shown the contributions of unacknowledged collaborators to texts attributed to single (and famous) authors (e.g., Stillinger, 1991). Composition researchers have studied aspects of collaborative writing, in which pairs or teams of writers produce a text, and have also studied the role of respondents, who do a special kind of reading.

Research focused on collaborative writing, such as that of Ede and Lunsford (1990), has addressed the role of reading as a text is produced. In much of this research, the term *reviewing* is used, as in the Flower–Hayes (1981) conception, and this reviewing is described as a critical reading by one of the collaborators. Particularly relevant to the present discussion is the work of Sharples et al. (1993), who identified three patterns of collaborative writing: parallel, sequential, and reciprocal. In parallel organization, different individuals write different sections at the same time, and these sections are subsequently combined. In sequential organization, one person writes a section and then passes it along to the next. In reciprocal organization, the pair or team members actually write together. There is also another organization for collaborative writing, discussed by Lowry, Curtis, and Lowry (2004), that appears as single-writer, with one person writing for the team. How does reviewing fit in these various kinds of collaborations described by Sharples et al. and Lowry et al.? At the very least, one could expect reviewing at the following points: In parallel writing, there would be reviewing of the various portions after they are written by different individuals so that the parts fit together and are consistent in style. In sequential writing, there would be reviewing of previous segments as the next is produced. In reciprocal writing, there would be reviewing and commenting by collaborators as they write. And in single-author writing, there would be reviewing with comments by team members on completion of a draft or sections of a draft.

Electronic technology facilitates collaborative writing for writers working in various contexts (e.g., Daiute, 2000). When creating the World Wide Web, Berners-Lee (2000) envisioned it as a means of collaboration, a "decentralized, organic growth of ideas, technology, and society" (p. 1). Today collaboration occurs across interlinked computers, and e-mail seems to be a common means of circulating drafts to be read. Technological developments have improved efficiency and speed of communication, but familiar challenges persist: keeping track of various versions, working from the appropriate version, and being able to identify contributors for various elements (Noel & Robert, 2004). In addition to planned and focused group writing, there are open collaborations on the Web, including some comprising multiple, unidentified authors who contribute to never-ending stories.

Besides collaborative writing itself, another collaborative element in discourse practices goes by the label *response*. Writers in various contexts—academic, occupational, political, personal, and others—often ask friends or colleagues to read drafts and to provide suggestions for improvement before the manuscript goes to the targeted audience. Respondents tend to go beyond being critical readers and actually do much of what is often considered to be composing—thinking about audience, deciding what is most appropriate for them, and considering rhetorical choices. Their role is distinct from that of formal reviewers, who assess the worth of a manuscript, determine its eventual fate, and provide commentary that supports their assessment. An illustration of response in disciplinary writing comes from a study that Reither and Vipond (1989) conducted of the process through which Hunt and Vipond (1986) went to publish an article on "evaluations in literary reading." Reither and Vipond focused to a great extent on the contributions of respondents, who were faculty colleagues of Hunt and Vipond. These trusted assessors provided not only critical commentary but also advice regarding audience, form, and emphasis for the text as it went through several versions.

Unlike authors, respondents do not receive credit or assume responsibility for the text. Instead they are given appreciation through acknowledgments, which was the case for the Hunt and Vipond's colleagues. Giannioni (2002), who has conducted text analyses of acknowledgments in research articles, pointed out that the "story" told in an acknowledgment provides much more than factual information. With "modesty, deference, and gratitude" (p. 4) authors indicate collegial relations with colleagues who assisted them and portray a "microcosm of intellectual harmony and empathy" (p. 23).

In literacy education, teachers often provide response for student writing. Sperling (1998) has described teachers as "situated readers," whose responses are shaped by the context of school and by schooling practices. Her research has shown that response can be a balancing act among the following: multiple social roles (e.g., critic, friend, authority), interpretive lenses (e.g., personal, academic), pedagogical aims (e.g., supportive, corrective), and evaluative stances (e.g., approving, disapproving). Teachers' responses are often given in conferences, which, as Ulichny and Watson-Gegeo's (1989) research showed, may follow a particular pattern: first, a reading of the text; second, a find-and-fix routine, in which the teacher identifies errors and students generate corrections; and, third, a conclusion with recommendations for next steps. Ulichny and Watson-Gegeo's study highlighted the authoritative-academic-corrective-(even) disapproving elements in the conferences they observed. Running throughout these conferences, as the researchers pointed out, were issues of power—authority exerted by teacher-readers and either cooperation or resistance by student-writers. Teachers' assertions of authority are also illustrated in studies of commentary on students' papers.

Reading the Writer

Despite the New Critics' warning against the intentional fallacy and the poststructuralists' declaration of the author's death, reading researchers have found that speculating about authorial intent is often an integral part of understanding a text (e.g., Gibbs, 2001). In discourse research the author concept is still viable, but not in the foundational sense that a writer has a particular meaning for a text that a reader must derive precisely if the reading is done "right." Now there is an acknowledgment that, even though authors' intentions cannot be *known* with any certainty, readers—some of them, anyway—do try to discern authorial intent as they read. Accomplished readers often seem to "read" (or invent or construct) the author, making inferences and assumptions, and their perceptions can influence their understanding of a text. Haas and Flower (1988) coined the term *rhetorical reading* for "readers actively trying to understand the author's intent, the context, and how other readers might respond" (p. 181). Studies have demonstrated that this reading of authors occurs in various disciplines by people who have expertise in their field. Geisler (1991), who focused on the discipline of philosophy, found that the philosophers in her study used author attributions to define positions taken on the reading topic and that their frequent references to author contrasted with students' inattention to this aspect of discourse. For scientists too, reading a text can be a matter of reading the author as well. Bazerman (1985) observed physicists as they read strategically to keep up with what others were doing in their field—actively looking for what was new in their research area.

In the discipline of literary studies, Hunt and Vipond conducted two related studies (Hunt & Vipond, 1986; Vipond & Hunt, 1984), one of which was discussed previously. The 1984 study was an investigation of a point-driven approach to reading taken by literary scholars. The sophisticated readers participating in the study "impute[d] motives" (p. 261) as they sought to discern what authors were getting at. In doing so, they were sensitive to the authors' evaluations—the indications they gave of the value that should be placed on certain elements. The 1986 inquiry, cited earlier, considered these evaluations in more detail—how writers lead readers to the points they want to make through such means as using nonstandard elements (e.g., nonchronological plot). In another study of literary reading, B. Graves and Frederiksen (1991) found patterns in the think-aloud protocols of literary scholars that seemed to concur with Haas and Flower's (1988) description of rhetorical reading. Author-oriented reading on the part of the experts contrasted with the reading of students, who gave little attention to author.

Notable for sustained scholarship into the issue of author-oriented reading is the educational psychologist Wineburg (e.g., 1991, 2001), who has focused much of his work on writing and reading in a single discipline, history. Particularly relevant here is the importance he found for author awareness on the part of historians as they read primary documents. In a study of the "breach" between the academy and the school, Wineburg (1991) found that, unlike students, who read for facts, historians saw texts as rhetorical artifacts written to meet an author's intentions and goals. They saw texts as human artifacts written by people who make assumptions and have biases, airs, and beliefs. As Wineburg explained, "It is a reading that leaps beyond the words authors use to the types of people authors are" (p. 499).

These studies have shown that attention to author characterizes the reading of people who are immersed in the discourse of their disciplines and that their reading contrasts with the fact-driven reading that students often do. What is the nature of development as individuals move from a fact-driven approach to one that is more rhetorical? To gain some insights into this process, Haas (1994) traced changes on the part of one student, a biology major, as she read texts in her field over a 4-year period. This young woman went from little awareness of the authors of the texts she read ("the book says") during her freshman year to recognition of texts as enscriptions of authors' choices and points of view when she was a junior. A major contribution to this development was her own participation in scientific practices.

For young readers, a number of pedagogical approaches are designed to develop the author concept and to enhance awareness of the person or persons who produced the text (e.g., Beck, McKeown, & Worthy, 1995; D. Graves & Hansen, 1983). However, not much is known about children's awareness of author in the absence of interventions, as Shanahan (1998) pointed out. Many of the reading experiences students have in school are with text-books, which seem to have little "voice," little authorial persona. These materials have sometimes been described as inconsiderate of readers—providing "facts" in listlike fashion with little guidance for a coherent understanding (Armbruster, 1984).

THE INTERTEXTUAL CONNECTION

A third, and ever-expansive, focus of research is the use that people as readers and writers make of the texts of others—texts they encounter through their reading as well as through oral language. As writing researchers have become increasingly aware, all writing is intertex-tual in that texts relate to other texts, and is social in that writers relate not only to their read-ers but also to writers of other texts. Gone is the image of a solitary writer producing a truly original work that is unaffected by the texts of others. Instead there is an awareness of inter-relatedness of texts and interrelatedness of writers because they are also readers. Influential here has been the theoretical work of Russian scholars, Volosinov (1973) and Bakhtin (1981), which was produced in the first half of the 20th century but published in English several decades later. As noted earlier, Volosinov argued that every utterance is a response to other utterances—is positioned relative to them. Also making this argument, Bakhtin claimed that "each utterance refutes, affirms, supplants, and relies on others, presupposes them to be known and somehow takes them into account" (p. 91). The poststructuralists associated with the Tel Quel group in France can be credited with first incorporating the notion of intertex-tuality into contemporary theory before the Russians' work was widely available. Especially important was Kristeva (1967/1986), who coined the term *intertextuality* and spoke of "a per-mutation of texts" (p. 30), and Barthes (1968/1977), who popularized the notion and spoke of a text as a "tissue of quotations drawn from innumerable centres of culture" (p. 146). (For a genealogy of the term *intertexuality,* see Bazerman, 2004.) Although Kristeva and Barthes focused on the text itself, apart from human agents, the concept of intertextuality has guided research into human activities of reading and writing.

Intertextual relations are manifested because of social relations among humans and the social practices in which they engage. Through listening and reading people experience the texts of others, and through speaking and writing they produce their own texts. Their own texts are tied to texts of others through repeated discourse features, repeated content, and similar orientations (Lemke, 1992). Although some poststructuralists consider intertextual-ity to be so complex that it is futile to try to trace bits of text to other bits of text, a growing number of writing researchers have sought to understand the transformations that writers make as they appropriate other texts and to see how those borrowings are sometimes acknowledged.

There are acts of writing in which people are in both roles, reader and writer—reader of texts produced by others as they are writers of their own. The phrases *writing from sources, reading to write,* and *writing from reading* have been used here. In acts of summarizing one text or synthesizing multiple texts, it might seem (to an observer) that a person reads and then writes. However, if comprehending and composing are both viewed as the making of meaning, it can be impossible to draw a line between comprehending the extant text(s) and composing the new text. A person makes meaning for his or her own text while reading the work of other writers and shapes meanings for that related work when writing the new text.

Writing Focused on One Other Text

Summarizing a text means reducing it to what is most essential for the use to which it will be put. Researchers have identified several operations that guide the compression process, such as deleting trivial and redundant information (cf. A. L. Brown & Day, 1983). It is important to note that, although the major emphasis in summary writing is on text compression, there are generative aspects to summary writing. People must, for instance, make inferences and create generalities that subsume more specific statements and terms. In much disciplinary discourse, writers produce their summaries in the form of abstracts, miniature versions of the text that are sometimes attached to the fuller text, as in a research article, and other times stand as separate texts, as in conference programs and databases. Berkenkotter and Huckin (1995) have argued that some abstracts can be seen as "promotional pieces" used to package texts and position authors. The text-in-miniature summary is not the only type, and it seems that different types of summaries serve different purposes. For instance, some summaries list topics addressed in the text and act as a kind of table of contents. Summarizing also plays a major role in much other writing, because it is a means by which writers incorporate others' and their own previously written material in the texts they compose.

Other practices in which writers tend to respond mainly to a single text are critiquing and translating. Critiquing requires some summarizing, but the major function is evaluating—assessing the value of the text. As Mathison (1996) showed in a study of students' critique writing in sociology, a critique is characterized by topic-comment patterns in which the writer presents aspects of the text as topics and makes evaluative comments about them. In disciplinary writing, evaluative commentary tends to be supported through reference to relevant knowledge in the field, which means referring to other relevant texts. Books are common objects of critique, and book reviews are important in community discourse. Hyland (2000), who has studied the book review in several disciplines, described it as an encounter not only with the book but also with its author, who is a "primary" audience. This researcher had two general findings: First, positive comments tend to address global aspects of the book, whereas negative comments address more specific aspects, and, second, reviewers tend to open with praise but the praise does not necessarily reflect the overall assessment. Although there are stand-alone critiques, critiquing, like summarizing, is a facet of much other writing.

Translating—changing a text from one language to another—requires a complex kind of interpretation as the translator tries to make a text accessible to a new linguistic community. Among scholars who focus on translation, issues abound regarding the matter of interpretation (e.g., Steiner, 1998). For instance, which is better: a translation that communicates the author's sense to people with another cultural frame but makes considerable changes in wording or a more literal translation that fails to communicate that sense? A translator, who can play a central role in communication, often tends to be hidden from view and is even sometimes omitted when bibliographic information is provided. Popularizations, which are also attempts to make texts more accessible to a different audience, might be considered a variant of translating. They too reflect the contributions of reading to the writing. Yet another kind of translation, resulting from a reader's interpretation, is what Bolter and Grusin (2000) have called *re-mediation*. Here there is a change in medium, which might be from linear text to hypertext, from written symbols to visual, and so on.

Writing and Positioning Relative to Multiple Texts

In much discourse activity, writers are positioned as readers of multiple texts, making use of other writers' work as they create their own. They write within a context of other texts, and their work often has identifiable intertextual relations with what they have read. Composition often entails summarizing a body of prior work and, in some cases, critiquing it to create an aperture for the new piece.

Discourse synthesis is the term I use for the integration of material from multiple textual sources as writers create their new texts. Studies into discourse synthesis have attended to three major kinds of transformations—organizational, selective, and connective—that writers make when they use other texts for their own purposes (Nelson, 2001; Spivey, 1984,

1990, 1997[1]; cf. Ackerman, 1991; Greene, 1993; Segev-Miller, 2004). In organizing, writers determine what goes with what and where it should go, and they provide an order or arrangement, which often means "dismantling" the texts that they read and generating new patterns. In selecting, writers attend to material that they consider relevant to the texts that they are creating. Sometimes they search for specific content to fill gaps or to make particular points, and other times they base their selections on what seems to be intertextually "important" in that it has been replicated across texts and there seems to be some agreement about its credibility. Writers also make selections on the basis of rhetorical factors, such as the personae they seek to create or the audience for whom they write. Still other transformations are connective. Writers generate connective links between propositions, ideas, and facts. They also generate links among authors, presenting some as agreeing among themselves and others as disagreeing. Studies with younger writers have shown some developmental progression associated with increases in maturity and instruction in writing. With age and instruction, students seem to do better with integrative connections (Spivey & King, 1989; cf. Many, Fyfe, Lewis, & Mitchell, 1996)) and to generate organizational patterns other than the novice "one document, one point, one sentence-next document, one point, one sentence" pattern (Young & Leinhardt, 1998).

In the scholarly writing and publishing associated with academic disciplines, use of others' texts is a social experience, in which writers connect with other writers and often indicate how they themselves are positioned relative to them. Kaufer and Geisler (1989) argued that academic writers must present the prior work in such a way that they make apparent what is new about their own. In presenting this prior work, they adjust their summaries to fit into the argument being developed. Writing in the context of other texts often requires evaluating the work of other authors, letting readers know how to interpret it, pointing to what should be valued, and even providing negative commentary to refute claims that are not consistent with the current work (cf. Baynham, 1999). However, there are disciplinary differences in the extent and nature of critique and are also cross-cultural differences in both, because pointing out deficiencies in prior work seems not to be conventional in all cultures.

Hypertext becomes relevant here too. Through hypertext, the interconnection of texts that was envisioned by Vannevar Bush (1945) has become actuality as well as virtuality. Hypertext is now a familiar tool for discourse synthesis in which a writer provides links to relevant texts, visual and audio as well as written, that are "included" (cf. Palumbo & Prater, 1993). In order to access these other texts, perhaps in their totality, all a reader has to do is click—which seems to be an easy move to make. With hypertext, as Burbules and Callister (1996) pointed out, there can be an instability in what is the *primary* text. Initially the (hyper)text being read would seem to be the primary text, providing links to other relevant texts. But the other texts can assume primary status if a reader moves into them and does not return, and thus that previously primary text would become merely a gateway.

Writers' appropriation of other writers' work is a topic that raises issues of ownership and ethics. The notion of authorship is surrounded by persistent questions: When must credit be given to other writers? How much transformation must occur before material "belongs" to the new author and not the previous authors? Although guidelines for avoiding plagiarism seem on the surface to be quite explicit, writing that is "original" but acknowledges others' work can be difficult to accomplish—not only by young writers but sometimes, it seems, by experienced writers as well. Cases of plagiarism abound in academe and other contexts. In recent years, the term *patchwriting* (Howard, 1999) has been applied to the practice of piecing together unattributed material from other sources. Now there is also *cyberplagiarism,* which refers, among other things, to putting together borrowed and unattributed material read on and drawn from the World Wide Web. As the National Research Council (2000) said, the Internet is "at once one of the world's largest libraries and surely one of the world's largest copying machines" (p. 23).

---

[1]Prior to 1998, I published under the name Nancy Nelson Spivey.

Citing Relevant Texts

This section would be incomplete without a consideration of citations, an important aspect of writing and of reading that has become a useful tool for researchers. Citations give an indication (though not a complete record by any means) of which texts and which people have been significant to writers when they were in the role of reader. There seem to be many reasons for citing particular authors and their texts: social, political, personal, and epistemological (cf. Cronin, 1984). Citations also provide a means of studying authoring identity. *Identity*, from *idem* ("the same"), refers to a sameness, not only within a writer's body of work (similar topics, similar issues, similar positions in the corpus) but also with other writers (similar topics, similar issues, similar positions to theirs). Through citations, a writer creates associations with others. Cronin and Shaw (2002), who applied the term *watermark* to a particular author's referencing style, pointed to two components of identity: *citation identity*, whom an author cites, and *citation image*, who cites that author. Another aspect of identity creation has to do more specifically with readers when they are writers— *cocitation*, with whom they associate a particular writer (Small, 2001).

Citations also provide a means of tracing shifts in the knowledge of discourse communities and seeing how and when one discourse group starts reading the work associated with another group and integrates that work in its own literature. For this epistemological process, McInnis (1996) used the term *discourse synthesis*—the same term I had used for reading and writing of individuals. He was speaking of *discourse* as a bounded body of knowledge at the community level and of *synthesis* as the community's bringing together two bodies of knowledge. An example mentioned earlier was the synthesis of story grammar into the discourse of cognitive psychology. As I have argued elsewhere (Nelson, 2001), the two kinds of discourse synthesis are related—are complementary. The synthesis at the community level happens because of synthesis at the individual reader–writer level. The synthesis between the discourse of story grammar and the discourse of cognitive psychology occurred through the reading and writing of David Rumelhart and others.

CONCLUSION: THE NEXUS

The issues addressed here—writing related to reading, writer related to reader, and text related to text—are central to written discourse. Much has been learned about these connections over the last decades, but discourse researchers had to cross some conceptual boundaries to view processes and roles in different ways. The cognitive connection was made by seeing reading and writing as having some parallels rather than being inverses of each other. Inquiries began to focus on shared aspects of the processes and on shared knowledge applied in performing them. The participant connection was made by seeing writers and readers as partners engaged in a mutual endeavor with blurred role distinctions rather than as separate and independent entities. The notions of author and audience became more complex as other participants, including respondents and entire discourse communities, were studied. The intertextual connection was made by seeing texts as incorporating other texts instead of standing alone as discrete units. This meant examining literate practices that include both reading and writing and also meant studying textual appropriations and intellectual lineages. With respect to all three connections, it was a matter of entering a contact zone and embracing the "other."

REFERENCES

Ackerman, J. (1991). Reading, writing, and knowing: The role of disciplinary knowledge in comprehension and composition. *Research in the Teaching of English, 25,* 133–178.

Allal, L., Chanquoy, L., & Largy, P. (Eds.). (2004). *Revision: Cognitive and instructional processes.* Dordrecht, the Netherlands: Kluwer.

Anderson, R. C., Reynolds, R. E., Schallert, D. L., & Goetz, E. T. (1977). Frameworks for comprehending discourse. *American Educational Research Journal, 14*, 367–382.

Armbruster, B. B. (1984). The problem of "inconsiderate text." In G. G. Duffy, L. R. Roehler, & J. Mason (Eds.), *Comprehension instruction: Perspectives and suggestions* (pp. 202–217). New York: Longman.

Bakhtin, M. M. (1981). *The dialogic imagination* (M. Holquist, Trans.; C. Emerson & M. Holquist, Eds.). Austin: University of Texas Press.

Barthes, R. (1977). *Image-music-text* (S. G. Heath, Ed. & Trans.). New York: Hill & Wang. (Original work published 1968)

Bartlett, F. C. (1932). *Remembering: A study in experimental and social psychology.* Cambridge, England: Cambridge University Press.

Baynham, M. (1999). Double-voicing and the scholarly "I": On incorporating the words of others in academic discourse. *Text, 19*, 485–504.

Bazerman, C. (1985). Physicists reading physics: Schema-laden purposes and purpose-laden schema. *Written Communication, 2*, 3–23.

Bazerman, C. (2004). Intertextualities: Volosinov, Bakhtin, literary theory, and literary studies. In A. Ball & S. W. Freedman (Eds.), *Bakhtinian perspectives on languages, literacy, and learning* (pp. 53–65). New York: Cambridge University Press.

Bazerman, C., & Paradis, J. (Eds.). (2001). *Textual dynamics and the professions: Historical and contemporary studies of writing in professional communities.* Madison: University of Wisconsin Press.

Beck, I. L., McKeown, M. G., & Worthy, J. (1995). Giving a text voice can improve students' understanding. *Reading Research Quarterly, 30*, 220–238.

Bereiter, C., & Scardamalia, M. (1984). Learning about writing from reading. *Written Communication, 1*, 163–188.

Berkenkotter, C., & Huckin, T. (1995). *Genre knowledge in disciplinary communication: Cognition/culture/power.* Hillsdale, NJ: Lawrence Erlbaum Associates.

Berners-Lee, T. (2000). *Weaving the web.* New York: HarperBusiness.

Blakeslee, A. (2001). *Interacting with audiences: Social influences on the production of scientific writing.* Mahwah, NJ: Lawrence Erlbaum Associates.

Bolter, J. D. (1991). *Writing space: The computer, hypertext, and the history of writing.* Hillsdale, NJ: Lawrence Erlbaum Associates.

Bolter, J. D., & Grusin, R. (2000). *Remediation: Understanding new media.* Cambridge, MA: MIT Press.

Bourdieu, P. (1977). *Outline of a theory of practice* (R. Nice, Trans.). Cambridge, England: Cambridge University Press.

Bracewell, R. J., Frederiksen, C. H., & Frederiksen, J. D. (1982). Cognitive processes in composing and comprehending discourse. *Educational Psychologist, 17*, 146–164.

Bransford, J. D., Brown, A. L., & Cocking, R. R. (2000). *How people learn: Brain, mind, experience, and school.* Washington, DC: National Academy Press.

Bransford, J. D., & Johnson, M. K. (1972). Contextual prerequisites for understanding. *Journal of Verbal Learning and Verbal Behavior, 11*, 717–726.

Bridwell, L. (1980). Revising strategies in twelfth grade students' transactional writing. *Research in the Teaching of English, 14*, 201–223.

Brown, A. L., & Day, J. D. (1983). Macrorules for summarizing texts; The development of expertise. *Journal of Verbal Learning and Verbal Behavior, 22*, 1–14.

Brown, J., Collins, A., & Duguid, P. (1989). Situated cognition and the culture of learning. *Educational Researcher, 18*, 32–42.

Burbules, N., & Callister, T. A., Jr. (1996). Knowledge at the crossroads: Some alternative futures of hypertext learning environments. *Educational Theory, 46*, 23–50.

Bush, V. (1945). As we may think. *Atlantic Monthly, 176*(1), 85–110.

Charney, D., & Carlson, R. (1995). Learning to write in a genre: What student writers take from model texts. *Research in the Teaching of English, 29*, 88–125.

Cronin, B. (1984). *The citation process.* London: Taylor Graham.

Cronin, B., & Shaw, D. (2002). Identity-creators and image-makers: Using citation analysis and thick description to put authors in their place. *Scientometrics, 54*, 31–49.

Daiute, C. (2000). Writing and communication technologies. In R. Indrisano & J. R. Squire (Eds.), *Perspectives on writing: Research, theory, and practice* (pp. 251–276). Newark, DE: International Reading Association.

Ede, L., & Lunsford, A. (1990). *Singular texts/plural authors: Perspectives on collaborative writing.* Carbondale: Southern Illinois University Press.

Flavell, J. H. (1966). Role-taking and communication skills in children. *Young Children, 21*, 164–177.

Flower, L., & Hayes, J. R. (1981). A cognitive process theory of writing. *College Composition and Communication, 32*, 365–387.

Geisler, C. (1991). Toward a sociocognitive model: Constructing mental models in a philosophical conversation. In C. Bazerman & J. Paradis (Eds.), *Textual dynamics and the professions: Historical and contemporary studies of writing in professional communities* (pp. 171–190). Madison: University of Wisconsin Press.

Giannoni, D. S. (2002). Words of gratitude: A contrastive study of acknowledgment texts in English and Italian research articles. *Applied Linguistics, 23*, 1–31.

Gibbs, R. W., Jr. (2001). Authorial intentions in text understanding. *Discourse Processes, 32*, 73–80.

Graves, B., & Frederiksen, C. H. (1991). Literary expertise in the description of a fictional narrative. *Poetics, 20*, 1–26.

Graves, D., & Hansen, J. (1983). The author's chair. *Language Arts, 60*, 176–183.

Greene, S. (1993). The role of task in the development of academic thinking through reading and writing in a college history course. *Research in the Teaching of English, 27*, 46–75.

Haas, C. (1994). Learning to read biology: One student's rhetorical development in college. *Written Communication, 11*, 43–84.

Haas, C., & Flower, L. (1988). Rhetorical reading strategies and the construction of meaning. *College Composition and Communication, 39*, 167–183.

Halliday, M. A. K. (1985). *An introduction to functional grammar.* London: Arnold.

Howard, R. M. (1999). *Standing in the shadow of giants: Plagiarists, authors, collaborators.* Stamford, CT: Ablex.

Hunt, R. A., & Vipond, D. (1986). Evaluations in literary reading. *Text, 6*, 53–71.

Hyland, K. (2000). *Disciplinary discourses: Social interactions in academic writing.* London: Longman.

Hyland, K. (2001). Bringing in the reader: Addressee features in academic writing. *Written Communication, 18*, 549–574.

Hyland, K. (2002). What do they mean? Questions in academic writing. *Text, 22*, 529–557.

Kaufer, D., & Geisler, C. (1989). Novelty in academic writing. *Written Communication, 6*, 286–311.

Kellogg, R. T. (1999). *The psychology of writing* (2nd ed.). New York: Oxford University Press.

Kintsch, W., & van Dijk, T. A. (1978). Toward a model of text comprehension and production. *Psychological Review, 85*, 363–394.

Knorr-Cetina, K. (1981). *The manufacture of knowledge: An essay on the constructivist and contextual nature of science.* Oxford, England: Pergamon.

Kristeva, J. (1986). Word, dialogue, and novel. In T. Moi (Ed.), *The Kristeva reader* (pp. 34–61). New York: Columbia University Press. (Original work published 1967)

Kroll, B. M. (1984). Writing for readers: Three perspectives on audience. *College Composition and Communication, 35*, 172–185.

Landow, G. (1992). *Hypertext: The convergence of contemporary theory and technology.* Baltimore: Johns Hopkins University Press.

Langer, J. A. (1986). *Children reading and writing: Structures and strategies.* Norwood, NJ: Ablex.

Lankshear, C. (1999). Literacy studies in education: Disciplined developments in a post-disciplinary age. In M. Peters (Ed.), *After the disciplines* (pp. 199–228). Westport, CT: Bergin & Garvey.

Lave, J., & Wenger, E. (1991). *Situated learning: Legitimate peripheral participation.* New York: Cambridge University Press.

Lemke, J. (1988). Genres, semantics, and classroom education. *Linguistics and Education, 1*, 81–99.

Lemke, J. (1992). Intertextuality and discourse research. *Linguistics and Education, 4*, 25–67.

Leontiev, A. N. (1981). *Problems of the development of mind* (M. Kopylova, Trans.). Moscow: Progress. (Original work published 1947)

Lowry, P. B., Curtis, A., & Lowry, M. R. (2004). Building a taxonomy and nomenclature of collaborative writing to improve interdisciplinary research and practice. *Journal of Business Communication, 41*(1), 66–99.

Many, J. E., Fyfe, R., Lewis, G., & Mitchell, E. (1996). Traversing the topical landscape: Exploring students' self-directed reading-writing-research processes. *Reading Research Quarterly, 31*, 12–35.

Mathison, M. A. (1996). Writing the critique: A text about a text. *Written Communication, 13*, 314–354.

McCutchen, D., Francis, M., & Kerr, S. (1997). Revising for meaning: Effects of knowledge and strategy. *Journal of Educational Psychology, 89*, 667–676.

McInnis, R. G. (1996). Introduction: Defining discourse synthesis. *Social Epistemology, 10*, 1–25.

Miller, C. R. (1984). Genre as social action. *Quarterly Journal of Speech, 70*, 151–167.

National Research Council. (2000). *The digital dilemma: Intellectual property in the information age.* Washington, DC: National Academies Press.

Nelson, N. (2001). Discourse synthesis: Process and product. In R. G. McInnis (Ed.), *Discourse synthesis: Studies in historical and contemporary social epistemology* (pp. 379–396). Westport, CT: Praeger.

Nelson, N., & Calfee, R. C. (1998). The reading–writing connection, viewed historically. In N. Nelson & R. C. Calfee (Eds.), *The reading–writing connection: Ninety-seventh yearbook of the National Society for the Study of Education* (pp. 1–52). Chicago: University of Chicago Press.

Nelson, N., & Kinneavy, J. (2003). Rhetoric. In J. Flood, D. Lapp, J. R. Squire, & J. M. Jensen (Eds.), *Handbook of research on teaching the English language arts* (pp. 786–798). Mahwah, NJ: Lawrence Erlbaum Associates.

Nielsen, J. (1990). *Hypertext and hypermedia*. San Diego, CA: Academic Press.

Noel, S., & Robert, J. M. (2004). Empirical study on collaborative writing: What do co-authors do, use, and like? *Computer-Supported Cooperative Work, 13,* 63–89.

Nystrand, M. (1986). *The structure of written communication: Studies in reciprocity between writers and readers.* Orlando, FL: Academic Press.

Palumbo, D. B., & Prater, D. (1993). The role of hypermedia in synthesis writing. *Computers and Composition, 9*(2), 59–70.

Piaget, J. (1932). *The language and thought of the child* (M. Gabain, Trans.). New York: Harcourt Brace. (Original work published 1923)

Porter, J. E. (1986). Intertextuality and the discourse community. *Rhetoric Review, 5,* 34–47.

Propp, V. (1968). *Morphology of the folktale* (2nd ed.). Austin: University of Texas Press. (Original work published 1928)

Reither, J. A., & Vipond, D. (1989). Writing as collaboration. *College English, 51,* 855–867.

Rubin, D. L. (1984). Social cognition and written communication. *Written Communication, 1,* 211–245.

Rumelhart, D. E. (1975). Notes on a schema for stories. In D. G. Bobrow & A. Collins (Eds.), *Representation and understanding: Studies in cognitive science* (pp. 211–236). New York: Academic Press.

Salomon, G. (Ed.). (1986). *Distributed cognitions: Psychological and educational considerations.* New York: Cambridge University Press.

Schnotz, W. (1984). Comparative instructional text organization. In H. Mandl, N. L. Stein, & T. Trabasso (Eds.), *Learning and comprehension of text* (pp. 53–74). Hillsdale, NJ: Lawrence Erlbaum Associates.

Schriver, K. A. (1992). Teaching writers to anticipate readers' needs: A classroom-evaluated pedagogy. *Written Communication, 9,* 179–208.

Segev-Miller, R. (2004). Writing from sources: The effect of explicit instruction on college students' processes and products. *L1 Educational Studies in Language and Literature, 4,* 5–33.

Shanahan, T. (1984). Nature of the reading–writing relation: An exploratory multivariate analysis. *Journal of Educational Psychology, 76,* 466–477.

Shanahan, T. (1998). Readers' awareness of author. In N. Nelson & R. C. Calfee (Eds.), *The reading–writing connection: Ninety-seventh yearbook of the National Society for the Study of Education* (pp. 88–111). Chicago: University of Chicago Press

Shanahan, T., & Lomax, R. G. (1986). An analysis and comparison of theoretical models of the reading–writing relationship. *Journal of Educational Psychology, 78,* 116–123.

Sharples, M., Goodlet, J., Beck, E., Wood, C., Easterbrook, S., & Plowman, L. (1993). Research issues in the study of computer supported collaborative writing. In M. Sharples (Ed.), *Computer supported collaborative writing* (pp. 9–28). London: Springer-Verlag.

Smagorinsky, P. (2001). If meaning is constructed, what is it made from? Toward a cultural theory of reading. *Review of Educational Research, 71,* 133–169.

Smagorinsky, P., & Smith, M. W. (1992). The nature of knowledge in composition and literary understanding: The question of specificity. *Review of Educational Research, 62,* 279–305.

Small, H. (2001). A journey through science. In R. G. McInnis (Ed.), *Discourse synthesis: Studies in historical and contemporary social epistemology* (pp. 143–194). Westport, CT: Praeger.

Sperling, M. (1998). Teachers as readers of student writing. In N. Nelson & R. C. Calfee (Eds.), *The reading–writing connection: Ninety-seventh yearbook of the National Society for the Study of Education* (pp. 131–152). Chicago: University of Chicago Press.

Spiro, R. J., Feltovich, P. J., Jacobson, M. J., & Coulson, R. L. (1992). Cognitive flexibility, constructivism and hypertext: Random access instruction for advanced knowledge acquisition in ill-structured domains. In T. M. Duffy & D. H. Jonassen (Eds.), *Constructivism and the technology of instruction* (pp. 57–76). Hillsdale, NJ: Lawrence Erlbaum Associates.

Spivey, N. N. (1984). *Discourse synthesis: Constructing texts in reading and writing* (Monograph). Newark, DE: International Reading Association.

Spivey, N. N. (1990). Transforming texts: Constructive processes in reading and writing. *Written Communication, 7,* 256–287.

Spivey, N. N. (1997). *The constructivist metaphor: Reading, writing, and the making of meaning.* San Diego, CA: Academic Press.

Spivey, N. N., & King, J. R. (1989). Readers as writers composing from sources. *Reading Research Quarterly, 24,* 7–26.

Steiner, G. (1998). *After Babel: Aspects of language and translation.* New York: Oxford University Press.

Stillinger, J. (1991). *Multiple authorship and the myth of solitary genius.* New York: Oxford University Press.

Stotsky, S. (1983). Research on reading/writing relationships: A synthesis and suggested directions. *Language Arts, 60,* 627–642.

Tierney, R. J., & Pearson, P. D. (1983). Toward a composing model of reading. *Language Arts, 60,* 568–580.

Ulichny, P., & Watson-Gegeo, K. A. (1989). Interactions and authority: The dominant interpretive framework in writing conferences. *Discourse Processes, 12,* 309–328.

van den Bergh, H., & Rijlaarsdam, G. (1999). The dynamics of idea generation during writing: An online study. In M. Torrance & D. Galbraith (Eds.), *Knowing what to write: Conceptual processes in text production* (pp. 99–120). Amsterdam: Amsterdam University Press.

Vipond, D., & Hunt, R. A. (1984). Point-driven understanding: Pragmatic and cognitive dimensions of literary reading. *Poetics, 13,* 261–277.

Volosinov, V. N. (1973). *Marxism and the philosophy of language* (L. Matejka & I. R. Titunik, Trans.). New York; Seminar Press.

Vygotsky, L. (1978). *Mind in society: The development of higher psychological processes* (M. Cole, V. John-Steiner, S. Scribner, & E. Souberman, Eds.). Cambridge, MA: Harvard University Press.

Vygotsky, L. S. (1986). *Thought and language* (A. Kozulin, Ed. & Trans.). Cambridge, MA: MIT Press. (Original work published 1934)

Wineburg, S. (1991). On the reading of historical texts: Notes on the breach between the school and academy. *American Educational Research Journal, 28,* 495–519.

Wineburg, S. (2001). *Historical thinking and other unnatural acts: Charting the future of teaching the past.* Philadelphia: Temple University Press.

Witte, S. P. (1983). Topical structure and revision: An exploratory study. *College Composition and Communication, 34,* 313–341.

Young, K. M., & Leinhardt, G. (1998). Writing from primary documents: A way of knowing in history. *Written Communication, 15,* 25–68.

CHAPTER 28

Writing and Cognition: Implications of the Cognitive Architecture for Learning to Write and Writing to Learn

Deborah McCutchen
Paul Teske
Catherine Bankston
University of Washington, Seattle

GENESIS OF COGNITIVE APPROACHES TO WRITING

Cognitive approaches to the study of writing have earlier roots (see Nystrand, 2006), but in the late 1970s the fields of cognitive psychology and process-oriented rhetoric converged with sustained impact on the campus of Pittsburgh's Carnegie Mellon University, spurred by work of Richard Young (e.g., Young & Becker, 1965) and spawning the influential cognitive model of writing developed by Dick Hayes and Linda Flower (Hayes & Flower, 1980). Influenced by the cognitive science zeitgeist, Hayes and Flower's initial conceptualizations drew heavily on expert–novice and artificial intelligence (AI) traditions and compared composing processes with problem solving (see also Collins & Gentner, 1980).

Like other contemporaneous studies of human problem solving in complex domains (e.g., Hayes, 1981; Hayes-Roth & Hayes-Roth, 1979; Larkin, McDermott, Simon, & Simon, 1980; A. Newell & Simon, 1972), Hayes and Flower's (1980) approach to writing followed the example of AI models, emphasizing constraint identification, problem decomposition, and hierarchical planning processes (i.e., developing goals with recursively nested subgoals and steps to attain them). The limitations of hierarchical planning for a full account of writing expertise have been articulated (McCutchen, 1984; Torrance, 1996a), and Hayes and Nash (1996) have also revisited the original model's emphasis on planning, concluding that planning is only one of several aspects of cognition that must be considered in an account of expertise in writing.

During the 1980s and 1990s, writing was examined through both cognitive and sociocultural lenses, and in 1996 Hayes substantially revised the 1980 model to augment the cognitive description with additional affective and social components (see Figure 28.1). Planning was subsumed under the broader label *reflection*, which encompasses problem solving (including planning), decision making, and inferencing. Translating was retitled *text production* and has been elaborated considerably by Chenoweth and Hayes (2001). The

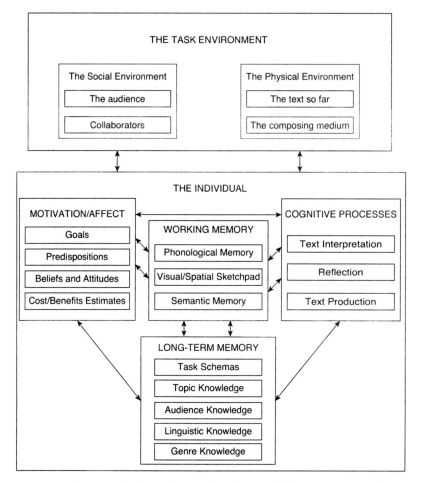

Figure 28.1. A revised version of the Hayes and Flower (1980) model.
(From Hayes, 1996).

original reviewing process was expanded to include *text interpretation* as well as embedded *reflection* and *text production* (see also Hayes, 2004). New in the 1996 model were specifications of affective goals, predispositions, and beliefs, as well as the social environment, although the model retained a decidedly cognitive character.

Another line of cognitive research on writing emerged simultaneously with the work of Hayes and Flower, one grounded more in the neo-Piagetian tradition than in AI. An alternative model offered by Bereiter and Scardamalia (1987) explored the writing strategies used by children, as well as the more sophisticated strategies available to experts. Bereiter and Scardamalia observed among children a strategy they termed "knowledge telling," which involves writers probing memory with a cue derived from either the writing assignment's topic or genre and retrieving relevant knowledge for the text. Bereiter and Scardamalia contrasted knowledge telling with a process they called "knowledge transformation," in which the process of writing initiates interactions between content and rhetorical knowledge, with the potential for transforming both. Although knowledge telling is frequently cited as a model of children's writing and knowledge transformation as a model of expert writing, Bereiter and Scardamalia argued that knowledge telling cannot necessarily be distinguished from knowledge transformation on the basis of text quality alone.

Skilled writers, they argued, may engage in knowledge telling and still produce a quality text (e.g., when writing about familiar material in a well-rehearsed context; see Torrance, 1996b), and experts and novices alike may engage in knowledge transformation yet still produce poor-quality text.

From the seminal models offered by Hayes and Flower (1980) and Bereiter and Scardamalia (1987) has emerged a substantial body of cognitive research in writing. In the review that follows, we selectively examine the issue of writing expertise in two ways. First we explore the development of expertise in writing (i.e., learning to write), examining aspects of cognitive processing that distinguish expert from novice writers. We focus on features of the cognitive architecture, specifically working memory and long-term memory, as they influence the three major processes described by Hayes and Flower (1980): planning, text production, and revising. We conclude with a discussion of the role of writing processes in the development of content expertise (i.e., writing to learn).

LEARNING TO WRITE: COGNITIVE PROCESS IMPLICATIONS FOR WRITING EXPERTISE

Task Schemata

Given the centrality of task schemata to theories of problem solving (e.g., A. Newell & Simon, 1972) and given the roots of cognitive models of writing in the problem-solving literature, it is not surprising that task schemata have been much discussed in relation to writing processes. Although task schemata were implicit in the original Hayes and Flower (1980) model, they were subsumed under the general control mechanism known as the "monitor." In light of the explicit attention allocated to task schemata by Hayes (1996), his colleagues (Chenoweth & Hayes, 2001; Wallace & Hayes, 1991; Wallace et al., 1996), and other writing researchers, we begin our review of cognitive processes in writing with an examination of the task schemata that coordinate them.

Task Schemata in Planning. In discussions of planning processes, task schemata constitute a key difference (although not the only difference, see Hayes & Nash, 1996) between novices and experts, specifically whether planning is devoted to generating content or to developing other sorts of goals. Task schemata employed by experts include goal formulation (e.g., to reach a given audience, to present a particular persona) and plans to achieve those goals (e.g., to adopt a particular genre or rhetorical stance, to include or avoid specific vocabulary), with clear distinctions between the plan and the text. Consider, for example, the protocol of a wine columnist of a major metropolitan newspaper as he began his weekly column. Before he wrote a word, the wine columnist laid out requirements for his opening sentence:

> Alright, so now you need a lead-in sentence and it's got to be something that's going to (1) catch the audience's eye, (2) given the way I usually write the column, it's got to be reasonably ornate, and (3) it's got to have something to do with the goddamn topic. (McCutchen, 1994, p. 4)

He continued a few minutes later to describe his plan for the remainder of the text:

> The general structure has got to be, we've got to give them some information about Chateau Latour, make it kinda real to them, give them something to chew on, and then we're going to go through the tasting notes because we had a tasting of Chateau Latour from 1924 to 1967, which means, you know, we have to save enough space to write about, you know, the wines themselves. (McCutchen, 1984, p. 228)

After articulating his plan (which involved audience and tone, as well as rhetorical structure), the writer then used it to regulate his writing throughout the writing session.

In contrast, the task schemata revealed in novice writing (derived from children primarily, but not exclusively) typically show little concern for conceptual planning, especially in advance of writing. Analyses of prewriting pauses reveal that children often begin writing within a minute of receiving a writing task, and they are often incredulous when told that some writers spend 15 minutes or more before they write (Bereiter & Scardamalia, 1987). Among adults, Breetvelt, Van den Bergh, and Rijlaarsdam (1996) found that writers who took longer to begin to put text on the page (because they presumably devoted some time to planning) wrote higher quality texts than writers who began to produce text very early in the writing session. Kellogg (1987b, 1988) also found that developing an outline before writing enabled college-age writers to produce higher quality texts.

The task schemata shaping the strategies of novice writers frequently focus on retrieving relevant content, and protocols produced by young writers often reveal them searching for content and saying aloud the words as they write, rather than developing conceptual plans (Bereiter & Scardamalia, 1987; McCutchen, 1988). Based on an analysis of protocols from children age 10 through 18, Bereiter and Scardamalia (1987) reported that approximately 90% of the statements produced by younger children involved either (a) generation of content or (b) explicit dictation or rereading, and even for adolescents, content generation comprised nearly half of the protocols (Bereiter & Scardamalia, 1987; see also Langer, 1986). Similar developmental differences in the conceptualization of writing were reported recently by Scheur, de la Cruz, Pozo, Huarte, and Sola (2006). These researchers noted that for kindergarten children, writing was primarily about transcribing letters, for first-grade children writing was primarily about transcribing words, and although text-level concerns began to emerge for fourth-grade children, those concerns still primarily involved retrieval of content.

Even when explicitly asked to plan, young children often have difficulty separating planning from writing (but see Cameron & Moshenko, 1996). When asked to make notes in advance of writing, Bereiter and Scardamalia (1987) found that 10-year-olds typically wrote what amounted to a first draft of the composition, whereas older children (ages 12 and 14) produced ideas that they later expanded into text. In addition, when evaluating paraphrases of main points taken from their texts, older children were far more likely than younger children to refer to their original intentions, that is, to their plans (Bereiter, Burtis, & Scardamalia, 1988).

It is not the case, however, that older writers' protocols always reveal a task schema focused on global planning, or that children never show evidence of a task schema that involves planning. Within meaningful contexts, even young children have shown signs of planning for a specific audience by adapting the texts they produced for audiences who were physically present or absent (Cameron & Wang, 1999; Littleton, 1998) or who varied in age or setting (Lee, Karmiloff-Smith, Cameron, & Dodsworth, 1998). Flower's (1979) description of *writer-based prose* suggests that even older novice writers can focus on content generation and fail to plan adequately for their readers. In addition, Torrance (1996b) found little evidence of advanced goal-directed planning among college students who nonetheless produced essays that were average or above in quality. In another study of college-age writers, Butcher and Kintsch (2001) found that prompts intended to support attention to audience and rhetorical goals affected planning (and text quality) only when provided well in advance of writing, while the students studied material that they were to use during their writing. In contrast, prompts intended to support attention to content consistently affected planning and text quality regardless of placement. Thus the task schemata that guide the planning process may reflect the skill level of the writer as well as the contexts in which writers find themselves and the goals they set within those contexts.

Task Schemata in Text Production.   Chenoweth and Hayes (2001) elaborated the translating (i.e., text production) process described originally by Hayes and Flower (1980;

Kaufer, Hayes, & Flower, 1986), proposing a detailed model of written language production in which a task schema directs cognitive processes. The control exerted by the task schemata may vary depending on the goal of the writer, as well as the skill level.

According to Chenoweth and Hayes (2001), the task schema orchestrates the cognitive processes involved in text production—initiating prelinguistic content retrieval by the *proposer,* setting levels of precision for the *translator* to clothe that content in actual words and the *transcriber* to spell those words accurately, and adjusting the threshold that allows the *reviser* to interrupt. For example, when engaged in freewriting or producing a rough draft, writers may set low precision requirements for the translator and transcriber and high thresholds for the reviser, all in order to get the general ideas and approximate spellings on the page without interruption. In contrast, when producing a final draft, the threshold for the reviser may be quite low, allowing the reviser to interrupt repeatedly and prompt the transcriber to ensure correct spellings or the translator to search for another word that more accurately expresses the semantic intent. As well as adjusting thresholds of subprocesses, the task schema may also be involved in distributing time allocation to text production across the writing session, which has been found to relate to writing quality (Breetvelt et al., 1996; Rijlaarsdam & Van den Bergh, 2006).

The nature of the task schemata employed by novice writers may be different from those employed by expert writers in even more fundamental ways. According to Bereiter and Scardamalia (1987), because children's initial experiences with discourse are largely conversational, their schema for text generation may be shaped by oral schemata. Prominent in conversational schemata is the concept of turn taking, that is, making room for and taking cues from the conversational partner. In contrast, text generation during writing often must operate without the interactive prompts provided by conversational partners. Bereiter and Scardamalia suggested that when young children transfer oral, conversational schemata to the generation of written text, they frequently write only a single conversational turn (i.e., the proposer does not self-prompt), with the resulting texts being short and incomplete. This suggestion has garnered empirical support from studies showing that children write longer texts, and texts of higher quality, when they are provided with a "conversational" partner during writing (Daiute, 1986; Daiute & Dalton, 1993) or even simple prompts to say more (Bereiter & Scardamalia, 1987). Indeed, effective writing instruction for young children frequently incorporates active collaboration and peer response (Boscolo & Ascorti, 2004; Calkins, 1986; Cameron, Hunt, & Linton, 1996; Graves, 1983), thereby emphasizing the implicit dialogue between writer and reader. Skilled writing, therefore, may require the development of a task schema that prompts more sustained cycles of text production than is common during oral language production.

Task Schemata in Revision.   Hayes (1996, 2004) has also elaborated the original description of the revision process offered by Hayes and Flower (1980). He proposed that revision, like planning and text production, is guided by an overall task schema that directs multiple cognitive processes, including critical reading, problem solving, and text production.

Wallace and Hayes (1991; Wallace et al., 1996) provided evidence supporting the existence of a revision task schema. Most writers (adults as well as children) seem to operate under a revision schema focused on surface features of the text, rather than the conceptual level, and thereby attend more to surface features of the text such as spelling, punctuation, and word choice (e.g., Butterfield, Hacker, & Plumb, 1994; Chanquoy, 2001; Faigley & Witte, 1981; Fitzgerald, 1987; McCutchen, Francis, & Kerr, 1997; Piolat, Roussey, Olive, & Amada, 2003). With very brief instruction, Wallace and Hayes (1991; Wallace et al., 1996) were able to reorient college writers to revise for meaning. Their instruction was so brief (8 minutes) that Wallace and colleagues argued they could not have taught students revision processes per se; rather, they argued they simply altered the students' revision schema by directing students' attention to meaning over mechanical features of texts (see also Graham, MacArthur, & Schwartz, 1995). If the task schema is indeed distinct from the cognitive processes it directs, then alterations in the task schema should have little effect in the absence of adequate revision-related cognitive processes. Data provided by Wallace et al. (1996) were again consistent with such a hypothesis; their brief schema-directed instruction did not increase meaning-based revision among struggling college writers.

Working Memory Resources

Task schemata coordinate cognitive processes during writing, but successful execution of those processes depends on the availability of sufficient resources within the limited capacity of working memory (Baddeley, 1998). Because all of the major writing processes (planning, text production, and revising) make demands on working-memory resources (Kellogg, 1988), working memory has received considerable attention from writing researchers (Alamargot & Chanquoy, 2001; Butterfield, Hacker, & Albertson, 1996; Levy & Ransdell, 1995; McCutchen, 1996, 2000; Piolat et al., 2003; Ransdell & Levy, 1996). Data as diverse as protocols (Flower & Hayes, 1980, 1981, 1984; Hayes & Flower, 1980; McCutchen, 1984, 1994), pause times (Chanquoy, Foulin, & Fayol, 1996; Schilperoord, 1996), and keystrokes (Levy & Ransdell, 1995) indicate that skilled writers continually juggle knowledge and process; but arguably the most systematic study of working memory has been the research of Kellogg (1987a, 1988, 1996).

Working Memory Influences in Planning. Kellogg (1987a, 1988) developed a secondary-task paradigm to monitor the cognitive effort reported by writers as they engaged in various writing processes, and he reported that planning generally required more processing resources than text production for college-age writers, and at times more than revision. Thus working-memory limitations can have serious consequences for the planning process. The writer needs to have sufficient working-memory resources to retain access to plans throughout the writing session, if those plans are going to guide later decisions. For example, the wine columnist described previously was well into his text, writing about the maturation of cabernet sauvignon grapes, when he stopped short:

> (typing) "It takes a long time for cabernet grapes to mature, to release the esters and—"
> Now I should say "esters and aldehydes," but if I did that, I'd have to explain about esters and aldehydes... Why not just talk about smells and flavors? (McCutchen, 1994, p. 5)

Because of his knowledge of audience and his plans for the flow of the column, the wine columnist chose not to include, as he put it, "a big dissertation and tell them a bit about some of the chemistry." The writer was able to access his text plan within working memory even in the midst of text generation, and his plan influenced the process of text generation by determining word choice. Because planning processes must compete for working-memory resources with other writing processes, it is critical that writers have adequate working-memory resources to allow the development and functional use of global planning (Dellerman, Coirier, & Marchand, 1996; McCutchen, 2000). Without adequate working-memory resources, writers may be unable to consult plans during writing, perhaps limiting themselves to the less sophisticated strategies described by Bereiter and Scardamalia (1987) and Flower (1979).

Working-Memory Influences in Text Production. Studies of working-memory constraints in text production have focused primarily on the operation of two subprocesses, *text generation* (under control of what Chenoweth & Hayes, 2001, called the translator), which involves the selection and refinement of a linguistic message, and *transcription*, which involves spelling and the physical act of getting the words onto the page (e.g., handwriting, keyboarding). Fluent text production can influence the writing process both directly and indirectly because inefficient text production can consume resources that might otherwise be devoted to higher level processes such as planning and revising (Marchand, Coirier, & Dellerman, 1996; McCutchen, 2000). Although text production requires working-memory resources even for adults (Kellogg, 1987b, 1988), the resource costs of text generation and transcription seem to decrease as fluency increases. Thus, working-memory constraints can be especially acute for children and struggling writers, for whom text production processes are less fluent.

Developmental differences in the working-memory demands of transcription were examined in a series of experiments by Bourdin and Fayol (1994), who varied response modality (spoken vs. written) in a serial-recall task. Bourdin and Fayol found that recall was significantly poorer in the written condition for children but not for adults. They reasoned that transcription processes of children are still relatively inefficient and draw on working-memory resources that could otherwise be devoted to the recall task. Bourdin and Fayol were able to interrupt adults' overlearned, highly fluent transcription processes by requiring them to write in cursive upper-case letters, with the result that adults then showed poorer recall when writing compared with speaking. In similar experiments, the task changed from serial recall to text recall (Bourdin, Fayol, & Darciaux, 1996) and text generation (Olive & Kellogg, 2002), with the consistent finding that transcription imposed higher working-memory costs for children than for adults.

The fluency of transcription processes generally increases with age (Berninger & Graham, 1998; Berninger & Swanson, 1994), theoretically decreasing demands on working memory and enabling resource allocation to other aspects of writing. Examining a wide range of component processes, Berninger and Swanson (1994) found that transcription measures accounted for more unique variance in composition quality among primary-grade children than among older shildren (see also Graham, Berninger, Abbott, Abbott, & Whitaker, 1997). Furthermore, improving handwriting fluency among children has led to general improvements in the fluency of their text generation (Berninger et al., 1997; Graham, Harris, & Fink, 2000). Hoskyn and Swanson (2003) found that transcription factors continued to contribute to age related-differences in text structure from adolescence to elder adulthood, and an independent measure of working memory accounted for additional unique variance in their text measures. Levy and Ransdell (1995) also documented that writers of higher quality texts wrote more fluently than writers of lower quality texts.

Other researchers have examined the working-memory demands of transcription by comparing the quality of written and dictated texts, reasoning that speaking and writing share text generation but not transcription processes. Children's written texts are typically shorter than their dictated texts (Bereiter & Scardamalia, 1987; McCutchen, 1987), whereas differences favoring dictation are not as consistent for adults (Gould, 1980; Grabowski, Vorwerg, & Rummer, 1994; Reece & Cumming, 1996), again suggesting that transcription is easier for adults than for children. In a seminal study, Bereiter and Scardamalia (1987) asked children to produce texts in three conditions: (a) writing, (b) regular dictation, and (c) slow dictation (i.e., a dictation rate indexed to the child's writing rate). Although dictation produced longer texts, quality ratings showed little difference across conditions. However, following simple prompts to produce more, children's written texts were rated higher in quality than those produced in either of the dictation conditions. Bereiter and Scardamalia concluded that the brevity of children's written texts is the primary factor contributing to the perception that children often speak better than they write, not the working-memory costs of transcription. They argued that by middle childhood, the processing cost associated with transcription is largely offset by other affordances of writing, if children simply persevere in generating longer texts.

Reece and Cumming (1996) argued that once transcription reaches minimal levels of fluency, part of the advantage of writing over conventional dictation results from the availability of a visible, developing text. Like Bereiter and Scardamalia (1987), Reece and Cumming found that texts written by 10- to 12-year-old children were shorter but higher quality than texts dictated in the conventional manner. However, when they asked children to dictate texts and simultaneously transcribed those texts for children to view on a computer screen, Reece and Cumming found that quality ratings were higher for the transcribed texts than for the handwritten texts.

For children with writing disabilities, transcription demands can be a persistent problem, extending well into adolescence. Graham (1990) replicated Bereiter and Scardamalia's (1987) procedures with children with learning disabilities and found quite different results. For children with learning disabilities, the working-memory demands imposed by transcription resulted in written essays that were consistently shorter and lower in quality than dictated essays, even after prompts to say more. In a partial replication of the study by Reece and Cumming (1996), MacArthur and Cavalier (2004) found that high school students with writing disabilities generated better texts when they dictated to speech recognition software compared to when they wrote by hand, and texts were better still when students dictated to a human scribe (who made no transcription errors). In contrast, MacArthur and Cavalier found no differences in writing mode for students without writing disabilities (see also Quinlan, 2004).

Thus, although comparisons between writing and traditional dictation may have been confounded by the absence of the visible text, data consistently indicate that transcription processes can impose measurable loads on working memory until writers gain sufficient handwriting fluency. Similar results emphasizing the importance of fluency have been reported in studies examining keyboarding as the transcription mode (Cochran-Smith, 1991; Dunn & Reay, 1989).

Working memory has also been related to text generation, text production's other major subprocess. Text generation, according to Chenoweth and Hayes (2001; see also Berninger & Swanson, 1994), is the mental production of a linguistic message, distinct from transcription of that message into written text. Like speech, text generation involves turning ideas into words, sentences, and larger units of discourse within working memory. As in speech, pauses in the stream of language generated during writing are influenced by syntactic junctures such as paragraph, sentence, and clause boundaries (Chanquoy et al., 1996); the larger the syntactic boundary (i.e., within vs. across clause, sentence, or paragraph boundaries), the larger demand on working memory, and the longer the average pause.

Working-memory spans have been linked to text generation in a number of studies. McCutchen, Covill, Hoyne, and Mildes (1994) showed that skilled elementary and middle school writers had larger working-memory spans, generated sentences more fluently during the span task, and accessed words in memory more quickly than less skilled writers (see also Ransdell & Levy, 1996). In a study with writers ranging in age from adolescents to elderly adults, Hoskyn and Swanson (2003) found that working-memory span predicted the structural complexity of texts even after reading skill, spelling, and handwriting speed were taken into account. Tetroe (1984; cited in Bereiter & Scardamalia, 1987) also linked working memory and text generation at the discourse level. Tetroe asked children to write stories that were to end with specific sentences, and she varied the number of constraints imposed by the ending sentences. Tetroe found a marked decrease in children's ability to honor the ending-sentence constraints as the number of constraints exceeded their working-memory spans. Similarly, Jeffrey and Underwood (1996) found a significant correlation between young writers' memory spans and their ability to coordinate ideas within a sentence and a similar (although nonsignificant) correlation between memory span and text quality. Bereiter and Scardamalia (1987) also found that the number of ideas children could coordinate within a single sentence was related to how well they defended a thesis in an expository writing task and attributed the relationship to the working-memory resources that each child had available. Dellerman et al. (1996) found that a similar coordination task predicted writing skill even for high school students.

Working-memory constraints may also make it difficult for writers to avoid or correct certain syntactic errors. For example, subject–verb agreement and other complex syntactic structures become more difficult to coordinate as working-memory load increases (Chanquoy & Negro, 1996), and Daiute (1984) found negative correlations between short-term memory capacity and the frequency of errors in students' texts. In addition, Fayol,

Largy, and Lemaire (1994) experimentally induced agreement errors by increasing writers' memory load.

Thus, working-memory demands imposed by text production processes (transcription and text generation) are sizable for novice writers, and although these demands decrease as writers gain fluency, text production seems to require working-memory resources even for skilled writers (Kellogg, 1987b, 1988, 1994; Ransdell & Levy, 1996).

Working-Memory Influences in Revision.   Revision entails multiple processes, each of which may also be constrained by available working-memory resources. Hayes (1996), building on models of revision proposed by Bereiter and Scadamalia (1987) and Hayes, Flower, Schriver, Stratman, and Carey (1987), argued that revision includes *critical reading* to interpret text and detect problems, *reflection* to identify the nature of the problem and define a solution, and *text production* to implement the solution, all operating under control of a task schema (described previously). Each aspect of revision poses challenges for novice writers (children and older novice writers alike), challenges that can be exacerbated by limitations in working memory.

Using a variant of Kellogg's (1988) dual-task paradigm, Piolat et al. (2004) found that the critical reading involved during revision required more working-memory resources for college students than reading simply to understand the text. Piolat and her colleagues directly linked working-memory limitations to problem detection, documenting that students with larger working-memory spans were more successful than students with smaller spans when correcting spelling errors (however, no effects of working-memory span were observed when the errors involved syntax or coherence problems).

McCutchen et al. (1997) linked text-level revision to working memory, arguing that writers' ability to read texts critically was related to the amount of text they were able to consider at any one time. In that study, we listened as middle school students worked collaboratively to revise texts within which we had created logical inconsistencies by reordering sentences, and we found that skilled and less skilled writers employed strategies that placed different demands on working memory. Skilled revisers developed a macrostructure of the text they were revising (see Kintsch, 1998) and considered the entire text as they worked, whereas less skilled revisers attended to one sentence or clause at a time. For example, even during their initial reading of the text, skilled writers readily recognized sentences that were out of place. The following exchange is typical of the strategy that skilled writers used as they worked to revise a text describing the initial voyage of Christopher Columbus:

> Student A: Wait—that should be somewhere on the top. Maybe after (reads) "However, Columbus also believed that the world was round. Many people laughed at this idea. They thought the world was flat." (Inserts and reads) "Columbus hoped to prove his theory, so he would sail west in order to reach the East."
> Student B: Yeah. That would work. Put that up there.

In contrast, we observed that less skilled writers used a more local, sentence-by-sentence strategy that interfered with their ability to consider the text's larger meaning. The following excerpt documents a less skilled writer revising the same Columbus text, examining each sentence individually, but completely missing the incongruous mention of the sailors' threatened mutiny:

> Student: (reads) "Christopher Columbus was determined to find an all water route to the East Indies, East Indies." That's good. (reads) "Discovering this could bring him fame and fortune. However, however, Columbus also believed that the world was round." OK. (reads) "Many people"—geez! (corrects spelling, reads) "laughed at this idea. They thought the world was flat." Next; that's good. (reads) "But still the sailors threatened to take over and turn, take over and turn back." That's good. (McCutchen et al., 1997, p. 673)

We concluded, like Hayes (1996, 2004), that sophisticated revision may depend on the ability to read texts critically, which in turn may make substantial demands on working memory by requiring attention to a text's macrostructure. In subsequent analyses of data not reported in the original publication (McCutchen et al., 1997), we found that less skilled writers in the study showed smaller working-memory spans than did skilled writers, further linking reading strategies to working-memory constraints.

Levy and Ransdell (1995) documented that revision required substantial working-memory resources. Although Levy and Ransdell found no systematic relationship between text quality and the working-memory resources employed by writers during revision, they found that writers of high-quality texts engaged in more reviewing and revising episodes than did writers of low-quality texts—*more* episodes but not necessarily longer episodes—requiring more frequent reallocation of processing resources.

Thus, working-memory limitations may affect revision processes in a number of ways. First, working-memory limitations may constrain the amount of text that writers are able to consider at any given point in time, enabling writers with more working-memory resources to consider text-level issues while forcing those with fewer available resources to focus on smaller sections of text. Working-memory limitations could thereby contribute to the well-documented tendency of novice writers to focus on surface-level revisions (Butterfield et al., 1994; Chanquoy, 2001; Faigley & Witte, 1981; Fitzgerald, 1987; McCutchen et al., 1997; Piolat et al., 2003). Second, working-memory limitations may reduce the writer's ability to shift between processes, inhibiting the writer's ability to initiate revision processes whenever needed (Kellogg, 1996).

Long-Term Memory Resources

For writers of all ages, knowledge stored in long-term memory is critical during writing. Hayes (1996) called attention to two sources of knowledge that have received considerable attention in writing research, knowledge of genre and knowledge of topic.

Genre Knowledge.   Familiarity with a genre can theoretically influence writing by providing access to an organized schema in long-term memory, which writers can use to structure content and assist ongoing processing. The protocol of the wine columnist discussed previously (McCutchen, 1984, 1994) revealed his genre knowledge in his detailed vision for the structural features of his column.

Issues of genre also extend into writers' broader knowledge of the disciplinary community for whom (or perhaps more appropriately *with* whom) they write. For example, writers generally learn the discourse forms and honor the rhetorical values of their respective academic disciplines (MacDonald, 1992; Myers, 1985). Skilled writers seem to have ready access to, if not explicit awareness of (Langer, 1992; Stockton, 1995), such rhetorical knowledge. This ready access is evidenced by the fact that genre and stylistic knowledge seem to influence many other processes, including lexical and syntactic choices (Barton, 1995; Bazerman, 1984; MacDonald, 1992; Vande Kopple, 1998). Thus, skilled writers seem to employ stored representations of text structures that may also include audience knowledge, in terms of the expectations of members of a disciplinary discourse community.

Genre knowledge develops from experience with a given text structure, and research documents a link between children's genre knowledge and writing skill. Due largely to children's broad early experience with narratives (Sulzby & Teale, 1987), even young children show signs of emergent narrative schemata (Stein & Glenn, 1979; Sulzby, 1985). Fitzgerald and Teasley (1986) provided evidence for a causal link between genre knowledge and writing skill, demonstrating that instruction in narrative structure improved the quality of children's written stories. Children's knowledge and use of expository genres generally develops later than knowledge of narrative (Englert, Stewart, & Hiebert, 1988; Langer, 1986), and comparisons reveal that children's written narratives are generally superior to their expositions (e.g., Cox, Shanahan, & Tinzmann, 1991; but see Langer, 1986;

McCutchen, 1987, for qualifications). Crammond (1998) found that students' skills with the argumentative genre continued to develop throughout high school, with marked differences remaining between high school students and expert adult writers (see also Meyer, Brandt, & Bluth, 1980; Wright & Rosenberg, 1993). Meyer and Poon (2001) showed that instruction in recognizing various expository genres (description, sequence, causation, problem/solution, and comparison) improved written summaries even for adults. It should be noted, however, that nontraditional text structures embodied in students' writing may reflect a purposeful genre selection, rather than lack of knowledge (Ball, 1992).

Children's use of genre knowledge during writing may be more implicit than that of expert writers. According to Bereiter and Scardamalia (1987), the knowledge-telling strategy uses cues from the assignment (genre and topic cues) to formulate memory probes. When children are more familiar with a genre, the memory probes generated as part of the knowledge-telling process will be more systematically related and should result in retrieval of more coherent content. Thus, although children may not use a genre-based plan as expert writers do, children's genre knowledge may influence their writing because it is incorporated within the knowledge-telling strategy.

Topic Knowledge. Instructional researchers have long argued that topic knowledge should improve writing (Calkins, 1986), and writing research supports that claim. Studies have shown that young writers who were more knowledgeable about their topic wrote better texts than did writers who were less knowledgeable (Langer, 1984; McCutchen, 1986). DeGroff (1987) linked topic knowledge to the quality of children's first drafts, as well as to their revision, finding that topic knowledge was especially important in children's ability to specify the nature of text problems during conferencing. We also examined the effects of topic knowledge in the revision study discussed previously (McCutchen et al., 1997). Participants revised two texts, one about Christopher Columbus (a familiar topic) and another about Margaret Mead (an unfamiliar topic). We found that both middle school and college students were more likely to detect and correct meaning-related problems with the familiar topic than the unfamiliar topic.

Topic knowledge contributes to writing quality even among high school and college students (Benton, Corkill, Sharp, Downey, & Khramtsova, 1995; Kellogg, 2001; Rowan, 1990; but see Kellogg, 1987a). Butterfield and his colleagues (1994) extended these findings to revision, documenting a positive relationship between adults' topic knowledge and their revising effectiveness.

Berninger, Fuller, and Whitaker (1996) documented the negative consequences of a lack of topic and genre knowledge in a study of graduate students working in a novel domain. Berninger et al. collected protocols as trainees in a school psychology program learned to write case reports, and they saw these relatively skilled writers resort to a linear writing process much like knowledge telling. As the trainees struggled to coordinate newly acquired knowledge (cognitive assessment) within a novel genre (the case report), many relied on the writing assignment to prompt step-by-step retrieval of relevant content. Thus, without the benefit of deep topic knowledge and a familiar genre, even skilled writers may resort to less mature strategies.

Long-Term Working-Memory Resources

Although distinctions between working memory and long-term memory are well recognized (e.g., Baddeley, 1998), the boundaries between them may not be as clear-cut as once imagined. Kintsch (1998) proposed an alternative account of the role of memory in complex real-world tasks, describing what he and Ericsson (Ericsson & Kintsch, 1995) called *long-term working memory* (LT-WM). Kintsch (1998) argued that a construct such as LT-WM is necessary to explain expertise in complex domains such as chess, medical diagnosis, and comprehension; and to that list we add the domain of writing (see also Kellogg, 2001; McCutchen, 2000).

According to Kintsch (1998), LT-WM comprises not only the limited number of elements activated in working memory as traditionally defined (what Kintsch called short-term working memory, or ST-WM), but also retrieval structures that link information in ST-WM to related elements in long-term memory (LTM). The items already activated within the capacity-limited ST-WM function as retrieval cues for those parts of LTM to which they relate. Thus, the information available in LT-WM is of two types: those items activated in ST-WM and relevant items in LTM reached via retrieval structures. The LTM elements are not actually stored within working memory, but they can be quickly retrieved whenever needed. Thus, LT-WM is an emergent feature of cognition resulting from an extensive knowledge base and efficient task-specific processing.

Unlike ST-WM, which has strict capacity limitations, the capacity of LT-WM is limited only by the nature of the encoding processes that build retrieval structures and by the extent of knowledge in LTM to which those structures relate. Kintsch's (1998) main focus was on comprehension, and in the case of comprehension, he characterized the encoding processes as the typical encoding processes of skilled comprehension (e.g., word recognition, syntactic parsing). In the case of writing, we suggest the encoding processes include fluent text production processes (text generation and transcription) operating in conjunction with relevant genre and topic knowledge. According to our view, emerging fluency in text production enables developing writers to begin to manage constraints imposed by ST-WM; and once text production becomes sufficiently fluent and knowledge bases sufficiently rich, writers can transcend the processing limits of ST-WM and capitalize on LT-WM. Fluent text production processes, combined with rich knowledge of genre and topic, enable skilled writers to link developing sentences to extensive knowledge stored in LTM. Thus, their sentence constructions (including word choice, syntax, semantic intent) can be influenced by earlier text choices (stored in an LTM text representation), by structural constraints for the chosen genre, by knowledge about a specific audience, and by knowledge about the general topic.

WRITING TO LEARN: COGNITIVE MECHANISMS AND RELATED EVIDENCE

Just as cognitive mechanisms play a role in learning to write, they also play a role in writing to learn. The cognitive processes described thus far may provide vehicles for students to synthesize new knowledge through the writing process itself. There have been several recent reviews of the writing-to-learn literature examining the evidence for claims that writing facilitates learning (Bangert-Drowns, Hurley, & Wilkinson, 2004, Bazerman et al., 2005; G. Newell, 2006), all documenting some positive effects on learning and many null results. Our goal in this section is not to reiterate the evidence evaluated in those or previous reviews (e.g., Ackerman, 1993). We adopt a goal more like that of Klein (1999), and we borrow the conceptual categories that he articulated; we are focused less on the question of under what conditions writing supports learning, and more on the question of, when writing does support learning, what cognitive mechanisms are theoretically involved.

As Ackerman (1993) noted, research designs in the writing-to-learn literature have varied considerably in their specification of what constitutes learning and the measures used to assess it. Consequently, activities examined in the writing-to-learn literature have run the gamut from informal (e.g., journaling, freewriting, electronic dialogues) to formal (e.g., analytic essays) writing events. These writing activities vary considerably, as do the cognitive mechanisms that would support their effects on learning.

The Role of Linguistic Expression

Most researchers source the contemporary writing-to-learn movement to discourse studies in the mid-1960s at the University of London done by Barnes, Britton, and Rosen (1969).

Britton's (1969) observation of knowledge construction during students' unstructured talk prompted him to theorize that unstructured writing, or *expressive* writing as he termed it, could also foster learning (Britton, 1970; Britton, Burgess, Martin, McLeod, & Rosen, 1975). According to Britton (1982), the act of specifying thoughts in language transforms otherwise tacit knowledge into explicit knowledge by "shaping [those thoughts] at the point of utterance."

Although Britton did not use such terminology, one might characterize the "shaping at the point of utterance" hypothesis as involving primarily interactions among the *proposer, translator,* and *transcriber,* to borrow the terminology of Chenoweth and Hayes (2001), with minimal intrusion from the *reviser.* Because the influence of writing on thought occurs in the act of expression according to Britton, too much self-monitoring and goal direction during writing can actually interfere with learning.

Some evidence in support of this view comes from research reported by Galbraith (1992, 1996). In studies of writers categorized as either high or low self-monitors, Galbraith found that low self-monitors reported more learning through writing (Galbraith, 1992) and generated more ideas when writing texts than when writing notes (Galbraith, 1996). Much other evidence offered in support of the "shaping at the point of utterance" hypothesis has been largely anecdotal (see Britton, 1970; Murray, 1978), and as Klein (1999) pointed out, the speech production literature does not provide much evidence of a feedback loop from lexical and syntactic levels back to the conceptual level.

Support From a Stable Text

Galbraith's (1992, 1996) theoretical stance on writing to learn extends beyond Britton's (1982) "shaping at the point of utterance" hypothesis to include also a role for the developing text in directing subsequent thought. Like previous researchers (e.g., Young & Sullivan, 1984), Galbraith argued that the relative permanence of the written text provides the writer an opportunity to return to ideas, develop and recombine ideas, and thereby create new understanding. In cognitive terms, the written text is presumed to extend the writer's working-memory capacity and provide grounds for further examination of current knowledge in long-term memory. Klein (1999) termed this theoretical perspective "forward search," suggesting that the written record of ideas within the text allows for examination of ideas that is not possible within the more temporary modality of speech.

The data Galbraith (1992, 1996) offered relating writers' dispositions toward self-monitoring with their perceived learning are as consistent with this theoretical account as with Britton's. Other data consistent with such a hypothesis come from the observation of Britton and his colleagues about the difficulties encountered in writing anything but the most straightforward text when they were unable to reread (Britton et al., 1975), a finding replicated with children in studies comparing texts dictated with and without written versions available for view (Quinlan, 2004; Reece & Cumming, 1996). In a study of children's learning in science, Klein (2000) documented that children's conceptual gains were related to the frequency with which they revisited the texts they had written about an experiment they had conducted. The evidence supporting this account of writing to learn is not extensive, but the inclusion of the written text as a source of feedback for the examination of knowledge solves the problem raised in relation to the "shaping at the point of utterance" hypothesis—that the speech production literature provides little evidence that lexical and syntactic choices flow backward to shape semantic intent. In the forward-search hypothesis, it is reexamination of the language of the text, not the initial linguistic formulation, that feeds back into conceptual considerations.

The Role of Genre

Although a number of genres have been advocated as ways to deepen learning (see Bazerman et al., 2005), the most compelling evidence is associated with analytic-essay writing. Theoretically, the genre of the text imposes a structure on the organization of ideas within the text, and when necessary, on the organization of knowledge itself. Such an account is consistent with an account of sophisticated writing processes that Bereiter and Scardamalia (1987) labeled *knowledge transformation,* during which rhetorical and content knowledge interact, leading to new understanding.

Langer and Applebee (1987) offered data indicating that writing analytic essays was more highly associated with student's meaning making and their engagement with ideas than were writing short answers to study questions or taking notes (see also Wiley & Voss, 1996). However, evidence on the effect of extended writing on simple *recall* of content is more mixed, as are results involving less structured genres (see Klein, 1999; G. Newell, 2006).

The Role of Goal Setting

As discussed previously, the model of sophisticated writing proposed by Hayes and Flower (1980) involves writers setting rhetorical goals and related subgoals that involve audience, personal voice, and text structure, all of which influence the generation of content to achieve those goals, often iteratively. Such a model suggests that there are goals and intentions that do not necessarily bubble up from the process of writing, but are known by the writer before the writing begins. Still, the iterative nature of goal satisfaction allows for the generation of ideas that were not part of the original plan for the text, leading Klein (1999) to refer to this and related theories under the label *backward search.* Indeed, it was the observation of writers' difficulties with neatly instantiating abstract plans within the specific constraints of language (recall the esters-and-aldehydes dilemma faced by the wine columnist) that prompted discussion of the limitations of characterizing writing as simply another instance of hierarchical planning and problem solving (McCutchen, 1984).

As Klein (1999) pointed out, there has been little explicit investigation of backward search as an account of writing to learn. Much of the data consistent with this view comes from protocol studies of expert writers at work (e.g., Flower & Hayes, 1980; Hayes & Flower, 1980). It is worth noting, however, that much of the evidence that supports the role of genre in fostering learning through writing is consistent with a view that incorporates text genre as one of several goals with which the writer begins.

CONCLUSION

Within this chapter, we have adopted a cognitive perspective and reviewed literature situated primarily within that theoretical frame. We have argued that writing, like other complex intellectual tasks, entails the coordination of multiple processes constrained by resource limitations in working memory and enhanced by relevant knowledge in long-term memory. We have described how task schemata direct the operation of cognitive processes involved in planning, text production, and revision. We have discussed how the cognitive architecture relates to the development of writing skill, arguing that as the processes of text production become more fluent, writers can transcend the limitations of working memory (traditionally defined) and recruit resources from long-term memory to support more sophisticated writing strategies. We have also explored how cognitive mechanisms might influence learning during writing.

Undoubtedly, writing also entails social and cultural aspects that go well beyond the focus of this chapter, and those topics are taken up elsewhere in this volume. Some researchers may even argue that cognitive accounts—rooted in problem-solving traditions and focused on the individual—cannot provide a complete description of a process so fundamentally social as writing (Cameron et al., 1996; Goldman, 1995; Klein, 1999). As Goldman pointed out, children's reliance on knowledge telling may be an adaptive response spawned as much by the social context of traditional classrooms as by working-memory limitations. When the teacher both determines the topic and serves as the sole audience for children's writing, it is logical for children to conclude the purpose of writing is something akin to knowledge telling. School contexts are so unlike the contexts in which experts write that when provided with typical school assignments, expert writers sometimes rebel (Freedman, 1984). Therefore, it should not surprise us that results from experiments (some of which also involve impoverished writing situations) indicate that children rarely employ expert writing processes.

Goldman (1995) warned of the dangers of the "expert trap" as a model of skill acquisition, a trap that inevitably casts the learner in terms of a deficit model. It was not our intention to characterize children's writing processes as deficient versions of expert processes, and this was the very trap that Bereiter and Scardamalia (1987) sought to avoid when they characterized knowledge telling as a process distinct from knowledge transformation, not necessarily a deficient version of it. Rather than standards that children fail to meet, we consider models of expert writing as indices of proximal development toward which we might scaffold children's writing (Vygotsky, 1978). For example, social aspects of expert writing are abundantly clear in cognitive models of expert performance: Expert writers develop models of their intended audience as part of planning, and they attend to possible interpretations of their audience as part of revising. Expert writing thus provides us with intuitions as to where we might most profitably invest efforts to support the development of writing skill, helping children develop the *intra*personal processes that characterize expert writing from their *inter*personal (i.e., social) experiences (e.g., Cameron et al., 1996).

Although we focused in this chapter on cognitive research, the study of writing is clearly cross-disciplinary. By their very nature, different disciplines have different canons of evidence, different questions of importance, and it is easy for researchers from different disciplines to talk past each other, never agreeing on the questions to ask or the methods to use. Although we have focused primarily on the cognitive literature in this chapter, the variety of disciplinary perspectives collected within this volume is an encouraging sign that writing is a phenomenon sufficiently robust to warrant—and even benefit from—multiple theoretical perspectives.

REFERENCES

Ackerman, J. M. (1993). The promise of writing to learn. *Written Communication, 10,* 334–370.

Alamargot, D., & Chanquoy, L. (Eds.). (2001). *Studies in writing: Vol. 9. Through the models of writing.* Boston: Kluwer.

Baddeley, A. D. (1998). *Human memory: Theory and practice.* New York: Allyn & Bacon.

Ball, A. F. (1992). Cultural preference and the expository writing of African-American adolescents. *Written Communication, 9,* 501–532.

Bangert-Drowns, R. L., Hurley, M. M., & Wilkinson, B. (2004). The effects of school-based writing-to-learn interventions on academic achievement: A meta-analysis. *Review of Educational Research, 74,* 29–58.

Barnes, D., Britton, J., & Rosen, H. (1969). *Language, the learner, and the school.* Harmondsworth, UK: Penguin.

Barton, E. L. (1995). Contrastive and non-contrastive connectives: Metadiscourse functions in argumentation. *Written Communication, 12,* 219–239.

Bazerman, C. (1984). Modern evolution of the experimental report in physics: Spectroscopic articles in *Physical Review,* 1893–1980. *Social Studies of Science, 14,* 163–196.

Bazerman, C., Little, J., Bethel, L., Charkin, T., Fouquette, D., & Ganufis, J. (2005). *Reference guide to writing across the curriculum.* West Lafayette, IN: Parlor.

Benton, S. L., Corkill, A. J., Sharp, J. M., Downey, R. G., & Khramtsova, I. (1995). Knowledge, interest, and narrative writing. *Journal of Educational Psychology, 87,* 66–79.

Bereiter, C., Burtis, P. J., & Scardamalia, M. (1988). Cognitive operations in constructing main points in written composition. *Journal of Memory and Language, 27,* 261–278.

Bereiter, C., & Scardamalia, M. (1987). *The psychology of written composition.* Hillsdale, NJ: Lawrence Erlbaum Associates.

Berninger, V. W., Fuller, F., & Whitaker, D. (1996). A process model of writing development. *Educational Psychology Review, 8,* 193–218.

Berninger, V. W., & Graham, S. (1998). Language by hand: A synthesis of a decade of research on handwriting. *Handwriting Review, 12,* 11–25.

Berninger, V. W., & Swanson, H. L. (1994). Modifying Hayes and Flower's model of skilled writing to explain beginning and developing writing. In J. S. Carlson (Series Ed.) & E. C. Butterfield (Vol. Ed.), *Advances in cognition and educational practice: Vol. 2. Children's writing: Toward a process theory of the development of skilled writing* (pp. 57–81). Greenwich, CT: JAI.

Berninger, V. W., Vaughan, K. B., Abbott, R. D., Abbott, S. P., Rogan, L. W., Brooks, A., et al. (1997). Treatment of handwriting problems in beginning writers: Transfer from handwriting to composition. *Journal of Educational Psychology, 89*, 652–666.

Boscolo, P., & Ascorti, K. (2004). Effects of collaborative revision on children's ability to write understandable narrative texts. In L. Allal, L. Chanquoy, & P. Largy (Eds.), *Studies in writing: Vol. 13. Revision: Cognitive and instructional processes* (pp. 157–172). Boston: Kluwer.

Bourdin, B., & Fayol, M. (1994). Is written language production more difficult than oral language production? A working memory approach. *International Journal of Psychology, 29*, 591–620.

Bourdin, B., Fayol, M., & Darciaux, S. (1996). The comparison of oral and written modes on adults' and children's narrative recall. In G. Rijlaarsdam, H. van den Bergh, & M. Couzijn (Eds.), *Studies in writing: Vol. 1. Theories, models, and methodology in writing research* (pp. 159–169). Amsterdam: Amsterdam University Press.

Breetvelt, I., van den Bergh, H., & Rijlaarsdam, G. (1996). Rereading and generating and their relation to text quality: An application of multi-level analysis ton writing process data. In G. Rijlaarsdam, H. van den Bergh, & M. Couzijn (Eds.), *Studies in writing: Vol. 1. Theories, models, and methodology in writing research* (pp. 10–21). Amsterdam: Amsterdam University Press.

Britton, J. (1969). Talking to learn. In Barnes, D., Britton, J., & Rosen, H. (Eds.), *Language, the learner and the school* (pp. 79–115). Harmondsworth, UK: Penguin.

Britton, J. (1970). *Language and learning*. London: Penguin.

Britton, J. (1982). Shaping at the point of utterance. In G. M. Prad (Ed.), *Prospect and retrospect: Selected esays of James Britton* (pp. 139–145). Montclair, NJ: Boynton/Cook.

Britton, J., Burgess, T., Martin, N., McLeod, A., & Rosen, H. (1975). *School councils research studies: The development of writing abilities*. London: Macmillan.

Butcher, K. R., & Kintsch, W. (2001). Support of content and rhetorical processes of writing: Effects on the written process and the written product. *Cognition and Instruction, 19*, 277–322.

Butterfield, E. C., Hacker, D. J., & Albertson, L. R. (1996). Environmental, cognitive, and metacognitive influences on text revision: Assessing the evidence. *Educational Psychology Review, 8*, 239–297.

Butterfield, E. C., Hacker, D. J., & Plumb, C. (1994). Topic knowledge, linguistic knowledge, and revision skill as determinants of text revision. In J. S. Carlson (Series Ed.) & E. C. Butterfield (Vol. Ed.), *Advances in cognition and educational practice: Vol. 2. Children's writing: Toward a process theory of the development of skilled writing* (pp. 83–141). Greenwich, CT: JAI.

Calkins, L. M. (1986). *The art of teaching writing*. Portsmouth, NH: Heinemann.

Cameron, C. A., Hunt, A. K., & Linton, M. (1996). Written expression in the primary classroom: Children write in social time. *Educational Psychology Review, 8*, 125–150.

Cameron, C. A., & Moshenko, B. (1996). Elicitation of knowledge transformational reports while children write narratives. *Canadian Journal of Behavioural Science, 28*, 271–280.

Cameron, C. A., & Wang, M. (1999). Frog, where are you? Children's narrative expression over the phone. *Discourse Processes, 28*, 217–236.

Chanquoy, L. (2001). How to make it easier for children to revise their writing: A study of text revision from 3rd to 5th grades. *British Journal of Educational Psychology, 71*, 15–41.

Chanquoy, L., Foulin, J. N., & Fayol, M. (1996). Writing in adults: A real-time approach. In G. Rijlaarsdam, H. van den Bergh, & M. Couzijn (Eds.), *Theories, models, and methodology in writing research* (pp. 36–43). Amsterdam: Amsterdam University Press.

Chanquoy, L., & Negro, I. (1996). Subject–verb agreement errors in written productions: A study of French children and adults. *Journal of Psycholinguistic Research, 25*, 553–570.

Chenoweth, N. A., & Hayes, J. R. (2001). Fluency in writing: Generating text in L1 and L2. *Written Communication, 18*, 80–98.

Cochran-Smith, M. (1991). Word processing and writing in elementary classrooms: A critical review of related literature. *Review of Educational Research, 61*, 107–155.

Collins, A., & Gentner, D. (1980). A framework for a cognitive theory of writing. In L. W. Gregg & E. R. Steinberg (Eds.), *Cognitive processes in writing* (pp. 51–72). Hillsdale, NJ: Lawrence Erlbaum Associates.

Cox, B. E., Shanahan, T., & Tinzmann, M. B. (1991). Children's knowledge of organization, cohesion, and voice in written exposition. *Research in the Teaching of English, 25*, 179–218.

Crammond, J. G. (1998). The uses and complexity of argument structures in expert and student persuasive writing. *Written Communication, 15*, 230–268.

Daiute, C. A. (1984). Performance limits on writers. In R. Beach & L. S. Bridwell (Eds.), *New directions in composition research* (pp. 205–224). New York: Guilford.

Daiute, C. A. (1986). Do 1 and 1 make 2? Patterns of influence by collaborative authors. *Written Communication, 3*, 382–408.

Daiute, C. A., & Dalton, B. (1993). Collaboration between children learning to write: Can novices be masters? *Cognition and Instruction, 10*, 281–333.

DeGroff, L. C. (1987). The influence of prior knowledge on writing, conferencing, and revising. *The Elementary School Journal, 88*, 105–116.

Dellerman, P., Coirier, P., & Marchand, E. (1996). Planning and expertise in argumentative composition. In G. Rijlaarsdam, H. van den Bergh, & M. Couzijn (Eds.), *Theories, models, and methodology in writing research* (pp. 182–195). Amsterdam: Amsterdam University Press.

Dunn, B., & Reay, D. (1989). Word processing and the keyboard: Comparative effects of transcription on achievement. *Journal of Educational Research, 82*, 237–245.

Englert, C. S., Stewart, S. R., & Hiebert, E. H. (1988). Young writer's use of text structure in expository text generation. *Journal of Educational Psychology, 80*, 143–151.

Ericsson, K. A., & Kintsch, W. (1995). Long-term working memory. *Psychological Review, 102*, 211–245.

Faigley, L., & Witte, S. (1981). Analyzing revision. *College Composition and Communication, 32*, 400–414.

Fayol, M., Largy, P., & Lemaire, P. (1994). Cognitive overload and orthographic errors: When cognitive overload enhances subject–verb agreement errors, a study in French written language. *Quarterly Journal of Experimental Psychology, 47*, 437–464.

Fitzgerald, J. (1987). Research on revision in writing. *Review of Educational Research, 57*, 481–506.

Fitzgerald, J., & Teasley, A. B. (1986). Effects of instruction in narrative structure on children's writing. *Journal of Educational Psychology, 78*, 424–432.

Flower, L. (1979). Writer-based prose: A cognitive basis for problems in writing. *College English, 41*, 19–37.

Flower, L., & Hayes, J. R. (1980). The dynamics of composing: Making plans and juggling constraints. In L. W. Gregg & E. R. Steinberg (Eds.), *Cognitive processes in writing* (pp. 31–50). Hillsdale, NJ: Lawrence Erlbaum Associates.

Flower, L. & Hayes, J. R. (1981). The pregnant pause: An inquiry into the nature of planning. *Research in the Teaching of English, 15*, 229–248.

Flower, L., & Hayes, J. R. (1984). Images, plans and prose: The representation of meaning in writing. *Written Communication, 1*, 120–160.

Freedman, S. W. (1984). The registers of student and professional expository writing: Influences on teacher responses. In R. Beach & L. S. Bridwell (Eds.), *New directions in composition research* (pp. 334–347). New York: Guilford.

Galbraith, D. (1992). Conditions for discovery through writing. *Instructional Science, 21*, 45–72.

Galbraith, D. (1996). Self-monitoring, discovery through writing and individual differences in drafting strategy. In G. Rijlaarsdam, H. van den Bergh, & M. Couzijn (Eds.), *Theories, models, and methodology in writing research* (pp. 121–141). Amsterdam: Amsterdam University Press.

Goldman, S. R. (1995). Writing as a tool for thinking and reasoning. *Issues in Education: Contribution From Educational Psychology, 1*, 199–204.

Gould, J. D. (1980). Experiments on composing letters: Some facts, some myths, and some observations. In L. W. Gregg & E. R. Steinberg (Eds.), *Cognitive processes in writing* (pp. 97–127). Hillsdale, NJ: Lawrence Erlbaum Associates.

Grabowski, J., Vorwerg, C., & Rummer, R. (1994). Writing as a tool for control of episodic representation. In G. Eigler & T. Jechle (Eds.), *Writing: Current trends in European research* (pp. 55–68). Freiburg, Germany: Hochschul Verlag.

Graham, S. (1990). The role of production factors in learning disabled students' compositions. *Journal of Educational Psychology, 82*, 781–791.

Graham, S., Berninger, V., Abbott, R., Abbott, S., & Whitaker, D. (1997). The role of mechanics in composing of elementary school students: A new methodological approach. *Journal of Educational Psychology, 89*, 170–182.

Graham, S., Harris, K. R., & Fink, B. (2000). Is handwriting causally related to learning to write? Treatment of handwriting problems in beginning writers. *Journal of Educational Psychology, 92*, 620–633.

Graham, S., MacArthur, C., & Schwartz, S. (1995). Effects of goal setting and procedural facilitation on the revising behavior and writing performance of students with writing and learning problems. *Journal of Educational Psychology, 87*, 230–240.

Graves, D. H. (1983). *Writing: Teachers & children at work*. Exeter, NH: Heinemann.

Hayes, J. R. (1981). *The complete problem solver*. Philadelphia: Franklin Press Institute.

Hayes, J. R. (1996). A new framework for understanding cognition and affect in writing. In C. M. Levy & S. Ransdell (Eds.), *The science of writing* (pp. 1–27). Mahwah, NJ: Lawrence Erlbaum Associates.

Hayes, J. R. (2004). What triggers revision? In L. Allal, L. Chanquoy, & P. Largy (Eds.), *Studies in writing: Vol. 13. Revision: Cognitive and instructional processes* (pp. 9–20). Boston: Kluwer.

Hayes, J. R., & Flower, L. S. (1980). Identifying the organization of writing processes. In L. W. Gregg & E. R. Steinberg (Eds.), *Cognitive processes in writing* (pp. 3–30). Hillsdale, NJ: Lawrence Erlbaum Associates.

Hayes, J. R., Flower, L. S., Schriver, K. A., Stratman, J. F., & Carey, L. (1987). Cognitive processes in revision. In S. Rosenberg (Ed.), *Advances in applied psycholinguistics: Vol. 2. Reading, writing, and language learning* (pp. 176–241). New York: Cambridge University Press.

Hayes, J. R., & Nash, J. G. (1996). On the nature of planning in writing. In C. M. Levy & S. Ransdell (Eds.), *The science of writing* (pp. 29–55). Mahwah, NJ: Lawrence Erlbaum Associates.

Hayes-Roth, B., & Hayes-Roth, F. (1979). A cognitive model of planning. *Cognitive Science, 3*, 275–310.

Hoskyn, M., & Swanson, H. L. (2003). The relationship between working memory and writing in younger and older adults. *Reading and Writing: An Interdisciplinary Journal, 16*, 759–784.

Jeffrey, G. C., & Underwood, G. (1996). The role of working memory in the development of writing skill: Learning to coordinate ideas within sentences. In G. Rijlaarsdam, H. van den Bergh, & M. Couzijn (Eds.). *Theories, models, and methodology in writing research* (pp. 268–282). Amsterdam: Amsterdam University Press.

Kaufer, D. S., Hayes, J. R., & Flower, L. (1986). Composing written sentences. *Research in the Teaching of English, 20*, 121–140.

Kellogg, R. T. (1987a). Effects of topic knowledge on the allocation of processing time and cognitive effort to writing processes. *Memory & Cognition, 15*, 256–266.

Kellogg, R. T. (1987b). Writing performance: Effects of cognitive strategies. *Written Communication, 4*, 269–298.

Kellogg, R. T. (1988). Attentional overload and writing performance: Effects of rough draft and outline strategies. *Journal of Experimental Psychology: Learning, Memory and Cognition, 14*, 355–365.

Kellogg, R. T., (1994) *The psychology of writing*. New York: Orford University Press.

Kellogg, R. T. (1996). A model of working memory in writing. In C. M. Levy & S. Ransdell (Eds.), *The science of writing* (pp. 57–71). Mahwah, NJ: Lawrence Erlbaum Associates.

Kintsch, W. (1998). *Comprehension: A paradigm for cognition*. New York: Cambridge University Press.

Kellogg, R. T. (2001). Long-term working memory in text production. *Memory & Cognition, 29*, 43–52.

Klein, P. (1999). Reopening inquiry into cognitive processes in writing-to-learn. *Educational Psychology Review, 2*, 203–270.

Klein, P. (2000). Elementary students' strategies for writing-to-learn in science. *Cognition and Instruction, 18*, 317–348.

Langer, J. A. (1984). The effects of available information on responses to school writing tasks. *Research in the Teaching of English, 18*, 27–44.

Langer, J. A. (1986). *Children reading and writing: Structures and strategies*. Norwood, NJ: Ablex.

Langer, J. A. (1992). Speaking and knowing: Conceptions of understanding in academic disciplines. In A. Herrington & C. Moran (Eds.), *Writing, teaching, and learning in the disciplines* (pp. 68–85). New York: Modern Language Association.

Langer, J. A., & Applebee, A. N. (1987). *How writing shapes thinking: A study of teaching and learning*. Urbana, IL: National Council of Teachers of English.

Larkin, J. H., McDermott, S., Dorthea P., & Simon, H. A. (1980). Models of competence in solving physics problems. *Cognitive Science, 4*, 317–345.

Lee, K., Karmiloff-Smith, A., Cameron, C. A., & Dodsworth, P. (1998). Notational adaptation in children. *Canadian Journal of Behavioural Science, 30*, 159–171.

Levy, C. M., & Ransdell, S. (1995). Is writing as difficult as it seems? *Memory & Cognition, 23*, 767–779.

Littleton, E. B. (1998). Emerging cognitive skills for writing: Sensitivity to audience presence in five- through nine-year-olds' speech. *Cognition and Instruction, 16*, 399–430.

MacArthur, C. A., & Cavalier, A. R. (2004). Dictation and speech recognition technology as test accommodations. *Exceptional Children, 71*, 43–58.

MacDonald, S. P. (1992) A method for analyzing sentence - level differences in disciplinary knowledge making. *Written Communication, 9*, 533–569.

Marchand, E., Coirier, P., & Dellerman, P. (1996). Textualization and polyphony in argumentative composition. In G. Rijlaarsdam, H. van den Bergh, & M. Couzijn (Eds.), *Theories, models, and methodology in writing research* (pp. 366–380). Amsterdam: Amsterdam University Press.

McCutchen, D. (1984). Writing as a linguistic problem. *Educational Psychologist, 19*, 226–238.

McCutchen, D. (1986). Domain knowledge and linguistic knowledge in the development of writing ability. *Journal of Memory and Language, 25*, 431–444.

McCutchen, D. (1987). Children's discourse skill: Form and modality requirements of schooled writing. *Discourse Processes, 10*, 267–286.

McCutchen, D. (1988). "Functional automaticity" in children's writing: A problem of metacognitive control. *Written Communication, 5*, 306–324.

McCutchen, D. (1996). A capacity theory of writing: working memory in composition. *Educational psychology Review, 8*, 299–324.

McCutchen, D. (2000). Knowledge acquisition, processing efficiency, and working memory: Implications for a theory of writing. *Educational Psychologist, 35*, 13–23.

McCutchen, D., Covill, A., Hoyne, S. H., & Mildes, K. (1994). Individual differences in writing: Implications of translating fluency. *Journal of Educational Psychology, 86*, 256–266.

McCutchen, D., Francis, M., & Kerr, S. (1997). Revising for meaning: Effects of knowledge and strategy. *Journal of Educational Psychology, 89*, 667–676.

Meyer, B. J. F., Brandt, D. M., & Bluth, G. J. (1980). Use of top-level structure in text: Key for reading comprehension of ninth grade students. *Reading Research Quarterly, 16*, 72–103.

Meyer, B. J. F., & Poon, L. W. (2001). Effects of structure strategy training and signaling on recall of text. *Journal of Educational Psychology, 93*, 141–159.

Murray, D. M. (1978). Internal revision: A process of discovery. In C. R. Cooper & L. Odell (Eds.) *Research on composing: Points of departure.* (pp. 85–103). Urbana, IL: National Council of Teachers of English.

Myers, G. (1985). Text as knowledge claims: The social construction of two biologists' proposals. *Written Communication, 2*, 219–245.

Newell, A., & Simon, H. (1972). *Human problem solving.* Englewood Cliffs, NJ: Prentice-Hall.

Newell, G. E. (2006). Writing to learn: How alternative theories of school writing account for student performance. In C. A. MacArthur, S. Graham, & J. Fitzgerald (Eds.), *Handbook of writing research* (pp. 235–247). New York: Guilford.

Nystrand, M. (2006). The social and historical context for writing research. In C. A. MacArthur, S. Graham, & J. Fitzgerald (Eds.), *Handbook of writing research* (pp. 11–27). New York: Guilford.

Olive, T., & Kellogg, R. T. (2002). Concurrent activation of high- and low-level production processing in written composition. *Memory & Cognition, 30*, 594–600.

Piolat, A., Roussey, J.-Y., Olive, T., & Amada, M.. (2003). Processing time and cognitive effort in revision: Effects of error type and of working memory capacity. In L. Allal, L. Chanquoy, & P. Largy (Eds.), *Studies in writing: Vol. 13. Revision: Cognitive and instructional processes* (pp. 21–38). Norwell, MA: Kluwer Academic.

Quinlan, T. (2004). Speech recognition technology and students with writing difficulties: Improving fluency. *Journal of Educational Psychology, 96*, 337–346.

Ransdell, S., & Levy, C. M. (1996). Working memory constraints on writing quality and fluency. In C. M. Levy & S. Ransdell (Eds.), *The science of writing* (pp. 93–105). Mahwah, NJ: Lawrence Erlbaum Associates.

Reece, J. E., & Cumming, G. (1996). Evaluating speech-based composition methods: Planning, dictation and the listening word processor. In M. C. Levy & S. Ransdell (Eds.), *The science of writing* (pp. 361–380). Mahwah, NJ: Lawrence Erlbaum Associates.

Rijlaarsdam, G., & van den Bergh, H. (2006). Writing process theory: A functional dynamic approach. In C. A. MacArthur, S. Graham, & J. Fitzgerald (Eds.), *Handbook of writing research* (pp. 41–53). New York: Guilford.

Rowan, K. E. (1990). Cognitive correlates of explanatory writing skill: An analysis of individual differences. *Written Communication, 7*, 316–341.

Scheuer, N., de la Cruz, M., Pozo, J. I., Huarte, M. F., & Sola, G. (2006). The mind is not a black box: Children's ideas about the writing process. *Learning and Instruction, 16*, 72–85.

Schilperoord, J. (1996). The distribution of pause time in written text production. In G. Rijlaarsdam, H. van den Bergh, & M. Couzijn (Eds.), *Theories, models, and methodology in writing research* (pp. 21–40). Amsterdam: Amsterdam University Press.

Stein, N. L., & Glenn, C. G. (1979). An analysis of story comprehension in elementary school children. In R. O. Freedle (Ed.), *Advances in discourse processing: Vol. 2. New directions in discourse processing* (pp. 53–120). Norwood, NJ: Ablex.

Stockton, S. (1995). Writing in history: Narrating the subject of time. *Written Communication, 12*, 47–73.

Sulzby, E. (1985). Kindergarteners as writers and readers. In M. Farr (Ed.), *Advances in writing research: Vol 1. Children's early writing development* (pp. 127–199). Norwood, NJ: Ablex.

Sulzby, E., & Teale, W. (1987). *Young children's storybook reading: Longitudinal study of parent child interactions and children's independent functioning* (Final Report to Spencer Foundation). Ann Arbor: University of Michigan Press.

Torrance, M. (1996a). Is writing expertise like other kinds of expertise? In G. Rijlaarsdam, H. van den Bergh, & M. Couzijn (Eds.), *Theories, models, and methodology in writing research* (pp. 3–9). Amsterdam: Amsterdam University Press.

Torrance, M. (1996b). Strategies for familiar writing tasks: Case studies of undergraduates. In G. Rijlaarsdam, H. van den Bergh, & M. Couzijn (Eds.), *Theories, models, and methodology in writing research* (pp. 283–298). Amsterdam: Amsterdam University Press.

Van de Kopple, W. J. (1998). Relative clauses in spectroscopic articles in the *Physical Review*, beginnings and 1980: Some changes in patterns of modification and a connection to possible shifts in style. *Written Communication, 15,* 170–202.

Vygotsky, L. (1978). *Mind in society: The development of of higher psychological processes* (M. Cole, V. John-Steiner, S. Scribner, & E. Souberman, Trans.). Cambridge, MA: Harvard University Press.

Wallace, D. L., & Hayes, J. R. (1991). Redefining revision for freshmen. *Research in the Teaching of English, 25,* 54–66.

Wallace, D. L., Hayes, J. R., Hatch, J. A., Miller, W., Moser, G., & Silk, C. M. (1996). Better revision in 8 minutes? Prompting first-year college writers to revise more globally. *Journal of Educational Psychology, 85,* 682–688.

Wiley, J., & Voss, J. F. (1996). The effects of "playing historian" on learning in history. *Applied Cognitive Psychology, 10,* S63–S72.

Wright, R. E., & Rosenberg, S. (1993). Knowledge of text coherence and expository writing: A developmental study. *Journal of Educational Psychology, 85,* 152–158.

Young, R., & Becker, A. (1965). Toward a modern theory of rhetoric: A tagmemic contribution. *Harvard Educational Review, 35,* 450–468.

Young, R., & Sullivan, P. (1984). Why write? A reconsideration. In R. J. Conners, L. S. Ede, & A. A. Lundsford (Eds.), *Essays on classical rhetoric and modern discourse* (pp. 215–225). Carbondale: Southern Illinois University Press.

CHAPTER 29

Writing and Communication Disorders Across the Life Span

Julie A. Hengst
Cynthia J. Johnson
University of Illinois, Urbana-Champaign

Viewing writing from the perspective of communication disorders highlights the intersections among physical, physiological, cognitive, linguistic, behavioral, and social dimensions of writing. Broadly, the field distinguishes between communication disorders that are acquired and those that are developmental. Research on *acquired communication disorders* addresses disruptions brought on by physiological or neurological damage (e.g., stroke, head injury, degenerative neurological diseases, head and neck cancer) and attends primarily to disorders acquired in adults. This research has been dominated by medical models and has focused on differential diagnosis among, and clinical interventions for, particular communication disorders (e.g., dysarthria, aphasia). In contrast, research on *developmental communication disorders* focuses on disruptions in children's developing language, learning, and communication abilities, including those with known causes (e.g., cerebral palsy, fetal alcohol syndrome) and those with as of yet unknown causes (e.g., autism, specific language impairment). Influenced by developmental psychology and education, research on developmental disorders documents deficits relative to typically developing children in early childhood (e.g., delays in attaining developmental milestones such as first words) and during the school years (e.g., delays in grade-level performance). In this chapter, we organize our review of research on writing and communication disorders around these two broad areas, looking first at acquired writing disorders and then at developmental writing disorders. In addition, we briefly review research on textually mediated augmentative and alternative approaches to spoken language for individuals with the most profound communication disorders.

WRITING AND ACQUIRED COMMUNICATION DISORDERS

Disruption or loss of an individual's ability to write as a direct result of brain damage is referred to as *dysgraphia* or *agraphia*. Much of the current research on dysgraphia has grown out of the 19th-century tradition of clinical neurological case studies, which involved correlating careful documentation of an individual patient's clinical symptoms with locations of brain damage, or *lesions* (see Benson, 1979). From this perspective, language is understood as a product of underlying physiological processes located in particular neurological structures, and thus, disruptions in language use (e.g., naming, repetition, understanding) across different modalities (e.g., spoken, written, reading, auditory comprehension) are interpreted as a direct reflection of differential damage to the neurological structures that house those processes. Although not without controversy, this line of research has documented relatively consistent neuroanatomical correlations for disruptions in spoken and auditory language modalities, supporting theories that localize specific language functions in the brain, and yielding clinically useful classifications for different types of *aphasia* (Benson, 1994). However, attempts to localize a writing center (or centers) based on neuroanatomical correlations with writing disturbances have not been as successful (Basso, 2003; Benson, 1979; Tseng & McNeil, 1997). Thus, dysgraphia has not emerged as a useful tool in the broader project of mapping particular functions onto specific areas of the brain, which, at least in part, helps to explain a relative lack of research interest into acquired writing disorders. The work that has been done has yielded better understandings of the impacts that neurological damage can have on an individual's ability to write and has begun to point to clinical interventions to support the (re)development of writing.

Documenting the Features of Acquired Dysgraphia

Focusing on writing as an ensemble of different brain functions, researchers adopted procedures for collecting multiple writing samples that would place different demands on the patient's production of written texts. Benson (1979), for example, outlined the following written samples that should be obtained: *automatic writing*—such as, patient signature, address; *copying*—including, meaningful and nonmeaningful material; *writing to dictation*—including, words and sentences; and *narrative or extended writing*—such as, description of the weather, picture description. The writing samples could then be analyzed for the quality and accuracy of both mechanical and linguistic elements, including: *handwriting*—including, completeness, size and neatness of letters, use of block or cursive script; *visual spatial attributes*— including, normal and consistent margins; consistent horizontal lines and vertical spacing; *spelling*— such as, letter substitutions, deletions, reversals; and, *word choice*—such as, semantic and syntactic errors.

Clinically, it is common for writing samples of individuals with acquired dysgraphia to display disruptions in both mechanical and linguistic elements. Disruptions to the linguistic elements of writing are routinely observed to co-occur with, and often assumed to be a symptom of, aphasia. Indeed, Benson (1979) claimed that "every individual with aphasia will show at least some degree of agraphia" (p. 121), and the linguistic deficits in writing will be generally consistent with those of the patient's spoken language (Benson, 1994). For example, patients with an *anterior nonfluent aphasia* will produce writing samples marked by sparse output, frequent phonetic spelling errors, and agrammatic or telegraphic phrases and sentences, whereas individuals with a *posterior fluent aphasia* will produce writing samples marked by omissions, reversals, and substitutions of letters, word choice errors, and grammatical or word-ordering errors. Disruptions to the mechanical elements are usually associated with disruptions in sensory or motor systems and frequently occur without an accompanying aphasia. For example, writing samples of patients with *left visual neglect* (common with lesions in the right hemisphere) may display a lack of attention to, or neglect of, the left side of the text. Thus, left margins may be large whereas right margins are small or absent; letters or words may have extra right-sided strokes whereas the dots on *i* and crosses on *t* may be missing; words, letters, and details on the left side of texts or drawings may be missing or incomplete (Benson, 1979; Myers, 1997). Individuals with reduced amplitude of movements (i.e., *hypokinesia*), typical of Parkinson's disease, often display excessively small script, referred to as *micrographia* (see Oliveira, Gurd, Nixon, Marshall, & Passingham, 1997). Although controversial, a pure motor, or *apraxic*, dysgraphia has also been proposed (e.g., Barriere & Lorch, 2003) in which motor programming specific to writing is selectively impaired. In the few documented cases, patients with normal auditory comprehension, spoken language, and reading had difficulty forming letters. The deficits can be so severe that patients are unable to write at all. In contrast, the differential sparing of writing in the face of disruptions to other modalities has also been documented. Perhaps the most striking example is *alexia without agraphia* in which patients have preserved abilities to produce and understand spoken language and can write normally, but have great difficulty reading. In severe cases, such patients display difficulty copying text and, often within moments of writing, are unable to read back what they have just written (Benson, 1979).

Researchers have argued that combining cognitivist approaches with neurological case studies will strengthen models of cognitive linguistic processes by holding cognitive science accountable to the anatomical and physiological understandings of the brain that have grown over the past two centuries (Lecours, 1999), and may further contribute to our understandings of the neural substrates of language (Balasubramanian, 2005). In the last few decades, cognitive models of writing have been used to theorize and assess acquired dysgraphia by using word- and spelling-level tasks designed to differentiate which underlying processes are impaired (Basso, 2003; Beeson, Rapcsak, Plante, Johnson, & Trouard, 2003). Researchers have posited distinct lexical and nonlexical (phonologic) cognitive routes for writing production, and identified three types of dysgraphia on these bases. With *lexical (or surface) dysgraphia,* patients can write to dictation nonwords and real words that conform to regular sound–letter correspondence rules, but make many plausible phonological errors in their attempts to write words with irregular spellings. On the other hand, with *phonological dysgraphia* patients are able to accurately write familiar irregular words, but cannot write nonwords that follow regular sound–letter correspondence rules. Finally, patients with *deep dysgraphia* evidence disruptions in both the lexical and nonlexical production routes. Whereas these cognitive models have in effect operationalized writing as transcription of language into alphabetic forms, a few researchers (influenced by clinical goals) have begun to describe disruptions in writing associated with higher order cognitive processes such as memory and executive functioning. In a longitudinal study of two individuals with Alzheimer's disease, researchers (Hillis, Benzing, & Lyketsos, 1995) found that patients' performance on spelling tasks deteriorated along with the more general cognitive decline associated with the disease. In another study, researchers (Wilson & Proctor, 2002) investigated the written discourse production of eight adolescents with deficits in memory, organization, and problem solving associated with brain damaged caused by a blow to the head, or a *closed head injury* (CHI). Comparing written picture descriptions of students with CHI to those of non-brain-damaged peers, researchers argued that texts produced by CHI students displayed planning and organizational deficits (e.g., repetitive and inaccurate sentences, poor use of cohesive ties) consistent with their cognitive deficits.

Intervention for Acquired Dysgraphia

In general, intervention for dysgraphia has been consistent with approaches used for aphasia more broadly (see Basso, 2003). Traditionally, aphasia therapy is provided on a one-to-one basis in clinical settings and is designed to target specific areas of deficit through drill-like activities presented in a series of increasingly more difficult or demanding tasks. Published studies on intervention for dysgraphia include detailed case reports of treatment programs (e.g., Robson, Pring, Marshall, Morrison, & Chiat, 1998), single-subject research designs (e.g., Beeson, 2002), and a few small-group experimental designs (e.g., Pizzamiglio & Roberts, 1967).

A recent line of writing intervention studies has focused on treating patients with chronic (e.g., often several years post brain injury) and severe aphasia (Alimonosa, McCloskey, Goodman-Schulman, & Sokol, 1993; Beeson, 1999, 2003; Clausen & Beeson, 2003; De Partz, 1995; Hillis, 1998; Jackson-Waite, Robson, & Pring, 2003; Murray & Karcher, 2000; Robson et al., 1998). Across these studies, patients showed improvements on word-level writing in direct response to treatment despite the prolonged and severe nature of their deficits. In some cases, the rationale for targeting writing in patients with such severe communication disorders was to stabilize a core set of written words that could be used to augment or support face-to-face communicative contexts (Beeson, 1999; Clausen & Beeson, 2003; Murray & Karcher, 2000; Robson et al., 1998). Despite some generalization from writing to spoken naming (Murray & Karcher, 2000), patients did not automatically transfer their success on word- and sentence-level writing tasks to use of writing in face-to-face communication. Researchers found that it was necessary, and effective, to directly teach the subjects to use their new (or renewed) writing skills functionally in conversational interactions (Robson et al., 1998; Beeson, 1999).

A few case studies have explored the use of technological supports to bypass specific writing deficits. For example, two case studies report successful use of voice recognition software (e.g., Bruce, Edmundson, & Coleman, 2003) and auditory feedback and word prediction software (e.g., Armstrong & MacDonald, 2000) for patients with chronic aphasia and dysgraphia to facilitate their everyday writing on computers (e.g., using e-mail). In addition to training technical use of the software and creating writing opportunities, the patient using the voice recognition software also needed direct instruction to develop a discourse style that supported speaking-to-write (e.g., preplanning and using templates to organize his dictated writing, listening back to and editing what he had just dictated). In both studies, the patients continued using the software after therapy ended (e.g., one client bought a computer and software to use at home) and expanded their everyday writing to meet new and personally meaningful goals (e.g., keeping a journal, writing stories).

A few researchers (Mortensen, 2004; Parr, 1996; Sohlberg, Ehlhardt, Fickas, & Sutcliffe, 2003) have argued for treating writing disorders in context by supporting clients to develop and use everyday writing practices. For example, Sohlberg and colleagues, using a participatory action research design, included their eight subjects in the development of specialized e-mail software designed to support both accessing and message construction, and then worked with them to implement a training program to support their use of e-mail as a means of maintaining social contact with family and friends. Using ethnographic methods, Parr (1992, 1994) documented the diverse everyday literate activities of adults and argued that choices to participate in particular activities were not simply a reflection of abilities—that is, participants with and without aphasia frequently did not participate in all possible activities. Drawing on Street's (1984) distinction between *autonomous* (i.e., socially neutral collection of measurable technical skills) and *social* (i.e., cultural practices) models of literacy, Parr (1995) juxtaposed autonomous and social assessments of literacy in aphasia and found that these two assessments could not be easily correlated. Indeed, specific linguistic impairments affecting writing could be masked in social literacy practices, and the problems patients had with literate activities could not be fully predicted by linguistic accounts of their dysgraphia. In addition, Parr argued that the functional improvements in literacy practices seen in adults with aphasia were often dependent on changes in their social roles, not simply on improvements in autonomous skills.

DEVELOPMENTAL DISORDERS AND WRITING

Language and learning disorders in childhood are often first identified by delays or disruptions in the typical developmental trajectories of language use, spoken and written. Children identified with learning disabilities (LD) may have problems with word recognition, such as dyslexia (e.g., Catts & Kamhi, 2005), as well as with writing (Nelson, Bahr, & Van Meter, 2004; Scott, 2005), and may present with writing disorders in later elementary school even without a history of other developmental or language disorders. Children identified with *specific language impairment* (SLI) (Leonard, 1998; Plante, 1998) can be identified as young as 2 years old, and may have deficits in many aspects of spoken language (e.g., vocabulary and concepts; word morphology and grammar; pragmatics and discourse such as storytelling and conversation; production and awareness of speech sounds) despite the absence of cognitive, neurological, sensory (e.g., hearing loss), or socioemotional (e.g., autism) disorders.

The bulk of the research on writing disorders in childhood has looked at elementary school children with LD, whereas very few studies have addressed writing in children with SLI. Many researchers (e.g., Flax et al., 2003; Nelson et al., 2004; Scott, 2002) argue that with respect to literacy there is substantial overlap between the SLI and LD populations, and that studies on LD often include children with concomitant language impairments (MacArthur, 2000). Therefore, given the questionable value of trying to differentiate writing disorders based on these two populations, in the following discussion we have integrated these two literatures in order to present a more general review of the research on childhood writing disorders (WD), looking first at research that primarily describes the features of childhood WD and then at research addressing intervention and teaching strategies designed to meet the needs of children with WD.

Describing Childhood Writing Disorders

Research comparing children with WD to their typically developing (TD) peers has consistently documented that children with WD display a wide range of deficits at every level, including handwriting and spelling; punctuation and capitalization; lexical, syntactic, and discourse features; and composition processes (for detailed reviews, see Graham & Harris, 2002; Nelson et al., 2004; Scott, 2002, 2004, 2005; Singer & Bashir, 2004). Over the last two decades, this research has been shifting from product-based to process-based analysis (Wong, 2000). However, due in part to the more linguistic nature of SLI, research focusing on children with SLI/WD continues to place an emphasis on linguistic components of texts (e.g., Fey, Catts, Proctor-Williams, Tomblin, & Zhang, 2004; Rubin, Patterson, & Kantor, 1991), often comparing spoken and written productions. In addition, group studies of SLI/WD often select control groups from TD children who match the WD children's spoken language ability (language-age, or LA, peers) instead of their chronological age or grade level. Using this approach, several studies (Gillam & Johnston, 1992; Mackie & Dockrell, 2004; McFadden & Gillam, 1996; Scott & Windsor, 2000; Windsor, Scott, & Street, 2000) have shown that for a number of product-oriented weaknesses (e.g., spelling, prepositions, pronouns, auxiliary verbs, grammatical morphemes, complex sentences), children with SLI/WD not only performed worse than their TD peers, but also worse than their LA peers. These researchers argue that such findings suggest that children with WD are not simply slow at developing writing skills, but may also be following different developmental trajectories.

Research has also compared the quantity of writing produced by children with WD and their TD peers, as well as the ease with which they produce written texts. Consistently, children with WD are found to write shorter texts, produce fewer words per minute, and take longer to finish a composition (Mackie & Dockrell, 2004; Scott & Windsor, 2000; Wong, 2000). In addition, parents of children with SLI report that, even during the preschool years, their children do not create as many written products per week or day, whether drawing pictures, writing letters of the alphabet, or writing words (Boudreau, 2005). Researchers who have reported observations of children's self-talk during writing tasks argue that due to their struggles with writing mechanics (i.e., handwriting, spelling) children with WD often greatly dislike writing and actively avoid it (Berninger, 2000; Graham & Harris, 1999; MacArthur, 2000; Ukrainetz, 1998). Consequently, children with WD have less practice and experience with writing than TD peers (Christenson, Thurlow, Ysseldyke, & McVicar, 1989; Graham & Harris, 2002; MacArthur, 2000). The implications of such findings are provocative, suggesting that these product- and process-based weaknesses might be accounted for, at least in part, by the lack of writing experience children with WD have, as well as by any specific linguistic or cognitive deficits.

Intervention for Childhood Writing Disorders

Writing process research was quickly extended to intervention, as researchers adapted and applied relatively well-recognized teaching strategies to address deficits displayed by children with WD (Wong, 2000). Much of the intervention research has focused on identifying effective classroom-based interventions for children with WD and has found that many of these children are able to improve their writing with process-targeted teaching and support. For example, one line of research has shown that for younger (e.g., first grade) children improving the automaticity of handwriting and spelling (through a variety of teaching strategies) often results in more fluent text generation and longer compositions (Berninger, 2000; Berniger et al., 1997, 1998; Graham & Harris, 2002; D. Jones & Christensen, 1999). Other researchers, drawing on *topoi* or heuristics (e.g., who, what, where, when) and scaffolded cuing strategies, have developed strategies and mnemonics that older (e.g., fourth through eighth grade) children with WD can learn to use to guide themselves through the planning, writing, and revising processes (see Bereiter & Scardamalia, 1987). Graham and colleagues (Berninger, 2000; Graham & Harris, 1999; Graham, Harris, & Troia, 2000; Singer & Bashir, 2004; Wong, 2000) have explored the use of such self-regulation strategies for older children with LD/WD. In comparison with control groups, this approach has been found effective in increasing children's engagement in the planning and revision processes and improving the length, completeness, logic, and quality of their texts.

Consistent with whole-language approaches to literacy, researchers have also explored interventions that bypass handwriting altogether, allowing children to engage in writing activities despite their deficits. For example, in one study fifth-, sixth-, and seventh-grade students with WD were taught to plan and write argument essays (De La Paz & Graham, 1997). Students were instructed to either write by hand or dictate their compositions. Students who planned and dictated their essays produced texts that were more than double the length of essays handwritten by a control group without training in planning. These dictated essays were judged to be higher in quality and more complete and coherent as well. In another study, dictated stories were composed 20 times and 9 times faster than typed or handwritten ones, respectively (MacArthur & Graham, 1987; Scott, 2005). In an interesting approach designed to bypass handwriting deficits in younger children, Ukrainetz (1998) taught second graders with WD to use pictography or "stick writing" to group and order their ideas as they drafted texts. Instead of writing words, the children were instructed to make a series of "quick and easy" stick-figure sketches to organize their thoughts, using arrows between the pictures to preserve the sequence for their narratives. In addition to organizing their own thoughts, by taking stick-writing notes, these students were better able to understand stories read to them. Perhaps the most important observation offered in this report addresses the issue of motivation and participation—that is, when using stick-writing, the children with WD, who often hated writing stories by hand, appeared to be willing as well as able to use this textual strategy productively to write and to read back what they had written.

Numerous studies have explored the benefits of using computer technology, particularly word-processing software and spell checkers, to offset the problems experienced by children with WD as they write (see MacArthur, 2000; MacArthur & Graham, 1987; MacArthur, Graham, Schwartz, & Schafer, 1995; Scott, 2005). Children with WD who have extensive word-processing experience and/or instruction are able to successfully use computers to write, and even in those cases when composing by computer is slower than by hand, typed compositions are usually of comparable or better quality than handwritten ones. Research has also shown that when children with WD are taught to use spell checkers and word prediction software, the number of spelling and grammatical errors is reduced, improving the overall quality of compositions (MacArthur, 1998, 2000; MacArthur, Graham, Haynes, & De La Paz, 1996). However, because spell checkers cannot detect errors that are real words or correct errors that are significantly different from the target word, over a third of students' spelling mistakes were missed, and correct spellings were offered for only just over half of the errors identified (MacArthur, 2000; MacArthur et al., 1996). These researchers argue that technology, though clearly useful, cannot stand alone as a simple solution to children's writing problems; rather, technology needs to be suited to the task and to the student's needs.

In a clinical intervention designed to enhance emergent writing abilities in young children with language impairments, Johnson and colleagues (2004) combined word processing, dictation, and collaborative writing. To circumvent encoding problems, specialized software was developed that included a personalized picture dictionary with recorded pronunciations where words could be found, heard, and dragged to a "sloppy copy," for later typing and illustration on a writing tablet. Intervention focused on supporting children in writing personal stories and producing books to take home, and during both structured writing and freewriting times, the clinician supported children's computer use. At the onset of this study, six kindergarten and first-grade children could write only their own names or short sentences formed from "sight" words. Across the 16 sessions of the study, they began to write personally meaningful, desired words, phrases, or sentences, with minimal adult assistance. Two children with severe language impairments (SLI and autism) began to write creative sentences or theme-based word lists (e.g., "My mom eats the birthday cake") illustrated with digital photos. In addition, when encouraged to dictate or collaboratively type personal stories they had told earlier during snack time, these children were able to produce even longer bona fide written stories such as the one that follows: "*NeNe's Bear.* I have a cousin. Her name is NeNe. She has a bear. It is his birthday. She let me play with her bear." (This story was accompanied by a scanned image of the child's stuffed bear.) This work suggests that with collaboration and enhanced access to desired words, children with WD can learn to write, at least in informal styles such as expressive writing and personal narratives, at much younger ages than previously demonstrated.

TEXTUALLY MEDIATED TALK—AUGMENTATIVE AND ALTERNATIVE COMMUNICATION (AAC)

For individuals with profound communication disorders, communicating through spoken and written modalities is extremely difficult or impossible, and traditional intervention approaches targeting specific areas of deficit are often only minimally effective. Taking up a multimodal perspective, augmentative and alternative communication (AAC) represents what is often referred to as a compensatory approach, with treatment efforts directed toward developing alternative modes and strategies to enhance, or substitute for, speech production. To support face-to-face communication, both unaided and aided techniques have been used. *Unaided techniques* rely on the user's own body to augment or substitute for speech, for example, the use of gestures and sign language. *Aided techniques* involve the use of technologies (e.g., communication boards, computers) external to the individual. Although not identified as "writing" per se, aided AAC techniques rely heavily on graphically or textually mediated means as users point to symbols on communication boards or type words on a computer to "speak" in face-to-face interactions.

AAC has a recent history with a broad interdisciplinary base including clinical fields (e.g., speech-language pathology, occupational therapy) and education, as well as engineering and assistive technology. Much of the AAC literature presents case accounts and rationales explicitly aimed at advocating for clinical, technical, and professional issues (see Zangari, Lloyd, & Vicker, 1994). In general, clinical and research attention focuses on identifying barriers, both internal (i.e., individual motor, sensory, cognitive, linguistic limitations) and external (i.e., physical and social contexts), that impede successful communication for individuals with profound disabilities, and on developing AAC technologies and strategies to overcome those barriers (see Beukelman & Mirenda, 1998; Glennen & DeCoste, 1997; Lloyd, Fuller, & Arvidson, 1997; M. Smith, 2005). Therefore, although the impact of physical disabilities is acknowledged, the AAC perspective shifts attention away from deficit models that focus on differentiating and treating specific disorders (e.g., dysgraphia, dysarthria, SLI, LLD) and modality-specific skills or abilities (e.g., writing, reading, auditory comprehension). Instead, ACC focuses attention on the functional systems that support successful communication. Therefore, interventions can be directed at any aspect of the functional system and can work to adapt not only AAC users to the technologies, but also the AAC technologies, the communication partners, and even the social and material contexts to the user's needs. Although this functional, multimodal approach to communication would seem to be ripe for situated and ethnographic studies, the emerging research more often draws on discipline-specific paradigms to address particular aspects of AAC systems and strategies. In this section, we provide a brief introduction to a portion of the AAC literature by focusing on several issues that have been raised with respect to the functional blending of oral and written modalities in the communicative practices of individuals with profound communication disabilities.

Augmenting Speech With Written Cues

For individuals with good language and literacy skills but poor intelligibility due to damage to the nerves and muscles that support motor production of speech (i.e., *dysarthria*), one approach to improving communication has been to supplement speech with writing. *Speech supplementation strategies* (see Hustad & Beukelman, 2000) offer a systematic approach in which speakers provide word-by-word written cues by pointing to the first letter of each word as they say it (e.g., point to C while saying "cantaloupe"), or provide periodic written cues by pointing to words or phrases depicting the topic of their spoken utterance (e.g., point to SHOPPING while saying "Jenny bought me a coat"). Drawing on models that depict *intelligibility* as a complex phenomenon influenced by speaker and listener variables, these researchers argue that written cues aid intelligibility by providing the listener with additional linguistic (e.g., alphabetic or semantic) context. Under controlled experimental conditions, listeners understand the audiotaped speech of dysarthric speakers better when supplemental visual cues are simultaneously provided (Hustad & Beukelman, 2001, 2002; W. Jones, Mathy, Azuma, & Liss, 2004). Improved intelligibility has also been documented during face-to-face interactions (Beukelman & Yorkston, 1977; Hustad, Jones, & Dailey, 2003).

Graphic Alternatives to Talk

For individuals with minimal language and literacy skills, the communicative value of graphic symbols has been explored. Several intervention case studies have found that patients with severe aphasia can learn to use drawing to augment face-to-face communication (e.g., Lyon, 1995; Sacchett, Byng, Marshall, & Pound, 1999; Ward-Lonergan & Nicholas, 1995). Sacchett and colleagues (1999) presented a conversationally based intervention with 10 clients with severe aphasia. In individual and group sessions, clinicians and clients together drew pictures relevant to the topic and used the drawings discursively during conversations. Although improvements were small, the participants maintained them after the end of therapy, and interviews with communication partners suggested that in many cases patients and their partners began to use communicative drawing to support communication at home.

Children with severely restricted expressive speech or language skills due to developmental disorders (e.g., autism) have also been taught to use manual signs (e.g., American Sign Language), graphic displays (e.g., photos or drawings), and/or speech generation devices (SGDs) to support communication (see chap. 9 in Beukelman & Mirenda, 1998). Driven by clinical concerns and grounded in didactic and behaviorist methods and theories, much of this research has focused on identifying the benefits and limitations of the various modes as well as on developing appropriate teaching procedures to shape and reinforce their use (e.g., Johnston, Nelson, Evans, & Palazolo, 2003; Sigafoos, Didden, & O'Reilly, 2003). Although providing children with a means of communicating their needs and wants has been shown to improve behavior, little attention has been given to the impact that such AAC approaches might have on the broader communication context or on long-term developmental outcomes. Based on a meta-analysis of research focusing on the use of AAC to support communication in children with autism specifically, Mirenda (2004) concluded that gestures, pictures, SGDs, as well as a combination of modes have all been used successfully, but there is no conclusive evidence supporting the benefits of one mode over another. As a caveat to interpreting this line of inquiry, Mirenda argues that, because AAC approaches are highly dependent on a combination of individual, instructional, and communicative partner/context variables, therapeutic success should ultimately be measured by the functional communicative outcomes for each individual, regardless of the mode or intervention approach applied.

Characteristics of Textually Mediated Discourse

In analyzing conversational interactions of individuals using AAC devices, a few researchers have begun to address issues of conversational management and social identity. It is well documented clinically that during interactions between aided speakers and unaided communication partners, aided speakers often take on a passive or subordinate role (see Collins & Markova, 1999; Collins, Markova, & Murphy, 1997; Muller & Soto, 2002). To explore these observations, Muller and Soto (2002) collected conversations of three adults who used computerized AAC devices with speech generation capabilities as their primary means of communication. Conversational dyads consisted of two aided speakers, or an aided speaker with an unaided speaker. Consistent with the clinical literature, this study documented that in conversations between aided and unaided speakers, the unaided speakers dominated. Specifically, unaided speakers asked frequent question to initiate topics, guessed at the aided speakers' responses (which often led to breakdowns and repair sequences), and generally did not allow the aided speakers time to input utterances into their devices. Surprisingly, however, the discourse patterns between two aided speakers were more egalitarian, with topics introduced by comments more often than questions, fewer breakdowns and repair sequences, and a slower interactional rate overall.

One of the most common issues raised by clinicians as well as AAC users and their communication partners relates to the management of the temporal dimensions of face-to-face interactions—for example, the time it takes for AAC users to access devices and for devices to produce a message; the lack of patience partners exhibit as they wait for AAC users to organize and produce a message; and the amount of time AAC users are willing to spend on face-to-face interactions (see Higginbotham & Wilkins, 1999). In a detailed case study, Higgenbothem and Wilkins used situated discourse analysis procedures to explore the complex ways that an AAC user, Jane, and her communication partners collaboratively managed the complexities of timing. They argue that textually mediated face-to-face interactions require active negotiation of an alternative temporal frame, and when such negotiations are successful, "it has the positive effect of socially constructing a dynamic, intelligent, communicatively competent individual" (p. 77).

Another key issue is the social acceptance of textually mediated talk. Adults who are faced with the loss or disruption of spoken language as a result of acquired communication disorders fairly readily accept textually mediated approaches. In fact, recent survey studies that reviewed case records of individuals with amytrophic lateral sclerosis (ALS, or Lou Gerhig's disease) have documented that the vast majority of these patients rely on a variety of AAC solutions to augment speech, including both low-tech (e.g., handwritten notes; pointing to alphabet boards) and high-tech (e.g., computer-based speech generation systems) solutions (Ball, Beukelman, & Pattee, 2004; Doyle & Phillips, 2001; Mathy, Yorkston, & Gutmann, 2000). However, acceptance of nonoral approaches in early childhood intervention has been more controversial. Fueled in part by parental desires for their children to be oral communicators and behaviorist theories that give prominence to imitation and reinforcement in verbal development, researchers, clinicians, and parents have raised questions about the impact that using alternate communicative modes may have on a child's natural speech development. However, recent reviews (Blischak, Lombardino, &

Dyson, 2003; Millar, Light, & Schlosser, 2000; Mirenda, 2004) conclude, based on evidence from clinical case studies (e.g., Johnston et al., 2003; Sigafoos et al., 2003) and group studies tracking natural language production along with other variables (e.g., DiCarlo, Stricklin, Banagee, & Reid, 2001), that the use of alternate modalities does not impede, and may in fact enhance, children's development of oral language production.

FUTURE DIRECTIONS

In this chapter, we have introduced the literatures on acquired and development communication disorders of writing and touched briefly on the use of written-graphic systems as an alternative or augmentative mode for oral communication. Research in each of these areas has highlighted the physical and physiological dimensions, as well as the variability and vulnerability, of writing. It has also documented that targeted treatment programs can improve writing skills, even in individuals with severe writing disorders. However, research in each area has been dominated by distinct models and concerns. Studies of developmental writing disorders have emphasized comparison with typically developing children on writing skills valued by school curricula. They have tended to document an array of deficits, as opposed to strengths, and to propose more intense pedagogical interventions. Studies of acquired writing disorders, on the other hand, have been dominated by a medical model, with attention to identifying neuroanatomical correlates to patterns of disrupted performance. Clinical interventions have taken the form of drills, on skills that tests suggest are disrupted. Use of writing as an augmentative or alternative means of oral communication has been dominated by the need to solve immediate communication problems in individuals' everyday interactions. It has viewed communication from a systems approach and worked to optimize whatever elements of the system seem amenable, not only the individual with the profound communication disorder, but also the technologies, communication partners, even the environments of interaction. Research in communication disorders has highlighted the physical and physiological dimensions of writing, a perspective that is often missing, or only minimally attended to, in social and even psychological research. Pushed by clinical demands, it has occasionally explored multimodal strategies to improve individuals' communication or asked how writing may contribute to the quality of individuals' everyday lives. However, the research so far has too often understood writing as transcription and been limited to clinical and educational writing tasks that address immediate concerns of diagnosis and treatment. We would argue that in the future, research on writing and communication disorders will need to expand outside of its institutional boundaries in order to address everyday writing practices. It will need to take up richer models of writing that attend to the complex interrelations between the physical, cognitive-linguistic and social: the ontogenesis, and ontogenetic remediation, of writing practices in the face of physical disruptions; the distributed functional systems that motivate and support writing in specific sociocultural settings; the diverse discourse practices that surround reading, writing, and language use; and the full range of individual and cultural variation in writing.

Beyond theoretical and methodological issues, researchers, clinicians, and individuals with communication disorders alike have pointed to the human costs, profound isolating effects, that long-standing communication disorders, in both spoken and written modalities, have on the lives of individuals (e.g., Clegg, Hollis, Mawhood, & Rutter, 2005). Given highly literate societies and now the shifting informational demands of the computer age, Smith (2005) argues that integrating literate practices into the everyday activities of individuals with communication disorders may be the key to (re)connecting them to social and vocational opportunities, providing them with tools for "minimizing the disabling effects of underlying speech and motor impairments and supporting participation in society" (p. 2). In the domain of writing, we conclude that much remains to be done to achieve such broad, but critical goals.

REFERENCES

Alimonosa, D, McCloskey, M., Goodman-Schulman, R., & Sokol, S. M. (1993). Remediation of acquired dysgraphia as a technique for testing interpretations of deficits. *Aphasiology, 7,* 55–69.

Armstrong, L., & MacDonald, A. (2000). Aiding chronic written language expression difficulties: A case study. *Aphasiology, 14*(1), 93–108.

Balasubramanian, V. (2005). Dysgraphia in two forms of conduction aphasia. *Brain and Cognition, 57,* 8–15.

Ball, L. J., Beukelman, D. R., & Pattee, G. L. (2004). Acceptance of augmentative and alternative communication technologies by persons with amytrophic lateral sclerosis. *AAC Augmentative and Alternative Communication, 20*(2), 113–122.

Barriere, I., & Lorch, M. (2003). Considerations on agraphia in light of a new observation of pure motor agraphia. *Brain and Language, 85,* 262–270.

Basso, A. (2003). *Aphasia and its therapy.* New York: Oxford University Press.

Beeson, P. M. (1999). Treating acquired writing impairment: Strengthening graphemic representations. *Aphasiology, 13*(9–11), 767–785.

Beeson, P. M. (2002). Successful single-word writing treatment: Experimental analyses of four cases. *Aphasiology, 16*(4/5/6), 473–491.

Beeson, P. M. (2003). Writing treatment for severe aphasia: Who benefits? *Journal of Speech, Language, and Hearing Research, 46,* 1038–1060.

Beeson, P. M., Rapcsak, S. Z., Plante, E., Johnson, S., & Trouard, T. P. (2003). The neural substrates of writing: A functional magnetic resonance imaging study. *Aphasiology, 17*(6/7), 647–665.

Benson, D. F. (1979). *Aphasia, alexia, and agraphia.* New York: Churchill Livingstone.

Benson, D. F. (1994). *The neurology of thinking.* New York: Oxford University Press.

Bereiter, C., & Scardamalia, M. (1987). *The psychology of written composition.* Hillsdale, NJ: Lawrence Erlbaum Associates.

Berninger, V. W. (2000). Development of language by hand and its connections with language by ear, mouth, and eye. *Topics in Language Disorders, 20*(4), 65–84.

Berninger, V. W., Vaughn, K., Abbott, R., Abbott, S., Rogan, L., Brooks, A., et al. (1997). Treatment of handwriting problems in beginning writers: Transfer from handwriting to composition. *Journal of Educational Psychology, 89,* 652–666.

Berninger, V. W., Vaughn, K., Abbott, R., Brooks, A., Abbott, S., Rogan, L., et al. (1998). Early intervention for spelling problems: Teaching functional spelling units of varying size with a multiple-connections framework. *Journal of Educational Psychology, 90,* 587–605.

Beukelman, D. R., & Mirenda, P. (1998). *Augmentative and alternative communication: Management of severe communication disorders in children and adults* (2nd ed.). Baltimore: Brooks.

Beukelman, D. R., & Yorkston, K. M. (1977). A communication system for the severely dysarthric speaker with an intact language system. *Journal of Speech and Hearing Disorders, 42,* 265–270.

Blischak, D. M., Lombardino, L. J., & Dyson, A. (2003). Use of speech-generating devices: In support of natural speech. *Augmentative and Alternative Communication, 19*(1), 29–35.

Boudreau, D. (2005). Use of a parent questionnaire in emergent and early literacy assessment of preschool children. *Language, Speech, and Hearing Services in the Schools, 36,* 33–47.

Bruce, C., Edmundson, A., & Coleman, M. (2003). Writing with voice: An investigation of the use of a voice recognition system as a writing aid for a man with aphasia. *International Journal of Language and Communication Disorders, 38*(2), 131–148.

Catts, H. W., & Kamhi, A. G. (Eds.). (2005). *Language and reading disabilities* (2nd ed.). Boston: Pearson.

Christenson, S., Thurlow, M., Ysseldyke, J., & McVicar, R. (1989). Written language instruction for students with mild handicaps: Is there enough quantity to ensure quality. *Learning Disability Quarterly, 12,* 219–229.

Clausen, N. S., & Beeson, P. M. (2003). Conversational use of writing in severe aphasia: A group treatment approach. *Aphasiology, 17*(6/7), 625–644.

Clegg, J., Hollis, C., Mawhood, L., & Rutter, M. (2005). Developmental language disorders—a follow-up in later adult life. Cognitive, language and psychosocial outcomes. *Journal of Child Psychology and Psychiatry, 46*(2), 128–149.

Collins, S., & Markova, I. (1999). Interaction between impaired and unimpaired speakers: Inter-subjectivity and the interplay of culturally shared and situation specific knowledge. *British Journal of Social Psychology, 38,* 339–368.

Collins, S., Markova, I., & Murphy, J. (1997). Bringing conversations to a close: The management of closings in interactions between AAC users and "natural" speakers. *Clinical Linguistics and Phonetics, 11,* 467–493.

De La Paz, S., & Graham, S. (1997). Effects of dictation and advanced planning instruction on the composing of students with writing and learning problems. *Journal of Educational Psychology, 89,* 203–222.

De Partz, M. (1995). Deficit of the graphemic buffer: Effects of a written lexical segmentation strategy. *Neuropsychological Rehabilitation, 5*, 129–147.

DiCarlo, C., Stricklin, S., Banagee, M., & Reid, D. (2001). Effects of manual signing on communicative verbalizations by toddlers with and without disabilities in inclusive classrooms. *Journal of the Association for personas with Severe Handicaps, 26*, 120–126.

Doyle, M., & Phillips, B. (2001). Trends in augmentative and alternative communication use by individuals with amytrophic lateral sclerosis. *AAC Augmentative and Alternative Communication, 17*, 167–178.

Fey, M., Catts, H. W., Proctor-Williams, K., Tomblin, J. B., & Zhang, X. (2004). Oral and written story composition skills of children with language impairment. *Journal of Speech, Language, and Hearing Research, 47*, 1301–1333.

Flax, J. F., Realpe-Bonilla, T., Hirsch, L. S., Brzustowicz, L. M., Bartlett, C. W., & Tallal, P. (2003). Specific language impairment in families: Evidence for co-occurrence with reading impairments. *Journal of Speech, Language, and Hearing Research, 46*, 530–543.

Gillam, R. B., & Johnston, J. R. (1992). Spoken and written language relationships in language/learning-impaired and normally achieving school-age children. *Journal of Speech and Hearing Research, 35*, 1303–1315.

Glennen, S. L., & DeCoste, D. C. (1997). *Handbook of augmentative and alternative communication*. San Diego, CA: Singular.

Graham, S., & Harris, K. R. (1999). Assessment and intervention in overcoming writing difficulties: An illustration from the self-regulated strategy development model. *Language, Speech, and Hearing Services in the Schools, 30*, 255–264.

Graham, S., & Harris, K. R. (2002). The road less traveled: Prevention and intervention with written language. In K. G. Butler & E. R. Silliman (Eds.), *Speaking, reading, and writing in children with language learning disabilities: New paradigms in research and practice* (pp. 199–218). Mahwah, NJ: Lawrence Erlbaum Associates.

Graham, S., Harris, K. R., & Troia, G. A. (2000). Self-regulated strategy development revisited: Teaching writing strategies to struggling writers. *Topics in Language Disorders, 20*(4), 1–14.

Higginbotham, D. J., & Wilkins, D. P. (1999). Slipping through the timestream: Social issues of time and timing in augmented interactions. In D. Kovarsky, J. Duchan & M. Maxwell (Eds.), *Constructing (in)competence: Disabling evaluations in clinical and social interactions* (pp. 49–82). Mahwah, NJ: Lawrence Erlbaum Associates.

Hillis, A. E. (1998). Treatment of naming disorders: New issues regarding old therapies. *Journal of the International Neuropsychological Society, 4*, 648–660.

Hillis, A. E., Benzing, L., & Lyketsos, C. (1995). Cognitive gains and losses of patients with Alzheimer's disease during frequent practice. *American Journal of Speech-Language Pathology, 4*(4), 152–158.

Hustad, K. C., & Beukelman, D. R. (2000). Integrating AAC strategies with natural speech in adults. In D. R. Beukelman, K. M. Yorkston, & J. Reichle (Eds.), *Augmentative and alternative communication for adults with acquired neurologic disorders*. Baltimore: Brooks.

Hustad, K. C., & Beukelman, D. R. (2001). Effects of linguistic cues and stimulus cohesion on intelligibility of severely dysarthric speech. *Journal of Speech, Language, and Hearing Research, 44*, 497–510.

Hustad, K. C., & Beukelman, D. R. (2002). Listener comprehension of severely dysarthric speech: Effects of linguistic cues and stimulus cohesion. *Journal of Speech, Language, and Hearing Research, 45*, 545–558.

Hustad, K. C., Jones, T., & Dailey, S. (2003). Implementing speech supplementation strategies: Effects on intelligibility and speech rate of individuals with chronic severe dysarthria. *Journal of Speech, Language, and Hearing Research, 46*, 462–474.

Jackson-Waite, K., Robson, J., & Pring, T. (2003). Written communication using a Lightwriter in undifferentiated jargon aphasia: A single case study. *Aphasiology, 17*(8), 767–780.

Johnson, C. J., Hengst, J. A., Donahue, M. L., Prior, P. A., Frame, S., Lin, L.-C., et al. (2004, August/September). *Narrative writing intervention with computers for early elementary-school children with expressive language difficulties*. Paper presented at the 26th World Congress of International Association of Logopedics and Phoniatrics, Brisbane, Australia.

Johnston, S., Nelson, C., Evans, J., & Palazolo, K. (2003). The use of visual supports in teaching young children with autism spectrum disorder to initiate interactions. *AAC Augmentative and Alternative Communication, 19*, 86–103.

Jones, D., & Christensen, C. (1999). The relationship between automaticity in handwriting and students' ability to generate written text. *Journal of Educational Psychology, 91*, 44–49.

Jones, W., Mathy, P.a, Azuma, T., & Liss, J. (2004). The effect of aging and synthetic topic cues on the intelligibility of dysarthric speech. *AAC Augmentative and Alternative Communication, 20*(1), 22–29.

Lecours, A. Roch. (1999). Frank Benson's teachings on acquired disorders of written language (with addenda). *Aphasiology, 13*(1), 21–40.

Leonard, L. B. (1998). *Children with specific language impairment*. Cambridge, MA: MIT Press.

Lloyd, L. L., Fuller, D. R., & Arvidson, H. H. (1997). *Augmentative and alternative communication: A handbook of principles and practices*. Boston: Allyn & Bacon.

Lyon, J. G. (1995). Drawing: Its value as a communication aid for adults. *Aphasiology, 9*(1), 33–94.

MacArthur, C. A. (1998). Word processing with speech synthesis and word prediction: Effects on the dialogue journal writing of students with learning disabilities. *Learning Disability Quarterly, 21*, 151–166.

MacArthur, C. A. (2000). New tools for writing: Assistive technology for students with writing difficulties. *Topics in Language Disorders, 20*(4), 85–100.

MacArthur, C. A., & Graham, S. (1987). Learning disabled students composing under three methods of text production: Handwriting, word processing, and dictation. *Journal of Special Education, 21*, 22–42.

MacArthur, C. A., Graham, S., Haynes, J. A., & De La Paz, S. (1996). Spelling checkers and students with learning disabilities: Performance comparison and impact on spelling. *Journal of Special Education, 30*, 35–57.

MacArthur, C. A., Graham, S., Schwartz, S., & Schafer, W. (1995). Evaluation of a writing instruction model that integrated a process approach, strategy instruction, and word processing. *Learning Disability Quarterly, 18*, 278–291.

Mackie, C., & Dockrell, J. E. (2004). The nature of written language deficits in children with SLI. *Journal of Speech, Language, and Hearing Research, 47*, 1469–1483.

Mathy, P., Yorkston, K. M., & Gutmann, M. L. (2000). AAC for individuals with amyotrophic lateral sclerosis. In D. R. Beukelman, K. M. Yorkston & J. Reichle (Eds.), *Augmentative and alternative communication for adults with acquired neurologic disorders* (pp. 183–232). Baltimore: Brookes.

McFadden, T. U., & Gillam, R. B. (1996). An examination of the quality of narratives produced by children with language disorders. *Language, Speech, and Hearing Services in the Schools, 27*(1), 48–56.

Millar, D. C., Light, J. C., & Schlosser, R. (2000). The impact of AAC on natural speech development: A meta-analysis. In *Proceedings of the 9th biennial conference of the International Society for Augmentative and Alternative Communication* (pp. 740–741). Washington, DC: ISAAC.

Mirenda, P. (2004). Toward functional augmentative and alternative communication for students with autism: Manual signs, graphic symbols, and voice output communication aids. *Language, Speech, and Hearing Services in the Schools, 34*, 203–216.

Mortensen, L. (2004). Perspectives on functional writing following acquired brain impairment. *Advances in speech-language pathology, 6*(1), 15–22.

Muller, E., & Soto, G. (2002). Conversation patterns of three adults using aided speech: Variations across partners. *AAC Augmentative and Alternative Communication, 18*, 77–90.

Murray, L. L., & Karcher, L.. (2000). A treatment for written verb retrieval and sentence construction skills. *Aphasiology, 14*(5/6), 585–602.

Myers, P. S. (1997). Right hemisphere syndrome. In L. L. LaPointe (Ed.), *Aphasia and related neurogenic language disorders* (2nd ed., pp. 201–225). New York: Thieme.

Nelson, N. W., Bahr, C. M., & Van Meter, A. M. (2004). *The writing lab approach to language instruction and intervention*. Baltimore: Brookes.

Oliveira, R. M., Gurd, J. M., Nixon, P., Marshall, J., & Passingham, R. E. (1997). Micrographia in Parkinson's disease: The effect of providing external cues. *Journal of Neurology, Neurosurgery, and Psychiatry, 63*, 429–433.

Parr, S. (1992). Everyday reading and writing practices of normal adults: Implications for aphasia assessment. *Aphasiology, 6*, 273–283.

Parr, S. (1994). Coping with aphasia. *Aphasiology, 8*, 457–466.

Parr, S. (1995). Everyday reading and writing in aphasia: Role change and the influence of pre-morbid literacy practice. *Aphasiology, 9*, 223–238.

Parr, S. (1996). Everyday literacy in aphasia: Radical approaches to functional assessment and therapy. *Aphasiology, 10*(5), 469–503.

Pizzamiglio, L., & Roberts, M. (1967). Writing in aphasia: A learning study. *Cortex, 3*, 250–257.

Plante, E. (1998). Criteria for SLI: The Stark and Tallal legacy and beyond. *Journal of Speech, Language, and Hearing Research, 41*, 951–957.

Robson, J., Pring, T., Marshall, J., Morrison, S., & Chiat, S. (1998). Written communication in undifferentiated jargon aphasia: a therapy study. *International Journal of Language and Communication Disorders, 33*(3), 305–328.

Rubin, H., Patterson, P. A., & Kantor, M. (1991). Morphological development and writing ability in children and adults. *Language, Speech, and Hearing Services in the Schools, 22*, 228–235.

Sacchett, C., Byng, S., Marshall, J., & Pound, C. (1999). Drawing together: Evaluation of a therapy programme for severe aphasia. *International Journal of Language and Communication Disorders, 34*(3), 265–289.

Scott, C. M. (2002). A fork in the road less traveled: Writing intervention based on language profile. In K. G. Butler & E. R. Silliman (Eds.), *Speaking, reading, and writing in children with language learning disabilities: New paradigms in research and practice* (pp. 219–237). Mahwah, NJ: Lawrence Erlbaum Associates.

Scott, C. M. (2004). Syntactic contributions to literacy learning. In C. A. Stone, E. R. Silliman, B. J. Ehren, & K. Apel (Eds.), *Handbook of language and literacy: Development and disorders* (pp. 340–362). New York: Guilford.

Scott, C. M. (2005). Learning to write. In H. W. Catts & A. G. Kamhi (Eds.), *Language and reading disabilities* (2nd ed., pp. 233–273). Boston: Pearson.

Scott, C. M., & Windsor, J. (2000). General language performance measures in spoken and written narrative and expository discourse of school-age children with language learning disabilities. *Journal of Speech, Language, and Hearing Research, 43*, 324–339.

Sigafoos, J., Didden, R., & O'Reilly, M. (2003). Effects of speech output on maintenance of requesting and frequency of vocalizations in three children with developmental disorders. *AAC Augmentative and Alternative Communication, 19*, 37–47.

Singer, B. D., & Bashir, A. S. (2004). Developmental variations in writing composition skills. In C. A. Stone, E. R. Silliman, B. J. Ehren, & K. Apel (Eds.), *Handbook of language and literacy: Development and disorders* (pp. 559–582). New York: Guilford.

Smith, M. (2005). *Literacy and augmentative and alternative communication.* Burlington, MA: Elsevier Academic.

Sohlberg, M. M., Ehlhardt, L. A., Fickas, S., & Sutcliffe, A. (2003). A pilot study exploring electronic (or e-mail) mail in users with acquired cognitive linguistic impairments. *Brain Injury, 7*(7), 609–629.

Street, B. (1984). *Literacy in theory and practice.* Cambridge, England: Cambridge University Press.

Tseng, C.-H., & McNeil, M. R. (1997). Nature and management of acquired neurogenic dysgraphias. In L. L. LaPointe (Ed.), *Aphasia and related neurogenic language disorders* (2nd ed., pp. 172–200). New York: Thieme.

Ukrainetz, T. A. (1998). Stickwriting stories: A quick and easy narrative representation strategy. *Language, Speech, and Hearing Services in the Schools, 29*, 197–206.

Ward-Lonergan, J. M., & Nicholas, M. (1995). Drawing to communicate: A case report of an adult with global aphasia. *European Journal of Disorders of Communication, 30*, 475–491.

Wilson, B., & Proctor, A. (2002). Written discourse of adolescents with closed head injury. *Brain Injury, 16*, 1011–1024.

Windsor, J., Scott, C. M., & Street, C. K. (2000). Verb and noun morphology in the spoken and written language of children with language learning disabilities. *Journal of Speech, Language, and Hearing Research, 43*, 1322–1336.

Wong, B. Y. L. (2000). Writing strategies instruction for expository essays for adolescents with and without learning disabilities. *Topics in Language Disorders, 20*(4), 29–44.

Zangari, C., Lloyd, L. L., & Vicker, B. (1994). Augmentative and alternative communication: An historic perspective. *AAC Augmentative and Alternative Communication, 10*, 27–59.

CHAPTER 30

Writing as Physical and Emotional Healing: Findings From Clinical Research

Jessica Singer
Arizona State University

George H. S. Singer
University of California, Santa Barbara

THE WRITTEN-DISCLOSURE PARADIGM

Educators have long assumed that writing is a healthy and important mode of communication. Medical research now confirms that brief structured writing sessions can significantly improve mental and physical health for some groups of people. Furthermore, these benefits accrue when people write for short periods of time (15–20 minutes) over 3 days. The surprising finding that short episodes of focused writing can improve physical and mental health has energized a research program among psychologists and medical scientists, but writing researchers have yet to join this community.

Pennebaker and Beall's (1986) seminal work in writing and affect established the written-disclosure paradigm from which the rest of this body of literature directly grows. Their initial intervention tested whether short sessions of writing about traumatic events affect health and whether such an effect might come from the release of emotion, statement of fact, or a combination of the two. Undergraduate students ($N = 46$) were randomly assigned to four conditions and participated in four consecutive experimental writing sessions of 20 minutes each. Participants in the control condition were told to write about a different trivial topic each evening (e.g., a description of their living room, the shoes they were wearing, etc.). The trauma-emotion participants were instructed to write about their feelings about a personally upsetting experience and were not to mention the details of what actually happened. Subjects in the trauma-fact condition were asked to describe the details of the event but no feelings. The trauma-combination subjects were instructed to describe both facts and feelings. Participants in all three trauma conditions were told they could write about the same traumatic event each session or a different upsetting event each day.

The researchers measured heart rate, blood pressure, and days of restricted activity due to health and self-reports of visits to a campus medical clinic over a 6-month period. Participants in the trauma-combination condition had relatively higher blood pressure and negative moods immediately following the writing but they had significantly fewer health center visits in the 6 months. All three trauma-writing conditions were linked to decreases in the number of days of restricted activity because of illness; however, those who wrote solely about the facts of the traumatic event did not have reduced medical visits (Pennebaker & Francis, 1996).

Researchers have continued to replicate and extend these findings over the past 20 years. One group of studies tested the efficacy of the expressive writing treatment on the physical health of patients with cancer, recent surgery, and chronic pelvic pain. A second set of studies examined its impact on psychological distress, such as depression, posttraumatic stress disorder, or bereavement. A third line of work examined its effect on individuals experiencing social adversity (e.g. violence, marital cheating, unemployment). Furthermore, recent studies have expanded the original paradigm by investigating possible positive health effects of writing about intensely positive emotional experience and the effect of other modes of writing such as e-mail. Finally, researchers have pursued inquiries designed to identify the mechanisms linking expressive writing to health benefits with a focus on the immune system.

POSSIBLE MECHANISMS FOR THE EFFECTS OF
WRITTEN EXPRESSIVE DISCLOSURE

Petrie, Booth, Pennebaker, Davison, and Thomas (1995) investigated whether written emotional expression of traumatic experiences influenced the immune response to a hepatitis B vaccination program. Forty medical students who tested negative for hepatitis B were randomly assigned to write about personally traumatic events or control topics during four consecutive daily sessions. The trauma disclosure condition wrote about their thoughts and feelings. Participants were vaccinated with hepatitis B injections 1 and 4 months following the intervention. Blood was collected after each vaccination and at a 6-month follow-up. Participants in the intervention group showed significantly higher antibody levels against hepatitis B at the 4- and 6-month follow-up periods, indicating better immune functioning than the control group.

HIV

HIV patients were the subjects of a second immunological study of expressive writing. Petrie, Funtanilla, Thomas, Booth, and Pennebaker (2004) examined how it affected the immune response of HIV-infected patients ($N = 37$). The intervention group wrote about the most traumatic and emotional experiences of their lives. They were encouraged to share their deepest thoughts and feelings about an event they had not previously disclosed. The control group wrote about their use of time using descriptive and objective language. The measures included a pretest for stress and self-reports about meaning attached to revealing emotions after each writing session. HIV viral load and CD4 lymphocyte count data were collected from 2 years prior to the study, and then were repeated 2, 3, and 6 weeks after the writing intervention. HIV viral load dropped immediately after the intervention in the experimental group and increased slightly in the control group. In the experimental group, the CD4 lymph counts, an indicator of the ability of the immune system to ward off infection, gradually increased over the 6-month follow-up, whereas the control group's level did not change. The emotion group rated their writing as more meaningful.

Verbal Versus Written Expression on Epstein-Barr Virus

An important question in this line of research is whether verbal disclosure and written expression have equal effects on the immune system. Esterling, Antoni, Fletcher, Marguiles, and Schneiderman (1994) studied the impact of written and oral emotion disclosure on (N 57) healthy Epstein-Barr virus seropositive undergraduates. The participants completed a personality inventory, provided blood samples, and were randomly assigned to three conditions: written disclosure of stressful events, verbal disclosure of stressful events, or a trivial writing condition. The experimental groups recalled and focused on an undisclosed stressful event about which they felt very guilty. Following the intervention, individuals provided a final blood sample. Both the verbal and written disclosure groups showed improved immune functioning but the verbal group had significantly better immune functioning than the written disclosure group. Subjects assigned to the written/stressful condition used more negative emotion words in their essays than the verbal/stressful and control groups and more positive emotion words than the verbal/stressful group at the same point. Thus, disclosure, whether spoken or written, improved immune functioning and verbal disclosure was most effective. Further analysis indicated that the verbal/stressful group exhibited the greatest improvements in cognitive change, self-esteem, and adaptive coping strategies. These findings suggest that writing about difficult experiences may not be preferable to verbal disclosure; however, it is still an effective alternative when verbal disclosure is not feasible.

The fact that participants who wrote rather than verbalized their traumas used a significantly higher number of negative words suggests something different may happen cognitively while writing than while speaking. Unfortunately, in the instructions, the researchers failed to ask the participants to write about their emotions and thoughts raising a question about the validity of their claims. Future research could benefit from the knowledge and practices of the writing studies community, which has long acknowledged the unique and beneficial impact of writing rather than speaking.

Blood Pressure

The writing intervention may affect other physical systems, including regulating blood pressure. A recent study, Beckwith McGuire, Greenberg, and Gevirtz (2005), evaluated blood pressure, heart rate variability, and skin conductance in participants ($N = 38$) randomly assigned to an expressive-writing intervention group and a control group. Measures included questionnaires assessing smoking, exercise habits, affect before and after each writing session, anger, blood pressure, skin conductance, and heart rate variability. A statistically significant drop in blood pressure took place for the intervention group over time and it reported more overall engagement with the writing than the control group. This study investigated anger levels as a possible mediator of writing and improvement of blood pressure. The subjects were given an assessment of anger-in, the degree to which a person is angry and directs it inward, a trait identified as a predictor of high blood pressure. After 4 months, the subjects who began the study with high levels of inhibited anger improved (lower blood pressure) whereas those with high inhibition in the control group got worse. The study provides evidence that emotionally inhibited individuals may disinhibit through writing. This outcome is consistent with Greenberg and Stone's (1992) finding that people who had not previously disclosed difficult experiences benefited the most from written disclosure. It appears that writing can bring feeling to the surface for those who typically inhibit emotion for external (social isolation) or internal reasons (anger-in).

Cancer

Three separate studies examined the effects of written disclosure on cancer patients (Moor et al., 2002; Rossenberg et. al., 2002; Zakowski, Ramati, Morton, Johnson, & Flanigan, 2004). Zakowski et al. investigated whether written emotional disclosure would reduce emotional distress among cancer patients ($N = 104$) and whether it would buffer the effects of high levels of social constraint on distress. The researchers define social constraint as "perceived inadequacy of social support resulting in a reluctance to express thoughts and feelings about a specific stressor" (p. 556). The dependent variable in this study was emotional distress rather than physical-health outcomes. The authors did not find stress was reduced after writing in the stress group, findings consistent with other studies conducted with cancer patients (Stanton & Danoff-Burg, 2002; Walker et al., 1999). There was, however, an important finding when the data was analyzed by taking into account social constraints. Patients who initially showed high levels of social constraint experienced a significant lowering of distress levels. These findings suggest that written emotional disclosure may be a helpful tool in assisting patients who are not able to express their feelings and thoughts about cancer to others because of social isolation.

Rosenberg et al. (2002) explored the feasibility and the efficacy of expressive disclosure in improving behavioral, medical, immunological, and emotional health outcomes in men ($N = 30$) with diagnosed prostate cancer who did not show improvements in psychological distress or in disease-relevant aspects of immunocompetence. However, compared to controls, patients in the expressive disclosure condition showed significant improvements in physical pain, suggesting a possible use of expressive writing in pain management. In a third cancer study, Moor et al. (2002) examined the affects of expressive writing on psychological and behavioral adjustment in patients enrolled in a trial of vaccine therapy for metastic renal cell carcinoma (MRCC), which is, they reported, the 10th leading cause of cancer-related death in the United States. Patients ($N = 42$) with MRCC were randomly assigned to an expressive-writing or neutral-writing group. The writing sessions took place during each of the first four clinic visits while patients waited to receive their vaccine treatment. The researchers found no significant differences between the intervention and control groups in symptoms of distress, perceived stress, or mood disturbance. However, "patients in the expressive writing group reported significantly less sleep disturbance, better sleep quality and sleep duration, and less daytime dysfunction compared with patients in the non-writing group" (p. 615). These results suggest that emotional written disclosure may be helpful as part of palliative care for terminally ill cancer patients.

Chronic Pelvic Pain

Norman, Lumley, Dooley, and Diamond (2004) examined the individual difference moderators of the effects of written disclosure among women with chronic pelvic pain. Forty-eight women with chronic pelvic pain completed three individual difference measures and then wrote for 3 days about stressful consequences of their pain (intervention group) or positive events (control group). The intervention group wrote specifically about how the pelvic pain had affected their lives and any problems and feelings associated with this discomfort. Participants also rated their essays for meaningfulness and how much they held back. The women rated their mood before and after each writing session as well as pain and ambivalence over emotional expression. The disclosure group experienced immediate significant increases in sadness, fear, anger, and guilt as well as decreased happiness after writing. By contrast, the disclosure group experienced significant reductions in pain whereas the control group's pain levels did not change, again suggesting that writing may be useful for pain reduction. More important, several baseline variables predicted who benefited. Women who were ambivalent about expressing their emotions prior to the intervention and engaged in catastrophizing or reported high levels of negative affect before the intervention, showed greatest signs of reduced pain or increased signs of positive affect 2 months after the intervention compared with women without these characteristics who wrote about stress, or women with these characteristics who wrote about positive events. It seems likely that people with ambiguous feelings about emotional disclosure tend to inhibit emotional expression and that writing provided an outlet or a way to access these feelings.

Physical Recovery From Surgery

A number of studies have investigated the effects of writing on the course of recovery prior to or post surgery, heart attacks, or short-term illness. Solano, Valentina, Pecci, Persichetti, and Colaci (2003) examined the impact of written emotional disclosure on the recovery of postoperative patients. Participants ($N = 40$) were inpatients of a urology ward waiting to undergo an endoscopic surgery on the bladder. The time between the first writing session and the operation varied from 3 to 4 days. Control subjects ($N = 20$) did not write. Participants who wrote stayed fewer days in the hospital after their surgery (30% less time) and had lower distress scores than participants who did not write. Study of interactions showed that the effect of writing was apparent only in participants who prior to the intervention were high in alexithymia. Patients from the writing group showed lower alexithymia levels than the control group. People who score high on measures of alexithymia often have difficulty putting emotional experience into words and exhibit difficulty in making sense of them. The authors appear to go beyond the evidence in concluding that expressive writing helped reticent individuals because language organizes and simplifies experience. Research on vision, for example, suggests that perceptions are organized at coherent but nonverbal levels and that language may not be necessary to make sense out of perception. This study differs from many of the others because it examines the impact of writing on individuals anticipating a stressful event and then recovering from it, rather than recalling a traumatic experience from the past.

In a departure from studies of patients, Barry and Singer (2000) examined the impact of journal writing on parents of infants served in a neonatal intensive care unit (NICU). These parents often experience extreme levels of stress linked to elevated symptoms of depression and posttraumatic stress. The participants ($N = 38$, women) had an infant hospitalized in the NICU in the previous 2 to 14 months prior to the intervention and were randomly assigned to either a waiting list or a treatment group. Dependent measures included a measure of depression and one of posttraumatic stress symptoms. At pretest, 37% of women in the intervention group exhibited clinical levels of psychological distress compared to 16% after writing expressively. The control group's levels of distress remained constant pre- and posttest with 37% reporting clinical levels of distress. This finding opens the way for research on parents whose children experience other stressful medical or behavioral stresses.

Schwartz and Drotar (2004) used linguistic analysis of written narratives of caregivers of chronically ill hospitalized adolescents in order to determine emotional and cognitive processes related to physical and psychological health outcomes following writing. The researchers designed this intervention to measure cognitive-processing language (Pennebaker, Mayne, & Francis, 1997), consisting of words that indicate reflection on the raw experiential memories and feelings related to the trauma event. The analysis of language is based on a computer program that matches words in the expressive writing to words that have been categorized into negative-emotion words (*frightened, horrified*), positive-emotion words (*relieved, helped*), and cognitive-processing words (*understand, make sense of*, etc.). The researchers found that the experimental group used significantly more negative-emotion and cognition-related words than the control group. The former was asked to write about the trauma and the latter about the events of the previous day. An increase on the physical-health measure was predicted by an increase in cognition-related words; change in negative-emotion-related words was not a significant predictor. This finding is consistent with other studies by Ullrich and Lutgendorf (2002) and Pennebaker et al. (1997) suggesting that cognitive processing of trauma thoughts and feeling may positively influence physical health. These findings further support the use of textual analysis (Esterling et al., 1994) to compare writing content as a measure for predicting future health outcomes. It is interesting to note that the essay's subject matter and content were not examined. Perhaps a more complex writing inquiry incorporating content analysis of written emotional-disclosure texts could help researchers understand the role of subject matter as well as affective word choice in influencing health outcomes.

Psychological Distress

In a series of studies, social scientists have examined the effects of expressive writing for individuals experiencing psychological rather than physical distress, such as depression, posttraumatic stress disorder (PTSD), and bereavement. Two studies (Snyder, Gordon, & Baucom, 2004; Stroebe, Stroebe, Schut, Zech, & Bout, 2002) extended the written-disclosure paradigm to determine how writing about different kinds of traumatic loss may produce positive effects. The Stroebe et al. experiment examined the effects of written disclosure on an individual's grieving the loss of a partner 3 months after bereavement. Participants ($N = 119$), all under the age of 70, were randomly assigned to four different conditions, one in which the focus was on deepest emotions associated with loss, one with a focus on problems due to the loss, a mixed condition that combined the problems and the emotions, and control groups made up of bereaved individuals who did not write. This study design assessed situational and individual differences that might influence the effect of disclosure on health, such as whether or not the loss was expected, previous disclosure, and need for disclosure.

Participants in the emotion group were instructed to write the feelings and emotions about the death of their husband or wife, which they had experienced that day. The problem group's instructions were to write as precisely as possible the problems experienced that day caused by changes in daily life resulting from the death of their husband or wife. The mixed group wrote about both their feelings and problems. All three writing conditions were instructed to write in a diary for 7 consecutive days for 10 to 30 minutes, a longer period of time than in previous studies. Participants completed pre- and posttest questionnaires as well as a 6-month follow-up questionnaire for depression, social dysfunction, anxiety, and sleep problems.

Surprisingly, this study revealed little evidence that writing benefits bereaved individuals. None of the experimental groups were better off at the follow-up than the two control groups. It was previously believed that people who had experienced a trauma, such as a sudden loss, benefited from written disclosure (Greenberg & Stone, 1992; Pennebaker et al., 2001). However, the findings of this study suggest otherwise. Researchers found no difference in the intervention results between participants who had expected the loss of a loved one and those who experienced a sudden unanticipated loss. The study did not find any significant difference between participants who had previously shared their emotions or problems connected with the loss and those who had disclosed prior to writing. In fact, the individuals who had not previously talked about their grief prior to the intervention actually suffered less from intrusive thoughts and had fewer visits to the doctor than high-disclosure participants. The researchers hypothesize from this data that "rather than facilitating adjustment, the extent to which the bereaved disclose their emotions may be a symptom of poor recovery" (p. 176). More research is needed to understand whether particular kinds of traumas require more time to overcome and why written emotional expression, in the case of the bereaved, does not reduce psychological distress.

The second study on loss represents a break from the traditional written-disclosure paradigm and investigates a form of counseling that uses writing to structure communication between distressed spouses. Snyder et al. (2004) examined the impact of emotional written expression on couples struggling to recover from an extramarital affair. The intervention took place in three stages: (a) dealing with the initial traumatic impact of the affair, (b) exploring contributing factors for the affair, and (c) reaching an informed decision about how to move on emotionally and behaviorally—either separately or while maintaining the relationship.

Letter writing was used as a therapeutic-intervention tool. At the beginning of the study, one spouse wrote a letter that summarized the impact of the partner's affair on how they viewed the marriage, their partner, and themselves. Drafts of the letter were shared with the couple's therapist, who provided feedback on the overall emotional content and tone. The letter was given to the participating partner 1 to 2 days prior to the couple's next therapy session. In the next session, the injured partner read the letter aloud to the other, who was encouraged to respond verbally. Following the session, the participating partner wrote a letter expressing his or her understanding and shared a draft of the letter with the therapist. In the second stage of the study, couples used letter writing to organize their understanding of why the affair happened.

Following treatment, injured spouses whose partner had participated in an extramarital relationship showed significant decreases in depression and PTSD-related symptoms, reductions in state anger and global marital distress, and decreases in negative assumptions and increases in forgiveness toward the partner. Effect sizes reflecting reductions in marital distress for injured spouses were moderate to large and generally exceeded average effect sizes for similar kinds of interventions without writing. In narratives after the final therapy session, the majority of the participants stated that the exchange of written disclosures produced greater understanding and affected a substantial shift in their attitudes toward their partners.

These findings are compelling because much of the research has emphasized intrapersonal processes and outcomes without attending to possible interpersonal applications of the written disclosure paradigm. Painful and traumatic experiences often take place in the context of intimate personal relationships; therefore, it is important to see how written emotional expression may impact these human connections. This study is a special case because of the reading by a partner and the facilitation of the letter exchange by a therapist. Here, there is a clear audience and writing is definitively a social act.

Social Adversity

Spera, Morin, Buhrfeind, and Pennebaker (1994) studied the impact of expressive written disclosure on recently unemployed individuals ($N = 63$). Prior to intervention, participants completed a questionnaire on health and transition. The writing group wrote about deepest thoughts and feelings about their layoffs and how their lives, both personal and professional, had been impacted. The control group wrote about their plans for that day and their activities in the job search. Following each 20-minute writing session, participants filled out a daily writing questionnaire. Participants wrote for 5 consecutive days, for 20 minutes each day. Surprisingly, the researchers found that the experimental group that wrote about the feelings and emotions associated with losing their jobs were significantly more likely to find reemployment. Expressive writing appeared to influence individuals' attitudes about their old jobs and about finding new work. Furthermore, the writing group drank less alcohol 6 weeks following the study than did the control subjects. Psychological processing through writing helped change some behaviors and helped gain new employment. This study takes a unique perspective because it examines the ways in which the written disclosure impacted participant's future actions and behaviors after disclosing the trauma, rather than a sole focus on health effects. The link between written expression and job hunting remains to be investigated. Future research might examine self-efficacy as a mediating variable. This study and others that seem to involve mysterious links between writing and outcomes could benefit from qualitative analysis of the content of the writing. Textual analysis may point to possible mediating variables.

Violence

A recent study (Koopman et al., 2005) examined the effects of expressive writing on depression, PTSD, and pain among women survivors of intimate-partner violence (IPV). Participants ($N = 47$, women) were randomly assigned to either an expressive-writing group or a control group. The researchers measured symptoms of pain, depression, and PTSD. The findings suggest that expressive writing may help reduce symptoms of depression in women recovering from intimate-partner abuse. Participants who reported greater pain prior to intervention, however, showed a greater reduction of pain symptoms if they participated in the control group. The reason for this finding is unclear. The intervention and control groups did not differ in levels of PTSD symptoms after the intervention. This study shows that narrative writing may serve as a cost-efficient, low-stress way to help alleviate depression for some women with high levels of depression who have experienced IPV. It may, however, not be helpful in treating other common post-IPV symptoms.

POSITIVE GROWTH FROM TRAUMA

A journaling intervention (Ullrich & Lutgendorf, 2002) compared the effects of emotional expression versus cognitive processing plus emotional expression during 1 month of journaling about a stressful or traumatic event. Journaling differs importantly from the brief writing sessions described so far because it involves writing over a longer period of time on a regular basis. This study examined a new variable, positive growth from trauma, as well as variables more typical in this series of studies. The cognitive-processing plus emotional-expression group subjects were given the following instruction:

> We are particularly interested in how you have tried to make sense of the situation and what you tell yourself about it to help you deal with it. If the situation does not make sense to you, or it is difficult to deal with, describe how you are trying to understand it, make sense of it, and deal with it and how your feelings may change about it. (p. 246)

Participants wrote at least twice a week for at least 10 minutes for 1 month. The measures for this study included an inventory of positive growth from trauma, infectious-illness episodes, and a linguistic word count of writing content. These measures were taken before and after the intervention. The researchers found that the writers focusing on both cognition and emotion developed greater awareness of the positive benefits of the stressful event than did the other two groups. Writers focusing on emotion alone reported more severe illness symptoms during the study than those other conditions. The ability to process what happened by both emoting and thinking allowed individuals to see the benefits of a difficult experience. This study points to the importance of the particular focus for journal writing in relation to trauma. Journaling that focuses on emotional expression and cognitive processing, an effort to both feel and make sense of an event, may offer greater benefits than journaling focused only on negative emotion.

HEALTH BENEFITS OF INTENSELY POSITIVE EXPERIENCES

All of the research discussed so far emphasized disclosure of traumatic experience. Recently, a movement within clinical psychology has raised research interest in positive experience and positive emotional disclosure. Burton and King's (2004) variation on Pennebaker's writing paradigm examined the implications of writing about an intensely positive experience for mood and physical health. Participants in this study ($N = 90$) were undergraduates randomly assigned to write about an intensely positive experience ($N = 48$) or a control topic ($N = 42$) for 20 minutes each day for 3 consecutive days. The following instructions were provided for the intervention group before each writing session:

> Think of the most wonderful experience or experiences in your life, happiest moments, ecstatic moments, moments of rapture, perhaps from being in love, or from listening to music, or [from] suddenly "being hit" by a book or painting or from some great creative moment. Choose one such experience or moment. Try to imagine yourself at that moment, including all the feelings and emotions associated with the experience. Now, write about the experience in as much detail as possible trying to include the feelings,

thoughts and emotions that were present at the time. Please try you best to re-experience the emotions involved. (Barton & King, 2004, p. 155)

The control group wrote about their plans for the day. Mood measures were taken before and after the writing sessions. The researchers found that participants in the intervention group wrote about a wide range of positive experiences including time spent with family and friends, graduations, birth of children, travel, and so on. A partial sample of a particularly positive essay from this study follows:

> I had so much adrenaline and excitement in me. I was very nervous before I started the hike, but right when we started one climb up it turned to excitement and I just couldn't wait to get to the top. Just looking around me as I climbed up was a pure joy because of how beautiful the surroundings were. It was a clear beautiful day and I could see forever in the distance. I could even see mountains in another country (Italy). When I finally got to the top after the long tough walk I was so happy. (p. 156)

Three months after the intervention, measures of health center visits for illness were collected. Writing about an intensely positive experience was associated with significantly fewer health center visits for illness and an increase in positive mood, suggesting that disclosure of positive emotional experience in writing has similar health benefits to writing about traumatic experience. Writing about positive experiences might be more acceptable, for example, in prevention-focused writing programs in public schools. If these findings are replicated, they will call into question explanations of expressive writing that rely on the assumption that there are unique processes of memory and cognition in traumatic experiences and trauma writing. It is possible that writing is effective when it releases and processes any powerful emotional experience whether intensely negative or intensely positive. These findings again are consistent with the hypothesis that expressive writing permits cognitive processing of feelings that are not in themselves language based.

A ROLE FOR COMPUTERS IN WRITTEN EMOTIONAL DISCLOSURE

The Internet and e-mail increasingly play a role in the way individuals learn about and receive health care. A recent study (Sheese, Brown, & Graziano, 2004) tested the effects of an e-mail-based writing intervention on undergraduates (N = 546; mean age 18.8 years) who were assessed with questionnaires for personality and dispositional mood and quality of social relations in addition to health outcomes. Participants were randomly assigned to one of three conditions: the control condition, which was asked to write about a non-emotional topic once a day for 3 days; the short-interval treatment condition, in which they were asked to write about a traumatic experience once a day for 3 days; or a long-interval condition, in which they wrote about a traumatic experience once a week for 3 weeks.

In contrast to previous written-disclosure research, all writing in this study took place via e-mail. Researchers found that the e-mail-based treatment improved health outcomes. Participants in the experimental conditions were more positive about the experiment than the control group and revealed that they had been happier since the writing treatment. Participants in the short-interval treatment were more likely to report that they were sad right after the intervention with later improvements in mood and health, consistent with previous findings (Pennebaker, Kiecolt-Glaser, & Glaser, 1988). This study shows that the use of e-mail to implement Pennebaker's written-disclosure paradigm can be effective for enhancing health outcomes, as well as for conducting large-scale writing intervention studies. The design did not allow a comparison of the effects of an e-mail intervention versus the tradition lab-based intervention. This study provides empirical support for Internet-mediated writing as a way to support undergraduates. The promise of e-mail as the medium for expressive writing is that it might allow access to groups of people who have difficulty coming to a clinic.

REPLICATION

In any program of research when there are several studies, some researchers do not find significant results. An example of this is Greenberg and Stone's (1992) extension of Pennebaker and Beall's (1986) original study. They hypothesized that people who had previously disclosed trauma experience would benefit less from writing than those subjects who disclosed for the first time in their writing. Rather than allowing participants to write about either previously disclosed or undisclosed problems, the researchers assigned participants randomly to three conditions: disclosed trauma, undisclosed trauma, and control groups. Sixty undergraduate psychology students participated in the study. This study failed to replicate the findings of Pennebaker and his colleagues (Pennebaker & Beall, 1986; Pennebaker et al., 1988) that writing about emotions related to past traumatic experiences is associated with positive health outcomes. The results were unexpected: There were no significant between-group differences on longer-term health utilization and physical symptom measures. Disclosed trauma and undisclosed trauma participants did not differ from each other on longer-term health measures of health and mood. However, there was one important finding. Participants who disclosed more severe traumas reported fewer physical symptoms following the intervention compared with low-severity trauma participants, and tended to report fewer symptoms than the control group. These findings are noteworthy because they suggest that health benefits occur when severe traumas are disclosed, regardless of whether previous disclosure has taken place. They also showed the need to further test the impact of expressive writing.

WRITTEN EMOTIONAL EXPRESSION IN SCHOOLS

A study by Soliday, Garofalo, and Rogers (2004) is unique in its examination of the written-disclosure paradigm in a public school with a young population. This research evaluated the effects of an expressive-writing intervention on adolescents' somatic symptoms, distress, and positive psychological functioning. Eighth-grade students ($N = 106$) from four suburban middle school health classes were randomly assigned to write about either an emotional or a neutral topic for 3 consecutive days. The writing instructions were slightly modified from Pennebaker and Beall's (1986) original protocol in order to accommodate the young age of participants and the classroom setting.

Students completed surveys of somatic symptoms, medical visits, psychological distress, and positive functioning at baseline, after completion of the intervention, and 2 and 6 weeks later. Somatic symptoms and medical visits were both unchanged as a result of the intervention. However, the researchers found that participants in the experimental group had significantly higher optimism scores and decreased negative-affect scores. The researchers did not analyze the essays for content, which, in future studies, could help reveal the kinds of topics and emotions adolescents take up with this kind of writing. Consistent with previous research with adult populations (Pennebaker, 1993), the positive impact of written disclosure became apparent over time. This study is significant because it points to the potential value of this kind of written disclosure and expression in the field of education. More research is needed to examine the impact of written emotional disclosure in the school setting on mental and physical health as well as learning.

WHAT PART OF EXPRESSIVE WRITING HAS THE MOST IMPACT?

Emotional Inhibition and Release

There is a long-standing tradition in psychology that emotional inhibition may bring about negative physical and psychological effects. The central assumption behind this theory is that withholding thoughts, feelings, and behavior connected to traumatic events is an active process, which leads to negative health outcomes and can be changed for the better through verbal therapy. The talking cure (Breuer & Freud, 1895/1966), which links cognition and affect, takes place when an individual who has experienced and withheld traumatic experience discloses the difficult memories linked to the traumatic event. A central aspect of this theory is the understanding that individuals who withhold memories about traumatic experience, whether consciously or unconsciously, actively influence their emotional and physical well-being through inhibition. Prior to Pennebaker and Beall (1986), the positive health benefits of emotional disclosure were investigated only through verbal communication. They were the first to examine whether or not disclosure through writing, rather than talking, leads to positive health outcomes. Over a period of 20 years, researchers have shown that Pennebaker and Beall's early hypothesis was well founded. The study by Burton and King (2004) also shows the benefits of release of intensely positive emotion through writing, challenging the focus on trauma as crucial to improving emotional and physical well-being.

Cognitive Theory

Cognitive theories related to written emotional disclosure examine the way an individual's processing of traumatic experience requires change in existing cognitive schemata, underlying assumptions central to an individual's general outlook (Janoff-Bulmann, 1992). Core assumptions include the belief that others are generally trustworthy, moral, compassionate, and that the world is basically a good place (Sloan & Marx, 2004). Cognitive adaptation is a process of reorganizing or developing new basic assumptions or finding ways of preserving the old ones taking into account the new traumatic experience. The process of cognitive adaptation to highly emotionally charged experiences involves disclosure that releases some of the emotion tied to memory and also involves making sense of the experience through conscious thought.

MacCurdy (2000) has summarized current neurophysiological explanations of trauma memory and its release. These have to do with the notion that trauma produces a mental picture that is stored but not accessible to the cerebral cortex. MacCurdy explains how traumas are sensory and that the body reacts to them whether or not the conscious mind can apprehend this information. Traumatic memories become locked in a part of the brain that is preverbal and are often accessed unexpectedly. These images "pop up sometimes unbidden when we smell, hear, see or touch something that takes us back to the time the traumatic event occurred. It is these images that must be accessed if a story about the trauma is to be told" (MacCurdy, 2000, p. 162). There are three layers of the brain, "the cerebellum, which controls the nervous system, the limbic system, which drives unconscious emotional responses, and the cerebrum, which allows cognitive functioning" (p. 163). When nonverbal images are put into words, the first layer of the brain passes on the feelings of fear, or perhaps other strong emotion, to the second layer, which makes an image, and the third turns it into something that can be manipulated by language. This process releases stress that otherwise may cause psychological and physical distress. Writing appears to be one valuable channel for linking nonverbal feelings and memories to language.

Pennebaker's (1997) view is much simpler. His belief is that memories are inhibited and, when expressed, the use of language organizes and integrates them into other cognitive structures. Once these memories are integrated, they then become more organized and manageable in the thought process. This theory does not require trauma, so it could be any kind of emotional inhibition. The notion behind the health benefits of emotional disclosure is that emotion held out of access to the conscious memory creates stress. The cognitive-adaptation model has generally been tested using linguistic analysis. These studies often measure the percentage of words used in the written essays that fall into preestablished categories, such as negative-emotion words, positive-emotion words, and cognition words. Pennebaker developed a computerized text analysis program, Linguistic Inquiry and Word Count (LIWC; Francis & Pennebaker, 1992; Pennebaker & Francis, 1996). "This program individually searches text files and computes the percentage of words that were earlier judged to reflect negative emotion, positive emotion, causation, and insight or self-reflection" (Pennebaker & Francis, 1996, p. 865). Studies using this methodology have shown that the more cognitive processing of language there is the more benefit people acquire (Pennebaker & Francis, 1996). Also, those who benefit the most tend to balance positive- and negative-emotion words. Merely stating the facts about emotion-laden experience does not have a beneficial impact because it does not activate the emotions or integrate them into comprehensible linguistic forms.

IMPLICATIONS FOR WRITING THEORY AND EDUCATIONAL PRACTICES

To date, theories of why written emotional expression works have come out of clinical psychology and have not been in touch with theories that frame writing research. We think that sociocultural analysis can provide some valuable insights and, thereby, link this line of research to other more familiar lines of work within the writing research community. Many of the findings in this review of the literature may support the social-cultural theory of writing as social action. Volosinov (1973) developed a theory of language as a system of signs that is only meaningful and necessary in a social world. "Consciousness becomes consciousness only once it has been filled with ideological (semiotic) content, consequently, only in the process of social interaction" (p. 11). The process of writing is one way that private, nonverbal mental experience is brought into the social realm where assistance from other people is available. Dewey (2001) provides further insight into the social nature of language: "Language is primarily a social thing, a means by which we give our experiences to others and get theirs again in return" (p. 35). From the evolutionary perspective, it is possible that in a highly social species dependent on communication for survival, the inhibition of personal experience might be detrimental and that selective advantage might accrue to individuals who were physiologically predisposed to be reinforced by verbal expression of experience. The ability to recount difficult or highly emotional material might relieve stress by bringing it into a social and, inevitably, cultural world in which cooperation from others could be recruited. This theory is consistent with findings about the effectiveness of expressive writing for people who are socially isolated (Zakowski et al., 2004).

If social disclosure is important for survival, one would expect cultures to develop social rituals and structures to allow such expression. From a sociocultural perspective, it is possible that writing can serve as a replacement for traditional cultural practices designed to aid individuals to obtain relief from the group, such as the practice of religious confession found in Christianity and some forms of Buddhism.

Research suggests a link between higher order linguistic and cognitive processing and the immune system. This line of work points to the potential value of neurophysiological research on writing in which the neural and biochemical mechanisms that connect language and somatic responses can be clarified. Given the apparent importance of cognitive processing and restructuring, acquisition of writing and thinking skills involved in reflective processing may have physical and mental health benefits that might link public health to writing education. Future studies might examine writing competence and its association with health in a population sample. If writing competence can help adults to process emotional experience in a way that improves physical and mental health, writing instruction in the public schools might function as a way to prevent or reduce stress related illness. Of particular interest in this respect is the study about eighth-grade students whose levels of optimism and positive affect improved from expressive writing (Soliday et al., 2004). Replication and extension of these findings deserves considerable research attention.

The findings from studies of the role of cognitive processing of memories and feelings are also relevant to an ongoing dispute in writing studies about the value of personal expression versus strictly academic prose. It appears that the more individuals can reflect on and structure difficult memories and emotions, the more likely they are to recover. This theory of the central role of cognitive processing suggests that formal academic writing skills may increase the effectiveness of personal expression. The two forms need not be mutually exclusive.

The expressive-writing paradigm continues to draw a great deal of research interest. Given the potential benefits, this line of clinical research promises to enhance and expand more traditional writing research and theory. The converse is also true; the extensive knowledge base generated by writing researchers should expand the theoretical and methodological tools available to clinical researchers. In the future, it is possible that interdisciplinary collaboration between writing and clinical research communities will create an important fusion of two discourse communities and open new vantage points for understanding writing in its social, psychological, and biological contexts.

REFERENCES

Barry, L., & Singer, G. (2000). Reducing maternal psychological distress after the NICU experience through journal writing. *Journal of Early Intervention, 24*(4), 287–297.

Beckwith McGuire, K. M., & Greenberg, M. A. (2005). Autonomic effects of expressive writing in individuals with elevated blood pressure. *Journal of Health Psychology, 10*, 197–209.

Breuer, J., & Freud, S. (1957). *Studios on hysteria* (J. Strachey, Trans.). New York: Baic Books. (Original work published 1895).

Burton, C. M., & King, L. A. (2004). The health benefits of writing about intensely positive experiences. *Journal of Research in Personality, 38*, 150–163.

Dewey, J. (2001). *The school and society & the child and the curriculum.* New York: Dover.

Esterling, B. A., Antoni, M. H., Fletcher, M. A., & Margulies, S. (1994). Emotional disclosure through writing or speaking modulates laten Epstein-Barr virus antibody titers. *Journal of Consulting and Clinical Psychology, 62*, 130–140.

Francis, M. E., & Pennebaker, J. W. (1992). Putting stress into words: Writing about personal upheavals and health. *American Journal of Health Promotion, 6*, 280–287.

Greenberg, M. A., & Stone, A. A. (1992). Emotional disclosure about traumas and its relation to health: Effects of previous disclosure and trauma severity. *Journal of Personality and Social Psychology, 63*, 75–84.

Janoff-Bulman, R. (1992). *Shattered assumptions: Towards a new psychology of trauma.* New York: The Free Press.

Koopman, C. L., Ismailji, T., Holmes, D., Classen, C. C., Palesh, O., Wales, T., et al. (2005). The effects of expressive writing on pain, depression and posttraumatic stress disorder symptoms in survivors of intimate partner violence. *Journal of Health Psychology, 10*, 211–221.

MacCurdy, M. (2000). From trauma to writing. In C. M. Anderson & M. MacCurdy (Eds.), *Writing and healing: Toward an informed practice* (pp. 159–200). Urbana, IL: National Council of Teachers of English.

Moor, C., Sterner, J., Hall, M., Warneke, C., Gilani, Z., Amato, R., et al. (2002). A pilot study of the effects of expressive writing on psychological and behavioral adjustment in patients with a phase II trail of vaccine therapy for metastic renal cell carcinoma. *Journal of Health Psychology, 21*, 615–619.

Norman, S. A., Lumley, M. A., Dooley, J. A., & Diamond, M. P. (2004). For whom does it work? Moderators of the effects of written emotional disclosure in a randomized trial among women with chronic pelvic pain. *Journal of Psychosomatic Medicine, 66*(2), 174–183.

Pennebaker, J. W. (1993). Putting stress into words: Health, linguistic and therapeutic implications. *Behaviour Research and Therapy, 31*, 539–548.

Pennebaker, J. W. (1997). Writing about emotional experiences as a therapeutic process. *Psychological Science, 8*, 162–166.

Pennebaker, J. W., & Beall, S. (1986). Confronting a traumatic event: Toward an understanding of inhibition and disease. *Journal of Abnormal Psychology, 95,* 274–281.

Pennebaker, J. W., & Francis, M. E. (1996). Cognitive, emotional, and language processes in disclosure. *Cognition and Emotion, 10,* 601–626.

Pennebaker, J. W., & Graybeal, A. (2001). Patterns of natural language use: Disclosure, personality, and social integration. *Current Directions in Psychological Science, 10,* 90–93.

Pennebaker, J. W., Kiecolt-Glaser, J. K., & Glaser, R. (1988). Disclosure of traumas and immune function: Health implications for psychotherapy. *Journal of Consulting and Clinical, 56,* 239–245.

Pennebaker, J. W., Mayne, T. J., & Francis, M. (1997). Linguistic predictors of adaptive bereavement. *Journal of Personality and Social Psychology, 72,* 863–871.

Petrie, K. J., Booth, R. J., Pennebaker, J. W., Davison, K. P., & Thomas, M. G. (1995). Disclosure of trauma and immune response to a Hepatitis B vaccination program. *Journal of Consulting and Clinical Psychology, 63,* 787–792.

Petrie, K. J., Fontanilla, I., Thomas, M. G., Booth, R. J., & Pennebaker, J. W. (2004). Effect of written emotional expression on immune function in patients with human immunodeficiency virus infection: A randomized trial. *The Journal of Psychosomatic Medicine, 66,* 272–275.

Rosenberg, H. J., Rosenberg, S. D., Ernstoff, M. S., Wolford, G. L., Amdur, R. J., Eshamy, M. R., et al. (2002). Expressive disclosure and health outcomes in a prostate cancer population. *International Journal of Psychiatry in Medicine, 32*(1), 37–53.

Schwartz, L., & Drotar, D. (2004). Linguistic analysis of written narratives of caregivers of children and adolescents with chronic illness: Cognitive and emotional process and physical and psychological health outcomes. *Journal of Clinical Psychology in Medical Settings, 11,* 291–301.

Sheese, B. E., Brown, E. L., & Graziano, W. G. (2004). Emotional expression in cyberspace: Searching for moderators of the Pennebaker disclosure effect via e-mail. *Journal of Health Psychology, 23,* 457–464.

Sloan, D. M., & Marx, B. P. (2004). Taking pen to hand: Evaluating theories underlying the written disclosure paradigm. *Clinical Psychology: Science and Practice, 11,* 121–137.

Snyder, D. K., Gordon, K. C., & Baucom, D. H. (2004). Treating affair couples: Extending the written disclosure paradigm to relationship trauma. *Clinical Psychology: Science and Practice, 11,* 155–159.

Solano, L., Donati, V., Pecci, F., Persichetti, S., Colaci, A. (2003). Post-operative course after papilloma resection: Effects of written disclosure of the experience in subjects with different alexithymia levels. *Psychosom Med, 65,* 477–84.

Solano, L., Donati, V., Pecci, F., Persichetti, S., & Colaci, A. (2003). Postoperative course after papilloma resection: Effects of written disclosure of the experience in subjects with different alexithymia levels. *Journal of Psychosomatic Medicine, 65,* 477–484.

Soliday, E., Garofalo, J. P., & Rogers, D. (2004). Expressive writing intervention for adolescents' somatic symptoms and mood. *Journal of Clinical Child and Adolescent Psychology, 33,* 792–801.

Spera, S., Buhrfeind, E., & Pennebaker, J. W. (1994). Expressive writing and coping with job loss. *Academy of Management Journal, 3,* 722–733.

Stanton, A. L., Danoff-Burg, S., Sworowski, L. A., Collins, C. A., Branstetter, A. D., Rodriguez-Hanley, A., et al. (2002). Randomized, controlled trial of written emotional expression and benefit finding in breast cancer patients. *Journal of Clinical Oncology, 20,* 4160–4168.

Stroebe, M., Stroebe, W., Schut, H., Zech, E., & Bout, J. (2002). Does disclosure of emotions facilitate recovery from bereavement? Evidence from two prospective studies. *Journal of Consulting and Clinical Psychology, 70*(1), 169–178.

Ullrich, P. M., & Lutgendorf, S. K. (2002). Journaling about stressful events: Effects of cognitive processing and emotional expression. *Annals of Behavioral Medicine, 24*(3), 244–250.

Volosinov, V. N. (1973). *Marxism and the philosophy of language.* Cambridge, MA: Harvard University Press.

Walker, B. L., Nail, L. M., & Croyle, R. T. (1999). Does emotional expression make a difference in the reaction to breast cancer? *Oncology Nursing Forum, 26,* 1025–1032.

Zakowski, S. A., Ramati, A., Morton, C., Johnson, P., & Flanigan, R. (2004). Written emotional disclosure buffers the effects of social constraints on distress among cancer patients. *Journal of Health Psychology, 23,* 555–563.

CHAPTER 31

Identity and the Writing of Culturally and Linguistically Diverse Students

Arnetha F. Ball
Pamela Ellis
Stanford University

Garcia (1992) predicted that "in the decades to come it will be virtually impossible for a professional educator to serve in a public school setting, and probably any private context, in which his or her students are not ... diverse—racially, culturally, and/or linguistically" (p. 66). As predicted by Garcia, American classrooms are becoming increasingly diverse. In 2000, 39% of the U.S. public school population was composed of students of color (National Center for Education Statistics, 2000–2001), an increase from 21% in 1971. The composition of the teaching force, however, has changed very little in comparison to the student demographic trends. In 2000, 90% of the U.S. public school teaching force was White, an increase from 88% in 1971 (National Education Association, 2001). As increasingly diverse student populations are coming together in classrooms taught by a predominantly White teaching force, culturally and linguistically complex contexts are created where cross-cultural communication and identity development are key factors in students' academic achievement. This is particularly evident in writing and composition classes, where the National Assessment of Educational Progress (NAEP) scores indicate that students from diverse backgrounds are not faring well. Results of the 2002 NAEP test scores indicate that there exists a significant gap in the academic writing skills of 4th-, 8th-, and 12th-grade African American and Latino students and their White peers. The 2002 NAEP results for 12th graders revealed that, whereas 79% of White students scored at or above the Basic level, only 59% of African American students and 64% of Latino students scored at or above the Basic level (National Center for Education Statistics, 2003). This gap in writing achievement scores for students from different racial and ethnic groups has led us to question possible relationships between writing achievement and how students of color see themselves—or identify—as writers. It has also motivated us to ask these questions: Can we do a better job of supporting and affirming students' identities of themselves as writers and whether affirmations lead to improved writing for students from diverse backgrounds? A review of the research on identity and on the writing of culturally diverse students will help us consider ways to assist students in developing a strong sense of themselves as writers and assist the current teaching force in supporting the academic achievement of students in culturally and linguistically complex classrooms.

To explore these issues, we draw connections between the research domains of identity, developing students' identities as writers, and teaching writing in culturally and linguistically diverse classrooms. We situate these distinct bodies of research together to foreground the complex reasoning needed to understand how identity is negotiated by students who write within today's complex learning environments and to explore the notion that when students begin to develop strong identities as writers, their writing performances will improve as well. In the closing section of this chapter, we consider the implications of research that focuses on using writing as a pedagogical tool for negotiating and strengthening the writing identities of students from diverse backgrounds and as a tool for enhancing their academic achievement.

RESEARCH ON IDENTITY

The research on identity spans several decades and crosses numerous disciplinary boundaries, including but not limited to anthropology, psychology, education, and sociology. One perspective has been to investigate anthropological views on how identity is linked to affiliations and systems of meaning (Davidson, 1996; Fordham & Ogbu, 1986; Holland, Lachicotte, Skinner, & Cain, 1998), whereas other perspectives have considered sociological and structural processes that determine identity and how society shapes the self and social behavior (Stryker, Owens, & White, 2000). These diverse perspectives have contributed to more dynamic and complex ways of thinking about the concept of identity where core issues center on static versus dynamic views of identity. Given that this body of literature is too extensive to cover exhaustively here, we provide a brief overview of some notable perspectives on identity and relevant theoretical frames as a way of setting the stage for our later discussions (see Carter & Goodwin, 1994; see also Kroger, 2000, for more references).

Erikson (1963), credited with focusing popular and scientific attention on identity from the mid-1950s, studied World War II veterans arguing that the psychological phenomenon of ego identity could be best understood through a study of those who had experienced a disruption in their ego identity. In his later work, Erikson (1968) elaborated further on the concept of identity, concluding that it is most predominantly formed in adolescence and then becomes a static characteristic. For Erikson, identity developed through tasks and optimal identity development was achieved when an individual found the role in society that best matched their biological and psychological capacities. Although most contemporary perspectives on identity view it as a fluid and dynamic entity, scholars who still rely on Erikson's work focus most often on the notion that identity is the key developmental task of adolescence, precisely the period of most writing instruction.

More recent psychological studies on identity have theorized that certain ways of being—or "self ways"—are afforded by cultural influences (Markus & Nurius, 1986). Consistent with contemporary research are two notions: that identities are negotiated through social relations and that identity is not merely an intrinsic quality. The work of researchers like Mehan, Hubbard, and Villanueva (1994), Nasir (2002), and Noguera (2003) confirm that student identities are not static—they can be constructed and reconstructed based on what goes on within the learning environment. According to Noguera, students generally achieve greater academic success when schools support and affirm their racial and cultural identities. The work of these researchers supports the notion that efforts to facilitate and support development of identities as writers for students of culturally and linguistically diverse backgrounds can result in greater academic success.

IDENTITIES WITHIN THE CLASSROOM SETTING

Insights provided by Gee (2001) can help to inform our understanding of the role identity can play in the writing of students from culturally diverse backgrounds. Gee proposes that identity can be used as an analytical lens for educational research. He argues that identity is not merely an internal state; rather, it is the recognition of being "a certain kind of person in a given context" (p. 99). Gee describes four interrelated perspectives on identity: nature, institutional, discourse, and affinity. Each of these four perspectives is described separately here to help us understand how identities within the classroom setting can be formed and sustained through the medium of writing, but that they are dynamic and interrelated.

From the nature perspective, identity is viewed as a naturally occurring state of being. In other words, an individual has certain characteristics that account for their ways of being. From this perspective, it is assumed that outside forces have little or no influence on identity—the identities of students and teachers are assumed to be constant and the personality traits of individuals in the classroom are not expected to vary significantly as a result of external forces, such as curricular content, social interactions, or pedagogy. According to Gee (2001), this nature perspective gains its force from the other three perspectives that constitute identity: institutions, discourses, and affinities. A person's nature is seen as their identity when it becomes recognized as a meaningful aspect of who the individual is as a person and neither individuals nor society has control over a person's identity.

From an institutional perspective, a person's identity is ascribed through authorization from an institution. In a classroom setting, an individual's identity would emerge through the power relationships that exist between students and teachers, such as institutionally defined by a teacher as authority and classroom leader. The students' identities are strongly influenced by their teacher's interactions with them, based on the authority teachers have been given by the school. From this perspective, students' identities are shaped by the teacher's performance, influenced by the teacher's power, and students' performances emerge in reaction to their teachers.

A discourse identity is an ascription that others give to an individual based on the way they talk and interact with that individual. Discourses refer to language interactions that are spoken and/or written. From this perspective, discursive interactions within a classroom setting can determine how students and teachers perform in that environment. In this case, identity is not based on intrinsic characteristics (nature) or institutional authority from the school administrators (institutional). Instead, identity is a result of interactions between individuals in that setting, and students either passively or actively take on an identity based on how the teacher and/or peers interact with them discursively. Research conducted from this perspective focuses on discursive interactions that are taking place in a classroom and on how individuals come to take on identities in response to those interactions. Dyson's (1985) work with student writers revealed that social interactions in a writing classroom influenced children's writing abilities. Within this environment, children shared their writing freely with teachers and peers and learned how to express who they were as individuals within the collective group.

Classroom researchers who conduct studies from an affinity perspective focus on the practices that take place and on the identities they foster. From an affinity perspective, taking on an identity as a writer requires that students have access to and participate in writing activities (the affinity group in this example). It is important to note that students' identity development as a writer can occur both inside and outside the classroom environment. This is why it is so important that teachers recognize how to capitalize on students' in- and out-of-school achievements. Mahiri (1998) and Ball (1997, 2000) found that students were engaging in out-of-school literacy practices, such as writing poetry, songs, and artistic expressions, that their school had not recognized, and Ball and Ellis (2004) actively sought ways to incorporate students' out-of-school literacy practices into the writing classroom environment so students could begin to identify these outside writing achievements as valuable to their academic writing identities. According to Gee (2001), access to and participation in affinity groups allows for a dynamic view of identity development and culture. This perspective differs from earlier static perspectives where culture was viewed as an innate identity that could not be changed by the individual or by society. Building on these last two perspectives—discourse and affinity—we can begin to gain an understanding of the important role that positive, constructive, and affirming interactions play in the shaping of students' identity development in classroom settings.

Gee (2001) proposes that important contemporary issues in education center on issues of access, networking, and mobility. With this in mind, it is critical that students be empowered with the discourses they need to communicate across cultural boundaries to gain access, networking, and mobility. According to Gee (1989), discourses are an important aspect of identity and he refers to discourses as identity kits. As a person comes to know the contexts for different discourses, they take on the identity kit that goes along with that discourse—including the words, syntax, and social characteristics that accompany that discourse. Gee (1989) grapples with how one attains and comes to control a discourse, distinguishing between acquired and learned discourses. Acquired discourses can be referred to as "dominant" if they provide access to social power. The primary discourse that most mainstream students control is a dominant discourse, which is reinforced in schools (see also Ball, 1992; Knoblauch & Johnston, 1990; Michaels, 1981; Rose, 1989). The primary discourse controlled by most nonmainstream students is different from the dominant discourse used in school settings. Consequently, many nonmainstream students are attaining the dominant discourse through "learning" rather than acquisition.

Gee (1989) describes the learning process as one that involves conscious knowledge gained through teaching and defines literacy as having control over the dominant discourse that is used in social institutions outside of home settings. To be most effective, this conscious knowledge and control of dominant discourses can be gained by combining learning and acquisition pedagogical approaches. Using writing as a pedagogical tool in classrooms is one way that social institutions can integrate learning with acquisition effectively. This process is also effective when helping students to develop strong identities as successful writers.

WRITING AND IDENTITY

Our review of the literature revealed that a limited amount of research looks at connections between writing and identity. Ivanic (1998) notes that writing is an act of identity in which people align themselves with socioculturally shaped possibilities for selfhood, playing their part in reproducing or challenging dominant practices and discourses, and the values, beliefs, and interest that they embody. The studies that we highlight herein focus specifically on writing and/or identity. The findings of the studies we reviewed challenge essentialist notions that identities are static; rather, they view identity as dynamic and shaped through dialogic processes like writing.

Drawing on a Bakhtinian perspective, Ivanic provided interesting insights when looking at cultural identity and the practices of individuals. Building on the theoretical premise that "the self" is often represented through language use, Ivanic (1994) investigated how writers positioned themselves through discourse in writing. She argued that identities are constructed in one's writing through what is said and through discourses in which the writer has already participated. Although Ivanic does not explicitly speak to cultural influences on writing, cultural practices are implicated in her work. Ivanic's study focused on a mature continuing education student and suggested that more research should be conducted using discourse-based interviews on identity among other age groups, both inside and outside of schools and in different cultural settings. In a related study, Ivanic (1994) found that certain values and beliefs of a writer are not easily relinquished. These findings are consistent with the work of Ball (1992), whose study also looked at learners within schools and in out-of-school settings.

Focusing on academic writing, Ivanic (1998) outlined four aspects of identity in relation to writing, which included the autobiographical self, discoursal self, self as author, and possibilities for selfhood. The first three aspects can be summarized as referring to the writer in relation to a particular text. Aspects of the autobiographical self suggest that writers bring a particular identity to their writing based on their life histories. The discoursal self is what writers convey about themselves or the impression that is made through one's writing. As Starfield (2002) has noted, whether consciously or not, writers convey a sense of who they are through the discursive practices they are able to draw on (p. 125). Somewhat similar to the discoursal self, the "self as author" refers to how a writer establishes authority in their writing. Central to our discussion is the fourth aspect, "possibilities for selfhood," which refers to those identities that are available within the sociocultural context of writing. Possibilities for selfhood are supported or discouraged by the context in which the writing occurs. Ivanic's first three aspects of identity in writing shape and are shaped by this fourth aspect. The teacher's pedagogical strategies, approaches to assessments, and the classroom context that these afford influence the identities that a student will take up in their writing.

Orellana (1999) also elaborates on the concept of "possibilities for selfhood" and captures the essence of how certain classroom contexts can foster a multiplicity of identities. Orellana considered gendered identities that were expressed through freewriting that allowed for the creation of multiple identities among the students in an elementary classroom. Orellana examined the freewriting narratives of approximately 30 elementary school, low-income, Latino students in Grades 1 to 3 and found that identity is performed and jointly constructed through choices about language forms. Orellana noted that the imagined writings of both boys and girls were closely tied to the realities and possibilities they perceived in their lives. Although these freewriting experiences had liberatory potential for both male and female students, the storytelling of girls in particular centered on issues of power and inequality.

Building on Gee's (2001) notions of discourse and affinity, cultural identity is viewed as a way of being, as a way of seeing oneself that is negotiated through communication and through one's participation in practices as a member of a group. Both of these perspectives suggest that identity development is a dynamic and fluid process, involving interactions across and among different social groups, and can be fostered through practices like writing. Cultural identity is internalized cultural consciousness—an identification with a distinct concept of reality, accepted by virtue of participation in it (Brock & Tulasiewicz, 1985). This cultural participation is not necessarily linked to physical traits but rather to ethnic and historical experiences (Kravetz, 1985). Within classroom settings, students can use writing to construct, negotiate, and maintain their cultural identities. In addition, the construction and negotiation of cultural identity can be examined and monitored through language practices such as writing.

DEVELOPING STUDENTS' IDENTITIES AS WRITERS

A student's sense of identity as a writer will be shaped and influenced by their home and community experiences, as well as by their school experiences. The nature of a student's home experiences, family makeup, and exposure to literacy practices early in life are all implicated in how students come to know themselves as literate individuals. The saliency of students' out-of-school experiences will influence the in-school experience of students in different ways. Mahiri (1998) notes the importance of out-of-school and in-school experiences as he emphasizes the point that students' youth culture cannot be ignored if we are to effect changes in their educational success. Looking at students struggling for voice through the development of writing skills and the support that teachers provide, he recommends that teachers must make viable connections between the students' street lives and their school lives to create more shareable cultural worlds for learning. Mahiri proposes that making these connections can lead to changes in classroom discourse, culture, and ways of reflecting diversity in the curriculum.

Davidson (1996) has also observed that students' out-of-school identities and school contexts exert a reciprocal influence on one another. As students enter the classroom environment, an important influence on identity development is how others validate, deny, or ignore aspects of their identity (Carter & Goodwin, 1994). Whether an individual sees him or herself as a writer will be influenced by whether others respond to them as if they are a writer. Particularly within the classroom context, teachers bear a heavy responsibility in confirming or disconfirming this identity for students. Simply stated, classrooms play a large role in how students come to see themselves as writers and how they come to perceive the role of writing in their daily lives. In culturally and linguistically complex classrooms, which are increasingly becoming the norm in today's schools, there is an increased possibility that cross-cultural conflicts can occur that negatively influence a student's identity development as a writer (Sperling & Freedman, 2001)—particularly when these students' expressions of individuality and cultural ways of communicating are suppressed.

Moya (2002) argues for a mobilizing of identities in classrooms, rather than suppressing the effects of identities in the classroom. This mobilizing of identities in the classroom requires that teachers see their students as complex individuals and that they move beyond the stereotyping of students. Teachers can begin to introduce alternative perspectives in curricular discussions and classroom activities that allow students to bring their own culturally influenced perspectives and identities into the classroom in critical ways. Students will then gain an understanding of alternative perspectives on a wide range of topics. Teachers must also begin to recognize how their own identities play a major role in classroom dynamics and pedagogical decision making. As teachers come to recognize the important role they play in this process, they can begin to strategically plan their classroom instructional practices and consider ways of implementing writing programs that engage students in the critical examination of the texts they encounter and the author's assumptions and perspective on issues of identity, gender, race, and class. For example, Blake (1998) used a critical reader response approach in an urban classroom to create cultural texts designed to encourage diverse readers to respond to texts that focused on cultural issues. As students wrote, they made links between the stories they read and the stories of their own lives, experiences, and the texts that shaped their identities. Blake proposed that responding critically to their own texts helped prepare students to become critical of other texts and to learn to challenge dominant societal discourses. Blake further proposed that this would help them to learn to use their own cultural resources to make connections with different people, times, and dilemmas and to challenge prevailing stereotypes. These are important steps in a student's identity development.

Ball (2002) asserts that, unfortunately, many students from culturally diverse backgrounds are confronted daily with demands to choose between their own cultural identities and those of the mainstream classroom culture. This assertion is consistent with the findings of other researchers who investigate the incongruencies that exist in the cultural identities of diverse students, the classroom cultures in most schools, and the negotiation of student identities that takes place within academic settings (Davidson, 1996; Ferguson, 2000; Fordham & Ogbu, 1986).

Fordham and Ogbu (1986) looked at cultural identities in relation to major structural features like race, gender, and nationality. Their work focused on African American students (referred to as involuntary minorities) in an urban high school (Ogbu, 1978). Fordham and Ogbu concluded that whereas most students bring their cultural identities with them into the classroom environment, African American students, in particular, must become raceless to be successful in American schools. For Fordham and Ogbu, these students' cultural identity played a major role in determining their academic success.

O'Connor (1997) provided a counterargument to the claims made by Fordham and Ogbu (1986) in her examination of African American students who are academically successful and still maintain their cultural identities. The group of resilient students that O'Connor studied was conscious of the race and class issues that surrounded them, which counters the claim that academic success for African American students equates to racelessness.

Davidson (1996) posited that there are many ways that students construct identities in schools. He problematized the notion that students mask their identities in order to perform well in school and noted that oppositional identities were not necessarily synonymous with academic failure as Fordham and Ogbu (1986) had suggested. Davidson agreed, however, that there were "strong links between conceptualizations of identity and engagement in school" (p. 213). In their work with college undergraduates, Steele and Aronson (1995) found that the dynamics within a school environment can lead to a disidentification of African American students with behaviors that the school defines as success. According to Steele and Aronson, this disidentification can occur as a defense mechanism when these students are confirming negative stereotypes. These studies imply that cultural identity can in fact be a motivation for academic success or a motivation for academic disengagement.

Within classroom settings, this research confirms that discourses and affinity groups play an important role in students' development of academic identities and that students' cultural identities play a major role in determining their academic success. In order to teach literacy effectively, to help students gain an understanding of the dominant discourses, and to support students in attaining academic success, an incorporation of what they have already acquired at home is critical for helping students to reach a meta level of a variety of discourses whereby they can develop powerful literacies that they can use to critique the discourses of power. Green (1997), Michaels (1981), and Ball and Ellis (2004) illustrate that this incorporation of the students' home discourses can begin to occur at the earliest stages of schooling, that is, kindergarten and first grade, and should continue to be incorporated throughout the middle and high school grades. Ball's urban writing course provided learning opportunities for African American, Latino, and Pacific Islander adolescents to become producers of knowledge rather than simply consumers of knowledge by valuing and building on their already acquired home literacy practices (Ball & Ellis, 2004). According to Ball (1992), these types of activities can help students build on and expand their repertoire of discourses to include those that schools want students to learn. In the case of writing, this process makes it possible for students to take on identities as successful writers. According to Ball (1998):

> "Successful learning environments allow participants to see themselves as responsible contributors in a dynamic language environment that allows them to question the status quo, give answers in areas where they feel a sense of accomplishment and achievement, respond without censure, absorb new knowledge through experience, and disseminate knowledge among accepting adults and peers". (pp. 243–244)

Within classrooms that use writing as a tool for teaching and learning, both opportunities and challenges exist for students to develop strong writing identities and to experience academic success. A number of researchers have noted that overall academic performance can be facilitated through writing that supports the development of strong academic identities. Building on Ivanic's (1998) argument that writing is shaped by and shapes a person's identity, teachers who want to shape students' identities as writers can do so by drawing on students' own experiences—by relating writing to students' personal and/or cultural experiences. For culturally and linguistically diverse students in particular, Ball and Ellis (2004) noted that these students often do not possess strong self-identities as academic writers and this, in turn, can lead to poor writing performance in school. Although this was initially the case with the students they worked with, they found that as students were encouraged to write more, they became more fluid in their writing, and found spaces to excel within supportive classroom environments where they could combine the diverse resources they already possess with the new academic resources they were gaining.

TEACHING WRITING IN CULTURALLY DIVERSE CLASSROOMS

A number of researchers have investigated how culture influences the teaching and learning of culturally diverse students. Michaels (1981) examined the interactions between a teacher and students in an integrated first-grade classroom. Focusing in on the "sharing time" activities within this classroom, Michaels showed that the cultural mismatches between the teacher's discourse and the home discourses of Black students can influence students' achievement. She also found that mismatches in the oral-discourse patterns of teachers and students can lead to students being denied important literacy-related experiences. In a similar vein, Green (1997) found that kindergarten students' unique approaches to literacy were influenced by their home discourse within an Appalachian community. Green, however, found that these students' home discourses were supported and honored within the classroom and resulted in positive learning outcomes.

Ball (1992) gathered writing samples from 102 ethnically diverse students attending urban schools and found that the African American students preferred to use organizational patterns commonly found in their culturally influenced oral-discourse patterns—including narrative interspersion and circumlocution. She also found that these organizational patterns received lower assessments than traditional academic organizational patterns preferred by classroom teachers. Ball's (1998) research involved a case study of the writing of an African American male high school student in which the African American Vernacular English (AAVE)–speaking student's writing contained features characteristic of AAVE oral language. Ball documented these features and concluded that the presence of a large percentage of AAVE oral features in this student's writing confirms the need for teachers to learn about the linguistic practices of their students. She also concluded that teachers should keep this information in mind when evaluating their students' writing and when planning instructional activities that broaden their students' writing experiences. The work of these researchers confirms the notion that students' personal identities and communicative practices from their home and community lives do influence their classroom writing practices. These findings also confirmed the need for teachers to learn about the discourse preferences and patterns of their students.

Other researchers have looked at the learning environment and the role it plays in the teaching and learning of writing to students from diverse backgrounds (Ball, 1995; Dyson, 1989; Mavrogenes & Bezruczko, 1993; Schneider, 2003; Sperling & Woodlief, 1997). Within the context of a second/third-grade classroom, Schneider (2003) examined the interplay of students' personal writing strategies and the teacher's instructional methods. Schneider suggested that teachers should move toward a freer, less constrained classroom setting where students can "think, write, and know in ways that make sense for them" (p. 371). Sperling and Woodlief (1997) examined two contrasting 10th-grade classrooms to find out how a sense of community was developed within the classroom to support student writing and identity development. Writing in these classrooms was used as a way for students to understand themselves. Sperling and Woodlief found that in addition to community building, several other factors shaped the students' writing, including course curriculum, kind of writing assigned, and the teacher's interests and methods for teaching writing. Likewise, in a longitudinal study of 1,255 low-income African American children in kindergarten to fourth-grade classrooms, Mavrogenes and Bezruczko found several consistent factors that were significantly correlated with writing ability: effort, attitude, teacher and student expectations, maturity, motivation, self-confidence, and behavior. All of these factors relate to a students' identity development. According to Mavrogenes and Bezruczko, changing teacher expectations would affect other factors—including students' development of identities as writers—in positive ways.

In a case study examination of a kindergarten classroom, Dyson (1985) focused on journal writing, community-building activities, and identity development of young writers, chronicling how culturally diverse students learned to write and share themselves through pictures and stories to their class. Dyson found that children's writing development was deeply embedded in the social practices that surrounded them as related to their peers, their own experiences, and how they view themselves.

These studies on teaching writing in culturally diverse classrooms have increased our understanding of factors that influence students' writing, including student and teacher effort, attitude, expectations, maturity, motivation, self-confidence, and behavior, as well as the importance of community building, curriculum development, and teachers' willingness to move toward freer, less constrained classroom settings that can build on students' performative skills. Other studies have been designed to enhance our understanding of why some culturally diverse students fare poorly on writing tasks in many classrooms (Ball, 1997; Dyson, 1989, 1993; Langer, 2001; Mavrogenes & Bezruczko, 1993; Needeols & Knapp, 1994; Schneider, 2003; Sperling & Woodlief, 1997). Still, the majority of these researchers have encouraged teachers to create assignments that build on student's community knowledge and make explicit links between students' writing, their lives outside of school, and what is being taught inside the classroom. Such assignments connect students' personal lives to their academic development and to writing in personally meaningful ways. Thus, this research implicitly links students' personal identities to their development as writers (see also Ball, 2002; Dyson, 1989; Heller, 1992).

Although this research confirms that assignments drawing on students' lives are most effective with these students, it is important to note that studies focusing on pedagogical strategies generally used to teach writing to culturally diverse students (Carbonaro & Gamoran, 2002; Davis, Clarke, & Rhodes, 1994; Needels & Knapp, 1994; Yeh, 1998) have found that students of color are disproportionately relegated to classrooms using drill exercises rather than interactive, meaningful approaches that require extended writing, reflection, and critical thinking. Whereas the studies reviewed in this chapter have all concluded that pedagogy and student achievement are closely linked when teaching students from culturally diverse backgrounds, the question remains: Why are most culturally and linguistically diverse students in poor and urban schools continuing to receive low-level drill-and-skill instruction when the research confirms that instruction that builds on students' background knowledge, builds a sense of community, is interactive and meaningful, and requires extended writing, reflection, and critical thinking is most effective with all students? Sperling and Freedman (2001) have concluded that acts of writing and writing instruction reflect broader social and cultural processes at work. Important connections can be drawn between students' identities as proficient writers and how they are instructed and assessed. Because every classroom has an identity of its own that either fosters or hinders students' identity development as writers, it is imperative that all classrooms provide students with interactive and meaningful curriculum that requires extended opportunities for writing, reflection, and critical thinking. In addition, having one's voice heard through their writing allows students to discover themselves through their writing (Ivanic, 1994).

Critical of teaching that relies excessively on the drill-and-skill approaches that are often overused in many writing programs, Davis et al. (1994) examined the effects of extending the writing opportunities for a diverse group of students in the fourth and fifth grades. These researchers found that in classrooms where there were extended opportunities to write, both students of color and White students fared better in the quality of the writing content and their usage of writing conventions. These researchers concluded that drill exercises, which often predominate in the instruction in classrooms that serve poor and culturally diverse students (Mavrogenes & Bezruczko, 1993), are not the best approach for improving the writing of students of color. Along the same lines, Needels and Knapp (1994) investigated 26 low-income fourth- and sixth-grade classrooms to observe differences in pedagogical strategies when using a sociocognitive model instead of the explicit drill-and-practice approaches that are often found in culturally diverse classrooms. These researchers found higher levels of writing abilities among students in those classrooms that used a sociocognitive model, which emphasized the use of authentic tasks and linkages to students' experiences and backgrounds. Coming from a very different perspective, Yeh's (1998) study of seventh graders in two different economically disadvantaged cities revealed the use of explicit instruction to be a key factor in improving students' writing skills. Yeh concluded that use of a heuristic as an instrumental tool led to improvements in the voices of students of color and provided a framework for students to think about the process of writing an argument. Though approaches that emphasized the use of authentic tasks and linkages to students' experiences and backgrounds and provided extended opportunities to write helped students develop identities as writers and improved the quality and content of their writing, explicit instruction is also needed and should be one part of a well-designed comprehensive writing program. Clearly, different instructional approaches should be examined closely to increase our understanding of why students of color fare poorly on most literacy achievement measures yet thrive in other kinds of writing environments.

Carbonaro and Gamoran (2002) proposed that the lower literacy achievements of students of color could be explained by differences in access to out-of-school and in-school resources. This study investigates the learning opportunities within the schools studied and found that when students were exposed to more intellectually challenging content in their language arts classes, for example, demanding different types of writing, this resulted in higher reading and writing achievement. Based on this research, we can conclude that all students should be challenged to engage in different types of demanding writing assignments if we want students to view themselves as accomplished writers and if we hope to close the current achievement gap.

In addition to research on the influence of instructional context, pedagogy, and curriculum on the writing of cultural and linguistically diverse students, Ball (1997) and Gabrielson, Gordon, and Engelhard (1995) have considered how the writing of culturally diverse students has been evaluated and found that assessments are a key tool that can affect students' views of themselves as writers. Looking at issues of assessment and the writing of students of color, Ball compared the scores assigned to the writing of students of color by a group of Euro-American and a group of African American teachers. Teachers rated the essays of ethnically diverse fifth- and sixth-grade students on qualities that included organizational structure, coherence, and mechanics. Ball found that teachers' assessments of the writing of students of color differed markedly between African American teachers and Euro-American teachers. This study revealed that teachers of color look at assessment from a perspective that is different from that of Euro-American teachers. The study also revealed that including the voice of teachers of color in dialogues on assessment is important for framing local and national policy. It should be noted that teachers' negative assessments of students' writing can negatively impact the development of students' identities as writers. Gabrielson et al. examined whether choice in writing tasks made a difference in students' writing performances and if that difference was related to students' race. Although Gabrielson et al. did not find that student choice in writing task made a difference in student performance, they did find a small indication that African American students had a greater sense of ownership when they chose the writing task.

Ball (1999) offered five principles that are important for creating successful writing and assessment contexts. Teachers should provide:

- Ample opportunities for students to talk, learn, and develop skills.
- Access to adult role models who hold high expectations for experimenting with dominant discourses and students' acquired discourses.
- Structured environments with interactive discourses and a variety of activities.
- Emphasis on collaboration, negotiation, responsibility, and commitment.
- Modeling of appropriate language use.

These principles were presented as factors that can be used to enhance the writing of diverse students. These studies remind us of the important role of teachers' assessment of students' writing, of students' choice, and of the need to give students opportunities to bring their own cultural resources into their classroom writing as we consider ways to help them write more fluidly and develop stronger identities as successful writers.

CONCLUSION

The studies reviewed in this chapter have implications for using writing as a pedagogical tool for negotiating and strengthening the cultural identities of students from diverse backgrounds and as a tool for enhancing these students' writing achievement. In *The Price of the Ticket*, James Baldwin (1985) reminds us that "it is exceedingly difficult for most of us to discard the assumptions of the society in which we were born, in which we live, to which we owe our identities" (p. 155). Building on this notion, we realize that students internalize the messages they receive from the society they live in and develop identities based on assumptions they glean from their interactions with individuals and from institutions in which they participate. If students receive messages from schools assuming that they will be successful writers, then it will be exceedingly difficult for them to discard those assumptions and identities as they grow. We can assist students in the development of these identities through an increased understanding of the research on identity, writing in cultural diverse classrooms, and the role that identity can play in the writing achievement of students in cultural and linguistically complex classrooms.

Building on this notion, Ball and Ellis (2004) conducted an exploratory study of the use of oral and written discourses in a small urban classroom where students came to know themselves and other students of color as writers and as producers of knowledge. This research was conducted with the thought in mind that students can and should be given numerous opportunities through the medium of writing to explore and negotiate who they are and who they have the possibility of becoming. All of the high school students who participated in this urban writing classroom had scored in the lower quartile on standardized achievement tests in the language arts. Ball and Ellis, along with one humanities teacher and three graduate students, designed their collaborative teaching around the notion that it is important to build a positive classroom cultural identity that is actively facilitated through the agency of student writers who engage with interesting and challenging materials. They designed the course around the notion that schools are a reflection of broader social and cultural processes that occur both inside and outside the classroom. The 22 students who participated in this high school elective writing class came from diverse cultural backgrounds and spoke several languages and dialects, including AAVE, Filipino, Samoan, Spanish, Spanglish, Tongan, and mainstream Standard English. Grounding the course in a curriculum that progressed from self-awareness, to social and community awareness, to global awareness, provided many opportunities for students to build a classroom community of writers, reinforced the development of students' identities as successful writers, and freed students to write at a level that was personally meaningful and intellectually challenging.

By honoring the community-based literacy skills that these urban adolescents brought from their home communities, we found that students displayed what we called generative literacy practices in their classroom writing. We use this term to describe the literacy practices that can occur in linguistically complex classrooms when students are allowed to freely bring their home and community literacy practices and personal cultural identities into the classroom, mixing them with the academic literacy practices that we were trying to teach. This resulted in the production of much richer hybrid texts.

Angela was a shy, 16-year-old Latina who rarely spoke in class. During the first half of the school year, all of Angela's writings were uninteresting and exclusively written in English, except the letters to her parents, which were always written in Spanish. As the year progressed, Angela's lexical density increased and there were more instances when her heritage language was integrated into her classroom writing. Hybrid forms of writing—which included culturally influenced stylistic features and Spanish and English excerpts where appropriate—emerged when Angela was allowed the flexibility to build bridges between her home communication practices and academic writing demands. Angela and many of the other students told us that sharing personal experiences was an activity that helped them to build their confidence and improve their writing.

The hybrid forms of writing we were receiving from the Latino, African American, Filipino, Samoan, and Tongan students in this culturally and linguistically complex classroom were, indeed, an improvement over the earlier writing we had received. The writing produced by the students later in the school year was richly textured, more descriptive, engaging, and elaborated. Mobilizing, rather than suppressing, the identities of the students in our classroom had empowered them to become producers of powerful literacies that shared alternative perspectives on content area topics and on topics teachers rarely have the privilege of reading about concerning the lives of their students.

As a result of our program, these students came to identify more closely with the behaviors of those who have control over a dominant discourse. The amount of their writing increased and their school attendance rates improved over the course of the year. As these students identified more with being "good students" and "members of our school community," their attitudes about themselves as students and as writers began to change as well.

As teachers, we demonstrated our valuing of these students' acquired literacy skills by allowing them numerous opportunities to bring their cultural identities into the classroom setting and into their writing (LeCourt, 2004). Through oral-history interviews, students shared and wrote about meaningful events in their lives and the lives of their family and community members. Banks (1998) affirms that teachers should help students examine and uncover the community and cultural knowledge they bring to school and to understand how it is similar to and different from school knowledge and the cultural knowledge of other students. This served as one of the core principles that guided our work in this culturally and linguistically complex classroom, which resulted in improved writing on the part of the students.

Once these students developed positive identities as writers within the context of a supportive classroom community, they went on to become more successful and more confident writers. One year after the course ended, we received follow-up reports from the school that a large proportion of the students who participated in our class had been admitted to college—a first for many of the families represented in this school. Though we realize that the success of these students was due to many factors, we feel that our class was one of the many positive contributing factors that led to these students' success. Based on our experiences with these students and the exit interviews we conducted with them, we found that it is indeed possible to use writing as a pedagogical tool for negotiating and strengthening the writing identities of students from diverse backgrounds and as a tool for enhancing their academic achievement. Although these students did not initially possess strong identities as successful academic writers, we found that drawing upon the cultural resources that students brought from home into these culturally and linguistically complex learning environments helped them to develop positive writing identities so that they eventually began to see themselves as good academic writers.

For culturally and linguistically diverse students in particular, we proposed that these students often do not self-identify as academically successful writers, and that this may lead to poor performance on writing tasks. A number of researchers have noted that overall academic performance can be supported by developing positive academic identities. We found that to help them do well involved helping them to relate writing to their personal and/or cultural experiences. We found that one important reason for the poor performance of students of color on academic performance measures is that they do not possess positive identities as successful academic writers. However, when students began to development strong identities as writers, their writing performances also improved. We concluded that students can develop an identity as a writer if teachers build on the resources they bring from home and value and include the students' voices in the curriculum. This can and did result in better performances as writers.

In this chapter, we looked at the research on identity in general and within classroom settings, writing and identity, and developing identities as writers within classrooms that successfully teach writing to culturally and linguistically diverse students. We concluded that all students can be successful academic writers, particularly if they are supported in the development of identities as successful writers and receive enjoyable instruction that builds on their background knowledge, builds a sense of community, is interactive and meaningful, and requires extended writing, reflection, and critical thinking. We have also concluded that this research has important implications that support the notion of using writing as a pedagogical tool for negotiating and strengthening the writing identities of students from diverse backgrounds and as a tool for enhancing the academic achievement of all students. This research supports the notion that if students in culturally and linguistically complex learning environments are allowed to write often, they will begin to see themselves as writers, and this can lead to improved writing achievement by students who have not been faring well historically.

Further research in this area is needed—research that focuses explicitly on the intersection between identity development and the writing of racially, ethnically, and linguistically diverse students. We need to know more about how writing can be used to strengthen students' identities of who they currently are and who they have the potential of becoming. In the meantime, we need to be acting on the knowledge that we already have by ensuring that all students receive engaging instruction that requires extended, reflective, critical writing and supports their developing identities as successful writers. We must also ensure that all students receive instruction that values the cultural identities and linguistic resources they bring into the classroom so they can develop powerful discourses that allow them to become contributors of knowledge in their own communities and in the larger society.

REFERENCES

Baldwin, J. (1985). The price of the ticket: Collected nonfiction, 1948–1985. New York: St. Martin's Press.

Ball, A. F. (1992). Cultural preference and the expository writing of African-American adolescents. Written Communication, 9(4), 501–532.

Ball, A. F. (1995). Community-based learning in urban settings as a model for educational reform. Applied Behavioral Science Review, 44(5), 127–146.

Ball, A. F. (1997). Expanding the dialogue on culture as a critical component when assessing writing. Assessing Writing, 4(2), 169–202.

Ball, A. F. (1998). Evaluating the writing of culturally and linguistically diverse students: The case of the African American vernacular English speaker. In C. R. Cooper & L. Odell (Eds.), Evaluating writing: The role of teachers' knowledge about text, learning, and culture (pp. 225–248). Urbana, IL: National Council of Teachers of English.

Ball, A. F. (2000). Empowering pedagogies that enhance the learning of multicultural students. Teachers College Record, 102(6), 1006–1034.

Ball, A. F. (2002). Three decades of research on classroom life: Illuminating the classroom communicative lives of America's at-risk students. In W. Secada (Ed.), Review of research in education (Vol. 26, pp. 71–111). Washington, DC: American Educational Research Association.

Ball, A. F., & Ellis, P. (2004). Investigating the writing practices of culturally and linguistically diverse students in complex classrooms. Unpublished manuscript, Stanford University, Stanford, CA.

Banks, J. A. (1998). The lives and values of researchers: Implications for educating citizens in a multicultural society. Educational Researcher, 27(7), 4–17.

Blake, B. (1998). "Critical" reader response in an urban classroom: Creating cultural texts to engage diverse readers. Theory Into Practice, 37(3), 238–243.

Brock, C., & Tulasiewicz, W. (1985). The concept of identity: Editor's introduction. In C. Brock & W. Tulasiewicz (Eds.), Cultural identity & educational policy (pp. 2–10). London: Croom Helm.

Carbonaro, W. J., & Gamoran, A. (2002).The production of achievement inequality in high school English. American Educational Research Journal, 39(4), 801–827.

Carter, R. T., & Goodwin, A. L. (1994). Racial identity and education. In L. Darling-Hammond (Ed.), Review of research in education (Vol. 19, pp. 291–336). Itasca, NY: Peacock.

Davidson, A. L. (1996). Making and molding identity in schools: Student narratives on race, gender, and academic engagement. Albany: State University of New York Press.

Davis, A., Clarke, M. A., & Rhodes, L. K. (1994). Extended text and the writing proficiency of students in urban elementary schools. Journal of Educational Psychology, 86(4), 556–566.

Dyson, A. H. (1985). Second graders sharing writing: The multiple social realities of a literacy event. Written Communication, 2(2), 189–215.

Dyson, A. H. (1989). Multiple worlds of child writers: Friends learning to write. New York: Teachers College Press.

Dyson, A. H. (1993). Social worlds of children learning to write in an urban primary school. New York: Teachers College Press.

Erikson, E. H. (1968). Identity, youth, and crisis. New York: Norton.

Ferguson, A. A. (2000). Bad boys: Public schools in the making of Black masculinity. Ann Arbor: University of Michigan Press.

Fordham, S., & Ogbu, J. U. (1986). Black students' school success: Coping with the burden of "acting White." Urban Review, 18(3), 176–206.

Gabrielson, S., Gordon, B., & Engelhard, G. (1995). The effects of task choice on the quality of writing obtained in a statewide assessment. Applied Measurement in Education, 8(4), 273–290.

Gee, J. P. (1989). What is literacy? Journal of Education, 171(1), 18–25.

Gee, J. P. (2001). Identity as an analytic lens for research in education. In W. Secada (Ed.), Review of research in education (pp. 99–125). Washington, DC: American Educational Research Association.

Green, C. R. (1997). Literacy development in an Appalachian kindergarten. Reading Horizons, 37(3), 215–232.

Heller, C. (1992). Written words: Students share culture through writing. Teaching Tolerance, 1(2), 36–43.

Holland, D. C., Lachiotte, W., Skinner, D., & Cain, C. (1998). Identity and agency in cultural worlds. Cambridge, MA: Harvard University Press.

Ivanic, R. (1994). I is for interpersonal: Discoursal construction of writer identities and the teaching of writing. Linguistics and Education, 6(1), 3–15.

Ivanic, R. (1998). Writing and identity: The discoursal construction of identity in academic writing. Amsterdam: Benjamins.

Knoblauch, C., & Johnston, P. (1990). Reading, writing, and the prose of the school. In R. Beach & S. Hynds (Eds.), Developing discourse practices in adolescence and adulthood (pp. 318–336). Norwood, NJ: Ablex.

Kravetz, N. (1985). United States educational policies and Black cultural identity. In C. Brock & W. Tulasiewicz (Eds.), Cultural identity & educational policy (pp. 286–303). London: Croon Helm.

Kroger, J. (2000). Identity development: Adolescence through adulthood. Thousand Oaks, CA: Sage.

Langer, J. A. (2001). Beating the odds: Teaching middle and high school students to read and write well. American Educational Research Journal, 38(4), 837–880.

LeCourt, D. (2001). Identity matters: Schooling the student body in academic discourse. Albany: State University of New York Press.

Markus, H. R., & Narius P. (1986). Possible selves. American Psychologist, 41(9), 954–969.

Mavrogenes, N. A., & Bezruczko, N. (1993). Influences on writing development. Journal of Educational Research, 86(4), 237–245.

Mehan, H., Hubbard, L., & Villanueva, I. (1994). Forming academic identities: Accommodation without assimilation among involuntary minorities. Anthropology and Education Quarterly, 42(5), 91–117.

Michaels, S. A. (1981). "Sharing time": Children's narrative styles and differential access to literacy. Language in Society, 10, 423–442.

Moya, P. M. L. (2002). Learning from experience: Minority identities, multicultural struggles. Berkeley: University of California Press.

Nasir, N. S. (2002). Identity, goals, and leaning: Mathematics in cultural practice. Mathematical Thinking and Learning, 4(2–3), 213–247.

National Center for Education Statistics. (2000–2001). State nonfiscal survey of public elementary/secondary education. Washington, DC: U.S. Government Printing Office.

National Center for Education Statistics. (2003). The nation's report card: Writing (NCES Report No. 2003-529). Washington, DC: U.S. Government Printing Office.

National Education Association. (2001). Status of the American public-school teacher. Washington, DC: Author.

Needels, M. C., & Knapp, M. S. (1994). Teaching writing to children who are underserved. Journal of Educational Psychology, 86(3), 339–349.

Noguera, P. (2003). City schools and the American dream: Reclaiming the promise of public education. New York: Teachers College Press.

O'Connor, C. (1997). Dispositions toward (collective) struggle and educational resilience in the inner city: A case analysis of six African-American high school students. American Educational Research Journal, 34(4), 593–629.

Ogbu, J. U. (1978). Minority education and caste: The American system in cross-cultural perspective. New York: Academic Press.

Orellana, M. F. (1999). Good guys and "bad" girls: Identity construction by Latina and Latino student writers. In M. Bucholtz, A. C. Liang, & L. A. Sutton (Eds.), Reinventing identities: The gendered self in discourse (pp. 65–82). New York: Oxford University Press.

Rose, M. (1989). Lives on the boundary: The struggles and achievements of America's underprepared. New York: Collier Macmillan.

Schneider, J. J. (2003). Contexts, genres, and imagination: An examination of the idiosyncratic writing performances of three elementary children within multiple contexts of writing instruction. Research in the Teaching of English, 37(3), 329–379.

Sperling, M., & Freedman, S. W. (2001). Research on the teaching of writing. In V. Richardson (Eds.), Handbook of research on teaching (4th ed., pp. 370–389). Washington, DC: American Educational Research Association.

Sperling, M., & Woodlief, L. (1997). Two classrooms, two writing communities: Urban and suburban tenth graders learning to write. Research in the Teaching of English, 31(2), 205–239.

Starfield, S. (2002). "I'm a second-language English speaker": Negotiating writer identity and authority in sociology one. Journal of Language, Identity, and Education, 1(2), 121–140.

Steele, C. M., & Aronson, J. (1995). Stereotype threat and the intellectual test performance of African Americans. Journal of Personality and Social Psychology, 69(5), 797–811.

Stryker, S., Owens, T. J., & White, R. W. (2000). Self, identity, and social movements. Minneapolis: University of Minnesota Press.

Yeh, S. S. (1998). Empowering education: Teaching argumentative writing to cultural minority middle-school students. Research in the Teaching of English, 33(1), 49–83.

CHAPTER 32

Multilingual Writing Development

Dwight Atkinson
Purdue University
Ulla Connor
Indiana University, Purdue University, Indianapolis

The world of writing is a broad and diverse one. The *multilingual* of our title is meant to signify an important part of that diversity: the writers who negotiate multiple linguistic and cultural repertoires, the processes they engage in, and the texts they produce. The *development* of our title marks a second major aspect of that diversity: the variable learning of skills, strategies, and identities—whether by adults, adolescents, or children—needed to succeed in multilingual contexts.

Yet it must be admitted that research on multilingual writing development has traditionally been rather limited—the bulk of studies have been conducted on English as a Second Language (ESL) contexts in Anglophone, and especially U.S., universities (Leki, Cumming, & Silva, 2005; see Reichelt, 1999, for exceptions). Reasons for this focus are obvious: the special attention given to writing instruction in the U.S. university over the past half century; the dominance of English as a world language; and the centrality of research (and especially the need to *do* research) in English-majority academic settings. Our aim in this chapter is therefore both to review the research so far done on multilingual writing development at different educational levels and in different professional settings, and then to point out where research still needs to be done. To this end, the chapter is divided into six main parts: (a) a review of situated case studies of multilingual writers, (b) a review of multilingual writing/literacy development in primary/secondary education, (c) a review of multilingual writing development in tertiary education, (d) a review of multilingual writing development in nonacademic contexts, (e) a review of work on the place of "culture" in multilingual writing development, and (f) a brief discussion of trends and future directions in multilingual writing development research.

CASE STUDIES OF MULTILINGUAL WRITERS

A substantial amount of research on multilingual writing development has adopted a positivistic, scientized approach—the description of trends among groups of writers that are explicitly or implicitly assumed to generalize to whole populations. Although such research has its value, and constitutes much of the work we review here, it downplays or ignores the most basic reality of all: that writers are individuals rather than aggregated types, and that "we can be led seriously astray" (Schegloff, 1993, p. 102) by mistaking the latter for the former. We therefore begin by highlighting the all-important case study literature on multilingual writers—we do so by reviewing three exemplar studies (Mishler, 1990), each from a different educational context, to give a sense of multilingual writers as individuals first and foremost.

Kenner (1997) described the emergent multilingual literacy of "Meera," a 4-year-old whose parents had immigrated from India's Gujarat state to London, England. At home, Meera's life centered around the family business, a neighborhood grocery store: Her play both at home and in kindergarten often involved imaginary service encounters. Meera's exposure to Gujarati literacy was at first limited to observing her mother read newspapers and write letters—her parents had decided to delay teaching her the Gujarati (Devanagari) script until she had mastered the English alphabet. However, things began to change when Meera's kindergarten, which actively sought to include the home literacies of its diverse student body in its curriculum, invited her mother to introduce Gujarati writing to the students. As her mother was demonstrating the script, Meera spontaneously climbed up next to her and pretended to write too, stating "I'm writing in Gujarati" (p. 79). Following this event, Meera often included proto-Gujarati script in her in-class writings/drawings, accompanied by such comments as "I write like my mum" (p. 80). By the end of the school year, Meera was producing bilingual texts featuring names, letters, and numbers in both English and Gujarati, and seemed well on her way to developing basic biliteracy.

Fu (1995) described the case of 14-year-old "Sy," the youngest of nine in a Laotian refugee family. The family had been reunited in the United States after years of separation in Thai refugee camps; as a result, Sy had received only 1 year of formal education. On first arriving in the United States, Sy had been moved from grade to grade, eventually ending up in Grade 3 at age 11. In his third year he was placed in seventh grade—a level more appropriate for his age. However, Sy struggled in his low-level mainstream classes, rarely spoke or joined in group activities, avoided eye contact, and was convinced that high school graduation was his educational limit. In terms of writing, he performed with minimal acceptability on knowledge-telling tasks such as story summaries, but found analytical writing impossible. Fu attributed such problems to both Sy's level of English and his overall lack of educational experience—like immigrant students in some other situated case studies (e.g., Valdés, 2001), she saw Sy headed for educational failure.

But something remarkable happened in the middle of the school year: Sy was introduced to freewriting, here used as shorthand for a simplified process pedagogy. Unable at first even to comprehend the idea, Sy eventually produced a short piece about his life in a refugee camp in Thailand, and quickly followed it with an imaginative story about Halloween, his first try at fiction. When the next freewriting unit began 4 months later, Sy immediately wrote a fairy tale, calling on his older sister for help translating. This was followed by a story titled "Lazy Cat," which he worked on intensively with his ESL tutor, Andy. Around this time, both Fu and Susan, Sy's classroom English teacher, began to see demonstrable changes in his behavior:

> From being markedly quiet in the class or ESL room … , he became quite animated with Andy and with his classmates in their small writing group during the free-writing periods. After Sy wrote "Lazy Cat," Susan also noticed Sy was beginning to emerge from his shell. She told me, "Sy has become very friendly to me recently. Whenever he sees me, he speaks to me loudly and clearly, and with a big smile on his face, 'Hi, Mrs. M. How are you doing today?' I feel really good about it." (p. 186)

Sy's writing skills and classroom involvement continued to develop during a 6-week unit of journal writing. By year's end, Sy had made substantially more progress than his three school-age siblings, and was first unbelieving but then thrilled at being promoted to the eighth grade. Although Sy's future educational path was by no means clear, his experience with process writing had proved transformative.

Finally, Leki (1999) described Jan, an American university student who had emigrated from Poland at age 17. In his first semester, Jan took 17 credits in a premedical program, failed a remedial ESL class, and ended up with an 0.65 grade point average (GPA); he spent the next 3 years digging himself out. Hardly an ideal student by educational standards, Jan nonetheless constructed his educational environment in a highly agentive way, choosing courses requiring little or no writing, reading strategically (and minimally), attending the writing center diligently to impress his composition teacher, recycling writing assignments in different classes, inventing content for experiential assignments, and setting up an elaborate lab report exchange ring. At the same time, Jan was unremittingly critical of his educational experience: He regarded most of his courses—and especially his ESL writing courses—as "B.S." Leki speculated on the degree to which Jan's first-semester experience colored his subsequent views, noting his obsessive concern with grades. She also mentioned Jan's full-time work schedule during his first 2 years of college, a point not to be underestimated. In sum, although Jan's experience as a university writer shared similarities with those of both his native and non-native English-speaking peers (e.g., Anderson, et al., 1990), his was first and foremost an *individual* experience, and Leki's account gives a lived feel for what that experience was like.

The three case studies just reviewed highlight the all-important individuality of the writers themselves; in so doing, they offer insights that other forms of research cannot provide. Leki's study, for example, reveals how the seemingly marginalized Jan cleverly and laboriously constructed his own educational experience, and in ways quite at variance with approved student behavior. For their part, both Kenner's and Fu's studies capture breakthrough moments that may have radically transformed their participants' multilingual development. Obviously, multilingual students also encounter failure (e.g., Johns, 1991; Valdés, 2001), as well as what can only be described as "mixed" formative experiences (e.g., Shen, 1989). But to understand these experiences as lived realities rather than statistical abstractions, rich and detailed individual description is required.

MULTILINGUAL WRITING AND BILITERACY DEVELOPMENT IN PRIMARY AND SECONDARY SCHOOL SETTINGS

According to the 2000 census, 18% of people in the United States 5 years or older spoke a language other than English at home (Pérez, 2004). Although most of these were Spanish speakers, more than 25 languages were widely spoken, the 4 most common being Vietnamese, Hmong, Cantonese, and Korean. These linguistically diverse populations lived in all parts of the United States, with the largest numbers in California, Puerto Rico, Texas, Florida, New York, Illinois, and Arizona. Although there is undoubtedly research being conducted on biliteracy around the world, the English-language literature focuses mainly on ESL settings in the United States. A notable exception is Hornberger (2003)—although many of its chapters deal with biliteracy in U.S. schools, the book also includes insightful discussions of biliteracy and language planning in Wales, India, South Africa, and Bolivia.

Here we focus specifically on child literacy/writing development in second or additional languages, usually English in the United States. Peregoy and Boyle (2005; see also Matsuda & De Pew, 2002) assert that although substantial research exists on such development in the first language, little has been done on early literacy/writing development in ESL, particularly among students who have not had literacy education in their home language. Notable exceptions include Edelsky (1982, 1986), Hudelson (1984), and Urzua (1987), whose case studies showed that ESL literacy development is similar in many respects to that of native English speakers, although there are also important differences. Research further shows that learners can benefit from ESL literacy instruction before developing full control of the oral language, and that students already literate in their first languages are more likely to transfer knowledge, skills, and attitudes to facilitate second-language (L2) literacy acquisition.

Much current research defines literacy not just as isolated reading and writing skills, but in terms of how meaning is constructed within specific sociocultural contexts. According to this perspective, functional literacy involves learning *multiple literacies* (Barton & Hamilton, 1998; Gee, 2000)—for school, church, work, community functions, everyday life, and so on. In this view, the development of first-language (L1) literacy is important both in itself and for its positive effects on L2 literacy development, as mentioned previously. A recent representative volume (Pérez, 2004) contains chapters on language/literacy acquisition in Native American, Puerto Rican, Vietnamese American, Mexican American, and Chinese American communities from a comparative perspective. Especially helpful in understanding the complexities of biliteracy is Dávila de Silva's (2004) case study of a Mexican second grader.

The multiple-literacies approach is currently being translated into classroom practice, as documented in Hawkins (2004). Most of the chapters in this book are based on Gee's (2004) notion of Discourse(s), which he defines there as follows:

> [Discourses are] ways of combining a specific social language with specific ways of acting-interacting-thinking-believing-valuing-feeling, as well as ways of coordinating, and getting coordinated by other people, various tools, technologies, objects, and artifacts, and various "appropriate" times and places in order to be recognized as enacting a socially-situated identity and an appropriately-related activity. (p. 24)

Gee argues that one never simply learns to read and write, but rather learns to read and write specific social languages within specific Discourses. He suggests that certain key elements are needed for the acquisition of Discourses—learning the right situated meanings, cultural models, identities, activities, and social languages. In order to go beyond simply being socialized into (and by) Discourses, however, Gee sees the need for two additional elements: *critical framing* and *transformed practice.* According to Gee:

> [Critical framing] involves juxtaposing the ways and values of different Discourses, and framing one Discourse within the ways and values of another. This process allows learners to compare and contrast different Discourses (and their values and their practices) as part and parcel of the learning process. (p. 29)

Transformed practice involves the learners not only learning the dominant Discourse but developing the power to critique and resist its various impositions when they are used to construct some as inferior; learners, according to Gee, need not only learn the game but also how to change the game.

Stein's action research (2004) sets out to use some of Gee's ideas in working with South African students in "a challenging and emotionally-laden project for both learners and their teachers" that "requires imaginative and culturally-sensitive pedagogical interventions" (p. 35). In an educational situation where writing in English is the dominant literacy practice, students come to school speaking English as their second, third, or even fourth language. The course described is designed to bring the students' "representational resources" (Kress, 1997)—their cross-cultural perspectives and diverse multiliteracies (oral, written, visual)—into the learning context of the classroom. Stein discusses teacher reactions to her work and writes:

> Some teachers think that the time devoted to developing multiliteracies (in this instance, the visual, oral and performance modes) is time wasted, time that should be spent on developing and sustaining students' skills in written academic English. My response is that literacy learning requires a social context in which learners' identities and histories are central to the formation of that context. (p. 49)

MULTILINGUAL WRITING DEVELOPMENT IN UNIVERSITY SETTINGS

Three comprehensive reviews chronicle the results of multilingual writing development research in tertiary settings. Silva's (1993) focus was on the attested differences between English as a first language (L1) writing and ESL (L2) writing as reported in 72 empirical research articles published in a variety of journals. Differences were found between L1 and L2 writers in terms of both their composing processes and their resulting texts. In the first case, L2 writers were found to do less planning, had more difficulty setting goals and organizing material, and reviewed and reflected less on their texts than L1 writers. In the second case, L2 texts were less fluent, accurate, and effective. Silva concluded that L1 and L2 writing are strategically, rhetorically, and linguistically different, and called for teaching approaches acknowledging these differences.

Cumming (2001) summarized findings from two decades of research on college-level ESL writing, employing three categories: quality of texts, composing processes, and specific sociocultural contexts of development. Text-based studies showed that, over time, multilingual writers developed more advanced, nativelike syntax, morphology, vocabulary, rhetorical structure, and means of signaling intertextuality. Process-based studies, many using think-aloud protocols, showed that L1 and L2 composing are basically similar processes, although multilingual writers exert more cognitive effort on formal issues, which may affect their ability to plan, as well as to perform other cognitive tasks. Yet the research also shows that:

> As people learn to write in a second language they gain greater control over their abilities to plan, revise and edit their texts, to search for appropriate words and phrases…, and to attend more often or intently to their ideas in respect to the forms of the second language. (p. 6)

For their part, contextually based studies have documented individual development of multilingual writing in various settings, as exemplified in the case studies described earlier.

In the third and most recent review, Polio (2003) divided second language writing studies into four categories:

1. Text-based studies, many of them quantitative which, have documented the development of writing over time and the role of task in writing performance.
2. Process-based studies which have been more qualitative in nature and have asked such questions as what the writing process is like, how L1 and L2 writing processes differ, what happens during peer review, how teacher feedback is interpreted, and how writing processes change over time and experience.
3. Writer-based studies which are virtually all done in the qualitative mode, have produced descriptions of students' experiences in ESL and content-area classes, their perspectives on plagiarism, and their coping strategies, and so on.
4. Research on social contexts which has studied writing development in the classroom, outside the classroom, and in writing programs.

The three reviews just described paint a picture of active research on ESL writing at the university level. This research has been driven mainly by the need for improved teaching methods. A primary motivation has been that teachers and researchers have not been content with borrowing methods from L1 composition without verifying their appropriateness. Next, we consider studies of the application of specific pedagogical techniques and domains in university-level multilingual settings.

Research on the Role of Feedback

Teacher feedback on student writing is considered a critical part of writing instruction. Such feedback can take different forms, for example, face-to-face dialogue in teacher–student writing conferences, or written comments at various points in the writing process. According to Ferris and Hedgcock (2005), empirical studies of teacher feedback represent three major categories: (a) descriptive studies of what teachers do when they respond, (b) research on the effects of teacher comments, and (c) surveys of student opinions about teacher feedback. The results in the first two categories have not been as consistent as those in the third, but Ferris and Hedgcock cite four relatively consistent results overall: (a) Students appreciate teacher feedback, (b) Students see value in teacher feedback in a number of areas, not just language errors, (c) Students are frustrated by teacher feedback that is cryptic and illegible, and (d) Students value a mix of encouraging and constructive criticism.

The other form of feedback recently receiving attention in L2 research is peer response. Stemming from developments in the social construction of knowledge and collaborative learning, peer response is an important part of L2 writing instruction in North American university contexts (see Levine, Oded, Connor, & Asons, 2002, for a rare study from a different context). L2 writing response groups involve varied and complex social relations, which have been researched in terms of distinct types of communication, intricate peer dynamics, and varied participant stances and roles (Mendonça & Johnson, 1994; Nelson, Carson, Danison, & Gajdusek, 1995). The research suggests that, in order to be implemented effectively in multilingual contexts, peer response should be extensively explained and modeled. Specific instruction, such as that involving videotaped group interaction or teaching politeness and communication strategies, can increase student understanding and acceptance of the activity (Liu & Hansen, 2002). Through preparation and training in such activities, students may gain appreciation of the methods and goals of peer response, thus enabling them to engage in it more effectively.

Although some earlier L2 studies (e.g., Connor & Asenavage, 1994) reported discouraging findings, more recent research indicates that both form and meaning revisions result from peer response, and that these revisions have positive effects on essay quality (e.g., Berg, 1999; Paulus, 1999). In addition, peer response boosts the performance and confidence of the responders (Leki, 1990). This is not to suggest, however, that peer response is trouble-free: Research has studied responders who focus only on surface errors or give vague or unkind comments, student doubts about the validity of the comments they receive, listening comprehension problems, and confusion over U.S. academic expectations (e.g., Ferris, 2003; Leki, 1990; Liu & Hansen, 2002). Some studies also suggest that differing cultural definitions of the situation limit the effectiveness of multilingual peer response (e.g., Carson & Nelson, 1996).

Research on the Role of Grammar

Historically, ESL teaching was largely grammar based; to some extent it continues to be so. It is no surprise, then, that, even recently, a substantial amount of research has investigated the role of grammar in L2 writing.

Error gravity studies—research on the effects of different error types on faculty members' evaluations of multilingual texts—have made important contributions. They respond, in part, to the increasing popularity of the Writing Across the Curriculum movement in the United States, where the goal is to integrate writing into all coursework. Santos (1988) studied the reactions of 178 U.S. university faculty from across fields to two 400-word compositions, one written by a Chinese student and the other by a Korean student. The results showed that: Content received lower ratings than language; professors found most errors comprehensible, unirritating, but still academically unacceptable; humanities/social science professors were more lenient than science professors; older professors were less irritated by errors than younger professors; and non-native English-speaking professors were usually more severe in their judgments. Janopoulos (1992) compared faculty members' tolerance for native speakers' and non-native speakers' errors, finding a generally greater tolerance for the latter. However, faculty judged different kinds of errors differently—for example, word order and relative clause errors were seen as major, whereas article and preposition errors were seen as minor.

In other grammar-focused research, Hinkel (2003) compared 1,083 academic texts written by L1 and L2 writers at U.S. universities. She found that advanced non-native speakers still used significantly higher median rates of simple syntactic and lexical features than newly admitted 1st-year native speaker students. In other words, non-native speakers' productive grammar and lexis is relatively unelaborated, consisting of everyday vocabulary and structures used in conversation.

Ferris (2002; Ferris & Hedgcock, 2005) comprehensively reviewed pedagogical approaches to grammatical error treatment in L2 writing. One important issue here is the claim that because research does not show substantial benefits for error correction, and because an error focus may actually detract from writing quality and language development, grammar should be downplayed in L2 writing instruction (e.g., Truscott, 1996; Zamel, 1982). Research on amount, type, and specificity of error treatment, however, provides interesting findings: Based on empirical work, Ferris and Roberts (2001) suggested that it is neither efficient nor possible for teachers to catch all errors—identifying patterns and marking only two or three major error types is more beneficial for students. Furthermore, research shows that explicit teacher correction does not provide students with any significant advantage in improving their written grammar. Instead, a minimalist approach in which teachers identify and code errors but do not correct them saves time, prevents student confusion, and leads to student improvement.

Text and Genre Analysis in Multilingual Writing Development

Linguistic and rhetorical text analysis was a popular approach in multilingual writing research in the 1980s and 1990s: Cohesion, coherence, top-level discourse structure, and metadiscourse were extensively studied as measures of writing development and performance. Connor and Kaplan (1987) and Connor (1996) included theoretical and empirical investigations of a variety of approaches to text analysis. Connor described three major schools of thought that have shaped linguistic text analysis in L2 writing research: The Prague School contributed the important concepts of *theme* and *rheme* to text analysis; systemic functional linguistics encouraged the analysis of texts at three levels: ideational, interpersonal, and textual; and, finally, the "new school of discourse analysis" has been more interdisciplinary and applied in its focus. This latter approach gave rise to the important NORDTEXT project in Scandinavia (Evensen, 1986) that has produced invaluable analyses of student writing. In addition, the new school has also combined linguistic and rhetorical analyses of student texts. An example is Connor and Lauer (1988), in which a multilevel analysis of persuasive essays by students was undertaken, focusing on both textual (e.g., cohesion and coherence) and rhetorical/persuasive (e.g., rhetorical appeals) features. The resulting text model was used to evaluate persuasive student essays in a number of empirical studies in the 1990s (e.g., Connor, 1990, 1991). More recently, Spicer-Escalante (2005) used Connor and Lauer's persuasive appeals model to study the essay writing of Mexican American or Spanish Heritage college students. She found it a useful tool for describing the strategies of these students' Spanish and English writing, and to distinguish their writing from that of monolingual native English- and Spanish-speaking students. The results showed that the Spanish Heritage Students used more appeals based on *logos* than did the native English- and Spanish-speaking students. When writing in both Spanish and English, the Spanish Heritage Students used more elements that construct rational appeals, such as analogies, testimonies, examples, and cause and effect. The results also showed that the Spanish Heritage Students in the study used more effective credibility and affective appeals than did the other students. Credibility was achieved through personal experiences; affective appeals included detailed, vivid stories and concrete, charged language.

However, as in mainstream rhetoric/composition studies, text analysis began to lose its luster when the social context of writing came to the fore in the late 1980s and 1990s. At the same time, as both L1 compositionists Barton and Stygall (2002) and L2 writing specialist Hyland (2003) argue, text analysis continues to have an important place in writing research. In addition, new developments in corpus linguistics make it easier to analyze, describe, and evaluate text (Biber, Conrad, & Reppen, 1998).

Contemporary text analysis, however, needs to go beyond simply studying texts, taking into account their contexts of production and consumption. Today, writing is increasingly regarded as socially situated, with each situation entailing considerations of audience, purpose, and form of presentation, and corresponding amounts of revision, collaboration, and attention to detail. The expectations and norms of discourse communities or communities of practice (cultural and disciplinary) obviously shape these expectations and practices. Instead of analyzing what texts mean, Bazerman and Prior (2004) proposed that we analyze what texts talk about, how they influence audiences, and how they come into being. Taking Bazerman and Prior's lead, Connor (2004) discussed ways to extend text analysis in L2 writing through observation, surveys, and miniethnographies.

Genre analysis began as a form of linguistically oriented text analysis (e.g., Swales, 1981; Tarone, Dwyer, Gillette, & Icke, 1981), and has had a major impact on English for Academic Purposes (EAP) and English for Specific Purposes (ESP) instruction. When the focus of analysis is on the structural regularities distinguishing one conventional kind of text from another, this is genre analysis. Inherent in the text-analytic approach to genre is the assumption that genres can be prototypically described from a linguistic/discourse perspective, and that the resulting descriptions can then be used to teach writing in academic and nonacademic settings. Swales' (1981, 1990) work on the rhetorical moves of the empirical research article was pioneering in this regard. Research on other genres—for example, letters, grant proposals, and business reports—has widened the scope of genre analysis, as reviewed in Swales (2004). Genre analysis in business and (nonacademic) professional contexts is further described below.

Hyon (1996) described two additional approaches to genre analysis: North American new rhetoric studies, and the Australian systemic functional approach. The former differs from the ESP approach in that it focuses more on the situational contexts in which genres occur and places emphasis on the social purposes or actions that these genres accomplish; but the new rhetoric approach has not had much impact on studies of multilingual writing. The Australian systemic functional approach has been actively used to research and teach genre conventions and expectations, especially (as its name implies) in Australia. Cope and Kalantzis (1993) and Johns (1997) have described the current and potential uses of this approach in Australia and North America, respectively.

WRITING IN MULTILINGUAL BUSINESS AND OTHER PROFESSIONAL SETTINGS

Ten years ago, the analysis of multilingual business writing dealt primarily with business letters and faxes. Abelen, Redeker, and Thompson (1993) analyzed the rhetorical strategies of American and Dutch fund-raising letters. They found that American letters were more overtly persuasive, used a more direct linguistic style, and were dominated by interpersonal relations. Yli-Jokipii's (1996) analysis of a large corpus of business letters and faxes of request written in Finnish, German, and British English was the first to show that, in corpus analysis, contexts of production has to be carefully considered to explain individual, cultural, and organizational variation in the letters. Louhiala-Salminen (1997) analyzed the genre moves of business faxes written in English in a Finnish company, and Connor (1999) conducted a miniethnography of faxing language by a Finnish fish broker and his multilingual buyers and sellers. In the latter study, all communication took place in English, and analysis revealed sociolinguistic accommodation by the fish broker depending on his role—buyer or seller—and on his evaluation of the interlocutor's English.

Common to all the aforementioned studies is their focus on the diversity of the audiences business writers need to persuade. Skills and strategies that multilingual writers may have after learning general English will need to be enhanced in global business environments.

As e-mail has become the preferred medium of international business communication, research has shifted accordingly. Nickerson (1999) studied the use of English in the e-mails of a Dutch manager of a multinational corporation. She found that English was used for communication outside the manager's own work group but that some Dutch lexis was used in the e-mails regardless of the native language of the recipient. She also found that e-mail openings and closings were in English, and remained so even when the rest of the message was in Dutch. Mulholland (1999) analyzed 76 e-mails collected over a 3-month period from secretaries and administrators at an Australian university, and the perceptions held by their senders and receivers. Polite expressions tended to occur only at the ends of e-mails, resulting in reader dissatisfaction.

Mulholland's (1999) and Nickerson's (1999) studies were some of the earliest on e-mail use in international business—they have been seminal in describing e-mail as a distinct genre. More recent studies of e-mailing in multilingual settings situate it as part of larger genre systems. Van Mulken and Van der Meer (2005), for example, studied the replies to customer inquiries by American and Dutch companies as the first component in the promotional sequence of sales: customer contact, reply, potential order, and after-sale correspondence. They mapped out the genre structure of the reply e-mails to customer inquiries and made both cross-national and cross-company comparisons.

Perhaps the most noteworthy development in studies of multilingual business writing has been the recognition of the constitutive role of spoken language in the construction of written texts. Researchers have realized that writing is intertextual and that much text production also involves speech (Gunnarsson, 1997; Loos, 1999). Following the lead of L1 professional writing researchers (e.g., Brown & Herndl, 1986; Smart, 1998), L2 researchers have embraced the case study method and ethnographic approaches in order to study the complexity of writing in international organizations.

Louhiala-Salminen (2002) described an ethnographic approach to studying international business communication in an international company in Finland with English as its main language of communication. The research methodology was developed by an international research group known as "INBUS." The method involves shadowing managers and allows for the analysis of communication through all phases of the genre system, including e-mail, faxes, face-to-face meetings, phone conversations, and so forth. The goal of the research was to generate descriptions of "slices of life" of managerial discourse in different languages and cultures. Written textual data were supplemented by transcriptions of taped speech; future research will benefit from videotaped data. Future research will also need to develop such data into corpora for ease of data manipulation and cross-cultural comparisons of multilingual writing. Such corpora will also provide useful knowledge for teachers and textbook writers about the actual language and writing needs of international business professionals.

The research on multilingual writing in business and industry, reviewed previously, has attempted to describe prototypical language and sequences of communicative events in English. The purpose has been to provide English-language standards for business communication instruction. The findings from international studies of business communication have shown that linguistic norms in today's business, conducted in English, may not be those of British, American, or other native-speaker Englishes. Instead, as Crystal (1997) has argued, "World Standard Spoken English," in which non-native varieties of English are used daily in international business negotiations, has emerged. Thus, in her study of the Finnish fish broker, Connor (1999) found that the broker did not judge his business associates based on their English-language ability or lack thereof: "As long as their fish is good and fresh and they can deliver in time, I'm happy," he said of his sellers. The point is that the broker could not have selected his business associates according to their English-language ability even if he had wanted to—"competition is too fierce and good suppliers are scarce, and so is the product, fresh fish" (p. 123). Scholars concerned with critical pedagogy, such as Modiano (2000, 2001), also argue for the recognition of non-native varieties of English.

Future research on second language writing in international business settings will need to collect data on varieties of English, and, even more important, on the choice of language by multilingual business writers. It will also need to become more corpus-based.

THE ISSUE OF "CULTURE" IN MULTILINGUAL WRITING DEVELOPMENT

The notion of culture has had a controversial recent history in studies of multilingual writing development. Much of the controversy concerns the degree to which such development is influenced by discrete cultural patterns, such as individualism versus collectivism, or inductive versus deductive styles of communication.

Proponents of cultural approaches to multilingual writing (e.g., Connor, 1996; Kaplan, 1966) originally emphasized received views of cultural difference that took discrete cultures as primary units of analysis. They hypothesized that these exercised direct causal influence on rhetorical patterning, expression of opinion, critical thinking, voice, originality, good writing, and attitudes toward both education in general and specific pedagogical techniques. They sometimes based their approaches on a substantial literature in cultural and cross-cultural communication (e.g., Heath, 1983; Hofstede, 1991).

Critics of cultural approaches, on the other hand, took their lead from newer understandings of culture influenced by critical theory and postmodernism, for example, Said's (1978) concept of Orientalism. Said argued that the broad distinction between East and West was a colonial invention that fit all colonial subjects to a set of dichotomous descriptions vis-à-vis their colonial masters, for example, emotional versus rational, group-oriented versus individualistic, imitative versus original. These mirror-image representations provided a broad sense-making framework by which colonialism could be justified; and, equally important, they continue to underpin justifications for neo-colonialism in the present day. Critics of cultural approaches to multilingual writing (e.g., Kubota, 1999; Pennycook, 1998) point to the correspondences between Orientalist stereotypes and researchers' generalizations about multilingual (especially East Asian–origin) writers. The latter, for example, are often characterized as inductive and imitative, with the implication that their native Western counterparts are their opposites in these regards. Such stereotyping has led at least one major researcher (Spack, 1997b) to argue that cultural explanation has no place in the study of multilingual writers.

Proponents of cultural explanation (e.g., Ramanathan & Atkinson, 1999b) have responded that cultural differences *do* exist and therefore need to be considered in research on multilingual writers. Though rejecting Orientalist stereotyping (e.g., Atkinson, 1999a), they point to the numerous studies that seem to show enduring patterns of cultural influence. They can also refer to work done by the critics themselves (e.g., Pennycook, 2001; Spack, 1997a), which sometimes also appeals to cultural influences in describing the characteristics of multilingual writers. At the same time, however, proponents of cultural explanation have become much more cautious about using cultural generalizations and dichotomies to describe individuals and whole groups (e.g., Atkinson, 1999b, 2004).

Contrastive Rhetoric

Originated by Robert Kaplan (1966), the concept of *contrastive rhetoric* (CR) has had a major impact on teaching multilingual writing worldwide. It is also, at present, a favorite target of critics of cultural approaches to multilingual writing development. Kaplan originally proposed CR to explain why writers in the university ESL program he administered were having trouble writing in a top-down, thesis-driven way. Basing his thinking on then-current trends in cultural anthropology, he made the assumption that each language had its own special logic, and that this logic was reflected directly in cultural styles of textual organization. Though Kaplan expressed this hypothesis in a generally careful and non-judgmental way, he also included a set of diagrams that has since become infamous—English rhetoric is represented as a straight line, Oriental rhetoric as a spiral, and various other cultural/linguistic rhetorics as zigzags, parallel lines linked by dotted lines, and so on. Much of the ensuing criticism has focused on the ethnocentric and stereotyping nature of these diagrams (e.g., Pennycook, 1998).

Various CR research efforts followed Kaplan's (1966) original proposal—the work of John Hinds in the 1980s is especially noteworthy (see also Connor & Kaplan, 1987). Hinds (e.g., 1983a, 1983b) identified four conventional patterns of expository prose in Japanese, one of which—the "ki-sho-ten-ketsu" pattern—seemed to differ maximally from English. Hinds further suggested that such patterns might be transferred to English academic writing by Japanese. In subsequent research, Hinds (1987) introduced the idea that different languages assume different levels of "reader versus writer responsibility" for explicitness; he also argued (1990) that the deductive versus inductive distinction commonly made between writing in English and some Asian languages was misguided, but that quasi-inductive rhetorical structures could be found in the latter.

In the 1990s, there were substantial developments in the study of CR, as documented by Connor (1996). Thus, genres beyond the student essay were recognized as falling into its domain, and, in terms of methodology, rhetorical analysis and genre analysis were added to CR's traditional text-analytic repertoire. CR research also moved beyond a focus on text per se to cultural influences on composition processes and pedagogy. Finally, as ESL classes in the United States began enrolling increasing numbers of Generation 1.5 students (i.e., students who had been born in or come to the United States at an early age but were raised in non-English-speaking home environments), researchers (e.g., Matsuda, 1997) argued that CR needed to offer dynamic models of multilingual development rather than viewing it in fixed and static terms.

Critics of CR, mostly the same scholars who have argued against cultural approaches to multilingual writing development in general, have focused on its use of single, broad generalizations to characterize whole cultural groups. Thus, in a lengthy series of publications, Kubota (e.g., 1999, 2002) has charged that CR *others*—that is, essentializes, homogenizes, and dichotomizes—East Asian writers along Orientalist lines. An earlier study (Kubota, 1997) questioned the prevalence of "ki-sho-ten-ketsu" in Japanese expository prose, arguing that no complex society—and certainly not one with Japan's history of importing Western knowledge—relies on single, pure approaches to writing. This was followed by an empirical study (1998), in which Kubota found both deductive and inductive organizational patterns in the Japanese and English essays of Japanese university students.

Other Culturally Focused Multilingual Writing Research

Additional studies provide rich descriptions of cultural contexts for writing. Such research is vital to understanding the backgrounds and educational experiences of multilingual writers, and hence their writing development in the additional language(s) being acquired.

The authors in Foster and Russell (2002) provided rich accounts of writing instruction in diverse national educational contexts, with a special focus on secondary school-to-university transitions. Muchiri (2002), for example, provided a knowledgeable insider's view of the role of English (the medium of instruction) writing in Kenyan higher education. Likewise, Li (2002) highlighted both continuity and change in education-sponsored writing in China—a dialectic that takes on immense importance considering China's rapid development along global capitalistic lines. Other recent research in this cross-national perspective tradition includes Canagarajah (2002a), Kobayashi and Rinnert (2002), and You (2005).

Hybridity and Transculturation in Multilingual Writing Development

Dissatisfaction with a focus on monolithic cultural identities, influences, and products has led to research and theory foregrounding the complex impurity of all cultural scenes (e.g., Bhabha, 1994; Pratt, 1991). Following this lead, multilingual writing researchers have begun to give the hybrid nature of multilingual writing their attention. Although it has been argued that *all* texts are multiply voiced (e.g., Bakhtin, 1986) and polygenetic (Patell, 1999), the assumption here is that because multilingual writers automatically access multiple linguistic and cultural knowledges, their writing will be an especially rich site for the production of hybrid forms and concepts. Canagarajah (e.g., 1999, 2002b), one of the main proponents of this approach, put it as follows:

> We now know that there is considerable interaction, borrowing, and fusion between cultures and communicative genres. The hybrid nature of cultures in the postmodern world creates considerable problems in defining which constructs of a particular culture are unique and native to one community and which are borrowed (or interactively shaped in contact with another culture). If the monolithic definition of cultures and genres is rejected, it becomes easy to see how students may move across cultures and texts in their communicative practice. Although students may come with certain preferred traditions and practices of text construction of their own, they can still creatively negotiate alternate structures they are introduced to (2002b).

One lens for looking at textual hybridity is *code-switching*—the practice of alternating elements of distinct linguistic codes within and across spoken utterances and written sentences. Taking a code-switching perspective, Buell (2004) argued for a three-pronged approach to researching hybridity in multilingual texts: interpretive analysis (i.e., of textual code features in terms of their functionality), intertextual analysis, and ethnographic analysis. She demonstrated this approach in analyzing the ESL writing of a student from the Ivory Coast.

Solsken, Willett, and Wilson-Kennan (2000) used the textual hybridity concept to analyze the discourse practices of a Puerto Rican–origin first grader in a U.S. primary school. From a normative, school-based standpoint, the child's texts appeared deficient; from the perspective of her home-based discourse practices, however, the child's texts richly interwove school- and home-based themes and genres, as well as mediated tensions between them. This analysis suggests the insurgent multiculturalism and transformative potential implicit in hybrid textual practices—for taking us beyond the currently limited and inequality-maintaining discourse practices of teachers and schools, ofttimes even those committed to multiculturalism.

Although the notion of textual/multicultural hybridity has begun to impact multilingual writing research, the cultural hybridity notion itself has come in for criticism. Young (1995), for example, pointed to the hidden foundationalist assumptions behind the notion—that is, a cultural "hybrid" can only be the combination of two purebreds—that is, two pure cultures. This criticism seems to extend to other concepts influencing cultural critique that have found their way into multilingual writing research, such as borderlands, contact zones, and third spaces. Transculturation (Pratt, 1991), in contrast, seems to avoid these foundationalist assumptions, although Zamel (1997), its original proponent in multilingual writing studies, has been criticized for arguing that textual regularities and conventions can simply be transcended (Canagarajah, 2002b).

TRENDS AND FUTURE DIRECTIONS

Regarding case studies, we believe that more research viewing writers as whole people rather than simply students or writers is needed to do justice to the multiple, complex identities and demands impacting multilingual writing development. This need is highlighted by the fact that even the case studies reviewed here were based on observations made mostly in school settings, whereas truly holistic accounts of writing development would have to go beyond such settings as well.

Relatedly, we call for studies that do not approach writing development as an activity taking place in isolation from other social activities. The integration of writers and writing into multiple social and social semiotic systems is a robust fact of life, and should therefore be foregrounded in future research. Literacy scholars (e.g., Gee, 1996) and L1 composition researchers (e.g., Bazerman, 1994, 1999) have led the way here, and multilingual writing development research should follow. Genre systems, activity systems, postprocess approaches, and enriched notions of discourse community all have a role to play here.

In pedagogically oriented research on multilingual writing development, there is a serious need for research on the effectiveness of needs analysis, which attempts to determine the needs of novice writers in order to guide pedagogical decisions, especially in the professional and advanced academic domains. Approaches to expanding needs analysis to include not only immediate, instrumental needs but also future lives and possible selves—for example, what Benesch (2001) called *rights analysis*—should also be innovated.

A further area in which research is needed involves the concept of multiliteracies (reviewed earlier). If literacy in the 21st century will involve the increasing integration of different symbolic sign systems—print, images, sounds, numbers, and graphic representations—then research needs to follow suit.

The study of cultural influences on multilingual writing development also needs to move forward. With help from new, dynamic definitions of culture (e.g., Atkinson, 2004), researchers should continue to focus on cultural influences on multilingual writing, but will need to complexify their views considerably vis-à-vis dichotomous distinctions such as linear versus nonlinear prose, Japanese versus Finnish writing, and individualist versus collectivist cultural orientations. Connor (2004) has proposed the term "intercultural rhetoric" to mark this new departure—it signifies the need to describe the vast complexities of cultural, social, and educational factors affecting multilingual writing situations.

Finally, the methodologies used to study multilingual writing development continue to evolve. The advent of corpus linguistics, for example, would seem to portend the possibility of charting the cross-time development of multilingual writing skills in ways that have yet to be envisioned. Likewise, the further development of sensitive and humane strategies for studying human beings in all their messy complexity—for example, situated qualitative research (Atkinson, 2005; Ramanathan & Atkinson, 1999a)—is needed.

ACKNOWLEDGMENTS

We would like to thank Marcia Buell, Suresh Canagarajah, Fred DiCamilla, Maggie Hawkins, John Hedgcock, Ilona Leki, Paul Kei Matsuda, Melinda Reichelt, Charlene Polio, Yoko Sabatini, and Miyuki Sasaki for their generosity in providing sources. We also thank Molly Anthony and Pilar Mur Dueñas for their comments and support during the writing of this chapter, and Ilona Leki, Paul Kei Matsuda, and Srikant Sarangi for their insightful reading of earlier drafts.

REFERENCES

Abelen, E., Redeker, G., & Thompson, S. (1993). The rhetorical structure of US–American and Dutch fund-raising letters. *Text, 13*(3), 323–350.

Anderson, W., Best, C., Black, A., Hirst, J., Miller, B., & Miller, S. (1990). Curricular underlife: A collaborative report on ways with academic words. *College Composition and Communication, 41*, 11–36.

Atkinson, D. (1999a). Response to R. Kubota, "Japanese Culture Constructed by Discourses: Implications for Applied Linguistics Research and ELT." *TESOL Quarterly, 33*, 745–749.

Atkinson, D. (1999b). TESOL and culture. *TESOL Quarterly, 33*, 625–654.

Atkinson, D. (2004). Contrasting rhetorics/contrasting cultures: Why contrastive rhetoric needs a better conceptualization of culture. *Journal of English for Academic Purposes, 3*, 277–289.

Atkinson, D. (2005). Situated qualitative research and second language writing. In P. Matsuda & T. Silva (Eds.), *Second language writing research: Perspectives on the process of knowledge construction* (pp. 49–64). Mahwah, NJ: Lawrence Erlbaum Associates.

Bakhtin, M. M. (1986). *Speech genres & other late essays*. Austin: University of Texas Press.

Barton, D., & Hamilton, M. M. (1998). *Local literacies: Reading and writing in one community*. London: Routledge.

Barton, E., & Stygall, G. (2002). *Discourse studies in composition*. Cresskill, NJ: Hampton.

Bazerman, C. (1994). Systems of genres and the enactments of social intentions. In A. Freedman & P. Medway (Eds.), *Genre and the new rhetoric* (pp. 79–101). London: Taylor & Francis.

Bazerman, C. (1999). *The languages of Edison's light*. Cambridge, MA: MIT Press.

Bazerman, C., & Prior, P. A. (Eds.). (2004). *What writing does and how it does it: An introduction to analyzing texts and textual practices*. Mahwah, NJ: Lawrence Erlbaum Associates.

Benesch, S. (2001). *Critical English for academic purposes: Theory, politics, and practice*. Mahwah, NJ: Lawrence Erlbaum Associates.

Berg, E. C. (1999). The effects of trained peer response on ESL students' revision types and writing quality. *Journal of Second Language Writing, 8*, 215–241.

Bhabha, H. (1994). *The location of culture*. London: Routledge.

Biber, D., Conrad, S., & Reppen, R. (1998). *Corpus linguistics: Investigating language structure and use*. Cambridge, England: Cambridge University Press.

Brown, R. L., & Herndl, C. G. (1986). An ethnographic study of corporate writing: Job status as reflected in written text. In B. Couture (Ed.), *Functional approaches to writing: Research perspectives* (pp. 11–28). London: Pinter.

Buell, M. (2004). Code-switching and second language writing: How multiple codes are combined in a text. In C. Bazerman & P. Prior (Eds.), *What writing does and how it does it: An introduction to analyzing texts and textual practices* (pp. 97–122). Mahwah, NJ: Lawrence Erlbaum Associates.

Canagarajah, A. S. (1999). *Resisting linguistic imperialism in English teaching*. Oxford, England: Oxford University Press.

Canagarajah, A. S. (2002a). *Critical academic writing and multilingual students*. Ann Arbor: University of Michigan Press.

Canagarajah, A. S. (2002b). *A geopolitics of academic writing*. Pittsburgh, PA: University of Pittsburgh Press.

Carson, J. G., & Nelson, G. L. (1996). Chinese students' perceptions of ESL peer group interaction. *Journal of Second Language Writing, 5*, 1–19.

Connor, U. (1990). Linguistic/rhetorical measures for international persuasive student writing. *Research in the Teaching of English, 24*(1), 67–87.

Connor, U. (1991). Linguistic/rhetorical measures for evaluating ESL writing. In L. Hamp-Lyons (Ed.), *Assessing ESL writing* (pp. 215–226). Norwood, NJ: Ablex.

Connor, U. (1996). *Contrastive rhetoric*. Cambridge, England: Cambridge University Press.

Connor, U. (1999). How like you our fish? Accommodation in international business communication. In M. Hewings & C. Nickerson (Eds.), *Business English: Research into practice* (pp. 71–99). Harlow, England: Longman.

Connor, U. (2004). Intercultural rhetoric research: Beyond texts. *Journal of English for Academic Purposes, 3*(4), 291–304.

Connor, U., & Asenavage, K. (1994). Peer response groups in ESL writing classes: How much impact on revision? *Journal of Second Language Writing, 3*, 257–276.

Connor, U., & Kaplan, R. B. (Eds.). (1987). *Writing across languages: Analysis of L2 text* (pp. 141–152). Reading, MA: Addison-Wesley.

Connor, U., & Lauer, J. (1988). Cross-cultural variation in argument. In A. C. Purves (Ed.), *Writing across languages and cultures* (pp. 138–159). San Francisco: Sage.

Cope, B., & Kalantzis, M. (Eds.). (1993). *The powers of literacy: A genre approach to teaching writing.* Pittsburgh, PA: University of Pittsburgh Press.

Crystal, D. (1997). *English as a global language.* Cambridge, England: Cambridge University Press.

Cumming, A. (2001). Learning to write in a second language: Two decades of research. *International Journal of English Studies, 1*(2), 1–23.

Dávila de Silva, A. D. (2004). Emergent Spanish writing of a second grader in a whole-language classroom. In B. Pérez (Ed.), *Sociocultural contexts of language and literacy* (2nd ed., pp. 247–274). Mahwah, NJ: Lawrence Erlbaum Associates.

Edelsky, C. (1982). Writing in a bilingual program: The relationship of L1 and L2 texts. *TESOL Quarterly, 16,* 211–228.

Edelsky, C. (1986). *Writing in a bilingual program: Había una vez.* Norwood, NJ: Ablex.

Evensen, L. S. (1986). *Nordic research in text linguistics and discourse analysis.* Trondheim, Norway: University of Trondheim, Tapir Press.

Ferris, D. R. (2002). *Treatment of error in second language student writing.* Ann Arbor: University of Michigan Press.

Ferris, D. R. (2003). *Response to student writing: Implications for second language students.* Mahwah, NJ: Lawrence Erlbaum Associates.

Ferris, D. R., & Hedgcock, J. S. (2005). *Teaching ESL composition. Purpose, process, and practice* (2nd ed.). Mahwah, NJ: Lawrence Erlbaum Associates.

Ferris, D. R., & Roberts, B. J. (2001). Error feedback in L2 writing classes: How explicit does it need to be? *Journal of Second Language Writing, 6,* 155–182.

Foster, D., & Russell, D. R. (Eds.). (2002). *Writing and learning in cross-national perspective: Transitions from secondary to higher education.* Urbana, IL: National Council of Teachers of English.

Fu, D. (1995). *"My trouble is my English": Asian students and the American dream.* Portsmouth, NH: Boynton/Cook.

Gee, J. P. (1996). *Social linguistics and literacies: Ideology in discourses* (2nd ed.). London: Falmer.

Gee, J. P. (2000). Discourse and sociocultural studies in reading. In M. Kamil, P. Mosenthal, P. Pearson, & R. Barr (Eds.), *Handbook of reading research* (Vol. III, pp. 195–207). Mahwah, NJ: Lawrence Erlbaum Associates.

Gee, J. P. (2004). Learning language as a matter of learning social languages within discourses. In M. R. Hawkins (Ed.), *Language learning and teacher education* (pp. 13–31). Clevedon, England: Multilingual Matters.

Gunnarsson, B. (1997). The writing process from a sociolinguistic viewpoint. *Written Communication, 14,* 139–188.

Hawkins, M. R. (Ed.). (2004). *Language learning and teacher education: A sociocultural approach.* Clevedon, England: Multilingual Matters.

Heath, S. B. (1983). *Ways with words: Language, life, and work in communities and classrooms.* Cambridge, England: Cambridge University Press.

Hinds, J. (1983a). Contrastive rhetoric: Japanese and English. *Text, 3,* 183–195.

Hinds, J. (1983b). Linguistics and written discourse in English and Japanese: A contrastive study (1978–1982). *Annual Review of Applied Linguistics, 3,* 78–84.

Hinds, J. (1987). Reader versus writer responsibility: A new typology. In U. Connor & R. B. Kaplan (Eds.), *Writing across languages: Analysis of L2 text* (pp. 141–152). Reading, MA: Addison-Wesley.

Hinds, J. (1990). Inductive, deductive, quasi-inductive: Expository writing in Japanese, Korean, Chinese, and Thai. In U. Connor & A. M. Johns (Eds.), *Coherence in writing: Research and pedagogical perspectives* (pp. 87–110). Alexandria, VA: Teachers of English to Speakers of Other Languages.

Hinkel, E. (2003). Simplicity without elegance: features of sentences in L1 and L2 academic texts. *TESOL Quarterly, 37*(2), 275–302.

Hofstede, G. (1991). *Cultures and organizations: Software for the mind.* London: McGraw-Hill.

Hornberger, N. H. (Ed.). (2003). *Continua of biliteracy: An ecological framework for educational policy, research, and practice in multilingual settings.* Clevedon, England: Multilingual Matters.

Hudelson, S. (1984). Kan yu ret and rayt en ingles: Children become literate in English as a second language. *TESOL Quarterly, 18,* 221–238.

Hyland, K. (2003). Genre-based pedagogies: A social response to process. *Journal of Second Language Writing, 12,* 17–29.

Hyon, S. (1996). Genre in three traditions: Implications for ESL. *TESOL Quarterly, 30,* 693–722.

Janopoulos, M. (1992). University faculty tolerance of NS and NNS writing errors: A comparison. *Journal of Second Language Writing, 1*(2), 109–122.

Johns, A. M. (1991). Interpreting an English competency exam: The frustration of an ESL science student. *Written Communication, 8,* 379–401.

Johns, A. M. (1997). *Text, role, and context: Developing academic literacies.* Cambridge, England: Cambridge University Press.

Kaplan, R. B. (1966). Cultural thought patterns in intercultural education. *Language Learning, 16,* 1–20.

Kenner, C. (1997). A child writes from her everyday world: Using home texts to develop biliteracy at school. In E. Gregory (Ed.), *One child, many worlds: Early learning in multicultural communities* (pp. 75–86). New York: Teachers College Press.

Kobayashi, H., & Rinnert, C. (2002). High school student perceptions of first language literacy instruction: Implications for second language writing. *Journal of Second Language Writing, 11,* 91–116.

Kress, G. (1997). *Before writing: Rethinking the paths to literacy.* London: Routledge.

Kubota, R. (1997). A reevaluation of the uniqueness of Japanese written discourse. *Written Communication, 14,* 460–480.

Kubota, R. (1998). An investigation of L1–L2 transfer in writing among Japanese university students: Implications for contrastive rhetoric. *Journal of Second Language Writing, 7,* 69–100.

Kubota, R. (1999). Japanese culture constructed by discourses: Implications for applied linguistics research and ELT. *TESOL Quarterly, 33,* 9–35.

Kubota, R. (2002). Japanese identities in written communication: Politics and discourses. In R. Donahue (Ed.), *Exploring Japaneseness: On Japanese enactments of culture and consciousness* (pp. 293–315). Westport, CT: Ablex.

Leki, I. (1990). Potential problems with peer responding in ESL writing classes. *CATESOL Journal, 3,* 5–19.

Leki, I. (1999). "Pretty much I screwed up": Ill-served needs of a permanent resident. In L. Harklau, K. M. Losey, & M. Siegal (Eds.), *Generation 1.5 meets college composition* (pp. 17–44). Mahwah, NJ: Lawrence Erlbaum Associates.

Leki, I., Cumming, A., & Silva, T. (2005). Second-language composition teaching and learning. In P. Smagorinsky (Ed.), *Research on composition: Multiple perspectives on two decades of change* (pp. 141–170). New York: Teachers College Press.

Levine, A., Oded, B., Connor, U., & Asons, I. (2002, December). Variation in EFL–ESL peer response. *TESL-EJ: Teaching English as a Second or Foreign Language, 6*(3). Retrieved September 1, 2005, from http://www-writing.berkeley.edu/tesl-ej/ej23/a1.html

Li, X.-M. (2002). "Track (dis)connecting": Chinese high school and university writing in a time of change. In D. Foster & D. R. Russell (Eds.), *Writing and learning in cross-national perspective: Transitions from secondary to higher education* (pp. 49–87). Urbana, IL: National Council of Teachers of English.

Liu, J., & Hansen, J. G. (2002). *Peer response in second language writing classrooms.* Ann Arbor: University of Michigan Press.

Loos, E. (1999). Intertextual networks in organizations: The use of written and oral business discourse in relation to context. In F. Bargiela-Chiappini & C. Nickerson (Eds.), *Writing business: Genres, media and discourses* (pp. 315–332). Harlow, England: Longman.

Louhiala-Salminen, L. (1997). Investigating the genre of a business fax: A Finnish case study. *Journal of Business Communication, 34*(3), 316–333.

Louhiala-Salminen, L. (2002). The fly's perspective: Discourse in the daily routine of a business manager. *English for Specific Purposes, 21*(3), 211–231.

Matsuda, P. K. (1997). Constrastive rhetoric in context: A dynamic model of L2 writing. *Journal of Second Language Writing, 6*(1), 45–60.

Matsuda, P. K., & De Pew, K. E. (2002). Early second language writing: An introduction [Special Issue]. *Journal of Second Language Writing, 11,* 261–268.

Mendonça, C. O., & Johnson, K. E. (1994). Peer review negotiations: Revision activities in ESL writing instruction. *TESOL Quarterly, 28,* 745–769.

Mishler, E. (1990). Validation in inquiry-guided research: The role of exemplars in narrative studies. *Harvard Educational Review, 60,* 415–442.

Modiano, M. (2000). Euro-English: Educational standards in a cross-cultural context. *European English Messenger, 9*(1), 33–37.

Modiano, M. (2001). A new variety of English. *English Today, 4*(17), 13–19.

Muchiri, M. N. (2002). An academic writer in Kenya: The transition from secondary school to university. In D. Foster & D. R. Russell (Eds.), *Writing and learning in cross-national perspective: Transitions from secondary to higher education* (pp. 242–271). Urbana, IL: National Council of Teachers of English.

Mulholland, J. (1999). E-mail: Uses, issues and problems in an institutional setting. In F. Bargiela-Chiappini & C. Nickerson (Eds.), *Writing business: Genres, media and discourses* (pp. 57–84). Harlow, England: Longman.

Nelson, G. L., Carson, J. G., Danison, N., & Gajdusek, L. (1995). Social dimensions of second-language writing instruction: Peer response groups as cultural context. In D. L. Rubin (Ed.), *Composing social identity in written language* (pp. 89–112). Hillsdale, NJ: Lawrence Erlbaum Associates.

Nickerson, C. (1999). The use of English in electronic mail in a multinational corporation. In F. Bargiela-Chiappini & C. Nickerson (Eds.), *Writing business: Genres, media and discourses* (pp. 25–34). Harlow, England: Longman.

Patell, C. R. K. (1999). Comparative American Studies: Hybridity and beyond. *American Literary History, 11*, 166–186.

Paulus, T. (1999). The effect of peer and teacher feedback on student writing. *Journal of Second Language Writing, 8*, 265–289.

Pennycook, A. (1998). *English and the discourses of colonialism*. London: Routledge.

Pennycook, A. (2001). *Critical applied linguistics: A critical introduction*. Mahwah, NJ: Lawrence Erlbaum Associates.

Peregoy, S. F., & Boyle, O. F. (2005). *Reading, writing and learning in ESL* (4th ed.). New York: Allyn & Bacon.

Pérez, B. (Ed.). (2004). *Sociocultural contexts of language and literacy* (2nd ed.). Mahwah, NJ: Lawrence Erlbaum Associates.

Polio, C. (2003). Research on second language writing: An overview of what we investigate and how. In B. Kroll (Ed.), *Exploring the dynamics of second language writing* (pp. 35–65). Cambridge, England: Cambridge University Press.

Pratt, M. L. (1991). Arts of the contact zone. *Profession, 91*, 33–40.

Ramanathan, V., & Atkinson, D. (1999a). Ethnographic approaches and methods in L2 writing research: A critical guide and review. *Applied Linguistics, 20*, 44–70.

Ramanathan, V., & Atkinson, D. (1999b). Individualism, academic writing, and ESL writers. *Journal of Second Language Writing, 8*, 45–75.

Reichelt, M. (1999). Toward a more comprehensive view of L2 writing: Foreign language writing in the U.S. *Journal of Second Language Writing, 8*, 181–204.

Said, E. W. (1978). *Orientalism*. New York: Vintage.

Santos, T. (1988). Professors' reactions to the academic writing of nonnative-speaking students. *TESOL Quarterly, 22*, 69–90.

Schegloff, E. A. (1993). Reflections on quantification in the study of conversation. *Research on Language and Social Interaction, 26*, 99–128.

Shen, F. (1989). The classroom and the wider culture: Identity as a key to learning English composition. *College Composition and Communication, 40*, 459–466.

Silva, T. (1993). Toward an understanding of the distinct nature of L2 writing. *TESOL Quarterly, 27*, 657–677.

Smart, G. (1998). Mapping conceptual worlds: Using interpretative ethnography to explore knowledge-making in a professional community. *The Journal of Business Communication, 35*(1), 111–127.

Solsken, J., Willett, J., & Wilson-Keenan, J.-A. (2000). Cultivating hybrid texts in multicultural classrooms: Promise and challenge. *Research in the Teaching of English, 35*, 179–212.

Spack, R. (1997a). The acquisition of academic literacy in a second language: A longitudinal case study. *Written Communication, 14*, 3–62.

Spack, R. (1997b). The rhetorical construction of multilingual students. *TESOL Quarterly, 31*, 765–774.

Spicer-Escalante, M. (2005). Writing in two languages/living in two worlds: A rhetorical analysis of Mexican-American written discourse. In M. Farr (Ed.), *Latino language and literacy in ethnolinguistic Chicago* (pp. 217–244). Mahwah, NJ: Lawrence Erlbaum Associates.

Stein, P. (2004). Re-sourcing resources: Pedagogy, history and loss in a Johannesburg classroom. In M. Hawkins (Ed.), *Language learning and teacher education: A sociocultural approach* (pp. 35–51). Clevedon, England: Multilingual Matters.

Swales, J. (1981). *Aspects of article introductions*. Birmingham, England: University of Aston.

Swales, J. (1990). *Genre analysis*. New York: Cambridge University Press.

Swales, J. (2004). *Research genres: Explorations and applications*. New York: Cambridge University Press.

Tarone, E., Dwyer, S., Gillette, S., & Icke, V. (1981). On the use of the passive in two astrophysics journal papers. *English for Specific Purposes, 1*, 123–140.

Truscott, J. (1996). The case against grammar correction in L2 writing classes. *Language Learning, 46*, 327–369.

Urzua, C. (1987). "You stopped too soon": Second language children composing and revising. *TESOL Quarterly, 21*, 279–304.

Valdés, G. (2001). *Learning and not learning English: Latino students in American schools*. New York: Teachers College Press.

van Mulken, M., & van der Meer, W. (2005). Are you being served? A genre analysis of American and Dutch company replies to customer inquiries. *English for Specific Purposes, 24*(1), 93–109.

Yli-Jokipii, H. (1996). An approach to contrasting languages and cultures in the corporate context: Finnish, British, and American business letters and telefax messages. *Multilingua, 15*(3), 305–327.

You, X. (2005). The conflation of rhetorical traditions: The formulation of Chinese writing instruction. *Rhetoric Review, 24*, 150–169.

Young, R. J. C. (1995). *Colonial desire: Hybridity in theory, culture and race*. London: Routledge.

Zamel, V. (1982). Writing: The process of discovering meaning. *TESOL Quarterly, 16*, 195–209.

Zamel, V. (1997). Toward a model of transculturation. *TESOL Quarterly, 31*, 341–352.

V

Writing as Text

Writing in its most practical sense is the inscription of language. Writers must work with language to transcribe and bring their thoughts and meanings into articulate shape so others can understand them. Linguistics, rhetoric, and communication studies have had had significant things to say about bringing the resources of language to bear on communicative tasks, and the effect of using these resources on the readers of the texts. Linguistically informed chapter 33 reviews the extensive work that has been done to understand the differences and similarities between written and spoken language, and by implication how language has been transformed by its transcription.

Grammar and syntax have long been part of writing and language instruction, dating back at least to the medieval trivium. Grammars have traditionally been produced for pedagogic purposes, distinct from the descriptive intent behind most current linguistically informed grammars. Chapter 34 presents the variety of grammatical analysis that has been applied to written texts and language instruction.

Larger forms of organization, considered as arrangement in classical rhetoric, have also been approached in linguistics under the topics of cohesion and genre. Chapter 36 examines issues of text organization as arising in both the linguistic and rhetorical traditions. One of the major functions of written language in both academic and public settings has been argument. Chapter 36 examines the intersection of classical rhetorical theory and contemporary communication research on argument.

Though design has always been an issue in the production of manuscripts and books, computers have extended the design tools available to the ordinary writer and the electronic media have facilitated the convenient transmission of multimedia documents. These developments have made design more than a specialized concern for typographers and book designers. Chapter 37 reviews what we currently know about design and points to the future of writing within enriched environments.

CHAPTER 33

Writing and Speaking

Douglas Biber
Northern Arizona University

Camilla Vásquez
University of South Florida

> Thought has always worked by opposition,
> Speech/Writing
> High/Low ...
> Does this mean something?

> —Cixous (1975, p. 90)

The past several decades have seen many shifts in perspective in the study of writing and speaking. In the early 20th century, a number of structural linguists (e.g., Sapir, Bloomfield) stressed the primacy of speech over writing, positing that writing was essentially an artifact of spoken language. Later scholars, working from a broader social perspective (e.g., Goody, 1968; Goody & Watt, 1968), documented the historical development and diffusion of different types of writing systems in various Western and non-Western cultures, and explored the social and cultural implications of the introduction of the technology of literacy, by analyzing some of the earliest functions of written texts. Other researchers in this tradition, most notably Olson and Ong, have argued that the introduction of literacy has had consequences for cognition, society, and language use. The work of Olson and Ong has come to be associated with an autonomous view of writing and with characterizations of writing as "detached, and self-contained" (Ong, 1982, p. 132) and "able to stand in as an unambiguous and autonomous representation of meaning" (Olson, 1977, p. 258).

At the same time, several early researchers suggested that the linguistic characteristics of speech and writing are fundamentally different. For example, DeVito (1967), Olson (1977), and Kay (1977) argued that the language of writing is more explicit, decontextualized, and therefore autonomous than speech, with referents being explicitly identified, and background assumptions and logical relations being overtly encoded in the text itself. Other researchers have claimed that writing is more structurally complex than speech, with longer sentences (or t-units) and a greater use of subordination (e.g., Chafe, 1982; O'Donnell, 1974).

Despite the many studies carried out in the 1970s and early 1980s, there was little agreement on the salient linguistic characteristics of the two modes. Several studies examined linguistic features such as sentence length, number of subordinate clauses, and the frequency of passive constructions in speech and writing (e.g., Chafe, 1982; Kay, 1977; Kroll, 1977; O'Donnell, 1974). These studies generally concluded that written language is structurally elaborated, complex, formal, and abstract, whereas spoken language is concrete, context-dependent, and structurally simple. Some studies, however, found almost no linguistic differences between speech and writing (Blankenship, 1962), whereas others (Halliday, 1979; Poole & Field, 1976) actually claimed that speech is more elaborated than writing (see the survey of research in Biber, 1988, chap. 3).

The 1980s saw a reaction to these earlier perspectives on literacy as opposed to orality (i.e., as autonomous, cognitive, and linguistic). During this decade, several studies appeared that called into question overgeneralizations made about speech and writing (e.g., Frawley, 1982; Tannen, 1982), and yet other more culturally or socially oriented studies focused less on the differences between oral and literate production and more on their diverse functions in particular social contexts (e.g., Heath, 1982; Street, 1984). And as the technical view of literacy as a mode of linguistic production independent of social context gradually came under increasing scrutiny, the work of Scribner and Cole (1981) also demonstrated that many of the cognitive effects that had been ascribed to literacy were instead the results of particular educational practices. A great deal of recent research on literacy—particularly anthropological and ethnographic approaches—has broadened the scope of inquiry, by viewing both oral and literate production as embedded in complex social practices. These anthropological, ethnographic, or ideological (Street, 1984) approaches to literacy have been useful in identifying the relationship between language and macrostructures (culture, power, etc.) and have therefore provided numerous insights into connections between literacy practices and schooling (e.g., Heath, 1982; Scribner & Cole, 1981; etc.); however, such studies have not been expressly concerned with specific linguistic differences between speaking and writing.

Over this same period, researchers in linguistics began to recognize the importance of linguistic differences within each mode and the inadequacy of simple dichotomous comparisons of spoken and written language. For example, Akinnaso (1982), Tannen (1982, 1985), and Beaman (1984) all argue that linguistic studies should be based on comparisons of the same task in speech and writing to isolate the effect of mode. That is, many earlier studies were based on a comparison of a single spoken variety to a single written variety, but these were often not matched for factors such as purpose and the amount of preplanning (e.g., a comparison of face-to-face conversation to a preplanned written essay). In contrast, the approach advocated by Tannen, Beaman, and others required that subjects perform the same task in speech and writing, usually producing spontaneous narratives. By controlling the task, researchers hoped to isolate the effect of the spoken versus written mode on linguistic form.

This line of research leads naturally to more general issues of register variation, where *register* is used as a cover term to refer to a language variety that is defined by situational characteristics and communicative purposes (examples of different registers include conversation, lectures, novels, biology research articles, etc.). Rather than focusing on the simple dichotomy of speech versus writing, the study of register variation entails a much broader scope of investigation; for example: To what extent do spoken registers differ from one another linguistically? That is, what are the patterns of linguistic variation among varieties within the spoken mode? Similarly, what kinds of linguistic differences exist among written registers? Studying the full range of registers within each mode (i.e., spoken and written) allows for a much more comprehensive framework to address the question of whether there are overall differences between speech and writing.

Research questions such as these motivated the development of multidimensional analysis (e.g., Biber 1986, 1988, 1995). Studies in this research tradition have used large corpora of naturally occurring texts to represent the range of spoken and written registers in a language. These registers are compared with respect to dimensions of variation, comprising constellations of linguistic features that typically co-occur in texts (see the section Multidimensional Analyses of Spoken and Written Register Variation). Each dimension is distinctive in three respects:

1. It is defined by a distinctive set of co-occurring linguistic features.
2. It is associated with distinctive communicative functions.
3. There are distinctive patterns of register variation associated with each dimension.

Several general patterns and conclusions about spoken and written language have emerged from multidimensional studies:

1. Some dimensions are strongly associated with spoken and written differences; other dimensions have little or no relation to speech and writing.
2. There are few, if any, absolute linguistic differences between spoken and written registers.
3. However, there are strong and systematic linguistic differences between stereotypical speech and stereotypical writing, that is, between conversation and written informational prose.
4. The spoken and written modes differ in their linguistic potential: They are not equally adept at accommodating a wide range of linguistic variation. In particular, there is an extremely wide range of linguistic variation among written registers, because writers can choose to employ linguistic features associated with stereotypical speech. In contrast, there is a more restricted range of linguistic variation among spoken registers, in part because the real-time production circumstances of the spoken mode make it difficult to employ many of the linguistic features associated with stereotypical informational writing.

In the next section, we survey the characteristic linguistic features of stereotypical speech and writing, showing how these two extremes of the spoken and written modes are dramatically different in their patterns of language use. Then, in the following section, we briefly survey the results of multidimensional studies to support the claim that the two modes differ in their linguistic potential, describing the overall linguistic relationship between speech and writing.

STEREOTYPICAL SPEECH AND WRITING: CONVERSATION VERSUS INFORMATIONAL PROSE

As noted previously, there are many different registers found within the spoken and written modes. However, it is possible to identify particular registers that are especially typical of each mode. Conversation and informational expository prose fit this description, and these two registers can thus be regarded as stereotypically spoken and written registers (see also Tannen, 1982; Biber, 1995, who use the terms *oral* and *literate* for this distinction).

The characterization of conversation as stereotypical speaking is not controversial: All languages and cultures have conversational interactions, and it can be considered the unmarked means of spoken communication universally. The communicative focus in conversation is typically on (inter)personal rather than informational concerns, and meaning can be clarified and jointly negotiated by participants. For these reasons, conversational interactions require fast, efficient communication, but they have relatively little need for a precise, dense packaging of information. These communicative priorities match the real-time production circumstances of the spoken mode. In other words, the real-time production of speech enables fast, easy communication, and facilitates direct interaction among participants, but it is less well-suited for highly informational or precise communication. (In contrast, the written mode would be slow and cumbersome for communication in face-to-face interactional situations.)

The characterization of informational expository prose as stereotypical writing is more controversial. Exposition differs from conversation in that it is not universal. Many speakers and cultures have literate competencies and traditions but lack expository registers. As a result, some researchers have claimed that expository registers are not representative of the written mode. For example, authors such as Street (1984, 1993) argue that academic exposition has been regarded as stereotypical writing simply because it is the most highly valued register of the intellectual elite in Western societies. According to this view, expository informational prose is not noteworthy for the way that it exploits the linguistic and communicative resources of the written mode; rather, the special status of expository prose is attributed to the fact that Western scholars have typically used this form of discourse for their own written communications. In contrast, we would argue that informational exposition is special in both its communicative/situational characteristics and its linguistic characteristics—because it maximally exploits the resources of the written mode. In particular, exposition maximally exploits the opportunities for carefully planned and revised expression made possible by the written mode, and thus it shows extreme characterizations of informational density, elaboration, and precision.

The communicative resources provided by the written mode are not necessarily obvious, to individual speakers or to developing cultures. As Goody (1977, 1986) and Stubbs (1980) point out, writers learn to exploit the resources of the written mode only gradually over time, in contrast to speakers' abilities to use the spoken mode, which appears to be native to all cultures. For example, Stubbs (1980) notes that it took nearly 100 years after the invention of printed books before page numbers were regularly added for the benefit of readers, and modern devices such as a table of contents and indexes appeared even later. Similarly, beginning readers do not immediately realize that written materials can be processed in different ways from speech. For example, written materials can be read at different speeds, depending on the difficulty of the material and the purposes of the reader. In addition, individuals can selectively process written materials in a nonlinear fashion, reading only those parts that are particularly interesting or relevant. It also takes time for writers to learn to exploit the production opportunities for planning and revision, in order to produce carefully integrated, informational prose.

We certainly would not claim that written exposition is in any sense better than other written registers, or that it is necessarily desirable for all cultures and speakers to develop proficiency in expository registers. However, we regard informational exposition as stereotypical writing in that it has the opposite situational and communicative characteristics from conversation: both exposition and conversation make maximal use of the communicative resources provided by their respective modes. As a result, a linguistic comparison/contrast of conversation and expository prose provides a description of the styles of expression associated with the exploitation of those communicative resources.

Linguistic Comparison/Contrast of Conversation and Academic Prose

One analytical approach that has been especially productive for studying register variation is corpus-based analysis, with its emphasis on the representativeness of the database, and its associated computational tools, which are used to investigate distributional patterns across registers and across discourse contexts in large text collections (for introductions to this analytical approach, see Biber, Conrad, & Reppen, 1998; Hunston, 2002; Kennedy, 1998; McEnery & Wilson, 1996; Meyer 2002). The recent *Longman Grammar of Spoken and Written English* (LGSWE; Biber, Johansson, Leech, Conrad, & Finnegan, 1999) applies corpus-based analyses to show how any grammatical feature can be described for both its structural characteristics and its patterns of use across spoken and written registers. The analyses in the *LGSWE* are based on texts from four registers: conversation, fiction, newspaper language, and academic prose. Although these are general registers, they differ in important ways from one another (e.g., with respect to mode, interactiveness, production circumstances, purpose, and target audience). The analyses were carried out on the Longman Spoken and Written English (LSWE) Corpus, which contains approximately 20 million words of text overall, with approximately 4 to 5 million words from each of these four registers.

Because the *LGSWE* systematically includes grammatical descriptions of conversation and academic prose, this reference work provides one of the most comprehensive surveys of the linguistic differences between stereotypical speech and writing. These two registers have been found to consist of dramatically different patterns of use for nearly every linguistic feature. Table 33.1 lists some of the features that are especially characteristic of conversation, whereas Table 33.2 lists features that are especially characteristic of academic prose. The Appendix provides examples and definitions for each of these features.

Many of the grammatical features typical of conversation, listed in Table 33.1, reflect a heavy reliance on verbs, adverbs, and pronouns rather than on complex noun phrases. These features result in the dense use of short, simple clauses. However, it also turns out that several dependent-clause features are much more common in conversation than in other registers. For example, complement clauses controlled by verbs, especially *that*-clauses and *WH*-clauses, are found frequently in conversation. (The complementizer *that* is frequently omitted in these structures.) Such grammatical features are often used to express speaker stance (personal attitudes or evaluations) in conversation: The controlling verb expresses the stance, whereas the complement clause contains the new information. The following excerpt from a conversation illustrates these features. Notice especially the dense use of verbs, pronouns, and *that* complement clauses. We have underlined the start of all *that*-clauses and WH-clauses, and inserted the symbol <> to mark places where the complementizer *that* has been omitted.

B: Well not the organizer surely, oh I <u>know </u>I would have <u>thought</u> you'd have to, [unclear] shoot it.
A: I'm <u>sure that</u> the social services require psychiatric or—
B: Mm, I would've thought so.
A: Obviously medical <unclear> <u>what</u> you're doing. Mhm, but they're to be qualified people involved. But I would have <u>expected that</u> the whole thing would have to be operated by, somebody who was qualified.
B: I don't know, because like, you know like the doctors <unclear>
A: <unclear> I <u>think</u> it sort of <u>depends how</u> big that you want to get involved in.

Taken together, these conversational features reflect two of the most important situational characteristics of typical speech: restriction to real-time production (resulting in a reliance on clausal structures rather than complex noun phrases), and a focus on personal involvement (resulting in the dense use of linguistic features to express stance).

In contrast, Table 33.2 lists major grammatical features that are especially common in academic prose. Three linguistic features are especially prevalent in this type of writing: nouns, adjectives, and prepositional phrases. In addition, there are many related specific features that are especially characteristic of academic prose (e.g., nominalizations, noun phrases with multiple modifiers). In contrast, verbs are much less common in academic prose than in conversation (although there are specific verb categories that are common in academic prose, such as the copula *be*, existence verbs, derived verbs, and passive-voice verbs.) The dense use of complex noun phrase structures reflect the informational/ideational focus of academic prose, together with the opportunity for careful crafting and revision of the text enabled by the written mode. The following short excerpt from a university textbook illustrates many of these features. We have underlined all nouns and marked prepositions in **bold**.

<u>Wildlife</u> <u>photography</u> represents the nonconsumptive <u>use</u> **of** <u>wildlife</u>, which is the <u>use</u>, **without** <u>removal</u> or <u>alteration</u>, **of** natural <u>resources</u>. **For** much **of** this <u>century</u>, the <u>management</u> **of** <u>wildlife</u> **for** the <u>hunter</u> has been emphasized **by** <u>wildlife</u> <u>managers</u>. **In** recent <u>years</u>, however, <u>management</u> **for** nonconsumptive <u>uses</u> **such as** <u>wildlife</u> <u>photography</u> and <u>bird-watching</u> has received more <u>attention</u>.

It is noteworthy that not all dependent-clause types are more common in informational written prose than in conversation. Rather, specific clause types have their own distributions, reflecting their primary communicative functions and apparently their production

TABLE 33.1
Grammatical Features That Are Especially Common in Conversation But Relatively
Rare in Academic Prose (based on a survey of the *Longman Grammar of Spoken and
Written English*, with page citations)

Feature	Specific pattern of use
Verbs and verb phrases:	
Lexical verbs: overall pp. 65, 359	Almost one third of all content words in conversation are lexical verbs
Mental verbs pp. 366, 368	E.g., *know, think, see, want, mean*
Phrasal verbs pp. 409, 424	E.g., *come on, get up, get off, find out, go on*
Present tense p. 456 ff.	Approximately 70% of all verb phrases in conversation are present tense
Progressive aspect p. 462 ff.	three times more common in conversation than in academic prose
Modal verbs p. 486 ff.	About twice as common in conversation than in the written registers; especially *can, will, would*
Semimodal verbs p. 486 ff.	Common only in conversation; especially *have to, (had) better, (have) got to, used to*
Adverbs:	
Simple adverbs p. 540–2, 560–3	Twice as common in conversation; e.g., *here, there, now, then, just, really*
Adjectival forms used as adverbs pp. 542–3	common only in conversation; e.g., *It's running <u>real good</u>*
Amplifiers pp. 564–6	Twice as common in conversation, especially *very, so, really/real, too*
Stance adverbs pp. 859, 867–71	Over twice as common in conversation, especially *really, actually, like, maybe*
Pronouns:	
Personal pronouns pp. 92, 235, 237, 333, 334	four times more common in conversation, especially *I, you, it*
Demonstrative pronoun *that* pp. 349–50	Extremely common only in conversation
Simple clause features:	
Questions pp. 211 ff.	Common only in conversation

TABLE 33.1 (*continued*)

Grammatical Features That Are Especially Common in Conversation But Relatively Rare in Academic Prose (based on a survey of the Longman Grammar of Spoken and Written English, with page citations)

Feature	Specific pattern of use
Imperatives pp. 221–220	Common only in conversation
Stranded prepositions in WH-questions pp. 106–107	Common only in conversation
Coordination tags pp. 116–7	Common only in conversation, e.g., *or something* (but note the use of *etc.* in writing)
Dependent clause features:	
Verb + *that* complement clause pp. 668–70, 674–5	Five times more common in conversation, especially think, *know, guess* + *that*-clause
Complementizer *that* omission (vs. retention) pp. 680–683	The preferred use in conversation (over 80% of all that-clauses omit the complementizer)
Verb + WH complement clauses pp. 688–9	Much more common in conversation, especially *know* + WH-clause
Conditional adverbial clauses p. 821 ff.	Twice as common in conversation

Note. Based on a survey of the Longman Grammar of Spoken and Written English, with page citations.

difficulty. For example, finite relative clauses are much more common in expository writing than in conversation; these clauses serve informational functions, being used for nominal specification and elaboration. In contrast, many complement clause types are considerably more common in conversation than in academic prose; these clauses are used primarily to express stance; thus they are a preferred structure in conversation, despite their apparent structural complexity. Many of these structures are formed through the use of lexical bundles: semifrozen recurrent multiword expressions such as *I don't know why* _____ (see *LGSWE*, chap. 13; Biber, Conrad, & Cortes, 2004). As a result, the dense use of these complement clause constructions does not pose a difficult production task in conversation.

MULTIDIMENSIONAL ANALYSES OF SPOKEN AND WRITTEN REGISTER VARIATION

Multidimensional (MD) analysis was developed as a corpus-based methodological approach to: (a) identify the salient linguistic co-occurrence patterns in a language, in empirical/quantitative terms, and (b) compare spoken and written registers in the linguistic space defined by those co-occurrence patterns. The approach was first used in Biber (1985, 1986) and then developed more fully in Biber (1988, 1995). As noted in earlier, MD analysis is based on the

TABLE 33.2
Grammatical Features That Are Especially Common in Academic
Prose But Relatively Rare in Conversation (based on a survey of the Longman
Grammar of Spoken and Written English)

Feature	Pattern of use
Nouns and noun phrases:	
Nouns: overall p. 65	Approximately 60% of all content words in academic prose are nouns
Nouns vs. pronouns pp. 235–236	Nouns are much more common than pronouns in academic prose, especially in object positions
Plural nouns pp. 291–229	Four times more common in informational writing than in conversation
Nominalizations pp. 322–3	Over 10 times more common in academic prose, especially nouns formed with –tion and –ity
Definite article the pp. 267–9	Three times more common in academic prose than in conversation
Noun phrases with modifiers p. 578	60% of all noun phrases in academic prose have a modifier
	In contrast, Approximately. 90% of the noun phrases in conversation are a single pronoun with no modifier
Nouns as premodifiers p. 589–596	Approximately. 10 times more common in academic prose (and newspapers)
Noun phrases with postmodifiers p. 606–608	Approximately. Six times more common in academic prose (and newspapers)
Noun phrases with multiple postmodifiers p. 640–644	Approximately. 10 times more common in academic prose
Appositive noun phrases as post-modifiers in noun phrases p. 606, 638–40	Approximately. Five times more common in academic prose (and newspapers)
Adjectives and adjective phrases:	
Adjectives: overall p. 65, 506	Adjectives are four times more common in academic prose than in conversation
Attributive adjectives p. 506, 589	Approximately Seven times more common in academic prose
Derived adjectives pp. 531–533	Approximately 10 times more common in academic prose, especially adjectives formed with –al
Verbs and verb phrases:	
Copula be Copular verb become pp. 359–360, 437–439	Twice as common in academic prose

TABLE 33.2 (*continued*)

Grammatical Features That Are Especially Common in Academic Prose But
Relatively Rare in Conversation (based on a survey of the Longman Grammar of Spoken and
Written English)

Feature	Pattern of use
Existence verbs (e.g., *include, involve, indicate*) pp. 366, 369, 419	Twice as common in academic prose
Verbs with inanimate subjects pp. 378–380	Common only in academic prose
Derived verbs pp. 400–403	Approximately Three times more common in academic prose, especially verbs formed with *re-* and *–ize*
Passive voice pp. 476–480, 937–40	Approximately 10 times more common in academic prose, especially the "short" passive (with no *by*-phrase)
Dependent Clause features:	
Relative clauses with the relative pronoun *which* pp. 609–612	Approximately 10 times more common in academic prose
Participle clauses as postmodifiers in noun phrases p. 606, 630–632	Approximately 10 times more common in academic prose (and newspapers)
That-clauses as noun complement clauses pp. 647–651	Over 10 times more common in academic prose, especially with the head nouns *fact, possibility, doubt, belief, assumption*
To-clauses as noun complement clauses pp. 647–51	over 10 times more common in academic prose (and newspapers), especially with the head nouns *attempt, ability, capacity, effort, right*
Abstract noun + *of* + *ing*-clause (e.g., *methods of assessing error*) pp. 653–655	over 10 times more common in academic prose, especially with the head nouns *way, method, possibility, effect, problem, process, risk*
Extraposed clauses pp. 672–5, 722–4	over 10 times more common in academic prose, especially *that*-clauses controlled by the adjectives *clear, (un)likely, and (im)possible*; and *to*-clauses controlled by the adjectives *(im)possible, difficult, hard, important, necessary*
Other features	
Prepositions p. 92	Over twice as common in academic prose
Of-phrases pp. 301–302	over 10 times more common in academic prose
Prepositional phrases as postmodifiers in noun phrases p. 606–608, 634–638	Over Five times more common in academic prose (and newspapers)
Dual Gender reference: pp. 316–317	Common only in academic prose e.g., *he or she, his or her, he/she*

Note.   Based on survey of the Longman Grammar of Spoken and Written English, with
page citations.

assumption that all registers have distinctive linguistic patterns of use (associated with their defining situational characteristics). Thus, MD studies of speech and writing set out to describe the linguistic similarities and differences among a range of spoken registers, and similarly among a range of written registers—and to then compare speech and writing within the context of a comprehensive analysis of register variation.

In the present chapter, we have space for only a brief summary of the major patterns of variation resulting from MD studies. Readers are referred to Biber (1988, 1995) or Conrad and Biber (2001; chaps. 1 and 2) for the details of these studies.

MD analysis uses factor analysis to reduce a large number of linguistic variables to a few basic parameters of linguistic variation. In MD analyses, the distribution of individual linguistic features is analyzed in a corpus of texts. Factor analysis is then used to identify the systematic co-occurrence patterns among those linguistic features—the dimensions—and then texts and registers are compared along each dimension. Each dimension comprises a group of linguistic features that usually co-occur in texts (e.g., nouns, attributive adjectives, prepositional phrases); these co-occurrence patterns are identified statistically using factor analysis. The co-occurrence patterns are then interpreted to assess their underlying situational, social, and cognitive functions. Many dimensions have positive and negative sets of co-occurring features. Rather than reflecting importance, the positive and negative signs identify two groupings of features that occur in a complementary pattern as part of the same factor. That is, when the features with positive loadings occur together frequently in a text, the features with negative loadings are markedly less frequent in that text, and vice versa.

For example, Dimension 1 in the 1988 MD analysis has both positive and negative features. The negative features include nouns, long words, prepositional phrases, type/token ratio, and attributive adjectives. These features reflect an informational focus, a careful integration of information in a text, and precise lexical choice. Text Sample 1 (technical academic prose) illustrates these co-occurring linguistic characteristics in an academic article:

> Apart from these general group-related aspects, there are also individual aspects that need to be considered. Empirical data show that similar processes can be guided quite differently by users with different views on the purpose of the communication.

This text sample is typical of written expository prose in its dense integration of information: frequent nouns and long words, with most nouns being modified by attributive adjectives or prepositional phrases (e.g., general group related aspects, individual aspects, empirical data, similar processes, users with different views on the purpose of the communication).

The set of positive features on Dimension 1 is more complex, although all of these features have been associated with interpersonal interaction, a focus on personal stance, and real-time production circumstances. For example, first- and second-person pronouns, WH-questions, emphatics, amplifiers, and sentence relatives can all be interpreted as reflecting interpersonal interaction and the involved expression of personal stance (feelings and attitudes). Other positive features are associated with the constraints of real-time production, resulting in a reduced surface form, a generalized or uncertain presentation of information, and a generally fragmented production of text; these include that deletions, contractions, proverb DO, the pronominal forms, and final (stranded) prepositions. Text Sample 2 (office hours—School of Business) illustrates the use of positive Dimension 1 features in a formal conversation (university office hours) from the T2K-SWAL Corpus:

Instructor: Now here's what you should do if you want me to go over your graduation papers—you gotta do it this semester because if you wait until the summer or the fall—

Student: Uh huh.

Instructor:	Then you'll have to go through somebody else and it'll just take longer.
Student:	Yeah, so I can do that then and what do I—do you just file?
Instructor:	You can go down to Rosemary's office and get the papers, two sets of papers one for the college of business and one for the university.
Student:	And I can do it now.
Instructor:	Mhm, you can do it this semester and if she says no, you tell her why.
Student:	OK.

Overall, Dimension 1 marks interactional, stance-focused, and generalized content (the positive features) versus high informational density and precise word choice (the negative features). Two separate communicative parameters seem to be represented here: the primary purpose of the writer/speaker (involved vs. informational), and the production circumstances (those restricted by real time constraints vs. those enabling careful editing possibilities). Reflecting both of these parameters, the interpretive label *Involved Versus Informational Production* was proposed for the dimension underlying this factor.

The 1988 MD analysis showed that English registers vary along five major dimensions associated with different functional considerations, including: interactiveness, involvement and personal stance, production circumstances, informational density, informational elaboration, narrative purposes, situated reference, persuasiveness or argumentation, and impersonal presentation of information. Two of these dimensions have no systematic relationship to speech and writing (Dimension 2: Narrative Discourse; and Dimension 4: Argumentation). However, the other three dimensions identify sharp distinctions between oral and literate registers, where the term *oral* is used to refer to stereotypical speech (i.e., conversation), and the term *literate* is used to refer to stereotypical writing (i.e., academic prose or other kinds of formal, informational prose). On Dimension 1: Involved Versus Informational Production, conversation is at one extreme, marked as extremely involved and restricted by real-time production circumstances; academic prose is at the other extreme, marked as extremely informational and carefully crafted and edited (see previous discussion). On Dimension 3: Elaborated Versus Situated Reference, conversation is at one extreme, marked as extremely situated in reference (frequent time and place adverbials); academic prose is at the other extreme, marked as extremely elaborated in reference (frequent relative-clause constructions). On Dimension 5, academic prose is at one other extreme, marked by impersonal styles of presentation (frequent passive constructions), whereas conversation is at the other extreme.

The 1988 MD analysis indicates that the spoken and written modes can be exploited in extreme ways, resulting in register characterizations not found in the other mode. There are fundamental differences in the production circumstances of speech and writing, and these differences provide the potential for styles of expression in writing that are not normally feasible in speech. In addition, spoken registers rarely adopt the extreme informational communicative focus of written expository registers. (Even classroom teaching is much more interactive and involved in purpose than typical written expository registers; see Biber, Conrad, Reppen, Byrd, & Helt, 2002). Thus, written academic prose and official documents are highly informational (Dimension 1), elaborated in reference (Dimension 3), and impersonal (Dimension 5)—extreme linguistic characterizations not found in any spoken register.

However, despite the existence of these oral/literate dimensions, no dimension identifies an absolute distinction between speech and writing. On Dimension 1, written registers can be involved (e.g., personal letters), whereas spoken registers can be moderately informational (e.g., prepared speeches). And on Dimensions 3 and 5, written registers such as fiction and personal letters are similar to conversation in being situated and not impersonal.

These same basic patterns have been found in the MD analyses of Somali and Korean: In both of these languages, there are several oral/literate dimensions that distinguish between conversation at one extreme and written informational prose at the other extreme. At the same time, there are few dimensions that define an absolute contrast between speech and writing. Rather, most dimensions show some overlap among spoken and written registers. The Lexical Elaboration dimension in the Somali analysis—consisting of once-occurring words, type–token ratio, nominalizations, and so on—comes the closest to defining an absolute spoken–written contrast: No spoken Somali register makes dense use of these features, whereas all written registers (except textbooks) rely extensively on these features.

Consideration of all MD analyses to date reveals an additional pattern that is less easily noticed: The range of linguistic variation among written registers is typically much greater than the range of variation among spoken registers. Written production gives the author maximum freedom to manipulate the linguistic characteristics of a text in response to numerous situational influences, including communicative purpose, interactiveness, personal involvement, and sometimes the desire to adopt a colloquial (even conversational) style. In contrast, spoken language is constrained by the need to produce language in real time. As a result, regardless of the speaker's focus on informational communicative purposes, spoken registers tend to be relatively oral with respect to all linguistic dimensions. For example, even classroom teaching is relatively oral in its MD profile (see Biber et al., 2002). In contrast, written registers show a much wider range of linguistic characteristics, because an author has ample time to exploit either oral or literate features depending on the primary communicative purposes. Thus, written registers like personal letters and e-mail messages tend to be oral in their MD profiles.

CONCLUSION

In this chapter, we have provided a brief and selective survey of previous research concerned with the linguistic differences between speech and writing. In illustrating some of the major linguistic differences found between stereotypical registers of the spoken and written modes of production, namely conversation and informational prose, we have argued that the modes differ considerably in their linguistic potential. The systematic differences associated with conversation and expository prose (as illustrated by numerous findings from the *LGSWE*) can be attributed to the defining situational characteristics as well as production circumstances of the two registers. Furthermore, although MD analyses have shown that there are few, if any, absolute linguistic differences between the spoken and written modes, there are strong and systematic linguistic differences between the registers of conversation and written informational prose—not only in English, but in other languages as well. In addition, MD analyses have revealed a more subtle difference between speech and writing: Spoken registers employ a restricted range of linguistic styles, whereas writers can shape their texts in whatever fashion that they want. These differences, we have argued, are clearly linked to the differing situational and production opportunities and constraints of the two modes. Thus, we conclude that any discussion of the linguistic differences between speech and writing must take into account the complex patterns of register variation within the two modes, while also recognizing the inherent restrictions on language production in the spoken mode relative to the written mode.

REFERENCES

Akinnaso, F. (1982). On the differences between spoken and written language. *Language and Speech, 25,* 97–125.

Beaman, K. (1984). Coordination and subordination revisited: Syntactic complexity in spoken and written narrative discourse. In D. Tannen (Ed.), *Spoken and written language: Exploring orality and literacy* (pp. 45–80). Norwood, NJ: Ablex.

Besnier, N. (1988). The linguistic relationships of spoken and written Nukulaelae registers. *Language, 64,* 707–736.

Biber, D. (1988). *Variation across speech and writing.* Cambridge, England: Cambridge University Press.

Biber, D. (1995). *Dimensions of register variation: A cross-linguistic comparison.* Cambridge, England: Cambridge University Press.

Biber, D., & Clark, V. (2000). Historical shifts in modification patterns with complex noun phrase structures: How long can you go without a verb? In T. Fanego, M. J. López-Couso, & J. Pérez-Guerra (Eds.), *English historical syntax and morphology* (pp. 43–66). Amsterdam: Benjamins.

Biber, D., & Conrad, S. (2001). Register variation: A corpus approach. In D. Schiffrin, D. Tannen, & H. Hamilton (Eds.), *The handbook of discourse analysis* (pp. 175–196). Oxford, England: Blackwell.

Biber, D., Conrad, S., & Cortes, V. (2004). *If you look at … :* Lexical bundles in university teaching and textbooks. *Applied Linguistics, 25,* 371–405.

Biber, D., Conrad, S., & Reppen, R. (1998). *Corpus linguistics: Exploring language structure and use.* Cambridge, England: Cambridge University Press.

Biber, D., Conrad, S., Reppen, R., Byrd, P., & Helt, M. (2002). Speaking and writing in the university: A multi-dimensional comparison. *TESOL Quarterly, 36*(1), 9–48.

Biber, D., & Finegan, E. (Eds.). (1994). *Sociolinguistic perspectives on register.* Oxford, Enjgland: Oxford University Press.

Biber, D., & Hared, M. (Eds.). (1994). Linguistic correlates of the transition to literacy in Somali: Language and adaptation in six press registers. In D. Biber & E. Finnegan (Eds.), *Sociolinguistic perspectives on register* (pp. 182–216). Oxford, England: Oxford University Press.

Biber, D., Johansson, S., Leech, G., Conrad, S., & Finnegan, E. (1999). *Longman grammar of spoken and written English.* London: Pearson.

Blankenship, J. (1962). A linguistic analysis of oral and written style. *Quarterly Journal of Speech, 48,* 419–422.

Chafe, W. (1982). Integration and involvement in speaking, writing, and oral literature. In D. Tannen (Ed.), *Spoken and written language: Exploring orality and literacy* (pp. 35–54). Norwood, NJ: Ablex.

Cixous, H. (1975). "Sorties" in La Jeune Née, Paris, Union Générale d'Editions, 10/12; English translation in E. Marks & I. de Courtivron (Eds.) (1980), *New French feminisms: An anthology.* Amherst: University of Massachusetts Press.

Conrad, S., & Biber, D. (Eds.). (2001). *Variation in English: Multi-dimensional studies.* London: Longman.

Coulmas, F., & Elich, K. (Eds.). (1983). *Writing in focus.* New York: Mouton.

DeVito, J. A. (1967, May). A linguistic analysis of spoken and written language. *Central States Speech Journal,* pp. 81–85.

Frawley, W. (Ed.). (1982). *Linguistics and literacy: Proceedings of the Delaware symposium on language studies.* New York: Plenum.

Goody, J., & Watt, I. (1968). The consequences of literacy. In J. Goody (Ed.), *Literacy in traditional societies* (pp. 27–68). Cambridge, England: Cambridge University Press.

Goody, J. (Ed.). (1968). *Literacy in traditional societies.* Cambridge, England: Cambridge University Press.

Goody, J. (1977). *The domestication of the savage mind.* Cambridge, England: Cambridge University Press.

Goody, J. (1986). *The logic of writing and the organisation of society.* Cambridge, England: Cambridge University Press.

Green, G. (1982). Colloquial and literary uses of inversions. In D. Tannen (Ed.), *Spoken and written language: Exploring orality and literacy* (pp. 119–154). Norwood, NJ: Ablex.

Halliday, M. A. K. (1979). Differences between spoken and written language: Some implications for literacy teaching. In G. Page, J. Elkins, & B. O'Connor (Eds.), *Communication through reading: Proceedings of the 4th Australian reading conference* (Vol. 2, pp. 000–000). Adelaide, South Australia: Australian Reading Association.

Heath, S. B. (1982). Protean shapes in literacy events: Ever-shifting oral and literate traditions. In D. Tannen (Ed.), *Spoken and written language: Exploring orality and literacy* (pp. 91–118). Norwood, NJ: Ablex.

Hunston, S. (2002). *Corpora and applied linguistics.* Cambridge, England: Cambridge University Press.

Kay, P. (1977). Language evolution and speech style. In B. G. Blount & M. Sanches (Eds.), *Sociocultural dimensions of language change* (pp. 21–33). New York: Academic Press.

Kennedy, G. (1998). *An introduction to corpus linguistics.* Harlow, England: Addison Wesley Longman.

Kim, Y., & Biber, D. (1990). A corpus-based analysis of register variation in Korean. In D. Biber & E. Finnegan (Eds.), *Sociolinguistic perspectives on register* (pp. 157–181). Oxford, England: Oxford University Press.

Kroll, B. (1977). Ways communicators encode propositions in spoken and written English: A look at subordination and coordination. In E. O. Keenan & T. Bennett (Eds.), *Discourse across time and space* (SCOPIL No. 5) (pp. 69–108). Los Angeles: University of Southern California.

Lakoff, R. T. (1982). Some of my favorite writers are literate: The mingling of oral and literate strategies in written communication. In D. Tannen (Ed.), *Spoken and written language: Exploring orality and literacy* (pp. 239–260). Norwood, NJ: Ablex.

McEnery, A. M., & Wilson, A. (1996). *Corpus linguistics.* Edinburgh, Scotland: Edinburgh University Press.

Meyer, C. (2002). *English corpus linguistics: An introduction*. Cambridge, England: Cambridge University Press.

O'Donnell, R. C. (1974). Syntactic differences between speech and writing. *American Speech, 49*, 102–110.

Olson, D. (1977). From utterance to text: The bias of language in speech and writing. *Harvard Educational Review, 47*(3), 257–281.

Olson, D. (1988). Mind and media: The epistemic functions of literacy. *Journal of Communications, 38*(3), 254–279.

Ong, W. (1967). *The presence of the word*. Minneapolis: University of Minnesota Press.

Ong, W. (1977). *Interfaces of the word*. Ithaca, NY: Cornell University Press.

Ong, W. (1982). *Orality and literacy: The technologizing of the word*. London: Methuen.

Poole, M. E., & Field, T. W. (1976). A comparison of oral and written code elaborations. *Language and Speech, 19*, 305–311.

Roberts, C., & Street, B. (1997). Spoken and written language. In F. Coulmas (Ed.), *The handbook of sociolinguistics* (pp. 168–186). Oxford, England: Blackwell.

Scribner, S., & Cole, M. (1981). *The psychology of literacy*. Cambridge, MA: Harvard University Press.

Street, B. (Ed.). (1984). *Literacy in theory and practice*. Cambridge, England: Cambridge University Press.

Street, B. (Ed.). (1993). *Cross-cultural approaches to literacy*. Cambridge, England: Cambridge University Press.

Stubbs, M. (1980). *Language and literacy: The sociolinguistics of reading and writing*. London: Routledge.

Tannen, D. (1982a). The oral/literate continuum in discourse. In D. Tannen (Ed.), *Spoken and written language: Exploring orality and literacy* (pp. 1–16). Norwood, NJ: Ablex.

Tannen, D. (Ed.). (1982b). *Spoken and written language: Exploring orality and literacy*. Norwood, NJ: Ablex.

Tannen, D. (1985). Relative focus on involvement in oral and written discourse. In D. R. Olson, N. Torrance, & A. Hildyard (Eds). *Literacy, language and learning: The nature and consequences of reading and writing*. Cambridge, England: Cambridge University Press.

CHAPTER 34

Grammar, the Sentence, and Traditions of Linguistic Analysis

Mary J. Schleppegrell
University of Michigan, Ann Arbor

The grammatical features of written texts are a frequent focus of writing researchers, as written texts get their structure and meaning from the language that constructs them. This chapter is concerned with studies that analyze the language of a written text at the level of the clause, by looking both at structure within the clause and at structures that enable movement from clause to clause within a text. The focus is on the language choices of the writer and what those language choices can reveal to writing researchers. We first review the theories and constructs that researchers use to approach the study of grammar in writing. Then the foci of this research are presented, showing how researchers have looked at differences between speaking and writing, at development of writing in first- and second-language students, at how language changes over time, and at functional variation related to genre and discipline. As it has become clear that grammar varies in ways that are functional for constructing texts of different types, research is increasingly oriented toward analysis of writing in particular contexts of use. In addition, this research is currently contributing to our understanding of how the choices of the writer construct different kinds of meanings in written text.

APPROACHES TO GRAMMATICAL ANALYSIS

The word *grammar* can refer both to the features of the language being studied and to the theoretical construct that informs the study, as researchers use the abstract constructs of grammatical theory in analyzing the language patterns in particular texts. The term *grammar*, rather than *syntax*, is used throughout this chapter, as the term *syntax* is associated with formal linguistics, where it is a level of analysis that contrasts with morphology, semantics, and so on. In the analysis of written texts, the goal is typically to investigate a text's complexity or to understand how it is constructed so that it can be compared with other texts or so that its features can become a focus of research or pedagogy. This makes analysis of text from a grammatical perspective a functional endeavor. The studies reviewed here start with a theory about what particular grammatical choices contribute to the meaning or structure of a text, and then analyze writing to see how those meanings are realized in different ways or in different types of texts. Some apply traditional grammatical labels (Quirk, Greenbaum, Leech, & Svartvik, 1972, 1985) to the parts of a clause or sentence and then compare the frequency of use of different structures in different kinds of texts. Functional linguistic theories typically inform this work, even where they are not explicitly evoked (Nystrand, Greene, & Wiemelt, 1993), contributing to grammatical approaches to analysis of writing by explaining the value of grammatical structures in the construction of discourse (e.g., Chafe, 1985; Chafe & Danielewicz, 1987; Mann & Thompson, 1992; S. Thompson, 1983, 1985). Under the influence of European functionalists from the Prague School (Vachek, 1966) and the London School (Butler, 1985), functional linguists have argued for understanding written language as a valid form in its own right, and not just as a way of representing speech. They take as basic principles that language should be studied in authentic instances of use, as whole texts, and comparatively across text corpora (Stubbs, 1996). These views, along with the notions that form and meaning are inseparable and that lexis and grammar are interdependent, have made functional approaches very relevant to researchers of written language. In particular, the Prague School linguists' notion of *theme/rheme* structure, referred to as *functional sentence perspective*, enabled analysis of the flow of information in a text as it moves from what is known to what is new. These linguists analyze transitivity options, nominal forms, and clause combining, focusing on information flow and constituent order and seeing discourse organization in terms of the grammatical patterns that construct texts.

The most elaborated framework for functional linguistic analysis has been developed by M. A. K. Halliday (Halliday & Matthiessen, 2004), who has been illustrating since the 1960s how a grammatical analysis of text, based on a functional theory of language, can help explain what makes a text the kind of text it is, and why certain texts are highly valued. Halliday comes to the analysis through the grammar; from the point of view of the systems internal to language. The *functionality* in his theory does not come from outside into the language by identifying social functions and then looking at how language construes these; instead, Halliday identifies the variations in meaning potential in the language itself, and then relates these to three abstract functions (*metafunctions*) of language. Halliday's theory of language, systemic functional linguistics (SFL), provides a framework for analyzing the contribution of each element of the clause to each of these three areas of meaning, *ideational* (how it constructs the "content" of the text), *interpersonal* (how it constructs the stance of the writer and interaction with the reader), and *textual* (how it contributes to the developing organization of the text), with each metafunction realized in grammatical selections from *systems* such as transitivity, modality, and information structure. This results in an extensive metalanguage, as each linguistic element can be labeled in three different ways. Aspects of SFL have been influencing writing researchers since the late 1960s, especially the theory of cohesion in text (Halliday & Hasan, 1976).

CONSTRUCTS FOR THE STUDY OF GRAMMAR IN WRITTEN TEXT

The *clause* is typically taken as the primary constituent in writing research from a grammatical perspective. Central to a clause is a *verb*, which can be finite (marked for tense) or nonfinite, and can be analyzed in terms of features such as *tense, voice,* and *modality*. The semantics of the verb is its key feature, as the semantics calls for a certain configuration of nominal or adjunct elements to be associated with the verb. Halliday and Matthiessen (2004) identify six categories of verbs, distinguished by type of process: *material, behavioral, verbal, mental, relational,* and *existential,* whereas Biber, Johansson, Leech, Conrad, and Finegan (1999), based on the categories of Quirk et al. (1985), recognize *public, private, suasive,* and *perception* categories. Verb semantics is important because the choice of verb brings with it both structural and semantic expectations for the rest of the clause (e.g., verbs of *saying* may have a whole clause as a complement; verbs of *action* do not). Analysis of verb semantics contributes to analysis of *transitivity*. *Nominal* elements, in their realizations as *subject* or clause *theme*, also referred to by some researchers as *topic*, have been a major focus of research, as have *connectors* and *conjunctions* that enable interclausal linkages. Each of these constructs is discussed in more detail next to show how they can be analyzed in their contributions to the presentation of ideas, the construction of the writer's stance, and the organization of the text as a whole.

Sentence, Clause, T-Unit, Clause Complex

A key issue in grammatical approaches to the analysis of writing has been the unit of analysis to take as primary. Although it might seem that *sentence* would be the obvious choice, and many studies do analyze sentences, the construct *sentence* presents difficulties for comparison of speech and writing, or for analysis of the texts of developing writers, where the notion of *sentence* may be irrelevant or its conventions still being learned. In fact, it has been argued that the construct *sentence* evolved with writing systems as an orthographic convention, and is not a unit of the grammar itself (Halliday & Matthiessen, 2004). When comparing speech and writing, or analyzing the writing of developing first- or second-language writers, taking each writer's capitalization and end punctuation as definitive of sentences may be unsatisfactory. Even in published texts, writers may use what are grammatically fragments to good effect, so analysts find that not all sentences are equal in their grammatical contributions to the text. For these reasons, the *clause* is the best basic unit of grammatical analysis of text.

Two constructs are typically employed to recognize clausal complexity, the *t-unit* and the *clause complex*. The t-unit was developed as a construct by Hunt (1965), influenced by the structural/transformational grammar that was in vogue in the 1950s and 1960s (Hunt cites Chomsky as a consultant on the project). In his study of schoolchildren's writing development, Hunt noted that many children do not use periods, chaining their clauses together with *and*. Counting these chained clauses as one sentence would make these students appear more mature, writing longer sentences, than their writing actually warranted. Hunt also found that editing the texts to divide them into sentences was unreliable; different people put periods in different places when punctuating a student's text, so making decisions about sentences was arbitrary. Hunt defined the t-unit as "one main clause plus all the subordinate clauses attached to or embedded within it" (Hunt, 1965, p. 141) and demonstrated that t-unit length was a better index of maturity in these terms than sentence length.

The *clause complex*, a construct of Hallidayan grammar, is similar to the t-unit in seeing the configuration of clauses related to each independent clause as a unit in the text, but differs in how it treats coordination (parataxis). T-unit analysis treats clauses linked with coordinating conjunctions as separate t-units, whereas the clause complex analysis treats them as part of the clause complex. The clause complex typically coincides with sentence in the analysis of written text, but, like the t-unit, can also serve in the analysis of spoken language, making it possible to adopt the same constructs in analyzing and comparing writing and speaking. Clause complexes are analyzed from a functional perspective in terms of the meaning relationships that are constructed between clauses, and not only in terms of the structural relationships (e.g., *hypotaxis, parataxis, embedding*) in the clause complex. For example, clauses that are projected through another clause, such as a clause of *saying*, are distinguished from those that are logically expanding the meaning of another clause through semantic relationships of *time, place, cause, manner*, and so on (Halliday & Matthiessen, 2004).

Conjunctions and *connectors* are often analyzed as indications of the structural and meaning relationships constructed between clauses, with a focus on what is subordinate and the syntactic function of the subordinate clause, as well as on the meaning contributed by the conjunction or connector. Subordination is not a unitary construct, however (Matthiessen & Thompson, 1987; S. Thompson, 1984). Different types of adverbial, nominal, and adjective clauses have different communicative functions (Biber, 1986), and embedded clauses differ from other kinds of subordinate clauses in their contribution to text structure. An embedded clause functions as a nominal element or part of a nominal element within another clause. The most frequently analyzed clause type in writing research is the *relative clause* (also called an *adjective clause*), but it is important to recognize that the *restrictive* and *nonrestrictive* relative clauses of structural grammar, although similar in form, have very different functions in a text. The restrictive relative clause (in, e.g., *The report that was read in class was inaccurate*) is embedded in and functions as part of a nominal group, whereas the nonrestrictive relative clause (in, e.g., *He was absent yesterday, which was really a shame*) contributes to the development of a text as an elaboration. Embedded relative clauses function as part of another nominal constituent and do not make independent contributions to the evolving structuring of a text. Nonrestrictive relative clauses, on the other hand, have discourse structuring functions. Identifying the clausal structure of a text is often the point of departure for text analysis.

Noun, Theme, Subject

Nouns and larger nominal elements are often the focus of linguistically oriented research on writing, as they are a key resource for constructing texts. Vande Kopple (1992), for example, finds that 83% of the total number of words in the scientific discourse he analyzes occurs in noun phrases. Researchers examine nominal elements to illuminate the construction of impersonality, agency, and abstraction in a text, as nominal groups present the actors, sayers, thinkers, and other semantic roles in the processes constructed by each clause. Nominal elements construe specific, generic, or technical meanings, and can be analyzed in terms of the judgment and value they contribute. Nominal expressions also establish and maintain reference and enable information to be expanded or distilled as a text develops. Structurally, nominal elements can be simple, without modification, or complex, sometimes including multiple pre- and postmodification with adjectives, other nouns, adverbs, *-ed/-ing* participles, prepositional phrases, and embedded clauses. The complexity of the nominal group is a frequent topic of research on writing.

Nominalization, the packaging of verbal or clausal meaning in a nominal element, is a pervasive feature of academic and scientific texts. Nominalization is defined differently by different researchers; some define all nouns with the suffixes *-tion*, *-ment*, *-ness*, or *-ity* as nominalizations (e.g., Biber, 1986; Hinkel, 2002), whereas Halliday (1998) discusses nominalization as an instance of *grammatical metaphor* and defines it as the reconstrual of *processes, relationships,* or *qualities* as *things* (nouns). When a process is nominalized, the modality and tense that are construed in the verb disappear from the clause, as does the agent of the action, so nominalization is often analyzed in studies of agency or the negotiability of information (Halliday, 1998). In text organizational terms, nominalization enables something that has been presented in a series of clauses to be distilled into one nominal element that can then participate in a chain of reasoning to be developed by the writer. This means that nominalization contributes both to the information density of a clause and to the internal structuring of a text, as it allows meanings to be condensed in nominal elements as information is developed. This structuring feature is also related to the role of nominal elements when they serve as clause *theme*, the first element of the clause. Analysis of *theme* illuminates issues important to many researchers—how information is structured, what is backgrounded and foregrounded, and how cohesion is created as a text moves from what is known to what is new. Nominalizations frequently appear in theme position in a clause, and in some kinds of texts, *theme* and *subject* also typically coincide.

The relationship between subject and theme is illuminated in Halliday's theory, where *subject* is seen as relevant to the interpersonal grammar (to what the writer has chosen to make the *modal participant* in the clause), whereas *theme* is a textual resource (the "point of departure" of the clause); in English, the element that comes first. Studies that show the value of *subject* as an organizing construct (e.g., MacDonald, 1992; Vande Kopple, 1994) are typically analyzing scientific or academic research writing, where the first element in a clause often coincides with *subject*. This analysis of clause subjects, then, is often comparable, seen from another perspective, to analyzing *theme*. Other research on nominal elements focuses on analysis of ideational functions such as *agency* or of interpersonal functions such as the way the writer is positioning him or herself (see later discussion).

A further relevant function of nominal elements is in establishing and maintaining *reference*. In particular, researchers are often interested in *deictic* reference, when a nominal element is pointing back to previous text, forward to coming text, or toward an element outside the text, in the immediate situation. This last function, common in spoken language where the interlocutors are copresent, is often relevant in the analysis of children's developing writing, where researchers may be interested in the child's ability to recognize the reader's need for explication of nonshared context (e.g., Cox & Sulzby, 1984). Intratextual deictic reference has been especially interesting to researchers looking at how a text is cohesively developed through deictic referrers such as *this* (e.g., *This demonstrates that...*) (McCarthy, 1994).

WHAT RESEARCH HAS SOUGHT AND FOUND

Research on writing from a grammatical perspective has compared spoken and written language, analyzed first- and second-language development, tracked language change, and demonstrated how variation in language is meaningful for construing knowledge in different ways. These issues have been approached using both quantitative and qualitative techniques.

Speaking and Writing

One major division that can be made in analyzing language is between speech and writing. During the 1980s, many studies were conducted to describe differences between language in the two modes, and key grammatical differences between (typical) speech and (typical) written language were proposed, creating a general consensus about the linguistic characteristics of spoken and written language (see Akinnaso, 1982, for review). Though all researchers hasten to include disclaimers about not wanting to posit a dichotomy between speech and writing, and suggest that the features they identify as characteristic of each are more appropriately seen as lying on a continuum, the mode of production, whether spoken or written, is generally seen to have an influence on the grammatical organization of language.

A comparison of reviews of differences between spoken and written language by Chafe and Danielewicz (1987) and Halliday (1987), both appearing in the same volume, and both taking functional orientations, demonstrates the consensus that emerged from this research. They both find that spoken language typically uses more everyday lexis, whereas in writing, on the other hand, clauses are more lexically dense, with more embedded structures and more information packed into each clause. The nominal group is the main site where information is compacted in the written clause, mainly through premodification and postmodification with prepositional phrases and embedded clauses. Nominalization is a key feature of written language, as "nominalizations are a principal means whereby a single clause can be constructed from what might otherwise have been several clauses" (Chafe & Danielewicz, 1987, p. 100). Chafe (1985) suggests that different ways of expanding and integrating ideas are characteristic of speech and writing. Using the construct *idea unit* (comparable to the *clause*), he finds that idea units in writing are significantly longer and more complex than those of speech, containing nominalizations, adjectives, participles, and prepositional phrases, with more dependent clauses, appositives, and participial clauses. Halliday (1987) characterizes spoken language as "dynamic," whereas written language is "synoptic," with high lexical density (the number of content words per nonembedded clause) and relatively simple sentence structure with frequent embedding. The dynamic style characteristic of spoken language has low lexical density and more complex clausal structure with frequent conjunctive links.

An empirical comparison of spoken and written language that appeared at about the same time is Biber (1986, 1988), which analyzed two major text corpora, the Lancaster-Oslo-Bergen (LOB) Corpus of British English and the London-Lund Corpus of Spoken English. Biber identified 481 spoken and written texts as belonging to particular "registers" such as scientific text, conversation, or fiction, comparing them along what he calls "dimensions" of linguistic variation. Biber's assumption is "that strong co-occurrence patterns of linguistic features mark underlying functional dimensions" (1988, p. 13). He used computer analysis to tag and count 67 linguistic features and then generate clusters of features that co-occur with high frequency. The clusters of features, or factors, are interpreted by identifying the "dimension" that constitutes the best interpretation of the functions of the features that constitute the factor. These dimensions are described by parameters such as *formal* versus *informal*, or *informational* versus *involved*, based on research that identifies the functional values of different linguistic features (e.g., Chafe, 1982, 1985; Chafe & Danielewicz, 1987; Quirk et al., 1985). Biber, like others who have studied this question, found that there are no absolute linguistic differences between speech and writing, but that "it is meaningful to discuss the typical or expected types of discourse in each mode, associated with the typical situational characteristics of speaking and writing" (Biber, 1988, p. 161). At the same time, it is clear that a general division of language into speech and writing has limitations, as differences between text types are often more important than differences in mode.

Language Development

Interest in developmental issues has stimulated grammar-based approaches to the analysis of student writing, as writing researchers have sought to identify grammatical structures that could be seen as indices of written language development so that students' writing could be described on a scale of complexity or maturity. Such studies typically analyze the ability of the writer to increase the amount of information in each clause through strategies of embedding and modification. Key constructs in language development studies have been the notions of *syntactic complexity* and *lexical density*, with studies generally showing increases in complexity and density as writers develop over time.

Syntactic complexity is typically defined as more dependent structures packed into a t-unit, following Hunt's (1965) frequently cited study analyzing the writing of students at three grade levels (4th, 8th, and 11th) to comprehensively describe changes in their grammar as they matured. Hunt found that the older students wrote more complex nominals, with more noun modifiers and more embedded clauses. This view of syntactic complexity, capturing the insight that more developed writing packs more information into each clause, and that this density of information is achieved by taking information that might be presented by a less mature writer in a whole clause and constructing it as a modifying element or subordinate clause, became very influential, stimulating other researchers to investigate syntactic complexity. Haswell's (2000) recent large-scale study, a reanalysis of 80 variables from studies of undergraduate writing using factor analysis to develop clusters of features that demonstrate maturity and development, also found increased length and density associated with postnominal modification, prepositional strings, and other structural features. The characterization of written language development as a movement from a more oral-like, clause-chaining style to a more writtenlike, dense clausal structure has been useful for researchers in analyzing the written language of developing writers (Crowhurst, 1990; Hinkel, 2002; Kress, 1994; Schleppegrell, 1996; Schleppegrell & Colombi, 1997; Scott, 1988).

Second-language writing in English is a more complex phenomenon, as second-language writers have different profiles in terms of their first-language development and experience with different kinds of writing in English. However, in a meta-analysis of 39 research studies on second- and foreign-language writing, Wolfe-Quintero, Inagaki, and Kim (1998) also found that the most consistent developmental indices of complexity reported in the studies were the number of clauses and complex nominals per t-unit.

Silva's (1993) summary of findings from studies comparing first- and second-language writing found that second-language writers wrote "more but shorter T units, fewer but longer clauses, more coordination, less subordination, less noun modification, and less passivization" (p. 668). They also used more conjunctions than did first-language writers. So, like first-language writers, second-language students also increase the amount of information that they incorporate into a clause or clause complex as they develop writing proficiency. Grammatical accuracy is another interest of second-language writing researchers, and in this regard Wolfe-Quintero et al.'s (1998) review found no general increase in accuracy over time for second-language writers, as learners vary in their accuracy even as their writing is developing. Schleppegrell (2002) demonstrates that this is related to the increasing demands of the disciplinary texts that second-language students need to write, and that students struggle with a tension between writing simply and avoiding errors, and engaging fully with an assignment in ways that result in more linguistic complexity and accordingly more grammatical errors.

As with the research comparing speech and writing, analysis of writing development gives more meaningful results when the texts that are being compared are of the same type, or when the genre, audience, or other aspects of variation are taken into consideration. A unidimensional view of complexity is untenable, as many researchers have pointed out (e.g., Crowhurst & Piche, 1979; Faigley, 1980; Witte & Davis, 1980). For example, Witte and Davis, exploring one college student's syntactic complexity, found that "different subject matters systematically elicit different ranges and kinds of syntactic structures and thus affect individual stability of mean T-unit length, even when the aim and the mode of the resultant discourse is controlled" (p. 14).

Based on these findings, language development research has moved away from overall measures of complexity to more targeted analysis of features of students' texts with a further focus on functional interpretations. Hinkel (2002), for example, brings a functional perspective to the structural analysis in her comparison of 1,500 essays by university second-language and native-speaker writers. Measuring the frequency with which 68 linguistic features are used, she shows that in expository writing the second-language writers are likely to provide personal stories as evidence for their arguments, reflected in their reliance on simple conjunctions, exemplification markers, and demonstrative pronouns for establishing text cohesion—devices appropriate to the personal stories they are telling, but different from the lexical ties used more frequently by native speakers as they provide evidence for their arguments. More generally, Hinkel shows that the second-language writers rely much more heavily on the grammar of everyday interaction, whereas even less academically experienced native speakers are using more highly valued features of academic registers.

Research on language development has also attempted to describe grammatical differences in developing writing in more contextualized ways, focusing not on cross-sectional analysis of complexity or density in comparing writers at different levels, but instead on how individual writers use increasingly sophisticated grammatical resources as they develop. Whether or not this research is based on a functional theory of language, the researchers typically recognize a natural relationship between the meaning and the linguistic realization. A frequently cited study of the development of one student writer (Berkenkotter, Huckin, & Ackerman, 1988) compares the student's use of certain grammatical features with use of the same features by his professor and composition theorists. They count the number of *I*'s, connectives, and discourse demonstratives per 50 t-units and suggest that the novice writer's "poor cohesion, disorganized paragraphs, [and] lack of focus" are constructed in part through heavy reliance on *I* at the beginning of sentences that more expert writers might begin with a logical connective or discourse demonstrative, making his prose "seem very writer-based and…more difficult for the reader to see how his ideas are linked" (Berkenkotter et al., 1988, p. 19). Such findings can be interpreted from a functional linguistic perspective as demonstrating how subject, theme, and conjunctive links contribute to interpersonal meaning and textual organization.

Using the tools of SFL, Christie (1998, 2002) describes the grammatical features that students need to learn as they move into the more complex writing demands of secondary school. She demonstrates how the use of embedded clauses and other means of expanding nominal groups are important for advanced literacy development. With developing maturity, students also use a greater variety of strategies for structuring their texts, incorporating a variety of clause dependencies. They use more processes of *being* of various kinds as they construct abstractions and generalizations, related to their emergent control of the incongruent ways of expressing meaning through grammatical metaphor that enable a writer to handle abstraction. Adverbs emerge late in students' development because they represent a facility for using language to express judgments. Other functional interpretations of the grammatical features of first- and second-language writing can be found in Couture (1986), Derewianka (2003), Schleppegrell and Colombi (2002), and Ravelli and Ellis (2004). Further explanation of first-language development from an SFL perspective can be found in the articles by Painter and Torr in Simon-Vandenbergen, Taverniers, and Ravelli (2003).

LANGUAGE CHANGE OVER TIME

The well-established finding that the clause increases in density of information with maturity, when the purposes for writing are held constant, holds not only for development in the individual, but also for the historical development of some genres of language. Linguistic resources for consolidating, condensing, and compacting information in a text develop in particular genres and disciplines as more is known and can be taken for granted by writers and readers.

The scientific research report has been a focus of analysis from the perspective of its development over time, and various approaches all point to similar conclusions. Atkinson's (1996) analysis of the *Philosophical Transactions of the Royal Society of London, 1675–1975*, based on Biber's multidimensional methodology, focuses on how authors represent or place themselves in their texts. He analyzes language that portrays affective states and psychological processes, stance markers, digressions, and politeness strategies, operationalized as linguistic features such as first-person pronouns and active verb constructions. He finds movement over the 300 years from *involved* to *informational* production, and from *narrative* to *non-narrative* presentation, with a tendency toward greater abstractness in the later texts.

This movement toward more technicality and abstraction over time is also found in Bazerman's (1988) and Vande Kopple's (1998) analyses of change over time in research reports in spectroscopy. As the field developed from the late 19th century to 1980, the percentages of "substantive active verbs" increased and of reporting verbs decreased, suggesting that the *finding* increased in importance in this field, whereas the *researcher* is more in the background (Bazerman, 1988). An increase in technicality and multiword noun phrases and a change in clause subjects over time from names of objects to abstractions also contributes to increased density and more focus on the theoretical import of the studies. An increase in noun and adverbial clauses that enable the construction of relationships between concepts indicates the increasing intellectual complexity of the discipline, even though syntactic complexity (operationalized as sentence length and percentage of simple vs. complex sentences) has not changed over time, providing additional evidence that quantitative measures of syntactic complexity are inadequate for analyzing and describing such disciplinary changes.

Interested in the functions of relative clauses in this same corpus, Vande Kopple (1998) found significantly more expansion of nominal elements with relative clauses in references to materials and results in the earlier texts, whereas by 1980, the most frequent postmodifying elements are reduced elements such as nonfinite clauses. Vande Kopple suggests that as information built up and became common knowledge in the field, more could be taken for granted by the writer about what could be commonly assumed. Vande Kopple (1992) shows that this condensation of linguistic structure also occurs *within* a scientific text, as writers use expanded nominal elements to introduce ideas and then condense these ideas into less elaborated nominals as the text develops (see Martin, 1999, for another perspective on this process called *logogenesis*).

Another study of changes in scientific language over time is reported in Halliday (1993), which describes the evolution of the grammatical features that characterize scientific English. Analyzing texts written by Chaucer (1391), Newton (ca. 1680), Priestley (1760), and 19th- and 20th-century scientists, Halliday illustrates how scientists took the grammatical resources available in English and exploited the potential of the nominal elements to create technical taxonomies as well as to distill and package processes in nominal elements so that given material could be backgrounded (as theme) or foregrounded. Verbal elements were increasingly drawn on to relate these nominalized processes to each other, or simply to construe natural processes as "happening" without explicit agency. This enabled scientists "to create a discourse that moves forward by logical and coherent steps, each building on what has gone before" (Halliday, 1993, p. 64). Halliday (1998) elaborates on this, illustrating how the development of science put pressure on the grammar of English that enabled it to expand its capacity to *refer* in the creation of technical taxonomies, and to exploit its capacity to relate one process to another to create *chains of reasoning*, both of these facilitated through grammatical metaphor and the nominal mode of construal. At the same time, some information is lost, as nominalization removes explicit conjunctive relations and grammatical agency in order to condense and structure information (Halliday, 2004; Halliday & Martin, 1993; Martin & Veel, 1998).

All of these studies, then, indicate that language change at the level of the grammatical choices scientists make in writing their research reports is related to the new kinds of knowledge and interpersonal relationships that develop over time. The role of the researcher, the assumptions the writer can make about knowledge in the field, and the kind of information that needs to be presented in a research report are constructed in the grammatical choices that the scientist makes in writing the research results, and the grammar itself is flexible in evolving in ways that are functional for the construction of new knowledge in the field.

VARIATION IN GENRE AND DISCIPLINE

Examining how different kinds of texts, or different disciplinary contexts, are realized in different ways in the grammar puts the focus on the functions of linguistic elements and how they construct different types of texts. Researchers who analyze differences in text types, focusing on grammar from a functional perspective, assume that the meanings created by the writer can be analyzed through a focus on the choice of forms. Contributions to such analyses have come from education-related research and research in discourse analysis.

Research on English for specific purposes (ESP) in the context of developing relevant approaches to teaching English as a foreign language in technical fields has made prominent contributions to this focus of study for several decades (e.g., Selinker, Tarone, & Hanzeli, 1981; Swales, 1971). Swales has been a major contributor to this line of research, demonstrating how grammatical structures contribute meaningfully to the construction of texts in different disciplines, especially scientific and academic texts. Swales is concerned with providing more functional explanations for how language is used than are available in traditional grammars, and suggests that these can be found by investigating the purpose of the components of texts in which a structure appears. In his most frequently cited work, he reviews grammatical features that have been analyzed in the context of research on the academic research article, concluding that "the different sections perform different rhetorical functions and thus require different linguistic resources to realize the functions" (Swales, 1990, p. 136). For example, he reports on the distribution of *that*-clauses across different parts of a research article, based on the idea that these are used to make claims. Swales looks for textual correlates of various "moves," for example, finding deictic references to the present text such as *this, the present*, and so on, when an author moves to *occupy the niche* that the research study addresses (Swales 1990). In more recent work, Swales (2004) explores theoretical and methodological issues in the study of genres and the role of language in them.

This approach, then, looks at the functions of a text in its social context and investigates the role of language in the functional moves within a text. Similarly, Hoey (1994) illustrates how verb form/tense, lexical choices, and the position of a clause in the text signal discourse moves, and Winter (1994) shows how analysis of the grammar of the clause, especially conjunctions and connectors, adverbials, verb forms, and other elements, enables analysis of clause relations and information structure. In analyzing student writing in history, McCarthy Young and Leinhardt (1998) provide examples of connecting elements that realize different text patterns, including conjunctions, verbs, and other linguistic elements that construct *lists, specified lists*, or *causal patterns*. Brandt analyzes exophoric referents, cohesive devices, and thematic structure in three passages by the same student writer to show how "functional text analysis can reveal how writers use the resources of written language to enact meanings in everyday discourse" (Brandt, 1986, p. 105). Schleppegrell (1998) takes this up in research on middle school students' texts, showing that relational processes, expanded nominal elements, certain verb tense choices, and exploitation of clause themes for organizing and structuring text are functional for writing a description, and Schleppegrell (2001, 2004) describes the linguistic features of the registers typical of schooling.

Other research that investigates grammar in writing seeks to compare the ways different text types are structured, or the ways different disciplines construct knowledge. Researchers have analyzed grammar to characterize distinctive patterns of conjunction in different genres (Morrow, 1989; Smith & Frawley, 1983); or different transitivity patterns and thematic structure (Christie, 1986). Rothery and Stenglin (1997) show how grammatical features distinguish different genres of narrative writing. Myers (1994) compares research articles with popularizations of the same scientific findings, showing how grammatical features construct different styles that enable different views of science to be constructed in these genres, with the scientific work presented as much more tentative. Using Biber's multidimensional approach to register variation, Conrad (1996) demonstrates how language features vary in a range of texts that students encounter, and Connor (1990) describes *abstract* and *situated* styles in second- and foreign-language writers' argumentative essays in grammatical terms.

Other grammatical analyses of written text have sought to compare the construction of knowledge in different disciplines. MacDonald (1992, 1994), for example, analyzes how psychology, history, and literary studies construct *particularism and abstraction, convention,* and *representations of agency* in the clause, with particular attention to the semantics of clause subjects, which she interprets as representing the ideologies and constructedness of the texts in the ways they give a sense of agency. She shows that subjects are important in "the ways knowledge claims are made and the relation of particular phenomena to conceptual abstractions" (1994, p. 149), and that this varies by discipline. MacDonald (1994) suggests that frequent epistemic subjects such as *reason, claim,* and *evidence* "have the effect of promoting disciplinary consensus because sustained attention to previous research and to claims of new knowledge can allow a thread of continuity to be built" (p. 172). She recognizes that the choice of subject has implications for the rest of the clause, working together with particular kinds of verbs and complements, and with tense and voice selections, to construct different kinds of disciplinary knowledge. For example, epistemic subjects function together with verbs like *be, suggest,* and *argue,* often with passive voice and *that*-clauses (e.g., *"comparison shows that X"*; MacDonald, 1994) to help construct a highly nominalized structure with a point-first organization. Grammatical differences between science and history in terms of the grammar that constructs texts of different types in these disciplines are also compared in Martin (1993), Schleppegrell (2004), and Unsworth (1999), with a focus on providing information to inform pedagogy in these subject areas.

Halliday's approach to showing the power of the grammar in construing meaning is illustrated in his analysis of William Golding's *The Inheritors* (Halliday, 1971), where he shows that syntactic patterns construe the underlying theme of the work at the same time they create the narrative flow. Analyzing the choice of verbs, the constellations of actors, and the expression of agency, he shows that the grammatical patterns that are foregrounded are significant in the way they represent the two different worldviews in the book: that of the people who are unable to preserve their way of life and that of the people who will be effective in taking over the world of the others. Halliday points out that the grammar of English makes a basic distinction between processes that are presented as due to an external cause and those that are not, and that these different syntactic options are meaningful in creating realizations of the different worlds of the novel.

J. R. Martin demonstrates how a discourse-semantics approach, based on SFL, reveals how meaning constructed at the clause level also redounds with meanings that are then realized at the level of the text (e.g., Martin, 1995; Martin & Rose, 2003). Martin (1999) shows how various grammatical features work together to enable Nelson Mandela to use the recounting of his life story to construe at the same time his vision of freedom and reconciliation, with the language resources working at many levels to construct a view of hope and change. Many scholars have used SFL to show, in contexts of schooling, how texts construct different kinds of knowledge, or to show why texts are valued in different ways. Veel (1998), for example, shows how a science textbook passage moves between abstract theoretical knowledge and contextualized explanation of physical features of ecosystems by drawing on grammatical metaphor to create cause-and-effect links; middle (ergative) and passive voice to elide agency; and theme, the nominal group, and relational processes to organize knowledge. Rose (1997) shows how obligation and causality are constructed in school texts in technical fields, and Unsworth (1997) demonstrates how a grammatical analysis can reveal why one text is a better explanation of a science topic than another. Hallidayan scholars have had a special interest in how meaning is constructed in the discourse of history, with the grammatical features that distinguish different genres of history discourse illustrated in Coffin (1997) and Martin (2002), who presents the genres as a kind of learner pathway into writing in history. SFL is currently being used in many approaches to discourse analysis (e.g., Gee, 1999; Martin & Rose, 2006; Martin & Wodak, 2003; Rampton, Roberts, Leung, & Harris, 2002; Young & Harrison, 2004).

CURRENT DIRECTIONS

Recent work on the grammatical features of various genres and disciplines has been fruitful, but much work remains to describe and analyze the grammar that constructs different kinds of knowledge in written text. This work is likely to continue to focus on the broader constellations of linguistic features that construct different kinds of meaning—for example, to look for text organization not just in connectors, but in all the resources that enable logical linking and the construction of information flow in a text. One area of current activity in this vein is research on the interpersonal stance the writer creates and projects.

Researchers have long been interested in the way a writer's voice is projected in a text and in how attitudes and evaluation are constructed. Features such as modality or pronouns have been used to analyze the attitudes or role relationships construed in a text, but recent studies exploring this area of meaning have shown that the stance and attitude of the writer are realized in a much broader range of grammatical resources. Myers (1989), for example, demonstrates how linguistic features typically considered conventions of scientific writing, such as certain pronouns, passives, and adverbs, have functional meaning as *politeness* strategies, and Myers (1992) shows how choice of verb and tense enable different kinds of assertions. Hyland (2004) and Hyland and Milton (1997) show how a range of linguistic features construe interpersonal meaning and demonstrate that developing writers' dependence on modal verbs and adverbs can result in assertions that are too strong and authoritative for their contexts and purposes.

Martin (2000) has shown that interpersonal meaning cannot be isolated in particular features, as it is constructed in various structures that create a prosody of evaluation. He provides a comprehensive overview of such structures through his appraisal theory (Martin, 2000), showing how the expression of values, manipulation of the strength of values, and the introduction and management of the voices to whom values are attributed are enabled through a wide range of grammatical resources. Using appraisal theory, Hood (2004) shows how *reporting verbs, concessive conjunctions, forms of citation,* and *tense* are implicated in the expression of values and attitudes, so that writers need to construct a stance through the dynamic establishment and management of a range of attitudinal meanings and evaluative resources. Other work using appraisal theory includes Coffin (2002, 2003) and Rothery and Stenglin (2000), and other recent work on evaluative meaning includes the chapters in Ravelli and Ellis (2004) and Hunston and Thompson (2000), as well as G. Thompson (1996), Martin and White (2005), and a special issue of *English for Academic Purposes* (2003, vol. 2).

Another trend in research on writing from a grammatical perspective is the growth in corpus analysis, especially of corpora designed to enable analysis of particular kinds of texts (see e.g., Coffin, Hewings, & O'Halloran, 2004; J. Flowerdew, 2002). Functional linguists are also developing tools for analysis of larger corpora (see http://www.wagsoft.com/Systemics/Software.html), and L. Flowerdew (2003) shows how a corpus analysis can work together with SFL. The Biber et al. (1999) recent grammar of English, based on corpus analysis and differentiating among contexts of use to provide probabilistic evidence about where a certain structure is typically more frequent than others, is likely to be cited frequently in future studies. Computer tools will likely continue to enable researchers to generalize about how grammatical structures contribute to meaning making in different contexts and types of texts.

CONCLUSION

This chapter has shown what can be learned about written texts from the analysis of the grammar that constructs them. Language varies along many dimensions, so grammatical analysis is an important means of characterizing the different ways writing is structured and of investigating how these differences are meaningful. The history of clause- and sentence-level approaches to the analysis of written discourse has been a continuing attempt to identify features that can be used as indicators of complexity, development, and maturity of expression; or, alternatively, that can characterize particular text types or show the evolution of language over time. Recently the focus has been on the structure of nominal elements, thematic organization at the clause level, and the construction of interpersonal meaning, as researchers recognize the roles of different linguistic resources in the construction of a text. Knowledge and information are constructed through deployment of linguistic features that are functional for meaning making in particular contexts, and approaches to the analysis of writing that recognize the complexity with which linguistic features interact in the construction of meaning are providing important new information about the challenges of language development, the construal of meaning in different fields and disciplines, and variation in the extent to which different features are drawn on in writing meaningful texts.

REFERENCES

Akinnaso, F. N. (1982). On the differences between spoken and written language. *Language and Speech, 25*(2), 97–125.

Atkinson, D. (1996). The *Philosophical Transactions of the Royal Society of London, 1675–1975*: A sociohistorical discourse analysis. *Language in Society, 25,* 333–371.

Bazerman, C. (1988). *Shaping written knowledge: The genre and activity of the experimental article in science.* Madison: University of Wisconsin Press.

Berkenkotter, C., Huckin, T. N., & Ackerman, J. (1988). Conventions, conversations, and the writer: Case study of a student in a rhetoric Ph.D. program. *Research in the Teaching of English, 22*(1), 9–44.

Biber, D. (1986). Spoken and written textual dimensions in English: Resolving the contradictory findings. *Language, 62*(2), 384–414.

Biber, D. (1988). *Variation across speech and writing.* Cambridge, England: Cambridge University Press.

Biber, D., Johansson, S., Leech, G., Conrad, S., & Finegan, E. (1999). *Longman grammar of spoken and written English.* London: Longman.

Brandt, D. (1986). Text and context: How writers come to mean. In B. Couture (Ed.), *Functional approaches to writing: Research perspectives* (pp. 93–107). London: Frances Pinter.

Butler, C. S. (1985). *Systemic linguistics: Theory and applications.* London: Batsford Academic and Educational.

Chafe, W. (1982). Integration and involvement in speaking, writing, and oral literature. In D. Tannen (Ed.), *Spoken and written language: Exploring orality and literacy* (pp. 35–54). Norwood, NJ: Ablex.

Chafe, W. (1985). Linguistic differences produced by differences between speaking and writing. In D. R. Olson, N. Torrance, & A. Hildyard (Eds.), *Literacy, language, and learning: The nature and consequences of reading and writing* (pp. 105–123). Cambridge, England: Cambridge University Press.

Chafe, W., & Danielewicz, J. (1987). Properties of spoken and written language. In R. Horowitz & F. J. Samuels (Eds.), *Comprehending oral and written language* (pp. 83–113). New York: Academic Press.

Christie, F. (1986). Writing in schools: generic structures as ways of meaning. In B. Couture (Ed.), *Functional approaches to writing: Research perspectives* (pp. 221–239). London: Pinter.

Christie, F. (1998). Learning the literacies of primary and secondary schooling. In F. Christie & R. Misson (Eds.), *Literacy and schooling* (pp. 47–73). London: Routledge.

Christie, F. (2002). The development of abstraction in adolescence in subject English. In M. Schleppegrell & M. C. Colombi (Eds.), *Developing advanced literacy in first and second languages: Meaning with power* (pp. 45–66). Mahwah, NJ: Lawrence Erlbaum Associates.

Coffin, C. (1997). Constructing and giving value to the past: an investigation into secondary school history. In F. Christie & J. R. Martin (Eds.), *Genre and institutions: Social processes in the workplace and school* (pp. 196–230). London: Cassell.

Coffin, C. (2002). The voices of history: Theorizing the interpersonal semantics of historical discourses. *Text, 22*(4), 503–528.

Coffin, C. (2003). Reconstruals of the past—settlement or invasion? The role of JUDGEMENT analysis. In J. R. Martin & R. Wodak (Eds.), *Re/reading the past: Critical and functional perspectives on time and value* (pp. 219–246). Amsterdam: Benjamins.

Coffin, C., Hewings, A., & O'Halloran, K. (Eds.). (2004). *Applying English grammar: Functional and corpus approaches.* London: Arnold.

Connor, U. (1990). Linguistic/rhetorical measures for international student persuasive writing. *Research in the Teaching of English, 24,* 67–87.

Conrad, S. M. (1996). Investigating academic texts with corpus-based techniques: An example from biology. *Linguistics and Education, 8*(3), 299–326.

Couture, B. (Ed.). (1986). *Functional approaches to writing research perspectives.* London: Pinter.

Cox, B., & Sulzby, E. (1984). Childen's use of reference in told, dictated, and handwritten stories. *Research in the Teaching of English, 18*(4), 345–365.

Crowhurst, M. (1990). The development of persuasive/argumentative writing. In R. Beach & S. Hynds (Eds.), *Developing discourse practices in adolescence and adulthood* (pp. 200–223). Norwood, NJ: Ablex.

Crowhurst, M., & Piche, G. L. (1979). Audience and mode of discourse effects on syntactic complexity in writing at two grade levels. *Research in the Teaching of English, 13*(2), 101–109.

Derewianka, B. (2003). Grammatical metaphor in the transition to adolescence. In A.-M. Simon-Vandenbergen, M. Taverniers, & L. Ravelli (Eds.), *Grammatical metaphor: Views from systemic functional linguistics* (pp. 185–219). Amsterdam: Benjamins.

Faigley, L. (1980). Names in search of a concept: Maturity, fluency, complexity, and growth in written syntax. *College Composition and Communication, 31,* 291–300.

Flowerdew, J. (Ed.). (2002). *Academic discourse*. Harlow, England: Pearson Education.

Flowerdew, L. (2003). A combined corpus and systemic-functional analysis of the problem–solution pattern in a student and professional corpus of technical writing. *TESOL Quarterly, 37*(3), 489–511.

Gee, J. P. (1999). *An introduction to discourse analysis: Theory and method*. London: Routledge.

Halliday, M. A. K. (1971). Linguistic function and literary style: An inquiry into the language of William Golding's *The Inheritors*. In S. Chatman (Ed.), *Literary style: A symposium*. Oxford, England: Oxford University Press. Reprinted in J. Webster (Ed.), *Linguistic studies of text and discourse* (Vol. 2 in *The Collected works of M. A. K. Halliday*, pp. 88–125). London: Continuum.

Halliday, M. A. K. (1987). Spoken and written modes of meaning. In R. Horowitz & J. Samuels (Eds.), *Comprehending oral and written language* (pp. 55–82). San Diego, CA: Academic Press.

Halliday, M. A. K. (1993). On the language of physical science. In M. A. K. Halliday & J. R. Martin (Eds.), *Writing science: Literacy and discursive power* (pp. 54–68). Pittsburgh, PA: University of Pittsburgh Press.

Halliday, M. A. K. (1998). Things and relations: Regrammaticising experience as technical knowlege. In J. R. Martin & R. Veel (Eds.), *Reading science: Critical and functional perspectives on discourses of science* (pp. 185–235). London: Routledge.

Halliday, M. A. K. (2004). *The language of science* (Vol. 5). London: Continuum.

Halliday, M. A. K., & Hasan, R. (1976). *Cohesion in English*. London: Longman.

Halliday, M. A. K., & Martin, J. R. (Eds.). (1993). *Writing science: Literacy and discursive power*. Pittsburgh, PA: University of Pittsburgh Press.

Halliday, M. A. K., & Matthiessen, C. M. I. M. (2004). *An introduction to functional grammar* (3rd ed.). London: Arnold.

Haswell, R. (2000). Documenting improvement in college writing: A longitudinal approach. *Written Communication, 17*(3), 307–352.

Hinkel, E. (2002). *Second language writers' text: Linguistic and rhetorical features*. Mahwah, NJ: Lawrence Erlbaum Associates.

Hoey, M. (1994). Signalling in discourse: a functional analysis of a common discourse pattern in written and spoken English. In M. Coulthard (Ed.), *Advances in written text analysis* (pp. 26–45). London: Routledge.

Hood, S. (2004). Managing attitude in undergraduate academic writing: A focus on the introductions to research reports. In L. J. Ravelli & R. A. Ellis (Eds.), *Analysing academic writing: Contextualized frameworks* (pp. 24–44). London: Continuum.

Hunston, S., & Thompson, G. (Eds.). (2000). *Evaluation in text*. Oxford, England: Oxford University Press.

Hunt, K. W. (1965). *Grammatical structures written at three grade levels*. Champaign, IL: National Council of Teachers of English.

Hyland, K. (2004). Patterns of engagement: dialogic features and L2 undergraduate writing. In L. J. Ravelli & R. A. Ellis (Eds.), *Analysing academic writing: Contextualized frameworks* (pp. 5–23). London: Continuum.

Hyland, K., & Milton, J. (1997). Qualification and certainty in L1 and L2 students' writing. *Journal of Second Language Writing, 6*(2), 183–205.

Kress, G. (1994). *Learning to write* (2nd ed.). London: Routledge.

MacDonald, S. P. (1992). A method for analyzing sentence-level differences in disciplinary knowledge making. *Written Communication, 9*(4), 533–569.

MacDonald, S. P. (1994). *Professional academic writing in the humanities and social sciences*. Carbondale: Southern Illinois University Press.

Mann, W. C., & Thompson, S. A. (Eds.). (1992). *Discourse description: Diverse linguistic analyses of a fund-raising text*. Amsterdam: Benjamins.

Martin, J. R. (1993). Life as a noun: Arresting the universe in science and humanities. In M. A. K. Halliday & J. R. Martin (Eds.), *Writing science: Literacy and discursive power* (pp. 221–267). Pittsburgh, PA: University of Pittsburgh Press.

Martin, J. R. (1995). Text and clause: Fractal resonance. *Text, 15*(1), 5–24.

Martin, J. R. (1999). Grace: The logogenesis of freedom. *Discourse Studies, 1*(1), 29–56.

Martin, J. R. (2000). Beyond exchange: Appraisal systems in English. In S. Hunston & G. Thompson (Eds.), *Evaluation in text: Authorial stance and the construction of discourse* (pp. 142–175). Oxford, England: Oxford University Press.

Martin, J. R. (2002). Writing history: Construing time and value in discourses of the past. In M. J. Schleppegrell & M. C. Colombi (Eds.), *Developing advanced literacy in first and second languages: Meaning with power* (pp. 87–118). Mahwah, NJ: Lawrence Erlbaum Associates.

Martin, J. R., & Rose, D. (2003). *Working with discourse*. London: Continuum.

Martin, J. R., & Rose, D. (2006). *Genre relations: Mapping culture*. London: Equinox.

Martin, J. R., & Veel, R. (Eds.). (1998). *Reading science: Critical and functional perspectives on discourses of science*. London: Routledge.

Martin, J. R., & White, P. R. R. (2005). *The language of evaluation*. New York: Palgrave Macmillan.

Martin, J. R., & Wodak, R. (Eds.). (2003). *Re/reading the past: Critical and functional perspectives on time and value*. Amsterdam: John Benjamins.

Matthiessen, C., & Thompson, S. A. (1987). *The structure of discourse and "subordination."* Marina del Rey, CA: Information Sciences Institute.

McCarthy, M. (1994). *It, this* and *that.* In M. Coulthard (Ed.), *Advances in written text analysis* (pp. 266–275). London: Routledge.

McCarthy Young, K., & Leinhardt, G. (1998). Writing from primary documents: A way of knowing in history. *Written Communication, 15*(1), 25–68.

Morrow, P. R. (1989). Conjunct use in business news stories and academic journal articles: A comparative study. *English for Specific Purposes, 8*(3), 239–254.

Myers, G. (1989). The pragmatics of politeness in scientific articles. *Applied Linguistics, 10*(1), 2–35.

Myers, G. (1992). "In this paper we report": Speech acts and scientific claims. *Journal of Pragmatics, 17*, 295–313.

Myers, G. (1994). Narratives of science and nature in popularizing molecular genetics. In M. Coulthard (Ed.), *Advances in written text analysis* (pp. 179–190). London: Routledge.

Nystrand, M., Greene, S., & Wiemelt, J. (1993). Where did composition studies come from? An intellectual history. *Written Communication, 10*(3), 267–333.

Quirk, R., Greenbaum, S., Leech, G., & Svartvik, J. (1972). *A grammar of contemporary English*. London: Longman.

Quirk, R., Greenbaum, S., Leech, G., & Svartvik, J. (1985). *A comprehensive grammar of the English language*. London: Longman.

Rampton, B., Roberts, C., Leung, C., & Harris, R. (2002). Methodology in the analysis of classroom discourse. *Applied Linguistics, 23*(3), 373–392.

Ravelli, L. J., & Ellis, R. A. (Eds.). (2004). *Analysing academic writing: Contextualized frameworks*. London: Continuum.

Rose, D. (1997). Science, technology and technical literacies. In F. Christie & J. R. Martin (Eds.), *Genre and institutions: Social processes in the workplace and school* (pp. 40–72). London: Cassell.

Rothery, J., & Stenglin, M. (1997). Entertaining and instructing: Exploring experience through story. In F. Christie & J. R. Martin (Eds.), *Genre and institutions: Social processes in the workplace and school* (pp. 231–263). London: Cassell.

Rothery, J., & Stenglin, M. (2000). Interpreting literature: The role of APPRAISAL. In L. Unsworth (Ed.), *Researching language in schools and communities: Functional linguistic perspectives* (pp. 222–244). London: Cassell.

Schleppegrell, M. J. (1996). Conjunction in spoken English and ESL writing. *Applied Linguistics, 17*(3), 271–285.

Schleppegrell, M. J. (1998). Grammar as resource: Writing a description. *Research in the Teaching of English, 32*(3), 182–211.

Schleppegrell, M. J. (2001). Linguistic features of the language of schooling. *Linguistics and Education, 12*(4), 431–459.

Schleppegrell, M. J. (2002). Challenges of the science register for ESL students: Errors and meaning making. In M. J. Schleppegrell & M. C. Colombi (Eds.), *Developing advanced literacy in first and second languages: Meaning with power* (pp. 119–142). Mahwah, NJ: Lawrence Erlbaum Associates.

Schleppegrell, M. J. (2004). *The language of schooling: A functional linguistics approach*. Mahwah, NJ: Lawrence Erlbaum Associates.

Schleppegrell, M. J., & Colombi, M. C. (1997). Text organization by bilingual writers: Clause structure as a reflection of discourse structure. *Written Communication, 14*(4), 481–503.

Schleppegrell, M. J., & Colombi, M. C. (Eds.). (2002). *Developing advanced literacy in first and second languages: Meaning with power*. Mahwah, NJ: Lawrence Erlbaum Associates.

Scott, C. M. (1988). Spoken and written syntax. In M. A. Nippold (Ed.), *Later language development: Ages 9 through 19* (pp. 49–95). Boston: College-Hill.

Selinker, L., Tarone, E., & Hanzeli, V. (Eds.). (1981). *English for academic and technical purposes: Studies in honor of Louis Trimble*. Rowley, MA: Newbury House.

Silva, T. (1993). Toward an understanding of the distinct nature of L2 writing: The ESL research and its implications. *TESOL Quarterly, 27*(4), 657–677.

Simon-Vandenbergen, A.-M., Taverniers, M., & Ravelli, L. (Eds.). (2003). *Grammatical metaphor: Views from systemic functional linguistics*. Amsterdam: Benjamins.

Smith, R. N., & Frawley, W. J. (1983). Conjunctive cohesion in four English genres. *Text, 3*(4), 347–374.

Stubbs, M. (1996). *Text and corpus analysis*. Oxford, England: Blackwell.

Swales, J. (1971). *Writing Scientific English*. London: Nelson.

Swales, J. (1990). *Genre analysis: English in academic and research settings*. Cambridge, England: Cambridge University Press.

Swales, J. (2004). *Research genres: Explorations and applications*. Cambridge, England: Cambridge University Press.

Thompson, G. (1996). Voices in the text: Discourse perspectives on language reports. *Applied Linguistics, 17*, 501–530.

Thompson, S. (1983). Grammar and discourse: The English detached participial clause. In F. Klein-Andreu (Ed.), *Discourse perspectives on syntax* (Vol. 43, pp. 43–65). New York: Academic Press.

Thompson, S. (1984). "Subordination" in formal and informal discourse. In D. Schiffrin (Ed.), *Meaning, form, and use in context: Linguistic applications* (pp. 85–94). Washington, DC: Georgetown University Press.

Thompson, S. (1985). Grammar and written discourse: Initial vs. final purpose clauses in English. *Text, 5*, 55–84.

Unsworth, L. (1997). "Sound" explanations in school sciences: A functional linguistic perspective on effective apprenticing texts. *Linguistics and Education, 9*(2), 199–226.

Unsworth, L. (1999). Developing critical understanding of the specialised language of school science and history texts: A functional grammatical perspective. *Journal of Adolescent and Adult Literacy, 42*(7), 508–521.

Vachek, J. (1966). *The linguistic school of Prague: An introduction to its theory and practice*. Bloomington: Indiana University Press.

Vande Kopple, W. J. (1992). Noun phrases and the style of scientific discourse. In S. P. Witte, N. Nakadate, & R. D. Cherry (Eds.), *A rhetoric of doing: Essays on written discourse in honor of James L. Kinneavy* (pp. 328–348). Carbondale: Southern Illinois University Press.

Vande Kopple, W. J. (1994). Some characteristics and functions of grammatical subjects in scientific discourse. *Written Communication, 11*(4), 534–564.

Vande Kopple, W. J. (1998). Relative clauses in spectroscopic articles in the *Physical Review*, beginnings and 1980: Some changes in patterns of modification and a connection to a possible shift in style. *Written Communication, 15*(2), 170–202.

Veel, R. (1998). The greening of school science: Ecogenesis in secondary classrooms. In J. R. Martin & R. Veel (Eds.), *Reading science: Critical and functional perspectives on discourses of science* (pp. 114–151). London: Routledge.

Winter, E. (1994). Clause relations as information structure: two basic text structures in English. In M. Coulthard (Ed.), *Advances in written text analysis* (pp. 46–68). London: Routledge.

Witte, S. P., & Davis, A. S. (1980). The stability of t-unit length: A preliminary investigation. *Research in the Teaching of English, 17*(1), 5–17.

Wolfe-Quintero, K., Inagaki, S., & Kim, H.-Y. (1998). *Second language development in writing: Measures of fluency, accuracy and complexity*. Manoa: Second Language Teaching and Curriculm Center, University of Hawaii.

Young, L., & Harrison, C. (2004). *Systemic functional linguistics and critical discourse analysis: Studies in social change*. London: Continuum.

CHAPTER 35

Form, Text Organization, Genre, Coherence, and Cohesion

Christine M. Tardy
DePaul University

John M. Swales
University of Michigan

Written texts are known to have culturally preferred shapes that structure their overall organization and influence their internal patterning. These shaping forces, at both general and local levels, are neither incidental nor accidental; rather, they exist to provide orientations for both readers and writers. This chapter therefore presents an evaluative overview of research into these organizational properties of written texts. We start with broad-level analyses of discourse structure, along with social orientations to generic form. We then proceed to discuss more local organizational features such as coherence and cohesion and phraseological patternings and finally close with some reflections on likely future directions for research into written text.

A great deal of the available research into written form has been motivated by pedagogical interests, particularly following the growth of applied research fields like rhetoric and composition and applied linguistics in the later decades of the 20th century. This is because research-oriented practitioners in these fields are often guided by a focus on helping developing writers succeed, and the underlying assumption of this focus is that a better understanding of texts and their structural properties has important applications to writing instruction and reading comprehension. Such applications might include systematic training in the use of structural elements that are favored within certain text types or genres, awareness-raising activities in which learners analyze texts themselves, and comparative work such as contrasting news items and feature articles in newspapers or introductions and discussions in research articles. In all cases, a greater understanding of textual form—including organizational and phraseological patterns—can provide instructors and students with tools for breaking down the complex construct of "writing" into more manageable and learnable parts. However, in general, the relative stress placed on analysis, awareness, and acquisition varies somewhat according to pedagogical circumstance. For example, Devitt, in her important book *Writing Genres* (2004), insists that for her U.S. undergraduates, awareness of textual form is the predominant aim. On the other hand, those responsible for helping disadvantaged writers—for example, minority children in the United States (Delpit, 1995), working-class kids in Australia (Christie, 1998), and speakers of English as a second language (ESL) or second dialect (Johns, 1997)—argue that analysis and awareness must be directly linked to acquisition. This latter position is particularly prevalent in the field of English for Specific Purposes, which provides specialized materials for professionals, academics, and students who are neither English specialists nor speakers of English as a first language.

Despite similar motivations for studying text across research fields, there is great diversity in approaches to studying text form. First, approaches may be variously historical, tracing the evolution of genres over time; ideological, unpacking, for instance, the so-called genres of power; or ethnographic, such as exploring multiple drafts of a particular text. Second, objects of analysis vary widely, ranging from the analysis of single paragraphs to multimillion-word corpora and from the study of monolingual samples to contrastive study of texts in multiple languages. In addition, technological innovations have made it possible to move from the laborious task of analyzing a text by hand to the use of computer software for uncovering patterns difficult to detect by simply eyeballing discourse. Methodological orientations are also wide-ranging, with approaches investigating text through structural features, intended social action and resulting text form, or word- and sentence-level devices used to create continuity within a given stretch of text.

Grabe and Kaplan (1996) argue that the diversity in text-based research on writing reflects both the broad range of interests with which scholars work and the broad range of purposes which work is designed to serve. In addition, scholarly fashion has its effect. For example, whereas earlier work in rhetoric and composition focused on discourse organization as a means of understanding the rhetorical functions of texts (e.g., Kinneavy, 1971; Moffett, 1968), text-based research has more recently fallen somewhat out of favor in contemporary rhetoric and composition (cf. Barton & Stygall, 2002). Currently, the bulk of such research has instead been conducted by applied linguists, who are also more likely to have been trained in methods of text and discourse analysis. Nevertheless, a great deal of text-based work today, particularly in the area of genre studies, blends and transcends traditional disciplinary boundaries, interfacing with such fields as information science, computational linguistics, and natural-language processing.

DISCOURSE STRUCTURES

One strand of research into the organizational properties of written text examines discourse structures at a cross-generic level, classifying texts along various dimensions. Much of this work grows out of functional linguistics, an orientation that is more prominent outside of the United States, where theoretical linguistics is still largely dominated by a Chomskyan generative approach. As a result, work in text and discourse analysis has come primarily from Europe, Australia, and, more recently, South America.

Macrogeneric Structure

One common classification scheme of discourse structure considers the broad function or aim of a text in a relatively decontextualized manner, somewhat akin to Kinneavy's (1971) modes of discourse. These classifications of structure are referred to through terms as diverse as instructional genres (Martin, 1993a), macrogenres (Grabe, 2002), and generic values (Bhatia, 2002) (see Table 35.1). What these schemes share is a relative independence from context, so that a macro-genre-like exposition might encompass text types as diverse as research papers, textbooks, and pamphlets. Nevertheless, proponents of such classification schemes argue that their value lies in differentiating the functions and purposes of text forms on a broad level. Grabe (2002), for example, provides persuasive empirical evidence for the distinctions between narrative and expository texts with regard to lexical and grammatical features, cohesion features, organizational structure, and reading comprehension. He and others argue that these higher level structures have great value for raising writers' awareness of discourse structure and for enhancing metalinguistic reflection.

TABLE 35.1
Alternative Classification Schemes for Macro Structures

Instructional genres Martin (1993a)	Macro-genres Grabe (2002)	Generic values Bhatia (2002)
Recounts	Narrative	Narration
Procedures	Expository	Description
Descriptions	...	Explanation
Reports		Evaluation
Explanations		Instruction
Expositions		...

Classifications of this sort have been adopted primarily in the study of school writing, particularly in K through 12 settings. In Australia, instructional genres have served as the basis for extensive curriculum reform (see Cope & Kalantzis, 1993). In the United States, the macrogenres like narrative, expository, and descriptive texts have served as operational categories for the study of literacy emergence at the elementary school level (Kamberelis, 1999; Reppen, 1994).

Somewhat comparable are studies of the internal rhetorical structure of supragenres. Those dealing with written text include problem–solution (Hoey, 1983) and general–specific patterns (Huckin & Olsen, 1991; Swales & Feak, 2004). For the first, Hoey shows that the prototypical arrangement of many administrative and technical texts (especially of a troubleshooting nature) is situation-problem-solution-evaluation. Here it should be stressed that the order is seen as being protypical rather than fixed; indeed, less common variants of this order can often be motivated and explained by reference to contextual or audience-design factors. The second pattern is common in many kinds of exposition, where a broad generalization (often of a definitional nature) is followed by narrowing ones, and then by details and/or examples, sometimes with some widening out at the end. For instance, many encyclopedia entries and other types of reference material adopt this pattern.

Information Structure

An even broader approach to textual analysis falls under the rubrics of information structure or information packaging. This has its origin in the Prague School's *functional sentence perspective* (Daneš, 1974), and has been further developed and modified by systemic-functional linguists. Sentences in most nonliterary written discourses will have a structure suited to the smooth presentation of information. In most normal circumstances (at least in English), the theme, as the point of departure for the sentence, will contain Given information, whereas the later rheme will contain the New information. However, it is worth pointing out that the Given information does not necessarily have to be actually "given," only that it can be recoverable from the discoursal context (Fries, 1994; Halliday, 1994). This recoverability, of course, makes it easier for the reader to link this part of the sentence to preceding discourse or to general knowledge and so sets the reader up for processing the New information to be contained in the postsubject part of the sentence. In this way, sentences tend to increase their "communicative dynamism" as they unfold (Firbas, 1992). Furthermore, this rise in dynamism frequently corresponds to the increasing complexity of the sentences constituent noun phases. This characteristic is sometimes known as "end weight," or, in Huckin and Olsen's (1991) terms, "light NPs before heavy NPs."

Although these unmarked theme–rheme, given–new packagings can be shown to operate over sequences of several sentences, inevitably numerous exceptions arise. First, there can be prethemes, such as subordinate clauses, which commonly occur in sentence-initial position. Second, writers have syntactic and other devices for giving certain pieces of information lesser or greater salience and focus. These include (a) the passive, (b) cleft constructions and extrapositions, (c) inversions, and (d) existential "there." To illustrate, consider the following sentence and its variants:

Unmarked: The students requested more tests.

(a) More tests were requested by the students.
(b) It was the students who requested more tests.
(c) More tests, the students requested.
(d) There was the strange case of the students' requesting more tests.

Although this lays out an outline of theme–rheme, more detailed but accessible treatments can be found in Bloor and Bloor (1995) and G. Thompson (1995).

GENRE AS SOCIAL ACTION

A second, livelier strand of discourse studies has examined and applied the notion of genre as a frame for communicative social action. Miller's (1984) definition of genre as social action provides the theoretical foundation for much of this work, which has been carried out within the fields of rhetoric and composition, professional writing, education, and applied linguistics. Genres, in this theoretical orientation, are described as typified patterns of language used to achieve rhetorical goals in regularly recurring situations. Examples of such text types therefore range from shopping lists to research articles to complaint letters. Formal regularities within a genre may include, for example, organizational structures, citation practices, quantity and location of detail, generalization, and transitions. A number of overlapping emphases have emerged within this strand of research, investigating the nature of genres and genre knowledge.

Dynamism and Durability

One such emphasis has examined the dynamism of genres, finding that their textual realizations, though typified, are not static entities; instead, they are better described as "stabilized-for-now" (Schryer, 1994). As changes occur in a community's ideologies, content knowledge, and discursive practices, so too must changes occur in the related genres (Kamberelis, 1995). Their situated and intertextual nature then leads genres to be sites of contention that are, paradoxically, both dynamic and durable. Historical investigations of academic genres (e.g., Bazerman, 1988; Gross, Harmon, & Reidy, 2003) have illustrated how texts like research articles evolve in relation to changes in social context and disciplinary ideology.

In addition to these temporal changes, geographic shifts greatly influence genre production and reception. Research in contrastive rhetoric, for example, illustrates how the textual realizations of genres like research articles or résumés vary across cultural-linguistic communities with regard to the presence or absence of various structural elements (Connor, 1996). Bhatia's (1993) work with job application letters shows that one genre may indeed function in different ways in different national settings. Because contrastive rhetoric research has often been accused of "essentializing" cross-cultural differences (e.g., Kubota, 1997), careful work by Burgess (2002) is particularly enlightening. She shows, for example, that rhetorical differences between article introductions in English and Hispanic studies written in English and Spanish are not largely ascribable to either area of specialization or to language of publication; rather, they can be more firmly linked to the size and nature of targeted discourse communities.

Cross-disciplinary research has found considerable genre variation among disciplines (Hyland, 2000; Samraj, 2002), again highlighting the contingent nature of genre texts. In recent years, many studies of this kind can be found in the pages of *English for Specific Purposes* and the *Journal of English for Academic Purposes*. Swales (2004) suggests that this disciplinary variation is in fact more striking in the methods sections of research articles than in introductions, results, or discussions. In some disciplines (e.g., social psychology), the methods are typically described in exhaustive and justificatory detail, whereas in others (e.g., biochemistry) they are largely standardized and can be taken for granted.

Generic Structure

A second area of emphasis within genre research has examined the text structure of genres or part genres. Systemic-functional linguistics views genres as structured in certain ways because the structure serves the social goals of the text; in other words, the organization is understood as revealing the text's purpose (Martin, 1993a) and the social world that is projected in the text (Hyland, 2000). Much research, primarily within applied linguistics, has concentrated on describing the structure of genres through a variety of models, including, most notably, moves and stages.

Move analysis attempts to identify rhetorical moves within a text, each move being made up of one or more steps. One early example of this type of analysis is the CARS model (Swales, 1981, 1990), which attempts to account for moves within research article introductions that create a research space. Move analysis has been used by researchers to investigate a wide range of written genres, such as job application letters (Bhatia, 1993), grant proposals (Connor & Mauranen, 1999), and company e-mail responses to customer inquiries (Van Mulken & Van der Meer, 2005). Even so, the primary emphasis in this research area remains concentrated on academic texts (textbooks, academic book reviews, theses and dissertations, and research articles), and this research has been largely undertaken by English for Academic Purposes (EAP) specialists.

Building on move analysis, Paltridge (1995) describes a relational approach, in which the relation *between* structural elements within a genre is explored. The notion of generic structure potential (Hasan, 1984) has also been applied in investigating not only the structural elements of a genre, but also the *possibilities* for structure (Paltridge, 1997). In other words, a relational analysis of a text genre reveals what elements must and can occur, where those elements must and can occur, and how often those elements occur.

A similar approach to investigating the structural elements of text genres has identified genre stages. Martin (1993b) describes stages as functional sequences in the structuring of genres. It is through the organization of text into stages that genres achieve their social purposes (Martin & Rothery, 1993). Staging is central to a literacy pedagogy used in Australia, in which the first goal for students is making conscious the staging of different genres.

More recent work in genre research has examined part genres, illustrating how these parts work somewhat as genres in their own right, encompassing particular socio-rhetorical functions and forms. For example, Dressen (2002) provides a comprehensive account of the *Geological Settings* in petrology articles, which occur between the introduction and the beginning of the analysis. These are essentially depictions of the terrain from which the rock samples have been extracted. Although once travelers' narratives, Dressen shows that today expertise in the locale is expressed via a short, expert, and conventionalized description of the site's geological record, in which the voice of the human geologist has been silenced.

In his important overview of developments in genre analysis, applied linguist Vijay Bhatia (2004) adopts a position that is considerably closer to those of the new rhetoricians. Bhatia traces an evolution from viewing genre as being concerned with textual space, to seeing it as being imbricated with sociocognitive space, and most recently with social space. Much of the impetus behind his thinking comes from his interest in promotional genres such as book blurbs, brochures, and fund-raising letters. With such discourses, descriptive, evaluative, and persuasive elements are conjoined. As he writes:

As a consequence, we often find a wide gap between genre analysis of texts in published literature, emphasizing the integrity and purity of individual genres, and the variety of rather complex and dynamic instances of hybridized genres that one tends to find in the real world. (p. xiv)

Bhatia calls for the use of integrated research methods in order to come to grips with these real-world genres.

Intertextuality

Genres, as tools for social action, rarely (if ever) function in isolation, instead interacting with other genres to form genre sets and systems (Bazerman, 1994; Devitt, 1991); these inter-generic networks form a third area of emphasis within recent genre research. Intertextuality, on one level, refers to the traces of prior texts that exist within any given text. Such dialogic overtones (Bakhtin, 1986), or intertextual components, might include: what has been said previously; what will be said in the future; what counts as knowledge, evidence, or value; what members of a group say (or do not say); and how they say it (Kamberelis, 1995; Porter, 1986). Many academic disciplinary genres explicitly draw on previous texts, as they construct and represent an intertext of prior research. As Bazerman's (1993) careful exploration of a biology article shows, the intertext is not simply a citational web, but can be more accurately thought of as a "crucial strategic weapon" (p. 37) used to control communal (disciplinary) memory.

A second, related level of intertextuality is the intermingling of genres into sets or systems of texts used to accomplish the various goals of a given community. Bazerman (1994) distinguishes genre sets and systems, describing sets as constituting the genres that one party encounters and systems as encompassing all of the genre sets between all of the multiple parties involved in the larger activity. More recently, Swales (2004) has added genre chains to this taxonomy, describing the chronological ordering of genres in which one genre is a required antecedent for the next. Research focusing on the reticulation of genres has expanded in recent years, as studies have examined the networks of genres in psychotherapy paperwork (Berkenkotter, 2001), electronic communities (Yates & Orlikowski, 2002), grant funding (Tardy, 2003), and academic-tenure files (Hyon & Chen, 2004). These genre networks work to organize activity, to help participants navigate the various nodes of community practice, and to help a community "cohere and define itself" (Devitt, 2004, p. 56). Within these networks, individual genres allow a limited range of appropriate generic responses, so that the genres influence one another in significant ways. In some cases, one genre may more or less dictate the form of another, as in grant writing, where the form of proposals is largely influenced by the funding agency's mission statement, proposal guidelines, and/or a proposal boilerplate. Considering the interrelatedness of genres in these ways has further highlighted the social nature of genres as they work together in order to accomplish a group's multiple goals and actions (Russell, 1997).

Social Interactions

A fourth area of genre research has revealed the integral relationship between social interactions and the development of genre exemplars. Work here has followed the textual practices of both experts and genre apprentices like graduate students, most often adopting case study and ethnographic methods that blend analysis of texts with rich qualitative data of oral interactions and commentary. These studies from applied linguistics, rhetoric and composition, and education have brought to light the role of negotiation and oral interventions in genre production. Academic and professional documents, for example, are not simply the product of one individual, but are instead shaped by a number of participants with multiple intentions and stakes in a genre's success (Beaufort, 2000; Prior, 1998). Genres thus pass through a chain of written and oral interactions including shared knowledge construction, feedback, negotiation, editing, and rewriting before reaching any sort of end point. Moreover, genre apprentices in school through professional contexts are subject to these same influences as they work with peers, teachers, and mentors to develop their genre repertoires (e.g., Chapman, 1994; Ivani_, 1998; Parks, 2000).

For many of those researching this social or developmental dimension of genre, activity theory has provided an important theoretical framework for studying the intercourse between individuals and the social worlds in which they act. The basic unit of analysis within this orientation is the activity system, defined as "any ongoing object-directed, historically conditioned, dialectically structured, tool-mediated human interaction" (Russell, 1997, p. 510). Within any activity system—such as a discipline, classroom, or workplace—individuals and groups use tools (e.g., oral or written communication) to work toward the accomplishment of shared motives. Through a theoretical integration of activity systems and genre theory, Russell (1997) illustrates how genre systems exist within complex activity systems, mediating both within and among those systems, as is often done between classrooms and disciplinary communities. An activity-system orientation to genre studies has been adopted in numerous studies of genre learning and use within classroom, workplace, and academic communities, particularly by scholars in professional writing and rhetoric and composition studies (e.g., Prior, 1998; Russell, 2002; Smart, 2000). Such work has led to valuable new insights into the ways in which groups and individuals both shape and are shaped by genres, although some (e.g., Swales, 2004) question whether the added complexity is worth the return.

Genre, Identity, and Originality

A fifth area of genre research has begun to examine not only the social interactions surrounding genres, but also the interplay between those interactions, the individuals involved, and the multiple ideologies and identities that individuals develop and invoke through genres. Genres are born out of the ideologies of a particular site or activity system, and those ideologies become inherent to the genre; enacting genres, therefore, becomes a process of enacting ideologies, and learning genres becomes a process of forming identities that align with those ideologies. Bazerman (2002) describes the process in this way: Individuals habituate places where particular genres are enacted; over time, they gain access to participation in those genres; eventually, they start writing in those genres, begin thinking in ways that result in the genre, and develop and commit to an identity within the genre's domain. Identities shaped by genres are continually developing, mediated through social interactions and participation in the larger activity system.

In some cases, newcomers to a community or activity system find the ideologies (and, thus, genres) to be at odds with their personal sense of identity. Studies of graduate student writers, for example, have illustrated that this new identity formation, or transformation, is an important part of genre learning—some writers may embrace their new identities, others may build a disembodied presence or a discursive self as a way to distance themselves from their textual identities, and still others may experience irresolvable conflicts and choose to leave the community altogether (Belcher, 1994; Berkenkotter, Huckin, & Ackerman, 1988; Casanave, 2002; Ivanic, 1998). In his study of Inuit social workers, Paré (2002) illustrates the conflicts faced when transporting the use of genres developed in urban Canada to the rural north. Participation in these genres, imbued with the ideological elements of the cultural context from which they originated, led the Inuit writers to develop a detached professional identity as a means of reconciling competing ideologies. Research within this emphasis of genre studies has convincingly shown that writers take on multiple, often conflicting, identities as they enact genres and participate in communities. Genres, however, not only shape individuals, but are also shaped by the individuals who enact them. With time, increased participation, and symbolic capital, writers may transform genres; both Bawarshi (2003) and Bazerman (2002) have thus viewed genres as sites of subject formation in which *both* socialization and transformation are at play.

Bawarshi (2003) extends a focus on the individual even further, exploring the interplay between genre and invention. Specifically, Bawarshi argues that writers' intentions and desires are always situated within genres, rather than being situated simply within the writer (as expressivist process approaches have tended to imply). In enacting genres, therefore, writers must negotiate their own intentions with the motives of the genre more broadly. Writers therefore act as "double agents" as they mediate these potentially conflicting sites of agency.

Genre Knowledge

Finally, genre studies have attempted to outline the dimensions or parameters of the genre knowledge required for communicative success. On the most salient level, this is knowledge of textual form, including elements such as text organization, disciplinary terminology, or citation practices (Beaufort, 1999). But genre knowledge extends to knowledge of content (Berkenkotter & Huckin, 1995; Johns, 1997), a less visible knowledge that requires writers to understand the discourse community's ideologies and discursive practices, as well as domain-specific knowledge. Content knowledge also requires understanding a text's rhetorical timing, surprise value, or *kairos*.

Because much of this knowledge appears to be based on interactions in local settings in which individual histories play an additional role, the development of genre knowledge is therefore often described as interactive, local, and historical (Casanave, 2002; Prior, 1998). Genre knowledge is likely developed over time through coparticipation (or intermental encounters) with experts, constituting a form of cognitive apprenticeship or legitimate peripheral participation (LPP; Lave & Wenger, 1991) in which newcomers gradually increase their participation in a community's activities (Belcher, 1994; Freedman, 1993; Winsor, 2001). At the same time, more recent research (e.g., Beaufort, 2000) has illustrated that although genre knowledge may be necessary for communicative success, it is unlikely to be sufficient. Users must also develop, for example, domain content knowledge and knowledge of procedures surrounding the use of genres. Furthermore, as some critics (e.g., Luke, 1996) have pointed out, an emphasis on mastery of genres overlooks the many other forms of symbolic capital (e.g., gender, race, and class) that influence social access and communicative success.

In sum, the interest in genre as a unit of text has flourished in recent decades, yielding a range of new and valuable insights into text structure. Genre studies have indeed been a fruitful site of interdisciplinarity, where the textual approaches of applied linguists have intersected with the social and developmental approaches of those in rhetoric, professional writing, and education. Together, these various studies have led to an increasingly richer view of the dynamic, intertextual, and interactive nature of genre.

COHERENCE AND COHESION

A third strand of research into written text has examined how texts "hang together," forming coherent and cohesive wholes. Text coherence has been used to describe the linking of ideas within a text to create meaning for readers. It is generally distinguished from cohesion as existing beyond surface-level patterns (like referential pronouns or demonstratives) to larger structural patterns. Growing out of the Prague School's work on theme and rheme discussed earlier, as well the study of argumentative discourse structure (e.g., Toulmin, 1958), research in coherence has examined the propositional units that make up a text and the ordering of those propositions (e.g., Kintsch & Van Dijk, 1978). Van Dijk (1997) defines coherence as encompassing both the microlevel (the semantic relationship of adjacent sentences, discussed later) and macrolevel (the meaning of the text of a whole). This macrolevel coherence centers around notions like topics or themes, which "define the overall 'unity' of discourse" (Van Dijk, 1997, p. 10).

One approach to researching text coherence has been topical structure analysis (developed by Lautamatti, 1978), which describes semantic relationships between topics of sentences and overall discourse. Topical structure analysis examines how topics are developed progressively through sentence sequencing; Lautamatti's three main pattern types include *parallel progression, sequential progression,* or *extended parallel progression*. This type of analysis has been used to study the relationship between topic structure patterns and essay ratings of native-English writers (e.g., Witte, 1983) and ESL writers (e.g., Schneider & Connor, 1990); in both cases, the high-and low-rated essays examined used significantly different structural patterns, suggesting a link between discourse structure and perceived quality. Other common schemes for analyzing structural patterns of coherence include problem–solution structures (Connor, 1987) and given–new structures (Cooper, 1988). The later scheme draws upon Clark and Haviland's (1977) model of a given–new contract between writer/speaker and reader/listener, in which unexpected structures are said to violate the contract and require the reader to infer the writer's intended meaning. These various methods of operationalizing coherence have offered a way for researchers and teachers to examine student writing at the discourse level, and indeed much interest in coherence has been driven by pedagogical motivations of helping students in this difficult area of writing (Bamberg, 1983; I. Lee, 2002).

Although coherence is related to cohesion, the presence of one does not seem to necessitate the presence of the other (Carrell, 1982; McCulley, 1985). Michael Halliday and Ruqaiya Hasan (1976) turned to the concept of cohesion to account for the semantic relationships that unify a text (distinguishing it from a random sequence of sentences). They define cohesion as "the range of possibilities that exist for linking something with what has gone before" (p. 10), and they describe five major types of cohesion, including *reference, substitution, ellipsis, conjunction,* and *lexical cohesion*. This framework laid out by Halliday and Hasan in the 1970s has provided the groundwork for a great deal of later writing research.

North American composition studies drew upon Halliday and Hasan's (1976) work in the 1980s, finding it to provide a useful scheme for analyzing continuity in student writing at the sentence level. It was adopted to study both the relationship between writing quality and cohesion (and coherence) in university student writing (Bamberg, 1983; McCulley, 1985; Witte & Faigley, 1981) and to create systematic ways for teachers to talk about structural elements with students (Fahnestock, 1983; Stotsky, 1983;). Interest in this structural orientation to writing coincided with an increased interest in audience and thus in how readers process texts (Phelps, 1985), often picking up on the work of Walter Kintsch (1974), Teun van Dijk (1980; Kintsch & Van Dijk, 1978), and Robert de Beaugrande (1984). Research in this area reiterated the need for a tangible approach to teaching these concepts that were so often used to evaluate student writing but were rarely approached systematically in the classroom.

Though interest in cohesion among rhetoric and composition scholars had largely abated by the 1990s, it has continued to be a focus of inquiry among applied linguists. Earlier work in the 1980s studied the differences in uses of cohesive devices among writers using English as a first or second language (e.g., Connor, 1984; Johns, 1984; Reid, 1992); findings here suggest fairly consistently that ESL writers tend to use various cohesive devices with different frequency than native-English writers and display a more limited repertoire of usage than native-English writers (e.g., Connor, 1984; Hinkel, 2001). Like compositionists, applied linguists have also studied the relationship between cohesion and overall writing quality, and have found cohesion (particularly referential and lexical) to be a good predictor of overall quality judgments (Bae, 2001; Chiang, 2003).

Although Halliday and Hasan's (1976) original work on cohesion illustrates the concept through literary text, the bulk of writing research thus far has applied the concept to student academic writing. Less interest has been shown in examining the cohesive properties of writing in professional contexts, although Campbell's (e.g., 1995) work is an important exception. Extending Halliday and Hasan's taxonomy to technical and scientific texts, she argues that similarity and proximity are additional principles of cohesion that establish continuity in discourse. With examples from numerous professional texts, she illustrates how these principles can involve not just semantic and syntactic relationships in texts, but also visual and auditory/phonological relationships. Rowley-Jolivet's (e.g., 2002) pioneering work in visual composition of scientific presentation slides similarly focuses on how spatial and temporal visual resources create textual cohesion and coherence. With a growth of interest in the nonverbal elements of text, particularly within professional writing studies, research into the unifying elements in multimodal documents will certainly continue to be a fruitful area of inquiry.

CORPUS LINGUISTICS AND PHRASEOLOGY

Although the first computerized corpus was constructed in America in the 1960s (Kucera & Francis, 1967), many of the important subsequent developments have taken place in Europe, especially in the United Kingdom and Scandinavia. Reasons for this shift are complex but include a more social—and less cognitive—approach to language study in Europe, the multilingual nature of the European Union, the greater availability of research grants, and the leadership roles of people like Sinclair and Leech in England, Svartvik in Sweden, and Johansson in Norway. However, a particularly strong impetus has come from major European-based educational publishers (especially those involved in ESL) who have underwritten many major research and development (R&D) projects. Outstanding achievements here include the British National Corpus (BNC), the *Collins COBUILD English Language Dictionary* (Sinclair, 1987), and the *Longman Grammar of Spoken and Written English* (Biber, Johansson, Leech, Conrad, & Finegan, 1999).

In retrospect, the 20th century will probably be seen as the era of large, relatively undifferentiated corpora, such as the Bank of English and the BNC. Though such corpora will continue to have important roles in lexicography (as in COBUILD and its offshoots), in natural-language-processing research, in lexical and phraseological approaches to foreign-language teaching (e.g., Aston, 2001), and in general grammatical descriptions of whole languages (as in the Longman Grammar), their immediate use as more specialized resources for writing research and development may be limited by their very large size and diffuseness. In effect, bigger may not always be better. Indeed, there are signs that the first decade of the new century will turn out to be the decade of fairly small, genre-specific or multigenre-specific corpora, such as a collection of 50 medical research articles. As D. Y. W. Lee (2001) notes:

> A small specialized corpus has the advantage of more homogeneity across the texts or transcripts in a corpus, which in turn makes the corpus more suitable for genre-based investigations or analyses that can take into account interactional, pragmatic and contextual features in addition to the purely linguistic ones. (p. 37)

In essence, corpus linguistics is a technology—a technology that enables a computer to store a collection of text files and then to apply software to those files in order to produce frequency lists, lists of key words, and, most usefully, strings of words showing which words co-occur (or collocate) with others. A corpus may also be part-of-speech tagged; indeed, today automatic taggers can reach very high rates of accuracy for standard modern prose. (They are less successful with speech or poetry.) Automatic pragmatic or discoursal-feature taggers are still a considerable way off.

This corpus technology is, however, not without certain methodological implications. It favors, for example, bottom-up approaches to textual analysis, especially those that investigate lexico-grammatical patterns and their relative frequencies. A corpus like Hyland's

(2000) collection of 240 research articles, 30 each from eight disciplines, will show, for example, 1,771 examples of *however,* 151 of *nevertheless,* and just four for *all the same.* Although this technology can easily and very quickly show *what* is linguistically occurring—and what is not occurring, as with *all the same*—and *how often,* it is less likely to be so effective at showing *where* these adversatives are occurring and *why.* A slow hand-analysis (eyeballing the text) of a corpus subset might be better at revealing whether or not these adversatives clustered around gap indications in introductions (as argued in Swales, 1990), or in limitations of the present research in discussions (as argued in Lewin et al., 2001).

Although the use of specialized corpora (such as that of Ken Hyland, 2000, mentioned ear;oer) has already proved to be of considerable use in various aspects of writing research, there are at least two further reasons why "irrational exuberance" in their regard might be resisted. The first is that the analyst still has to rely on her or his intuitions as to what is worth exploring, and common experience suggests that many lines of investigation wither away for lack of sufficiently interesting patterns in the data or for the difficulty of coming up with plausible explanations for any patterns that may be discerned. The second is the stubborn issue of context. Stubbs (2001) argues that context in corpus work consists of cotext (the words around the sample item) and intertext (i.e., "repeated occurrences, often a large number, of similar patterns across different, independent texts" (p. 157)). To many writing scholars, of course, Stubbs's position will seem reductive. After all, it is not hard to conceive of situations where we can legitimately require information (say) about the author, the setting, the intended audience, or the relationship of the text under investigation to previous texts. It looks as though corporist approaches to genre provide a useful tool for the analyst, but not a complete tool kit.

To date, much of this corpus-informed work has been devoted to academic and research writing. There have been studies of article usage in complex noun phrases in medical papers (Luzon Marco, 2000), of collocations in the introductions in a similar corpus (Gledhill, 2000), and of modals in agriculture PhD dissertations (P. Thompson, 2002). However, the most extensive studies have been conducted by Hyland. In his *Disciplinary Discourses* (2000), for example, he examined citation practices across research articles, praise and blame in book reviews, and the move structure in abstracts, in all cases from eight fields consisting of cell biology, electronic engineering, mechanical engineering, applied linguistics, marketing, philosophy, sociology, and physics. Because of his sustained interest in the social interactions in academic writing, he has continued to investigate the vexed question of metadiscourse in academic writing (Hyland & Tse, 2004). This study uses a corpus of 4 million words in order to sort out the empirical confusion as to what counts as metadiscourse, and goes on to argue that the study of metadiscourse provides a way of better understanding the rhetorical and social distinctiveness of academic writers.

A very different area where corpus work has continued to make a contribution to writing research is the construction and analysis of "learner corpora." The leader here has been Granger in Belgium and the compilation and use of the *International Corpus of Learner English (ICLE),* a 2-million-word corpus of upper-intermediate EFL (English as a first language) writers drawn from 11 first-language backgrounds (Granger, 1998). The basic approach is to see whether non-native English speaker (NNES) learners writing essays overuse or underuse certain structures or phrases in comparison to their native speaker counterparts. Among the findings reported in Granger (1998) are overuse of the verb *think* and the conjunction *but* and a general tendency to incorporate in their writing more features of spoken English. Although there are theoretical and methodological issues with regard to learner corpora, their scale and use will certainly increase in the years ahead, especially with the increasing use of computers in schools. At present, the number of genres investigated is limited, although a number of universities are now collecting corpora of native English speaker (NES) and NNES undergraduate and graduate student writing. One intriguing recent development is that reported by Lee and Swales (2006) where, in an experimental class of doctoral students from the sciences, they helped the students to develop a corpus of their own disciplinary writing and one of published articles from their own subfield and then, using Wordsmith Tools, to search for similarities and differences. Other areas where genre-based writing research has been aided by corpora are in translation studies (e.g., Partington, 1988) and in contrastive rhetoric (e.g., Moreno, 2004).

To sum up this section, there is currently a large amount of corpus-based analysis that is directly or indirectly relevant to writing research. Its main adherents to date, however, have been linguists (Biber et al., 1999), applied linguists (Hunston, 2002), and practitioners in languages for specific purposes (Bowker & Pearson, 2002). It remains surprising (at least to us) that those in rhetoric and composition in the United States have apparently been little interested in taking advantage of corpora; in fact, the only group of U.S. English specialists to do so has been those interested in the history of the English language.

FUTURE RESEARCH DIRECTIONS

Study of the organizational properties of written text has developed over the past decades to encompass a broader understanding of text structure and, in many cases, an increasingly multidisciplinary approach to text investigation. Both corpus-based research and genre analysis are now often complemented by oral-interview data (e.g., Connor, 2000; Hyland, 2000) in order to provide an emic perspective into the study of texts; similarly, research methods that mix ethnography with text-based analysis (e.g., Prior, 1998; Swales, 1998) have added to an understanding of the social interactions that give rise to text form. Newer mul- timethod studies that blend methodologies as diverse as ethnography, readability analysis, genre analysis, interview data, and/or critical discourse analysis (e.g., Schryer, 2000; Scollon, Bhatia, Li, & Yung, 1999) build an ever more complex view of textual form.

Recent trends across writing-related disciplines suggest several future directions for research into written texts. One direction will likely be more attention paid to reception rather than production histories. Closer study of writer–audience considerations may shed further light on the causes of alternative rhetorical patterns found in texts from different national and linguistic cultures. More specifically, Paul, Charney, and Kendall (2001) argue that analysis of scientific texts by rhetoricians has, somewhat ironically, concentrated on the writer and the production of texts while neglecting the reader and the reception. Yet research into these latter elements is needed if we are to understand a text's power and acceptance within its intended community—both at the moment of production and beyond. Mixed- method research using longitudinal ethnography and/or discourse-based interviews are an area of research that we believe will gain momentum in the coming years. Several likely developments in corpus linguistics have already been mentioned in the previous section; here we only additionally note that corpus-based research will continue to elucidate the stylistic features of various genres, producing results both expected and unexpected.

To this point, the study of text structure has overwhelmingly viewed texts as mono- modal, paper-based entities. Yet, with the growth of technology, texts continue to develop into increasingly multimodal forms, relying more and more on the visual, and often exist- ing solely in the digital medium. The work of Kress (2003) and Kress and Van Leeuwen (1996) offer persuasive evidence that multimodal and digital texts rely on different (nonlin- ear) logic than do verbal, paper-based texts. Rhetoric and composition scholars have been eager to explore visual elements of text (see chap. 37, this volume), and applied linguists are beginning to expand research in this area as well (e.g., Baldry, Thibault & Lemke, 2006; Ventola, Charles, & Kaltenbacher, 2004); Kress and Van Leeuwen's work offers a spring- board for continued study of the structural and semantic relationships between image and text. In addition, growing interest in digital texts and hypertext (Bazerman, 2002; Lemke, 2002) promises insights into the influence of new technologies on the organizational prop- erties of text in a variety of media.

Finally, as the English language continues to globalize in its functions as a language of research, education, business, and technology, we are likely to see forms and structures of texts evolve as they are adopted and adapted in both local and international communities.

To this point, much of the interest in English as an international language has been in the area of spoken language (e.g., Jenkins, 2000), whereas research of written texts has tended toward the study of local varieties of academic and professional genres (written for local audiences). As the global and local become increasingly intertwined—with Chinese scientists presenting papers in Finland, or Indian and German executives forming joint cventures—we suspect that an interest in the effects of *glocalization* (Mauranen, 2001) on written texts will grow in the coming decades.

REFERENCES

Aston, G. (Ed.) (2001). *Learning with corpora*. Bologna, Italy: CLUEB.

Bae, J. (2001). Cohesion and coherence in children's written English: Immersion and English-only classes. *Issues in Applied Linguistics, 12,* 51–88.

Bakhtin, M. M. (1986). *Speech genres and other late essays* (V. W. McGee, Trans.; C. Emerson & M. Holquist, Eds.). Austin: University of Texas Press.

Baldry, A., Thilbault, P. J. & Lemke, J. (2006). *Multimodal transcription and text analysis*. London: Equinox.

Bamberg, B. (1983). What makes a text coherent? *College Composition and Communication, 34,* 417–429.

Barton, E., & Stygall, G. (2002). *Discourse studies in composition*. Cresskill, NJ: Hampton.

Bawarshi, A. (2003). *Genre and the invention of the writer: Reconsidering the place of invention in composition*. Logan: Utah State University Press.

Bazerman, C. (1988). *Shaping written communication: The genre and activity of the experimental article in science*. Madison: University of Wisconsin Press.

Bazerman, C. (1993). Intertextual self-fashioning: Gould and Lewontin's representations of the literature. In J. Selzer (Ed.), *Understanding scientific prose* (pp. 20–41). Madison: University of Wisconsin Press.

Bazerman, C. (1994). Systems of genres and the enactment of social intentions. In A. Freedman & P. Medway (Eds.), *Genre and the new rhetoric* (pp. 79–101). Bristol, PA: Taylor & Francis.

Bazerman, C. (2002). Genre and identity: Citizenship in the age of the internet and the age of global capitalism. In R. Coe, L. Lingard, & T. Teslenko (Eds.), *The rhetoric and ideology of genre* (pp. 13–37). Cresskill, NJ: Hampton.

Beaufort, A. (1999). *Writing in the real world: Making the transition from school to work*. New York: Teachers College Press.

Beaufort, A. (2000). Operationalizing the concept of discourse community: A case study of one institutional site of composing. *Research in the Teaching of English, 31,* 486–529.

Belcher, D. (1994). The apprenticeship model to advanced academic literacy: Graduate students and their mentors. *English for Specific Purposes, 13,* 23–34.

Berkenkotter, C. (2001). Genre systems at work: DSM–IV and rhetorical recontextualization in psychotherapy paperwork. *Written Communication, 18,* 326–347.

Berkenkotter, C., & Huckin, T. N. (1995). *Genre knowledge in disciplinary communication*. Hillsdale, NJ: Lawrence Erlbaum Associates.

Berkenkotter, C., Huckin, T. N., Ackerman, J. (1988). Conventions, conversations, and certainty: Case study of a student in a rhetoric Ph.D. program. *Research in the Teaching of English, 22,* 9–44.

Bhatia, V. K. (1993). *Analysing genre: Language use in professional settings*. New York: Longman.

Bhatia, V. K. (2002). Applied genre analysis: Analytical advanced and pedagogical procedures. In A. M. Johns (Ed.), *Genre in the classroom: Multiple perspectives* (pp. 279–283). Mahwah, NJ: Lawrence Erlbaum Associates.

Bhatia, V. K. (2004). *Worlds of written discourse: A genre-based view*. London: Continuum.

Biber, D., Johansson, S., Leech, G., Conrad, S., & Finegan, E. (1999). *The Longman grammar of spoken and written English*. Harlow, England: Pearson Education.

Bloor, T., & Bloor, M. (1995). *The functional analysis of English: A Hallidayan approach*. London: Arnold.

Bowker, L., & Pearson, J. (2002). *Working with specialized corpora: A practical guide to using corpora*. London: Routledge.

Burgess, S. (2002). Packed houses and intimate gatherings: Audience and rhetorical structure. In J. Flowerdew (Ed.), *Academic discourse* (pp. 196–215). Harlow, England: Longman.

Campbell, K. S. (1995). *Coherence, continuity, and cohesion: Theoretical foundations for document design*. Mahwah, NJ: Lawrence Erlbaum Associates.

Carrell, P. L. (1982). Cohesion is not coherence. *TESOL Quarterly, 16,* 479–488.

Casanave, C. P. (2002). *Writing games: Multicultural case studies of academic literacy practices in higher education*. Mahwah, NJ: Lawrence Erlbaum Associates.

Chapman, M. L. (1994). The emergence of genres: Some findings from an examination of first-grade writing. *Written Communication, 11,* 348–380.

Chiang, S. (2003). The importance of cohesive conditions to perceptions of writing quality at the early stages of foreign language learning. *System, 31,* 471–484.

Christie, F. (1998). Learning the literacies of primary and secondary schooling. In F. Christie & R. Misson (Eds.), *Literacy and schooling* (pp. 47–73). London: Routledge.

Clark, H. H., & Haviland, S. E. (1977). Comprehension and the given–new contract. In R. O. Freedle (Ed.), *Discourse production and comprehension* (pp. 1–39). Westport, CT: Ablex.

Connor, U. (1984). A study of cohesion and coherence in ESL students' writing. *Papers in Linguistics: International Journal of Human Communication, 17,* 301–316.

Connor, U. (1987). Argumentative patterns in student essays: Cross-cultural differences. In U. M. Connor & R. B. Kaplan (Eds), *Writing across languages: Analysis of L2 text* (pp. 73–87). Reading, MA: Addison-Wesley.

Connor, U. (1996). *Contrastive rhetoric: Cross-cultural aspects of second-language writing.* Cambridge, England: Cambridge University Press.

Connor, U. (2000). Variation in rhetorical moves in grant proposals of US humanists and scientists. *Text, 20,* 1–28.

Connor, U., & Mauranen, A. (1999). Linguistic analysis of grant proposals: European Union research grants. *English for Specific Purposes, 18,* 47–62.

Cooper, A. (1988). Given–new: Enhancing coherence through cohesiveness. *Written Communication, 5,* 352–367.

Cope, B., & Kalantzis, M. (Eds.). (1993). *The powers of literacy: A genre approach to teaching writing.* Pittsburgh, PA: University of Pittsburgh Press.

Daneš, F. (Ed.). (1974). *Papers on functional sentence perspective.* The Hague, Netherlands: Mouton.

De Beaugrande, R. (1984). *Text production: Toward a science of composition.* Norwood, NJ: Ablex.

Delpit, L. (1995). *Other people's children: Cultural conflict in the classroom.* New York: The New Press.

Devitt, A. J. (1991). Intertextuality in accounting. In C. Bazerman & J. Paradis (Eds.), *Textual dynamics of the professions* (pp. 336–357). Madison: University of Wisconsin Press.

Devitt, A. J. (2004). *Writing genres.* Carbondale: Southern Illinois University Press.

Dressen, D. F. (2002). *Accounting for fieldwork in three areas of modern geology: A situated analysis of textual silence and salience.* Unpublished doctoral dissertation, University of Michigan, Ann Arbor.

Fahnestock, J. (1983). Semantic and lexical coherence. *College Composition and Communication, 34,* 400–416.

Firbas, J. (1992). *Functional sentence perspective in written and spoken communication.* Cambridge, England: Cambridge University Press.

Freedman, A. (1993). Show and tell? The role of explicit teaching in the learning of new genres. *Research in the Teaching of English, 27,* 222–251.

Fries, P. H. (1994). On theme, rheme and discourse goals. In M. Coulthard (Ed.), *Advances in written text analysis* (pp. 229–249). New York: Mouton de Gruyter.

Gledhill, C. (2000). The discourse function of collocation in research article introductions. *English for Specific Purposes, 19,* 115–135.

Grabe, W. (2002). Narrative and expository macro-genres. In A. M. Johns (Ed.), *Genre in the classroom: Multiple perspectives* (pp. 249–267). Mahwah, NJ: Lawrence Erlbaum Associates.

Grabe, W., & Kaplan, R. B. (1996). *Theory and practice of writing.* New York: Addison Wesley Longman.

Granger, S. (1998). *Learner English on computer.* London: Longman.

Gross, A. G., Harmon, J. E, & Reidy, M. (2003). *Communicating science: The scientific article from the 17th century to the present.* Oxford, England: Oxford University Press.

Halliday, M. A. K. (1994). *An introduction to functional grammar.* London: Edward Arnold.

Halliday, M. A. K., & Hasan, R. (1976). *Cohesion in English.* London: Longman.

Hasan, R. (1984). The nursery tale as a genre. *Nottingham Linguistic Circular, 13,* 71–102.

Hinkel, E. (2001). Matters of cohesion in L2 academic texts. *Applied Language Learning, 12,* 111–132.

Hoey, M. (1983). *On the surface of discourse.* London: Allen & Unwin.

Huckin, T. N., & Olsen, L. A. (1991). *Technical writing and professional communication* (2nd ed.). New York: McGraw-Hill.

Hunston, S. (2002). *Corpora in applied linguistics.* Cambridge, England: Cambridge University Press.

Hyland, K. (2000). *Disciplinary discourses.* Harlow, England: Longman.

Hyland, K., & Tse, P. (2004). Metadiscourse in academic writing: A reappraisal. *Applied Linguistics, 25,* 156–177.

Hyon, S., & Chen, R. (2004). Beyond the research article: University faculty genres and EAP graduate preparation. *English for Specific Purposes, 23,* 233–263.

Ivanic, R. (1998). *Writing and identity: The discoursal construction of identity in academic writing.* Philadelphia: Benjamins.

Jenkins, J. (2000). *The phonology of English as an international language: New models, new norms, new goals.* Oxford, England: Oxford University Press.

Johns, A. M. (1984). Textual cohesion and the Chinese speaker of English. *Language Learning and Communication, 3*, 69–74.

Johns, A. M. (1997). *Text, role, and context: Developing academic literacies*. Cambridge, England: Cambridge University Press.

Kamberelis, G. (1995). Genre as institutionally informed social practice. *Journal of Contemporary Legal Issues, 6*, 115–171.

Kamberelis, G. (1999). Genre development and learning: Children writing stories, science reports, and poems. *Research in the Teaching of English, 33*, 403–460.

Kinneavy, J. (1971). *A theory of discourse*. Englewood Cliffs, NJ: Prentice-Hall.

Kintsch, W. (1974). *The representation of meaning in memory*. New York: Wiley.

Kintsch, W, & van Tijk, T. A. (1978). Toward a model of text comprehension and production. *Psychological Review, 85*, 363–394.

Kress, G. (2003). *Literacy in the new media age*. London: Routledge.

Kress, G., & van Leeuwen, T. (1996). *Reading images: The grammar of visual design*. London: Routledge.

Kubota, R. (1997). A reevaluation of the uniqueness of Japanese written discourse: Implications for contrastive rhetoric. *Written Communication, 14*, 460–480.

Kucera, H., & Francis, W. N. (1967). *Computational analysis of present-day American English*. Providence, RI: Brown University Press.

Lautamatti, L. (1978). Observations on the development of the topic of simplified discourse. In V. Kohonen & N. E. Enkvist (Eds.), *Text linguistics, cognitive learning, and language teaching* (pp. 71–104). Turku, Finland: Afinla.

Lave, J., & Wenger, E. (1991). *Situated learning: Legitimate peripheral participation*. Cambridge, England: Cambridge University Press.

Lee, D. Y. W. (2001). Genres, registers, text-types, domains, and styles: Clarifying the concepts and navigating a path through the BNC jungle. *Language Learning and Technology, 5*, 37–72.

Lee, D. Y. W., & Swales, J. M. (in press). A corpus-based EAP course for NNS doctoral students: Moving from available corpora to self-complied corpora. *English for Specific Purposes, 25*, 56–75.

Lee, I. (2002). Teaching coherence to ESL students: A classroom inquiry. *Journal of Second Language Writing, 11*, 135–159.

Lemke, J. L. (2002). Travels in hypermodality. *Visual Communication, 1*, 299–325.

Lewin, B. A., Fine, J., & Young, L. (2001). *Expository discourse: A genre-based approach to social science research texts*. London: Continuum.

Luke, A. (1996). Genres of power? Literacy education and the production of capital. In R. Hasan & G. Williams (Eds.), *Literacy in society* (pp. 308–338). New York: Longman.

Luzon Marco, M. J. (2000). Collocational frameworks in medical research papers: A genre-based study. *English for Specific Purposes, 19*, 63–86.

Martin, J. R. (1993a). A contextual theory of language. In B. Cope & M. Kalantzis (Eds.), *The powers of literacy: A genre approach to teaching writing* (pp. 116–136). Pittsburgh: University of Pittsburgh Press.

Martin, J. R. (1993b). Genre and literacy—modeling context in educational linguistics. *Annual Review of Applied Linguistics, 13*, 141–172.

Martin, J. R., & Rothery, J. (1993). Grammar: Making meaning in writing. In B. Cope & M. Kalantzis (Eds.), *The powers of literacy: A genre approach to teaching writing* (pp. 137–153). Pittsburgh, PA: University of Pittsburgh Press.

Mauranen, A. (2001). Descriptions or explanations? Some methodological issues in contrastive rhetoric. In M. Hewings (Ed.), *Academic writing in context* (pp. 43–54). Birmingham, England: University of Birmingham Press.

McCulley, G. A. (1985). Writing quality, coherence, and cohesion. *Research in the Teaching of English, 19*, 269–282.

Miller, C. R. (1984). Genre as social action. *Quarterly Journal of Speech, 70*, 151–167.

Moffett, J. (1968). *Teaching the universe of discourse*. Boston: Houghton Mifflin.

Moreno, A. I. (2004). Retrospective labelling in premise–conclusion metatext: An English–Spanish contrastive study of research articles on business and economics. *Journal of English for Academic Purposes, 3*, 321–340.

Paltridge, B. (1995). Analyzing genre: A relational perspective. *System, 24*, 503–511.

Paltridge, B. (1997). *Genre, frames and writing in research settings*. Philadelphia: Benjamins.

Paré, A. (2002). Genre and identity: Individuals, institutions, and ideology. In R. Coe, L. Lingard, & T. Teslenko (Eds.), *The rhetoric and ideology of genre* (pp. 57–71). Cresskill, NJ: Hampton.

Parks, S. (2000). Professional writing and the role of incidental collaboration: Evidence from a medical setting. *Journal of Second Language Writing, 9*, 101–122.

Partington, A. (1998). *Patterns and meanings: Using corpora for English language research and teaching.* Amsterdam: Benjamins.

Paul, D., Charney, D., & Kendall, A. (2001). Moving beyond the moment: Reception studies in the rhetoric of science. *Journal of Business and Technical Communication, 15,* 372–399.

Phelps, L. W. (1985). Dialectics of coherence: Toward an integrative theory. *College English, 47,* 12–29.

Porter, J. E. (1986). Intertextuality and the discourse community. *Rhetoric Review, 5,* 34–47.

Prior, P. A. (1998). *Writing/disciplinarity: A sociohistoric account of literate activity in the academy.* Mahwah, NJ: Lawrence Erlbaum Associates.

Reid, J. (1992). A computer text analysis of four cohesion devices in English discourse by native and nonnative writers. *Journal of Second Language Writing, 1*(2), 79–107.

Reppen, R. (1994). A genre-based approach to content writing instruction. *TESOL Journal, 4*(2), 32–35.

Rowley-Jolivet, E. (2002). Visual discourse in scientific conference papers: A genre-based study. *English for Specific Purposes, 21,* 19–40.

Russell, D. R. (1997). Rethinking genre in school and society: An activity theory analysis. *Written Communication, 14,* 504–554.

Russell, D. R. (2002). The kind-ness of genre: An activity theory analysis of high school teachers' perception of genre in portfolio assessment across the curriculum. In R. Coe, L. Lingard, & T. Teslenko (Eds.), *The rhetoric and ideology of genre* (pp. 225–242). Cresskill, NJ: Hampton.

Samraj, B. (2002). Introductions in research articles: Variations across disciplines. *English for Specific Purposes, 21,* 1–18.

Schneider, M., & Connor, U. (1990). Analyzing topical structure in ESL essays: Not all topics are equal. *Studies in Second Language Acquisition, 12,* 411–427.

Schryer, C. F. (1994). The lab vs. the clinic: Sites of competing genres. In A. Freedman & P. Medway (Eds.), *Genre and the new rhetoric* (pp. 105–124). Bristol, PA: Taylor & Francis.

Schryer, C. F. (2000). Walking a fine line: Writing negative letters in an insurance company. *Journal of Business and Technical Communication, 14,* 445–497.

Scollon, R., Bhatia, V., Li, D., & Yung, V. (1999). Blurred genres and fuzzy identities in Hong Kong public discourse: Foundational ethnographic issues in the study of reading. *Applied Linguistics, 20,* 22–43.

Sinclair, J. (Ed.). (1987). *Collins COBUILD English language dictionary.* London: Collins ELT.

Smart, G. (2000). Reinventing expertise: Experienced writers in the workplace encounter a new genre. In P. Dias & A. Paré (Eds.), *Transitions: Writing in academic and workplace settings* (pp. 223–252). Cresskill, NJ: Hampton.

Stotsky, S. (1983). Types of lexical cohesion in expository writing: Implications for developing the vocabulary of academic discourse. *College Composition and Communication, 34,* 430–446.

Stubbs, M. (2001). Text, corpora, and problems of interpretation: A response to Widdowson. *Applied Linguistics, 22,* 149–172.

Swales, J. M. (1981). *Aspects of article introductions.* Birmingham, England: Language Studies Unit, Aston University.

Swales, J. M. (1990). *Genre analysis: English in academic and research settings.* Cambridge, England: Cambridge University Press.

Swales, J. M. (1998). *Other floors, other voices: A textography of a small university building.* Mahwah, NJ: Lawrence Erlbaum Associates.

Swales, J. M. (2004). *Research genres: Explorations and applications.* Cambridge, England: Cambridge University Press.

Swales, J. M., & Feak, C. B. (2004). *Academic writing for graduate students* (2nd ed.). Ann Arbor: University of Michigan Press.

Tardy, C. M. (2003). A genre system view of the funding of academic research. *Written Communication, 20,* 7–36.

Thompson, G. (1995). *Introducing functional grammar.* London: Arnold.

Thompson, P. (2002). Academic writers putting modal verbs to work. In G. Aston & L. Burnard (Eds.), *Corpora in the description and teaching of English* (pp. 25–43). Bologna: CLUEB.

Toulmin, S. (1958). *Uses of argument.* New York: Cambridge University Press.

van Dijk, T. A. (1980). *Macrostructures: An interdisciplinary study of global structures in discourse, interaction, and cognition.* Hillsdale, NJ: Lawrence Erlbaum Associates.

van Dijk, T. A. (1997). The study of discourse. In T. A. van Dijk (Ed.), *Discourse as structure and process* (pp. 1–34). London: Sage.

van Mulken, M., & van der Meer, W. (2005). Are you being served? A genre analysis of American and Dutch company replies to customer inquiries. *English for Specific Purposes, 24,* 93–109.

Ventola, E., Charles, C., & Kaltenbacher, M. (Eds.). (2004). *Perspectives on multimodality*. Philadelphia: Benjamins.

Winsor, D. (2001). Learning to do knowledge work in systems of distributed cognition. *Journal of Business and Technical Communication, 15*, 5–28.

Witte, S. (1983). Topical structure and revision: an exploratory study. *College Composition and Communication, 34*, 313–341.

Witte, S. P., & Faigley, L. (1981). Coherence, cohesion, and writing quality. *College Composition and Communication, 32*, 189–204.

Yates, J., & Orlikowski, W. (2002). Genre systems: *Chronos* and *kairos* in communicative interaction. In R. Coe, L. Lingard, & T. Teslenko (Eds.), *The rhetoric and ideology of genre* (pp. 103–121). Cresskill, NJ: Hampton.

CHAPTER 36

Persuasion, Audience, and Argument

Carolyn R. Miller
North Carolina State University

Davida Charney
University of Texas, Austin

A writer writes in order to influence readers, to change their beliefs, attitudes, or behaviors. Readers make judgments about validity and plausibility; they ask questions about importance, relevance, and interest; and they decide whether action is warranted. The authors and readers who interact by way of a written text operate from specific sociohistorical contexts, contexts that may differ in time, location, and culture. Writing is thus a complex, dynamic, and situated mode of communication, and persuasion—the aim to influence—is a dimension of all writing, not a distinct type or genre of discourse that can be separated from "informative" or "expressive" or other supposedly nonpersuasive types. Researchers who seek to understand these dimensions of writing—the interactions of writer, reader, context, and text—enter the province of rhetoric, the classical art of choosing from among the available means of persuasion. As Kennedy (1998) describes it, rhetoric is "a form of mental and emotional energy" (p. 3) aimed at affecting a situation.

Although valuable work on the interactions of readers, writers, and texts has been conducted by educational psychologists (see chap. 27, this volume), much of it has been confined to factors affecting comprehension and recall. In the United States, the rhetorical perspective has been explored mainly by scholars in communication studies, those in English with specializations in composition studies (including rhetoric, technical and professional communication, electronic media), and occasionally in other disciplines, such as history, sociology, psychology, and philosophy. Comprehensive introductions to the field of rhetoric are provided by two recent encyclopedias, Enos (1996) and Sloane (2001). Questions raised from the rhetorical perspective have been approached with a variety of historical, speculative, analytical, observational, and experimental methods, and there are several useful guides to methods of analysis and research in the areas we cover. For rhetorical analysis and rhetorical criticism, Barton and Stygall (2001) include a chapter by Fahnestock and Secor, Bazerman and Prior (2004) include a chapter by Selzer, and Jasinski (2001) includes a long entry on criticism in contemporary rhetorical studies. For other modes of textual and verbal data analysis, Barton and Stygall, Bazerman and Prior, and Geisler (2003) provide detailed guidance.

In this chapter, after providing a brief orientation, we synthesize rhetorical research into current questions about the central issues of audience and argument, focusing on studies of three kinds: analysis of textual features, inquiry-based experimentation, and pedagogical application.

ORIENTATION: THE RHETORICAL APPROACH TO WRITING

Historically, rhetoric emerged in response to the communicative demands of governance in ancient Greece and Rome, where citizens and leaders conducted public business in public forums and assemblies. Public discourse was seen as an event or performance, not an artifact or text; as dialogue or deliberation, not as monologue; and as subject to standards of effectiveness or expedience, not of form or correctness. Rhetorical theories were developed and refined over the centuries by pedagogues such as the Sophists, Plato, Aristotle, and later Cicero. These theories assumed that a (typically male) speaker was physically present in a large assembly and appealed directly to hearers by drawing on his knowledge of the community and its values and by making skillful use of performative gestures and vocal qualities as well as verbal language and argument (for an accessible history, see Kennedy, 1999). In these societies, persuasion was understood and valued as "an instrument of power," as "a political tool" (Vernant, 1982, p. 49).

Traditionally, then, theories of rhetoric developed under an instrumental and intentional model: Persuasion was assumed to be a purposive function centered in the speaker and under his or her conscious control. This model has undergirded a substantial line of empirical research in communication studies and social psychology that we cannot cover here. The model has also been subject to postmodern critique, pressed particularly by Gaonkar (1997), who characterizes classical rhetoric as an "ideology of human agency" that views the speaker "as the seat of origin rather than a point of articulation." In many ways, Gaonkar's critique was anticipated by Burke (1969). In conceptualizing a "new rhetoric," Burke replaces "persuasion" as the key term with "identification," which takes into account tacit persuasive influences such as social cohesion, courtship, and class relationships in addition to deliberate design.

The presumption that persuasion depends on a proximate audience and an oral modality weakened with the advent of writing as a central force in Western culture (Olson & Torrance, 2001; Ong, 1982). Even in classical Greece, rhetorical theorists recognized that the written modality would affect an author's persuasive options and composing process. The pivotal figure framing the debate was Plato (1998b, 1998a), who paradoxically rejected both persuasion and writing, denouncing rhetoric as a threat to social order. For Plato, persuasion is dangerous because it derives from partial and partisan interests and it seeks advantage rather than truth. Writing is dangerous because it reduces the mental discipline necessary for composing, memorizing, and delivering an address on the one hand, and for comprehending and critiquing a speech on the other. Ironically enough, Plato's own use of the written modality made his critique so durable and influential that it may well have dampened scholarly interest in the role that persuasion plays in writing for centuries.

Writing changes the concept of communication. First, writing transforms the particularity of an oral situation into a decontextualized and universalized space. As Ong (1982) emphasizes, the evanescence of the spoken word is replaced by the fixity and durability of the text, which can be introduced into any situation. Second, writing transforms persuasion into logic. Writing directs the attention beyond what an immediate audience is willing to accept to what any rational hearer *should* accept (see Barker, 2000; Crosswhite, 1996). Scholars even argue that Aristotle's conceptualization of the syllogism, the basis of deductive logic, was fostered by his use of the written modality (Lentz, 1989; Ong, 1982). Third, writing transforms an audience into readers. An audience, as Ong (1975) notes, is a present and participating collectivity, but readers are a distant and fragmented plurality, and readership is a decontextualized abstraction. Ricoeur (1981, 202) calls this transformation the "exemplary" achievement of writing, that it "explodes" the "narrowness of the dialogical relation" into a universality of address. And fourth, writing transforms performance into text. Text fixes meaning in the sense that discourse ceases to be an event and becomes a proposition. Written text dissociates propositional meaning from authorial intention, thus achieving a kind of autonomy (Ricoeur, 1981).

To study the persuasive dimension of writing, therefore, scholars must recapture its qualities as situated, addressed, performative, and ethical—qualities that are obscured by writing. Rhetoric calls for a dynamic recontextualization of a text within a history, discourse tradition, published literature, or set of social conventions. Only then do the elements of situation, timing, audience, action, and ethics become central, allowing us to ask questions about the nature and effects of writing that would not otherwise be possible.

QUESTIONS CONCERNING AUDIENCE

With its roots in orality, rhetoric has a bias for viewing audiences as particular: the jury in *this* trial, the citizens of *this* city-state, the students in *this* classroom. For Kenneth Burke (1969), understanding rhetoric depends on seeing "its nature as *addressed*, since persuasion implies an audience" (p. 38). As Aristotle (1991) put it, "The persuasive is persuasive to someone" (I.ii.11). One sign of the centrality of audience for Aristotle is that his basic taxonomy of speeches grows out of the hearers' purpose (*telos*): to decide policy (deliberative speeches), conduct an inquiry (forensic speeches), or perform a ceremony (epideictic speeches) (I.iii.1). In the *Phaedrus*, Socrates says that because the function of speech is "to influence men's souls," the speaker must have knowledge of the different types of souls and the ways each type can be persuaded of different things (Plato, 1998b, 271d). For recent reviews and guides to the literature on audience within rhetorical studies, see the entries in Sloane (2001), Jasinski (2001), and Enos (1996).

In contrast to rhetoric, writing has a bias for an abstract or generalized conception of audience which is reflected in the literary tradition. Among literary scholars, only historicist and "reader response" critics make a point of focusing on delimited groups of readers. Likewise, few empirical studies have focused on the effects of writing for particular audiences. In many academic writing tasks, the designated audience is a remote and unknowable abstraction: "general" readers, "peers," "educated" readers, "younger adults," local leaders. Because writing so easily transcends its moment of composition, the rhetorical study of audience in writing must engage both ways of thinking about audience, the particular and the generalized.

In this section, we connect the available research to rhetorical conceptions of audience. We begin by examining ways of defining audience. Then we consider how audience affects the production of a text and how writers learn to accommodate an audience.

What Counts as an Audience and What Audience Counts?

In *The New Rhetoric,* Perelman and Olbrechts-Tyteca (1969) define audience as "the ensemble of those whom the speaker wishes to influence by his argumentation" (p. 19). This seemingly simple definition raises at least three difficulties. First, by invoking the speaker's "wishes," it raises a host of questions about intentionality. We alluded to some of these questions in the introduction and return to this issue in the section on argument. Second, this definition puts no limits on the "ensemble" that an author may "wish to influence," allowing it to range from a list of specific living people (a realist conception of audience) to the widest assemblage a speaker can imagine across time and space (a constructivist conception). Third, the definition leaves open the issue raised by arguing in the written modality, between the particularity of rhetoric and the universalism of writing.

Perelman and Olbrechts-Tyteca (1969) take on this last problem explicitly by defining the universal audience as "the whole of mankind, or at least, of all normal, adult persons" (p. 30) of which a particular audience is an unrepresentative subset. For this reason, a particular audience can be persuaded, whereas the universal audience must be convinced; particular audiences can be approached by way of values, whereas the universal audience (which transcends partisan values) must be approached with facts, truths, and presumptions, in other words, with what the society regards as "the real." Thus, writing to the universal audience aims at a higher standard, providing a "norm for objective argumentation" (p. 31); it is in effect a representation of the faculty of reason. Dillon (1991) points out that writing to an academic audience at the postsecondary level is often equated with writing to this kind of timeless universal audience, rather than to the general public of the writer's time.

Convincing the universal audience is commonly portrayed as ethically superior to persuading a particular audience. The appeal of the universal audience derives from its transcendence of time, space, and other limitations and thus, presumably, of the possibilities for manipulation and deception. In contrast, the need to accommodate a particular audience can conflict with a commitment to truth or justice and can promote the very prejudices that give the audience its particularity. This is why Plato condemned rhetoric as flattery. But the "universal" audience can be a projection or idealization by a particular writer or by an academic community that will be understood as particular by audiences who cannot identify with it.

In fact, for Perelman and Olbrechts-Tyteca (1969), particular and general audiences do not correspond to "real" and "constructed" audiences respectively. They treat both universal and particular audiences as constructions of the speaker, maintaining that "each individual, each culture, has... its own conception of the universal audience" and "everyone constitutes the universal audience from what he knows of his fellow men" (p. 33; see also chap. 3 of Gross & Dearin, 2003). Other constructivist conceptions of audience are Black's (1970) "second persona," Booth's (1961) "implied reader" in fiction, Charland's (1995) "constituted" audience, Ede and Lunsford's (1984) "audience invoked," and Ong's (1975) treatment of the audience as a "fiction." The constructed audience can emphasize the writer's point of view, as a part of what the writer has to create and control, or the reader's point of view, as a role that the reader must be willing to assume in order to take on the writer's perspective. Black, for example, refers to the textualized second persona as "a model of what the rhetor would have his real auditor become" (p. 113).

Acknowledging these difficulties, Crosswhite (1996, p. 151) offers a reading of the universal audience that makes it both "concrete and universal" by being an emergent ideal built specifically in local situations from particular materials.

Discussions of particular audiences often have a realist rather than constructivist conception. But realism involves its own complications. Does it refer to the set of living people to whom the text is literally addressed or to the people who actually sit down and read it? Ede and Lunsford (1984) use the term "audience addressed" to focus on actual living people who can be identified yet who serve as an audience only when rhetorically constituted, such as by receiving the text. As part of his highly influential discussion of the rhetorical situation, Lloyd Bitzer (1968) conceives of audience as specific real persons who are "capable of being influenced by discourse and of being mediators of change" (p. 8). Bitzer explicitly raises the possibility that the argument will fail if it is made at the wrong time or addressed to the wrong people.

A somewhat broader realist conception describes ongoing societies and associations that evolve and change their memberships over time and that continually revisit some sets of issues. Examples of these audiences include academic disciplines or professions, advocacy and interest groups, and loose associations of neighbors. This kind of audience has been described both as discourse community (e.g., Porter, 1992) and as public (e.g., Hauser, 1999). Both concepts differ from particular audiences by representing durable (though evolving) structures of interests and values that are manifested through real people, people who could become audiences (or rhetors) in a given rhetorical situation. Discourse communities and publics constrain and enable rhetorical agents as well as authorizing them and their arguments (Miller, 1993). The discourse community is thus similar to the linguistic concept of a speech community, as explained by Nystrand (1982), who contrasts it with the audience: "Speakers address their udiences...*through particular texts* but become members of their speech communities by learning the ways-of-speaking of these groups, and especially the *potential for making many texts*" (p. 15; emphasis original).

A final dimension of audience concerns difference, those who oppose the author's argument, those whom the author ignores, and those who are denied a role in the discourse (Lunsford & Ede, 1996). Wander's (1984) concept of the "third persona," for example, "focuses on audiences negated through the 'text'—the language, the speaking situation, the established order shaping both" (p. 216). Roberts-Miller (2004) analyzes the various ways a society can set its communicative purpose and its tolerance of dissent, ranging from societies devoted to free-ranging bull-sessions to tight homogeneous enclaves of true believers who squelch dissent. Roberts-Miller's analysis is especially useful to compositionists because she explicitly relates these possibilities to the different ways in which the writing classroom has been conceptualized.

How Do a Writer's Assumptions About Audience Affect the Production of a Text?

Of all the ideas an adult writer has while composing a text, only a small percentage makes it into the final draft (Bereiter & Scardamalia, 1987). A writer's decisions about the form and content of a text are strongly influenced, for good or for ill, by considerations of audience. Writers decide how much to elaborate on their ideas on the basis of what they think their readers know. Researchers have found that when writing to readers they see as knowledgeable, familiar, and sympathetic, writers omit important details that they assume are shared knowledge. For example, in a study of middle school students, Cohen and Riel (1989) found writers wrote less engagingly and descriptively for their instructor than for a peer cohort overseas who could not be presumed to know about local events, athletes, and customs. Without knowing the intended audience, both the instructors and independent raters gave higher evaluations to the essays for peers.

Writers also tailor the development of their claims according to perceived levels of agreement with the audience. Wolfe (2002) found that when college students wrote on an issue to an audience they perceived as committed to a position, they included more reasons and evidence, whereas when writing to a general audience, they spent more time simply summarizing and describing the issue.

Effects of audience seem to arise only when students take the putative audience seriously. In a study following a set of engineering students over two semesters, Herrington (1985) found that the plausibility of the audience seemed to lead to large differences in their writing. When enrolled in a design class working on projects for hypothetical clients, the students frequently discussed their audience's needs. In contrast, they rarely considered any audience other than the instructor in a traditional laboratory class; they simply followed the strictures for a lab report, even though their syllabus directed them to write with a similar hypothetical client audience in mind. Consistent with these findings, Winsor (1996) found that students gave much less attention to audience considerations in classroom projects than when interning in the workplace.

Students also have difficulty accommodating audiences with whom they cannot identify. Hays and Brandt (1992) observed that college students who were asked to present arguments to audiences opposed to their positions (e.g., appealing to bartenders to support stricter drunk-driving regulations) resorted more often to hectoring their readers, sometimes in pejorative terms.

How Do Writers Approach Indifferent or Resistant Readers?

In any real-world context, writers must assume that readers may question or disagree with any given point, including assumptions that are left implicit in a text. Readers can respond by challenging the validity (or facticity) of a claim, by challenging its value (or quality), and/or by being unwilling to adopt the reader role constructed for them or to accept unstated assumptions. Considering the audience, therefore, is not simply a matter of selecting the information that readers need to understand the argument. Instead, writers must anticipate objections and questions and develop persuasive appeals, including building on common ground, refuting opposing claims, offering an acceptable reader–writer relationship, and presuming upon appropriate beliefs and values.

In the classical period when rhetorical theory was developed, the citizenry was far more homogeneous than today. For this reason, some classical strategies seem reactive, based on fairly simple inferences about what the audience knows, agrees, expects. But today's academic, civic, and commercial settings are far more complex, particularly because written texts are available to readers who are distant in both time and location from the writer. It is far more difficult for a writer today to accommodate readers' beliefs and attitudes.

Audience resistance is especially common when a writer advances new ideas that are likely to overturn current beliefs or desires. The concept of novelty relates to an historical context, either the one in which the writer makes an argument or the many in which a reader may engage with the written text. Writers who wish to contribute to an ongoing debate over an issue must be able to tell whether their positions are new or old (Kaufer & Geisler, 1989; Ong, 1975). Otherwise, the writer is very likely to come across as naive, uninformed, or boring. Knowing what is new also means knowing what has already been said and how it was received. That is, writers must situate new ideas carefully in the context of older ones, as documented in published articles in journals, newspapers, company records, and so on. Novelty is essentially rhetorical because *new* and *old* can be defined only in relation to a given community at a given time.

Swales (1990) explored how research writers position their work between the old and the new to maximize interest and minimize resistance. After analyzing hundreds of introductions to academic journal articles, Swales found a consistent pattern that scholars use to establish the topic area, review previous work, expose a gap or inconsistency in this work, and introduce their new study as a way to address the gap. His "create a research space" (CARS) model has been used to investigate the expectations that academic readers bring to a text and the evolution of research issues over time (Paul, 2004; Paul & Charney, 1995). Miller (1992) connects the CARS model to the classical Greek concept of *kairos*, which captures the writer's imperative to seize the most opportune moment for a message.

Authors of academic journal articles have been observed putting considerable effort into gaining insider status to aid them in anticipating audience responses and making every aspect of the text as persuasive as possible. In Myers's (1990) study of two senior biologists writing grant proposals, the one with an ongoing research project looked for ways to heighten the novelty and interest of the project, whereas the other, who was attempting to branch into a new area of biology, had to adopt a new set of discourse conventions to persuade researchers in the new area to take him seriously. Similarly, Blakeslee (2001) observed that physicists who wanted to persuade chemists to consider a new statistical modeling technique relied on direct interactions with audience members to learn about audience knowledge and concerns.

In many situations, such as election campaigns, several writers with opposing positions compete to persuade an audience whose members are undecided. In these situations, differences in the way the writers characterize the audience can affect their success. For example, Kaufer and Butler (1996) argue that part of Abraham Lincoln's success in his famous debates with Stephen Douglas derived from his recognition that residents of Illinois were following the speeches by reading transcripts in newspapers. Lincoln took advantage of his audience's growing familiarity with his position to move his arguments along from speech to speech. In contrast, Douglas' addresses repeated points with which the audience was already familiar. However, most audiences are too complex to characterize easily. Kirsch (1990) found vast differences in characterizations when three experienced writers were asked to appeal to the same intended audience. Furthermore, despite their extensive rhetorical efforts to shake up the preconceptions of their audience of evolutionary biologists,

Stephen Jay Gould's and R. C. Lewontin's readers were apparently quite successful in using standard scientific reading strategies (D. H. Charney, 1993; Gragson & Selzer, 1993).

Researchers have also investigated what writers do when addressing readers in differential power relations. Winsor (2003) reports on a careful study of communication within and across levels of a workplace hierarchy. Like others, Winsor found that organizational hierarchies are reflected in many aspects of written communication between supervisors and subordinates. However, she also found that workers at each level enjoyed some agency that shaped their less official communications with others.

How Do Writers Learn to Accommodate an Audience?

The difficulties that undergraduates have in accommodating audiences have been recognized for many years, after Flower (1979) vividly described students producing "writer-based" rather than "reader-based" prose. As the complexity of writing to academic, civic, and professional audiences became apparent in the 1980s, researchers began to focus on students' conceptions of audience and how to enrich them. What kinds of audiences should students be asked to address? What pedagogical practices would help students learn to adapt to a wide variety of audiences? What courses or combinations of courses would be most effective: general composition courses, courses in Writing Across the Curriculum (WAC) or writing in Writing in the Disciplines (WID)?

A series of observational case studies suggests that writers learn to make major adjustments to audience across their college, graduate, and professional careers. First-year college students were observed in several studies having difficulty adopting an authoritative stance without becoming authoritarian or denying the possibility of uncertainty or dissent (Berkenkotter, 1984; Haas, 1994; Penrose & Geisler, 1994; Smagorinsky, 1997). Even within the period of one academic term, Herrington (1992) observed two undergraduates in an anthropology class developing stances more appropriate for their discipline after oscillating between personal narrative and impersonal authoritarianism. As revealed by studies employing think-aloud protocols (Geisler, 1994; Penrose & Geisler, 1994), some student writers mistakenly believe that their own insights and experiences have no place in academic writing, perhaps overapplying strictures intended to promote research.

A similar struggle to create an appropriate relationship to a disciplinary audience seems to take place during graduate school (Belcher, 1994; Berkenkotter, Huckin, & Ackerman, 1988; Blakeslee, 2001; Dong, 1996). Blakeslee observed a physics professor taking great pains to convince a postdoctoral student that the audience would not be interested in a long passage of technical background information that the student had spent a long time developing. Belcher (1994) and Dong (1996) both observed graduate students (in this case, non-native English speakers) having difficulty learning which articles deserved citation in their drafts so that readers would perceive them as knowledgeable. Beyond graduate school, Myers (1995) has shown that biological and medical researchers who are experienced in accommodating their disciplinary audiences may have difficulty in addressing the expectations of patent examiners.

Studies such as these have led to calls for writing instruction to focus on addressing actual audiences (Blakeslee, 2001), rather than universal or constructed audiences. Other instructional techniques that increase awareness of audience involve presenting writers with feedback from representative readers (Schriver, 1992; Sitko, 1993).

QUESTIONS CONCERNING ARGUMENT

At different points in its 2,500-year history, rhetoric has been conceptualized as a truth-seeking, power-seeking, or justice-seeking interaction, with each conceptualization in ascendance at different times and each leading to different theories of argument and argumentation. These different conceptualizations are of deep concern to writing instructors and scholars today. Does the ability to argue empower students (especially those who are traditionally marginalized) to act more effectively in civic, academic, and professional forums? Or does it simply enmesh them within cultural and political systems that are inequitable and immoral? These questions do not have simple answers, but recent theory and research supports the former position. In this section, we describe these alternative conceptualizations of argument and summarize the relevant research.

It is beyond our scope to discuss the elements of argumentation theory in detail. Van Eemeren, Grootendorst, and Henkemans (1996) provide a comprehensive guide to argumentation theory, Cox and Willard (1982) provide an extensive though dated review, and useful entries appear in Enos (1996), Jasinski (2001), and Sloane (2001). Crosswhite (1996) offers a reconstruction of argument theory that accounts for the philosophical issues, ethical requirements, and the needs of higher education and the writing classroom.

How Is Argument Conceptualized?

Sophists in ancient Greece reportedly offered to teach students to prevail in decision making and to acquire power through rhetoric. Plato disparaged rhetoric precisely because it afforded evil and good people the same access to power and subverted the quest for truth. The quest for a valid method of decision making led literate Western civilization, from Plato through the Enlightenment and into most of the 20th century, to valorize logic over persuasion. In this prescriptive tradition, argument is confined to the rational component of persuasion (in Aristotelian terms, appeals to *logos*), whereas persuasive appeals to emotion and character (Aristotelian *pathos* and *ethos*, respectively) are set aside as the nonrational components. Syllogistic logic is taken as the normative standard for argument, under the assumption that logical validity guarantees the truth of the result. The quest for logical validity has in turn been repudiated as unjust because the truth of the powerful is often imposed on the powerless; in a deliberative democracy, argument can be seen as a quest for justice.

The challenge to this traditional conception of argument is due primarily to the publication in 1958 of two works, Perelman and Olbrechts-Tyteca's (1969) *The New Rhetoric* (French publication 1958) and Toulmin's (1958) *The Uses of Argument*. At the outset of *The New Rhetoric*, Perelman and Olbrechts-Tyteca reject the standard of logical demonstration, "which has set its mark on Western philosophy for the last three centuries" (p. 1), in favor of studying "the discursive techniques allowing us to induce or to increase the mind's adherence to the theses presented for its assent" (p. 4). Similarly, Toulmin dismissed the "abstract and formal criteria relied on in mathematical logic" (p. viii) that were characteristic of British philosophy of the time in favor of studying applied logic or practical reasoning to understand and assess argumentation in everyday contexts.

An additional challenge to the standard of logical demonstration came from studies of the course of scientific debates, which were presumed to be based entirely on reason. Thomas Kuhn (1962) observed that scientific change often was not governed by logic but was influenced by technological innovations, social factors, personal values, aesthetics, and dogma, rather than by the steady building of claim upon claim. Theory choice is often a generational conflict, because new theories often do not prevail until the defenders of older dogmas die off and a younger generation can control the debate. Later sociologists of science such as Bruno Latour (1987) investigated the effects of power relationships among individual scientists, research teams, and funding sources, concluding that what comes to be called truth may be whatever claim a group's most powerful members choose. In the strongest versions of critical theory, which Karl Popper (1971) terms radical skepticism, it is impossible for the validity of alternative claims to be evaluated objectively, so argument can only be about power and not truth (Charney, 1996).

Rejecting the goal of certainty through logical demonstration might seem to require embracing the unpredictability of "anything goes" relativism. To avoid both extremes, some theorists retain the quest for an absolute transcendent truth as an ideal that can be approached only via constructivist or intersubjective truths based on the best evidence that can be obtained. Popper (1971) emphasizes this point:

> The fallibility of our knowledge—or the thesis that all knowledge is guesswork, though some consists of guesses which have been most severely tested—must not be cited in support of skepticism or relativism. From the fact that we can err, and that a criterion of truth which might save us from error does not exist, it does not follow that the choice between theories is arbitrary or non-rational: that we cannot learn, or get nearer to the truth: that our knowledge cannot grow. (p. 375)

For Popper, it is crucial that all scientific claims and findings remain open to scrutiny and challenge from the community, a condition he calls "the inter-subjectivity of scientific method." Hannah Arendt (1990; see also Roberts-Miller, 2002) conceived of political deliberation in a similar way, advocating that each person subject his or her own beliefs to the same rigorous challenges that they raise against others.

This emphasis on the process of argumentation has led to a lively interest in what is called "deliberative democracy," pursued in studies of political theory and sociology as well as rhetoric, to investigate whether and how argumentation can serve truth, justice, and power at the same time (Benhabib, 1996; Delli Carpini, Cook, & Jacobs, 2004; Pellizzoni, 2001).

Are There Criteria for Valid or Effective Argument?

Truth-seeking theories of argumentation have traditionally had a strong prescriptive bias, indicating what *ought* to be effective, based on criteria for rationality or logical validity. Scholars in philosophy and informal logic work toward articulating such criteria and toward identifying impediments to reasoning, or fallacies (Kahane, 1980; Lumer, 2000). Much of this work is devoted to explaining why a given pattern of reasoning is "fallacious" in some circumstances and valid or acceptable in others. Walton discusses many such patterns in detail, including the slippery-slope argument (1992b), the argument from authority (1997), and the use of emotion (Walton, 1992a), among others. Fulkerson (1996a) includes a discussion of major fallacies adapted to the needs of writing instructors, but Crosswhite (1996) finds the identification of fallacies in writing instruction to be harmful. He characterizes the work of the informal logicians as a futile attempt to apply a "logical model of rationality" to practical human affairs. Similarly, Secor (1987) argues against identifying practical strategies of argumentation as fallacies, claiming that the notion of "fallacy" itself is often a "question-begging epithet."

Others have sought different kinds of criteria for evaluating arguments, for example, ethical standards relating the rhetor to the audience; such approaches usually focus more on empowerment and justice than on truth. Johnstone (1982) offers the principle of bilaterality, which says that "the arguer must use no device of argument he could not in principle permit his interlocutor to use" (p. 95). Bilateral communication is humanizing and "reflective," meaning that interlocutors can reflect on the argument and revise it (p. 100). A similar proposal that has been more widely discussed in composition studies is Young, Becker, and Pike's (1970) "Rogerian" argument, which seeks to reduce audience resistance to alternative ideas by reducing the sense of threat they may pose. Writers using the Rogerian strategy, which is based on principles developed by psychotherapist Carl Rogers for oral discourse, acknowledge the validity of the interlocutor's position and emphasize mutual understanding and shared values. Brent (1991, 1996) reviews the sources and criticisms of Rogerian rhetoric, concluding that it provides a basis for an ethical pedagogy that emphasizes not "winning" but rather social understanding and cooperation.

Feminists have also been concerned about the criteria for argumentation. Reacting to the agonistic model of argument as a tool of power, some have reached the extreme position that all argument is coercive, an "act of violence" (Gearhart, 1979). Persuasion, as an attempt to influence others, is viewed as aggressive, competitive, and patriarchal. Foss and Griffin (1995) present an alternate, corrective model they call "invitational rhetoric," designed to promote "equality, immanent value, and self-determination," a model with similarities to Rogerian rhetoric (Young et al., 1970) and bilaterality (Johnstone, 1982). Fulkerson (1996b) reviews the feminist debate about argument with an eye to its pedagogical implications and proposes replacing the conceptual metaphor of argument as war (Lakoff & Johnson, 1980) with a view of argument as partnership.

In contrast to these various prescriptive approaches to evaluating argument are a number of descriptive approaches, which focus on how actual audiences evaluate or respond to argumentation. Perhaps the basic feature of these approaches is multiplicity, because different audiences at different times and places with different needs, beliefs, and values will respond to argument in different ways. Crosswhite's (1996) rhetoric of reason bases the evaluation of arguments in the audience, understood as the emergent universal audience (described previously). Although there are prescriptive universalizing tendencies to this conception, it does allow for multiple, transversal forms of rationality grounded in local conditions. Audience-based text evaluation methods (surveys, focus groups, comprehension tests, and other methods of user testing and market research) can be used to obtain descriptive information about the effectiveness of arguments on specific audiences.

Toulmin's (1958) concept of argument fields provides a rationale for these descriptive approaches. Toulmin (1958) proposed that in assessing arguments, we must distinguish between field-invariant and field-dependent criteria, that is, between criteria applicable to any argument and those appropriate for and operative in a court of law, a scientific journal, and Euclidean geometry, to use his initial examples. Loosely, the criteria of evaluation that are field-invariant (or universal) are formal or analytical, and those that are field-dependent are substantive or material, but even the manner of applying field-invariant criteria will vary from field to field. Although arguments in different fields use the same elements (claims, warrants, etc.), fields have different goals for argumentation, degrees of formality and precision, and modes of resolution, with the consequence that evaluative judgments should be made within fields, not between fields (Toulmin, Rieke, & Janik, 1979) and are best made by members or practitioners within the field. Argument fields were the subject of much discussion among scholars of argumentation and forensics in the 1980s, who described them variously as based in disciplines (or subject matters), communities, situations, forums, and audiences (Willard, 1982; see also Jasinski, 2001; Zarefsky, 2001).

How Can Students Learn to Argue Productively?

In the wake of reviving interest in classical rhetoric in the 1950s and 1960s, some undergraduate writing classes began focusing on argument with the goal of empowering students to act more effectively in civic, academic, and professional contexts (Lunsford, Moglen, & Slevin, 1990; Roberts-Miller, 2004; Yeh, 1998). However, those who understand argument primarily as power seeking have opposed teaching argument in the writing classroom altogether. Others have sought alternative models of argument that deemphasize the competitive nature of argument in favor of cooperation, a conceptualization of argument that may be termed justice seeking.

Perry's (1970) well-known model of how undergraduates progress through stages of sociocognitive development suggests a process of how students might learn truth-seeking argument, with the goal of instruction to move them along from unreflective absolutist views of truth, through the stages of multiplicity and relativism, to the final "committed relativist" stage, when they find it possible to evaluate competing claims against a framework of beliefs, methods, and standards of evidence and even to evaluate alternative frameworks (much as Popper, 1971, advocates). But some researchers have argued that a stage model is inappropriate for describing epistemological development. Newman (1993; Charney, Newman, & Palmquist, 1995), for example, developed a more complex model in which three dimensions (which Newman terms absolutism, relativism, and evaluativism) can co-occur; in his studies of undergraduates, Newman found a low level of absolutism that remained fairly constant for 1st-year and upper-division students, but higher levels of relativism and evaluativism that shifted over time. He also found different mixes of dimensions for students in different disciplines. This research suggests that descriptive pedagogies that teach students to recognize common fallacies and to challenge a claim's validity can be worthwhile. The ability to test conjectures against evidence has been found to improve with more advanced schooling (Crammond, 1998; Felton & Kuhn, 2001; Klein, 2004); studies of descriptive instructional pedagogies have also been shown to increase students' abilities to supply evidence and generate counterarguments (Crowhurst, 1991; Yeh, 1998).

An instructor's conceptualization of argument has strong effects on classroom dynamics, which in turn will shape students' willingness to understand and accept the goals of intersubjective truth and justice for their academic arguments. The effects of these pedagogies deserve more careful study. Roberts-Miller (2004) considers a wide range of college-level writing pedagogies and the elements they incorporate from various social and political discourse models (e.g., liberal political theory, interest-group politics, communitarianism, and public deliberation). She argues that some classroom practices, those that emphasize deliberation and a fair degree of agonism, are likeliest to foster classroom cultures that stimulate the most productive dissent. Lynch, George, and Cooper (1997) describe a classroom approach designed around cooperative approaches to argument with an emphasis on inquiry. They report that students in two 1st-year composition courses were able to engage in argument-based inquiry, rather than hardening their own predetermined positions on an issue, and to produce work that focused on the complexities of the issues involved rather than on seeking power by winning a case.

Some feminist scholars challenge the view that agonistic argument is necessarily masculinist or counter to feminist goals (Dingwaney & Needham, 1992; Fulkerson, 1996b). Researchers who investigate gender differences in argumentation style have also argued against gender-based essentialism. Wolfe (1999, 2002) has studied face-to-face and computer-mediated discussions in several small classrooms investigating whether students typically viewed as marginalized participate more effectively with alternative media. Wolfe (1999) found that male and female college students participated equally in an online argumentative discussion; however, women were more likely to feel that their responses were ignored. An analysis of the conversational turns suggests that women changed the subject after a respondent disagreed, whereas men took more turns to defend their positions. This finding suggests that women may especially benefit from heuristics that help students generate counterarguments (Crowhurst, 1991; Leitão, 2003; Yeh, 1998).

In recent years, a growing number of researchers have investigated argumentation in academic disciplines, some spurred by universities promoting WID programs, and the concept of field-dependent criteria has been supported by many of these. Comparisons of the argument structures in the sciences, social sciences, and humanities have identified differences at many levels, including sentence structure, citation patterns, stases, and topoi. Some of these studies are textual analyses (Fahnestock & Secor, 1988, 1991; MacDonald, 1994), including historical studies of the evolution of disciplinary genres (Atkinson, 1999; Bazerman, 1988; Wilder, 2005). In a comparative textual study of differences between the ways students and academics developed arguments, Barton (1993) delineates multiple differences between academic argument and public argument, particularly a marked tendency of students to use generalizations to frame problems, construct their persona, cite sources, and support their claims. Another strand of this work focuses on students learning disciplinary argumentation (Herrington, 1992; Wilder, 2002), including studies of non-native English speakers (Belcher & Braine, 1995; Dong, 1996). In a 4-year study of an undergraduate biology major, Haas (1994) observed progress in the student's recognition that authors of scientific research articles were presenting arguments within a discipline. Noting that most of this research employs observational and text analytic methods, Paul, Charney, and Kendall (2001) call for studies that explore the real-time responses of readers, test the effects of rhetorical strategies on readers, and track the course of acceptance or rejection over time.

Considerable research has also been conducted on argumentation in workplace and public-policy contexts. For example, Stratman (2000) studied voters' perceptions of bias in informational materials for a Colorado ballot referendum; Herndl, Fennell, and Miller (1991) examine the contrasting topoi of managers and engineers in the Three Mile Island and Challenger disasters; Miller (2005) describes the different argumentative topoi and other strategies used by biological and physical scientists conducting electromagnetic field research; Schiappa (1995) provides case studies illustrating epistemic, ethical, and political criteria in public-policy debates; and Ellis and Maoz (2002) compare the argument patterns of Israeli-Jewish and Palestinian participants in group dialogues.

CONCLUSION

Persuasion, audience, and argument are all inherent dimensions of writing, and they are all related to each other. That there are different intellectual and research traditions treating each of these concepts is perhaps a necessary sin of analysis. Worse, however, is the danger when a narrow or parochial outlook distorts the dynamic nature of rhetorical practice. In this chapter, we have treated persuasion as a master term, the underlying essence of human communicative language use, and have focused attention on audience and argument as distinct traditions of conceptualization and research. Both are relevant to contemporary writing research, and when they connect, they provide some of our deepest insights into the nature of writing.

REFERENCES

Arendt, H. (1990). Philosophy and politics. *Social Research, 57*(1), 73–103.

Aristotle. (1991). *On rhetoric: A theory of civic discourse* (G. A. Kennedy, Trans.). New York: Oxford University Press.

Atkinson, D. (1999). Scientific discourse in sociohistorical context: *The Philosophical Transactions of the Royal Society of London, 1675–1975*. Mahwah, NJ: Lawrence Erlbaum Associates.

Barker, S. (2000). The end of argument: Knowledge and the internet. *Philosophy and Rhetoric, 33*(2), 154–181.

Barton, E. L. (1993). Evidentials, argumentation, and epistemological stance. *College English, 55*(7), 745–769.

Barton, E., & Stygall, G. (Eds.). (2001). *Discourse studies in composition*. Cresskill, NJ: Hampton.

Bazerman, C. (1988). *Shaping written knowledge*. Madison: University of Wisconsin Press.

Bazerman, C., & Prior, P. (Eds.). (2004). *What writing does and how it does it*. Mahwah, NJ: Lawrence Erlbaum Associates.

Belcher, D. (1994). The apprenticeship approach to advanced academic literacy: Graduate students and their mentors. *English for Special Purposes, 13*, 23-34.

Belcher, D., & Braine, G. (1995). *Academic writing in a second language: Essays on research and pedagogy*. Norwood, NJ: Ablex.

Benhabib, S. (Ed.). (1996). *Democracy and difference: Contesting the boundaries of the political*. Princeton, NJ: Princeton University Press.

Bereiter, C., & Scardamalia, M. (1987). *The psychology of written composition*. Hillsdale, NJ: Lawrence Erlbaum Associates.

Berkenkotter, C. (1984). Student writers and their sense of authority over texts. *College Composition and Communication, 35*, 156-168.

Berkenkotter, C., Huckin, T. H., & Ackerman, J. (1988). Conventions, conversations and the writer: Case study of a student in a rhetoric Ph.D. Program. *Research in the Teaching of English, 22*(1), 9–44.

Bitzer, L. F. (1968). The rhetorical situation. *Philosophy and Rhetoric, 1*(1), 1–14.

Black, E. (1970). The second persona. *Quarterly Journal of Speech, 56*(2), 109–119.

Blakeslee, A. M. (2001). *Interacting with audiences: Social influences on the production of scientific writing*. Mahwah, NJ: Lawrence Erlbaum Associates.

Booth, W. (1961). *The rhetoric of fiction*. Chicago: University of Chicago Press.

Brent, D. (1991). Young, Becker and Pike's "Rogerian" rhetoric: A twenty-year reassessment. *College English, 53*, 452–466.

Brent, D. (1996). Rogerian rhetoric: Ethical growth through alternative forms. In B. Emmel, P. Resch, & D. Tenney (Eds.), *Argument revisited; argument redefined: Negotiating meaning in the composition classroom* (pp. 73–96). Thousand Oaks, CA: Sage.

Burke, K. (1969). *A rhetoric of motives.* Berkeley: University of California Press.

Charland, M. (1995). *The constitution of rhetoric's audience.* In S. Jackson (Ed.) *Argumentation and Values: Proceedings of the Ninth SCA/AFA Conference on Argumentation* (pp. 12–15). Alta, Utah: Speech Communication Association.

Charney, D. (1993). A study in rhetorical reading. In J. Selzer (Ed.), *Understanding scientific prose* (pp. 203–231). Madison: University of Wisconsin Press.

Charney, D. (1996). Empiricism is not a four-letter word. *College Composition and Communication, 47*(4), 567–593.

Charney, D., Newman, J. H., & Palmquist, M. (1995). "I'm just no good at writing": Epistemological style and attitudes toward writing. *Written Communication, 12*(3), 298–329.

Cohen, M., & Riel, M. (1989). The effect of distant audiences on students' writing. *American Educational Research Journal, 26,* 143–159.

Cox, J. R., & Willard, C. A. (Eds.). (1982). *Advances in argumentation theory and research.* Carbondale: Southern Illinois University Press.

Crammond, J. G. (1998). The uses and complexity of argument structures in expert and student persuasive writing. *Written Communication, 15*(2), 230–268.

Crosswhite, J. (1996). *The rhetoric of reason: Writing and the attractions of argument.* Madison: University of Wisconsin Press.

Crowhurst, M. (1991). Interrelationships between reading and writing persuasive discourse. *Research in the Teaching of English, 25*(3), 314–338.

Delli Carpini, M. X., Cook, F. L., & Jacobs, L. R. (2004). Public deliberation, discursive participation, and citizen engagement: A review of the empirical literature. *Annual Reviews of Political Science, 7,* 315–344.

Dillon, G. L. (1991). *Contending rhetorics.* Bloomington: Indiana University Press.

Dingwaney, A., & Needham, L. (1992). Feminist theory and practice in the writing classroom: A critique and a prospectus. In M. Secor & D. Charney (Eds.), *Constructing rhetorical education* (pp. 6–25). Carbondale: Southern Illinois University Press.

Dong, Y. R. (1996). Learning how to use citations for knowledge transformation: Non-native doctoral students' dissertation writing in science. *Research in the Teaching of English, 30,* 428–457.

Ede, L., & Lunsford, A. (1984). Audience addressed/audience invoked: The role of audience in composition theory and pedagogy. *College Composition and Communication, 35*(2), 155–171.

Ellis, D. G., & Maoz, I. (2002). Cross-cultural argument interactions between Israeli-Jews and Palestinians. *Journal of Applied Communication Research, 30*(2), 181–194.

Enos, T. (Ed.). (1996). *Encyclopedia of rhetoric and composition: Communication from ancient times to the information age.* New York: Garland.

Fahnestock, J., & Secor, M. (1988). The stases in scientific and literary argument. *Written Communication, 5*(4), 427–443.

Fahnestock, J., & Secor, M. (1991). The rhetoric of literary criticism. In C. Bazerman & J. Paradis (Eds.), *Textual dynamics of the professions: Historical and contemporary studies of writing in professional communities* (pp. 76–96). Madison: University of Wisconsin Press.

Felton, M., & Kuhn, D. (2001). The development of argumentative discourse skill. *Discourse Processes, 32*(2–3), 135–153.

Flower, L. (1979). Writer-based prose: A cognitive basis for problems in writing. *College English, 41*(1), 19–37.

Foss, S. A., & Griffin, C. L. (1995). Beyond persuasion: A proposal for an invitational rhetoric. *Communication Monographs, 62*(1), 2–18.

Fulkerson, R. (1996a). *Teaching the argument in writing.* Urbana, IL: National Council of Teachers of English.

Fulkerson, R. (1996b). Transcending our conception of argument in light of feminist critiques. *Argumentation and Advocacy, 32*(4), 199–118.

Gaonkar, D. P. (1997). The idea of rhetoric in the rhetoric of science. In A. G. Gross & W. M. Keith (Eds.), *Rhetorical hermeneutics: Invention and interpretation in the age of science* (pp. 25–85). Albany: State University of New York Press.

Gearhart, S. M. (1979). The womanization of rhetoric. *Women's Studies International Quarterly, 2,* 195–201.

Geisler, C. (1994). *Academic literacy and the nature of expertise.* Mahwah, NJ: Lawrence Erlbaum Associates.

Geisler, C. (2003). *Analyzing streams of language: Twelve steps to the systematic coding of text, talk, and other verbal data.* New York: Longman.

Gragson, G., & Selzer, J. (1993). A study in rhetorical reading. In J. Selzer (Ed.), *Understanding scientific prose* (pp. 180–202). Madison: University of Wisconsin Press.

Gross, A. G., & Dearin, R. D. (2003). *Chaim Perelman*. Albany: State University of New York Press.

Haas, C. (1994). Learning to read biology: One student's rhetorical development in college. *Written Communication, 11,* 43–84.

Hauser, G. A. (1999). *Vernacular voices: The rhetoric of publics and public spheres.* Columbia: University of South Carolina Press.

Hays, J. N., & Brandt, K. S. (1992). Socio-cognitive development and students' performance on audience-centered argumentative writing. In M. Secor & D. H. Charney (Eds.), *Constructing rhetorical education* (pp. 202–229). Carbondale, IL: Southern Illinois University Press.

Herndl, C. G., Fennell, B. A., & Miller, C. R. (1991). Understanding failures in organizational discourse: The accident at Three Mile Island and the shuttle Challenger disaster. In C. Bazerman & J. Paradis (Eds.), *Textual dynamics of the professions: Historical and contemporary studies of writing in professional communities* (pp. 279–305). Madison: University of Wisconsin Press.

Herrington, A. (1985). Writing in academic settings: A study of writing in two college chemical engineering classes. *Research in the Teaching of English, 19,* 331–359.

Herrington, A. J. (1992). Composing one's self in a discipline: Students' and teachers' negotiations. In M. Secor & D. H. Charney (Eds.), *Constructing rhetorical education* (pp. 91–115). Carbondale: Southern Illinois University Press.

Jasinski, J. (2001). *Sourcebook on rhetoric: Key concepts in contemporary rhetorical studies.* Thousand Oaks, CA: Sage.

Johnstone, H. (1982). Bilaterality in argument and communication. In J. R. Cox & C. A. Willard (Eds.), *Advances in argumentation theory and research* (pp. 95–102). Carbondale: Southern Illinois University Press.

Kahane, H. (1980). The nature and classification of fallacies. In J. A. Blair & R. H. Johnson (Eds.), *Informal logic: The first international symposium* (pp. 31–40). Inverness, CA: Edgepress.

Kaufer, D. S., & Butler, B. (1996). *Rhetoric and the arts of design.* Mahwah, NJ: Lawrence Erlbaum Associates.

Kaufer, D. S., & Geisler, C. (1989). *Novelty in academic writing. Written Communication, 6,* 286–311.

Kennedy, G. A. (1998). *Comparative rhetoric: An historical and cross-cultural introduction.* New York: Oxford University Press.

Kennedy, G. A. (1999). *Classical rhetoric and its Christian and secular tradition from ancient to modern times* (2nd ed.). Chapel Hill: University of North Carolina Press.

Kirsch, G. (1990). Experienced writers' sense of audience and authority: Three case studies. In G. Kirsch & D. H. Roen (Eds.), *A sense of audience in written communication* (Vol. 5, pp. 216–230). Newbury Park, CA: Sage.

Klein, J. (2004). The contribution of higher education to the development of objective and subjective judgment in day-to-day decision-making. *Higher Education in Europe, 29*(2), 255–269.

Kuhn, T. S. (1962). *The structure of scientific revolutions.* Chicago: University of Chicago Press.

Lakoff, G., & Johnson, M. (1980). *Metaphors we live by.* Chicago: University of Chicago Press.

Latour, B. (1987). *Science in action: How to follow scientists and engineers through society.* Milton Keynes: Open University Press.

Leitão, S. (2003). Evaluating and selecting counterarguments: Studies of children's rhetorical awareness. *Written Communication, 20*(3), 269–306.

Lentz, T. M. (1989). *Orality and literacy in Hellenic Greece.* Carbondale, IL: Southern Illinois University Press.

Lumer, C. (2000). Reductionism in fallacy theory. *Argumentation, 14,* 405–423.

Lunsford, A. A., & Ede, L. (1996). Representing audience: "Successful" discourse and disciplinary critique. *College Composition and Communication, 47,* 167–179.

Lunsford, A. A., Moglen, H., & Slevin, J. (Eds.). (1990). *The right to literacy.* New York: Modern Language Association.

Lynch, D. A., George, D., & Cooper, M. M. (1997). Moments of argument: Agonistic inquiry and confrontational cooperation. *College Composition and Communication, 48*(1), 61–85.

MacDonald, S. P. (1994). *Professional academic writing in the humanities and social sciences.* Carbondale: Southern Illinois University Press.

Miller, C. R. (1992). Kairos in the rhetoric of science. In S. Witte, N. Nakadate, & R. Cherry (Eds.), *A rhetoric of doing: Essays in honor of James L. Kinneavy.* Carbondale: Southern Illinois University Press.

Miller, C. R. (1993). Rhetoric and community: The problem of the one and the many. In T. Enos & S. C. Brown (Eds.), *Defining the new rhetorics* (Vol. 7, pp. 79–94). Newbury Park, CA: Sage.

Miller, C. R. (2005). Novelty and heresy in the debate on nonthermal effects of electromagnetic fields. In R. A. Harris (Ed.), *Rhetoric and incommensurability* (pp. 464–505). West Lafayette, IN: Parlor.

Myers, G. (1990). *Writing biology: Texts in the social construction of scientific knowledge.* Madison: University of Wisconsin Press.

Myers, G. (1995). From discovery to invention: The writing and rewriting of two patents. *Social Studies of Science, 25,* 57–105.

Newman, J. H. (1993). *A structural investigation of intellectual development and epistemological style in young adults*. Unpublished doctoral dissertation, Pennsylvania State University, University Park.

Nystrand, M. (1982). Rhetoric's "audience" and linguistics' "speech community": Implications for understanding writing, reading, and text. In M. Nystrand (Ed.), *What writers know: The language, process, and structure of written discourse* (pp. 1–28). New York: Academic Press.

Olson, D., & Torrance, N. (Eds.). (2001). *The making of literate societies*. Malden, MA: Blackwell.

Ong, W. J. (1975). The writer's audience is always a fiction. *PMLA: Publications of the Modern Language Association of America, 90*(1), 9–20.

Ong, W. J. (1982). *Orality and literacy: The technologizing of the word*. London: Methuen.

Paul, D. (2004). Spreading chaos: The role of popularizations in the diffusion of scientific ideas. *Written Communication, 21*(1), 32–67.

Paul, D., & Charney, D. H. (1995). Introducing chaos into science and engineering: Effects of rhetorical strategies on scientific readers. *Written Communication, 12*, 396–438.

Paul, D., Charney, D. H., & Kendall, A. (2001). Moving beyond the moment: Reception studies in the rhetoric of science. *Journal of Business and Technical Communication, 15*, 372–399.

Pellizzoni, L. (2001). The myth of the best argument: Power, deliberation, and reason. *British Journal of Sociology, 52*(1), 59–86.

Penrose, A., & Geisler, C. (1994). Reading and writing without authority. *College Composition and Communication, 45*, 505–520.

Perelman, C., & Olbrechts-Tyteca, L. (1969). *The new rhetoric: A treatise on argumentation* (J. Wilkinson & P. Weaver, Trans.). Notre Dame, IN: University of Notre Dame Press.

Perry, W. G., Jr. (1970). *Forms of intellectual and ethical development during the college years: A scheme*. New York: Holt, Rinehart and Winston.

Plato. (1998a). *Gorgias* (J. H. Nichols, Jr., Trans.). Ithaca, NY: Cornell University Press.

Plato. (1998b). *Phaedrus* (J. H. Nichols, Jr., Trans.). Ithaca, NY: Cornell University Press.

Popper, K. R. (1971). *The open society and its enemies* (5th ed.). Princeton, NJ: Princeton University Press.

Porter, J. E. (1992). *Audience and rhetoric: An archaeological composition of the discourse community*. Englewood Cliffs, NJ: Prentice-Hall.

Ricoeur, P. (1981). The model of the text: Meaningful action considered as a text. In J. B. Thompson (Ed.), *Hermeneutics and the human sciences* (pp. 197–221). Cambridge, England: Cambridge University Press.

Roberts-Miller, P. (2002). Fighting without hatred: Hannah Arendt's agonistic rhetoric. *JAC: A Journal of Composition Theory, 22*(3), 585–601.

Roberts-Miller, P. (2004). *Deliberate conflict: Argument, political theory, and composition classes*. Carbondale: Southern Illinois University Press.

Schiappa, E. (Ed.). (1995). *Warranting assent: Case studies in argument evaluation*. Albany: State University of New York Press.

Schriver, K. (1992). Teaching students to anticipate readers' needs: A classroom evaluated pedagogy. *Written Communication, 9*, 179–208.

Secor, M. J. (1987). How common are fallacies? *Informal Logic, 9*(1), 41–48.

Sitko, B. (1993). Exploring feedback: Writers meet readers. In A. Penrose & B. Sitko (Eds.), *Hearing ourselves think: Cognitive research in the college writing classroom* (pp. 170–187). New York: Oxford University Press.

Sloane, T. O. (Ed.). (2001). *Encyclopedia of rhetoric*. Oxford, England: Oxford University Press.

Smagorinsky, P. (1997). Personal growth in social context: A high school senior's search for meaning in and through writing. *Written Communication, 14*(1), 62–85.

Stratman, J. (2000). Readers' perception of bias in public education documents: The case of ballot booklets. *Written Communication, 17*, 520–578.

Swales, J. M. (1990). *Genre analysis: English in academic and research settings*. Cambridge, England: Cambridge University Press.

Toulmin, S. E. (1958). *The uses of argument*. Cambridge, England: Cambridge University Press.

Toulmin, S., Rieke, R., & Janik, A. (1979). *An introduction to reasoning*. New York: Macmillan.

van Eemeren, F. H., Grootendorst, R., & Henkemans, F. S. (1996). *Fundamentals of argumentation theory: A handbook of historical backgrounds and contemporary developments*. Mahwah, NJ: Lawrence Erlbaum Associates.

Vernant, J.-P. (1982). *The origins of Greek thought*. Ithaca, NY: Cornell University Press.

Walton, D. (1992a). *The place of emotion in argument*. University Park: Pennsylvania State University Press.

Walton, D. (1992b). *Slippery slope arguments*. Oxford, England: Clarendon.

Walton, D. (1997). *Appeal to expert opinion: Arguments from authority*. University Park: Pennsylvania State University Press.

Wander, P. (1984). The third persona: An ideological turn in rhetorical theory. *Central States Speech Journal, 35*(4), 197–216.

Wilder, L. (2002). "Get comfortable with uncertainty": A study of the conventional values of literary analysis in an undergraduate literature course. *Written Communication, 19*, 175–221.

Wilder, L. (2005). "The rhetoric of literary criticism" revisited: Mistaken critics, complex contexts, and social justice. *Written Communication, 22*(1), 76–119.

Willard, C. A. (1982). Argument fields. In J. R. Cox & C. A. Willard (Eds.), *Advances in argumentation theory and research* (pp. 24–77). Carbondale: Southern Illinois University Press.

Winsor, D. (1996). *Writing like an engineer.* Hillsdale, NJ: Lawrence Erlbaum Associates.

Winsor, D. (2003). *Writing power: Communication in an engineering center.* Albany: State University of New York Press.

Wolfe, J. (1999). Why do women feel ignored? Gender differences in computer-mediated interaction. *Computers and Composition, 16*, 153–166.

Wolfe, J. (2002). Marginal pedagogy: How annotated texts affect a writing-from-sources task. *Written Communication, 19*(2), 297–333.

Yeh, S. S. (1998). Empowering education: Teaching argumentative writing to cultural minority middle-school students. *Research in the Teaching of English, 33*(1), 49–83.

Young, R. E., Becker, A. L., & Pike, K. L. (1970). *Rhetoric: Discovery and change.* New York: Harcourt, Brace.

Zarefsky, D. (2001). Argument fields. In T. O. Sloane (Ed.), *Encyclopedia of rhetoric* (pp. 37–40). New York: Oxford University Press.

CHAPTER 37

Seeing the Screen: Research Into Visual and Digital Writing Practices

Anne Frances Wysocki
Michigan Technological University

Responsibility for the visual aspects of printed pages belonged once to graphic designers: because our history of printing technologies and books (see chaps. 2, 3, and 4, this volume) has separated responsibilities in the production of pages, writers have used rhetorical and subject knowledge to produce and arrange words whereas designers have used knowledge about readability, aesthetics, and the technologies of the printing press to give those words visual shape. Though it has been possible for writers to have say in the look of their words (Mallarmé's *Un Coup de Dés,* 1998; Derrida's *Glas,* 1990; Ronell's *The Telephone Book,* 1991), with digitization, "graphics, moving images, sounds, shapes, spaces, and texts...become computable; that is, they comprise simply another set of computer data" (Manovich, 2001, p. 20); when photographs, video, animation, and sound become—in digital memory—equivalent to words, practices once limited to the arrangement and production of one mode can be tested with others, as when composition teachers include visual and aural along with verbal texts in their classes or when rhetorical analyses similarly include the visual.

Although my preceding narrative describes computer technologies as encouraging the currently broadening attention to visuals in writing research, in what follows I first consider how writing research has addressed the visual aspects of texts, because such research—emerging primarily in response to advertising—precedes digitization; then I turn to digitality's various reframings of writing research. It is fitting to end the Handbook with the visual and digital, for they return us to the considerations of the Handbook's opening chapters, that our practices cannot be understood without eyes open to their variously historically bound material structures.

THE VISUAL ASPECTS OF WRITTEN AND MULTIMODAL TEXTS

That we live in a time that places "a premium on rendering experience in visual form" (Mirzoeff, 1998, p. 6)—and it doesn't take much looking to see how many texts explain us back to ourselves in material we are meant to see rather than touch or smell—explains this nonexhaustive, unordered list of disciplines of and perspectives for shaping research into the visual: art, art history, aesthetics, the gaze, ocularcentrism and scopic regimes, gender, ethnicity, the visual unconscious, technologies of visual production, advertising, color, perspective, photography, painting, drawing, film, theater, animation, comics, scientific and data visualization, graphic design, typography, book design, architecture, fashion, the physiology of the eye, anthropology of the senses, culture, histories of seeing, visual literacy, visual rhetoric, visual argument, visual semiotics, ekphrasis, visual tropes, iconography. These disciplines and perspectives provide their own (often unparallel and sometimes unreconcilable) understandings of our texts, and their number indicates that any comprehensive take on the visual aspects of texts is quixotic.

The context of this Handbook, however, provides one frame for cutting through the aforementioned list: I focus in this chapter on approaches to visual research that have developed out of or that parallel approaches to writing research. There is in what follows therefore no or little reference to approaches for understanding photography on its own, for example, or the visual aspects of quotidian human activity; my focus instead is on research into the texts with which those in writing research are likely to be familiar, texts in which the verbal is entwined with other visual traces, as well as into how theories once limited to the written stretch to other modalities.

THE OBJECTS OF RESEARCH IN TEXTS THAT INCORPORATE WRITING AND VISUAL ELEMENTS

"The marijuana of the nursery, the bane of the bassinet, the horror of the house, the curse of the kids, and a threat to the future ..."

Those words—from a 1948 radio debate on the value of comics that also characterized comics as "the lowest, most despicable, and harmful form of trash," because they made reading "too easy" (Nyberg, 1999, p. 44)—echo with Habermas' concerns (1989) that "variegated type and layout and ample illustration" make reading "easy at the same time that its field of spontaneity in general is restricted by serving up the material as a ready-made convenience, patterned and pre-digested" (pp. 168–169). Writing studies research into the visual aspects of texts is shaped by a continuing belief that the interpretation of words, unadorned and unaccompanied by illustrations, is what produces the steadily rational beings we often believe we ought to be. Note that in the quotations what keeps us from engaging appropriately with words is the intrusion of both pictures and layout: The latter category is often elided from discussions of what constitutes a page's elements, but appear later in this chapter. For now, I foreground discussions about the pictures that mix with text or, as the two categories of objects are often named, *words and images*.

Mitchell (1984), for example, considers *word* and *image* in the writings of G. E. Lessing to show how Lessing equated women, ornamentation, silence, and painting while attributing to poetry—and words—the masculine potentials of theory and action. Under such splitting of attributes, Mitchell (1994) writes that the "image is the medium of the subhuman, the savage, the 'dumb' animal, the child, the woman, the masses" (p. 24). Mitchell assumes that none of us are comfortable with Lessing's equation of image and Others, and thus Mitchell argues that *word* and *image* cannot be treated as fixed categories that reliably align with qualities such as the serious or the subhuman. Instead, Mitchell (1984) argues that any tension or difference we see between *word* and *image* is a "struggle that carries the fundamental contradictions of our culture into the heart of theoretic discourse itself"; we ought therefore to examine the tension between the terms to "see what interests and powers it serves" (p. 44; see also Steiner, 1982).

Demonstrating how words and pictures have served particular interests at particular times, other researchers argue that, in the development of comic books, the tension between word and picture is that of class. Nineteenth-century British educational magazines, such as the *Penny Magazine* and *Penny Cyclopeida* produced by the Society for the Diffusion of Really Useful Knowledge, were published for the working classes; as Johns (1998) describes, the Society, worried that working-class people who read what the upper classes did would get ideas about what their lives should be, provided the lower classes with magazines of simplified information—more illustration than words—about natural history and mathematics. Roger Sabin (1996) observes that contemporary story magazines were similarly "designed for a working class audience" (p. 14) and were at one time "feared to be so politically subversive that a censorship campaign was initiated to ban them" (p. 14). Similarly, Kress and Van Leeuwen (1996) argue that the late-19th-century differentiation between serious newspapers and illustrated popular media is grounded in class, with the popular media shaped for—and not by—its audience and meant to keep that audience visually aware of its place. If illustrations and layout are now seen as less serious than pages of type alone, this is not because of intrinsic differences between the modalities but rather because they have been differentiated to serve different ends (see also Drucker, 1994; and Lanham, 1993, on the historicity of text-only pages; see McCloud, 1993, for the potential of the comic-form for complex argument).

To see visual aspects of pages treated instead as serious, we can look to medieval illuminated manuscript pages. These pages' visual designs, Carruthers (1998) argues, functioned not to explain the texts but rather to support readers in remembering and thinking: "Visual coding, like writing, allows the memory to be organized securely for accurate recollection of a sort that permits not just reduplication of the original material, but sorting, analysis, and mixing as well, genuine learning, in short" (p. 9). The illustrations in such books could also provide visual training in habits needed for understanding: of the "Chi-rho" page in the Book of Kells, for example, Carruthers writes that "this page is designed to make one meditate upon it, to look and look again, and remake its patterns oneself; the process of seeing this page models the process of meditative reading which the text it introduces will require" (p. 257). Regarding more recent texts, Wysocki (2001) shows, by comparing two interactive digital media pieces, that the argumentative work of the two is contained more in their visual structures—their screen and temporal arrangements, colors, typography, and use of photography—than in their verbal.

As we research what make our pages, then, we need to move gingerly in claiming any essential functions for words or other visible elements. We need, in fact, to be alert to a potential bias we may have simply from working within a word-bound field: Some literacy researchers, for example, claim that the general lack of attention to the visual in writing studies helps keep the definition of literacy functional, attentive to apparently neutral skills; these researchers remind us that literacy is always ideological, tied to what counts as a culture's favored communication modes or technologies and to bound by and reproductive of larger cultural practices (Kress & Van Leeuwen, 1996; Mignolo, 1994a, 1994b; Street, 1984). Composition studies provides an example in support of these claims, in the many articles published in the 1960s and early 1970s about incorporating visuals into writing classrooms and encouraging teachers to teach production of creative texts in different media; the arguments in support of this work articulate to contemporary arguments for expressivism and to the events of the late 1960s, and the work disappeared as cognitivist approaches valuing schematized abstract thinking over material production and creativity gained prominence (George, 2002; Jasken, 2005).

THE RESEARCH METHODS AND OBJECTS OF SEMIOTICS

If the distinction between words and the other visual elements on pages does not simply involve description of natural relations, then the distinction between words and images—as Mitchell's arguments imply—has material consequences. Psychologist Robert Romanyshyn (1993) argues that emphasizing words as serious and the visual as trivial has particular embodied results: It splits "the mind from flesh, reason from emotion" and so "first creates a mindless body and its needs for distraction, and then produces the means to do it" (p. 348) with easily-consumed TV. Under such a telling, it is easy to understand why (prior to desktop publishing and multimedia software) the texts in which we most often encountered visually inflected words together with photographs or illustrations are advertisements, and why an early and continuing line of research into the interactions of *word* and *image* has focused on advertising.

Berger's (1972) *Ways of Seeing* focuses on the tradition of oil painting and its encouragement of a gendered kind of seeing, that of fixing one's property before one's eyes. The book's final chapter is about how advertising—publicity—draws on oil painting's traditions: Oil painting, Berger argues, was "a celebration of private property," equating identity with possession, and so, for Berger, it "is a mistake to think of publicity supplanting the visual art of post-Renaissance Europe; it is the last moribund form of that art" (p. 139). Berger's examples of advertising photographs using oil painting's arrangements show that we cannot look at photographs as functioning simply to represent objects in the world; photographs work only within our historically situated ways of seeing.

Barthes (1997) applied the structural tools of semiotics to advertisements to consider how photographs work alone and in concert with words. Barthes argues that, alone, photographs have the meanings they do because they function in a two-fold manner: Photographs (seem to) function simply as references to objects; they also suggest to us chains of cultural associations, as when spaghetti and vegetables suggest freshness and "Italianicity." The words in an advertisment can fix (or "anchor") the chain of associations we might make in response to a photograph; for Barthes, then, words thus have "a repressive value" and "it is at this level that the morality and ideology of a society are above all invested" (p. 40)—but the apparently natural referentiality of the photographs then works to make the words seem natural and therefore innocent. (Barthes also speaks of a relationship of "relay" between words and photographs, in which one does not fix the other but in which, rather, the two work together to create a message.) Judith Williamson (1978) used semiotic analysis to show the importance of the arrangements of words and photographs in print advertising. Describing an advertisement using photographs of a luxury car and a pack of cigarettes, Williamson describes how the placement of the headline and the car carries the advertisement's words about "luxury" and the car's visible luxury value "into" the pack of cigarettes. Williamson concludes that her examples "prove that it is structure which signifies in ads: not genuinely 'significant' things, but things arranged so as to transfer significance from themselves to something else" (p. 168). For Williamson, as for Barthes, the words in a specific layout of an advertisement are as engaged in the seduction of consumers as the photographs (see Meyers, 1994, for a semiotic focus on how words function in advertisements; see Messaris, 1997 or Crow, 2003, for more recent explications of Barthes and of Pierciean semiotic approaches to the visual).

These considerations argue that photographs are not capturings of reality; our understandings of advertisements depend on the particular—and carefully arranged—interplay of the words and photographs. Neither words nor photographs have precedence but can be placed to achieve a particular formal relation and so a particular effect. These semiotic methods for researching advertising have threaded out in at least two, more recent, directions: the field of visual culture and a social semiotic approach to visual and multimodal texts.

VISUAL CULTURE AND SOCIAL SEMIOTICS

Visual culture, as the name suggests, considers visual texts through cultural studies approaches and so extends the potentially formally constrained one-size-fits-all interpretations of earlier semiotic approaches into the responses of audiences situated within differing contexts. As Rogoff (1998) writes, "In visual culture, the history becomes that of the viewer or that of the authorizing discourse rather than that of the object" (p. 20). The visual culture readers proliferating in the mid-1990s shared emphasis on the "modern tendency to picture or visualize existence" (Mirzoeff, 1998, p. 6) and on how seeing is gendered, raced, and articulated to other power-inscribing practices; as Rogoff asks, "What are the visual codes by which some are allowed to look, others to hazard a peek, and still others forbidden to look altogether?" (p. 20). (For an elaborated geneaology of visual culture, see Dikovitskaya, 2005.) Visual-culture approaches, therefore, remind us that just as there is no one way to write or speak, there is no one way to see or be seen and no one standard to be applied in the production or judgment of any text. One shortcoming of visual culture, however, is its sometimes focus on a limited range of texts. Elkins (2003), for example, argues that "visual culture is predominantly about film, photography, advertising, video including television, and the Internet" (p. 36), missing practices and texts such as heraldry, the designs of household furnishings, visualization equipment, or writing systems (p. 197). (See also Emmison & Smith's arguments 2000, about visual research in general being restricted to photography.)

The social semiotic approach to visual texts, however, has been alert to children's books, toothbrush holders, charts, interior design, sculptures—and advertisements. As with visual culture, this approach augments the formal codes of semiotics with attention to social practices: Kress and Van Leeuwen (1996), for example, claim that representation, alphabetic or visual, arises from the "cultural, social, and psychological history of the sign-maker, and [is] focused by the specific context in which the sign is produced" (p. 6). They offer a grammar for understanding how textual semiotic systems do their representing and cohere into singular texts, providing as an example a reading of a child's painting in which the child "fuses her thinking, her cognitive work, with her affects in an active process of working through some of the problems connected with her identity and subjectivity" (p. 267). Although the grammar offered does encourage systematic description of relations among a text's elements, it does not yet provide schemata for constructing such readings, because the reading depends on the writers knowing the girl-compositionist's particular life. Kress and Van Leeuwen (2001) also argue that, when digitized, the modes of communication "become the same at some level of representation," so that the same semiotic principles can be applied across the modes (p. 2). To establish these principles, they distinguish between the content and the expression of any communication; content is divided into discourse and design and expression into production and distribution: the four "strata" each contribute to signification. Discourses are "socially situated forms of knowledge about (aspects of) reality" (p. 20) that are shaped abstractly before being materially produced and distributed; "particular ensembles of discourses appearing in texts [produce] effects for which we use the term ideology" (p. 34). In addition, Kress and Van Leeuwen (2001) emphasize that the physical materials used in textual production contribute to the signifying force of a text when media become "modes," when "their principles of semiosis begin to be conceived…as 'grammars'" (p. 22). Paralleling Barthes' argument that we understand photographs through a mix of perception and culturally-tied associations, Kress and Van Leeuwen describe how our bodily experiences of the world mix with the cultural associations we have with a text as we build understandings. Although social semiotics encircles more than the visual, it reminds us that when we work with the visual aspects of texts our understandings must stitch the particular form and content of visual work together with the experiences of particular bodies. In addition, the acknowledgment of production's signifying weight argues for attention to production in the study of visual texts.

PRODUCTIVE LITERACIES

The New London Group (2000) formed with the "objective of creating the learning conditions for full social participation" given changes in work and in public and personal lives brought about by globalization and digitization (pp. 9–10). The New London Group (NLG) argues that we should consider pedagogy as "design" because "design" holds together both process and product, bridges work and classroom, and helps us consider how literacy practices shape our futures. The NLG proposes that we understand all text creation to involve three elements: engagement with Available Designs (existing social systems of conventions, grammars, and genres), on which text composers rely in Designing new texts— the Redesigned—which in turn become Available Designs. These elements show how, for the NLG, literacy practices are social and hence can be socially transformative for those who design texts if in the process they "reconstruct and renegotiate their identities" (p. 23). Toward that end, the NLG develops a pedagogy of multiliteracies to help students work with available literacies (visual, linguistic, audio, spatial, and gestural) so that students become "creative and responsible makers of meaning" (p. 36). Such a pedagogy necessarily involves students not only consuming and analyzing a wide range of texts, but also producing; as Buckingam argues (2004), "to become an active participant in public life necessarily involves making use of the modern media" (p. 5) and engagement in multi-modal production provides a "basis for more democratic and inclusive forms of media production in the future" (p. 14). When they articulate current communication technologies within their social and political contexts, researchers understand production also to be a form of research into the relations producers build with their audiences—and this opens up the need to examine approaches to the consumption and production of visual texts, including notions of visual literacy.

For the NLG, what counts as being multiliterate requires engagement in transformative practice, and this requires both the technical abilities and the understanding necessary for communicative agency. For literacy researchers in general, however, the definition of *literacy* is no less contested when the word is preceded by *multi* or *visual* as when it stands alone. Messaris (1994) characterizes positive claims for teaching visual literacy as, first, that systematic learning about visual texts "may lead to a general enhancement of cognitive abilities" (p. 3), and, second, that knowledge of how advertisements or other visual texts are composed will necessarily or automatically render viewers aware of and so resistant to such texts' manipulations. Messaris counters those claims, at least for visual texts using representational modes such as photography and film, by arguing that we easily understand such texts because their compositional structures are "based on perceptual habits a viewer can be expected to have developed in everyday, real-world experience, even without any previous exposure to visual media" (p. 9), and because he believes we do not use images with the same culturally constructed—and learned—systematicity as we do verbal language. Messaris therefore hones visual literacy into having aesthetic and ideological value only: The former supports us in judging "quality of execution" of any text; the latter "equips the viewer for drawing inferences about the broader social implications of images" (p. 138).

Other approaches to visual literacy can overlook the ideological aspects of visual work and can assume that learning visual composition—without explicit instruction in the cultural grounds of composition—equips one to function adequately in the visual world, a tendency that can align with the autonomous notion of literacy critiqued by Brian Street (1984). Such approaches to visual literacy appear in books aimed at helping readers produce visual texts through learning and manipulating a basic vocabulary of elements and compositional syntax to compose specific effects with more or less attention to the cultural—which perhaps can be explained by their emphasis on the bodily basis of perception. Dondis (1973), for example, grounds her instruction in visual literacy in the claim that the "most important psychological as well as physical influence on human perception is man's need for balance" such that "equilibrium, then, is man's firmest and strongest visual reference" (p. 22). Similarly, Bang (1991) approaches visual composition strictly through our bodily responses to space. (For similar approaches to visual composition for onscreen and four-dimensional texts, see Block, 2001, or Zettl, 2004.) Both Dondis and Bang refer to gestalt principles of perception and arrangement, and so reference Rudolf Arnheim, whose book, *The Power of the Center* (1982), proposes that we understand visual compositions because of universal experiences of gravity. These approaches to visual literacy and composition, then, can be seen as a working out of those aspects of Barthes, Kress and Van Leeuwen, and Messaris that speak of how bodily experiences translate into shapes and arrangements in the materials of communication. Although these visual-literacy and visual-composition approaches are useful for helping us make compositional choices in producing texts, they for the most part lack attention or give quick turns to the specificity of experience for different bodies and to any cultural base for physical experience (see Wysocki, 2004, for further critique).

PRODUCTIVE RHETORICS

Because rhetoric is attentive to context as well as text and audience, rhetorical approaches to the visual aspects of texts can attend to the experiences of specific audiences within cultural milieus; production can still be seen as an isolated task, however, rather than as a kind of analysis, and relegated to what is perceived as the most practical of rhetorical exertions.

For example, with control over the visible features of printed pages more easily extended to writers with desktop publishing than with the technologies of the printing press, visual rhetoric has easily aligned with the practical concerns of technical communication: How do readers use pages of documentation and instructions (Bernhardt, 1996)? Bernhardt (1993), for example, directs attention to how the material constructions of computer screens and the possible arrangements of words and other visible elements on them shape how readers read. Kostelnick and Roberts (1998) offer four levels for delineating and so analyzing visual aspects of texts, moving from typography through paragraph features and then photographs, charts, and graphs to the level of the features that make a text seem unified. This focus on the surface functioning of documents can be balanced in technical communication by attentions to how visual design is temporally tied, as Schriver (1996) carefully documents in timelines and studies of how different audiences apply texts in everyday tasks or as Kostelnick and Hassett (2003) show how texts only make sense within the range of cultural conventions shaping both textual production and consumption; Brasseur (2003) argues that technical communication ought to supplement its often singular cognitive approach to technical visuals with more sociologically based approaches.

Such attentions to the functionings of pages are necessary for understanding how particular texts articulate with our ways of seeing and being in culture; those attentions complement other areas of rhetoric, where researchers have been expanding the original scope of the visual, which at least since Cicero and Quintilian has been within the office of delivery, such that orators studied the visible bodily aspects of speaking. Within the last decades the space in which such rhetoric happens—whether that space be literary or physical—has also entered into study, as in Mountford's writing on pulpits and their potentials for shaping character, audience response, and gender (2001); Mountford argues for a notion of rhetorical space in which spaces carry "a physical representation of relationships and ideas" (p. 42). Other visible structures have been brought into rhetoric's purview: battlefield monuments (Halloran, 2001), tourism (Clark, 2004), design of city streets (Fleming, 1998), quilts (Rohan, 2004), Web pages (Hocks, 2003), prisons (Marback, 2004), picturesque manners of seeing (Groenendyk, 2000), film (Blakesley, 2004), as well as photography (Finnegan, 2001, (as in 2001) Lucaites & Harriman, 2003). These analyses consider how space is formed into visible shapes as well as into places in and over which eyes and bodies move; the analyses consider how such shapings encourage attitudes and responses from differing audiences within specific cultural contexts. For example, in line with the other writers listed previously, Dickinson (2002) analyzes the visible details of a typical franchise to show how Starbucks hides what might be unsettling contradictions for its consumers; Blair, Jepperson, and Pucci (1991) argue for the postmodernity of the Vietnam War Memorial, its design and placement refusing modernist inclinations toward closure and grand narratives by creating spaces in which different audiences can ask differing questions and so sustain the unsettled national response to the war.

Their attentions to the Memorial, however, suggest to C. Blair et al. (1991) questions for rhetoric itself: They note how their analysis asks us to rethink authority and political work in texts and rhetorical criticism. Similarly, in his first of two articles on visual argument, J. A. Blair (2004) claims only that visual argument might be possible, given a definition of *argument* tied explicitly to verbally stated propositions; several years later, reconsidering the persuasiveness of visual texts, he concludes that visual propositions are possible—if different from—the written precisely because we use the visual and the written differently. The changing uses of hand-stitched samplers—in which threaded words cannot be separated from their material visibility or from the positions of women—suggest to Goggin (2004) that rhetorical attention to print texts "severely limits what counts as rhetorical practices and who counts in its production, performance, and circulation" (p. 88; see also Foss, 2004).

When researchers using rhetorical theory look to the visible materiality and functioning of a range of texts, then, they do not simply broaden rhetoric's objects of study; they ask instead why persuasion, argument, audiences, and authors—and the workings of the visual—have been so narrowly conceived as to have made those objects, and their producers and consumers, previously invisible. Such openings suggest how rhetoric might potentially expand the "invention of social futures," to use Hauser's expression (1999). For example, in a book about empirical studies of public representations, Hauser compares hasty televised representations of public opinion in the United States with Habermas' reflective interpretations of changing public action after the Berlin Wall's destruction; Hauser asks how public opinion can be better seen and heard, how publics and public spheres can be more inclusive. This is a matter of both visibility and audibility; researching rhetorical constructions of televised and advertising visuality—or the view of our pages—can help us see previously unnoticed limitations of rhetoric as well as approaches for producing differing patterns of visibility and representation. By researching how visual practices ask us to see each other, we can learn to see differently.

RESEARCHING DIGITAL WRITING AND READING

That we even discuss researching visual practices is a result, in part, of digitality, an opening observation of this chapter, and it is to research openings into digital reading and writing practices that I now turn and into which I carry my observations about the visual materiality of those practices. I stress, however, that current digital composing practices do not result simply from the ease of inserting photographs or using color in writing: The shape and functioning of texts that can be produced digitally differs from the traditional press, and the distribution of writing no longer requires a press or even a mimeograph. Given the (momentary) shape of the Internet, with open-source access and peer-to-peer and one-to-many connectivity, savvy writers can modify the terrains of online writing while audiences form and disperse quickly for play, politics, or mourning. Questions about what constitutes writing—who writes it, who owns it, what it is—show that, as with research into the visual aspects of texts, research into the effects of digitization on writing (and on writing studies) demonstrates that expanding the objects of research can give perspective for seeing the materialities of our practices.

The earliest researchers into writing with computers understood that computers were not elaborate typewriters (Hawisher, LeBlanc, Moran, & Selfe, 1996). Not only did researchers recognize how the face of writing was changing with both the screen's emphasis on textual visuality and the ease of mixing words with other visuals (Bolter, 1998; Faigley, 1997; Stafford, 1996), but researchers also noted how computer-based writings—such as hypertext—could be structured in variations not easy or not possible in print. Some (Bolter, 1992; Landow, 1997) hailed hypertext as instantiation of postmodern or deconstructionist literary theories: Hypertexts encourage multiple, unclosed readings, apparently placing more responsibility on readers than on writers for constructing meaning. Some (Douglas, 1994; Johnson-Eilola, 1994) quickly pointed to how hypertexts could give even more control to writers than printed texts, whereas others (Bernstein, 1991) noted how readers could easily lose place in such texts. In addition, some researchers noted how screen interfaces reinforce existing ideologies, encouraging the participation of some readers while excluding others (Selfe & Selfe, 1994). What the appearance of such texts also showed, then, was how much our reading and writing habits articulated to (the look of) the printed page (Bolter, 1991) and how readers needed new strategies for reading new digital (and digitally designed print) texts.

What seems to differentiate online writing and reading possibilities even more from book culture than its look, however, is computer networking. With the early spread of asynchronous (e-mail and Listservs) and synchronous (Internet Relay Chat or Daedalus Interchange™) online communication, only possible with networked computers, researchers observed (as they had with hypertext) that such communication supported theories about the identity's fragmentation in postmodernity (Faigley, 1992) and they saw how certain identity markers appeared to be invisible onscreen, leading potentially to egalitarian communication among people who could not see each other's race, gender, or class (Cooper & Selfe, 1990). Further research showed, however, that markers of race, gender, class, and other usually visible qualities were still present and that networked communication could reify hierarchical relations among writers just as firmly as face-to-face conversation (Kolko, Nakamura, & Rodman, 2000; Romano, 1993; Takayoshi, 1994). Once optimism about these online environments was tempered, much remained useful to writing teachers and researchers: In such environments, students were writing, and the temporality and surface anonymity of such environments did encourage participation from otherwise silent students; in addition, students could be connected with writers in other cities and countries, providing more concrete sense of audience and wider response to writing. Newer environments, such as the text-based immersive environments of MOOs and MUDs, kept the useful-to-writing-instruction features of e-mail and synchronous discussion, but because they allowed participants to construct features of the environment (or even the environment itself), they allowed researchers to experiment with how online environments encourage written collaboration and community formation (Day, 1996; Holmevik & Haynes, 2000).

MOOs and MUDs have particular strengths and limitations, open as they are only to those who log in to a particular space, with the conceptual place of the environment being a small core to which others can only add. Still newer writing environments—such as blogs (Hourihan, 2002) and wikis ("Wiki," n.d.)—are open to the whole Internet; in theory, anyone can link to any other blog or edit any wiki, encouraging expansive social networks and knowledge building. These writing environments have given rise to the nomenclature of *social software* (Allen, 2004), online environments that support interactions among groups. Although these environments have been the subject of conference panels and of reflexive blog entries, blogs are starting to receive formal academic attention within writing studies for their possibilities in classrooms (Barrios, 2005; Ratliff, 2005), for the kinds of writing—mixed public and private (Miller & Shepherd, 2004)—and community building (Lindgren, 2005; Wei, 2004) they encourage, and for how they change journalistic practice (Gillmor, 2004). Similarly, wikis are being used in writing and literature classrooms (Romantic Audience Project, 2003; "Web Logs and Wikis," 2004) and are just starting to be the subject of (print) research as examples of collaborative writing and knowledge building.

The linking between Web pages that underlies the publicness of blog writing has also given rise to *social bookmarking* or *folksonomy* ("Folksonomy," 2005). Sites such as flickr.com or del.icio.us—in which individuals apply descriptive categorical tags to their photographs or to others' Web pages—are "collaborative systems for building a shared database of items, developing a metadata vocabulary about the items, performing metadata-driven queries, and monitoring change in areas of interest" (Udell, 2004), "enabling groups of people to remember things together" (Joshua Schacter; cited in Samuel, 2005). By encouraging readers to tag and link information they believe matters, applications like blogs and flickr encourage readers to see writing not as individual effort or ever finalized but as intertextual and social, always collaborative to some degree and ongoing (Johnson-Eilola, 2004).

Such shifts in conceptions of writing can induce plagiarism anxiety for those who believe writing arises from a singular individual; for others, this is an instantiation of arguments that writing is indeed social, arising out of and responding to shared concerns and knowledge. For the latter set of researchers, the anxiety is about intellectual property: These researchers point to the restrictive and often punitive responses of corporations to the easy copying and dissemination of digitized media and the threat to fair use and the public domain by such responses (Lessig, 2004; Porter & Rife, 2005). Debates about digital copyright exist in the tension between notions of individuality and property tied to book culture and those notions in emerging digital reading and writing processes.

For those who value the word as what links us, the rise of gaming culture (such that a recently released online game has 4 million subscribers worldwide; Schiesel, 2005) can be disturbing—but researchers into the narrative structures of writing, for example, have migrated to studying how games engage players in narrative and how narrative reshapes in gaming (Aarseth, 1997; Murray, 1998; Ryan, 2001); those interested in how writing constructs identity study identity formation in gaming (Cassell & Jenkins, 2000; Taylor, 2003); questions about the value of affective engagement and pleasure in reading and literacy resurface in game research (Gee, 2004; Woods, 2004). Although gaming is receiving attention from those grounded in writing research (Wardrip-Fruin & Harrigan, 2004), the speed of online change challenges academic publishing's pace (Kücklich, 2004), suggesting how all aspects of production of words have been shaped by a book culture whose grounds and objects now shift.

REFERENCES

Aarseth, E. J. (1997). *Cybertext: Perspectives on ergodic literature.* Baltimore: Johns Hopkins University Press.

Allen, C. (2004). *Tracing the evolution of social software.* Retrieved September 24, 2005, from http://www.lifewithalacrity.com/2004/10/tracing_the_evo.html

Arnheim, R. (1982). *The power of the center: A study of composition in the visual arts.* Berkeley: University of California Press.

Bang, M. (1991). *Picture this: Perception & composition.* Boston: Little, Brown.

Barrios, B.. (2005). *Blogs, a primer.* Computers and Composition *online.* Retrieved August 12, 2005, from http://www.bgsu.edu/departments/english/cconline/bap/

Barthes, R. (1997). The rhetoric of the image. In S. Heath (Trans.), *Image, music, text* (pp. 32–51). New York: Hill & Wang.

Berger, J. (1972). *Ways of seeing.* London: British Broadcasting Corporation and Penguin.

Bernhardt, S. A. (1993). The shape of text to come: The texture of print on screens. *College Composition and Communication, 44,* 151–175.

Bernhardt, S. A. (1996). Visual rhetoric. In T. Enos (Ed.), *Encyclopedia of rhetoric and composition* (pp. 746–748). New York: Garland.

Bernstein, M. (1991). The navigation problem reconsidered. In E. Berk & J. Devlin (Eds.), *Hypertext/hypermedia handbook* (pp. 285–297). New York: McGraw-Hill.

Blair, C., Jeppeson, M. S., & Pucci, E. (1991). Public memorializing in postmodernity: The Blair, J. A. (1996). The possibility and actuality of visual arguments. *Argumentation and Advocacy, 33,* 23–39.

Blair, J. A. (2004). The rhetoric of visual arguments. In C. Hill & M. Helmers (Eds.), *Defining visual rhetorics* (pp. 41–61). Mahwah, NJ: Lawrence Erlbaum Associates.

Blakesley, D. (2004). Defining film rhetoric: The case of Hitchcock's *Vertigo.* In C. Hill & M. Helmers (Eds.), *Defining visual rhetorics* (pp. 111–133). Mahwah, NJ: Lawrence Erlbaum Associates.

Block, B. (2001). *The visual story: Seeing the structure of film, TV, and new media.* Boston: Focal.

Bolter, J. D. (1991). *Writing space: The computer, hypertext, and the history of writing.* Hillsdale, NJ: Lawrence Erlbaum Associates.

Bolter, J. D. (1992). Literature in the electronic writing space. In M. C. Tuman (Ed.), *Literacy online: The promise (and perils) of reading and writing with computers* (pp. 19–42). Pittsburgh, PA: University of Pittsburgh Press.

Bolter, J. D. (1998). Hypertext and the question of visual literacy. In D. Reinking, M. C. McKenna, L. D. Labbo, & R. D. Kieffer (Eds.), *Handbook of literacy and technology: Transformations in a post-typographic world* (pp. 3–14). Mahwah, NJ: Lawrence Erlbaum Associates.

Brasseur, L. (2003). *Visualizing technical information: A cultural critique.* Amityville, NY: Baywood.

Buckingham, D. (2004). *Media education: Literacy, learning, and contemporary culture.* Cambridge, England: Polity.

Carruthers, M. (1998). *The book of memory: A study of memory in medieval culture.* Cambridge, England: Cambridge University Press.

Cassell, J., & Jenkins, H. (2000). *From Barbie® to Mortal Kombat: Gender and computer games.* Cambridge, MA: MIT Press.

Clark, G. (2004). *Rhetorical landscapes in America: Variations on a theme from Kenneth Burke.* Columbia: University of South Carolina Press.

Cooper, M., & Selfe, C.L. (1990). Computer conferences and learning: Authority, resistance, and internally persuasive discourse. *College English, 52,* 1–23.

Crow, D. (2003). *Visible signs: An introduction to semiotics.* Toronto, Ontario, Canada: AVA.

Day, M. (Coordinator). (1996). Pedagogies in virtual spaces: Writing classes in the MOO. *Kairos, 1*(2). Retrieved August 12, 2005, from http://english.ttu.edu/kairos/1.2/coverweb.html

Derrida, J. (1990). *Glas* (J. P. Leavey & R. Rand, Trans.). Omaha: University of Nebraska Press.

Dickinson, G. (2002). Joe's rhetoric: Finding authenticity at Starbucks. *Rhetoric Society Quarterly, 32*(4), 5–27.

Dikovitskaya, M. (2005). *Visual culture: The study of the visual after the cultural turn.* Cambridge, MA: MIT Press.

Dondis, D. A. (1973). *A primer of visual literacy.* Cambridge, MA: MIT Press.

Douglas, J. Y. (1994). How do I stop this thing?: Closure and indeterminacy in interactive narratives. In G. P. Landow (Ed.), *Hyper/text/theory* (pp. 159–188). Baltimore: Johns Hopkins University Press.

Drucker, J. (1994). *The visible word: Experimental typography and modern art, 1909–1923.* Chicago: University of Chicago Press.

Elkins, J. (2003). *Visual studies: A skeptical introduction.* New York: Routledge.

Emmison, M., & Smith, P. (2000). *Researching the visual: Images, objects, contexts, and interactions in social and cultural inquiry.* London: Sage.

Evans, J., & Hall, S. (Eds.). (1999.) *Visual culture: The reader.* London: Sage.

Faigley, L. (1992). *Fragments of rationality.* Pittsburgh, PA: University of Pittsburgh.

Faigley, L. (1997). Literacy after the revolution. *College Composition and Communication, 48,* 30–43.

Finnegan, C. A. (2001). Documentary as art in U.S. camera. *Rhetoric Society Quarterly, 31*(2), 3–67.

Fleming, D. (1998). The space of argumentation: Urban design, civic discourse, and the dream of the good city. *Argumentation, 12,* 147–166.

Folksonomy. (2005). In *The motive Internet glossary.* Retrieved September 23, 2005, from http://www.motive.co.nz/glossary/folksonomy.php

Foss, S. K. (2004). Framing the study of visual rhetoric: Toward a transformation of rhetorical theory. In C. Hill & M. Helmers (Eds.), *Defining visual rhetorics* (pp. 303–314). Mahwah, NJ: Lawrence Erlbaum Associates.

Gee, J. P. (2004). *What video games have to teach us about learning and literacy.* New York: Palgrave Macmillan.

George, D. (2002). From analysis to design: Visual communication in the teaching of writing. *College Composition and Communication, 54,* 11–39.

Gillmor, D. (2004). *We the media: Grassroots journalism by the people, for the people.* Sebastopol, CA: O'Reilly.

Goggin, M. D. (2004). Visual rhetoric in pens of steel and inks of silk: Challenging the great visual/verbal divide. In C. Hill & M. Helmers (Eds.), *Defining visual rhetorics* (pp. 87–110). Mahwah, NJ: Lawrence Erlbaum Associates.

Groenendyk, K. L. (2000). The importance of vision: Persuasion and the picturesque. *Rhetoric Society Quarterly, 30*(1), 9–28.

Habermas, J. (1989). *The structural transformation of the public sphere: An inquiry into a category of bourgeois society* (T. Burger, Trans.). Cambridge, MA: MIT Press.

Halloran, M.S. (2001). Text and experience in a historical pageant: Toward a rhetoric of spectacle. *Rhetoric Society Quarterly, 31,* 5–17.

Hauser, A. G. (1999). *Vernacular voices: The rhetorics of publics and public spheres.* Columbia: University of South Carolina Press.

Hawisher, G., LeBlanc, P., Moran, C., & Selfe, C. L. (1996). *Computers and the teaching of writing in American higher education, 1979–1994: A history.* Norwood, NJ: Ablex.

Hocks, M. (2003). Understanding visual rhetoric in digital environments. *College Composition and Communication, 54*(4), 629–656.

Holmevik, J. R., & Haynes, C. (2000). *MOOniversity: A student's guide to online learning environments.* Boston: Allyn & Bacon.

Hourihan, M. (2002). *What we're doing when we blog.* Retrieved August 15, 2005, from http://www.oreillynet.com/pub/a/javascript/2002/06/13/megnut.html

Jasken, J. (2005). *Designing composition: Textbooks, teaching, and identity in the digital age.* Unpublished doctoral dissertation, Michigan Technological University, Houghton.

Johns, A. (1998). *The nature of the book: Print and knowledge in the making.* Chicago: University of Chicago.

Johnson-Eilola, J. (1994). Reading and writing in hypertext: Vertigo and euphoria. In C. L. Selfe & S. Hilligoss (Eds.), *Literacy and computers: The complications of teaching and learning with technology* (pp. 195–219). New York: Modern Language Association.

Johnson-Eilola, J. (2004). Reading and writing in hypertext: Vertigo and euphoria. In A. F.Wysocki, J. Johnson-Eilola, C. Selfe, & G. Sirc (Eds.), *Writing new media: Theory and applications for expanding the teaching of composition* (pp. 199–235). Logan: Utah State University Press.

Kolko, B., Nakamura, L., & Rodman, G. (Eds.). (2000). *Race in cyberspace.* New York: Routledge.

Kostelnick, C., & Hassett, M. (2003). *Shaping information: The rhetoric of visual conventions.* Carbondale: Southern Illinois University Press.

Kostelnick, C., & Roberts, D. D. (1998). *Designing visual language: Stategies for professional communicators.* Boston: Allyn & Bacon.

Kress, G., & van Leeuwen, T. (1996). *Reading images: The grammar of visual design.* London: Routledge.

Kress, G., & van Leeuwen, T. (2001). *Multimodal discourse: The modes and media of contemporary communication.* London: Edward Arnold.

Kücklich, J. (2004). *Review of first person: New media as story, performance, and game.* Retrieved September 22, 2005, from http://www.dichtung-digital.com/2004/2/Kuecklich/

Landow, G. P. (1997). *Hypertext 2.0: The convergence of contemporary critical theory and technology.* Baltimore: Johns Hopkins University Press.

Lanham, R. (1993). *The electronic word: Democracy, technology, and the arts.* Chicago: University of Chicago Press.

Lessig, L. (2004). *Free culture: How big media uses technology and the law to lock down culture and control creativity.* New York: Penguin.

Lindgren, T. (2005). Blogging places: Locating pedagogy in the whereness of Weblogs. *Kairos, 10*(1). Retrieved September 1, 2005, from http://english.ttu.edu/kairos/10.2/binder2.html?coverweb/lindgren/index.htm

Lucaites, J., & Hariman, R. (2003). Public identity and collective memory in U.S. iconic photography: The image of "Accidental Napalm." *Critical Studies in Media Communication, 20,* 35–66.

Mallarmé, S. (1998). *Oeuvres completes I* [The complete works I] (B. Marchai, Ed.). Paris: Gallimard.

Manovich, L. (2001). *The language of new media.* Cambridge, MA: MIT Press.

Marback, R.. (2004). The rhetorical space of Robben Island. *Rhetoric Society Quarterly, 34*(2), 7–27.

McCloud, S. (1993). *Understanding comics.* New York: HarperPerennial.

Messaris, P. (1994). *Visual literacy: Image, mind, and reality.* Boulder, CO: Westview.

Messaris, P. (1997). *Visual persuasion: The role of images in advertising.* Thousand Oaks, CA: Sage.

Meyers, G. (1994). *Words in ads.* New York: St. Martin's.

Mignolo, W. D. (1994a). Literacy and the colonization of memory: Writing histories of people without history. In D. Keller-Cohen (Ed.), *Literacy: Interdisciplinary conversations* (pp. 91–114). Cresskill, NJ: Hampton.

Mignolo, W. D. (1994b). Signs and their transmission: The question of the book in the new world. In E. Boone & W. D. Mignolo (Eds.), *Writing without words: Alternative literacies in Mesoamerica and the Andes* (pp. 220–270). Durham, NC: Duke University Press.

Miller, C. R., & Shepherd, D. (2004). Blogging as social action: A genre analysis of the Weblog. In L. J. Gurak, S. Antonijevic, L. Johnson, C. Ratliff, & J. Reyman (Eds.), *Into the blogosphere: Rhetoric, community, and culture of Weblogs.* Retrieved August 13, 2005, from http://blog.lib.umn.edu/blogosphere/blogging_as_social_action_a_genre_analysis_of_the_weblog.html

Mirzoeff, N. (1998). What is visual culture? In N. Mirzoeff (Ed.), *The visual culture reader* (pp. 3–13). London: Routledge.

Mitchell, W. J. T. (1984). *Iconology: Images, texts, ideology.* Chicago: University of Chicago Press.

Mitchell, W. J. T. (1994). *Picture theory.* Chicago: University of Chicago Press.

Mountford, R. (2001). On gender and rhetorical space. *Rhetoric Society Quarterly, 31*(1), 41–71.

Murray, J. (1998). *Hamlet on the holodeck: The future of narrative in cyberspace.* Cambridge, MA: MIT Press.

New London Group. (2000). A pedagogy of multiliteracies: Designing social futures. In B. Cope & M. Kalantzis (Eds.), *Multiliteracies: Literacy learning and the design of social futures* (pp. 9–37). London: Routledge.

Nyberg, A. K. (1999). Comic book censorship in the United States. In J. A. Lent (Ed.), *Pulp demons: International dimensions of the postwar anti-comics campaign* (pp. 42-68). Cranbury, NJ: Associated University Presses.

Porter, J., & Rife, M. (2005). MGM v. Grokster: *Implications for educators and writing teachers.* Retrieved September 21, 2005, from http://www.wide.msu.edu/widepapers/grokster/

Ratliff, C. (2005). *Using Weblogs in your writing courses*. Retrieved September 1, 2005, from http://culturecat. net/node/915

Rogoff, I. (1998). Studying visual culture. In N. Mirzoeff (Ed.), *The visual culture reader* (pp. 14–26). London: Routledge.

Rohan, L. (2004). I remember mamma: Material rhetoric, mnemonic activity, and one woman's turn-of-the-twentieth-century quilt. *Rhetoric Review, 23*(4), 368–387.

Romano, S. (1993). The egalitarian narrative: Whose story? Which yardstick? *Computers and Composition, 10*(3), 5–28.

Romantic Audience Project. (2003). Retrieved July 21, 2005, from http://ssad.bowdoin.edu:8668/space/ snipsnap-index

Romanyshyn, R. (1993). The despotic eye and its shadow: Media image in the age of literacy. In D. M. Levin (Ed.), *Modernity and the hegemony of vision* (pp. 339–360). Berkeley: University of California Press.

Ronell, A. (1991). *The telephone book: Technology, schizophrenia, electric speech*. Omaha: University of Nebraska.

Ryan, M. L. (2001). Beyond myth and metaphor: The case of narrative in digital media. *Game Studies, 1*. Retrieved June 1, 2002, from http://www.gamestudies.org/0101/ryan/

Sabin, R. (1996). *Comics, comix, and graphic novels: A history of comic art*. London: Phaidon.

Samuel, A. (2005). Today in the *Toronto Star*: Tagging. Retrieved September 23, 2005, from www. alexandrasamuel.com/20050516/ today-in-the-toronto-star-tagging

Schiesel, S. (2005). Conqueror in a war of virtual worlds. *The New York Times*. Retrieved September 6, 2005, from http://www.nytimes.com/2005/09/06/arts/design/06worl.html?pagewanted=print

Schriver, K. A. (1996). *Dynamics in document design: Creating text for readers*. New York: Wiley.

Selfe, C. L., & Selfe, R. (1994). The politics of the interface: Power and its exercise in electronic contact zones. *College Composition and Communication, 45*(4), 480–504.

Stafford, B. M. (1996). *Good looking: Essays on the virtue of images*. Cambridge, MA: MIT Press.

Steiner, W. (1982). *The colors of rhetoric: Problems in the relation between modern literature and painting*. Chicago: University of Chicago Press.

Street, B. V. (1984). *Literacy in theory and practice*. Cambridge, England: Cambridge University Press.

Takayoshi, P. (1994). Building new networks from the old: Women's experiences with electronic communications. *Computers and Composition, 11*, 21–36.

Taylor, T. L. (2003). Multiple pleasures: Women and online gaming. *Convergence, 9*(1), 21–46.

Udell, J. (2004). Collaborative knowledge gardening. *Infoworld*. Retrieved August 15, 2005, from http://www.infoworld.com/article/04/08/20/34Opstrategic_1.html

Wardrip-Fruin, N., & Harrigan, P. (2004). *First person: New media as story, performance, and game*. Cambridge, MA: MIT Press.

Web Logs and Wikis: New Writing Spaces for Advancing Writers. (2004). Retrieved July 21, 2005, from http://199.17.178.148/%7Emorgan/cgi-bin/blogsAndWiki.pl?CourseDescription

Wei, C. (2004). Formation of norms in a blog community. In L. J. Gurak, S. Antonijevic, L. Johnson, C. Ratliff, & J. Reyman (Eds.), *Into the blogosphere: Rhetoric, community, and culture of Weblogs*. Retrieved August 13, 2005, from http://blog.lib.umn.edu/blogosphere/blogging_as_social_action_a_genre_analysis_of_the_ weblog.html

Wiki. (n.d.). In *Wikipedia*. Retrieved September 25, 2005, from http://en.wikipedia.org/wiki/Wiki

Williamson, J. (1978). *Decoding advertisement: Ideology and meaning in advertising*. London: Boyars.

Woods, S. (2004). Loading the dice: The challenge of serious videogames. *Game Studies, 4*(1). Retrieved July 10, 2005, from http://www.gamestudies.org/0401/woods

Wysocki, A. F. (2001). Impossibly distinct: On form/content and word/image in two pieces of computer-based interactive multimedia. *Computers and Composition, 18*, 209–234.

Wysocki, A. F. (2004). The sticky embrace of beauty. In A. F. Wysocki,, J. Johnson-Eilola, C. Selfe, & G. Sirc (Eds.), *Writing new media: Theory and applications for expanding the teaching of composition* (pp. 147–197). Logan: Utah State University Press.

Zettl, H. (2004). *Sight, sound, motion: Applied media aesthetics*. New York: Wadsworth.

Author Index

A

Aarseth, E. J., *604*
Abbott, J. A., 404, *410*
Abbott, R., 294, *303*, 453, *463*
Abbott, R. D., 294, *303*, 453, *462*
Abbott, S., 294, *303*, 453, *463*, 472, *477*
Abbott, S. P., 453, *462*
Abelen, E., 518, *524*
Ackerman, J., 441, *442*, 551, 567, *557*, 573, 585, *590*
Ackerman, J. M., 458, *461*
Adam, C., *229*
Adams, T., 76, *77*
Adburgham, A., 209, *212*
Addison, J., 256, *261*
Adler, M., 27, 29, *31*
Afflerbach, P., 369, *375*
Ainslie, R., 204, *212*
Akinnaso, F., 532, *542*
Akinnaso, F. N., 548, *557*
Alamargot, D., 452, *461*
Albers, M. J., 222, *227*
Albertini, J. A., 390, *391*
Albus, V., 25, *31*
Ali, S., 387, *391*
Alimonosa, D., 469, *477*
Allal, L., 301, *302*, 433, *442*
Allen, C., 603, *604*
Allen, C. K., 132, *136*
Allen, H. B., 349, *356*
Allen, N., 219, *227*, 366, *375*
Allen, N. J., 218, *227*
Allen, R., 193, 194, *199*
Allen, S., 211, *213*
Almasi, J., 369, *375*
Altheide, D., 211, *212*
Altschull, J. H., 202, *212*
Alvermann, D., 418, *426*
Alvermann, D. E., 418, 419, 420, *426*
Alvesson, M., 266, *275*
Amada, M.., 451, 452, 455, 456, *465*
Amato, R., 483, 484, *494*
Amdur, R. J., 483, *494*
American Association of Colleges for Teacher Education, 419, *426*
American Association of University Women, 258, *261*
American Heritage Dictionary, *31*
Anastasi, A., 368, *375*

Andersen, J., 174, *185*
Anderson, B., 65, 77, 158, *168*, 178, *185*, 203, 212
Anderson, D., 387, *392*
Anderson, G., 425, *426*
Anderson, L. M., 298, *303*
Anderson, M., 408, *410*
Anderson, P. J., 205, *212*
Anderson, R. C., 432, *443*
Anderson, W., 513, *524*
Anderson-Yockel, J., 426, *427*
Andrade, H. G., 373, *375*
Andrews, A., 157, *168*, 201, *212*
Angell, N., 202, *212*
Annas, P. J., 252, *261*
Anson, C. M., 219, 224, *227*, 328, 337, *339*
Anthony, H. M., 298, *303*
Antoni, M. H., 482, 485, *493*, *494*
Anzaldua, G., 257, *261*
Applebee, A. N., 295, 296, *302*, 307, 310, 311, 312, 313, 314, 315, 316, 317, *323*, 350, *356*, 460, *464*
Applebee R., 349, *359*
Aram, D., 291, 292, *302*
Arendt, H., 587, *590*
Aristotle, 87, 88, *92*, 343, *356*, 581, *590*
Armbruster, B. B., 439, *443*
Armstrong, L., 470, *477*
Arnaoutoglou, I., 126, *136*
Arnheim, R., 600, *604*
Aronson, J., 501, *509*
Arvidson, H. H., 473, *479*
Aschauer, M. A., 219, *230*
Ascorti, K., 451, *462*
Asenavage, K., 516, *524*
Asher, J. W., 328, *341*
Ashley, H., 384, 385, 390, *392*
Asons, I., 516, *526*
Assmann, J., 65, 66, *77*
Astin, A. W., 338, *339*
Astington, J. H., 281, *287*
Astington, J. W., 284, *287*
Aston, G., 570, *573*
Atkinson, D., 160, *168*, 219, *227*, 520, 523, *524*, 527, 552, *557*, 589, *590*
Atkinson, P. A., 116, *120*
Atton, C., 205, *212*
Atwell, N., 313, *323*, 350, *356*
Auerbach, E., 426, *427*

Ayalon, A., 205, *212*
Azuma, T., 474, *478*

B

Baake, K., 90, *92*
Bachman, L. F., 362, *375*
Backhouse, R., 103, *107*
Baddeley, A. D., 452, 457, *461*
Bae, J., 569, *573*
Bagdikian, B. H., 77
Baghban, M., 399, 406, *410*
Bahn, P., 8, *20*
Bahr, C. M., 470, 471, *479*
Bailey, J., 390, *393*
Bain, A., 348, *356*
Baines, J., 126, *136*
Bakan, J., 101, *106*
Baker, E., 362, 367, 370, 377, *378*
Baker, E. A., 404, *410*
Baker, E. L., 370, *380*
Baker, J. H., 131, *136*
Baker, L., 426, *427*
Baker, S., 389, *392*
Baker, T., 372, *375*
Bakhtin, M., 116, *120*, 299, *302*
Bakhtin, M. M., 434, 439, *443*, 522, *524*, 566, *573*
Balasubramanian, V., 469, *477*
Baldasty, G. J., 202, *212*
Baldry, A., 572, *573*
Baldwin, J., 505, *507*
Ball, A., *375*
Ball, A. F., 497, 498, 500, 501, 502, 503, 504, 505, *507*
Ball, C., 368, *380*
Ball, L. J., 475, *477*
Ballaster, R., 210, *212*
Ballenger, C., 399, *410*
Balsamo, A., 257, *261*
Bamberg, B., 569, *573*
Banagee, M., 476, *478*
Bang, M., 600, *604*
Bangert-Drowns, R., 331, *339*
Bangert-Drowns, R. L., 458, *461*
Banks, J. A., 506, *507*
Bardel, J., 211, *212*
Bardine, B., 389, *392*
Barker, N., 76, *77*
Barker, R. T., 220, *228*
Barker, S., 580, *590*
Barlett, P., 272
Barneby, N., 61, *64*
Barnes, D., 458, *461*
Barnes, L., 256, *263*
Baron, D., 23, *31*, 84, *93*
Baron, N., 28, 30, *31*
Baron, N. S., 221, *228*
Baron, S., 203, *213*
Barriere, I., 468, *477*
Barrios, B., 603, *604*
Barron, S., 369, *378*

Barron, S. I., 369, *380*
Barry, L., 485, *493*
Barthes, R., 81, *93*, 439, *443*, 598, *604*
Bartholomae, D., 390, *392*
Bartlett, C. W., 471, *478*
Bartlett, F. C., 432, *443*
Barton, D., 233, 242, 247, *248*, 398, *410*, 424, *427*, 514, *524*
Barton, E., 517, 518, *524*, 562, *573*, 579, *590*
Barton, E. L., 456, *461*, 589, *590*
Barton, P., 421, *427*
Barzun, P., 285
Basham, C. S., 364, *375*
Bashir, A. S., 471, 472, *480*
Bass, A. S., 402, 405, 407, *413*
Basso, A., 468, 469, *477*
Batalio, J. T., 160, *168*
Bate, J., 234, 237, *248*
Bate, W. J., 198, *199*
Baucom, D. H., 486, *494*
Baudrillard, J., 211, *212*
Bauer, D., 251, *261*
Bauman, R., 18, *20*
Bawarshi, A., 568, *573*
Bayliss, M., 13, *20*
Bayly, C. A., 65, *77*
Baynham, M., 441, *443*
Bazerman, C., 81, 82, 83, 90, 91, *93*, 100, 101, 102, *106*, 116, *120*, 140, *151*, 155, 160, 161, 164, 167, *168*, *169*, 223, 225, *228*, 266, 267, 275, 299, 300, *302*, 330, *339*, 435, 438, 439, *443*, 456, 458, 459, *461*, 518, 523, *524*, 552, 557, 564, 566, 567, 568, 572, *573*, 579, 589, *590*
Beach, R., 317, *323*, 418, *427*
Beal, W. E., *494*
Beall, S., 481, 490, 491, *494*
Beaman, K., 532, *542*
Bear, D., 401, *410*
Beard, R., 374, *375*
Beatty, S., 347, *357*
Beaufort, A., 85, *93*, 218, 219, 224, 225, 226, 227, 228, *339*, 372, *375*, 566, 568, *573*
Beck, E., 436, *445*
Beck, I., 285, *288*
Beck, I. L., 438, *443*
Becker, A., 447, *465*
Becker, A. L., 586, *593*, *594*
Beckwith McGuire, K. M., 483, *493*
Beder, H., 422, 423, 424, *427*
Beers, J., 401, *412*
Beeson, P. M., 469, 470, *477*
Beetham, M., 210, *212*
Begay, K., 294, *303*
Behnken, K. L., 401, *412*
Belcher, D., 387, *392*, 567, *573*, 585, 589, *590*
Belenky, M. F., 254, *261*
Belfiore, M. E., 112, *120*
Bell, A., 207, *212*
Bell, B., 210, *213*

Bell, K., 283, *287*
Bell, M., 206, *212*
Bell, R., 370, *378*
Bellis, M., 24, 30, *31*
Belsey, A., 207, *212*
Belzer, A., 426, *427*
Benesch, S., 523, *524*
Bénet, J., 210, *216*
Benfield, X., 168, *169*
Benhabib, S., 587, *590*
Beniger, J. R., 109, 112, *120*
Benjamin, W., 86, *93*, 112, *120*, 195, *199, 248*
Bennett, R. A., *261*
Bennett, T., 90, *93*
Bennion, S. C., 210, *212*
Benson, D. F., 467, 468, 469, *477*
Benton, S. L., 298, *302*, 457, *461*
Benzing, L., 469, *478*
Berdan, F., 142, 143, *151*
Bereiter, C., 290, 296, 297, 298, *302, 305*, 313, *323*, 434, *443*, 448, 449, 450, 451, 452, 453, 454, 455, 457, 460, 461, *461*, 472, *477*, 583, *590*
Berent, G. P., 390, *392*
Berg, E. C., 516, *524*
Berg, M., 116, *121*
Bergamini, J., 371, *379*
Berger, J., 598, *604*
Berger, P. L., 207, *212*
Berkenkotter, C., 90, *93*, 223, 225, *228*, 270, 271, 275, 299, *302*, 440, *443*, 551, *557*, 566, 567, 568, *573*, 585, *590*
Berlin, J., 309, *323*
Berlin, J. A., 348, *356*
Berners-Lee, T., 437, *443*
Bernhardt, S. A., 222, *228*, 601, *604*
Berninger, V., 453, *463*
Berninger, V. W., 290, 294, 298, *302, 303, 305*, 453, 454, 457, *461, 462, 463*, 471, 472, *477*
Bernstein, M., 602, *604*
Berridge, V., 202, 204, *212*
Besnier, N., 88, *93*, 241, *248, 542*
Besse, J. M., 400, 401, *410*
Bessie S., 208, *212*
Best, C., 513, *524*
Besterman, T., 174, *185*
Bethel, L., 330, *339*, 458, 459, *461*
Beukelman, D. R., 473, 474, 475, *477, 478*
Bezruczko, N., 502, 503, *508*
Bhabha, H., 522, *524*
Bhagwati, J., 103, *106*
Bhatia, V. K., 562, 563, 564, 565, 572, *573, 576*
Biagioli, M., 85, *93*, 155, 161, *169*
Biancarosa, G., 419, 420, *427*
Biber, D., 518, *524*, 532, 533, 534, 537, 540, 541, *543*, 546, 548, 550, 556, *557*, 570, 572, *573*
Bill, M., *64*
Billig, M., 207, *212*
Binder, J. C., 405, *411*
Binfield, K., 239, *248*

Binns, H. B., *249*
Birch, C., 233, *249*
Bird, N. K., 351, *356*
Bird, S. E., 208, *212*
Bird, V., 233, *249*
Bissex, G., 403, *410*
Bissex, G. L., 290, *303*
Bissonnette, V., 401, *412*
Bitzer, L. F., 582, *590*
Bizzell, P., 256, *261*, 344, 345, 346, 347, 348, 354, *356*
Black, A., 513, *524*
Black, E., 582, *590*
Black, K., 368, *375*
Black, L., 373, *375*
Black, P., 371, *375*
Blair, C., 601, *604*
Blair, H., 347, 348, *356*
Blair, H. A., 408, *410*
Blair, J. A., 601, *604*
Blake, B., 500, *507*
Blakeslee, A., 435, *443, 573*
Blakeslee, A. M., 167, *169*, 223, *228*, 584, 585, *590*
Blakesley, D., 372, *375*, 601, *604*
Blalock, G., 327, *340*
Blankenship, J., 532, *543*
Blischak, D. M., 475, *477*
Bliven, B., Jr., 27, *32*
Block, B., 600, *604*
Bloodgood, J., 401, *410*
Bloom, H., 269, *275*
Bloom, L. Z., 253, *261*
Bloor, M., 273, *275*, 564, *573*
Bloor, T., 273, *275*, 564, *573*
Blum, R., 174, 175, *185*
Blumer, H., 113, *121*
Blumler, J., 209, *212*
Bluth, G. J., 457, *464*
Blyer, N. R., 227, *228*
Boardman, K., 253, *263*
Bodde, D., 128, *136*, 149, *151*
Bodkin, R., 105, *106*
Boehmer, R., 15, *20*
Bogoch, B., 129, *136*
Bolker, J., 252, 253, *261*
Bolter, J. D., 92, *93*, 178, 182, 183, 184, *185*, 436, 440, *443*, 602, 603, *604*
Boltz, W. G., 16, *20*
Bonfante, L., 15, *21*
Boone, E., 143, *151*
Booth, R. J., 482, *494*
Booth, W., 582, *590*
Bordia, P., 334, *339*
Borzone de Manrique, A. M., 400, *410*
Boscolo, P., 290, 293, 296, 297, 300, *303, 304*, 399, 441, 451, *462*
Boston Women's Health Collective, 259, *261*
Boudreau, D., 471, *477*
Bourdieu, P., 193, *199*, 211, *212*, 233, *248*, 271, *275*, 434, *443*

Bourdin, B., 453, *462*
Bourne, G., 244, *248*
Bourne, H. R. F., 157, *169*
Bout, J., 486, *494*
Bovino, T. D., 403, *412*
Bowers, C., 424, *427*
Bowey, J. A., 401, *414*
Bowker, G., 90, *93*
Bowker, L., 572, *573*
Bowman, A., 90, *93*
Boyce, D., 268, *275*
Boyce, G., 206, *212*, *213*
Boyd, D. H., *213*
Boyle, O. F., 513, *527*
Bracewell, R. J., 433, *443*
Braddock, R., 308, 310, 313, *323*
Braddock, R. R., 328, *339*
Bradley, D. H., 404, *410*
Braine, G., 589, *590*
Brake, L., 210, *213*
Brandt, D., 92, *93*, 233, 234, 237, 242, 243, 244, 247, *248*, 396, 554, *557*
Brandt, D. M., 457, *464*
Branscomb, A. W., 29, 30, *32*
Branscombe, N. A., 401, *411*
Bransford, J. D., 432, 433, *443*
Branston, G., 211, *213*
Brasseur, L., 601, *605*
Brazeal, D. K., 28, *32*
Breetvelt, I., 450, 451, *462*
Breland, H., 363, *375*
Breland, H. H., 365, *375*
Breland, H. M., 361, *375*
Brenneman, K., 402, *411*
Brent, D., 587, *590*, *591*
Brewer, J., 72, *77*
Briand, P. L., 333, *339*
Brice Heath, S., 246, 247, *248*
Bridgeman, B., 363, 364, 365, 369, *375*, *376*, *377*
Bridwell, L., 314, *324*, 432, *443*
Bridwell-Bowles, L., 254, 255, *261*
Briggs, A., 241, *248*
Bright, G. W., 333, *341*
Britton, J., 92, *93*, 458, 459, *462*
Britton, J. N., 321, *324*
Broad, B., 329, *339*
Broad, R., 373, *375*
Broad, W., 161, *169*
Broadfoot, P., 371, *376*
Broadhead, G. J., 218, *228*
Brock, C., 499, *507*
Brock, M. N., 328, *339*
Brockliss, L., 156, *169*
Brockmann, R. J., 157, *169*, *228*
Brodkey, L., 337, *340*
Brooke, R., 330, *340*
Brookfield, F., 349, *356*
Brookfield, S., 425, *427*
Brooks, A., 294, *303*, 453, *462*, 472, *477*
Brooks, C., 193, *199*

Brooks, D., 70
Brooks, K., 210, *214*
Brossell, G. C., 368, *376*
Brown, A., 365, *376*
Brown, A. L., 433, 440, *443*
Brown, C. J., 71, *77*
Brown, E. L., 489, *494*
Brown, J., 434, *443*
Brown, J. D., 365, 368, *376*
Brown, R. L., 219, 227, *228*, 519, *524*
Brown, S. C., 352, 354, *356*
Brown, V., 103, 104, *106*
Brown, V. J., 338, *340*
Bruce, B., 92, *93*, 418, *427*
Bruce, C., 470, *477*
Brugger, W., 135, *136*
Brumburger, E. R., 222, *228*
Brumm, D., 209, *213*
Bruning, R., 290, *303*
Brunschwig, J., 145, *151*
Bryant, P., *287*
Brzustowicz, L. M., 471, *478*
Buckingham, D., 600, *605*
Buckland, M. K., 182, *185*
Buckland, W. W., 127, 128, *136*
Buell, M., 522, *524*
Buell, M. J., 405, *411*
Bugbee, B. W., 157, *169*
Burbules, N., 441, *443*
Burgess, S., 564, *573*
Burgess, T., 92, *93*, 321, *324*, 459, *462*
Burgh, J., 347, *356*
Burke, C. L., 397, 399, 400, 401, 402, 403, 404, 405, 406, *412*, *414*
Burke, K., 89, *93*, 106, *106*, 580, 581, *591*
Burke, P., 180, *185*
Burnett, J., 236, 239, *248*
Burns, A., 28, *32*
Burns, M. S., 405, *411*
Burns, T. J., 404, *411*
Burrell, G., 266, *275*
Burris, N. A., 401, *414*
Burrows, E., 13, *21*
Burstein, 374, *380*
Burtis, P. J., 450, *461*
Burton, C. M., 488, 491, *493*
Bush, V., 182, *185*, 441, *443*
Butcher, K. R., 450, *462*
Butler, B., 584, *592*
Butler, C. S., 546, *557*
Butler, J., 257, *261*
Butterfield, E. C., 451, 452, 456, 457, *462*
Byng, S., 474, *479*
Byrd, P., 541, *543*

C

Cain, C., 496, *508*
Calfee, R. C., 431, *444*
Calkins, L. M., 350, *356*, 404, *411*, 451, 457, *462*
Callaghan, M., 299, *303*

Callahan, S., 371, *376*
Callister, T. A., Jr., 441, *443*
Camargo, M., 89, *93*, 346, *356*
Cameron, C. A., 450, 451, 460, *461, 462, 464*
Cameron, D., 207, *213*
Camp, R., 363, 364, 367, 371, 372, *375, 376*
Campbell, D. T., 314, *324*
Campbell, G., 347, 348, *356*
Campbell, K., 203, *213*
Campbell, K. S., 570, *573*
Campbell, P., 425, *427*
Campbell, W. J., 208, *213*
Canagarajah, A. S., 168, *169*, 522, 523, *524*
Capell, F., 368, *379*
Capella, M., 346, *357*
Carbonaro, W. J., 503, 504, *507*
Carey, J., 202, *213*
Carey, L., 455, *463*
Carini, P. F., 373, *376*
Carino, P., 335, *340*
Carley, K., 140, *152*
Carlson, R., 434, *443*
Carlson, S., 364, 365, 369, *375*
Carlson, S. B., 363, *376*
Carpenter, M., 85, *93*
Carr, J. F., 348, *357*
Carr, N., 367, *376*
Carr, S. L., 348, *357*
Carrell, P. L., 569, *574*
Carrillo, R., 419, *429*
Carroll, K., 364, *379*
Carruthers, M., 597, *605*
Carson, J., 369, *377*
Carson, J. G., 516, *524, 527*
Carter, C., 211, *213*
Carter, R. T., 496, 500, *507*
Carter, T., 24, 26, *32*
Carter, T. F., 149, *151*
Caruso, L., 365, 366, *380*
Casanave, C. P., 567, 568, *574*
Casbergue, R., 405, *411*
Cassell, J., 604, *605*
Casson, L., 174, *185*, 307, *324*
Castro-Klaren, S., 205, *213*
Catts, H. W., 470, 471, *477, 478*
Cavalier, A., 389, *392*
Cavalier, A. R., 454, *464*
Cavallo, G., 65, *77*
Caywood, C., 253, *261*
Ceccarelli, L., 167, *169*
Cervero, R., 421, 423, 425, *427, 428*
Chadwick, J., 18, *21*
Chadwick, R., 207, *212*
Chafe, W., 531, *543*, 546, 548, 549, 550, *557*
Chalaby, J. K., 202, *213*
Chalhoub-Deville, M., 365, *376*
Chall, J. S., 281, 286, *287*
Chandleer-Olcott, K., 418, *427*
Chandler, A. D., 111, *121*
Chanquoy, L., 433, *442*, 451, 452, 454, 456, *461, 462*

Chapman, M. L., 300, *303*, 403, 405, *411*, 567, *574*
Charkin, T., 458, 459, *461*
Charland, M., 582, *591*
Charles, C., 165, *169*, 572, *577*
Charney, D., *230*, 434, *443*, 572, *576*,
    585, 586, 588, *591*
Charney, D. H., 584, 589, *593*
Chartier, A.-M., 282, 284, 286, *287*
Chartier, R., 68, *78*, 111, *121*, 161, *169*, 175, *185*
Chassagnard, G., 18, *21*
Chasteen, J. C., 205, *213*
Chavkin, T., 330, *339*
Chen, R., 566, *575*
Chenoweth, N. A., 447, 449, 450, 451,
    452, 454, 459, *462*
Cherry, R., 367, *381*
Chesler, A., 168, *169*
Cheville, J., 426, *427*
Chiang, S., 569, *574*
Chiat, S., 469, 470, *479*
Chiser-Strater, E., 355, *358*
Cho, Y., 367, *376*
Chodorow, N., 254, *261*
Chomsky, N., 86, *93*, 187, *199*, 206, 209, *214*
Chou, C., 368, *379*
Chouliaraki, L., 265, *275*
Christensen, C., 472, *478*
Christenson, S., 471, *477*
Christians, C. G., 207, *213*
Christie, F., 299, *303*, 552, 554, *557*, 561, *574*
Christin, A.-M., 65, *78*
Cicero, 345, *357*
Cicourel, A. V., 116, *121*
Ciechanowski, K. M., 419, *429*
Cisotto, L., 293, *303*
Cixous, H., 531, *543*
Claggett, M., 142, *151*
Clair, R., 266, *276*
Clanchy, M., 84, *93*
Clanchy, M. T., 129, 131, *136*, 234, *248*, 346, *357*
Clark, C. M., 388, *392*
Clark, G., 601, *605*
Clark, H. H., 569, *574*
Clark, I. L., 298, *303*, 335, *340*
Clark, R., 425, *427*
Clark, V., *543*
Clarke, J., 207, 208, *213*
Clarke, M. A., 503, *507*
Classen, C. C., 487, *493*
Clausen, N. S., 469, *477*
Clay, M., 397, 399, 400, 401, *411*
Clay, M. M., 290, *303*
Clegg, J., 476, *477*
Clifford, J., 85, *93*, 167, *169*
Clinchy, B. M., 254, *261*
Clyde, J. A., 402, 405, 406, *411*
Cochran-Smith, M., 454, *462*
Cocking, R. R., 433, *443*
Cody, C., 284, *287*
Coe, M., 16, *21*

Coffin, C., 555, 556, *557*
Coffman, W., 363, 368, *377*
Coffman, W. E., 319, *324*
Cohen, A., 370, *379*
Cohen, A. D., 329, *340*
Cohen, J., 322, *324*
Cohen, M., 583, *591*
Coing, H., *136*
Coirier, P., 452, 453, 454, *463*, *464*
Coker, I. H. E., 204, *213*
Colaci, A., 484, *494*
Colander, D., 102, *106*
Colder, M., *494*
Cole, G. D. H., 242, *248*
Cole, M., 88, *95*, 140, *152*, 532, *544*
Cole, S. W., *493*
Coleman, K. B., 294, *303*
Coleman, M., 470, *477*
Collazo, T., 419, *429*
College Board, 374, *376*
College English, 252, *261*
Collins, A., 373, 374, *376*, 434, *443*, 447, *462*
Collins, R., 140, *151*
Collins, S., 475, *477*
Collison, R., 180, *185*
Colls, R., 236, *248*
Colombi, M. C., 550, 552, *559*
Comings, J., 426, *427*
Conboy, M., 202, 209, *213*, 405, 406, *411*
Condon, W., 370, *377*
Conference on College Composition and
    Communication, 327, *340*, 368, 374, *376*
Conley, T. M., 344, 345, *357*
Connell, I., 208, *213*, 267, 271, *275*
Connery, C. L., 147, *151*
Connery, L. C., 110, 111, 115, *121*
Connor, U., 321, *324*, 516, 517, 518, 519,
    520, 521, 523, *524*, *526*, 554, *557*, 564,
    565, 569, 572, *574*, *576*
Connors, R., 81, *93*, 354, *357*
Connors, R. J., 217, *228*, 329, 330, 331,
    340, 348, 353, *357*
Conrad, S., 518, *524*, 533, 534, 537, 540, 541, *543*,
    546, 556, *557*, 570, 572, *573*
Conrad, S. M., 554, *557*
Cook, B. F., 15, *21*
Cook, F. L., 587, *591*
Cook-Gumperz, J., 221, 223, *228*
Cooper, A., 569, *574*
Cooper, C., 105, *106*, 319, *324*
Cooper, H., 314, *324*
Cooper, J. S., 13, *21*
Cooper, M., 603, *605*
Cooper, M. M., 589, *592*
Cope, B., 225, *228*, 296, 299, *303*, 518, *525*, 563, *574*
Copeland, D. A., 204, *213*
Corbett, E. P. J., 353, 354, *360*
Corbett, H. D., 363, *376*
Cordasco, F., 346, *357*
Corkill, A. J., 457, *461*

Cortes, V., 537, *543*
Coulmas, F., 18, 23, 24, 26, *32*, 83, *93*, 142, *151*, *543*
Coulson, R. L., 436, *445*
Couture, B., 218, *228*, 552, *557*
Covill, A., 454, *464*
Cowley, M., 81, 91, 92, *93*
Cox, B., 549, *557*
Cox, B. E., 456, *462*
Cox, J. R., 586, *591*
Crammond, J. G., 457, 589, *591*
Cranfield, G., 202, *213*
Cranton, P., 426, *427*
Crawford, V. M., 418, *428*
Cray, E., 386, *392*
Crick, J., 235, *248*
Crisp, R., 353, *358*
Critcher, C., 207, 208, *213*
Cronbach, L. J., 286, *288*
Cronin, B., 442, *443*
Cronin, F. C., 218, *231*
Cross, G., 85, *93*
Crosswhite, J., 580, 582, 586, 587, 588, 589, *591*
Crow, D., 598, *605*
Crowhurst, M., 368, *376*, 550, 551, *557*, 589, *591*
Crowley, S., 92, *93*
Crump, J., 89, *93*
Crystal, D., 234, 235, *248*, 519, *525*
Cumming, A., 365, *376*, 511, 515, *525*, *526*
Cumming, G., 453, 454, 459, *465*
Cummins, G., 371, *380*
Curran, J., 26, 27, *32*, 204, *213*
Currie, P., 386, *392*
Currie Martin, G., 238, 242, *248*
Curtin, G., 294, *303*
Curtis, A., 436, *444*
Curtis, M., 339, *340*
Cushman, E., *248*

D

Dagenais, B., 209, *215*
Dahl, K., 294, *304*
Dahl, K. L., 292, 293, *303*
Dahlgren, P., 208, *213*
Daiker, D., 373, *375*
Dailey, S., 474, *478*
Daiute, C., 220, *228*, 437, *443*
Daiute, C. A., 451, 454, *462*
Daley, K. E., 407, *414*
Dalton, B., 451, *462*
Daly, M. E., 350, *359*
Daneš, F., 563, *574*
Danet, B., 129, *136*
Danielewicz, J., 546, 549, 550, *557*
Daniels, A., 210, *216*
Danison, N., 516, *527*
Darciaux, S., 453, *462*
Darnton, R., 75, 76, *78*, 161, *169*, 204, *213*
Daub, M., 105, *106*
Dautermann, J., 221, *228*
Davenport, N., 355, *357*

Davidson, A. L., 496, 499, 500, *507*
Dávila de Silva, A. D., 514, *525*
Davis, A., 503, *507*
Davis, A. S., 551, *560*
Davison, K. P., 482, *494*
Dawson, M., 109, *121*
Day, H. N., 348, *357*
Day, J. D., 440, *443*
Day, M., 603, *605*
De Beaugrande, R., 255, *261*, 569, *574*
De Bury, P., 284
De Fonenai, A., 51, *64*
De Goes, C., 291, *303*
De l'Aune, W., 388, *393*
de la Cruz, M., 450, *465*
De La Paz, S., 472, *477, 479*
De Montigny, G. A. J., 116, *121*
De Partz, M., 469, *478*
De Pew, K. E., 513, *526*
De Vries, W., 101, *107*
Dear, P., 160, *169*
Dearin, R. D., 582, *591*
DeBaryshe, B. D., 405, *411*
Debs, M. B., 227, *228*
DeCoste, D. C., 473, *478*
DeFrancis, J., 16, *21*
Degener, S., 421, *429*
Degenhart, R. E., 321, *324*
DeGroff, L. C., 457, *462*
Deleuze, G., 266, *275*
Dellerman, P., 452, 453, 454, *463, 464*
Delli Carpini, M. X., 587, *591*
Delpit, L., 384, *392*, 561, *574*
Deoe, T. A., 112, *120*
Derewianka, B., 548, 552, *557*
Derrida, J., *21*, 595, *605*
Desai, M., 102, *107*
Despain, L., 370, *376*
DeTemple, J., 426, *427*
DeVilliers, P., 390, *392*
DeVito, J. A., 531, *543*
Devitt, A. J., 224, 226, *228*, 561, 566, *574*
Dewey, J., 206, *213*, 492, *493*
Diamond, M. P., 484, *494*
Dias, P., 224, 226, *228*
DiCarlo, C., 476, *478*
Dice, C. P., 331, *342*
Dickinson, D., 426, *427*
Dickinson, G., 601, *605*
Didden, R., 474, *480*
Diederich, P., 319, *324*, 362, *376*
Dierick, S., 371, 373, *377*
Dikovitskaya, M., 598, *605*
Dillon, G. L., 582, *591*
Dingwaney, A., 589, *591*
DiPardo, A., 332, *340*
Dirkx, J., 426, *427*
Dochy, F., 332, *340*, 371, 373, *377*
Dockrell, J. E., 471, *479*
Dodsworth, P., 450, *464*

Doheny-Farina, S., 218, 219, 223, 224, 227, *228, 229*
Dolet, É., 86, *93*
Donahue, M. L., 473, *478*
Donati, V., 484, *494*
Dondis, D. A., 600, *605*
Dong, Y. R., 585, 589, *591*
Donovan, C. A., 403, *411, 414*
Dooley, B., 203, *213*
Dooley, J. A., 484, *494*
Dorff, D. L., *229*
Dorgg, D. L., 218
Dorner, L., 426, *429*
Dorsey-Gaines, C., 426, *429*
Dorsey-Gaines, D., 407, *414*
Dorthea P., 447, *464*
Douglas, J. Y., 602, *605*
Douglas, W., 351, *357*
Douglass, F., 238, *248*
Dowling, N., 370, *379*
Downey, R. G., 457, *461*
Downing, J. D., 205, *213*
Doyle, M., 475, *478*
Dreher, M. J., 401, *412*
Dressen, D. F., 565, *574*
Dreyer, G., 15, *20*
Drotar, D., 485, *494*
Drucker, J., 597, *605*
Dryden, J., 86, *93*
Du Bois, W. E. B., 384, *392*
Dudley-Evans, T., 103, *107*
Duffy, T. M., 226, *231*, 286, *288*
Duguid, P., 76, *78*, 434, *443*
Duin, A. H., *229*
Duke, N. K., 300, *303*
Dukerich, J., 268, 269, *275*
Dunbar, S. B., 362, *378*
Dunham, D. E., 368, *380*
Dunn, B., 454, *463*
Duran, R., 374, *376*
Durer, A., 162, *169*
Durst, R. K., 328, *340*
Dutton, I., 268, 269, *275*
Dwyer, S., 518, *527*
Dyer, M., 349, *359*
Dyson, A., 88, *93*, 398, 399, 400, 402, 404, 405, 407, 408, *411*, 475, *477*
Dyson, A. H., 497, 502, 503, *508*
Dyson, H. A., 289, 290, 292, *303*

E

Eagleton, T., 203, *213*
Easley, A., 210, *213*
Easterbrook, S., 436, *445*
Ebest, S. B., 355, *357*
Ede, L., 85, *95*, 255, *263*, 353, *357*, 436, *443*, 582, 583, *591, 592*
Edelsky, C., 513, *525*
Edmondson, J., 246, *248*
Edmundson, A., 470, *477*
Educational Testing Service, 374, *376*

Ehlhardt, L. A., 470, *480*
Ehringhaus, C., 422, *427*
Eichorn, J., 251, *261*
Eisenhower, D. D., 164, *169*
Eisenstein, E., 65, 71, *78*, 111, *121*
Eisenstein, E. L., 26, *32*, 155, 158, 159, 164, *169*, 178, *185*
Eisenstein, P., 285
Elbow, P., 253, *261*, 352, *357*, *463*
Eldred, J. C., 244, *248*
Elias, D., 332, *342*
Elich, K., *543*
Elkins, J., 92, 93, 599, *605*
Ellickson, R., 125, *136*
Elliott, D. L., 286, *288*
Ellis, D. G., 590, *591*
Ellis, L., 419, *429*
Ellis, P., 501, 505, *507*
Ellis, R. A., 552, *559*
Ellsworth, E., 424, *427*
Elman, B., 90, *93*
Emig, J., 92, *93*, 253, 254, 256, *261*, *263*, 295, *303*, 313, *324*, 350, *357*
Emmison, M., 599, *605*
Encyclopaedia, *185*
Engelhard, G., 385, *392*, 504, *508*
Engeström, Y., *94*
Englert, C. S., 298, *303*, *305*
Enos, R. L., 344, 345, *357*
Enos, T., 257, *261*, 352, 354, *356*, 579, 581, 582, 586, *591*
Epstein, R., 105, *107*
Equipped for the Future Project, 424, *427*
Erard, M., 20, *21*
Erdosy, M. U., 365, 366, *376*
Eresh, J., 370, *378*
Ericsson, K. A., 457, *463*
Ericsson, P. G., 374, *376*
Erikson, E. H., 496, *508*
Ernst, M. L., 29, 30, *32*
Ernstoff, M. S., 483, *494*
Escarpit, R., 74, *78*
Eshamy, M. R., 483, *494*
Eskritt, M., 283, *288*
Esterling, B. A., 482, 485, *493*
Etzkowitz, H., 157, *169*
Eubanks, P., 89, *94*
Evans, B., 307, 308, 309, 310, *324*
Evans, J., 474, 476, *478*, *605*
Evans, P. J. A., 366, *376*
Evans, R. J. W., 155, *169*
Evensen, L. S., 517, *525*

F

Faber, B., 266, 267, 271 273, *275*
Fahnestock, J., 160, *169*, 223, *229*, 569, *574*, 589, *591*
Faigley, L., 217, 226, *229*, 451, 456, *463*, 551, *557*, 569, 577, 602, 603, *605*
Fairclough, N., 118, 119, *121*, 207, *213*, 265, 267, 270, 272, 273, *275*, 424, 425, *427*

Fairclough, P. 268, 271, 272, 273
Falick, T. G., 390, *392*
Faludi, S., 258, *261*
Fang, I., 23, 24, 25, 26, 27, 28, 29, *32*
Fang, Z., 405, *411*
Farnsworth, E. A., 131, *136*
Farrell, T., 252, *261*
Farris, S., 251, *261*
Fayol, M., 291, *304*, 452, 453, 454, *462*, *463*
Feak, C. B., 563, *576*
Febvre, L., 72, *78*
Fecho, B., 418, *427*
Federico, P. J., 157, *169*
Felton, M., 589, *591*
Feltovich, P. J., 436, *445*
Fennell, B. A., 223, *229*, 590, *592*
Fenton, S., 87, *94*
Ferber, M., 102, *107*
Ferguson, A. A., 500, *508*
Ferreira-Buckley, L., 238, *248*
Ferreiro, E., 291, 292, *304*, *305*, 397, 400, 401, 402, *411*
Ferretti, R., 389, *392*
Ferris, D. R., 516, 517, *525*
Fetter, W., 105, *107*
Fey, M., 471, *478*
Feyerabend, P., 266, 267, *275*
Fickas, S., 470, *480*
Field, T. W., 532, *544*
Fillion, B., 297, *305*
Finders, M., 92, *94*, 258, *261*
Finders, M. J., 418, *428*
Fine, J., *574*
Finegan, E., 543, 546, 556, *557*, 570, 572, *573*
Fingeret, A., 425, 426, *428*
Fink, B., 453, *463*
Finkelstein, D., *78*, 210, *213*
Finnegan, C. A., 601, *605*
Finnegan, E., 534, *543*
Firbas, J., 563, *574*
Firestone, S., 259, *261*
Fisher, J., 421, 423, *429*
Fitch, J. D., 402, 405, 407, *413*
Fitzgerald, J., 331, *340*, 451, 456, *463*
Fitzgerald, S. M., 390, *393*
Flach, J., 362, 367, *381*
Flanigan, R., 483, 492, *494*
Flannery, K., 142, *151*
Flavell, J., 283, *288*
Flavell, J. H., 435, *443*
Flax, J. F., 471, *478*
Fleck, C., 367, *379*
Fleming, D., 345, *357*, 601, *605*
Fleming, S., 408, *411*
Fletcher, M. A., 482, 485, *493*
Fliegelman, J., 159, *169*
Flinsbee, S., 112, *120*
Flower, F., 438, *444*
Flower, L., 89, *94*, 432, 436, *443*, 452, 460, 585, *591*
Flower, L. S., 256, *261*, 294, *304*, 313, *324*, 447, 448, 449, 450, 451, 452, 455, 460, *463*

Flowerdew, J., 168, *169*, 556, *558*
Flowerdew, L., *558*
Flowers, L., 338, *340*
Flynn, E., 251, 255, 259, *261*
Fontanilla, I., 482, *494*
Fordham, S., 496, 500, 501, *508*
Forsberg, L. L., 219, 224, *227*
Fortune, R., 221, *229*
Foss, S. A., 588, *591*
Foss, S. K., 602, *605*
Foster, D., 327, *340*, 361, *376*, 521, *525*
Foster, J. B., 109, *121*
Foster, S., 389, *392*
Foucault, M., 90, *94*, 114, *121*, 266, *275*
Foulin, J. N., 452, 454, *462*
Fouquette, D., 330, *339*,
    458, 459, *461*
Fowler, R., 118, *121*, 207, *213*, 272, *275*
Fowles, M. E., 367, *379*
Fox, J. D., *248*
Fox, R., 352, *358*
Fracasso, A., 103, *107*
Frame, S., 473, *478*
Francis, M., 432, *444*, 451, 455, 456,
    457, *464*, 485, 492, *493*, *494*
Francis, M. E., 482, 492, *494*
Francis, W. N., 570, *575*
Frank, J., 203, *213*
Franklin, B., *213*
Franklin, P., 351, *357*
Frawley, W., 532, *543*
Frawley, W. J., 552, *559*
Frazer, E., 210, *212*
Fredericksen, J., 373, 374, *376*
Frederiksen, C. H., 433, 438, *443*, *444*
Frederiksen, J. D., 433, *443*
Freed, R. C., 218, *228*
Freedman, A., 224, 226, *228*, *229*, 299,
    304, 368, *376*, 568, *574*
Freedman, S. W., 227, *229*, 318, *324*,
    325, 332, *340*, 364, 365, 366, *376*,
    461, *463*, 500, 503, *509*
Freiberger, P., 29, 30, *32*
Freire, P., 245, *248*
French, H., 20, *21*
Freppon, P., 294, *304*
Fresch, M. J., *304*, 401, *411*
Frey, O., 253, *262*
Friedman, M., 102, *107*
Fries, P. H., 563, *574*
Frohmann, B., *185*
Frost, J., 349, *357*
Fry, P. G., 351, *358*, 369, *378*
Frye, N., 194, *199*
Fu, D., 512, *525*
Fulkerson, R., 587, 588, 589, *591*
Fuller, D. R., 473, *479*
Fuller, F., 290, *302*, 457, *461*
Furner, M., 166, *169*
Fyfe, R., 399, *413*, 441, *444*

G

Gabriel, Y., 269, *275*
Gabrielson, S., 385, *392*, 504, *508*
Gagarin, M., *136*
Gage, J. T., 352, *357*
Gajdusek, L., 516, *527*
Galasinski, D., 267, 271, *275*
Galbraith, D., 459, *463*
Galison, P., 85, *93*, 161, *169*
Gallas, K., 402, 408, *411*
Gambell, T., 387, 388, *392*
Gamoran, A., 315, *325*, 503, 504, *507*
Ganufis, J., 458, 459, *461*
Gaonkar, D. P., 580, *591*
Garcia, A., 155, *169*
Gardiner, A. H., 162, *169*
Gardner, P. W., 236, *248*
Garfield, E., *185*
Garofalo, J. P., 490, 493, *494*
Garufis, J., 330, *339*
Garwood, K., 116, *122*, *171*
Gaynor, J., *375*
Gearhart, M., 367, 370, 371, *377*
Gearhart, S. M., 254, *262*, 587, *591*
Gebhardt, R. C., 353, *357*
Gedin, P., *78*
Gee, J. P., 225, *229*, 384, *392*, 398, 406, *411*,
    418, *428*, 496, 497, 498, 499, *508*, 514,
    523, *525*, 555, *558*, 604, *605*
Gee, T. C., 317, *324*
Geertz, C., 167, *169*
Geisler, C., 221, 227, *229*, 438, 441, *444*,
    579, 584, 585, *591*, *592*, *593*
Gelb, I. J., 17, *21*
Gelman, R., 402, *411*
Genberg, H., 103, *107*
Gentner, D., 447, *462*
Gentry, J. R., 401, *411*
Gentzler, E., 87, *94*
Genung, J. F., 348, *357*
George, D., 589, *592*, 597, *605*
George, T. J. S., 205, *213*
Gere, A. R., 243, 246, *248*, 256, 257, *262*
Gergen, K., 167, *170*, *171*
Gernet, J., 26, *32*
Gerrig, J., 223, *230*
Gersten, R., 389, *392*
Ghosh, S., 87, *94*
Giannoni, D. S., 437, *444*
Gibbons, T., 347, *357*
Gibbs, R. W., Jr., 438, *444*
Gielen, S., 371, 373, *377*
Gilani, Z., 483, 484, *494*
Gilbert, P., 418, *428*
Gilbert, S., 192, *199*
Gilbert-Levin, E., 258, *262*
Gilbertson, M. K., 225, *230*
Gilgamesh, 24, *32*
Gillam, R. B., 471, *478*, *479*

Gilles, R., 372, *379*
Gillespie, M., 233, 245, *248*
Gillette, S., 518, *527*
Gilligan, C., 254, *262*
Gillispie, C. C., 162, *169*
Gillmor, D., 603, *605*
Giltrow, J., 116, *121*
Gimenez, J. C., 221, *229*
Gipps, C., 371, *377*
Gipps, P., 373, *377*
Giroux, H., 269, *275*, 424, *428*
Gitelman, L., 27, *32*
Gitomer, D., 373, *377*
Gladwell, M., 220, *229*
Glaser, R., 489, 490, *494*
Glasser, T., 207, *213*
Gledhill, C., 571, *574*
Glenn, C., 256, *262*, 344, 354, *357*
Glenn, C. G., 456, *465*
Glennen, S. L., 473, *478*
Glew, M., 366, *379*
Gluck, S. B., 256, *262*
Godshalk, F., 363, 368, *377*
Godshalk, F. I., 319, *324*
Goetz, E. T., 432, *443*
Goetzmann, W., 100, 101, *107*
Goffman, E., 85, *94*
Goggin, M. D., 347, 351, 352, *357*, 602, *605*
Goldberger, N. R., 254, *261*
Golding, P., *214*
Goldman, S. R., 460, 461, *463*
Goldthwaite, M. A., 354, *357*
Golub-Smith, M., 368, *377*
Gombert, J. E., 291, *304*
González-Pérez, A., 205, *213*
Goodlet, J., 436, *445*
Goodman, A. D. J., 330, *340*
Goodman, Y., 397, 398, 399, *411*, *414*
Goodman-Schulman, R., 469, *477*
Goodwin, A. L., 496, 500, *507*
Goodwin, C., 156, *169*
Goodwin, J., 369, *380*
Goody, J., *21*, 65, *78*, 87, *94*, 97, *98*, 99, 100, *107*, 109, 110, 111, *121*, 139, 140, *151*, *152*, 173, 174, 176, *186*, 531, 533, *543*
Gordon, B., 385, *392*, 504, *508*
Gordon, K. C., 486, *494*
Gordon, W. T., *21*
Gorman, T. P., 321, *324*
Goswami, D., 219, *230*
Gottschalk, K., 354, *357*
Gould, J. D., 453, *463*
Grabe, W., 562, 563, *574*
Grabowski, J., 453, *463*
Graff, G., 166, *169*
Graff, H., 279, *288*
Graff, H. J., 235, 236, 238, 239, *248*
Grafton, A., 155, *170*
Gragson, G., 585, *591*

Graham, B., 238, *248*
Graham, P., 270, 271, *275*
Graham, S., 290, 297, 298, *304*, 389, 392, 451, 453, 454, *461*, *463*, 468, 471, 472, 477, *478*, 479
Graumann, C. F., 167, *170*
Graves, B., 438, *444*
Graves, D., 404, 408, *412*, 439, *444*
Graves, D. H., 295, *304*, 350, *357*, 451, *463*
Graves, F. P., 346, *357*
Gray, J., 258, *262*
Gray, N., 54, *64*
Gray-Schlegel, M. A., 408, *412*
Gray-Schlegel, T., 408, *412*
Graziano, E. E., 181, *186*
Graziano, W. G., 489, *494*
Greco, A., 75, *78*
Green, C. R., 400, *412*, 501, 502, *508*
Green, G., *543*
Greenbaum, S., 545, 546, 550, *559*
Greenberg, K., 368, *377*
Greenberg, M. A., 483, 486, 490, *493*
Greene, S., 81, *95*, 441, *444*, 545, *559*
Greenspan, E., 76, *78*
Greenwood, C., 362, *381*
Gregory, D., 105, *107*
Gregory, E., 405, *412*
Gregory, G., 245, *248*
Gress, E., 54, *64*
Grice, P., 282, *288*
Grieve, R., 401, *414*
Griffin, C. L., 588, *591*
Griffith, W., 423, *428*
Griffiths, G., 192, *199*
Grimes, B., *21*
Grimes, J., *21*
Gripsrud, J., 208, *213*
Groenendyk, K. L., 601, *605*
Grogan, P. R., 292, 293, *303*
Grootendorst, R., 586, *593*
Gross, A. G., 160, 161, *170*, 564, *574*, 582, *591*
Grossi, E. P., 400, 401, *412*
Grossman, L. K., 211, *213*
Grusin, R., 92, 93, 440, *443*
Guattari, F., 266, *275*
Guba, E., *377*
Gubar, S., 192, *199*
Guerlac, H., 159, *170*
Guinan, H., 388, *392*
Gunnarsson, B., 519, *525*
Gunnarsson, B. L., 101, *107*, 160, 161, *170*
Gurak, L. J., 259, *262*
Gurd, J. M., 468, *479*
Gurevitch, M., 209, *212*
Gutas, D., 86, *94*
Guthrie, J., 369, *375*
Gutman, L. M., 405, *412*
Gutmann, M. L., 475, *479*
Guy, K., 90, *94*

H

Haakonssen, K., 105, *107*
Haas, C., 218, 220, 222, 226, *229, 231*, 339, *340*, 438, *444*, 585, 589, *592*
Haas, N. S., 377
Haavelmo, T., *107*
Haber, L. F., 163, *170*
Habermas, J., 203, *213*, 114, *121*, 596, *605*
Hacker, D. J., 451, 452, 456, 457, *462*
Hacking, I., 90, *94*
Hague, R., 57, 58, *64*
Hairston, M., 350, *357*
Haladyna, T. M., *377*
Halas, M., 390, *392*
Hale, G., 369, *377*
Hale, M., 133, *136*
Hall, D. D., 70, *78*
Hall, M., 483, 484, *494*
Hall, S., 207, 208, *213, 605*
Halliday, M. A., 118, *121*
Halliday, M. A. K., 160, *170*, 434, *444*, 532, *543*, 546, 547, 548, 549, 553, 555, *558*, 563, 569, *574*
Halliday, P., 272, 273
Halloran, M., 233, 236, *248*, 601, *605*
Hamadache, A., 423, *428*
Hamel, C., 389, *392*
Hamilton, H. E., 118, *122*
Hamilton, L., 364, 369, 374, *377, 378*
Hamilton, M., 233, 237, 242, 247, *248, 249*, 398, *410*, 424, *427*
Hamilton, M. M., 514, *524*
Hammer, C., 426, *428*
Hamp-Lyons, L., 364, 366, 370, *377*
Haney, M. R., 401, *412*
Haney, W., 363, *377*
Hanna, K., 221, 223, *228*
Hannon, P., 233, *249*
Hansen, J. G., 516, *526*
Hansen, J., 439, *444*
Hansen, K., 226, *229*, 355, *357*
Hansen, V., 100, *107*
Hanzeli, V., 553, *559*
Hapke, T., 180, *186*
Haraway, D., 257, *262*
Harcup, T., 207, *213*
Harding, S., 256, *262*
Hardt, H., 202, *213*
Hardy, C., 268, *275*
Hared, M., *543*
Hariman, R., 601, *606*
Haring-Smith, T., 354, *357*
Harman, D., 422, *428*
Harmon, J. E., 160, 161, *170*, 564, *574*
Harper, R., 101, *107*
Harper, R. H. R., 30, *33*, 220, *231*
Harquail, C., 268, *275*
Harrigan, P., 604, *607*
Harris, D. E., 337, *340*

Harris, D. P., 390, *391*
Harris, K. H., 290, 297, 298, *304*
Harris, K. R., 453, *463*, 471, 472, *478*
Harris, M., 203, *213*, 352, *358*
Harris, M. H., 176, 177, *186*
Harris, R., 82, 83, 87, *94*, 555, *559*
Harris, W. V., 65, *78*
Harrison, C., 272, 273, *276*, 555, *560*
Harrison, J. F. C., 237, 238, 242, 245, 247, *249*
Harste, J. C., 397, 399, 400, 401, 402, 403, 404, 405, 406, *412, 414*
Hartfiel, V. F., 366, *378*
Hart-Landsberg, S., 217, *229*
Hartley, J., 208, *213*
Harvey, E., 372, *375*
Harwood, J. T., 217, *229*
Hasan, R., 118, *121*, 272, *276*, 546, *558*, 565, 569, *574*
Haskins, E., 89, *94*
Hassett, M., 168, *170*, 601, *606*
Haswell, R., 366, *377*, 550, *558*
Haswell, R. H., 327, 330, 334, 338, *340*, 374, *376*
Hatch, J. A., 330, *340*, 449, 451, *465*
Hauser, A., 195, *199*
Hauser, A. G., 602, *605*
Hauser, G. A., 582, *592*
Hauser, R. M., 361, 362, *377*
Havelock, E., 65, *78*, 87, *94*, 139, 145, *152*
Havelock, E. A., *21*
Haviland, S. E., 569, *574*
Hawhee, D., 89, *94*
Hawisher, G., 92, *95*, 255, 263, 602, *605*
Hawisher, G. E., 257, *262*, 334, *340*
Hawkins, M. R., 514, *525*
Hay, D., 239, *249*
Hayes, D. L., 355, *358*
Hayes, E., 421, *428*
Hayes, J., 89, *94*
Hayes, J. R., 256, *261*, 294, *304*, 313, *324*, 330, *340*, 432, 436, 443, 447, 448, 449, 450, 451, 452, 454, 455, 456, 459, 460, *462, 463, 465*
Hayes, K., 251, *261*
Hayes-Roth, B., 447, *463*
Hayes-Roth, F., 447, *463*
Hayhoe, R., 167, *170*
Haynes, C., 603, *605*
Haynes, J. A., 472, *479*
Haynes, W., 426, *427*
Hazeltine, H. D., 129, *136*
Headrick, D. R., 179, *186*
Healey, J., 15, *21*
Healey, P., 157, *169*
Heath, C., 91, *94*
Heath, R., 268, *276*
Heath, S., 426, *428*
Heath, S. B., 225, *229*, 405, 406, 407, *412*, 520, *525*, 532, *543*
Heaton, L. B., 331, *342*
Hebrand, J., 282, *287*
Hebron, S., 210, *212*

Hedengren, B. F., 354, *358*
Hedgcock, J. S., 516, 517, *525*
Hedges, L. V., 314, 323, *324*
Heffernan, L., 399, 408, *412*
Heilbroner, R., 102, 103, *107*
Hein, K., 270, *276*
Helgerson, R., 158, *170*
Heller, C., 503, *508*
Heller, J., 371, *380*
Helt, M., 541, *543*
Henderson, E., 401, *412*
Henderson, W., 103, *107*
Hengst, J. A., 473, *478*
Henkemans, F. S., 586, *593*
Henkin, R., 408, *412*
Henning, G., 370, *377*
Henry, G. H., 349, *356*
Henry, J., 219, *229*
Hepburn, J., *78*
Herd, H., 202, *214*
Herman, E., 206, 209, *214*
Herman, J., 367, 370, *377*
Hermes, J., 210, *214*
Hernandez, A., 251, *261*
Herndl, C. C., 223, *229*
Herndl, C. G., 219, 227, *228*, 519, *524*, 590, *592*
Herrington, A., 219, *230*, 374, *379*, 585, *592*
Herrington, A. J., 329, 339, *340*, 589, *592*
Herse, R., 401, *413*
Herzberg, B., 256, *261*, 344, 345, 346, 347, 348, 354, *356*
Herzberg, T., 388, *392*
Hesford, W., 259, *262*
Heubert, J. P., 361, 362, *377*
Hewings, A., 556, *557*
Hiatt, M. P., 252, 253, *262*
Hidi, S., 290, *304*
Higginbotham, D. J., 475, *478*
Higgins, E., 334, *341*
Hildreth, G., 400, *412*
Hilgers, T., 367, 368, 370, 372, *376, 377*
Hill, A. S., 348, *358*
Hill, C., 134, *136*
Hill, D. J., 348, *358*
Hilliard, C., 245, *249*
Hilligoss, S., 256, *261*
Hillis, A. E., 469, *478*
Hillocks, G., 81, *94*, 318, 319, *324*
Hillocks, G., Jr., 289, 295, *304*, 308, 311, 312, 313, 314, 315, 316, 317, 318, 321, 322, *324*, 328, 331, *341*, 350, *358*, 369, 371, *377*, 426, *428*
Hinchman, K. A., 418, *426*
Hinds, J., 521, *525*
Hinkel, E., 517, *525*, 548, 550, 551, *558*, 569, *574*
Hirsch, L. S., 471, *478*
Hirst, J., 513, *524*
Hirvela, A., 386, 387, *392, 393*
Hitti, P., 85, *94*
Hjortshoj, K., 354, *357*
Hobsbawm, E., 233, *249*

Hobson, A., 25, *32*
Hobson, E. H., 335, *341*
Hocks, M., 601, *605*
Hodge, B., 118, *121*
Hodge, R., 118, *121*, 207, *214*, 272, *275*
Hodges, C., 384, 391, *393*
Hoey, M., 118, *121*, 554, *558*, 563, *574*
Hoffert, D. E., 210, *214*
Hofstede, G., 520, *525*
Hogan, P. C., 187, 189, *199*
Hoggart, R., 208, *214*, 245, *249*
Holland, D. C., 496, *508*
Holland, P., 366, *375*
Hollis, C., 476, *477*
Hollis, P., 204, *214*
Holmes, D., 487, *493*
Holmes, J., 347, *358*
Holmevik, J. R., 603, *605*
Homburg, T. J., *377*
Hood, S., 556, *558*
Hook, J. N., 349, 350, 353, *356, 358*
Horn, C., 290, *303*
Horn, P., 237, *249*
Hornberger, N. H., 513, *525*
Horner, W. B., 238, *248*
Horowitz, R., 283, *288*
Horton, W., 221, 222, *229*
Houben, J., 144, *152*
Hourihan, M., 603, *605*
House, J., 86, *94*
Hovde, M. R., 218, *229*
Howard, R. M., 85, *94*, 441, *444*
Howard, U., 234, 236, 237, 238, *239, 240, 241, 242, 243, 244, 247, 249*
Howard, X., 168, *169*
Howe, F., 252, *262*
Howell, M. E., 338, *340*
Hoyles, M., 245, *249*
Hoyne, S. H., 454, *464*
Hoyrup, J., 15, *21*
Huarte, M. F., 450, *465*
Hubbard, L., 496, *508*
Hubbard, R., 402, *412*
Huckin, T., 270, 271, *275*, 440, *443*
Huckin, T. H., 585, *590*
Huckin, T. N., 225, *228*, 299, *302*, 551, *557*, 563, 567, *573, 574*
Hudelson, S., 513, *525*
Hudson, F., 202, *214*
Huff, T. E., 149, *152, 167, 170*
Hughes, A., 235, *249*
Hughes, C. F., *494*
Hughes, J. A., 112, *121*
Hughes, R., 240, *249*
Hughes, R. E., 363, *378*
Hughes, T. P., 163, *170*
Hughey, J. B., 366, *378*
Hull, D., 266, *276*
Hull, G., 217, 222, 225, *229*, 247, *249*, 368, *380*, 418, *428*

Humphreys, K. W., 175, *186*
Humphries, T., 389, *392*
Hunsberger, M., 333, *341*
Hunston, S., 533, *543*, 556, *558*, 572, *574*
Hunt, A. K., 451, 460, 461, *462*
Hunt, K., 313, *324*
Hunt, K. W., 328, 338, *341*, 547, 550, *558*
Hunt, R. A., 437, 438, *444*, *446*
Hunter, D., 27, *32*, 387, 388, *392*
Hunter, J., 112, *120*, 210, *214*
Hunting, R. S., *358*
Huntsman, J. F., 307, *324*
Huntzicker, W. E., 208, *214*
Hunwick, J., 151, *152*
Huot, B., 319, *324*, 337, *342*, 361, 362,
    365, 369, *378*, *379*
Hurewitz, A., *494*
Hurley, M. M., 331, *339*, 458, *461*
Hussey, E., 372, *377*
Hustad, K. C., 474, *478*
Hutton, F., 205, *214*
Hyland, K., 436, 440, *444*, 518, *525*,
    556, *558*, 565, 571, 572, *574*
Hyon, S., 518, *525*, 566, *575*
Hyun, T., 86, *94*

I

Icke, V., 518, *527*
Iedema, R., 92, *94*, *121*
Illinois State Board of Education, 320, *324*
Impey, O., 158, *170*
Inagaki, S., 550, 551, *560*
Ingalls, D., 193, *200*
Inman, J. A., 334, *341*
Introna, L. D., 183, *186*
Ismailji, T., 487, *493*
Isocrates, 344, *358*
Ivani, R., 424, *427*, *428*, 567, *575*
Ivanic, R., 92, *94*, 233, *248*, 498, 501, 503, *508*

J

Jackson, B. S., 126, *136*
Jackson, K., 210, *214*
Jackson, N. S., 112, *120*, *121*
Jackson, P., 210, *214*
Jackson, R., 352, 354, *356*
Jackson-Waite, K., 469, *478*
Jacob, C., 25, *32*
Jacob, M. C., 159, *170*
Jacobs, H. L., 366, *378*
Jacobs, L. R., 587, *591*
Jacobs, P., 353, *358*
Jacobson, E., 421, *429*
Jacobson, M. J., 436, *445*
Jahandarie, K., *21*
James, L., 208, *214*
James, S., 116, *122*
Jameson, F., 266, *276*
Jamieson, A., 348, *358*

Janik, A., 588, *593*
Janks, H., 425, *428*
Janoff-Bulman, R., 491, *493*
Janopoulos, M., 365, *378*, 517, *525*
Jarratt, S., 268, *276*
Jarratt, S. C., 251, 253, 254, 257, *261*, *262*
Jasinski, J., 579, 581, 586, 588, *592*
Jasken, J., 597, *606*
Jaszi, P., 85, *96*
Jauss, H. R., 198, *200*
Jefferson, T., 207, 208, *213*
Jeffrey, G. C., 454, *463*
Jencks, C., 322, *324*
Jenkins, H., 604, *605*
Jenkins, J., 573, *575*
Jenkins, L., 421, *427*
Jennings, C., 370, *378*
Jeppeson, M. S., 601, *604*
Jevons, W. S., 102, *107*
Johannessen, L., 316, *325*
Johanson, G., 69, *78*
Johansson, S., 534, *543*, 546, 556, 557, 570, 572, *573*
Johns, A., 65, *78*, 159, *170*, 596, *606*
Johns, A. M., 513, 518, *525*, *526*, 561, 568, 569, *575*
Johns, L. C., 218, *230*
Johnson, A. F., 37, 46, *64*
Johnson, C. J., 473, *478*
Johnson, C. S., 161, *170*
Johnson, E. D., 177, *186*
Johnson, K. E., 516, *526*
Johnson, M., 236, *249*, 588, *592*
Johnson, M. K., 432, *443*
Johnson, N., 348, *358*
Johnson, P., 483, 492, *494*
Johnson, R., 237, *249*
Johnson, S., 83, *94*, 469, *477*
Johnson, T. R., 331, *342*, 354, *358*, 351, *358*
Johnson, T. S., 369, *378*
Johnson, W., 128, *136*
Johnson-Bailey, J., 421, 425, *428*
Johnson-Eilola, J., 602, 603, *606*
Johnson-Eiola, J., 92, *96*
Johnston, D., 127, 128, *136*
Johnston, J. R., 471, *478*
Johnston, P., 498, *508*
Johnston, S., 474, 476, *478*
Johnstone, H., 587, 588, *592*
Jolliffe, D., 217, *230*
Jones, C., 337, *341*
Jones, D., 472, *478*
Jones, I., 404, 405, *412*
Jones, R., 363, *375*
Jones, R. F., 155, *170*
Jones, R. J., 365, *375*
Jones, T., 474, *478*
Jones, W., 474, *478*
Jones-Quarty, K. A. B., 204, *214*
Jonker, G., 13, *21*
Jorn, L. A., 219, *230*
Juel, C., 294, *304*

Junker, C., 252, 255, *262*
Jurmo, P., 425, *428*
Juska, J., 349, *359*
Justeson, J. S., 19, *21*
Justice, L. M., 401, *414*

K

Kachur, R., 315, *325*
Kaell, A., *494*
Kaganoff, T., 369, *380*
Kahane, H., 587, *592*
Kahn, E., 316, *325*
Kalantzis, M., 225, *228*, 296, 299, *303*,
    518, *525*, 563, *574*
Kallinikos, J., 111, *121*
Kalman, J., 88, *94*, 247, *249*
Kaltenbacher, M., 572, *577*
Kamberelis, G., 88, *94*, 290, *304*, 403,
    412, 563, 564, 566, *575*
Kamhi, A. G., 470, *477*
Kamii, C., 400, 401, *412*
Kanfer, F., 372, *378*
Kantor, M., 471, *479*
Kantor, R., 369, *377*
Kaplan, R., 387, 391, *393*
Kaplan, R. B., 517, 520, 521, *524, 526*, 562, *574*
Karcher, L.., 469, 470, *479*
Karmiloff-Smith, A., 450, *464*
Kärreman, D., 266, *275*
Kasoma, F. P., 204, *214*
Katula, R. A., 344, *358*
Katz, A. M., 332, *340*
Katz, B., 179, *186*
Katz, S. M., 223, *230*
Kaufer, D. S., 584, *592*
Kaufer, D., 140, *152*, 441, *444*
Kaufman, T., 19, *21*
Kaul, C., 205, *214*
Kay, P., 531, *543*
Kazemek, F., 422, 423, *428*
Keane, J., 209, *214*
Keating, P., *78*
Keeble, R., 209, *214*
Keech, C. L., 365, 366, *378*
Keightley, D. N., 16, *21*
Keith, S., 369, *378*
Kellogg, R. T., 433, *444*, 450, 452, 453,
    455, 456, 457, *464, 465*
Kelly, A. B., 390, *392*
Kemeny, M. E., *493*
Kenan, L., 86, *94*
Kendall, A., 572, *576*, 589, *593*
Kennedy, G., 89, *94*, 268, *276*, 533, *543*
Kennedy, G. A., 344, 345, *358*, 579, 580, *592*
Kennedy, M. M., *358*
Kenner, C., 399, 400, 402, *412*, 512, *526*
Kerr, S., 432, *444*, 451, 455, 456, 457, *464*
Ketter, J., 369, *378*
Keynes, J. M., 102, 103, 105, *107*
Khramtsova, I., 457, *461*

Khurshodov, A., 25, 29, 31, *32*
Kiecolt-Glaser, J. K., 489, 490, *494*
Kieran, M., 207, *214*
Killingsworth, M. J., 225, *230*
Kim, H.-Y., 550, 551, *560*
Kim, Y., *543*
Kimball, B. A., 346, *358*
King, C., 134, *136*
King, J. R., 419, *428*, 441, *445*
King, L. A., 488, 491, *493*
Kinkead, J., 335, *341*
Kinneavy, J., 435, *444*, 562, *575*
Kinneavy, J. L., 298, *304*
Kintgen, E. R, *248*
Kintsch, W., 432, *444*, 450, 455, 457,
    458, *462, 463, 464*, 568, 569, *575*
Kinzer, C., 364, *379*
Kirsch, G., 256, *263*, 584, *592*
Kirsch, G. E., 256, 259, *262*
Kirsop, W., 69, *78*
Kittler, F., 211, *214*
Kitzhaber, A. R., 338, *341*,
    348, 352, *358*
Klamer, A., 103, *107*
Klare, G. R., 218, *231*
Klein, J. T., 165, *170*
Klein, J., 589, *592*
Klein, L., 105, *106, 107*
Klein, P. D., 331, *341*
Klein, P., 458, 459, 460, *464*
Klein, S., 370, *378*
Kluwin, T. N., 390, *392*
Knapp, M. S., 503, *508*
Knapp, P., 299, *303*
Knoblauch, C., 498, *508*
Knorr-Cetina, K., 90, *94*
Knorr-Cetina, K., 435, *444*
Knowledge Analysis Technologies, *378*
Knudson, R., 385, *392*
Kobayashi, H., 365, *378*, 522, *526*
Koenig, A. J., 388, *392*
Kolinsky, R., 282, *288*
Kolko, B., 603, *606*
Kolko, B. E., *262*
Köll, E., 100, *107*
Koopman, C. L., 487, *493*
Kopelson, K., 257, *262*
Korat, O., 407, *412*
Koretz, D., 369, 370, *378*
Korkeamaki, R.-L., 401, *412*
Kostelnick, C., 168, *170*, 601, *606*
Kötz, H., 134, *137*
Kozol, W., 259, *262*
Krahn, H., 339, *341*
Kramarae, C., 210, *215*,
    257, 260, *262*
Kramer, K., 419, *429*
Kramer, S. N., 141, *152*
Kras, R., 25, *31*
Kravetz, N., 499, *508*

Kress, G., 118, *121*, 207, *214*, 247, *249*, 272, *275*, 399, 402, 403, 405, 406, *412*, 514, *526*, 550, *558*, 572, *575*, 597, 599, *606*

Krishnamurty, N., 205, *214*

Kristeva, J., 439, *444*

Kroger, J., 496, *508*

Kroger, R., 272, *276*

Kroll, B., 369, *377*, 531, *543*

Kroll, B. M., *248*, 435, *444*

Kromer, B., 15, *20*

Kronick, D. A., 160, *170*, 181, *186*

Krugman, P., 103, *107*

Kruidenier, J., 423, *428*

Kruse, O., 164, *170*

Kubler, G. A., 25, 26, 27, *32*

Kubota, R., 383, 384, 387, *392*, 520, 521, *526*, 564, *575*

Kucera, H., 570, *575*

Kücklich, J., 604, *606*

Kuhn, D., 589, *591*

Kuipers, C. M., 191, *200*

Kumar, K., 286, *288*

Kumar, M., *494*

Kunde, B., 30, *32*

Kutner, M., 422, *428*

Kwachka, P. E., 364, *375*

L

Labbo, L., 399, 405, *412*

Labercane, G. D., 333, *341*

Lachiotte, W., 496, *508*

Lacqueur, T. W., 236, 237, 239, *249*

LaFollette, M., 161, *170*

Lakoff, G., 90, *94*, 588, *592*

Lakoff, R., 253, *262*

Lakoff, R. T., *543*

Lamb, C., 254, *262*

Lamb, D., 204, *214*

Lambert, D. A., 218, *231*

Lambrou, A., 23, 25, *32*

Lancaster, L., 399, 400, 402, 405, *412*

Land, R. E., 368, *380*

Landow, G., 436, *444*

Landow, G. P., 602, *606*

Lane, H., 389, *392*

Lange, P. C., 336, *341*

Langer, J., 364, *378*, 403, *412*

Langer, J. A., 433, *444*, 450, 456, 457, 460, *464*, 503, *508*

Langman. L., 30, *32*

Langston, C. A., 390, *392*

Lanham, R., 597, *606*

Lankshear, C., 424, *428*, *429*, 434, *444*

Largy, P., 433, *442*, 454, *463*

Larkin, J. H., 447, *464*

Larson, J., 407, *413*

Lassen, P., 273

Latour, B., 19, 85, 90, *94, 21*, 104, *107*, 111, *121*, 266, 271, *276*, 586, *592*

Latterell, C. G., 354, *358*

Lau, D. C., 193, *200*

Lauer, J. M., 328, *341*

Lauer, J., 257, *262*, 321, *324*, 517, *524*

Lautamatti, L., 569, *575*

Lavallée, D., 65, *78*

Lave, J., 224, *230*, 398, *413*, 434, *444*, 568, *575*

Lavoie, M., 101, *108*

Law, J., 335, *341*, 352, *359*

Lawall, S., 188, *200*

Lawrence, T., 268, *275*

Lawson, J., 347, *358*

Lawson, L. L., 292, 293, *303*

Lazare, G., 285, *288*

Lder, N., 367, *379*

Lea, M. R., 336, *341*

Leahy, R., 352, *358*

LeBlanc, P., 334, *340*, 602, *605*

Lebvre, L., *32*

Lechtman, H., 65, *78*

Lecours, A. Roch., 469, *478*

LeCourt, D., 256, *263*, 506, *508*

Lee, A. J., 203, *213, 214*

Lee, A. M., 202, *214*

Lee, D. Y. W., 570, *575*

Lee, I., 569, *575*

Lee, K., 450, *464*

Lee, T. H. C., 148, *152*

Leech, G., 534, *543*, 545, 546, 550, 556, 557, *559*, 570, 572, 573

LeFevre, J.-A., 407, *414*

Leff, G., 154, *170*

Leinhardt, G., 441, *446*, 554, *559*

Leitão, S., 589, *592*

Leki, I., 511, 512, 516, *526*

LeMahieu, P., 370, *378*

Lemaire, P., 454, *463*

Lemke, J., 92, *95*, 267, 273, *276*, 398, 407, *413*, 434, 439, *444*

Lemke, J. L., 572, *575*

Lentz, T. M., 580, *592*

Leonard, L. B., 470, *479*

Leonard, P., 424, *429*

Leontiev, A. N., 434, *444*

Lerner, F., 179, *186*

Lerner, N., 332, *341*

Leroi-Gourhan, A., 8, *21*

Leroi-Gourhan, S., 8, *21*

Lesko, N., 418, *428*

Lessig, L., 604, *606*

Lethaby, W. R., 58, *64*

Leung, C., 555, *559*

Levin, I., 291, 292, 302, *304*, 305, 407, *412*

Levine, A., 516, *526*

Levine, J. M., 155, *170*

Levinson, P., 30, *32*

Levis, Q. D., 280, 281, *288*

Levy, C. M., 452, 453, 455, 456, *464, 465*

Levy, D., 101, *108*

Lewin, B. A., *574*

Lewis, G., 399, *413*, 441, *444*

Lewis, M. E., 110, *121*
Lewison, M., 399, 408, *412*
Li, D., 572, *576*
Li, H., 389, *392* Lindgren, E., *393*
Li, X.-M., 522, *526*
Libanius, 345, *358*
Lichtenberg, J., 206, *214*
Lichtheim, M., 142, *152*, 188, 198, *200*
Lievrouw, L. A., 157, *170*
Light, J. C., 476, *479*
Lillis, T. M., 338, *341*
Lin, L.-C., 473, *478*
Lin, S. C., 177, *186*
Lincoln, Y., *377*
Lindemann, E., 353, *358*
Lindgren, T., 603, *606*
Lingard, L., 116, *122*, 156, *171*
Linn, R., 362, *378*
Linton, M., 451, 460, 461, *462*
Lisberg, B. C., 222, *227*
Liss, J., 474, *478*
Little, J., 330, *339*, 458, 459, *461*
Littleton, A. C., 156, *170*
Littleton, E. B., 450, *464*
Liu, H., 189, *200*
Liu, J., 195, *200*, 516, *526*
Livingston, S., 367, *378*
Livingstone, A., 66, *78*
Lloyd, G. D., 145, *151*
Lloyd, L. L., 473, *479*, *480*
Lloyd-Jones, R., 308, 313, 320, *323*, *324*, 328, *339*
Logan, S., 256, *263*
Lomax, R. G., 433, *445*
Lombardino, L. J., 475, *477*
Long, R., 400, 401, *412*
Lonsdale, M., 420, *428*
Loofbourrow, P., 369, *378*
Loos, E., 519, *526*
Lorch, M., 468, *477*
Lord, A. B., 188, *200*
Louhiala-Salminen, L., 519, *526*
Lounsbury, F., 16, *21*
Lowry, M. R., 436, *444*
Lowry, P. B., 436, *444*
Loy, D., 106, *108*
Lu, C., *186*, *200*
Lu, G., 148, *152*
Lu, X., 89, *95*
Lucaites, J., 601, *606*
Lucas, R., 102, *108*
Luckman, T., 207, *212*
Luff, P., 91, *94*
Luke, A., *428*, 568, *575*
Luke, C., 426, *429*
Lumer, C., 587, *592*
Lumley, M. A., 484, *494*
Lundmark, T., 27, 28, *32*
Lunsford, A., 85, *95*, 255, 256, 257, 259, *263*, 436, 443, 582, *591*
Lunsford, A. A., 329, *340*, 583, 588, *592*

Lunsford, K., 88, *95*
Luo, S., 149, *152*
Lutgendorf, S. K., 485, 488, *493*, *494*
Lutz, J. A., 220, *230*
Luzon Marco, M. J., 571, *575*
Lyketsos, C., 469, *478*
Lynch, D. A., 589, *592*
Lynch, J. J., 307, 308, 309, 310, *324*
Lynch, J. P., 146, *152*
Lyon, J. G., 474, *479*
Lyotard, J. F., 266, *276*
Lysaker, J., 405, *413*

M

Ma, Z., 86, *95*
Mabrito, M., 219, *230*
MacArthur, C., 389, *392*, 451, *463*
MacArthur, C. A., 297, *304*, 454, *464*, 471, 472, *479*
MacCurdy, M., 491, *494*
MacDonald, A., 470, *477*
MacDonald, M. L., 69, *78*
MacDonald, S. P., 167, *170*, 548, 554, *558*, 589, *592*
Mace, J., 245, 247, *249*
MacGillivray, L., 408, *413*
MacGregor, A., 158, *170*
Machado, S. F., 402, *411*
Macherel, C., 72, *78*
Mack, M., 188, *200*
Mackie, C., 471, *479*
Mackler, K., 426, *427*
Macrorie, K., 253, *263*
Mahar, D., 418, *427*
Mahiri, J., 258, *263*, 418, *429*
Maier, M., 407, *413*
Makdisi, G., 151, *152*
Mallam, D., 334, *341*
Mallarmé, S., 595, *606*
Malthus, T., 102, *108*
Mann, W. C., 546, *558*
Manning, M., 400, 401, *412*
Manovich, L., 82, *95*, 182, *186*, 595, *606*
Mansbridge, A., 242, *248*
Many, J. E., 399, *413*, 441, *444*
Manyak, P., 407, *413*
Manzer, B. M., 181, *186*
Maor, F. S., 259, *262*
Maoz, I., 590, *591*
Marback, R., 601, *606*
Marchand, E., 452, 453, 454, *463*, *464*
Marckwardt, A. H., 349, *356*
Marcus, G., 85, *93*
Marcus, G. E., 167, *169*
Marcus, J., 142, *151*
Margulies, S., 482, 485, *493*
Markkanen, R., 336, *341*
Markoe, G. E., 15, *21*
Markoff, J., 30, *32*
Markova, I., 475, *477*
Markus, H. R., 496, *508*
Marschark, M., 390, *392*

Marsella, J., 368, *376*
Marshall, A., 103, *108*
Marshall, J., 468, 469, 470, 474, *479*
Marshall, O., 205, *214*
Martens, P., 398, *414*
Martens, P. A., 401, 406, *413*
Martin, D., 363, *379*, 423, *428*
Martin, H., 23, 24, 25, *32*
Martin, H.-J., 65, 72, *78*, 111, *121*
Martin, J., 90, *95*, 272, *276*
Martin, J. R., 160, *170*, 553, 555, 556,
        558, *559*, 563, 565, *575*
Martin, L., 421, 423, *429*
Martin, N., 92, *93*, 321, *324*, 459, *462*
Martin, R., 424, 426, *429*
Martin, S., 24, 26, *32*
Martin, S. E., 204, *213*
Martinez, A. M., 408, *413*
Martinez, M. G., 292, *305*
Martin-Jones, M., 425, *427*
Martlew, M., 291, *303*
Marwah, K., 105, *106*
Marx, B. P., 491, *494*
Marx, K., 102, *108*
Mason, L., 300, *303, 304*, 399, *413*
Massey, C., 402, *411*
Massey, L., 259, *262*
Matheson, D., 207, *214*
Matheson, N., 422, *428*
Mathews, P., 143, *152*
Mathison, M. A., 440, *444*
Mathy, P., 475, *479*
Mathy, P. A., 474, *478*
Matsuda, P. K., 513, 521, *526*
Matsuhashi, A., 313, *324*, 367, *378*
Matthias, S., 366, *377*
Matthiessen, C., 547, *559*
Matthiessen, C. M. I. M., 546, 547, *558*
Mauranen, A., 565, 572, *574, 575*
Mauss, M., 72, *78*
Mavrogenes, N. A., 502, 503, *508*
Mawhood, L., 476, *477*
Maxwell, M. M., 390, *392*
May, T., 116, *121*
Mayall, D., 236, 239, *248*
Mayer, C., 401, *413*
Mayne, T. J., 485, *494*
McArthur, T., 158, *170*
McAuliffe, S., 408, *413*
McCabe, B. J., 308, *325*
McCaffrey, D., 370, *378*
McCalman, I., *77*
McCann, T., 316, *325*
McCarry, S., 258, *263*
McCarthey, S., 418, *429*
McCarthy Young, K., 554, *559*
McCarthy, L., 223, *230*
McCarthy, L. P., 116, *121*, 336, *341*
McCarthy, M., 549, *559*
McCartney, S., 29, *32*

McChesney, R. W., 109, *122*
McCleery, A., *78*
McCloskey, D., 89, *95*, 103, 104, *107, 108*, 167, *170*
McCloskey, M., 469, *477*
McCloud, S., 597, *606*
McCoy, L., 117, *122*
McCracken, E., 210, *214*
McCulley, G. A., 569, *575*
McCurry, D., 420, *428*
McCutchen, D., 290, *304*, 432, *444*, 447, 449, 450,
        451, 452, 453, 454, 455, 456, 457, 460, *464*
McDermott, S., 447, *464*
McDonald, P., *78*, 203, 210, *214*
McEnery, A. M., 533, *543*
McFadden, T. U., 471, *479*
McGann, J., 76, *78*, 196, *200*
McGee, S.J., 259, *261*
McIlwaine, I. C., 180, *186*
McInnis, R. G., 442, *444*
McIntyre, E., 294, *304*
McIsaac, C., 219, *230*
McKee, H., 334, *341*
McKenzie, D. F., *79*
McKeon, M., 195, *200*
McKeown, M., 285, *288*
McKeown, M. G., 438, *443*
McKerrow, R. B., *79*
McKinney, J. G., 355, *358*
McLachlan, S., *214*
McLane, J. B., 290, *304*
McLaren, P., 424, *428, 429*
McLendon, L., 421, 423, *429*
McLeod, A., 92, *93*, 321, *324*, 459, *462*
McLeod, W. R., *213*
McLuhan, M., *21*, 65, *79*, 195, *200*, 207, 211, *214*
McLuskey, K., 109, 115, *122*
McManus, H. R., 207, *214*
McNeil, M. R., 468, *480*
McNelly, M. E., 365, 366, *378*
McRobbie, A., 258, *263*
McVicar, R., 471, *477*
Meade, R. A., 349, *356*
Meadow, C., 29, 30, 31, *32*
Meath-Lang, B., 390, *391*
Medina, P., 422, *427*
Medway, P., 222, 224, 226, *228, 230*, 299, *304*
Megarry, R., 133, *136*
Mehan, H., 422, *429*, 496, *508*
Meier, W. A., *79*
Mellon, J., 313, *325*
Meltzer, N. S., 401, *413*
Mendonça, C. O., 516, *526*
Merritt, D., 207, *214*
Merryman, J. H., 135, *136*
Mersand, J., 349, *356*
Merton, R. K., 161, *170*
Messaris, P., 598, 600, *606*, 598, *606*
Messick, S., 362, 363, 364, *378, 379*
Meyer, B. J. F., 457, *464*
Meyer, C., 533, *544*

Meyer, C. A., 372, *379*
Meyer, D., 205, 211, *214*
Meyer, E. A., 128, *136*
Meyer, M., 118, *122*
Meyer, P.R., 352, *356*
Meyer, V., 422, *429*
Meyers, M., 211, *214*
Meyers, P., 256, *263*
Meza, M., 426, *429*
Michaels, S. A., 498, 501, *508*
Michon, J., *79*
Mignolo, W. D., 597, *606*
Miksa, F. L., 181, *186*
Mildes, K., 454, *464*
Mill, J. S., 102, *108*
Millar, D. C., 476, *479*
Miller, B., 513, *524*
Miller, C., 299, *304*
Miller, C. R., 116, *122*, 223, *229*, 434, *444*, 564, *575*,
    582, 584, 590, *592*, 603, *606*
Miller, S., 513, *524*
Miller, T. P., 217, *229*
Miller, W., 449, 451, *465*
Milner, A., *79*
Milton, J., 556, *558*
Miner, K. N., *493*
Mirenda, P., 473, 474, 476, 477, *479*
Mirzoeff, N., 595, 598, *606*
Mischel, T., *325*
Mishler, E., 511, *526*
Mitch, D. F., 233, 239, 243, *249*
Mitchell, E., 399, *413*, 441, *444*
Mitchell, F., 329, *341*
Mitchell, K., 369, *378*
Mitchell, R., 372, *379*
Mitchell, W. J. T., 596, *606*
Mlynarczyk, R., 333, *341*
Modern Language Association, 327, *341*
Modiano, M., 520, *526*
Moffett, J., *263*, 562, *575*
Moglen, H., 588, *592*
Moje, E. B., 418, 419, *429*
Mokhtari, K., 404, *413*
Mollier, J.-Y., *79*
Montgomery, S. L., 86, *95*
Mookerji, K. R., 144, 145, *152*
Moon, P., 87, *94*
Moor, C., 483, 484, *494*
Moore, D. W., 418, *426*, *429*
Moore, M. T., 368, *380*
Moore, R. H., 352, *358*
Moore, T., 219, *227*
Moorey, P. R. S., 13, *21*
Moos, M. E., *21*
Morahan, S., 354, *358*
Morais, J., 282, *288*
Moran, C., 334, *340*, 374, *379*, 602, *605*
Moreno, A. I., 572, *575*
Mores, E. R., 48, *64*
Morgan, A., 346, *358*

Morgan, M., 219, *227*, 372, *379*
Morison, S., 42, 43, 44, 45, 50, 58, *64*
Morley, C., 349, *358*
Morley, D., 245, *249*
Morris, C., 128, *136*
Morris, M., 363, *375*
Morrison, S., 469, 470, *479*
Morrow, P. R., 554, *559*
Mortensen, L., 470, *479*
Mortensen, P., 244, *248*, 256, *263*
Morton, C., 483, 492, *494*
Mosco, V., 109, *122*
Moser, G., 449, 451, *465*
Moshenko, B., 450, *462*
Moskos, E., 401, *413*
Moss, P., 373, *379*
Mott, F. L., 201, *214*
Mountford, R., 601, *606*
Mouradian, V., 390, *392*
Moya, P. M. L., 500, *508*
Muchiri, M. N., 522, *526*
Mulholland, J., 519, *526*
Muller, E., 475, *479*
Müller, J.-D., *79*
Mumby, D., 266, 268, *276*
Mumby, F. A., 25, 26, 27, *32*
Munger, R., 224, *230*
Murphy, C., 335, *341*, 352, 353, 354, *358*, *359*
Murphy, J., 475, *477*
Murphy, J. J., 344, 346, 347, 348, *358*, *359*
Murphy, S., 363, 364, 369, 370, 371, *379*, *380*
Murray, D., 175, *186*, 253, *263*, 295, *304*
Murray, D. E., 221, *230*
Murray, D. M., 352, 355, *359*
Murray, J., 604, *606*
Murray, J. E., Jr., 131, *136*
Murray, L. L., 469, 470, *479*
Myers, G., 83, 85, 90, *95*, 160, 161, *170*,
    223, *230*, 266, *276*, 456, *464*, 554, 555,
    556, *559*, 584, 585, *592*
Myers, N., 354, *360*
Myers, P. S., 468, *479*

N

Nagelhout, E., 328, *341*
Nagin, C., 349, *359*
Nagy, C., 17, *21*
Nakamura, L., 603, *606*
Narius P., 496, *508*
Nash, J. G., 447, 449, *463*
Nasir, N. S., 496, *508*
Natarajan, J., 205, *214*
Natelson, R. G., 130, *136*
Nathan, R., 401, *414*
National Assessment of
    Educational Progress, 320, *325*
National Center for Education Statistics, 495, *508*
National Center for Learning Disabilities, 389, *392*
National Council of Teachers of English, 252, *263*
National Education Association, 495, *508*

National Research Council, 441, *444*
National Writing Project, 349, *359*
Neal, L., 101, *108*
Needels, M. C., 503, *508*
Needham, J., 26, *32*, 148, *152*
Needham, L., 589, *591*
Negro, I., 454, *462*
Nelms, G., 339, *341*
Nelson, C., 474, 476, *478*
Nelson, C. H., 363, *378*
Nelson, G. L., 516, *524, 527*
Nelson, J., 102, *107*, 337, *341*
Nelson, N., 298, *304*, 431, 435, 440, *444*
Nelson, N. W., 470, 471, *479*
Nelson, T., 182
Nevitt, M., 210, *215*
New London Group, 424, *429*, 599, *606*
Newell, A., 447, 449, *464*
Newell, G. E., 458, 460, *464*
Newkirk, P., 205, *215*
Newkirk, T., 258, *263*, 296, *304*, 329,
    333, *341*, 402, 405, 408, *413*
Newman, J. H., 588, *591, 592*
Newman, S. P., 348, *359*
Nicholas, M., 474, *480*
Nickerson, C., 519, *527*
Nickoson-Massey, L., 259, *262*
Niditch, S., 13, *21*
Nielsen, J., 436, *445*
Nietz, J. A., 286, *288*
Nissenbaum, H., 183, *186*
Nixon, P., 468, *479*
Noble, G., 299, *303*
Noegel, S. B., 66, *79*
Noel, S., 437, *445*
Noguera, P., 496, *508*
Nolen, S. B., 300, *304, 377*
Nord, D. P., 202, *215*
Norman, S. A., 484, *494*
Norris, E. A., 404, *413*
North, J., 154, *170*
North, S. M., *341*, 352, *359*
Northend, C., 349, *359*
Nowell, A., 323, *324*
Nunberg, G., 109, *122*
Nunes, T., 287
Nunez, A., 371, *380*
Nyberg, A. K., 596, *606*
Nystrand, M., 81, *95*, 225, *230*, 315, *325*, 370, *379*,
    435, *445*, 447, *464*, 545, 559, 582, *592*

O

O'Brien, D. G., 419, *428*
O'Conner, D., 142, *152*
O'Connor, C., 500, *508*
O'Connor, M., 188, *200*
O'Donnell, R. C., 531, *544*
O'Halloran, K., 556, *557*
O'Heeron, R., *494*
O'Neill, P., 369, *379*

O'Reilly, M., 474, *480*
O'Rourke, R., 245, *249*
O'Shea, M. V., 328, *342*
Oakley, A., 256, *263*
Oded, B., 516, *526*
Odell, L., 219, *230*, 363, *379*
Oettinger, A. G., 29, 30, *32*
Ogbu, J. U., 496, 500, 501, *508*
Okamura, K., 221, *231*
Okolo, C., 389, *392*
Olbrechts-Tyteca, L., 89, *95*, 581, 582, 586, *593*
Olive, T., 451, 452, 453, 455, 456, *465*
Oliveira, R. M., 468, *479*
Oliver, J.-P., 65, *79*
Oliver, L., 131, *136*
Olsen, L. A., 225, 227, *230*, 563, *574*
Olsen, T., 233, *249*
Olson, D., 81, 83, 87, *95*
Olson, D. R., *21*, 111, *122*, 281, 283, 284, 286,
    288, 283, *288*, 283, *288*, 284, 287, 292,
    296, *304*, 531, *544*, 580, *593*
Olson, H. A., 181, *186*
Olson, J. L., 402, *413*
Olson, M., 363, *379*
Ong, W., 83, 87, *95*, 266, *276*, 531, *544*
Ong, W. J., 65, *79*, 139, *152*, 187, 189,
    193, *200*, 580, 582, 584, *593*
Oppenheim, A. L., 83, 90, *95*
Orellana, M., 426, *429*
Orellana, M. F., 499, *509*
Orlikowski, W., 566, *577*
Orlikowski, W. J., 219, 221, 224, 226, *230, 231*
Ormerod, P., 102, *108*
Osterlind, S., 338, *340*
Overing, G., 253, *261*
Owens, T. J., 496, *509*
Owocki, G., 398, *414*

P

Padden, C., 389, *392*
Padmore, S., 247, *249*
Page, E., 374, *379*
Pahl, K., 233, *249*, 399, 402, *413*
Palazolo, K., 474, 476, *478*
Palesh, O., 487, *493*
Palmer, A. S., 362, *375*
Palmquist, M., 588, *591*
Paltridge, B., 565, *576*
Palumbo, D. B., 441, *445*
Pan, J., 167, *170*
Pandit, L., *199*
Paradis, J., 435, *443*
Parasnis, I., 389, *392*
Pardoe, S., 337, *341*
Paré, A., 116, *122*, 223, 224, 226, 228, *230*, 567, *576*
Parella, A., 426, *427*
Park, R. E., 202, *215*
Parker, R., 103, *108*
Parker, R. G., 349, *359*
Parker, R. P., 350, *359*

Parker, W. R., 166, *170*, 351, *359*
Parks, S., 567, *576*
Parr, S., 470, *479*
Partington, A., 572, *576*
Parton, J., 202, *215*
Parvin, V. E., 284, 285, *288*
Pascarella, E., 338, *340*
Passingham, R. E., 468, *479*
Patai, D., 256, *262*
Patell, C. R. K., 522, *527*
Pattee, G. L., 475, *477*
Patterson, P. A., 471, *479*
Patthey-Chavez, G. G., 335, *341*
Paul, D., *230*, 572, *576*, 584, 589, *593*
Paul, P., 390, *393*
Paul, P. V., 390, *393*
Paulson, F. L., 372, *379*
Paulson, P. P., 372, *379*
Paulukonis, S., 371, *380*
Paulus, T., 516, *527*
Pavlik, J. V., 211, *215*
Payne, D. G., 221, *231*
Pearson, J., 572, *573*
Pearson, P. D., 432, *446*
Pecci, F., 484, *494*
Pedersen, O., 156, *170*
Peet, R., 101, *108*
Pellizzoni, L., 587, *593*
Pemberton, M. A., 335, *341*
Pennebaker, J. W., 481, 482, 485, 489, 490, 491, 492, *493*, *494*
Pennycook, A., 520, 521, *527*
Penrose, A., 585, *593*
Pera, M., 160, *171*
Peregoy, S. F., 513, *527*
Perelman, C., 89, *95*, 581, 582, 586, *593*
Pérez, B., 513, 514, *527*
Perez, S., 404, *413*
Perl, S., 350, *359*
Perrett, R. W., 144, *152*
Perry, W. G., 283, *288*
Perry, W. G., Jr., 588, *593*
Persichetti, S., 484, *494*
Pesaran, M. H., 105, *108*
Pestalozzi, J. H., 348, *359*
Petersen, N. S., 374, *379*
Peterson, M., 168, *171*
Peterson, S., 408, *413*
Petraglia, J., 296, *305*
Petrie, K. J., 482, *494*
Petroski, H., 24, *32*
Peyton, J. K., 390, *393*
Pezzolo, L., 100, *108*
Phelps, L., 82, *95*
Phelps, L. W., 253, 254, *263*, 569, *576*
Phelps, S. F., 418, *426*
Phillips, B., 475, *478*
Phillips, J., 372, *378*
Phillips, M., 322, *324*
Phillips, N., 268, *275*

Phippen, A. R., 349, *359*
Piaget, J., 435, *445*
Pianko, S. H., *325*
Piazza, C., 369, *380*
Piche, G. L., 368, *376*, *379*, 551, *557*
Pierson, C. T., 338, *340*
Pike, K. L., 587, 588, *594*
Piolat, A., 451, 452, 455, 456, *465*
Pipher, M., 258, *263*
Pizzamiglio, L., 469, *479*
Plante, E., 469, 470, 477, 470, *479*
Plato, 23, 31, 32, 33, 83, 87, 95, 343, 344, *359*, 580, 581, *593*
Plowman, L., 436, *445*
Plucknett, T. F. T., 130, 131, 132, *136*
Plumb, C., 451, 452, 456, 457, *462*
Pohl, M., 17, *21*
Polio, C., 366, 367, *379*, 515, *527*
Pontecorvo, C., 291, *305*, 400, *413*
Pool, J., 369, *378*
Poole, M. E., 532, *544*
Poon, L. W., 457, *464*
Pope, K., 17, *21*
Popkin, J. D., 204, *215*
Popper, K. R., 586, 587, 588, *593*
Porter, J., 604, *607*
Porter, J. E., 434, *445*, 566, *576*, 582, *593*
Porter, T. M., 162, 167, *171*
Posner, E., 173, *186*
Possehl, G., 15, *21*
Poster, C., 260, *263*
Potter, S. J., 204, *215*
Pound, C., 474, *479*
Poursat, J.-C., 15, *21*
Powell, B. B., 195, *200*
Power, B. M., 403, 407, *413*
Powers, D. E., 367, *379*
Powers-Stubbs, K., 251, *261*
Pozo, J. I., 450, *465*
Prater, D., 441, *445*
Pratt, M. L., 522, *527*
Prendergast, C., 92, *95*, 315, *325*
Price, L., 76, *79*
Priestley, J., 347, *359*
Pring, T., 469, 470, 478, *479*
Pringle, I., 368, *376*
Prior, L., 118, *122*
Prior, P., 83, 85, 88, *95*, 167, *171*, 579, *590*
Prior, P. A., 473, 478, 518, 524, 566, 567, 568, 572, *576*
Proctor, A., 469, *480*
Proctor, M., 283, *288*
Proctor-Williams, K., 471, *478*
Propp, V., 432, *445*
Pucci, E., 601, *604*
Purcell-Gates, V., 407, *413*, 421, 425, 426, *429*
Purves, A. C., 321, 323, *324*, *325*
Purvis, J., 238, 239, *249*

Q

Quellmalz, E., 368, *379*
Quellmalz, E. S., 370, *380*
Quick, D., *230*
Quinlan, T., 454, 459, *465*
Quintilian., 89, *95*, 348, *359*
Quirk, R., 545, 546, 550, *559*

R

Raboy, M., 209, *215*
Ramanathan, V., 387, 391, *393*, 520, 523, *527*
Ramati, A., 483, 492, *494*
Rampton, B., 555, *559*
Rankin, H. D., 268, *276*
Ransdell, S., 452, 453, 454, 455, 456, *464, 465*
Rapcsak, S. Z., 469, *477*
Raphael, T. E., 298, *303, 305*
Raskind, M. H., 334, *341*
Ratliff, C., 603, *607*
Ravelli, L., 552, *559*
Ravelli, L. J., 552, *559*
Raymond, J., 157, *171*, 203, *215*
Rayward, W. B., 180, 182, *186*
Readence, J. E., 418, *429*
Realpe-Bonilla, T., 471, *478*
Reay, D., 454, *463*
Redeker, G., 518, *524*
Reder, S., 217, *229*
Redish, J. C., 222, *230*
Reece, J. E., 453, 454, 459, *465*
Reed, B. S., 205, *214*
Reed, D., 70, *79*
Reed, J., 259, *263*
Reedy, D., 298, *305*, 404, *413*
Reese, C., 368, *377*
Reichard, C., 404, *413*
Reichelt, M., 511, *527*
Reid, D., 476, *478*
Reid, J., 367, *379*, 569, *576*
Reidy, M., 160, 161, *170*, 564, *574*
Reither, J. A., 437, *445*
Renfrew, C., 139, *152*
Reymond, E., 142, *152*
Resnick, L., 372, *380*
Reppen, R., 386, *393*, 518, *524*, 533,
    541, *543*, 563, *576*
Reymond, E., 142, *152*
Reynolds, D., 386, *393*
Reynolds, E., 372, *375*
Reynolds, J., 15, *21*, 426, *429*
Reynolds, L. D., 175, *186*
Reynolds, N., 354, 355, *356, 359*
Reynolds, R. E., 432, *443*
Rhodes, L. K., 503, *507*
Ricardo, D., 102, *108*
Riccardi, A., 87, *95*
Rich, A., 252, *263*
Richards, I., 83, *95*
Richards, J. M., *494*
Richardson, S., 87, *95*

Richman, P., 192, *200*
Ricoeur, P., 580, *593*
Ridder-Symoens, H., 154, *171*
Rieke, R., 588, *593*
Riel, M., 583, *591*
Rife, M., 604, *607*
Rigg, P., 422, *428*
Rijlaarsdam, G., 433, *446*, 450, 451, *462, 465*
Riley, J., 298, *305*, 404, *413*
Rinnert, C., 365, *378*, 522, *526*
Ritchie, J., 253, 255, 256, *262, 263*, 344, *359*
Robb, K., 126, 127, *136*
Robbins, R., 349, *359*
Robbins, S., 349, *360*
Robert, J. M., 437, *445*
Roberts, B., 207, 208, *213*, 401, *413*
Roberts, B. J., 517, *525*
Roberts, C., *544*, 555, *559*
Roberts, D. D., 601, *606*
Roberts, J., 167, *171*
Roberts, M., 469, *479*
Roberts-Miller, P., 583, 587, 588, 589, *593*
Robertson, A. J., 130, *136*
Robertson, L. R., 336, *342*
Robinson, D., 86, *95*
Robson, J., 469, 470, *478, 479*
Robson, J. M., 202, *215*
Robyns, A., 364, *379*
Rock, D., 363, *375*
Roderick, G. W., 238, *250*
Rodman, G., 603, *606*
Rodriguez, C., 205, *215*
Rogan, L., 294, *303*, 472, *477*
Rogan, L. W., 453, *462*
Rogers, D., 490, 493, *494*
Rogers, H., 18, *21*
Rogers, P., 271, *276*
Rogers, R., 246, *249*
Rogoff, I., 598, *607*
Rohan, L., 601, *607*
Rohman, D. G., 295, *305*
Romano, S., 603, *607*
Romano, T., 350, *359*
Romantic Audience Project, 603, *607*
Romanyshyn, R., 597, *607*
Ronald, K., 256, *263*, 344, *359*
Ronan, C. A., 148, *152*
Ronell, A., 595, *607*
Rooney, P., 371, *379*
Rose, D., 555, 558, *559*
Rose, J., 76, *78*, 233, 236, 237, 238, 241, *249*
Rose, M., 70, 71, 72, *79*, 222, *230*,
    248, 269, *276*, 498, *509*
Rosen, H., 92, 93, 321, *324*, 459, *462*
Rosenberg, H. J., 483, *494*
Rosenberg, S., 457, *465*
Rosenberg, S. D., 483, *494*
Ross, D., 167, *171*
Rothery, J., 554, 556, *559*, 565, *575*
Rouncefield, M., 112, *121*

Roussey, J.-Y., 451, 452, 455, 456, *465*
Rowan, K. E., 457, *465*
Rowbotham, S., 245, *249*
Rowe, D. W., 399, 402, 405, 406, 407, *413*
Rowley-Jolivet, E., 570, *576*
Rowntree, J. W., *249*
Royer, D., 372, *379*
Royster, J. J., 244, *249*, 256, *263*, 384, 391, *393*
Rozendal, M. S., 404, *410*
Rubin, D. C., 139, *152*, 189, 192, *200*
Rubin, D. L., *379*, 435, *445*
Rubin, H., 471, *479*
Rubin, J. S., 29, 30, *32*
Rude, G., 239, *249*
Ruegg, W., 158, 165, *171*
Rumelhart, D. E., 432, *445*
Rummer, R., 453, *463*
Rupier, A., 354, *360*
Russell, D., 90, *95*, *106*, 225, 230, 296, *305*, 361, *376*
Russell, D. R., 225, *230*, 330, 336, 337, 342,
    521, *525*, 566, 567, *576*
Russo, A., 210, *215*
Ruth, L., *379*
Rutter, M., 476, *477*
Rutz, C., 328, *341*
Ryan, L., 354, *359*
Ryan, M. L., 604, *607*
Ryle. G., 119, *122*
Rymer, J., 218, *228*
Rymes, B., 418, *429*

S

Sabin, R., 596, *607*
Sablo, S., 418, *429*
Sacchett, C., 474, *479*
Sachs, J., 103, *108*
Sadker, D., 257, *263*
Sadker, M., 257, *263*
Sager, C., 316, *325*
Said, E. W., 520, *527*
Salmon, R., *215*
Salomon, G., 434, *445*
Samar, V. J., 390, *392*
Samraj, B., 565, *576*
Samuel F. B. Morse preview, 29, *33*
Samuel, A., 603, *607*
Samuels, W., 103, *108*
Samuelson, P., *108*
Sanders, K., *215*
Sanderson, M., 235, 237, 239, 243, *249*
Sanford, K., 408, *410*
Santos, T., 365, *379*, 516, *527*
Sarangi, S., 119, *122*
Sassoon, R., 5
Sauer, B., 116, *122*, 223, *230*
Sauer, E. H., 350, *359*
Scalia, A., 132, *136*
Scardamalia, M., 290, 296, 297, 298, *302*, *305*, 313,
    323, 434, *443*, 448, 449, 450, 451, 452, 453, 454,
    455, 457, 460, 461, *461*, 472, 477, 583, *590*

Scarre, C., 139, *152*
Schafer, W., 369, *375*, 472, *479*
Schaffer, S., 159, 160, *171*
Schaible, R., 337, *340*
Schallert, D. L., 432, *443*
Scharer, P. L., 292, 293, *303*
Schegloff, E. A., 511, *527*
Schele, L., 143, *152*
Schell, E. E., 257, 258, *263*
Scher, D., 426, *427*
Scherff, L., 369, *380*
Scheuer, N., 405, *415*, 450, *465*
Schiappa, E., 590, *593*
Schick, K., 354, *360*
Schickedanz, J. A., 406, *413*
Schieffelin, B., 88, *95*
Schiesel, S., 604, *607*
Schiffrin, A., *79*
Schiffrin, D., 118, *122*
Schiller, D., 109, *122*, 206, *215*
Schilperoord, J., 452, *465*
Schirmer, B. R., 390, *393*
Schleppegrell, M. J., 550, 551, 552, 554, *559*
Schlesinger, M., 204, *215*
Schlosser, R., 476, *479*
Schmandt-Besserat, D., 8, *22*, 13, *21*, 65, *79*
Schmidt, L. Z., 251, *263*
Schneider, J. J., 404, *414*, 502, 503, *509*
Schneider, M., 569, *576*
Schneider, 174, 175, See pp. 174, 175.
    Not in list. Initial? Please add.
Schneiderman, N., *494*
Schneirov, M., *79*
Schnotz, W., 432, *445*
Schoer, L., 308, 313, *323*, 328, *339*
Schofield, R., *249*
Schon, D. A., 372, *380*
Schriver, K., 585, *593*
Schriver, K. A., 222, *230*, *231*, 435,
    445, 455, *463*, 601, *607*
Schroder, H., 336, *341*
Schryer, C., 270, *276*
Schryer, C. F., 116, 119, *122*, *171*, 223,
    225, *231*, 564, 572, *576*
Schudson, M., 206, *215*
Schulman, L., 372, *380*
Schultz, J. R., 222, *231*
Schultz, K., 225, 229, 404, 405, *414*, 418, *428*
Schultz, L. M., 348, *357*, *359*
Schulz, K., 247, *249*
Schumacher, G. M., 218, *231*
Schumpeter, J., 102, *108*
Schut, H., 486, *494*
Schwartz, L., 485, *494*
Schwartz, S., 451, *463*, 472, *479*
Schwiebert, J. E., 337, *339*
Schwinges, R. C., 154, *171*
Scogin, H. T., Jr., 128, *136*
Scollon, R., 572, *576*
Scott, B. T., 218, *231*

Scott, C. M., 470, 471, 472, *480*, 550, *559*
Scott, L., 363, *377*
Scott, T., 371, *380*
Screpanti, E., 102, *108*
Scribner, S., 88, *95*, 140, *152*, 532, *544*
Scurlock, J. A., 13, *22*
Seagal, J. D., *494*
Seccareccia, M., 101, *108*
Secor, M., 223, *229*, 589, *591*
Secor, M. J., 587, *593*
Segal, J. Z., 224, *231*
Segers, M., 332, *340*
Segev-Miller, R., 441, *445*
Selfe, C., 92, *95, 96*, 255, 256, *263*
Selfe, C. L., 334, *340*, 602, 603, *605, 607*
Selfe, R., 603, *607*
Selinker, L., 553, *559*
Sellen, A., 30, *33*
Sellen, A. J., 220, *231*
Selzer, J., 218, *231*, 585, *591*
Senechal, M., 407, *414*
Senner, W., *22*
Serfaty, V., 211, *215*
Seymor, S., 177, *186*
Shanahan, T., 433, 439, *445*, 456, *462*
Shandler, S., 258, *263*
Shapin, S., 159, 160, *171*
Share, D. L., 291, *304*
Sharp, J. M., 457, *461*
Sharp, L. K., *494*
Sharples, M., 436, *445*
Shatil, E., 291, *304*
Shattock, J., 210, *215*
Shaughnessy, M., 352, *359*
Shaw, D., 442, *443*
Shaw, P., 168, *171*
Shea, W., 160, *171*
Sheehan, M. M., 129, *136*
Sheese, B. E., 489, *494*
Sheingold, K., 371, *380*
Shen, F., 513, *527*
Shepard, L., 370, *380*
Shepherd, D., 603, *606*
Sheridan, D., 244, 245, *249, 250*
Sheridan, T., 347, *359*
Sheridan-Rabideau, M., 92, *95*
Sheridan-Rabideau, M. P., 258, 259, *262, 263*
Sherman, S., 203, *215*
Shermis, M. D., 374, *380*
Sherwin, J. S., 328, *342*
Sherwood, S., 335, *341*, 354, *359*
Sherzer, J., 18, *20*
Shevelow, K., 210, *215*
Shils, E., 167, *171*
Shinn, N., 59, *64*
Shipka, J., 89, *96*
Sholle, D., 23, 30, 31, *33*
Shor, I., 423, 424, *429*
Short, K. G., 404, *414*
Shotter, J., 167, *171*

Siebert, F. S., 203, 206, *215*
Siegel, M., 402, *414*
Sigafoos, J., 474, *480*
Signorini, A., 400, *410*
Silk, C. M., 330, *340*, 449, 451, *465*
Silva, T., 511, 515, *526, 527*, 551, *559*
Silverman, D., 142, *152*
Silzer, B. J., 339, *341*
Simmons, J., 367, *380*, 408, *414*
Simmons, W., 372, *380*
Simon, H., 447, 449, *464*
Simon, H. A., 447, *464*
Simon-Vandenbergen, A.-M., 552, *559*
Sims, B. R., 221, *231*
Sinclair, J., 570, *576*
Singer, B. D., 471, 472, *480*
Singer, G., 485, *493*
Sipe, L., 400, 404, 405, *414*
Siraisi, N., 154, *171*
Sirc, G., 92, *96*
Sitko, B., 585, *593*
Skidelsky, R., 102, 105, *108*
Skinner, D., 496, *508*
Slaughter, M. M., 160, *171*
Slevin, J., 588, *592*
Sloan, B., 208, *215*
Sloan, D. M., 491, *494*
Sloan, W. D., 202, *215*
Sloane, T. O., 579, 581, 586, *593*
Slobin, D., 282, *288*
Sluijsmans, D., 332, *340*
Smagorinsky, P., 312, 316, *325*, 351, *358, 359*, 369, *378*, 433, 434, *445*, 585, *593*
Small, H., 442, *445*
Smart, G., 101, 103, 104, 105, *108*, 224, *231*, 519, *527*, 567, *576*
Smith, A., 105, *108*, 347, *359*
Smith, A. D., 207, 208, *215*
Smith, D., 91, *96*
Smith, D. E., 109, 110, 111, 117, 118, 119, *122*, 183, *186*
Smith, E., 355, *359*
Smith, G. R., 241, *250*
Smith, L. S., 370, *380*
Smith, M., 349, 355, *359*, 473, 476, *480*
Smith, M. L., 363, *380*
Smith, M. W., 258, *263*, 312, 316, *325*, 433, *445*
Smith, P., 286, 599, *605*
Smith, R. N., 552, *559*
Smith, S., 337, *342*
Smith, W. L., 366, 368, *380*
Smolkin, L. B., 403, *411, 414*
Smyth, J. M., *494*
Snow, C., 219, *227*
Snow, C. E., 419, 420, *427*
Snow, R., 211, *212*
Snyder, D. K., 486, *494*
Sohlberg, M. M., 470, *480*
Sokol, S. M., 469, *477*
Sola, G., 450, *465*

Solan, L. M., 132, *136*
Solano, L., 484, *494*
Soldi, A.-M., 65, *78*
Soliday, E., 490, 493, *494*
Solow, R., 103, *107*
Solsken, J., 398, 403, 407, 408, *414*, 522, *527*
Sommers, J., 373, *375*
Sommerville, C. J., 157, *171*
Sommerville, J., 203, *215*
Song, B., 365, 366, *380*
Soricone, L., 426, *427*
Sosnoski, J., *33*
Soto, G., 475, *479*
Sowers, S., 404, *414*
Soyland, A. J., 167, *171*
Spack, R., 520, *527*
Spafford, M., 116, *122, 171*
Sparks, B., 425, *429*
Sparks, C., 208, 209, *213*
Spaulding, E., 371, *380*
Speck, B. W., 329, 331, *342*
Spender, D., 253, *263*
Sperling, M., 318, 319, *325*, 329, *342*,
    437, 445, 500, 502, 503, *509*
Spicer-Escalante, M., 517, *527*
Spilka, R., 218, 226, *231*
Spinuzzi, C., 271, *276*
Spiro, R. J., 436, *445*
Spivey, G., 269, *276*
Spivey, N. N., 290, *305*, 440, 441, *445*
Splichal, S., 205, *215*
Spoel, P., 116, *122*
Spooner, M., 221, *231*
Spufford, M., 235, *250*
Squire, J. R., 281, 286, *287*, 349, *359*
Stafford, B. M., 602, *607*
Stafford, K., 355, *357*
Stahl, S. A., 292, 293, *305*
Stallard, C. K., 313, *325*
Stanley, C. E., *342*
Stanley, J. C., 314, *324*
Stanovich, K. E., 293, *305*
Star, S., 90, *93*
Starck, K., 207, *215*
Starfield, S., 385, 387, *393*, 499, *509*
Starr, P., 115, *122*
Stecher, B., 370, *378*
Stecher, B. M., 369, *380*
Steele, C. M., 501, *509*
Stein, N. L., 456, *465*
Stein, P., 514, *527*
Stein, S., 422, 424, *429*
Steiner, G., 440, *445*
Steiner, W., 596, *607*
Steinhaus, K., 368, *377*
Stenglin, M., 554, 556, *559*
Stephens, M. D., 238, *250*
Stephens, W. B., 236, *250*
Stern, N., 29, *33*
Sterner, J., 483, 484, *494*

Sternglass, M. S., 339, *342*
Stevens, D. D., 298, *303*
Stevens, J., 208, *215*
Stevens, L. P., 418, *429*
Stevenson, N., 210, *214*
Stewart, D. C., 351, 352, 353, *359*
Stewart, P. L., 352, 353, *359*
Sticht, T., 422, 423, *429*
Stiglitz, J., 103, *108*
Stillinger, J., 436, *445*
Stirling, J., 347, *360*
Stitt-Bergh, M., 372, *377*
Stock, B., 100, *108*, 110, 111, 112, 114, 115, 120, *122*
Stock, M., 242, 245, *250*
Stock, P., 257, 258, *263*
Stockton, S., 456, *465*
Stokstad, E., 17, *22*
Stone, A. A., 483, 486, 490, *493, 494*
Storms, B. A., 371, *380*
Stormzand, M. J., 328, *342*
Stotsky, S., 433, *446*, 569, *576*
Stough, L. M., 388, *392*
Stratman, J., 590, *593*
Stratman, J. F., 226, *231*, 455, *463*
Street, B., 470, *480*, 532, 533, *544*
Street, B. V., *250*, 336, 337, *341*, 398, *414*, 597, 600, *607*
Street, C. K., 471, *480*
Stricklin, S., 476, *478*
Stroebe, M., 486, *494*
Stroebe, W., 486, *494*
Strong, W., 313, 316, *325*
Stryker, S., 496, *509*
Stubbs, M., 533, *544*, 546, *559*, 571, *576*
Stygall, G., 223, *231*, 373, *375*, 517, 518, *524*, 562,
    573, 579, *590*
Suarez, M. F., *78*
Sullivan, A., 401, *414*
Sullivan, F., 364, *380*
Sullivan, K., *393*
Sullivan, P., 459, *465*
Sullivan, P. A., 256, 257, *262, 264*
Sulzby, E., 291, 292, *305*, 397, 400, 405, *412, 414*,
    456, *465*, 549, *557*
Surrency, E. C., 132, *136*
Susser, B., 334, *342*
Sutcliffe, A., 470, *480*
Svartvik, J., 545, 546, 550, *559*
Swaine, M., 29, 30, *32*
Swales, J., 90, *96*, 103, *108*, 167, 168, *171*,
    271, *276*, 518, *527*, 553, 554, *560*
Swales, J. M., 225, *231*, 563, 565, 566, 567,
    571, 572, *576*, 584, *593*
Swanson, H. L., 294, 302, 453, 454, *462*
Sweedler-Brown, C. O., 365, 366, *380*
Swindells, J., 234, 243, *250*
Swineford, E., 363, 368, *377*
Swineford, F., 319, *324*
Swiss, T., 31, *33*
Symonds, J. A., 37, *64*
Synder, P. A., 355, *357*

T

Takayoshi, P., 255, 260, *264*
Takayoshi, P., 603, *607*
Tallal, P., 471, *478*
Tannen, D., 118, *122*, 258, *264*, 532, 533, *544*
Tardibuono, J., *393*
Tardy, C. M., 566, *576*
Tarone, E., 518, *527*, 553, *559*
Tarule, J. M., 254, *261*
Tate, G., 328, *342*, 353, 354, *360*
Taverniers, M., 552, *559*
Tawney, R. H., 245, *250*
Taylor, C., 233, *249*, 369, *377*
Taylor, D., 407, *414*, 426, *429*
Taylor, J. B., 401, *411*
Taylor, S., 118, *123*
Taylor, S. E., *493*
Taylor, S. O., 252, *264*
Taylor, T. L., 604, *607*
Teale, W., 397, 407, *414*, 456, *465*
Teale, W. H., 292, *305*
Tebeaux, E., 157, *171*, 219, *231*
Teberosky, A., 291, 292, *304*, 397, 400, 401, 402, *411*
Tedick, D. J., 364, *380*
Temple, C., 401, *414*
Temple, F., 401, *414*
Templeton, S., 401, *410*
Thayer, D., 366, *375*
Thilbault, P. J., 572, *573*
Thomas, E. M., 407, *414*
Thomas, I., 204, *216*
Thomas, M. G., 482, *494*
Thomas, R., 127, *137*
Thomas, W. I., 240, *250*
Thompson, D., 84, 85, *96*
Thompson, E. P., *216*, 234, 237, 239, 240, *250*
Thompson, F., 241, *250*
Thompson, G., 556, *558, 560*, 564, *576*
Thompson, J. W., 176, *186*
Thompson, L., 351, *358*, 369, *378*
Thompson, P., 571, *576*
Thompson, S., 518, *524*, 546, 547, *560*
Thompson, S. A., 546, 547, *558, 559*
Thompson, T., 242, *250*
Thonus, T., 335, *342*, 386, *393*
Thorland, C., 125, *136*
Thornton, T. P., *5*
Thralls, C., 266, *276*
Thurlow, M., 471, *477*
Thurschwell, P., 27, *33*
Tierney, R. J., 432, *446*
Tiersma, P., 128, 129, *137*
Tiffin, H., 192, *199*
Tinbergen, J., *108*
Tinzmann, M. B., 456, *462*
Tisdell, E., 426, *429*
Titscher, S., 118, *122*
Tobin, L., 296, *304*
Tolchinsky, L., 401, *414*

Tolchinsky Landsmann, L., 291, *305*
Tolmie, P., 112, *121*
Tomblin, J. B., 471, *478*
Too, Y. L., 87, 89, *96*
Torrance, M., 447, 449, *465*
Torrance, N., *21*, 580, *593*
Toulmin, S., 89, *96*, 568, *576*, 588, *593*
Toulmin, S. E., 316, *325*, 586, 588, *593*
Toury, G., 85, *96*
Tower, C., 399, 404, *414*
Trachsel, M., 361, 362, *380*
Traill, H. D., 201, *216*
Trappel, J., *79*
Tremmel, R., 351, *360*
Trew, T., 118, *121*, 272, *275*
Troia, G. A., 472, *478*
Trouard, T. P., 469, *477*
Troyer, C., 405, *414*
Truscott, J., 517, *527*
Truss, L., 31, *33*
Tschichold, J., *64*
Tse, P., 571, *574*
Tseng, C.-H., 468, *480*
Tsui, L., 338, *342*
Tucher, A., 208, *216*
Tuchman, G., 210, *216*
Tulasiewicz, W., 499, *507*
Tulloch, J., 209, *215*
Tunmer, W. E., 401, *414*
Turner, J., 337, *341*
Turner, S., 117, *122, 123*
Tylecote, M., 238, *250*

U

Udell, J., 603, *607*
Ukrainetz, T. A., 471, 472, *480*
Ulichny, P., 437, *446*
Ullrich, P. M., 485, 488, *494*
Underwood, G., 454, *463*
Underwood, T., 369, 370, *379, 380*
Unsworth, L., 555, *560*
Updike, D. B., 39, 40, 42, *64*
Urban Institute, The, 421, *429*
Urton, G., 24, *33*
Urzua, C., 513, *527*

V

Vacca, R. T., 419, *429*
Vachek, J., 546, *560*
Vadeboncoeur, J., *430*
Valdés, G., 426, *430*, 512, 513, *527*
Van de Kopple, W. J., 456, *465*
van de Mieroop, M., 99, *108*
van den Bergh, H., 433, *446*, 450, 451, *462, 465*
van der Meer, W., 519, *528*, 565, *577*
van Dijk, T., 207, *216*, 272, *276*
van Dijk, T. A., 118, 119, *123*, 432, *444*, 568, 569, *577*
van Eemeren, F. H., 586, *593*
van Leeuwen, T., 119, *123*, 572, *575*, 597, 599, *606*

Van Meter, A. M., 470, 471, *479*
van Mulken, M., 519, *528*, 565, *577*
van Nostrand, A. D., 164, *171*
van Sluys, K., 408, *414*
van Tijk, T. A., 568, 569, *575*
van Zoonen, L., 210, *216*
Vanburen Wilkes, G., 267, *276*
Vande Kopple, W., 266, *276*
Vande Kopple, W. J., 548, 552, *560*
Vanstiphout, H. L. J., 141, *152*
Varble, M. E., 293, *305*
Varnum, R., 349, *360*
Vaughan, K., 294, *303*
Vaughan, K. B., 453, *462*
Vaughn, K., 472, *477*
Veblen, T., 111, *123*
Veel, R., 90, *95*, 553, 555, *558, 560*
Velterop, J., 168, *171*
Venezky, R., 285, *288*
Venezky, R. L., 285, 286, *288*
Ventola, E., 572, *577*
Venuti, L., 86, *96*
Verger, J., 154, *171*
Vernant, J.-P., 580, *593*
Vernon, S. A., 292, *305*
VerSteeg, R., 125, *137*
Versteegh, K., 150, *152*
Vertut, J., 8, *20*
Vetter, E., 118, *122*
Veysey, L. R., 166, *171*
Vicinus, M., 239, *250*
Vicker, B., 473, *480*
Vickers, B., *360*
Vickery, B. C., 178, 181, *186*
Villaneuva, I., 496, *508*
Vincent, D., 233, 234, 235, 236, 237,
        239, 240, 241, 242, 244, *248, 250*
Vipond, D., 437, 438, *444, 445, 446*
Visscher, B. R., *493*
Vogelzang, M. E., 141, *152*
Volosinov, V. N., 435, 439, *446*, 492, *494*
von Glahn, R., 100, *108*
von Hayek, F., 102, *108*
Vorwerg, C., 453, *463*
Voss, J. F., 460, *465*
Voss, P. J., 203, *216*
Vygotsky, L., 371, *380*, 434, *446*, 461, *465*
Vygotsky, L. S., 434, *446*

W

Waanders, J., 363, *376*
Wacquant, L., 271, *275*
Wade, N., 161, *169*
Waff, D. R., 418, *426*
Wagner, K., 112, *123*
Waines, D., 192, *200*
Wales, T., 487, *493*
Walker, C. B. F., 15, 18, *22*
Walker, C. P., 332, *342*

Wallace, D. L., 449, 451, *465*
Wallace, R., 370, *378*
Wallace, V. L., 369, *380*
Waller. R., 286, *288*
Walsh, L., *593*
Walsham, A., 235, *248*
Walton, D., 587, *593*
Wander, P., 583, *593*
Wang, M., 450, *462*
Ward, J., 347, *360*
Warde, B., *64*
Ward-Lonergan, J. M., 474, *480*
Wardrip-Fruin, N., 604, *607*
Waring, M., 102, *108*
Warneke, C., 483, 484, *494*
Warner, M., 159, *171*
Washington State Critical
        Thinking Project, 373, *380*
Watson, G., *171*, 388, *393*
Watson, R., 116, 117, *123*
Watson-Gegeo, K. A., 437, *446*
Watt, I., 195, *200*, 531, *543*
Weaver, A., 24, *33*
Web Logs and Wikis, 603, *607*
Webb, L., 422, *428*
Weber, 111, *123*
Webster, A., 157, *169*
Wegner, D., 116, *123*
Wei, C., 603, *607*
Weigle, S. C., 364, 365, *380*
Weinberg, B. H., 182, *186*
Weintraub, E. R., 167, *171*
Weisbord, S., 205, *216*
Welch, K., 81, 89, *96*
Welch, O., 384, 391, *393*
Wellcome Trust, 168, *171*
Welsch, J. G., 401, *414*
Wenger, E., 224, *230*, 398, *413*, 434, *444*, 568, *575*
Wenger, M. J., 221, *231*
Werchado, B., 399, *415*
Wertheimer, M. M., 344, *360*
West, J. L. W., III, *79*
Westbrook, R., 125, 126, *137*
Westenholz, J. G., 13, *22*
Wetherell, M., 118, *123*
Weymouth, A., 205, *212*
Whately, R., 348, *360*
Whitaker, D., 290, *302*, 453, 457, 461, *463*
White, C. L., 209, *216*
White, E., 366, *380*
White, E. M., 320, *325*, 354, *360*
White, G., 267, *276*
White, P. R. R., 556, *559*
White, R. W., 496, *509*
Whitelock, D., 129, *137*
Whitenack, J. W., 404, *410*
Whiting, M. E., 351, *359*
Whitmore, K. F., 398, *414*
Whitt, W. D., 15, *22*

Whittaker, A., 370, *377*
Wiegand, W. A., 181, *186*
Wiemelt, J., 81, *95*, 545, *559*
Wiki, 603, *607*
Wikler, J., 29, 30, *32*
Wilder, L., 589, *593*, *594*
Wiley, J., 460, *465*
Wilford, J. N., 24, *33*
Wilhelm, J., *430*
Wilhelm, J. D., 258, *263*
Wilhoit, S., 355, *360*
Wilhoit, S. W., 354, *360*
Wilkins, D. P., 475, *478*
Wilkinson, B., 331, *339*, 458, *461*
Willard, C. A., 586, 588, 591, *594*
Willett, J., 403, *414*, 522, *527*
William, D., 371, *375*
Williams, C. L., 402, 405, *414*
Williams, J., 83, *96*, 386, *393*
Williams, J. D., 296, *305*
Williams, J. H., 202, *215*
Williams, L., 101, *107*
Williams, R., *79*, 208, *216*,
    233, 235, *250*
Williamson, J., 598, *607*
Williamson, M., 362, 366, 369,
    372, 374, *379*, *380*, *381*
Williamson, M. M., 337, *339*
Willis, A. I., 418, *430*
Wilson Logan, S., 243, *250*
Wilson, A., 533, *543*
Wilson, B., 469, *480*
Wilson, B. L., 363, *376*
Wilson, K., 362, *381*
Wilson, N. G., 175, *186*
Wilson-Keenan, J.-A., 403, *414*, 522, *527*
Windsor, J., 471, *480*
Wineburg, S., 438, *446*
Wingate, P., *213*
Winsor, D., 116, *123*, 219, *231*, 271,
    276, 568, 577, 583, 585, *594*
Winsor, D. A., 218, *231*
Winston, B., 28, *33*
Winter, D., 349, *360*
Winter, E., 554, *560*
Winters, L., 367, 370, *380*, *381*
Wiseman, A. M., 399, 404, 405, *414*
Witte, S., 92, *96*, 362, 367, *381*,
    451, 456, *463*, 569, *577*
Witte, S. P., 218, 225, 226, *231*, 432,
    446, 551, *560*, 569, *577*
Witty, F. J., 181, *186*
Wodak, R., 118, *122*, 555, *559*
Woledge, G., 175, *186*
Wolf, D. P., 372, *381*
Wolf, S., 371, *377*
Wolfe, J., 589, *594*
Wolfe-Quintero, K., 550, 551, *560*
Wolford, G. L., 483, *494*

Wollman-Bonilla, J. E., 399, 403, 404,
    405, 406, *414*, *415*
Wong, B. Y., 294, 298, *305*
Wong, B. Y. L., 471, *480*
Wood, C., 436, *445*
Wood, G., 383, *393*
Wood, J., 101, *108*
Wood, L., 272, *276*
Woodham, J. M., 25, *31*
Woodin, T., 245, 246, 247, *250*
Woodlief, L., 502, 503, *509*
Woodmansee, M., 85, *96*
Woods, M. C., 89, *96*, 346, *360*
Woods, S., 604, *607*
Woodward, A., 286, *288*
Woodward, V. A., 397, 399, 400, 401,
    402, 403, 405, 406, *412*
Woolf, G., 90, *93*
Woolf, V., 83, *96*
Woolgar, S., 90, *94*, 112, *123*
Woolley, C. L., 13, 14, *22*
Wootton-Don, L., 330, *342*
Wormald, P., 131, *137*
Wormuth, D. R., 366, *378*
Worpole, K., 245, *249*
Worsham, L., 253, 255, *262*, *264*
Worth, V., 86, *96*
Worthy, J., 438, *443*
Wouters, P., 182, *186*
Wright, E., 233, 236, *248*
Wright, H. C., 173, 174, *186*
Wright, R. E., 457, *465*
Wright, V., 388, *393*
Wyatt, E., 30, *32*
Wyplosz, C., 103, *107*
Wyse, E., 388, *393*
Wysocki, A., 92, *96*
Wysocki, A. F., 597, 601, *607*

X

Xerox, 29, *33*

Y

Yaden, D., *393*
Yagelski, R. P., 334, *342*
Yancey, K., 221, *231*
Yancey, K. B., 337, *342*, 371, 372, *379*, *381*
Yates, J., 91, *96*, 101, *108*, 156, *171*,
    221, 225, *231*, 566, *577*
Yates, J. A., 219, 221, 224, 226, *230* *231*
Yates, S., 118, *123*
Yeh, S. S., 316, 317, *325*, 503, *509*, 588, 589, *594*
Yeo, S., 245, 246, *250*
Yli-Jokipii, H., 518, *528*
Yoon, H., 386, *393*
Yorkston, K. M., 474, 477, *479*
You, X., 522, *528*
Young, J., 418, *429*
Young, K. M., 441, *446*

Young, L., 272, 273, *276*, 555, *560*, *574*
Young, R., 447, 459, *465*
Young, R. E., 586, *593*, *594*
Young, R. J. C., 522, *528*
Ysseldyke, J., 471, *477*
Yung, V., 572, *576*
Yunis, H., 88, *96*

Z

Zachry, M., 266, *276*
Zakowski, S. A., 483, 492, *494*
Zamagni, S., 102, *108*
Zamel, V., 517, 522, *528*
Zangari, C., 473, *480*
Zarefsky, D., 588, *594*

Zawacki, T. M., 254, *264*
Zech, E., 486, *494*
Zecker, L. B., 400, 403, *415*
Zettl, H., 600, *607*
Zhang, X., 471, *478*
Zhang, Y., 389, *393*
Zifcak, L., 220, *228*
Zimmerman, B. B., 222, *231*
Zimmerman, D., 116, *123*
Zimmerman, J., 284, *288*
Zinkgraf, S. A., 366, *378*
Znaniecki, F., 240, *250*
Zuboff, S., 111, *123*
Zucchermaglio, C., 291, *305*, 400, 405, *413*, *415*
Zweigert, K., 134, *137*

Subject Index

A

Academic prose   389, 497, 538–543, 545
Access 122, 196, 215, 303, 387, 456, 460, 494, 508
    educational 170–171, 249, 387, 391–395, 501–502
    to knowledge 143, 146–148, 155, 157 162–163,
        167–168, 172, 183–185, 188
    to publication 153, 263
    to writing 239, 241, 245, 410–413
Accountability 368, 378, 429–430
Accounting 12–13, 97, 174, 177, 230
Acknowledgments 441
Activity systems 229, 527, 571
Adjectives 539, 542–544, 552–553
Adolescent development biological model of 422
    sociocultural model of 422–423, 428
Adolescent literacy 421–424, 433
    federal legislation 423–424, 430
Adult literacy 249, 252–253, 379, 421, 424–433, 564
    basic skills instruction 426
    critical literacy instruction 428–429
    education 252, 421, 427–431, 433
    federal legislation 424–426, 430
    functional literacy 427, 518
    identity 424, 428, 430
    programs 432–433
Adult schools 241
    Quaker-led 242
Adult-child interactions 409
Adverbs 539–540, 552, 556, 560
Advertising 54, 59–61, 70, 277, 599, 601–603, 606
Aesthetics 51, 57, 83, 203, 599, 604
Affect 120, 222, 224–225, 328, 352, 367,
        369, 378, 387–388, 399, 401, 485,
        487–488, 494–495, 497, 556
Affordances of 83, 457
African American communities 247–248,
        250, 388, 425, 499, 504–506, 508, 510
Age-appropriate composition textbooks 353
Age of Steam 69
Agency 71, 227, 238, 240, 262, 277–278, 389,
        391, 394–395, 509, 552–553, 557–559, 604
Agent 129, 134, 269, 271, 274, 552, 586
Agonism/agonistic 591, 593
Agraphia (see also dysgraphia) 471–473
Alexandrian library 178
Alexia 473
Alliance for Excellent Education 423
Allusion 198
Alphabetic principle 298, 404

Alphabetic scripts 199
Alphabets 7, 15, 65
Americans with Disabilities Act (ADA) 393
Anglo-Saxons 133
Aphasia 471–474, 478
Appraisal theory 560
Appropriation 75, 445–446
Archaeology 8
Archives 9, 85, 97, 134, 136, 143, 161, 162, 169,
        177–178, 180–181, 186–187, 288,
Argument 88–89, 99, 107, 164, 257–259,
        266, 320, 348, 366–367, 371–372, 533,
        583–594, 600–601, 605–606
    fields 592
Argumentation 95, 258, 270, 302, 313, 545, 589–594
Arrangement 81, 89, 222, 313, 349–350, 404, 445,
        533, 567, 602, 604
Art 7–9, 12–13, 25, 37, 44, 46–47, 49–52, 56–59,
        91–92, 117, 191–193, 195–197, 199–201
Assessment 83, 281, 296–297, 323–327, 365–369,
        371, 373–379, 391–392, 425–428, 430, 508
    alternative 378, 427
    authentic 366, 373
    Chinese 90,
    curriculum embedded 374
    direct 367–368
    formative 375
    high-stakes 90
    holistic 323–324, 326, 339, 367–370, 372
    indirect 366–367
    methods 365, 373–374, 378
    portfolios 316, 325, 373–376
    self-assessment 376–377
    state 315–316, 325, 373, 375, 389
    topic 370, 432
Assignments 88, 249, 262, 284, 304, 305, 315–316,
        318, 321, 322, 341, 342, 413,
        424, 461, 507–508
Assistive technologies 393
Athens 130, 150
Audience 197, 211–215, 223, 285, 316, 371–372, 376,
        390–391, 395, 407–410, 413–414, 439–441,
        444–446, 452–454, 464–465, 576–577, 584–594,
        601–602, 604–607
    addressed 586, 595
    awareness 333, 335, 372, 408, 589
    invoked 586
    knowledge 452, 456, 460, 588
    particular 439, 462, 585–586, 592
    universal 585–586, 592

Auditing tools 104
Augmentative and alternative
    communication (AAC) 477
Author audience relations 439
Authoritative texts 71, 135, 137, 158, 289
Authority 71, 77, 84, 114–116, 118–119, 136–137,
    162–163, 186, 251, 256, 286, 288–291, 389, 503
Authorship 70–71, 76–77, 83–86, 92,
    99, 165, 223, 343, 374
    authenticity 83–84
    ghostwriting 85
    in the Industrial age 74
    Medieval 71
    payment system 73
    Renaissance definitions 70–71
    trust 77
Autobiographical self 502–503
Autobiography 100, 146, 192, 241–242

B

Beadle Brothers 70
Belletristic tradition 351–352
Bereavement 486, 490
Bible 26, 35–40, 47, 51, 60, 66–68, 100, 118, 130,
    179–180, 182, 196, 198, 200–201, 238, 284
Bich, Marcel 25
Bilaterality 591–592
Biliteracy 84, 516–518
Blogging 251
Blogs 210, 215, 262, 337, 607
Bonds 104
Book collections 44, 155, 181–182
Book design 46–48, 65, 285, 533, 599, 601
    textbooks 289–291
Book learning 160, 182, 288
Book publishing, trade 67, 74–75, 155, 182, 289
Bookkeeping 104, 160
Braille 392, 395
British East India Company 105
Bureaucracy/atic 91, 104, 113, 124, 145,
    151–154, 166–167, 277, 288
Business communications 223, 225–226, 230

C

Canons, Chinese 90, 151–152
Canons, educational 285, 465
Canons, legal 158–159
Canons, literary 193–201, 203
Canons, rhetorical 81, 89, 199, 349
Capitalism,discursive
    formation of 105–106, 108–110
CARS model 569, 588
Caselaw: *see* judicial opinions
Caste 148
Census lists 104
Cheques (Checks) 104
Children's genre knowledge 415, 460–461

China 7–8, 16, 19–20, 23–24, 26, 35,
    65, 84, 86, 89–91, 104, 114, 132,
    151–153, 171, 180–181
Chronic pain 488
Cite/Citation 130, 160, 165, 186,
    228, 446, 568, 570, 572,
    575, 589, 593
Civil service 16, 145, 151–153
Claim 74, 85, 92, 134, 160, 163–165,
    278, 287–288, 321, 367, 375,
    439–440, 445, 558, 587–588, 590–593
Clause 277–278, 317, 320, 458–459,
    521, 539–541, 543, 545, 549–560
    dependent 539–540, 543
    embedded 551–554, 556
    relative 521, 541, 545, 552
    subordinate 535, 551, 554, 568
    that-clause 539, 541, 543, 557
Closed head injury (CHI) 473
Code switching 526,
Code Napoleon 139
Codes: *see also* legislation 65,
    129–132, 135, 138–139, 160,
Codification 115, 139, 148, 180
Cognition 202, 278, 295, 437–439,
    451, 462, 492–493, 495,
    distributed 223, 228, 230, 438
    situated 230, 438
Cognitive adaptation 495–496
Cognitive models 202, 451, 453, 465, 473
Cognitive process(es) 88–89, 202, 230, 300–301,
    331, 436, 452–453, 455–456
Cognitive Instruction in Writing (CSWI) 302
Coherence 301, 459, 508, 521, 572–574
Cohesion 278, 334, 342, 394, 407, 521, 550, 552, 555,
    562, 563, 565–566, 572–574
Collaborative writing 85, 222–223, 230, 259, 409,
    440–441, 477, 607
Colonialism 171, 196, 524
Comic books 75, 600
Comments, teacher 315, 321–323, 333,
    368, 375, 520
Comments, peer 296, 410, 441
Communication 7, 23–24, 28–31, 56, 65–66, 68,
    74–77, 82, 97, 115, 178, 203, 224–226, 269–272,
    274, 278, 537, 583–584, 589, 601, 603, 605–607
    circuit 75–76
    disorders 471–480
    technologies 84, 91, 186–189, 263, 604
Community learning 240, 242
Composition 255–261, 287, 293–294, 298, 301–302,
    304, 311–314, 318, 320–323, 325–326, 475–476
    courses 287, 334, 391, 593
    extracurriculum of 250, 261
    research 222, 233, 260, 332, 424, 435
    scholars 256, 259, 261, 573, 576
    textbook 353, 357
Compositor 27, 60
Computer-mediated communication 259, 593

Computers 19–20, 51, 60–61, 77, 86, 116–118, 124,
    185–186, 224–225, 332, 337–340, 393–394, 441,
    474, 476–477, 605–607
development of 29–31
Conference on College Composition and
    Communication (CCCC) 355, 372, 378
Conferences [student-teacher] 299, 319, 322–323,
    328, 331, 333, 336–337, 441, 520
Confucian arts 152
Constructivism 258, 293, 297, 302–306, 436,
    585–586, 591
Context(s) 227–231, 269–278, 437–438,
    453–454, 464–465, 518–520,
    and assessment 366–367, 370–371, 373, 377–379
    complex 499
Contracts 84–85, 104, 129, 131–135,
    138, 146, 159, 168, 238
Contrastive rhetoric 525, 568, 576
Convention 58, 401–408, 411, 413–414, 428, 603
Conversation 455, 536–546, 554, 593
Cooperation 591–592
Copyright 69–73, 75–76, 85, 161, 608
Core concept 271–272
Corporate organization 116–117
Corpus linguistics 522, 527, 574, 576
Counterargument 593
Counting 8, 12
Craft 36–37, 47, 54, 60–61, 63, 83–84, 146
Crisis definition 213
Criteria [for evaluating writing] 283, 296,
    317–320, 324, 326, 341, 333, 341,
    369, 373, 377–378
Critique, critiquing 444–445
Cues and Constraints 193–194
Cultural change 67, 74, 269–272
Cultural identities 209, 500, 502–505, 509
Cultural traditions 195, 200–201, 203
Culture 410–411, 413–414, 503–505,
    515, 524–527, 583
Cuneiform 15, 18, 20, 23, 25, 66, 103, 129, 190
Currency 104
Curricula 152, 158–160, 162, 169–170,
    201, 283, 325, 340–342

D

Dame schools 240–241, 284
Decipherment 16, 18–19
Deeds 104, 133–134, 146
Deficit 427, 465, 471–478, 480
Deictic/Deixis 553, 558
Delay 471, 474
Deliberation 84, 87, 584, 591, 593
Delivery 89, 349, 351, 605
Democracy 119, 139, 207–208, 590–591
Demonstration 164, 297, 409–410
    logical 590
Descriptions 104, 129, 149, 162–164,
    166–167, 313, 567

Design, designing (see also book design) 5, 226,
    264, 533, 599, 601, 603–605
    typeface 50–64
Development [growth in writing performance]
    334, 336, 339, 341, 430, 506, 515
Development Principles 192–195, 199–201
Developmental
    models 303, 421–422, 424–426,
        453, 459, 465, 473, 480, 525
    sequences 293, 295, 300, 303, 305, 334, 404
    of writing systems 19
    trajectories 474–475
Diacritics 16
Diagnosis 471, 480
Dialectic 88–89, 154, 348, 350,
Dictate, dictation 88, 192, 224, 298, 301, 454,
    457–458, 463, 472–474, 476–477
Dictionaries 37, 162, 183
Digital libraries 187–188
Digitial literacies 423
Digitial technology 42, 63, 74–75, 200, 225, 379
Digitization 84, 187, 264, 599, 603, 606
Disciplinarity 81–82, 84–85, 89–92
Disciplinary discourse 103, 439, 444, 460
Disciplinary genres, academic 570, 593
Disciplinary styles 333
Disciplinary writing 340, 441, 444, 575
Discourse analysis 91, 120, 122–123,
    211, 276, 340, 428, 479, 521, 559, 566
Discourse, constructive 269–275
Discourse communities 228–230, 388, 402,
    438–439, 446, 460, 522, 527, 572, 586
Discourse knowledge 435, 437
Discourse practices 338, 435, 441, 526
Discourse structure(s) 521,565–566, 572–573
Discourses, economic 106–107
Discourses, scientific 82–83, 90, 144, 163–165, 168,
    171, 184–185, 270, 277, 552,
Disorder 392, 399, 471–475, 477–480
Disruption 273, 278
Dissemination of written knowledge 159, 163, 165,
    179–181, 183, 186
Dissent 143, 587, 589, 593
Document design 226, 577
Documentary governance 116–117, 124
Documentary society 97, 113–124
Documentation 115, 117, 120, 122,
    177, 184, 222, 227
Drafting 90, 335, 408
Drawing 12, 19, 55, 59–61, 225, 287,
    293, 295, 406, 408, 413, 475, 478
stick writing 476
Dutch East India Company 105
Dysgraphia 471–474, 477

E

Earl of Stanhope 27
Economic activity 97, 103–105, 107, 109, 281

Economic models 106, 109
Economics 9, 19, 103, 105–108, 166, 169–171
  discursive construction of 105–107
  Keynsian 106, 109
Ecriture feminine 258–259
Eduba 145
Egypt 15, 18, 23–24, 65–66, 84, 103–104, 129–131,
    145–146, 150, 154, 179–180, 192
Eight-legged essay 151
Elaboration 324–326, 342, 538, 541, 545
Electronic media 31, 109, 199–200, 290, 533
Electronic networks 105
Electronic texts 82, 105
E-mail 20, 30–31, 225, 230, 251, 332, 337, 407, 441,
    474, 493–494, 523, 607
Emergent literacy 293–295, 304, 401–402, 405
Emotional expression 486, 488, 490–492, 494, 496
Encyclopedias 151, 165, 183–184, 186, 189
England 25–29, 45–49, 51, 58–61, 133–137, 139,
    160–163, 165, 169, 183, 206–207, 210, 238–239,
    241–242, 244, 284, 365
English 136–141, 565–569, 573–577
  departments 255, 261, 341, 351, 356
  as language of schooling 172, 353, 518
  as language of science 172, 557
  as language of scholarship 162–163,
      172, 574, 576
  as a Second Language 331, 369, 387–390,
      515–519, 521–526, 554, 565
  for specific purposes (ESP) 522, 557, 569
ENIAC 29
Entertainment 97, 191–203
Epithets 193–194
Error 312, 315, 333–335, 337–338, 340, 354, 367,
    369, 390, 394, 426, 458–459, 476,
    520–521, 543, 555
Essentialism 259, 593
Ethics 211, 377, 445, 585
  in journalism 211
Ethnographic approaches 85, 88, 90, 120–121, 124,
    231, 255, 260, 262, 322, 523, 576
Ethnomethodology 120–121
Ethos 107, 590
Eulogy 192
Evidence 227, 287, 324, 326, 340–341, 367, 373, 555,
    558, 587, 592–593
Examinations 198, 286, 325, 365
  Chinese Imperial 91, 151–153
Expert writers 228–229, 300, 317, 436, 451–453, 455,
    461, 464–465, 555, 570–572
Explanation 302, 313, 317, 567
Exposition, expository prose 300–303, 313–314,
    325, 372, 389, 458, 460–461, 537–538, 541,
    544–546, 555, 566–567
  Japanese 525
Expression 23, 97–98, 133, 237, 243, 270,
    395, 496, 603
Expressive writing 463, 477, 486–489, 491, 493–494,
    496–497
Extracurriculum 250, 261–262

F

Facsimile machine 29
Fair use 608
Fallacy(ies) 591, 593
Familiarity 196–197, 200–202, 303, 317, 460
Feedback 228, 299, 305, 319, 321, 323, 367, 375–377,
    393, 408, 422, 519–520
Feminism 249, 255–258, 260, 263
Financial institutions 105, 107
Financial markets 104, 105, 107
Financial statements 105
First-year composition 357
First-year writing programs 339–340, 342
Floating documents/texts 118–119
Focus of instruction 293, 317–320
Folksonomy 607
Fount (font) 42–64, 68
Forgery 134, 241
Formulae 143, 194
Fourth estate 210
Freewriting 319–320, 335, 455, 462, 503, 516
Freire, Paolo 249, 428–429
French 37, 47, 51, 75, 133, 163, 166, 169–170, 183,
    208, 331, 405
feminists 258–259
Functional analysis 279, 304, 562, 577
Future of writing 19, 20, 533

G

Gain [in writing ability] 318–322, 324, 332,
    334–335, 338, 341–342
Gay, lesbian, bisexual, transgender, and
    gender-questioning 266, 387–388, 391
Gender differences 223, 247, 257, 260,
    274, 327, 377, 392, 412, 593
Gender-questioning 387
Gender and writing 255–264
Gendered identities 262, 264, 503
Generation 1.5 525
Generative literacy practices 509
Genre
  academic 568
  analysis 521–522, 525, 569–570, 576
  conventions 227, 522
  features 226, 228, 407–408
  knowledge 188, 274–275, 407, 452,
      460–461, 568, 572
  learning 304, 571
  moves 523
  research 569–571
  social interactions 303, 407, 409–410, 570–571
  structure 523, 565–569, 572, 575–576
  systems 90, 229, 523, 527, 571
  teaching 302–303
  theory 82, 571
  wheel model of teaching 303
Genre vs text type 302–303
Genres, scientific 90, 229

Gestalt 335, 604
Girls Studies 262
Global capitalism 425
Global communication 63–64, 113, 116
Glyphs 16–17, 146
Governance 84, 110, 114–117, 120, 123, 124, 584
Graduate programs in rhetoric
    and composition 356, 358
Graduate students 171, 224, 357–359, 461, 509,
    570–571, 575, 589
Grammar 18, 122, 145, 148, 154, 155, 158,
    243, 311–312, 316–321, 334–337, 349, 350,
    352–354, 367–368, 520–521, 540–543,
    549–555, 557–561, 603
  error treatment 521
  as prerequisite to writing 311
  role in second language writing 388, 392, 394
  textbooks 246, 288, 311–312, 350, 352, 538
Grammatical metaphor 276–277, 552, 556–557, 559
Greece 15, 18, 24, 67, 84, 87, 88, 130, 149, 201,
    347–348, 584
Group methods of instruction 283, 286
Gutenberg, Johannes 26–27, 35–40, 51, 67

H

Hammurabi's Code 129–130, 145
Handwriting 5, 46, 50, 132, 333, 393, 456–458, 472
  children's 295, 298, 401, 408, 457, 475–476
Healing 485–497
Hebrew diaspora 86, 147
Heroic tragi-comedy 192
Heuristic 320, 335, 348, 439, 476, 507, 593
Hieroglyphics 18–19, 65–66, 129
Historical roots 237
History of knowledge 179
Hoe, Richard 27
Holistic assessment 323–324,
    326, 339, 367–370, 372
Horizons of Expectation 202
Human activity 110, 189
Hybrid forms of writing 509–510, 526
Hybridity in multilingual
    writing development 526
Hypertext 30, 85, 168, 186, 188, 200, 225, 226, 260,
    337–338, 440, 444–445, 576, 606–607

I

IBM 20, 29–30
Ideal Reader 197, 200
Identification 89, 208–209, 215, 584
Identities, construction of 207–209, 211, 214
Identity 70, 83, 117, 196, 200–203, 239–240, 244,
    247, 269, 272–274, 333, 342, 387–395, 411–412,
    422, 428, 430, 446 499–511, 571, 607–608
  development 394, 499–507, 511
  kits 502
Ideology 568
Illustration 600–601

Image 7–9, 36–37, 115, 117, 162, 264, 269, 272–274,
    599–601, 604
Imagined reader 197, 199, 207–208
Imitation 83, 143, 151, 335, 349, 352, 438
Immigrants 68, 244, 247, 353
Immigration 244, 247, 387, 390
Immune functioning 486–487
Impact of technology 5, 19, 224
Impairment 392, 471, 474, 477, 480
Indenture 134
Individuality 202, 391, 504, 517
Industrial Revolution 54, 65, 69, 105, 161, 184, 239
Influence 75, 76, 108, 109, 200–201, 325,
    583–587, 590, 592
Informal schooling 241
Informated systems 117
Information society (age) 28, 92, 113,
    115–116, 168, 263
Information structure 550, 558, 567
Informational density 538, 545
Inhibition 487–488, 495–496
Ink 24–26, 29, 35–36, 43–44, 51, 55–56,
    61, 63, 65, 83, 90
Innovation 196, 202
Inquiry 319–321, 583, 585, 593
Inscription 5, 13–14, 18–19, 82–83, 90, 103, 110,
    129–130, 145–146, 148, 160,
    164, 172, 192–193, 533
Institutional ethnography 121
Institution [post-secondary] 331–332, 340–343
Institutions 97–99, 105, 107, 113–115, 121, 143–144,
    147, 154–155, 157, 159, 163, 170, 177, 179–183,
    211, 221, 241–242, 269, 281, 283, 285, 501–502
Instruction [or teacher practice] 161, 241, 283,
    285–286, 293, 296–306, 311–323, 326, 331–342,
    348–350, 352–353, 356–358, 373, 389–395, 403,
    408, 413, 424–430, 437, 445, 455, 460–461, 497,
    506–508, 511, 517, 520–523, 589
Intellectual property 71, 75, 115, 263, 608
Intention 35, 118, 401–402, 439, 572, 584
Intentionality 403, 585
Inter-subjectivity 591
Interaction 122, 230, 276, 303–304, 332, 401–402,
    407, 409–414, 480, 570–571, 583, 588–589
Interdisciplinarity 256, 263, 572
Interdisciplinary 86, 91, 171, 212, 255–256, 258,
    262–263, 340–341, 435
Interdiscursivity 123
Intermediaries (see also sponsors and significant
    others) 238, 243
International Association for the Evaluation of
    Educational Achievement 325
Internet 30–31, 105, 109, 118, 161, 172, 186–188,
    210, 215, 251, 338, 445, 606–607
Interpersonal communication 115, 224
Interpersonal stance 559
Interpretation 26, 52, 63, 68, 73, 97, 99, 112,
    136–137, 139, 158, 203, 213, 273
Intertextuality 188, 222, 229–230, 443, 519, 570
Intervention 298, 437, 471–480, 485–494

Invention 81, 89, 92, 313–314, 339, 349–350, 352, 572
Islam 85, 99, 181, 196
Islamic world 84, 153–155, 157–158
Israel 66, 129–130, 147
Italic 46–47, 50–51, 60

J

Jacquard's loom 29
Journal writing 335, 474, 489, 492, 506, 516
Journalism 98, 161, 165, 205–216, 284
Journals 69–70, 75, 92, 117–118, 169–172,
    188–189, 246–248, 285, 337, 394, 588
    personal 195, 320, 334–335, 462, 474,
        489, 492, 516
    scientific 164–165, 167, 185, 592
Judicial opinions 133, 137–138
Justice 120, 586, 589–593
Justinian 131, 139, 158, 180

K

Kairos 572, 588
Khipu (or Quipu) 24
Knowledge 23, 30, 66–67, 77, 82–84, 86–87, 90–91,
    97–98, 118, 143–155, 157–172, 177–189, 197,
    228–231, 257, 259, 270, 288–291
    abstract versus practical 143–144, 146–147, 149,
        151, 153, 160–161, 170
    agricultural 147, 149, 151–152, 170
    astronomical 147, 149–150, 152, 153
    based industries, ascension of 30, 165
    botanic 162–164, 169
    bureaucratic 145, 153, 159, 166–167, 169
    civic, political 162
    colonial 162, 166
    commercial 160–162
    definition 143, 263
    economic 107, 109, 145, 161–162, 165–166,
        169–172
    future of 171–172
    geographical 146, 150–151, 155, 162–163
    genre *see* genre, knowledge
    governmental 145–147, 149–153, 160,
        165–170, 172
    historical 153
    legal 145–147, 158–160, 162, 177, 180, 182
    linguistics 144, 149, 152, 154, 162, 170
    mathematical 145, 148–152, 154
    medical 146–147, 149, 152, 154–155, 157–158,
        160, 166
    military 146–147, 149, 152, 166–169, 172
    nationalism as 162–163, 169
    oral 143–144, 148, 150, 161, 177–178
    patents as 161
    pharmacological 155
    philology 152, 169–170
    philosophic 144, 149, 150, 154–155,
        160, 163, 169

production 152, 157, 168, 184
public (open) access 119, 168, 172, 188
rhetorical 452, 460
secrecy 152–153, 161, 166–168, 172, 245
secular 144, 147–149, 154–155, 159, 169–170
surgical 149, 158, 160
technical 166
telling 300, 452–453, 461, 464–465
transforming, transformation 300–301, 305,
    452–453, 461, 464–465
value 159, 161, 165, 171–172, 179, 184
zoological 151, 162–163
Koenig steam press 27, 70
Koran (Quran) 85, 154, 180

L

Land deeds 104, 134
Language 17–20, 82–83, 144, 162–164, 256–259,
    471–473, 496, 517–525, 535–537, 546–547,
    553–560
    change over time 556–557
    development 521, 553–556, 560
    disorders 474–475
    of science, scientific 172, 557
Large-scale organization 118, 121
Laslo, Josef Biro 25
Latin 15, 18, 35, 47, 133, 150–151, 157–158,
    179–181, 311, 349–352
Law 104, 129–139, 145, 147, 150–152, 158–160, 173,
    180, 263, 356, 362, 363
    canon 158
    civil 138–139, 158, 180
    common 133–139
    Roman 131–133, 138–139
Learning disability (LD) 392
Legal status of personhood 105
Legal systems 87, 104, 130, 133, 139, 230
Legibility 54, 57
Legislation 129–131, 135, 136, 139
Lesbian 387, 391
Letter-writing 244–245
Letterpress 26–27, 43, 51, 55, 59
Letters 15, 18, 19, 26–28, 50, 51, 82, 87–90,
    104, 120, 131, 146, 160, 166, 195, 214,
    222, 225, 227, 243–248, 350
Lexical density 553–554
Libraries 25, 30, 44, 154–155, 160, 177–189
    imperial 146, 181
    monastary 179, 182–183
    university 66, 182–183
Library
    classification 184–185
    history 146–147, 177–189
Linguistic analysis 211, 489, 496, 549–560
Linguistic differences between speech
    and writing 536, 546, 554
Linguistic features 535–537, 539,
    544, 554–556, 558–560
Linguistic turn 211–212

Linguistics 81, 86, 88, 144, 152, 154, 170, 191, 257, 536, 549–550, 565–566, 568–570
Lists 88, 104, 135, 143, 145–146, 178
Literacy (*see also* Adult literacy, Adolescent literacy) 87–88, 144, 149, 180, 191, 237–243, 246–251, 281, 283–285, 288–289, 399–400, 502, 535–553
    emergent 293–295, 304, 401–402, 405
    learning 248, 295–297, 303, 306, 401
    practices 238–239, 247–251, 262, 341, 366, 390, 501, 503, 505, 509, 603
    visual 599, 604
Literary agent 73
Literary classics 153, 198
Literary market 181, 197, 199
Literary modeling 198
Literary paradigms 201
Literary texts 13, 86, 97–98, 145, 351
Literary Theory 203
Literary works 191–195, 198, 199, 203, 365
Literate culture 24, 103, 149, 195, 202
Literate institutions 143, 283
Literate practices 88–89, 91, 105, 110
Literature, distribution and production 193–195, 197, 199–201
Lithography and offset lithography 27
Litigation 132, 161
Logic 150, 157–159, 311, 313, 326, 350–351, 584, 590–591
Logographic scripts 15, 199
Logos 521, 590
Long-term memory (LTM) 298, 300, 452–453, 460–464
Long-term working memory (LT-WM) 461
Longitudinal 304, 342–343, 473, 506, 576

M

Managerial invention 313
Manufacturing companies 105, 221, 225
Manuscript culture 65–66, 71
Manutius, Aldus 37, 42–45, 49, 61, 67–68
Marriage register 239
Mass education 84, 283, 285–286, 289
Master printer 37
Material tools 187–188
Materiality documents/texts 5, 115–116, 119, 123, 606
Mathematical plainness of style 285
Measurement of literacy 240
Mechanics Institutes 242
Media 28–31, 73–75, 77, 109–110, 119, 208–215, 225–226, 601, 604
    mass 115–119
    globalization 74–75
Mediation 92, 124, 274, 295–296
Medical visits 486, 494
Medieval period 117, 158, 161, 349–350
Memex 168, 186
Memorandum 105, 133–135

Memory (*see also* Working memory) 19, 29, 33, 65, 66, 93, 94, 143, 192, 286–287, 311, 349, 599, 601
Men's movement 261–262
Mental discipline 311, 584
Mesoamerica 5, 7–8, 16–17, 144, 146
Mesopotamia 7–15, 17–19, 23–24, 65–66, 103–104, 129, 145
Meta-analysis, research synthesis 318–321
Metadiscourse 82–83, 89, 437, 521, 575
Metaphor 198
Methods of inquiry 89
Micrographia 472
Military-industrial-academic-complex 168
Mimeograph machine 28, 105
Minorities 201, 504, 565
Mishnah 147
Misinterpretation 270, 287
Mobilizing identities 504, 510
Modality 276–278, 550, 552, 559
Mode 7, 536–539, 545–546, 553–555, 599, 601, 603–604
    of instruction 158, 293, 299–300, 318–319
Models 151, 303, 313, 316, 320, 326, 335, 349–350, 438
Modern Language Association (MLA) 256, 355
Monastic Age 66, 68
Monetary vouchers 104
Morse, Samuel B. 28–29
Motivation to write 239–242, 296, 306
Multiculturalism 526
Multidimensional analysis 536
Multilingual business writing 522–523
Multiliteracies 229, 430, 518, 527, 604
Multimodality 82, 92, 406–407, 422–423, 477–478, 480, 574, 576, 602, 604
Multiple-choice testing 323–324, 367–368
Mutual improvement societies 242–243, 249–250

N

Name writing 404–405, 413
Narration 302, 313, 567
Narrative(s) 104, 269, 272–274, 489, 491
    of personal experience 317, 322, 326
Nation states (and literacy) 288,
National heritages 162–163, 169
National languages 162–163
National Assessment of Educational Progress (NAEP) 324, 354, 379, 499
National Defense Education Act (NDEA) 353
National Writing Project (NWP) 322, 353
Needs analysis 527
Networking, computer 337, 394, 607
New Media 31, 92, 199–200, 225–226, 263–264, 424
Newspapers 28, 54, 65, 68–70, 118, 160, 161, 205–215, 285, 588
Nominalization 223, 228, 277, 539, 542, 546, 552–553, 557
Notaries 89, 138, 159
Note taking 284, 286–287

Noun/Nominal 541, 550–560
Noun phrases 539, 542–543, 552, 556
Novel 75, 199, 202–203, 284, 559
Novelty 194–195, 202, 588
Number of languages in the world 21
Numeracy 243, 288, 425–426
Numerical tables 103–104

O

Online discussion 338, 593, 606–607
Open access publications 172, 188
Oppositional identities 505
Oral composition 192–195
Oral culture(s) 114, 143, 177–178, 195, 202, 284
Oral rhetoric 351
Orality 191–192, 194, 199, 585
   and literacy 87–88, 194
Organization of knowledge 178, 182, 184,
   186, 188, 464
Orientalism 524
Orthography 7, 295, 404

P

Pain 486, 488, 491
Paper 17–18, 35–37, 51, 65, 115, 146,
   148, 224, 286, 338
   development of; advances in 24–31
   currency 104, 153
Paperbacks 70
Papyrus 15, 24–25, 31
Parchment 15, 24–27
Participant relations 435, 438–440
Participation 84–85, 88, 172, 207, 211, 215, 401–402,
   410–411, 480, 501, 503, 571–572, 607
Patent archives 161
Pathos 590
Patronage 71–73, 163, 169, 199
Peciae 66
Pedagogy 89, 169, 256–259, 341, 347–352, 354–360,
   390, 421–422, 507–508, 603–604
Peer response 316, 455, 520
Performance 366–367, 371, 375–377, 584, 606
Personal involvement 539, 546
Persuasion 88, 107, 119, 313, 348, 583–585, 587,
   590–591, 594, 606
Petitions 88, 243, 250
Phonics vs. whole-language approach 294,
   296–298
Photography 599–601, 603–605
Pictography 12
Plagiarism 85, 165, 338, 342, 445, 608
Plain-meaning rule 136
Planning 222, 224, 298–302, 393, 408, 414, 436, 451,
   453–457, 461, 464–465, 476, 519, 538
Plato's Academy 150, 348
Playwrights 71
Poetry 13, 17, 67, 73, 114, 145, 148, 182, 201–202,
   243, 249, 313, 349, 501

Popular journalism 166, 208, 212–213
Popular science 165
Popularization 52, 444
Portfolios 325–326, 358, 371, 373–376
Positive health outcomes 494–495
Post graduation 326, 343
Post-process 527
Postal Systems 25–26, 28, 74, 244
Postcolonialism 86, 208–209, 261
Postmodernism 85, 212, 261, 291, 524
Posttraumatic Stress 486, 489–490, 497
Power 270, 584, 589–593
Practice(s) 81–84, 86, 88–92, 435,
   438–439, 441–444, 446
Prayer 13, 146, 192
Precedent: *see* judicial opinions
Press 35–37, 43–44, 47, 51,
   53–56, 58–61, 63
Presentational teaching 299, 319
Prestige 197
Presupposition 276–278
Prewriting 225, 299–300, 315–317,
   320, 335, 393, 454
Primary trait 326
   scales 324
Print 35–37, 42–43, 54, 56, 65, 68, 70–71, 73–79, 82,
   85, 115–116, 199–200, 206–208, 212–215,
   378–379, 404–405, 413–414, 527, 606–608
Print Communication Practices 68–69
Print Culture 71, 75, 186, 206, 214
Printing 5, 18, 26–31, 35–37, 42–45, 47–48,
   50–51, 54–56, 58–61, 65–71, 73–74,
   76–77, 152–153, 159, 182
   development of 26, 67–69, 182
   history of 60, 205, 220
   invention of 26, 35, 65, 68, 115,
      136, 152–153, 199,
   houses 44, 68, 153, 159
Printing press 5, 23, 26–27, 51, 55, 63,
   67–69, 84, 153
   effects of 26, 31, 153, 159, 163
Procedural facilitation 300–302
Procedures 104, 129, 143, 167, 283, 567
Process approach 299, 301–303
   natural 299
Process-based analysis 294, 475, 519
Process writing 408, 413, 516
Product-based 294, 475
Production 599, 601, 603–606, 608
   circumstances 537–538, 544–546
Professional writing 166, 221–222, 228–230,
   355, 568, 571–572, 574
Progress report 105
Progymnasmata 151, 349–350
Promissory notes 104
Pronouns 372, 440, 539–540, 542, 544,
   555–556, 559–560, 572
Proofreader 36
Property 129, 131, 133–134
Prototypes 192–193, 195, 197, 200–201

Psychology 169–170, 258–259, 262, 352, 446, 494–496
Public argument 593
Public discourse 163, 211, 248, 258, 584
Public domain 109, 608
Public journalism 211
Public Sphere 70, 98, 116–118, 123, 163, 170, 205–216
Publics 98, 118, 209, 215, 284, 586, 606
Publishers 27, 44, 46–47, 60, 69–75, 163, 188–189, 312, 358
Punches 35, 47, 50

Q

Quadrivium 158, 311, 350
Quantification 165–166
Quill 25
Quipu (*see* Khipu)
Qussas 196–197

R

Race 338, 387–389, 391, 393–394, 402, 422, 429, 504, 508, 602, 607
Railroad 28, 105, 117
Rater 323–324, 369–370, 374
Rationality 591–592
Reader-based prose 589
Readers 206, 208, 210, 212, 214, 284–285, 287, 290–291, 583–589, 593, 604–607
  and assessment 368–369, 376
  ideal 197, 200
  implied 586
Readership 72, 114, 197, 199, 205–208, 211–214, 284, 370, 584
Reading 30, 38, 68, 115, 121, 124, 224, 283, 283–291, 435–446
  comprehension 295, 323, 390, 435, 565–566
  process 437
  public 66, 71–72, 183, 210, 239, 284–285, 287, 289
  research 435–436
  to write 443
Receipts 103, 146
Recitation 132, 148, 180, 193, 318–319, 349
Recovery 488–490
Reference 552–553, 556, 558
Reflective practice 81–84
Reflective processing 497
Reformation 26, 68, 100, 159, 169, 183, 315
Register 554–555, 558
  variation 536, 538, 541, 544, 546, 558
Rehearsal 408–409
Reliability 318, 323–324, 365, 370, 374, 377
Remediation 339, 430
  textual 92
Renaissance 25, 29, 36, 57–58, 68, 70–71, 84, 86, 104–105, 110, 150–151, 159, 161, 166, 181–183, 350
Reaumur, Rene 27

Representing morphemes 17
Representing syllables 17
Republic of Letters 159
Research 81–85, 87–88, 91–92
  article introductions 568–569
  method 332
  synthesis 318
Resistance 588, 591
Response 439–441, 443
Reviewing, revision 452, 460
Revision 300–301, 305, 316, 318, 320–322, 333, 336, 338–339, 390, 408–409, 436, 455, 456, 459–461
Rhetoric 81, 84, 87–92, 151, 248, 269–272, 274, 277, 302, 311–313, 347–352, 566–569, 583–586, 589–594, 605–606
  ars dictaminis (manuals of letter writing) 89, 159, 350,
  canons 89, 349
  Chinese 89
  comparative/global 88–90
  contrastive 525, 568, 576
  eighteenth century 313
  European 81
  Greek 81, 84, 88, 90
  invitational 592
  medieval   81, 89, 349–350
  public speaking 84, 87–88, 99
Rhetorical models 151, 438
Rhetorical moves 522, 569
Rhetorical reading 442
Rhetorical theory 229, 588, 606
Rogerian 591–592
Roles, writing 402–403, 408–409, 411–412, 414
Roman 15, 20, 24–26, 42–48, 50–54, 131–133, 138–139, 149–151, 157–158, 160, 179–180, 348–349
Roman Codex 24
Rome 15, 24–25, 52, 84, 131, 149–151, 584
Ruling relations 113, 115–116, 124

S

Sans serif 54, 57–59, 61
Scales 318–321, 323–325, 333, 371
Schemata 317, 453–456, 460, 464, 495
Scholarly societies 163–164
Scientific journals 164, 185
Scientific language 172, 557
Scientific revolution 153
Scientific writing 164, 560
Scoring 324–326, 337–338, 365, 368, 370–371, 374–378, 430
Scottish Common Sense Philosophers 311
Scribes 15, 24–25, 66, 88, 145–148, 238, 245–246, 251
Script 7, 15–20, 65–67
  hieroglyphic 18
Scriptorium 26, 66, 181
Scripts, schemata 317

Second language learners (ESL) 387–390, 394–395, 425, 515–517, 519–520, 525–526
    writing 369, 391, 519, 524, 554–556
Secular Age 66
Self-help 241–243, 246
Self-improvement 165, 246
Self-regulated strategy development (SRSD) 301
Semiotics 81, 92, 600
    social 602–603
Sentence 549–551, 560, 566–568
    combining 317–320, 335, 437
Sentences 312–314, 316–320
Serif 53–54, 57–59
Shareholder newsletters 105
Sholes and Glidden Type Writer 27
Signatures 71, 136, 138, 227, 238–240, 244
Significant others (*see also* sponsors and intermediaries) 248, 251
Signification 603
Situated 438, 441
    qualitative research 527
Skilled writers 453, 456, 458–462
Skills 293–294, 297–299, 305–306, 320, 331–332, 334, 336, 340–343
Small-group discussion 319
Smith, Adam 105–106, 109, 351
Social activity 246, 269, 293–294, 366, 388
    adversity 486, 491
    change 269–271, 273, 275–279
    class 238–243, 246–250
    cognition 437, 439
    communication 65, 74, 77
    constraint 487–488
    constructionism 107, 259
    context 269, 271, 274–276, 278, 333, 435, 438, 441, 444–445
    groupings 216
    interaction 402, 407, 409–410
    movements 205–216, 239
    organization 82, 90–92, 105, 187
    power 270, 502
    practice 212, 237, 275, 413, 506, 536
    protest 243–244
    theories of the press 206
    turn 438
Socialization 82–83, 228, 230, 258, 572
    of the text 76
Society, text-mediated 116
Sociocultural perspectives 410–413
Socrates 23, 31, 87, 149, 348, 585
Spatialization [learning space] 332, 339
Specific language impairment (SLI) 474
Speech 535–539, 544–546, 553–555, 584–586
    generation devices 478
    supplementation strategies 478
Spell check 476
Spelling 152, 295, 297–298, 393–394, 405, 407–409, 411, 413–414, 427, 455–456, 472–473, 476
Sponsor(s) (*see also* significant others and intermediaries) 238, 248, 251

Spread of writing 8, 13, 19
Spreadsheet 105
Stance 539–541, 544–545, 550–551, 556, 559–560
State assessments 315–316, 324–326
Statute of Frauds 133, 135
Statutes: *see* legislation
Stereotyping 27
Stock reports 105
Stocks 104
Stories 193–196, 198
Strategies 293–294, 296–299, 301–302, 306, 334–336, 405, 408–409, 452, 454, 456, 459–461, 464, 475–478
Stress 486–490, 492, 495–497
Stylus 10, 15, 23, 25
Subject 550, 552, 555, 558, 591–593
Summary, summarizing 443–445
Sunday schools 241
Surveillance 283
Syllogism 584
Symbolic capital 275, 571–572
Symbols 7–8, 16–17, 19
Syntactic complexity 371, 439, 554–556
Systemic-functional linguistics 550, 567

T

Task schema 452, 453–456, 459, 464
Taxation roll 104
Teacher feedback 519–520
Teacher-peer conference 299, 319, 322–323, 332–333, 336–337, 339
Teacher preparation 354–355, 357, 359
Teacher response-reliability 333
Teacher response or commentary 319, 333, 352, 376
Teacher and student beliefs 306
Teaching strategy 334–336, 475–476
Technical documentation 120
Techinical writing 161, 221, 223
Technocratic discourse 277–278
Technologies of writing 115
Technology 191, 193, 195–196, 200, 261–263, 337–339, 393, 441, 476
    and assessment 378–379
Telegraph 27–28, 74, 105, 225
Tests and testing 283, 286–287, 291, 315–316, 323–327, 331–332, 355, 365–368, 370–371, 373–374, 377–378
Text(s) 85–89, 103–107, 110, 113–116, 118–124, 583–588, 603–605
    design 291
    floating 118–119
    generation 455–459
    production 450–459
    transmission of 146, 182
        Islamic role 153–154
Textbooks 18, 185, 284–291, 311–316, 318, 331, 335, 352–358, 374, 443
Texts-in-action 122

Text-reader conversation 114, 121
Textual analysis 231, 332, 489, 491, 567, 574
Textual authority 114, 119
Textual communities 114, 116–120, 124
Textualism 136
Textuality 114, 119, 440
Textually mediated talk 477–479
Theme 276–278, 550, 552–553, 559
Third persona 587
Topic choice 335, 370, 408
Topic knowledge 452, 461–462
Topic sentences 286, 312–314
Topics 315–316
Topoi 476, 593–594
Toulmin model of argument 320
Trajectory 401, 404, 407
Transcription 456–459, 462
Transculturation in multilingual writing
    development 526
Transgender 387, 391
Translating 451, 454
Translation 83–87, 91
Trauma writing 485, 493
Tropes 89–90
Trivium 158, 311, 350
Truth 584, 586, 589–593
Ts'ai Lun 24
T-unit 317, 371, 551, 554–555
Tutorial 336
Tutors 246, 339–340, 346, 356, 390
Twelve Tables 131
Typeface 45–46, 50–51, 54–55, 57–63, 226
Typing 27, 30, 91, 222, 477
Typography 35–64, 599, 601, 605

U

Undergraduates 287, 589, 592–593
Universities 47, 66, 144, 155, 158–163, 168–175,
    182–183, 255–256, 273–275, 277–278, 289,
    331–343, 515
    curricula 158, 160, 162
    four faculties 158
    French 158, 169–170, 331
    German 169–170, 331
    Islamic 153–155
    origin 66, 158
    post-colonial 171
    research 168–171
    United States 159, 168, 171, 515

V

Validity 281, 318, 365–379, 587, 590–591, 593
    consequential 367, 374, 378
    construct 366–369, 373
    content 366,
    systemic 378
    threats to 367
    Vellum 24, 35, 37, 47

Verb(s) 539–543, 550, 552, 556–560, 575
Virtual capitalism 113
Virtual organization 117
Virtual society 113, 115–117
Visual argument 600, 605
Visual composition 574, 604
Visual culture 77, 602–603
Visual design 226, 579, 601, 605, 610
Visual literacy 599, 604, 608–610
Visual neglect 472
Visual rhetoric 263, 605
Visual semiotics 600
Voice 202, 257–259, 343, 387–389, 391–392, 394,
    412, 443, 503, 507–508, 558–559
    recognition 338, 395, 474

W

Warrant 122, 592
Waterman, Lewis Edson 25
Weaponry 153, 167–168
Wikipedia 186–187
Wikis 607
Wills 104, 130–134, 138
Women's clubs 247
Women's journalism 213–214
Word processors 29–30, 393
Working memory (WM) 298, 452–453, 456–464
Workplace 120, 243, 264, 341, 424–427,
    587, 589, 594
    writing 81, 221–231, 376
Writer-based prose 454
Writing across the curriculum
    (WAC) 171, 334, 520, 589
Writing center(s) 332, 336, 338–340,
    356, 390, 472, 517
Writing in the community 237–251
Writing development 297, 300, 312, 336, 407,
    421–430, 506, 515, 517, 519, 521, 523–527
Writing forms 295, 402–404, 407, 409, 419
Writing functions 103–105, 113, 116,
    227, 261, 274, 290–291
Writing instruction 239, 241, 297–299, 301–302,
    305–306, 315–316, 318, 321, 331, 335–336,
    338, 340–342, 352, 355–357, 371, 390–392,
    394–395, 408, 413, 424–425, 428, 455,
    497, 500, 507, 520–521
Writing instructions 487, 490, 492, 494
Writing materials 193, 240–241,
    403, 410, 413–414
Writing and mathematical tools 104, 106
Writing practices 237–238, 240, 244–251, 264, 395,
    402, 410–412, 414, 474, 480, 605–607
Writing process(es) 91–92, 221–224, 226,
    230, 299–300, 317, 320, 322, 335, 354,
    393, 395, 402, 408–410, 413–414,
    436–437, 453, 456, 461–462,
    464–465, 519–520
Writing purposes 372, 403, 413
Writing from reading 443

Writing from sources 443
Writing studies 82–84, 87, 91–92, 487, 497, 519, 527, 574, 600–601, 606–607
Writing system(s) (*see also* scripts) 7–8, 15–16, 18–20, 66,84, 129, 198–199, 296, 535, 551, 603
Writing task 368–369, 371–372
Writing, transmission of 83
Writing tutors 246, 339–340, 346, 356, 390

Written culture 65, 187
Written disclosure paradigm 485, 487–488, 490–491, 493–494, 498

X

Xerography 29
Xylography 26

CPSIA information can be obtained at www.ICGtesting.com

234209LV00004B/3/P